SIPRI Yearbook 1999

Armaments, Disarmament and International Security

sipri

Stockholm International Peace Research Institute

SIPRI is an independent international institute for research into problems of peace and conflict, especially those of arms control and disarmament. It was established in 1966 to commemorate Sweden's 150 years of unbroken peace.

The Institute is financed mainly by the Swedish Parliament. The staff and the Governing Board are international. The Institute also has an Advisory Committee as an international consultative body.

The Governing Board is not responsible for the views expressed in the publications of the Institute.

Adam Daniel Rotfeld, Director, *Yearbook Editor and Publisher*
Connie Wall, *Managing Editor*
Coordinators
Eric Arnett, Gennady Chufrin, Elisabeth Sköns
Editors
Billie Bielckus, Jetta Gilligan Borg, Eve Johansson
Editorial Assistant
Rebecka Charan

sipri

Stockholm International Peace Research Institute
Signalistgatan 9, S-169 70 Solna, Sweden
Cable: SIPRI
Telephone: 46 8/655 97 00
Telefax: 46 8/655 97 33
E-mail: sipri@sipri.se
Internet URL: http://www.sipri.se

SIPRI Yearbook 1999

Armaments, Disarmament and International Security

sipri
Stockholm International Peace Research Institute

OXFORD UNIVERSITY PRESS
1999

Oxford University Press, Great Clarendon Street, Oxford OX2 6DP
Oxford New York
Athens Auckland Bangkok Bogotá Buenos Aires Calcutta
Cape Town Chennai Dar es Salaam Delhi Florence Hong Kong Istanbul
Karachi Kuala Lumpur Madrid Melbourne Mexico City Mumbai
Nairobi Paris São Paulo Singapore Taipei Tokyo Toronto Warsaw
and associated companies in Berlin Ibadan

Oxford is a trade mark of Oxford University Press

Published in the United States
by Oxford University Press Inc., New York

Yearbooks before 1987 published under title
'World Armaments and Disarmament:
SIPRI Yearbook [year of publication]'

British Library Cataloguing in Publication Data

Data available

ISSN 0953–0282

ISBN 0-19-829646-0

Library of Congress Cataloging in Publication Data

Data available

ISSN 0953–0282

ISBN 0-19-829646-0

Typeset and originated by Stockholm International Peace Research Institute
Printed and bound in Great Britain by
Biddles Ltd., Guildford and King's Lynn

Contents

Part III. Non-proliferation, arms control and disarmament, 1998

Annexes

Preface

The Stockholm International Peace Research Institute presents in this volume the 30th edition of the SIPRI Yearbook. In the Preface to the first edition, *SIPRI Yearbook of World Armaments and Disarmament 1968/69*, Robert Neild, the Institute's first Director, wrote: 'The Yearbook was designed to fill a gap. Until now there has been no authoritative international source which provided—in one place—an account of recent trends in world military expenditure, the state of the technological arms race, and the success or failure of recent attempts at arms limitations or disarmament'. This goal has been achieved. Over the years the teams of researchers have changed, the methodology has evolved and the scope of the research has widened, particularly since the end of the cold war, but the premises on which SIPRI's reputation rests—competence and professionalism in the collection of data and facts, in analyses and in the presentation of solid research based on open sources—have remained unchanged.

The Introduction to the present volume addresses the need to rethink the contemporary international security system.

In Part I, *Security and conflicts,* the first two chapters contain data and critical assessments of the major armed conflicts of 1998 and of efforts in the field of conflict prevention, management and resolution. There are also detailed accounts of the conflicts in Kashmir, Kosovo and Tajikistan as well as the Good Friday Agreement for Northern Ireland. In chapters on regional security, the problems of the Middle East, Russia and its programme of military reform, the Caspian Sea Basin and the European security process are thoroughly analysed.

Part II, *Military spending and armaments,* presents the research results of several of SIPRI's flagship projects—military expenditure, arms production, military research and development, and transfers of major conventional weapons—as well as special studies of China's military spending and of the nuclear tests conducted by India and Pakistan.

Part III, *Non-proliferation, arms control and disarmament*, deals with weapons of mass destruction (nuclear, chemical and biological) and conventional weapons, and their respective control regimes, with appendices on nuclear explosions since 1945 and the ban on anti-personnel mines. The final chapter of this Yearbook analyses the multilateral dimension of non-cooperative responses to proliferation and the multilateral arms and technology export control regimes.

All but two of the chapters and several appendices reflect the results of research conducted at SIPRI. I would like to acknowledge and express our appreciation to Bernard Adam, Alexei Arbatov, William M. Arkin, Malcolm Dando, Robert S. Norris, Stefan Troebst, Peter Wallensteen and the Uppsala Conflict Data Project, Shaoguang Wang, Sten Widmalm and Irina Zviagelskaya for sharing with us their knowledge and expertise.

In addition to the authors at SIPRI, I wish to thank all the other members of the staff for the great amount of support needed for the production of such a volume. The Yearbook editorial team—Billie Bielckus, Jetta Gilligan Borg, Eve Johansson and Rebecka Charan, editorial assistant—led by Connie Wall, provided the authors with invaluable assistance. My thanks also go to Gerd Hagmeyer-Gaverus, information technology manager; Billie Bielckus, cartographer; and Peter Rea, indexer.

Adam Daniel Rotfeld, Director
June 1999

Acronyms

Acronyms for UN observer, peacekeeping and electoral operations and weapon systems are given in appendix 2A and appendix 11B, respectively. Acronyms not defined in this list are defined in the chapters of this volume.

ABM	Anti-ballistic missile
ACM	Advanced cruise missile
ACV	Armoured combat vehicle
ADM	Atomic demolition munition
AG	Australia Group
AIFV	Armoured infantry fighting vehicle
ALCM	Air-launched cruise missile
AMU	Arab Maghreb Union
APC	Armoured personnel carrier
APM	Anti-personnel mine
ARF	ASEAN Regional Forum
ARV	Armoured recovery vehicle
ASEAN	Association of South-East Asian Nations
ASEAN–PMC	ASEAN Post Ministerial Conference
ATBM	Anti-tactical ballistic missile
ATC	Armoured troop carrier
ATTU	Atlantic-to-the-Urals (zone)
AWACS	Airborne warning and control system
BIC	Bilateral Implementation Commission
BMD	Ballistic missile defence
BTWC	Biological and Toxin Weapons Convention
BW	Biological weapon/ warfare
CBM	Confidence-building measure
CBSS	Council of the Baltic Sea States
CBW	Chemical and biological weapon/warfare
CCW	Certain Conventional Weapons (Convention)
CD	Conference on Disarmament
CEE	Central and Eastern Europe
CFE	Conventional Armed Forces in Europe (Treaty)
CFSP	Common Foreign and Security Policy
CIO	Chairman-in-Office
CIS	Commonwealth of Independent States
CivPol	Civilian police
CJTF	Combined Joint Task Forces
CPC	Conflict Prevention Centre
CPI	Consumer price index
CSBM	Confidence- and security-building measure
CSCAP	Council for Security Cooperation in the Asia Pacific
CTBT	Comprehensive Nuclear Test-Ban Treaty
CTBTO	Comprehensive Nuclear Test-Ban Treaty Organization
CTR	Cooperative Threat Reduction
CW	Chemical weapon/ warfare

CWC	Chemical Weapons Convention
DOD	Department of Defense
DOE	Department of Energy
DPKO	Department of Peacekeeping Operations
EAEC	European Atomic Energy Community (Euratom)
EAPC	Euro-Atlantic Partnership Council
ECOMOG	ECOWAS Monitoring Group
ECOSOC	Economic and Social Council
ECOWAS	Economic Community of West African States
EFTA	European Free Trade Association
Enmod	Environmental modification
ESDI	European Security and Defence Identity
ETA	Euzkadi Ta Azkatasuna
EU	European Union
Euratom	European Atomic Energy Community (EAEC)
FMT	Fissile Material Treaty
FSC	Forum for Security Co-operation
FY	Fiscal year
G7	Group of Seven
G8	Group of Eight
G-21	Group of 21
GDP	Gross domestic product
GLCM	Ground-launched cruise missile
GNP	Gross national product
HACV	Heavy armoured combat vehicle
HCNM	High Commissioner on National Minorities
HEU	Highly enriched uranium
HLTF	High Level Task Force
IAEA	International Atomic Energy Agency
ICC	International Criminal Court
ICBL	International Campaign to Ban Landmines
ICBM	Intercontinental ballistic missile
ICJ	International Court of Justice
ICTR	International Criminal Tribunal for Rwanda
ICTY	International Criminal Tribunal for the Former Yugoslavia
IDC	International Data Centre
IFOR	Implementation Force
IFV	Infantry fighting vehicle
IGAD	Inter-Governmental Authority on Development
IMF	International Monetary Fund
INF	Intermediate-range nuclear forces
IPTF	International Police Task Force
IRA	Irish Republican Army
IRBM	Intermediate-range ballistic missile
JCC	Joint Consultative Commission
JCG	Joint Consultative Group
JCIC	Joint Compliance and Inspection Commission
KLA	Kosovo Liberation Army
LCA	Light Combat Aircraft
LDC	Least developed country

MBT	Main battle tank
MD	Military District
MER	Market exchange rate
MERCOSUR	Mercado Común del Sur
MIRV	Multiple independently targetable re-entry vehicle
MNLH	Maximum National Levels for Holdings
MOD	Ministry of Defence
MOU	Memorandum of Understanding
MTCR	Missile Technology Control Regime
MTM	Multinational technical means (of verification)
NAC	North Atlantic Council
NACC	North Atlantic Cooperation Council
NAM	Non-Aligned Movement
NATO	North Atlantic Treaty Organization
NBC	Nuclear, biological and chemical (weapons)
NGO	Non-governmental organization
NIC	Newly industrialized countries
NMD	National missile defence
NPT	Non-Proliferation Treaty
NSG	Nuclear Suppliers Group
NSIP	NATO Security Investment Programme
NTM	National technical means (of verification)
NWFZ	Nuclear weapon-free zone
OAS	Organization of American States
OAU	Organization of African Unity
OCCAR	Organisme Conjoint de Coopération en Matière d'Armement
ODIHR	Office for Democratic Institutions and Human Rights
OECD	Organisation for Economic Co-operation and Development
OIC	Organization of the Islamic Conference
O&M	Operation and maintenance
OPANAL	Agency for the Prohibition of Nuclear Weapons in Latin America and the Caribbean
OPCW	Organisation for the Prohibition of Chemical Weapons
OPEC	Organisation of Petroleum Exporting Countries
OSCC	Open Skies Consultative Commission
OSCE	Organization for Security and Co-operation in Europe
P5	Permanent Five (members of the UN Security Council)
PA	Palestinian Authority
PFP	Partnership for Peace
PJC	Permanent Joint Council (NATO–Russia)
PLO	Palestine Liberation Organization
PPP	Purchasing power parity
PrepCom	Preparatory Committee
PTB(T)	Partial Test Ban (Treaty)
R&D	Research and development
RDT&E	Research, development, testing and evaluation
RPV	Remotely piloted vehicle
RV	Re-entry vehicle

SADC	Southern African Development Community
SAM	Surface-to-air missile
SCC	Standing Consultative Commission
SDR	Strategic Defence Review
SFOR	Stabilization Force
SLBM	Submarine-launched ballistic missile
SLCM	Sea-launched cruise missile
SLV	Space launch vehicle
SNDV	Strategic nuclear delivery vehicle
SNF	Short-range nuclear forces
SRAM	Short-range attack missile
SRBM	Short-range ballistic missile
SRCC	Sub-Regional Consultative Commission
SRBM	Short-range ballistic missile
SSBN	Nuclear-powered, ballistic-missile submarine
SSM	Surface-to-surface missile
START	Strategic Arms Reduction Talks/Treaty
THAAD	Theater High-Altitude Area Defense
TLE	Treaty-limited equipment
TMD	Theatre missile defence
TNF	Theatre nuclear forces
UNCLOS	UN Convention on the Law of the Sea
UNDP	UN Development Programme
UNHCR	UN High Commissioner for Refugees
UNROCA	UN Register of Conventional Arms
UNSCOM	UN Special Commission on Iraq
WA	Wassanaar Arrangemenet
WEAG	Western European Armaments Group
WEAO	Western European Armaments Organization
WEU	Western European Union
WMD	Weapon of mass destruction
WTO	Warsaw Treaty Organization (Warsaw Pact)
WTO	World Trade Organization
XFOR	Extraction Force

Glossary

RAGNHILD FERM and CONNIE WALL

The main terms and organizations discussed in this Yearbook are defined in the glossary. For acronyms that appear in the definitions, see page xvi; for the arms control and disarmament agreements mentioned in the glossary, see annexe A.

Agency for the Prohibition of Nuclear Weapons in Latin America and the Caribbean (OPANAL)	Established by the 1967 Treaty of Tlatelolco to resolve, together with the IAEA, questions of compliance with the treaty.
Anti-ballistic missile (ABM) system	*See* Ballistic missile defence.
Anti-personnel mine (APM)	A landmine designed to be exploded by the presence, proximity or contact of a person and that will incapacitate, injure or kill one or more persons.
Arab League	The League of Arab States, established in 1945, with Permanent Headquarters in Cairo. Its principal objective is to form closer union among Arab states and foster political and economic cooperation. An agreement for collective defence and economic cooperation among the members was signed in 1950. *See* the list of members.
Arab Maghreb Union (AMU)	Established in 1989 among five North African states to ensure regional stability, enhance policy coordination and promote common defence. *See* the list of members.
Asia–Pacific region	The Pacific rim states of Asia, North and South America, and Oceania. It is defined differently by the membership of different Asia–Pacific organizations.
Association of South-East Asian Nations (ASEAN)	Established in 1967 to promote economic, social and cultural development as well as regional peace and security in South-East Asia. The seat of the Secretariat is in Jakarta. The ASEAN Regional Forum (ARF) was established in 1993 to address security issues in a multilateral forum. The ASEAN Post Ministerial Conference (ASEAN–PMC) was established in 1979 as a forum for discussions of political and security issues with Dialogue Partners. *See* the lists of the members of ASEAN, ARF and ASEAN–PMC.
Atlantic-to-the-Urals (ATTU) zone	Zone of application of the 1990 CFE Treaty and the 1992 CFE-1A Agreement, stretching from the Atlantic Ocean to the Ural Mountains. It covers the entire land territory of the European NATO states (excluding part of Turkey); the former non-Soviet WTO states; and Armenia, Azerbaijan, Belarus, Georgia, Moldova and Ukraine. It also includes the territory of Russia and Kazakhstan west of the Ural River.

Australia Group (AG)	Group of states, formed in 1985, which meets informally each year to monitor the proliferation of chemical and biological products and to discuss chemical and biological weapon-related items which should be subject to national regulatory measures. *See* the list of members.
Balkan states	States in south-eastern Europe bounded by the Adriatic, Aegean and Black seas: Albania, Bosnia and Herzegovina, Bulgaria, Croatia, Greece, the Former Yugoslav Republic of Macedonia, Romania, Slovenia, Turkey and Yugoslavia (Serbia and Montenegro).
Ballistic missile	Missile which follows a ballistic trajectory (part of which may be outside the earth's atmosphere) when thrust is terminated.
Ballistic missile defence (BMD)	Weapon system designed to defend against a ballistic missile attack by intercepting and destroying ballistic missiles or their warheads in flight.
Baltic Council	Established in 1990 for the promotion of democracy and development of cooperation between the three Baltic states, it consists of the Baltic Assembly (established in 1991, for cooperation between the three parliaments) and the Baltic Council of Ministers (established in 1994, for cooperation between the governments). The Baltic Council Secretariat is in Riga. *See* the list of members.
Baltic states	Estonia, Latvia and Lithuania, three Baltic Sea littoral states in north-eastern Europe.
Binary chemical weapon	A shell or other device filled with two chemicals of relatively low toxicity which mix and react while the device is being delivered to the target, the reaction product being a super-toxic chemical warfare agent, such as a nerve agent.
Biological weapon (BW)	Weapon containing infectious agents or living organisms, or infective material derived from them, when used or intended to cause disease or death in humans, animals or plants, as well as their means of delivery.
Central and Eastern Europe (CEE)	Bulgaria, the Czech Republic, Hungary, Poland, Romania, Slovakia and Slovenia. The term is sometimes also taken to include the European former Soviet republics—Armenia, Azerbaijan, Belarus, Georgia, Moldova, the European part of Russia and Ukraine—and sometimes also the Baltic states.
Central Asia	Kazakhstan, Kyrgyzstan, Tajikistan, Turkmenistan and Uzbekistan.
Chemical weapon (CW)	Chemical substances—whether gaseous, liquid or solid—when used or intended for use in weapons because of their direct toxic effects on humans, animals or plants, as well as their means of delivery.
Combined Joint Task Forces (CJTF)	Concept declared at the June 1996 meeting of NATO foreign ministers to facilitate NATO contingency operations, including the use of 'separable but not separate' military capabilities in operations which might in future be led by the European Union/Western European Union, with the participation of states outside the NATO Alliance.

Common Foreign and Security Policy (CFSP)	Institutional framework, established by the 1992 Maastricht Treaty, for consultation and development of common positions and joint action on European foreign and security policy. It constitutes the second of the three 'pillars' of the European Union. The CFSP is further elaborated in the 1997 Amsterdam Treaty. *See also* European Union.
Commonwealth of Independent States (CIS)	Established in 1991 as a framework for multilateral cooperation among former Soviet republics. *See* the list of members.
Comprehensive Nuclear Test-Ban Treaty Organization (CTBTO)	Established by the 1996 CTBT to resolve questions of compliance with the treaty and as a forum for consultation and cooperation among the states parties. Its seat is in Vienna.
Conference on Disarmament (CD)	A multilateral arms control negotiating body, based in Geneva, composed of states representing all the regions of the world and including the permanent members of the UN Security Council. The CD reports to the UN General Assembly. *See* the list of members under United Nations.
Confidence- and security-building measure (CSBM)	Measure undertaken by states to promote confidence and security through military transparency, openness, constraints and cooperation. CSBMs are militarily significant, politically binding, verifiable and, as a rule, reciprocal.
Confidence-building measure (CBM)	Measure undertaken by states to help reduce the danger of armed conflict and of misunderstanding or miscalculation of military activities.
Conventional weapon	Weapon not having mass destruction effects. *See also* Weapon of mass destruction.
Conversion	Term used to describe the shift in resources from military to civilian use. It usually refers to the conversion of industry from military to civilian production.
Council for Security Cooperation in the Asia Pacific (CSCAP)	Established in 1993 as an informal, non-governmental process for regional confidence building and security cooperation through dialogue, consultation and cooperation in Asia–Pacific security matters. *See* the list of members.
Council of Europe	Established in 1949, with its seat in Strasbourg. The Council is open to membership of all the European states which accept the principle of the rule of law and guarantee their citizens human rights and fundamental freedoms. Among its organs is the European Court of Human Rights. *See* the list of members.
Council of the Baltic Sea States (CBSS)	Established in 1992 to promote common strategies for political and economic cooperation and development among the states bordering on the Baltic Sea as well as Iceland and Norway. The seat of the Secretariat is in Stockholm. *See* the list of members.
Counter-proliferation	Measures or policies to prevent the proliferation or enforce the non-proliferation of weapons of mass destruction.

Cruise missile	Guided weapon-delivery vehicle which sustains flight at subsonic or supersonic speeds through aerodynamic lift, generally flying at very low altitudes to avoid radar detection, sometimes following the contours of the terrain. It can be air-, ground- or sea-launched (ALCM, GLCM and SLCM, respectively) and carry a conventional, nuclear, chemical or biological warhead.
Dual-capable	Term that refers to a weapon system or platform that can carry either conventional or non-conventional explosives.
Dual-use technology	Technology that can be used for both civilian and military applications.
Economic Community of West African States (ECOWAS)	A regional organization established in 1975, with its Executive Secretariat in Lagos, Nigeria, to promote cooperation and development in economic activity, improve relations among its member countries and contribute to development in Africa. In 1981 it adopted the Protocol on Mutual Assistance in Defence Matters. The ECOWAS Cease-fire Monitoring Group (ECOMOG) was established in 1990. *See* the list of members.
Euro-Atlantic Partnership Council (EAPC)	Established in 1997, the EAPC provides the overarching framework for cooperation between NATO and its PFP partners, with an expanded political dimension. *See* the list of members under North Atlantic Treaty Organization.
European Atomic Energy Community (Euratom or EAEC)	Based on the 1957 Treaty Establishing the European Atomic Energy Community (Euratom Treaty), Euratom was established to promote common efforts between EU member states in the development of nuclear energy for peaceful purposes. Euratom is located in Brussels. It has an agreement with the IAEA for joint application of safeguards in the territories of the Euratom member states.
European Security and Defence Identity (ESDI)	Concept aimed at strengthening the European pillar of NATO while reinforcing the transatlantic link. Militarily coherent and effective forces, capable of conducting operations under the control of the European Union/Western European Union, are to be created.
European Union (EU)	Organization of European states, with its headquarters in Brussels. The 1992 Treaty on European Union (Maastricht Treaty), which created the EU, entered into force in 1993. The 1997 Treaty of Amsterdam Amending the Treaty on European Union, which entered into force on 1 May 1999, strengthens the political dimension of the EU and prepares it for enlargement. At the June 1999 European Council meeting, the General Affairs Council was tasked with preparing the conditions and measures for including in the EU those functions of the WEU which will be necessary for the EU to fulfil its new responsibilities in the area of the Petersberg tasks. The three EU pillars are: cooperation in economic and monetary affairs and Euratom; the common foreign and security policy (CFSP); and cooperation in justice and home affairs. *See also* Petersberg tasks, and *see* the list of members.

Fissile material	Material composed of atoms which can be split by either fast or slow (thermal) neutrons. Uranium-235 and plutonium-239 are the most common fissile materials.
Group of Seven (G7)	Group of leading industrialized nations which have met informally, at the level of heads of state or government, since the 1970s. *See* the list of members. From 1997 Russia has participated with the G7 in meetings of the G8.
Group of 21 (G-21)	Originally 21, now 30, non-aligned CD member states which act together on proposals of common interest. *See* the list of members under Conference on Disarmament.
Intercontinental ballistic missile (ICBM)	Ground-launched ballistic missile with a range greater than 5500 km.
Intermediate-range nuclear forces (INF)	Theatre nuclear forces with a range of 1000–5550 km.
International Atomic Energy Agency (IAEA)	An intergovernmental organization within the UN system, with headquarters in Vienna. The IAEA is endowed by its Statute, which entered into force in 1957, to promote the peaceful uses of atomic energy and ensure that nuclear activities are not used to further any military purpose. It has also cooperated with the UN Special Commission on Iraq (UNSCOM) in carrying out the removal of nuclear weapon-usable material from Iraq. Under the NPT and the nuclear weapon-free zone treaties, non-nuclear weapon states must accept IAEA nuclear safeguards to demonstrate the fulfilment of their obligation not to manufacture nuclear weapons. *See* the list of IAEA members under United Nations.
International Court of Justice (ICJ)	The principal juridical organ of the United Nations, set up in 1945 and located in The Hague. It settles legal disputes submitted to it by states and gives advisory opinions on legal questions referred to it by international organs and agencies.
International Criminal Tribunal for the Former Yugoslavia (ICTY)	The international tribunal, with its seat in The Hague, established in 1993 to prosecute persons responsible for war crimes committed since 1991 in the former Yugoslavia.
International Criminal Tribunal for Rwanda (ICTR)	The international tribunal, with its seat in Arusha, Tanzania, established in 1994 to prosecute persons responsible for crimes of genocide committed in 1994 in Rwanda or by Rwandan citizens in neighbouring states.
Joint Consultative Group (JCG)	Established by the 1990 CFE Treaty to promote the objectives and implementation of the treaty by reconciling ambiguities of interpretation and implementation.
Joint Compliance and Inspection Commission (JCIC)	Established by the 1991 START I Treaty to resolve questions of compliance, clarify ambiguities and discuss ways to improve implementation of the treaty. It convenes at the request of at least one of the parties.
Landmine	An anti-personnel or anti-vehicle mine, emplaced on land.

Maghreb	An Arabic term for north-western Africa, referring to the areas of Algeria, Morocco and Tunisia that lie between the Atlas Mountains and the Mediterranean Sea. *See also* Arab Maghreb Union.
Mine	A munition placed under, on or near the ground or other surface area, designed to be detonated or exploded by the presence, proximity or contact of a person or vehicle. A mine may be directly emplaced or remotely delivered (by artillery, rocket, mortar or similar means or dropped from an aircraft).
Minsk Group	Group of states created in 1992 which act together in the OSCE for political settlement of the conflict in the Armenian enclave of Nagorno-Karabakh in Azerbaijan. *See* the list of members under Organization for Security and Co-operation in Europe.
Missile Technology Control Regime (MTCR)	An informal military-related export control regime, established in 1987, which produced the Guidelines for Sensitive Missile-Relevant Transfers. Its goal is to limit the spread of weapons of mass destruction by controlling their delivery systems. *See* the list of members.
Multiple independently targetable re-entry vehicles (MIRVs)	Re-entry vehicles, carried by a single ballistic missile, which can be directed to separate targets along separate trajectories.
National technical means (NTM) of verification	Technical means of intelligence, under the national control of a state, which are used to monitor compliance with an arms control treaty to which the state is a party.
NATO–Russia Permanent Joint Council (PJC)	Established by the 1997 NATO–Russia Founding Act on Mutual Relations, Cooperation and Security for consultation and cooperation.
NATO–Ukraine Commission	The North Atlantic Council meets periodically with Ukraine as the NATO–Ukraine Commission, to ensure that NATO and Ukraine are implementing the provisions of the 1997 NATO–Ukraine Charter on a Distinctive Partnership.
Non-Aligned Movement (NAM)	Group established in 1961, sometimes referred to as the Movement of Non-Aligned Countries. The NAM is a forum for consultations and coordination of positions on political and economic issues. The Coordinating Bureau of the Non-Aligned Countries (also called the Conference of Non-Aligned Countries) is the forum in which the NAM coordinates its actions within the UN. *See* the list of members.
Non-conventional weapon	*See* Weapon of mass destruction.
Non-governmental organization (NGO)	A national or international organization of individuals or organizations whose aim is to provide advice and present positions to national and international bodies and to inform the public about specific issues. Some NGOs are accredited by international organizations such as the UN and the OSCE, which seek their advice and assistance.
Non-strategic nuclear forces	*See* Theatre nuclear forces.

Nordic Council	Political advisory organ for cooperation between the parliaments of the Nordic states, founded in 1952 and with its Secretariat in Copenhagen. The Nordic Council of Ministers, established in 1971, is an organ for cooperation between the governments of the Nordic countries and between these governments and the Nordic Council. *See* the list of members.
North Atlantic Treaty Organization (NATO)	Established in 1949 by the North Atlantic Treaty as a defence alliance. NATO has 19 member nations (17 European states, the USA and Canada) and its headquarters are in Brussels. *See* the list of members.
Nuclear Suppliers Group (NSG)	Also known as the London Club and established in 1975, the NSG coordinates multilateral export controls on nuclear materials. In 1977 it agreed the Guidelines for Nuclear Transfers (London Guidelines, subsequently revised). The Guidelines contain a 'trigger list' of materials which should trigger IAEA safeguards when exported for peaceful purposes to any non-nuclear weapon state. In 1992 the NSG agreed the Guidelines for Transfers of Nuclear-Related Dual-Use Equipment, Material and Related Technology (Warsaw Guidelines, subsequently revised). *See* the list of members.
Open Skies Consultative Commission (OSCC)	Established by the 1992 Open Skies Treaty to resolve questions of compliance with the treaty.
Organisation for Economic Co-operation and Development (OECD)	Established in 1961, its objectives are to promote economic and social welfare by coordinating policies among the member states. Its headquarters are in Paris. *See* the list of members.
Organisation for the Prohibition of Chemical Weapons (OPCW)	Established by the 1993 Chemical Weapons Convention to resolve questions of compliance with the convention. Its seat is in The Hague.
Organisme Conjoint de Coopération en Matière d'Armement (OCCAR)	Established in 1996 as a management structure for international cooperative armaments programmes between France, Germany, Italy and the UK. It is also known as the Joint Armaments Cooperation Organization (JACO).
Organization for Security and Co-operation in Europe (OSCE)	Established in 1973 as the Conference on Security and Co-operation in Europe (CSCE), which adopted the Helsinki Final Act in 1975. In 1995 it was transformed into an organization, as a primary instrument for early warning, conflict prevention and crisis management in the OSCE region. The OSCE is concerned with implementation of the principles guiding relations between the member states, human rights, pluralistic democracy (election monitoring), and economic and environmental security. Its Forum for Security Co-operation (FSC) deals with arms control and CSBMs. The OSCE comprises several institutions, all located in Europe. *See* the list of members.

Organization of African Unity (OAU)	A union of African states established in 1963 to promote African international cooperation and harmonization of *inter alia* defence policies. The seat of the Secretary-General is in Addis Ababa. *See* the list of members.
Organization of American States (OAS)	Group of states in the Americas which adopted a charter in 1948, with the objective of strengthening peace and security in the western hemisphere. The General Secretariat is in Washington, DC. *See* the list of members.
Organization of the Islamic Conference (OIC)	Established in 1971 by Islamic states to promote cooperation among the member states and to support peace, security and the struggle of the people of Palestine and all Muslim people. Its Secretariat is in Jedda, Saudi Arabia. *See* the list of members.
Pact on Stability in Europe	The French proposal presented in 1993 as part of the cooperation in the framework of the EU Common Foreign and Security Policy (CFSP). Its objective is to contribute to stability by preventing tension and potential conflicts connected with border and minorities issues. The Pact was adopted in 1995, and the instruments and procedures were handed over to the OSCE.
Partnership for Peace (PFP)	Launched in 1994, the PFP is the programme for political and military cooperation between NATO and the partner states within the framework of the EAPC. It is open to all OSCE states able to contribute to the programme. The Enhanced PFP programme, adopted in 1997, is intended to strengthen political consultation, develop a more operational role, and provide for greater involvement of partners in PFP decision making and planning. *See* the list of members under North Atlantic Treaty Organization.
Peaceful nuclear explosion (PNE)	A nuclear explosion for non-military purposes, such as digging canals or harbours or creating underground cavities. The USA terminated its PNE programme in 1973. The USSR conducted its last PNE in 1988.
Petersberg tasks	Tasks emanating from the 1992 meeting of the WEU Council at Petersberg, Germany. Under a UN mandate, WEU member states will engage in humanitarian and rescue tasks, peacekeeping tasks and tasks of combat forces in crisis management, including peacemaking. The 1997 Amsterdam Treaty provides the EU with access to an operational capability in the context of the Petersberg tasks. *See also* European Union.
Re-entry vehicle (RV)	The part of a ballistic missile which carries a nuclear warhead and penetration aids to the target. It re-enters the earth's atmosphere and is destroyed in the final phase of the missile's trajectory. A missile can have one or several RVs and each RV contains a warhead.
Safeguards agreements	*See* International Atomic Energy Agency.
Short-range nuclear forces (SNF)	Nuclear weapons, including artillery, mines, missiles, etc., with ranges of up to 500 km.

Southern African Development Community (SADC)	Established in 1992 to promote regional economic development and fundamental principles of sovereignty, peace and security, human rights and democracy. The Secretariat is in Gaborone, Botswana. *See* the list of members.
Standing Consultative Commission (SCC)	Established by a 1972 US–Soviet Memorandum of Understanding. The parties to the 1972 ABM Treaty refer issues regarding implementation of the treaty to the SCC.
Strategic nuclear weapons	ICBMs and SLBMs with a range usually of over 5500 km, as well as bombs and missiles carried on aircraft of intercontinental range.
Subcritical experiments	Experiments designed not to reach nuclear criticality, i.e., there is no nuclear explosion and no energy release.
Submarine-launched ballistic missile (SLBM)	A ballistic missile launched from a submarine, usually with a range in excess of 5500 km.
Sub-Regional Consultative Commission (SRCC)	Established by the 1996 Agreement on Sub-Regional Arms Control (Florence Agreement) as a forum for the parties to resolve questions of compliance with the agreement.
Tactical nuclear weapon	A short-range nuclear weapon which is deployed with general-purpose forces.
Theatre missile defence (TMD)	Weapon systems designed to defend against non-strategic nuclear missiles by intercepting and destroying them in flight.
Theatre nuclear forces (TNF)	Nuclear weapons with ranges up to and including 5500 km. Also referred to as non-strategic nuclear forces.
Toxins	Poisonous substances which are products of organisms but are not living or capable of reproducing themselves, as well as chemically created variants of such substances. Some toxins may also be produced synthetically.
Treaty-limited equipment (TLE)	Five categories of equipment on which numerical limits are established by the 1990 CFE Treaty: battle tanks, armoured combat vehicles, artillery, combat aircraft and attack helicopters.
United Nations Register of Conventional Arms (UNROCA)	A voluntary reporting mechanism set up in 1992 for UN member states to report annually their imports and exports of seven categories of weapons or systems: battle tanks, armoured combat vehicles, large-calibre artillery systems, attack helicopters, combat aircraft, warships, and missiles and missile launchers.
Visegrad Group	Group of states comprising the Czech Republic, Hungary, Poland and Slovakia, formed in 1991 with the aim of intensifying subregional cooperation in political, economic and military areas and coordinating relations with multilateral European institutions.
Warhead	The part of a weapon which contains the explosive or other material intended to inflict damage.

Warsaw Treaty Organization (WTO)	The WTO, or Warsaw Pact, was established in 1955 by the Treaty of Friendship, Cooperation and Mutual Assistance between eight countries: Albania (withdrew in 1968), Bulgaria, Czechoslovakia, the German Democratic Republic, Hungary, Poland, Romania and the USSR. The WTO was dissolved in 1991.
Wassenaar Arrangement (WA)	The Wassenaar Arrangement on Export Controls for Conventional Arms and Dual-Use Goods and Technologies was formally established in 1996. It aims to prevent the acquisition of armaments and sensitive dual-use goods and technologies for military uses by states whose behaviour is cause for concern to the member states. *See* the list of members.
Weapon of mass destruction	Nuclear weapon and any other weapon, such as chemical and biological weapons, which may produce comparable effects.
Western European Union (WEU)	Established by the 1954 Protocols to the 1948 Brussels Treaty of Economic, Social and Cultural Collaboration and Collective Self-Defence among Western European States. The seat of the WEU is in Brussels. Within the EU Common Foreign and Security Policy (CFSP) and at the request of the EU, the WEU is to elaborate and implement EU decisions and actions which have defence implications. The Western European Armaments Group (WEAG) is the WEU armaments cooperation forum. The Western European Armaments Organization (WEAO) was established in 1997 (as a subsidiary body of the WEU) to provide a legal framework for the cooperative armaments activities of WEAG. Its main task is the management of WEAG military research and technology activities. *See also* European Union, and *see* the list of members.
Yield	Energy released in a nuclear explosion measured in equivalent kilotons or megatons of trinitrotoluene (TNT).
Zangger Committee	Established in 1971, the Nuclear Exporters Committee, called the Zangger Committee after its first chairman, is a group of nuclear supplier countries that meets informally twice a year to coordinate export controls on nuclear materials. *See* the list of members.

Membership of international organizations

The UN member states and organizations within the UN system are listed first, followed by all other organizations in alphabetical order. Note that not all the members of organizations are UN member states.

United Nations members and year of membership

Afghanistan, 1946
Albania, 1955
Algeria, 1962
Andorra, 1993
Angola, 1976
Antigua and Barbuda, 1981
Argentina, 1945
Armenia, 1992
Australia, 1945
Austria, 1955
Azerbaijan, 1992
Bahamas, 1973
Bahrain, 1971
Bangladesh, 1974
Barbados, 1966
Belarus, 1945
Belgium, 1945
Belize, 1981
Benin, 1960
Bhutan, 1971
Bolivia, 1945
Bosnia and Herzegovina, 1992
Botswana, 1966
Brazil, 1945
Brunei Darussalam, 1984
Bulgaria, 1955
Burkina Faso, 1960
Burundi, 1962
Cambodia, 1955
Cameroon, 1960
Canada, 1945
Cape Verde, 1975
Central African Republic, 1960
Chad, 1960
Chile, 1945
China, 1945
Colombia, 1945
Comoros, 1975
Congo (Brazzaville), 1960
Congo, Democratic Republic of the, 1960
Costa Rica, 1945
Côte d'Ivoire, 1960
Croatia, 1992
Cuba, 1945
Cyprus, 1960
Czech Republic, 1993
Denmark, 1945
Djibouti, 1977
Dominica, 1978
Dominican Republic, 1945
Ecuador, 1945
Egypt, 1945
El Salvador, 1945
Equatorial Guinea, 1968
Eritrea, 1993
Estonia, 1991
Ethiopia, 1945
Fiji, 1970
Finland, 1955
France, 1945
Gabon, 1960
Gambia, 1965
Georgia, 1992
Germany, 1973
Ghana, 1957
Greece, 1945
Grenada, 1974
Guatemala, 1945
Guinea, 1958
Guinea-Bissau, 1974
Guyana, 1966
Haiti, 1945
Honduras, 1945
Hungary, 1955
Iceland, 1946
India, 1945
Indonesia, 1950
Iran, 1945
Iraq, 1945
Ireland, 1955
Israel, 1949
Italy, 1955
Jamaica, 1962
Japan, 1956
Jordan, 1955
Kazakhstan, 1992
Kenya, 1963
Korea, Democratic People's Republic of (North Korea), 1991
Korea, Republic of (South Korea), 1991
Kuwait, 1963
Kyrgyzstan, 1992
Lao People's Democratic Republic, 1955
Latvia, 1991
Lebanon, 1945
Lesotho, 1966
Liberia, 1945
Libya, 1955
Liechtenstein, 1990
Lithuania, 1991
Luxembourg, 1945
Macedonia, Former Yugoslav Republic of (FYROM), 1993
Madagascar, 1960
Malawi, 1964
Malaysia, 1957
Maldives, 1965
Mali, 1960
Malta, 1964
Marshall Islands, 1991
Mauritania, 1961
Mauritius, 1968
Mexico, 1945
Micronesia, 1991
Moldova, 1992
Monaco, 1993
Mongolia, 1961
Morocco, 1956
Mozambique, 1975
Myanmar (Burma), 1948
Namibia, 1990
Nepal, 1955
Netherlands, 1945
New Zealand, 1945
Nicaragua, 1945
Niger, 1960
Nigeria, 1960
Norway, 1945
Oman, 1971
Pakistan, 1947
Palau, 1994
Panama, 1945
Papua New Guinea, 1975
Paraguay, 1945
Peru, 1945
Philippines, 1945
Poland, 1945
Portugal, 1955
Qatar, 1971
Romania, 1955
Russia, 1945[a]
Rwanda, 1962

Saint Kitts (Christopher) and Nevis, 1983
Saint Lucia, 1979
Saint Vincent and the Grenadines, 1980
Samoa, Western, 1976
San Marino, 1992
Sao Tome and Principe, 1975
Saudi Arabia, 1945
Senegal, 1960
Seychelles, 1976
Sierra Leone, 1961
Singapore, 1965
Slovakia, 1993
Slovenia, 1992
Solomon Islands, 1978
Somalia, 1960
South Africa, 1945
Spain, 1955
Sri Lanka, 1955
Sudan, 1956
Suriname, 1975
Swaziland, 1968
Sweden, 1946
Syria, 1945
Tajikistan, 1992
Tanzania, 1961
Thailand, 1946
Togo, 1960
Trinidad and Tobago, 1962
Tunisia, 1956
Turkey, 1945
Turkmenistan, 1992
Uganda, 1962
UK, 1945
Ukraine, 1945
United Arab Emirates, 1971
Uruguay, 1945
USA, 1945
Uzbekistan, 1992
Vanuatu, 1981
Venezuela, 1945
Viet Nam, 1977
Yemen, 1947
Yugoslavia, 1945[b]
Zambia, 1964
Zimbabwe, 1980

[a] In Dec. 1991 Russia informed the UN Secretary-General that it was continuing the membership of the USSR in the Security Council and all other UN bodies.

[b] A claim by Yugoslavia (Serbia and Montenegro) in 1992 to continue automatically the membership of the Socialist Federal Republic of Yugoslavia was not accepted by the UN General Assembly. It was decided that Yugoslavia should apply for membership, which it had not done by 1 Jan. 1999. It may not participate in the work of the General Assembly, its subsidiary organs, or the conferences and meetings it convenes.

UN Security Council

Permanent members (the P5): China, France, Russia, UK, USA

Non-permanent members in 1998 (elected by the UN General Assembly for two-year terms; the year in brackets is the year at the end of which the term expires): Bahrain (1999), Brazil (1999), Costa Rica (1998), Gabon (1999), Gambia (1999), Japan (1998), Kenya (1998), Portugal (1998), Slovenia (1999), Sweden (1998)

Note: Argentina, Canada, Malaysia, Namibia and the Netherlands were elected non-permanent members for 1999–2000.

Conference on Disarmament (CD)

Members: Algeria, Argentina, Australia, Austria, Bangladesh, Belarus, Belgium, Brazil, Bulgaria, Cameroon, Canada, Chile, China, Colombia, Congo (Democratic Republic of), Cuba, Egypt, Ethiopia, Finland, France, Germany, Hungary, India, Indonesia, Iran, Iraq, Israel, Italy, Japan, Kenya, Korea (North), Korea (South), Mexico, Mongolia, Morocco, Myanmar (Burma), Netherlands, New Zealand, Nigeria, Norway, Pakistan, Peru, Poland, Romania, Russia, Senegal, Slovakia, South Africa, Spain, Sri Lanka, Sweden, Switzerland, Syria, Turkey, UK, Ukraine, USA, Venezuela, Viet Nam, Yugoslavia,* Zimbabwe

* Yugoslavia (Serbia and Montenegro) has been suspended since 1992.

Members of the Group of 21 (G-21): Algeria, Bangladesh, Brazil, Cameroon, Chile, Colombia, Congo (Democratic Republic of), Cuba, Korea (North), Egypt, Ethiopia, India, Indonesia, Iraq, Iran, Kenya, Mexico, Mongolia, Morocco, Myanmar, Nigeria, Pakistan, Peru, Senegal, South Africa, Sri Lanka, Syria, Venezuela, Viet Nam, Zimbabwe

International Atomic Energy Agency (IAEA)

Members: Afghanistan, Albania, Algeria, Argentina, Armenia, Australia, Austria, Bangladesh, Belarus, Belgium, Bolivia, Bosnia and Herzegovina, Brazil, Bulgaria, Burkina Faso, Cambodia, Cameroon, Canada, Chile, China, Colombia, Congo (Democratic Republic of), Costa Rica, Côte d'Ivoire, Croatia, Cuba, Cyprus, Czech Republic, Denmark, Dominican Republic, Ecuador, Egypt, El Salvador, Estonia, Ethiopia, Finland, France, Gabon, Georgia, Germany, Ghana, Greece, Guatemala, Haiti, Holy See, Hungary, Iceland, India, Indonesia, Iran, Iraq, Ireland, Israel, Italy, Jamaica, Japan, Jordan, Kazakhstan, Kenya, Korea (South), Kuwait, Latvia, Lebanon, Liberia, Libya, Liechtenstein, Lithuania, Luxembourg, Macedonia (Former Yugoslav

Republic of), Madagascar, Malaysia, Mali, Malta, Marshall Islands, Mauritius, Mexico, Moldova, Monaco, Mongolia, Morocco, Myanmar (Burma), Namibia, Netherlands, New Zealand, Nicaragua, Niger, Nigeria, Norway, Pakistan, Panama, Paraguay, Peru, Philippines, Poland, Portugal, Qatar, Romania, Russia, Saudi Arabia, Senegal, Sierra Leone, Singapore, Slovakia, Slovenia, South Africa, Spain, Sri Lanka, Sudan, Sweden, Switzerland, Syria, Tanzania, Thailand, Tunisia, Turkey, Uganda, UK, Ukraine, United Arab Emirates, Uruguay, USA, Uzbekistan, Venezuela, Viet Nam, Yemen, Yugoslavia,* Zambia, Zimbabwe

* Yugoslavia (Serbia and Montenegro) has been suspended since 1992. It is deprived of the right to participate in the IAEA General Conference and the Board of Governors' meetings but is assessed for its contribution to the budget of the IAEA.

Note: North Korea was a member of the IAEA until Sep. 1994.

Arab League

Members: Algeria, Bahrain, Comoros, Djibouti, Egypt, Iraq, Jordan, Kuwait, Lebanon, Libya, Mauritania, Morocco, Oman, Palestine, Qatar, Saudi Arabia, Somalia, Sudan, Syria, Tunisia, United Arab Emirates, Yemen

Arab Maghreb Union (AMU)

Member: Algeria, Libya, Mauritania, Morocco, Tunisia

Association of South-East Asian Nations (ASEAN)

Members: Brunei, Indonesia, Laos, Malaysia, Myanmar (Burma), Philippines, Singapore, Thailand, Viet Nam

ASEAN Regional Forum (ARF)

Members: The ASEAN states plus Australia, Cambodia, Canada, China, European Union (EU), India, Japan, Korea (South), Mongolia, New Zealand, Papua New Guinea, Russia, USA

ASEAN Post Ministerial Conference (ASEAN–PMC)

Members: The ASEAN states plus Australia, Canada, European Union (EU), Japan, Korea (South), New Zealand, USA

Australia Group (AG)

Members: Argentina, Australia, Austria, Belgium, Canada, Czech Republic, Denmark, Finland, France, Germany, Greece, Hungary, Iceland, Ireland, Italy, Japan, Korea (South), Luxembourg, Netherlands, New Zealand, Norway, Poland, Portugal, Romania, Slovakia, Spain, Sweden, Switzerland, UK, USA

Observer: European Commission

Baltic Council

Members: Estonia, Latvia, Lithuania

Commonwealth of Independent States (CIS)

Members: Armenia, Azerbaijan, Belarus, Georgia, Kazakhstan, Kyrgyzstan, Moldova, Russia, Tajikistan, Turkmenistan, Ukraine, Uzbekistan

Council for Security Cooperation in the Asia Pacific (CSCAP)

Members: Australia, Canada, China, European Union (EU), Indonesia, Japan, Korea (North), Korea (South), Malaysia, Mongolia, New Zealand, Philippines, Russia, Singapore, Thailand, USA, Viet Nam

Associate member: India

Council of Europe

Members: Albania, Andorra, Austria, Belgium, Bulgaria, Croatia, Cyprus, Czech Republic, Denmark, Estonia, Finland, France, Germany, Georgia, Greece, Hungary, Iceland, Ireland, Italy, Latvia, Liechtenstein, Lithuania, Luxembourg, Macedonia (Former Yugoslav Republic of), Malta, Moldova, Netherlands, Norway, Poland, Portugal, Romania, Russia, San Marino, Slovakia, Slovenia, Spain, Sweden, Switzerland, Turkey, UK, Ukraine

Observers: Canada, Holy See, Japan, USA

Council of the Baltic Sea States (CBSS)

Members: Denmark, Estonia, European Commission, Finland, Germany, Iceland, Latvia, Lithuania, Norway, Poland, Russia, Sweden

Economic Community of West African States (ECOWAS)

Members: Benin, Burkina Faso, Cape Verde, Côte d'Ivoire, Gambia, Ghana, Guinea, Guinea-Bissau, Liberia, Mali, Mauritania, Niger, Nigeria, Senegal, Sierra Leone, Togo

European Union (EU)

Members: Austria, Belgium, Denmark, Finland, France, Germany, Greece, Ireland, Italy, Luxembourg, Netherlands, Portugal, Spain, Sweden, UK

Group of Seven (G7)

Members: Canada, France, Germany, Italy, Japan, UK, USA

Missile Technology Control Regime (MTCR)

Members: Argentina, Australia, Austria, Belgium, Brazil, Canada, Czech Republic, Denmark, Finland, France, Germany, Greece, Hungary, Iceland, Ireland, Italy, Japan, Luxembourg, Netherlands, New Zealand, Norway, Poland, Portugal, Russia, South Africa, Spain, Sweden, Switzerland, Turkey, UK, Ukraine, USA

Non-Aligned Movement (NAM)

Members: Afghanistan, Algeria, Angola, Bahamas, Bahrain, Bangladesh, Barbados, Belize, Benin, Bhutan, Bolivia, Botswana, Brunei, Burkina Faso, Burundi, Cambodia, Cameroon, Cape Verde, Central African Republic, Chad, Chile, Colombia, Comoros, Congo (Brazzaville), Congo (Democratic Republic of), Côte d'Ivoire, Cuba, Cyprus, Djibouti, Ecuador, Egypt, Equatorial Guinea, Eritrea, Ethiopia, Gabon, Gambia, Ghana, Grenada, Guatemala, Guinea, Guinea-Bissau, Guyana, Honduras, India, Indonesia, Iran, Iraq, Jamaica, Jordan, Kenya, Korea (North), Kuwait, Laos, Lebanon, Lesotho, Liberia, Libya, Madagascar, Malawi, Malaysia, Maldives, Mali, Malta, Mauritania, Mauritius, Mongolia, Morocco, Mozambique, Myanmar (Burma), Namibia, Nepal, Nicaragua, Niger, Nigeria, Oman, Pakistan, Palestine, Panama, Papua New Guinea, Peru, Philippines, Qatar, Rwanda, Saint Lucia, Sao Tome and Principe, Saudi Arabia, Senegal, Seychelles, Sierra Leone, Singapore, Somalia, South Africa, Sri Lanka, Sudan, Suriname, Swaziland, Syria, Tanzania, Thailand, Togo, Trinidad and Tobago, Tunisia, Turkmenistan, Uganda, United Arab Emirates, Uzbekistan, Vanuatu, Venezuela, Viet Nam, Yemen, Yugoslavia,* Zambia, Zimbabwe

* Yugoslavia (Serbia and Montenegro) has not been permitted to participate in NAM activities since 1992.

Nordic Council

Members: Denmark (including the Faroe Islands and Greenland), Finland (including Åland), Iceland, Norway, Sweden

North Atlantic Treaty Organization (NATO)

Members: Belgium, Canada, Czech Republic, Denmark, France,* Germany, Greece, Hungary, Iceland, Italy, Luxembourg, Netherlands, Norway, Poland, Portugal, Spain,* Turkey, UK, USA

* France and Spain are not in the integrated military structures of NATO; in December 1997 the Government of Spain approved Spain's full participation.

Euro-Atlantic Partnership Council (EAPC)

Members: The NATO states plus Albania, Armenia, Austria, Azerbaijan, Belarus, Bulgaria, Estonia, Finland, Georgia, Kazakhstan, Kyrgyzstan, Latvia, Lithuania, Macedonia (Former Yugoslav Republic of), Moldova, Romania, Russia, Slovakia, Slovenia, Sweden, Switzerland, Tajikistan, Turkmenistan, Ukraine, Uzbekistan

Partnership for Peace (PFP)

Partner states: Albania, Armenia, Austria, Azerbaijan, Belarus, Bulgaria, Estonia, Finland, Georgia, Kazakhstan, Kyrgyzstan, Latvia, Lithuania, Macedonia (Former Yugoslav Republic of), Moldova, Romania, Russia, Slovakia, Slovenia, Sweden, Switzerland, Tajikistan, Turkmenistan, Ukraine, Uzbekistan

Nuclear Suppliers Group (NSG)

Members: Argentina, Australia, Austria, Belgium, Brazil, Bulgaria, Canada, Czech Republic, Denmark, Finland, France, Germany, Greece, Hungary, Ireland, Italy, Japan, Korea (South), Latvia, Luxembourg, Netherlands, New Zealand, Norway, Poland, Portugal, Romania, Russia, Slovakia, South Africa, Spain, Sweden, Switzerland, UK, Ukraine, USA

Organisation for Economic Co-operation and Development (OECD)

Members: Australia, Austria, Belgium, Canada, Czech Republic, Denmark, Finland, France, Germany, Greece, Hungary, Iceland, Ireland, Italy, Japan, Korea (South), Luxembourg, Mexico, Netherlands, New Zealand, Norway, Poland, Portugal, Spain, Sweden, Switzerland, Turkey, UK, USA

The European Commission participates in the work of the OECD.

Organization for Security and Co-operation in Europe (OSCE)

Members: Albania, Andorra, Armenia, Austria, Azerbaijan, Belarus, Belgium, Bosnia and Herzegovina, Bulgaria, Canada, Croatia, Cyprus, Czech Republic, Denmark, Estonia, Finland, France, Georgia, Germany, Greece, Holy See, Hungary, Iceland, Ireland, Italy, Kazakhstan, Kyrgyzstan, Latvia, Liechtenstein, Lithuania, Luxembourg, Macedonia (Former Yugoslav Republic of), Malta, Moldova, Monaco, Netherlands, Norway, Poland, Portugal, Romania, Russia, San Marino, Slovakia, Slovenia, Spain, Sweden, Switzerland, Tajikistan, Turkey, Turkmenistan, UK, Ukraine, USA, Uzbekistan, Yugoslavia*

* Yugoslavia (Serbia and Montenegro) has been suspended since 1992.

Members of the Minsk Group in 1998: Armenia, Azerbaijan, Belarus, Finland, France, Germany, Italy, Poland, Russia, Sweden, Turkey, USA

Partners for Co-operation: Algeria, Egypt, Israel, Japan, Jordan, Korea (South), Morocco, Tunisia

Organization of African Unity (OAU)

Members: Algeria, Angola, Benin, Botswana, Burkina Faso, Burundi, Cameroon, Cape Verde, Central African Republic, Chad, Comoros, Congo (Brazzaville), Congo (Democratic Republic of), Côte d'Ivoire, Djibouti, Egypt, Equatorial Guinea, Eritrea, Ethiopia, Gabon, Gambia, Ghana, Guinea, Guinea-Bissau, Kenya, Lesotho, Liberia, Libya, Madagascar, Malawi, Mali, Mauritania, Mauritius, Mozambique, Namibia, Niger, Nigeria, Rwanda, Western Sahara (Saharawi Arab Democratic Republic, SADR*), Sao Tome and Principe, Senegal, Seychelles, Sierra Leone, Somalia, South Africa, Sudan, Swaziland, Tanzania, Togo, Tunisia, Uganda, Zambia, Zimbabwe

* The Western Sahara was admitted in 1982, but its membership was disputed by Morocco and other states. Morocco withdrew from the OAU in 1985.

Organization of American States (OAS)

Members: Antigua and Barbuda, Argentina, Bahamas, Barbados, Belize, Bolivia, Brazil, Canada, Chile, Colombia, Costa Rica, Cuba,* Dominica, Dominican Republic, Ecuador, El Salvador, Grenada, Guatemala, Guyana, Haiti, Honduras, Jamaica, Mexico, Nicaragua, Panama, Paraguay, Peru, Saint Kitts (Christopher) and Nevis, Saint Lucia, Saint Vincent and the Grenadines, Suriname, Trinidad and Tobago, Uruguay, USA, Venezuela

* Cuba has been excluded from participation since 1962.

Permanent observers: Algeria, Angola, Austria, Belgium, Bosnia and Herzegovina, Bulgaria, Croatia, Cyprus, Czech Republic, Egypt, Equatorial Guinea, European Union (EU), Finland, France, Germany, Ghana, Greece, Holy See, Hungary, India, Israel, Italy, Japan, Kazakhstan, Korea (South), Latvia, Lebanon, Morocco, Netherlands, Pakistan, Poland, Portugal, Romania, Russia, Saudi Arabia, Spain, Sri Lanka, Sweden, Switzerland, Thailand, Tunisia, Turkey, UK, Ukraine, Yemen

Organization of the Islamic Conference (OIC)

Members: Afghanistan, Albania, Algeria, Azerbaijan, Bahrain, Bangladesh, Benin, Bosnia and Herzegovina, Brunei, Burkina Faso, Cameroon, Chad, Comoros, Djibouti, Egypt, Gabon, Gambia, Guinea, Guinea-Bissau, Indonesia, Iran, Iraq, Jordan, Kazakhstan, Kuwait, Kyrgyzstan, Lebanon, Libya, Malaysia, Maldives, Mali, Mauritania, Morocco, Mozambique, Niger, Nigeria, Oman, Pakistan, Palestine, Qatar, Saudi Arabia, Senegal, Sierra Leone, Somalia, Sudan, Suriname, Syria, Tajikistan, Tunisia, Turkey, Turkmenistan, Uganda, United Arab Emirates, Uzbekistan, Yemen

Southern African Development Community (SADC)

Members: Angola, Botswana, Congo (Democratic Republic of), Lesotho, Malawi, Mauritius, Mozambique, Namibia, Seychelles, South Africa, Swaziland, Tanzania, Zambia, Zimbabwe

Wassenaar Arrangement (WA)

Members: Argentina, Australia, Austria, Belgium, Bulgaria, Canada, Czech Republic, Denmark, Finland, France, Germany, Greece, Hungary, Ireland, Italy, Japan, Korea (South), Luxembourg, Netherlands, New Zealand, Norway, Poland, Portugal, Romania, Russia, Slovakia, Spain, Sweden, Switzerland, Turkey, UK, Ukraine, USA

Western European Union (WEU)

Members: Belgium, France, Germany, Greece, Italy, Luxembourg, Netherlands, Portugal, Spain, UK

Associate Members: Czech Republic, Hungary, Iceland, Norway, Poland, Turkey

Associate Partners: Bulgaria, Estonia, Latvia, Lithuania, Romania, Slovakia, Slovenia

Observers: Austria, Denmark, Finland, Ireland, Sweden

Members of WEAG and WEAO: Belgium, Denmark, France, Germany, Greece, Italy, Luxembourg, Netherlands, Norway, Portugal, Spain, Turkey, UK

Zangger Committee

Members: Argentina, Australia, Austria, Belgium, Bulgaria, Canada, China, Czech Republic, Denmark, Finland, France, Germany, Greece, Hungary, Ireland, Italy, Japan, Korea (South), Luxembourg, Netherlands, Norway, Poland, Portugal, Romania, Russia, Slovakia, South Africa, Spain, Sweden, Switzerland, UK, USA

Conventions

. .	Data not available or not applicable
–	Nil or a negligible figure
( )	Uncertain data
b.	Billion (thousand million)
km	Kilometre (1000 metres)
kt	Kiloton (1000 tonnes)
m.	Million
Mt	Megaton (1 million tonnes)
th.	Thousand
tr.	Trillion (million million)
$	US dollars, unless otherwise indicated

Introduction
Rethinking the contemporary security system

ADAM DANIEL ROTFELD

Ten years have passed since profound changes began in the international security system. In spite of all the fairly common expectations cherished at the threshold of the 1980s and still in the 1990s, uncertainty and unpredictability remain as the most serious threats to international security.[1] The course of events in 1998 confirmed this. Although there were fewer major armed conflicts than in 1989, world security has not made significant progress since the cold war ended. New concerns are generated by both internal and international factors. On the one hand, some states, unable to provide basic governance and protection for their own populations, have brought about bloody domestic conflicts and thus undermine security in different parts of the world; on the other hand, the proliferation of weapons of mass destruction and the spread of dangerous technologies pose a great potential threat to global stability and security.[2] The nuclear tests carried out by India and Pakistan in May 1998 posed a serious threat to the non-proliferation regime,[3] all the more serious because since their independence and partition India and Pakistan have fought three wars. These events placed on the international agenda the urgent need to rethink some basic axioms about the objectives of nuclear arms control. All this calls for an integrated approach by the international community in its search for a new security system and a new agenda for future arms control and disarmament.

The most formidable challenge to the international security system at the global and regional levels is the fragility and erosion of the states which are not capable of managing developments on their territory. Mass violations of human and minority rights and ethnic cleansing resulting from aggressive nationalism have become a matter of grave concern in different parts of the world. The strength and effectiveness of state institutions and structures are reduced most often in poor countries torn apart by civil wars and centrifugal tendencies. In some situations the availability of small arms contributes to instability or even state collapse.[4]

[1] UN, Annual report of the Secretary-General on the work of the organization 1998, UN document A/53/1, 27 Aug. 1998, para. 1.

[2] Binnendijk, H. and Gompert, D. C., 'Foreword', in *1998 Strategic Assessment: Engaging Power for Peace* (National Defense University, Institute for National Strategic Studies: Washington, DC, 1998), p. vii.

[3] See chapters 9 and 12 in this volume.

[4] According to the UN Secretary-General, 90% of those killed or wounded by light weapons are civilians. UN (note 1), para. 50.

I. Old questions, new problems

Against the background of these and other adverse developments, and especially of the evolution of the situation in the Balkans and NATO's military intervention in Yugoslavia, some questions that seemed to be forgotten or irrelevant are returning to the political agenda. One is: Is major war obsolete? This question has touched off a serious debate.[5]

It is not a new question. A hundred years ago, Jan Bloch argued that war had become impossible from the military, economic and political points of view. He considered war to be an 'impracticable operation' which would inevitably result in catastrophe.[6] His book inspired the Russian Tsar and the Queen of the Netherlands to convene the international Peace Conferences at the Hague in 1899 and 1907. His reasoning, which turned out to be prophetic in the light of the course and outcome of World War I, led statesmen to realize that war was an anachronistic way of settling conflicts between states since the costs were higher than the potential benefits of victory. Bloch is acknowledged as a classic writer. His view, after two world wars, is still noteworthy.

Mandelbaum argues that a major war is unlikely but not unthinkable: 'it is obsolete in the sense that it is no longer in fashion'. In fact, his definition of 'major war' describes what is known as total war: 'a war fought by the most powerful members of the international system, drawing on all their resources and using every weapon at their command, over a period of years, leading to an outcome with revolutionary geopolitical consequences including the birth and death of regimes, the redrawing of borders and the reordering of the hierarchy of sovereign states'.[7] The majority of present-day wars recorded in the SIPRI Yearbook are not major wars according to this definition.

What is more important, NATO's intervention in Yugoslavia illustrates that future wars, even if waged on a mass scale, will not, for many reasons, be like the wars of the past. However, definitions of 'major', 'obsolete' or 'fashionable' apart,[8] every war spreads destruction and death.

[5] Mandelbaum, M., 'Is major war obsolete?', *Survival*, vol. 40, no. 4 (winter 1998/99), pp. 20–38. In reply to Mandelbaum's article, 3 comments were published under the rubric 'Is major war obsolete? An exchange': Kagan, D., 'History is full of surprises'; Cohen, E. A., 'The "major" consequences of war'; and Doran, C. F., 'The structural turbulence of international affairs', *Survival*, vol. 41, no. 2 (summer 1999). Mandelbaum responded in 'Learning to be warless', *Survival*, vol. 41, no. 2 (summer 1999), pp. 139–52.

[6] 'The dimensions of modern armaments and the organization of society have rendered its prosecution an economic impossibility.' Bloch, I. S., *Is War Now Impossible?* An abridgement of *The War in the Future in Its Technical, Economic and Political Relations* (Grant Richards: London and Boston, 1899; reprinted by Gregg Revivals with the Department of War Studies, King's College, London: Aldershot, 1991), p. xi. First published in Poland as *Przyszla wojna pod wzgledem technicznym, politycznym i ekonomicznym* (Warsaw, 1899–1900), 6 vols.

[7] Mandelbaum (note 5), p. 20.

[8] One of Mandelbaum's opponents argues that we must face 'the real possibility that major war may yet again come into fashion'. Kagan (note 5), p. 142. A second argues that wars can still occur 'that affect the lives of millions of people, that can inflict many casualties, and that can change regional politics without fitting Mandelbaum's unusual definition of the word "major"'. Cohen (note 5), p. 144. A third argues that the probability of a major war 'declines for some states, but increases for others'. Doran (note 5), p. 148.

International military interventions: legal, illegal and non-legal

Vexing and troublesome questions keep recurring. Who has the right to intervene militarily on behalf of the international community in defence of a law that has been broken, and in what circumstances? What is the relationship between states' commitments to respect human rights and the rights of minorities, on the one hand, and the principles of sovereignty and non-intervention in internal affairs, on the other? The answer is unambiguous: the international community cannot tolerate mass violations of the rights of human beings and groups. It remains an open question, however, who should be entitled or authorized to decide how states may be coerced into respecting the rights that are being violated, including the rights of their own citizens.

The sovereign equality and integrity of states remain the main foundation of international law. This does not mean that sovereignty is absolute. In exercising their sovereign rights towards their own citizens within their respective territories, states are limited by commitments they have adopted under international law. These include the principles and norms of the 1948 Universal Declaration of Human Rights and the two 1966 International Covenants—on Civil and Political Rights and on Economic, Social and Cultural Rights.[9] These three instruments, along with the UN Charter and many other treaties, conventions and agreements, constitute the indisputable pillars of the existing international system. On this basis, states undertake to recognize the inherent dignity and the equal and inalienable rights of all members of the human family as 'the foundation of freedom, justice and peace in the world'.[10]

The provisions of these documents and their implementation under national law mean that a significant limitation has been introduced on sovereignty and the principle of non-intervention in internal affairs. As a rule states today do not question that the obligation to respect human rights and the rights of minorities is an integral part of international law. The agreement in 1998 to establish a permanent International Criminal Court in The Hague is a significant step on the road to creating an international system based on universal human rights and the rule of law.[11] However, coercion or the enforcement of law in international relations is different from enforcing respect for the law domestically. This is a particularly complex matter when it comes to violations of international law by the constitutional authorities of a sovereign state. Coercive measures taken by the international community should also be proportional to the crime and 'not additionally increase the suffering of victims'.[12]

[9] US Congress, House of Representatives, Committee on Foreign Affairs, *Human Rights Documents: Compilation of Documents Pertaining to Human Rights* Committee Print (US Government Printing Office: Washington, DC, Sep. 1983), pp. 69–99.

[10] Preamble of the 1948 Universal Declaration of Human Rights. *Human Rights Documents: Compilation of Documents Pertaining to Human Rights* (note 9), p. 63.

[11] The Statute of the Court, approved at a UN Diplomatic Conference of 160 countries and 200 NGOs in Rome on 17 July 1998. On the International Criminal Court, see chapter 2, section II in this volume.

[12] Symonides, J., 'New human rights dimensions, obstacles and challenges: introductory remarks', ed. J. Symonides, *Human Rights: New Dimensions and Challenges* (UNESCO/Ashgate: Aldershot, 1998), p. 37.

Major disagreements exist as to who can apply coercion and under what conditions it can be applied to a state which has violated human rights on a mass scale, used ethnic cleansing as official state policy or had recourse to genocide vis-à-vis its own population.

The decision to stand up to such behaviour cannot be an arbitrary decision by one or more states. It should be taken in accordance with agreed procedures and norms. No state in the international system has the monopoly on enforcing international law. According to the UN Charter (Articles 41 and 42), only the Security Council may decide what measures are to be employed. If it considers that measures that do not involve the use of armed force would be inadequate or have proved to be inadequate to restore peace and security, it may decide to take military action. However, because of the requirement of unanimity among the five permanent members (P5) of the Security Council when such a decision is adopted, the Security Council's ability to act effectively may be hamstrung by one of the P5. Moreover, their motives in disagreeing over military action may differ. They are often guided more by their national interests than by the need to restore peace or defend international law.

In effect, a situation has evolved in which the United Nations is almost helpless. In his statement to the 55th session of the UN Commission on Human Rights, Secretary-General Annan noted: 'When civilians are attacked and massacred because of their ethnicity, as in Kosovo, the world looks to the United Nations to speak up for them'. Consequently, he raised the question: 'Will we say that rights are relative, or that whatever happens within borders shall be of concern to an organizations of sovereign States? No one that I know of can today defend that position. Collectively, we should say no. We will not, and we cannot accept a situation where people are brutalized behind national boundaries'.[13] The time is ripe for a new and just world order which not only embraces declarations of respect for human and minority rights but also defines procedures and mechanisms for the restoration of rights that have been violated.

Military interventions must be mandated and legitimized by broad acceptance of the international community of states ('a critical mass of nations').[14] It has been said that 'If power is used to do justice, law will follow'.[15]

In sum, the international security system that is taking shape today includes legal actions in accordance with binding treaties, UN Security Council decisions and customary law, and actions and means which are morally justified and not illegal but are not yet legally regulated (non-legal ones). There are lacunae in contemporary international law where the regulation of humanitarian intervention is concerned.

The debate on the establishment of a new and just international order has been aimed more at streamlining the existing institutions and creating new

[13] 'Secretary-General calls for renewed commitment in new century to protect rights of man, woman, child—regardless of ethnic, national belonging', UN Press release SG/SM/6949, 7 Apr. 1999.

[14] Glennon, M. J., 'The new interventionism: the search for a just international law', *Foreign Affairs*, vol. 78 (May/June 1999), p. 7.

[15] Glennon (note 14).

ones than at putting into effect the existing norms and principles. It has hitherto concerned particularly the regional and subregional security organizations and structures in Europe.

II. A cooperative security order

In the search for a new security system, fundamental change is observable in three new phenomena: (*a*) globalization and new transnational networks prove that power and wealth are no longer determined by territorial authority; (*b*) human rights, the protection of minorities and the rule of law are not called into question as the common values of the contemporary world order; and (*c*) political leaders are held to be individually responsible under international criminal law. All these are important elements of new world governance, a part of which is the international security system. The norms of this system cannot, however, be imposed unilaterally by any power or alliance without the approval of the international community within the UN system.

A future security regime should be based on the concept of common, comprehensive and cooperative security. These adjectives are perhaps to be understood as criteria which the new security system should meet rather than as its guiding principles. A new order will have to take account of the new reality. Three years ago the Report of the Independent Working Group established by SIPRI identified four principal categories of risk: (*a*) a resurfacing of ethnic and religious conflicts in situations where democratic institutions are lacking and there are no institutions of self-government capable of accommodating the new problems of ethnic, national, religious and language groups; (*b*) political instabilities associated with the transformation of a totalitarian, one-party system to a pluralistic democracy based on the rule of law; (*c*) social tensions stemming from the transformation of centrally planned economies to market economies; and (*d*) environmental hazards.[16]

The report recommended that to the decalogue of the 1975 Helsinki Final Act be added a commitment to democracy in connection with security and the right to what might be called 'cooperative intervention' under the authority of the UN Security Council. The relationship between the existing principles of sovereignty and non-intervention should be reinterpreted or redefined in the light of a new principle—that of international *solidarity*. There is also an urgent need to redefine the relationship between the principle of state integrity and the right to self-determination (which is not to be identified with the right to secession or independent statehood).

In short, a new security regime should be based on shared values and the rule of law. 'The risks posed by a universal system that provides no escape from lawfully centralized coercion remain greater than the risks of a system that lacks coercive enforcement mechanisms.'[17]

[16] A Future Security Agenda for Europe: The Report of the Independent Working Group established by the Stockholm International Peace Research Institute (SIPRI), SIPRI, Stockholm, Oct. 1996.

[17] Glennon (note 14), p. 5.

III. Strategic perspectives

Five features characterize the international security environment which has taken shape in recent years.

First, it is marked by instability, of which the main source is the number of weak or failed states and their governments' quite frequent lack of democratic legitimacy. Although states remain the main subjects of the international system, the legitimacy of some is called into question. This becomes a source of uncertainty and, consequently, unpredictability.[18] Crises and conflicts in the contemporary world are predominantly an outcome of the weakness of states. It is clear that some governments are unable to control the territory which is under their sovereignty. This weakness combined with undemocratic governance results in the internationalization of crises which, as a rule, are in their origin of a local or domestic character.

Second, the trends of globalization and internationalization, mainly in the economic and information technology sphere, are in conflict with those of fragmentation and regionalization in the political and civilizational dimensions.

A third key element in the strategic perspective is the new role of the United States, both globally and regionally. It holds a position of power unequalled by any other country by virtue of its economic and technological potential, its military might and the associated political ability to shape the international security system. This makes it difficult for it to withstand the temptation to conduct security policy on a hegemonic basis, often called a 'unipolar world' policy.[19] Its alternative is partnership with other states.

A fourth factor is weapons of mass destruction (WMD).[20] For the members of the Atlantic Alliance the fundamental purpose of their nuclear forces is political.[21] For India and Pakistan their purpose is different. The two countries remain in conflict over Kashmir. Continued or suspected cases of nuclear, biological and chemical (NBC) weapon proliferation by Iraq, North Korea and Libya raise the question how best to prevent the spread of WMD, the materials for producing them and their means of delivery.[22] Regional non-proliferation efforts are of special significance in three regions: the Korean peninsula, the Middle East and South-East Asia. The US Cooperative Threat Reduction programme (the Nunn–Lugar programme) has helped Belarus, Kazakhstan and Ukraine to become non-nuclear weapon states. It also helps

[18] Delman, R., *The Rosy Future of War* (The Free Press: New York and London, 1995), pp. 124–25.

[19] 'We will continue to exercise our leadership in the world in a manner that reflects our national values and protects the security of this great nation.' 'A national security strategy for a new century', The White House, Washington, Oct. 1998, p. 59.

[20] 'The existence of powerful nuclear forces outside the Alliance and the proliferation of NBC weapons and their means of delivery remain a matter of serious concern' states the basic document adopted by the NATO Washington summit meeting. *The Alliance's Strategic Concept*, Washington, 23–24 Apr. 1999, paras 21–22.

[21] *The Alliance's Strategic Concept* (note 20), para. 62.

[22] 'A national security strategy for a new century' (note 19), p. 11.

Russia in meeting its obligations under the START I treaty[23] but sizeable quantities of fissile materials in Russia remain unprotected. The profound economic crisis in Russia as well as the decisions taken recently by President Boris Yeltsin to increase the readiness of the Russian strategic nuclear forces[24] may undermine some of the progress already made.

The relative diminution of the significance of nuclear weapons, paradoxically, poses a danger and generates pressure on the highly industrialized countries to begin a process of qualitative conventional rearmament. If that happens, some of the nuclear weapon powers might feel forced to increase rather than reduce their reliance on nuclear defence.[25] One signal of the risk of such a situation developing is the effort to streamline and modernize anti-ballistic missile (ABM) defence systems. Not only would the 1972 ABM Treaty be undermined; the global situation would be destabilized if only one nuclear superpower were capable of ensuring strategic immunity for itself.[26]

The fifth issue that raises special concern is small arms. It is true that for the peaceful resolution of crises democratic institutions, the rule of law and the socio-economic condition of a country are decisive.[27] However, in the search for security for conflict-prone regions, especially in those where state structures are fragile, steps need to be taken 'to curb the flow of small arms circulating in civil society'.[28]

IV. SIPRI findings

The authors of this edition of the SIPRI Yearbook present original data, facts and analyses of developments in 1998 in security and conflicts; military spending and armaments; and non-proliferation, arms control and disarmament.

Conflicts.[29] In 1998 there were 27 major armed conflicts in 26 locations throughout the world. All but two—those between India and Pakistan and between Eritrea and Ethiopia—were internal. The increases in the numbers of conflicts and of conflict locations are accounted for by those on the African continent.

Conflict prevention, management and resolution.[30] There were several major successes in armed conflict prevention, management and resolution in 1998.

[23] The 1991 US–Russian Treaty on the Reduction and Limitation of Strategic Offensive Arms.

[24] For the revision of the Russian nuclear strategy, see *Izvestiya*, 27 Apr. 1999, p. 1. See also 'Report on cooperative approaches to halt Russian nuclear proliferation and improve openness of nuclear disarmament', Congressional Budget Office Memorandum, CBO: Washington, DC, May 1999.

[25] The 5 recognized nuclear weapon powers still possess some 36 000 nuclear warheads. *Disarmament Forum* (UN Institute for Disarmament Research, Geneva), no. 1 (1999), p. 3.

[26] 'Meanwhile, many countries continue to develop long-range missiles, which may well rekindle a new global arms race in ballistic missile defence systems, not to mention additional missile proliferation. If we factor in the element of new technologies, the dynamics of these various arms races could well evolve into extraterrestrial dimensions, resulting in the weaponization of outer space'. See note 25.

[27] Harris, P. and Reilly, B., *Democracy and Deep-Rooted Conflict: Options and Negotiations* (International Institute for Democracy and Electoral Assistance (IDEA): Stockholm, 1998).

[28] UN (note 1), para. 50.

[29] See chapter 1 in this volume.

[30] See chapter 2 in this volume.

Attempts by the UN and regional organizations to support peace settlements or processes were notably successful in the Central African Republic, Eastern Slavonia and Guatemala; precarious in Bosnia and Herzegovina, Georgia, Sierra Leone and Tajikistan; and ineffective in Angola. Armed conflict subsided with regionally monitored agreements in Guinea-Bissau and Kosovo, was stalemated in an uneasy truce between Ethiopia and Eritrea, and escalated into regional war in the Democratic Republic of Congo. Fighting continued or was resumed in a number of other countries. The largest peace enforcement/peacekeeping mission was the NATO-led Stabilization Force (SFOR) in Bosnia and Herzegovina—at 33 000 troops twice as large as all UN operations put together.

Northern Ireland.[31] Since 1969 over 3250 people have died in politically motivated attacks in Northern Ireland. The Good Friday Agreement of April 1998 was overwhelmingly approved in simultaneous referendums in the Republic of Ireland and Northern Ireland. It created a framework in which a political settlement to the conflict could be found, but did not in itself resolve the underlying issues.

The Middle East.[32] Many issues that confronted the Middle East in 1998 remained as 1999 began. These included: the position of a new Israeli Government on resumption of the peace process with both the Palestinians and Syria; the possible Palestinian declaration of statehood, and the response of Israel and the rest of the world to such an announcement; the continuing bloodshed in Algeria; the stability of President Mohammad Khatami's Government and his quest to liberalize Iran; and the situation in Iraq. Any one of these issues would be a serious challenge to peace and stability in most regions. The Middle East must deal with them all at the same time.

Russia.[33] The drive for military reform in the Russian Federation has been led by economic pressures and the need for savings on operations and for modernization of the armed forces rather than by changes in Russia's threat assessments. With the continuing shrinking of the Russian economy and after the financial crisis of August 1998 it is unlikely that Russia will now meet its target for reduction in troop numbers to 1.2 million by 1999 or achieve the change to all-professional forces.

The Caspian Sea region.[34] The regional security situation has been strongly influenced by growing competition among regional and extra-regional countries over the vast oil and gas reserves believed to be in the Caspian Sea Basin. Among major obstacles to the use of those resources are the dispute over the existing Caspian Sea legal regime and the different approaches to it of the littoral states (Azerbaijan, Iran, Kazakhstan, Russia and Turkmenistan) and the problem of the transport of oil and gas to outside consumers. The security of oil and gas transport routes passing across or close to zones of local conflict

[31] See appendix 2B in this volume.
[32] See chapter 3 in this volume.
[33] See chapter 4 in this volume.
[34] See chapter 5 in this volume.

(in Abkhazia, Chechnya and Nagorno-Karabakh) has become increasingly linked to the resolution of these conflicts.

Europe.[35] The process of adapting the European security organizations to the post-cold war environment made further progress in 1998: the Czech Republic, Hungary and Poland joined NATO; formal negotiations were opened with six candidates for membership of the European Union (EU); and the Organization for Security and Co-operation in Europe (OSCE) underwent further evolution as the primary instrument of conflict prevention, crisis management and post-conflict rehabilitation. The European security debate focused to a great extent on the future missions and mandates of the major security institutions—NATO, the EU, the Western European Union (WEU) and the OSCE—and their interrelationships as well as on the role of the great powers within these organizations. The December 1998 British–French Joint Declaration on European Defence, the Saint-Malo initiative, presented some 'fresh thinking' on and mapped out the future direction of common European defence within the EU.

Military expenditure.[36] In 1998 world military expenditure amounted to roughly $745 billion—$125 per capita and 2.6 per cent of world gross national product (GNP) on average. The downward trend initiated after the end of the cold war continued in 1998 (after a slight increase in 1997) but this was due almost entirely to sharp cuts in Russian military expenditure and a reduction in US military spending. Actual military expenditure of the Russian Federation fell by 55 per cent in real terms in 1998, in sharp contrast to the 9 per cent increase planned, although this was due to economic difficulties rather than government priorities. US military expenditure dropped by 4 per cent in 1998 according to NATO data. The US defence plan for the next five years foresees a change into growth in the budget for fiscal year 2000/01.

China's military expenditure.[37] Chinese military expenditure is estimated to be roughly 75 per cent higher than the official defence budget—156 billion yuan for 1998, or 1.9 per cent of gross domestic product (GDP) rather than the official figure of 1.1 per cent.

Arms production.[38] The general decline in arms production worldwide has ceased. The top 100 arms-producing companies had combined arms sales of $156 billion in 1997 and accounted for roughly 75 per cent of total world arms production. Russian arms production in 1997 was 10 per cent of what it had been in 1991, but during 1998 grew by 5 per cent in real terms. For the first time, the SIPRI Yearbook gives an estimate of the total value of world arms production—$200 billion (± $5 billion) in 1996.

Arms transfers.[39] The SIPRI trend-indicator value for major conventional arms transfers in 1998 was $21.9 billion in constant 1990 prices. That was not much higher than the level in 1994 ($20 billion—the lowest since 1970). The

[35] See chapter 6 in this volume.
[36] See chapter 7 in this volume.
[37] See appendix 7D in this volume.
[38] See chapter 10 in this volume.
[39] See chapter 11 in this volume.

global reduction in 1998 was not primarily an effect of the financial crisis in Asia in 1997 but the result of procurement decisions made several years before.

The adoption by the EU member states of a Code of Conduct for Arms Exports in 1998 constitutes an important step in a difficult political process towards the creation of common arms export regulations.

Light weapons.[40] The success of the campaign to ban anti-personnel landmines gave some encouragement to the non-governmental organizations, international bodies and some national governments that were seeking improved control of light weapons, but the progress achieved was limited. Cooperation developed at a practical level in southern Africa.

Research and development.[41] Events in 1998 pointed up more starkly than before the central issues of military technology in the post-cold war era. For the industrialized states on close terms with the USA, the issue is whether to compete with or complement US technological advantages. Further, these states must decide how much they are willing to invest in equipping themselves to use military force for missions other than homeland defence.

Nuclear tests by India and Pakistan.[42] While the 1998 nuclear tests focused international attention on the problems of war and nuclear risk in South Asia, they may be more a reminder or warning of related problems than a cause of instability in themselves. The greatest risk of nuclear war in South Asia arises from Pakistan's long-standing strategy of using the threat of early first use of nuclear weapons to deter conventional war. As long as Indian military planners believe that their own nuclear capability will deter Pakistani first use, and therefore leaves them the option of launching a punitive conventional war, the risk of nuclear escalation not only is real but also stems directly from the perfectly logical designs of the states involved. No clear decision to expand its nuclear capabilities has yet been made by either government.

Nuclear arms control.[43] The nuclear tests carried out by India and Pakistan did not encourage other states to promptly follow suit; however, they highlighted weaknesses in the nuclear non-proliferation regime, in particular its lack of universal adherence and legitimacy. Together with renewed suspicions about secret North Korean and Iraqi nuclear weapon programmes, the tests contributed to a growing sense that the nuclear non-proliferation regime was under siege by an unprecedented series of challenges.

It was a largely disappointing year for nuclear arms control efforts. The 1996 Comprehensive Nuclear Test-Ban Treaty (CTBT) did not enter into force. Negotiations in the Conference on Disarmament on a global ban on the production of fissile material for nuclear explosives did not start and the START II Treaty[44] remained stalled in the Russian Duma, thereby blocking progress towards deeper reductions in the still sizeable US and Russian

[40] See appendix 11E in this volume.
[41] See chapter 8 in this volume.
[42] See chapter 9 in this volume.
[43] See chapter 12 in this volume.
[44] The 1993 US–Russian Treaty on Further Reduction and Limitation of Strategic Offensive Arms.

nuclear arsenals within the framework of a START III accord. In addition, the controversy over a US national ballistic missile defence system and the future of the ABM Treaty jeopardized support for deeper cuts in the US strategic nuclear forces and threatened to reverse the progress made in recent years in reducing those forces.

Chemical and biological arms control.[45] There is definite progress in the development of strong disarmament regimes for chemical and biological weapons (CBW). At the end of 1998, there were 121 states parties and 48 signatories to the 1993 Chemical Weapons Convention (CWC). Moreover, 90 states parties submitted their initial declarations to the Organisation for the Prohibition of Chemical Weapons (OPCW). A total of 384 inspections in 28 countries were carried out by OPCW inspectors. Progress in adding a verification protocol to the 1972 Biological and Toxin Weapons Convention (BTWC) has been limited, but successes in implementing the CWC should help increase faith in the goal of universal disarmament in the area of biological weapons (BW) as well.

The United Nations Special Commission on Iraq (UNSCOM) experienced serious setbacks during 1998, culminating in the air strikes on Iraq by the UK and the USA. UNSCOM's inability to declare Iraq free from non-conventional weapons meant that sanctions against Iraq would continue, despite the opposition of China, France and Russia to such measures.

Biotechnology and genetic engineering.[46] Concern about the proliferation and possible use of BW increased in the 1990s. Both national and international medical associations have warned that future scientific and technological advances could be misused. The BTWC does not restrain beneficial research designed to achieve medical advances.

Conventional arms control.[47] Talks on the adaptation of the 1990 Treaty on Conventional Armed Forces in Europe (the CFE Treaty) were still deadlocked in 1998. Only in early 1999 was headway made. A new deadline for both the latter and confidence- and security-building measures (CSBMs) was set for the OSCE summit meeting in Istanbul in November 1999. The entry into force of the 1992 Open Skies Treaty remained stalemated.

On the regional level within Europe the successful implementation of the 1996 Agreement on Sub-Regional Arms Control (the Florence Agreement) contrasted with the lack of progress in other fields. Efforts to get talks under way on a regional military balance for the Balkans resulted in an agreement on the mandate for negotiations on regional stabilization, but because of the conflict in Kosovo no negotiations are in sight.

CSBMs in Europe.[48] Adaptations suggested during 1998 for the 1994 Vienna Document on CSBMs aim to enhance transparency, predictability and cooperation and emphasize deeper security cooperation suited to regional differences. Compliance was reported with the 1996 Agreement on CSBMs in

[45] See chapter 13 in this volume.
[46] See appendix 13A in this volume.
[47] See chapter 14 in this volume.
[48] See appendix 14A in this volume.

Bosnia and Herzegovina, in contrast to the mixed record of implementation of the civilian provisions of the 1995 General Framework Agreement for Peace in Bosnia and Herzegovina (the Dayton Agreement).

Landmines.[49] Progress towards a total ban on landmines was made in 1998. Although none of its major opponents had signed the 1997 Convention on the Prohibition of the Use, Stockpiling, Production and Transfer of Anti-Personnel Mines and on their Destruction (the APM Convention), with the required 40 ratifications achieved in September the convention entered into force on 1 March 1999. The Landmine Monitor got off to a promising start with the aim of reporting on all activities related to the implementation of a total ban.

Non-cooperative responses to proliferation.[50] In spite of efforts to achieve NBC disarmament through cooperation leading to verifiable legal commitments by governments to disarm, events in 1998 underlined that no comprehensive arms control and disarmament agenda has been achieved. Actual or suspected cases of NBC weapon proliferation continued. Possible responses include the threat or use of force, sanctions or technology denial. In 1998 there were cases of the threat and actual use of force along with sanctions in response to breaches of its disarmament commitments by Iraq.

The international community's response to the nuclear tests by India and Pakistan was largely based on a combination of diplomacy (increased efforts to persuade them to join the CTBT) and narrowly focused export controls (introducing technical barriers and raising the costs to them of nuclear weapon development).

V. Conclusions

The events, arrangements and processes discussed in this volume permit the following conclusions.

First, the existing international security frameworks, institutions and structures are not effective in eliminating new risks or meeting challenges.

Second, a new cooperative security system should in equal measure take into account the specific features of states and regions and the needs of the global community as a whole. It should help the new states in transition to build democratic institutions, promote the rule of law, develop respect for human rights and the protection of minorities, and prevent the proliferation of weapons of mass destruction and the growth of conventional armaments.

Third, the transformation and adaptation of the international security system and its institutions to new tasks calls not only for a change of procedures and mechanisms, but also for a bold embracing of new principles and norms adequate to the new needs and requirements.

[49] See appendix 14B in this volume.
[50] See chapter 15 in this volume.

Part I. Security and conflicts, 1998

1. Major armed conflicts

MARGARETA SOLLENBERG, PETER WALLENSTEEN and ANDRÉS JATO

I. Global patterns of major armed conflicts, 1989–98

In 1998 there were 27 major armed conflicts in 26 locations throughout the world. Both the number of major armed conflicts and the number of conflict locations were higher than the previous year (in 1997 there were 25 major armed conflicts in 24 locations). However, both figures for 1998 are lower than those for 1989, the first year of the period covered in the conflict statistics. The rise in the number of conflicts and locations in 1998 is accounted for by the conflicts on the continent of Africa. The conflicts and locations for 1998 are presented in the table in appendix 1A.

A 'major armed conflict' is defined as prolonged use of armed force between the military forces of two or more governments,[1] or of one government and at least one organized armed group, incurring the battle-related deaths of at least 1000 people during the entire conflict and in which the incompatibility concerns government and/or territory.[2] A conflict 'location' is the territory of at least one state. Since certain countries are the location of more than one conflict, the number of conflicts reported is greater than the number of conflict locations.[3] A major armed conflict is removed from the table when the contested incompatibility has been resolved and/or when there is no recorded use of force related to the incompatibility between the parties during the year. The same conflict may reappear in the table for subsequent years if there is any renewed use of armed force between the same parties. In cases where one of the parties to a conflict splits into new factions, these groups constitute new parties to a new conflict.[4]

All but two of the conflicts in 1998 were internal, that is, the issue concerned control over the government or territory of one state. The two interstate conflicts in 1998 were those between India and Pakistan and between Eritrea and Ethiopia. The conflict between India and Pakistan over Kashmir continued from previous years and intensified during the summer of 1998. Bilateral talks resumed in July, after having been cancelled in May after the Indian and Pak-

[1] The government of a state is that party which is generally regarded as being in central control even by those organizations seeking to assume power. If this criterion is not applicable, the government is the party which controls the capital. In most cases the 2 criteria coincide.

[2] See appendix 1A for definitions of the criteria. See also Heldt, B. (ed.), *States in Armed Conflict 1990–91* (Department of Peace and Conflict Research, Uppsala University: Uppsala, 1992), chapter 3, for the full definitions.

[3] Some countries may also be the location of minor armed conflicts. The table in appendix 1A presents only the major armed conflicts in the countries listed.

[4] E.g., in 1998 this occurred in the Northern Ireland conflict with the formation of the Real IRA.

istani nuclear tests were conducted, but little progress was made on the Kashmir issue.[5] The fighting between Eritrea and Ethiopia started in May over their common border, which has been contested since Eritrea gained independence in 1993 (see section IV).

In at least six of the conflicts the intensity of the fighting in 1998 increased to a higher level than in the previous year. Thirteen of the major armed conflicts in 1998 incurred at least 1000 deaths during the year—Afghanistan, Algeria, Angola, Burundi, Colombia, the Democratic Republic of Congo, Eritrea–Ethiopia, Guinea-Bissau, Rwanda, Sierra Leone, Sri Lanka, Sudan and Yugoslavia (Serbia and Montenegro). Five of these were also recorded for 1997 as incurring over 1000 deaths during the year—Afghanistan, Algeria, Sri Lanka, Sudan and Zaire (now the Democratic Republic of Congo).

In addition to the 27 major armed conflicts, many international crises led to the brink of armed conflict or to armed action across borders in 1998.[6]

Other states contributed regular troops in three of the conflicts: Angola, Chad, Namibia, Rwanda, Uganda and Zimbabwe in the Democratic Republic of Congo (formerly Zaire); Guinea and Senegal in Guinea-Bissau; and ECOMOG (the Economic Community of West African States [ECOWAS] Monitoring Group) forces comprising mainly troops from Ghana and Nigeria in Sierra Leone.[7]

Section II of this chapter examines the conflict developments in 1998 and section III the regional patterns over the past 10 years. The most dramatic conflict developments in 1998 occurred in Africa, discussed in section IV. Appendix 1A presents the conflict data for 1998. Appendices 1B–D present full accounts of developments in the conflicts in Kashmir, Kosovo and Tajikistan, respectively.

II. Changes in the table of conflicts for 1998

New conflicts

There were six new conflicts in 1998: one in Europe and five on the African continent.

In *Yugoslavia (Serbia and Montenegro)*, the ethnic Albanian Kosovo Liberation Army (KLA, or Ushtria Clirimtare e Kosoves, UCK) had announced its campaign for the independence of Kosovo in November 1997. Fighting with Serbian forces began in earnest in February 1998.[8]

Angola reappeared in the table of conflicts because the 1994 Lusaka Protocol broke down at the end of 1998. Since 1994 there had been sporadic ceasefire breaches which escalated dramatically in 1998, finally resulting in both parties abandoning the peace accord. Events in the neighbouring Democratic

[5] See appendix 1B in this volume.
[6] Some of these crises are discussed in other chapters in this volume.
[7] When an intra-state conflict involves forces from other states on the side of either of the internal parties, it is treated in this chapter as an intra-state conflict.
[8] See appendix 1C and chapter 2 in this volume.

Republic of Congo, where both Angola and the National Union for the Total Independence of Angola (UNITA) had intervened on opposite sides in this internal conflict, exacerbated the tension and violence. The border war between *Ethiopia and Eritrea* and the army rebellion in *Guinea-Bissau* are discussed in section IV. The conflict in *the Democratic Republic of Congo* is registered as a new conflict because of the new party constellations formed in 1998. In *Rwanda*, violence had continued after the victory of the Rwandan Patriotic Forces (RPF) in the armed conflict of 1990–94. Forces from the ousted government, the former Rwandan Armed Forces and Hutu Interahamwé militias which had been active in the Rwandan genocide launched attacks on the present government as well as the civilian population.

Conflicts recorded in 1997 that were not recorded for 1998

Three conflicts recorded in 1997 do not appear in the table for 1998.

In *Northern Ireland* a peace agreement involving all the major parties was signed on 10 April 1998.[9] However, implementation of the agreement ran into other obstacles during the year, mainly concerning the disarming of the Provisional Irish Republican Army (Provisional IRA) and the Omagh bomb attack on 15 August.[10]

A peace agreement for the Chittagong Hill Tracts in *Bangladesh* was signed on 2 December 1997. Implementation of the agreement began in February 1998, when the Shanti Bahini began to disarm. However, the peace agreement gave rise to internal political crisis and riots. The opposition in Dhaka rallied against the government for having signed the agreement and argued that the granting of autonomy to the Chittagong Hill Tracts was an act of betrayal against the state.

The armed conflict in *Congo (Brazzaville)*, which was fought between the forces of then President Pascal Lissouba and the forces of Denis Sassou-Nguesso with support from Angola, ended in the overthrow of Lissouba in October 1997 and Sassou-Nguesso declaring himself president. Violence erupted again in 1998 between Lissouba's militiamen and the army of the present government supported by Angola, but it is not clear whether this fighting was politically motivated.

III. Regional patterns of major armed conflicts, 1989–98

The regional distribution of major armed conflicts and conflict locations over the period 1989–98 is shown in tables 1.1 and 1.2.

As table 1.1 shows, the number of major armed conflicts in *Europe* has declined since the peak in 1993. Since Northern Ireland was not recorded as a

[9] See appendix 2B in this volume.

[10] Since the Real IRA, a breakaway group from the Provisional IRA which claimed responsibility for the bombing, was not previously recorded as a party to this conflict, these deaths are not included in the total number of deaths. Since no battle-related deaths were incurred in the conflict between the British Government and the Provisional IRA, the armed conflict in Northern Ireland is not included in the table.

Table 1.1. Regional distribution of locations with at least one major armed conflict, 1989–98[a]

Region[b]	1989	1990	1991	1992	1993	1994	1995	1996	1997	1998
Africa	9	10	10	7	7	6	6	5	8	11
Asia	11	10	8	11	9	9	9	10	9	8
Central and South America	5	5	4	3	3	3	3	3	2	2
Europe	1	1	2	4	5	4	3	2	1	1
Middle East	5	5	5	4	4	5	4	4	4	4
Total	**31**	**31**	**29**	**29**	**28**	**27**	**25**	**24**	**24**	**26**

Table 1.2. Regional distribution, number and types of major armed conflicts, 1989–98[a,b]

	1989		1990		1991		1992		1993		1994		1995		1996		1997		1998	
Region[a]	G	T	G	T	G	T	G	T	G	T	G	T	G	T	G	T	G	T	G	T
Africa	7	3	8	3	8	3	6	1	6	1	5	1	5	1	4	1	7	1	9	2
Asia	6	8	5	10	3	8	5	9	4	7	4	7	4	8	4	7	3	7	3	6
Central and South America	5	–	5	–	4	–	3	–	3	–	3	–	3	–	3	–	2	–	2	–
Europe	–	1	–	1	–	2	–	4	–	6	–	5	–	3	–	2	–	1	–	1
Middle East	1	4	1	4	2	5	2	3	2	4	2	4	2	4	2	4	2	2	2	2
Total	**19**	**16**	**19**	**18**	**17**	**18**	**16**	**17**	**15**	**18**	**14**	**17**	**14**	**16**	**13**	**14**	**14**	**11**	**16**	**11**
Total	**35**		**37**		**35**		**33**		**33**		**31**		**30**		**27**		**25**		**27**	

G = Government and T = Territory, the two types of incompatibility.

[a] The total annual number of conflicts does not necessarily correspond to the number of conflict locations in table 1.1 or table 1A, appendix 1A, since there may be more than 1 major armed conflict in each location. Note that the figure for Europe for 1989 in both tables has been revised (see *SIPRI Yearbook 1998,* p. 20, where 2 conflicts are recorded for Europe): after closer examination of the armed conflict in Romania, the number of deaths was revised to below 1000.

[b] Only those regions of the world in which a conflict was recorded for the period 1989–98 are included in the tables.

Source: Uppsala Conflict Data Project.

conflict in 1998, the only active armed conflict in Europe in 1998 was theKosovo conflict in Yugoslavia (Serbia and Montenegro). This was the first new conflict in Europe since the conflict in Russia (Chechnya) began in late 1994. The conflicts in Georgia (last recorded in 1994), Azerbaijan (last recorded in 1994) and Russia (last recorded in 1996), for all of which there are ceasefires, have shown little progress towards comprehensive peace agreements. The ceasefires in Russia (Chechnya) and Georgia (Abkhazia) looked increasingly unstable during 1998, and Abkhazia experienced several incidents of violence between forces of the self-proclaimed Republic of Abkhazia and pro-Georgian militias.

The *Middle East* region shows little variation in the number of major armed conflicts during this period. As was the case in 1997, there was no recorded activity between the government of Iraq and Iraqi Kurdish groups or between the government of Iran and Iranian Kurdish groups,[11] although neither conflict was resolved. The conflict between the Kurdish Workers' Party (PKK) and Turkey continued, with Turkey making large-scale offensives into Iraq to strike at PKK bases. The Turkish conflict also affected relations between Turkey and Syria, one of the PKK's most loyal supporters over the years, which contributed to a high level of tension between the two states.

Asia has had the highest number of major armed conflicts every year in the period 1989–97. However, in 1998 the number of conflicts in Asia declined slightly and there were fewer conflicts in that region than in Africa for the first time in the past 10 years. There were no new conflicts in the region during 1998. Conflicts in Asia were fought on a comparatively low level of intensity, with the exception of Afghanistan, India (Kashmir) and Sri Lanka. The situations deteriorated in these three conflicts in different respects. In Afghanistan, Iran was on the brink of becoming a warring party after the execution of Iranian diplomats captured in northern Afghanistan in August. Large-scale massacres in northern Afghanistan, mainly of Shi'ite Hazaras, exacerbated the tension with Iran. The conflict in Kashmir escalated, which increased insecurity on the border. In Sri Lanka, the government's series of offensives continued unabated, leading to very high casualty figures. As in the Middle East, little progress was made towards resolving the conflicts in Asia. In Cambodia, Prince Ranariddh and Prime Minister Hun Sen were reconciled after Hun Sen's coup in 1997, which deposed Ranariddh from the government. The Khmer Rouge became increasingly weaker during the year and, as 1998 ended, all the major leaders had defected to the government, leaving the movement on the verge of dissolution. Indonesia experienced a turbulent year with an unprecedented level of economic crisis accompanied by a political crisis which led to the resignation of President Suharto. The crisis in Indonesia might for the first time provide an opportunity to settle the conflict in East

[11] As was the case in 1997, there are indications of possible activity in the Kurdish–Iranian conflict. However, since none of the reports could be verified, the conflict is not included in the table. Iraqi Kurdistan continued to be controlled by rival Kurdish factions whose intermittent fighting, which escalated in 1994, continued during 1998.

Timor, where UN-led negotiations are being held between Indonesia and Portugal.

Over the entire period 1989–98 there was only one region with an overall trend of declining numbers, *Central and South America*. The same armed conflicts were active in 1998 as in 1997. In Colombia, the level of intensity remained high, with some of the largest guerrilla offensives of the entire conflict. However, the new president, Andrés Pastrana, initiated talks with the Revolutionary Armed Forces of Colombia (FARC) during the summer of 1998, leading to a meeting in early 1999 which was the first direct talks ever between a Colombian president and the leaders of FARC. The armed conflict between Peru and Sendero Luminoso saw only isolated incidents of violence in 1998.

The number of conflicts in *Africa* increased sharply in 1997 and 1998, after a period of declining numbers in 1992–96. The developments in Africa were dramatic in 1998, as discussed in section IV.

IV. Conflict patterns in Africa

There were very negative developments in Africa in 1998. There were 11 armed conflicts on the continent (10 in sub-Saharan Africa)—as many as in 1990 and 1991, the previous peak years of the period 1989–98 (see table 1.2). The hopes for an 'African renaissance' expressed in 1997 were dashed and the outlook is now pessimistic. Africa is the most conflict-ridden region of the world and the only region in which the number of armed conflicts is on the increase.[12]

Major armed conflicts in Africa in 1998

Seven years after having won the struggle together against the Mengistu regime in Addis Ababa, the successor governments of Ethiopia and Eritrea were at war with each other. The conflict primarily concerned their undefined common border. The current conflict can also be traced to the profound differences between the ruling People's Front for Democracy and Justice (formerly the Eritrean People's Liberation Front) of Eritrea and the ruling Ethiopian People's Revolutionary Democratic Front of Ethiopia concerning such questions as economic policy and the constitutional rights of national minorities. Heavy fighting was reported in May and June 1998, especially around Badme in the Yirga Triangle. A mediation effort by the US Administration resulted in an agreement to halt air strikes, but no peace agreement has been reached.

The conflict between Ethiopia and Eritrea directly affected the strategic situation in the war in Sudan. Ethiopia and Eritrea were, together with Uganda, the main supporters of the National Democratic Alliance (NDA), which is fighting the Islamist regime in Sudan. The NDA brings together several southern and northern opposition organizations of which the Sudan People's Liber-

[12] For other detailed discussions of Africa, see chapter 2, section V, and chapter 7, section II.

ation Movement (SPLM), led by John Garang, is the largest. In 1997 the National Islamic Front (NIF) regime in Sudan was under heavy military pressure from the armed opposition. The conflict between Ethiopia and Eritrea thus weakened the strategic position of the NDA.

The Democratic Republic of Congo (DRC), then Zaire, had experienced an insurrection between October 1996 and May 1997, when rebels supported by Rwanda and Uganda overthrew President Mobuto Sese Seko. A new insurrection started in the DRC in August 1998. It was sparked by ethnic tension in the eastern part of the country and the July expulsion of Rwandan troops who had helped the government of President Laurent-Désiré Kabila to power in 1997. Since August 1998 at least six states have been directly militarily involved in the DRC conflict. Angola, Chad, Namibia and Zimbabwe have sided with Kabila, while Rwanda and Uganda are fighting alongside the rebels. The main rebel movement, the Congo Liberation Movement (RCD), led by Jean-Pierre Bemba, was in control of large parts of eastern DRC by the end of 1998.

In Burundi and Rwanda, the deep-rooted conflict between the Hutus and the Tutsis continued to claim victims on a large scale. However, the new round in the Arusha peace process, initiated in June 1998, constituted a serious effort to end the violence in Burundi. The Hutu rebels from Burundi and Rwanda coordinated their activities during the year. On several occasions Hutu rebels from Rwanda, including the former FAR (Forces Armée Rwandaises) and the Interahamwé militia, joined with the rebels from Burundi, including the National Council for the Defence of Democracy (CNDD), the Party for the Liberation of the Hutu People (Palipehutu) and the National Liberation Front (Frolina). The massacre at Bujumbura airport in early 1998, in which over 250 people were killed, was a coordinated attack by Burundian and Rwandan guerrillas.

During 1998 the Angolan peace process initiated in the Zambian capital Lusaka in 1994 broke down. After several months of low-intensity confrontation between the government and what was often called 'UNITA remnants', intense armed conflict broke out between the government and Jonas Savimbi's UNITA. Both parties are backed by heavily equipped armies, and a military victory for either side seems unlikely. The breakdown of the Lusaka Protocol is a major setback for the United Nations Observation Mission in Angola (MONUA). UN sanctions against UNITA remained in place.

In Uganda the conflict continues between the government and the main rebel movements—the Lord's Resistance Army (LRA), led by Joseph Kony, and the Allied Democratic Front (ADF); compared to the level of conflict in 1997, the fighting has intensified. The civilian population, particularly in the northern part of the country, live under the constant threat of terrorist attacks. The rebels continue to attract support from the government in Sudan.

Sierra Leone suffered from the armed conflict involving the coalition of the Armed Forces Revolutionary Council (AFRC) and the Revolutionary United Front (RUF). The AFRC had overthrown President Ahmad Tejan Kabbah in a coup in May 1997 and took power together with the RUF. ECOMOG troops,

Figure 1.1. Map of Africa

together with the local Kamajor militia, succeeded, after heavy fighting, in capturing the capital Freetown and reinstalled President Kabbah in March. However, the conflict continued. Heavy fighting was reported in December, when the rebels unsuccessfully tried to retake the capital. Systematic terror against the civilian population has been an integral part of the AFRC–RUF struggle to keep, and at a later stage retake, power.

In Guinea-Bissau a former army chief of staff, Ansumane Mane, supported by most of the armed forces of Guinea-Bissau, rebelled in June 1998, aiming at the removal of President João Bernardo Vieira and the holding of new elections. An agreement to end the conflict was signed in Cape Verde on 26 August, but sporadic fighting continued. On 1 November a second agreement, which included plans for a government of national unity and elections in March 1999, was signed in Abuja, Nigeria. Still, sporadic clashes were reported during the remainder of the year.

Senegal saw a continuation of the conflict in Casamance which had begun in the early 1980s. Although calls for peace came from the leader of the rebel group Movement of Democratic Forces of Casamance (MFDC), Augustin Diamacoune Senghor, fighting continued as the split widened between a northern faction favouring negotiation and a southern faction favouring continued armed struggle.

The conflict in Algeria between the government and Islamists continued in 1998, with massive violence by organized as well as unorganized groups that claimed thousands of lives, as in previous years.[13] The beginning of the year saw intense fighting and widespread massacres, especially at the time of Ramadan. The only remaining group fighting the government, although reportedly fragmented, was the Armed Islamic Group (GIA). The Islamic Salvation Front (FIS), which had initiated the rebellion in 1992, had announced a ceasefire in October 1997 and its military wing, the Islamic Salvation Army (AIS), was to have disbanded. The FIS issued calls for an investigation of who was responsible for the continuous massacres of civilian villagers but no comprehensive, objective investigation had been initiated by the end of 1998.

Conflict complexes

The conflicts in *sub-Saharan Africa* are increasingly becoming regionalized and are hence difficult to analyse in isolation from each other. Many conflicts in the subregion are connected through cross-border interests and actors, and there is an increase of various types of external military involvement in the internal conflicts. Three types of external military involvement can be seen: (*a*) external military assistance, including either arms sales or direct military support to a government (e.g., Zimbabwe's involvement in the DRC); (*b*) direct military intervention of foreign troops directed against a government (e.g., Rwanda's and Uganda's intervention in the DRC); and (*c*) indirect external intervention, that is, support of various kinds to rebel groups operating against a government (e.g., Sudan's support of the LRA and the ADF in Uganda in the form of arms and logistic assistance).[14] A fourth type of external involvement, that by countries outside Africa, has become less explicit since the end of the cold war, although it still exists. For example, Eritrea, Ethiopia and Uganda still attract US military aid in their struggle against the National Islamic Front regime in Sudan.

[13] See also chapter 3, section III, in this volume.

[14] Including allowing training and combat bases.

In *Central Africa* the dynamics of conflict in the region have come to centre around the Democratic Republic of Congo. There is a clear connection between the war in the DRC and the domestic situation in Burundi and Rwanda. The armed conflict in the DRC, which started in the eastern part of the country (the Kivu regions), was sparked by the ill-treatment of the Banyamulenge, a Tutsi people who have resided in the DRC for several hundred years. Anti-Tutsi sentiments in the capital Kinshasa put pressure on President Kabila to send home Rwandan soldiers who had helped bring him to power in 1996–97, which in turn provoked a military intervention from Rwanda. To bolster the military strength of the DRC, Kabila actively supports the Hutu rebels from Burundi and Rwanda and is thus indirectly intervening in the internal affair of his two eastern neighbours. The volatile situation in the DRC poses a threat to several actors in the region. At present at least six states—Angola, Chad, Namibia, Rwanda, Uganda and Zimbabwe—are directly involved militarily in the conflict. Angola's military assistance to the government in Kinshasa is linked to the Angolan Government's struggle against UNITA. By keeping Kabila in power, Angola hopes to prevent UNITA from using DRC territory as a springboard for its operations into Angola. Uganda in turn, has sided with the anti-Kabila rebels, partly in order to contain LRA, ADF and Sudanese interests.

Zimbabwe has sent at least 6000 troops to assist Kabila. Its interests in the DRC are to a large extent economic.[15]

The conflicts in *West Africa* also have a strong subregional dimension, involving Guinea-Bissau, Liberia, Nigeria, Senegal and Sierra Leone. In Sierra Leone, Liberian soldiers have been operating alongside the RUF/ARFC rebels. Liberian President Charles Taylor, who was instrumental in the creation of the RUF in the early 1990s, when he was the leader of the rebel group National Patriotic Forces of Liberia, denies any official military involvement in the neighbouring country. He describes his armed compatriots in Sierra Leone as mercenaries. Diplomatic relations between Nigeria, in the role of the dominant force in ECOMOG and on the side of the civilian government in Sierra Leone, and Liberia have deteriorated as a result of alleged Liberian involvement on the side of the RUF/AFRC rebels. The armed rebellion in Guinea-Bissau was related to the armed conflict in neighbouring Senegal. Mane's suspension in early 1998 over alleged arms smuggling to the Casamance separatists sparked a rebellion by the Guinea-Bissau Army. Senegalese and Guinean troops supported the Guinea-Bissau Government and the Casamance Movement of Democratic Forces (MFDC) supported the rebellion.

Assessment

A root cause of the conflict developments in Africa is to be found in the weakness of many of its states, which became especially obvious after the cold war. Corruption, the lack of efficient administration, the poor infrastructure and

[15] *Africa Research Bulletin*, 1–31 Dec. 1998, p. 13370.

weak national coherence make governance both difficult and costly. At the same time several states in sub-Saharan Africa have vast natural resources. The combination of weak states and rich natural resources has resulted in a dangerous structural environment fuelling conflicts throughout the subcontinent. Natural resources have become a cause for war as well as a necessary source of wealth for keeping the conflicts going. The main actors in the struggle for Africa's natural resources are now primarily African, although foreign companies play a role. In several parts of sub-Saharan Africa semi-political actors are fighting for the control of natural resources without any wider political ambitions.[16]

In Angola the conflict has come to focus more on oil and diamonds than on ideology. Revenue from the sale of diamonds—according to some estimates amounting to $500 million per year[17]—allows UNITA to maintain its armed forces. The Angolan Government is in turn financing the war by selling out oil concessions to foreign multinational companies.[18] In Sierra Leone control of the diamond mines is a key to power and wealth. Liberian soldiers in Sierra Leone, fighting alongside the RUF/AFRC, are paid in diamonds. The primary motive behind Zimbabwe's intervention in the DRC seems to be the protection of natural resources belonging to the leaders in Harare.[19]

[16] For further discussion of these developments in Africa, see e.g. Cilliers, J. and Mason, P. (eds), *Peace, Profit or Plunder? The Privatization of Security in War-Torn African Societies* (Institute for Strategic Studies: Midrand, 1999).

[17] Reuters News Service, 30 Jan. 1998.

[18] *Africa Confidential*, vol. 39, no. 10 (15 May 1998).

[19] *Africa Confidential*, vol. 39, no. 24 (4 Dec. 1998), p. 1.

Appendix 1A. Major armed conflicts, 1998

MARGARETA SOLLENBERG, STAFFAN ÅNGMAN, YLVA BLONDEL, ANN-SOFI JAKOBSSON and ANDRÉS JATO*

The following notes and sources apply to table 1A. Note that, although some countries are also the location of minor armed conflicts, the table lists only the major armed conflicts in those countries. Reference to the tables of major armed conflicts in previous SIPRI Yearbooks is given in the list of sources.

[a] The stated general incompatible positions. 'Govt' and 'Territory' refer to contested incompatibilities concerning government (type of political system, a change of central government or in its composition) and territory (control of territory [interstate conflict], secession or autonomy), respectively.

[b] 'Year formed' is the year in which the incompatibility was stated. 'Year joined' is the year in which use of armed force began or recommenced.

[c] The non-governmental warring parties are listed by the name of the parties using armed force. Only those parties which were active during 1998 are listed in this column.

[d] The figure for 'No. of troops in 1998' is for total armed forces (rather than for army forces, as in the *SIPRI Yearbooks 1988–1990*) of the government warring party (i.e., the government of the conflict location), and for non-government parties from the conflict location. For government and non-government parties from outside the location, the figure in this column is for total armed forces within the country that is the location of the armed conflict. Deviations from this method are indicated by a note (*) and explained.

[e] The figures for deaths refer to total battle-related deaths during the conflict. 'Mil.' and 'civ.' refer, where figures are available, to *military* and *civilian* deaths, respectively; where there is no such indication, the figure refers to total military and civilian battle-related deaths in the period or year given. Information which covers a calendar year is necessarily more tentative for the last months of the year. Experience has also shown that the reliability of figures improves over time; they are therefore revised each year.

[f] The 'change from 1997' is measured as the increase or decrease in the number of battle-related deaths in 1998 compared with the number of battle-related deaths in 1997. Although based on data that cannot be considered totally reliable, the symbols represent the following changes:

+ +	increase in battle deaths of > 50%
+	increase in battle deaths of > 10 to 50%
0	stable rate of battle deaths (± 10%)
–	decrease in battle deaths of > 10 to 50%
– –	decrease in battle deaths of > 50%
n.a.	not applicable, since the major armed conflict was not recorded for 1996.

Note: In the last three columns ('Total deaths', 'Deaths in 1998' and 'Change from 1997'), '. .' indicates that no reliable figures, or no reliable disaggregated figures, were given in the sources consulted.

* S. Ångman was responsible for the conflict locations Colombia, Peru, Sri Lanka, Turkey and Yugoslavia; Y. Blondel for Algeria; A.-S. Jakobsson for Israel; and A. Jato for Angola, Burundi, the Democratic Republic of Congo, Eritrea–Ethiopia, Rwanda, Sierra Leone, Somalia, Sudan and Uganda. M. Sollenberg was responsible for the remaining conflict locations.

Sources: For additional information on these conflicts, see the chapters on major armed conflicts in the *SIPRI Yearbooks 1987–1998*.

Reference literature, research reports on specific conflicts, and other information available in the Department of Peace and Conflcit Research, at SIPRI and on the Internet were used as sources.

In addition, the following journals, newspapers and news agencies were consulted: *Africa Confidential* (London); *Africa Events* (London); *Africa Reporter* (New York); *Africa Research Bulletin* (Oxford); *AIM Newsletter* (London); *Asian Defence Journal* (Kuala Lumpur); *Asian Recorder* (New Delhi); *Balkan War Report* (London); *Burma Focus* (Oslo); British Broadcasting Company (BBC) Monitoring Service (London); *Burma Issues* (Bangkok); *Conflict International* (Edgware); *Dagens Nyheter* (Stockholm); Dialog Information Services Inc. (Palo Alto); *The Economist* (London); *Facts and Reports* (Amsterdam); *Far Eastern Economic Review* (Hong Kong); *Financial Times* (Frankfurt); *Fortnight Magazine* (Belfast); *The Guardian* (London); *Horn of Africa Bulletin* (Uppsala); *Jane's Defence Weekly* (Coulsdon, Surrey); *Jane's Intelligence Review* (Coulsdon, Surrey); *The Independent* (London); *International Herald Tribune* (Paris); *Kayhan International* (Teheran); *Keesing's Contemporary Archives* (Harlow, Essex); *Latin America Weekly Report* (London); *Le Monde Diplomatique* (Paris); *Mexico and Central America Report* (London); *Middle East International* (London); *Monitor* (Washington, DC); *Moscow News* (Moscow); *New African* (London); *New Times* (Moscow); *New York Times* (New York); *Newsweek* (New York); *OMRI (Open Media Research Institute) Daily Digest* (Prague); *Pacific Report* (Canberra); *Pacific Research* (Canberra); *Reuters Business Briefing* (London); *Prism* (Washington, DC); *RFE/RL (Radio Free Europe/Radio Liberty) Research Report* (Munich); *S.A. Barometer* (Johannesburg); *Selections from Regional Press* (Institute of Regional Studies: Islamabad); *Southern African Economist* (Harare); *Southern Africa Political & Economic Monthly* (Harare); *SouthScan* (London); *Sri Lanka Monitor* (London); *The Statesman* (Calcutta); *Sudan Update* (London); *Svenska Dagbladet* (Stockholm); *Tehran Times* (Teheran); *The Times* (London); *Transition* (Prague); *World Aerospace & Defense Intelligence* (Newtown, Conn.).

Table 1A. Table of conflict locations with at least one major armed conflict in 1998

Location	Incompat-ibility[a]	Year formed/ year joined[b]	Warring parties[c]	No. of troops in 1998[d]	Total deaths[e] (incl. 1998)	Deaths in 1998	Change from 1997[f]
Europe							
Yugoslavia*			Govt of Yugoslavia	115 000	1 000–2 000	1 000–2 000	n.a.
	Territory	1997/1998	*vs.* UCK	5 000–10 000			
UCK: Ushtria Clirimtare e Kosoves (Kosovo Liberation Army, KLA)							
* Yugoslavia refers to the Federal Republic of Yugoslavia (FRY), also referred to as Yugoslavia (Serbia and Montenegro).							
Middle East							
Iran			Govt of Iran	500 000–550 000*	. .	. .	. .
	Govt	1970/1991	*vs.* Mujahideen e-Khalq	. .			
* Including the Revolutionary Guard.							
Iraq			Govt of Iraq	430 000	. .	. .	. .
	Govt	1980/1991	*vs.* SAIRI	. .			
SAIRI: Supreme Assembly for the Islamic Revolution in Iraq							
Israel			Govt of Israel	170 000–180 000	1948–:	100 (mil.)	–
	Territory	1964/1964	*vs.* Non-PLO groups*	. .	> 13 000	50 (civ.)	
PLO: Palestine Liberation Organization							
* Examples of these groups are Hamas, Hizbollah and Amal.							
Turkey			Govt of Turkey	800 000*	> 30 000	> 800	–
	Territory	1974/1984	*vs.* PKK	5 000–6 000			
PKK: Partiya Karkeren Kurdistan, Kurdish Workers' Party, or Apocus							
* Including the Gendarmerie/National Guard.							

Asia

Afghanistan			Govt of Afghanistan	25 000–50 000	. .	> 2 000	0
	Govt	1992/1992	*vs.* Jumbish-i Milli-ye Islami,	40 000			
			Jamiat-i-Islami,	. .			
			Hezb-i-Wahdat	. .			
Cambodia			Govt of Cambodia	140 000*	> 25 500**	. .	. .
	Govt	1979/1979	*vs.* PDK	1 000–3 000			

PDK: Party of Democratic Kampuchea (Khmer Rouge)

* Including all militias.

** For figures for battle-related deaths in this conflict prior to 1979, see *SIPRI Yearbook 1990*, p. 405, and note *p*, p. 418. Regarding battle-related deaths in 1979–89, i.e., not only involving the Govt and PDK, the only figure available is from official Vietnamese sources, indicating that 25 300 Vietnamese soldiers died in Cambodia. An estimated figure for the period 1979–89, based on various sources, is > 50 000, and for 1989 >1000. The figures for 1990, 1991 and 1992 were lower.

India			Govt of India	1 175 000	> 20 000*	> 800	+
	Territory	. . /1989	*vs.* Kashmir insurgents**	. .			
	Territory	. . /1992	*vs.* BdSF	. .			
		1982/1988	*vs.* ULFA	. .			

BdSF: Bodo Security Force
ULFA: United Liberation Front of Assam

* Only the Kashmir conflict.

** Several groups are active, some of the most important being the Jammu and Kashmir Liberation Front (JKLF), the Hizb-ul-Mujahideen and the Harkat-ul-Ansar.

India–Pakistan			Govt of India	1 175 000	. .	> 300	. .
	Territory	1947/1996	*vs.* Govt of Pakistan	587 000			

Location	Incompatibility[a]	Year formed/ year joined[b]	Warring parties[c]	No. of troops in 1998[d]	Total deaths[e] (incl. 1998)	Deaths in 1998	Change from 1997[f]
Indonesia	Territory	1975/1975	Govt of Indonesia *vs.* Fretilin	500 000* 100–200	15 000– 16 000 (mil.)	50–200	+
Fretilin: Frente Revolucionára Timorense de Libertação e Independência (Revolutionary Front for an Independent East Timor) * Including paramilitary forces.							
Myanmar	Territory	1948/1948	Govt of Myanmar *vs.* KNU	300 000–400 000 2 000–4 000	1948–50: 8 000 1981–88: 5 000–8 000	. .	. .
KNU: Karen National Union							
Philippines	Govt	1968/1968	Govt of the Philippines *vs.* NPA	110 000 6 000–7 000	21 000– 25 000	< 50	–
NPA: New People's Army							
Sri Lanka	Territory	1976/1983	Govt of Sri Lanka *vs.* LTTE	110 000 6 000–8 000	> 45 000	> 4 000	0
LTTE: Liberation Tigers of Tamil Eelam							
Africa							
Algeria	Govt	1993/1993	Govt of Algeria *vs.* GIA	270 000* . .	40 000– 100 000**	> 1 500 (mil.) > 2 500 (civ.)	. .***
GIA: Groupe Islamique Armée (Armed Islamic Group) * Including the Gendarmerie, the National Security Forces and Legitimate Defence Groups (local militias).							

** Note that this figure includes deaths in the fighting since 1992 in which other parties than those listed above also participated, notably the Front Islamique du Salut (FIS), or Islamic Salvation Front..
*** The minimum number of deaths is > 4000, but it has not been possible to determine the change from 1997.

Angola			Govt of Angola	110 000	. .	> 1 000	n.a.
	Govt	1975/1998	*vs.* UNITA	30 000			

UNITA: Uniao Nacional Para a Independencia Total de Angola (National Union for the Total Independence of Angola)

Burundi			Govt of Burundi	40 000	> 2 000*	1 000	+
	Govt	1994/1994	*vs.* CNDD	3 000–10 000			
		. . / . .	vs. Palipehutu	2 000			

CNDD: Conseil national pour la défense de la démocratie (National Council for the Defence of Democracy)
Palipehutu: Parti pour la libération du peuple Hutu (Party for the Liberation of the Hutu People)
* Political violence in Burundi since 1993, involving other groups than the CNDD, has claimed a total of at least 100 000 lives.

Congo, Dem. Rep. of			Govt of Dem. Rep. of Congo,	50 000*	> 2 000	> 2 000	n.a.
			Angola,	4 000			
			Namibia,	1 000			
			Zimbabwe,	6 000			
			Chad	1 000			
	Govt	1998/1998	*vs.* RCD,	60 000			
			MLC,	. .			
			Rwanda,	4 000			
			Uganda	6 000			

RCD: Rassemblement Congolaises pour la Démocratie (Congolese Democratic Rally)
MLC: Mouvement de libération Congolais (Congolese Liberation Movement)
* The total number of armed individuals fighting for the Government of the DRC is likely to be 100 000.

Location	Incompat-ibility[a]	Year formed/ year joined[b]	Warring parties[c]	No. of troops in 1998[d]	Total deaths[e] (incl. 1998)	Deaths in 1998	Change from 1997[f]
Eritrea–Ethiopia			Govt of Eritrea	40 000–55 000	> 1 000	> 1 000	n.a.
	Territory	. . /1998	*vs.* Govt of Ethiopia	80 000			
Guinea-Bissau			Govt of Guinea-Bissau,	3 000–6 000*	> 1 000	> 1 000	n.a.
			Senegal,	2 000–3 000			
			Guinea	1 000–1 500			
	Govt	1998/1998	*vs.* Military faction	3 000–6 000			
* Including the Gendarmerie.							
Rwanda			Govt of Rwanda	55 000	. .	> 1 500	n.a.
	Govt	. . /1997	*vs.* Opposition alliance*	50 000–65 000			
* Consisting of former government troops of the Forces Armées Rwandaises (Rwandan Armed Forces) and the Interahamwé militia.							
Senegal			Govt of Senegal	13 000	> 1 000	> 250	0
	Territory	1982/1982	*vs.* MFDC	500–1 000			
MFDC: Mouvement des forces démocratiques de la Casamance (Casamance Movement of Democratic Forces)							
Sierra Leone			Govt of Sierra Leone,	30 000*	> 5 000	> 1 500	+ +
			ECOMOG	10 000–15 000			
	Govt	1991/1991	*vs.* RUF, AFRC	15 000			
ECOMOG: ECOWAS (Economic Community of West African States) Monitoring Group AFRC: Armed Forces Revolutionary Council RUF: Revolutionary United Front * The figure is for the Kamajors, the militia acting as the government armed forces.							

Sudan			Govt of Sudan	90 000	37 000–	> 2 500	–
	Govt	1980/1983	*vs.* NDA*	50 000	40 000 (mil.)**		

NDA: National Democratic Alliance

* The June 1995 Asmara Declaration forms the basis for the political and military activities of the NDA. The NDA is an alliance of several southern and northern opposition organizations, of which the SPLM (Sudan People's Liberation Movement) is the largest, with 30 000–50 000 troops. SPLM leader John Garang is also the leader of the NDA.

** Figure for up to 1991.

Uganda			Govt of Uganda	45 000–60 000	> 2 000	> 800	+ +
	Govt	1993/1994	*vs.* LRA	6 000			
		1996/1996	*vs.* ADF	1 500			

LRA: Lord's Resistance Army
ADF: Alliance of Democratic Forces

Central and South America

Colombia			Govt of Colombia	140 000	. .*	1 000–1 500	+
	Govt	1949/1978	*vs.* FARC	10 000			
		1965/1978	*vs.* ELN	3 500			

FARC: Fuerzas Armadas Revolucionarias Colombianas (Revolutionary Armed Forces of Colombia)
ELN: Ejército de Liberación Nacional (National Liberation Army)

* In the past 3 decades the civil wars of Colombia have claimed a total of some 30 000 lives.

Peru			Govt of Peru	125 000	> 28 000	25–100	–
	Govt	1980/1981	*vs.* Sendero Luminoso	250–500			

Sendero Luminoso: Shining Path

Appendix 1B. The Kashmir conflict

STEN WIDMALM*

I. Introduction

The conflict in the Indian state of Jammu and Kashmir continues despite attempts over the past three years to revitalize democratic institutions. When India and Pakistan carried out nuclear tests in May 1998, concern was expressed regarding the implications for the Kashmir conflict of the proliferation of nuclear arms in South Asia. This appendix describes the background to the conflict and summarizes more recent events in the region.[1] Section II sketches the historical background to the conflict, and the violence in the 1990s is examined in section III. The evolution of the conflict in 1998 is recapitulated in section IV, which also touches upon its role in the broader context of nuclear proliferation in the region.[2] The conclusions are presented in section V.

II. Background to the conflict

Kashmir at the time of independence

Lord Mountbatten's decision, as the last Viceroy of India, to bring forward the date of independence for India and Pakistan was probably intended to be seen as a sign of strength and decisiveness. Instead of 1948, India and Pakistan would become independent in August 1947. This decision, however, proved fateful, since far too few aspects of the complexity of partition received sufficient consideration. The new borders were immediately disputed and the migration of Hindus to India and Muslims to Pakistan caused fighting and indescribable suffering. Kashmir, one of some 600 princely states in the British Indian Empire, remained an unsolved problem even after August 1947.[3]

As British India was coming to its end, what was commonly referred to as Kashmir included six regions: the Vale of Kashmir, Jammu, Poonch, the Gilgit Agency, Baltistan and Ladakh (see figure 1B.1). Since the turn of the century, Sunni Muslims had

[1] In addition to the literature cited in the footnotes, this appendix is based on reports and articles from *Asian Age, Daily Star, Dawn, Frontline, The Hindu, Hindustan Times, The Independent, India Today, Indian Express, The Muslim, The Nation, National Herald, The News, The Patriot, The Pioneer, Seminar, Statesman, The Telegraph* and *Times of India* from 1975 onwards. It is also based on interviews with, among others, Amanullah Khan, Syeed Ali Shah Geelani, Gunnar Jarring and Farooq Abdullah, carried out in the preparation of Widmalm, S., *Democracy and Violent Separatism in India: Kashmir in a Comparative Perspective* (doctoral dissertation, Department of Government, Uppsala University: Uppsala, 1997). Journalists Harinder Baweja at India Today and Syed Shujaat Bukhari at The Hindu were particularly helpful in the preparation of this appendix.

[2] For more details of the nuclear tests see chapters 9 and 15 and appendix 12B in this volume.

[3] One-third of British India consisted of princely states under the indirect control of the British rulers. The status and number of princely states in India are discussed in Lamb, A., *Birth of a Tragedy: Kashmir 1947* (Roxford Books: Hertingfordbury, 1994), p. 413; and Thomas, R. G. C., *Perspectives on Kashmir: The Roots of Conflict in South Asia* (Westview Press: Boulder, Colo., 1992), pp. 82–83, 169, 208.

* Anna Fornstedt and Stefan Ernlund, research assistants at the Council for Development and Assistance Studies at Uppsala University, assisted in researching this appendix.

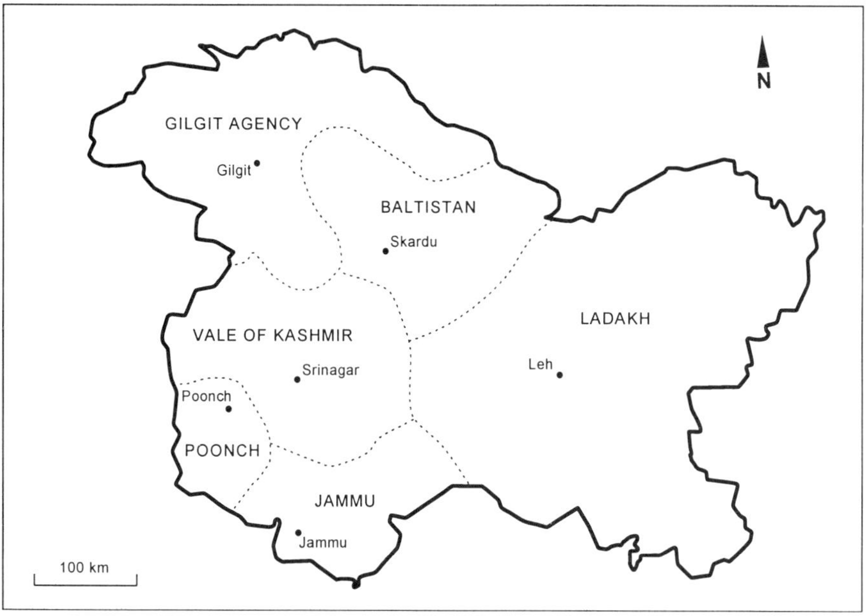

Figure 1B.1. The regions of Kashmir, 1947

Source: Based on Lamb, A., *Kashmir: A Disputed Legacy, 1846–1990* (Roxford Books: Hertingfordbury, 1991), map 2.

been the dominant group in the area, but these regions are also populated by Gujjars, Bakerwals, Sikhs, Sudhans, Hindus and Twelver Shia Muslims. The Vale of Kashmir is the most densely populated region and has a majority of Muslims. In Jammu the Hindus are in the majority with a strong Dogra community. The main languages spoken are Urdu, Kashmiri and Dogri. The label 'Muslim' for Kashmir's majority population slightly obscures the historical interaction between Hinduism and Islam and the influence of Islamic mystics—the Rishi Silsilah—which have given the region a unique character. This heterogeneous region was ruled at the time of partition by the Dogra Maharaja Hari Singh. Like other princely rulers, he was given the choice of joining either India or Pakistan, but even after August 1947 he could not make up his mind. As a result, the political elite in Delhi increasingly saw Sheikh Abdullah, the leader of a regional party, the Jammu and Kashmir National Conference, and a strong opponent of the Maharaja, as a more attractive ally.

The Maharaja's indecisiveness gave way to panic when Pathan tribal forces invaded Kashmir in October 1947.[4] It is far from clear when he signed the letter of accession to India, but Indian troops were sent in to stop the invasion.[5] Mountbatten

[4] By necessity, this is a simplification. The background to this event, especially its connection with the Poonch Revolt and the question of the extent to which the Pakistani Government was involved, is very complicated and far from uncontroversial among researchers. For further discussion, see, e.g., Jha, P. S., *Kashmir 1947: Rival Versions of History* (Oxford University Press: Delhi, 1996); and Lamb (note 3).

[5] Whether or not the instrument of accession was signed before, after or indeed at all by the Maharaja (it has also been argued that the signature is a complete forgery) is also intensely debated. Two of the main opponents in the debate are the columnist and writer Prem Shankar Jha and the historian Alastair Lamb. Jha (note 4); Lamb (note 3); Lamb, A., *Kashmir: A Disputed Legacy, 1846–1990* (Roxford

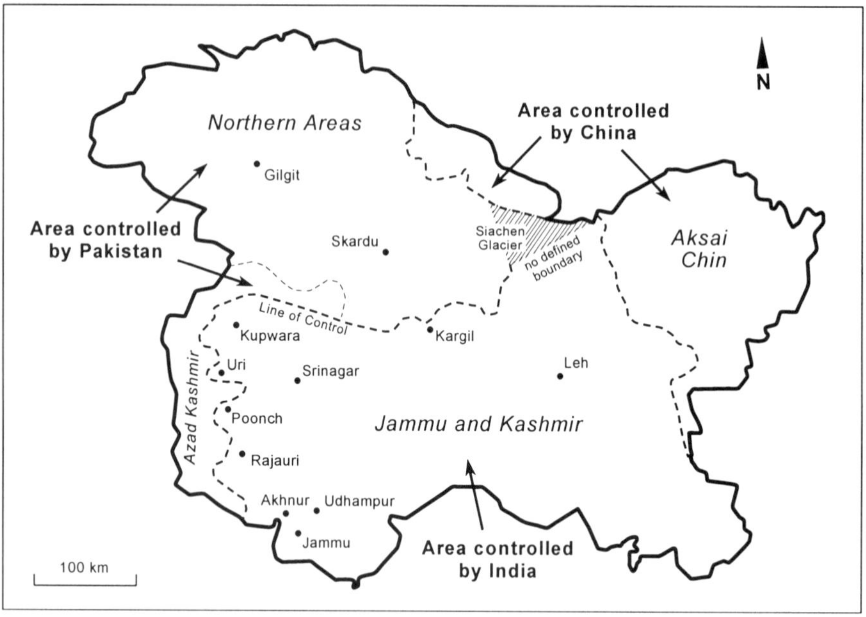

Figure 1B.2. Kashmir in 1998

agreed that Kashmir's accession was to be seen as a temporary solution and that a plebiscite would be held on whether Kashmir should belong to Pakistan or India when the situation had calmed down.[6] However, peace was far away. The controversy and fighting over Kashmir soon escalated into a full-scale war between India and Pakistan.

Although the Indian forces halted the tribal invaders close to Srinagar, regular army forces gradually became more involved from both India's and Pakistan's side. The conflict was discussed in the United Nations in January 1948,[7] and in July the same year the United Nations Commission for India (UNCIP)[8] arrived with an observer force; on 1 January 1949 a ceasefire agreement came into effect. A ceasefire line—the Line of Control—was established on 27 July 1949, which is the de facto border in Kashmir between India and Pakistan today.[9] It starts to the west of Jammu and Akhnur and wriggles north, to the west of Poonch and Uri, makes a turn eastwards north of Kupwara and continues to a point just north of Kargil. Then the line makes a northward turn and ends in the Siachen Glacier area, where no defined ceasefire line

Books: Hertingfordbury, 1991); and Lamb, A., *Incomplete Partition: The Genesis of the Kashmir Dispute 1947–1948* (Roxford Books: Hertingfordbury, 1997) contain most of the central arguments.

6 Akbar, M. J., *Kashmir: Behind the Vale* (Viking Penguin India: New Delhi, 1991), pp. 112–17; and Letter from Mountbatten to Maharaja Hari Singh, 27 Oct. 1947, reproduced in Grover, V., *The Story of Kashmir: Yesterday and Today, Vol. 3* (University of Delhi: Delhi, 1995), p. 109.

7 The 4 UN Security Council resolutions on Kashmir that were passed in winter/spring 1948 (UN Resolutions S/651, 17 Jan. 1948; S/654, 20 Jan. 1948; S/726, 21 Apr. 1948; and S/819, 3 June 1948) are described in Lamb 1997 (note 5).

8 UNCIP was replaced in 1951 by the United Nations Military Observer Group in India and Pakistan (UNMOGIP), which is still active in the area today.

9 Lamb 1991 (note 5), pp. 161–65; Dawson, P., *The Peacekeepers of Kashmir: The UN Military Observer Group in India and Pakistan* (Popular Prakashan: Bombay, 1995), p. 36; and Karim, A., *Kashmir: The Troubled Frontier* (Uppal Publishing House: New Delhi, 1994), p. 10.

exists. The one-third of the area of Kashmir over which Pakistan has taken de facto control is divided into two parts, officially called Azad Kashmir (Free Kashmir) and the Northern Areas (see figure 1B.2).[10] The region controlled by India is officially named Jammu and Kashmir and in the 1990s about 64 per cent of the population were Muslims and 32 per cent were Hindus.[11]

After the first war between India and Pakistan, the military presence and tension remained high and were among the reasons given for not holding the plebiscite in Kashmir as provided by the discussions held by leaders of the Indian Interim Government in October 1947. The temporary solution of letting Kashmir accede to India gradually came to be seen more as a permanent solution.

Kashmir between interstate conflicts

The post-independence era began with a war over Kashmir and continued confrontations shaped the political climate and the institutions in the area. Sheikh Abdullah replaced the Maharaja as the leader of Kashmir and led the first emergency government of Jammu and Kashmir and, as a consequence of the way the terms of accession were formulated, the Indian Constituent Assembly adopted the crucial Article 370 that gave a unique status to Kashmir. The Indian Government was given powers only with regard to defence, foreign affairs and communications. In other respects Kashmir would function as an autonomous unit until a plebiscite eventually determined the future. Kashmir might have entered on a path to stability with this arrangement, but instead the opposite occurred.

The cold war in particular helped to breed suspicion between India and Pakistan and it was feared that Sheikh Abdullah was about to demand complete independence for Kashmir with the support of the United States.[12] Abdullah was jailed in 1953 and replaced by political forces in the state more loyal to the Indian Government. Also, the autonomy clauses in Article 370 of the constitution were amended and diluted, both formally and even more so in practice. Pakistan brought the Kashmir issue to the UN General Assembly in 1956 and to the UN Security Council in 1957, but without significant results. Attempts to bring in third-party mediators in the conflict did little to decrease the tension.[13]

Subsequently, tension in South Asia began to rise: in 1961 Indian forces were sent to Goa and in 1962 India was at war with China. Again, the Kashmir question was brought to the UN Security Council but with no tangible results. Border clashes between India and Pakistan in 1965 led to large-scale confrontations.[14] However, as

[10] This area is commonly referred to as 'Pakistani-occupied Kashmir' by India. The constitutional status of the Northern Areas is somewhat unclear in comparison with that of Azad Kashmir.

[11] Butler, D., Lahiri, A. and Roy, P., *India Decides: Elections 1952–1991* (Living Media Books: New Delhi, 1991), p. 110. Jammu and Kashmir is referred to by Pakistan as 'Indian-occupied Kashmir'. It should be added that the easternmost part of the state, the Aksai Chin, is controlled by China. To some extent the ceasefire line coincides with a linguistic boundary. Kashmiri is most common in the Vale of Kashmir (in Jammu and Kashmir) while various Punjabi dialects are spoken in Azad Kashmir. Rose, L., 'The politics of Azad Kashmir', ed. Thomas (note 3), p. 248.

[12] The Indian Government discovered that Sheikh Abdullah had discussed the independence option with the US Ambassador in 1950 and with US Democrat leader Adlai Stevenson in 1953. Lamb 1991 (note 5), pp. 182–213; and Gopal, S., *Jawaharlal Nehru: A Biography*, vol. 3 (Oxford University Press: Delhi, 1984), pp. 131–33.

[13] Interviews by the author in 1993, 1994, and 1996 with the Swedish diplomat Gunnar Jarring, who was the mediator between India and Pakistan in 1957.

[14] Blinkenberg, L., *India–Pakistan: The History of Unsolved Conflicts*, Dansk Udenrigspolitisk Instituts Skrifter no. 4 (Munksgaard: Copenhagen, 1972), pp. 238–64.

the fighting increased, so did the pressure to stop the conflict by China, the USA and the UK. A UN-proposed ceasefire was accepted in September, and, as a result of an initiative by the Soviet Union, the Tashkent Declaration of 10 January 1996, signed by India and Pakistan, established peaceful relations.[15]

By the end of the 1960s, however, both India and Pakistan were internally politically and economically unstable. The relationship between East and West Pakistan had remained unstable since partition, and in November 1970 the government in West Pakistan was charged with not giving adequate support to the victims of the cyclone that hit East Pakistan. In the general election in December the outcome was in favour of Sheikh Mujibur Rahman and the Awami League, the dominant party in East Pakistan. However, Rahman was not allowed to form the new government and he therefore demanded independence from West Pakistan. West Pakistan responded with a military assault on Dhaka in March 1971, which resulted in a flood of refugees moving from East Pakistan to India. Indira Gandhi subsequently expressed her support for those demanding independence, and by the end of 1971 India and Pakistan were again involved in a war that included hostilities along the Punjab border and the ceasefire line. Fighting stopped on 17 December 1971, Bangladesh was created and in July the following year India's Prime Minister Indira Gandhi met Pakistani President Zulfikar Ali Bhutto in Simla, where a new peace agreement was signed. The 1972 Simla Agreement stated that the ceasefire line was to be seen as a 'Line of Control',[16] in other words, the de facto border in Kashmir between India and Pakistan. The war in December 1971 had a strong impact on the political climate in Jammu and Kashmir. Support for Pakistan was weak and when Sheikh Abdullah re-emerged as the regional leader he saw the demand for a plebiscite as impossible to pursue after the recent clashes between India and Pakistan. Instead preservation of the autonomy of Jammu and Kashmir was seen as the main priority.[17]

The road to democracy and peace

An often overlooked aspect of Jammu and Kashmir's historical, institutional and political heritage is that it has been deprived of the democratic consolidation process experienced by almost all other parts of India since the 1950s. While a democratic culture was allowed to take root in the Indian Union, all the elections in Jammu and Kashmir were corrupted. The hostile relationship with Pakistan and the geo-strategic location of Jammu and Kashmir are naturally two of the main reasons for this. The Indian Government often found the strong Kashmiri identity difficult to handle in this volatile context. It was feared that political freedoms would only lead to increased demands for a separate state or accession to Pakistan. The democratic climate was choked for more than two decades, but as Sheikh Abdullah gave up the demand for a plebiscite an opening for democratic reforms appeared. In return, and as an outcome of the Delhi Accord that had been finalized in 1975,[18] the Indian Government agreed

[15] The text of the 1996 Tashkent Declaration is reproduced in Grover (note 6), pp. 322–23.

[16] The text of the 1972 Simla Agreement on Bilateral Relations between the Government of India and the Government of Pakistan is reproduced in Smith, C., SIPRI, *India's* Ad Hoc *Arsenal* (Oxford University Press: Oxford, 1994), pp. 229–30.

[17] Kadian, R., *The Kashmir Tangle: Issues and Options* (Vision Books: New Delhi, 1992), p. 135; Bhattacharjea, A., *Kashmir the Wounded Valley* (UBS Publishers: New Delhi, 1994), pp. 223–37; and Akbar (note 6), pp. 185–90.

[18] Lamb 1991 (note 5), pp. 308–13. The February 1975 Delhi Accord, also known as the Kashmir Accord, is reproduced in Grover (note 6), pp. 327–28.

to retain Article 370. The National Conference was reformed and soon proved itself to be a strong political force that could act independently in the region. A process of democratic consolidation had finally begun in Jammu and Kashmir.

In 1977 Prime Minister Morarji Desai secured the transition to democracy by declaring that anyone who attempted to corrupt the elections in Jammu and Kashmir would be severely punished. The state assembly election that followed is widely recognized as the most democratic ever held in Jammu and Kashmir.[19] The National Conference won a majority of the seats in the state parliament, followed by the Janata Dal and Congress (I). A significant feature of this election was the low support for Hindu as well as Muslim nationalist parties. From a historical perspective, it seems that the decade between 1974 and 1984 saw a process not only of democratic consolidation but also of national consolidation. The demand for a separate state or accession to Pakistan was at its weakest when democratic institutions worked.[20] Moreover, at this time religion did not significantly affect patterns of political competition.[21] These consolidation processes were, however, to be halted and reversed, and it seems that the trouble began when Sheikh Abdullah died in 1982.

Institutional breakdown in Jammu and Kashmir, 1982–89

Pakistan supported the uprising in Jammu and Kashmir, especially during the 1990s, by, for example, allowing separatists to establish training facilities close to the Line of Control. The root causes of the conflict that escalated rapidly at the end of the 1980s and in the early 1990s are, however, to be found by studying the acts of the political elite in Kashmir and the Indian Government and the institutional breakdown during the 1980s.[22]

Sheikh Abdullah left behind an internally divided and weak National Conference.[23] His son, Farooq Abdullah, was inexperienced and not very skilful in politics, and he had difficulty in handling internal power conflicts. He also began his term as Chief Minister of Jammu and Kashmir by alienating Indira Gandhi's government and by making political liaisons with her enemies around the country. After the comfortable victory by the National Conference in the 1983 state election,[24] by early 1984 Farooq Abdullah's government was under constant attack internally from rival forces and externally from Indira Gandhi. In July the new Governor of Jammu and Kashmir, Jagmohan Malhotra, declared that Farooq Abdullah had lost his majority, and a new

[19] Widmalm, S., 'The rise and fall of democracy in Jammu and Kashmir', *Asian Survey*, vol. 37, no. 11 (Nov. 1997), pp. 1006–1007.

[20] In the 1977 election, the Jamaat-e-Islami, which advocates accession to Pakistan, only won 1 seat. When the leader of the Jammu and Kashmir Liberation Front (JKLF), Amanullah Khan, tried to recruit for an armed uprising in the area in 1983, he failed simply because there was no interest in or support for such a campaign. Widmalm (note 19), pp. 1007–1008.

[21] At this time, Hindu nationalists could work in alliance with Muslim-dominated party forces at local levels of politics. Widmalm, S., 'The rise and fall of democracy in Jammu and Kashmir, 1975–1989', eds A. Basu and A. Kohli, *Community Conflicts and State in India* (Oxford University Press: Delhi, 1998), pp. 154–55.

[22] Most of the events discussed here are described in more detail in Widmalm (note 1); Widmalm (note 19); and Widmalm (note 21). In particular the role of Pakistan's involvement is discussed in Widmalm (note 1), pp. 109–14.

[23] Before he died Sheikh Abdullah decided to make his son Farooq Abdullah his heir to power. The rival to this choice was Ghulam Mohammed Shah, Sheikh Abdullah's son-in-law, but he was considered too arrogant. When Sheikh Abdullah died, this created a rift in the National Conference and from then on Shah did all he could to dethrone Farooq Abdullah.

[24] It should be mentioned that this election, although considered by many as free and fair, was plagued by an increase in violence and fraud.

state government including National Conference 'defectors' was created, supported by Congress (I). This action was widely condemned as unconstitutional and undemocratic.

The process of democratic consolidation came to a halt in 1984. Some of the damage done could have been repaired at this point but a number of events worsened the situation. Rajiv Gandhi, who took over the Congress (I) leadership after the assassination of Indira Gandhi, found that the National Conference defectors were unpredictable and hardly added to stability in Jammu and Kashmir. However, he found Farooq Abdullah a more reasonable political partner. In 1986 Abdullah was reinstalled as Chief Minister. The Congress (I) and National Conference formed an alliance for the 1987 state election which won almost all the votes.[25] Furthermore, to ensure that almost no seats were lost, Congress (I) and the National Conference engaged in widespread fraud in the few constituencies where opponents had established some sort of stronghold. In contrast to the 1977 and 1983 elections, almost all the institutions designed to guard the election process and prevent rigging had been brought under the direct control of the National Conference or Congress (I) in 1987. Consequently, courts refused to act on allegations of electoral fraud and the police seem to have participated actively in carrying out the orders of the two leading parties. The election commission also remained silent. In the aftermath of these events, when the political protests grew, Congress (I) and the National Conference passed the Jammu and Kashmir Special Powers (Press) Bill in the Legislative Assembly in 1989, bringing almost full press censorship to Jammu and Kashmir.

These events reversed the democratization process in Jammu and Kashmir. As the popular political support for democracy was lost and the non-violent avenues for expressing discontent were closed, sympathies for groups advocating armed struggle as the main resource for making Jammu and Kashmir independent, or a part of Pakistan, increased radically. The Jamaat-e-Islami formed the Muslim United Front, where most of the supporters of joining Pakistan were gathered. The pro-independence Jammu and Kashmir Liberation Front (JKLF) also gained support and found no problem in recruiting youths for the armed struggle.[26] This breakdown of democratic institutions led to growing polarization between Hindus and Muslims in the state.[27] In 1989, the severe tension in the state led to the violent phase which has continues to this day.

III. A decade of violence

Estimates of the number of lives claimed by the conflict in Jammu and Kashmir, including civilians, military personnel, border security forces and separatists, vary greatly. Some of the observations that might be described as comparatively neutral suggest around 25 000 casualties between 1989 and 1996.[28] It is natural to use 1989 as the starting date since there was a rapid escalation in the use of violence by all parties to the conflict in Jammu and Kashmir at this time.

[25] In fact, what could be called an 'election cartel' was created. Widmalm (note 19).

[26] I.e., contrary to the experience of Amanullah Khan in the early 1980s.

[27] The logic of polarization corresponds well to the patterns described in Kohli, A., *Democracy and Discontent: India's Growing Crisis of Governability* (Cambridge University Press: New York, 1990).

[28] See, e.g., the reports provided by the United News of India, or Brown, M., *International Dimensions of Internal Conflict* (MIT Press: Cambridge, Mass., 1996), p. 5.

Almost immediately after Vishwanath Pratap Singh became Prime Minister of the Janata Dal Government in 1989, he visited Punjab as a conciliatory move. Any impression that separatism was abating, however, was countered by an abduction by 'Kashmiri terrorists' and subsequent widespread demonstrations in Jammu and Kashmir supporting separatism. The Indian Government came increasingly to rely on the use of security forces against any 'anti-national' activities in the state, and the 'spiral of violence' was entered.

Every move to suppress the support for separatists by force seems to have had the opposite result. During the winter of 1989–90 the separatist movement grew rapidly in strength and support. When governor's rule was introduced in January 1990 and Jagmohan took direct control of the state, the harsh measures employed to fight the supporters of the 'Kashmir uprising' resulted in an increase in reports of human rights violations. In particular the border security forces were alleged to be using methods far outside the constitutional limits. At this time the relationship with Pakistan was at an all-time low, and it seems that the crisis in Kashmir seriously jeopardized the peace between India and Pakistan.[29] Since January 1990, violence has continued to plague the state and surprisingly few changes have occurred in the conflict during the past 10 years. The most important characteristics of the conflict can be summarized in four points.

1. Although the levels of violence have varied greatly from year to year, fighting in Jammu and Kashmir has been continuous since 1989. Although president's rule was lifted before the September 1996 election in Jammu and Kashmir, the violent conflict continues.

2. The separatists are only united in one way: they have all agreed to fight against the Indian Government. Otherwise the separatist movement suffers from internal divisions. The All-Party Hurriyat Conference (the Hurriyat) has been the leading 'umbrella organization' for many of the separatist organizations in the state during the 1990s, but it has always been deliberately vague about whether it advocates independence or accession to Pakistan.[30] The dominating organization within the Hurriyat is the Jamaat-e-Islami, which has always advocated accession to Pakistan.[31] The JKLF has been a part of the Hurriyat periodically during the 1990s, and it has also been plagued by severe internal power struggles. Unlike the Jamaat-e-Islami, the JKLF has consistently advocated independence. The picture of separatism in Kashmir became even more complicated as groups referred to in India as foreign mercenaries became more involved in the conflict during the 1990s.[32]

[29] Bobb, D. and Chengappa, R., 'War games: tension between India and Pakistan raises the threat of another conflict', *India Today*, 28 Feb. 1990, pp. 14–19; Jain, M., 'Raising the stakes: Nobody wants war but political compulsions restrict the options', *India Today*, 28 Feb. 1990, pp. 19–21; and Hersh, S. M., 'On the nuclear edge', *New Yorker*, vol. 69, no. 6 (29 Mar. 1993), pp. 56–73.

[30] In 1994 the Hurriyat had 34 organizations as members.

[31] The Jamaat-e-Islami has a military branch, the Hizb-ul Mujaheddin, which has also suffered from internal divisions. For much of the 1990s the Hurriyat was led by the son of the assassinated Mirwaiz Maulvi Farooq, Mirwaiz Maulvi Umar Farooq, although a council of leaders representing the largest or most important organizations in the Hurriyat exercised de facto power. Now the organization is chaired by the leader of the Jamaat-e-Islami, Ali Shah Geelani (see section IV). The Hurriyat also suffers from internal rivalry between the dominant Sunnis and the minority Shia representatives.

[32] Some of them originate from Afghanistan and fought during the war there in the 1980s. The war in Afghanistan contributed significantly to the proliferation of arms in the region and thereby to the escalation of violence. In some cases these groups have appeared in Jammu and Kashmir fighting for organizations such as the Harqut Al-Ansar and possibly the Al Faran, which carried out the kidnapping

3. The policies of the Indian Government during the 1990s have for the most part relied on one simple formula: meet violence with violence. The number of troops in Jammu and Kashmir was estimated at half a million in 1995 and the military presence remains high today. Political moves initiated by the Indian Government have had little effect on the overall situation in Jammu and Kashmir so far.[33]

4. Events during the 1990s show how the conflict in Jammu and Kashmir is entangled in the poor relationship between India and Pakistan. The internal conflict in Jammu and Kashmir in 1990 nearly escalated into a new war between India and Pakistan. Therefore, a diplomatic solution to the conflict in Kashmir would almost certainly need to include the settlement of the border disputes and the status of the Line of Control and the Siachen Glacier.[34] So far, however, there have been no talks between India and Pakistan that could significantly stabilize the relationship between the two states in a longer perspective, and India has rejected any suggestion of bringing in a third party to act as a mediator.

IV. The Kashmir conflict in 1998

The decision to introduce a democratically elected government in Jammu and Kashmir in October 1996 was regarded as everything from an over-optimistic belief in the inherent capacity of democratic institutions to alleviate political tension to a cynical gesture aimed only at creating a democratic façade to abate international criticism on the Kashmir question. Nevertheless, the state assembly election in 1996 was carried out under heavy surveillance and in the presence of armed forces, and Farooq Abdullah managed to establish a new government. After his first year in office the number of 'insurgency-related' incidents dropped, according to some sources by more than 40 per cent. For a while it seemed that Jammu and Kashmir was recovering from the violence and that the strategy was to some extent successful. However, the following year hopes that violence would end were dashed. By the end of 1998 Jammu and Kashmir had lived through one of the most violent periods of the decade. This section recapitulates the evolution of the Kashmir conflict in 1998.

Farooq Abdullah, Kashmir and the Bharatiya Janata Party Government

It is difficult to say whether the election that gave Farooq Abdullah back his post as Chief Minister was corrupted to the same degree as the elections in 1987. The level of violence, the obstrusive presence of military and security forces, the high level of activity by the separatists and the limits put on freedom of information in the state because of the circumstances, combined with the outright fear that plagued the citizens, makes it, to say the least, difficult to classify it as 'free and fair'.[35] The problems

of 5 Western tourists in 1995. Most reports suggest that these 'foreign' troops have only reached Jammu and Kashmir with active support from outside India, and primarily from Pakistan.

[33] Minor incidents have been dealt with by more creative political initiatives, such as the occupation of the Hazratbal mosque in 1993. However, there is no party outside Jammu and Kashmir, or on the national level, that can be characterized as 'taking the side of the Kashmiris', which adds to the alienation of Kashmiris from India. The Indian political context in general was characterized by increased polarization between Hindus and Muslims during the 1990s.

[34] Eventually a political solution should also take into account the Chinese-controlled Aksai Chin.

[35] Official sources claim that the voter turnout was 50–60% in the various regions. This would indicate a 'normal' voter turnout. However, eyewitnesses describe how voters were forced to participate

of trying to rebuild democracy in Jammu and Kashmir are also illustrated by the failure to hold Panchayat, or village-level, elections. Since 1996, Panchayat elections have been planned and then cancelled on three occasions.

Nonetheless, Farooq Abdullah returned to power and managed, in cooperation with the United Front Government, to reduce tension to some extent in the state. Hopes were raised that Hindus who had migrated in large numbers, in particular from the Kashmir Valley, would be able to move back. These hopes were dashed when 23 Pandits, or Kashmiri Brahmins, were killed on 25 January 1998 in an attack by separatists in Wandhama village. Wandhama is a part of Abdullah's constituency and the act was carried out the day before the Indian Republic Day. The symbolic message was clear: Farooq Abdullah could be attacked in his own 'backyard' and Kashmir should not be seen as a part of India. The new year could not have started more badly and from this point onwards the situation in Jammu and Kashmir was to deteriorate further.

As in 1984 and 1990, Abdullah was charged by his opponents with having lost control over Jammu and Kashmir. The Lok Sabha, or national, election carried out in February–March 1998 further weakened his position. In the state assembly in October 1996 the National Conference had won a clear majority. In the Lok Sabha election Abdullah's party won three of the six seats, which was widely seen as a sign of weakening support.[36] Furthermore, the Anantnag seat was won by Congress (I), which was seen as a particularly hard blow to the National Conference, and the two remaining seats were won by the Bharatiya Janata Party (BJP). Political change on the national level would also challenge Abdullah's position. The national election brought the BJP to power. Farooq Abdullah therefore found that from his weakened position in the state, trying to represent a Muslim-dominated population, he was forced to cooperate with the Hindu nationalist party. The BJP has the assimilation of Jammu and Kashmir, and 'abolishing Article 370', which guarantees Jammu and Kashmir's autonomy in the constitution, on its main agenda. This would prove to be an almost impossible balancing act for Abdullah.

At first, the situation did not look too gloomy. The fact that the BJP had to form a minority government had the effect of moderating some of its more radical positions. Most significant was that the demand regarding Article 370 was not pursued and it seemed for a while that the BJP and the National Conference had managed to find a formula for coexistence. Farooq Abdullah managed to keep the peace with the BJP Government by making the National Conference Lok Sabha members abstain from voting against the new government. To the surprise of many, Abdullah also supported the Indian nuclear tests carried out in May, and was rewarded by being allowed to accompany Prime Minister Atal Bihari Vajpayee on the highly publicized visit to the Pokhran test site. In sum, the spring was to some extent characterized by consolidation on the elite level of politics with regard to the situation in Jammu and Kashmir. The situation became more complicated when regional political forces reacted against Abdullah's association with the Hindu nationalists and when other voices within the BJP were raised concerning the Kashmir issue.

In Jammu and Kashmir Farooq Abdullah's cooperation with the BJP was condemned by, among others, the Hurriyat. After the BJP formed the new government the Hurriyat elected a new chairperson. The former chairperson, who was regarded as

in the election in, e.g., Anantnag and Baramulla. Baweja, H., 'Voting under coercion', *India Today*, 15 June 1996, pp. 48–51.

[36] The Srinagar seat was won by Farooq Abdullah's son Omar Abdullah.

a more moderate leader, was replaced on 24 April by Ali Shah Geelani, the long-time leader of the Jamaat-e-Islami who has always advocated accession of Jammu and Kashmir to Pakistan. How this will affect the JKLF's membership of the Hurriyat remains to be seen since the JKLF clearly advocates independence for Jammu and Kashmir. The significant change was that the largest umbrella organization for the separatist organizations chose a leader who was politically as far away as possible from the BJP.

Within the BJP, too, the positions were less accommodating. Home Minister Lal Krishna Advani, widely known to be a 'hardliner' on issues regarding Kashmir and Pakistan, announced after the government's first meeting on Kashmir, on 18 May, that Pakistan would have to pay 'dearly' for its interference in Jammu and Kashmir.[37] In his speeches Advani has made a direct connection between India's nuclear tests and India's policy on Kashmir. Such statements were quoted by Pakistan's Prime Minister Nawaz Sharif in his speeches on the tension with India. Advani was also quoted as supporting a policy of allowing Indian troops to follow separatists beyond the Line of Control.[38] At this point the relationship between India and Pakistan entered a critical phase and, according to some observers, the tension that developed in the late spring and early summer of 1998 was as high as in 1990, when war was imminent. Advani's position towards Pakistan was regarded as central to the polarization. Furthermore, Advani ruled out any negotiations with separatists, including the Hurriyat, and Defence Minister George Fernandes was asked to cancel a planned meeting with Geelani.[39] In spite of the growing tension, Farooq Abdullah continued to avoid antagonizing the BJP Government and he endorsed Advani's four-point plan on Jammu and Kashmir that was launched in May.

The four-point plan included strengthening the democratic process, a strategy to isolate the militants, a more proactive approach by the security forces and a programme for development.[40] Under the 'development programme' the Indian Government promised to reimburse the Jammu and Kashmir state government for some of the high security expenses. Costs relating to the conflict had certainly put a halt to many of the development projects planned in the state, and in 1998 the state deficit was so high that Jammu and Kashmir was described as bankrupt.[41] The proactive approach included giving freer rein to the military and the security forces and to some extent there were 'success stories', such as when the Jammu and Kashmir Police Special Operations Group in a joint action with the security forces carried out its attack on the Hizbul Mujaheedin leader Ali Mohammed Dar in August.[42] Nevertheless, only three months after Advani's plan had been launched it was evaluated as having had no positive impact.[43] The main reason for this conclusion was the escalation of violence.

[37] Baruah, A., 'The South Asian nuclear mess', *Frontline*, vol. 15, no. 12 (6–19 June 1998), URL <http://www.the-hindu.com/fline/fl1512/15120040.htm>.

[38] Strategies including 'hot pursuit' were, however, rejected by Defence Minister George Fernandes and, by the end of the year, by Advani himself.

[39] It should be noted that Fernandes' political background is in the Janata Party and not the BJP.

[40] Some of those steps clearly resemble some of the actions taken by the Indian Government when dealing with the problem of the Punjab.

[41] Mojumdar, A., 'Funds crunch hampering J&K development: Farooq Abdullah', *The Statesman* (Delhi), 28 Nov. 1998.

[42] Dar and several of his aides were killed in the attack.

[43] See, e.g., Bhan, R., 'Centre's big plans make no dent on militancy in Kashmir', *Indian Express* (New Delhi), 23 Aug. 1998.

Violence in Kashmir in 1998

Both separatist-related violence and cross-border firing increased in 1998. Much of the separatist violence was claimed to be the result of foreign insurgency operations. As described in section III, forces from as far away as Afghanistan were reported as being active in the state.[44] Both 1997 and 1998 saw an increase in militants crossing the border and new infiltration routes were used, especially further south in Jammu. Intelligence agencies estimated that 400 militants crossed the border in 1997 from Jammu as compared to 100 in 1996. May 1998, however, was reported to have seen a higher number of border crossings by separatists than ever before.[45]

As the border crossings increased, so did the violence. The attack on Pandits in January was followed by more attacks on Hindus and more separatist-related violence followed from April onwards.[46] Violence that was previously confined to the Kashmir Valley spread to Jammu and in particular the areas around Rajauri, Poonch and Udhampur.[47] By August observers claimed that Jammu and Kashmir had gone through one of the most violent periods of the whole decade.[48] It is far too easy to explain the increase by focusing on the 'foreign mercenaries' alone. The inclination to support and join the separatists' movement also seemed to increase inside the state.[49]

Many of the assessments that violence increased in 1998 also take into account the cross-border firing by the Indian and Pakistani military forces. Firing at various places along the Line of Control intensified after the Indian and Pakistani nuclear tests in May and culminated in July with an intense exchange lasting for two weeks with as many as 150 casualties, mostly civilian, on both sides together.[50] Firing across the Line of Control often 'coincides' with diplomatic talks, and this time the crescendo was reached when Atal Bihari Vajpayee and Nawaz Sharif met in Colombo at the end of July. The intensity of shelling across the border was the highest since the war in 1971. The heightened tension was also reflected by several decisions made by the Indian Government to send more troops to Jammu and Kashmir.

Against this background the continued failure to establish a constructive dialogue between India and Pakistan is a cause for concern. Talks at the foreign-secretary level from 1990 onwards provided no solutions to or improvements in the problems in Kashmir. In November 1998 the positions were as far apart as they had ever been. Pakistan's Foreign Minister Sartaj Aziz stated that recognition of the 'right of self-determination of the people' is the prerequisite for any solution of the Kashmir problem. This is interpreted by India as meaning that Pakistan will only negotiate if India agrees to a plebiscite, and this will not be accepted by India. It should be added that the plebiscite Pakistan may have in mind does not include the JKLF's position on

[44] Baweja, H., 'Hired guns', *India Today*, 4 May 1998, pp. 26–27.

[45] Swami, P., 'Tackling terror', *Frontline*, vol. 15, no. 10 (9–22 May 1998), URL <http://www.the-hindu.com/fline/fl1510/15100650.htm>.

[46] Chengappa, R., 'The no-win situation', *India Today*, 6 July 1998, pp. 16–17.

[47] Ramakrishnan, V., 'A new front in the proxy war', *Frontline*, vol. 15, no. 13 (20 June–3 July 1998), URL <http://www.the-hindu.com/fline/fl1513/15130180.htm>.

[48] 'J&K most violent spell in decade', *Hindustan Times*, 11 Aug. 1998; and Swami, P., 'The tales of a bloody November', *Frontline*, vol. 15, no. 25 (5–18 Dec. 1998), URL <http://www.the-hindu.com/fline/fl1525/15250360.htm>.

[49] According to Joshi, B., 'Police in Kashmir upset as more locals join insurgents', *Economic Times* (New Delhi), 12 Oct. 1998.

[50] Swami, P., 'Flashpoint Kashmir', *Frontline*, vol. 15, no. 17 (15–28 Aug. 1998), URL <http://www.the-hindu.com/fline/fl1517/15170040.htm>.

independence.[51] India also continued to adhere to the demand that no third party should be allowed to take part in negotiations on the Kashmir problem. The nuclear tests carried out in May highlighted the importance of the Kashmir issue in the broader context of nuclear proliferation in the region. The UN Secretary-General and a number of state leaders around the world urged India and Pakistan to try to settle the dispute. Continued talks on Kashmir were expected in February 1999 but there was little to indicate a change in the positions mentioned here. Bilateral negotiations between India and Pakistan on Kashmir have provided few solutions over the past 50 years.

V. Conclusions

The political heritage in Kashmir has certainly worked against democratic development. The repeated military confrontations with neighbouring states led the Indian Government to give priority to security rather than the democratic consolidation that the rest of the country experienced. The changes after the 1975 Delhi Accord paved the way for the introduction of free and fair elections and, for one decade, democracy was perceived as an alternative far more attractive than violence for pursuing political demands. This changed during the 1980s as the political elite in Jammu and Kashmir and the state government took advantage of the system for short-term gains. This led to a process of deinstitutionalization, resulting in a polarization along religious divides, the fall of democracy by the end of 1989 and the outbreak of widespread separatist violence.

The 1990s has been a decade of violence for Kashmir during which the relationship between India and Pakistan has continued to be volatile. In 1998 no political or diplomatic solutions to the conflict were in sight. The two countries have not been able to agree on significant measures to decrease tension and no third-party intervention has been allowed. The nuclear tests worsened the relationship between India and Pakistan and were followed by a drastic increase in firing across the Line of Control and an escalation of violence in Jammu and Kashmir. If the attempt to reinstall democratic institutions had some effects in decreasing tension in Jammu and Kashmir in 1996 and 1997, all such processes were reversed in 1998. The separatist movement, although internally divided, continues its war against the Indian Union.

Clearly, peace in South Asia is most threatened by the conflict between Pakistan and India, and Kashmir is one of the main causes of the tension. The risk of full-scale war cannot be neglected, and the use of nuclear arms cannot be ruled out. Despite military and diplomatic tension, however, there is no evidence that either India or Pakistan is currently planning an offensive attack on its neighbour. The risk of seeing the use of nuclear arms in South Asia seems remote from a rational perspective. Nevertheless, the conflict in Kashmir undoubtedly adds to instability in the region in that a war could be set off by mistake. There is no comprehensive security arrangement for the region, and border confrontations and internal fighting continue. The Line of Control, which runs through the Kashmir region, is the most volatile area in South Asia.

[51] Joshi, M., 'Terms of engagement', *India Today*, 2 Nov. 1998, URL <http://www.india-today.com./itoday/02111998/diplo.html>.

Appendix 1C. The Kosovo conflict

STEFAN TROEBST

I. Introduction

The province of Kosovo—Kosova, in Albanian—is today an administrative unit of 10 887 square kilometres consisting of 29 municipalities in the south-western part of the Republic of Serbia within the Federal Republic of Yugoslavia (FRY).[1] According to incomplete official Serbian statistics, of the 1 954 747 inhabitants of Kosovo in 1991, 1 607 690 (82.2 per cent) were Albanians, 195 301 (10.0 per cent) Serbs, 57 408 (2.9 per cent) southern Slav-speaking Muslims, 42 806 (2.2 per cent) Roma, 20 045 (1.0 per cent) Montenegrins, 10 838 (0.6 per cent) Turks, and 8161 (0.4 per cent) Croats.[2] An estimated 85 per cent of the population in Kosovo are Muslims and the rest Christian Orthodox and Catholic. By the end of 1995, 340 700 Kosovar Albanians had sought political asylum outside the FRY.[3] In 1998 the armed conflict in Kosovo resulted in the flight of another 98 100 Kosovar Albanians: 42 000 to Montenegro, 20 500 to Albania, 20 000 to other parts of Serbia, 8600 to Bosnia and Herzegovina, 3000 to Macedonia, 2000 to Slovenia and 2000 to Turkey; in addition, 200 000 were displaced within Kosovo.[4] There were also population movements of non-Albanians in Kosovo. In 1991–96 some 19 000 Serbian refugees from Bosnia and Herzegovina, Krajina and other parts of Croatia were resettled in Kosovo,[5] while in 1998 the war caused about 20 000 Kosovo Serbs to flee to the interior of Serbia.[6] By the spring of 1997 nearly the entire Croat population of Kosovo had emigrated to Croatia.[7]

Between February and October 1998 a major armed conflict took place in central and western Kosovo between the Kosovar Albanian guerrilla formation called the Kosovo Liberation Army (KLA, known as the Ushtria Clirimtare e Kosoves, UCK, in Albanian) and regular units of the Army of Yugoslavia (Vojska Jugoslavije, VJ), regular Serbian police as well as three specialized police forces of the Public Security Service within the Ministry of the Interior of the Republic of Serbia (Sluzba javne bezbednosti Ministerstva unustrasnjih poslova Republike Srbije, MUP)—that is, the Special Purposes Police Units (Jedinice posebne namjene policije, JPNP), also called the Red Berets; the Special Anti-Terror Units (Specialne antiteroristicke jedinice, SAJ); and the Special Police Unit (Posebna jedinica milicije, PJM).[8] Fighting resulted in the death of over 100 Serbian police officers, some 40 army soldiers, and an

[1] Yugoslavia (Serbia and Montenegro) was formally established as the FRY on 27 Apr. 1992.

[2] Pushka, A. (translated by M. Hamiti), *Kosova and its Ethnic Albanian Background: An Historical–Geographical Atlas* (Qendra per Informim e Kosoves: Pristina, 1996), tables 14–15, pp. 21–22.

[3] Council of Europe, Parliamentary Assembly, 1996 Ordinary Session, 5th Sitting, Resolution 1077 (1996) on Albanian asylum seekers from Kosovo, Strasbourg, 24 Jan. 1996, para. 3.

[4] United Nations High Commissioner for Refugees, 'UN inter-agency update on Kosovo situation report period covered: 14–20 Oct. 1998', Pristina, 22 Oct. 1998, p. 4, URL <http://www.reliefweb.int>.

[5] Malcolm, N., *Kosovo: A Short History* (Macmillan and New York University Press: London/New York, 1998), pp. 352–53.

[6] Dinmore, G., 'Kosovo Serbs flee war in their ancestral homes', *Financial Times*, 21 May 1998, p. 2.

[7] Vickers, M., *Between Serb and Albanian: A History of Kosovo* (C. Hurst and Columbia University Press: London/New York, 1998), pp. 307–308.

[8] Federation of American Scientists, FAS Intelligence Resource Program, 'Serbia intelligence and security agencies', URL <http://www.fas.org/irp/world/serbia>.

Figure 1C. Map of Kosovo

unknown number of Montenegrin and Serbian civilians as well as about 1500 casualties on the Albanian side.[9] Estimates of the number of houses rendered uninhabitable vary between 20 000 and 45 000.[10]

The next section of this appendix presents a brief background to the present conflict, followed in section III by an account of the armed conflict in the period February–October 1998. Section IV describes the period of the informal ceasefire, agreed on 12 October 1998, up to the end of the year. Section V presents the conclusions.

[9] Rüb, M., 'Im Kosovo sind ganze Landstriche entvölkert' [Entire areas depopulated in Kosovo], *Frankfurter Allgemeine Zeitung*, 6 Oct. 1998, p. 3. See also Loza, T., 'A Milosevic for all seasons', *Transitions*, vol. 5, no. 10 (Oct. 1998), p. 38; and Council for the Defence of Human Rights and Freedoms in Prishtina, 'Report on the violation of human rights and fundamental freedoms in Kosova during October 1998', Pristina, 6 Nov. 1998, URL <http://albanian.com/kmdlnj/showdoc.cgi?/file=english/mujore/10en.htm>.

[10] Hiatt, F., 'Strong talk about Kosovo was just talk', *International Herald Tribune*, 1 Sep. 1998, p. 8; and Rüb (note 9).

II. Background

The current conflict between Serbs and Kosovar Albanians over the province of Kosovo is a territorial one, albeit with strong ethno-political, cultural and language factors. Economic, religious and ethnic identity factors are considerably less prominent. The claims on the entire territory of Kosovo by the present Serbian regime are based on arguments of history going back to the 12th century, when the territory of today's Kosovo formed the core of medieval Serbia. Albania and the Kosovar Albanian elite also argue in terms of history, referring to an ancient state called Illyria that covered the entire territory of Kosovo. In addition, both sides stress ethno-demographic factors such as continuous Serbian settlement from the time of the major migrations of the 5th century to the 1990s and the continuous Albanian settlement from classical antiquity to the present day.

The conflict is also a consequence of a wider Albanian question in the southern Balkan region. This knot of territorial and ethno-political problems emerged in the late 19th century as a by-product of the disintegration of the Ottoman Empire. Since the Albanian lands as well as the Albanian political elite were much more firmly integrated into the Sultan's realm than were their Greek, Slav or other neighbours, they developed a national movement much later than the others. When 'Turkey-in-Europe' was finally divided up among the Balkan states in the Balkan Wars of 1912 and 1912–13, Albanians were the last to achieve their own nation-state. The Kingdom of Albania, established in 1913, was about the size of today's Republic of Albania and nearly half the Albanian population remained outside its borders. Considerable Albanian-speaking minorities lived in Montenegro, southern Serbia, western Macedonia, north-western Greece, southern Italy and, in particular, in Kosovo.[11] From 1912 to the present day, Kosovo and its Albanian majority have been under harsh Serbian rule which has periodically resembled that of an apartheid regime. Thus, inter-ethnic Serbian–Albanian relations in Kosovo were permanently tense.[12] The exception was the period of full territorial autonomy granted to Kosovo in 1974 and lasting until the 1980s. However, Serbian President Slobodan Milosevic withdrew the autonomy step-by-step from 1988 to 1991 and reinstalled Serbian rule over the province. The Albanian majority reacted by establishing a 'parallel state' with its own educational, fiscal, health, media and other structures.[13]

In 1991 the efforts of the Kosovar Albanian leadership to obtain recognition by the outside world as a Yugoslav successor state along with Bosnia and Herzegovina,

[11] Schukalla, K.-J., 'Nationale Minderheiten in Albanien und Albaner im Ausland' [National minorities in Albania and Albanians abroad], ed. K.-D. Grothusen, *Albanien* (Südosteuropa-Handbuch, VIII), (Vandenhoeck & Ruprecht: Göttingen, 1993), pp. 505–28; and Troebst, S., 'Still looking for an answer to the "Albanian Question"', *Transition*, vol. 3, no. 4 (Mar. 1997), pp. 24–27, and the figure 'Ethnic Albanians in Southeastern Europe', p. 25.

[12] Reuter, J., *Die Albaner in Jugoslawien* [The Albanians in Yugoslavia] (R. Oldenbourg: Munich, 1982); and Roux, M., *Les Albanais en Yougoslavie: Minorité nationale, territoire et développement* [The Albanians in Yugoslavia: national minority, territory and development] (Editions de la maison des sciences de l'homme: Paris, 1992).

[13] Lukic, R. and Lynch, A., SIPRI, *Europe from the Balkans to the Urals: The Disintegration of Yugoslavia and the Soviet Union* (Oxford University Press: Oxford, 1996), pp. 143–62; Schmidt, F., 'Kosovo: the time bomb that has not gone off', Radio Free Europe/Radio Liberty, *RFE/RL Research Report*, vol. 2, no. 39 (1993), pp. 21–29; Reuter, J., 'Die politische Entwicklung in Kosovo 1992/93: Andauernde serbische Repressionspolitik' [Political developments in Kosovo 1992/93: continuous Serb policy of repression], *Südosteuropa*, vol. 43 (1994), pp. 18–30; and Kostovicova, D., *Parallel Worlds: Response of Kosovo Albanians to Loss of Autonomy in Serbia, 1986–1996*, Keele European Research Centre Research Papers: Southeast Europe Series, 2 (Keele University: Keele, 1997).

Croatia, Macedonia, Slovenia, and later the FRY had failed. According to the Economic Community (EC) Conference on Yugoslavia held in The Hague in 1991, the secession of Kosovo from the FRY would constitute a one-sided change of international borders and thus be a violation of international law.[14] In spite of severe political repression and systematic violations of human rights by Belgrade, under the influence of the Democratic League of Kosova (Lidhja Demokratike e Kosoves, LDK) and its chairman Ibrahim Rugova, the Kosovar Albanian elite did not turn to violence to pursue their aim of independence but instead proclaimed non-violence as its main tactic. The peculiar dualism of an official Serbian state and a Kosovar Albanian 'parallel state' on the same territory began to erode with the 1995 General Framework Agreement for Peace in Bosnia and Herzegovina (the Dayton Agreement).[15] Since the Kosovo problem was not addressed in this agreement, the Kosovar Albanians were deeply disappointed and considered themselves as 'the Forgotten of Dayton'. From early 1996 influential intellectuals challenged Rugova's tactics of non-violent resistance by opting for a proactive intifada-type protest movement.[16] The radicals formed an underground movement which turned to violent means in fighting the Serbian regime. In the autumn of 1997 these activist and militant wings were reinforced by a student movement which staged mass demonstrations. At this point, the asymmetrical conflict between the Serbian state, with its firm security and military structures, and the Kosovar Albanian majority population, with its feeble 'parallel institutions', spiralled towards inter-ethnic warfare.

III. The war over Kosovo

In January and February 1998 a Serbian military build-up took place in Kosovo in preparation for a strike against the still *in statu nascendi* KLA guerrilla force. According to Albanian, Serbian and Western estimates, there were some 15 000 regular police and SAJ, JPNP and PJM forces in Kosovo as well as about 15 000 VJ troops.[17] The mobile components of the 52nd Army Corps in Pristina (Prishtina)[18] consisted of 140 tanks and 150 armoured vehicles.[19] The strength of the KLA was estimated at 350–1500 fighters in the beginning of 1998[20]—a figure which was said to have risen to 5000–30 000 members in the late spring.[21] Throughout the war, except when they occasionally captured Yugoslav Army tanks and artillery, KLA

[14] Ramcharan, B. G. (ed.), *The International Conference on the Former Yugoslavia: Official Papers*, vol. 1 (Kluwer Law International: The Hague, London, Boston, 1997), p. 3.

[15] For the text, see *SIPRI Yearbook 1996: Armaments, Disarmament and International Security* (Oxford University Press: Oxford), 1996), appendix 5A, pp. 232–50.

[16] Schmidt, F., 'Teaching the wrong lesson in Kosovo', *Transition*, vol. 2, no. 14 (July 1996), pp. 37–39.

[17] US Department of State, 'Off-Camera Daily Press Briefing, DPB #119, Thursday, October 29, 1998', URL <http://www.fas.org/man/dod-101/ops/docs/981029db.html>; and *KD-arta*, 2 Mar. 1998, URL <http://www.koha.net/ARTA/ drenica.htm>.

[18] At the first mention, the names of towns are given in Serbian, with the Albanian name in parentheses; thereafter, the Serbian names are used. Where only one name is given, it is identical in Albanian and Serbian.

[19] Jovanovic, V., '"Adut" za kasnije pregovore: Priprema li se ogranicen udar na Drenicu?' ['Advance move' for later negotiations: Is a limited strike against Drenica in the making?], *Nedeljna Nasa Borba*, 31 Jan.–1 Feb. 1998, p. 2.

[20] Kusovac, Z., 'Another Balkans bloodbath?', *Jane's Intelligence Review*, no. 2 (1998), pp. 13–16.

[21] Stavljanin, D., 'Kosovo crosses the brink', *Transitions*, vol. 5, no. 7 (July 1998), p. 64.

armaments remained poor and insufficient.[22] The underground army was said to be 'organized in small compartmentalized cells rather than a single large rebel movement and is divided between a manoeuvrable strike nucleus of a few hundred trained commandos and the much larger number of locally organized members active throughout the region'.[23] Up to the October 1998 ceasefire, the degree of coordination between the KLA supreme command, the various field commanders and individual units was low because of a 'rather horizontal command structure'.[24]

On 28 February a battle between KLA fighters on the one side and SAJ, JPNP and PJM units on the other, equipped with 20 helicopter gunships and 30 armoured personnel carriers, took place near the Drenica village of Likosan (Likoshan). The incident was triggered by the killing of four Serbian policemen in a KLA ambush. During the next three days, more than 16 Albanian guerrillas were killed.[25] On 2 March Serbian riot police equipped with armoured vehicles, water canons, tear gas and batons attacked a large crowd of Albanian demonstrators in Pristina and injured at least 289 persons.[26] On 4–7 March the Serbian security forces directed a second attack, on the Drenica villages of Donji Prekaz (Prekaz i Ulet) and Lausa (Llausha), in which entire extended families and clans were executed.[27] In what the Kosovar Albanians later called the Drenica Massacre, some 80 Albanians, among them 25 women and children, were killed.[28] Thus the stage was set for the seven months of war to come.

At the same time the stage was set for reactions by the international community. By March 1998, owing to what was called a 10-year 'pattern of neglect',[29] neither the Organization for Security and Co-operation in Europe (OSCE), the European Union (EU), the United Nations or NATO nor individual great powers had adopted or even

[22] Steele, J., 'Kosovo fighters set no-go areas', *Guardian Weekly*, 17 May 1998, p. 4; Federation of American Scientists, FAS Intelligence Resource Program, 'Kosovo Liberation Army KLA', URL <http://www.fas.org/irp/world/para/kla.htm>. By the end of 1998, however, the KLA was said to be in possession of 'significant amounts of anti-tank rockets, anti-aircraft guns, shoulder-fired Stinger anti-aircraft missiles, and long-barrelled sniper rifles that can pierce armoured vehicles . . . from three-quarters of a mile away'. Associated Press, 20 Dec. 1998, citing 'unnamed foreign experts' in 'Quotes of the week', *Radio Free Europe/Radio Liberty Balkan Report*, vol. 2, no. 51 (30 Dec. 1998), URL <http:www.rferl.org/balkan-report/index-html>.

[23] 'Quotes of the week' (note 22).

[24] Quoted by Garton Ash, T., 'Cry, the dismembered country', *New York Review of Books*, vol. 46, no. 1 (Jan. 1999), p. 30.

[25] International Crisis Group, 'Again, the visible hand: Slobodan Milosevic's manipulation of the Kosovo dispute', Belgrade, 6 May 1998, URL <http://www.intl-crisis-group.org/projects/sbalkans/reports/you02rep. htm'exe>.

[26] Hedges, C., 'Serb riot police beat protesters in edgy Kosovo', *International Herald Tribune*, 3 Mar. 1998, p. 1; and Rüb, M., 'Bewunderung für die Befreiungsarmee der Kosovo-Albaner' [Admiration for the KLA], *Frankfurter Allgemeine Zeitung*, 4 Mar. 1998, p. 5.

[27] Dinmore, G., '30 killed in Serb clashes with Albanian rebels', *Financial Times*, 2 Mar. 1998, pp. 1, 20; Hedges, C., 'Serbia tries to stamp out an ethnic Albanian rebellion in Kosovo', *International Herald Tribune*, 3 Mar. 1998, p. 5; Dinmore, G., 'Serbian forces accused of slaughter', *Financial Times*, 3 Mar. 1998, p. 2; Robinson, A., 'Alarm bell sounds over Kosovo', *Financial Times*, 4 Mar. 1998, p. 2; Hedges, C., 'After the rampage: bodies of 14 Kosovo Albanians return home', *International Herald Tribune*, 5 Mar. 1998, p. 7; and 'The Kosovo cauldron', *The Economist*, 14 Mar. 1998, pp. 33–34.

[28] *Kosovo Spring: The International Crisis Group Guide to Kosovo* (International Crisis Group: Brussels, 1998), p. 8; and Hedges, C., 'Bodies attest to fury of Serb attack on town', *International Herald Tribune*, 10 Mar. 1998, p. 6.

[29] Caplan, R., 'International diplomacy and the crisis in Kosovo', *International Affairs*, vol. 74, no. 4 (Oct. 1998), p. 747.

formulated a Kosovo policy. Instead, international actors kept repeating their 'deep concern' over what was happening in Kosovo.[30]

At its London meeting of 9 March 1998, the six-power Contact Group,[31] which in the autumn of 1997 had emerged as the main coordinating body for handling the Kosovo crisis, was unable to arrive at a unanimous position. While the USA and the UK opted for a swift and harsh reaction, France, Italy and Russia refused to agree to such a move, and Germany tried to mediate. This resulted in a statement by the UN Security Council calling for no more than 'a comprehensive arms embargo against the FRY, including Kosovo',[32] 'a refusal to supply equipment to the FRY which might be used for internal repression, or for terrorism', the 'denial of visas for senior FRY and Serbian representatives responsible for repressive action by FRY security forces in Kosovo' and 'a moratorium on government financed credit support for trade and investment, including government financing for privatisation, in Serbia'.[33] Russia dissociated itself from the last two measures. By making some concessions, Milosevic succeeded in widening the gap between the Contact Group members and thus achieved a five-day extension of the deadline that had been fixed on 9 March: within 10 days Milosevic was to take specific steps to stop the violence as well as engage in a commitment to find a political solution through dialogue.[34] When the Contact Group met on 25 March in Bonn, the then long-expired deadline was extended another four weeks,[35] even though on the previous day a new Serbian revenge attack on three villages near the town of Decani (Decan) on the border with Albania resulted in the death of over 40 Kosovar Albanians.[36]

At the next Contact Group meeting, held in Rome on 29 April 1998, it was established that 'crucial requirements set out in the Contact Group's statements of 9 and 25 March' had not yet been met by Milosevic, and a freeze of funds held abroad by the FRY and the Serbian governments was put into effect. However, the Contact Group announced that it would 'immediately reverse this decision' if by 9 May the parties to the conflict had set up a 'framework for dialogue' and adopted a 'stabilization package'. Should Belgrade fail to comply by that date, the Group's Western members threatened 'action to stop new investment in Serbia'.[37]

[30] Troebst, S., *Conflict in Kosovo: Failure of Prevention? An Analytical Documentation, 1992–1998*, ECMI Working Paper no. 1 (European Centre for Minority Issues: Flensburg, 1998), pp. 21–71, also available on the Internet at URL <http:// www.ecmi.de/wp_r.htm#Conflict in Kosovo>.

[31] Formally established in Apr. 1994, the Contact Group on Bosnia and Herzegovina originally consisted of France, Germany, Russia, the UK and the USA, represented by their foreign ministers. In May 1996 it was enlarged to include Italy. Contact Group meetings are usually also attended by representatives of the EU Presidency, the EU Commission, the OSCE Chairman-in-Office and the Office of the High Representative (the OHR was established to monitor implementation of the Dayton Agreement).

[32] On 31 Mar. the Security Council adopted this proposal and decided on an embargo of 'arms and related *materiel* of all types, such as weapons and ammunition, military vehicles and equipment and spare parts for the aforementioned'. UN Security Council Resolution 1160, 31 Mar. 1998.

[33] 'Contact Group meeting, statement on Kosovo, London, 9 March 1998', URL <http://www.ohr.int/docu/d980309a.htm>.

[34] 'Kosovo and the allies', *International Herald Tribune*, 21–22 Mar. 1998, p. 6.

[35] 'Contact Group statement on Kosovo, Bonn, 25 March 1998', URL <http://www.ohr.int/docu/d980325b. htm>.

[36] Drozdiak, W., 'US faces uphill battle on Kosovo', *International Herald Tribune*, 25 Mar. 1988, p. 7; 'Tote bei Kämpfen in Kosovo' [Deaths in clashes in Kosovo], *Frankfurter Rundschau*, 26 Mar. 1998, p. 1; and 'Rugova fordert mehr Engagement der Kontaktgruppe' [Rugova calls for greater commitment from the Contact Group], *Frankfurter Allgemeine Zeitung*, 28 Mar. 1998, p. 2.

[37] 'Contact Group statement, Rome, 29 April 1998', URL <http://www.ohr.int/docu/ d980429a.htm>.

In mid-April 1998 clashes took place between Yugoslav border guards and KLA fighters crossing into Kosovo from Albania,[38] where the underground army had set up a training and stockpiling base in the Albanian border village of Tropoje.[39] The Albanian Government in Tirana, which tried to remain neutral in the Kosovo conflict, was unable to effectively control the northern part of its country. Thus, Kosovar Albanian volunteers from Western Europe, with armaments and equipment, freely crossed into northern Albania and from there into the FRY. The fighting on the border soon spread into western Kosovo. On 22 April Serbian security forces shelled the Decani village of Babaloc (Baballoc),[40] and on 23 April 1998—the day a referendum on international mediation in the Kosovo conflict was held throughout Serbia[41]—a two-day battle began near the border village of Kozare between some 200 KLA guerrillas and Yugoslav troops, resulting in the death of 23 Kosovar Albanians.[42] During the following days, newly brought-in VJ units shelled villages with artillery and tanks, while KLA fighters attacked police posts in the Djakovica (Gjakova) region to the south of Decani.[43]

Although only lightly armed, the steadily growing KLA now became a military problem for the inflexible Soviet-style Yugoslav Army, with its poor morale, low night-fighting ability and lack of counter-insurgency experience.[44] From May the KLA expanded its activities into central Kosovo by attacking police posts on the region's main traffic artery, the highway leading west from Pristina to Pec (Peja) and further into Montenegro.[45]

The increasing strength of the KLA was exploited by US diplomacy to pressure LDK chairman Rugova to agree to direct negotiations with the FRY. On 15 May Milosevic received Rugova in Belgrade for the first round of what was supposed to become an institutionalized dialogue.[46] The meeting did not bring any concrete results but seriously damaged the reputation of Rugova, who was accused of treason by some Kosovar Albanians.[47] Milosevic, on the other hand, profited from the 'photo opportunity' with Rugova by demonstrating his willingness to find a political solution to the conflict and thus regaining goodwill in the West. Accordingly, with the con-

[38] 'Zwischenfall an der Grenze Jugoslawiens zu Albanien' [Incident on Yugoslavia's border with Albania], *Neue Zürcher Zeitung*, 21 Apr. 1998, p. 3.

[39] 'International Crisis Group, The view from Tirana: the Albanian dimension of the Kosovo crisis, Tirana–Sarajevo, 10 July 1998', URL <http://www.intl-crisis-group.org/projects/sbalkans/reports/kosrep03.htm#1>.

[40] 'Berichte über Gefechte im Westen Kosovos' [Report on fighting in western Kosovo], *Neue Zürcher Zeitung*, 23 Apr. 1998, p. 2.

[41] With a turnout of some 73%, 95% answered 'No' to the question 'Do you approve of the participation of foreign representatives in the solution of the problems in Kosovo and Metohija?'. 'Milosevic triumphiert—Erhöhte Kriegsgefahr in Kosovo' [Milosevic triumphs—increased danger of war in Kosovo], *Neue Zürcher Zeitung*, 25–26 Apr. 1998, p. 3.

[42] 'Clash on Albanian border is reported as Serbs vote', *International Herald Tribune*, 24 Apr. 1998, p. 5; and Dinmore, G., 'Yugoslavs say Albania aids "terrorists"', *Financial Times*, 25–26 Apr. 1998, p. 2.

[43] 'Clash breaks out on Kosovo border', *International Herald Tribune*, 27 Apr. 1998, p. 5; Dinmore, G. and Barber, L., 'Kosovo violence "spinning out of control"', *Financial Times*, 28 Apr. 1998, p. 2; 'Berichte über anhaltende Gefechte in Kosovo' [Report on continuous fighting in Kosovo], *Neue Zürcher Zeitung*, 4 May 1998, p. 1; 'Terror und Gegenterror in Kosovo' [Terror and counter-terror in Kosovo], *Neue Zürcher Zeitung*, 6 May 1998, pp. 1–2; and Dinmore, G., 'Kosovo adversaries dig in for final showdown', *Financial Times*, 7 May 1998, p. 3.

[44] 'Kosovo: it's war', *The Economist*, 2 May 1998, p. 34.

[45] Dinmore, G., 'Rebels in Kosovo attack police patrol', *Financial Times*, 12 May 1998, p. 4.

[46] Dinmore, G., 'Kosovo leader in first talks with Milosevic', *Financial Times*, 16–17 May 1998, p. 2.

[47] Rüb, M., 'Rugova "Kapitulation" vorgeworfen' [Rugova accused of 'capitulation'], *Frankfurter Allgemeine Zeitung*, 15 May 1998, p. 6.

currence of the USA on 23 May, the Contact Group cancelled the 9 May decision by its Western members to impose a ban on investment in the FRY.[48]

With the danger of Western sanctions averted, Milosevic ordered an offensive in the Decani region to destroy the KLA's new base of operations by cutting off its supply routes to Albania. On 24 May villages along the Pec–Djakovica highway were attacked by tanks and artillery and depopulated by scorched-earth tactics. The regional centre Decani was reduced to rubble and its 20 000 inhabitants had to flee. The KLA stronghold Junik, a village near Decani, was reported to have been bombed on 5 June by four Serbian military aircraft.[49] Several Serbian policemen and up to 100 Kosovar Albanians were killed. Villagers fled by the tens of thousands into the neighbouring Kosovo regions around Djakovica and Malisevo (Malisheva), 7000 into Montenegro and another 11 000 to Albania, while some 20 000 were trapped between the front lines.[50] The aim of the offensive was 'to have an eight to 10 kilometre-wide stretch where no neutral people live'.[51] In addition, the Yugoslav Army planted landmines in the new cordon sanitaire along the 130-km border with Albania.[52]

By early June it became obvious that the KLA counter-strategy of defending entire villages against superior Serbian firepower instead of flexibly withdrawing and striking again at night was causing disastrous results.[53] On 13 June 1998 Western media reported that '9000 to 11 000 Yugoslav troops . . . surged into Kosovo, backed by 175 tanks, 200 armoured personnel carriers and 120 artillery batteries, as well as 7000 to 10 000 police or paramilitary troops'.[54] The Serbian side exploited the growing weakness of the KLA by launching a major attack on villages west of Djakovica where tens of thousands of refugees had sought shelter. On 11 June Serbian shelling of the town of Djakovica itself and its immediate surroundings began and lasted for several days.[55]

In late May Western disappointment with Milosevic—who had met Rugova and then again attacked Kosovo Albanian villages—caused the UK, which then held the EU Presidency, and in particular the USA to shift their focus. Because of the Russian obstruction of efforts in the Contact Group, the UK and the USA started acting through Western institutions such as NATO and the EU instead of relying on the

[48] Erlanger, S., 'G-7 nations halt Serbia investment', *International Herald Tribune*, 11 May 1998, p. 5.

[49] 'Aufforderung zum Kampf in Kosovo' [Appeal to fight in Kosovo], *Neue Zürcher Zeitung*, 8 June 1998, p. 1.

[50] Dinmore, G., 'Serbs launch attack on Albanian rebels', *Financial Times*, 25 May 1998, p. 1; 'Mindestens dreizehn Tote bei Kämpfen in Kosovo' [At least 13 killed in clashes in Kosovo], *Neue Zürcher Zeitung*, 27 May 1998, p. 2; '6 killed in Kosovo, ethnic Albanians say', *International Herald Tribune*, 1 June 1998, p. 7; 'Berichte über Gefechte in Kosovo' [Reports on fighting in Kosovo], *Neue Zürcher Zeitung*, 2 June 1998, p. 1; 'Hundreds flee as toll rises in Kosovo', *International Herald Tribune*, 2 June 1998, pp. 1, 6; Buchan, D., 'Serbs step up crackdown in Kosovo', *Financial Times*, 4 June 1998, p. 1; 'Serbian forces claim heavy strikes against Kosovo separatists', *International Herald Tribune*, 4 June 1998, p. 8; 'Schwere Kämpfe im Westen Kosovos' [Fierce battles in western Kosovo], *Neue Zürcher Zeitung*, 5 June 1998, p. 1; Dinmore, G., 'Parallels with Srebrenica found in destruction of Decane', *Financial Times*, 11 June 1998, p. 3; and Steele, J., 'Learning to live with Milosevic', *Transitions*, vol. 5, no. 9 (Sep. 1998), pp. 19–20.

[51] Hedges, C., 'Milosevic starts sweep to crush Kosovo rebels', *International Herald Tribune*, 3 June 1998, pp. 1, 7.

[52] Hedges, C., 'Serbs laying minefields', *International Herald Tribune*, 13–14 June 1998, pp. 1, 4.

[53] Hedges, C., 'For Kosovo rebels, fading hopes', *International Herald Tribune*, 10 June 1998, p. 5.

[54] Myers, S. L., 'NATO action in Kosovo would face new pitfalls', *International Herald Tribune*, 13–14 June 1998, p. 2.

[55] Dinmore, G., 'Serb gunners defy West's "outrage"', *Financial Times*, 12 June 1998, p. 2; and Hedges, C., 'Serbs laying minefields', *International Herald Tribune*, 13–14 June 1998, pp. 1, 4.

Contact Group or the UN.[56] On 9 June the EU banned new investments in Serbia—a decision that in particular affected Greece and Italy[57]—while NATO stepped up its military presence in Albania and Macedonia .[58] On 15 June, some 80 aircraft from 15 NATO countries embarked on exercise 'Determined Falcon', a five-hour show of force in Albania and Macedonia at a distance of 20 km from the border with the FRY. This move was severely criticized by Russia, which pressed for a political solution of the Kosovo conflict.[59]

On the same day, Milosevic countered NATO's demonstration of unity by increasing the number of troops, artillery and anti-aircraft missiles in the region bordering on Albania as well as by paying an official visit to Moscow.[60] His meeting with President Boris Yeltsin on 16 June resulted in an announcement that diplomats accredited in the FRY as well as humanitarian and medical non-governmental organizations would be given unimpeded access to Kosovo, that the return of refugees would not be hindered, and that the Serbian security forces and army would abstain from any repressive actions against the Kosovar Albanian population. Milosevic also repeated his readiness to contribute to a political solution of the conflict and to meet again with Rugova.[61]

Until mid-June, the Serbian supply route from Pristina via Prizren to the western border region had been safe, while the main Kosovo traffic artery, Pristina–Pec, was firmly controlled by the KLA. Now, however, the KLA, from its southern stronghold Malisevo, started to set up temporary checkpoints on the Pristina–Prizren road. In a counter-move, army and special police were concentrated around Suva Reka (Suhareka) and Stimlje (Shtim).[62] In the face of NATO air strikes, however, Milosevic was biding his time until he saw an opportune moment to deliver what was intended to be the *coup de grâce* for the KLA. This moment came when the KLA, ill-coordinated as it still was, began to overstretch its capabilities. In Junik and other places in western Kosovo, battles took place between the Yugoslav Army and the KLA from fixed front-line positions in trenches and bunkers—a type of warfare from which the Serbian side was clearly profiting.[63] Nonetheless, on 24 June the KLA refused to agree to the regional ceasefire offered by US Special Envoy Richard Hol-

[56] Firchett, J., 'NATO draws line on Kosovo', *International Herald Tribune*, 28 May 1998, pp. 1, 8; and Buchan, D., 'NATO prepares for Kosovo explosion', *Financial Times*, 29 May 1998, p. 2.

[57] 'European Union Statement on Kosovo, Brussels, London, 9 June 1998', URL <http://europa.eu.int/abc/doc/off/bull/en/9806/p104023.htm>. See also Barber, L. and Dinmore, G., 'Kosovo crisis prompts EU ban on new investments in Serbia', *Financial Times*, 9 June 1998, p. 16.

[58] 'Statement on Kosovo issued at the meeting of the North Atlantic Council in Defence Ministers Session, Press Release M-NAC-D-1(98)77, 11 June 1998', URL <http://www.nato.int/douc/pr/1998/p98-077e.htm>. See also Drozdiak, W., 'NATO plans air activity as warning to Milosevic', *International Herald Tribune,* 12 June 1998, pp. 1, 12.

[59] Spolar, C., 'NATO planes warn Serbs to halt Kosovo assault', *International Herald Tribune*, 16 June 1998, pp. 1, 4; Dinmore, G., 'Serbs ignore Nato exercise to continue Kosovo attacks', *Financial Times*, 16 June 1998, pp. 2, 18. See also 'Statement by NATO Secretary General, Dr. Javier Solana, on Exercise "Determined Falcon"', Press Release (98)80, 13 June 1998, URL <http://www.nato.int/docu/pr/1998/p98-080e.htm>.

[60] 'Russlands ambivalente Haltung auf dem Balkan' [Russia's ambivalent position on the Balkans], *Neue Zürcher Zeitung*, 16 June 1998, p. 2.

[61] Thornhill, J., 'Yeltsin claims breakthrough on Kosovo', *Financial Times*, 17 June 1998, p. 1; and Hoffman, D., 'Milosevic agrees to talks with Kosovars', *International Herald Tribune*, 17 June 1998, pp. 1, 6.

[62] 'Krieg der Worte und der Waffen in Kosovo' [War of words and weapons in Kosovo], *Neue Zürcher Zeitung*, 19 June 1998, p. 1; and 'Strategien des Kleinkriegs in Kosovo' [Battle strategies in Kosovo], *Neue Zürcher Zeitung*, 23 June 1998, pp. 1, 4.

[63] Dinmore, G., 'Casualties mount as Kosovo conflict starts to spread', *Financial Times*, 10 July 1998, p. 3.

brooke to the KLA field commander, Lum Haxhiu.[64] Instead, the guerrilla army opened up more and more fronts: it started to ethnically cleanse Serbian villages in central Kosovo, stepped up its attacks on the Pristina–Prizren road as well as in the Djakovica region and staged a surprise attack on the strategically important open-pit coal mine of Belacevac (Bardh i Madh) near Pristina.[65] The KLA supreme command and the field commanders in the western part of Kosovo and the Drenica region clearly acted in an uncoordinated fashion.[66] On 29 June Serbian forces resumed operations in several parts of Kosovo and by 30 June had recaptured the Belacevac mine.[67] In Western Kosovo, however, the KLA profited from its capture of arsenals of anti-tank and anti-aircraft weapons and inflicted heavy casualties on the Yugoslav Army.[68]

On the diplomatic front Milosevic was again gaining terrain since NATO, taken by surprise by the KLA forays, began to significantly step down its pressure on Belgrade.[69] The Serbian regime even achieved goodwill in the West: on 6 July a Kosovo Diplomatic Observer Mission (KDOM), launched by Russia and the USA, started to operate.[70] Soon reaching a strength of 200 members, this mission functioned under the political guidance of a coordinating group consisting of the ambassadors of the Contact Group countries in Belgrade as well as the ambassadors of Austria (representing the EU Presidency) and Poland (representing the OSCE Chairman-in-Office). The international community has since then officially monitored the Kosovo conflict.[71]

By mid-July the Yugoslav Army and special police forces were being heavily attacked by the KLA. On 17 July the underground army launched a strike on the town of Orahovac (Rahovec) in south-western Kosovo and captured it. The attack was paralleled by the unsuccessful attempt of 1000 KLA fighters to cross the Albanian–Serbian border into Kosovo.[72] After four days of heavy fighting, Serbian forces reconquered Orahovac; 110 people, among them 34 KLA guerrillas, were said to have died during the fighting and 25 000 inhabitants fled the town.[73]

The success of the strike on Orahovac encouraged Milosevic to carry out his *coup de grâce* scheme according to a two-phase scenario: first, KLA communication and supply lines had to be severed while Serbian ones would be restored; and second, the

[64] Dinmore, G., 'Holbrooke meets the Kosovo fighters', *Financial Times*, 25 June 1998, p. 2.

[65] Hedges, C., 'Rebels start attacking Serb minority', *International Herald Tribune*, 25 June 1998, p. 6; and 'Pendeldiplomatie Holbrookes in Jugoslawien' [Holbrooke's pendulum diplomacy in Yugoslavia], *Neue Zürcher Zeitung*, 27–28 June 1998, pp. 4, 5.

[66] Judah, T., 'Impasse in Kosovo', *New York Review of Books*, vol. 45, no. 15 (Oct. 1998), pp. 4–5.

[67] Hedges, C.,'Holbrooke fails in Kosovo talks; attack expected', *International Herald Tribune*, 27–28 June 1998, pp. 1, 4; Dinmore, G. and Barber, L., 'EU softens line on Serbs as fighting intensifies', *Financial Times*, 30 June 1998, pp. 1–2; Hedges, C., 'Serb troops attack Kosovo positions', *International Herald Tribune*, pp. 1, 10; 'Harter Kampf um eine Kohlegrube in Kosovo' [Fierce battles over coal mine in Kosovo], *Neue Zürcher Zeitung*, 1 July 1998, p. 1; and 'Serbs seize strategic Kosovo mine', *International Herald Tribune*, 1 July 1998, p. 10.

[68] Hedges, C., 'Kosovo rebels get flood of arms', *International Herald Tribune*, 13 July 1998, p. 5.

[69] Myers, S. L., 'NATO backs away from Kosovo strike', *International Herald Tribune*, 17 July 1998, p. 7.

[70] See also chapter 2 and table 2A in appendix 2A in this volume.

[71] 'Kosovo Diplomatic Observer Mission, Fact Sheet released by the Bureau of European and Canadian Affairs of the US Department of State, Washington, DC, 8 July 1998', URL <http://www.state.gov/www/regionsd/eur>.

[72] 'Dozens die as a town in Kosovo is ensnared', *International Herald Tribune*, 20 July 1998, pp. 1, 7; Buchan, D., 'Serbs retaliate as KLA launch bold offensive', *Financial Times*, 20 July 1998, p. 3; and 'Intensivierung der Kampfhandlungen in Kosovo' [Intensified clashes in Kosovo], *Neue Zürcher Zeitung*, 21 July 1998, pp. 1, 2.

[73] 'Serbian forces said to kill 34 Kosovo rebels', *International Herald Tribune*, 22 July 1998, p. 8.

remaining KLA strongholds in central and western Kosovo should be destroyed completely. Immediately after the retaking of Orahovac, Serbian forces attacked KLA posts along the Pristina–Pec and Pristina–Prizren highways and destroyed them completely.[74] The KLA's 'liberated territory' in central Kosovo was now split into two parts.[75] On 28 July Serbian forces marched from three different directions into the town of Malisevo, where the KLA supreme command was located. The KLA did not make a serious attempt to defend the town but retreated in disarray together with several tens of thousands of inhabitants and refugees.[76] In military as well as political terms, this was the turning point of the conflict. The myth of the KLA as a modern, omnipresent and ultimately superior force and as such the nucleus of a new nation-state of Kosovar Albanians was seriously damaged.

During the first half of August, the Serbian side succeeded in crushing the remaining KLA strongholds in Drenica and in the west—among them the strategic villages of Likovac (Llikovc) on 6 August and Junik on 15 August.[77] By taking a step-by-step approach, Belgrade ensured that the campaign did not provoke strong reactions on the part of the international community. According to Western observers, the new Serbian tactic was 'a village a day keeps NATO away'.[78] On 17 August regional KLA leaders in the Pec area and Serbian forces agreed on a ceasefire mediated by the KDOM in order to allow international aid agencies to reach civilians who were displaced and wounded in recent fighting.[79]

The KLA had to admit that it was losing the war. Kosovo's elder statesman Adem Demaci, who on 13 August took over the function of KLA's political representative, declared the strategy of defending liberated territories against superior Serbian firepower a 'fatal mistake' and announced the readoption of 'classic guerrilla warfare tactics'.[80] In fact, the KLA was in urgent need of a long break to streamline its chains of command, train its many new members and improve its armaments and equipment in order to effectively counter the Serbian side in a prospective second round of the war.[81]

The fall of Junik triggered a twofold Serbian operation throughout Kosovo. Its first component consisted in further military action against pockets of KLA resistance in

[74] 'Grossoffensive gegen die UCK-Guerilla in Kosovo' [Major offensive against the KLA guerrilla in Kosovo], *Neue Zürcher Zeitung*, 27 July 1998, p. 1; Buchan, D.,'Serbs claim KLA stronghold taken', *Financial Times*, 28 July 1998, p. 2; 'Durchbruch der serbischen Truppen in Kosovo' [Breakthrough of Serbian troops in Kosovo], *Neue Zürcher Zeitung*, 28 July 1998, p. 1; and Rüb, M., 'Im Kosovo Zehntausende auf der Flucht vor den serbischen Truppen' [10 000 flee from Serbian troops in Kosovo], *Frankfurter Allgemeine Zeitung*, 30 July 1998, pp. 1, 2.

[75] Rüb, M., 'Serbische Polizei rückt auf das Hauptquartier der UCK vor' [Serbian police marches on the UCK headquarters], *Frankfurter Allgemeine Zeitung*, 4 Aug. 1998, p. 3; 'Fierce fighting reported in Kosovo', *International Herald Tribune*, 7 Aug. 1998, p. 5; and 'Serb forces overrun rebels' former base', *International Herald Tribune*, 8–9 Aug. 1998, p. 2.

[76] 'Serbs deliver blow to Kosovo guerrillas', *Financial Times*, 29 July 1998, p. 3; and 'Vormarsch der Serben in Zentral-Kosovo' [Serbs gain ground in central Kosovo], *Neue Zürcher Zeitung*, 29 July 1998, p. 2.

[77] 'Kein Ende der Kämpfe in Kosovo' [No end to the battles in Kosovo], *Neue Zürcher Zeitung*, 3 Aug. 1998, p. 1; 'Wichtige UCK-Bastion in Kosovo gefallen' [Important KLA bastion in Kosovo sieged], *Neue Zürcher Zeitung*, 17 Aug. 1998, p. 3; and O'Connor, M., 'In big drive, Serbs send Kosovo Albanians reeling and burn villages', *International Herald Tribune*, 17 Aug. 1998, pp. 5, 8.

[78] Stelzenmüller, C., 'Zögernder Falke' [Hesitant falcon], *Die Zeit*, 15 Oct. 1998, p. 7.

[79] Dinmore, G., 'Kosovo rebels and Serbs in partial truce', *Financial Times*, 18 Aug. 1998, p. 2; and Dinmore, G., 'Ceasefire allows aid for Kosovo refugees', *Financial Times*, 19 Aug. 1998, p. 3.

[80] International Crisis Group, 'Kosovo's long hot summer: briefing on military, humanitarian and political developments in Kosovo', Pristina–Sarajevo, 2 Sep. 1998, URL <http://www.crisisweb.org/projects/sbalkans/reports/kosrep05.htm>.

[81] Perlez, J., 'Kosovo rebels learn from mistakes', *International Herald Tribune*, 12 Nov. 1998, p. 4.

strategically important locations such as the airport near Pristina as well as along the Pristina–Prizren, Pristina–Pec, Prizren–Pec and Pristina–Mitrovica highways.[82] The second part of the operation was characterized by the increasing role of the Serbian judiciary in Kosovo in the repression of politically active Kosovar Albanians. According to Belgrade, by 4 October, when Serbian security forces and army started to retreat to their barracks and garrisons, 1242 ethnic Albanians had been officially charged with 'terrorist acts'.[83]

The humanitarian catastrophe caused by the internal displacement of some 200 000 Kosovar Albanians, including approximately 50 000 'forest people' living in woods and hills,[84] as well as by the unusually early snowfall on 28 September[85] kept the attention of the international community focused on Kosovo. News of a massacre at Gornje Obrinje (Obri e Eperme) in the Drenica region, in which 16 ethnic Albanian civilians had been killed on 25 September, had the same effect.[86]

Once again, on 24 September, NATO stepped up pressure on Milosevic by issuing an Activation Warning for both a limited air option and a phased air campaign.[87] In doing so NATO was able to count on the political support of the UN. In Resolution 1199 of 23 September 1998, the UN Security Council—with China abstaining, but with Russia voting—required the FRY to implement a ceasefire, withdraw forces deployed in Kosovo during the war and return those already in the province to their garrisons, allow complete access for humanitarian workers to deal with displaced persons and cooperate with the UN tribunal to investigate war crimes in Kosovo.[88]

IV. The informal ceasefire

The approaching winter and the threat of a humanitarian catastrophe among the 'forest people' caused the international community to press for a ceasefire in order to allow people to return and to rebuild their destroyed homes. On 8 October the foreign ministers of the Contact Group decided to send US Special Envoy Holbrooke to Belgrade 'with the full authority of the Contact Group' to demand compliance with Reso-

[82] Dinmore, G., 'Serbian fire pushes back Kosovo rebels', *Financial Times*, 25 Aug. 1998, p. 2; 'Anhaltende Kämpfe in Kosovo' [Fighting continues in Kosovo], *Neue Zürcher Zeitung*, 26 Aug. 1998, p. 1; Dinmore, G., 'Kosovo fighting overshadows progress in talks', *Financial Times*, 4 Sep. 1998, p. 3; 'Serbische Offensive gegen die letzten UCK-Bastionen' [Serb offensive against the last KLA bastion], *Neue Zürcher Zeitung*, 23 Sep. 1998, p. 2; and 'Serbs attack again, ignoring NATO', *International Herald Tribune*, 28 Sep. 1998, p. 5.

[83] 'Federal Republic of Yugoslavia: human rights developments', Human Rights Watch World Report 1999, URL <http://www.hrw.org/hrw/worldreport99/europe/yugoslavia.html>. See also 'Welle von Verhaftungen in Kosovo' [Wave of arrests in Kosovo], *Neue Zürcher Zeitung*, 4 Sep. 1998, p. 7.

[84] Smith, R. J., 'Kosovo war spawns a refugee disaster', *International Herald Tribune*, 3 Aug. 1998, p. 5.

[85] Perlez, J., 'Living amid mud, Kosovo refugees fear winter', *International Herald Tribune*, 30 Sep. 1998, p. 5.

[86] 'KDOM Daily Report, Released by the Bureau of European and Canadian Affairs, Office of South Central European Affairs, US Department of State, Washington, DC, 28 Sep. 1998', URL <http://www.state.gov/www/regions/eur/rpt_980928_kdom.html>; and Dinmore, G., 'Massacre overshadows Serb ceasefire claim', *Financial Times*, 30 Sep. 1998, p. 3.

[87] 'Statement by the Secretary General following the ACTWARN decision', Press Statement, Vilamoura, 24 Sep. 1998, URL <http://www.nato.int/docu/pr/1998/p980924e.htm>. See also Myers, S. L., 'NATO raises pressure on Serbs, dangling specter of Kosovo intervention', *International Herald Tribune*, 23 Sep. 1998, p. 6; and 'NATO allies warn Milosevic of air strikes over atrocities', *Financial Times*, 2 Oct. 1998, p. 1.

[88] UN Security Council Resolution 1199, 23 Sep. 1998.

lution 1199.[89] His mission was paralleled by a renewed military threat by NATO and by Russian approval of OSCE verification on the ground. This combination made Milosevic accept the Contact Group's mediation and engage in negotiations with Holbrooke. On 12 October, at the peak of a dramatic build-up of military pressure by NATO, Milosevic agreed to a ceasefire, to an OSCE presence of 2000 unarmed verifiers in Kosovo combined with unarmed NATO verification by aerial reconnaissance, and to a political solution of the conflict in the form of an increased degree of internal self-determination for Kosovo.[90] However, no formal document seems to have been signed by Milosevic—at least none was made public.

On the evening of 12 October, Holbrooke briefed NATO on Milosevic's intention to comply with the resolution, and on 13 October the Yugoslav President for the first time since the 1995 Dayton Agreement appeared on Serbian television to inform his compatriots in vague terms about the 'accords we have reached' which 'eliminate the danger of military intervention against our country'.[91] Kosovo was to remain an integral part of the Republic of Serbia, that is, it was not going to become a third republic of the FRY or gain self-determination. In addition, the massive presence of the Serbian security forces and Yugoslav Army in Kosovo was to be perpetuated at the high level of the beginning of the armed conflict in the spring of 1998. While Holbrooke had been pressing for a maximum of 17 500 police and army troops to be permanently stationed in Kosovo, Milosevic succeeded in securing a ceiling of 15 000 VJ troops and 10 000 MUP forces.[92]

On 13 October, a few hours after having been briefed by Holbrooke on the agreement with Milosevic and thus being relieved of the obligation to live up to its military threat against Belgrade, the North Atlantic Council decided to turn the Activation Warning of 24 September into Activation Orders for both limited air strikes and a phased air campaign in Yugoslavia.[93] Meeting a wish of Holbrooke, the 48-hour deadline for the execution of these measures was extended to 96 hours.[94] This new deadline coincided with the one set for Milosevic by Holbrooke to comply with the ceasefire agreement. On 16 October NATO extended its previous deadline another 10 days.[95] This was done because on 15 October NATO's Supreme Allied Commander in Europe, US General Wesley Clark, and the VJ Chief of Staff, General Momcilo Perisic, had in Belgrade signed an agreement providing for the establishment of a NATO Air Verification Mission over Kosovo (Operation 'Eagle Eye'). The agreement established a Mutual Safety Zone composed of Kosovo and a

[89] 'Foreign Secretary of State Robin Cook, Contact Group discussion on Kosovo, Thursday, 8 Oct. 1998', URL <http://www.mod.uk/news/kosovo/news/fco081098.htm>.

[90] 'The Holbrooke Agreement', News, background and images on Kosovo from the UK Ministry of Defence and the Foreign & Commonwealth Office, URL <http://www.mod.uk/news/kosovo/agreemnt/index.htm>.

[91] 'President Milosevic announces accord on peaceful solution', Yugoslav Daily Survey—Special Issue, 13 Oct. 1998, URL <http://www.mfa.gov.yu/Bilteni/Engleski/si131098_1_e.html>.

[92] 'Serbische Truppen ziehen aus dem Kosovo ab' [Serb troops withdraw from Kosovo], *Frankfurter Allgemeine Zeitung*, 28 Oct. 1998, p. 1; 'Ungebrochene Gewaltbereitschaft im Kosovo' [Unchanged readiness to use violence in Kosovo], *Neue Zürcher Zeitung*, 14–15 Nov. 1998, URL <http://www.nzz.ch/online/02_dossiers/kosovo/kos981114awy.htm>; and Rüb, M., 'Viele "Waldmenschen" haben wieder ein Dach über dem Kopf' [Many 'forest people' have a roof over their heads again], *Frankfurter Allgemeine Zeitung*, 7 Nov. 1998, p. 7.

[93] 'Statement to the press by the Secretary General following decision on the ACTORD', NATO HQ, 13 Oct. 1998, URL <http://www.nato.int/docu/speech/1998/s981013a.htm>.

[94] 'Transcript of the Press Conference by Secretary General, Javier Solana', NATO HQ, Brussels, 13 Oct 1998, URL <http://www.nato.int/docu/speech/1998/s981013b.htm>.

[95] 'Statement by the NATO Spokesman on the NAC of 16 Oct. 1998', URL <http://www.nato.int/docu/speech/1998/s981016a.htm>.

25-km corridor extending beyond its boundaries. Unarmed NATO aircraft were allowed free rein over Kosovo.[96]

On 16 October OSCE Chairman-in-Office Bronislaw Geremek of Poland went to Belgrade to sign an agreement on an OSCE Kosovo Verification Mission (KVM). The mission's aim was defined as being 'to verify compliance by all parties in Kosovo with UN Security Council Resolution 1199, and report instances of progress and/or non-compliance to the OSCE Permanent Council, the United Nations Security Council and other organizations'.[97] In order to do so, the mission was given the possibility to 'travel throughout Kosovo to verify the maintenance of the ceasefire by all elements. It will investigate reports of ceasefire violations. Mission personnel will have full freedom of movement and access throughout Kosovo at all times'.[98] The mission was to consist of unarmed verifiers from OSCE member states and could 'be augmented with technical experts provided by OSCE'.[99] Its headquarters were to be set up in Pristina, whereas outside Pristina the mission was entitled to establish coordination centres in the capitals of each municipality as well as sub-stations in other towns and villages.[100] On 17 October Geremek appointed US diplomat William G. Walker, a former head of the UN Transitional Administration for Eastern Slavonia (UNTAES), as head of the KVM.[101]

The UN Security Council endorsed the KVM on 24 October through Resolution 1203. It demanded that the FRY abide by its agreements and commitments concerning the OSCE presence in Kosovo as well as NATO air verification over Kosovo and reminded the FRY of its 'primary responsibility for the safety and security of all diplomatic personnel accredited to the Federal Republic of Yugoslavia, including members of the OSCE Verification Mission'.[102] On 26 November NATO inaugurated a Kosovo Verification Coordination Centre in the Macedonian town of Kumanovo on the border with the FRY. Its purpose was to coordinate the activities of the NATO Air Verification Mission for Kosovo with the OSCE KVM in Pristina.[103] On 2 December the Macedonian Government approved the stationing of a French-led NATO Extraction Force (XFOR, 'Operation Joint Guarantor') of 1700 personnel from several NATO countries in Kumanovo, and on 5 December the Activation Order for XFOR was issued. Its mandate was to 'extract' individual or all members of the OSCE KVM or other designated persons from Kosovo in an emergency.[104]

[96] 'Press Points by Secretary General, Dr. Javier Solana', Belgrade, 15 Oct. 1998, URL <http://www.nato.int/docu/speech/1998/s981015a.htm>; and 'The US mission to NATO, Defense spokesman outlines Kosovo verification regime', Washington, DC, 15 Oct. 1998, URL <http://www.natio.int/usa/dod/ s981015a.htm>.

[97] 'Agreement on the Kosovo Verification Mission', Belgrade, 16 Oct. 1998, Part II, Article 1, URL <http://www.osceprag.cz/news/kosovo.htm>. See also chapter 2 in this volume.

[98] 'Agreement on the Kosovo Verification Mission' (note 97), Part III, Article 1.

[99] 'Agreement on the Kosovo Verification Mission' (note 97), Part IV, Article 2.

[100] 'Agreement on the Kosovo Verification Mission' (note 97), Part IV, Article 3, and Part V, Articles 1 and 2.

[101] 'OSCE appoints head of Kosovo Verification Mission', OSCE Secretariat Press Release no. 64/98, Warsaw, 17 Oct. 1998, URL <http://www.osceprag.cz/inst/secret/presrel/pr64-98.htm>.

[102] UN Security Council Resolution 1203, 24 Oct. 1998.

[103] 'Remarks by Javier Solana, Secretary General of NATO, at the Inauguration of the Kosovo Verification Coordination Centre (KVCC)', 26 Nov. 1998, URL <http://www.nato.int/docu/speech/s981126a.htm>.

[104] NATO Press Statement. Press Release (98)139, 5 Dec. 1998, URL <http://www.nato.int/docu/pr/1998/p98-139e.htm>; and 'Frankreich will Nato-Einsatz führen' [France wants to lead NATO operation], *Frankfurter Allgemeine Zeitung*, 6 Nov. 1998, p. 8.

In spite of some 170 incidents, resulting in the death of about 200 people,[105] the ceasefire of 12 October held for two months. On 14 December, however, a serious clash between Yugoslav border guards and KLA fighters trying to cross into Kosovo from Albania near Prizren resulted in the death of 37 Kosovar Albanians. On the same day, in a revenge attack six Serbs were assassinated in Pec.[106] The tension escalated further on 21 December, when the Yugoslav Army staged an artillery attack on the town of Podujevo (Podujeva) in eastern Kosovo.[107] On 24 December the worst fighting since the ceasefire broke out in the Llap region near Podujevo. The Serbian side deployed up to 100 tanks and killed 14 Kosovar Albanians,[108] and more than 5000 people were displaced internally.[109] On 28 December outgoing OSCE Chairman-in-Office Geremek announced that if the fighting continued 'the OSCE would have to reconsider the forms of its activities' in Kosovo by withdrawing its then 600 verifiers.[110] Yet, on 27 December 1998 the head of the KVM succeeded in mediating a ceasefire in the Podujevo region which lasted into the new year.[111]

In his New Year Message to the citizens of the FRY, Yugoslav President Milosevic took a fierce stand against 'pressures, which . . . are being exerted with the aim of ensuring such a level of self-governance for Kosovo and Metohija, so that its full secession from Serbia, that is, from Yugoslavia be easy and logical'. He demanded that 'the year 1999 should be devoted to the preservation of the sovereignty of Yugoslavia' as well as to the 'affirmation of the truth about our history and present'[112]—not very promising statements with regard to the prevention of a flare-up of inter-ethnic warfare in the country's troubled south-west or to a lasting solution of the Kosovo problem.

V. Conclusions

The recent history of the Kosovo conflict teaches a sad lesson. During the entire first half of the 1990s, the Kosovar Albanians exercised non-violent resistance but were ignored by both Belgrade and the international community. In turning increasingly to violent resistance from 1996, the conflict acquired an international dimension, involving other countries and multilateral organizations. In 1998, however, when the conflict escalated to full-fledged warfare, it required a tremendous amount of political

[105] Dieterich, J., 'Ihr müsst nett sein' [You have to be nice], *Die Woche*, 24 Dec. 1998, p. 22; and 'KDOM Progress Report, Prishtina, 8 Dec. 1998', URL <http://www.usia.gov/regional/eur/balkans/kosovo/heading/1208prog.htm>.

[106] Tuhina, G., 'Tenuous cease-fire', *Transitions*, vol. 6, no. 2 (Feb. 1999), pp. 12–13.

[107] 'Ogata besorgt über Lage im Kosovo' [Ogata concerned about situation in Kosovo], *Frankfurter Allgemeine Zeitung*, 22 Dec. 1998, p. 10; and 'OSZE mit Belgrad nicht zufrieden' [OSCE dissatisfied with Belgrade], *Frankfurter Allgemeine Zeitung*, 23 Dec. 1998, p. 2.

[108] 'Four days of clashes in Kosova', *Radio Free Europe/Radio Liberty NewsLine, Southeastern Europe*, 28 Dec. 1998, URL <http://www.rferl.org/newsline/4-see.html>; and Rüb, M., 'Waffenstillstand im Kosovo faktisch zusammengebrochen' [Armistice in Kosovo actually collapsed], *Frankfurter Allgemeine Zeitung*, 28 Dec. 1998, p. 4.

[109] 'UNHCR looks for displaced persons', *Radio Free Europe/Radio Liberty NewsLine, Southeastern Europe*, 29 Dec. 1998, URL <http://www.rferl.org/newsline/4-see.html>.

[110] 'Future of monitoring in doubt', *Radio Free Europe/Radio Liberty NewsLine, Southeastern Europe*, 29 Dec. 1998, URL <http://www.rferl.org/newsline/4-see.html>.

[111] 'Yugoslavia: OSCE monitors say truce restored in Kosovo', *Radio Free Europe/Radio Liberty Features*, 28 Dec. 1998, URL <http://www.rferl.org/nca/features/1998/12/F.RU.981228163834.html>.

[112] 'Yugoslav President Milosevic's New Year message to the nation, Belgrade, 31 Dec. 1998', Yugoslav Daily Survey—Special Issue, 31 Dec. 1998, URL <http://www.mfa.gov.yu/Bilteni/Engleski/si311298_e.html>.

will and energy on the part of the international actors to at least contain the fighting within the borders of the FRY. While both sides in the conflict included outside political factors in their calculations, the actual impact of the international community on the development of military events on the ground throughout 1998 was modest at best. With the KLA deliberately striving for an escalation of the conflict in order to provoke military intervention by NATO, Milosevic sought to contain the conflict at a level that would avoid such intervention. His meeting with Rugova on 15 May 1998, his announcement in Moscow on 16 June and his acceptance of some of the demands of Resolution 1199 in the ceasefire agreement of 12 October served this purpose.

By the end of 1998 the long-term solutions to the Kosovo conflict favoured by the Serbian and the Kosovar Albanian sides were even more complex and difficult to reconcile than they were at the beginning of the year. The Serbian regime wants to preserve the status quo, including the continued outward migration of Kosovar Albanians—which has occurred as a result of political repression, economic crisis or ethnic cleansing. Should full Serbian control of all of Kosovo be unrealistic, the Milosevic regime would settle for a partition of Kosovo paralleled by an ethnic separation of the region along the new border. The Kosovar Albanians, on the other hand, can no longer accept a future within Serbia, and even the 'third-republic option'—Kosovo as a constituent republic of the FRY alongside Serbia and Montenegro—is now less likely to be acceptable to them. Both Rugova's LDK and the KLA opt for complete independence.

In justifying their strategic aims, the two sides apply different political arguments. The FRY depicts the conflict as an internal affair between legitimate state organs and an illegal separatist movement using terrorist means. Accordingly, it rejects any attempt to internationalize the conflict or any discussion of 'enhanced status', 'meaningful autonomy' or 'third republic'. The Kosovar Albanian political actors, on the other hand, strive to achieve a multilateralization of the conflict in the form of either foreign military intervention or 'track one', diplomatic, third-party mediation resulting in the deployment of peacekeepers. Serbian rule over Kosovo is depicted by them as an occupation regime that denies basic human rights to the Albanian majority in Kosovo.

The Serbian and the Kosovar Albanian points of view concerning the future of Kosovo seemed at the end of 1998 to be too far apart to be bridged by any compromise solution. There were, however, indications on both sides of a willingness to leave the controversial issue of the ultimate status of Kosovo unanswered for the time being and to overcome the deadlock of 1998 by concentrating on the establishment of a joint Serbian–Kosovar Albanian interim administration for the province with international support or even under international control. This requires that the moderates of both sides succeed in keeping their respective radicals in check.

Appendix 1D. The Tajikistan conflict

IRINA ZVIAGELSKAYA

I. Introduction

Although the five-year civil war in Tajikistan between the Tajik Government and the United Tajik Opposition (UTO)[1] ended in June 1997 with the signing of the General Agreement on Peace and National Accord,[2] there were tensions and armed conflict in Tajikistan in 1998. Several factors hindered the reconciliation process: (*a*) the rivalry between clans and regions of Tajikistan; (*b*) inter-ethnic tensions; and (*c*) ideological differences between the government and the opposition.[3]

All these factors were present in 1998, although their relative importance changed. While the weight of the ideological factor diminished, the inter-regional and inter-ethnic controversies came to the foreground, as did certain international factors.

In 1998 the situation in Tajikistan was characterized by both the post-conflict reconciliation process and new confrontations. Despite many difficulties, reconciliation between the Tajik Government and the UTO has dominated the political scene. On the one hand, the government and the UTO implemented a number of the measures in the General Agreement on Peace and National Accord, the March 1997 Protocol on Military Issues[4] and the May 1997 Protocol on Political Issues.[5] The National Reconciliation Commission (NRC), established in February 1997, played a significant role in monitoring the process to ensure implementation of these agreements.[6] On the other hand, mutual mistrust persisted between the two main parties to the reconciliation process, and there were acute crises in their relations. While the main priority of the Tajik Government was the implementation of the military aspects of the agreements, above all the disarmament of the UTO armed groups, the UTO leadership was most concerned with the political aspects, primarily with achieving a share of the power. Despite the attempts by the government and the NRC to stabilize the situation, they were unable to curb the terrorist acts, bandit attacks and armed skirmishes which contributed to keeping the level of tension relatively high.

In November 1998 the government and the UTO were challenged by a rebellion in the Leninabad region of northern Tajikistan. The rebellion can be attributed to the reconciliation policy itself because, in bringing together two political minorities—the

[1] The UTO is composed of the Islamic Revival Party, the Democratic Party, the Lali Badakhshan Party and Rastohez (National Revival).

[2] For the text see *Paiki Oshty (Sanadho).Vesti o Mire: Documenty* [News on peace: documents] (Nashriyoti Oli Somon: Dushanbe, 1998), pp. 72–115 (in Tajik and in Russian).

[3] For the background to the conflict see Amer, R. *et al.*, 'Major armed conflicts', *SIPRI Yearbook 1993: World Armaments and Disarmament* (Oxford University Press: Oxford, 1993), pp. 104–107. For recent developments in the conflict see Baranovsky, V., 'Russia: conflicts and its security environment', *SIPRI Yearbook 1997: Armaments, Disarmament and International Security* (Oxford University Press: Oxford, 1997), pp. 118–20; and Baranovsky, V., 'Russia: conflicts and peaceful settlement of disputes', *SIPRI Yearbook 1998: Armaments, Disarmament and International Security* (Oxford University Press: Oxford, 1998), pp. 135–37.

[4] For the text see *Diplomaticheskiy Vestnik*, no. 4 (Apr. 1997), pp. 45–46.

[5] For the text see *Diplomaticheskiy Vestnik*, no. 6 (June 1997), pp. 39–40.

[6] The NRC was established for a transitional 12- to 18-month period and consists of representatives of the government and the UTO. Its work will be terminated after the parliamentary elections to be held in the second half of 1999.

Figure 1D. Map of Tajikistan

government and the UTO, which predominantly represent the southern regions—it has a narrow regional basis and excludes Leninabad from the power-sharing process. The resentment of the inhabitants of Leninabad was seriously increased by the efforts of representatives of the Kulyab region, who have dominated the administrative bodies, to establish control in the north. The rebellion had the effect of changing the configuration of the conflict, giving it a north–south dimension. It also aggravated the situation between Tajikistan and neighbouring Uzbekistan.

Section II outlines the political issues in the reconciliation process and the conflict, and section III provides the background to the Leninabad rebellion. The military issues are described in section IV and developments in the mandated return of refugees from Afghanistan in section V. Section VI discusses terrorism and drug trafficking in Tajikistan. Sections VII–IX describe three of the external influences on the conflict, the Afghan and Uzbek factors and the Russian presence, respectively. Section X presents the conclusions.

II. The political issues

In 1998 a substantial breakthrough was made in one of the most controversial problems, namely, the division of power according to a December 1996 agreement by which 30 per cent of the Tajik Government posts were to be reserved for the UTO.[7]

[7] Agreement between the President of the Republic of Tajikistan E. Sh. Rakhmonov and the Leader of the United Tajik Opposition S. A. Nuri on the Results of the Meeting held in Moscow on 23 December 1996. For the text of the agreement and the Additional Protocol on the Main Functions and Powers of the Commission on National Reconciliation, see *Paiki Oshty (Sanadho)*, (note 2), pp. 75, 87.

At a meeting on 23 January 1998 Tajik President Imomali Rakhmonov and UTO Chairman Said Abdullo Nuri agreed on the appointment of UTO Deputy Chairman Hoji Akbar Turajonzoda, who was considered the UTO's main political strategist, to the post of first deputy prime minister. At the same meeting, Nuri handed the president a complete list of UTO nominees for government posts.[8] On 12 February Rakhmonov issued decrees on the appointments of representatives of the opposition to government positions, accepting the UTO's proposals.[9]

On 27 February 1998 Turajonzoda returned to the Tajik capital, Dushanbe, after five years of political exile in Iran and Afghanistan. Addressing a mass welcome rally and a news conference, he outlined five UTO priorities: (*a*) parallel implementation of the 1997 military and political protocols; (*b*) revival of the Tajik state and of Islam; (*c*) the holding of a referendum on an amendment to the 1994 Tajik Constitution that would replace the term 'secular government' with 'popular government';[10] (*d*) the introduction of a mixed economy and market relations; and (*e*) the maintenance of good and 'balanced' relations with Uzbekistan, other Central Asian countries, Iran and Russia, 'so that Tajikistan becomes no one's protectorate'.[11]

Although some aspects of this programme of priorities were unacceptable to both the government and radicals within the UTO, Turajonzoda's return to the capital was seen as a symbol of the political success of the UTO and a sign of both parties' serious intentions to pursue national reconciliation.

Implementation of the decision on amnesty for political opponents of the government, which was part of the Protocol on Political Issues, had lagged behind the accelerating political process but was stepped up during the year. On 1 February 1998 Tajikistan's procurator-general publicly announced that charges of criminal actions, arrests and police searches of UTO leaders—including Nuri, Turajonzoda and Davlat Usmon—would be lifted.[12]

Despite these achievements, implementation of the political aspects of the agreements faced many difficulties during the year. Tensions and misunderstandings repeatedly arose between the parties. They were caused by the hostility engendered by the bloody civil war, which has not been completely settled, by new political events and by post-conflict developments.

A May 1998 agreement concluded by the presidents of Russia, Tajikistan and Uzbekistan on resisting 'the advance of Islamic fundamentalism' in Afghanistan, Tajikistan and Central Asia in general was one of the factors that led to intensified differences between the government and the UTO.[13] In joining the agreement, Rakhmonov seemed to be proceeding from a wish to strengthen relations with the two main external powers—Russia and Uzbekistan—that have a direct bearing on the situation in Central Asia and are especially important for Tajikistan as well as from a desire to obtain additional leverage over his Islamic opponents. However, he obvi-

[8] *Jumkhuriyat*, 7 Feb. 1998 (in Tajik); and *Biznes i Politika*, no. 6 (6 Feb. 1998), (in Russian).

[9] *Kurier Tadzhikistana*, 13 Feb. 1998 (in Russian).

[10] Formally, the UTO proposed the referendum in order to allow equal political participation by secular and religious parties, but the real aim was to avoid becoming tied down by constitutional provisions that exclude the introduction of the norms of the Shariat in the event of the Islamists, who seek to create an Islamic state, coming to power.

[11] *Jamestown Monitor* (Washington, DC), vol. 4, no. 41 (2 Mar. 1998).

[12] *Kurier Tajikistana*, 6 Feb. 1998 (in Russian).

[13] The agreement, which has not been published, was signed in Moscow on 6 May 1998 by Russia and Uzbekistan; Tajikistan became a party to the agreement shortly thereafter. *Jamestown Monitor* (Washington, DC), vol. 4, no. 91 (12 May 1998).

ously overestimated the possibilities of using this agreement to weaken the opposition and as a result created additional domestic difficulties for himself.

On 16 May 1998 Rakhmonov accused the main party of the UTO, the Islamic Revival Party (IRP), of aiming to turn Tajikistan into an 'Islamic state'. He described the IRP as extremist and fundamentalist, pointed out that the 1994 ban on the IRP remained in effect and charged that the party's attempts to resume political activities violated that ban.[14]

The UTO saw Rakhmonov's signing of the 'troika agreement' of 6 May as the abandonment of earlier commitments, especially in light of the fact that his reminder of the ban started a chain reaction. The Tajik Parliament, which has treated the opposition badly in spite of the peace agreements, perceived Rakhmonov's statement as a call for action. Thus on 23 May 1998 the parliament took a decision which expanded the legal basis of the 1994 ban to include not only existing such parties but also the future formation of all religious parties and all organizations and parties formed on a regional basis.[15] This affected not only the IRP but also other factions of the UTO, in particular the Lali Badakhshan Party, representing the Gorno-Badakhshan region, and National Revival, a bloc of movements representing the Leninabad region and supporting Abdumalik Abdulladzhanov, a former prime minister and the main rival of the president.[16]

The Tajik Parliament also invalidated the appointment of opposition leaders Akbar Turajonzoda as first deputy prime minister and Davlat Usmon as minister of the economy and foreign trade. UTO Chairman Nuri warned that the UTO would withdraw from the reconciliation process unless President Rakhmonov vetoed the parliament's decision.[17]

These parliamentary decisions provoked reactions from other states. Russia, one of the guarantors of the settlement in Tajikistan, could not allow the country to slide back into chaos and military confrontation. Yevgeniy Belov, Russian Ambassador to Tajikistan, pointed out that the decision of the parliament would make further development of the reconciliation process difficult.[18] In a statement distributed in Dushanbe on 29 May 1998, the US State Department urged Rakhmonov to veto the parliament's ban on parties of a religious character. It further urged Rakhmonov, his government and the Tajik Parliament to accelerate the appointment of UTO representatives to government positions and pointed out that the 1997 peace agreements call for the free operation of political parties and the allotment of government positions to the opposition.[19]

The crisis between the government and the UTO was not resolved until November 1998, after their victory over the rebels in Leninabad (see section III).

During 1998 both Rakhmonov and the UTO initiated campaigns to mobilize supporters for the forthcoming presidential and parliamentary elections.[20] In order to expand the electorate of Rakhmonov, who is considered an exponent of the interests of the Kulyab area, and to present him as a national leader, attempts were made to

[14] *Jamestown Monitor* (Washington, DC), vol. 4, no. 95 (18 May 1998).

[15] The ban has been formally in force since 1994. In the 1997 General Agreement on Peace and National Accord, however, both parties agreed to work towards the goal of lifting the ban.

[16] *Jamestown Monitor* (Washington, DC), vol. 4, no. 101 (27 May 1998).

[17] ITAR-TASS, 31 May 1998.

[18] *Biznes i Politika*, no. 24 (12 June 1998), (in Russian).

[19] *Jamestown Monitor* (Washington, DC), vol. 4, no. 104 (1 June 1998).

[20] The elections were scheduled to be held in 1998 but have been postponed until the second half of 1999.

rally citizens around the concept of the creation of a secular as opposed to an Islamic state. The reduction of confrontations between the government and the UTO was seen by Rakhmonov's advisers as the most effective means of securing nationwide support for him. A 'presidential party' was formed when, on 18 April, at the congress of the Popular Democratic Party (PDP), set up in 1996, Rakhmonov was elected its chairman. He took over as PDP leader from Abdulmajid Dostiev, first vice-chairman of both the parliament and the NRC.[21] The PDP presents itself as left-of-centre, cautious about market reforms, Russia-oriented and a champion of secularism. It is still narrowly based in southern Tajikistan, primarily in the Kulyab region, the native area of the group which dominates the central government. Conversion of the PDP to 'a party of power' will require at least a formal expansion of its regional base.

III. The rebellion in Leninabad: a new balance of forces

The attempted march into the Leninabad region on 4 November 1998, led by Mahmoud Khudoberdiev, in effect created a new balance of forces within and around the Tajikistan conflict. Leninabad—the most advanced region of the country and one from which *nomenklatura* cadres in Tajikistan traditionally came—has since 1992–93 diminished in importance. The people of the region are particularly resentful of the government's appointment of Kulyabis to the main government positions—a reversal of the hierarchy during the Soviet era, in which the agricultural region of Kulyab had a low profile.

The rise of the Kulyabi cannot be attributed to intrigue. Since the political and military defeat of the Islamist–Democratic opposition in 1992, the Kulyabi have been very dynamic, exhibiting a capacity to mobilize and adapt to new conditions. By contrast, the Leninabadi elite made no attempt to rise to power in times of trouble, preferring to wait in the belief that, with stabilization, they would again obtain the leading positions and that the country could not do without them. This was an illusion. The Kulyabi were not interested in sharing power with the Leninabadi, their former ally, but in consolidating their position and leadership in all the organs of power.

President Rakhmonov failed to mobilize supporters in the Leninabad region, where a leading role is played by his political opponents, primarily former prime minister Abdumalik Abdulladzhanov, who stood for the presidency during the 1994 elections. The distribution of government positions by a close circle of people at the top excluded Abdulladzhanov and his supporters from power.

With its significant Uzbek population, the secular Leninabad region is considered by Uzbekistan as a natural ally. The region borders on Uzbekistan and has close economic ties with it. Leninabad's participation in the power structures could have countered the influence of the Islamists, who are a source of irritation and concern for the Uzbek Government. On 28 February 1998 Uzbek Foreign Minister Abdulaziz Kamilov pointed out that a reconciliation process which involves only two sides—the government and the UTO—to the exclusion of Leninabad 'will not bring any stability to the country' and stated that it was necessary to include representatives of the Leninabad region in the government.[22] While there is some justification for this position, it also reflects Uzbekistan's interests in strengthening its influence. In Tajik

[21] *Jumkhuriyat*, 25 Apr. 1998 (in Tajik).
[22] ITAR-TASS, 28 Feb. 1998.

society, where regional self-identification prevails, stability depends on a balanced representation of the different regions in the government.

The exclusion of Leninabad promoted a further heightening of inter-regional tensions and led to the aborted coup. Khudoberdiev demanded: (*a*) the formation of a new government giving the Leninabad region a 40 per cent representation; (*b*) the holding of a special session of the parliament in Khujand to settle major political issues; (*c*) the creation of a 'national council' which would include all the political forces and a balanced regional representation; and (*d*) an opportunity for Abdulladzhanov to address the country on television.[23] The government rejected these demands and the opportunity to negotiate with the rebels.

The government and the UTO managed to crush the rebellion after several days of fighting. There are two main reasons for their success. First, the rebels failed to rouse the northern Tajiks and ethnic Uzbeks in the Leninabad region against the central government. After several years of civil war people were tired of violence, and the military methods used by Khudoberdiev scared them off. Second, for the first time government forces acted in collaboration with the UTO—fighters of the UTO, commanded by Mirzo Zioev, assisted the government forces.[24] Thus a new alliance was set up against Leninabad which changed the configuration of the conflict.

The balance was further changed with the accusation by Tajik officials that Uzbekistan and Uzbek President Islam Karimov had organized the rebellion. It was reported that Khudoberdiev had enjoyed sanctuary in Uzbekistan since 1997, invaded the Leninabad region from Uzbek territory and been well equipped with combat hardware. It was also said that among the rebels were Uzbeks who formerly belonged to the forces of General Abdul Rashid Dostum, the military leader of Uzbeks in Afghanistan.[25] President Rakhmonov even described the rebellion as external aggression against Tajikistan by Uzbekistan.[26] This unusually strong government reaction can be explained not so much by any firm evidence of Uzbekistan's involvement as by the government's fear of coming under Uzbekistan's tutelage.

As a result of the new situation in November 1998 the parliament approved for government positions nearly the same list of nominees as the UTO had presented in February. It confirmed Akbar Turajonzoda as first deputy prime minister, Zokir Vazirov as deputy prime minister and Davlat Usmon as minister of the economy and foreign trade. The parliament also agreed to consider a revised draft law on the operation of political parties.[27]

IV. The military issues

Resolution of the military issues remained one of the major preconditions for stability and progress in the political field in 1998.[28] Both sides were interested in a speedy

[23] *Jamestown Monitor* (Washington, DC), vol. 4, no. 205 (5 Nov. 1998). Allegations have been raised that Abdulladzhanov, the president's chief rival, may have played a role in the rebellion. In the course of investigations of accusations that his party, the National Unity Party, was engaged in such activities as tax evasion, evidence was presented that implicated the party in the rebellion. It was subsequently banned by the Supreme Court of Tajikistan. *Biznes i Politika,* 11 Dec. 1998.

[24] *Jamestown Monitor* (Washington, DC), vol. 4, no. 207 (9 Nov. 1998).

[25] Radio Dushanbe, 6–8 Nov. 1998.

[26] *Jamestown Monitor* (Washington, DC), vol. 4, no. 213 (17 Nov. 1998).

[27] ITAR-TASS, 15–16 Nov. 1998; and *Sadoi Mardum*, 5 Dec. 1998 (in Tajik).

[28] Implementation of the 1997 Protocol on Military Issues is to be carried out in 4 stages: (*a*) assembly of the UTO military units at special points and transfer of the fighters from Afghanistan; (*b*) formation of regular military detachments on the basis of the UTO units and the taking of an oath of

solution, although for different reasons: the UTO strove to resettle its members in Tajikistan as quickly as possible, and the government to disarm them within the shortest possible time. According to UTO Chairman Nuri, by the summer of 1998 more than 3000 UTO fighters were prepared to be integrated into the national army in accordance with the 1997 Protocol on Military Issues.[29] The last UTO armed group, numbering 160 men, was transferred from Afghanistan in late September 1998.[30] Thus one of the tasks stipulated in the peace agreements had been formally accomplished.

Implementation of the protocol requires the allocation of substantial financial resources for this purpose. The retraining of soldiers and members of UTO armed groups, their medical care and socio-economic rehabilitation will be provided at a reintegration centre that will function under NRC auspices. The World Bank has allocated a special grant of $165 000 to Tajikistan for implementation of the military provisions in 1998–99.[31]

Despite these measures, armed confrontations between government and UTO forces continued in 1998. In March, bloody battles raged in the Kofarnikhon district, 25 km from Dushanbe. The NRC press secretary reported that artillery was being used, with government forces using helicopters to fire on the positions of the UTO armed groups.[32] On 30 March a joint commission consisting of government and UTO representatives and members of the UN Mission of Observers in Tajikistan (UNMOT) visited the battle zone.[33] The conflict was resolved through joint efforts: captured government troops were returned, and the question of the withdrawal of heavy military equipment along with units of the ministries of defence and the interior was discussed.[34] After the Kofarnikhon battles the Special Representative of the UN Secretary-General commented that the UTO leadership had to explain the situation clearly to its supporters. 'Those who shoot at militiamen today, in fact, shoot at the government of which representatives of the opposition are already a part'.[35] This comment illustrates the reasons for many of the confrontations. Field commanders do not perceive the division of power as something that directly applies to them and, in the new conditions, are carrying on with the same policy they applied in the period of severe military and political hostility.

Another common example of such confrontations is the clashes between the government forces and armed opposition groups that occurred in a suburb of Dushanbe in early May, in which the victims were the inhabitants of nearby villages. The government and the UTO interpreted the reasons for the confrontation differently and blamed each other for using military force. Subsequently, public support for both the government and the UTO fell steeply. People throughout the country asked why neither of the parties had prevented the confrontations, the scale of which was reminiscent of the worst times of the civil war in the capital.

allegiance by personnel; (*c*) certification of personnel of reintegrated UTO detachments by a joint commission and selection of those who are fit for military service, with demobilization of the rest; and (*d*) complete integration of former UTO formations in the government military structures.

[29] *Kurier Tajikistana*, 26 June 1998 (in Russian).

[30] *Vostochny Ekspres*, 25 Sep. 1998 (in Russian).

[31] *Biznes i Politika*, no. 12 (20 Mar. 1998), (in Russian).

[32] *Jamestown Monitor* (Washington, DC), vol. 4, no. 61 (30 Mar. 1998).

[33] UNMOT was established in 1994 to monitor the situation in Tajikistan and the activities of the Russian-led Collective Peacekeeping Forces. Eckstein, S., 'Multilateral peace missions', *SIPRI Yearbook 1998* (note 3), p. 77. See also chapter 2, section III, in this volume.

[34] *Vecherniy Dushanbe*, 3 Apr. 1998 (in Russian).

[35] *Narodnaya Gazeta*, 3 Apr. 1998 (in Russian).

The lines of confrontation run not only between the two former opponents but also within both camps. The complexity of the situation lies in the fact that neither the government nor the UTO fully controls the military groups that are formally under its command. The government forces are not monolithic, their loyalty is dictated primarily by the commanders, and relations between the commanders are not always friendly. In addition, soldiers and policemen use their positions for personal advancement.

The situation is no better in the UTO, where the notions of subordination and discipline are rather abstract. Many field commanders (from the legal opposition units) are preoccupied with their own struggle for control over individual areas and do not pin too much hope on the efforts to obtain a share of power in the highest echelons. There were several confrontations between UTO groups. In the Kofarnikhon district, battles continued for two days in July 1998 between two armed UTO groups, with numerous victims, including civilians. Significantly, the fighting took place after members of these armed groups took military oaths of allegiance when they were prepared to be integrated into the government armed forces.[36] The battles attested to the fact that the Protocol on Military Issues is not perceived by all field commanders as binding, which seriously hinders the implementation of the peace agreements.

The illegal armed groups that are not formally subordinated to either side and are active in various regions of Tajikistan present the greatest challenge for the government and the UTO. On the whole, their activity is the result of a general criminalization of the society, which has been one of the consequences of the conflict. This criminalization is caused by many factors, including the impoverishment and marginalization of the population, the abundance of unregistered weapons, the lack of jobs, and ambitions for personal advancement among the heads of armed groups and field commanders.

New measures in the struggle against illegal armed groups were taken in the autumn of 1998. The coordination of government and UTO action in this field was strengthened and they began jointly to take more resolute steps. An ultimatum presented by the government and the UTO in early October to Saidmukhtar Yerov and Ravshan Gafurov, the heads of two illegal armed groups, demanding an immediate surrender of weapons and disbandment of troops, served as a warning to other field commanders engaged in robbery and extortion. After the expiry of the ultimatum, the Tajik authorities gave the order to apply military measures. Both of these armed groups, which had terrorized the inhabitants of Dushanbe and its suburbs for many months, were encircled by government troops. As a result of the military operation, some members of the groups were killed and others taken prisoner.[37]

V. The return of refugees

In the General Agreement on Peace and National Accord, special attention is given to the repatriation of refugees. Although the return and rehabilitation of refugees have not caused any notable clashes between the Tajik Government and the UTO, there are many technical and economic problems which must be solved before peace can be established in Tajikistan. According to data presented by the chairman of the NRC Subcommission on Refugees, Shukurjon Zukhurov, 60 000 people had returned from

[36] *Sadoi Mardum*, 17 July 1998 (in Tajik); and *Jumkhuriyat*, 18 July 1998 (in Tajik).
[37] Interfax, 12 Oct. 1998.

Afghanistan by 1998—that is, all those who had fled there during the civil war.[38] Those who had migrated to the territories of other CIS states (Kyrgyzstan, Russia and Turkmenistan) are reluctant to return to their ruined homes as are any who have managed to settle, find work or begin to study. Among the refugees, many are from non-titular groups (e.g., of the 16 000 migrants to Kyrgyzstan, 13 000 are Kyrgyz who had been living in Tajikistan).

Considerable effort is required to establish normal conditions for repatriated refugees in Tajikistan. This includes help not only in the construction of housing but also in finding employment and retraining where necessary. The financial resources for the accommodation of refugees have come from international organizations, in particular the World Bank.

The problem is especially acute in the case of former fighters who cannot find their place in civilian life and who take up arms again.[39] On the whole, the situation concerning the repatriation of refugees remains unsatisfactory. At an NRC meeting on 5 March 1998 it was pointed out that many people who returned received neither housing nor money and that the land given to them by the government (by a decree of the president 25 000 hectares were allocated to the refugees) is being taken away from them by armed groups. The people who return are not provided with even a minimum of security and, having no means of existence and no rights, they suffer from the arbitrary rule of the local authorities to a much greater degree than the rest of the population of Tajikistan. The NRC has recommended that a special commission be created consisting of the officials of the ministries of defence and the interior to work out mechanisms for the protection of refugees. However, in 1998 the situation in this respect did not change significantly.[40]

VI. Challenges to security: terrorism and drug trafficking

In 1998 terrorist actions in Tajikistan added tension to the situation, undermining the trust of the population in the parties involved in the process of national reconciliation and calling into question their ability to control the situation.

On 3 February, by a decree of the president, a special group was formed to ensure the security of UN representatives during their stay in Tajikistan.[41] Despite the creation of this detachment, four UNMOT employees were killed in a terrorist attack on 20 July on the Dushanbe–Tavildara highway. The head of UNMOT, Jan Kubis, announced that the military observers and civil UN staff from all the regions of the republic would be withdrawn to Dushanbe. He also let it be understood that more radical measures might be taken in coordination with UN headquarters.[42]

The attack on the UN employees was regarded as a serious setback to the process of national reconciliation. The Tajik Government and the UTO were united in their assessment of the matter: for both parties the terrorist act against the UN staff dealt a serious blow to their prestige, especially since it was carried out in an area with a high concentration of opposition armed groups. As Rakhmonov put it, this terrorist act had

[38] *Biznes i Politika*, no. 9 (27 Feb. 1998), (in Russian).
[39] *Biznes i Politika*, no. 9 (27 Feb. 1998), (in Russian).
[40] *Informatsionny Listok MNOONT* [UNMOT Information Bulletin], 8 Mar. 1998 (in Russian).
[41] *Sadoi Mardum*, 6 Feb. 1998 (in Tajik).
[42] *Jumkhuriyat*, 25 July 1998 (in Tajik).

a clear political motive—to disrupt the peace process and the progress of post-conflict reconstruction. The UTO's reaction was also sharp and immediate.[43]

Another blow to the process came on 22 September, with the murder of one of the most prominent UTO leaders, Otakhon Latifi, in Dushanbe. Latifi played an appreciable political role in Tajikistan and was deputy head of the UTO at the 1997 Inter-Tajik negotiations. He was also head of the NRC Subcommission on Legal Issues.[44] The UTO's demand that those responsible be found and punished nearly led to another in a series of crises in relations between the UTO and the government. The UTO announced a suspension of the activity of its representatives in the NRC and the government, and only at a special meeting between Rakhmonov and Nuri was it possible to prevent a further escalation of the crisis. This was facilitated by the elaboration of additional measures for stepping up the peace process, to which a special statement of 28 September 1998 was dedicated. These measures included the introduction of additional steps to ensure the security of UTO representatives in the NRC and the Tajik Government; acceleration of the process of reforming the Tajik Government and other power structures by according the UTO a 30 per cent quota of the government posts; and the creation of a joint rapid-response unit in order to intensify the struggle against crime and ensure the observance of military discipline in the armed units.[45]

Crime in Tajikistan is closely connected with the illegal drug trade. The acuteness of the problem has a direct relation to the conflict in Tajikistan since money received from drug sales is used to buy weapons and for criminal purposes. In the opinion of many experts, the drug business contributes to instability because, where the law enforcement bodies cannot exert full control, drug dealers enjoy impunity and receive huge profits on a stable basis. The law enforcement bodies are able to apprehend only a small number of them. Tajik drug dealers provide an important link in an international network for the processing, sale and delivery of drugs.

During 1997 about 2000 tons of raw opium and 2 tons of heroin were concentrated in the north-eastern provinces of Afghanistan awaiting delivery to Tajikistan and further into countries of the Commonwealth of Independent States (CIS) and Western Europe. A significant amount of the opium drugs smuggled into Tajikistan is produced in the north-western provinces of Pakistan. Between January and March 1998 alone, border guards intercepted 391 kilograms of drugs, including 60 kg of heroin.[46] The problem of interception is complicated by the fact that border guards are fired on from both Afghanistan and Tajikistan. As testified by the commander of the troops of the Russian Federal Border Guard Service in Tajikistan, President Rakhmonov and Chairman Nuri are united in their opposition to the smuggling of drugs into Tajikistan.

While the unity of views of the Tajik leadership is necessary for the fight against drug trafficking, it is not the only condition. Law enforcement bodies, often characterized by corruption, must be strengthened. In war-ravaged Tajikistan bribery is rampant and actively exploited by drug dealers, and it is often their hired couriers rather than the drug bosses themselves who are apprehended, allowing the drug business to continue to flourish.

[43] *Vecherniy Dushanbe*, 31 July 1998 (in Russian).

[44] Panfilova, V., 'Pogib Otakhon Latifi' [Otakhon Latifi lost his life], *Nezavisimaya Gazeta*, 23 Sep. 1998 (in Russian).

[45] *Jumkhuriyat*, 2 Oct. 1998 (in Tajik).

[46] *Biznes i Politika*, no.11 (13 Mar. 1998), (in Russian).

VII. The Afghan factor

One of the most important external influences on developments in Tajikistan in 1998 was the situation in Afghanistan. The Taleban offensive in the north of the country in August 1998 caused considerable anxiety among the Tajik leadership and led President Rakhmonov to ask Russian President Boris Yeltsin to call an urgent meeting of the CIS Council of Ministers of Defence in order to confirm the validity of the 1992 Tashkent Treaty on Collective Security.[47] The Taleban advance also caused concern among the UTO leaders, since there were still 160 opposition fighters in Afghanistan at the time. According to the chairman of the NRC Military Subcommission, Khabib Sanginov, the UTO and Taleban leaders had reached an understanding on the security of the UTO fighters. However, the UTO fighters urgently needed foodstuffs, medicines and other aid, since a malaria epidemic had broken out in areas where they were stationed. Sanginov insisted on an immediate evacuation of the fighters, without the help of the UN observers.[48]

Some believed that Rakhmonov's anxiety was dictated not so much by real fears that the Taleban might cross the border as by a desire to attract the attention of Russia and other CIS states to the situation, so that they would provide aid and take additional measures to strengthen border security. Using Russian border guard troops, reserve rapid-response groups were prepared in order to prevent an uncontrollable breakthrough and possible provocations. However, in September 1998 the Russian military and border troop commanders questioned the need for any special response to the developments in Afghanistan, arguing that Taleban attacks were unlikely and that the situation on the border was not threatening.[49]

At the same time the events in Afghanistan remain a serious external factor which clearly affects Tajikistan. The absence of law and order in Afghanistan creates favourable conditions for arms and drug trafficking. A spillover of violence and the spread of religious extremism might have a negative impact on the situation in Tajikistan, undermining the fragile stabilization process.

VIII. The Uzbek factor

The recent accusations against Uzbekistan made by Rakhmonov and other Tajik officials concerning interference in the internal affairs of Tajikistan highlight the role of the Uzbek factor.[50] There is no doubt that Uzbekistan has its own interests in the region and is very much concerned by developments in bordering Tajikistan. The two countries have a significant measure of interdependence because of their historic and cultural ties as well as their ethnic composition. The noticeable worsening of their interstate relations plays a negative role in that it can only impede the process of stabilization in Tajikistan.

[47] As a signatory to the treaty, Tajikistan is eligible for military assistance from the other CIS members, provided they view the situation as a threat from 'external aggression'. For the text see *Izvestiya*, 16 May 1992, p. 3.

[48] Panfilova, V., 'Dushanbe obespokoyen priblizheniem talibov' [Dushanbe is concerned over Taleban advance], *Nezavisimaya Gazeta*, 13 Aug. 1998 (in Russian).

[49] *Jamestown Monitor* (Washington, DC), vol. 4, no. 162 (4 Sep. 1998).

[50] See, e.g., Panfilova, V., 'Protivorechiya imeyut glubokie korni' [Contradictions are deep-rooted], *Nezavisimaya Gazeta*, 25 Nov. 1998 (in Russian).

IX. The Russian presence

The CIS Collective Peacekeeping Forces (CPF),[51] whose composition and financing are mainly Russian, continued to play an important role in safeguarding the peace process in Tajikistan in 1998.[52] They participated in the implementation of the military–political decisions and assisted with the repatriation of refugees. The predominance of the Russian contingent became even more obvious after the November coup in Leninabad when the Uzbek battalion left Tajikistan. This was also another indication of the escalation of tension in relations between Tajikistan and Uzbekistan.[53]

The Russian border forces have also played a significant role in the maintenance of security in Tajikistan, especially taking into account the instability in Afghanistan. As distinct from the CPF, a large number of Tajiks (approximately 80 per cent of the troops) serve in the ranks of the Russian border forces, some of whom are draftees and the others serving on a contract basis.[54]

The presence of the Russian border guards is viewed positively by the supporters of both Rakhmonov and the UTO. Both parties recognize that, without a reliable force to protect the Tajik–Afghan border, the country would face constant challenges to its security which the Tajik authorities are unable to deal with on their own. In addition, service in the border troop units provides a large number of local inhabitants with work and steady earnings which, in the present conditions, is an important factor.

The Russian presence in Tajikistan serves as a stabilizing factor not only within Tajikistan but also in the region by preventing the export of violence from this conflict-ridden area to other countries. It has also eased implementation of the Tajik peace agreements. The CPF were the first to come to Tajikistan at a time when no other peacekeeping force was prepared to stop the bloodshed. It was not a presence imposed on the Tajiks but one they wished to have.

In spite of debate in Russian political circles on whether the military presence in Tajikistan is necessary, it seems that it is also in Russia's own security interests since it provides protection for the most troublesome borders (drugs from Afghanistan and Pakistan pass through Tajikistan to Russia) and prevents the eventual increase of confrontation in the country.

X. Conclusions

Major changes occurred in the military–political situation in Tajikistan in 1998. The efforts to achieve a division of power laid the foundation for a gradual transformation of the government. However, the process of post-conflict reconciliation has proved to be complicated and contradictory. The rebellion in Leninabad and ensuing reactions

[51] In late 1997 the total number of the CIS Collective Peacekeeping Forces was *c.* 8000. Zavarin, V., 'Mirotvorcheskiye sily v Tadzhikistane' [Peacekeeping forces in Tajikistan], *Nezavisimoye Voyennoye Obozreniye*, no. 41 (31 Oct.–13 Nov. 1997), p. 2. The CPF are composed of *c.* 8000 officers and servicemen mainly from the Russian 201st Motor Rifle Division. See also chapter 2, section V, in this volume.

[52] Baranovsky, *SIPRI Yearbook 1998* (note 3), p. 136.

[53] *Vostochny Ekspres*, 27 Nov. 1998 (in Russian).

[54] In Nov. 1998 the Russian Federal Border Guard troops numbered 11 500; in addition, 6687 troops serve in the 201st MRD. 'Russian border service' in Foreign Broadcast Information Service, *Daily Report–Central Eurasia: Military Affairs (FBIS-UMA)*, FBIS-UMA-98-302, 29 Oct. 1998.

of the government and the UTO signified a new emerging balance of forces. For the first time the government and the opposition were united in their efforts to suppress a ‘third force’. Aggravation of relations with neighbouring Uzbekistan as a result of the failed coup in Leninabad might accentuate the ethnic dimension of the conflict, thus making it more intractable. The bilateral accommodation between the government and the UTO may promote peace and stability in the short term but could well become destabilizing in the medium term if the two partners continue to exclude the Leninabad region from a share of the power. By the end of the year the UTO had still not received a 30 per cent share of government positions. At the same time, it is practically impossible to embark on a redistribution of power now, when the two main parties are still bargaining. What should be done as fast as possible in order to ensure stability is to remove from administrative posts in Leninabad those nominees of the government who have caused the greatest resentment in the region. Efforts should be made to strengthen economic, political and cultural ties between the regions with a special emphasis on Leninabad. The main problem for Tajikistan lies in its fragmentation, which may cause new crises and upheavals.

2. Armed conflict prevention, management and resolution

JAANA KARHILO*

I. Introduction

Decades of attempts at conflict resolution finally culminated in the signing of a historic peace agreement in 1998 among all the major parties to the intractable conflict in Northern Ireland.[1] The Basque separatist movement ETA (Euzkadi Ta Azkatasuna, Basque Homeland and Liberty) announced a 'total and indefinite' truce in its 30-year terrorist campaign for independence from Spain. Regionally monitored peace accords brought an end to two other long-standing armed conflicts, waged over the border between Ecuador and Peru and over the secessionist ambitions of the island of Bougainville in Papua New Guinea. The pursuit of definitive peace settlements continued between Russia and Japan and North and South Korea, while China and Taiwan had their highest-level formal contact since 1949. The last pending China–Kazakhstan and Argentina–Chile border disputes were settled by mutual accord. Ceasefires held or were quickly re-established in Azerbaijan, Chechnya (Russia), Abkhazia and South Ossetia (Georgia), Moldova and Nagaland (India), and a partial truce was attained in Chad. Exploratory peace talks opened in Colombia against the backdrop of continuing civil war.

The record was mixed, as always, on the implementation of peace accords recently achieved between former adversaries in armed conflict. Among the most successful were the settlements in the Central African Republic, Eastern Slavonia, Guatemala and the Philippines, although all faced formidable challenges. Despite progress in some areas, the high expectations engendered by the ongoing or resuscitated peace processes in Bangladesh, Bosnia and Herzegovina, Cambodia, Liberia, the Middle East and Tajikistan remained unfulfilled. In Sierra Leone, the reinstatement of the elected president failed to secure the peace process, whereas in Angola the deeply troubled peace unravelled completely and the country returned to civil war.

Serious destabilizing intra-state armed conflicts broke out in 1998: an externally supported insurgency in the Democratic Republic of Congo (DRC) escalated into a regional war in Central Africa, while the armed resistance of ethnic Albanians to Serb repression in the Kosovo province of the Federal Republic of Yugoslavia (FRY) rekindled Balkan animosities. An armed rebellion in

[1] For details of the 1998 Good Friday/Belfast Agreement for Northern Ireland, see appendix 2B in this volume. For the major armed conflicts in 1998 see chapter 1 and appendix 1A in this volume.

* Johan Sjöberg of the SIPRI Project on Peacekeeping and Regional Security assisted in researching this chapter.

West African Guinea-Bissau subsided with a regionally monitored peace accord. Fighting continued or was renewed in Afghanistan, Algeria, Angola, Burundi, Chad, western China, Comoros, Colombia, Congo (Brazzaville), India, Myanmar, Rwanda, Senegal, Sierra Leone, Somalia, Sri Lanka, Sudan and Tajikistan. Armed uprisings and isolated clashes continued in the Chiapas region in Mexico, Nepal, Nicaragua, Peru and Yemen while ethnic violence erupted in Indonesia and Kenya. The main separatist group on Corsica ended a truce and escalated its campaign of bomb explosions. In the Great Lakes Region in Africa, new protagonists appeared—such as the Former Uganda National Army (FUNA) and the revived West Nile Bank Front (WBNF) in Uganda—to fuel the obscure small-scale insurgencies which operated across borders.

A fratricidal interstate conflict surprised the world when Ethiopia and Eritrea engaged in a land and air campaign over disputed border areas in the Horn of Africa. The nuclear testing by India and Pakistan heightened regional tensions, manifested in exceptionally heavy fire across the India–Pakistan border. Turkey threatened Syria with military force unless Kurd leader Abdullah Öcalan was extradited. Afghanistan and Iran were brought back from the brink of war after they had gathered massive troop concentrations along their border following the killing of Iranian diplomats in Afghanistan.

This chapter examines efforts by global and regional organizations to prevent, manage or resolve armed conflict in 1998. While often equally instrumental to success, initiatives by individual states, statesmen and non-governmental organizations (NGOs) are beyond the scope of the chapter and, together with the international humanitarian and development assistance crucial to peace building, are excluded from detailed examination. Section II surveys the activities of the United Nations, the main multilateral actor. Section III focuses on peacekeeping while section IV provides an overview of the UN role in enforcement action. The role of regional and other multilateral organizations is analysed in section V. Section VI comments on the emerging interrelationships and division of labour between the world body and regional organizations. Appendix 2A presents a table of multilateral peace missions in 1998.

II. The United Nations

UN Secretary-General Kofi Annan entered his second year in office with a clear mandate to continue his 'quiet revolution' of institutional reforms. With a new Deputy Secretary-General, Canadian Louise Fréchette, directing the implementation of the reform agenda, Annan was keen to refocus the attention of the 185 member states on the substantive agenda of the world body. The UN remained involved in a wide range and number of conflict prevention, management and resolution efforts, both alone and increasingly in cooperation with regional or other organizations.

The Secretary-General and the Secretariat

The Secretary-General continued to devote considerable attention to issues of peace and security, including the provision of good offices and mediation. During the year Annan was personally involved *inter alia* in Africa, the Balkans and, above all, Iraq. The most visible of his travels to trouble spots was the high-profile mission to Baghdad in February, where he averted a military showdown by brokering an agreement with Iraq over the conduct of inspections by the UN Special Commission on Iraq (UNSCOM). The limits of his office became apparent later as the splits within the Security Council precluded a unified approach to the conduct of diplomacy with Iraq.

During 1998 the Secretary-General and/or his representatives also continued their efforts to settle conflicts in Angola, Afghanistan, Burundi, Cambodia, Cyprus, the DRC, East Timor, the Middle East, Rwanda, Somalia, South Asia and Western Sahara.[2] Several of the new special envoys were appointed to overcome particular hurdles—Prakash Shah in Iraq to circumvent the stalemate between national authorities and the UN, and Lakhdar Brahimi in Angola to prevent a total collapse of the peace process. In Burundi a senior UN adviser supported regional peacemaking efforts. To break the political stalemate in Burma, UN Assistant Secretary-General for Political Affairs Alvaro de Soto offered the government $1 billion in incremental aid conditional upon progress in negotiations with the opposition. Formulated together with the World Bank, this venture into 'dollar diplomacy' represents the UN's first attempt to include international financial institutions directly in political negotiations.[3] A UN Political Office was established in Bougainville, the first of its kind in the south Pacific, and the first UN Peace-building Support Office opened in Liberia.

The prospects for peaceful resolution of the East Timor conflict brightened with a breakthrough in the tripartite talks held between Indonesia and Portugal under UN auspices in August. The resignation on 21 May of Indonesian President Suharto opened a window of opportunity for the government to reverse its long-standing intransigence, with new President Bacharuddin Jusuf Habibie's offer to grant Special Region status to East Timor.[4] Although rejected by East Timorese leaders favouring independence, such as Nobel Peace Prize laureate José Ramos-Horta, the offer sparked off a hectic series of round-robin meetings with the parties by UN Special Envoy Jamsheed Marker. The tripartite meeting in New York agreed to intensify negotiations on Indonesia's proposal for 'wide-ranging autonomy', which for the first time offers the territory power to control everything except foreign affairs, external

[2] UN, Annual report of the Secretary-General on the work of the organization, UN document A/53/1, 27 Aug. 1998.

[3] Crampton, T., 'UN links Burma aid to political dialogue', *International Herald Tribune*, 26 Nov. 1998.

[4] 'East Timor is offered special status', *Jane's Defence Weekly*, vol. 29, no. 24 (17 June 1998), p. 14.

defence, and monetary and fiscal policy.[5] The East Timorese, still excluded from direct negotiations, failed to agree on a common demand for self-determination at the fourth meeting of the All-Inclusive Intra-East Timorese Dialogue (AIETD) held near Vienna in early November.[6] Ramos-Horta announced that the National Council of the Timorese Resistance (CNRT) would no longer participate in the AIETD and called for future meetings in Timor in a different format.[7]

Lakhdar Brahimi, supported by the UN Special Mission to Afghanistan (UNSMA), failed to disengage interested regional powers from the Afghan conflict despite intense shuttle diplomacy. Persuaded by visiting UN Ambassador Bill Richardson in the highest-level US intervention in 20 years, the Afghan factions convened in Islamabad in April under the auspices of the UN and the Organization of the Islamic Conference (OIC).[8] However, calling on the UN to find a new basis for negotiations, the Taleban withdrew from the talks and expanded their control to 90–95 per cent of Afghanistan in a summer offensive. Renewed guerrilla warfare by the remnants of the northern alliance promised no early end to the fighting.[9] While outside powers reached common positions on the conflict in March, the inflow of arms continued and volunteers from neighbouring countries fought alongside the parties.[10] UNSMA attempted to coordinate UN activities within a new strategic framework for Afghanistan, but humanitarian efforts had to be suspended several times during the year.[11]

UN member states gleaned some insight from two fact-finding missions established by the Secretary-General into conflicts that remain impervious to outside scrutiny. An eminent panel led by former Portuguese President Mario Soares visited Algeria in July–August at the invitation of the government, the first international body allowed to gather information inside Algeria on the prolonged violence. Restricted in its ability to conduct independent investigations, the panel nevertheless recommended increased accountability of law enforcement and security forces and a change of mentality in the judiciary.[12] The Secretary-General's Investigative Team (SGIT) in the DRC had to be withdrawn in April before it had concluded its mandate to examine allegations

[5] Richardson, M., 'Jakarta details partial autonomy for East Timor', *International Herald Tribune*, 29 July 1998; Mydans, S., 'In Timor, terror and hope intertwined', *International Herald Tribune*, 22 July 1998; and UN Press Release SG/SM/6666, 5 Aug. 1998.

[6] RDP Antena 1 (Lisbon), 3 Nov. 1998, in 'Portugal: No accord on Timorese resistance document at Austria meet', Foreign Broadcast Information Service, *Daily Report–West Europe (FBIS-WEU)*, FBIS-WEU-98-307, 5 Nov. 1998; and UN Press Release SG/2049, 29 Oct. 1998.

[7] RDP Antena 1 (Lisbon), 3 Nov. 1998, 'Austria: Timorese leader causes rift at Austria meeting', FBIS-WEU-98-307, 5 Nov. 1998.

[8] Davis, A., 'An elusive peace', *Jane's Defence Weekly*, vol. 29, no. 19 (13 May 1998), p. 15. The OIC members are listed in the glossary in this volume.

[9] 'The Taliban: in charge, again', *The Economist*, vol. 348, no. 8083 (29 Aug. 1998); and UN Press release SC/6608, 8 Dec. 1998.

[10] United States Information Service (USIS), 'Ambassador Burleigh's General Assembly speech on Afghanistan', *Washington File* (US Embassy: Stockholm, 9 Dec. 1998).

[11] UN, Report of the Secretary-General, The situation in Afghanistan and its implications for international peace and security, UN document S/1998/1109, 23 Nov. 1998.

[12] UN, *Algeria: Report of Eminent Panel July–August 1998* (Department of Public Information, 1998).

of large-scale atrocities during the past five years. Despite persistent obstruction by local authorities, the team managed to document instances of gross violations of human rights, possibly even of genocide, and called for further scrutiny by independent investigation and an international tribunal.[13]

On the 50th anniversary of the Universal Declaration of Human Rights, the UN conducted its human rights work on less than 2 per cent of its resources, including a vast expansion in operational activities.[14] Requests for technical assistance alone strained the capacity of the Office of the UN High Commissioner for Human Rights (OHCHR), which carried out some 45 projects to support national human rights in over 25 states during 1997–98. Another nine projects were implemented at the regional level and nine at the global level.[15] Human rights field presences had been set up in 22 countries over just a few years. In Rwanda, where violence continued and some 125 000 detainees awaited trial, human rights observation suffered a severe setback when the oldest field operation was terminated in July after the government refused to accept a monitoring function for the mission.[16]

The Secretariat continued to provide electoral assistance and advice on strengthening national electoral institutions. The global interest in good governance was illustrated by the UN's report that it had received over 140 such requests since 1989.[17] In 1997–98 the UN responded to calls for long- and short-term electoral assistance from Armenia, Cameroon, the Central African Republic, El Salvador, Equatorial Guinea, Guinea, Guyana, Honduras, Lesotho, Mauritius, Nicaragua, Swaziland, the Former Yugoslav Republic of Macedonia (FYROM) and Togo. The UN also helped to coordinate and support international observation of the National Assembly elections held in Cambodia in July.[18]

Reform of its leadership and management structure had improved coordination of conflict management within the UN. A new Strategic Planning Unit, established in August as a policy-generating body, supported decision making by the heads of departments and offices in the Senior Management Group. Managing one of the four core areas of UN activity, the Executive Committee for Peace and Security focused particularly on improving the level of coordination and collaboration in post-conflict peace building.[19] The Department of Political Affairs in turn initiated a review of its internal structure to improve

[13] UN, Letter dated 29 June 1998 from the Secretary-General addressed to the President of the Security Council, UN document S/1998/581, 29 June 1998.

[14] UN, Report of the United Nations High Commissioner for Human Rights, UN document A/53/36, 9 Oct. 1998, para. 62.

[15] UN, Report of the Secretary-General, Support by the United Nations system of the efforts of governments to promote and consolidate new or restored democracies, UN document A/53/554, 29 Oct. 1998, para. 17.

[16] UN, Human rights field operation in Rwanda, UN document A/53/367, 11 Sep. 1998; and 'Rwanda bleeds on', *The Economist,* vol. 347, no. 8069 (1998), 23 May 1998.

[17] UN document A/53/554 (note 15), para. 34.

[18] UN document A/53/1 (note 2), para. 120.

[19] The 4 thematic areas are peace and security, development cooperation, international economic and social affairs, and humanitarian affairs. Human rights is a 5th, cross-cutting issue.

its ability to develop a system-wide strategic framework for UN assistance to countries responding to and recovering from crisis.[20]

The Secretary-General also pursued the implementation of reforms to consolidate UN activities both at headquarters and in the field. The Department of Humanitarian Affairs (DHA) was divested of operational responsibilities and reconstituted as the Office for the Coordination of Humanitarian Affairs (OCHA) in January.[21] At the country level, the aim was to unify the UN presence in common premises under the leadership of a UN Resident Coordinator. 'UN Houses' were established in Algeria, Lebanon, Malaysia and South Africa with an additional 32 countries approved to follow suit.[22] For further unity of relief and political efforts, some resident coordinators were also appointed humanitarian coordinators and in two cases Deputy Special Representatives of the Secretary-General.[23]

Despite widespread agreement on the advantages of conflict prevention both globally and regionally, practical advances remained negligible. A report by the prestigious Carnegie Commission urged the UN to conduct its first serious review of preventive measures and to institute regular meetings with regional organizations to discuss preventive regional strategies. Annan conceded that such strategies and the requisite political will were lacking throughout the UN system.[24] The third meeting between the UN and regional organizations, devoted to conflict prevention, noted that cooperation most often took the form of consultation and diplomatic support. A UN liaison officer was to be appointed at the Organization for African Unity (OAU) headquarters to improve coordination, a model to be replicated with other organizations.[25]

The Security Council and the General Assembly

The Security Council, while continuing to remain seized of a multitude of peace and security issues, met most frequently to consider the conflicts in Iraq, the former Yugoslavia and Angola, as well as others on the African continent. Overcoming long-standing conservatism about intervention in internal conflict, the council established two new UN peacekeeping operations in 1998, in the Central African Republic and in Sierra Leone. China continued through abstentions to oppose peace operations it considered as involving interference in the internal affairs of a state, but no vetoes were cast in 1998.

The persistent Iraqi challenge to the authority of the Security Council evoked the most acrimonious divisions among its members. The greatest num-

[20] UN, Report of the Secretary-General, Status of implementation of actions described in the report of the Secretary-General entitled 'Renewing the United Nations: a programme for reform', UN document A/53/676, 18 Nov. 1998, p. 4.

[21] UN, Report of the Secretary-General, Triennial comprehensive policy review of operational activities for development of the United Nations system, UN document A/53/226/Add.1, 12 Aug. 1998, para. 115.

[22] UN Press Release DSG/SM/40, 8 Dec. 1998.

[23] UN document A/53/226 (note 21), para. 122.

[24] Deen, T., 'Annan slams UN failure to prevent ethnic wars', *Jane's Defence Weekly*, vol. 29, no. 7 (18 Feb. 1998), p. 6.

[25] UN, Press Release SG/SM/6653, 27 July 1998.

ber of meetings in 1997–98 and largest volume of correspondence were devoted to ensuring Iraq's compliance with its obligations to let UNSCOM conduct its verification and monitoring duties to determine that Iraq had destroyed its weapons of mass destruction and long-range missile programmes.[26] The first of many crises was defused when Iraq reconfirmed its acceptance of all relevant Security Council resolutions in a Memorandum of Understanding signed on 23 February, and inspections of presidential sites could proceed under special procedures. In August Iraq suspended cooperation with UNSCOM after disagreement over continued inspections, whereupon the council cancelled a planned comprehensive review of the sanctions regime.[27] Iraq's decision in October to cease cooperation with UNSCOM and limit International Atomic Energy Agency (IAEA) activities provoked the council, acting under Chapter VII of the UN Charter, to condemn Iraq for flagrant violations of UN resolutions.[28] With US bombers already on their way, Iraq indicated that UNSCOM and the IAEA could resume their work. The council remained ready to proceed with the sanctions review once Iraq had returned to full cooperation, but UNSCOM's 15 December report concluded that it had not.[29] Before the council had debated three possible responses suggested by the Secretary-General, two of its permanent members had put into effect their threat to launch military strikes against Iraq. Heated informal consultations within the council revealed deep rifts between the UK and the USA and other permanent members on the appropriate response to Iraqi non-compliance. As Iraq announced its opposition to any future return of UNSCOM, the Security Council's authority was further eroded by allegations that US agents had worked under cover on UNSCOM teams to gather independent intelligence, possibly used in planning the bombing raids.[30]

Regarding some of the most acute conflicts to erupt in 1998, the Security Council opted to 'contract out' diverse peace missions and/or mediation to regional organizations and groupings. In September the Security Council endorsed prior initiatives by numerous actors resulting in international monitoring in Kosovo by the European Community Monitoring Mission (ECMM) and the Kosovo Diplomatic Observer Mission (KDOM).[31] In October it endorsed the Organization for Security and Co-operation in Europe (OSCE) verification mission in and NATO air surveillance over Kosovo, the terms of which had been negotiated directly between those organizations and the FRY.[32] Following mediation by Gambia, the Community of Portuguese-

[26] UN, Report of the Security Council to the General Assembly 16 June 1997–15 June 1998, UN document A/53/2, 9 Sep. 1998, p. 166.

[27] UN Security Council Resolution 1194, 9 Sep. 1998. On the activities of UNSCOM see also chapters 3, 13 and 15 in this volume.

[28] UN Security Council Resolution 1205, 5 Nov. 1998.

[29] UN, Letter dated 15 Dec. 1998 from the Secretary-General addressed to the President of the Security Council, UN document S/1998/1172, 15 Dec. 1998.

[30] 'A little light eavesdropping', *The Economist*, vol. 350, no. 8101 (9 Jan. 1999), p. 45.

[31] UN Security Council Resolution 1199, 23 Sep. 1998 (adopted by 14–0–1 with China abstaining).

[32] UN Security Council Resolution 1203, 24 Oct. 1998 (adopted by 13–0–2 with China and Russia abstaining).

Speaking Countries (Comunidade dos Países de Língua Portuguesa, CPLP)[33] and the Economic Community of West African States (ECOWAS) in the violent conflict in Guinea-Bissau, the council endorsed the deployment there of a border monitoring force by the ECOWAS Monitoring Group (ECOMOG).[34] In the Eritrea–Ethiopia border dispute the council initially supported mediation by the subregional Inter-Governmental Authority on Development (IGAD), Rwanda and the USA; in June it called for a halt to the use of force and offered the good offices of the Secretary-General.[35] The council remained passive but supportive of regional mediation with regard to the conflict in the DRC, announcing only in December its readiness to 'consider active involvement' of the UN in holding a peace conference together with the OAU. While it did reactivate the International Commission of Inquiry charged with investigating the illegal flow of arms to former government forces of Rwanda and in the Great Lakes Region, the council failed to act on the suggestion of the SGIT that it pursue an independent investigation into allegations of human rights violations in the DRC.[36] The council's interest in the conflict over Kashmir, mentioned for the first time in decades in a resolution condemning the nuclear tests by India and Pakistan, was briskly rebuffed by India, which reiterated its refusal to accept any third-party mediation in the 50-year dispute.[37]

The Security Council's attention to Africa was given a more operative focus by the Secretary-General's analytical report on the causes of conflict on the continent, discussed by 52 states, organizations and observers in an open debate at the council in April.[38] An Ad Hoc Working Group was charged with preparing specific proposals for action for the council's second ministerial meeting on Africa in September. Six sub-groups reviewed the Secretary-General's main recommendations on strengthening arms embargoes; enhancing Africa's peacekeeping capacity; regional cooperation; developing an international mechanism to secure refugee camps; stemming illicit arms flows; and improving the council's capacity to monitor activities authorized by it. The council further committed itself to assessing progress at the ministerial level on a biennial basis.[39]

Through thematic discussions, the council sought to develop the modalities of UN post-conflict peace building as a tool for conflict settlement. Recognizing the need for coordination, sustained political will and a long-term

[33] The CLCP member states are Angola, Brazil, Cape Verde, Guinea-Bissau, Mozambique, Portugal, and Sao Tome and Principe.

[34] UN Security Council Resolution 1216, 21 Dec. 1998.

[35] UN Security Council Resolution 1177, 26 June 1998.

[36] UN Press Release SC/6626, 12 Jan. 1999.

[37] 'UN defied over resolution of Kashmiri issue', *Jane's Defence Weekly*, vol. 29, no. 24 (17 June 1998), p. 13. The Kashmir conflict is discussed in appendix 1B in this volume.

[38] UN, Report of the Secretary General on the causes of conflict and the promotion of durable peace and sustainable development in Africa, UN document S/1998/318, 13 Apr. 1998.

[39] UN Security Council Resolution 1170, 28 May 1998. The recommendations made by the sub-groups are given in resolutions S/RES/1196, 16 Sep. 1998, S/RES/1197, 18 Sep. 1998, S/RES/1208 and S/RES/1209, 19 Nov. 1998, and presidential statements S/PRST/1998/28, 16 Sep. 1998 and S/PRST/1998/35, 30 Nov. 1998.

approach in UN decision making, the council announced a future policy, where appropriate, of integrating clearly identified peace-building elements into the mandates of peacekeeping operations. Their exit strategy was to include recommendations to other UN bodies on the transition to post-conflict peace building.[40] In its first-ever meeting on children, 2 million of whom have been killed in armed conflicts over the past decade, the council vowed to focus more attention on their plight and to give special consideration to the disarmament, demobilization and reintegration into society of child soldiers.[41]

After five years of effort, reform of the Security Council remained as elusive as ever. The non-aligned states, previously intent on enlarging the permanent membership, adopted a 'fall-back' position proposing an initial increase only in the number of elective seats in order to move the process forward.[42] While no substantive agreement was in evidence, the General Assembly resolved not to adopt any decision on council reform without the affirmative vote of at least two-thirds of the member states.[43] Meanwhile, the council moved to increase its transparency through open debates and briefings.[44]

The General Assembly continued its consideration of the situation in east Jerusalem under the Uniting for Peace resolution in its 10th emergency session but failed to advance the issue. The assembly also prolonged by a year the mandate of the largest and most important UN peace-building operation, the UN Verification Mission in Guatemala (MINUGUA).[45]

International legal mechanisms

The International Court of Justice (ICJ) witnessed states acquiring a 'law habit' as four new contentious cases and one request for an advisory opinion were added to its docket in 1998. The court delivered four judgements, deciding to proceed to the merits in three cases and finding that it lacked jurisdiction in one. Faced with an expanded caseload of great geographical diversity, the court bemoaned the shortage of staff and funds that were causing a backlog in its work.[46]

Paraguay instituted proceedings against the USA in a dramatic case in April, claiming that a Paraguayan national on 'death row' had not been properly advised of his right to consular assistance. Although the court called on the USA to 'take all measures at its disposal' to prevent the execution pending its final decision, the Governor of Virginia allowed it to proceed following a US

[40] UN Security Council Presidential Statement, UN document S/PRST/1998/38, 29 Dec. 1998.

[41] UN Security Council Presidential Statement, UN document S/PRST/1998/18, 29 June 1998.

[42] Cohen, M., 'Simplistic to write off NAM', SAPA (Johannesburg), 5 Sep. 1998, in 'South Africa: Analyst: "Simplistic" to view non-aligned meet as worthless', Foreign Broadcast Information Service, *Daily Report–Sub-Saharan Africa (FBIS-AFR)*, FBIS-AFR-98-248, 9 Sep. 1998.

[43] UN General Assembly Resolution 53/30, 1 Dec. 1998.

[44] UN document A/53/2 (note 26), pp. 331 and 360.

[45] UN General Assembly Resolution A/RES/53/93, 7 Dec. 1998.

[46] UN, Report of the International Court of Justice, 1 August 1997–31 July 1998, UN document A/53/4, 4 Sep. 1998, pp. 82–95.

Table 2.1. Cases before the International Court of Justice, 1998[a]

- Maritime Delimitation and Territorial Questions between Qatar and Bahrain (Qatar v. Bahrain)
- Questions of Interpretation and Application of the 1971 Montreal Convention arising from the Aerial Incident at Lockerbie (Libyan Arab Jamahiriya v. United Kingdom)
- Questions of Interpretation and Application of the 1971 Montreal Convention arising from the Aerial Incident at Lockerbie (Libyan Arab Jamahiriya v. United States of America)
- Oil Platforms (Islamic Republic of Iran v. United States of America)
- Application of the Convention on the Prevention and Punishment of the Crime of Genocide (Bosnia and Herzegovina v. Yugoslavia)
- Gabcíkovo-Nagymaros Project (Hungary/Slovakia)
- Land and Maritime Boundary between Cameroon and Nigeria (Cameroon v. Nigeria)
- Fisheries Jurisdiction (Spain v. Canada)
- Kasikili/Sedudu Island (Botswana/Namibia)
- Vienna Convention on Consular Relations (Paraguay v. United States of America)[b]
- Difference relating to immunity from legal process of a Special Rapporteur of the Commission on Human Rights (ECOSOC)*
- Request for Interpretation of the Judgment of 11 June 1998 in the Case concerning the Land and Maritime Boundary between Cameroon and Nigeria (Cameroon v. Nigeria), Preliminary Objections (Nigeria v. Cameroon)
- Sovereignty over Pulau Litigan and Pulau Sipadan (Indonesia/Malaysia)
- Ahmadou Diallo (Republic of Guinea v. Democratic Republic of the Congo)

[a] Cases listed as 1 party versus another are those in which 1 party (the first mentioned) brought to the ICJ a case against another party; the others are cases where both parties jointly sought a court ruling. Cases marked with an asterisk (*) are those in which an advisory opinion has been sought by 1 party.

[b] The case was removed from the Court's list in Nov. 1998 at the request of Paraguay.

Supreme Court ruling that the decision was his alone.[47] A new case arose out of Nigeria's request for an interpretation of the court's ruling in June, 14 votes to 3, that it had jurisdiction to adjudicate the case brought by Cameroon concerning the land and maritime boundary between the two states. Although the court had opined that the exact scope of the dispute could not yet be determined, Nigeria sought clarification of which alleged incidents in areas of contested sovereignty should form part of the merits of the case.[48] Indonesia and Malaysia jointly seized the court of a dispute concerning sovereignty over two islands in the Celebes Sea whereas Guinea brought a case against the DRC for alleged unlawful treatment of a Guinean businessman.[49] The Economic and Social Council (ECOSOC) asked the court for an advisory opinion on the applicability of the 1946 Convention on the Privileges and Immunities of the United Nations after the Special Rapporteur of the Commission of Human

[47] International Court of Justice (ICJ): Case concerning the Vienna Convention on Consular Relations (Paraguay v. United States of America), 9 Apr. 1998, in 37 International Legal Materials (ILM) 4 (1998), pp. 810–23; and ICJ, Communiqué no. 98/36, The Hague, 11 Nov. 1998.

[48] ICJ, Case concerning the land and maritime boundary between Cameroon and Nigeria (Cameroon v. Nigeria), Judgment 11 June 1998, at URL <http://www.icjij.org/icjwww/idocket/icn/icnjudgment/icn_ijudgment-980611_frame. htm>; and ICJ, Communiqué no. 98/34, The Hague, 29 Oct. 1998.

[49] ICJ, Communiqués no. 98/35, The Hague, 2 Nov. 1998, and no. 98/46, The Hague, 30 Dec. 1998.

Rights on the independence of judges and lawyers had been sued for defamation in Malaysian courts despite his immunity from legal process.[50]

In a matter with potentially explosive legal implications, the court ruled in February that it had jurisdiction to hear the virtually identical Lockerbie cases between Libya and the UK and the USA, respectively, and that Libya's claims were admissible.[51] As the case proceeds, with the respondents arguing *inter alia* the primacy of Security Council resolutions over the 1971 Montreal Convention, the court will have its first opportunity to address the question whether it possesses review power over council decisions. The court concluded in December by 12 votes to 5 that it had no jurisdiction in the dispute relating to the pursuit, arrest and detention by Canadian officials of the Spanish fishing vessel *Estai* on the high seas in 1995, as it came under the terms of a reservation contained in Canada's declaration accepting the compulsory jurisdiction of the court.[52] By an order released in March, the court accepted as admissible a US counter-claim concerning alleged unlawful military actions by Iran in 1987–88 in the Oil Platforms case between the two states.[53] Slovakia filed a request for an additional judgement in the dispute concerning the Gabcíkovo–Nagymaros dam project on the Danube River, citing Hungary's unwillingness to implement the judgement delivered in 1997.[54]

The two international ad hoc tribunals pursued their path-breaking work in the development of international humanitarian law by trying individuals suspected of war crimes and gross violations of human rights. Fully operational after four years of 'institution building', the International Criminal Tribunal for the Former Yugoslavia (ICTY) witnessed unprecedented levels of litigation with three trials under way, seven cases in the pre-trail stages and three appeals pending as of November 1998.[55] In a seminal judgement, and the first involving multiple defendants and non-Serbs, the tribunal provided the first elucidation of the doctrine of command responsibility since the Nuremberg and Tokyo trials, finding it to encompass not only military commanders but also civilians holding positions of authority, whether *de jure* or de facto.[56] The judgement also included the ICTY's first conviction for sexual assault as a war crime. Adjudicating the first case to focus exclusively on rape as a war crime, the tribunal found the prohibition against torture to have attained the

[50] ICJ, Communiqué no. 98/26, The Hague, 10 Aug. 1998.

[51] In the former case, the court voted 13–3 on jurisdiction and 12–4 on admissibility, in the latter 13–2 and 12–3. ICJ, Case concerning questions of interpretation and application of the 1971 Montreal Convention arising from the aerial incident at Lockerbie (Libyan Arab Jamahiriya v. United Kingdom), Judgment, 27 Feb. 1998, URL <http://www.icj-cij.org/icjwww/idocket/iluk/ilukjudgment/iluk_ijudgment>; and ICJ, Case concerning questions of interpretation and application of the 1971 Montreal Convention arising from the aerial incident at Lockerbie (Libyan Arab Jamahiriya v. United States of America), Judgment, 27 Feb. 1998, in 37 ILM 3 (1998), pp. 587–652.

[52] ICJ, Communiqués nos 98/41 and 98/41 bis, The Hague, 4 Dec. 1998.

[53] ICJ, Case concerning oil platforms (Islamic Republic of Iran v. United States of America). Counter-claim Order 10 Mar. 1998, at URL <http://www.icj-cij.org/icjwww/idocket/iop/ioporders/iop_iorders_toc.htm>.

[54] ICJ, Communiqué no. 98/28, The Hague, 3 Sep. 1998.

[55] Address to the UN General Assembly by Judge Gabrielle Kirk McDonald, President of ICTY, 19 Nov. 1998, URL <http://www.un.org/icty/pressreal/speechP.htm>.

[56] International Criminal Tribunal for the Former Yugoslavia, Celebici case: the judgement of the trial chamber, official summary, ICTY document CC/PIU/364-E, 16 Nov. 1998.

status of *jus cogens*, a peremptory norm from which no derogation is permitted.[57] The first person to have been convicted by the tribunal in 1996 of crimes against humanity was resentenced in March 1998 after being allowed on appeal to plead to the lesser war crimes charge and was transferred to serve his prison term.[58] With a threefold annual increase in the number of detainees in custody, the Security Council approved the establishment of a third Trial Chamber and the election of three additional judges who took up their duties in November.[59]

The Stabilization Force (SFOR) continued to accompany tribunal teams in the execution of search warrants in Bosnia and Herzegovina and accelerated the pace of arrests, prompting several indictees to surrender voluntarily. The success in both areas inundated the Office of the Prosecutor, which refocused resources on the major offenders and withdrew all charges against 14 suspects.[60] By December, 26 detainees were in custody at The Hague, including a three-star general charged with genocide perpetrated in Srebrenica and arrested under sealed indictment, but some 30 public indictments remained outstanding. The FRY refused to hand over indictees on its territory and remained the only signatory of the 1995 General Framework Agreement for Peace in Bosnia and Herzegovina (the Dayton Agreement) not to have adopted legislation to facilitate cooperation with the tribunal. Its contempt became more pronounced as the Security Council asked the tribunal to gather information on the violence in Kosovo. The chief prosecutor was able to dispatch small investigative teams over the summer but was unceremoniously rebuffed in November in her attempt to lead a fact-finding mission on the ground herself.[61] At year's end the president and chief prosecutor of the tribunal bluntly pronounced the FRY to be in violation of international law and challenged the council to enforce its own mandate.[62]

The International Criminal Tribunal for Rwanda handed down two historic sentences for genocide, thereby recognizing that the crime had occurred in Rwanda in 1994.[63] The landmark judgement of 2 September 1998 was the first time an international court has ever applied and interpreted the 1948 Genocide Convention, determined individual responsibility for genocide and recognized

[57] International Criminal Tribunal for the Former Yugoslavia, Furundzija case: the judgement of the trial chamber, official summary, ICTY document JL/PIU/372-E, 10 Dec. 1998.

[58] UN, Fifth annual report of the International Tribunal for the prosecution of persons responsible for serious violations of international humanitarian law committed in the territory of the former Yugoslavia since 1991, UN document A/53/219, S/1998/737, 10 Aug. 1998, paras 22–25.

[59] The UN General Assembly elected David Anthony Hunt (Australia), Patrick Lipton Robinson (Jamaica) and Mohamed Bennouna (Morocco) from among 9 candidates. ICTY Press Release CC/PIU/354-E, 19 Oct. 1998, URL <http://www.un.org/icty/pressreal/p354-e.htm>.

[60] Rafferty, P., 'Tribunal frees 14 Serb suspects despite evidence of war crimes', *UN Observer and International Report*, vol. 20, no. 6 (June 1998), p. 8.

[61] Truehart, C., 'Yugoslavia bans UN mission to Kosovo', *International Herald Tribune*, 6 Nov. 1998.

[62] ICTY Press Release JL/PIU/371-E, Judge Gabrielle Kirk McDonald, President of the International Criminal Tribunal for the Former Yugoslavia, addresses the UN Security Council, 8 Dec. 1998.

[63] For background on the tribunal, see Karhilo, J., 'The establishment of the International Tribunal for Rwanda', *Nordic Journal of International Law,* vol. 64, no. 4 (1995), pp. 683–713.

that rape and sexual violence can constitute genocide.[64] Former mayor Jean-Paul Akayesu was sentenced in October to three life terms in prison for genocide and crimes against humanity related to extermination.[65] Jean Kambanda, Prime Minister of the interim government in Rwanda in April 1994, became in May 1998 the first person ever to plead guilty to genocide and be found guilty of it by an international jurisdiction, thereby also confirming that the genocide had been planned and organized at the highest levels.[66] Two more trials were under way, some eight were in pre-trial stages and in December a leader of the notorious Interahamwe Hutu militia became the second defendant to plead guilty to genocide.[67] Numerous states cooperated with the tribunal in apprehending suspects, and 31 of the 43 indictees, all formerly in positions of authority, were taken into custody. In the light of the increased caseload, the Security Council established a third Trial Chamber and decided to hold elections for the judges of all chambers together for a term to expire in 2003.[68] Despite managerial and procedural reform, problems persisted with inefficiency in hiring and procurement, weaknesses in the witness protection scheme, delays in the proceedings and shortcomings in the dissemination of public information.[69] A Swedish judge resigned before the expiry of his term in apparent frustration with administrative inefficiency and mismanagement.[70]

Decades of planning culminated in 1998 in a historic agreement to establish a permanent International Criminal Court (ICC) to deter and punish the most heinous crimes. After five weeks of deliberations in Rome, the UN Diplomatic Conference, attended by 160 states and some 200 NGOs, adopted the ICC Statute on 17 July with 120 votes for, 7 against and 20 abstentions.[71] The outcome of compromises negotiated primarily between a group of some 50 'like-minded' countries aiming for a strong, independent court and a group led by great powers seeking restrictions in favour of national sovereignty, the statute attracted criticism from human rights groups. Yet it failed to allay US fears

[64] International Criminal Tribunal for Rwanda: Prosecutor v. Akayesu, 2 Sep. 1998, in 37 ILM 6 (1998), pp. 1399–410.

[65] 'Rwandan mayor gets 3 life terms for genocide', *International Herald Tribune,* 3–4 Oct. 1998.

[66] The first person ever to be sentenced for genocide, Kambanda was sentenced to life imprisonment on 4 Sep. International Criminal Tribunal for Rwanda, Prosecutor v. Kambanda, 4 Sep. 1998 in 37 ILM 6 (1998), pp. 1411–26.

[67] UN, Third annual report of the International Criminal Tribunal for the prosecution of persons responsible for genocide and other serious violations of international humanitarian law committed in the territory of Rwanda and Rwandan citizens responsible for genocide and other such violations committed in the territory of neighbouring states between 1 January and 31 December 1994, UN document A/53/429–S/1998/857, 23 Sep. 1998; and 'Rwandan militia leader admits to genocide and related crimes', *International Herald Tribune*, 15 Dec. 1998.

[68] Judges Laïty Kama (Senegal), Yakov Ostrovskiy (Russian Federation), Navanethem Pillay (South Africa) and William Sekule (Tanzania) were re-elected and Pavel Dolenc (Slovenia), Mehmet Güney (Turkey), Dionysios Kondylis (Greece), Erik Mose (Norway) and Lloyd George Williams (Jamaica) were newly elected from a list of 18 candidates. UN Press Release GA/9495, 3 Nov. 1998.

[69] Amnesty International, *International Criminal Tribunal for Rwanda: Trials and Tribulations*, Report IOR 40/03/98, Apr. 1998.

[70] Säll, O., 'Svensk hoppar av Rwandatribunal' [Swede leaves the Rwanda tribunal], *Svenska Dagbladet*, 18 July 1998.

[71] The 7 states to vote against were China, Iraq, Israel, Libya, Qatar, the USA and Yemen. UN, Rome Statute of the International Criminal Court adopted July 17, 1998, in 37 ILM 5 (1998), pp. 999–1069.

that its armed forces operating overseas could be exposed to the court's jurisdiction.[72] The ICC will have only prospective jurisdiction over war crimes, crimes against humanity, genocide and aggression (provided it can later be defined), although states can 'opt out' of accepting the war crimes jurisdiction for seven years.[73] Civil wars are brought into its competence, increasing its relevance to future armed conflicts. The ICC will consist of 18 judges, a prosecutor and a registrar and will comprise an appeals, a trial and a pre-trial division. The prosecutor has the power, upon approval from a pre-trial chamber, to initiate investigations, which may, however, be hampered by weak provisions on state cooperation that mostly delegate the collection of evidence to local authorities. Cases can also be referred to the court by states parties or the Security Council. Unlike the ad hoc tribunals, the ICC does not have priority over but complements national courts, acting only when they are 'unwilling or unable genuinely' to do so. For the long-awaited court to become a reality, 60 ratifications of its statute are required and a preparatory commission must successfully draft the legal infrastructure.[74]

A special Arbitral Tribunal established by the Dayton Agreement ruled in March on the situation of Brcko in Bosnia and Herzegovina, deciding to continue to keep it under temporary international supervision pending a final arbitration phase, postponed until 1999, rather than handing it to the Bosnian Serbs or the Government of Bosnia and Herzegovina.[75]

III. UN peacekeeping operations

The United Nations commemorated the 50th anniversary of peacekeeping by honouring the more than 1500 peacekeepers who have died in the course of their international duty. Beginning with the deployment of 36 unarmed observers in the Middle East in May 1948, the UN has established 49 peacekeeping operations, 36 of them since 1988. Over 750 000 military and civilian police personnel as well as thousands of other civilians, from 118 different countries, have served under the UN flag. The total cost of this enterprise for the past 50 years has amounted to approximately $18 billion.[76]

The first post-cold war decade has witnessed both the much-publicized resurgence and the continuing retrenchment of UN peacekeeping. Costs had plummeted from nearly $3.3 billion in 1994, when the UN fielded more than 70 000 troops, to barely $1 billion in 1998. In December the approximately 14 500 UN peacekeepers deployed around the world represented less than half the number serving under NATO command in the world's largest peace opera-

[72] Public Diplomacy Query (PDQ), 'Scheffer on why the U.S. opposed International Criminal Court', 23 July 1998, URL <http://pdq2.usia.gov>.

[73] Ronzitti, N., 'Is the Rome Statute of the International Criminal Court a real breakthrough in international law?', *International Spectator*, vol. 33, no. 3 (1998), p. 12.

[74] UN, Note by the Secretary-General: establishment of an International Criminal Court, UN document A/53/387, 19 Sep. 1998.

[75] *UN Chronicle*, no. 2 (1998), p. 67.

[76] UN Press Release SG/SM/6732, PKO/74, 6 Oct. 1998; and Garval, K., 'FN markerar 50 års fredsinsatser' [UN marks 50 years of peace efforts], *FN Information* (UN Information Centre for the Nordic Countries, Copenhagen), Nov. 1998, p. 7.

tion, in Bosnia and Herzegovina. A West African subregional operation in Sierra Leone also outranked in size the largest UN operation, the UN Interim Force in Lebanon (UNIFIL). Indeed, UN-endorsed intervention by regional organizations and multinational coalitions had become a growing trend as the world body implemented lessons learned from the setbacks in Bosnia and Herzegovina, Rwanda and Somalia and shed operational responsibility for large-scale enforcement missions.

The 16 UN operations deployed at the end of the year comprised five carried over from the cold war period, unable as yet to fulfil their mandates; remnants or spin-offs of previously large-scale missions; small observer missions, three of which—in Georgia, Tajikistan and Sierra Leone—also monitored a regional or subregional force they were co-deployed with; two purely civilian police (CivPol) missions in Haiti and Bosnia and Herzegovina; and one new multi-dimensional operation in Central Africa. CivPols were included in 9 of the 16 extant missions; a tenth, the Police Support Group established for a transitional nine months following the liquidation of a larger UN operation in Eastern Slavonia, handed over its tasks to an OSCE mission in October.

The UN's operational involvement in conflict management was revived in 1998 with the establishment of two new peacekeeping operations. Having delegated peacekeeping in the Central African Republic and Sierra Leone to subregional forces in 1997, the Security Council now deemed both countries to be stable enough for the entry of UN peacekeepers. Except for the temporary expansion of the mandate of the human rights monitoring mission in Guatemala in 1997, these operations have the only genuinely new peacekeeping mandates since 1994. Having overcome its aversion to operations in Africa, the Security Council was unanimous in authorizing the first new missions on the continent since the ill-fated ones in Somalia and Rwanda. Its members, however, emphasized the importance of prior regional action to restore stability and of continued African involvement in support of both peace-building efforts.[77] Furthermore, the US Administration reportedly decided to override congressional objections to expenditure on the Central African mission because President Bill Clinton was in Africa at the time the decision was made. Even so, France and Kenya, which negotiated the creation of the force, only managed to achieve agreement on an initial three-month mandate instead of the longer one proposed by the Secretary-General.[78]

The UN Mission in the Central African Republic (Mission des Nations Unies en République centrafricaine, MINURCA) was established on 27 March to replace the Inter-African Mission to Monitor the Implementation of the Bangui Agreements (MISAB), in place since February 1997.[79] The Security Council determined that the situation in the country continued to constitute a

[77] UN Security Council, Provisional Verbatim Records, UN documents S/PV.3867, 27 Mar. 1998, and S/PV.3902, 13 July 1998.

[78] *Africa Research Bulletin*, vol. 35, no. 3 (1–31 Mar. 1998), p. 13049.

[79] For background on MISAB, see Findlay, T., 'Armed conflict prevention, management and resolution', *SIPRI Yearbook 1998: Armamaments, Disarmament and International Security* (Oxford University Press: Oxford, 1998), pp. 31–74.

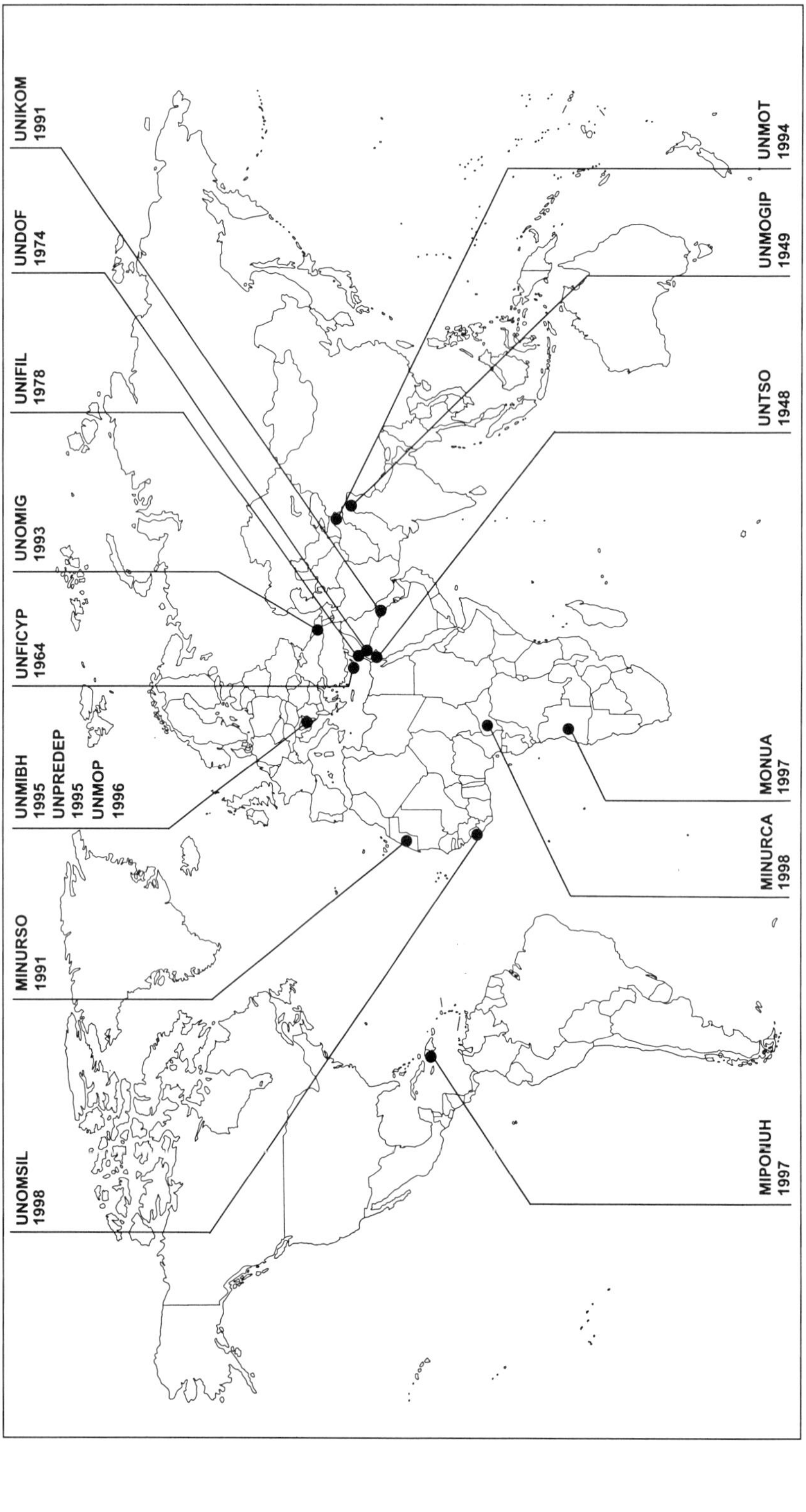

Figure 2.1. UN peacekeeping operations in the field, as of 31 December 1998

threat to international peace and security in the region but stopped short of giving MINURCA the explicit Chapter VII mandate for self-defence accorded to its predecessor. With up to 1350 military personnel, the mission was to maintain security in and around the capital Bangui, assist national security forces in maintaining law and order, monitor disarmament and control weapon storage, ensure security and freedom of movement of UN personnel, assist and advise on training and restructuring the national police, and support national electoral bodies in planning legislative elections initially scheduled for August/September.[80] Despite a tight schedule, the force was operational in mid-April thanks to an advance UN transition team which set up the new mission headquarters and the transfer by six countries of their contingents from MISAB to MINURCA.[81] By July over 1200 troops and 8 of the 24 authorized civilian police officers were deployed.[82] MINURCA's mandate was expanded in October to comprise provision of security for the monitoring of the postponed elections, the transport of electoral materials and equipment, and limited electoral observation.[83] Supplemented by 150 Central African troops, the contingents were deployed in five sites throughout the provinces where security remained precarious as the continued inflow of small arms from neighbouring conflict zones led to an upsurge in banditry.[84] The legislative elections, however, were completed without incident in December, encouraging the Secretary-General to propose an extension of MINURCA's mandate beyond February 1999 to cover scheduled presidential elections.[85]

On 13 July the Security Council authorized another new operation, the UN Observer Mission in Sierra Leone (UNOMSIL), having slowly expanded the UN's role after elected President Ahmad Tejan Kabbah had been reinstated by ECOMOG.[86] With an authorized strength of up to 70 military observers and a small medical unit, UNOMSIL was mandated to monitor the military and security situation, respect for international humanitarian law and the disarmament and demobilization of some 33 000 former combatants and members of the militia-based Civil Defence Forces (CDU).[87] Co-deployed with ECOMOG, the mission would also monitor ECOMOG's role in the provision of security and in the collection and destruction of arms in secure areas. By December five CivPol advisers were working closely with the Commonwealth Police Development Task Force for Sierra Leone to provide advice on the reform and restructuring of the police force and on police practice, training and recruit-

[80] UN Security Council Resolution 1159, 27 Mar. 1998 (adopted by 14–0–1 with China abstaining).

[81] *UN Chronicle*, vol. 35, no. 2 (1998), p. 59; and UN, Report of the Secretary-General on the United Nations Mission in the Central African Republic, UN document S/1998/540, 19 June 1998.

[82] UN, Second report of the Secretary-General on the United Nations Mission in the Central African Republic, UN document S/1998/783, 21 Aug. 1998.

[83] UN Security Council Resolution 1201, 15 Oct. 1998.

[84] UN, Third report of the Secretary-General on the United Nations Mission in the Central African Republic, UN document S/1998/1203, 18 Dec. 1998, para. 9; and Panafrican News Agency (PANA), 18 Nov. 1998, URL <http://www.africanews.org/PANA/news/>.

[85] UN document S/1998/1203 (note 84); and *Daily Highlights* (UN Department of Public Information), 22 Dec. 1998.

[86] UN Security Council Resolution 1181, 13 July 1998.

[87] UN, First progress report of the Secretary-General on the United Nations Observer Mission in Sierra Leone, UN document S/1998/750, 12 Aug. 1998, para. 28.

ment. The Human Rights Unit of the mission faced the thankless task of addressing human rights needs in the country and reporting on violations in inaccessible areas under rebel control.[88] Atrocities increased in the last quarter of the year on a par with the escalation of rebel offensives, which disrupted the demobilization of mutinous members of the former army who were reinducted into combat in five battalions to fight alongside ECOMOG.[89] To drum up support for ECOMOG and humanitarian assistance, the UN convened a special conference with ECOWAS and donor countries in July.[90] It also set up a joint task force with international and local actors for the demobilization of child combatants, over 4000 of whom had been forcibly recruited to fight on either side of the conflict, as part of a UN pilot project for post-conflict reconstruction.[91]

A decade of UN involvement in the Angolan conflict unravelled during 1998 as the UN Observer Mission in Angola (Missao de Observação das Nações Unidas em Angola, MONUA), mandated to observe the last transitional phase of the 1994 Lusaka Protocol, instead witnessed the descent of the country back into civil war. Although legalized as a political party following limited demobilization of its former combatants, the National Union for the Total Independence of Angola (União Nacional para a Independência Total de Angola, UNITA) refused to relinquish all areas under its control to state authority.[92] Before his death in an unexplained plane crash in the Côte d'Ivoire on 26 June, the Secretary-General's Special Representative Alioune Blondin Beye tried to reverse the decline in intensive consultations with President Jos Eduardo dos Santos and UNITA leader Jonas Savimbi. As the security situation deteriorated, intervention by UN Special Envoy Lakhdar Brahimi failed to reinvigorate the Joint Commission charged with overseeing the transition to peace. Efforts by new Special Representative Issa Diallo and the three observer countries to the peace process—Portugal, Russia and the USA—to revive negotiations between the parties proved equally futile.[93] UNITA's firm retaliations to a government offensive in December vindicated long-standing reports that it had managed to circumvent sanctions, purchase arms with proceeds from diamond sales and maintain a force of about 30 000–50 000 based in neighbouring countries.[94] As MONUA regrouped to safer

[88] UN, Second progress report of the Secretary-General on the United Nations Observer Mission in Sierra Leone, UN document S/1998/960, 16 Oct. 1998, para. 22.

[89] UN, Third progress report of the Secretary-General on the United Nations Observer Mission in Sierra Leone, UN document S/1998/1176, 16 Dec. 1998, para. 35.

[90] Hule, J., PANA, 'UN hosts conference on Sierra Leone', 29 July 1998.

[91] UN, Fifth report of the Secretary-General on the situation in Sierra Leone, UN document S/1998/486, 9 June 1998, para. 23; Eziakonwa, A., 'Aiding child victims in Sierra Leone', *Africa Recovery,* vol. 12, no. 1 (Aug. 1998), p. 27; and AFP (Paris), 3 Oct. 1998, in 'Sierra Leone: Sierra Leone–UNICEF head deplores child-drafting in war', FBIS-AFR-98-276, 6 Oct. 1998.

[92] UN, Report of the Secretary-General on the United Nations Observer Mission in Angola, UN document S/1998/333, 16 Apr. 1998.

[93] PANA, 'UN mediator confers with observer countries', 26 Nov. 1998.

[94] 'Renewed war in Angola: a threat of regional conflict', *Strategic Comments* (IISS), vol. 4, no. 7 (Aug. 1998); Säll, O., 'Flyktingkatastrof hotar Angola' [Refugee catastrophe threatens Angola], *Svenska Dagbladet,* 20 Dec. 1998; and Daley, S., 'Ink long dry on Angola pact, but peace hasn't set', *New York Times*, 24 May 1998.

areas and UN aircraft came under attack, the Secretary-General concluded that the conditions for a meaningful UN peacekeeping role had ceased to exist.[95]

Despite initial momentum in the identification of voters for a scheduled December referendum on independence, the UN Mission for the Referendum in Western Sahara (MINURSO) found itself bogged down in an old quagmire. While the vast majority of applicants from non-contested tribal groups had been identified by September and demining completed of areas needed for future expanded deployment of the mission, the parties remained deadlocked over the last intractable issue, the treatment of some 65 000 contested applications.[96] A flurry of diplomatic effort by the Secretary-General's Special Representative and Special Envoy preceded the intervention by Kofi Annan himself with an arbitration package proposing the identification of individual contested applications simultaneously with an appeals process, effective refugee repatriation and a revised transitional schedule leading up to a referendum at the end of 1999.[97] At the end of the year the future viability of the mission remained in question as Morocco still weighed the UN proposals which had been approved by Algeria, Mauritania and the Popular Front for the Liberation of Saguía el-Hamra and Rio de Oro (Frente Popular para la Liberacíon de Saguía el-Hamra y del Río de Oro—known as the Polisario Front).[98]

The UN Peacekeeping Force in Cyprus (UNFICYP) continued to keep the peace amid multifarious diplomatic efforts to revive a stalemated political dialogue. The UN's hands were tied in facilitating a solution alone; there were no fewer than 11 special envoys to the negotiations in March from interested states and international organizations.[99] With tensions exacerbated by the European Union (EU)–Cyprus accession talks, and continued military upgrading by both sides, efforts to bring the parties to direct negotiations, implement UNFICYP confidence-building measures or reinvigorate bi-communal activities all remained at a standstill.[100] Meanwhile, UNFICYP was restructured with responsibility for inter-communal liaison, and economic and humanitarian tasks consolidated in a new Civil Affairs Branch.[101] In September the Secretary-General announced a new initiative of confidential 'shuttle talks' with the leaders of both communities within the framework of his Mission of Good Offices, privately characterized as aiming to stave off the proposed

[95] UN, Report of the Secretary-General on the United Nations Observer Mission in Angola, UN document S/1999/49, 17 Jan. 1999, para. 39.

[96] UN, Report of the Secretary-General on the situation concerning Western Sahara, UN document S/1998/997, 26 Oct. 1998.

[97] UN Press Release SG/SM/6789, 10 Nov. 1998; and UN, Report of the Secretary-General on the situation concerning Western Sahara, UN document S/1998/1160, 11 Dec. 1998.

[98] UN Security Council Resolution 1215, 17 Dec. 1998; and PANA, 'Ben Ali, Kofi Annan hold talks', 3 Dec. 1998.

[99] United Nations Association of the United States of America, *A Global Agenda: Issues Before the 53rd General Assembly of the United Nations* (Rowman & Littlefield: Lanham, Md., 1998), p. 33.

[100] UN, Report of the Secretary-General on the United Nations operation in Cyprus, UN document S/1998/488, 10 June 1998; and 'Instability in the Eastern Mediterranean: a Cypriot crisis in the making', *Jane's Intelligence Review*, Special Report no. 17, 1998.

[101] UN, Report of the Secretary-General on the United Nations operation in Cyprus, UN document S/1998/1149, 7 Dec. 1998.

deployment, opposed by Turkey, of a Russian S-300 anti-aircraft missile system on the island.[102] After a US diplomatic campaign in December, the Cypriot Government agreed to store the missiles on the Greek island of Crete, thus giving new impetus to the pursuit of a political settlement.[103]

The effectiveness of two small UN observer missions co-deployed with Commonwealth of Independent States (CIS) peacekeeping forces in the Caucasus and Central Asia was called into question as security threats hampered their operations and challenged their very viability. The UN Mission of Observers in Tajikistan (UNMOT) continued to assist in the sluggish implementation of a transitional peace process, bedevilled with difficulties in reintegrating opposition fighters into the armed forces and legalizing opposition parties. The security situation remained volatile, with incidents of hostage-taking and harassment of international personnel. After consent was withheld by the opposition for a proposed CIS escort and by the government for a UN infantry battalion, a joint force of the parties was slowly being trained to provide protection for UNMOT, delaying its planned expansion towards an authorized strength of 120.[104] The size of the mission was abruptly reduced from 83 to 33 and all field activities were suspended following the brutal murders of three observers and a Tajik interpreter on 20 July.[105] The functions of the UN Observer Mission in Georgia (UNOMIG) were also severely curtailed by a freeze on all operational patrolling after four observers were temporarily taken hostage in February.[106] Limited patrolling resumed in May, but intermittent attacks, ambushes and highjackings directed at both UNOMIG and CIS forces continued to jeopardize their operations. After the proposed deployment of a 294-strong self-protection unit was vetoed by the Abkhazians, the UN decided to recruit more international security personnel as a partial solution to sustaining the mission.[107]

The UN presence in the republics of the former Yugoslavia was reduced in 1998 as one mission out of four, the UN Transitional Administration for Eastern Slavonia, Baranja and Western Sirmium (UNTAES), was terminated on 15 January with the handover of the Croatian Serb-occupied area to Croatian government control. To consolidate the fragile reintegration of the region achieved under robust administrative powers conferred on and utilized by UNTAES, a 180-strong support group of CivPols remained to monitor the

[102] UN, Letter dated 14 Dec. 1998 from the Secretary-General addressed to the President of the Security Council, UN document S/1998/1166, 14 Dec. 1998; and Khatzikiriakos, A., 'Hercus: secrecy is her recipe', *O Fileleftheros* (Nicosia), 15 Oct. 1998, in 'Cyprus: Limited success prospect seen in UN procedure on Cyprus', FBIS-WEU-98-288, 16 Oct. 1998.

[103] Fitchett, J., 'Deployment of missiles is scrapped by Cyprus', *International Herald Tribune*, 30 Dec. 1998.

[104] UN, Interim report of the Secretary-General on the situation in Tajikistan, UN document S/1998/754, 13 Aug. 1998, paras 18–23.

[105] UN, Report of the Secretary-General on the situation in Tajikistan, UN document S/1998/1029, 3 Nov. 1998, para. 38.

[106] UN, Report of the Secretary-General concerning the situation in Abkhazia, Georgia, UN document S/1998/375, 11 May 1998.

[107] UN, Report of the Secretary-General concerning the situation in Abkhazia, Georgia, UN document S/1998/1012, 29 Oct. 1998; and UN, Security Council Presidential Statement, UN document S/PRST/1998/34, 25 Nov. 1998.

Croatian police in the Danube region, particularly with regard to the return of refugees, for a single nine-month period.[108] Bilateral talks opened between Croatia and the FRY on the disputed ownership of the Prevlaka peninsula, where the UN Mission of Observers in Prevlaka (UNMOP) witnessed continued violations of the demilitarized zone and unauthorized civilian attempts to make commercial use of parts of the UN-controlled zone.[109] The deteriorating situation in Kosovo had a direct impact on the UN Preventive Deployment Force (UNPREDEP) deployed across the border in the FYROM. Due to be withdrawn in August, the mission was instead extended until 28 February 1999, its strength was returned to 1050, and new observation posts were established along the Kosovo and Albanian borders.[110] The largest of the four Yugoslav missions, the UN Mission in Bosnia and Herzegovina (UNMIBH) comprising civilians and the International Police Task Force (IPTF), was entrusted with the new task of running a court monitoring programme as part of a larger project of legal reform.[111] The strength of the IPTF was brought up to 2057 to carry out intensive training programmes for the local police in specialized fields, such as the management of critical incidents and the fight against corruption, organized crime and drugs.[112] On the canton level, new police assessment teams evaluated compliance with integration of minority officers into the multi-ethnic police forces.[113]

According to an independent evaluation, the UN Civilian Police Mission in Haiti (Mission de police civile des Nations Unies en Haïti, MIPONUH) had proved effective in training the Haitian National Police, but the international investment would fail unless it was sustained.[114] Despite progress made in professionalizing the force, which according to an opinion poll had gained the confidence of 70 per cent of the population, the institution remained fragile with absenteeism, crime, corruption and drug trafficking rife among its ranks.[115] Faced with prolonged political paralysis and economic stagnation, Haitian President René Préval requested an extension of the MIPONUH mandate, overriding the preference of lawmakers for local instructors.[116] In November the Security Council authorized a one-year non-renewable extension at the mission's current strength of 300 CivPols and foresaw a transition

[108] UN, Final report of the Secretary-General on the United Nations Police Support Group, UN document S/1998/1004, 27 Oct. 1998.

[109] UN, Report of the Secretary-General on the United Nations Mission of Observers in Prevlaka, UN document S/1998/939, 12 Oct. 1998; and *UN Chronicle*, vol. 35, no. 3 (1998), p. 47.

[110] UN Security Council Resolution 1186, 21 July 1998; and UN, Report of the Secretary-General on the United Nations Preventive Deployment Force, UN document S/1998/644, 14 July 1998.

[111] UN Security Council Resolution 1184, 16 July 1998.

[112] UN Security Council Resolution 1168, 21 May 1998.

[113] UN, Report of the Secretary-General on the United Nations Mission in Bosnia and Herzegovina, UN document S/1998/491, 10 June 1998, paras 3–8.

[114] UN, Report of the Secretary-General on the United Nations Civilian Police Mission in Haiti, UN document S/1998/796, 24 Aug. 1998.

[115] UN, Report of the Secretary-General on the United Nations Civilian Police Mission in Haiti, UN document S/1998/1064, 11 Nov. 1998.

[116] 'UN police extend mission to Haiti', *International Herald Tribune*, 27 Nov. 1998; and Radio Metropole Network (Port-au-Prince), 28 Oct. 1998, in 'Haiti: Parliament debates MIPONUH mandate renewal', Foreign Broadcast Information Service, *Daily Report–Latin America (FBIS-LAT)*, FBIS-LAT-98-301, 30 Oct. 1998.

to other forms of international assistance thereafter.[117] Already part of a multi-agency peace-building effort, the mission's links with one of its main partners was reinforced with the Secretary-General's novel decision to appoint the United Nations Development Programme (UNDP) Resident Representative as deputy head of mission.[118]

Continuing peacekeeping reforms

A debate erupted in 1998 on the short- and long-term implications of the changing nature of peacekeeping for those charged with its management. The UN Department of Peacekeeping Operations (DPKO) was most affected by the 1997 decision of the General Assembly to phase out gratis personnel throughout the Secretariat by the end of February 1999.[119] In a comprehensive review of its total human resource requirements, called for by the General Assembly, the DPKO concluded that its existing structure was generally sound but needed minor modifications—the Situation Centre would be transferred to the Office of Operations and the 'lessons learned' function consolidated with the Policy and Analysis Unit. However, given the loss of these seconded officers, the 279 authorized staff posts were deemed inadequate for the anticipated workload, which included the management of larger volumes of activity and credible contingency planning.[120] Divided as to the long-term repercussions of the recent decline in peacekeeping, the Special Committee on Peacekeeping Operations called for a more fundamental review to determine appropriate structures for periods of both low and high intensity in UN peacekeeping.[121] The UN's powerful Advisory Committee on Administrative and Budgetary Questions (ACABQ) also took a sceptical stance towards the DPKO submissions and approved only 43 of 106 positions, requested in replacement of 134 gratis personnel.[122]

There was more agreement on the need to support the potential 'growth industry' within peacekeeping, the civilian police. With capabilities for mobilizing, training, equipping and sustaining police field operations outstripped by recent requirements, an academic study found the DPKO staffing levels

[117] UN Security Council Resolution 1212, 25 Nov. 1998 (adopted by 13–0–2 with Russia and China abstaining). Both favoured other forms of training and economic assistance. UN Security Council Provisional Meeting Record, UN document S/PV.3949, 25 Nov. 1998.

[118] UN, Situation of human rights in Haiti, UN document A/53/355, 10 Sep. 1998.

[119] UN, Report of the Secretary-General, Gratis personnel provided by governments and other entities, UN document A/C.5/52/54/Rev.1, 10 July 1998.

[120] UN, Report of the Secretary-General, Administrative and budgetary aspects of the financing of the United Nations peacekeeping operations: financing of the United Nations peacekeeping operations, UN document A/52/837, 20 Mar. 1998.

[121] UN, Comprehensive review of the whole question of peacekeeping operations in all their aspects. Report of the Special Committee on Peacekeeping Operations, UN document A/53/127, 21 May 1998, para. 66.

[122] The ACABQ recommended another 18 posts for redeployment from within the Secretariat. UN, Support account for peacekeeping operations. Report of the Advisory Committee on Administrative and Budgetary Questions, UN document A/53/418, 22 Sep. 1998, paras 7 and 67.

'woefully insufficient' to manage the 3000 CivPol personnel in the field.[123] The size of the Civilian Police Unit has remained constant as the five seconded officials within it were replaced.[124] Meanwhile, analytical work continued on developing the manifold roles of civilian police as the public security arm of multi-dimensional peace missions, an exit strategy for the military and a key component of post-conflict peace building. A detailed concept of operations for civilian police components was under preparation while the recruitment procedures for international CivPols had been improved with routine selection and training assistance. The Training Unit of the DPKO compiled additional training support material, including selection and training standards for CivPols.[125] In view of the expanding volume of police functions in peacekeeping operations, the Special Committee called for further improvements in the differentiation of police and military tasks, the integration of CivPol elements in the planning phase of new operations, a modification of the peacekeepers' code of conduct for CivPols and a broader geographical base for selecting police commissioners.[126]

The DPKO assumed the role of coordinator for several new tasks. The Training Unit established a focal point for African peacekeeping training and started building an information database on national activities to strengthen African capacity for peacekeeping. The department was also promoting the development of a common policy on mine action after the UN Mine Action Service within the DPKO had become the focal point for the coordination of demining in the UN system.[127] It will be supported by a new International Center for Humanitarian Demining in the collection, collation and distribution of available information. Authorized by the Swiss Federal Council, the Center in Geneva was due to become fully operational by the year 2001.[128]

The UN continued to battle the increasing violence directed against its peacekeeping and other field personnel. By mid-year, the civilian death toll had exceeded that of the military for the first time in UN history.[129] The Secretary-General was particularly perturbed that no one had ever been charged with or tried for causing the death of a UN staffer. Hampered by a shortage of funds, UN recruitment of security professionals had been limited to fewer than 100 to support deployment of more than 30 000 field staff. Instead, the UN attempted to raise security awareness through training while insisting that violence against its staff should be considered a war crime under

[123] Oakley, R. *et al.* (eds), *Policing the New World Disorder: Peace Operations and Public Security* (National Defence University Press: Washington, DC, 1998), p. 516.

[124] UN document A/53/418 (note 122), paras 18 and 38.

[125] UN, Report of the Secretary-General on the implementation of the recommendations of the Special Committee on Peacekeeping Operations, UN document A/AC.121/42, 27 Mar. 1998, para. 40.

[126] UN document A/53/127 (note 121), paras 93–98.

[127] UN document A/AC.121/42 (note 125), para. 30.

[128] Khansari, H., 'New humanitarian center in Geneva to collate world data on landmines', *UN Observer and International Report,* vol. 20, no. 1 (Jan. 1998), pp. 4 and 13.

[129] Crossette, B., 'Toll of UN's civilian workers overtakes the military deaths', *New York Times,* 28 July 1998. Since July 1997, 23 staff members have died in deliberate attacks, 31 in plane crashes, and 33 have been taken hostage and 60 local UN personnel have been reported detained or missing. Guest, I., 'Who will stand up for menaced UN workers?', *International Herald Tribune*, 27 Nov. 1998.

the Statute of the new ICC.[130] In September Japan announced a donation of $1 million in memory of an UNMOT observer who had been killed, to support measures for protecting UN personnel.[131] By the end of the year one such measure, the Convention on the Safety of UN and Associated Personnel, had finally been ratified by the requisite 22 countries to enter into force on 15 January 1999 but did not yet bind any African states, for example.[132] As governmental authority is patently lacking in many conflict zones, its effect on reducing violence against non-combatants remains doubtful.

In a bid to improve the standard of conduct of UN personnel, the Secretary-General set minimum age requirements for peacekeepers. Governments contributing personnel to UN operations were asked not to send civilian police or military observers younger than 25 years, while troops in national contingents should preferably be at least 21 years old and not younger than 18.[133] A pro-active measure taken to promote the rights of the child, the age limit was also viewed as a better guarantee that UN missions would be staffed with 'experienced, mature and well trained' people.[134] Guidelines for adherence to international humanitarian law by all personnel associated with UN peace-keeping operations were under preparation, while standard directives were approved for Special Representatives of the Secretary-General in charge of multidimensional peacekeeping operations to provide a common framework for implementing mission mandates.[135] A proposal that all new UN programmes and mandates be subjected to time limits was hotly debated in the General Assembly, partly for fear that it could lead to future scrutiny of long-standing peacekeeping commitments.[136]

Lack of funding was holding up the establishment of a Rapidly Deployable Mission Headquarters (RDMHQ), intended to accelerate deployment of future peace operations. Voluntary contributions totalling $475 100 had been pledged or received from six countries, falling far short of the $3.2 million estimated as necessary for the first two years of its operation.[137] Forming the core of a three-tiered structure, eight officers had been identified to serve full-time on the RDMHQ. An additional 29 were to be earmarked from Secretariat personnel and 24 from national establishments to serve in their regular positions until deployment. Giving outright approval to only one-fourth of the Secretary-

[130] Deen, T., 'Death toll of UN civilians exceeds military figures', *Jane's Defence Weekly*, vol. 30, no. 6 (12 Aug. 1998), p. 6; and Crossette (note 129).

[131] Kyodo (Tokyo), 21 Sep. 1998, in 'Japan: Obuchi announces "Akino Fund" for UN peacekeepers', Foreign Broadcast Information Service, *Daily Report–East Asia (FBIS-EAS)*, FBIS-EAS-98-264, 25 Sep. 1998.

[132] Information from the Swedish Foreign Ministry, 26 Jan. 1999.

[133] UN, Secretary-General decides to set minimum age requirements for UN peacekeepers, SG/SM/6777, PKO/79 (UN Information Centre for the Nordic Countries: Copenhagen, 29 Oct. 98).

[134] Crossette, B., 'UN imposes minimum age for its soldiers', *International Herald Tribune*, 2 Nov. 1998.

[135] UN document A/53/127 (note 121), para. 80; and UN document A/53/676 (note 20), p. 2.

[136] *Washington Weekly Report*, vol. 24, nos 24 and 25 (18 and 25 Sep. 1998), URL <http://www.unausa.org/publications>. Pakistan rejected the application of 'sunset provisions' to the continuance of UNTSO and UNMOGIP. 'Time limits may force early end to peacekeeping', *Jane's Defence Weekly*, vol. 29, no. 19 (13 May 1998), p. 3.

[137] UN document A/52/837 (note 120), paras 9–12.

General's funding request for the core group, the ACABQ criticized what it viewed as a fragmented approach to planning functions within the DPKO, calling for their streamlining and consolidation.[138]

The UN Stand-by Arrangements System (UNSAS), which permits states to make conditional offers of contributions to future peacekeeping missions, attracted a substantial number of additional pledges. As of 1 January 1999, 82 countries, including 10 additional African states, had volunteered a total of 104 300 personnel, but only 33 countries had provided more detailed information on their contributions. Eight more countries—Finland, Germany, Ireland, Kyrgyzstan, Lithuania, the Netherlands, Nigeria and Romania—joined the 13 which had signed a Memorandum of Understanding with the UN confirming their participation in the system.[139] Member states continued to offer more operational than support units, resulting in a particular dearth of key specialized resources such as airlift and sea-lift services, logistical support, communications, civilian police, medical staff and engineers.[140] Despite its limitations, DPKO staff had found the UNSAS database helpful in the deployment of the two new African missions and planning for operations in Angola, Congo (Brazzaville), the FYROM, Georgia, Guatemala, Haiti, Eastern Slavonia and Western Sahara.[141]

Recommendations by the Office of Internal Oversight Services (OIOS) and the Board of Auditors were implemented to standardize rules and procedures governing support for field operations. Following an OIOS audit of all peacekeeping operations, the lessons learned from the liquidation and closure of missions in Haiti, Liberia and the former Yugoslavia were institutionalized.[142] A new field assets control system, being tested in UNOMIG, UNTSO, UNFICYP and the UN Logistics Base in Brindisi, improved inventory control, enabling management at headquarters and the field to have a nearly real-time, global view of peacekeeping assets.[143] It was used in support of a new peacekeeping operation for the first time when start-up kit equipment and other assets were deployed with MINURCA.[144] While the reorganized UN Procurement Division had improved its performance with staff training and finalized new procurement guidelines, the OIOS still recommended strengthening fast-track procurement procedures and greater delegation of financial authority.[145] As of March 1998 the supplier roster had been expanded to include vendors from a total of 102 countries, but in practice the USA remained over-

[138] UN document A/53/418 (note 122), paras 10–17. UN, Report of the Fifth Committee. Administrative and budgetary aspects of the financing of the United Nations peacekeeping operations: financing of the United Nations peacekeeping operations, UN document A/53/522, 19 Oct. 1998, p. 3.

[139] UN, Monthly Status Report, UN Standby Arrangements, 1 Jan. 1999.

[140] UN document A/53/127 (note 121), para. 99.

[141] Mentzen, R. T. (Cdr), UN Department of Peacekeeping Operations, Annual update briefing to member states on Standby Arrangements, 4 Nov. 1998, at URL <http://www.un.org/Depts/dpko/rapid>.

[142] UN document A/53/1 (note 2), para. 218.

[143] UN, Report of the Secretary-General, Implementation of the recommendations of the Board of Auditors concerning United Nations peacekeeping operations for the period ended 30 June 1997, UN document A/52/879, 30 Apr. 1998.

[144] UN document A/53/127 (note 121), para. 75.

[145] UN, Report of the Secretary-General on the activities of the Office of Internal Oversight Services, UN document A/53/428, 23 Sep. 1998.

represented, with 61 per cent of all contracts in 1997.[146] Irked by the US non-payment of its arrears, other member states passed a resolution in the General Assembly to study the restriction of UN procurement to countries not in debt to the organization as well as increased transparency and contract opportunities for developing countries.[147]

Peacekeeping finance

Although the UN's financial outlook had stabilized with the adoption of two successive zero-growth biennial budgets, its cash position was getting weaker with the persistent decline in peacekeeping assessments. Following the liquidation of large and complex missions, the peacekeeping cash balance at the end of the year had decreased steadily for four years from $923 million in 1995 to a projected $761 million in 1998. Since cross-borrowing from peacekeeping accounts continued to cover structural year-end shortfalls in the regular budget, the UN's overall cash balance fell accordingly, from $728 million in 1995 to a projected $577 million in 1998. The General Assembly has failed to establish a revolving credit fund to relieve such cash flow pressures through temporary advances against unpaid assessed contributions.[148] The proposal was treated with scepticism by the two biggest contributors and in any case viewed as an insufficient measure to deal with the problem.[149] While a growing number of member states were paying more or all of their assessments, fewer of them did so on time in 1998.[150]

A UN International Partnership Trust Fund was established to manage the allocation to UN projects of media mogul Ted Turner's 10 annual donations of $100 million each. As of mid-September, a total of 39 projects in the amount of some $55 million had been approved for funding in the areas of population, environment and health, traditionally paid for by voluntary contributions.[151] Thus the availability of this new and additional financial resource failed to alleviate the overall UN financial situation or its cash flow problems.

The USA remained the largest peacekeeping debtor, owing the UN $975 million out of a total of $1.6 billion at the end of 1998, followed by Ukraine, Russia and Japan.[152] The UN owed the largest reimbursements during

[146] UN document A/AC.121/42 (note 125), para. 15; and US General Accounting Office (GAO), Briefing report to congressional requesters. United Nations. Financial issues and US arrears, GAO/NSIAD-98-201BR, June 1998, p. 41.

[147] *UN Chronicle*, no. 2 (1998), p. 17.

[148] UN General Assembly Resolution 53/205, 18 Dec. 1998; and UN Press Release GA/AB/3270, 23 Nov. 1998.

[149] *Washington Weekly Report*, vol. 24, no. 16 (12 June 1998), URL <http://www.unausa.org/publications>.

[150] UN document A/53/1 (note 2), para. 201; and GAO/NSIAD-98-201BR (note 146), pp. 14–19.

[151] UN, Report of the Secretary-General, United Nations Fund for International Partnerships, UN document A/53/700, 24 Nov. 1998.

[152] UN, Status of outstanding contributions to the regular budget, international tribunals and peacekeeping operations as at 31 December 1998 (United Nations Information Centre for the Nordic Countries: Copenhagen, Jan. 1999).

the year for equipment and services to France and the USA, and for troops to Bangladesh, Finland and Pakistan. Among the top debtors, Russia had paid some $300 million of its past unpaid assessments over a three-year period, whereas financial hardship had prevented payments from Belarus, Brazil and Ukraine. Only the USA did not pay its arrears for policy reasons.[153]

In October the US Congress approved the administration's request for nearly full funding for regular dues ($325 million) and peacekeeping expenses ($231 million) for fiscal year 1999. The release of a further $475 million in arrears was made contingent on authorization and fulfilment of numerous conditions and therefore did not take place.[154] A three-year plan for payment of over $800 million in arrears had been included in a State Department authorization bill passed in April, but, based on the conditions agreed in 1997 by senators Jesse Helms and Joseph R. Biden, Jr, it contained a ban on the use of funds to lobby foreign governments to change their abortion laws and was vetoed by President Clinton in October. By continuing not to pay its arrears, the USA was in danger of losing its voting privilege in the General Assembly in 1999 but squeaked by with a payment of $357 million to the UN in November.[155] For the first time, the USA failed to make its full contribution to the international ad hoc tribunals under an earlier congressional directive not to pay the share of those assessments charged at the higher peacekeeping 'premium'.[156]

The problem was set to recur, however, as Congress seemed locked in a persistent game of 'Catch-22', having lost the opportunity to bring about some of the very changes it had demanded as a precondition for release of the arrears funding. The USA missed its chance to renegotiate the level of its contributions to the regular budget from 25 to 22 per cent when the special, one-time offer by other member states to reconsider the scale of assessments, already fixed for 1998–2000, expired in the absence of arrears payments.[157] The USA also failed to regain a seat on the ACABQ, as demanded by lawmakers, for the same reason.[158] Meanwhile the State Department admitted that the outstanding arrears issue had led to a 'loss of influence and prestige of the United States within all the bodies of the United Nations'.[159]

[153] GAO/NSIAD-98-201BR (note 146), pp. 23–35.

[154] 'Congress adjourns with no resolution of arrears to UN and international organizations', *Washington Weekly Report,* vol. 24, no. 28 (22 Oct. 1998); and 'FY 1999 spending for international organizations near request—no settlement of UN arrears', *Washington Weekly Report,* vol. 24, no. 29 (1 Nov. 1998), both at URL <http://www.unausa.org/publications>.

[155] Under Article 19 of the UN Charter, a member state which is in arrears exceeding its assessments for the previous 2 years loses its right to vote in the General Assembly. US arrears were projected to exceed its biennial assessments of $1.28 billion by the end of 1998.

[156] Laurenti, J., 'Losing America's vote at the United Nations', 29 June 1998, at URL <http://www.unausa.org/issues/losevote.htm>.

[157] 'Administration requests just over $1 billion for arrears to international organizations; political obstacles remain', *Washington Weekly Report,* vol. 24, no. 2 (10 Feb. 1998), URL <http://www.unausa.org/publications>.

[158] 'US not elected again to key UN budget committee', *Washington Weekly Report,* vol. 24, no. 29 (16 Nov. 1998), URL <http://www.unausa.org/publications>.

[159] GAO/NSIAD-98-201BR (note 146), p. 60.

National and cooperative efforts to improve capability

National and cooperative efforts outside the UN framework also promised increased effectiveness of personnel and interoperability of units to be used in UN peace operations. For instance, the joint peacekeeping task force operating under the auspices of the NATO–Russia Permanent Joint Council (PJC) decided to shift its discussions from doctrine to operational cooperation.

Joint peacekeeping units were established at an accelerating pace at the subregional and regional levels. Hungary and Romania agreed to set up a joint peacekeeping battalion, as did Bulgaria and Greece.[160] The Multinational Land Force, a joint 4500-strong Italian–Slovene–Hungarian brigade, was established with a focus on operations in mountainous terrain.[161] Austria, Hungary, Romania, Slovakia and Slovenia signed a letter of intent to set up a joint force in two years within the framework of the Central European Nations Cooperation in Peacekeeping (CENCOOP).[162] Complex US-sponsored negotiations culminated in an agreement in September to establish a Multilateral Peacekeeping Force for Southeastern Europe (MPFSEE) at brigade level by Albania, Bulgaria, Greece, Italy, the FYROM, Romania and Turkey.[163] A new proposal for a multinational force in the Black Sea region was made by Greece and Romania in December.[164]

Older peacekeeping partnerships took more steps towards operability during the year. Denmark, Finland, Norway and Sweden had assembled nearly a complete brigade under the Nordic Coordinated Arrangement for Military Peace Support (Nordcaps) and pursued joint training.[165] Plans for the Baltic Battalion, composed of Estonian, Latvian and Lithuanian units, to go on independent peacekeeping duty in Bosnia and Herzegovina were cancelled following concerns about its readiness, but its platoons continued to serve with Nordic units in SFOR.[166] Polish–Ukrainian and Polish–Lithuanian battalions continued training with a view to becoming operational in early 1999.[167]

[160] Kossuth Radio (Budapest), 20 Mar. 1998, in 'Hungary: Hungary, Romania sign accord on joint peacekeeping force', Foreign Broadcast Information Service, *Daily Report–East Europe (FBIS-EEU)*, FBIS-EEU-98-079, 23 Mar. 1998; and Sharabov, G., 'Strobe Talbott travels along the Balkan paths of the CIA', *Trud* (Sofia), 20 Mar. 1998, in 'Bulgaria: Talbott visit, rapid reaction force initiative viewed', FBIS-EEU-98-079, 23 Mar. 1998.

[161] Kante, L. *et al.*, 'Blunders and misunderstandings', *Delo* (Ljubljana), 2 June 1998, in 'Slovenia: Article presents trilateral peacekeeping corps', FBIS-EEU-98-153, 4 June 1998.

[162] TASR (Bratislava), 19 Mar. 1998, in 'Slovakia: Central European defense ministers sign cooperation pact', FBIS-EEU-98-078, 20 Mar. 1998.

[163] It is also known as the Multinational Peace Force Southeastern Europe. AFP (Paris), 26 Sep. 1998, in 'FYROM: Four Balkan states agree to form peacekeeping force', FBIS-EEU-98-269, 29 Sep. 1998.

[164] 'The Romanian and Greek defense ministries initiated a new regional project "Peacekeeping Force in the Black Sea Region"', Azi (Bucharest), 23 Dec. 1998, in 'Romania: Greek, Romanian ministers propose Black Sea peacekeepers', FBIS-EEU-98-357, 28 Dec. 1998.

[165] Vainio, R., 'Nordic countries augment their rapid response force', *Helsingin Sanomat* (Helsinki), 10 Dec. 1998, in 'Finland: Joint Nordic rapid response force changes', FBIS-WEU-98-344, 14 Dec. 1998.

[166] Rich, V., 'Delays as BALTBAT proves ineffective', *Jane's Intelligence Review,* Mar. 1998, p. 2; and 'Swedish accord grants guns, training aid to Baltic states', *Jane's Defence Weekly,* vol. 30, no. 21 (25 Nov. 1998), p. 6.

[167] Lentowicz, Z., 'Army: the shadow of Kosovo; soldiers on call', *Rzeczpospolita* (Warsaw), 14 Oct. 1998, in 'Poland: Polish readiness for peacekeeping missions viewed', FBIS-EEU-98-287, 16 Oct. 1998.

Argentina decided to contribute 300 troops to the Multinational United Nations Stand-by Forces High Readiness Brigade (SHIRBRIG), while Romania and Spain joined its steering committee and Portugal signed a letter of intent to join.[168] The modest expansion of its membership was insufficient, however, to quell other member states' criticism of the elitist nature of the venture.

Major Western powers continued to evaluate their role in and responsibility for past peacekeeping failures. Italy disciplined 12 military officers for failing to protect Somalis from abusive Italian UN troops in 1992–94.[169] A parliamentary report critical of Belgian action at the time of the 1994 genocide in Rwanda led to disciplinary action against three officers, although a later confidential report by the Belgian armed forces exonerated all senior officers of the general staff.[170] The first French parliamentary inquiry to venture into the presidential domain of foreign policy asserted that France would not have been able to prevent the Rwandan genocide, but it remained inconclusive about the alleged delivery of French arms to the government after April 1994 in violation of the international embargo.[171] In the Netherlands, the defence minister launched two new investigations into accusations that Netherlands troops guarding the UN 'safe area' of Srebrenica had actively participated in the Serb programme of ethnic cleansing and subsequently destroyed the evidence.[172]

New countries and coalitions with an interest in peacekeeping continued to appear. Viet Nam initiated a study for the first time to consider participation in UN peacekeeping.[173] The Dominican Republic and Haiti affirmed their determination to contribute, while Georgia announced plans for a peacekeeping battalion.[174] The CPLP agreed to develop joint training with a view to creating a Lusophone peace force.[175]

Joint multinational training was becoming routine. Large-scale peacekeeping exercises were held under NATO's Partnership for Peace (PFP) programme in Albania, the FYROM, Hungary, Romania, Ukraine and the Baltic Sea, with Russia participating for the first time in 'Cooperative Jaguar-98', held in Denmark in May (see table 2.2). The Central Asian Battalion exercised

[168] Its other members are Austria, Canada, Denmark, the Netherlands, Norway, Poland and Sweden. Telam (Buenos Aires), 12 Feb. 1998, in 'Argentina: Dominguez, Haekkerup on creation of multinational force', FBIS-LAT-98-043, 15 Feb. 1998.

[169] *Horn of Africa Bulletin,* vol. 10, no. 3 (May/June 1998), p. 22.

[170] Vidal, K., 'This is an insult to Parliament', *De Morgen* (Brussels), 9 Dec. 1998, in 'Belgium: Parliament reacts angrily to army's Rwanda report', FBIS-WEU-98-343, 11 Dec. 1998.

[171] 'Les leçons d'un rapport' [Lessons of a report], *Le Monde*, 17 Dec. 1998, p. 15; and Braeckman, C., 'The report which washes whiter', *Le Soir* (Brussels), 16 Dec. 1998, in 'Belgium: Arms deliveries not mentioned in French Rwanda report', FBIS-WEU-98-350, 17 Dec. 1998.

[172] AFP (Paris), 29 Aug. 1998, in 'Netherlands: General: Minister had "damning" evidence on Srebrenica', FBIS-WEU-98-241, 1 Sep. 1998.

[173] 'Vietnam considers peacekeeping', *Jane's Defence Weekly*, vol. 30, no. 4 (29 July 1998), p. 17.

[174] Radio Nationale (Port-au-Prince), 23 June 1998, in 'Preval, Fernandez sign cooperation accord', FBIS-LAT-98-174, 25 June 1998; and Interfax (Moscow), 13 May 1998, in 'Russia: NATO Central Asian exercise planning meeting taking place', *Daily Report–Central Eurasia (FBIS-SOV),* FBIS-SOV-98-133, 14 May 1998.

[175] Mascarenhas, E., 'Foundation for Lusophone force', *Diario de Noticias* (Lisbon), 22 July 1998, in 'Portugal: Lusophone countries to extend military cooperation', FBIS-WEU-98-203, 23 July 1998.

Table 2.2. Peacekeeping exercises held under PFP auspices in 1998

Exercise	Host nation/ location (date)	Type of exercise	Participation
'Cooperative Jaguar-98'	Denmark (May)	Joint air, sea and land exercise	> 3000 servicemen from 17 NATO and PFP countries
'Cooperative Lantern-98'	Hungary (May)	Command and communications	750 officers from 19 countries
'Cooperative Partner-98'	Romanian coast (June)	Naval peacekeeping	Military units from 11 countries
'Cooperative Assembly-98'	Albania (Aug.)	Joint air, sea and land exercise	1700 servicemen from 11 NATO countries, Albania, Lithuania, Russia
'Cooperative Best Effort-98'	FYROM (Sep.)	Multinational coordination	> 1500 troops from 26 NATO and PFP countries
'Peace Shield-98'	Ukraine (Sep.)	Computer-based HQ exercise	400 servicemen from > 20 countries
'Sea Breeze-98'	Black Sea (Oct.)	Maritime relief operations	Military units from 11 countries
'Baltic Challenge-98'	Lithuanian coast (July)	Joint air, sea and land exercise	4600 servicemen from the USA and 11 European countries
Central Asian Battalion (Centrasbat)	Kyrgyzstan and Uzbekistan (Sep.)	Joint regional exercise	> 1440 servicemen from Azerbaijan, Georgia, Kazakhstan, Kyrgyzstan, Russia, Turkey, USA, Uzbekistan
'Nordic Peace'	Sweden (Sep./Oct.)	Joint air, sea and land exercise	2000 servicemen and civilians from the Baltic states, Finland, Denmark, Norway, Sweden

together for the second time in September while the second 'Nordic Peace' PFP exercise involved civilian organizations as a new feature.[176] French, Italian, Portuguese and Spanish troops exercised together under 'EOLE 98' in June to assess the capability of the Euroforces in discharging a humanitarian peacekeeping mandate.[177] The US and select South American armies sought to improve regional peacekeeping cooperation in exercises hosted by Guatemala in May and Paraguay in July.[178] Argentina and the UK sponsored a peacekeeping training seminar for military and police officers and policy makers from 25 Latin American countries in March.[179] Numerous countries also paired up for joint training, and peacekeeping was included in training provided by the

[176] Radio Tallinn (Tallinn), 21 Sep. 1998, in 'Estonian troops leave for peacekeeping exercises in Sweden', FBIS-SOV-98-264, 25 Sep. 1998; and ELTA (Vilnius), 28 Sep. 1998, in 'Lithuanian military join international maneuvers in Sweden', *Daily Report–Central Eurasia: Military Affairs (FBIS-UMA)*, FBIS-UMA-98-271, 29 Sep. 1998.

[177] AFP (Paris), 2 June 1998, in 'France: Four-nation military exercise begins', FBIS-WEU-98-153, 3 June 1998.

[178] ABC Color (Asuncion), 17 July 1998, in 'Paraguay: Country hosts international peacekeeping exercises', FBIS-LAT-98-198, 20 July 1998.

[179] Telam (Buenos Aires), 17 Mar. 1998, in 'Argentina: UK sponsor UN peacekeeping seminar', FBIS-LAT-98-076, 19 Mar. 1998.

major Western powers through bilateral arrangements in their outreach programmes.[180]

France, the UK and the USA pursued their nominally coordinated training initiatives designed to strengthen African capabilities to undertake peacekeeping tasks on the continent. Seven countries had signed on to the US-sponsored African Crisis Response Initiative (ACRI); of the regional powers, South Africa was supportive without participating, while Nigeria continued to reject Western proposals of assistance.[181] Exercise 'Guidimakha 98', involving 3700 troops from eight West African countries, was staged in March with logistics and command support from France, the UK and the USA to test the French concept known as Reinforcement of African Peacekeeping Capacities (RECAMP).[182] France financed the 'Compienga 98' exercises held in Togo in April, which aimed to familiarize the nine participating countries with techniques of peace restoration.[183] In East Africa, 2000 military personnel from Kenya, Tanzania and Uganda included US participants in a peacekeeping and humanitarian exercise in June.[184]

IV. UN peace-enforcement measures

Sanctions

A plethora of sanctions regimes remained in place in 1998 against Iraq, Libya, Liberia, Somalia, Sudan and non-governmental forces in Rwanda.[185] The existing oil and arms embargo on UNITA in Angola was supplemented with a call on states to freeze UNITA's assets abroad, suspend official contacts with its leadership, and prohibit the unauthorized import of diamonds from Angola and sale of mining equipment to areas outside state control.[186] The oil embargo on Sierra Leone was terminated and the arms embargo restricted to non-governmental forces with the exception of the UN and ECOMOG.[187] Travel restrictions remained in force against leading members of the former military junta and their associates. Sanctions were imposed on the FRY in response to the repression in Kosovo, prohibiting the sale of arms and related *matériel* of all types as well as arming and training for terrorist activities.[188] Following

[180] E.g., joint peacekeeping training was conducted between the US forces and the Russian Army. Sasaki, Y., 'The day when the Sea of Okhotsk will turn into a "sea of peace"', AERA (Tokyo), 27 Jan. 1998, in 'Japan: Tokyo–Moscow military situation viewed', FBIS-EAS-98-027, 29 Jan. 1998.

[181] *The Star* (Johannesburg), 28 Apr. 1998, in 'South Africa: Country not ready to join US-driven African peace force', FBIS-AFR-98-118, 30 Apr. 1998; and Radio France Internationale (Paris), 1 Mar. 1998, in 'Nigeria: Nigeria "rejects" Western aid proposal for African Force', FBIS-AFR-98-060, 5 Mar. 1998. For background on ACRI see Findlay (note 79).

[182] Blanche, E., 'Tug-of-war over West African peacekeeping', *Jane's Defence Weekly*, vol. 29, no. 12 (25 Mar. 1998), p. 16.

[183] Radio France Internationale (Paris), 10 July 1998, in 'Chad: African military chiefs of staff take stock', FBIS-AFR-98-191, 13 July 1998.

[184] Western European Union Assembly, Peacekeeping and Security in Africa: Colloquy (Lisbon, 15 Sep. 1998), p. 36.

[185] See also chapters 11 and 15 in this volume.

[186] UN Security Council Resolutions 1173 and 1176, 12 and 24 June 1998.

[187] UN Security Council Resolutions 1156 and 1171, 16 Mar. 1998 and 5 June 1998.

[188] UN Security Council Resolution 1160, 31 Mar. 1998 (adopted by 14–0–1 with China abstaining).

Libya's agreement, in principle, to allow the two suspects in the 1988 Lockerbie bombing to stand trial before a Scottish court sitting in the Netherlands, the Security Council announced its intention to suspend sanctions immediately after they had been handed over while the OAU decided to disregard the UN sanctions regime altogether.[189]

While the seven-year sanctions regime against Iraq was retained,[190] the oil-for-food programme, which allows Iraq to sell oil under UN supervision to buy food and other humanitarian goods for its population, was expanded in February. The new plan, renewed for six months in November, increased the authorized Iraqi oil sales from $2000 million to $5256 million.[191] An allowance of $300 million was made for material needed to rebuild the oil industry, whose dilapidated state was now a hindrance to increasing oil revenue beyond $3000 million.[192] Disappointed with the enlarged programme as still grossly insufficient to meet the needs of the Iraqis, the UN Humanitarian Coordinator for Iraq, Denis Halliday, resigned in September, criticizing the entire sanctions regime as a blunt instrument contrary to basic human rights provisions.[193]

Meanwhile a policy debate continued at the UN on improved targeting of economic sanctions. An ad hoc group of experts proposed a set of guidelines for assessing the impact of sanctions and providing international assistance to affected third states.[194] The Sixth Committee of the General Assembly advocated greater access to the sanctions committees by third states and the non-permanent members of the Security Council called for similar access to the council prior to its imposing a sanctions regime.[195] In the opinion of the Secretary-General, however, the trend towards 'smarter' sanctions could not obscure the fact that sanctions were a tool of enforcement, the goals of which could not easily be reconciled with humanitarian and human rights policy.[196]

Military enforcement

In 1998 four UN or UN-authorized missions—the Iraq–Kuwait Observation Mission (UNIKOM) on the Iraq–Kuwait border, SFOR in Bosnia and Herzegovina, UNTAES in Eastern Slavonia and MISAB in the Central African Republic—were mandated to use force under Chapter VII, the enforcement chapter of the UN Charter. UNTAES and MISAB were terminated and

[189] UN Security Council Resolution 1192, 27 Aug. 1998; and *Africa Research Bulletin*, vol. 35, no. 6 (1–30 June 1998), p. 13134.

[190] For details on the sanctions against Iraq in 1998, see chapters 13 and 15 in this volume.

[191] UN Security Council Resolution 1153, 20 Feb. 1998.

[192] UN Security Council Resolution 1210, 24 Nov. 1998; and USIS, 'UN Security Council renews Iraqi oil-for-food program', *Washington File* (US Embassy: Stockholm, 24 Nov. 1998).

[193] Aaron, C., 'UN official resigns over Iraqi sanctions', *In These Times*, 15 Nov. 1998, p. 4; and Friends Committee on National Legislation (FCNL), *Washington Newsletter*, no. 627 (Dec. 1998), p. 3.

[194] UN, Report of the Secretary-General, Implementation of provisions of the Charter related to assistance to third states affected by the application of sanctions, UN document A/53/312, 27 Aug. 1998.

[195] UN, Press Release GA/L/3102, 19 Nov. 1998.

[196] UN document A/53/1 (note 2), paras 62–64.

UNIKOM fulfilled its mandate in 1998 without incident.[197] SFOR, with a 12-month extension of its mandate in June, became more active in the arrest of war criminals and occasionally used harsh measures in their apprehension as well as in providing security in the Republika Srpska. Its new Multinational Specialized Unit was also forceful in exercising crowd control.

The Security Council also acted under Chapter VII in endorsing the establishment of the OSCE Kosovo Verification Mission (KVM) and NATO Air Verification Mission over Kosovo under the terms agreed between the respective organizations and the FRY. However, it failed to provide direct authorization for enforcement action by them or the NATO Extraction Force (XFOR). At best, it affirmed that 'action may be needed' to ensure the safety and freedom of movement of the KVM.[198]

Controversial military action was taken by the UK and the USA in December in response to the Iraqi refusal to fully comply with its obligations under Security Council resolutions. In the air strikes launched under operation 'Desert Fox', the two permanent members sought to degrade the Iraqi programme of weapons of mass destruction and to reduce its ability to threaten its neighbours.[199] Justifying their action on the basis of previous resolutions, they argued that the council's earlier determination that Iraqi non-compliance constituted a violation of ceasefire Resolution 687 (1991) ending the Persian Gulf War had implicitly revived the authorization to use force under Security Council Resolution 678 (1990), passed after the invasion of Kuwait.[200] This interpretation was contested by many council members and totally rejected by China and Russia, which considered the action a gross violation of the UN Charter and international law. In contrast to the USA, which claimed to uphold the authority of the council by enforcing compliance with its dictates, the Russian representative rejected the right of any one nation 'to act independently on behalf of the United Nations, still less assume the functions of a world policeman'.[201]

V. Regional and other multilateral organizations

Efforts by regional organizations to prevent, manage and resolve conflicts in 1998 were accelerated with the support and blessing of the UN in most cases; some began to stretch the limits of Chapter VIII of the UN Charter.[202] Institutional initiatives proliferated particularly within the organized European struc-

[197] As of 23 Sep., there had been 1 serious incident involving the highjacking at gunpoint of a UNIKOM patrol vehicle. UN, Reports of the Secretary-General on the United Nations Iraq–Kuwait Observation Mission, UN documents S/1998/269 and S/1998/889, 25 Mar. 1998 and 24 Sep. 1998.

[198] UN Security Council Resolution 1203, 24 Oct. 1998, para. 9 (adopted by 13–0–2 with China and Russia abstaining.).

[199] USIS, *Washington File* (US Embassy: Stockholm, 20 Dec. 1998).

[200] UN, Letter dated 16 Dec. 1998 from the Chargé d'Affaires A.I. of the United States Mission to the United Nations addressed to the President of the Security Council, UN document S/1998/1181, 16 Dec. 1998.

[201] UN Security Council Verbatim Records, S/PV.3955, 16 Dec. 1998.

[202] Chapter VIII of the UN Charter regulates the relationship between the UN and regional arrangements and asserts the primacy of the Security Council in decisions on enforcement action.

tures, but there were also a number of missions from regional and subregional organizations in Africa. Asian and Latin American organizations maintained their primary focus on conflict prevention and peace building.

Europe and the CIS

The flare-up in 1998 of the hostility and repression which had smouldered in the Yugoslav province of Kosovo, the cradle and symbol of the Balkan crises of the 1990s, presented the European security organizations with perhaps their greatest challenge yet. Although kept in reserve by security planners, a worst-case scenario for the break-up of Yugoslavia had long included a crisis such as the one which erupted in February with a Serb crackdown on the ethnic Albanian guerrilla organization, the Kosovo Liberation Army (KLA). With its potential to destabilize neighbouring Albania, Bosnia and Herzegovina, and the FYROM, draw in Greece and Turkey, and evolve into a confrontation engulfing south-eastern Europe, the crisis held the attention of the continent and created complex dilemmas with repercussions beyond the region.

NATO leaders, haunted by the Balkan humiliations of 1991–94, were more determined to halt the violence in Kosovo, protect the progress in Bosnia and Herzegovina, and defend the credibility of their organization. Having ruled out partition as an outcome in Bosnia and Herzegovina the Western powers could hardly accept a precedent-setting Kosovan secession, but their preferred solution, greater autonomy within the federation, was unacceptable both to the Kosovar Albanians and to the Serbs, now polarized in their positions. While the international community was broadly united behind the pursuit of negotiated autonomy, if not the means for achieving it, the apparent concessions made by the parties during the year failed to resolve the underlying issue or stop the fighting.[203] Yet military measures to deter, contain or compel fell under the domain of enforcement action for which the UN under its Charter retained prime responsibility as the FRY was a sovereign state conducting repression within its own borders. Consistent Chinese and Russian opposition to the use of force precluded authorization by the Security Council for the military pressure Western powers came to favour as an adjunct to diplomacy, prompting NATO to take a historic decision to go it alone.

Following the initial outbreak of conflict, the main regional organizations—*NATO*, the *EU*, the *OSCE* and the *Western European Union* (WEU)—took measures, albeit small ones and slowly, to contain the fighting to Kosovo. Differences of strategy regarding the conflict itself were thrashed out within the six-nation Contact Group, which had emerged in 1997 as the prime coordinating and mediating body.[204] Its efforts were supported by the EU and the OSCE whose own joint representative, former Spanish Prime Minister Felipe Gonzalez, was rebuffed by the FRY for its suspension from the OSCE. Concern for regional destabilization led the OSCE to enhance the capabilities of its

[203] For an account of the conflict in Kosovo and the conduct of diplomatic negotiations see appendix 1C in this volume.

[204] The Contact Group comprises France, Germany, Italy, Russia, the UK and the USA.

Presence in Albania and its Spillover Monitor Mission in Skopje. With a widened mandate, the former set up eight temporary field offices in March to allow for adequate observation of the border with Kosovo, ineffectively patrolled by only 200 guards. Working closely with the ECMM, it also facilitated the work of humanitarian organizations in the area. Temporary border monitors were added to the Skopje mission in June.[205] NATO, similarly, initially focused on preventing spillover by strengthening neighbouring countries within the PFP framework. After holding its first-ever PFP '16+1' emergency consultations on 11 March 1998, NATO agreed to assist Albania to cope with the effects of the crisis—especially in managing refugee inflows, improving border security, and securing munitions and weapons dumps—and decided to open an office in Tirana to coordinate its activities.[206] The WEU extended and expanded the mandate of its Multinational Advisory Police Element (MAPE) in Albania to include advice, training and equipment to improve the Albanian police's capacity to monitor and control the border area.[207] A PFP package drawn up for the FYROM comprised mainly training assistance and equipment. Both countries hosted PFP exercises in August and September.

Despite the strategic importance of the region and firm US rhetoric from as far back as 1992, NATO military planning for a 'Kosovo contingency' seems to have been sketchy at best. Taken by surprise by the third Balkan war of the decade, NATO leaders prevaricated on their desired course of action should diplomacy fail. Confident in their newly established machinery for conflict management, WEU officials indicated that the organization could do more than advise police in Albania; but a major role for the WEU, sidelined in the Albanian crisis in 1997, was again ruled out when Germany and the UK among others preferred to see NATO and the USA in the lead.[208] The countries of the region also turned to NATO, requesting preventive troop deployments or, in the case of the FYROM, involvement in UNPREDEP. Within NATO, the idea of a preventive force in Kosovo had been raised sporadically but with no follow-up.[209] An Albanian request for NATO peacekeepers, supported by Italy, was turned down.[210] It was not until mid-May 1998, on the eve of a Serb offensive timed to coincide with the positive publicity generated by President Slobodan Milosevic's meeting with Kosovar Albanian leader Ibrahim Rugova, that the North Atlantic Council (NAC) instructed the Political Coordination Group to study the possibility of setting up a 'security belt' around the borders of Kosovo. Meeting in Luxembourg on 28 May, NATO foreign ministers formally commissioned military advice on preventive deployments in Albania

[205] OSCE Secretary-General, *Annual Report 1998 on OSCE Activities (1 December 1997–30 November 1998)*, OSCE document SEC.DOC/2/98 (OSCE: Vienna, 2 Dec. 1998), pp. 7 and 25.

[206] Buchan, D., 'Albania to get NATO advisers', *Financial Times*, 28–29 Mar. 1998; Rogers, M., 'Kosovo puts PfP to the NATO test', *Jane's Defence Weekly*, vol. 29, no. 12 (25 Mar. 1998); and *Atlantic News*, vol. 32, no. 2998 (25 Mar. 1998) and no. 3008 (8 May 1998).

[207] The mandate was extended until Apr. 1999. *Atlantic News*, vol. 32, no. 3009 (13 May 1998).

[208] Rogers, M., 'Kosovo dilemma: Europe still seeks a plan', *Jane's Defence Weekly*, vol. 29, no. 21 (27 May 1998), p. 5; and Rogers, M., 'Identity crisis', *Jane's Defence Weekly*, vol. 29, no. 22 (3 June 1998), pp. 46–55.

[209] *Atlantic News*, vol. 32, no. 2993 (4 Mar. 1998).

[210] *Atlantic News*, vol. 32, no. 3008 (8 May 1998).

and the FYROM.[211] Subsequent assessment teams sent to the rugged 'Damned Mountains' in northern Albania, a lawless region under the virtual control of forces supporting the KLA, reported that the logistically complicated mission requiring 7000–23 000 troops would be nearly impossible to carry out.[212] The plan was criticized because it would put the KLA at a disadvantage if its mule traffic of weapons were to be cut off, not to mention that by June any deterrent effect was lost.[213]

As the Serbs intensified their anti-insurgency campaign, a debate within the Contact Group, NATO and the UN got under way in June on the possibility and desirability of using military options to intervene directly in Kosovo. British Prime Minister Tony Blair opined that 'we must be prepared to use force decisively' at an early stage, and in the USA a meeting between State Department and Pentagon officials on 8 June produced agreement to present air strikes as a real option.[214] Even the UN Secretary-General favoured diplomacy backed up by firmness and force 'when necessary', seemingly prodding the Security Council to take charge.[215] In the US view, existing UN resolutions on the FRY provided sufficient authority for any military measures, but France, Germany and Russia among others insisted on a new decision authorizing the use of force in Kosovo before any NATO action was possible.[216] A draft of such a resolution, circulated by the UK in the Security Council in June, failed to gain support.[217]

NATO defence ministers nevertheless directed the military authorities to draw up a 'full range of options' and to accelerate the planning already under way.[218] Priority was to be given to options which were 'effective and readily available'—such as air strikes, which General Klaus Naumann, head of NATO's Military Committee, had come to believe could achieve an end to the fighting, as in Bosnia and Herzegovina.[219] Critics pointed out that in 1995 air strikes had been accompanied by a Croat–Muslim ground offensive. The possible deployment of ground forces was now among the options to be studied,

[211] NATO, Statement on Kosovo issued at the Ministerial Meeting of the North Atlantic Council held in Luxembourg on 28 May 1998, Press Release M-NAC-1(98)61, 28 May 1998.

[212] 'Another Balkan crisis', *Strategic Comments* (IISS), vol. 4, no. 5 (June 1998); Drozdiak, W., 'NATO plans air activity as warning to Milosevic', *International Herald Tribune*, 12 June 1998; and Rogers, M., 'NATO moves may support possible Kosovo ceasefire', *Jane's Defence Weekly*, vol. 30, no. 5 (5 Aug. 1998), p. 3.

[213] Husarka, A., 'It's too late for a "preventive deployment" in Kosovo', *International Herald Tribune*, 13–14 June 1998.

[214] 'The descent into another Balkan war', *The Economist*, vol. 347, no. 8072 (13 June 1998).

[215] Spolar, C., 'NATO planes warn Serbs to halt Kosovo assault', *International Herald Tribune*, 16 June 1998; and Annan, K., 'Kosovo hold key to peace and war in and beyond Balkans, *UN Observer and International Report*, vol. 20, no. 7 (July 1998), p. 5.

[216] '8 big powers back NATO in warning to Milosevic', *International Herald Tribune*, 13–14 June 1998; and 'Bonn wants mandate', *International Herald Tribune*, 11 June 1998.

[217] Whitney, C., 'Milosevic under more pressure on Kosovo', *International Herald Tribune*, 11 June 1998; and Youngs, T., 'Kosovo: The diplomatic and military options', House of Commons Research Paper 98/93 (27 Oct. 1998), p. 11.

[218] Planning had started for possible support for UN and OSCE monitoring activity and for preventive deployments in Albania and the FYROM. NATO, Statement on Kosovo issued at the Meeting of the North Atlantic Council in Defence Ministers Session, Press Release M-NAC-D-1(98)77, 11 June 1998.

[219] Drozdiak, W., 'NATO plans air activity as warning to Milosevic', *International Herald Tribune*, 12 June 1998.

as was the imposition of a no-fly zone over Kosovo, both requested by Rugova.[220] An air exercise, 'Determined Falcon', was undertaken in mid-June to demonstrate NATO's capability to project power rapidly into the region,[221] but the deployment of troops would have required some lead time. As the preliminary 'study of options' became 'contingency planning' by the end of June, NATO sources indicated that only 1000 troops could be sent within days of a possible political decision; 80 days would be needed to deploy 20 000 troops in or around Kosovo.[222] Despite continuing political reluctance to contemplate using them, NATO planning still included measures requiring the presence of ground troops, either to implement a negotiated solution or even to impose peace.[223] The former was estimated to require up to 50 000 troops.[224]

While NATO continued to refine its options over the summer as the fortunes of battle turned first for and then against the KLA, international mediators and military planners had the benefit of real-time information gathered by the KDOM, inaugerated on 6 July by Russia and the USA. One of many Contact Group demands, its establishment had been furthered in mid-June by a meeting in Moscow between Russian President Boris Yeltsin and President Milosevic, who promised foreign diplomats full freedom of movement in Kosovo.[225] Under the political guidance of a diplomatic coordination group, the KDOM, composed of personnel from numerous embassies in Belgrade, was to observe and report on NGO and foreign government access throughout Kosovo, security conditions and activities in Kosovo, and the situation of internally displaced persons and refugees.[226] Initially comprising fewer than 50 observers, it expanded to over 400 by December.[227]

There was no consensus or real momentum to activate military threat as a tool of coercive diplomacy until the successful Serbian summer offensives had displaced 70 000 ethnic Albanians outside and almost 200 000 inside Kosovo, including 50 000 outdoors, raising the spectre of a humanitarian catastrophe with the early onset of winter.[228] Several factors contributed to its emergence as a serious policy option by September: NATO had completed its contingency planning, the Bosnian elections were completed successfully and internal unrest broke out in Albania.[229] Meanwhile President Milosevic had played

[220] *Atlantic News*, vol. 32, no. 3018 (12 June 1998).

[221] *Atlantic News*, vol. 32, no. 3020 (16 June 1998).

[222] *Atlantic News*, vol. 32, no. 3023 (26 June 1998).

[223] *Atlantic News*, vol. 32, no. 3027 (10 July 1998).

[224] NATO itself released no official figures. 'NATO officer predicts 50 000 needed in Kosovo', *Defense News*, vol. 13, no. 37 (14–20 Sep. 1998).

[225] Interfax (Moscow), 16 June 1998, in 'Russia: Primakov reads joint statement by Yeltsin, Milosevic', FBIS-SOV-98-167, 17 June 1998.

[226] The coordination group consisted of the ambassadors of the Contact Group countries in Belgrade as well as the ambassadors of Austria and Poland, representing the EU and the OSCE. 'Kosovo Diplomatic Observer Mission', Fact sheet released by the Bureau of European and Canadian Affairs, US Department of State, 8 July 1998.

[227] US Department of State, Bureau of European and Canadian Affairs, *Kosovo Progress Report*, Washington, DC, 8 Dec. 1998.

[228] UN, Report of the Secretary-General prepared pursuant to Resolution 1160 (1998) of the Security Council, UN document S/1998/834, 4 Sep. 1998.

[229] NATO plans covered 3 categories of options: preventive deployment in Albania; airborne operations ranging from limited actions to substantial campaigns; and deployment of ground troops backed by

a skilful game of qualified concessions but never complying with the demand to cease hostilities and ethnic cleansing, repeated on 23 September by the UN Security Council, which viewed the deterioration of the situation as a threat to peace and security in the region.[230] Informal consultations having been conducted in August, NATO decided to step up the pressure by publicizing its 'Activation Warning', asking allies to volunteer assets for a potential military strike.[231] The Yugoslav Government's announcement on 28 September of an end to its military campaign, with concurrent news of brutal slaughter in the Drenica region, failed to convince the UN Secretary-General, whose opinion on compliance was awaited by NATO. He concurred with the Contact Group that time for preventing humanitarian disaster was running out, but a Security Council meeting on 6 October reached no agreement on further action against Belgrade.[232] As US Special Envoy Richard Holbrooke embarked on a Contact Group mission to obtain Yugoslav compliance with the earlier UN demands, NATO was building the required consensus for air strikes.[233] Able to reassure the allies on 12 October of the outlines of an agreement, Holbrooke argued for the maintenance of continued pressure to ensure compliance with outstanding requirements.[234] A few hours later, in the knowledge that a diplomatic solution was imminent, the NAC decided unanimously to issue Activation Orders for both limited air operations and a phased air campaign in the FRY.[235] Initially deferred for four days, their execution was postponed for another 10 days to allow for continued negotiations and signs of compliance before the threat was suspended on 27 October; it remained in effect.

The agreement between Holbrooke and Milosevic broke new ground in providing for a joint NATO–OSCE monitoring regime: unimpeded NATO air surveillance was coupled with the deployment in Kosovo of up to 2000 unarmed OSCE 'verifiers' to ensure compliance with UN Resolution 1199. The arrangement was confirmed in two separate verification agreements, concluded between the respective organizations and the FRY, and endorsed by the UN.[236] Politically, the deal was fragile—the FRY agreed, in principle, to pull

air support in Kosovo to implement a ceasefire or peace agreement. *Atlantic News*, vol. 32, no. 3038 (11 Sep. 1998).

[230] UN Security Council Resolution 1199, 23 Sep. 1998 (adopted by 14–0–1 with China abstaining).

[231] NATO, 'Statement by the Secretary General following the ACTWARN decision', Press Statement, Vilamoura, 24 Sep. 1998, at URL <http://www.nato.int./docu/pr/1998/p980924e.htm>; and 'Analysts: NATO threat to Serbia is bluff', *Defense News*, vol. 13, no. 39 (28 Sep.–4 Oct. 1998), p. 2.

[232] UN, Report of the Secretary-General prepared pursuant to resolutions 1160 (1998) and 1199 (1998) of the Security Council, UN document S/1998/912, 3 Oct. 1998; *Survey of Current Affairs* (Foreign and Commonwealth Office, London), vol. 28, no. 10 (Oct. 1998), p. 356; and Youngs (note 217), p. 13.

[233] In Holbrooke's opinion, President Clinton 'brought [the incoming German Chancellor Gerhard] Schröder around and the Germans delivered NATO'. Hirsh, M., 'Holbrooke's game of chicken', *Newsweek*, vol. 132, no. 17 (26 Oct. 1998), p. 17.

[234] *Atlantic News*, vol. 32, no. 3049 (14 Oct. 1998).

[235] NATO, Secretary-General's Press Conference, 13 Oct. 1998, information by e-mail from <natodoc @hq.int>. Italy and Germany were the last 2 countries to approve the use of force on 12 Oct. Youngs (note 217), p. 14.

[236] The agreement between NATO and the FRY was signed on 15 Oct. and between the OSCE and the FRY on 16 Oct. UN, Letter dated 22 Oct. 1998 from the Chargé d'Affaires A.I. of the Mission of the United States of America to the United Nations addressed to the President of the Security Council, UN

back its troops and special police, allow refugees to return, hold local elections and establish an Albanian-dominated police force—as the ultimate status of the province remained to be determined in later negotiations.[237] Vigorous mediation efforts by US Ambassador Christopher Hill in the last months of 1998 failed to bring the parties closer to an interim solution.

The KVM was charged with monitoring compliance on the ground—verifying the maintenance of the ceasefire, investigating violations and reporting on hindrances to the return of refugees. It was 10 times bigger than any other OSCE mission, and this was the first time the OSCE had undertaken such tasks, ordinarily discharged by military observers. It did so because the deployment of NATO forces had been resisted by Milosevic.[238] Established for one year by the OSCE Permanent Council, the mission was also to stay informed on movements of forces, to accompany police units, and ultimately to assist with the supervision of elections due in nine months and with police force development in Kosovo.[239] The existing KDOM, pulled out during the threat of air strikes, was to be absorbed by the KVM, once operational. The former head of UNTAES, Ambassador William Walker of the USA, was appointed to head the KVM, while two-thirds of the mission staff were to be recruited from EU countries.[240] Following delays caused by administrative and logistical difficulties, some 500 international verifiers were deployed in December with a projected increase to 1500 by mid-January 1999.[241] Their work was complemented from the air by some 20 unarmed NATO surveillance aircraft based in the FYROM. Their flights over Kosovo and a surrounding 40-km mutual security zone started after an activation order was issued in early November.[242] Russia was expected to join 'Operation Eagle Eye' and cooperate with NATO for the first time in the sensitive area of intelligence.[243]

While the FRY had assumed responsibility for the day-to-day security of the unarmed verifiers under the OSCE–FRY agreement, NATO wanted a rapid reaction force available to ensure their safety in case the Belgrade agreements were not met.[244] Canada, whose suggestion that the OSCE verifiers be provided with armed bodyguards was ruled out by Walker, demanded a new UN resolution to authorize NATO protection for the KVM but was opposed by

document S/1998/991, 23 Oct. 1998; UN, Letter dated 19 Oct. 1998 from the Permanent Representative of Poland to the United Nations addressed to the Secretary-General, UN document S/1998/978, 20 Oct. 1998; and UN Security Council Resolution 1203, 24 Oct. 1998.

[237] For further details on the agreement, see appendix 1C in this volume.

[238] The anticipated battle with the US Congress over using NATO troops had apparently also been a factor favouring the OSCE. Hirsh (note 233), p. 18.

[239] UN document S/1998/978 (note 236); and OSCE document SEC.DOC/2/98 (note 205), p. 27.

[240] OSCE Press Release, no. 64/98, 17 Oct. 1998.

[241] UN, Report of Report of the Secretary-General prepared pursuant to resolutions 1160 (1998), 1199 (1998) and 1203 (1998) of the Security Council, UN document S/1998/1147, 4 Dec. 1998; and Van Velthem, E., 'Kosovo: OSCE wants to step up its presence', *Le Soir* (Brussels), 4 Dec. 1998, in 'Norway: Derycke confirms Belgian role in OSCE Kosovo mission', FBIS-WEU-98-338, 7 Dec. 1998.

[242] Rogers, M., 'Contingency plan set for evacuating Kosovo monitors', *Jane's Defence Weekly*, vol. 30, no. 19 (11 Nov. 1998).

[243] AFP (Paris), 22 Oct. 1998, in 'Kosovo: NATO approves plan for air surveillance of Kosovo', FBIS-EEU-98-295, 23 Oct. 1998.

[244] Bender, B. and Clayton, A., 'Surveillance vital to Kosovo deal', *Jane's Defence Weekly*, vol. 30, no. 16 (21 Oct. 1998), p. 3.

Russia.[245] The Security Council did recognize that, in the event of an emergency, 'action might be needed' to ensure their safety.[246] According to a concept of operations approved by NATO in early November, XFOR would only be used 'in extremis' at the request of the OSCE for individual extractions, emergency evacuation, hostage rescue or full-scale extraction of the KVM. Following host country approval and activation orders from NATO, the 1500-strong French-led force began to deploy in the FYROM in early December.[247] The USA provided satellite transmission cover and potential reinforcements in an emergency with US forces 'on the horizon' if not on the ground.[248] Planning coordination and liaison between the NATO and OSCE missions was provided by a Kosovo Verification Coordination Centre (KVCC), inaugurated near Skopje on 26 November by NATO.[249] However, Milosevic warned that, were they to cross over into Kosovo, NATO troops would be treated as aggressors.[250] The position of the verifiers was indeed precarious since the ceasefire was violated by both the Serbs and the reinvigorated KLA before the end of the year. Even as the ceasefire was restored with KVM mediation, warnings were issued by the OSCE of the possible need to reconsider its mission if violence worsened and by NATO of its continued readiness to use force.[251]

The international community remained committed to the re-establishment of a stable multi-ethnic society in neighbouring Bosnia and Herzegovina, where the largest international peace operation, the NATO-led Stabilization Force, hunkered down to face the sobering reality that peace and reconciliation cannot be achieved within set time limits. Its extension past June 1998, when the original 18-month mandate expired, became possible with President Clinton's announcement of a continued commitment despite cuts in US troop levels. NATO, and ultimately the US Congress, accepted the argument that SFOR's presence was a necessary albeit insufficient condition for nation building—a multi-agency effort to be driven by an end-state, not an end-date. NATO decided to review the situation semi-annually with a view to achieving both 'progressive reductions in the size, role and profile of the force' and the transfer of responsibilities to other institutions.[252] The USA had identified

[245] AFP (Paris), 22 Oct. 1998, in 'Kosovo: Western leaders disagree on security for verifier mission', FBIS-EEU-98-295, 23 Oct. 1998; and Whitney, C., 'NATO generals to confront Milosevic', *International Herald Tribune*, 24–25 Sep. 1998.

[246] UN Security Council Resolution 1203, 24 Oct. 1998.

[247] NAC statement 8 Dec. 1998; Statement to the press by the Secretary-General, 8 Dec. 1998. France also provided up to half of the troops. Whitney, C., 'France offers to lead Kosovo force', *International Herald Tribune*, 6 Nov. 1998; and *Kosovo Progress Report* (note 227).

[248] Fredet, J.-G., 'Kosovo, Europe's strategic test lab', *Le Nouvel Observateur* (Paris), 12 Nov. 1998, in 'France: Kosovo force seen sowing EU defense identity seed', FBIS-WEU-98-316, 16 Nov. 1998; and Seigle, G., 'NATO's Kosovo rescue force set for deployment', *Jane's Defence Weekly*, vol. 30, no. 22 (2 Dec. 1998), p. 4.

[249] 'KVCC—up and running', Allied Forces Southern Europe (AFSOUTH) Press Release no. 98–49, 1 Dec. 1998, URL <http://www.afsouth.nato.int/LATEST/1998releases.htm#98-49>.

[250] 'Yugoslav leader defies NATO', *International Herald Tribune*, 14 Dec. 1998.

[251] 'Calm prevails in Kosovo', *International Herald Tribune*, 30 Dec. 1998.

[252] *Atlantic News*, vol. 32, no. 2990 (21 Feb. 1998). NATO foreign ministers approved the new Operation Plan 'Joint Forge' in May. NATO, Statement on Bosnia and Herzegovina issued at the Ministerial Meeting of the North Atlantic Council, Luxembourg, 28 May 1998. The UN Security Council

'benchmarks' for assessing progress towards enduring peace, and NATO attempted to develop criteria to link them with force restructuring and reduction.[253] The largest of four follow-on options presented by NATO's Military Committee,[254] the new SFOR operated at its existing strength until it was temporarily augmented from 31 700 in August to 36 100 during the general elections in September.[255] US contingents, reduced to 6900 by mid-July, peaked at 10 500–11 300 in mid-September and dropped back to 6900 by November.[256]

The major novelty and one of the most contentious issues of the extended SFOR was the establishment of a 600- to 800-strong Multinational Specialized Unit (MSU) to address the infamous 'security gap' between the civilian and military aspects of the implementation of the Dayton Agreement. Operating under SFOR rules of engagement, its main tasks were the maintenance of public order, especially crowd control, and policing functions which fell outside the mandates of the SFOR military contingents or the unarmed UN IPTF and the capability of the local police.[257] Although the USA initially proposed the MSU to ensure that European countries took a leading role in assuring the transition to a peacetime environment upon SFOR's withdrawal, the Supreme Allied Commander Europe (SACEUR) confirmed by June that the MSU would eventually leave Bosnia before or at the same time as SFOR combat units.[258] With officers from Argentina and Italy, the first MSU battalion became operational in August with a second battalion due to be deployed during the spring of 1999.[259]

Although most of the military tasks assigned to the NATO-led force under the Dayton Agreement had long since been completed, the maintenance of a secure environment remained at the heart of the SFOR mission. In 1998 SFOR assisted the factions in mine-clearance *inter alia* by initiating 'mine lifting' operations that were focused on refugee return areas for which mine records were available. More responsibility for the process was assumed locally as the UN Mine Action Centre became the Bosnia-Herzegovina Mine Action

authorized the extension of SFOR's mandate and enforcement powers for 12 months. UN Security Council Resolution 1174, 15 June 1998.

[253] US General Accounting Office (GAO), Report to the Chairman, Committee on Foreign Relations, US Senate: Bosnia Peace Operation. Mission, Structure, and Transition Strategy of NATO's Stabilization Force, GAO/NSIAD-99-19 (Oct. 1998), pp. 45–47; and *Atlantic News*, vol. 32, no. 3007 (6 May 1998).

[254] Option A proposed the total withdrawal of SFOR; B a limited deterrence force mainly deployed outside Bosnia; C a mobile and geographically concentrated enhanced deterrence force of 20 000–25 000; and D maintaining a force equivalent to SFOR. *Atlantic News*, vol. 32, no. 2989 (18 Feb. 1998).

[255] The new SFOR was reduced from 27 to 26 battalions; 17 were provided by NATO members and 9 by non-member countries. *Atlantic News*, vol. 32, no. 3005 (25 Apr. 1998).

[256] GAO/NSIAD-99-19 (note 253), pp. 3 and 14.

[257] Rogers, M., 'NATO agrees plans to extend Bosnian force', *Jane's Defence Weekly*, vol. 29, no. 19 (13 May 1998).

[258] Starr, B., 'USA prompts NATO over new Bosnia peace force', *Jane's Defence Weekly*, vol. 29, no. 5 (4 Feb. 1998); and GAO/NSIAD-99-19 (note 253), p. 20.

[259] Contributions from the Czech Republic, Hungary, Poland and Spain were due in 1999. *Atlantic News*, vol. 32, no. 3059 (20 Nov. 1998).

Centre.[260] Free movement throughout Bosnia became easier as SFOR reopened railway lines and dismantled unauthorized checkpoints on the roads together with the IPTF.[261] The SFOR Commander exercised tight control over 'Specialist Police' paramilitary forces whose restructuring in the Republika Srpska began slowly under the new, more pro-Western government.[262]

While there was no change in the official SFOR policy only to detain the indicted war criminals it came across, the force became much more active with US involvement in apprehending suspects in 1998. Having previously provided only back-up support, US forces captured an indictee for the first time in January.[263] By October, SFOR had detained nine suspects and enjoyed greater mutual understanding with the ICTY, which now applauded it for giving appropriate cooperation.[264] Most arrests took place without incident, but some led to a backlash, as when UN IPTF and OSCE field offices were attacked in June.[265] Official statements were scarce on NATO's possible intentions to apprehend the most wanted war criminals, Bosnian Serb wartime political and military leaders Radovan Karadzic and Ratko Mladic, but press reports indicated that by mid-year the USA had dropped its clandestine plans for their arrest.[266]

The future of the new SFOR had become explicitly linked to the success of the civilian implementation of the Dayton Agreement, committed to the elusive aim of forging a functioning state of Bosnia and Herzegovina out of its constituent entities, the Federation of Bosnia and Herzegovina and the Republika Srpska. A self-sustaining peace was the declared goal but not yet the reality. Critical problems included endemic corruption, tension around Brcko, problematic implementation of the municipal election results and strained relations between Bosniacs and Croats, especially in Mostar and central Bosnia and Herzegovina.[267] Parallel illegal structures within the federation continued to exist, the most serious threat to its integrity being posed by the attitude of Croatia. In August Croatian President Franjo Tudjman informed US Secretary of State Madeleine Albright that he refused to stop subsidizing Croatian forces or to prohibit the use of the Croatian flag in the federation.[268]

[260] Starr, B., 'NATO rethinks mine clearance in Bosnia', *Jane's Defence Weekly*, vol. 29, no. 24 (17 June 1998), pp. 27–29.

[261] Clark, W., 'Building a lasting peace in Bosnia and Herzegovina', *Review of International Affairs*, vol. 49, no. 1066 (1998), p. 10.

[262] Kitfield, J., 'Bosnia forever', *National Journal* (5 Sep. 1998), pp. 2018–19; and Biden, J., 'Bosnia: why the United States should finish the job', *SAIS Review*, vol. 18, no. 2 (summer/fall 1998), p. 4.

[263] Smith, J., 'U.S. soldiers seize Serb for war crimes', *International Herald Tribune*, 23 Jan. 1998.

[264] Taylor, D., 'Interview with Judge Arbour, ICTY Prosecutor', *SFOR Informer*, no. 49 (25 Nov. 1998).

[265] Office of the High Representative (OHR), Report of the High Representative for implementation of the Peace Agreement to the Secretary-General of the United Nations, 14 Oct. 1998, para. 78.

[266] E.g., Weiner, T., 'U.S. drops plan to nab accused Serbs', *International Herald Tribune*, 27 July 1998.

[267] OHR, Report of the High Representative for implementation of the Peace Agreement to the Secretary-General of the United Nations, 9 Apr. 1998.

[268] Viotta, P. H., 'Implementing the Dayton Accord: the role of NATO and SFOR. A military and personal perspective', Paper presented at the Third Pan-European International Relations Conference and Joint Meeting with the International Studies Association, Vienna, 16–19 Sep. 1998, pp. 7–8.

The September 1998 general elections, conducted under the supervision of the OSCE and with security assistance from SFOR, brought cautious hope for advancing the common institutions of state under a more constructive presidency, as the obstructionist Serb incumbent was replaced with a more moderate candidate for the first time since the Dayton Agreement. Hailed by Western observers as the most democratic and peaceful in the country's history, the elections showed a general trend towards greater moderation and pluralism in Bosnian politics.[269] The one notable exception was the election to the Republika Srpska presidency of Nikola Poplasen, leader of the extreme nationalist Serbian Radical Party, who replaced the more moderate leader Biljana Plavsic.[270]

In the autumn, SFOR turned its attention to providing more vigorous assistance to the return of refugees and internally displaced persons, viewed by High Representative Carlos Westendorp as the 'litmus test' of reconciliation in Bosnia. The results, however, fell short of expectations for 1998. A total of 140 000 people returned (compared with 170 000 in 1997), of whom 40 000 were members of minority groups.[271] Only 2000 out of a promised 70 000 Croat and Muslim refugees returned to the Republika Srpska, while in Sarajevo international assistance to the Bosniac sectors was suspended for their failure to support large flows of refugees back to the city.[272] The United Nations High Commissioner for Refugees (UNHCR) and other organizations had implemented numerous innovative programmes to promote return, but progress was hampered most notably by the harassment and intimidation of minority groups and the systematic violation of property rights.[273] At its first biannual review in December NATO deemed the progress to be insufficient to warrant any substantial reduction of SFOR, although there was scope for short-term efficiency measures.[274]

While engaging in its most ambitious and high-profile activities in Kosovo, the OSCE also maintained its various field missions designed to prevent, manage or resolve conflict, adding a new Advisory and Monitoring Group to support democratic institutions in Belarus and opening up liaison centres in Kazakhstan, Kyrgyzstan and Turkmenistan.[275] In Croatia, the OSCE also broke

[269] OHR (note 265), 14 Oct. 1998; and US Department of State, Ambassador Robert S. Gelbard, Special Representative of the President and the Secretary of State for Implementation of the Dayton Peace Accords: On-the-record briefing on results of the Bosnian elections and status of Dayton Accord implementation, 25 Sep. 1998.

[270] Kostovic, D., 'Republika Srpska: Dayton and democracy', *Transitions*, vol. 5, no. 11 (Nov. 1998), p. 14.

[271] OHR, Report of the High Representative for implementation of the Peace Agreement to the Secretary-General of the United Nations, 12 Feb. 1999, para. 58.

[272] 'Bosnia: putting it right', *The Economist*, vol. 349, no. 8095 (21 Nov. 1998); and Viotta (note 268).

[273] Cox, M., 'The right to return home: international intervention and ethnic cleansing in Bosnia and Herzegovina', *International and Comparative Law Quarterly*, vol. 47 (July 1998), p. 623.

[274] NATO, Statement on Bosnia and Herzegovina issued at the Ministerial Meeting of the North Atlantic Council, Brussels, 8 Dec. 1998.

[275] OSCE document SEC.DOC/2/98 (note 205). For details of OSCE missions see appendix 2A in this volume.

new ground by deploying police monitors in the Danube region, many of whom had already participated in the earlier UN Police Support Group.[276]

Other regional organizations in Europe lagged behind NATO and the OSCE in operational activity and preparedness for conflict management. The WEU, commemorating the 50th anniversary of the signing of the Treaty of Brussels, set up a new military structure, activated its military committee and continued to cooperate with NATO.[277] However, its hitherto limited role in conflict management remained unclear in the light of a Franco-British initiative in December to develop the EU's capacity for autonomous action in response to crises, 'backed up by credible military forces'.[278] Delays in ratifications of the 1997 Amsterdam Treaty held up the further operationalization of the EU's foreign policy apparatus, including the appointment of a High Representative for the Common Foreign and Security Policy (CFSP) and the establishment of a new Policy Planning and Early Warning Unit.[279]

The Commonwealth of Independent States

The CIS continued to maintain two troubled peace operations, in Abkhazia (Georgia) and in Tajikistan, both assisted and monitored by accompanying UN missions, UNOMIG and UNMOT, respectively.[280] President Eduard Shevardnadze cast doubt on the future of the Collective Peacekeeping Forces (CPF) in Georgia by continuing to call for their replacement with international peacekeepers and for enforcement along the lines of a 'Bosnian model' to compel the breakaway region of Abkhazia to peace.[281] The conflict worsened after the CIS summit meeting in April endorsed a plan for the repatriation of Georgians to the Gali district of Abkhazia under a 'temporary administration' including UN and OSCE representation. The CPF, extended until 31 July 1998, was to be redeployed from the internal Abkhaz–Georgian border to the entire territory of Gali.[282] A Georgian guerrilla attack, which followed Abkhazian condemnation of the summit declaration, sparked the fiercest fighting in the region in five years and claimed up to 300 lives.[283] A new Protocol on a Ceasefire signed at Gagra on 25 May provided for the establishment of special groups composed of representatives of the parties, UNOMIG and the CPF to

[276] Eide, E., 'Regionalizing intervention? The case of Europe in the Balkans', ed. A. McDermott, *Sovereign Intervention,* PRIO Report 2/99 (International Peace Research Institute: Oslo, 1999), p. 80.

[277] *Atlantic News*, vol. 32, nos 3002 (9 Apr. 1998) and 3008 (8 May 1998).

[278] Fitchett, J., 'Britain and France call for EU military capability for crises', *International Herald Tribune*, 5–6 Dec. 1998. For further discussion of the initiative see chapter 6 and for the text of the British–French Joint Declaration on European Defence, 4 Dec. 1998, see appendix 6A in this volume.

[279] 'Europe juggles its jobs', *The Economist,* vol. 350, no. 8180 (2 Jan. 1999).

[280] Russian peacekeepers remained involved in joint operations with the parties in South Ossetia and Moldova under bilateral, not CIS, agreements. For details of the conflict in Tajikistan see appendix 1D in this volume.

[281] The plan was rejected by the Abkhaz leadership and Russian officials. Radio Free Europe/Radio Liberty, *RFE/RL Caucasus Report,* vol. 1, no. 8 (21 Apr. 1998); Interfax (Moscow), 5 Jan 1998, in 'Georgia: Fears voiced for Bosnian-style peacekeeping in Abkhazia', FBIS-SOV-98-005, 6 Jan. 1998; and 'President is not pleased with Russian peacekeeping', *New Europe*, 8–14 Feb. 1998.

[282] *RFE/RL Caucasus Report,* vol. 1, no. 10 (5 May 1998).

[283] Cohen, J., 'Peace postponed', *Transitions,* vol. 5, no. 7 (July 1998); and 'Another defeat for Georgia', *Strategic Comments* (IISS), vol. 4, no. 6 (July 1998).

monitor the truce.[284] A series of UN-sponsored peace negotiations facilitated by Russia with the assistance of the OSCE and the Friends of Georgia (France, Germany, Russia, the UK and the USA) failed to produce agreement on a protocol on the repatriation of ethnic Georgians to Abkhazia.[285] The mandate of the CPF, of indeterminate status since August, was to be renewed at a CIS summit meeting postponed until early 1999.[286]

Africa

The Organization of African Unity

The principal regional organization in Africa, the OAU[287] faced formidable challenges as it struggled to revitalize itself and cooperate with subregional organizations to tackle both new and ongoing breaches of African peace and security. No sooner had President Clinton hailed the 'beginning of a new African renaissance', during the most extensive tour of the continent ever made by a US leader, than the 'new African leaders', expected to provide a bloc of stability, launched into battle in a great arc of conflict stretching from the Horn of Africa to the Great Lakes. Subregional organizations took the lead in attempting to manage many of these crises, and the OAU Council of Ministers proposed formalizing an embryonic peacekeeping structure with the creation of subregional brigades under OAU command and control.[288] The 34th OAU summit meeting, held in Ouagadougou, Burkina Faso, failed to endorse the plan but decided to make peace, security and political stability in Africa a pre-occupation of the highest order and to cooperate with the UN in conflict management.[289] South Africa's outgoing President Nelson Mandela questioned the OAU's doctrine of non-intervention in the face of tyrannical regimes and challenged Africa to find another way, if the OAU's Mechanism for Conflict Prevention, Management and Resolution was not working, to take charge of its own security.[290]

The UN sought to regularize its assistance to the OAU for building African institutional and operational capacity in conflict management. In April, the UN established a political liaison office with the OAU in Addis Ababa and was ready to appoint liaison officers to UN-authorized African peacekeeping operations as well as the headquarters of subregional organizations, subject to sufficient funding. Several high-level meetings between the two secretariats had as yet produced few tangible improvements to the OAU Situation Room,

[284] The freeze on UNOMIG patrolling was partially lifted to enable it to participate in the implementation of the Protocol. UN, Report of the Secretary-General concerning the situation in Abkhazia, Georgia, UN document S/1998/497, 10 June 1998, para. 4.

[285] 'Western diplomats to speed up Abkhaz deal', *New Europe,* 6–12 Dec. 1998; and *RFE/RL Caucasus Report,* vol. 1, no. 43 (23 Dec. 1998).

[286] *RFE/RL Caucasus Report,* vol. 2, no. 3 (20 Jan. 1999).

[287] For a list of OAU member states see the glossary in this volume.

[288] *Africa Research Bulletin,* vol. 35, no. 3 (1–31 Mar. 1998), p. 13030.

[289] *Africa Research Bulletin,* vol. 35, no. 6 (1–30 June 1998), pp. 13134–35.

[290] Address of the President of the Republic of South Africa, Nelson Mandela, to the Summit Meeting of the OAU Heads of State and Government, Ouagadougou, Burkina Faso, 8 June 1998, at URL <http://www.oau-oua.org/oau_info/burkdoc/mandela.htm>.

still an empty office, but plans were under way to arrange for the short-term secondment of current or previous DPKO personnel to provide expertise to the OAU Conflict Management Centre. In May the UN Secretariat convened an African Peacekeeping Training Strategy Session to develop training goals and conducted a peacekeeping mission management seminar in Zambia in February, a training assistance visit to Swaziland in March and a logistics training course in Kenya in June. The UN was also represented at a two-week regional course for police officers from Southern African Development Community (SADC) countries held in South Africa in November.[291] Seed money for African conflict management remained scarce with only one contribution, from the UK, to the UN Trust Fund established in 1996.[292] In November, the EU pledged a grant of about $1 million to support the OAU mechanism.[293]

As part of its tool kit for coping with ongoing African crises, the OAU continued to maintain two small observer missions in 1998, in Burundi and Comoros. A handful of civilian observers in *Burundi*, the most costly conflict for the OAU to date, were able to witness substantial progress in June as 17 factions signed a ceasefire declaration. For the first time in nearly five years of conflict, the government, armed groups, and both majority and opposition parties agreed to open peace talks.[294] A schedule was drawn up for at least six rounds of negotiations with the intention of having a peace agreement ready for signature in August 1999.[295] In November mediating Tanzanian President Julius Nyerere recommended that subregional leaders suspend economic sanctions against Burundi, an appeal repeated by the OAU.[296] The UN was considering Burundi's request for the establishment of an international criminal tribunal for Burundi provided the peace process was successful.[297]

Conditions were less auspicious in *Comoros*, where OAU observers had deployed on the islands of Grande Comore and Mohéli but not secessionist Anjouan, which reaffirmed its sovereignty in a constitutional referendum in February.[298] The OAU, committed to the territorial integrity of the tiny Indian Ocean state, called for the resolution of the conflict with 'all means necessary'; but its mediation was rebuffed in March as demonstrators denied an OAU ministerial delegation access to the secessionist leadership.[299] Ironically, the self-proclaimed Anjouan leader himself sought French and OAU mediation after coming under attack from a rival secessionist for reconsidering

[291] For a list of the SADC member states see the glossary in this volume.

[292] UN, Enhancement of African peacekeeping capacity, Report of the Secretary-General, UN document S/1999/171, 12 Feb. 1999.

[293] PANA, 'News in brief', 30 Nov. 1998.

[294] The Burundi crisis alone had cost the OAU *c.* $10.1 million out of a total of $13.9 million spent on preventive diplomacy missions. Ejime, P., PANA, 'African conflicts gulp OAU Peace Fund', 5 June 1998; *Africa Research Bulletin*, vol. 35, no. 6 (1–30 June 1998), p. 13151; and *UN Chronicle*, no. 3 (1998), p. 54.

[295] PANA, 'Six negotiation rounds required for Burundi peace', 13 Nov. 1998.

[296] *Africa Research Bulletin*, vol. 35, no. 11 (1–30 Nov. 1998), p. 13366; and PANA, 'OAU urges lifting of sanctions against Burundi', 19 Dec. 1998.

[297] *Africa Research Bulletin*, vol. 35, no. 5 (1–31 May 1998), p. 13126.

[298] 'A separatist vote in Comoros', *International Herald Tribune*, 27 Feb. 1998.

[299] Cornwell, R., 'Africa Watch. Anjouan: a spat in the Indian Ocean', *African Security Review*, vol. 7, no. 3 (1998), pp. 60–61.

confederation with Grande Comore. As fighting broke out on Anjouan in December, the OAU called on its members to respond to a Comoran Government request for military intervention, but none volunteered to send troops.[300]

The OAU had also provided special grants to the UN-mandated regional African peacekeeping force MISAB, which completed its mission in the *Central African Republic* in mid-April following France's decision to withdraw all its troops and vital logistical support. The force had successfully assisted in the implementation of the 1997 Bangui Agreements intended to pacify the country after recent army mutinies. MISAB had recovered almost all heavy weapons, but only half the number of light weapons taken from state armouries had been handed over by former mutineers, militias and the civilian population.[301] With the establishment of MINURCA, the MISAB troop contributors—Burkina Faso, Chad, Gabon, Mali, Senegal and Togo—transferred their contingents from Gabonese military command to that of the UN.[302]

The Southern African Development Community

The greatest challenge for the OAU—in cooperation with the SADC, the UN and regional leaders—was to prevent a regional conflagration in the *Democratic Republic of Congo* from turning into Africa's 'first world war'. Sparked by President Laurent Désiré Kabila's decision to expel the foreign troops and remaining Rwandan military trainers who had helped him to power in 1996–97, a mutiny erupted on 2 August among the mainly Congolese Tutsi (Banyamulenge) soldiers of the ethnically riven army in the eastern part of the country.[303] The amorphous rebel movement, the Congolese Rally for Democracy (Rassemblement Congolais pour la Démocratie, RCD), aimed to unseat Kabila and came to comprise civilian oppositionists, ethnic Tutsi and numerous government troops.[304] Concerned about continuing raids on their territory by Hutu and Ugandan militants from bases inside the DRC, neighbouring Rwanda and later Uganda deployed troops in support of the rebellion although both initially denied involvement. Kabila, who for months portrayed the crisis purely as a foreign invasion, appealed to the UN, the OAU and the SADC to condemn and expel the aggressors.[305]

Even as the OAU and the SADC each sent early consultative missions to the country, rifts appeared over the handling of the crisis within the 14-member

[300] PANA, 'OAU appeals to member states to intervene in Comoros', 8 Dec. 1998; *Africa Research Bulletin*, vol. 35, no. 12 (1–31 Dec. 1998), p. 13366; and 'Comoros appeal for help', *BBC News*, 13 Dec. 1998, at URL <http://news2.thdo.bbc.co.uk/hi/english/world/africa>.

[301] UN, Letter dated 11 March 1998 from the Secretary-General addressed to the President of the Security Council, UN document S/1998/221, 12 Mar. 1998, paras 14 and 17.

[302] UN Security Council Resolution 1152, 5 Feb. 1998; and UN Security Council Resolution 1155, 16 Mar. 1998.

[303] Heitman, H., 'DRC rebels move to oust President Kabila', *Jane's Defence Weekly*, vol. 30, no. 6 (12 Aug. 1998), p. 7; and 'Renewed danger in the Congo', *Strategic Comments* (IISS), vol. 4, no. 6 (July 1998).

[304] 'Turning the tables', *Africa Confidential*, vol. 39, no. 17 (28 Aug. 1998), pp. 4–5.

[305] Hule, J., PANA, 'Kabila appeals for help to remove foreign troops', 11 Aug. 1998.

development community which the DRC had recently joined.[306] Six of nine SADC defence ministers present at a meeting in Harare declared support for the embattled government. Consequently, Zimbabwean President Robert Mugabe, as head of the contested SADC Organ on Politics, Defence and Security, argued that a mandate existed for military intervention on Kabila's behalf under SADC auspices. South Africa, as chair of the SADC, initially denied that Mugabe had the authority since the role of the SADC Organ had yet to be approved; but, surprisingly, Mandela, mandated by an SADC summit meeting to seek an immediate ceasefire, soon endorsed the military assistance, presumably to encourage the SADC leaders to close ranks.[307] By the end of August, a large-scale intervention by Angolan and Zimbabwean forces with logistical support from Namibia had forced the withdrawal of the rebels from the far west of the country, where they had quickly opened a second front.[308] While the UN called for a ceasefire, political dialogue and the withdrawal of all foreign forces, Kabila announced that he would launch a counter-offensive in the east.[309]

Regional leaders pursued the elusive quest for a ceasefire in numerous meetings without the direct participation of the rebels, who were spurned by Kabila as 'pawns' of neighbouring countries. The SADC summit meeting in Mauritius favoured dialogue and failed to pass Kabila's draft motion condemning Rwanda and Uganda for aggression.[310] Regional efforts took on renewed urgency with the escalation of the conflict in mid-October after rebel success prompted a summit decision by the three pro-Kabila allies, who had deepening economic interests in the conflict, to commit more troops for a counter-offensive.[311] At least Chad and Sudan were also fighting with the government while a new rebel group with more popular support, the Congo Liberation Movement (MLC), appeared in the north-east.[312] As President Mandela stepped up his mediation efforts through meetings with representatives of Namibia, Rwanda, Uganda and the rebels, another round of peace talks was held in Lusaka on 26–27 October, sponsored by the SADC and the OAU.[313] The meeting, which set up a committee to conduct proxy talks with

[306] Cornwell, R. and Potgieter, J., 'Africa Watch: a large peace of Africa?', *African Security Review*, vol. 7, no. 6 (1998), pp. 75–76; and Mulenga, M., PANA, 'Defence chiefs discuss instability in SADC region', 12 Aug. 1998;

[307] Cornwell and Potgieter (note 306), pp. 76–78.

[308] *Africa Research Bulletin*, vol. 35, no. 8 (1–31 Aug. 1998), pp. 13221–25; and Heitman, H., 'Loyalty split remains as Congo fighting intensifies', *Jane's Defence Weekly*, vol. 30, no. 9 (2 Sep. 1998), p. 19.

[309] UN, Security Council Presidential Statement, UN document S/PRST/1998/26, 31 Aug. 1998.

[310] *Africa Research Bulletin*, vol. 35, no. 9 (1–30 Sep. 1998), p. 13243; and Cornwell and Potgieter (note 306), p. 83.

[311] 'Zimbabwe and Congo: down with war', *The Economist*, vol. 349, no. 8093 (7 Nov. 1998); and AFP (Paris), 22 Oct. 1998, in 'Congo-Kinshasa: AFP reports Zimbabwe starts troop build-up in DR Congo', FBIS-AFR-98-295, 23 Oct. 1998.

[312] Kabila was reportedly also supported openly or tacitly by the Central African Republic, Egypt, Eritrea, Libya and Niger and the rebels by Burundi, which denied involvement. By Dec. a new rebel splinter group, RCD-Renovated, was formed in Belgium. *Africa Research Bulletin*, vol. 35, no. 10 (1–31 Oct. 1998), p. 13293; *Africa Research Bulletin*, vol. 35, no. 11 (1–30 Nov. 1998), p. 13312; and *Africa Research Bulletin*, vol. 35, no. 12 (1–31 Dec. 1998), p. 13371.

[313] PANA, 'Crucial meeting on Congo begins', 26 Oct. 1998.

the rebels, adopted an unsigned draft ceasefire agreement.[314] Consultations continued between regional actors and the OAU to prepare the modalities of an eventual framework accord. One obstacle to mediation was removed in early November when Vice-President Paul Kagame admitted for the first time that Rwandan troops were involved, albeit for reasons of national security.[315]

Limited progress was finally made with UN assistance at the 20th Franco-African summit meeting, in Paris. On 28 November French President Jacques Chirac announced that the presidents of the DRC, Rwanda, Uganda and Zimbabwe had agreed to a ceasefire 'in principle', but the deal was denounced as irrelevant by the rebels.[316] Although the agreement was not signed at the OAU conflict resolution meeting in Ouagadougou on 17–18 December, the warring parties relaxed their positions in favour of 'proximity talks'.[317] The rebels, now in control of one-third of the DRC territory, accepted the principles of a ceasefire if linked to negotiations, even by proxy. Kabila no longer demanded the 'immediate' departure of Rwandan and Ugandan troops and accepted a Zimbabwean plan to pursue the orderly retreat of foreign forces after a ceasefire.[318] Absent from the OAU summit meeting, Rwanda and Uganda continued to insist on a ceasefire negotiated with the rebels to ensure security along their borders. The UN Secretary-General in turn confirmed UN preparedness to assist with a peacekeeping force in the DRC once all the countries involved chose to honour a ceasefire.[319]

The regional peacebroker, South Africa, tarnished its military reputation in an ill-conceived intervention in *Lesotho* in September to put down an army mutiny which followed allegations of electoral fraud. The 600 troops deployed in the first wave of 'Operation Boleas', soon joined by 200 Botswanan troops, came under unexpectedly heavy attack and were powerless to intervene against the looters and arsonists who subsequently destroyed central Maseru.[320] Six days of fighting did restore control to the elected government but resulted in over 80 deaths. Criticized within the South African National Defence Force (SANDF) for poor planning, intelligence and operational coordination, the operation also failed to live up to the principles and procedures set out in a new White Paper for South African participation in international peace missions.[321]

[314] Chaired by Zambia, the committee includes representatives of the UN, OAU, SADC, Mozambique, South Africa and Tanzania. PANA, 'DRC rebels spurn SADC ceasefire plan', 28 Oct. 1998. *Africa Research Bulletin*, vol. 35, no. 10 (1–31 Oct. 1998), pp. 13293–94; and AFP (Paris), 30 Oct. 1998, in 'Tanzania: Tanzania says Rwanda obstacle to DR Congo peace', FBIS-AFR-98-303, 2 Nov. 1998.

[315] Rwanda denied having set up a joint command with Uganda, as reported, to prosecute the war. By Dec. they disagreed about the conduct of the war and relations with the new MLC in the north. Duke, L., 'Rwanda admits its troops are in Congo', *International Herald Tribune*, 7–8 Nov. 1998; and 'A hard war to stop—or win', *The Economist*, vol. 349, no. 8097 (5 Dec. 1998), pp. 51–52.

[316] Ben Bouzza, B., PANA, 'Chirac announces ceasefire agreement in DRC', 28 Nov. 1998.

[317] Gaye, S., PANA, 'African conflicts task OAU's capacity to maintain peace', 30 Dec. 1998.

[318] *Africa Research Bulletin*, vol. 35, no. 12 (1–31 Dec. 1998), pp. 13369–70.

[319] 'UN willing to form force for DRC', *Jane's Defence Weekly*, vol. 30, no. 24 (16 Dec. 1998).

[320] *Africa Research Bulletin*, vol. 35, no. 9 (1–30 Sep. 1998), p. 13239.

[321] 'Report by Israel Mogale', SAPA (Johannesburg), 2 Nov. 1998, in 'South Africa: RSA: SANDF says government lacks clear security policy', FBIS-AFR-98-306, 3 Nov. 1998; and White Paper on

The southern African subregion had yet to finalize its procedures for responding to conflicts within the area. Legitimacy for the South African intervention, dubbed a 'SADC Task Force', was derived alternatively from Lesotho's request for military assistance, from a decision of the Southern African Inter State Defence and Security Committee not to tolerate military *coups d'état* in SADC member states, and from a 1994 SADC decision to appoint Botswana, South Africa and Zimbabwe as guarantors of the return of democracy to Lesotho.[322] However, no explicit authorization or mandate for Operation Boleas would seem to have been approved at the SADC summit meeting in September. The SADC Organ on Politics, Defence and Security remained in suspended animation as the conflicting views on its structuring put forward by South Africa and Zimbabwe were not even included in the agenda, much less resolved, at the summit.[323] Consequently, the validity of decisions taken under its auspices remained open to question, as did the legitimacy of enforcement measures, whether in the DRC or Lesotho, taken without UN authorization.

The Inter-Governmental Authority on Development

African and international observers were taken aback by the intensity of the fratricidal border dispute which erupted between *Ethiopia* and *Eritrea* in May 1998. Building on tension over economic and fiscal policies, a minor and probably unplanned skirmish on 6 May suddenly escalated into battle in the rugged and remote 'Yirga Triangle' in north-western Ethiopia. Ethiopia accused Eritrea of aggression while Eritrea claimed to be retaking its own territory, a disputed area still under review by a bilateral border commission.[324] By early June the war had widened to three fronts with air raids by both sides until US President Clinton persuaded the protagonists to institute a moratorium.[325] US representatives, Rwandan officials and Djibouti's President Gouled Aptidon, Chairman of the IGAD, intervened after Eritrea suggested international mediation on 14 May.[326] Ethiopia accepted a US–Rwandan peace plan, which called for: (*a*) renunciation of the use of force; (*b*) withdrawal of Eritrean forces to positions held before 6 May, return of the previous civilian administration and deployment of observers; (*c*) binding border delimitation and demarcation; and (*d*) demilitarization of the entire common border.[327] Eritrea balked at the proposed pull-out of troops, demanding a more regional

South African participation in international peace missions, Approved by Cabinet, Pretoria, 21 Oct. 1998.

[322] Hough, M., 'SADC's new intervention', *Jane's Sentinel Pointer*, vol 5, no. 11 (Nov. 1998), p. 14.

[323] Malan, M., *Regional Power Politics under Cover of SADC: Running Amok with a Mythical Organ*, Occasional Paper no. 35 (Institute for Security Studies: Pretoria, Oct. 1998).

[324] 'Murder in the family', *Africa Confidential*, vol. 39, no. 11 (29 May 1998), p. 1; and *Horn of Africa Bulletin*, vol. 10, no. 3 (May/June 1998), pp. 7–8.

[325] Esterhuysen, P., 'Eritrea–Ethiopia: family feud', *Africa Insight*, vol. 28, no. 1/2 (1998), pp. 90–92; and *Horn of Africa Bulletin*, vol. 10, no. 3 (May/June 1998), p. 10.

[326] President Aptidon was the first to mediate in the crisis. Salter, M., 'The Horn's broken hopes', *New Routes*, no. 3 (1998), pp. 26–29.

[327] Cornwell, R., 'Africa Watch. Ethiopia and Eritrea: fratricidal conflict in the Horn', *African Security Review*, vol. 7, no. 5 (1998), p. 66.

solution, but the annual OAU summit meeting in Burkina Faso on 10 June decided to build on the Rwandan–US plan.[328] It was also tacitly endorsed by the Security Council, which called on the parties to cease hostilities.[329] Meanwhile both parties continued their rearmament, military build-up along the frontier, expulsion of each other's citizens and hostile propaganda.[330] Two missions to each country and a special summit meeting in November organized by the OAU mediation committee—comprising Burkina Faso, Djibouti, Rwanda (initially) and Zimbabwe—met with continued Eritrean refusal to withdraw.[331] Three trips to the region in November–December by US Presidential Envoy Anthony Lake to further the OAU plan also proved inconclusive.[332] On 17 December the Central Organ of the OAU mechanism endorsed a framework agreement calling for redeployment of all troops and demilitarization of the border supervised by OAU military observers.[333]

Armed conflict between two of its key members complicated the efforts of the IGAD to further negotiations between the Sudanese Government and the large southern rebel movement, the Sudan People's Liberation Movement/Army (SPLM/A), to bring an end to the 15-year civil war in *Sudan*.[334] With approval by the National Democratic Alliance (NDA), comprising the largest southern and northern opposition groups, of the 1994 Declaration of Principles on Peace drafted by the IGAD, all the major actors in the civil war had accepted the IGAD's role as mediator.[335] The peace talks, resumed on 4 May in Kenya, reached agreement on an internationally supervised referendum on self-determination for the south of the country at an unspecified date. However, the parties disagreed on the region's boundaries and the issue of religion and state.[336] The SPLM demanded a secular state and viewed the concurrent nationwide referendum on a new constitution, confirming Sudan's status as a federation based on Islamic Sharia law, as an obstacle to the peace process. Further IGAD-sponsored talks in Addis Ababa in early August failed to resolve the outstanding issues. A meeting in Egypt of the NDA opposition

[328] *Africa Research Bulletin*, vol. 35, no. 6 (1–30 June 1998), p. 13136; *Horn of Africa Bulletin*, vol. 10, no. 3 (May/June 1998), p. 1; and UN, Letter dated 10 June 1998 from the Permanent Representative of Kenya to the United Nations addressed to the President of the Security Council, UN document S/1998/494, 10 June 1998.

[329] UN, Security Council Resolution 1177, 26 June 1998; and *Africa Research Bulletin*, (vol. 35, no. 6 (1–30 June 1998), p. 13135.

[330] Salter (note 326); and 'Eritrea and Ethiopia: spit and slug', *The Economist*, vol. 348, no. 8086 (19 Sep. 1998).

[331] PANA, 'OAU foreign ministers to discuss Ethiopia–Eritrea report', 29 July 1998; *Horn of Africa Bulletin*, vol. 10, no. 4 (July/Aug. 1998), pp. 6–8; PANA, 'African leaders attempt to mediate in border dispute' and 'No breakthrough yet at Eritrea–Ethiopia talks', 8 Nov. 1998; *Africa Research Bulletin*, vol. 35, no. 11 (1–30 Nov. 1998), p. 13315; and AFP (Paris), 9 Nov. 1998, in 'Ethiopia: Ethiopia accepts OAU peace plan on conflict with Eritrea', 10 Nov. 1998.

[332] PANA, 'US envoy meets Meles over border conflict', 15 Jan. 1999.

[333] *Africa Research Bulletin*, vol. 35, no. 12 (1–31 Dec. 1998), pp. 13349–50.

[334] The member states of the IGAD are Djibouti, Eritrea, Ethiopia, Kenya, Somalia, Sudan and Uganda.

[335] *Horn of Africa Bulletin*, vol. 10, no. 2 (Mar./Apr. 1998), pp. 27–29.

[336] *Horn of Africa Bulletin*, vol. 10, no. 3 (May/June 1998), p. 25; and PANA, 'Sudan peace talks end in deadlock', 7 May 1998.

groups called for an expansion of the IGAD process.[337] Meanwhile, fighting continued in southern Sudan amid mutually denied allegations of Eritrean, Ethiopian and Ugandan support for the SPLA and Chadian support for the government forces.[338] An attempt to persuade rebel leader Colonel John Garang to join the five other factions which had signed a 1997 peace accord with the government ended in failure.[339] Instead, the SPLA, one of the most organized guerrilla armies in Africa, gained control over more territory than at any time during the insurgency.[340] With the IGAD in disarray over the border dispute in the Horn of Africa, the initiative for negotiating a ceasefire was passed on to its Western partner countries. In July British Foreign Office Minister Derek Fatchett brokered a three-month 'humanitarian truce' between the government and the SPLA to establish corridors of tranquillity in famine-stricken areas.[341] A further agreement, reached in November under the auspices of an inter-agency Technical Committee at the behest of the IGAD, permitted aid agencies to deliver food by road for the first time across lines separating SPLA and government forces.[342] This was expected to reduce reliance on the biggest food-drop operation in world history, which tried to reach the over 2 million Sudanese who risked starvation.[343]

The IGAD shifted gears in its attempts to promote peace in *Somalia*, abandoning the pursuit of 'top–down' leadership conferences in favour of 'bottom–up' approaches that rewarded regions for maintaining peace. Two rival peace initiatives, the 1997 Sodere Declarations backed by Ethiopia (mandated to mediate by the IGAD and the OAU) and the 1997 Cairo Accord brokered by Egypt, had bestowed important roles on the Darod clan and the Mogadishu-based Hawiye clan, respectively, each to the exclusion of important leaders of the other clan. As delegations from the principal leaders of Mogadishu, Hussein Aideed and Ali Mahdi Mohamed, courted regional capitals for support for the Cairo Accord, criticized by the IGAD, the UN called on the international community to speak with one voice in confronting the civil war. Egypt was invited for the first time to attend a meeting of the IGAD in May where host nation Italy worked towards bridging the gaps between the two peace proposals.[344] In August Aideed announced that he welcomed Ethiopia's help in facilitating the delayed national reconciliation conference, to be held in

[337] *Horn of Africa Bulletin*, vol. 10, no. 4 (July/Aug. 1998), pp. 27 and 29; and Reuters, 'Sudanese rebels claim Egypt's support', 18 Aug. 1998.

[338] *Africa Research Bulletin*, vol. 35, no. 10 (1–31 Oct. 1998), p. 13302; and 'Sudan's rebels change their spots', *The Economist*, vol. 346, no. 8061 (28 Mar. 1998).

[339] *Horn of Africa Bulletin*, vol. 10, no. 3 (May/June 1998), p. 27.

[340] *Africa Research Bulletin*, vol. 35, no. 2 (1–28 Feb. 1998), p. 13019; and Byron, J., 'Dossier: Sudan', *Cantilevers*, vol. 5 (summer 1998), pp. 11–15.

[341] *Horn of Africa Bulletin*, vol. 10, no. 4 (July/Aug. 1998), p. 27; Hassan, Y., PANA, 'Britain offers to help settle Sudan conflict', 16 July 1998; and 'Southern Sudan's starvation', *The Economist*, vol. 348, no. 8077 (18 July 1998).

[342] *Africa Research Bulletin*, vol. 35, no. 11 (1–30 Nov. 1998), pp. 13337–38.

[343] *WFP Emergency Report*, no. 46 (20 Nov. 1998), at URL <http://www.wfp.org/ereport/981120.html>; and Public Diplomacy Query (PDQ), 'Sudan relief to surpass Berlin airlift aid, Rice says', 29 July 1998, URL <http://pdq2.usia.gov>.

[344] *Horn of Africa Bulletin*, vol. 10, no. 3 (May/June 1998), p. 17; and *Africa Research Bulletin*, vol. 35, no. 2 (1–28 Feb. 1998), p. 13018.

early 1999 and aimed at establishing a three-year transitional central government.[345] While the search for peace was frayed by conflicting regional agendas and factional bickering over the reconciliation conference, the IGAD urged greater participation in the process by Somalian civil society in its March summit meeting and turned its attention to burgeoning regional initiatives as the building blocks of a federated Somalia.[346] Relative peace reigned in the north-western self-proclaimed Somaliland, and in July clan leaders in north-eastern Puntland elected a president in a move to form an administration with a constitution, attracting donor interest.[347] In talks hosted by Kenya in April and by Libya in July, rival leaders Aideed and Ali Mahdi agreed to set up a joint administration in the Benadir region around Mogadishu, which was due to open the port and airport in December and deploy a new police force with Arab support.[348] With two Mogadishu warlords hostile to the Benadir arrangement, Aideed's stronghold in Baidoa under attack and plans for a south-western Jubaland administration frustrated by continued fighting over Kismayo in December, the future of decentralization remained in doubt.[349]

The Economic Community of West African States

The pioneering West African peacekeeping force, ECOMOG, remained in *Liberia* beyond the date scheduled for its withdrawal in February, at the request of its erstwhile foe, former warlord President Charles Taylor. A Status of Forces Agreement (SOFA), signed between the government and ECOMOG in June, stipulated that the force would help provide security and maintain law and order as well as assist in restructuring Liberia's army and police.[350] The latter had already proved a sore point with the continued recruitment of Taylor's former fighters into the police, the Presidential Special Security Service and the army and charges by ECOMOG that they had been rearmed in violation of the UN arms embargo.[351] Disagreements over responsibility for the restructuring persisted despite the SOFA, with Taylor's insistence that requests for assistance would have to come from Liberia after a government committee on army reorganization had completed its work.[352] In the absence of an accompanying protocol detailing its desired size and exact role, ECOMOG kept a low profile during security incidents and transferred its headquarters as well as all but 800 of its troops to Sierra Leone. ECOWAS heads of state

[345] Hagos, G., PANA, 'Aideed accepts Ethiopia's mediation in Somalia', 30 Aug. 1998.

[346] *Horn of Africa Bulletin,* vol. 10, no. 2 (Mar./Apr. 1998), p. 1; and *UN Chronicle*, vol. 35, no. 3 (1998), p. 52.

[347] *Horn of Africa Bulletin,* vol. 10, no. 4 (July/Aug. 1998), pp. 16–18.

[348] PANA, 'Somali warlords produce another peace deal', 10 Apr. 1998; and *Africa Research Bulletin,* vol. 35, no. 7 (1–31 July 1998), p. 13192.

[349] 'Somalia: no nation, new regions', *Africa Confidential,* vol. 39, no. 25 (18 Dec. 1998), p. 7.

[350] Eziakonwa, A., 'Donors back Liberia's reconstruction', *Africa Recovery,* vol. 12, no. 1 (Aug. 1998), p. 26.

[351] Whelan, L., 'Controversy and concern over restructuring', *Jane's Sentinel Pointer*, vol. 5, no. 4 (Apr. 1998), p. 12; and Sannah, T., PANA, 'Insecurity, human rights abuse abound in Liberia', 31 July 1998.

[352] Davies, D., 'Liberia: special report: the security dilemma', *West Africa,* no. 4196 (28 Sep.–11 Oct. 1998), pp. 716–19.

failed to reach agreement on Liberia's request for a new protocol on ECOMOG's mandate and returned the matter to its secretariat and the government for drafting.[353]

In neighbouring *Sierra Leone*, Nigerian ECOMOG contingents resorted to force in early February to implement the 1997 Conakry Agreement intended to reinstate ousted President Kabbah. After a week of fighting, the remnants of the mutinous Armed Forces Ruling Council (AFRC) and its supporters of the Revolutionary United Front (RUF) withdrew on a rampage into north-eastern Sierra Leone.[354] President Kabbah's return to Freetown in March was welcomed by the UN, the OAU and ECOWAS, although the Nigerians had failed to inform the UN Secretary-General or even their ECOMOG partners of the offensive in advance.[355] Allegations that 'Operation Sandstorm' had been carefully planned, with British Government support, by Kabbah, the Nigerian military and the London-based security company Sandline, which had shipped arms into the country in contravention of the UN embargo, caused an uproar in the UK.[356] In May the UN deployed eight military liaison officers to assist ECOMOG in planning its future objectives. With a prolonged mandate from the ministerial meeting in Yamoussoukro, ECOWAS Chiefs of Staff had defined these as the attainment of peace, the training of a new army, disarmament and demobilization of former combatants, and humanitarian assistance.[357] Although captured rebels were disarmed by ECOMOG and the UNOMSIL observers deployed in July, some 8000 fighters continued a brutal campaign of terror in the diamond-rich areas in the north and east, mutilating villagers as 'messages' to the government. Backed by a US pledge of $3.9 million and logistic support, ECOMOG sought to augment its force of 10 000–12 000 with a further 6000 troops to decisively defeat the RUF.[358] By year's end, these veterans of a 1991 rebellion advanced again on Freetown and continued to find supplies and recruits in Liberia, now governed by their former ally.[359] Taylor denied involvement and agreed to work with Guinea and

[353] Radio Nigeria (Lagos), 2 Nov. 1998, in 'Nigeria: Nigeria–ECOWAS summit ends, adopts resolutions', FBIS-AFR-98-306, 3 Nov. 1998; and Olowo, B. and Whiteman, K., 'ECOWAS: an action-packed summit', *West Africa*, no. 4199 (7–20 Dec. 1998), pp. 858–59.

[354] 'ECOMOG troops seize Sierra Leone's capital', *Jane's Defence Weekly*, vol. 29, no. 7 (18 Feb. 1998), p. 6; and 'Fighting over, Sierra Leone now faces other woes', *New York Times*, 17 Feb. 1998.

[355] 'Nigeria does it again' and 'Sierra Leone: Putting a country together again', *The Economist*, vol. 346, no. 8056 (21 Feb. 1998); Ejime, P., PANA, 'Ecowas congratulates Ecomog on arrest of military junta', 15 Feb. 1998; *Africa Research Bulletin*, vol. 35, no. 2 (1–28 Feb. 1998), p. 12993; and UN Security Council Resolution 1156, 16 Mar. 1998.

[356] 'Freetown fracas', *Africa Confidential*, vol. 39, no. 5 (6 Mar. 1998), p. 8; and 'The Freetown fall-out', *Africa Confidential*, vol. 39, no. 10 (15 May 1998), pp. 1–2.

[357] ECOWAS foreign ministers authorized the continued exercise by ECOMOG of its mandate to secure the reinstatement of the legitimate government, the return of peace and security, and a solution to the refugee problem. *Fraternité Matin* (Abidjan), 14–15 Mar. 1998, in 'Côte d'Ivoire: ECOWAS meeting ends; Communiqué issued', FBIS-AFR-98-074, 17 Mar. 1998; UN Security Council Resolution 1162, 17 Apr. 1998; and UN, Fifth report of the Secretary-General on the situation in Sierra Leone, UN document S/1998/486, 9 Jun. 1998, paras 17–23.

[358] 'The Freetown fall-out', *Africa Confidential*, vol. 39, no. 10 (15 May, 1998), p. 1; 'Sierra Leone: grisly message', *The Economist*, vol. 348, no. 8080 (8 Aug. 1998); and 'Sierra Leone: war without end', *The Economist*, vol. 349, no. 8095 (21 Nov. 1998), pp. 49–50.

[359] Rupert, J., 'As peacekeepers bog down, Sierra Leone rebels step up fight', *International Herald Tribune*, 18 Dec. 1998.

Sierra Leone to restore peace at an extraordinary summit meeting, convened to rejuvenate the three-member Mano River Union.[360] The ECOWAS summit meeting advocated a dual-track approach to the conflict whereby efforts to strengthen ECOMOG would be accompanied by the opening of dialogue with the rebels.[361] Even as Liberia publicly called for such dialogue, the USA joined Ghana, Nigeria, Sierra Leone and the EU in claiming to have found clear proof of Taylor's material and logistical support for the RUF.[362]

The involvement of ECOMOG was sought in a third West African conflict after an army rebellion broke out in *Guinea-Bissau* in early June. The well-armed rebels were led by Brigadier Ansumane Mane, who had been sacked as army chief of staff on suspicion of smuggling arms to the Movement of the Democratic Forces of the Casamance (Mouvement des forces démocratiques de Casamance, MFDC) battling for autonomy in southern Senegal. The governments of Guinea and Senegal, which immediately sent over 2000 troops under bilateral defence agreements to help the elected but unpopular regime of President João Bernardo Vieira, joined him in calling for air strikes and intervention by ECOMOG.[363] Instead, ECOWAS foreign ministers favoured the use of sanctions to end the conflict and established a committee of seven nations to mediate.[364] Meanwhile Portugal led initial diplomatic efforts to broker a ceasefire. Having established a contact group on Guinea-Bissau at its second-ever summit in Cape Verde, the CPLP secured a truce on 27 July. The rebels supported the CPLP's offer to set up a buffer force to oversee its implementation.[365] Each backed by one of the parties, the two rival groups of mediators had to iron out their differences before a formal ceasefire accord was signed in Praia, Cape Verde, under joint mediation in August.[366] The details on a buffer force were still to be negotiated when an outbreak of heavy fighting in October led to the rebels taking virtual control of the country. Having offered a unilateral ceasefire, the president signed a peace accord with the rebel leader on 1 November on the sidelines of the ECOWAS summit meeting in Nigeria. It provides for rule by a government of national unity until general elections are held under ECOWAS and CPLP observation as well as the replacement of foreign troops by ECOMOG, mandated to guarantee security along the Sene-

[360] *Africa Research Bulletin,* vol. 35, no. 1 (1–30 Nov. 19981), p. 13314.

[361] As of Dec. troops were provided by Ghana, Guinea and Nigeria. Benin, Côte d'Ivoire, Gambia, Mali and Niger had promised to contribute. Olowo and Whiteman (note 353), p. 859; and UN, Third progress report of the Secretary-General on the United Nations Observer Mission in Sierra Leone, UN document S/1998/1176, 16 Dec. 1998.

[362] 'West Africa according to Mr. Taylor', *Africa Confidential*, vol. 40, no. 2 (22 Jan. 1999), p. 2; and AFP (Paris), 29 Dec. 1998, in 'Liberia: Liberia's Taylor urges sides to talk in Sierra Leone', FBIS-AFR-98-363, 30 Dec. 1998.

[363] 'Guinea-Bissau, the confession', *Jeune Afrique* (Paris), 24 July 1998, in 'Guinea-Bissau: Paper reveals ECOWAS military heads minutes', FBIS-AFR-98-205, 28 July 1998; 'Guinea-Bissau: instant war', *The Economist*, vol. 347, no. 8073 (20 June 1998); and 'Rebels and loyalists in Guinea-Bissau exchange shellfire', *New York Times*, 16 June 1998.

[364] The members of the committee are Burkina Faso, Côte d'Ivoire, Gambia, Ghana, Guinea, Nigeria and Senegal. Niger and Togo were included in Oct. PANA, 'Ecowas put out plan to end Bissau mutiny', 5 July 1998; and PANA, 'Guinea-Bissau crisis tasks ECOWAS leaders', 1 Nov. 1998.

[365] The CPLP contact group comprises Angola, Brazil, Cape Verde, Mozambique, Portugal, and Sao Tome and Principe.

[366] *Africa Research Bulletin,* vol. 35, no. 8 (1–31 Aug. 1998), pp. 13225–26.

galese border and separate the belligerent parties.[367] Benin, Gambia, Niger and Togo pledged a total of 1450 troops to ECOMOG, and Senegal pledged to repatriate its troops once the force was in place.[368] The UN Security Council approved the implementation of ECOMOG's mandate 'in conformity with UN peacekeeping standards'.[369]

With cumulative experience in regional peacekeeping, the West African states decided to establish their own conflict management mechanism based on ECOMOG.[370] An old division between Anglophone and Francophone states, brought into starker relief after Nigeria's use of force in Sierra Leone, prevented consensus on its transformation into a standing force. Instead, trained contingents would be ready to act in crises on authorization from a proposed nine-member ECOWAS security council. The modalities of a command and control structure were spelled out. A new department of peacekeeping and humanitarian affairs was to be created within the ECOWAS Secretariat, replacing ad hoc committees, to prevent, manage and resolve regional conflicts with the help of four early-warning 'observatories'.[371] While fears persisted about the inevitable dominance of the mechanism by regional heavyweight Nigeria, the country's incipient moves towards democracy triggered apprehension about its continued commitment to regional military ventures.

Latin America

The Military Observer Mission to Ecuador/Peru (MOMEP), comprising observers from the four guarantors of the 1942 Rio Protocol—Argentina, Brazil, Chile and the USA—and from the two parties to the conflict, successfully monitored the 1995 ceasefire accord until a peace agreement signed on 26 October by the presidents of Peru and Ecuador brought an end to the most dangerous border dispute extant in Latin America. The comprehensive settlement followed agreement by the two legislatures to respect a solution proposed by the guarantor states.[372] An earlier ominous flare-up of military tension in the disputed region in August had been defused with the creation of a

[367] Clewlow, A., 'Peace pact may mark end to Guinea-Bissau crisis', *Jane's Defence Weekly,* vol. 30, no. 19 (11 Nov. 1998); RDP Antena 1 Radio Network (Lisbon), 2 Nov. 1998, in 'Guinea-Bissau: Guinea-Bissau minister on peace accord', FBIS-AFR-98-306, 3 Nov. 1998; and *Africa Research Bulletin,* vol. 35, no. 11 (1–30 Nov. 1998), p. 13331.

[368] According to press reports, Senegal initially sent over 1500 and Guinea 320 troops to Guinea-Bissau. By the end of the year they had *c.* 2500 and 600 troops there, respectively. PANA, 'President Vieira to stay in power', 19 Nov. 1998; and AFP (Paris), 26 Nov. 1998, in 'Guinea-Bissau: Four West African countries pledge troops for Bissau', FBIS-AFR-98-330, 30 Nov. 1998.

[369] UN Security Council Resolution 1216, 21 Dec. 1998.

[370] The ECOWAS Mechanism for Conflict Prevention, Management and Resolution, Peacekeeping and Security was adopted at the ECOWAS summit meeting in Abuja, Nigeria, on 30–31 Oct. 1998.

[371] The 4 observatories were to be set up in Benin, Burkina Faso, Gambia and Liberia. AFP (Paris), 29 Oct. 1998, in 'Nigeria: AFP details proposed ECOWAS draft treaty on peacekeeping', FBIS-AFR-98-302, 30 Oct. 1998; 'Guinea-Bissau peace accord is highlight of ECOWAS summit', *Africa Recovery,* vol. 12, no. 2 (Nov. 1998), p. 30; and PANA, 'ECOWAS goes tough on small arms', 1 Nov. 1998.

[372] 'Peace in the Andes', *The Economist,* vol. 349, no. 8092 (31 Oct. 1998); and US Department of State, Bureau of Inter-American Affairs, 'Fact Sheet: Commissions to resolve the Ecuador–Peru border dispute', 18 Feb. 1998.

second MOMEP-patrolled demilitarized zone.[373] The observers continued their patrol and flight missions in the demilitarized border areas pending the presentation of a demarcation plan in early 1999.[374] MOMEP was also charged with preparing guidelines for the removal of the estimated 10 000 mines planted during the decades-long dispute, due to be cleared with US training assistance under the umbrella of the *Organization of American States* (OAS).[375]

While the Second Summit of the Americas, held in Santiago de Chile on 18–19 April, called on participating governments to increase their cooperation with the UN in its peacekeeping efforts and entrusted the OAS to revitalize hemispheric security arrangements, peace building remained at the heart of regional conflict management.[376] Argentina revived its White Helmets initiative of international humanitarian assistance by launching a special fund of $500 000 within the OAS, most of it earmarked for mine-clearance in Central America, already under way with support from the world's oldest albeit obscure security organization, the Inter-American Defense Board (IADB).[377] In October the OAS Unit for the Promotion of Democracy organized a forum on peace building to assess lessons learned from special missions in Haiti, Nicaragua and Suriname as well as from programmes to strengthen democratic institutions and human rights in numerous countries. As one step in the consolidation of democracy, the OAS had monitored 37 elections in 15 countries of the hemisphere between 1989 and December 1997.[378]

A joint venture of the OAS and the UN, the International Civilian Mission to Haiti (MICIVIH), continued to assist the Haitian authorities in the tasks of institution building, especially human rights promotion and verification. Despite the persistent political stalemate, and with a limited staff of 40 observers from each organization, MICIVIH documented and helped redress the most serious shortcomings of the dysfunctional justice and penal systems although its calls for corrective action went unheeded. Awaiting progress on judicial reform, the mission focused its human rights training programmes increasingly on the police, prison system and judiciary.[379]

[373] US Department of State, Bureau of Inter-American Affairs, 'Background Notes: Ecuador', Nov. 1998, at URL <http://www.tradeport.org/ts/countries/ecuador/bnotes.shtml>; 'Drawing back from the brink', *Latin American Weekly Report* (18 Aug. 1998), p. 377; and Information from the US Embassy in Lima, Peru, 2 Feb. 1999.

[374] *El Comercio* (Quito), 16 Nov. 1998, in 'Peru: MOMEP Official: Plan to remove mines from border ready', FBIS-LAT-98-320, 17 Nov. 1998; and Bender, B., 'Ecuador–Peru peace plan progresses', *Jane's Defence Weekly*, vol. 30, no. 23 (9 Dec. 1998).

[375] *El Universo* (Guayaquil), 16 Dec. 1998, in 'Ecuador: Peru denies planted mines along Ecuadorian border', FBIS-LAT-98-350, 17 Dec. 1998; and 'Transcript: Cohen laudes success of Peru-Ecuador peace process', USIS, *Washington File* (US Embassy: Stockholm, 2 Dec. 1998).

[376] OAS, Office of Summit Follow-up, 'Plan of Action of the Second Summit of the Americas', Santiago de Chile, Chile, 18–19 Apr. 1998.

[377] 'Argentina has launched regional humanitarian assistance fund', OAS News Release, 19 May 1998; and 'At 56, Inter-American Defense Board, world's oldest regional security organization reviews its contribution', OAS News Release, 31 Mar. 1998.

[378] 'OAS peace-building forum opens in Washington', OAS News Release, 20 Oct. 1998; and 'Peru invites OAS to monitor October polls', OAS New Release, 19 May 1998.

[379] UN, The situation of democracy and human rights in Haiti, Report of the Secretary-General, UN document A/53/564, 18 Nov. 1998. The UN General Assembly extended the MICIVIH mandate until 31 Dec. 1999. UN, Press Release GA/9529, 8 Dec. 1998.

Asia

The last outsider of the 10 countries of the region, Cambodia failed again in 1998 to gain admission into Asia's principal regional organization, the *Association of South-East Asian Nations* (ASEAN). Modifying its long-standing policy of non-interference in 'internal affairs', ASEAN formed a task force to press for free elections after Second Prime Minister Hun Sen had ousted his power-sharing First Prime Minister Prince Norodom Ranariddh in 1997.[380] Having rebuffed ASEAN offers to mediate, Hun Sen agreed to a Japanese peace plan under international pressure and a ceasefire in February with forces loyal to the prince.[381] However, Prince Ranariddh's return after complicated arrangements in April failed to stabilize the conduct of the campaign leading up to the first elections since 1993, marred as it was by political violence, extra-judicial killings and intimidation, or to guarantee the opposition representation on the election administration.[382] The July election results, which fell just short of giving the opposition a majority in the National Assembly and failed to allow Hun Sen to govern alone, were quickly denounced for fraud by the main opposition parties.[383] Their leaders' four-month flight from a government crackdown ended when King Norodom Sihanouk brokered a settlement whereby Hun Sen remained sole prime minister and the prince entered a coalition government as President of the National Assembly.[384] The UN subsequently let Cambodia take up its seat in the General Assembly after a 15-month absence, but ASEAN, struggling with the regional economic crisis, remained deeply divided in its attitude towards the new government. Hun Sen's position was further strengthened by the surrender in December of the last main fighting force of the Khmer Rouge; the notorious Pol Pot had died in April of seemingly natural causes.[385] Although the government had shown little interest in prosecuting the former offenders, the UN sent an expert team to assess the prospects of creating an effective international tribunal—on

[380] Eng, P., 'Cambodian democracy: In a bleak landscape, strong signs of hope', *Washington Quarterly*, vol. 21, no. 3 (summer 1998), pp. 71–91.

[381] 'Cambodia: foul and unfair?', *The Economist*, vol. 346, no. 8053 (31 Jan. 1998); and 'The trial of Cambodia's prince', *The Economist*, vol. 346, no. 8058 (7 Mar. 1998).

[382] Sanderson, J. and Maley, M., 'Elections and liberal democracy in Cambodia', *Australian Journal of International Affairs*, vol. 52, no. 3 (1998), pp. 241–53.

[383] Some 15 000 Cambodian and 700 international observers monitored the polling process. US Department of State, Testimony by Ralph A. Boyce, Deputy Assistant Secretary for East Asian and Pacific Affairs, before the House International Relations Committee, Subcommittee on Asia and the Pacific, Washington DC, 28 Sep. 1998; and 'Cambodia: unhappy returns', *The Economist*, vol. 349, no. 8088 (3 Oct. 1998).

[384] 'Cambodia: royal assent', *The Economist*, vol. 349, no. 8095 (21 Nov. 1998); 'Trouble in Cambodia', *International Herald Tribune*, 12 Sep. 1998; and Thayer, N., 'State of fear', *Far Eastern Economic Review*, vol. 161, no. 41 (8 Oct. 1998), pp. 28–29.

[385] Thayer, N., 'Nowhere to hide', *Far Eastern Economic Review*, vol. 161, no. 17 (23 Apr. 1998), pp. 12–14, and 'Dying breath', *Far Eastern Economic Review*, vol. 161, no. 18 (30 Apr. 1998), pp. 18–21.

which the Chinese position was non-committal—to scrutinize the brutal 1975–79 Khmer Rouge rule over Cambodia.[386]

A regionally monitored peace accord was achieved in the south Pacific when talks facilitated by New Zealand brought an end to nine years of secessionist fighting on the Papua New Guinea island province of Bougainville. On 23 January the warring parties signed the Lincoln Agreement on Peace, Security and Development on Bougainville, which provided for the phased withdrawal of government forces, amnesty for the secessionists, provincial elections, and the deployment of a regional Peace Monitoring Group (PMG) to monitor compliance with a permanent ceasefire.[387] This came into effect with the signing at Arawa, Papua New Guinea, of an Agreement Covering Implementation of the Ceasefire on 30 April, when the Australian-led PMG replaced the Truce Monitoring Group deployed since December 1997 under New Zealand command.[388] The same four countries—Australia, Fiji, New Zealand and Vanuatu—provided civilian and military personnel to the 300-strong unarmed force. The largest contributor, with 240 personnel, Australia also took the lead in assisting in rebuilding the province.[389] Together with New Zealand it provided trainers for an auxiliary police training programme to address public security problems on Bougainville.[390]

VI. Conclusions

The main successes in armed conflict prevention, management and resolution in 1998 were the new peace accords in Northern Ireland, in Papua New Guinea, and between Ecuador and Peru as well as the steady implementation of previous settlements in the Central African Republic, Eastern Slavonia and Guatemala. Peace implementation by the UN and regional organizations was slower and more precarious in Bosnia and Herzegovina and Haiti; beset with security problems in Georgia, Sierra Leone and Tajikistan; and beyond repair in Angola. Both new and previously unresolved conflicts in Africa, the Balkans and Iraq proved challenging for international organizations.

While the UN and regional bodies lamented the dearth of effective means, political will and adequate funding for conflict prevention, one promising development was the rapid proliferation of human rights field operations by the OHCHR. Although no substitute for a comprehensive early-warning

[386] Thayer, N., 'End of story?', *Far Eastern Economic Review*, vol. 161, no. 51 (17 Dec. 1998), pp. 23–24; and Seper, C., 'Can the Khmer Rouge be tried?', *International Herald Tribune*, 12 Nov. 1998.

[387] UN, Letter dated 31 Mar. 1998 from the representative of Papua New Guinea addressed to the President of the Security Council, UN document S/1998/287, 31 Mar. 1998.

[388] UN, Letter dated 2 June from the Secretary-General addressed to the President of the Security Council, UN document S/1998/506, 15 June 1999; and Regan, A., 'Bougainville—a new spirit and a new deal?', *The Courier*, no. 171 (Sep./Oct. 1998), pp. 24–27.

[389] 'Australia to command Peace Monitoring Group on Bougainville', Australian Department of Foreign Affairs and Trade, Joint Media Release FA 53, 30 Apr. 1998; and Young, P., 'Exclusive interview: The New Zealand Minister of Defence The Honourable Max Bradford', *Asian Defence Journal*, Aug. 1998, p. 19.

[390] *Foreign Affairs and Trade Record*, vol. 2, no. 4 (Dec. 1998), p. 12.

mechanism, such missions could nonetheless alert the UN to incipient conflicts as well as consolidate post-conflict peace building. The development of international humanitarian law through the growing jurisprudence of the ad hoc international tribunals, to be joined by a permanent International Criminal Court, served the same dual function in the long term.

The UN remained central to integrated conflict prevention, management and resolution efforts, but its load was lightened by regional bodies that undertook many demanding operations. The two new peacekeeping initiatives, in the Central African Republic and Sierra Leone, built on previous subregional attempts to stabilize the conflicts. Ironically, and even as reform of peacekeeping procedures continued, the organization was in danger of losing the hard-won lessons it had learned from previous operations by dismantling the capacity accumulated at the DPKO. Diminished credibility was likely to hamper the UN's ability to give conflicting parties the benefit of its 50 years of peacekeeping experience.

The trend towards greater operational regionalization had various implications, some better addressed than others. The UN, the regions and individual states continued to focus attention on building institutional and professional capacity for conflict management, particularly on the war-torn African continent, although developing the appropriate organizational culture, training for interoperability and raising sufficient resources were a slow process. The need for collective and comprehensive responses to crises was another lesson the reformed UN was attempting to integrate by developing its peace-building tools, increasing coordination among its departments and programmes, and starting up liaison arrangements with regional bodies. The UN and European organizations had trimmed their skills in integrated peace implementation in the Bosnian 'laboratory', and a new level of operational cooperation was thrust upon NATO and the OSCE in Kosovo. However, the increase in the activities of regional bodies, while indispensable as partners to the UN, also posed a challenge to its authority in the absence of agreed oversight procedures to ensure that their action in furtherance of peace and security conforms to common standards.

The first post-cold war decade was drawing to a close on a note of uncertainty about the effective primacy of the Security Council, eroded from within by more pronounced dissension among its permanent members. Its failure to agree on a common policy against Serb repression in Kosovo or Iraqi non-compliance with its dictates prompted not only unilateral action by the most powerful Western states but also a united pronouncement from NATO members that ethnic cleansing in Europe would not be tolerated. If the Security Council, the body with primary responsibility for international peace and security, is to ensure that it is not circumvented, it needs to reclaim its authority so as not to deprive some of the most acute conflicts, such as the regional entanglement in the Great Lakes Region, of the attention they deserve.

Appendix 2A. Multilateral peace missions, 1998

JOHAN SJÖBERG

Table 2A lists the multilateral observer, peacekeeping, peace-building and combined peacekeeping and peace-enforcement missions initiated, continuing or terminated in 1998, by international organization and by starting date. Six groups of mission are presented. The 21 run by the United Nations are divided into two sections: UN peacekeeping operations (18) are those so designated by the UN itself, although they may include some missions more properly described as observer missions; the other 3 UN operations comprise missions not officially described by the UN as peacekeeping operations (2 of these are operated in cooperation with the Organization of American States, OAS). Of the remaining missions, 14 are run by the Organization for Security and Co-operation in Europe (OSCE), 4 by the Commonwealth of Independent States (CIS)/Russia (2 by the CIS and 2 in accordance with special arrangements with Russia as the main peacekeeping force contributer), 3 by the Economic Community of West African States (ECOWAS) Monitoring Group (ECOMOG), and 15 by other organizations or ad hoc groups of states. Peace missions comprising individual negotiators or teams of negotiators not resident in the mission area or subregional operations with a vague mandate, such as the interventions in the Democratic Republic of Congo and Lesotho by members of the Southern African Development Community (SADC), are not included.

Legal instruments underlying the establishment of an operation, such as relevant resolutions of the UN Security Council, are cited in the first column.

The names of missions that ended in 1998 and of individual countries and organizations that ended their participation in 1998 are italicized, while new missions and individual countries and organizations participating for the first time in 1998 are listed in bold text. Numbers of civilian observers and international and local civilian staff are not included.

Mission fatalities are recorded from the beginning of the mission until the last reported date for 1998 ('to date'), and as a total for the year ('in 1998'). Information on the approximate or estimated annual cost of the missions ('yearly') and the approximate outstanding contributions ('unpaid') to the operation fund at the close of the 1998 budget period (the date of which varies from operation to operation) is given in millions of current dollars. In the case of UN missions, unless otherwise noted, UN data on contributing countries and on numbers of troops, military observers and civilian police as well as on fatalities and costs are as of 31 December 1998. UN data on total mission fatalities ('to date') are for all UN missions since 1948.

Figures on the number of personnel in/for OSCE missions are totals for each mission, and include both military and civilian staff in 1998.

Table 2A. Multilateral peace missions

Acronym/ (Legal instrument[a])	Name/type of mission[b]	Location	Start date	Countries contributing troops, military observers (mil. obs) and/or civilian police (CivPol) in 1998	Troops/ Mil. obs/ CivPol	Deaths: To date In 1998	Cost: Yearly Unpaid
United Nations (UN) peacekeeping operations[1] (18 operations) (UN Charter, Chapters VI and VII)					10 708[2] 921 2 718	1 580[3] 31	890.2[4] 1 593[5]
UNTSO (SCR 50)[6]	UN Truce Supervision Organization (O)	Egypt/Israel/ Lebanon/Syria	June 1948	Argentina, Australia, Austria, Belgium, Canada, Chile, China, Denmark, Estonia, Finland, France, Ireland, Italy, Netherlands, New Zealand, Norway, Russia, **Slovakia, Slovenia,** Sweden, Switzerland, USA	– 157 –	38 –	26.4[7] –
UNMOGIP (SCR 91)[8]	UN Military Observer Group in India and Pakistan (O)	India/Pakistan (Kashmir)	Jan. 1949	Belgium, Chile, Denmark, Finland, Italy, South Korea, Sweden, Uruguay[9]	– 45 –	9 –	7.8[10] –
UNFICYP (SCR 186)[11]	UN Peacekeeping Force in Cyprus (PK)	Cyprus	Mar. 1964	Argentina, Australia, Austria, Canada, Finland, Hungary, Ireland, **Netherlands,** Slovenia, UK	1 238 – 35	168 –	45.3[12] 16.5[13]
UNDOF (SCR 350)[14]	UN Disengagement Observer Force (O)	Syria (Golan Heights)	June 1974	Austria, Canada, Japan, Poland, **Slovakia**	1 053 –[15] –	39 –	35.4[16] 52.9[17]
UNIFIL (SCR 425, 426)[18]	UN Interim Force in Lebanon (PK)	Lebanon (Southern)	Mar. 1978	Fiji, Finland, France, Ghana, **India,** Ireland, Italy, Nepal, *Norway*, Poland[19]	4 528 – –	227 5	143[20] 112.9[21]
UNIKOM (SCR 689)[22]	UN Iraq–Kuwait Observation Mission (O)	Iraq/Kuwait (Khawr 'Abd Allah water-way and UN DMZ)[23]	Apr. 1991	Argentina, Austria, Bangladesh, Canada, China, Denmark, Fiji, Finland, France, Germany, Ghana, Greece, Hungary, India, Indonesia, Ireland, Italy, Kenya, Malaysia, Nigeria, Pakistan, Poland, Romania, Russia, Senegal, Singapore, Sweden, Thailand, Turkey, UK, USA, Uruguay, Venezuela	905 194 –	13 3	52.1[24] 14.8[25]
MINURSO (SCR 690)[26]	UN Mission for the Referendum in Western Sahara (O)	Western Sahara	Sep. 1991	Argentina, Austria, Bangladesh, Canada, China, Egypt, El Salvador, France, Ghana, *Greece*, Guinea, Honduras, India, Ireland, Italy, Kenya, Malaysia, Nigeria, **Norway,** Pakistan, Poland, Portugal, Russia, South Korea, *Sweden*, USA, Uruguay, **Venezuela**	183 202 26	9 2	58.9[27] 64.7[28]

UNOMIG (SCR 849, 858)[29]	UN Observer Mission in Georgia (O)	Georgia (Abkhazia)	Aug. 1993	*Albania*, Austria, Bangladesh, Czech Rep., Denmark, Egypt, France, Germany, Greece, Hungary, Indonesia, Jordan, South Korea, Pakistan, Poland, Russia, Sweden, Switzerland, Turkey, UK, USA, Uruguay	– 100 –	3 –	19.4[30] 8.4[31]
UNMOT (SCR 968)[32]	UN Mission of Observers in Tajikistan (O)	Tajikistan	Dec. 1994	Austria, Bangladesh, Bulgaria, **Czech Rep.**, Denmark, Ghana, Indonesia, Jordan, **Nepal**, Nigeria, Poland, *Switzerland*, Ukraine, Uruguay	– 31 2	7 6	20[33] 9.2[34]
UNPREDEP (SCR 983)[35]	UN Preventive Deployment Force (PK)	Macedonia	Mar. 1995	Argentina, Bangladesh, Belgium, Brazil, Canada, Czech Rep., Denmark, Egypt, Finland, Ghana, Indonesia, Ireland, Jordan, Kenya, Nepal, New Zealand, Nigeria, Norway, Pakistan, Poland, Portugal, Russia, Sweden, Switzerland, Turkey, Ukraine, USA	846 35 25	4 –	50.1[36] 20.3[37]
UNMIBH (SCR 1035)[38]	UN Mission in Bosnia and Herzegovina (CP)	Bosnia and Herzegovina	Dec. 1995	Argentina, Austria, Bangladesh, Bulgaria, Canada, Chile, Denmark, Egypt, Estonia, **Fiji,** Finland, France, Germany, Ghana, Greece, Hungary, Iceland, India, Indonesia, Ireland, Italy, Jordan, **Kenya, Lithuania,** Malaysia, Nepal, Netherlands, Nigeria, Norway, Pakistan, Poland, Portugal, **Romania,** Russia, Senegal, Spain, Sweden, Switzerland, Thailand, Tunisia, Turkey, UK, Ukraine, USA	3 – 1 982	6 2	189.5[39] –
UNTAES (SCR 1037)[40]	*UN Transitional Administration for Eastern Slavonia, Baranja and Western Sirmium (PK)*	*Croatia*	*Jan. 1996*	*Argentina, Austria, Bangladesh, Belgium, Brazil, Czech Rep., Denmark, Egypt, Fiji, Finland, Ghana, Indonesia, Ireland, Jordan, Kenya, Lithuania, Nepal, New Zealand, Nigeria, Norway, Pakistan, Poland, Russia, Slovakia, Sweden, Switzerland, Tunisia, Ukraine, USA*	86[41] – 223	11 1	23[42] –
UNMOP (SCR 1038)[43]	UN Mission of Observers in Prevlaka (O)	Croatia	Jan. 1996	Argentina, Bangladesh, Belgium, *Brazil*, Canada, Czech Rep., Denmark, Egypt, Finland, Ghana, Indonesia, Ireland, Jordan, Kenya, Nepal, New Zealand, Nigeria, Norway, Pakistan, Poland, *Portugal*, Russia, Sweden, Switzerland, Ukraine	– 26 –	– –	–[44] –
MONUA (SCR 1118)[45]	UN Observer Mission in Angola[46] (O)	Angola	July 1997	**Argentina,** Bangladesh, Brazil, Bulgaria, Congo, Egypt, France, **Gambia, Ghana,** Guinea-Bissau, Hungary, India, Jordan, Kenya, Malaysia, Mali, Namibia, New Zealand, Nigeria, Norway, Pakistan, Poland, Portugal, Romania, Russia, Senegal, Slovakia, **Spain,** Sweden, Tanzania, Ukraine, Uruguay, Zambia, Zimbabwe	590 90 337	14[47] 9	130.8[48] 101.2[49]

Acronym/ (Legal instrument[a])	Name/type of mission[b]	Location	Start date	Countries contributing troops, military observers (mil. obs) and/or civilian police (CivPol) in 1998	Troops/ Mil. obs/ CivPol	Deaths: To date In 1998	Cost: Yearly Unpaid
MIPONUH (SCR 1141)[50]	UN Civilian Police Mission in Haiti[51] (CP)	Haiti	Nov. 1997	Argentina, Benin, Canada, France, India, Mali, Niger, Senegal, Togo, Tunisia, USA	– – 284	– –	29.9[52] 17.9[53]
UNPSG (SCR 1145)[54]	***United Nations Police Support Group (CP)***	***Croatia***	***Jan. 1998***	***Argentina, Austria, Denmark, Egypt, Fiji, Finland, Indonesia, Ireland, Jordan, Kenya, Lithuania, Nepal, Nigeria, Norway, Poland, Russia, Sweden, Switzerland, Tunisia, Ukraine, USA***	– – 114[55]	1 1	7.5[56] –
MINURCA (SCR 1159)[57]	**UN Mission in the Central African Republic (PK)**	**Central African Republic**	**Apr. 1998**	**Benin, Burkina Faso, Canada, Chad, Côte d'Ivoire, Egypt, France, Gabon, Mali, Portugal, Senegal, Togo, Tunisia**	1 347[58] – 22	2 2	29.1[59] –
UNOMSIL (SCR 1181)[60]	**UN Observer Mission in Sierra Leone (O)**	**Sierra Leone**	**July 1998**	**China, Egypt, India, Kenya, Kyrgyzstan, Lithuania, Namibia, New Zealand, Norway, Pakistan, Russia,** ***Sweden,*** **UK, Zambia**	15 41 5	– –	22[61] 12.5[62]
Other United Nations (UN) operations (3 operations)[63]							
MICIVIH (GAR 47/20B)[64]	International Civilian Mission to Haiti (O)	Haiti	Feb. 1993	Argentina, Barbados, **Brazil**, Canada, Colombia, Chile, El Salvador, Grenada, Jamaica, Mexico, Nicaragua, Paraguay, Peru, Saint Lucia, Trinidad and Tobago, USA[65]	– 80[66] –	– –	10.4[67] . .
UNSMA (GAR 48/208)[68]	UN Special Mission to Afghanistan	Afghanistan/ Pakistan	Mar. 1994	China, France, Ghana, Ireland, Italy, Japan, Jordan, Malaysia, Russia, Uganda, UK, USA[69]	– 6[70] –	1 1[71]	4[72] . .
MINUGUA (GAR 48/267)[73]	UN Verification Mission in Guatemala	Guatemala	Oct. 1994	Argentina, Brazil, Canada, Colombia, **El Salvador,** Italy, **Norway, Portugal,** Spain, Sweden, Uruguay, Venezuela[74]	– 20[75] 51	7 7[76]	31.5[77] . .
Organization for Security and Co-operation in Europe (OSCE) (14 operations)[78]							
– (CSO 18 Sep. 1992)[79]	OSCE Spillover Mission to Skopje (O)	Former Yugoslav Rep. of Macedonia	Sep. 1992	Germany, Italy, Norway, Slovakia, Sweden, UK, USA	– 7[80] –	– –	0.4[81] . .

– (CSO 6 Nov. 1992)[82]	OSCE Mission to Georgia (O)	Georgia (S. Ossetia; Abkhazia)[83]	Dec. 1992	Bulgaria, Czech Rep., Denmark, France, Germany, Hungary, Ireland, Moldova, Norway, Poland, Slovakia, Spain, Sweden, Switzerland, Ukraine, USA	– 22[84] –	1 –	1.7[85] . .
– (CSO 13 Dec. 1992)[86]	OSCE Mission to Estonia (O)	Estonia	Feb. 1993	Denmark, Finland, Germany, Sweden	– 4[87] –	– –	0.5[88] . .
– (CSO 4 Feb. 1993)[89]	OSCE Mission to Moldova (O)	Moldova	Apr. 1993	France, Germany, Netherlands, Poland, Slovakia, USA	– 6[90] –	– –	0.5[91] . .
– (CSO 23 Sep. 1993)[92]	OSCE Mission to Latvia (O)	Latvia	Nov. 1993	France, Germany, Norway, Poland, UK	– 5[93] –	– –	0.6[94] . .
– (1 Dec. 1993)[95]	OSCE Mission to Tajikistan (O)	Tajikistan	Feb. 1994	Austria, Bulgaria, France, Norway, Romania, Russia	– 9[96] –	– –	1.1[97] . .
– (CSO 15 June 1994)[98]	OSCE Mission to Ukraine (O)	Ukraine	Nov. 1994	Finland, Georgia, USA	– 3[99] –	– –	0.5[100] . .
– (11 Apr. 1995)[101]	OSCE Assistance Group to Chechnya (O)	Chechnya	Apr. 1995	Czech Rep., Moldova, Norway, Poland, Romania	– 5[102] –	– –	1.6[103] . .
– (10 Aug. 1995)[104]	The Personal Representative of the Chairman-in-Office on the Conflict Dealt with by the OSCE Minsk Conference (O)	Azerbaijan (Nagorno-Karabakh)[105]	Aug. 1995	Czech Rep., Germany, Hungary, Poland, Ukraine	– 5[106] –	– –	0.7[107] . .
– (8 Dec. 1995)[108]	OSCE Mission to Bosnia and Herzegovina (O)	Bosnia and Herzegovina[109]	Dec. 1995	Austria, Belarus, Belgium, Bulgaria, Canada, Czech Rep., Denmark, Finland, France, Georgia, Germany, Greece, Hungary, Ireland, Italy, Netherlands, Norway, Poland, Portugal, Romania, Russia, Spain, Sweden, Switzerland, Turkey, Ukraine, UK, USA	– 170[110] –	– –	27.2[111] . .

Acronym/ (Legal instrument[a])	Name/type of mission[b]	Location	Start date	Countries contributing troops, military observers (mil. obs) and/or civilian police (CivPol) in 1998	Troops/ Mil. obs/ CivPol	Deaths: To date In 1998	Cost: Yearly Unpaid
– (18 Apr. 1996)[112]	OSCE Mission to Croatia (CP, O)	Croatia	July 1996	Armenia, Austria, Belarus, Belgium, Bulgaria, Canada, Czech Rep., Denmark, Finland, Former Yugoslav Republic of Macedonia, France, Georgia, Germany, Greece, Ireland, Italy, Japan, Lithuania, Netherlands, Norway, Poland, Portugal, Romania, Russia, Spain, Sweden, Switzerland, Turkey, Ukraine, UK, USA	– 258[113] –	– –	22.5[114] . .
– (27 Mar. 1997)[115]	OSCE Presence in Albania (O)	Albania	Apr. 1997	Austria, Bulgaria, Georgia, Germany, Ireland, Italy, Lithuania, Netherlands, Norway, Poland, Sweden, Switzerland, UK, USA	– 27[116] –	– –	1.6[117] . .
– **(18 Sep. 1997)**[118]	**OSCE Advisory and Monitoring Group in Belarus (O)**	**Belarus**	**Feb. 1998**	**France, Germany, Moldova, Switzerland, USA**	– 5[119] –	– –	0.8[120] . .
– **(15 Oct. 1998)**[121]	**Kosovo Verification Mission (O)**	**Former Republic of Yugoslavia (Kosovo)**[122]	**Oct. 1998**	**Belgium, Canada, Denmark, Finland, France, Germany, Greece, Hungary, Italy, Kazakhstan, Lithuania, Norway, Poland, Romania, Russia, Sweden, Switzerland, Turkey, Ukraine, UK, USA**	– 745[123] –	– –	204[124] . .
CIS/Russia (4 operations)							
– (Bilateral agreement)[125]	'South Ossetia Joint Force' (PK)	Georgia (S. Ossetia)	July 1992	Georgia, Russia, North and South Ossetia[126]	1 236[127] – –	. . . .	. .[128] . .
– (Bilateral agreement)[129]	'Joint Control Commission Peace-keeping Force' (PK)	Moldova (Trans-Dniester)	July 1992	Moldova, Russia, 'Trans-Dniester Republic', **Ukraine**[130]	1 700[131] 10 –	. . 3[132]	. .[133] . .
– (CIS 24 Sep. 1993)[134]	CIS 'Collective Peacekeeping Force' (PK)	Tajikistan (Afghan border[135])	Aug. 1993	Kazakhstan, Kyrgyzstan, Russia, *Uzbekistan*[136]	8 000[137] – –	. .[138] . .	. .[139] . .
– (CIS 15 Apr. 1994)[140]	CIS 'Peacekeeping Forces in Georgia' (PK)	Georgian–Abkhazian border	June 1994	Russia	1 690[141] – –	57[142] 6[143]	. .[144] . .

ECOMOG (3 operations)							
ECOMOG (ESMC 7 Aug. 1990)[145]	ECOWAS[146] Monitoring Group (PK)	Liberia	Aug. 1990	*Benin*, *Burkina Faso*, *Côte d'Ivoire*, *Gambia*, *Ghana*, *Guinea*, *Mali*, *Niger*, Nigeria, *Sierra Leone*	800[147] – –	. . . .	. .[148] . .
ECOMOG (OAU mandate)[149]	ECOWAS Monitoring Group (PK)	Sierra Leone	May 1997	Ghana, Guinea, **Mali**, Nigeria[150]	14 000[151] – –	. . . .	. .[152] . .
ECOMOG (Abuja Agt 1998)[153]	**ECOWAS Ceasefire Monitoring Group in Guinea-Bissau (PK)**	**Guinea-Bissau**	**Dec. 1998**	**Togo**[154]	112[155] – –	. . . .	. .[156] . .
Other (15 operations)							
NNSC (Armistice Agreement)[157]	Neutral Nations Supervisory Commission (O)	North Korea/ South Korea	July 1953	Sweden, Switzerland[158]	– 10[159] –	– –	0.7[160] . .
MFO (Protocol to treaty)[161]	Multinational Force and Observers in the Sinai (O)	Egypt (Sinai)	Apr. 1982	Australia, Canada, Colombia, Fiji, France, Hungary, Italy, New Zealand, Norway, Uruguay, USA	1 896[162] – –	37 2[163]	51[164] . .
ECMM (Brioni Agreement)[165]	European Community Monitoring Mission (O)	Former Yugoslavia/ Albania	July 1991	Austria, Belgium, Denmark, Finland, France, Germany, Greece, Ireland, Italy, Luxembourg, Netherlands, Norway, Portugal, Slovakia, Spain, Sweden, UK	– 320[166] –	7 1[167]	20[168] . .
OMIB[169] (OAU 1993)	OAU Mission in Burundi (O)	Burundi	Dec. 1993	. .	– 3[170] –	1 –	2.4[171] . .
MOMEP (Decl. of Itamaraty)[172]	Mission of Military Observers Ecuador/ Peru (O)	Ecuador/Peru	Mar. 1995	Argentina, Brazil, Chile, Ecuador, Peru, USA[173]	– 34[174] –	– –	5[175] . .
SFOR (SCR 1088)[176]	NATO Stabilization Force (PK)	Bosnia and Herzegovina	Dec. 1996	Albania, Austria, Belgium, Bulgaria, Canada, Czech Rep., Denmark, Egypt, Estonia, Finland, France, Germany, Greece, Hungary, Iceland, Ireland, Italy, Jordan, Latvia, Lithuania, Luxembourg, Malaysia, Morocco, Netherlands, Norway, Poland, Portugal, Romania, Russia, Slovenia, Spain, Sweden, Turkey, UK, Ukraine, USA[177]	33 000[178] – –	600[179] 66[180]	. .[181] . .

Acronym/ (Legal instrument[a])	Name/type of mission[b]	Location	Start date	Countries contributing troops, military observers (mil. obs) and/or civilian police (CivPol) in 1998	Troops/ Mil. obs/ CivPol	Deaths: To date In 1998	Cost: Yearly Unpaid
TIPH 2 (Hebron Protocol)[182]	Temporary International Presence in Hebron (O)	Hebron	Jan. 1997[183]	Denmark, Italy, Norway, Sweden, Switzerland, Turkey	– 110[184] –	– –	2.3[185] . .
MISAB (S/1997/561, SCR1125)[186]	*Inter-African Mission to Monitor the Implementation of the Bangui Agreements*[187] *(PK)*	*Central African Republic*	*Feb. 1997*	*Burkina Faso, Chad, Gabon, Mali, Senegal, Togo*	800[188] – –	. .[189] . .	. .[190] . .
MAPE (authorized by WEU Council 2 May 1997)[191]	Multinational Advisory Police Element for Albania (CP)	Albania	May 1997	Bulgaria, Czech Rep., Denmark, Estonia, Finland, France, Germany, Greece, Hungary, Italy, Latvia, Lithuania, Luxembourg, Netherlands, Norway, Poland, Portugal, Romania, Slovenia, Spain, Sweden, Turkey, UK[192]	– – 87[193]	. . –	4.1[194] . .
OMIC (OAU 1997)[195]	OAU Observer Mission in the Comoros (O)	Comoros	Nov. 1997	Egypt, Nigeria, Senegal, Tunisia[196]	– 20 –	– –	. .[197] . .
TMG (Burnham Decl. 1997)[198]	*Bougainville Truce Monitoring Group (PK)*	*Papua New Guinea*	*Nov. 1997*	*Australia, Fiji, New Zealand, Vanuatu*[199]	328 – –	– –	. .[200] . .
PMG (Lincoln Agt 1998)[201]	**Bougainville Peace Monitoring Group (PK)**	**Papua New Guinea**	**May 1998**	**Australia, Fiji, New Zealand, Vanuatu**[202]	301[203] – –	– –	. .[204] . .
CPDTF (Edinburgh Summit, Oct. 1997)[205]	**Commonwealth Police Development Task Force (CP)**	**Sierra Leone**	**July 1998**[206]	**Canada, Sri Lanka, UK, Zimbabwe**[207]	– – 6[208]	– –	. .[209] . .
KDOM (Moscow Decl. 1998)[210]	***Kosovo Diplomatic Observer Mission (O)***	***Kosovo (FRY)***	***July 1998***	***European Union, Russia, USA***	– 400[211] –	– –	. .[212] . .
XFOR (SCR 1203)[213]	**NATO Extraction Force (PK)**	**Former Yugoslav Republic of Macedonia**	**Dec. 1998**	**France, Germany, Italy, Netherlands, UK**[214]	1 800[215] – –	– –	. .[216] . .

Notes for table 2A

[a] CSO = OSCE Committee of Senior Officials (now the Senior Council); GAR = UN General Assembly Resolution; PC.DEC = OSCE Permanent Council Decision; SCR = UN Security Council Resolution; UNGA = UN General Assembly; UNSC = UN Security Council

[b] O = observer; PK = peacekeeping; CP = civilian police

[1] Sources for this section, unless otherwise noted: UN, Department of Peacekeeping Operations, Monthly summary of troop contributions to peace-keeping operations; and UN Information Centre for the Nordic Countries, Copenhagen.

[2] As of 30 Nov. 1998. Operational strength varies from month to month because of rotation.

[3] Casualty figures are valid as of 31 Dec. 1998 and include military, civilian police and civilian international and local staff. The figures, from the UN Situation Centre, are based on information from the Peace-Keeping Data-Base covering the period July 1949–Dec. 1998, and hence include both completed and current missions. This database is still under review and there may be some errors or omissions.

[4] 16 of the 18 UN peacekeeping operations conducted or under way in 1998 are financed from their own separate accounts on the basis of assessments legally binding on all member states in accordance with Article 17 of the UN Charter. UNTSO and UNMOGIP are funded from the UN regular budget. Some missions are partly funded by voluntary contributions. Figures are annualized budget estimates in US$ m., but the period covered differs between missions. Specific funding details are noted in the footnotes.

[5] It has only been possible to present comparable information on the outstanding contributions for some missions. Thus the figures given in this column do not add up to the total figure of $1539 m. for all peacekeeping operations as of 31 Dec. 1998. UN, Status of outstanding contributions to the Regular Budget, International Tribunals and Peacekeeping Operations as at 31 Dec. 1998, UN Information Centre for the Nordic Countries, Copenhagen, 1999.

[6] UNTSO provided UNIFIL and UNDOF with military observers. Mandate maintained during 1998.

[7] Initial budget appropriation for 1998.

[8] After heavy shelling by Indian and Pakistani forces during summer 1998 there were requests for a stronger mandate for UNMOGIP (partly from Pakistan), but no decision was taken. Interview with Brig.-Gen. Sergio Hernán Espinosa Davies, UNMOGIP Chief Military Observer in Kashmir, *Jane's Defence Weekly*, 16 Sep. 1998, p. 32.

[9] In Mar. 1998 Sergio Hernán Espinosa Davies was appointed Chief Military Observer of UNMOGIP. He returned to Chile in the autumn when appointed Inspector General of the Chilean Army. In Sep.–Oct. allegations were directed against him of human rights violations in Chile under Pinochet's regime and he was replaced by Col Johansen of Denmark. The mandate was maintained during 1998. UN Press Release SG/A/675, BIO/3145, 11 Mar. 1998; Daily Press Briefing of Office of Spokesman for Secretary-General, 11 Nov. 1998; 'UN observer Chief leaves his post', *Hindustan Times*, 13 Nov. 1998; and Human Rights Watch Press Release, 9 Oct. 1998, URL <http://www.hrw.org/hrw/press98/oct/chile09.htm>.

[10] Initial budget appropriation for 1998.

[11] The mandate was extended twice: until 31 Dec. 1998 (SCR 1178, 29 June 1998) and 30 June 1999 (SCR 1217, 22 Dec. 1998). A new Civil Affairs Branch was established comprising both civilian and military personnel. UN, Report of the Secretary-General on the United Nations Operations in Cyprus, UN document S/1998/1149, 7 Dec. 1998.

[12] Appropriated amount for the period 1 July 1998–30 June 1999. This amount includes the voluntary contributions of one-third of the cost of the force, and the annual amount of $6.5 m. contributed by the Government of Greece. UN document S/1998/1149 (note 11).

[13] As at 30 Nov. 1998. For the period 16 June 1993–31 Dec. 1998. UN document S/1998/1149 (note 11).

[14] The mandate was extended 3 times: until 31 May 1998 (SCR 1139, 21 Nov. 1997), 30 Nov. (SCR 1169, 27 May 1998) and 31 May 1999 (SCR 1211, 25 Nov. 1998).

[15] During 1998 UNTSO provided UNDOF with *c.* 80 military observers. UN, Report of the Secretary-General on the United Nations Disengagement Observer Force, UN document S/1998/1073, 14 Nov. 1998.

[16] Appropriated amount for the period 1 July 1998–30 June 1999. UN document S/1998/1073 (note 15).

[17] As at 5 Nov. 1998 for the period from the establishment of the force to 30 Nov. 1998. UN document S/1998/1073 (note 15).

[18] During 1998 the mandate was extended twice: until 31 July (SCR 1151, 30 Jan. 1998) and until 31 Jan. 1999 (SCR 1188, 30 July 1998).

[19] After having provided UNIFIL with troops for more than 20 years the Norwegian unit was replaced by an Indian battalion in late Nov. 1998. UN, Report of the Secretary-General on the United Nations Interim Force in Lebanon, UN document S/1999/61, 19 Jan. 1999.

[20] Appropriated amount for the period 1 July 1998–30 June 1999. UN document S/1999/61 (note 19).

[21] As at 31 Dec. 1998. For the period from the inception of the force to 31 Jan. 1999. UN document S/1999/61 (note 19).

[22] The mandate was maintained during 1998.

[23] Demilitarized zone (DMZ).

[24] Appropriated amount for the period 1 July 1998–30 June 1999. Two-thirds of the cost of the mission, equivalent to $33.5 m., is funded through voluntary contributions from the Kuwaiti Government. UN, Report of the Secretary-General on the United Nations Iraq–Kuwait Mission, UN document S/1998/889, 24 Sep. 1998.

[25] As at 22 Sep. 1998. For the period from the start of the mission through 31 Oct. 1998. UN document S/1998/889 (note 24).

[26] On 26 Jan. 1998 the UNSC approved the deployment of additional units to MINURSO for demining activities (SCR 1148, 26 Jan. 1998). The mandate was extended 5 times in 1998: until 20 July (SCR 1163, 17 Apr. 1998), 21 Sep. (SCR 1185, 20 July 1998), 31 Oct. (SCR 1198, 18 Sep. 1998), 17 Dec. (SCR 1204, 30 Oct. 1998), and finally until 31 Jan. 1999 (SCR 1215, 17 Dec. 1998).

[27] Appropriated amount for the period 1 July 1998–30 June 1999. In June the UNGA appropriated $21.6 m. for the period 1 July–31 Oct. 1998. In Nov. an additional $37.3 m. was appropriated for 1 Nov. 1998–30 June 1999. UN, Report of Secretary-General on the situation concerning Western Sahara, UN document S/1998/997, 26 Oct. 1998; and UN, Report of the Secretary-General on the situation concerning Western Sahara, UN document S/1998/1160, 11 Dec. 1998.

[28] As at 8 Dec. 1998. For the period from the start of the mission to 8 Dec. 1998. UN document S/1998/1160 (note 27).

[29] During 1998 the security situation did not improve. After a hostage-taking incident in Feb. all operational patrolling by UNOMIG was suspended, making it difficult to implement the mandate. In May the situation deteriorated with open hostilities but it improved by the end of the month. A ceasefire agreement was signed and a special group composed of representatives of the parties, UNOMIG and the CIS was established to monitor the ceasefire and thus UNOMIG resumed limited patrolling. A helicopter was assigned to the mission in June and in Nov. additional armoured vehicles arrived, enhancing the personal security of the mission staff. In Aug. a joint Investigation Group was established composed of representatives from the parties, UNOMIG and the CIS to investigate different criminal acts and violations of the agreements. On 25 Nov. the UNSC authorized an increase of UNOMIG's security contingent for the protection of the mission members as proposed by the Secretary-General. UN Press Release SC/6602, 1998; and UN, Reports of the Secretary-General concerning the situation in Abkhazia, Georgia, UN documents S/1998/647, 14 July 1998; S/1998/375, 11 May 1998; S/1998/497, 10 June 1998; and S/1998/1012, 29 Oct. 1998. The mandate was extended twice: until 31 July 1998 (SCR 1150, 30 Jan. 1998) and 31 Jan. 1999 (SCR 1187, 30 July 1998).

[30] Appropriated amount for the period 1 July 1998–30 June 1999. In addition, the Secretary-General obtained a commitment authorization from the Advisory Committee on Administrative and Budgetary Questions in the amount of $1.5 m. for the strengthening of the internal security of UNOMIG. UN, Report of the Secretary-General concerning the situation in Abkhazia, Georgia, UN document, S/1999/60, 20 Jan. 1999.

[31] As at 31 Dec. 1998. For the period from the start of the mission until 31 Dec. 1998. UN document, S/1999/60 (note 30).

[32] During 1998 UNMOT continued to assist in the implementation of the General Agreement on the Establishment of Peace and National Accord in Tajikistan, signed on 27 June 1997, and to fulfil its other obligations according to the initial mandate. However, as a consequence of the killing of 4 UN personnel in July, the UN suspended all its field activities for the remainder of 1998. On 12 Nov. 1998 the mandate was extended until 15 May 1999 (SCR 1206, 12 Nov. 1998).

[33] Appropriated amount for the period 1 July 1998–30 June 1999. GAR 53/19, 2 Nov. 1998.

[34] As at 15 Oct. 1998. For the period from the start of the mission to 31 Oct. 1998. UN document S/1998/1029 (note 32).

[35] The phased reduction of the force to 750 was completed in June pending the intended termination of the mission on 31 Aug. pursuant to SCR 1142 (4 Dec. 1997). UN, Report of the Secretary-General on the United Nations Preventive Deployment Force pursuant to Security Council Resolution 1142 (1997), UN document S/1998/454, 1 June 1998. However, because of continuing hostilities in Kosovo UNPREDEP had been given additional tasks, such as monitoring and reporting on illicit arms transfers in

accordance with sanctions imposed in Mar. 1998 (SCR 1160, 31 Mar. 1998). UN, Report of the Secretary-General on the United Nations Preventive Deployment Force, UN document S/1998/644, 14 July 1998. Pursuant to the Secretary-General's recommendations the UNSC extended the mandate until 28 Feb. 1999 and increased the troop strength to 1050 (SCR 1186, 21 July 1998).

[36] Appropriated amount for the period 1 July 1998–30 June 1999. UN, Report of the Secretary-General on the United Nations Preventive Deployment Force Pursuant to Security Council Resolution 1186 (1998), UN document S/1999/161, 12 Feb. 1999. The assessment of $16.7 m. for 1 Mar.–30 June 1999 was subject to the decision of the UNSC to extend the mandate of the force. However, on 25 Feb. the UNSC decided not to extend the mandate beyond 28 Feb. 1999. UN, Security Council Press Release SC/6648, 25 Feb. 1999.

[37] As at 31 Jan. 1999. For the period from the start of the mission to 31 Jan. 1999. UN document S/1999/161 (note 36).

[38] The International Police Task Force (IPTF) was authorized in accordance with Annex 11 of the 1995 General Framework Agreement for Peace in Bosnia and Herzegovina (the Dayton Agreement) (SCR 1035, 21 Dec. 1995), together with a civilian mission as proposed by the Secretary-General in Dec. 1995. UN, Report of the Secretary-General on Former Yugoslavia, UN document S/1995/1031, 13 Dec. 1995. The mission was later given the name UNMIBH. UN, Further report of the Secretary-General pursuant to Security Council resolutions 1025 (30 Nov. 1995) and 1026 (1995), UN document S/1996/83, 6 Feb. 1996. The mandate was extended until 21 June 1998 (SCR 1144, 19 Dec. 1997) and until 21 June 1999 (SCR 1174, 15 June 1998). Pursuant to SCR 1168 (21 May 1998) the authorized strength of IPTF was increased to 2057 police monitors. The UNMIBH mandate was expanded to include the establishment of a monitoring and evaluating programme for the court system in Bosnia and Herzegovina (SCR 1184, 16 July 1998). UN, Report of Secretary-General on the United Nations Mission in Bosnia and Herzegovina, UN document S/1998/1174, 16 Dec. 1998.

[39] Appropriated amount for the period 1 July 1998–30 June 1999. Covers the maintenance of UNMIBH, UNMOP, as well as central support services to the operations in the former Yugoslavia, and the United Nations liaison offices in Belgrade and Zagreb. GAR 52/243, 30 July 1998.

[40] The mandate of UNTAES was extended for a final period ending 15 Jan. 1998 (SCR 1120, 14 July 1997). The establishment of a United Nations Police Support Group (UNPSG) was later authorized (SCR 1145, 19 Dec. 1997). See UNPSG (note 54).

[41] Strength as of 28 Feb. 1998. A 2-phase exit strategy allowed the progressive reduction of UNTAES personnel and resources. Complete withdrawal was expected not later than 31 May 1998. UN, Report of the Secretary-General on the United Nations Transitional Administration for Eastern Slavonia, Baranja and Western Sirmium, UN document S/1998/59, 22 Jan. 1998.

[42] Appropriated amount for the liquidation of UNTAES and the maintenance of UNPSG for the period 16 Jan.–30 June 1998. GAR 52/244, 26 June 1998.

[43] During 1998 the mandate was extended twice: until 15 July 1998 (SCR 1147, 13 Jan. 1998) and until 15 Jan. 1999 (SCR 1183, 15 July 1998). For the first time Croatia allowed UNMOP foot patrols in Dec. 1998 in former restricted areas in the demilitarized zone. UN, Report of the Secretary-General on the United Nations Mission of Observers in Prevlaka, UN document S/1999/16, 6 Jan. 1999.

[44] Cost included in UNMIBH (note 39).

[45] MONUA was authorized as a follow-on mission to UNAVEM III for an initial 4-month period (SCR 1118, 30 June 1997), later extended until 30 Jan. 1998 (SCR 1135, 29 Oct. 1997). Due to be completed by 1 Feb. 1998, the mission mandate was extended until 30 Apr. (SCR 1149, 27 Jan. 1998). The UNSC also authorized the resumption of a gradual decrease of MONUA personnel and an increase in the number of civilian police observers (SCR 1157, 20 Mar. 1998). The mandate was then extended until 30 June (SCR 1164, 29 Apr. 1998), and the UNSC endorsed the Secretary-General's recommendation to withdraw all but a small contingent of troops and observers by the end of June while deploying an additional 83 civilian police observers. For a short period the UNSC requested the Secretary-General to temporarily redeploy the personnel to provide assistance in the extension of state administration throughout the country (SCR 1173, 12 June 1998), but following a deterioration in the security situation a decision was taken to resume the withdrawal. In addition the Secretary-General was requested to reconsider the deployment of civilian police observers (SCR 1180, 29 June 1998). In Sep. the Secretary-General authorized MONUA to 'adjust its deployment as needed, to ensure the safety and security of MONUA personnel' (SCR 1195, 15 Sep. 1998). During June–Dec. the mandate was extended 5 times, most recently until 26 Feb. 1999 (SCR 1213, 3 Dec. 1998). In Dec. all MONUA personnel were withdrawn to safer areas and in early/mid-Jan. 1999 their deployment and rotation were stopped. UN, Report of the Secretary-General on the United Nations Observer Mission in Angola (MONUA),

UN document S/1999/49, 17 Jan. 1999.

[46] MONUA (Missao de Observação das Nações Unidas em Angola, in Portuguese).

[47] In addition, on 26 Dec. 1998 a UN aircraft was shot down; 1 military observer, 2 police observers and 2 soldiers were missing. 2 more soldiers have been missing since a second aircraft crashed on 2 Jan. 1999. UN document S/1999/49 (note 45).

[48] Appropriated amount for the period 1 July 1998–30 June 1999. UN document S/1999/49 (note 45).

[49] As at 31 Dec. 1998. Unpaid assessed contributions to MONUA and its predecessor UNAVEM. UN document S/1999/49 (note 45).

[50] SCR 1141 (28 Nov. 1997) authorized the establishment of MIPONUH as a follow-on mission to UNTMIH, for a single 12-month period ending 30 Nov. 1998. However, the Secretary-General reported that terminating the mandate in Nov. 1998 would 'jeopardize the very real achievements of the Haitian National Police and have a negative effect on the efforts of the country to reinforce its institutions'. He also suggested additional tasks for MIPONUH to reinforce and strengthen the training programme. UN, Report of the Secretary-General on the United Nations Civilian Police Mission in Haiti, UN document S/1998/1064, 11 Nov. 1998. On 15 Nov. the UNSC followed the recommendations and extended the mandate until 30 Nov. 1999 (SCR 1212, 15 Nov. 1998).

[51] MIPONUH (Mission de police civile des Nations Unies en Haïti, in French).

[52] Estimated budget for the period 1 July 1998–30 June 1999. UN, Draft resolution by UNGA Fifth Committee, UN document A/C.5/53/L.40, 16 Mar. 1999.

[53] As at 28 Feb. 1999. For the period from the establishment of MIPONUH's predecessor UNSMIH (est. July 1996) to 30 June 1998. UN document A/C.5/53/L.40 (note 52).

[54] A civilian police force (UN Police Support Group) was established for the period 16 Jan. until 16 Oct. 1998 to monitor the performance of the Croatian Police in the Danube region after UNTAES (SCR 1145, 19 Dec. 1997). By 16 Oct. 1998 the OSCE took over the monitoring task. See OSCE Mission in Croatia (note 112).

[55] Strength as of 30 Sep. 1998. With an authorized strength of 180, the mission peaked in June with 179 police monitors and began to decrease in Aug. to 114 in Sep.

[56] Appropriated additional amount for the maintenance and liquidation of UNPSG for the period 1 July–30 Nov. 1998. The initial amount of $23 m. appropriated covered the termination of UNTAES and the maintenance of UNPSG for the period 16 Jan.–30 June 1998. The estimated costs included personnel expenses covering the 180 civilian police and their support by 53 international and 165 local civilian personnel. GAR 52/244, 26 June 1998.

[57] MINURCA (Mission des Nations Unies en République centrafricaine) was established on 27 Mar. 1998 to replace MISAB (note 186) with an initial mandate to assist in maintaining and enhancing security and stability, assist in maintaining law and order, supervise and monitor the collection and destruction of arms, ensure security and freedom of movement for UN personnel, and assist in training programmes for police and electoral assistants. The electoral assistants' mandate was later expanded to include direct support for the conduct of the legislative elections (SCR 1201, 15 Oct. 1998). The authorized strength of the MINURCA military units was not to exceed 1350 members (SCR1159, 27 Mar. 1998). A contingent of *c.* 20 civilian police officers started deploying in May 1998 and began its first training session around mid-Aug. with the aim of training *c.* 120 gendarmes before the elections (held Nov./Dec., initially scheduled for Aug./Sep.). UN, Second Report of the Secretary-General on the United Nations Mission in the Central African Republic, UN document S/1998/783, 21 Aug. 1998. The UNSC welcomed the deployment of additional troops (150) from the Central African Armed Forces to monitor the elections, operating under the control of MINURCA (SCR 1201). Some 70 more troops from France and 16 from Canada were also deployed. Report of the Secretary-General to the Security Council, UN, Third Report of the Secretary-General on the United Nations Mission in the Central African Republic, UN document S/1998/1203, 18 Dec. 1998. MINURCA was initially established for 3 months and then extended until 25 Oct. 1998 (SCR 1182, 14 July 1998) and 28 Feb. 1999 (SCR 1201).

[58] By 30 Apr. 1998, 1218 troops had been deployed and in May 9 police officers were deployed; the number of officers increased in subsequent months to *c.* 20.

[59] Appropriated amount for the period 1 July–30 Nov. For the establishment and operation of the mission for the period 27 Mar.–30 June, the UNGA appropriated $18.6 m. The cost of maintaining the mission from 1 Dec. 1998 to 26 Feb. 1999 was *c.* $18.1 m. and that for the mission beyond 26 Feb. 1999, if the mandate were to be extended, to the end of Dec. 1999 was *c.* $62.1 m. GAR 52/249, 29 Sep. 1998. UN, Third Report of the Secretary-General on the United Nations Mission in the Central African Republic (Addendum), UN document S/1998/1203/Add.1, 14 Jan. 1999.

[60] The UN Observer Mission to Sierra Leone (UNOMSIL) was established on 13 July for an initial 6 months, comprising military observers, a 15-member medical unit and 5 police monitors to be deployed later. The mandate included monitoring the security and military situation in Sierra Leone and monitoring ECOMOG in its role of providing

security and collecting and destroying arms. The first deployment phase, consisting of 40 military observers and the 15 members of the medical unit, was completed at the end of Aug. UN, Second progress report of the Secretary-General on the United Nations Observer Mission in Sierra Leone, UN document S/1998/960, 16 Oct. 1998. In Oct. 3 police officers were deployed (2 more were being recruited). Because of a deteriorating situation in Sierra Leone the remaining group of observers was not deployed in 1998. UN, Third progress report of the Secretary-General on the United Nations Observer Mission in Sierra Leone, UN document S/1998/1176, 16 Dec. 1998. In Jan. 1999 the UNSC extended the mandate until 13 Mar. 1999 (SCR 1220, 12 Jan. 1999).

[61] Appropriated amount for the period 13 July 1998–30 June 1999. The resources provided by the UNGA covered the mission's start-up costs as well as its maintenance at the authorized full strength. UN, Fifth Report of the Secretary-General on the United Nations Observer Mission in Sierra Leone, UN document S/1999/237, 4 Mar. 1999.

[62] As at 15 Feb. 1999. For the period from the start of the mission to 15 Feb. 1998. UN document S/1999/237 (note 61).

[63] Comprises substantial UN peace missions (2 in cooperation with the Organization of American States, OAS) not officially described by the UN as peacekeeping.

[64] Joint UN participation with the OAS was authorized by the resolution. The OAS mandate was extended until 31 Dec. 1999. Information provided by Senior Specialist Pablo Zuniga, Unit for the Promotion of Democracy, General Secretariat of the Organization of American States, Washington, DC.

[65] Information provided by Zuniga (note 64).

[66] As of 31 Dec. 1998 the mission consisted of 40 UN and 40 OAS observers. Information provided by Zuniga (note 64).

[67] OAS budget for 1998: $4.5 m.; UN estimated total expenditures for 1998: $5.9 m. Information from Zuniga (note 64); and UN document A/C.5/53/39, 30 Nov. 1998.

[68] UNSMA maintained a temporary headquarters in Islamabad, Pakistan. During 1998 there were no changes in the legal mandate and it was extended on 18 Dec. 1998 by the Secretary-General. Information from Kiyotaka Kawabata, Asia and the Pacific Division, UN Department of Political Affairs, New York. In SCR 1214 (8 Dec. 1998) the UNSC supported the establishment within the mission of a civil affairs unit with the primary objective of monitoring different aspects of human rights in Afghanistan. The proposed unit would consist of 12 civilian monitors who, conditions permitting, would be deployed in major centres in Afghanistan. UN Press Release SC/6608, 8 Dec. 1998. After the killing of 2 local UN workers in July and of an UNSMA military adviser in Aug., the UN decided to withdraw all UN agency workers from Afghanistan. UN, Report of the Secretary-General on the situation in Afghanistan and its implications for the international peace and security, UN document S/1998/913, 2 Oct. 1998.

[69] Officials from the first 6 countries participated in the mission as political officers, and officials from the other countries participated as military advisers during 1998. Information from Kawabatak (note 68).

[70] 2 political affairs officers and 4 military advisers. Information from Kawabatak (note 68).

[71] 1 military adviser was killed in Aug. Information from Kawabata (note 68).

[72] Information from Kawabata (note 68).

[73] In Mar. 1997 the mandate of MINUGUA was renewed until 31 Mar. 1998 with expanded responsibilities, enabling the mission to verify all agreements signed by the parties in Dec. 1996. GAR 51/198B, 27 Mar. 1997. In a report to the UNGA the Secretary-General recommended that the mandate be extended until the end of 1999 to conform with the 3rd phase of the Agreement on the Implementation, Compliance and Verification Timetable for the Peace Agreements (signed on 29 Dec. 1996) timetable. GAR 52/554, 31 Oct. 1997. The UNGA extended the mandate until 31 Dec. 1998 and then 31 Dec. 1999. GAR 52/175, 24 Feb. 1998, and UN document A/53/L.20, 30 Oct. 1998.

[74] Countries providing military observers and civilian police monitors in 1998. In addition several countries contributed with civilian personnel: 133 international staff and 229 local staff. Information from Maria José Torres, Political Affairs Officer, Americas and Europe Division, UN Department of Political Affairs, New York.

[75] Figures as approved by the UNGA for the period 31 Mar.–31 Dec. 1998 (UN document A/C.5/52/21 and Add.1). Information from Torres (note 74).

[76] On 17 Mar. in a helicopter crash on official duty, 7 staff members of MINUGUA were killed and 3 injured. Information from Torres (note 74).

[77] Information from Torres (note 74).

[78] The mission to Kosovo, Sandjak and Vojvodina, expelled 28 June 1993, could not be redeployed in the absence of agreement on its extension. Unless otherwise stated, all missions were extended until 31 Dec. 1998. Sources for all OSCE missions: *Survey of OSCE Long-Term Missions and other OSCE Field Activities* (Conflict Prevention Centre, CPC: Vienna, 10 Aug. 1998); *Annual Report 1998 on OSCE Activities* (1 Dec. 1997–30 Nov. 1998); *Overview of Deployment (by mission)* (CPC: Vienna, 11 Jan. 1999).

[79] Decision to establish the mission taken at 16th CSO meeting, 18 Sep. 1992, Journal no. 3, Annex 1. Authorized by the Government of the Former Yugoslav Republic of Macedonia (FYROM) through Articles of Understanding (corresponding to an MOU) agreed by exchange of letters, 7 Nov. 1992.

[80] Authorized strength: 8 members. Supplemented by 2 monitors from the European Community Monitoring Mission under operational command of OSCE Head of Mission. In Mar. 1998 in relation to the escalating crisis in Kosovo the mandate was temporarily widened to include border monitoring (Kosovo border). PC.DEC/218, 11 Mar. 1998.

[81] Budget adopted for 1998 by the Permanent Council (ATS 5.27 m.).

[82] Decision to establish the mission taken at 17th CSO meeting, 6 Nov. 1992, Journal no. 2, Annex 2. Authorized by Government of Georgia through MOU, 23 Jan. 1993 and by 'Leadership of the Republic of South Ossetia' by exchange of letters on 1 Mar. 1993. Mandate expanded on 29 Mar. 1994 to include *inter alia* monitoring of Joint Peace-keeping Forces in South Ossetia.

[83] The mission is based in Tbilisi. In Apr. 1997, a branch office in Tskhinvali became operational.

[84] The authorized strength increased by 2 officers when the branch office in Tskhinvali became operational.

[85] Budget adopted for 1998 (ATS 20.55 m.).

[86] Decision to establish the mission taken at 18th CSO meeting, 13 Dec. 1992, Journal no. 3, Annex 2. Authorized by Estonian Government through MOU, 15 Feb. 1993.

[87] Authorized strength: 6 members.

[88] Budget adopted for 1998 (ATS 6.35 m.).

[89] Decision to establish the mission taken at 19th CSO meeting, 4 Feb. 1993, Journal no. 3, Annex 3. Authorized by Government of Moldova through MOU, 7 May 1993. An 'Understanding of the Activity of the CSCE Mission in the Pridnestrovian [Trans-Dniester] Region of the Republic of Moldova' came into force on 25 Aug. 1993 through an exchange of letters between the Head of Mission and the 'President of the Pridnestrovian Moldovan Republic'.

[90] Authorized strength: 8 members.

[91] Budget adopted for 1998 (ATS 5.93 m.).

[92] Decision to establish the mission taken at 23rd CSO meeting, 23 Sep. 1993, Journal no. 3, Annex 3. Authorized by Government of Latvia through MOU, 13 Dec. 1993.

[93] Authorized strength: 7 members.

[94] Budget adopted for 1998 (ATS 7.03 m.).

[95] Decision to establish the mission taken at 4th meeting of the Council, Rome (CSCE/4-C/Dec. 1), Decision I.4, 1 Dec. 1993. No MOU signed. In Apr. 1998 an OSCE presence was established in the Garm Region, temporarily suspended for 6 weeks until early Sep. as a response to the killing of 4 UNMOT members, and the opening of a field office in Leninabad province was authorized by the OSCE Permanent Council (PC).

[96] Authorized strength: 11 members.

[97] Budget adopted for 1998 (ATS 12.56 m.).

[98] Decision to establish the mission taken at 27th CSO meeting, 15 June 1994, Journal no. 3, Decision (c). Ukrainian Government authorization through MOU, 24 Jan. 1995.

[99] Authorized strength: 4 members.

[100] Budget adopted for 1998 (ATS 5.99 m.).

[101] Decision to establish the mission taken at 16th meeting of the PC, 11 Apr. 1995, Decision (a). No MOU signed.

[102] Initially, the group consisted of 6 members. The OSCE Chairman-in-Office in consultation with the Russian Federation has the authority to decide on the membership.

[103] Budget adopted for 1998 (ATS 19.17 m.).

[104] In Aug. 1995 the OSCE Chairman-in-Office appointed a Personal Representative (PR) on the Conflict Dealt with by the OSCE Minsk Conference. The Minsk Conference, planned for since 1992 by the Minsk Group (consisting of the conflict parties and 10 more states) with the purpose of negotiating a peaceful settlement to the Nagorno-Karabakh conflict, has so far not been held because of the absence of agreement by the conflict parties. However, the Minsk Group has continued to hold meetings. The PR's mandate consists of assisting the Minsk Group in planning possible peacekeeping operations, assisting the parties in confidence-building measures (e.g. the use of OSCE radio

equipment permitting direct contact between local commanders) and in humanitarian matters, and to cooperate with other international organizations. With 5 Field Assistants, appointed by the OSCE Chairman-in-Office, to conduct the activities, the PR is responsible for monitoring the ceasefire, monitoring military activities in the border area between Azerbaijan and Nagorno-Karabakh and Azerbaijan and Armenia, and for carrying out field visits to Armenian-occupied areas in Azerbaijan. The monitoring activities take place once a month. Because of a shooting incident in Feb. 1998, the monitoring activities were temporarily suspended and did not resume until May.

[105] The headquarters for the PR and the Field Assistants is based in Tbilisi. In addition, 3 branch offices exist for the conduct of the operational activities; in Baku, Yerevan, and Stepanakert.

[106] The 5 Field Assistants are assisted during visits outside the Headquarters by 3 locally recruited personnel (liaison person, driver and security guard).

[107] Budget adopted for 1998 (ATS 9.2 m.).

[108] Decision to establish the mission taken at 5th meeting, Ministerial Council, Budapest, 8 Dec. 1995 (MC(5).DEC/1) in accordance with Annex 6 of the Dayton Agreement. The former OSCE mission to Sarajevo is now included in OSCE Mission to Bosnia and Herzegovina.

[109] The Head of the Mission is based in Sarajevo with an additional office in Brcko and 5 regional centres and 20 field offices throughout Bosnia and Herzegovina.

[110] The authorized strength is 246 members. In connection with the elections on 12 and 13 Sep. about 2600 international supervisors were deployed and 12 long-term observers joined by 150 short-term observers from the Office for Democratic Institutions and Human Rights (ODIHR). OSCE prepares for elections in Bosnia and Herzegovina, OSCE Press Release, no. 48/98, Sep. 1998.

[111] Budget adopted for 1998 (ATS 322.77 m.). In addition the budget adopted for the 1998 election was $41.25 m. (ATS 488.96 m.).

[112] Decision to establish the mission taken by the PC, 18 Apr. 1996, Journal no. 65 (PC.DEC/112). Adjustment of the mandate by the Permanent Council, 26 June 1997, Journal no. 121 (PC.DEC/176). On 15 Oct. the UNPSG mandate in the Croatian Danubian region expired and OSCE civilian police monitors assumed the responsibilities (PC.DEC/239, 25 June 1998). This was the first time the OSCE deployed civilian police monitors.

[113] The mission was authorized to increase its personnel, starting July 1997, to a ceiling of 250 expatriates with a view to full deployment by 15 Jan. 1998. PC.DEC/176, 26 June 1997. In addition a maximum of 120 OSCE police monitors were being deployed as of Oct. 1998.

[114] Budget adopted for 1998 (ATS 268.01 m.). The civilian police monitors are seconded by the OSCE member states which are responsible for their respective costs. No financial implications were envisaged for the Croatian mission's budget for 1998.

[115] Decision to establish the mission taken at 108th meeting of the Permanent Council, 27 Mar. 1997. PC.DEC/160. Mandate adjusted on 11 Dec. 1997. Journal no. 193 (PC.DEC/206). The mandate was temporarily widened in Mar. 1998 to include border monitoring (Kosovo border). PC.DEC/218, 11 Mar. 1998.

[116] On 11 Mar. 1998, the PC temporarily enhanced the monitoring capabilities of the mission, 'to allow for adequate observation of the borders with Kosovo, the Former Republic of Yugoslavia (FRY), and prevention of possible crisis spillover effects', by adding 30 members.

[117] Budget adopted for 1998 (ATS 1.55 m.). In addition supplementary budgets were approved by the PC because of the temporarily enhanced monitoring capabilities with $1.06 m. (ATS 12.58 m.) covering the period 17 Mar.–16 Sep. PC.DEC/220, 17 Mar. 1998; PC.DEC/223, 7 Apr. 1998; PC.DEC/226, 14 May 1998; PC.DEC/228, 4 June 1998.

[118] Decision to establish the mission taken at the 129th meeting of the PC, 18 Sep. 1997. PC.DEC/185. The mission could not take up its activities until Feb. 1998, because of the delay of parts of an agreement between the OSCE and the Government of Belarus on the practical modalities of the work. The mission's mandate is to 'assist the Belorussian authorities in promoting democratic institutions and in complying with other OSCE commitments and to monitor and report on this process'. As part of the activities the Advisory and Monitoring Group (AMG) requested the Belorussian Government to set up special groups to cooperate in different fields: political questions; laws on human rights and fundamental freedoms; practical applications of bills in the field of human rights; democratic institutions; and education in human rights. It has also tried to support and provide legal advice to individuals concerning human rights issues. In addition discussions, seminars and conferences with the opposition, other Belorussian institutions, NGOs, and experts from other OSCE countries have taken place within the framework of the AMG's activities. There has been no limitation on the duration of the mission.

[119] The mission comprises the Head of the AMG and 4 experts on the relevant aspects of the mission. The AMG is often supported by experts from international organizations and member countries.

[120] Budget adopted for the period 15 Jan.–31 Dec. 1998 (ATS 9.8 m.).

[121] Decision to establish the Kosovo Verification Mission (KVM) taken by the PC, 25 Oct. 1998 (PC.DEC/263), after its endorsement by SCR 1203 (24 Oct. 1998). On 16 Oct. the OSCE and FRY signed an agreement on the creation of the KVM for 1 year, with the possibility of extension. Its mandate is to verify FRY compliance with SCR 1160 (31 Mar. 1998) and SCR 1199 (23 Sep. 1998). Two regional centres were fully operational in Dec. and 3 more were to be established in Jan. 1999. The inclusion of the Kosovo Diplomatic Observer Mission (see note 210) in the KVM, statuted in the 16 Oct. agreement, was almost complete in Dec. and the strength of the KVM was *c.* 1100 staff members (including local staff). It was reduced to 745 members on 12 Jan. 1999. 'Tense Christmas in Kosovo', *OSCE Newsletter,* vol. 5, no. 12 (Dec. 1998).

[122] Headquarters established in Pristina and a liaison office in Belgrade.

[123] Deployment as of 12 Jan. 1999. Authorized strength: 2000 verifiers.

[124] Approximate budget for KVM for a 1-year period. OSCE Kosovo Verification Mission, OSCE Internet site, URL <http://www.osce.org/e/kvm-fact.htm#7>.

[125] Agreement on the Principles Governing the Peaceful Settlement of the Conflict in South Ossetia, signed in Dagomys, 24 June 1992, by Georgia and Russia. A Joint Monitoring Commission with representatives of Russia, Georgia, and North and South Ossetia was established to oversee the implementation of the agreement.

[126] The composite force has a Russian commander. Georgiyev, V., *Nezavisimoye Voyennoye Obozreniye* (Moscow), no. 23, 26 June–2 July 1998, p. 2, in 'Russia: Rotation of peacekeeping forces through Southern Ossetia', Foreign Broadcast Information Service, *Daily Reports–Central Eurasia: Military Affairs (FBIS-UMA)*, FBIS-UMA-98-197, 16 July 1998.

[127] In Mar. 1998 the total number of peacekeeping troops was 1236. Semiryaga, V., 'Peacekeeping is common task', *Pravda* (Moscow), 13 Mar. 1998, pp. 1–2, in 'Russia: General interviewed on CIS peacekeeping', Foreign Broadcast Information Service, *Daily Reports–Central Eurasia: (FBIS-SOV)*, FBIS-SOV-98-075, 16 Mar. 1998. The peacekeeping forces in the Tskhinvali region were being cut back during autumn 1998. Tsagareishvili, K., 'Interview with Irakliy Machavariani, personal representative of the President of Georgia for political problems of national security and conflict settlement', *Svobodnaya Gruziya* (Tbilisi), 25 Oct. 1998, p. 6, in 'Georgia: Machavarian: details progress on Ossetia', FBIS-SOV-98-315, 11 Nov. 1998.

[128] For 1998, the calculated expenditures for Russia concerning all 4 peacekeeping operations, in Abkhazia, Moldova, South Ossetia and Tajikistan, were *c.* \$39.1 m. (512.4 m. roubles in accordance with the average 1998 exchange rate: \$1=13.09 roubles). Georgiyev (note 126).

[129] Agreement on the Principles Governing the Peaceful Settlement of the Armed Conflict in the Trans-Dniester Region, signed in Moscow, 21 July 1992 by the presidents of Moldova and Russia. A Joint Control Commission with representatives of Russia, Moldova and Trans-Dniester was established to coordinate the activities of the joint peace-keeping contingent.

[130] The 'Trans-Dniester Republic' is the breakaway part of Moldova east of the Dniester River and not recognized by any country as an independent state. On 16 Nov. 10 Ukrainian Military Observers joined the peacekeeping force in accordance with the Odessa Agreement of 20 Mar. 1998 to monitor the Security Zone between Moldova and Trans-Dniester. Information from Lt Col RNLA J. J. Marseille, Military Mission Member, OSCE Mission to Moldova.

[131] In accordance with the Moldova–Trans-Dniester Odessa Agreement, troop withdrawal was scheduled to begin in July 1998. Before the withdrawal Moldova had 800 troops in the security zone, the Trans-Dniester region 900 and Russia 500. On 30 June the Joint Control Commission ruled that Moldova and Trans-Dniester would cut their peacekeeping forces to 500 persons, and in Nov. Moldova unilaterally withdrew *c.* 150 troops. At the end of 1998 Russia, Moldova and Trans-Dniester had *c.* 500 troops each in the security zone and Ukraine had *c.* 10 military observers. Outside the security zone, but considered part of the Trans-Dniestrian contingent, there was an addiional battalion of *c.* 200 personnel. Information from Marseille (note 130); Basapress (Chisinau), 23 Nov. 1998, in 'Moldova: Mediators satisfied with Moldova's troop cuts in Dniester', FBIS-SOV-98-328, 24 Nov. 1998; and Basapress (Chisinau), 1 July 1998, in 'Chisinau, Tiraspol to cut peacekeeping troops to 500 men', FBIS-SOV-98-182, 1 July 1998.

[132] Information from Marseille (note 130).

[133] See note 128.

[134] CIS Agreement on the Collective Peace-keeping Forces and Joint Measures on their Logistical and Technical Maintenance, signed in Moscow, 24 Sep. 1993. The operation is the first application of the Agreement on Groups of Military Observers and Collective Peacekeeping Forces in the CIS, signed in Kiev, 20 Mar. 1992.

[135] The Russian border troops and other CIS forces stationed or operating elsewhere in Tajikistan are not part of this operation.

[136] On 16 Nov. Uzbekistan withdrew its peacekeeping battalion, *c.* 140–150 troops, from Tajikistan. On 19 Feb. 1999 Kyrgyzstan followed the Uzbek example and decided to withdraw its battalion. ITAR-TASS (Moscow), 17 Nov. 1998, in 'Uzbekistan: Uzbek peacekeepers leave deployment position in Tajikistan', FBIS-UMA-98-321, 17 Nov. 1998; and Interfax (Moscow), 11 Mar. 1999, in 'Kyrgyz official justifies border reinforcement', FBIS-SOV-1999-0311, 11 Mar. 1999.

[137] The Russian 201st Motorized Rifle Division (MRD) constitutes the core of the CIS Collective Peacekeeping Forces (CPF). In the second half of 1998 the Russian part of the CPF consisted of *c.* 7000 servicemen. In late Aug. discussions were held between Russian military leaders concerning the need to increase the number of troops within the 201st MRD to 10 000. However, no increase of troops was made. The Kyrgyz part of the CPF and the Kazakh part each consisted of a battalion comprising *c.* 500 troops. Radio Tajikistan (Dushanbe), 13 Oct. 1998, in 'CIS peacekeeping head backs extension of Tajik mandate', FBIS-UMA-98-287, 14 Oct. 1998; *Sodruzhesto, NG* (Supplement to *Nezavisimaya Gazeta*), no. 10 (Nov. 1998), p. 6; Interfax (Moscow), 11 Mar. 1999, 'Kyrgyz official justifies border reinforcement', FBIS-SOV-1999-0311, 11 Mar. 1999; and Interfax (Moscow), 20 Aug. 1998, 'Russian, Central Asian defense ministers to meet early Sep.', FBIS-SOV-98-232, 20 Aug. 1998.

[138] 100 peacekeepers were killed between the beginning of the operation and Apr. 1995. Interfax (Moscow), 20 Apr. 1995, in 'CPF Commander Partikeyev holds press conference—says 100 CIS soldiers killed since 1993', FBIS-SOV-95-077, 20 Apr. 1995. More than 60 Russians were killed during 1995–96. 'Suspect sentenced to death for killing Russian soldiers', *Open Media Research Institute (OMRI) Daily Digest*, no. 24, part I (4 Feb. 1997). In Apr.–May 1998, 3 people were killed in 2 incidents. Zhukov, V., ITAR-TASS (Moscow), 25 May 1998, in 'Tajikistan: Russian serviceman killed in Tajikistan', FBIS-UMA-98-145, 25 May 1998; and ITAR-TASS (Moscow), 11 Apr. 1998, in 'Tajikistan: Peacekeeping forces' jet crashes in Tajikistan', FBIS-UMA-98-101, 11 Apr. 1998.

[139] National contingents are fully financed by the state sending them. Only the command of the collective force and combat support units are financed from a joint budget, shared as follows: Kazakhstan 15%; Kyrgyzstan 10%; Russia 50%; Tajikistan 10%; and Uzbekistan 15%. 'Press conference with the commander of the CIS peacekeeping force in Tajikistan', Radio Tajikistan (Dushanbe), 13 Oct. 1998, in 'Tajikistan: CIS peacekeeping head backs extension of Tajik mandate', FBIS-UMA-98-287, 14 Oct. 1998; O'Prey, K., *Keeping the Peace in the Borderlands of Russia*, Occasional paper no. 23 (Henry L. Stimson Center: Washington, DC, July 1995), p. 38; and note 128.

[140] Georgian–Abkhazian Agreement on a Cease-fire and Separation of Forces, signed in Moscow, 14 May 1994. Mandate approved by heads of states members of the CIS Council of Collective Security, 21 Oct. 1994. Endorsement by the UNSC through SCR 937 (21 July 1994). On 7 Feb. 1998 the Russian peacekeeping mandate expired and on 29 Apr. the Council of Heads of State of the CIS decided to extend the mandate, with the consent of the parties involved, until 31 July 1998. UN, Report of the Secretary-General concerning the situation in Abkhazia, Georgia, UN document S/1998/375, 11 May 1998. At the same summit a draft decision was taken extending 'the zone of jurisdiction of the CIS peacekeeping force currently deployed along the internal border between Abkhazia and the rest of Georgia to cover the entire territory of Gali'. Fuller, L., Radio Free Europe/Radio Liberty, *Caucasus Report,* vol. 1, no. 10 (5 May 1998), URL <http://www.rferl.org/caucasus-report/1998/05/10-050598.html>. Although called for by some factions in Georgia, no official Georgian demands were made for a Russian troop withdrawal from Abkhazia. *Rezonansi* (Tbilisi), 29 Oct. 1998, p. 7, in 'Georgia demands Russian troop withdrawal from Abkhazia', FBIS-UMA-98-303, 30 Oct. 1998. There has been no summit or decision since 30 July and hence the mandate has been neither revoked nor extended. Osokin, M., NTV (Moscow), 30 Dec. 1998, in 'Georgia: Moscow TV reports on Russian peacekeepers in Georgia', FBIS-SOV-98-365, 31 Dec. 1998.

[141] Estimated number of troops in Sep. 1998 was *c.* 1690 (for 1997: 1600). Yurkin, A., ITAR-TASS (Moscow), 22 Sep. 1998, in 'Georgia: Abkhaz Government welcomes Russian peacekeeping troops role', FBIS-SOV-98-265, 22 Sep. 1998.

[142] During the period 1994–May 1998. UN, Report of the Secretary-General concerning the situation in Abkhazia, Georgia, UN document S/1998/375, 11 May 1998.

[143] During May–Oct. 1998, 6 peacekeepers were killed and several wounded. Kuchuberiya, A., ITAR-TASS (Moscow), 19 Oct. 1998, in 'Georgia: Abkhazia: another Russian peacekeeper killed', FBIS-SOV-98-292, 19 Oct. 1998; 'In brief', *Jane's Defence Weekly,* vol. 29, no. 16 (22 Apr. 1998), p. 14; vol. 30. no. 3 (22 July 1998), p. 12; vol. 30, no. 4 (29 July 1998), p. 5; Kuchuberiya, A., ITAR-TASS (Moscow), 23 Oct. 1998, in 'Russian command protests killing of peacekeeper in Abkhazia', FBIS-SOV-98-297, 24 Oct. 1998; and Interfax (Moscow), 28 Nov. 1998, in 'Georgia: Anti-tank mine explosion injures 6 peacekeepers in Abkhazia', FBIS-SOV-98-332, 28 Nov. 1998.

[144] From the outset the peacekeeping mission has been paid for by the regions from which the peacekeepers were sent. Osokin, M., NTV (Moscow), 30 Dec. 1998, in 'Georgia: Moscow TV reports on Russian peacekeepers in Georgia', FBIS-SOV-98-365, 31 Dec. 1998. See also note 128.

[145] Decision A/DEC.1/8/90 on the ceasefire and establishment of an Economic Community of West African States (ECOWAS) Monitoring Group (ECOMOG) for Liberia. Economic Community of West African States, First Session of the Community Standing Mediation Committee, Banjul, 6–7 Aug. 1990. The ECOWAS Standing Mediation Committee (ESMC) comprises Gambia, Ghana, Guinea, Mali, Nigeria, Sierra Leone and Togo. On 5 June 1998 ECOMOG and the Liberian Government signed an agreement extending the mandate but with no fixed end date. Henceforth, ECOMOG's tasks were to assist the government in providing security in the country, maintaining law and order, and restructuring the army and police. Eziakonwa, A., 'Donors back Liberia's reconstruction: governance and refugee resettlement high on the agenda', *Africa Recovery,* Aug. 1998, p. 26. At the ECOWAS High Authority of Heads of States and Government summit in Abuja, Nigeria, on 30–31 Oct., Liberian President Charles Taylor asked for an extension of the mandate resulting in a request, included in the final communiqué, from the summit participants that the Liberian President and the executive director of ECOWAS should work out procedures for a continuation of ECOMOG in Liberia. 'Conferences: ECOWAS: conflict resolution', *Africa Research Bulletin,* vol. 35, no. 11 (Nov. 1998), p. 13314.

[146] ECOWAS member states 1998: Benin, Burkina Faso, Cape Verde, Côte d'Ivoire, Gambia, Ghana, Guinea, Guinea-Bissau, Liberia, Mali, Mauritania, Niger, Nigeria, Senegal, Sierra Leone and Togo.

[147] In Aug. 1996 ECOWAS decided to end the ECOMOG mandate in Liberia and complete the withdrawal by 2 Feb. 1998. Sannah, T., 'Mandate of ECOMOG ends', Panafrican News Agency (PANA), 2 Feb. 1998, URL <http://www.africanews.org/PANA/news/>. ECOMOG troops were cut from *c.* 10 000 at the end of 1997 to *c.* 5000–6000 by spring 1998. 'Liberia: Taylor adamant over forces', *Africa Research Bulletin*, vol. 35, no. 4 (Apr. 1998), p. 13081. However, after the signing of a new agreement in June (note 145) *c.* 90% of ECOMOG's troops in Liberia were relocated to Freetown, Sierra Leone. Ejime, P., 'Bissau conflict high on ECOWAS agenda', PANA, 29 Oct. 1998. The remaining force was deployed in Monrovia. Davies, D., 'Liberia's unique position [Interview with Liberian President Charles Taylor]', *West Africa*, no. 4196 (28 Sep.–11 Oct. 1998), p. 712. In Dec. 1998 there were only 800 ECOMOG troops left in Liberia (all in Monrovia). Olowo, B. and Whiteman, K., 'An action-packed summit', *West Africa,* no. 4199 (7–20 Dec. 1998), p. 858. In early Jan. 1999, after repeated accusations from ECOMOG (Nigeria) that Liberia supported rebels in Sierra Leone, the remaining ECOMOG troops, consisting of Nigerian soldiers, began withdrawing from Liberia. Benin, Côte d'Ivoire, Gambia and Guinea had already left during Jan.–Mar. 1998. Kahler, P., 'Nigerian troops leave Liberia', PANA, 15 Jan. 1999; 'World: Africa ECOMOG quits Liberia', BBC News, 17 Jan. 1999, URL <http://www.ews2.thdo.bbc.co.uk/hi/english/world/africa/newsid_256000/256740.stm>; and Davies, D., 'The security dilemma', *West Africa,* no. 4196 (28 Sep. 11–Oct. 1998), p. 716.

[148] Originally financed by ECOWAS countries with additional voluntary contributions from UN member states through the Trust Fund for the Implementation of the Cotonou Agreement. At the summit meeting of the Heads of State and Government of ECOWAS, held in Abuja, 28–29 Aug. 1997, the ECOWAS leaders decided that the costs of the continued ECOMOG presence in Liberia will be financed mainly by the Government of Liberia. UN, Final report of the Secretary-General on the United Nations Observer Mission in Liberia, UN document S/1997/712, 12 Sep. 1997.

[149] Following a military coup on 25 May 1997 ECOMOG peacekeeping forces intervened in Sierra Leone on 2 June 1997. Authorization was given by the OAU at the 33rd annual summit in Harare, 2–4 June 1997. 'Zimbabwe: OAU gives "green light" to use force in Sierra Leone', SAPA (Johannesburg), 3 June 1997, in Foreign Broadcast Information Service, *Daily Report–Sub-Saharan Africa (FBIS–AFR),* FBIS-AFR-97-155, 4 June 1997. The decision of the OAU was supported by the UNSC and by the Secretary General of the Commonwealth (Sierra Leone has been a member since 1961). UN document S/PRST/1997/36, 11 July 1997; and 'ECOMOG forces seize Freetown', *Pointer*, Apr. 1998. The Conakry Agreement signed in Guinea, 23 Oct. 1997, by the ECOWAS Committee of Five on Sierra Leone and a delegation representing Major Johnny Koroma, Chairman of the Armed Forces Revolutionary Council (AFRC) regime in Sierra Leone, called for a ceasefire to be monitored by ECOMOG forces. UN, Second Report of the Secretary-General on the situation in Sierra Leone, UN document S/1997/958, 5 Dec. 1997. During the ECOWAS summit meeting in the beginning of Nov. 1998 it was decided to recommend an extension of the mandate of ECOMOG in Sierra Leone and additional manpower and logistics. Voice of Nigeria (Lagos), 2 Nov. 1998, in 'Nigeria: ECOMOG commander on extending force mandate', FBIS-AFR-98-307, 3 Nov. 1998.

[150] Benin, Côte d'Ivoire, Gambia and Niger promised to contribute with troops during 1998 but owing to lack of sufficient logistical support no deployment of troops took place. Olowo and Whiteman (note 147), p. 858. Guinea temporarily withdrew its forces to Guinea for some time during spring/summer 1998 to protect its own citizens from attack by Sierra Leone rebels. 'Sierra Leone: hundreds mutilated by rebels', *Africa Research Bulletin,* vol. 35, no. 6 (June 1998), p. 13156; and Information from Halima

Ahmed, Head of Division, Legal Affairs ECOWAS Secretariat, Abuja.

[151] Between June 1997 and June 1998 the troops were reinforced with 7400 bringing their number to *c.* 12 000. *Keesing's Record of World Events*, vol. 43, no. 6 (June 1997), p. 41672; and UN, Fifth Report of the Secretary-General on the Situation in Sierra Leone, UN document S/1998/486, 9 June 1998. In Nov. the number had decreased to *c.* 9000. 'Jackson brings message of hope and reconciliation to Sierra Leone', *USIS Washington File*, 13 Nov. 1998. At the end of Dec. 1998 the troops had once again been reinforced, bringing numbers to 14 000. 'Nigerian envoy seeks UN support for Sierra Leone', PANA, 31 Dec. 1998; and 'Sierra Leone: Rebels step up fight', *African Research Bulletin*, vol. 35, no. 12, (Dec. 1998), p. 13375.

[152] Financed by ECOWAS countries with additional voluntary contributions from UN member states, to a large extent the UK and the USA. In May the USA contributed $3.9 m. Voice of Nigeria (Lagos), 2 Nov. 1998, in 'Nigeria: ECOMOG commander on extending force mandate', FBIS-AFR-98-307, 3 Nov. 1998; and 'Sierra Leone: grisly message', *The Economist*, vol. 348, no. 8080 (8 Aug. 1998).

[153] According to the Abuja Peace Agreement of 1 Nov. 1998 negotiated by ECOWAS, to be implemented by ECOMOG, the monitoring group's role is 'aimed at guaranteeing security along the Guinea-Bissau–Senegal border, keeping apart the parties in the conflict' and guaranteeing access for humanitarian organizations. The deployment of ECOMOG was endorsed by the UNSC (SCR 1216, 21 Dec. 1998).

[154] 'Benin, The Gambia, and Niger to send troops later', AFP (Paris), 26 Nov. 1998, in 'Guinea-Bissau: Four West African countries pledge troops for Bissau', FBIS-AFR-98-330, 26 Nov. 1998.

[155] On 26 Dec. 1998, the first contingent consisting of an advance team of 112 soldiers from Togo arrived. 'Togolese troops in Guinea-Bissau', PANA, 28 Dec. 1998; and information from Ahmed (note 150). The authorized strength was 1450 soldiers. Earlier Togo pledged an additional 420 men, Niger 500, Gambia 150 and Benin 300 (note 154).

[156] Financial, technical and logistical support provided on a voluntary basis from UN member states through a UN trust fund for Guinea-Bissau. SCR 1216 (21 Dec. 1998); and UN Press Release SC/6614 (21 Dec. 1998).

[157] Agreement concerning a military armistice in Korea, signed at Panmunjom on 27 July 1953 by the Commander-in-Chief, UN Command; the Supreme Commander of the Korean People's Army; and the Commander of the Chinese People's Volunteers. Entered into force on 27 July 1953. No change of mandate during 1998. Information from Lt Col Christer Svärd, Swedish delegation to the NNSC, Panmunjom, South Korea.

[158] The Neutral Nations Supervisory Commission (NNSC) entrusted to oversee the armistice agreement originally consisted of representatives from Czechoslovakia, Poland, Sweden and Switzerland. The Czech delegation was forced to leave in Apr. 1993 and was still absent in 1998. No replacement had been nominated. The Polish delegation was forced to leave in Feb. 1995. Poland, however, remains a member, maintaining an office in Warsaw, and 3–4 times per year the Polish delegation travels to Panmunjom to participate in the work of the NNSC. Information from Svärd (note 158).

[159] 5 from Sweden and 5 from Switzerland. Information from Svärd (note 158).

[160] Approximate costs: Sweden $112 000 (SEK 883 000, salaries excluded), Switzerland $500 000, USA $40 000 (food). Information from Svärd (note 158).

[161] 1981 Protocol to the Treaty of Peace between Egypt and Israel, signed 26 Mar. 1979. Established following the withdrawal of Israeli forces from Sinai. Deployment began 20 Mar. and mission commenced 25 Apr. 1982. 'The Multinational Force and Observers', Report from the Office of Personnel and Publications, MFO, Rome, June 1993.

[162] Strength as of Nov. 1998. Annual Report of the Director General, MFO, Rome, Jan. 1999.

[163] 2 Hungarian MFO members were killed in a vehicle accident. Annual Report of the Director General (note 162).

[164] Operating budget for FY 1998. Force funded by Egypt, Israel and the USA (*c.* 32% each). Voluntary contributions from Germany (since 1992), Japan (since 1989) and Switzerland (since 1994) amounted to *c.* $1.5 m. in 1998. Annual Report of the Director General (note 162).

[165] Mission established by the Brioni Agreement, signed at Brioni (Croatia), 7 July 1991 by representatives of the European Community (EC) and the governments of Croatia, Slovenia and FRY. Mandate confirmed by the EC meeting of foreign ministers, The Hague, 10 July 1991. Mission authorized by the governments of Croatia, Slovenia and FRY through MOU, 13 July 1991. In 1997 an MOU was signed with Albania which was later extended. On 21 Dec. 1998 a new MOU was signed with Croatia. Information from Sven Linder, Head of the Swedish delegation to the ECMM, Sarajevo.

[166] Of a total of 490 personnel 320 are observers. Information from Linder (note 165).

[167] A non-observer mission member was killed in a traffic accident in 1998. Information from Linder (note 165).

[168] Information from Linder (note 165).

[169] MIOB (Mission de l'OUA au Burundi, in French). Both names are official.

[170] Following the 1996 coup in Burundi, the Organization of African Unity (OAU) decided to withdraw the 87-strong military component of OMIB and to reinforce the civilian component. This latter decision had not been implemented by Dec. 1998 when the number of observers was 3, of which 2 were civilian observers and 1 was a medical officer assisting in humanitarian matters. Head of the mission was the Special Envoy of the Secretary-General of the OAU to Burundi (the Great Lakes region). Information from Niang Cheikh, Information Officer, OAU mission, Brussels.

[171] Funded by the regular budget of the OAU and voluntary contributions. The monthly cost for the mission was $200 000. Information from Niang Cheikh (note 170).

[172] The first article of the Declaration, dated 17 Feb. 1995, states the willingness of the guarantor countries of the 1942 Protocol of Rio de Janeiro—Argentina, Brazil, Chile and the USA—to send an observer mission to the region in conflict, as well as the acceptance of this offer by the conflicting parties. During a sensitive time in the peace talks in Aug. 1998 MOMEP's mandate was extended to include monitoring of an additional part of the border, thereby easing the military tensions in the area. In addition, MOMEP has been monitoring the demining process in the border region. Information from Ambassador Dennis C. Jett, Embassy of the United States of America, Peru.

[173] In Jan. 1998, MOMEP coordinator Gen. Luis Zeldao Da Silva handed over to another Brazilian, Gen. Sergio Coelho Lima. Voz de los Andes (Quito), 7 Jan. 1998, in 'Brazilian general named new MOMEP co-ordinator', Foreign Broadcast Information Service, *Daily Reports–The Americas (FBIS-LAT),* FBIS-LAT-98-013, 13 Jan. 1998.

[174] In addition, 110 personnel from Argentina, Brazil, Chile and the USA provide logistical and communications support. Information from Jett (note 172).

[175] The cost was divided between the governments of Ecuador and Peru. Brazil provided helicopter support and also contributed to significant separate expenses during 1998. Information from Jett (note 172).

[176] SFOR's mandate was to expire on 20 June 1998. However, the North Atlantic Council Defence Ministers Session in Brussels on 20 Feb. and 11 June 1998 decided to extend the mandate. On 15 June the UNSC authorized a continuation of the operation for another 12-month period (SCR 1174, 15 June 1998). SFOR's operation from its start in Dec. 1996 until 19 June 1998 was called Operation Joint Guard. On 20 June the name was changed to Operation Joint Forge. The new NATO mandate, with no end date fixed, called for half-yearly reviews with a view to achieving a gradual reduction in the size, role and profile of the operation. NATO Press Release (98) 18, 20 Feb. 1998; Final Communiqué, Meeting of the North Atlantic Council in Defence Ministers Session in Brussels on 11th June 1998; and SCR 1174 (15 June 1998).

[177] Iceland provided medical support.

[178] Information from 10 Dec. 1998. UN, Letter from the Secretary-General addressed to the President of the Security Council, UN document S/1998/1167, 15 Dec. 1998.

[179] The total number of casualties since the establishment of the Implementation Force (IFOR) in Dec. 1995. Includes both battle and non-battle fatalities. Information from SFOR, Sarajevo.

[180] Fatalities since 23 June 1997.

[181] Costs divided between all contributing states. Each state is responsible for the costs associated with its troop contribution.

[182] Protocol Concerning the Redeployment in Hebron, signed 15 Jan. 1997.

[183] In May 1996, a group of Norwegian observers were sent to Hebron. After Israel and the Palestinian Authority signed and implemented the Hebron Protocol in Jan. 1997, the mission was expanded to include observers from 5 additional countries. On 30 June 1998 the TIPH mandate was extended for a further 6 months. In mid-July 1998 the command of TIPH 2 was changed. The Head of Mission since Nov. 1997, Trond Prytz (Norway), left the chair to his Norwegian colleague Arne Huuse. No change of mandate was made during 1998. Information from Ambassador Mona Juul, Royal Ministry of Foreign Affairs, Oslo, Norway.

[184] Information from Juul (note 183).

[185] Approximate cost for 1998. Information from Juul (note 183).

[186] MISAB was originally set up by the presidents of Burkina Faso, Chad, Gabon and Mali (original mandate in UN, identical letters dated 18 July 1997 from the chargé

d'affaires A.I. of the Permanent Mission of the Central African Republic to the United Nations addressed to the Secretary-General and to the President of the Security Council, UN document S/1997/561, 22 July 1997, Appendix I), to monitor the implementation of the Bangui Agreements signed on 25 Jan. 1997 (S/1997/561, Appendixes III–VI). Upon request (UN, Letter dated 7 July 1997 from the President of Gabon addressed to the Secretary-General, UN document S/1997/543, 14 July 1997), the UNSC authorized MISAB in SCR 1125 (6 Aug. 1997). The mandate was later extended to 6 Feb. 1998 (SCR 1136, 6 Nov. 1997) and 16 Mar. (SCR 1152, 5 Feb. 1998). After a last extension it ended on 15 Apr. 1998 and was replaced by the United Nations Mission in the Central African Republic (MINURCA), (SCR 1155, 16 Mar. 1998 and SCR 1159, 27 Mar. 1998).

[187] MISAB (Mission Interafricaine de Surveillance des Accords de Bangui, in French).

[188] Since 8 Feb. 1997, MISAB was deployed in Bangui, comprising *c.* 800 troops under the military command of Gabon and with French logistical and financial support. UN, Report of the Secretary-General pursuant to SCR 1136 (6 Nov. 1997) concerning the situation in the Central African Republic, UN document S/1998/61, 23 Jan. 1998.

[189] MISAB suffered some casualties in particular during confrontations in Bangui in Mar. and June 1997. UN document S/1998/61 (note 188).

[190] The cost of the mission was borne on a voluntary basis (SCR 1136, 6 Nov. 1997). In addition, a trust fund for the Central African Republic was established by the UN Secretary-General. The Organization of African Unity supported MISAB with special grants. UN document S/1998/61 (note 188).

[191] Established under the authority of the Western European Union (WEU) Council, 2 May 1997. On 24 June 1997 an MOU between the Government of Albania and the WEU was signed, enabling the deployment of MAPE to be completed by early July 1997. MAPE's mission is to 'rebuild the Albanian police by modernizing it and gradually to hand over the training responsibilities to the Albanian police'. The mandate was extended in Apr. 1998 until 12 Apr. 1999. 'The WEU multinational police element for Albania', WEU Fact Sheet, no. 1/98, 12 Nov. 1998.

[192] MAPE is under French command. 'The WEU multinational police element for Albania' (note 191).

[193] With the extension in mandate from 12 Oct. 1997 until 12 Apr. 1998, there was an increase in the number of officers from 25 to *c.* 60. With the latest extension in mandate in Apr. an increase to *c.* 100 was approved. On 12 Nov. the number of officers was 87. 'The WEU's multinational advisory police element in Albania', *Nato's Sixteen Nations*, Special Supplement 1998, p. 60; and 'The WEU multinational police element for Albania' (note 191).

[194] The 1998–99 budget allocated for logistics and equipment support for the Albanian police (4.8 m. ECU). 'The WEU multinational police element for Albania' (note 191).

[195] Mission established by decision of the OAU at its 36th Ordinary Session at Ambassadorial Level in Addis Ababa, Ethiopia, 22 Aug. 1997. Information from OAU Political Department, Addis Ababa, Ethiopia. The mission continued during 1998 with the same number of military observers as in 1997. SAPA (Johannesburg), 6 July 1998, in 'South Africa: Nation donates non-lethal military equipment to OAU', FBIS-AFR-98-187, 6 July 1998; SAPA (Johannesburg), 11 Dec. 1998, in 'South Africa: RSA: OAU fact-finding mission to Comoros returns 11 Dec.', FBIS-AFR-98-345, 11 Dec. 1998; and information from Niang Cheikh (see note 170).

[196] Observers from Egypt, Nigeria and Senegal under a Tunisian commander. Gaye, S., 'When a nation just one-fifth of Gambia's size crumbles', PANA, 25 Feb. 1999; and Information from Niang Cheikh (note 170).

[197] Monthly operational cost estimated at $160 000. Information as of 1998 from Niang Cheikh (170).

[198] The TMG was established in order to monitor the implementation of the Burnham Truce signed by the Government of Papua New Guinea and the Bougainville parties (the Bougainville Transitional Government, the Bougainville Interim Government and the Bougainville Revolutionary Army) at Burnham, New Zealand, 1–10 Oct. 1997. The TMG was replaced on 30 Apr. 1998 by a Peace Monitoring Group (PMG) (note 201).

[199] The TMG was headed by New Zealand.

[200] See note 204.

[201] The PMG was established on 30 Apr. 1998 in accordance with the Lincoln Agreement signed by the Government of Papua New Guinea and the Bougainville parties at a meeting in Lincoln, New Zealand, 19–23 Jan. 1998. The PMG mandate included monitoring the ceasefire, promoting confidence, providing information, and assisting in the democratization and development process in accordance with the agreement. Information from Second Secretary Matthew Broadhead, New Zealand Embassy in Sweden.

[202] The PMG is headed by Australia.

[203] The 301 PMG personnel (end 1998) are both civilian and military. Information from Broadhead. (note 201) In Nov. 1998 the PMG consisted of 250 Australian, 30 New

Zealand, 10 Fijian, 15 Vanuatan troops and 19 civilians. Australian Defence Force: Operation Bel Isi, URL <http://www.defence.gov.au/belisi/details.htm#anchor476444>.

[204] Australia is the major contributor to the PMG. The Australian estimated budget for FY 1998/99 (July–July) is $23.6 m., personnel-related costs excluded. URL <http://www.dod.gov.au/budget/budget.html>. In addition AusAID contributes $1.3 m. for the civilian component of Australia's participation in the Truce and Peace Monitoring exercises covering the period Sep. 1997 to Dec. 1998. URL <http://www.ausaid.gov.au/country/png/peace.html>. New Zealand's approximate cost in 1998 was TMG $2.1 m. (NZ$4 m.) and for PMG $1.3 m. (NZ$2.4 m.) and consists of support to New Zealand Defence Force. Fiji's and Vanuatu's contributions were included in New Zealand's budget. Information from Broadhead (note 201).

[205] The Task Force forms part of the Commonwealth's reconstruction programme for Sierra Leone initiated at the Oct. 1997 Commonwealth Heads of Government summit according to the Harare Declaration. It was established by the Commonwealth Secretary-General following the Sierra Leone President's request to the Commonwealth Ministerial Action Group (CMAG). In cooperation with the Sierra Leone Police Force and in consultation with the UN and other international agencies the aim of the Task Force is to 'develop a strategic plan for the reorganisation of the SLPF'. Initial deployment was for 2 months with the possibility of an extension. Information from Chief Programme Officer Sandra Pepera, Commonwealth Political Affairs Division; and 'Commonwealth helps to rebuild Sierra Leone Police Force', *Commonwealth Currents*, no. 3 (1998), p. 5.

[206] Phase 1 from July 1998 until mid-Dec. 1998. Phase 2 from Oct. 1998 until the end of Feb. 1999. Information from Pepera (note 205).

[207] Neither the head of the Task Force, the retired Assistant Inspector of Constabulary from the UK nor the other Task Force members is currently an active member of their respective police forces, but senior former police officers. 'Commonwealth helps to rebuild Sierra Leone Police force' (note 205), p. 5.

[208] Three police experts from the UK and 1 officer from each of the other 3 countries. Information from Pepera (note 205).

[209] The Task Force members are provided by their respective governments. Additional operational and logistical support to the group as a whole is provided by the British Government (£500 000). Information from Pepera (note 205); and 'Commonwealth helps to rebuild Sierra Leone Police force' (note 205), p. 5.

[210] On 16 June 1998 President Yeltsin, authorized by the other members of the Contact Group, and President Milosevic issued a joint statement, in which Milosevic agreed to Contact Group demands that Serbian forces allow free movement to diplomats throughout the region. The mission started on 6 July to observe and report on such issues as general freedom of movement, human rights, and the humanitarian and general security situation in Kosovo, and to be present in the area to facilitate confidence in the region. The KDOM is under the political guidance of a coordination group consisting of the Contact Group, EU Presidency and OSCE Chairman-in-Office. By late Dec. 1998 its inclusion in the OSCE KVM, as statuted in the 16 Oct. OSCE–FRY agreement, was virtually complete. 'Tense Christmas in Kosovo' (note 121); Kosovo Diplomatic Observer Mission, Fact Sheet released by the Bureau of European and Canadian Affairs, US Department of State, Washington, DC, 8 July 1998; and 'Milosevic agrees to talks with Kosovars' *International Herald Tribune,* 17 June 1998.

[211] Total number of personnel from all the member countries as at 8 Dec. 1998. All KDOM members are accredited embassy personnel in Belgrade. The EU and US components were temporarily withdrawn in Oct. following an expected NATO adoption of an activation order enabling air strikes on targets in Yugoslavia. *Kosovo Progress Report,* Bureau of European and Canadian Affairs, US Department of State, Washington, DC, 8 Dec. 1998; and AFP (Paris), 12 Oct. 1998, in 'Kosovo: Russian observers make no plans to withdraw from Kosovo', Foreign Broadcast Information Service, *Daily Reports–East Europe, Central Eurasia (FBIS-EEU)*, FBIS-EEU-98-285, 12 Oct. 1998.

[212] Each Embassy retains control over its staff and decides the size of its contribution according to its own resources. Kosovo Diplomatic Observer Mission (note 210).

[213] On 4 Dec. the North Atlantic Council authorized the activation of the NATO Extraction Force 'Operation Joint Guarantor'. The mission is to 'extract OSCE verifiers or other designated persons from Kosovo in the event all other measures are unsuccessful and at OSCE request'. 'AFSOUTH activates NATO Extraction Force', AFSOUTH Press Release, no. 98–51, 16 Dec. 1998; Press Statement, NATO Press Release (98) 139, 5 Dec. 1998; and Allied Forces Southern Europe, 'Operation Determined Guarantor', AFSOUTH Internet site, URL <http://www.afsouth.nato.int/\\detforce\force.htm>.

[214] The commander of XFOR is French Army Brig.-Gen. Marcel Valentin. Several other NATO countries including the USA contribute with equipment and staff personnel.

[215] Between Oct. and Dec. 1998 there were *c.* 1500–1800 troops. Information from AFSOUTH Public Information Office, Naples.

[216] Costs divided between all contributing states. Each state is responsible for its troops and the associated costs.

Appendix 2B. The Northern Ireland Good Friday Agreement

IAN ANTHONY

I. Introduction

Between 1969 and 1998 over 3250 people (2500 of them non-military) were killed by politically motivated attacks of one kind or another carried out in the context of disagreement over the legal and political status of the north-eastern part of the island of Ireland.[1] These deaths occurred as a result of attacks carried out in Northern Ireland, elsewhere in the United Kingdom and on mainland Europe. This was the most violent period in a centuries-old conflict between Ireland and Britain. On 10 April 1998 multi-party talks concluded with an agreement, known as the Good Friday Agreement or the Belfast Agreement, which is part of a wider effort to ensure that political arrangements in Northern Ireland will not be decided through a 'dialogue of violence'.

Ten political parties, which together represent around 80 per cent of the electorate of Northern Ireland, signed the Good Friday Agreement.[2] The agreement was then endorsed by simultaneous referendums in the Republic of Ireland and Northern Ireland on 22 May 1998. In the Republic the agreement received a virtually unanimous endorsement. In Northern Ireland 81 per cent of qualified voters participated in the referendum, of which 71 per cent endorsed the agreement. Most elements of the agreement have a maximum two-year timetable for implementation.

Although it should (if implemented) prevent the use of force for political ends, in another sense the Good Friday Agreement is not a peace settlement.[3] The issue underpinning the conflict—the legal status of the territory of Northern Ireland—has not been resolved, and the positions of the two main political groupings remain mutually exclusive. The group known as 'nationalists' (including the hard-line subgroup of 'republicans') still believe that the north-eastern part of Ireland should be governed as part of a unified Irish state entirely separate from the UK. The group known as 'unionists' (including the hard-line subgroup of 'loyalists') still believe that Northern Ireland should maintain its existing status of political union with the rest of the UK.[4]

[1] Security statistics published by the Northern Ireland Office in Apr. 1998 updated through press reports through to the end of 1998, URL <http://www.nio.gov.uk/secstats0498.htm>. From Oct. 1968 civil rights marches and activity by, in particular, militant student organizations increased in intensity. In Jan. 1969 a civil rights march was attacked in Derry/Londonderry. Following continued violence the British Army was deployed in increased numbers in Northern Ireland. This upsurge in violence is taken as the date when the latest conflict was joined.

[2] Citations in this appendix from the Good Friday/Belfast Agreement are based on the text published by the Northern Ireland Office on the Internet, URL <http://www.nio.gov.uk/agreement.htm>.

[3] For a broader discussion of the conflict and efforts to resolve it, see Dunn, S. (ed.), *Facets of the Conflict in Northern Ireland*, (Macmillan: Basingstoke, 1995); Alexander, Y. and O'Day, A. (eds), *Terrorism in Ireland* (Croom Helm: London, 1984); and Arthur, P. and Jefferey, K., *Northern Ireland since 1968* (Basil Blackwell: Oxford, 1996).

[4] In 1922 the Irish Free State, comprising 26 of the island's 32 counties, was established as a dominion of the British Commonwealth. In 1949 the Republic of Ireland was formally declared and the British Government passed the Ireland Act, which declared (*a*) that the Republic of Ireland was not a

The concern remains that if and when it becomes undeniable to one or other paramilitary grouping that its political objectives cannot be reached, the organized use of force may reappear.

The multi-party talks, which began in June 1996, were part of a wider peace process in which the role of actors not present at the talks was important. These actors were of different kinds. Two political parties, the Democratic Unionist Party (DUP) and the tiny United Kingdom Unionist Party (UKUP), left the talks in mid-1997 but continued to exert an influence on events.[5] Republican and loyalist paramilitary forces were excluded from direct participation at the talks, but their political representatives were present and their contribution was heavily influenced by the perspectives of these armed groups. External actors, in particular the United States, also played an important role in shaping the wider peace process although they were not officially involved in negotiating the agreement.

This appendix is not a survey of the Northern Ireland peace process but concentrates more narrowly on the contents of the Good Friday Agreement.[6]

II. Constitutional issues and new institutional arrangements

The Good Friday Agreement does not change the fundamental legal or constitutional status of Northern Ireland. The agreement includes a declaration that Northern Ireland in its entirety remains part of the United Kingdom and shall not cease to do so without the consent of a majority of the people of Northern Ireland. At the same time it is also declared that if the wish expressed by a majority is that Northern Ireland should cease to be part of the United Kingdom, the British and Irish governments will consult about what steps to take.

At the same time the Irish Government agreed to introduce legislation changing the contents of the Irish Constitution in a way which gave up any claim to legal jurisdiction over the entire island.

In the amended version, the will of 'the Irish nation' is not identified as synonymous with decisions by the Irish Government but has a more general frame of reference, including people of Irish descent both on the island of Ireland and in the diaspora beyond.[7] The agreed language states that the will of this 'Irish nation' is to unite all the people who share the territory of the island of Ireland but recognizes that, until unification can be brought about by consent, laws enacted by the Republic of Ireland will not apply throughout the island.

To summarize, a change in the legal and constitutional arrangements to take Northern Ireland out of the UK is possible by consent. If consent for a change is obtained, the provisions are worded in a way that points to a unified Irish state.[8]

British dominion, and (*b*) that Northern Ireland should not cease to be part of the UK without the consent of the Northern Ireland Parliament.

[5] The DUP and UKUP together represent around 20% of the electorate of Northern Ireland.

[6] The peace process is surveyed in Bloomfield, D., 'Northern Ireland', eds P. Harris and B. Reilly, *Democracy and Deep-Rooted Conflict: Options for Negotiators* (Institute for Democracy and Electoral Assistance (IDEA): Stockholm, 1998). The general political and religious background to the conflict in Northern Ireland is described by the CAIN (Conflict Archive on the Internet) Project conducted by the University of Ulster, URL <http://cain.ulst.ac.uk>. A recent summary article examining the wider peace process is Lloyd, J., 'Ireland's uncertain peace', *Foreign Affairs*, vol. 77, no. 5 (Sep./Oct. 1998), pp. 109–22.

[7] Irish nationhood is thereby comparable to the idea of a German 'Volk'.

[8] It is unclear from the agreement whether the creation of a separate independent state in Northern Ireland is a possible outcome. This outcome is not explicitly ruled out.

The agreement creates new institutions which can be described under four broad groupings: arrangements for Northern Ireland, arrangements for the island of Ireland, arrangements between different parts of the British Isles, and arrangements between the governments of the Republic of Ireland and the UK.

Arrangements for Northern Ireland

The agreement provides for a democratically elected assembly in Northern Ireland which is 'inclusive in its membership, capable of exercising executive and legislative authority, and subject to safeguards to protect the rights and interests of all sides of the community'.[9]

The 108-member assembly is to take over authority for all matters now the responsibility of six Northern Ireland departments currently within the British Government. This authority includes the right to pass laws (both primary and secondary legislation) which would then apply in Northern Ireland. Responsibility for all areas not specifically ceded to the authority of the assembly remains with a minister of the British Government.[10]

The assembly includes an Executive Committee led by a First Minister and including a Deputy First Minister and 10 ministers with departmental responsibilities. The First Minister and Deputy First Minister are elected jointly by the assembly voting on a 'cross-community' basis.[11]

There will not be an adversarial system in which a government and opposition form according to party affiliation. Ministerial posts are allocated to parties by reference to the number of seats each party has in the assembly, and ministerial posts will be allocated to both unionist and nationalist members. In December 1998 a final agreement was reached on the number of departments and distribution of the ministerial posts between parties.[12]

The Executive Committee will provide 'a forum for the discussion of, and agreement on, issues which cut across the responsibilities of two or more ministers, for prioritizing executive and legislative proposals and for recommending a common position where necessary (e.g., in dealing with external relationships)'.[13] Therefore, ministers exercise jurisdiction within their own departments and over questions which fall under the authority of their departments.

[9] The Good Friday/Belfast Agreement (note 2), section 3, Strand One, Democratic Institutions in Northern Ireland, para. 1.

[10] The delegated responsibilities include responding to crime through an effective policing framework, crime prevention measures (including social programmes aimed to prevent offending behaviour), administration of the criminal law, providing support to victims of crime and the prison system. The assembly is also responsible for spending aimed at the broad socio-economic development of Northern Ireland including, for example, support for projects to improve community relations.

[11] Apart from their political party affiliation, each member of the assembly must register as a 'nationalist' or a 'unionist'. Cross-community voting means that any decision must have either 'parallel consent' (which means that a majority of those members present and voting, including a majority of the unionist and nationalist designations present and voting, support it) or a 'weighted majority' (which means that 60% of members present and voting, including at least 40% of each of the nationalist and unionist designations present and voting, support it). By agreement among the parties in the assembly, the First Minister is the leader of the largest unionist party (David Trimble of the Ulster Unionist Party) while the first Deputy First Minister is a representative of the largest nationalist party (Seamus Mallon of the Social Democratic and Labour Party).

[12] de Breádún, D., 'Six new North–South bodies agreed in principle', *Irish Times* (Internet edition), 18 Dec. 1998, URL <http://www.irish-times.ie>.

[13] The Good Friday/Belfast Agreement (note 2), section 3, Strand One, Democratic Institutions in Northern Ireland, para. 19.

This is not the first Northern Ireland Parliament. From 1922 to 1972 a system of devolved government operated in Northern Ireland, but for all of this period one party (the Ulster Unionist Party) was dominant. The exclusive preservation of power in one party was considered untenable after the upsurge in political violence after 1969. Permanent one-party government could not lead to stability because it was manifestly unacceptable to the nationalist community of Northern Ireland. In 1972 'direct rule' (administration of Northern Ireland by a minister in London) was instituted as a temporary measure while a new system of devolved government was developed. Under this new system executive powers were not to be concentrated in elected representatives from one community only. A system known as 'power-sharing' was elaborated in 1973 and introduced in 1974. However, this system collapsed after only five months of sustained opposition by the unionist community and direct rule was resumed.

To avoid a repeat of these failed attempts at devolution the present agreement was submitted to the general population in both Northern Ireland and the Republic of Ireland in a referendum. However, the agreement also includes 'safeguards' intended 'to protect the rights and interests of all sides of the community' by reassuring nationalists that their interests will be taken into account even if they receive a minority share of the vote in elections.

For nationalists the main safeguards are the cross-community voting procedures noted above and the allocation of committee chairs, ministers and committee membership in proportion to party strength rather than by a decision of the largest party. For some unionists this system creates a concern that Sinn Féin, a nationalist political party intimately tied to the proscribed Provisional Irish Republican Army (IRA), will almost certainly receive two of the 10 ministerial posts (as will the anti-agreement DUP) and so assume full authority for the issues falling under those ministerial portfolios.

Arrangements for the island of Ireland

The Good Friday Agreement envisages the establishment of a North/South Ministerial Council 'to bring together those with executive responsibilities in Northern Ireland and the Irish Government, to develop consultation, cooperation and action within the island of Ireland'.[14]

Northern Ireland is to be represented on the council by the First Minister, Deputy First Minister and any relevant ministers (depending on the agenda for the council meeting). The Irish Government is represented by the Prime Minister (known as the Taoiseach, phonetic pronunciation 'teeshok') and relevant ministers.

The council is to meet in plenary format (twice a year) and to consider specific issues ('on a regular and frequent basis').

The tasks of the council are 'to exchange information, discuss and consult with a view to co-operating on matters of mutual interest within the competence of both Administrations, North and South'.[15]

[14] The Good Friday/Belfast Agreement (note 2), section 4, Strand Two, North/South Ministerial Council, para. 1.

[15] The Good Friday/Belfast Agreement (note 2), section 4, Strand Two, North/South Ministerial Council, para. 5(i). Twelve areas are listed in the agreement as being within this competence: agriculture; education; transport; environment; waterways; social security/social welfare; tourism; relevant EU programmes such as the European Interregional Cooperation Programme (INTERREG), Leader II and their successors; inland fisheries; health; urban development; and rural development.

The council has some decision authority but will take all decisions by agreement (i.e., a consensus is required). Implementation of any agreement is to be carried out separately in each jurisdiction. With the consensus rule a danger is perceived that unionists (who will always be represented under present circumstances) can block all decisions by the council not because of substantive disagreement but to prevent the council from functioning. It is not known how nationalists would respond if unionists seemed to be acting in bad faith.

Arrangements between different parts of the British Isles

The agreement envisages the creation of a British–Irish Council (BIC) 'to promote the harmonious and mutually beneficial development of the totality of relationships among the peoples of these islands'.[16] The BIC will comprise representatives of the Irish and British governments, devolved institutions in Northern Ireland, Scotland and Wales, and possibly elsewhere in the United Kingdom, together with representatives of the Isle of Man and the Channel Islands.

The tasks and procedures for the BIC are not defined in detail but only discussed in general terms and as decisions in principle since they depend on other political processes that have not been completed.[17]

Arrangements between the Irish and British governments

In 1985 a bilateral agreement between the governments of the UK and the Republic of Ireland (the 'Anglo-Irish Agreement') established a framework for regular dialogue. Under the Good Friday Agreement a new British–Irish Intergovernmental Conference is envisaged to 'bring together the British and Irish Governments to promote bilateral co-operation at all levels on all matters of mutual interest'.[18]

Regular and frequent meetings are envisaged to discuss matters that are not devolved to the authority of the other bodies established by the agreement. The conference will also facilitate cooperation in security matters in their all-island or cross-border aspects and review the Good Friday Agreement, including a formal published review three years after the agreement comes into effect.

III. Security

After 1969 the political violence in Northern Ireland led to the development of security measures that are not normal for the UK as a whole. These measures include the presence of large numbers of British armed forces. While the armed forces maintained a garrison in Northern Ireland before 1969, the scale of the deployment was usually around 2500 personnel; in 1997 about 17 000 personnel were stationed in

[16] The Good Friday/Belfast Agreement (note 2), section 5, Strand Three, British–Irish Council, para. 1.

[17] Northern Ireland Information Service, news release, 'British–Irish Council: ministers look forward to close cooperation', 16 Dec. 1998, URL <http://www.nio.gov.uk/981216c-nio.htm>. In 1997–98 the British Labour Government had a range of proposed reforms in various stages of discussion, definition and implementation. These include devolved government in Scotland and Wales, creation of some form of new executive administration in large cities (beginning with London) and embryonic proposals for a revised system of local and regional government in England.

[18] The Good Friday/Belfast Agreement (note 2), section 5, Strand Three, British–Irish Intergovernmental Conference, para. 1.

Northern Ireland.[19] Moreover, the British Government has exercised emergency powers in Northern Ireland that allow practices not allowed elsewhere in the UK.

The Good Friday Agreement notes that the development of a peaceful environment 'can and should mean a normalization of security arrangements and practices',[20] including a reduction in the numbers and role of the armed forces deployed in Northern Ireland, the removal of security installations and the lifting of emergency powers.

The armed forces in Northern Ireland have acted as an aid to the civilian authorities. The police (the Royal Ulster Constabulary, RUC) have responsibility for policing while the armed forces offer different kinds of assistance in performing policing duties. This can include providing protection to the RUC in areas of high threat, patrolling police bases, supporting counter-terrorist operations and specialist support—including bomb disposal and providing other special equipment and skills that the police do not have.

Restoration of normal security conditions depends on the level of perceived threat of political violence and the extent to which the civilian police are able to perform their functions. This issue is discussed below. In 1997–98 the number of armed forces in Northern Ireland has been reduced and their operational procedures have been altered. This has been criticized by unionists, who argue that there have not yet been tangible signs of a reduced threat from armed groups.

IV. Arms decommissioning

One tangible signal that the use of force to achieve political objectives is no longer contemplated in Northern Ireland is considered to be the decommissioning of illegally held arms in the possession of paramilitary groups.

Unionist and some British politicians have given this issue the highest priority. For example, on 14 September 1998, speaking in the new Northern Ireland Assembly, Nigel Dodds of the DUP observed that:

> the most important issue is that of decommissioning and whether IRA/Sinn Féin are going to be admitted into the Government of Northern Ireland while still armed to the teeth. Mr Flanagan, the Chief Constable of the RUC, has made it very clear that while troop levels are reduced and military patrols are withdrawn in Belfast, such paramilitary organizations are still intact, they still have access to arms and ammunition, they continue to pose a grave threat to peace, and they are still capable of carrying out atrocities such as the Omagh bombing.[21]

By the end of 1997 a report by retired Canadian General John de Chastelain provided an outline of how decommissioning might be approached.[22] This was accepted by the governments of the Republic of Ireland and the UK, and in mid-1998 an Independent Commission was established under de Chastelain to monitor, review and verify progress on decommissioning of illegal arms.[23]

[19] This figure of 17 000 was itself lower than during some periods after 1969.

[20] The Good Friday/Belfast Agreement (note 2), section 8, Security, para. 1.

[21] Verbatim report of statement in the Northern Ireland Assembly, 14 Sep. 1998. Publications of the Northern Ireland Assembly are archived on the Internet at URL <http://www.ni-assembly.gov.uk>. The bomb detonated in the town of Omagh on 15 Aug. 1998 led to the largest number of deaths from a single attack since 1969.

[22] Burns, J., 'N. Ireland report omits weapons timetable', *Financial Times*, 2 Dec. 1997, p. 10.

[23] Northern Ireland Information Service, news release, 'Decommissioning scheme introduced', 29 June 1998, URL <http://www.nio.gov.uk/980629g-nio.htm>.

All participants in the agreement are committed to 'use any influence they may have to achieve the decommissioning of all paramilitary arms within two years' of the referendums on the agreement.

In May Billy Hutchinson of the Progressive Unionist Party (PUP) was appointed as the point of contact and liaison with the Ulster Volunteer Force (UVF), an armed loyalist organization.[24] In early September 1998 Martin McGuinness of Sinn Féin was appointed as a point of contact and liaison between the decommissioning body and the IRA.[25] The choice of these high-profile individuals was interpreted by de Chastelain as a positive indication that parties were prepared to use their influence to bring about decommissioning.

In December 1998 the first arms were decommissioned when a small UVF offshoot organization—the Loyalist Volunteer Force—turned over a consignment of rifles, sub-machine guns, sawn-off shotguns, revolvers, ammunition, pipe bombs and explosives.[26]

However, the leader of Sinn Féin, Gerry Adams, suggested that no rapid progress could be expected from the main republican paramilitary organizations. He stated that the immediate priority must be 'to avoid stalemates, cul-de-sacs, brinkmanship, broken promises or bad faith. The decommissioning issue is a cul-de-sac, a dead end issue. It was thoroughly discussed and negotiated during the talks process.'[27] Significant numbers of unionists, however, insist on at least a beginning of IRA decommissioning before Sinn Féin can take their seats in the Executive Council.[28] By extension, the main loyalist paramilitary organization also seems unlikely to decommission significant quantities of arms in the near term.

V. Review of criminal procedures, policing and justice

Issues of police and criminal justice are among the most sensitive and important issues that will be dealt with in the wider peace process. The RUC is currently responsible for policing Northern Ireland. The Good Friday Agreement envisages reform of the existing policing arrangements and in practical terms the future of the RUC will be highly contentious. The agreement states that it is:

> essential that policing structures and arrangements are such that the police service is professional, effective and efficient, fair and impartial, free from partisan political control; accountable, both under the law for its actions and to the community it serves; representative of the society it polices, and operates within a coherent and co-operative criminal justice system,

24 Monaghan, E., 'Decommissioning Chief sees N. Irish guns handed in', Reuters, 25 May 1998, URL <http://customenews.cnn.com/cnews>.

25 Burns, J., 'Hope of a breakthrough on weapons', *Financial Times*, 5–6 Sep. 1998, p. 5.

26 Northern Ireland Information Service, news release, 'Dr Mowlam welcomes LVF decommissioning', 18 Dec. 1998, URL <http://ww.nio.gov.uk/981218b-nio.htm>.

27 'Decommissioning is a dead end issue', Sinn Féin statement dated 21 Sep. 1998, URL <http://sinnfein.ie/index.html>.

28 The Sinn Féin position on decommissioning created a problem for British Prime Minister Tony Blair in that during the weeks before the referendum in Northern Ireland he gave commitments to unionists that the process of decommissioning would have to begin before Sinn Féin representatives would be allowed to sit on the Executive Council of the new Northern Ireland Assembly. The Ulster Unionist Party campaigned for the agreement on this basis under attack from the Democratic Unionist Party. When the legislation was introduced in the House of Commons the language of the bill did not make any such linkage, leading the Conservative Party to oppose the legislation on the basis that present arrangements required the unionist community to make 'a huge leap of faith'. Halligan, L. and Burns, J., 'Blair accused over arms pledge', *Financial Times*, 30 May 1998.

which conforms with human rights norms. The participants also believe that those structures and arrangements must be capable of maintaining law and order including responding effectively to crime and to any terrorist threat and to public order problems. A police service which cannot do so will fail to win public confidence and acceptance.[29]

There is no agreement on how to create such a force and an independent commission has been established 'to make recommendations for future policing arrangements in Northern Ireland'.[30] The commission will be led by Chris Patten, until 1997 the British Governor of Hong Kong and previously a cabinet minister in successive Conservative governments.[31]

Nationalists see the RUC as both a symbol and the main instrument of British rule, while RUC officers and their families were high-priority and regular targets for attacks by the IRA and other nationalist armed groups.[32] Addressing a meeting of RUC officers before the referendum in Northern Ireland, British Prime Minister Tony Blair pledged that the RUC would be reformed but not disbanded. Moreover, the continued existence of the RUC is envisaged in recent British legislation. In part 1, paragraph 1 of the 1998 Police (Northern Ireland) Act it is stated that 'there shall continue to be a body corporate known as the Police Authority for Northern Ireland', and in paragraph 2 it is stated that this Police Authority 'shall continue to consist of (*a*) the Royal Ulster Constabulary; and (*b*) the Royal Ulster Constabulary Reserve'.[33]

In September 1998 Sinn Féin published its submission to the independent Commission on Policing, which opens with the statement: 'Policing, like democratic structures of government and an equality ethos, is one of those issues which lie at the heart of conflict resolution. The RUC is not a police service. Its history, behaviour, make-up and ethos make it unacceptable to nationalists and republicans. Reform is not an option'.[34]

There will also be a review of criminal justice according to terms of reference published in the agreement. On 27 June 1998 the Review of Criminal Justice in Northern Ireland commenced 'to develop the criminal justice system in Northern Ireland in a direction which commands the support and confidence of all parts of the community'.[35]

One controversial element of the criminal justice review is the approach taken in the agreement to implementation of provisions on release of individuals currently in prison convicted of so-called 'scheduled offences'. These are offences under legislation related specifically to the political status of Northern Ireland. In the agreement the British and Irish governments envisage 'mechanisms to provide for an accelerated programme for the release of prisoners'. However, 'prisoners affiliated to

[29] The Good Friday/Belfast Agreement (note 2), section 9, Policing and Justice, para. 2.

[30] The terms of reference of the commission are stated in the Good Friday/Belfast Agreement (note 2), section 9, Policing and Justice, Annex A, Commission on Policing for Northern Ireland.

[31] The commission will also include law enforcement and police reform experts from the United States and South Africa.

[32] By mid-1998 over 300 RUC officers and reserve officers had been killed in politically motivated attacks.

[33] The text of the Police (Northern Ireland) Act, 24 July 1998, is published on the Internet at URL <http://www.hmso.gov.uk/acts/acts1998/19980032.htm>.

[34] A Policing Service for a New Future, Sinn Féin Submission to the Commission on Policing, Sep. 1998. Sinn Féin documents are archived at the Sinn Féin website, URL <http://sinnfein.ie/index.html>.

[35] Northern Ireland Information Service, news release, 'Secretary of State publishes Review of Criminal Justice System consultation paper', 27 Aug. 1998, URL <http://www.nio.gov.uk/980827b-nio.htm>.

organizations which have not established or are not maintaining a complete and unequivocal ceasefire are not eligible for release'.

No specific timetable for release is included in the agreement beyond the statement that 'should the circumstances allow it, any qualifying prisoners who remained in custody two years after the commencement of the scheme would be released at that point'.[36]

The timetable for prisoner release is a contentious issue in particular for unionists. Unionists, many of whom are uncomfortable with the idea of people convicted of armed attacks receiving early release, have criticized the decision to release large numbers of prisoners before arms decommissioning has begun, arguing that when both arms and those trained to use them are at large in society the security risk is increased and not reduced.[37]

For nationalists, many of whom do not accept that 'scheduled offences' are legitimate in law, those in jail are seen as political prisoners held as a result of the British–Irish conflict rather than criminals. Release of these prisoners is therefore seen as 'a necessary part of the search for peace and reconciliation in Ireland'.[38]

VI. Conclusions

On 20 May 1998 *The Boston Globe* reported that 'the war in Northern Ireland is over. It ended in 1994, when the main paramilitary groups called ceasefires. Since then there have been spurts of violence, which will continue. But the war is over.'[39] This statement was written on the eve of the referendums that endorsed the Good Friday Agreement at a time of great optimism. Both unionist and nationalist political leaders had difficulty convincing their respective constituencies that the agreement was in their best interests and, given the complexity of the process, a more cautious assessment seems appropriate. Mike Smith of the University of London has observed that 'although the accord has been extolled as heralding a springtime of peace, to echo President Clinton's words, most of the participants know that the reality will be tougher'.[40]

The suspicion, mistrust and dislike among different parts of the community in Northern Ireland remain very deep. The Good Friday Agreement can only be successful, therefore, as part of a wider peace process in which much remains to be done to achieve a reconciliation between the parties to the conflict and the communities with which they identify.

As noted in the introduction, one significant strand of unionist political opinion—led by the Democratic Unionist Party—did not sign the agreement, and there is real

[36] The Good Friday/Belfast Agreement (note 2), section 10, Prisoners, para. 3.

[37] The leader of the DUP, Reverend Ian Paisley, expressed this feeling as follows: '[The Prime Minister] consciously and deliberately deceived the people of Northern Ireland regarding the early release of prisoners and the surrender of terrorist arms. Mr. Blair's gimmicky pledge to the people of Northern Ireland designed to influence the referendum result has already been exposed as a blatant lie, for there has been absolutely no linkage between prisoner releases and arms decommissioning, and yet some unrepentant and unreformed terrorist murderers are already being released'. 'The fruits of appeasement', Speech by Reverend Ian Paisley, 3 Sep. 1998, URL <http://www.dup.org.uk/scripts/dup_s/sitedetails.idc?article_ID=214>.

[38] 'Prisoner releases welcomed', Press statement by Martin Ferris, Sinn Féin, 22 Dec. 1998. Sinn Féin press releases are archived at the Sinn Féin website, URL <http://sinnfein.ie/index.html>.

[39] Cullen, K., 'At the end of the day, this is an island of strangers', *Boston Globe Online*, 20 May 1998, URL <http://www.boston.com/globe/turning_point>.

[40] Smith, M. L. R., 'Peace in Ulster? A warning from history', *Jane's Intelligence Review*, July 1998, pp. 4–6.

concern that the 28 DUP representatives in the Northern Ireland Assembly could disrupt the work of the body.[41]

No paramilitary faction has disbanded and a few armed groups continue, actively or passively, to reject the peace process and the agreement. The Irish National Liberation Army (INLA) did not declare a ceasefire until August 1998. Two breakaway groups from the Provisional IRA—the 'Continuity IRA' and the 'Real IRA'—continue to reject the peace process because the agreement does not include a commitment to end the political union with the UK.[42]

It is unclear how Sinn Féin will develop in a peacetime context. Whereas the larger unionist parties have participated in administration and decision making, Sinn Féin has never fully developed policies on many issues as its agenda (in many ways its *raison d'être*) has been dominated by ending the political union with the rest of the United Kingdom. Sinn Féin now faces the challenge of forming policies on the issues under the authority of the Northern Ireland Assembly. How successful it will be in this remains unclear.

Under the Good Friday Agreement it is envisaged that the Secretary of State for Northern Ireland in the British Government may hold a poll to test whether there is consent by a majority of the people of Northern Ireland to maintain a political union with the rest of the United Kingdom. The Secretary of State is to hold this poll 'if at any time it appears likely to him that a majority of those voting would express a wish that Northern Ireland should cease to be part of the United Kingdom and form part of a united Ireland'.

Only if and when the circumstances arise to call such a poll can the question of whether peace has been established in Northern Ireland be answered.

[41] If 30 members request a judicial review of a decision of the Northern Ireland Assembly such a review must be conducted. If the 28 DUP members were supported by individual unionist members from the Ulster Unionist Party (several of whom are known to be sceptical about the peace process) the work of the assembly could be very much delayed or even paralysed.

[42] Many unionists suspect that these groups are not breakaway factions at all but a tactic by which the IRA can appear to be in compliance with the peace process while retaining the option of use of force.

3. The Middle East

PETER JONES and ANDERS JÄGERSKOG

I. Introduction

Developments in the Middle East in 1998 were largely negative. Although the Israeli–Palestinian peace process made progress, it failed to achieve the measures called for by the schedule of the Oslo agreements.[1] There was no observable progress on the Israeli–Syrian or the Israeli–Lebanese tracks of the peace process and violence continued in Lebanon. The situation in the Persian Gulf remained tense and the Iraqi stand-off led to a US–British bombing campaign. Algeria's bloody civil war continued, although progress was made in 1998 in planning for elections to restore a modicum of civilian rule.

Section II of this chapter assesses the peace process. Section III reviews events in the North Africa/Mediterranean subregion, and section IV outlines the developments in the Persian Gulf. Section V presents the conclusions. Appendix 3A contains the 1998 Wye River Memorandum.

II. The peace process

The Middle East peace process began at the Madrid Conference in 1991. Two tracks were established: bilateral discussions between Israel and the neighbouring states with which it had not signed peace treaties; and multilateral discussions aimed at addressing long-term problems affecting the region. While each track has produced considerable achievements, the process has slowed dramatically since the election of Israeli Prime Minister Benjamin Netanyahu in 1996. His government includes factions which do not accept the basic philosophy of the peace process: that Israel should trade land it has captured from the Arabs and receive peace from them in return. Netanyahu's personal views are not well known. He may be more concerned with balancing his precarious coalition than with any philosophical position on the peace process as such. Of course, the difficulties are not solely Israel's responsibility. Statements and actions by several other Middle East leaders indicate that they do not subscribe to the notion that Israel should be permitted to live in peace after it has traded land, and some Palestinian movements continue to actively sponsor terrorist acts against Israel. However, there is a general sense that

[1] The 13 Sep. 1993 Declaration of Principles on Interim Self-Government Arrangements (known as the DOP or Oslo Agreement) and the 28 Sep. 1995 Israeli–Palestinian Interim Agreement on the West Bank and the Gaza Strip (known as the Interim Agreement or Oslo II) are together known as the Oslo agreements. The DOP is reproduced in *SIPRI Yearbook 1994* (Oxford University Press: Oxford, 1994), pp. 117–22. Excerpts from The Interim Agreement are reproduced in Jones, P., 'The Middle East peace process', *SIPRI Yearbook 1996: Armaments, Disarmament and International Security* (Oxford University Press: Oxford, 1996), pp. 191–202.

Israel is primarily responsible for the slowdown of the peace process since 1996.

Netanyahu's coalition broke up in December 1998, but not before his attempt to retain power by reconciling fundamentally contradictory positions had seriously damaged the peace process. Nonetheless, some progress was made in the Israeli–Palestinian talks in 1998 and a crucial agreement, the Wye River Memorandum, was reached.[2] These limited achievements were offset by the failure to implement previous agreements and the downward spiral in trust. The other tracks of the peace process made no discernible progress in 1998.

The Israeli–Palestinian track

In December 1997 President Bill Clinton invited Netanyahu and President Yasser Arafat to visit Washington separately at the beginning of 1998.[3] The peace talks had broken off in February 1997 because of a new Israeli settlement initiative at Har Homa, a suburb of Jerusalem.[4] Israel had not made a series of long-overdue deployments from the West Bank that were called for in the Oslo agreements. US mediator Dennis Ross travelled to the Middle East on the eve of the Washington meetings carrying a message that Israel must hand over a 'credible' amount of land in return for enhanced Palestinian efforts to combat terrorism.

The situation was complicated by Israel's internal politics. Foreign Minister David Levy, regarded as one of the 'doves' of the Likud cabinet, resigned in a dispute over the budget just days before Ross arrived. It was widely speculated that this strengthened the cabinet 'hawks', although Netanyahu may have used the situation to delay making decisions he wished to avoid.[5] Ross left without announcing progress, but Netanyahu took pains to say that the visit was part of a long process which would achieve success.[6]

On 9 January Israel announced a plan to expand Jewish settlements in disputed areas of the West Bank. Although a long-range plan, the announcement cast a pall over the Washington meeting,[7] and it may have been linked to Netanyahu's need to appeal to the political right wing on the eve of a no-confidence vote which the government narrowly survived.[8] The cabinet

[2] For the text of the Wye River Memorandum see appendix 3A in this volume.

[3] Jones, P. and Flodén, G., 'The Middle East peace process', *SIPRI Yearbook 1998: Armaments, Disarmament and International Security* (Oxford University Press: Oxford, 1998), p. 97.

[4] Jones and Flodén (note 3), pp. 92–93. Israel calls the suburb Har Homa; the Palestinians call it Jabal Abu Ghneim.

[5] For more on the internal situation in Israel see 'Netanyahu down, but not out—yet', *Mideast Mirror*, vol. 12, no. 1 (5 Jan. 1998), pp. 2–8; and Schmemann, S., 'Netanyahu's hold on power is hurt as minister quits', *New York Times*, 5 Jan. 1998, p. A1.

[6] Associated Press, 'Clinton envoy seeks promise by Netanyahu on pullback', *International Herald Tribune*, 7 Jan. 1998, p. 7; Dempsey, J., 'US envoy in new Mideast peace drive', *Financial Times*, 7 Jan. 1998, p. 4; and *al-Ayyam* (Ramallah) (Internet version), 11 Jan. 1998, 'West Bank: Palestinians accuse Netanyahu of foiling Ross mission', in Foreign Broadcast Information Service, *Daily Report–Near East and South Asia* (*FBIS-NES*), FBIS-NES-98-014, 15 Jan. 1998.

[7] Sharrock, D., 'Israel plans to double settler homes', *The Guardian*, 10 Jan. 1998, p. 5.

[8] Reuters, 'Israeli leader survives a no-confidence vote', *International Herald Tribune*, 13 Jan. 1998, p. 6.

also decided to refuse further withdrawals from the West Bank unless the Palestinians met a new series of obligations concerning security. These included demands which many argued Arafat could not meet and still retain the support of his own political power base (e.g., a request that 34 Palestinians wanted by Israel for terrorism be extradited from Palestinian-controlled areas to Israel).[9] Israel also restated its position that the Palestine Liberation Organization (PLO) Charter be revised, a requirement many believed the Palestinians had already fulfilled,[10] and for the Palestinian Authority (PA) to take greater action to fight terrorism and bring its extensive security forces into line with the limitations of the Oslo agreements.

Perhaps because of perceived Israeli intransigence and new demands, speculation grew that the reportedly difficult relationship between the Netanyahu Government and the Clinton Administration was deteriorating, including the personal relations between the two leaders. This began in 1997. As the Washington meeting approached there was also speculation that Clinton held Netanyahu responsible for the impasse and would adopt a cool approach.[11] Arafat awaited developments, in the hope that Clinton would force Netanyahu to compromise. The beginning of a progressive US tilt towards a more balanced relationship between the USA and the Palestinians and Israel was apparent and intensified throughout 1998.[12] Netanyahu retaliated by meeting with US right-wing political opponents of Clinton immediately upon his arrival in Washington, even before he met the president.[13] Netanyahu's boldness may have been inspired by the scandal which had developed around Clinton.

The Washington meetings and their aftermath

Clinton met with Netanyahu on 20–21 January, and with Arafat on 20 January. An Israeli proposal for a three-phase withdrawal from an additional 10 per cent of the West Bank in return for Palestinian security measures was reportedly discussed. Netanyahu maintained that his cabinet would not agree to more and reiterated demands that the Palestinians take additional steps to fight terrorism.[14] However, the relationship between the Palestinian actions

[9] Embassy of Israel, Stockholm, 'Myths and facts about the conversion law', *PMR* [Prime Minister's Report], vol. 2, no. 13 (14 Jan. 1998); Embassy of Israel, Stockholm, 'Cabinet communiqué', 14 Jan. 1998; and Schmemann, S., 'Israel announces stringent terms for withdrawal', *New York Times*, 14 Jan. 1998, p. A1.

[10] Jones and Flodén (note 3), p. 94.

[11] Gellman, B., 'Clinton's "snub diplomacy"', *International Herald Tribune*, 21 Jan. 1998, p. 1.

[12] Schmemann, S., 'Arafat trims his hopes and pins them on Clinton', *New York Times*, 18 Jan. 1998, p. D3.

[13] Kettle, M. and Borger, J., 'Netanyahu meets US far-right', *The Guardian*, 20 Jan. 1998, p. 7.

[14] Erlanger, S., 'US and Israel talk mainly of more talks', *New York Times*, 22 Jan. 1998, p. A6; Harris, J. F., 'An initial meeting of Clinton and Netanyahu yields little progress', *International Herald Tribune*, 21 Jan. 1998, p. 1; Clark, B., 'Israeli PM offers troops pull-out', *Financial Times*, 21 Jan. 1998, p. 8; Ehud Ya'ari report from the White House, Israel Television Channel 1 Network (Jerusalem), 20 Jan. 1998, in 'Israel: Netanyahu interviewed on Clinton meeting', FBIS-NES-98-020, 23 Jan. 1998; Radio Monte Carlo (Paris), 21 Jan. 1998, in 'West Bank: PA's Sha'th views Washington meetings', FBIS-NES-98-021, 23 Jan. 1998; and Briefing for Israeli correspondents by Israeli Prime Minister, IDF

and Israel's withdrawals was not made clear publicly, nor was the question of who would assess compliance. Based on past experience, the Palestinians suspected that Israel would unilaterally halt the process whenever Netanyahu's political requirements made such a move necessary. Because the type of land to be turned over was not specified, the Palestinians also had concerns about the quality of the land and the degree of autonomy that they would enjoy. There is also serious concern that the Palestinian areas are developing into a patchwork of separated islands in the West Bank which will not be economically viable. These issues had been the subject of bitter debate previously. The plan offered by Netanyahu in Washington was rejected by Arafat a few days later.[15]

The talks then entered a lengthy phase of public pessimism. There was no sign of new momentum before April 1998. In the meantime, secret meetings were held and various compromises examined. In early February Palestinian negotiators went to Washington to discuss a detailed plan for a phased Israeli withdrawal.[16] Direct meetings between Israeli and Palestinian negotiators continued during this period to develop proposals.[17]

Publicly, during this period Israel announced additional settlement plans for the West Bank (to the annoyance of the USA and the Palestinians).[18] US Secretary of State Madeleine Albright commented that the USA might abandon the peace process if the two sides were unprepared to make the necessary compromises.[19] Violence recurred with tragic consequences,[20] and Israel antagonized the European Union (EU). The latter event was the culmination of increasing European frustration with Israel and the limited EU role in the process.[21] The catalyst was the visit by British Foreign Secretary Robin Cook, representing the EU Presidency, to Har Homa. The visit was a debacle as

Radio (Tel Aviv), 21 Jan. 1998, in 'Israel: Netanyahu describes meetings, denies US "package deal"', FBIS-NES-98-021, 23 Jan. 1998.

[15] Borger, J., 'Arafat spurns withdrawal plan', *The Guardian*, 2 Feb. 1998, p. 7.

[16] Report from Palestine by Mazin Sa'adah, *al-Ra'y* (Amman), 5 Feb. 1998, in 'Jordan: paper on "US" ideas to unblock peace process', FBIS-NES-98-038, 11 Feb. 1998.

[17] Schiffer, S., *Yedi'ot Aharonot* (Tel Aviv), 17 Feb. 1998, in 'Israel: Netanyahu holds "long secret meeting" with Arafat envoys', FBIS-NES-98-048, 21 Feb. 1998; and Kaspit, B., Limor, Y. and Drucker, R., *Ma'ariv* (Tel Aviv), 25 Mar. 1998, p. 2, in 'Israel: Netanyahu's bureau drafts "secret" plan to promote talks', FBIS-NES-98-084, 27 Mar. 1998.

[18] Dempsey, J., 'Israel confirms new settlement plans', *Financial Times*, 5 Feb. 1998, p. 10.

[19] Bar-Yosef, A., Dudkevitch, M. and Najib, M., 'US may suspend Oslo mediation efforts', *Jerusalem Post* (Internet version), 12 Feb. 1998, URL <http://www.jpost.com/com/Archive/12.Feb.1998/News/Article-2.html>; and Schmemann, S., 'Israelis worry that peace effort is dead', *New York Times*, 4 Feb. 1998, p. A8.

[20] Greenberg, J., 'Martyrs' rites in West Bank town for men Israelis killed', *New York Times*, 12 Mar. 1998, p. A3.

[21] The EU is the largest financial donor to the peace process, but it has a marginal role in the bilateral discussions, which are effectively run by the USA. Both Europe and the Arabs (who suspect a US bias towards Israel) are displeased with this state of affairs. However, Europe's inability to develop a clear foreign policy works against its leadership in the peace process. Nevertheless, EU leaders have repeatedly called for a greater role, beyond simply making a financial contribution. Walker, M., 'EU seeks bigger role in Middle East peace', *The Guardian*, 17 Jan. 1998, p. 5; and Barber, L., 'Santer seeks new EU role in Mideast', *Financial Times*, 6 Feb. 1998, p. 4.

Israeli security forces and settlers clashed with the EU delegation. Netanyahu abruptly cancelled several events with Cook.[22]

Netanyahu's conflict with the EU and his courting of Clinton's political opponents appear to have been primarily motivated by domestic political concerns as he signalled to his right-wing supporters that he would promote Israel's 'interests' against foreign pressure to compromise. These actions perhaps enabled Netanyahu to maintain his coalition a few months longer, but they risked damaging Israel's relations with the USA and Europe.

In late March Ross again visited the region. For the first time, the figure of 13.1 per cent was publicly discussed as the US proposal for Israel's next redeployment from the West Bank. This figure appears to have been largely inspired by a desire on the part of the USA to ensure that the amount of land transferred would be sufficiently large so that Arafat could face his constituents and maintain that he had achieved a substantial further withdrawal on the road to eventual control over most of the West Bank. The Israeli Government was reported to have offered less and to have insisted on various Palestinian concessions in other areas. The Palestinians responded that Israel was obligated to make further withdrawals and could not reopen previous agreements by demanding new Palestinian actions in order for Israel to live up to those agreements. Albright said that important ideas had been explored, and the Palestinians seemed to view the Ross mission as useful.[23] A few days later, Israel sought Ross's return to discuss ideas for allowing an apparent increase in the amount of land that Israel would hand over so that the 13 per cent goal could be achieved while ensuring that some of that land would not actually come under Palestinian control for security purposes.[24] Meanwhile, violence continued.

British Prime Minister Tony Blair brokered the next significant step. In a visit to the Middle East in April, Blair, acting in coordination with Washington, invited Netanyahu and Arafat to London for talks. In accepting, both made clear that their core positions were not open to compromise. Separate meetings were to be held between each leader and Albright and Blair. Opponents on both sides expected little progress to be made, and each side accused the other of stalling.[25]

The London meetings

The London meetings began on 4 May. Albright promoted the US proposal of an Israeli withdrawal from 13 per cent of the area of the West Bank and

[22] Dempsey, J., 'Cook to visit Har Homa in defiance of Israeli protests', *Financial Times*, 17 Mar. 1998, p. 5.

[23] Machlis, A., 'Israel drags feet on West Bank handover', *Financial Times*, 30 Mar. 1998, p. 5; Reuters, 'Albright stresses gains of Ross's Mideast trip', *International Herald Tribune*, 1 Apr. 1998, p. 6; and Radio Monte Carlo (Paris), 31 Mar. 1998, in 'West Bank: Palestinian minister notes Ross mission's positive points', FBIS-NES-98-090, 2 Apr. 1998.

[24] Kaspit, B. and Ben-Horin, Y., *Ma'ariv* (Tel Aviv), 3 Apr. 1998, p. 2, in 'Israel: new ideas reported to end deadlock', FBIS-NES-98-093, 6 Apr. 1998.

[25] Greenberg, J., 'Albright to see Netanyahu and Arafat in London', *New York Times*, 21 Apr. 1998, p. A3; and Ward, L., 'Blair's peace breakthrough', *The Guardian*, 21 Apr. 1998, p. 3.

acceleration of the Final Status talks.[26] She was unsuccessful. Press reports speculated that the main obstacle had been Netanyahu's unwillingness to move beyond 9 per cent of the West Bank for fear that his cabinet would not approve such a proposal and his coalition would collapse.[27] At the end of the meetings, Albright invited Netanyahu and Arafat to Washington if there was anything for them to discuss. She also stated that the process was in danger of being irreparably damaged and that the USA would reconsider its involvement unless progress was made soon. Albright did not threaten to abandon the peace process but said that the USA would revise its approach if the two sides could not move forward. She also hinted that in future blame would be publicly apportioned, and the US delegation made a point of leaking news of the fact that Arafat had accepted the US proposal.[28]

There was no meeting in Washington, and no discernible progress was made in the summer although there were reports of secret meetings between emissaries of Arafat and Netanyahu to lay the foundation of an eventual compromise.[29] Arafat made several trips abroad to increase pressure on Israel and called for an Arab summit meeting.[30] Although his actions did not influence Israel, the international community expressed increasing sympathy. In a 'personal' comment in May, US First Lady Hillary Clinton stated, 'It would be in the longer term interest of the Middle East for Palestine to be an independent state'.[31] In July, by a large vote, the UN General Assembly increased the level of the PLO's representation. Although falling short of granting them full representation as a state, Palestinian representatives are now able to take part in debates in ways not open to other observers.[32]

[26] These issues include the status of the Palestinian Government, Jerusalem, Israeli settlements, borders, water, security arrangements and the rights of return of Palestinian refugees.

[27] A few days later Ariel Sharon publicly stated that any handover exceeding 9% would constitute 'a grave security threat to Israel' and that he would bring down the government if Netanyahu tried to do so. Whether this was staged or not, is another question. Barne'a, N. and Eichner, I., *Yedi'ot Aharonot* (Tel Aviv), 12 May 1998, p. 2, in 'Israel: Sharon criticizes Netanyahu on FRD, comments on talks', FBIS-NES-98-132, 13 May 1998.

[28] 'London yields conditional invitation to Washington', *Mideast Mirror*, vol. 12, no. 84 (5 May 1998), pp. 2–10; Buchan, D. and Gardner, D., 'Albright warns of last chance for Oslo accords', *Financial Times*, 7 May 1998, p. 1; and Black, I., 'US sets ultimatum for peace progress', *The Guardian*, 6 May 1998, p. 1.

[29] Channel 2 Television Network (Jerusalem), 17 July 1998, in 'Israel: Israel–PA security cooperation resumes after "secret" talks', FBIS-NES-98-198, 20 July 1998; *al-Aswaq* (Amman), 14 Sep. 1998, p. 1, in 'West Bank & Gaza Strip: Urayqat confirms secret talks, meetings with Israelis', FBIS-NES-98-257, 15 Sep. 1998; and Dickey, C., Contreras, J. and Masland, T., 'Back at the table', *Newsweek*, 26 Oct. 1998, pp. 20–23.

[30] Dempsey, J. and Huband, M., 'Arafat calls for Arab summit talks', *Financial Times*, 21 May 1998, p. 8.

[31] 'Hillary Clinton: eventual Palestinian state important for Middle East peace', *Mideast Mirror*, vol. 12, no. 86 (7 May 1998), p. 9.

[32] 'UN vote seen taking Palestine a (symbolic) step closer to statehood', *Mideast Mirror*, vol. 12, no. 129 (8 July 1998), pp. 9–14; Crossette, B., 'Palestinians UN role widened: US "no" vote is overwhelmed', *New York Times*, 8 July 1998, p. A1; and Silber, L. and Dempsey, J., 'PLO granted greater rights at the UN', *Financial Times*, 8 July 1998, p. 1. According to an Israeli newspaper, the USA refused to intervene at the UN to try to prevent this and did so to signal its displeasure at Netanyahu's policies. Schiffer, S., *Yedi'ot Aharanont* (Tel Aviv), pp. 4, 5, in 'Israel: new US approach to Netanyahu outlined', FBIS-NES-98-177, 29 June 1998.

During this period Arafat began to talk of unilaterally declaring statehood for Palestine on 4 May 1999, the deadline for the close of the Oslo process, unless the negotiations were completed. Israel took the view that such a declaration would fundamentally prejudge the outcome of the Final Status talks and stated that such an action would have dire consequences. The Palestinians responded that Israel's refusal to address the issues was a strategy to delay the peace process until it was too late to reach an agreement under the Oslo guidelines and then end it.[33] At a meeting in Gaza on 24 September the Palestinian leadership formally announced its intent to declare statehood on 4 May 1999.[34] However, this may be a ploy to gain concessions from Israel and benefits from Europe and the USA in return for not doing so before talks have concluded.

Throughout the summer Israel announced further settlement activity, particularly around Jerusalem,[35] and the government coalition suffered further stress.[36] Arafat suffered political difficulties when polls showed that Palestinians were disillusioned with the peace process and with Arafat; a decrease in the standard of living since the beginning of the process was cited as the primary cause of discontent.[37] In August a respected member of Arafat's Government, Hanan Ashrawi, resigned because of alleged systematic corruption among Arafat supporters. This followed numerous reports of corruption over several years.[38]

In August Israel made a written offer of a 13 per cent withdrawal from the West Bank. However, there were various conditions, and it was uncertain what the 13 per cent actually represented. Israel linked the figure to a requirement that 3 per cent of the land would become a nature reserve, and thus only available for that use.[39] Although the PA refused, this offer became the basis of the Wye agreement after detailed negotiation. Further discussion took place in September, and Ross and Albright visited the Middle East in the autumn. An agreement was reached to hold open-ended talks at Wye Plantation, Maryland, beginning on 15 October with President Clinton acting as 'chairman', as needed. Significantly, US Central Intelligence Agency (CIA) Director George Tenet took part in the pre-Wye discussions and pledged to assist both sides in implementing an eventual agreement. The CIA had assisted the two sides in

[33] Abd-al-Jabbar, A., *al-Sharq al-Awsat* (London), 8 May 1998, p. 8, in 'West bank: preparing for Palestine state must start now', FBIS-NES-98-128, 11 May 1998; and Schmemann, S., 'Arafat likely to declare statehood in '99', *New York Times*, 8 July 1998, p. A8.

[34] *al-Ayyam* (Ramallah) (Internet version), 25 Sep. 1998, in 'West Bank & Gaza Strip: "text" of PA leadership's 24 Sep. statement', FBIS-NES-98-268, 28 Sep. 1998.

[35] Skafi, I., *al-Ayyam* (Ramallah) (Internet version), 25 May 1998, in 'West bank: report notes Israeli plan to change Jerusalem's demography', FBIS-NES-98-147, 29 May 1998; Sharrock, D. and Kettle, M., 'Fury greets new Israeli expansion', *The Guardian*, 22 June 1998, p. 1; Silber, L., 'UN hits at plan to enlarge Jerusalem', *Financial Times*, 15 July 1998, p. 4; and 'Number of settlers grows to nearly 170 000', *Mideast Mirror*, vol. 12, no. 171 (7 Sep. 1998), p. 3.

[36] 'Beginning of the end?', *The Economist*, 1 Aug. 1998, pp. 36–37.

[37] *al-Hayah al-Jadidah* (Gaza) (Internet version), 29 May 1998, in 'West Bank: poll shows people's support for peace process, PA declining', FBIS-NES-98-153, 3 June 1998.

[38] Borger, J., 'Ashrawi quits over crookery in Arafat ranks', *The Guardian*, 7 Aug. 1998, p. 9.

[39] 'Israel is said to give written pullout offer to Palestinians', *International Herald Tribune*, 22–23 Aug. 1998, p. 3.

dealing with their disputes over terrorism since 1997, but that role was about to grow substantially.[40]

The Wye River Memorandum

Prior to the Wye Plantation talks Netanyahu announced that the hardliner Ariel Sharon would be his new foreign minister and lead the Israeli delegation in the upcoming Final Status talks. There was speculation in Israel that Netanyahu had done this to strengthen his right-wing support, and Palestinians regarded the step as a sign that Netanyahu was not serious about the peace process. Some felt that Netanyahu's ultimate ambition was to use the Wye talks to set the stage for an early election.[41]

The talks were held on 15–23 October, and the Wye River Memorandum was signed on 23 October 1998. It was immediately criticized as a 'sell-out' by opponents on both sides and worries persisted over whether the resulting deal would be observed.[42] Jordan's King Hussein participated, interrupting medical treatment to attend. Palestinian opponents of the process staged a terrorist attack in hope of forcing Netanyahu to leave the talks. They did not succeed, although they strengthened his hand in calling for stringent security measures as part of the agreement.[43]

The Wye River Memorandum is wide-ranging and will represent compromises by both sides if it is implemented. An attachment established a time line for the various steps of the memorandum. The Wye River Memorandum also signalled the continuation of a change in the relationship between the USA and Israel and the Palestinians with respect to the peace process.

The 'further redeployments' section calls for a 13 per cent transfer of land from area C—territory on the West Bank under exclusive Israeli control—to areas A (1 per cent) and B (12 per cent).[44] This means that 13 per cent more land will come under varying degrees of PA control, although at least 3 per

[40] Lippman, T. W., 'Israel and Palestinians finally make progress', *International Herald Tribune*, 8 Oct. 1998, p. 6; and Dempsey, J., 'Albright upbeat after Mideast talks', *Financial Times*, 8 Oct. 1998, p. 4.

[41] Although some pointed out that Sharon's appointment could be beneficial to the process if he used his influence to push for a deal. 'FM Sharon need not be a bane, says *Al-Ahram* editor', *Mideast Mirror*, vol. 12, no. 196 (12 Oct. 1998), p. 11; Dempsey, J., 'Israeli hardliner to lead peace delegation', *Financial Times*, 10–11 Oct. 1998, p. 3; and Contreras, J., 'One step forward . . .', *Newsweek*, 19 Oct. 1998, p. 23.

[42] IDF Radio (Tel Aviv), 16 Oct. 1998, in 'Israel: "lack of confidence" between parties noted at summit', FBIS-NES-98-289, 19 Oct. 1998; Erlanger, S., 'Clinton returns to Mideast summit in Maryland', *New York Times*, 18 Oct. 1998, p. A.16; *al-Sharq al-Awsat* (London), 19 Oct. 1998, p. 3, in 'West Bank & Gaza Strip: accords reached, but Netanyahu leaves Arafat "fuming"', FBIS-NES-98-292, 20 Oct. 1998; 'Israel threatens to break off talks at peace summit', *International Herald Tribune*, 22 Oct. 1998, pp. 1, 6; and Dempsey, J., 'Clinton urges Israel to accept terms of security document', *Financial Times*, 22 Oct. 1998, p. 14.

[43] 'Beersheba terror attack hangs over Wye summit', *Mideast Mirror*, vol. 12, no. 201 (19 Oct. 1998), pp. 2–9; and Hockstader, L., 'Terrorist wounds dozens', *International Herald Tribune*, 20 Oct. 1998, pp. 1, 4.

[44] Wye River Memorandum, section I. Area A consists of those zones for which the Palestinians will have full responsibility for internal security and public order as well as for civil affairs (the cities of Bethlehem, Jenin, Nablus, Qalqilya, Ramallah and Tulkarem, in addition to Jericho) and parts of the city of Hebron outside specific areas where the Israeli Army will be responsible for security. Area B consists of Palestinian towns and villages on the West Bank in which the PA has civil authority but shares security responsibility with Israel. Area C consists of those areas of the West Bank under Israeli control.

cent of that 13 per cent must be set aside as a nature reserve. There is also a promise that 14.2 per cent of the current area B will become part of area A and thus under exclusive Palestinian control. Although attention was focused on the 13 per cent issue, the 14.2 per cent transfer from area B to area A was also significant. At the end of the process the PA will have full control over 17.9 per cent of the West Bank and partial control over 22.9 per cent.[45]

In terms of 'security and security cooperation', Arafat resisted Netanyahu's demand that Palestinians wanted for terrorism be handed over to Israel but accepted US monitoring to ensure that they would be prosecuted and held by the PA.[46] Israel agreed to resume the release of Palestinian political prisoners as called for under the Oslo agreements. Each side recommitted itself to fight terrorism, cooperate and prevent incitement of violence. The CIA will play a large role as a formal partner and (to some extent) a go-between for the Israeli and Palestinian security services.[47] The involvement of a credible third party may make it difficult for Israel to unilaterally claim that the PA has not lived up to its commitments as a pretext for stalling, provided that the PA does so.

On the issue of the Palestinian Police Israel had argued, with justification, that they have grown to a number and capability far in excess of that permitted by the Oslo agreements. The Wye River Memorandum states that the PA will cut the number of Palestinian Police in order to come into 'conformity with the prior agreements'.[48] No mention was made of what would happen to policemen made redundant, and it seems likely that they will remain on the PA payroll in some capacity. The PA also agreed to confiscate excess weapons held by Palestinians, although no commitment exists to turn them over to Israel.

On the revoking of the PLO Charter, Netanyahu had long argued that the steps taken by the PLO during the Rabin–Peres era were insufficient (although they were deemed adequate by Israel and the USA at the time). A process was established in the Wye River Memorandum to gather the Palestinian National Council (PNC) and others in order to make the necessary further changes, and it was specified that this would happen four to six weeks after the Wye River Memorandum came into effect. The document stated that President Clinton would address this meeting, a politically significant gesture.[49]

On economic issues, both sides stated their intention to reactivate the economic cooperation committees.[50] They agreed to resolve the 'safe passage' issue (i.e., unimpeded passage for Palestinians between Gaza and the areas of the West Bank under PA control). The two sides committed themselves to open the Gaza Port, the Gaza Industrial Estate and the Gaza Airport, and target dates were set. Both sides pledged support for continuous and uninterrupted

[45] The different categories of land are discussed in Jones (note 1) pp. 169–71

[46] Wye River Memorandum, section II, subsections A and B.

[47] Yasin, N., *al-Quds al-Arabi* (London), 27 Oct. 1998, p. 8, in 'West Bank & Gaza Strip: role of CIA in Palestinian–Israeli accord', FBIS-NES-98-301, 30 Oct. 1998; and Dempsey, J., 'CIA thrust into role of Mideast's honest broker', *Financial Times*, 26 Oct. p. 3.

[48] Wye River Memorandum, section II, subsection C, para. 1.

[49] Wye River Memorandum, section II, subsection C, para. 2.

[50] Wye River Memorandum, section III.

Final Status talks and stated their desire to achieve a settlement by 4 May 1999.[51] This is a highly ambitious goal.

The final section of the Wye River Memorandum stated that neither side 'shall initiate or take any steps that will change the status of the West Bank and the Gaza Strip in accordance with the Interim Agreement'.[52] This section has been interpreted in two ways. Israel argues that it precludes a unilateral declaration of statehood by the PA. The Palestinians use it to declare settlement activity illegal. In strictly legal terms, the Palestinian position is tenuous as this section addresses only the legal status of the area. Politically, however, the PA's arguments were strengthened when Israel announced plans for settlements.

Israel and the USA also signed a separate memorandum which promises to give Israel greater access to US resources in fields such as missile defence and defence against threats of use of non-conventional weapons.[53] It may have been designed to lessen Israeli concerns about long-term security threats as Israel takes risks to make peace with the Palestinians.

The implementation of the Wye River Memorandum

Not surprisingly, implementation of the Wye River Memorandum was not smooth since Arafat and Netanyahu faced stinging criticism. On 2 November Netanyahu announced that 'normal' settlement construction would continue. This enraged the Palestinians, who stated that it violated the Wye River Memorandum. The announcement also brought harsh criticism from the USA.[54] Meanwhile, the PA began a substantial crackdown against Hamas, which itself threatened Arafat.[55] Netanyahu phoned Arafat on 2 November to request a delay in implementing the Wye River Memorandum. Although pledging to respect the timetable, Netanyahu was reluctant to put the memorandum to his cabinet because he was not sure that it would be accepted. Ironically, he had no such fears in parliament generally as the opposition Labour Party had stated that it would vote with the government. Arafat accepted the delay,[56] the first of many. At the same time, Israel lifted a 'closure' on the West Bank and Gaza that had been in effect for 50 days.

On 6 November, two Palestinian bombers killed themselves in Jerusalem and injured 25 others. The incident took place as the Israeli Cabinet met to vote on the Wye River Memorandum. Netanyahu immediately suspended discussion and made additional demands on the PA, the first of several. In addition to new security conditions, he also stated that the PLO Charter must be

[51] Wye River Memorandum, section IV.

[52] Wye River Memorandum, section V.

[53] US–Israel Memorandum of Agreement, reprinted in *Strategic Assessment*, Jaffee Centre for Strategic Studies, vol. 4, no. 1 (Jan. 1999), p. 9.

[54] A US Government official stated 'we are angry about these statements . . . They are not conducive to fostering confidence in the [Wye] accord'. Dempsey, J., 'Israelis defiant on settlements', *Financial Times*, 3 Nov. 1998, p. 4.

[55] Hockstader, L., 'Hamas issues a threat to Arafat', *International Herald Tribune*, 2 Nov. 1998, pp. 1, 8. Hamas is an Islamic movement active in the West Bank and Gaza Strip.

[56] Sharrock, D., 'Arafat takes delay with good grace', *The Guardian*, 3 Nov. 1998, p. 7.

revoked by a formal vote (the procedure whereby the PA would revoke the charter had not been specified at Wye).[57] Both steps presented Arafat with political problems. As time passed it became obvious that the demands had less to do with the PA than with Netanyahu's need to shore up his coalition.[58]

On 11 November the Israeli Cabinet approved the Wye River Memorandum. The vote in the 17-member cabinet was 8 for, 4 against and 5 abstentions (2 cabinet members were abroad). However, the cabinet attached more conditions. For example, each withdrawal called for in the memorandum is to be brought before the cabinet for a vote on whether the Palestinians are fulfilling their obligations. On the other hand, the cabinet promised to authorize and expedite the opening of the Gaza Airport and to begin the release of Palestinian prisoners.[59] The addition of new requirements angered the Palestinians and the rhetoric again turned harsh. Particularly notable was a statement made by Foreign Minister Sharon to a group of settlers urging 'Everyone [to] take action . . . run, grab more hills. Whatever is seized will be ours. Whatever isn't seized will end up in their [Palestinian] hands'.[60] Sharon made this statement as Netanyahu was castigating Arafat for statements which appeared to prejudge the outcome of the Final Status talks.

The peace process further deteriorated when Israel released 250 of the 750 prisoners called for in the Wye River Memorandum. Most of them were criminals, not Palestinians incarcerated for political activities.[61] Netanyahu's statement that the agreement on prisoners did not specify the type of prisoners to be freed is legally correct but ran counter to the manner in which previous Israeli governments had interpreted the term 'prisoner release'. Hundreds of Palestinian prisoners began a hunger strike and trust deteriorated further when rioting again broke out.[62] In contrast to this, the first redeployment called for in the Wye River Memorandum took place on 20 November, as Israel pulled out of 500 square kilometres on the northern West Bank, between Jenin and Nablus.[63]

President Clinton visited the West Bank and Gaza in late December. Reports had circulated that senior Israeli officials tried to dissuade him from making the trip. Clinton arrived in Israel on 13 December and made a round of high-profile appearances before continuing to Gaza on 14 December. He participated in a session of the Palestinian National Council that voted to void those parts of the PLO Charter which denied Israel's right to exist. The trip was highly symbolic and marked the continuation of improving relations between

[57] 'Gov't suspends debate on Wye deal after Jerusalem car bomb', *Mideast Mirror*, vol. 12, no. 215 (6 Nov. 1998), pp. 6–10; and Dempsey, J., 'Suicide car bomb attack sets back Israel peace deal', *Financial Times*, 7–8 Nov. 1998, p. 1

[58] Dempsey, J., 'US angered as Israelis erect another Wye accord obstacle', *Financial Times*, 10 Nov. 1998, p. 4.

[59] 'Israeli cabinet approves deal on pullout, but adds conditions', *International Herald Tribune*, 12 Nov. 1998, pp. 1, 10.

[60] 'Verbal sparring escalates, but Wye implementation seems inevitable', *Mideast Mirror*, vol. 12, no. 221 (16 Nov. 1998), p. 3.

[61] Sharrock, D., 'Israel frees hundreds of prisoners', *Guardian Weekly*, 29 Nov. 1998, p. 3.

[62] Hockstader, L., 'Protests intensify in Israeli jails', *Guardian Weekly*, 13 Dec. 1998, p. 15.

[63] Dempsey, J., 'Israeli cabinet agrees to return land', *Financial Times*, 20 Nov. 1998, p. 10.

the USA and the Palestinians. Netanyahu, on the other hand, perhaps sensing that a new election would soon be called, made a number of harsh comments about the process. The meetings that were held did not go well, particularly one with Netanyahu and Arafat just before Clinton's departure.[64]

These events formed the backdrop to the disintegration of the Israeli Government. The religious right-wing in the cabinet no longer supported Netanyahu, and in the latter part of November and December Netanyahu made frantic attempts to shore up the government.[65] Faced with a choice between honouring commitments or scrapping them to appeal to his supporters, Netanyahu chose the latter. Nevertheless, a vote of no-confidence was passed by the Knesset on 21 December. Netanyahu remained in office as a caretaker prime minister but was unlikely to honour any of the remaining sections of the Wye River Memorandum as he prepared for 17 May 1999 elections.

In the final weeks of 1998 Arafat embarked upon a strategy to portray himself to the international community as a moderate in the run-up to the endgame leading to 4 May 1999. He made a speech in Stockholm on 5 December in which he called for a new basis for relations between the two sides and laid out positions intended to appeal to moderate Israelis and the USA.[66]

The Israeli–Syrian and Israeli–Lebanese tracks

No discernible progress was made in either the Israeli–Syrian or Israeli–Lebanese tracks of the peace process in 1998, although there were rumours of secret emissaries and meetings.[67] Syrian President Hafez-al Assad continued to refuse discussions with Israel unless it accepts the principle that all the area of the Golan Heights be returned,[68] which strengthened his standing in the Arab world. The failure of the peace process added to Assad's lustre as the Arab leader who refused to 'be tricked' by Netanyahu.[69] However, Netanyahu maintained his position that Israel would not enter talks that required the return of all of the Golan Heights in exchange for peace.

Although not related directly to the peace process, Syria's and Israel's relations with Turkey were of relevance. Israel continued to develop ties with

[64] 'Wye deal on rocks as Clinton heads home and Netanyahu braces for Monday's no-confidence test', *Mideast Mirror*, vol. 12, no. 242 (15 Dec. 1998), pp. 2–9.

[65] 'PM swings rightward, shooting down Wye to shore up his coalition', *Mideast Mirror*, vol. 12, no. 237 (8 Dec. 1998), pp. 2–8; Hockstader, L., 'Netanyahu's scramble to gain support', *International Herald Tribune*, 26 Nov. 1998, pp. 1, 10; and Sharrock, D., 'Israel faces meltdown over peace deal', *Guardian Weekly*, 13 Dec. 1998, p. 1.

[66] Palestinian National Authority Official Website, 'Speech of HE President Yaser Arafat–Stockholm, 5 Dec. 1998', URL <http://nmopic.pna.net/speeches/stockholm_051298.html>.

[67] All of which were denied. Abbud, A., *al-Ittihad* (Abu Dhabi), 24 July 1998, in 'Syria: Syrian sources deny secret Syrian–Israeli contacts', FBIS-NES-98-206, 28 July 1998; and IDF Radio (Tel Aviv), 17 Nov. 1998, in 'Israel: Ross said trying to renew Israeli–Syrian track', FBIS-NES-98-321, 18 Nov. 1998, which also mentions EU efforts to broker a resumption of the talks. For reports of a secret meeting in Europe to discuss possible Israeli withdrawal from south Lebanon see Rabin, E. and Kaspit, B., *Ma'ariv* (Tel Aviv), 29 Nov. 1998, p. 3, in 'Israel: *Ma'ariv* reports on Israeli–Syrian talks on withdrawal', FBIS-NES-98-333, 1 Dec. 1998.

[68] Gardner, D., 'Assad insists Israel must hand back Golan Heights', *Financial Times*, 16 July 1998, p. 12.

[69] 'Syria: at the centre?', *The Economist*, 27 June 1998, p. 44.

Turkey, to the annoyance of the Arab states, particularly Syria.[70] A dispute between Syria and Turkey was resolved by Egyptian mediation, unfavourably for Syria.[71] While Israel was not involved, the wider strategic implications of its relations with Turkey were clear.

The stand-off in south Lebanon continued with weekly killings on both sides. The Israeli Cabinet came under increasing pressure from the public to unilaterally withdraw from the self-proclaimed Israeli security zone in Lebanon. Netanyahu repeatedly offered to do so if a credible force would replace the Israeli Army and provide security for Israel's northern border or at least if Syria would guarantee peace on the border. The idea was unacceptable to Lebanon's real ruler, Syria, which regards the bloody situation as a way of punishing Israel for its refusal to resume peace negotiations on acceptable terms.[72]

The situation appears stalemated, at least on the basis of public statements. Unless secret talks are being held in which a compromise is being considered, it seems unlikely that progress will occur in the absence of political change in either Israel or Syria. If the Israeli death toll in Lebanon becomes too high, Israel may be pressured to withdraw unilaterally, but this appears unlikely.

The Israeli–Jordanian track

The steady process of implementing the 1994 Israel–Jordan peace treaty continued.[73] Various committees conducted their work but received little publicity. Although the treaty is increasingly unpopular in Jordan in the light of the lack of progress on the Israeli–Palestinian track,[74] Jordan and Israel are committed to it.[75] The USA is also committed to this process and its warm relations with Jordan have intensified. Jordan continues to urge Israel to honour its commitments to the Palestinians. Events on this track were overshadowed by the death of King Hussein. In September he made a broadcast from a US hospital, where he was undergoing treatment for cancer, to inform his subjects of the situation. He held out hope, but his condition deteriorated and he died on

[70] Syrian Arab Television Network (Damascus), 23 Apr. 1998, in 'Syria: Damascus reports on Israel, Turkey, Jordan military ties', FBIS-NES-98-113, 27 Apr. 1998; and Rodan, S., 'Turkey, Israel enhance ties', *Defense News*, 1–7 June 1998, p. 28.

[71] De Bellaigue, C. and Machlis, A., 'Mubarak seeks to defuse spat between Syria and Turkey', *Financial Times*, 5 Oct. 1998, p. 5; and Fitchett, J., 'Syrian pledge seen as victory for Turkish military', *International Herald Tribune*, 23 Oct. 1998, p. 12. Iran is also mentioned as a mediator.

[72] Machlis, A., 'Israeli losses fuel calls for Lebanon pullout', *Financial Times*, 4 Mar. 1998, p. 7; 'Israel calls on Annan to push Lebanon plan', *International Herald Tribune*, 25 Mar. 1998, p. 3; Khalaf, R., 'It's just a political manoeuvre, say the Lebanese and Syrians', *Financial Times*, 3 Apr. 1998, p. 7; and Radio Lebanon (Beirut), 20 Apr. 1998, in 'Lebanon: Lebanese Defence Minister views Israeli offer, others', FBIS-NES-98-110, 21 Apr. 1998.

[73] For the text of the Treaty of Peace Between the State of Israel and the Hashemite Kingdom of Jordan , 26 Oct. 1994, see Kemp, G. and Pressman, J., 'The Middle East: continuation of the peace process', *SIPRI Yearbook 1995: Armaments, Disarmament and International Security* (Oxford University Press: Oxford, 1995), pp. 197–203.

[74] See, e.g., the generally negative analysis in al-Tahir, G., *Jordan Times* (Amman) (Internet version), 23 Nov. 1998, in 'Jordan: analysis on 5 years of Jordan–Israel peace', FBIS-NES-98-327, 24 Nov. 1998.

[75] Radio Jordan Network (Amman), 23 Nov. 1998, in 'Jordan: Hasan, Israel's Sharon, Sharansky discuss co-operation', FBIS-NES-98-327, 24 Nov. 1998.

7 February 1999. The loss of an outstanding and experienced leader is a great blow to Jordan and the region. Shortly before his death the King replaced Prince Hassan bin Talal as his successor with his eldest son, Abdullah. Although King Abdullah appears popular with the army and the people, he is not so politically experienced as Hassan.

The multilateral track

The multilateral track of the peace process has been effectively frozen since 1997.[76] A few technical meetings of the refugee, water and environment working groups took place in 1998, but none of the plenaries met, nor did the steering committee. Rumours that the Wye River Memorandum would lead to resumption of work were never tested because that agreement was shelved.

III. North Africa and the Mediterranean

In Algeria the killing of civilians continued. In January 1998, during Ramadan, more than 1000 civilians were killed, with more than 400 people dying in a single incident.[77] The crisis began in 1992 when the military, fearing that the Islamic Salvation Front (FIS) was headed for victory, stopped the elections and seized power. The FIS was banned by the military, which set the stage for clashes. The killings have occurred at a steady rate since 1992, with increases each year during Ramadan. However, the number of killings declined in 1998, especially towards the end of the year. Between 1992 and 1998 approximately 65 000–120 000 people were killed.[78]

When violence escalated in early 1998 the international community intervened by sending observer missions from the EU and the UN. They were met with scepticism by the Algerian Government, which continued to blame the FIS for the violence. Suspicion grew in 1998 that the government was using the problem as an excuse to slow down the democratization process. The government dismissed reports that its security forces were involved in the killings. International human rights organizations called for independent investigations

[76] The multilateral talks are discussed in Jones (note 1), pp 181–88; Jones, P., 'The Middle East peace process', *SIPRI Yearbook 1997: Armaments, Disarmament and International Security* (Oxford University Press: Oxford, 1997), pp. 97–100; and Jones and Flodén (note 3), pp. 101–102.

[77] 'Algeria's awful slaughter', *The Economist*, 10 Jan. 1998, p. 12; Truehart, C., 'A new height in carnage is confirmed by Algerians', *International Herald Tribune*, 5 Jan. 1998, p. 7; '22 killed in Algerian attack', *International Herald Tribune*, 13 May 1998, p. 4; 'Train bomb kills 12 and wounds 21 in rural Algeria', *International Herald Tribune*, 12 June 1998, p. 7; and '45 butchered in attack on Algeria town', *International Herald Tribune*, 10 Dec. 1998, p. 2

[78] Dickey, C., 'The house is on fire: a blood-soaked country is being torn apart', *Newsweek*, 19 Jan. 1998, p. 30; Benmiloud, Y., 'It's the generals, stupid: how the outside world has failed Algeria', *Newsweek*, 19 Jan. 1998, p. 31, estimates 80 000–100 000 dead. Khouri, R. G., 'Algeria's terrifying but unsurprising agony', *Meria*, vol. 2, no. 1 (Mar. 1998), estimates 80 000–120 000 dead. The figures are uncertain since the death toll seldom is confirmed by the authorities The Algerian press, the source in most cases, is unable to work freely; and many of the attacks happen in remote villages. See also chapter 1 in this volume.

into the killings, but these were also rejected by the government.[79] In July Algeria gave in to pressure and allowed a UN mission to visit Algeria. Its cautious report called for a reinforcement of the civilian government in Algeria and increased privatization of the economy, but it did not touch on the issue of complicity by government security forces in the bloodshed.[80]

Algerian Prime Minister Ahmed Ouyahia resigned in December, responding to demands by opposition parties which accused him of failing to stop election fraud in the 1997 local elections and end the violence.[81] Presidential elections will be held in April 1999 to choose current President Liamine Zeroual's successor. There is hope that a civilian president will be elected who will promote reconciliation.[82]

In Morocco a significant change in government took place in mid-March 1998. For the first time since independence in 1956 the government is not led by the candidate of the monarchy. It is, however, too early to assess the administration of Prime Minister Abderrahman Youssofi, the leader of the Union Socialiste des Forces Populaires. Youssofi has pledged to work for social justice and to reform the administration and justice systems, which are obstacles to foreign investment in Morocco.[83]

Efforts to resolve the dispute over the western Sahara, which is claimed by both Morocco and the Polisario Front (backed by Algeria), continued in 1998. The parties agreed in 1991 to hold a referendum to choose between integration or separation, but it has not taken place because of disputes over who would be eligible to vote. UN Secretary-General Kofi Annan was involved in efforts to resolve the dispute, but it remains unresolved.[84]

The EU's Euro-Mediterranean Partnership (also known as the Barcelona Initiative) continued its meetings.[85] There was no significant progress in 1998,

[79] Whitney, C. R., 'Burdened by history, France balks at wading into Algerian strife', *New York Times*, 13 Jan. 1998, p. A4; Khalaf, R. and Tucker, E., 'Algiers snubs EU bid to end bloodshed', *Financial Times*, 15 Jan. 1998; Khalaf, R., 'Euro MPs to pursue peace in Algeria', *Financial Times*, 9 Feb. 1998, p. 4; Zoubir, Y., 'Algeria in crisis', *Jane's Defence Weekly*, vol. 50, no. 7 (Aug. 1998), p. 22; al-Madani, K. S., *al-Sharq al-Awsat* (London), 12 Apr. 1998, p. 3, in 'Algeria: Algerian minister on violence, EU mediation', FBIS-NES-98-106, 17 Apr. 1998; 'Algerian massacres: the case for an international inquiry', *Mideast Mirror*, vol. 12, no. 9 (15 Jan. 1998), pp. 16–19; and 'Why international intervention is the lesser evil in Algeria', *Mideast Mirror*, vol. 12, no. 17 (27 Jan. 1998), pp. 19–21.

[80] Khalaf, R., 'UN panel's report on Algeria seen as "feeble"', *Financial Times*, 16 Sep. 1998; Clayton, A., 'UN probe into massacres in Algeria', *Jane's Defence Weekly*, vol. 30, no. 4 (July 1998), p. 19; Jones and Flodén (note 3), p. 106; UN Department of Public Information, 'Report of the panel appointed by the Secretary-General of the United Nations to gather information on the situation in Algeria in order to provide the international community with greater clarity on that situation', July–Aug. 1998, URL <http://www.UN.org/NewLinks/dpi2007/>; and 'Algeria: a tale of terror', *Mideast Mirror*, vol. 12, no. 192 (6 Oct. 1998), pp. 15–17.

[81] Khalaf, R., 'Algerian premier quits over election fraud', *Financial Times*, 15 Dec. 1998, p. 6; and 'Algerian Prime Minister quits', *International Herald Tribune*, 15 Dec. 1998, p. 7.

[82] Tuquoi, J.-P., 'Algerian PM bows out after allies desert', *Guardian Weekly*, 20 Dec. 1998, p. 19.

[83] Khalaf, R., 'Kiss that tells so much about Morocco's new prime minister', *Financial Times*, 13 May 1998, p. 4; and Khalaf, R., 'King Hassan brings in opposition', *Financial Times*, 16 Mar. 1998, p. 4.

[84] Khalaf, R., 'Annan in drive to resolve Sahara dispute', *Financial Times*, 9 Nov. 1998, p. 4; and 'Annan turns to Western Sahara', *International Herald Tribune*, 30 Nov. 1998, p. 5.

[85] On 28 Nov. 1995, in Barcelona, the EU and 12 Mediterranean participants (Algeria, Cyprus, Egypt, Israel, Jordan, Lebanon, Malta, Morocco, the Palestinian Authority, Syria, Tunisia and Turkey) signed a

but the participants reconfirmed the 1995 decision to work towards the creation of a 'stability charter' for the Mediterranean. The efforts to create a free-trade zone are also progressing slowly.[86]

IV. The situation in the Persian Gulf

The situation in the Persian Gulf remained unstable in 1998. In Iran the struggle between the moderates and the conservatives persisted, and in Iraq the United Nations Special Commission on Iraq (UNSCOM) continued to experience disruption of its inspection efforts.

The situation in Iran

President Mohammad Khatami continued efforts to liberalize Iran. However, conservative forces, including Iran's supreme leader Ayatollah Khamenei, continued to regard such moves with suspicion and sought to block many of Khatami's programmes. An indication of the tension was the arrest and sentencing of moderate Tehran mayor Gholam-Hossein Karbaschi to five years' imprisonment, a large fine and 60 lashes. Much of the sentence was later commuted, but the conviction stood. Karbaschi was found guilty of embezzlement but many believed the ruling to be 'political' and a signal to the reformers. The judiciary in Iran is dominated by conservatives who oppose the changes advocated by Khatami.[87]

The continuing struggle between moderates and conservatives raises doubts about Khatami's ability to implement reforms. Newspapers were closed and their publishers arrested if they challenged the conservatives too openly.[88] The conservatives won a majority in October elections for the Assembly of Experts, Iran's supreme constitutional authority. Many viewed the vote as rigged by the conservative Council of Guardians, which denied many moderates the right to stand. As a result, many Khatami's supporters abstained from voting.[89] In November and December several Iranian reformist authors and prominent politicians critical of the clerical establishment were murdered. The Ministry of Information and Security, the Iranian intelligence ministry,

declaration concerning the new Euro-Mediterranean Partnership which creates a framework for political, economic, cultural and social ties between the partners.

[86] Peters, J., 'The Arab–Israeli multilateral peace talks and the Barcelona process: competition or convergence?', *International Spectator*, vol. 33, no. 4 (Oct./Dec. 1998), pp. 63–76; Jones (note 1), Jones (note 76), and Jones and Flodén (note 3).

[87] 'Too bold', *The Economist*, 25 July 1998, p. 46; Borger, J., 'Tehran's mayor jailed', *Guardian Weekly*, 2 Aug. 1998, p. 3; 'Mayor of Tehran denounces accusers', *International Herald Tribune*, 8 June 1998, p. 7; and 'Are the rival Iranian factions heading for "all-out war"?', *Mideast Mirror*, vol. 12, no. 74 (20 Apr. 1998), pp. 18–19; and 'Tehran mayor expected to be freed after tensions spill onto the streets', *Mideast Mirror*, vol. 12, no. 71 (15 Apr. 1998), pp. 17–18.

[88] Hirst, D., 'Iran paper bounces back', *Guardian Weekly*, Aug. 1998, p. 5; and Huband, M., 'Pressure on Iran media grows', *Financial Times*, 24 Sep. 1998, p. 4.

[89] 'Iranians vote for assembly dominated by conservatives', *International Herald Tribune*, 24–25 Oct. 1998, p. 4; Allen, R., 'Conservatives triumph in Iran elections', *Financial Times*, 26 Oct. 1998, p. 3; and Gardner, D., 'Mulahs' election ploy backfires', *Financial Times*, 28 Oct. 1998, p. 4.

later admitted that some of its members had carried out the killings, suggesting that Khatami had at least been able to get them to accept responsibility.[90]

In addition to the political struggle between the moderates and the conservatives Iran also faces growing economic problems. With .5–1 million new entrants into the labour market every year Iran is in desperate need of economic reform and greater openness. However, given the corrupt nature of the economy, economic reform is directly tied to political changes.[91]

In July Iran tested the Shahab 3 missile, which is capable of reaching Israel, the Gulf region, large parts of Turkey and some parts of Russia. This alarmed Israel and the USA, which accuse Iran of seeking weapons of mass destruction and supporting terrorism.[92] In contrast, Khatami's call for a 'dialogue of civilizations' bore modest fruit in 1998 in the form of sports exchanges and academic meetings. The call for dialogue was made by Khatami in an interview on the Cable News Network (CNN).[93] In June US Secretary of State Albright responded to Khatami. Although the speech was measured and held the promise of a 'new beginning' for US–Iranian relations, it was received without enthusiasm in Iran.[94] Both Albright and Iranian Foreign Minister Kamal Kharrazi were scheduled to attend a 22 September UN meeting on the civil war in Afghanistan. This would have been the highest level of contact between the two countries in more than 20 years, but Kharrazi did not attend and instead sent a deputy.[95] In September Khatami made his first trip to the USA, where he addressed the UN General Assembly in a speech that was relatively

[90] 'Political killings unnerve Iran', *Financial Times*, 15 Dec. 1998, p. 6; Allen, R., 'Iran's political murders widen the gulf between reformist moderates and Islamic hardliners', *Financial Times*, 25–26 Dec. 1998, p. 4; Jehl, D., 'Iran's leaders praise admission of killings', *International Herald Tribune*, 7 Jan. 1999, p. 2; Allen, R., 'Khatami on top as ministry admits murder links', *Financial Times*, 7 Jan. 1999, p. 4; and 'Iran's religious hardliners deemed seeking eradicate secular influence', *Mideast Mirror*, vol. 12, no. 246 (21 Dec. 1998), pp. 22–23.

[91] 'Reaching out, if he can', *The Economist*, 8 Aug. 1998, p. 37; Chubin, S. and Green, J. D., 'Engaging Iran: a US strategy', *Survival*, vol. 40, no. 3 (1998), p. 155; and Faruqui, M. D., 'Iran: renegotiating a "revolutionary" identity', *Economic and Political Weekly*, 1 Aug. 1998, p. 2074.

[92] Hoffman, D., 'Russia to finish Iranian reactor: it will expand role despite US and Israeli objections', *International Herald Tribune*, 23 Feb. 1998; Blanche, E., 'Shahab 3 launch success spurs Israeli response', *Jane's Defence Weekly*, 12 Aug. 1998, p. 18; 'Iran tests medium-range ballistic missile', *Disarmament Diplomacy*, no. 29 (Aug./Sep. 1998), pp. 54–55; Quiring, M., *Die Welt* (Berlin) (Internet version), 3 Nov. 1998, in 'Germany: Russian expert cited on Iran's missile program', Foreign Broadcast Information Service, *Daily Report–West Europe* (*FBIS-WEU*), FBIS-WEU-98-307, 5 Nov. 1998; and Howe, H., *Yedi'ot Aharonot* (Tel Aviv), 24 Apr. 1998, pp. 2, 3, in 'Israel: details of missile base in western Iran', Foreign Broadcast Information Service, *Daily Report–Arms Control* (*FBIS-TAC*), FBIS-TAC-98-114, 27 Apr. 1998.

[93] Interview with President Mohammad Khatami, CNN, 8 Jan. 1998; Bourbeau, H., 'Amateur wrestlers get to grips with a thaw in US–Iran hostilities', *Financial Times*, 11–12 Apr. 1998, p. 2; and 'US Mideast experts help "crack the wall of mistrust" with Iran', *Mideast Mirror*, vol. 12, no. 37 (24 Feb. 1998), p. 19.

[94] Dunne, N., 'US welcomes Iranian call for dialogue', *Financial Times*, 9 Jan. 1998, p. 4; Erlanger, S., 'US aides warm up to informal Iran ties', *New York Times*, 10 Jan. 1998, p. A6; Sciolino, E., 'Clinton hails overture, but isolation policy is unchanged', *New York Times*, 16 Dec. 1998, p. A8; 'Long live Khatami, down with Saddam!', *Mideast Mirror*, vol. 12, no. 115 (18 June 1998), pp. 16–17; and 'US olive branch will help Khatami fend off opponents', *Mideast Mirror*, vol. 12, no. 116 (19 June 1998), p. 18.

[95] 'Albright meets with Iranian minister on Afghan crisis', *International Herald Tribune*, 22 Sep. 1998, p. 4; and 'Sitting down with the Great Satan', *The Economist*, 26 Sep.–2 Oct. 1998, p. 42.

uncritical of the USA.[96] However, a thaw in relations on the official level remains unlikely, and both Khatami and Khamenei have called such a step inappropriate.[97] Khatami's views may be motivated largely by domestic considerations in Iran.

Relations between Iran and the EU improved in 1998, after having reached a low point in 1997 when a German court ruled that Iran had sponsored assassinations of political opponents in Germany.[98] Khatami said that the fatwa (death threat) on British author Salman Rushdie is no longer the desire of the Iranian Government, which paved the way for continued improvement. Although the British and Iranian governments said that they consider the Rushdie case closed, there are still Islamic groups that believe the fatwa should be carried out.[99]

Tension between Iran and Afghanistan increased in 1998. Iran views the Taleban Government in Afghanistan as a source of potential instability in the region. The Taleban have also mistreated the Shi'a minority in Afghanistan. The situation worsened in August when the Taleban seized the city of Mazar-i-Sharif and killed 11 Iranian diplomats and journalists who had taken refuge in the Iranian consulate. In September Iran staged military exercises involving 500 000 troops, and there was talk of confrontation between Afghanistan and Iran. The tension along the border eased, but the possibility of confrontation remains.[100]

The situation in Iraq[101]

Iraq continued its efforts to end UNSCOM's inspection activities and have the sanctions against it removed. Although UNSCOM has reported that Iraq has not revealed the full extent of its weapons of mass destruction programmes, Iraq has stressed the considerable suffering of its people as an argument for the removal of sanctions. Baghdad has neglected to mention that it is respon-

[96] IRNA (Tehran) (Internet version), 21 Sep. 1998, in 'Iran: Khatami addresses UN General Assembly', FBIS-NES-98-264, 25 Sep. 1998.

[97] Sciolino, E., 'Iranian dismisses all hope for now of political thaw', *New York Times*, 23 Sep. 1998, p. A1.

[98] *Tehran Times*, 18 May 1998, pp. 1, 15, in 'Iran: Iranian Majles deputies support expansion of Iran–EU ties', FBIS-NES-98-146, 29 May 1998.; and Jones and Flodén (note 3), p. 103.

[99] Black, I., 'Cook softens line on Iran', *The Guardian*, 14 Jan. 1998, p. 6; Black, I., 'Britain gets closer to Iran', *The Guardian*, 8 Sep. 1998, p. 6; and Crossette, B., 'Iran drops Rushdie death threat, and Britain renews Teheran ties', *New York Times*, 25 Sep. 1998, p. A1.

[100] Davis, A., 'Endgame in Afghanistan', *Jane's Defence Weekly*, vol. 30, no. 8 (1998), p. 22; Huband, M., 'Iran puts 500 000 troops on alert in warning to Taliban', *Financial Times*, 16 Sep. 1998, p. 20; 'Iran shows might in border drills', *Jane's Defence Weekly*, vol. 30, no. 19 (1998), p. 22; 'Holier than thou: behind the Iranian–Afghan rift', *New York Times*, 7 Sep. 1998, p. A3; 'Taleban–Iran showdown "would turn into Sunnite–Shiite conflict"', *Mideast Mirror*, vol. 12, no. 176 (14 Sep. 1998), pp. 12–14; and 'Iran's unpalatable options in tackling the Taleban challenge', *Mideast Mirror*, vol. 12, no. 179 (17 Sep. 1998), pp. 17–20. The differences between the Iranian revolution and the Taleban are discussed in Howeidi, F., *al-Majalla*, excerpted in 'The main points of difference between Iran's Islamic Revolution and Afghanistan's Taleban', *Mideast Mirror*, vol. 12, no. 230 (27 Nov. 1998), pp. 12–15.

[101] See also chapters 13 and 15 in this volume.

sible for the continuation of the sanctions.[102] Throughout 1998 the UK and the USA argued that the threat of force was the only way to ensure Iraqi compliance. The other three permanent members of the UN Security Council, China, France and Russia, opposed the use of force. France and Russia were apparently motivated by economic considerations as Iraq has large debts to both countries.[103] Arab states were generally reluctant to support the use of force against Iraq in 1998, although they do not support Iraqi President Saddam Hussein. The lack of support is, in part, a response to the suffering of the Iraqi people, but it also stems from the low credibility of the USA in the Arab world because of the perceived failure of the USA to press Israel to honour its commitments to the Palestinians.[104]

After repeated crises, the USA and the UK launched air strikes against Iraq on 17 December. They were intended to weaken Iraq's military capability, particularly its weapons of mass destruction capability. The air strikes were also intended to erode support for Saddam Hussein in Iraq. Whether either goal was met is debatable, but the air strikes appear to have destroyed any chance for UNSCOM to continue its work. Moreover, the air strikes highlighted the rift in the Security Council as China, France and Russia strongly criticized the bombing. Even in the USA, critics questioned Clinton's motives as the air strikes coincided with impeachment hearings.[105] Arab reactions to the air strikes were mixed. Some argued that they violated international norms while others blamed the Iraqi regime.[106]

It is unclear what the long-term British–US strategy will be against Iraq, aside from bombing whenever Saddam Hussein acts in a manner of which the UK and USA disapprove. The gap between US policy goals (to eliminate Iraq's weapons of mass destruction and bring about a regime change) and the means to realize them is wider than ever.[107] At the end of 1998 there were verbal confrontations between Iraq and several Arab states. Iraq strongly criticized those states for collaborating with the UK and the USA in the air strikes

[102] Silber, L., 'UN deeply divided over the use of force', *Financial Times*, 7–8 Feb. 1998, p. 4; and Crossette, B., 'Iraqis are told to prepare for "holy war" on UN sanctions', *New York Times*, 19 Jan. 1998, p. A3.

[103] Silber, L., 'Russia tries to head off action against Iraq', *Financial Times*, 27 Jan. 1998, p. 5; Goshko, J. M., 'US battles Russia and China on Iraq', *International Herald Tribune*, 24–25 Jan. 1998, p. 3; and SIPRI, 'Iraq: the UNSCOM experience', *Fact Sheet*, Oct. 1998, available at URL <http://www.sipri.se/pubs/Factsheet/unscom.html>.

[104] Huband, M., 'Arab world detects US double standard', *Financial Times*, 18 Dec. 1998, p. 3; 'Arab foxes in defense of Iraq', *Mideast Mirror*, vol. 12, no. 21 (2 Feb. 1998), pp. 16–18; 'US counseled not to pick a fight with Iraq and overhaul UNSCOM', *Mideast Mirror*, vol. 12, no. 152 (10 Aug. 1998), pp. 13–14; and 'Arab governments lag behind public opinion over Iraq', *Mideast Mirror*, vol. 12, no. 219 (12 Nov. 1998), pp. 13–18.

[105] Buchan, D., 'Russia and China head global critic', *Financial Times*, 18 Dec. 1998, p. 1; Nicoll, A. and Fidler, S., 'Deterrence only option in future', *Financial Times*, 19–20 Dec. 1998, p. 2; Littlejohns, M., 'Butler denies being creature of Washington', *Financial Times*, 19–20 Dec. 1998, p. 2; and Apple, R. W., Jr, 'The reservoir of credibility runs dry', *International Herald Tribune*, 18 Dec. 1998, pp. 1, 4.

[106] 'The "big lie" of Arab support for the Anglo-Saxon assault on Iraq', *Mideast Mirror*, vol. 12, no. 245 (18 Dec. 1998), pp. 17–22; and 'Iraq inquest: who won, and what it to be done?', *Mideast Mirror*, vol. 12, no. 247 (22 Dec. 1998), pp. 10–11.

[107] Erlanger, S., 'With bombing finished, hunt for a policy begins', *International Herald Tribune*, 21 Dec. 1998, pp. 1, 3.

and made threats against several neighbouring states. Some Arab countries went so far as openly to call for the removal of the current regime in Iraq.[108]

V. Conclusions

Many issues that confronted the Middle East in 1998 remained open as 1999 began. These included: the position of a new Israeli Government on resumption of the peace process with both the Palestinians and the Syrians; the possible Palestinian declaration of statehood on 4 May 1999, and the response of Israel and the rest of the world to such an announcement; the continuing bloodshed in Algeria; the stability of President Khatami's Government and his quest to liberalize Iran; and the situation in Iraq. Any of these issues would be a serious challenge to peace and stability in most regions. The Middle East must deal with them all at the same time.

Although each issue commands attention and concern, the Palestinian question appears to hold the greatest potential either to usher in a new era of reconciliation in the Middle East or a new period of confrontation. Each of the other problems, with the possible exception of the Algerian situation, will be made more complex and dangerous if the peace process fails, although the success of that process will not, in itself, guarantee solutions to the other problems. After eight years of peacemaking, 1999 is the critical year. The schedule in the Oslo agreements established 4 May 1999 as the date by which the basis of a new relationship between Israel and the Palestinians should be achieved. It was always an ambitious deadline, but it now seems impossible since Israel's election will take place on 17 May. The 4 May 1999 date could be changed by the mutual consent of the parties, but it seems unlikely that the Palestinians will agree to do so in the absence of a concession that Israel will find difficult to make in time. A full declaration of sovereignty on 4 May by the Palestinians is not the only possible outcome, but the interests of both parties must be served if another interim step is to succeed. This sense is lacking at the present time.

Ultimately, the Middle East requires a new approach to security if it is to move beyond the confrontations and bloodshed which characterized 1998. The successful conclusion of the peace process is a sine qua non of the establishment of a new approach.

[108] Hirst, D. and Black, I., 'Kuwait on alert as Gulf tension rises', *Guardian Weekly,* 17 Jan. 1999, p. 1; Fitchett, J., 'Saudi Arabia is denounced by Baghdad', *International Herald Tribune,* 13 Jan. 1999, pp. 1, 8; Republic of Iraq Network (Baghdad), 5 Jan. 1999, in 'Iraq: Aziz article attacks Saudi Arabia, Egypt', FBIS-NES-99-006, 7 Jan. 1999; MENA (Cairo), 4 Jan. 1999, in 'Egypt: MENA slams Iraq's Aziz, Baghdad's poor propaganda', FBIS-NES-99-004, 5 Jan. 1999; 'Are Washington and London serious about acting to overthrow Saddam?', *Mideast Mirror*, vol. 12, no. 223 (18 Nov. 1998), pp. 8–10; and 'Focus on Arab propaganda wars as Iraq braces for further attacks', *Mideast Mirror*, vol. 13, no. 3 (6 Jan. 1999), pp. 11–12.

Appendix 3A. Documents on the Middle East peace process

THE WYE RIVER MEMORANDUM

Washington, DC, 23 October 1998

The following are steps to facilitate implementation of the Interim Agreement on the West Bank and Gaza Strip of September 28, 1995 (the 'Interim Agreement') and other related agreements including the Note for the Record of January 17, 1997 (hereinafter referred to as 'the prior agreements') so that the Israeli and Palestinian sides can more effectively carry out their reciprocal responsibilities, including those relating to further redeployments and security respectively. These steps are to be carried out in a parallel phased approach in accordance with this Memorandum and the attached time line. They are subject to the relevant terms and conditions of the prior agreements and do not supersede their other requirements.

I. Further redeployments

A. Phase One and two further redeployments

1. Pursuant to the Interim Agreement and subsequent agreements, the Israeli side's implementation of the first and second FRD [further redeployment] will consist of the transfer to the Palestinian side of 13% from Area C as follows:

1% to Area (A)
12% to Area (B).

The Palestinian side has informed that it will allocate an area/areas amounting to 3% from the above Area (B) to be designated as Green Areas and/or Nature Reserves. The Palestinian side has further informed that they will act according to the established scientific standards, and that therefore there will be no changes in the status of these areas, without prejudice to the rights of the existing inhabitants in these areas including Bedouins; while these standards do not allow new construction in these areas, existing roads and buildings may be maintained

The Israeli side will retain in these Green Areas/Nature Reserves the overriding security responsibility for the purpose of protecting Israelis and confronting the threat of terrorism. Activities and movements of the Palestinian Police forces may be carried out after coordination and confirmation; the Israeli side will respond to such requests expeditiously.

2. As part of the foregoing implementation of the first and second FRD, 14.2% from Area (B) will become Area (A).

B. Third Phase of further redeployments

With regard to the terms of the Interim Agreement and of Secretary Christopher's letters to the two sides of January 17, 1997 relating to the further redeployment process, there will be a committee to address this question. The United States will be briefed regularly.

II. Security

In the provisions on security arrangements of the Interim Agreement, the Palestinian side agreed to take all measures necessary in order to prevent acts of terrorism, crime and hostilities directed against the Israeli side, against individuals falling under the Israeli side's authority and against their property, just as the Israeli side agreed to take all measures necessary in order to prevent acts of terrorism, crime and hostilities directed against the Palestinian side, against individuals falling under the Palestinian side's authority and against their property. The two sides also agreed to take legal measures against offenders within their jurisdiction and to prevent incitement against each other by any organizations, groups or individuals within their jurisdiction.

Both sides recognize that it is in their vital interests to combat terrorism and fight violence in accordance with Annex I of the Interim Agreement and the Note for the Record. They also recognize that the struggle against terror and violence must be comprehensive in that it deals with terrorists, the terror support structure, and the environment conducive to the support of terror. It must be continuous and constant over a long-term, in that there can be no pauses in the work against terrorists and their structure. It must be cooperative in that no effort can be fully effective without Israeli–Palestinian cooperation and the continuous exchange of information, concepts, and actions.

Pursuant to the prior agreements, the Palestinian side's implementation of its responsibilities for security, security cooperation, and other issues will be as detailed below during the time periods specified in the attached time line:

A. Security actions

1. Outlawing and combating terrorist organizations

a. The Palestinian side will make known its policy of zero tolerance for terror and violence against both sides.

b. A work plan developed by the Palestinian side will be shared with the US and thereafter implementation will begin immediately to ensure the systematic and effective combat of terrorist organizations and their infrastructure.

c. In addition to the bilateral Israeli–Palestinian security cooperation, a US–Palestinian committee will meet biweekly to review the steps being taken to eliminate terrorist cells and the support structure that plans, finances, supplies and abets terror. In these meetings, the Palestinian side will inform the US fully of the actions it has taken to outlaw all organizations (or wings of organizations, as appropriate) of a military, terrorist or violent character and their support structure and to prevent them from operating in areas under its jurisdiction.

d. The Palestinian side will apprehend the specific individuals suspected of perpetrating acts of violence and terror for the purpose of further investigation, and prosecution and punishment of all persons involved in acts of violence and terror.

e. A US–Palestinian committee will meet to review and evaluate information pertinent to the decisions on prosecution, punishment or other legal measures which affect the status of individuals suspected of abetting or perpetrating acts of violence and terror.

2. Prohibiting illegal weapons

a. The Palestinian side will ensure an effective legal framework is in place to criminalize, in conformity with the prior agreements, any importation, manufacturing or unlicensed sale, acquisition or possession of firearms, ammunition or weapons in areas under Palestinian jurisdiction.

b. In addition, the Palestinian side will establish and vigorously and continuously implement a systematic program for the collection and appropriate handling of all such illegal items in accordance with the prior agreements. The US has agreed to assist in carrying out this program.

c. A US–Palestinian–Israeli committee will be established to assist and enhance cooperation in preventing the smuggling or other unauthorized introduction of weapons or explosive materials into areas under Palestinian jurisdiction.

3. Preventing incitement

a. Drawing on relevant international practice and pursuant to Article XXII (1) of the Interim Agreement and the Note for the Record, the Palestinian side will issue a decree prohibiting all forms of incitement to violence or terror, and establishing mechanisms for acting systematically against all expressions or threats of violence or terror. This decree will be comparable to the existing Israeli legislation which deals with the same subject.

b. A US–Palestinian–Israeli committee will meet on a regular basis to monitor cases of possible incitement to violence or terror and to make recommendations and reports on how to prevent such incitement. The Israeli, Palestinian and US sides will each appoint a media specialist, a law enforcement representative, an educational specialist and a current or former elected official to the committee.

B. Security cooperation

The two sides agree that their security cooperation will be based on a spirit of partnership and will include, among other things, the following steps:

1. Bilateral cooperation

There will be full bilateral security cooperation between the two sides which will be continuous, intensive and comprehensive.

2. Forensic cooperation

There will be an exchange of forensic expertise, training, and other assistance.

3. Trilateral committee

In addition to the bilateral Israeli–Palestinian security cooperation, a high-ranking US–Palestinian–Israeli committee will meet as required and not less than biweekly to assess current threats, deal with any impediments to effective security cooperation and coordination and address the steps being taken to combat terror and terrorist organizations. The committee will also serve as a forum to address the issue of external support for terror. In these meetings, the Palestinian side will fully inform the members of the committee of the results of its investigations concerning terrorist suspects already in custody and the participants will exchange additional relevant information. The committee will report regularly to the leaders of the two sides on the status of cooperation, the results of the meetings and its recommendations.

C. Other issues

1. Palestinian Police Force

a. The Palestinian side will provide a list of its policemen to the Israeli side in conformity with the prior agreements.

b. Should the Palestinian side request technical assistance, the US has indicated its willingness to help meet these needs in cooperation with other donors.

c. The Monitoring and Steering Committee will, as part of its functions, monitor the implementation of this provision and brief the US.

2. PLO Charter

The Executive Committee of the Palestine Liberation Organization and the Palestinian Central Council will reaffirm the letter of 22 January 1998 from PLO Chairman Yasir Arafat to President Clinton concerning the nullification of the Palestinian National Charter provisions that are inconsistent with the letters exchanged between the PLO and the Government of Israel on 9/10 September 1993. PLO Chairman Arafat, the Speaker of the Palestine National Council, and the Speaker of the Palestinian Council will invite the members of the PNC, as well as the members of the Central Council, the Council, and the Palestinian Heads of Ministries to a meeting to be addressed by President Clinton to reaffirm their support for the peace process and the aforementioned decisions of the Executive Committee and the Central Council.

3. Legal assistance in criminal matters

Among other forms of legal assistance in criminal matters, the requests for arrest and transfer of suspects and defendants pursuant to Article II (7) of Annex IV of the Interim Agreement will be submitted (or resubmitted) through the mechanism of the Joint Israeli–Palestinian Legal Committee and will be responded to in conformity with Article II (7) (f) of Annex IV of the Interim Agreement within the twelve week period. Requests submitted after the eighth week will be responded to in conformity with Article II (7) (f) within four weeks of their submission. The US has been requested by the sides to report on a regular basis on the steps being taken to respond to the above requests.

4. Human rights and the rule of law

Pursuant to Article XI (1) of Annex I of the Interim Agreement, and without derogating from the above, the Palestinian Police will exercise powers and responsibilities to implement this Memorandum with due regard to internationally accepted norms of human rights and the rule of law, and will be guided by the need to protect the public, respect human dignity, and avoid harassment.

III. Interim committees and economic issues

1. The Israeli and Palestinian sides reaffirm their commitment to enhancing their relationship and agree on the need actively to promote economic development in the West Bank and Gaza. In this regard, the parties agree to continue or to reactivate all standing committees established by the Interim Agreement, including the Monitoring and Steering Committee, the Joint Economic Committee (JEC), the Civil Affairs Committee (CAC), the Legal Committee, and the Standing Cooperation Committee.

2. The Israeli and Palestinian sides have agreed on arrangements which will permit the timely opening of the Gaza Industrial Estate. They also have concluded a 'Protocol Regarding the Establishment and Operation of the International Airport in the Gaza Strip During the Interim Period'.

3. Both sides will renew negotiations on Safe Passage immediately. As regards the southern route, the sides will make best efforts to conclude the agreement within a week of the entry into force of this Memorandum. Operation of the southern route will start as soon as possible thereafter. As regards the northern route, negotiations will continue with the goal of reaching agreement as soon as possible. Implementation will take place expeditiously thereafter.

4. The Israeli and Palestinian sides acknowledge the great importance of the Port of Gaza for the development of the Palestinian economy, and the expansion of Palestinian trade. They commit themselves to proceeding without delay to conclude an agreement to allow the construction and operation of the port in accordance with the prior

agreements. The Israeli–Palestinian Committee will reactivate its work immediately with a goal of concluding the protocol within sixty days, which will allow commencement of the construction of the port.

5. The two sides recognize that unresolved legal issues adversely affect the relationship between the two peoples. They therefore will accelerate efforts through the Legal Committee to address outstanding legal issues and to implement solutions to these issues in the shortest possible period. The Palestinian side will provide to the Israeli side copies of all of its laws in effect.

6. The Israeli and Palestinian sides also will launch a strategic economic dialogue to enhance their economic relationship. They will establish within the framework of the JEC an Ad Hoc Committee for this purpose. The committee will review the following four issues: (1) Israeli purchase taxes; (2) cooperation in combating vehicle theft; (3) dealing with unpaid Palestinian debts; and (4) the impact of Israeli standards as barriers to trade and the expansion of the A1 and A2 lists. The committee will submit an interim report within three weeks of the entry into force of this Memorandum, and within six weeks will submit its conclusions and recommendations to be implemented.

7. The two sides agree on the importance of continued international donor assistance to facilitate implementation by both sides of agreements reached. They also recognize the need for enhanced donor support for economic development in the West Bank and Gaza. They agree to jointly approach the donor community to organize a Ministerial Conference before the end of 1998 to seek pledges for enhanced levels of assistance.

IV. Permanent status negotiations

The two sides will immediately resume permanent status negotiations on an accelerated basis and will make a determined effort to achieve the mutual goal of reaching an agreement by May 4, 1999. The negotiations will be continuous and without interruption. The US has expressed its willingness to facilitate these negotiations.

V. Unilateral actions

Recognizing the necessity to create a positive environment for the negotiations, neither side shall initiate or take any steps that will change the status of the West Bank and the Gaza Strip in accordance with the Interim Agreement.

Attachment: Time line

This Memorandum will enter into force ten days from the date of signature.

For the Government of the State of Israel: Benjamin Netanyahu

For the PLO: Yasser Arafat.

Witnessed by: William J. Clinton, The United States of America.

Time line

Note: Parenthetical references below are to paragraphs in 'The Wye River Memorandum' to which this time line is an integral attachment. Topics not included in the time line follow the schedule provided for in the text of the Memorandum.

1. Upon entry into force of the Memorandum:

Third further redeployment committee starts (I (B))

Palestinian security work plan shared with the US (II (A) (1) (b))

Full bilateral security cooperation (II (B) (1))

Trilateral security cooperation committee starts (II (B) (3))

Interim committees resume and continue; Ad Hoc Economic Committee starts (III)

Accelerated permanent status negotiations start (IV)

2. Entry into force–week 2:

Security work plan implementation begins (II (A) (1) (b)); (II (A) (1) (c)) committee starts

Illegal weapons framework in place (II (A) (2) (a)); Palestinian implementation report (II (A) (2) (b))

Anti-incitement committee starts (II (A) (3) (b)); decree issued (II (A) (3) (a))

PLO Executive Committee reaffirms Charter letter (II (C) (2))

Stage 1 of FRD implementation: 2% C to B, 7.1% B to A. Israeli officials acquaint their Palestinian counterparts as required with areas; FRD carried out; report on FRD implementation (I (A))

3. Week 2–6:

Palestinian Cen tral Council reaffirms Charter letter (weeks two to four) (II (C) (2))

PNC and other PLO organizations reaffirm Charter letter (weeks four to six) (II (C) (2))

Establishment of weapons collection program (II (A) (2) (b)) and collection stage (II (A) (2) (c)); committee starts and reports on activities.

Anti-incitement committee report (II (A) (3) (b))

Ad Hoc Economic Committee: interim report at week three; final report at week six (III)

Policemen list (II (C) (1) (a)); Monitoring and Steering Committee review starts (II (C) (1) (c))

Stage 2 of FRD implementation: 5% C to B. Israeli officials acquaint their Palestinian counterparts as required with areas; FRD carried out; report on FRD implementation (I (A))

4. Week 6–12:

Weapons collection stage II (A) (2) (b); II (A) (2) (c) committee report on its activities.

Anti-incitement committee report (II (A) (3) (b))

Monitoring and Steering Committee briefs US on policemen list (II (C) (1) (c))

Stage 3 of FRD implementation: 5% C to B, 1% C to A, 7.1% B to A. Israeli officials acquaint Palestinian counterparts as required with areas; FRD carried out; report on FRD implementation (I (A))

5. After week 12:

Activities described in the Memorandum continue as appropriate and if necessary, including:

Trilateral security cooperation committee (II (B) (3))

(II (A) (1) (c)) committee

(II (A) (1) (e)) committee

Anti-incitement committee (II (A) (3) (b))

Third Phase FRD Committee (I (B))

Interim Committees (III)

Accelerated permanent status negotiations (IV)

End of Attachment

Sources: Israel Ministry of Foreign Affairs, 'The Wye River Memorandum', URL <http://www.mfa.gov.il/mfa/go.asp?MFAH07o10>; and United States Information Agency, 'The Wye River Memorandum', URL <http://www.usia.gov/regional/nea/summit/agree.htm>.

4. Russia: military reform

ALEXEI G. ARBATOV*

I. Introduction

The profound economic and political transformation of the Russian Federation which has been going on since 1991, and which is often indiscriminately called democratic reform, has deeply and controversially affected its military establishment. On the one hand, the tectonic changes in Russia's domestic ways of life and in its external relations, above all with the West, have created an absolute requirement for comprehensive military reform as part and parcel of the overall economic and political reforms. This is particularly so because of the major role that threat assessments, defence requirements and the military establishment have played in Russian and Soviet history, and most of all in its seven decades of communist rule, which built the greatest military empire in the world.

Pressure for military reform was essentially pressure on resources—the yawning gap between the size of the armed forces and the funding available in a situation of increasing economic difficulty, the crisis in the defence industry, poor morale in the armed forces, and the need for savings on operations and maintenance and for investment in new equipment.

Russia's new external security conditions and defence requirements were less clearly understood as motives for reform. Even if the external situation had not changed radical military reform in Russia would have been needed in any case because of the domestic transformation. Military reform has become much more than a method of adjusting Russian defence to the post-cold war security environment (as is the case in the USA): it is rather the only way of saving it from final and irreversible collapse. Moreover, radical military reform is not just the means to provide for Russia's future national defence and external security, but most importantly the route to avoiding an extremely dangerous domestic destabilization and the only way to establish civilian control over the armed forces and defence policy in general, provide an ultimate guarantee of Russia's further democratic development and bring its defence in line with its security requirements and economic resources.

Earlier attempts at military reform during 1993–97 foundered because of the lack of political leadership on the part of President Boris Yeltsin and the resistance of the military bureaucracy under former ministers of defence Pavel

* The author is grateful to Col (ret.) P. B. Romashkin for help in gathering statistical data, to Dr A. S. Kozlova for collecting latest reference material on the subject and to Col (ret.) V. E. Yarynich for technical support and refinement of this chapter. Some of the material on which it is based appeared in the author's article on 'Military reform in Russia: dilemmas, obstacles, and prospects', *International Security*, vol. 22, no. 4 (spring 1998), pp. 83–134.

Grachev and Igor Rodionov, despite declarations of progress and success. It was the appointment of Marshal Igor Sergeyev as Defence Minister in May 1997 and subsequent major changes among top military officials which provided the impetus for progress. Paradoxically, the particular type of economic reform and political developments in Russia in 1992–98, culminating in the 'Great Crash' of 17 August 1998, have been seriously counter-productive where military reform is concerned and in many respects severely hampered it.

'Military reform' is usually treated in Russia as a more comprehensive notion than 'reform of the armed forces'. The latter includes doctrine and strategic missions and the structure, composition, force levels, equipment and training of the armed services and armed forces of the Ministry of Defence (MOD). 'Military reform' includes all these and reform of other troops and formations,[1] of the defence industries and war mobilization assets, of the recruitment system and social security for the military, of the division of powers and authority between the branches of the government on military matters, of the system of funding defence and security, and of the organization of the executive branch and the MOD itself. The law 'On military reform', approved by the Duma (the lower house of the Russian Parliament) on 2 December 1998,[2] interprets it as a complex of political, economic, legal, military, military–technical, social and other measures designed to transform the armed forces, other troops and military formations, military executive agencies, defence production assets and their administrative organizations, with the purpose of providing a sufficient level of national defence within the limits of available resources.

This chapter focuses on the reform of the armed forces and the defence industry and the term 'military reform' is used here to mean these two items.

II. The new domestic and external security environment

Two principal factors have direct implications for Russia's defence posture and provide powerful incentives for reform: the profound changes in Russia's military requirements and in the economic resources available for defence.

Russia's military requirements

The Russian military doctrine still largely derives from the document approved at the session of the Security Council of the Russian Federation on 2 November 1993.[3] On the same day the 'Principal guidance on the military doctrine of the Russian Federation' was embodied in Presidential decree

[1] According to the Law on Defence (Federal law N61-FZ of 31 May 1996), clause 1, 'other troops' consist primarily of the Federal Border Guards, Ministry of the Interior troops, Railway Troops and troops of the presidential Federal Agency on Governmental Communications and Information; and 'military formations' are the engineering, technical and road-building military formations attached to the 'federal bodies of executive power'. *Rossiyskaya Gazeta*, 9 Oct. 1992.

[2] The law was not yet approved by the Council of the Federation at the time of writing (Feb. 1999).

[3] *Krasnaya Zvezda*, 4 Nov. 1993, p. 1.

no. 1833.[4] This document was refined into a newer version in 1998. Another important official directive on this subject is 'The basics (concept) of the state policy of the Russian Federation on military development until the year 2005', Presidential directive no. 1068-Pr, of 30 July 1998.[5] Among other things, it postulated that national defence must receive not less than 3.5 per cent of gross national product (GNP).

These documents reflect crucial changes in Russia's military environment and requirements. The Soviet armed forces were built up and deployed according to the strategic missions of fighting and limiting damage in a global nuclear war with any combination of the other four nuclear powers, winning wars in Europe and the Far East in a large-scale multi-theatre war, and conducting subregional operations in support of its Third World clients. Now to the west and south Russia faces a new security environment in the former Soviet republics. They are characterized by a high degree of internal instability, very open to influence from outside and in several cases in conflict with each other, with Russia or with their own secessionists, even to the extent of open armed conflict. Russia's borders with them are mostly symbolic and largely open to illegal migration and massive smuggling.

It is thus unlikely that Russia's armed forces will be called on to fight a large-scale theatre-wide war in the foreseeable future. The principal threats in the next 5–10 years are local conflicts, which could occur in several places simultaneously. It is also widely recognized that they are unlikely to be used against any of the other former Soviet republics, however severe Russia's contradictions with them might become in future. However, they may be employed in local relief and peacekeeping operations, both in the post-Soviet space and outside it under UN mandate.

In the past the USSR and its allies were militarily superior to any hostile neighbouring country or alliance to the west, south or east, and only US power counterbalanced Soviet preponderance in Eurasia. Now and in the foreseeable future adjacent nations will possess—individually or in some combination—military forces either comparable or clearly superior to Russia's. Although none of them are at present open opponents of Russia, this is not guaranteed in the future. In addition to Russia's growing economic inferiority, this military imbalance may cast a long shadow over developments in the post-Soviet space and eventually on Russia's own national security.

After the addition of the Czech Republic, Hungary and Poland, the next wave of NATO enlargement will probably bring NATO much closer to the borders of Russia. During the next 10 years, in addition to superiority in conventional arms in Europe by a ratio of between 2 : 1 and 3 : 1, NATO will have substantial superiority over Russia in both tactical and strategic nuclear

[4] *Izvestiya,* 18 Nov. 1993, pp. 1–4. A translation into English was published in *Jane's Intelligence Review*, Special Report, Jan. 1994.

[5] The document was not published.

forces.[6] This is a major shift in the military balance in Europe. Only 10 years ago the Warsaw Pact had three times as many conventional forces as NATO, twice as many theatre and tactical nuclear weapons, and the same numbers of strategic nuclear forces. In Europe alone the USSR was twice as strong in conventional forces as all the European NATO states together.[7] If factors of a qualitative nature, such as training, combat readiness, command and control, morale of troops, and technical sophistication of weapons and equipment are taken into account, the balance is presently and will in the future be even more favourable to NATO.

Such a rapid and fundamental shift away from the traditional environment is making Russia extremely uncomfortable, regardless of all other circumstances. Nevertheless, Russia also recognizes that conventional or nuclear war with NATO is unthinkable, whatever the new political tensions between it and the West resulting from NATO enlargement and NATO's use of force outside its area of responsibility. Moreover, because of economic, demographic and geopolitical limitations, Russia cannot even attempt to match NATO in nuclear or conventional forces. If its relations with an enlarging NATO are not settled politically, Russia will have to rely on the doctrine of 'extended nuclear deterrence', much as NATO did in the 1950s and 1960s.

Afghanistan, Pakistan and Turkey, and less likely Iran, may present a security problem individually or in some combination during next decade or two. Here, too, Russia feels much less certain than it did. Iran and Turkey combined have armed forces numerically equal to Russia's and together with Pakistan 50 per cent more.[8] The quality of these forces is not high, but even here the former Russian advantage will probably be eroded. These states are unlikely to threaten Russia in a united front or in a direct way; rather, a threat might materialize through their support of regimes, movements or policies in the Transcaucasus and Central Asia which are directed against Russia or Russian allies or, still worse, might take the form of encouraging ethnic and religious separatism in the Russian northern Caucasus and Volga regions. The political shifts of national forces in the region should not be underestimated as the background to possible paramilitary activities and clashes.

This general reorientation of Russia's threat perceptions over the past few years, from west to south and east, might be changed by NATO enlargement. The threat of military action by NATO in the Kosovo conflict in Yugoslavia (Serbia and Montenegro) and the US–British air strikes against Iraq in late 1998 aroused the highest anti-US sentiment in Russia since the worst times of the cold war and revived some of the traditional fears and suspicions.

In the Far East China and Japan may present a threat to Russia in future decades. Japan's offensive conventional capabilities which could be used

[6] Arbatov, A., *Military Reform in Russia: Dilemmas, Obstacles and Prospects* (Harvard University, John F. Kennedy School of Government, Center for Science and International Affairs: Cambridge, Mass., Sep. 1997), p. 18.

[7] Konovalov, A., [Towards a new division of Europe? Russia and the North Atlantic Alliance], *Nezavisimaya Gazeta*, 7 Dec. 1994.

[8] International Institute for Strategic Studies, *The Military Balance 1997/98* (Oxford University Press: Oxford, 1997), pp. 67, 125, 159.

against Russia are limited, and will be so at least for the next decade, although for the first time since 1945 its forces are numerically comparable to Russian deployments in the Russian far east and much better in quality. An attempt by Japan to take the southern Kurile Islands or Sakhalin by force is hardly conceivable, and the USA, whose support would be essential, is highly unlikely to encourage such a policy. However, the remilitarization of Japan (including its acquisition of nuclear weapons) and a revival of its expansionist strategies cannot be ruled out.

China is another major uncertainty in Russia's security environment and requirements. Its current military build-up, geo-strategic situation and long history of territorial disputes with Russia and the USSR make it impossible for Moscow to exclude any threat scenarios, despite the present cooperation, border agreements and mutual troop reduction agreements with Beijing. With active armed forces twice as large as Russia's, in a decade or two China will most probably achieve conventional offensive superiority along the borders with Transbaikal and Primorskiy Krai (Maritime Province).[9] It may also come much closer to Russia in terms of the sophistication and size of its nuclear arsenal, thus making even nuclear deterrence a dubious reassurance for Russia.

Financial resources for the military

Where resources available for defence are concerned, the changes of the past decade are even greater than the shifts in global and regional, nuclear and conventional military balances. There is no question of Russia being able to mount a defence effort in peacetime resembling that of the former USSR.

Table 4.1 shows the amounts budgeted for 'national defence' since 1994.[10] This budget heading excludes other troops and force structures, domestic functions and protection of the borders, the costs of which have been at a level of 1.5–2 per cent of GNP and 6–9 per cent of federal budget expenditure since 1994.[11] Regardless of the state of the national economy or finances, it is highly unlikely that the government will raise the share of defence appropriations to more than 3.5 per cent of GNP and 20 per cent of the federal budget. Only major changes in the external security environment or in Russia's political regime could lead to much higher military spending.

These comparative figures do not reveal the whole picture of the severe limitation on the resources available for defence. Since 1992 the Russian Federation has been undergoing a deep and protracted economic and social crisis, the end of which is still far from sight. As a result of the programme of 'shock therapy' in 1992–93 and 'macroeconomic stabilization' in 1994–98,

[9] *The Military Balance 1997/98* (note 8), pp. 176, 181.

[10] For detals of what is included in the 'national defence' budget heading, see Cooper, J., 'The military expenditure of the USSR and the Russian Federation', *SIPRI Yearbook 1998: Armaments, Disarmament and International Security* (Oxford University Press: Oxford, 1998), pp. 248–49.

[11] Russian State Duma, Committee on Defence, 'Reference information on the 1997 federal budget law and 1997 federal budget sequestering draft law', Moscow, Dec. 1996, June 1997. Unpublished.

Table 4.1. Russian 'national defence' as a share of GNP and of the federal budget, 1994–99

Figures in italics are percentages.

	'National defence' budget (current roubles)	'National defence' as share of GNP (%)	'National defence' as share of federal budget (%)
1994	40 626.0 tr.	*5.60*	*20.89*
1995	59 378.8 tr.	*3.76*	*20.85*
1996	82 462.3 tr.	*3.59*	*18.92*
1997	104 317.5 tr.	*3.82*	*19.76*
1998	81 765 b.[a]	*2.97*	*17.32*
1999	93 703 b.[a]	*2.34*	*16.29*

[a] The rouble was redenominated on 1 Jan. 1998, at the rate of 1 new rouble = 1000 old.

Source: Successive laws 'On the federal budget', 1994–99.

which culminated in the economic and financial crash of August 1998, Russia has suffered an unprecedented decline in production and investment, which has hit not only heavy and defence industries but even harder agriculture, consumer goods production and housing.

According to generally accepted figures, between 1992 and 1998 Russia's GNP declined by at least half, to a level of 15 per cent of that of the USA if measured by the market exchange rate (MER). The crash of August 1998 resulted in a devaluation of the rouble to roughly one-third of its previous value and further economic decline. This devaluation largely reflected the collapse of the banking system, default on domestic debt and inflation expectations, which are producing exaggerated demand for hard currency as the most reliable value 'deposit'. Prices rose by 50–70 per cent by the end of 1998. Almost 80 per cent of Russian industry and agriculture is standing idle or has transferred to barter and money surrogates.[12] The rest—20 per cent, which provides the remaining revenue base—is probably the same size as the 'shadow economy' which is the result of absurd taxation and comprehensive corruption. Hence, the whole productive economy is possibly seven to eight times bigger than the statistics would indicate. Even this, however, does not disguise the magnitude of the economic crisis and the failure of the reforms, which primarily affect the federal budget and its functions, including defence.

'National defence' allocations for 1999 are planned at about $5 billion at the market exchange rate (93.7 billion roubles plus an uncertain 8 billion roubles from individual income tax).[13] It is true that the domestic purchasing power of the rouble in the defence sector is higher than the MER would indicate. Still, even with such corrections Russia's defence budget would probably be no higher than $10–15 billion in purchasing-power parity terms. Hence, since the

[12] Unpublished estimates of the Yabloko bloc.

[13] Romashkin, P., 'Voyenny byudzhet Rossiyskoy Federatsii na 1999 god' [Military budget of the Russian Federation for 1999], *Yadernoye Rasprostraneniye* (Carnegie Centre: Moscow), vo. 26 (Nov. 1998), pp. 23–28.

mid-1980s Soviet/Russian defence expenditure has declined by roughly a factor of 10 in constant prices.

There is consensus, supported by the greater part of the new Russian political elite and strategic community, on the need for Russia to maintain a sufficiently strong defence for the foreseeable future, which would address real threats and conceivable contingencies but would not overburden the economy.[14] The main puzzle is how to get from here to there. Maintaining the existing armed forces of over 1.2 million men with huge stockpiles of arms and equipment (including about 10 000 nuclear weapons and 40 000 tons of chemical munitions) while radically reforming, reducing and reorganizing them—all for $5 billion per year—is an unprecedented challenge even in Russia, whose history is so full of striving for impossible goals.

III. The basic principles of the military reform

Although opinions differ on infinite details, during the past few years some consensus has appeared in Russia on the basic principles of the military reform.

First is the need to sacrifice quantity—numbers of personnel, military units, weapons, defence sites and military production facilities—for much better quality. This implies better arms and equipment, housing and material standards of living, training and combat readiness, efficiency of maintenance and supply, command and control and information-gathering systems, and so on.[15] Part of this principle, although much more controversial and accepted by many only with serious reservations, is the need to change progressively from massive conscript forces to smaller all-volunteer/professional forces better suited to operate modern weapons and fight wars of new types.[16]

Second, resulting from the changes in Russia's security environment discussed in section II, is the need to redirect the armed forces from preparing for global or large-scale protracted nuclear and conventional wars to local and regional conflicts of much shorter duration.

Third, also arising from changes in threat perceptions and supported by a majority but not a predominant part of the political–military elite, there is a need to redirect the main effort in strategic contingency planning from the traditional global or West European theatres to the southern (meaning the Transcaucasus and Central Asia) and later the Far Eastern theatres.

Finally, a point of almost universal agreement is that the nuclear forces should have highest priority in the Russian defence posture. This is considered as a compensation for the absolute and relative weakening of the country's conventional capabilities and the new vulnerability of its geopolitical situation. It is also seen as an 'umbrella' for implementing military reform and the only remaining heritage of the Soviet superpower status and role in world affairs.

[14] Arbatov, A., 'Army reform in the midst of disaster', *Moscow News*, no. 3 (20–26 Jan. 1995).

[15] Lebed, A., [Russia has the army, but is it indeed an army?], *Nezavisimaya Gazeta*, 16 Nov. 1994.

[16] Lopatin, V., [A professional army instead of an armed nation], *Novaya Yezhednevnaya Gazeta*, 26 May 1994.

Although, with very few exceptions, no one seriously envisions any threat of large-scale external aggression against Russia in the foreseeable future, most politicians, military and researchers prefer to retain a reliable material guarantee in the form of viable nuclear forces in order to ensure that they are not proved wrong by events.

However, high priority for nuclear deterrence does not imply a need for a crash missile build-up or a hair-trigger employment strategy. Rather it is mostly conceived in terms of 'inherent extended deterrence'. The nuclear force levels envisaged (approximately 1000 warheads or less on strategic forces by the years 2008–2010) are lower than those of the USA or those implied by the agreed START II and START III ceilings.[17] Despite bitter controversies over START II, arms control retains broad support as a viable element of the national security strategy. The revival of the nuclear first-strike concept since 1993 has been largely a declaratory move and has not in any way affected either command and control system architecture and functioning or force operation, the modernization programme or the exercise pattern.

This is a far cry from the former Soviet strategic posture, with its strong flavour of counterforce first-strike operational planning and the avowed goal of maintaining 'strategic parity', commonly interpreted as superiority in nuclear weapons over all opponents combined.

IV. Reduction and reorganization of the armed forces

The basic point of departure for military reform has been the need for deep reductions in the armed forces to generate savings on their maintenance, which allegedly could be used to improve their quality under the same budget ceilings. Presently, the budget item for funding this reduction is labelled 'military reform', although the reduction itself is clearly not a reform but rather its first step and a precondition.

From the USSR Russia inherited 2.7 million armed forces, of which 0.6 million were deployed beyond Russia's borders. They were reduced to 2.1 million by 1994 through force withdrawal and natural wastage.[18] In early 1997 the authorized strength of Russia's armed forces was 1.6 million military and 0.6 million civilian employees[19]—roughly equal to US forces (1.5 million military and 0.8 million civilians). However, the actual number of civilian employees was at least 50 per cent higher and there were many more military paid by the defence budget but not included in actual strength (such as those engaged in quality control at military production facilities, the Baikonur space range and so on).

[17] Maslyukov, Yu., 'Nas ne poimut, esli my seychas otkazaemsya ot SNV-2' [No one will understand us if we refuse START II now], *Krasnaya Zvezda*, 20 Oct. 1998.

[18] Baev, P., 'Russia's armed forces: spontaneous demobilization', *Bulletin of Arms Control*, no. 13 (Feb. 1994), pp. 8–13.

[19] 'Reference information on the 1997 federal budget law and 1997 federal budget sequestering draft law' (note 11).

It is safe to assume that by 1997 the actual personnel level of the Russian armed forces was around 1.8 million. This does not include 'other troops and military formations', which are funded by their own budget and employed about 1 million personnel. In terms of major classes of weapon, with few exceptions, Russia still had 10–30 per cent more than the USA[20] (although these figures do not reflect the quality or effectiveness of their military equipment). Its armed forces were still composed of the five services (the Strategic Rocket Forces, Ground Forces, Air Force, Air Defence and Navy), three independent armed forces (the Military–Space Forces, Missile–Space Defence and the Paratroop Forces), 8 military districts, 4 fleets and 30 divisions, with 4700 combat aircraft, 370 large combat ships and submarines, and 10 000 strategic and tactical nuclear warheads, as well as industrial assets for their maintenance and equipment.

The yawning gap between the size of the armed forces and the resources available had created a crisis of staggering proportions. The original budget request for 'national defence' in 1997 was more than twice eventual appropriations,[21] and in the spring of 1997 the senior military openly challenged the political leadership when Defence Minister Rodionov, supported by the then chairman of the Duma Defence Committee, Lev Rokhlin, publicly dissented from presidential policy. Sergeyev replaced Rodionov and major changes followed among the top military officials. During the next year and a half reform gained momentum and made great strides.

According to the plan of the Ministry of Defence, the strength of the armed forces was to be cut by 0.6 million military and 0.4 civilian personnel down to about 1.2 million and 0.5 million, respectively, by January 1999.[22]

Two armed services—the Air Force and Air Defence—were merged into one, the Air Force in 1998. Another powerful armed service—the Ground Forces—was deprived of its Supreme Command and directly subordinated to the General Staff.[23] By the year 2005 it is envisaged to change to a triad—the Ground Forces, Navy and Air Force (which will include the strategic forces).

The Military–Space Forces and Missile–Space Defence were integrated into the Strategic Rocket Forces. The Defence Minister has made public a plan to integrate all elements of the strategic forces into a single Strategic Deterrent

[20] The balance between Russia and the USA in 1997 was 10 000 : 7000 in tanks, 20 000 : 12 000 in armoured combat vehicles, 4700 : 3200 in combat aircraft, 3200 : 4500 in combat helicopters, 270 : 235 in large combat ships, 101 : 96 in large submarines, and 10 000 : 9000 in strategic and tactical nuclear warheads.

[21] Rogov, S., *Military Reform and the Defense Budget of the Russian Federation,* Report no. CIM 527 (Center for Naval Analyses: Alexandria, Va., Aug. 1997), pp. 15–16; and Cooper, J., 'The military expenditure of the USSR and the Russian Federation, 1987–97', *SIPRI Yearbook 1998: Armaments, Disarmament and International Security* (Oxfrod University Press: Oxford, 1998), p. 247.

[22] Sergeyev, I., [The new stage of the military development in Russia, press conference], *Krasnaya Zvezda*, 13 Aug. 1998.

[23] Oparin, M., [The prospects of long-range aviation], *Krasnaya Zvezda*, 5 Mar. 1998; and Georgiev, V., [The reform of the Ground Forces would not be confined to reductions], *Nezavisimoye Voyennoye Obozreniye*, no. 11 (26 Mar. 1998).

Forces Command, which is to integrate their operational control, supply, maintenance, training and modernization programmes.[24]

In 1998 the Transbaikal Military District (MD) was merged with the Siberian MD, reducing the number of military districts from 8 to 7. In future this number will most probably be further reduced through merging the Ural and Volga MDs and eventually transforming all of the above into operational–strategic commands.[25]

It is also planned to cut the number of Ground Force units from 30 to 9–10 divisions. It is possible that two of the four fleets—the Black Sea and the Baltic—will be reduced to flotilla or even squadron scale. There will be drastic reductions in air/air defence armies and other structural elements of the armed forces.

Although the present reform programme of the MOD, approved by the president, does not go further than 1999 in personnel reduction (down to 1.2 million), there is a general consensus among the supporters of reform that by the end of the year 2000 force levels should be reduced to about 1 million military personnel. This is the first stage of the reform, at which substantial savings on maintenance should be achieved. At this stage the programme of conversion should also be revived, research and development (R&D) centres and programmes must be supported, and procurement should be kept at a necessary minimum in order to save industries needed for the future in the military production sector.

At the second stage, by the year 2005, depending on economic and other factors, the armed forces could be further reduced to 0.8 million, mostly through the retirement of officers, the curtailment of conscription and the expanded use of contracts. This should produce a more reasonable proportion of officers to privates, provide a larger number of fully manned combat-ready units and permit improvement of the quality of life and training of the military. If by that time the Russian economy takes off and budget revenues go up, the armed forces may transfer to an all-volunteer basis. At the third stage, by the year 2010, the armed forces should transfer fully to a contract/professional basis. By this time the reorganization and redeployment of the forces should be finalized and the revived defence industry should complete equipping them with new weapons and technology.

V. The crash of 1998 and military reform

Quite early it became clear to experts that even simply reducing the armed forces—to say nothing of really reforming, redeploying, retraining and rearming them—would not be free of charge.

The paradox is that for the first few years substantially reducing the armed forces is more expensive than maintaining them without change at the same

[24] Sokut, S., [Russia will gather nuclear forces in a single fist], *Nezavisimoye Voyennoye Obozreniye*, no. 40 (29 Oct. 1998).

[25] Korbut, A., [Four military districts will be eliminated], *Nezavisimoye Voyennoye Obozreniye*, no. 21 (18 June 1998).

austere level of funding. By the laws 'On the status of military servicemen' and 'On military duty and military service'[26] a retiring officer is entitled to 22 months' salary, an apartment or house (if he or she does not have one) and some additional payments for the costs of removal. On average this means costs of the order of 80 000–120 000 roubles ($15 000–20 000 before August 1998) for a single middle-rank officer. His or her continuing in service during the first year would cost half or one-third of this, depending on details of rank, job, years of service and so on.

Hence, the gist of the concept of radical reform, which was brought in by the new leadership of the MOD and shared by its supporters in parliament and the strategic community, was as follows. Within two to three years deep reductions in force levels would generate sufficient savings on personnel costs, which could be redistributed, within a constant level of funding for 'national defence', to take care of qualitative factors of maintenance (training and higher standards of living and service) and to enhance defence investment (R&D, procurement of better equipment and construction). All this would have to be implemented while seriously restructuring and transforming the army in line with the above doctrinal and strategic guidelines. Last but not least, to launch the whole process some up-front funding would be required, since starting deep reductions would initially imply higher costs than just maintaining them at the same force levels.

In order not to increase the defence budget and to make sure that money was not spent for purposes other than force reductions, it was proposed to provide the necessary funding under a special federal budget section labelled 'military reform', separate from the section on 'national defence'. This was brought in by the law adopted in March 1998 amending the law 'On the budget classification'.[27] In addition, this law spelled out a breakdown of the national defence budget into more than 100 lines. Indeed, in the original version of the 1998 federal budget, 'military reform' was separated as a special item (although inside the defence budget, since the law was late in entering into force for that budget) and funded at a level of 4 billion roubles (about $700 million at the exchange rate of the time).

Unfortunately, the budget crisis of spring 1998 and then the crash of August severely undercut the implementation of the military reform when it was finally gaining great momentum. In the spring of 1998 planned defence fund-

[26] 'O statuse voyennosluzhashchikh' [On the status of military servicemen], Federal law no. 76-FZ, *Rossiyskaya Gazeta*, 27 May 1998; and 'O voinskoy obyazannosti i voyennoy sluzhbe' [On military duty and military service], Federal law no. 53-FZ, *Rossiyskaya Gazeta*, 2 Apr. 1998.

[27] 'O byudzhetnoy klassifikatsii Rossiyskoy Federatsii' [On the budget classification of the Russian Federation), *Sobraniye Zakonodatelstva Rossiyskoy Federatsii* [Collection of legislative acts of the Russian Federation], Federal law no. 34 (1996), article 4030; and 'O vnesenii izmenemii i dopolnenii v Federalny Zakon "O byudzhetnoy klassifikatsii Rossiyskoy Federatsii" v chasti detalizatsii i unifikatsii statei raskhodov federalnogo byudzheta na obespechenie oborony, bezopasnosti i pravookhranitelnoy deyatelnosti gosudarstva' [On the making of changes and additions to the Federal Law 'On the budget classification of the Russian Federation' concerning the elaboration and unification of the items of expense on the provision of defence, security and law enforcement activity of the state], *Sobraniye Zakonodatelstva Rossiyskoy Federatsii* (Collection of legislative acts of the Russian Federation], Federal Law no. 13 (1998), article 1462.

ing was reduced by the Cabinet of then Prime Minister Sergey Kiriyenko from 82 billion to 61 billion roubles. After the August crisis it was further curtailed and by the end of the year 'national defence' expenditure was implemented only to a level of about 38 billion roubles, that is, less than 50 per cent of the initial plan.[28]

This not only took away all resources for up-front investment for reductions; even worse, it also greatly reduced even the baseline defence budget within which money for reform was allocated and savings on maintenance had to be generated to be channelled into qualitative improvements.

Since it was difficult to reduce maintenance outlays proportionally, the drastic cuts hit R&D and procurement most of all. Those were funded at a level of only 14 per cent (4 billion instead of the planned 28.5 billion roubles). This has further exacerbated the crisis in the defence industry and undermined the technical standards of the armed forces. Only about 20 per cent of their arms and equipment are modern, while the rest are obsolete and not provided with needed repairs and spare parts. For the first time in a long history, in 1998 the defence industry did not supply the armed forces with a single tank, armoured personnel carrier, artillery piece, tactical or anti-aircraft missile, combat ship, submarine or aircraft.

The material level and morale of the armed forces deteriorated further. The 60–70 per cent inflation in the second half of 1998 brought a large part of the military (up to the rank of captain-major) below the poverty level and payment of salaries was delayed by two to three months. Training and exercises in the Ground Forces, Navy and Air Force virtually stopped: for instance, average flying time for a pilot went down to 8–12 hours per year, whereas the minimum formal requirement is 180 hours, and in NATO 300 hours. The crime rate, desertions and suicides in the army reached an unprecedented level.

Support of the key and most advanced branches and enterprises of the defence industry, which is considered the principal avenue of military reform, deteriorated still further. As a result of cuts in contracts the number of defence enterprises fell spontaneously from 1800 in 1991 to 500 by 1997 and their aggregate military and civilian output fell by 82 per cent. At the same time, the Federal Programme of Conversion in 1992–97 was funded on average to only 10 per cent of the plan, and in 1998 funding stopped altogether.

Very few of those lost 1300 enterprises were converted efficiently for civilian production. Most were simply mothballed, disintegrated or have been prolonging their agony by selling stocks and equipment, leasing space, surviving on small contracts and shifting to a partial working week. On average, wages in the defence industries are 60 per cent of the overall industrial level and delays in payment of wages are as long as six or nine months. Moreover, since traditionally in many cities the whole social infrastructure (housing, hospitals, recreation facilities, kindergartens, schools and so on) was built and supported from the profits of key (sometimes only one or two) defence enter-

[28] Mukhin, V., [The military budget '99 as a mirror of the crisis], *Nezavisimaya Gazeta*, 12 Dec. 1998.

prises, their collapse means total social degradation and the criminalization of whole urban areas.

Of large defence programmes only the development and deployment of new strategic SS-27 intercontinental ballistic missiles (ICBMs) (called Topol-M in Russia) was proceeding more or less steadily and the first 10 missiles were put on a combat-ready status on 28 December 1998.[29]

As a result of the financial crisis and budget cuts, together with the accumulated debt for the two years 1996–97 (about 25 billion roubles) the debt of the federal budget to the armed forces and defence industries reached 70 billion roubles by January 1999.[30]

The progress of military reform also suffered badly. Although the reorganization, integration and streamlining of the forces and command structures as described above went on, the most important direction—personnel reductions—was hindered by financial cuts. The only item that was funded fully was the payment of dues to retiring officers. However, this was done at the cost of cuts in funding for the maintenance of the remaining forces, including personnel outlays, and the most acute and important part of the programme of reductions—housing entitlements—was virtually destroyed by the financial crash.

For most demobilized officers housing was provided through the programme of housing certificates which were financially secured by the federal government: in the regions where officers went to live after service those certificates were to be accepted by the local authorities as payment for housing of a particular size, quality and cost. In 1998–2002 around 210 000 citizens were to be provided with such certificates. In 1998 the funding of those was planned at 5 billion roubles. However, because of the financial crash and the upsurge of inflation after August 1998 (including housing costs) these certificates lost much of their value. By the end of the year the MOD had issued 13 000 of them, instead of 40 000 planned. Those already issued cannot provide adequate housing to those who have not yet redeemed them. About 11 000 officers demobilized in 1998 were left without homes and 9000 more, who have already been laid off, cannot vacate their army apartments as they have no other home to go to. At the same time about 90 000 serving officers are not provided with proper MOD housing.[31]

All in all, because of the financial crisis and above all the collapse of the housing programme, the planned reduction in the armed forces' military personnel to 1.2 million was not completely fulfilled by January 1999. As a result slightly fewer than 1.3 million remain in the army and further cuts next year do not seem likely. This means that the whole concept of reducing numbers, generating savings, improving quality and reforming will disintegrate.

[29] Yakovlev, V., [Effectiveness, costs, feasibility: interview with S. Sokut], *Nezavisimoye Voyennoye Obozreniye*, no. 41 (11 Nov. 1998).

[30] Mukhin (note 28).

[31] [On the implementation of the programme of housing certificates], Resolution of the State Duma, Draft introduced by the Duma Defence Committee, 27 Nov. 1998.

One other important aspect of military reform fell victim to the financial crisis—the transfer to an all-volunteer or contract service. At the peak of the presidential election campaign in May 1996, Boris Yeltsin signed Presidential decree no. 723 on the change to all-volunteer armed forces by the year 2000.[32] This would have effectively solved the problems of manpower shortage, morale, the prestige attached to military service, abuse of soldiers and quality of personnel.

There were two principal conditions for implementation of this change. First was the deep reduction in force levels. It was calculated that all-volunteer armed forces of 0.8 million would cost in maintenance about the same as the 1.6 million, including conscripts, of early 1997.[33] Second, while funding the reductions separately, it was necessary to keep at least the same defence budget baseline, since a contract soldier is paid much more than a conscript one. In the course of a few years a contract force might bring some savings because the term of service is longer and the massive annual cost of transport and initial training of conscripts would disappear. Even so, maintenance costs could be higher, in particular if it were decided to increase the salaries of contract soldiers in order to attract a higher quality of personnel, raise officers' salaries accordingly and allocate more to training, housing and social benefits.

When the real reforms started in 1997, out of 1.6 million authorized personnel about 0.4 million were drafted privates, 0.3 million contract soldiers, and 0.9 million officers and non-commissioned officers. (By normal standards an army of 0.7 million privates would need only 0.3 million officers.) Deep reductions in the number of officers would generate big savings on maintenance in the end, as was desired, but would be costly initially, as has been seen. Major reductions in the number of privates would be cheap and would alleviate the problem of draft evasion. On the other hand, it would not generate serious savings on maintenance and would exacerbate still further the distorted ratio between officers and privates.

Since the funding of reductions from the very beginning was insufficient, it was decided to emphasize reductions in the number of contract soldiers, who would be cheap to lay off (the law did not make them eligible for housing and other payments) but would generate some savings on maintenance, since their salaries were much higher than those of draftees (normally five times as much or even 10 times as much in combat areas). Hence, of the savings made in 1997–98, at least 40 per cent were achieved by cutting down on contracts and setting aside one of the main generally accepted principles of reform. The crisis of 1998 did away with this concept for a long time.

[32] 'O perekhode k komplektovaniyu dolzhnostey ryadovogo i serzhantskogo sostava Vooruzhennykh Sil i drugich voysk Rossiyskoy Federatsii na professionalnoy osnove' [On the transition to recruiting privates and sergeants in the Armed Forces and other troops of Russian Federation on a professional basis], Presidential decree no. 722, 16 May 1996, *Sobraniye Zakonodatelstva Rossiyskoy Federatsii* [Collection of legislative acts of the Russian Federation], no. 21 (1996), article 2466.

[33] Karaganov, S., Arbatov, A. and Tretyakov, V., 'Rossiyskaya voyennaya reforma' [Russia's military reform: Report of the Council on Foreign and Defense Policy], *Nezavisimoye Voyennoye Obozreniye*, no. 25 (12–19 July 1997), pp. 1–7.

The change of government in September 1998 and the numerous statements of the new Prime Minister, Yevgeny Primakov, on the need for a 'New Deal' for Russia to replace the failed shock therapy and macroeconomic stabilization roused great hopes of a general revision of economic policy and in particular of radical improvements in the areas of defence policy and military reform. However, the first budget draft law proposed by the new government in December 1998 produced the effect of a cold shower on this optimism.

VI. The draft 1999 budget and military reform

The 1999 federal budget was elaborated in the midst of unprecedented economic and financial crisis, during the transition from one cabinet to another, and under huge pressure of the external debt, and was called an emergency budget. It was unique in another sense. Introduced by Primakov's coalition government with heavy representation of leftist parties, it was even more stringent than the preceding budgets of the liberal governments of Viktor Chernomyrdin and Kiriyenko, which reflected liberal–monetarist economic policy and the philosophy of macroeconomic stabilization. The main parameters were: GNP 4000 billion roubles; federal budget revenues 473.7 billion roubles; expenditure 575 billion roubles; deficit 101.3 billion roubles; planned printing of banknotes 32 billion roubles; projected inflation 32 per cent during the year; and an average rouble : dollar exchange rate of 21.5 : 1.

The main reason for this was Russia's dependence on the Western financial institutions, above all the International Monetary Fund (IMF) and the World Bank. Russia's accumulated foreign debt of almost $170 billion (including over $100 billion debt inherited from the USSR) implies paying $17.5 billion to service the debt in 1999.[34] After the August 1998 crash and the fall of the rouble (from 6 : 1 to the US dollar to 20 : 1 in December 1998) this would be over 70 per cent of projected federal budget revenues (350 billion roubles). Since this would mean nothing less than final financial collapse, and thus was unacceptable, restructuring of the debt to postpone and reformulate payments became Russia's highest economic priority. To secure the agreement of the West for the debt restructuring and new credits to service the debt, the most stringent budget was elaborated for 1999 and quickly approved by the Duma by an overwhelming majority, with only one party (Yabloko) voting against. The position of the Duma was another unique feature of that budget, and it reflected the vote as a purely political vote of support for Primakov and his coalition government.

It is beyond the scope of this chapter to discuss the 1999 federal budget, but its 'national defence' section implied bad news for the maintenance of Russia's defence capability and the military reform.

Total appropriations for 'national defence' were set at 93.7 billion roubles, that is, 2.34 per cent of GNP instead of 3.5 per cent as implied by 'The basics (concept) of the state policy of the Russian Federation on military develop-

[34] *The Economist*, 6 Feb. 1999, p. 21.

ment until the year 2005'. Fulfilling this directive would mean allocating 140 billion roubles to defence—hence the shortage of funding was about 58 billion roubles. In clear violation of the 1996 law 'On the budget classification'[35] the defence budget was introduced under a veil of secrecy: it was represented by only three lines instead of 120: (*a*) maintenance and development of the armed forces; (*b*) the military programme of the Ministry of Atomic Energy; and (*c*) mobilization activities. Clearly, this was done to cover up the inadequacy of the defence budget, which in constant prices would be 50 per cent lower than that initially planned for 1998. Higher inflation, which is highly likely in the opinion of the majority of experts, would bring it to a still lower level.

Through other budget items and sources of revenues it is intended to bring defence expenditure up to about 120 billion roubles (i.e., 3.2 per cent of GNP). This is done by statistical games: items such as military pensions and international activities are artificially added to the defence budget. The sources for the additional funding (part of the revenue from individual income tax, savings from reduction of central government expenditures, and so on) are also fairly doubtful.

The section 'military reform' is completely absent from both the federal budget and the 'national defence' category of the budget. Instead, in a section 'task budget funds' there is a 'task fund for the support of the reform', setting outlays at 2.9 billion roubles, of which the MOD is entitled to only 1.1 billion roubles. It is unclear what are the sources for that fund, and it is still much less than the funding for military reform in 1998 (4 billion roubles).

First of all this means that follow-on reductions of the force levels will not happen. The funding envisioned for reform will be barely sufficient to provide housing and other benefits to those already demobilized in 1998 but denied their proper entitlements for financial reasons. Even fulfilment of the goal originally set—cuts to 1.2 million military personnel—will be difficult and the much deeper reductions, down to 0.9–0.8 million, which are needed to improve the situation radically will clearly not be feasible. This means that the core concept of generating savings on maintenance through reductions to enhance quality and defence investment will fail.

This is all the more so because it is envisioned to raise military salaries by 150 per cent in January 1999 and double payment for military rank in July 1999. This is necessary but would not tangibly improve the well-being of officers, in particular if inflation is higher than projected, and would increase the share of maintenance costs in expenditure, thus partly negating the savings from the radical personnel reductions in 1997–98. What is worse, it is apparently not included in the draft budget: allocations for personnel payments are planned at 28.7 billion roubles, while the rise would mean an annual salary bill of 35 billion roubles. On top of this, there are outstanding salary payments

[35] See note 27.

which by the end of 1998 had reached 14.4 billion roubles, and these are not included in the budget either.[36]

Hence, much less would be left for raising the living standards of personnel, better training, repairs and spare parts for equipment, R&D, procurement and military construction. Further reorganization of the armed forces, redeployment and integration of units, and storage and utilization of arms would be much more difficult. Even such high-priority programmes as deployment of the SS-27s, maintenance of command and control and early-warning systems, and safety of nuclear arms would suffer seriously through shortage of funding.

Further degradation of even the most advanced branches of the defence industry is unavoidable. By early 1998 the accumulated debt of the MOD to the industry was 19 billion roubles.[37] Of the 28.5 billion roubles allocated for R&D and procurement in 1998 only 4 billion roubles were actually provided. By the end of the year the debt had grown to about 40 billion roubles.[38] Since in 1999 allocations for R&D and procurement are about the same as in 1998 in current prices, they will not be sufficient even to pay for the accumulated debt. As for new contracts, realistically projected inflation (at the minimum 100 per cent between September 1998 and December 1999) would cut the planned funding by half in real terms.

Although not included in the 'national defence' or the 'task fund for the support of the reform' sections of the budget, another item gives reason for much concern—the elimination of nuclear and chemical weapons and the dismantling of decommissioned nuclear submarines. In 1998 implementation of the 1993 Chemical Weapons Convention was funded only to 20 per cent of the plan, which implies that it is now lagging behind the schedule in the treaty by four years. In the 1999 budget only 1.7 billion roubles are provided for the implementation of international treaties, while the minimum requirement is 7.4 billion. No money is allocated for the elimination of decommissioned nuclear submarines (there are at present around 100 with their nuclear reactors still not extracted), while the minimum requirement is 1.2–1.4 billion roubles per year.

VII. Conclusions

Changing military requirements and resource limitations have provided a double incentive for radical military reform in Russia since the early 1990s. However, the deepening economic decline, constant financial shortages and gross mismanagement deadlocked the implementation of reform until mid-1997. The breakthrough achieved since then came to an almost full stop as a result of the crash of August 1998. Russia has arrived at the ultimate paradox of desperately lacking money either to support its existing defence establish-

[36] Romashkin, P., 'Voyenny byudzhet Rossiyskoy Federatsii na 1999 god' [Military budget of the Russian Federation for 1999], *Yadernoye Rasprostraneniye* (Carnegie Center, Moscow), vol. 26 (Nov. 1998).

[37] Romashkin (note 36).

[38] Romashkin (note 36).

ment or to radically reduce and restructure it in line with its limited resources and new military requirements. All in all, the 1999 defence budget will mean deeper degradation of the armed forces and defence industries, as well as curtailment of the military reform. That in turn would exacerbate still further the crisis in Russia's defence capacity and could bring about serious social and political consequences.

The printing of money, even if it results in higher inflation, so long as it is properly managed seems an acceptable price for saving the Russian defence establishment from final collapse and for continuing military reform, disarmament programmes and cooperation with the West. Both the domestic stability of Russia and the security of its near and more distant neighbours would certainly greatly benefit from this.

5. The Caspian Sea Basin: the security dimensions

GENNADY CHUFRIN

I. Introduction

In 1998 the Caspian Sea Basin continued to gain in prominence in international affairs. This process, initiated by a combination of political, economic and strategic factors, started in the early 1990s when, with the collapse of the Soviet Union, its former constituent republics in this region (Azerbaijan, Kazakhstan and Turkmenistan) became sovereign states. Occupying a central strategic position in the Transcaucasus and Central Asia they began to assume an important role in a new geopolitical setting, inviting the growing interest of major international actors.

The security dimensions of the Caspian Basin are closely related to the oil and gas reserves of the region, and these are discussed in section II. The legal regime regulating the jurisdiction and use of the Caspian Sea is described in section III, and section IV discusses the existing and potential pipeline routes for transporting oil and gas from the region. Section V examines the threat of militarization of the Caspian Basin, and a summary of the local conflicts in the region is given in section VI. The conclusions of the chapter are presented in section VII.

II. Caspian oil and gas reserves

Apart from its strategic significance the Caspian Basin has attracted the interest of the outside world because of the vast reserves of natural oil and gas claimed to be in the region.[1] Estimates of the actual size of these reserves vary widely. Some, including those made by Iran and the USA, indicate the ultimately recoverable reserves in the Caspian Basin to be some 160–200 billion barrels of oil equivalent, suggesting that this region is the third largest storehouse of oil and gas after the Middle East and western Siberia.[2]

According to more conservative estimates, largely corresponding to data quoted in various Russian sources, the proven reserves of oil and gas in the Caspian Basin are about 100 billion barrels of oil equivalent—still twice the

[1] The Caspian Sea Basin comprises territory of the 5 Caspian littoral states: Azerbaijan, Iran, Kazakhstan, Russia and Turkmenistan.

[2] *Inside (and Beyond) Russia and the FSU*, vol. 6, no. 15 (15 Apr. 1998), p. 8; Sarir , M., 'Utilisation of oil and gas in the Caspian region', *Amu Darya* (Tehran), vol. 2, no. 1 (1997), p. 14; and Gafarly, M., 'Neft Kaspiya—problema i politiki i ekonomiki' [Caspian oil—both a political and an economic problem], *Sodruzhestvo NG* [supplement to *Nezavisimaya Gazeta*], no. 4 (Apr. 1998).

size of those of Northern Europe.[3] However, these evaluations have been claimed by British experts to grossly overrate the Caspian Basin reserves and it has been suggested that the recoverable reserves of oil in this region are in the range of only 25–35 billion barrels. No estimates of gas reserves have been given.[4]

Since no comprehensive geological surveys of the Caspian seabed or of the maritime region have been carried out since the dissolution of the USSR it is difficult to evaluate the above estimates with any certainty. Although there is no doubt that the Caspian Basin contains substantial oil and gas reserves, estimates are clearly influenced by political and economic interests. Those made by the littoral states are obviously intended to attract foreign investments that could help turn the oil and gas potential of the Caspian region into a major sustainable source of economic prosperity. As Azerbaijan, Kazakhstan and Turkmenistan could not expect any other economic sector to offer real prospects for development in the foreseeable future, it was logical for them to orientate their domestic economic strategies and foreign policies towards this goal. Since Russia, their main economic partner in the Soviet times, was either unable or unwilling to assist them in a rapid and massive development of their oil and gas resources it was natural for these countries to seek new economic partners.

The new geopolitical and geo-economic situation in the Caspian Basin also attracts the interest of a large group of outside actors. Not only is there growing involvement of a number of international oil corporations (e.g., Chevron, Mobil Oil, UNOCAL and Texaco of the USA; British Petroleum and British Gas of the UK; Agip of Italy; Total of France; and Statoil of Norway) in local oil and gas development projects, but Caspian Sea affairs are also given a high profile in the foreign policy of a number of extra-regional countries. While energy issues are among the most important behind the policies of a number of international actors in the Caspian Basin, however, they are not the only reasons for their presence there.

This can be seen most clearly from the US policy in the region. In the 1990s it has shifted from a benevolent but rather passive support of the sovereignty of newly emerging states to a clearly formulated and active engagement in a wide range of political, security and economic issues in the region. In 1998, the major aims of US policy in the Caspian region were outlined as follows: (*a*) to strengthen modern political and economic institutions and advancing market democracy; (*b*) to resolve conflicts within and between countries of the region; (*c*) to promote security cooperation with the regional states; and (*d*) to

[3] 'Central Asia survey', *The Economist*, vol. 346, no. 8054 (7–13 Feb. 1998), p. 6; Shutov, A., 'Rossiya, Zakavkazye i neft Kaspiya' [Russia, Transcaucasus and Caspian oil], *Diplomaticheskiy Vestnik*, no. 1 (Jan. 1998), p. 65; and interview with Valery Garipov, Russian Deputy Minister of Fuel and Energy, in ITAR-TASS (Moscow), 28 Apr. 1998, in 'Russia: Russian official: Caspian resources less than claimed', Foreign Broadcast Information Service, *Daily Report—Central Eurasia (FBIS-SOV)*, FBIS-SOV-98-118, 28 Apr. 1998.

[4] Quoted among the sources used by the International Institute for Strategic Studies (IISS) in reaching these estimates were the *Oil and Gas Journal* and British Petroleum's *Statistical Review of World Energy*. IISS, *Strategic Survey 1997/98* (Oxford University Press: Oxford, 1998), p. 24.

promote energy development and the creation of an east–west transport corridor.[5]

The new strategic situation in the Caspian Basin after the disintegration of the USSR, as well as their own growing energy requirements, strongly motivated a number of European and Asian countries to activate their policies in the region, too. This was especially true of Turkey, whose annual natural gas requirements were projected to increase almost fourfold by 2005 and to double again by 2010.[6] The Caspian region was high on Turkey's list of sources of energy supplies to meet these domestic requirements. In addition to its interest in free access to Caspian energy resources, Turkey also wanted to use its historical, cultural and ethnic ties to many of the Caspian Basin countries to re-establish its political influence in the region.

Several Asia–Pacific countries—in particular China, Japan and South Korea—were also attracted to the region because their own energy self-sufficiency level was expected to fall from 43 per cent in 1995 to 29 per cent in 2015.[7] The worst hit would be China, whose energy consumption could equal that of all the European countries of the Organisation for Economic Co-operation and Development (OECD) combined in the first decade of the 21st century.[8] Logically, access to the energy resources of the Caspian Basin was given high priority in China's policy in the East Caspian (Central Asian) subregion.

III. The Caspian Sea legal regime

The existing legal regime of the Caspian Sea presents a major obstacle to the unimpeded use of the Caspian oil and gas resources. It is still based on the 1921 Treaty of Friendship between the RSFSR (Russian Soviet Federative Socialist Republic) and Iran (Persia) and on the 1940 Soviet–Iranian Trade and Navigation Agreement, which do not reflect the recent geopolitical changes in this area. While the need to establish a new and mutually acceptable legal regime for the Caspian Sea is recognized by all the littoral states, their radically different approaches have made this difficult to achieve.

Iran and Russia, supported in the first half of the 1990s by Turkmenistan, opted for a 'condominium' principle, according to which a 45-nautical mile coastal zone would fall under the jurisdiction of the respective littoral countries and the rest would be used jointly. Treating the Caspian Sea in accordance with the provisions of the 1982 United Nations Convention on the Law of the Sea (UNCLOS) as a lake (since it has no outlet to another sea or

[5] US policy toward the Caucasus and Central Asia, Statement by Ambassador-at-Large and Special Adviser to Secretary of State Stephen Sestanovich at the House of Representatives International Relations Committee, 30 Apr. 1998.

[6] Larrabee, F. S., 'US and European policy toward Turkey and the Caspian Basin', *Allies Divided: Transatlantic Policies for the Greater Middle East*, RAND reprint (RAND Corporation: Santa Monica, Calif., 1998), p. 155.

[7] Dupont, A., *The Environment and Security in Pacific Asia* (Oxford University Press: New York, 1998), p. 28.

[8] Dupont (note 7), p. 27.

the ocean), Iran and Russia insisted that its legal regime could not be governed by the convention.[9] Therefore, in their view, such categories as 'territorial waters', 'continental shelf' or 'exclusive economic zones' envisaged by UNCLOS were not applicable to the Caspian. Azerbaijan and Kazakhstan, however, claimed that in accordance with the existing international practice the legal regime of lakes surrounded by two or more coastal states was to be decided in each particular case by these states themselves and insisted on a sectoral division of the Caspian Sea. In order to bridge their differences, the littoral countries held intensive bilateral consultations in 1998.

After consultations in February and March, Azerbaijan and Turkmenistan agreed on the need to divide the Caspian seabed into national sectors. They held different positions on how such a division should be carried out, however, and were unable to resolve their dispute over the sovereignty of several major oilfields, including the Kapaz (Serdar) and Chirag oilfields.[10] This dispute intensified after Turkmenistan announced that it was inviting international tenders for the rights to explore the Kapaz oilfield, with estimated reserves of 1–1.3 billion barrels of oil. When it was announced in June that the tender had been won by an international consortium headed by the US Mobil company, this was flatly rejected by the Azerbaijani Government. Azerbaijan even threatened to impose economic sanctions on the foreign oil companies if they started exploiting the Kapaz oilfield before the ownership dispute was resolved.[11]

There were also significant changes in Russia's position on the legal status of the Caspian Sea. During negotiations with Azerbaijan at the end of March 1998, Russia agreed that rights to mineral resources located beneath the Caspian Sea should be demarcated by the median line through the centre of the sea. Although it accepted the principle of dividing the Caspian Sea into national sectors, Russia insisted on joint use of the Caspian Sea waters to allow free navigation and to facilitate the solution of the environmental problems.[12] This stand had also been taken by Russia at the intergovernmental consultations in February with another littoral country, Kazakhstan. Agreement was reached on the division of the Kazakh–Russian part of the Caspian Sea seabed into national sectors as well as on the need for common use of the Caspian waters for navigation and fishing.[13] These principles were upheld and further expanded at the meetings of presidents Boris Yeltsin and Nursultan Nazarbaev in April and July, which resulted in the Russia–Kazakhstan Agreement on

[9] For the definition of 'enclosed or semi-enclosed seas' see the 1982 United Nations Convention on the Law of the Sea, Part IX, article 122. *The Law of the Sea* (United Nations: New York, 1983).

[10] Turan (Baku), 9 Feb. 1998, 'Azerbaijan: Azeri, Turkmen teams agree "basic points" on Caspian Sea', FBIS-SOV-98-040, 11 Feb. 1998; and Turan (Baku), 30 Mar. 1998, in 'Azerbaijan: Azeri President, Turkmen Foreign Minister on Caspian talks', FBIS-SOV-98-089, 2 Apr. 1998.

[11] ITAR-TASS (Moscow), 18 June 1998, in 'Azerbaijan: Azerbaijan, Turkmenistan disagree over oilfield ownership', FBIS-SOV-98-169, 19 June 1998; and Radio Free Europe/Radio Liberty, *RFE/RL Newsline*, vol. 2, no. 116, part I (18 June 1998).

[12] Interfax (Moscow), 29 Mar. 1998, in 'Russia: Russia, Azerbaijan sign Caspian Sea legal status protocol', FBIS-SOV-98-088, 29 Mar. 1998; and Interfax (Moscow), 31 Mar. 1998, 'Russia: Moscow, Baku agree on median line Caspian mineral division', FBIS-SOV-98-090, 2 Apr. 1998.

[13] *RFE/RL Newsline*, vol. 2, no. 128, part I (7 July 1998).

Division of the Northern Caspian Seabed. According to this agreement, only the seabed and its mineral resources were to be divided along the median line, while the Caspian waters and biological resources should remain in common use. In the opinion of the Kazakh and Russian presidents these principles were not only of bilateral significance but could also constitute the basis for a convention on the legal status of the Caspian Sea which, they proposed, should be concluded by all the littoral states.

These ideas met with strong reservations from Azerbaijan, however, which insisted on dividing not only the seabed but also the surface of the sea. Turkmenistan, which fundamentally revised its stand on the legal status of the Caspian Sea during 1998, also opposed the Kazakh–Russian proposal and assumed a position similar to that of Azerbaijan.[14]

The strongest opposition to the Kazakh–Russian proposal came from Iran. In the course of Iranian–Russian consultations held in Tehran in July, and during the visits of the Iranian Foreign Minister to Azerbaijan, Kazakhstan and Turkmenistan in August, Iran reiterated its resistance to any division of the Caspian Sea into national sectors, whether of the seabed or of the surface, until a comprehensive agreement on its legal status was reached by all five littoral states. Until such an agreement is signed, Iranian officials maintained, the 1921 and 1940 treaties, which did not envisage such a division of the Caspian Sea, should remain in force.[15] Further clarifying the Iranian attitude towards possible changes in the existing legal regime, Hojatoleslam Hassan Rowhani, Secretary of Iran's Supreme National Security Council, stated in September that although Iran was prepared and willing to divide the Caspian Sea fairly it would endorse an agreement on this issue only if: (*a*) it was reached with the consensus of all the littoral states; (*b*) it ensured the protection of the environment; and (*c*) the non-militarized character of the Caspian Sea was preserved. He also emphasized that Iran would not tolerate any interference by foreign countries in this process.[16]

IV. Oil and gas routes from the Caspian Sea

Apart from determining the legal status of the Caspian Sea and the ownership of oil deposits, the littoral states were confronted with another serious problem, that is, the determination of routes for transporting oil and gas from the Caspian Basin to outside consumers. The dispute over this problem is pro-

[14] *RFE/RL Newsline*, vol. 2, no. 94, part I (19 May 1998). This accord met with criticism even in Russia since it was regarded as an unacceptable concession of Russian national interests in the Caspian. With the weakening of President Yeltsin's authority following the financial crash in Russia in Aug. 1998 his political opponents threatened to block ratification of the agreement in the State Duma. Tesemnikova, E., 'Moskva snova poshla na ustupki' [Moscow yielded again], *Nezavisimaya Gazeta*, 11 Apr. 1998; Aleksandrov, A., 'Komu vygoden razdel Kaspiya' [Who gains from the Caspian division?], *Nezavisimaya Gazeta*, 23 Sep. 1998; and IRNA (Tehran), 7 Nov. 1998, in 'Iran: Doubts over Russian Duma approval of Caspian agreement', Foreign Broadcast Information Service, *Daily Reports—Near East and South Asia (FBIS-NES)*, FBIS-NES-98-311, 7 Nov. 1998.

[15] *RFE/RL Newsline*, vol. 2, no. 137, part I (20 July 1998); vol. 2, no. 155, part I (13 Aug. 1998); vol. 2 , no. 156, part I (14 Aug. 1998); and vol. 2, no. 157, part I (17 Aug. 1998).

[16] IRNA (Tehran), 27 Sep. 1998, in 'Iran: Rowhani calls for unanimous legal regime for Caspian', FBIS-NES-98-270, 29 Sep. 1998.

bably the single most important cause of growing political tension in the area surrounding the Caspian Sea and especially in the Transcaucasus region. The conflict of interests arose from the fact that by the beginning of 1998 all Caspian oil and gas pipelines (except for a new gas pipeline from Turkmenistan to Iran commissioned in late December 1997)[17] ran through Russia. While Russia obviously wanted to retain this pre-eminent position, with the oil and gas pipelines passing mainly if not exclusively through its territory, other Caspian states, which were all land-locked, wanted to change this situation and their excessive dependence on Russia.

They considered alternative routes to bypass Russia: a western route via Georgia to the Black Sea and on to Europe either across Ukraine, via Romania or via Bulgaria and Greece; a south-western route from Azerbaijan to Georgia and on to the Mediterranean Sea via Turkey; southern routes through Iran, either to Europe via Turkey, to the Persian Gulf or via Afghanistan to Pakistan; and eastern routes from Kazakhstan and Turkmenistan to China.

Each of these routes was supported or opposed not only on economic but also on political grounds. Laying gas and oil pipelines through war-torn Afghanistan raised obvious security concerns. The proposed pipelines from Kazakhstan and Turkmenistan, passing through Xinjiang province in western China, besides being extremely long (2500–3000 km), could be vulnerable to terrorist acts by Uighur separatists. There were also serious reservations about plans to establish routes through Iran and fears that Iran would not be able to exercise control over international pipelines passing across its territory.[18]

Despite US Government objections the Iranian route came to be seen by the littoral countries, Kazakhstan and Turkmenistan in particular, as a very attractive one, both logistically and commercially, for the transport of their oil and gas to the world market. The geographical proximity of Iran to major oil and gas deposits in the Caspian Basin, together with access by the littoral countries to the extensive existing pipeline network on Iranian territory and Iranian oil terminals in the Persian Gulf, made the cost of transporting oil and gas across Iran comparatively low. As well as the Caspian states, US oil companies such as Mobil also increasingly favoured the Iranian route. It was also openly supported by a number of major West European oil companies and governments, far less adverse than the US Government to the political implications of dealing with Iran. However, even though the first signs of a thaw in the then highly strained US–Iranian relations appeared in 1998, the US Administration continued to oppose the laying of pipelines across Iran, motivating its opposition by the need to reduce US oil dependence on the Persian Gulf states. For its part Iran announced plans to construct an oil pipeline from the Caspian port

[17] Gafarly, M., 'Pervy gazoprovod v yuzhnom napravlenii' [First gas pipeline in a southern direction], *Nezavisimaya Gazeta*, 27 Jan. 1998.

[18] United States Information Service (USIS), 'Kalicki details US policies, interests in Caspian oil', *Washington File* (US Embassy: Stockholm, 25 Feb. 1998).

of Neka to Tehran's refinery that would help to divert the oil flow from the Caspian Basin to Iran.[19]

Another serious conflict of interests between different Caspian as well as several extra-regional states was recorded in 1998 in connection with Georgia's plans, actively supported by Azerbaijan and Turkey, to lay oil pipelines through its territory, either to Supsa on its west coast or southwards to Turkey.[20] In turn Turkey, supported by the USA, expressed its preference for a 1730-km pipeline from Baku via Georgia to Ceyhan, a terminal on its Mediterranean coast.[21]

Plans to construct the Baku–Ceyhan pipeline received strong backing from the US Government. Under Secretary of State Stuart Eizenstat stated in the US Senate Appropriations Subcommittee that this pipeline 'will provide a diversification of oil routes [from the Caspian Basin], will allow Caspian oil to get to the world markets without transiting Iran and will avoid putting more oil through the Bosporus'.[22]

The USA also strongly supported plans for a trans-Caspian pipeline to transport oil and gas from Kazakhstan and Turkmenistan and help establish an east–west transit corridor for oil and gas exports from the Caspian region. This position was influenced not so much by economic considerations (especially as the minimum cost for laying such a pipeline was projected to be at least $2 billion) as by political ones since, if realized, the trans-Caspian route would seriously undermine Russian influence in the Caspian Basin.

Russia's attitude towards these plans was clearly negative. While trying to raise Azerbaijan's and Kazakhstan's interest in northern oil routes (from Baku to Novorossiysk and from the Tengiz oilfield in western Kazakhstan to Novorossiysk), Russia strongly objected to laying a pipeline across the Caspian seabed, ostensibly on ecological grounds.[23] There was clear support from Iran, whose Foreign Minister Kamal Kharrazi stated that his government rejected existing plans to lay a trans-Caspian pipeline as one-sided and violating the rights of other littoral states.[24] The Iranian support was critical since, in the face of joint Russian–Iranian opposition, it would be practically impossible to construct a pipeline across the Caspian Sea.

However, other Russian efforts to resist solving the Caspian oil transport problem by establishing multiple routes were less successful. The strategic situation in the Caspian Basin had changed so fundamentally since the

[19] IRIB Television (Tehran), 3 Sep. 1998, in 'Iran: Iranian minister on tenders for Caspian oil projects', FBIS-NES-98-246, 4 Sep. 1998.

[20] In the view of Georgian President Shevardnadze, 'Georgia should serve as one of the major transit routes for transporting Caspian oil to Western Europe'. Interfax (Moscow), 12 Feb. 1998, in 'Georgia: Shevardnadze—main Caspian oil pipeline to cross Georgia', FBIS-SOV-98-043, 17 Feb. 1998.

[21] *RFE/RL Newsline*, vol. 2, no. 48, part I (11 Mar. 1998).

[22] United States Information Service (USIS), 'Eizenstat testimony on energy issues in Caspian region, testimony to Senate Appropriation Subcommittee on March 31, 1998', *European Washington File* (US Embassy: Stockholm, 7 Apr. 1998).

[23] Gadzizade, A., 'Kak delit Kaspiy' [How to divide the Caspian], *Nezavisimaya Gazeta*, 2 Apr. 1998.

[24] IRNA (Tehran), 22 Apr. 1998, in 'Iran: Kharrazi: Iran, Russia oppose pipeline on Caspian sea bed', FBIS-NES-98-112, 28 Apr. 1998.

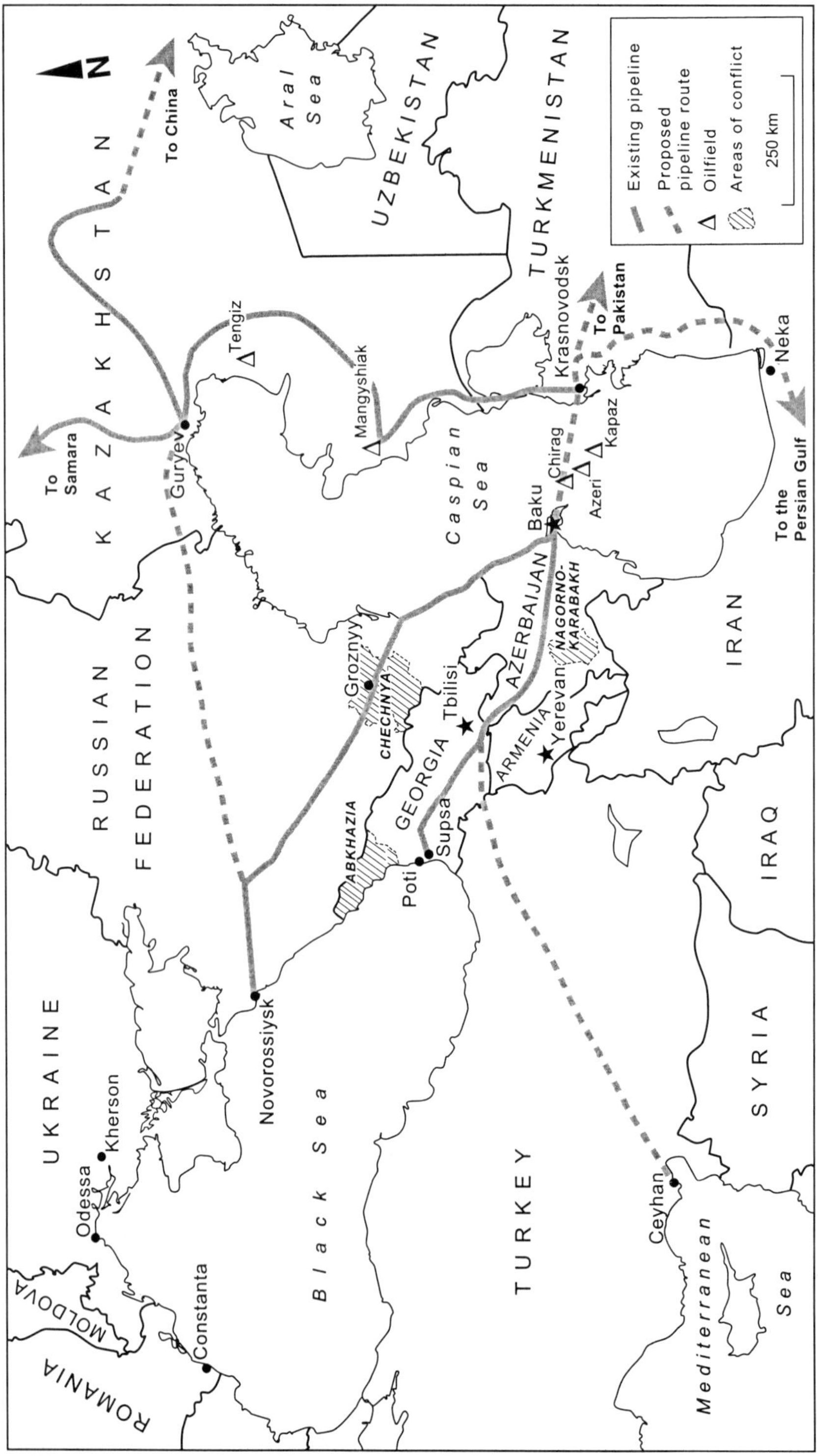

Figure 5.1. Map showing the routes of existing and planned oil pipelines from the Caspian Basin

disintegration of the USSR that most of the littoral states now favoured alternative routes for political as well as for economic reasons.

Responding to the US request, Azerbaijan announced its official endorsement of the trans-Caspian project 'not only for economic but also for strategic reasons'.[25] When it openly sided with Georgia and Turkey in favour of the Baku–Ceyhan pipeline, Azerbaijan's support was politically motivated. Economic incentives offered by Russia to use the northern route were turned down. In October in Ankara the presidents of Azerbaijan, Georgia, Kazakhstan, Turkey and Uzbekistan signed a political declaration in support of the Baku–Ceyhan route. The document was also signed by US Secretary of Energy Bill Richardson.[26] Both Iran and Russia reacted negatively to this declaration. The Russian Foreign Ministry issued a statement warning against 'excessive politicizing' of the issue of the Baku–Ceyhan route and affirming that Turkish threats to bar an increase in tanker traffic through the Bosporus straits were a violation of international norms.[27] Iran was even more blunt in its negative attitude towards the declaration and accused the US Government of exerting pressure on Caspian countries to sign an accord which sought to prevent them from using routes through Iran.[28] However, the future of the Baku–Ceyhan pipeline was put in serious doubt not so much because of Russian and Iranian objections to it as because of the fall of world oil prices in 1998. Even before that, construction of the pipeline was estimated to be very costly ($2.5–3.3 billion),[29] while its commercial operation under existing conditions on the world market became even more questionable.

Azerbaijan and Georgia were also considering a more economically viable outlet for Caspian oil to the world market—the 920-km Baku–Supsa pipeline that would bypass Russia. During 1998 they continued to repair and reconstruct it and to build an oil terminal at Supsa on the Georgian Black Sea coast. Although postponed several times for financial, technical and security reasons, it was expected to be commissioned in early 1999.[30]

Turkmenistan's stand on the future of oil and gas transport from the Caspian Basin also underwent serious changes, as became clear after President Saparmurat Niyazov's first state visit to the USA in April 1998. A number of agreements on US–Turkmen cooperation in oil and gas exploration were signed in Washington and a grant of $750 000 was offered to Turkmenistan for carrying out a technical and economic feasibility study regarding the con-

[25] Interfax (Moscow), 16 Apr. 1998, in 'Azerbaijan: Azeri president gives go-ahead to Transcaspian oil project', FBIS-SOV-98-106, 20 Apr. 1998.

[26] Tesemnikova, E. and Broladze, N., '"Ankarskaya deklaratsiya" prinyata' [Ankara declaration adopted], *Nezavisimaya Gazeta*, 30 Oct. 1998.

[27] *RFE/RL Newsline*, vol. 2, no. 210, part I (30 Oct. 1998).

[28] IRNA (Tehran), 31 Oct. 1998, in 'Iran: Tehran Times: Experts say Caspian Sea accord doomed', FBIS-NES-98-304, 31 Oct. 1998.

[29] Alimov, G., 'Trabzon skrepil "troystvenny soyuz"' [Trabzon sealed 'trilateral union'], *Izvestiya*, 28 Apr. 1998; and Blandy, C., 'The impact of Baku oil on Nagorny Karabakh. Waxing Western influence: waning Russian power', Conflict Studies Research Centre, S33, Royal Military Academy, Sandhurst, Camberly, Dec. 1997, p. 5. The cost of the project may even reach $4 billion according to recent published estimates. *RFE/RL Newsline*, vol. 2, no. 205, part I (22 Oct. 1998).

[30] *RFE/RL Newsline*, vol. 2, no. 127, part I (3 July 1998). In fact the pipeline became operational in early Jan. 1999.

struction of a trans-Caspian pipeline.[31] On his return from the USA Niyazov affirmed his support for the proposed pipeline but emphasized that its construction would be contingent on resolving the dispute between Azerbaijan and Turkmenistan over the delineation of their respective sectors of the Caspian Sea.[32] These developments signalled not only a thaw in relations between Ashkhabad and Washington, previously seriously strained over human rights in Turkmenistan, but also a further weakening of Russia's influence in the Caspian Basin.

Another step in strengthening Turkmen–US cooperation on energy issues could have been made when plans to start the construction of the 1271-km gas pipeline across Afghanistan and Pakistan before the end of 1998 were announced.[33] However, these plans were seriously set back by the US missile attack on alleged terrorist camps in Afghanistan in August. There were strong negative reactions from Islamic radicals in both Afghanistan and Pakistan, threatening retaliation against US interests. Consequently the US UNOCAL corporation, which had initiated the Pakistani–Turkmen gas pipeline project, announced the suspension of all its activities on the proposed pipeline.[34]

Meanwhile, Ukraine extended support to the east–west transport corridor project. Dissatisfied with the commercial terms offered by Russia for the transit of Turkmen gas across its territory, Ukraine invited international oil companies to invest in an alternative transport route for oil and gas from the Caspian Basin to Europe via the Black Sea and Ukraine. This proposal included the construction of an oil terminal with an estimated annual capacity of 40 million tonnes, a 670-km Odessa–Brody oil pipeline from the Black Sea coast to the Lviv region and modernization of the existing Drogobych, Kherson, Nadvirnian and Odessa refineries. The total cost of the project was estimated at $600–800 million.[35]

Another European country which joined the multinational gamble concerning the Caspian oil was Romania, which offered its own well-developed system of oil terminals, refineries and pipelines to receive Caspian oil in the Black Sea port of Constanta from Novorossiysk—and at a later stage from Supsa as well—for transport to Western Europe.[36] If approved, this route would not only help to side-step Turkey's objections to any further increase of oil deliveries through the Bosporus but would also put the future of the proposed Baku–Ceyhan route in doubt.

However, the Baku–Ceyhan route would lose almost all economic viability if yet another Caspian oil transport project, put forward by Greece for economic and even more for anti-Turkish political reasons, were to be realized. It

[31] Mikhailov, V. and Smolnikov, G., 'Washington priznal Ashgabat' [Washington recognized Ashkhabad], *Nezavisimaya Gazeta*, 29 Apr. 1998.

[32] *RFE/RL Newsline*, vol. 2, no. 94, part I (19 May 1998).

[33] *RFE/RL Newsline*, vol. 2, no. 157, part I (17 Aug. 1998).

[34] *RFE/RL Newsline*, vol. 2, no. 161, part I (21 Aug. 1998).

[35] Interfax (Moscow), 9 June 1998, in 'Ukraine: Ukraine plans Caspian oil transit consortium', FBIS-SOV-98-160, 9 June 1998.

[36] Nesterova, M., 'Bolshaya igra v neft' [Big oil game], *Sodruzhestvo NG* [supplement to *Nezavisimaya Gazeta*], no. 7 (July 1998).

envisaged transporting oil across the territories of Bulgaria and Greece to the Aegean Sea and was supported by a strong US–Greek lobby in the USA.[37]

With economic prospects for the Baku–Ceyhan pipeline rather bleak the only realistic options for Caspian oil and gas routes bypassing Russia in the southern and western directions remained that from Baku to Supsa or possible routes via Iran.

V. The threat of militarization of the Caspian Basin

Rejection of the 'condominium' principle by the majority of the littoral states and their clear preference for dividing the Caspian Sea into national sectors created a new security agenda in the region.

Without waiting for an international agreement establishing a legal regime for demarcation of national sectors Kazakhstan decided to start patrolling part of the Caspian Sea, which it arbitrarily included into its national territory, and a completely new security situation began to evolve in the region. In January 1998 Kazakhstan established a special naval patrol force, 'Snow Leopard', armed with high-speed gunboats and military helicopters. Its duties were officially defined as protecting the safety of territorial waters and guarding oil-rich fields there against potential intruders. It was reported in the press, however, that in future those duties were to be extended to include the protection of oil transports from the Tengiz field in western Kazakhstan to oil terminals in Azerbaijan via the Caspian Sea.[38]

The establishment of such a force, with duties exceeding the regular functions of a border patrol service, set a precedent with far-reaching consequences. Although the Snow Leopard force did not change the existing military balance in the Caspian Basin in any significant way, the Kazakh motives that led to its creation were not lost on other Caspian littoral states. This was the first time since the break-up of the Soviet Union that one of the newly emerged states had created its own naval capability in the Caspian Basin. If other new Caspian states were provoked into following this example, and decided to defend their own unilaterally defined national sectors and economic zones by force and patrol communication lines prior to any agreement regulating such activities, this could seriously destabilize the security situation in the Caspian Basin.

Caspian Basin security became increasingly influenced not only by national developments in the littoral states but also by their growing military cooperation with outside powers, in particular after some of them began regular participation in NATO's Partnership for Peace (PFP) programme and became recipients of military aid from NATO countries. Within the framework of this cooperation Turkey and the USA continued to assist Azerbaijan and Georgia

[37] Suponina, E., 'Rossiya, Bolgariya i Gretsiya pristupili k proyektirovke svoego marshruta dlya kaspiyskoy nefti' [Russia, Bulgaria and Greece started their own Caspian oil transport project], *Nezavisimaya Gazeta*, 26 June 1998.

[38] Mukhin, V., 'Kazakhstan ukreplyayet voyennoye prisutstviye na Kaspii' [Kazakhstan strengthens its military presence in the Caspian], *Nezavisimaya Gazeta*, 19 May 1998.

in 1998 in training their armed forces and in carrying out arms modernization programmes. In June, as part of this assistance, Turkey donated $5.5 million to Georgia.[39] In March, Georgia had concluded an agreement on military and security cooperation with the USA which envisaged financial assistance for the purchase of military and communications equipment.[40]

In the East Caspian (Central Asian) subregion, too, Kazakhstan, according to its newly declared military doctrine, regarded increased cooperation with the NATO countries as an important element of the common European–Central Asian security system which it wanted to develop. Although it continued to be party to the 1992 Commonwealth of Independent States (CIS) Treaty on Collective Security[41] Kazakhstan wanted to enlarge the number of its security partners. It believed that this would not only strengthen regional security but also help to 'minimise the reliance of the Central Asian republics on Russia and consequently mitigate Russian domination in the region'.[42] Along with Kyrgyzstan and Uzbekistan, therefore, Kazakhstan was strengthening its military cooperation with Turkey and the USA within the framework of the PFP programme. This included joint military manoeuvres in the Caspian Basin;[43] another round of such exercises was organized by the US Central Command in September 1998 in Kyrgyzstan and Uzbekistan. Servicemen from Azerbaijan and Georgia were included for the first time in 1998.[44]

Russia interpreted these tendencies and developments in the East Caspian subregion as another challenge to its already waning influence there, now in security affairs. For their part Chinese strategic analysts saw the sending of US paratroopers to Central Asia for manoeuvres as a logical consequence of NATO's eastward expansion and 'indicated that the struggle between the big powers has spread from economic and political fields to military and security fields'.[45]

In the West Caspian (Transcaucasus) subregion too, Turkey and the USA seemed unwilling to confine their role in security affairs to providing military supplies and training the armed forces. According to statements made in 1998 by such high-ranking officials as, for instance, US Ambassador to Georgia

[39] Anatolia (Ankara), 12 June 1998, 'Turkey: Turkey donates $5.5 million to Georgian Army', Foreign Broadcast Information Service, *Daily Report–West Europe (FBIS-WEU)*, FBIS-WEU-98-163, 12 June 1998.

[40] *RFE/RL Newsline*, vol. 2, no. 58, part I (25 Mar. 1998); and Broladze, N., 'Amerikano-gruzinski dialog' [American–Georgian dialogue], *Nezavisimaya Gazeta*, 4 Apr. 1998.

[41] The Tashkent Treaty on Collective Security was signed on 15 May 1992 by Armenia, Kazakhstan, Kyrgyzstan, Russia, Tajikistan and Uzbekistan. It was later joined by Azerbaijan, Belarus and Georgia. The text of the treaty is reproduced in *Izvestiya*, 16 May 1992, p. 3.

[42] Kasenov, O., 'Military aspects of security in Central Asia: national and regional strategies of security', ed. S. N. MacFarlane, *Regional Security in Central Asia* (Centre for International Relations, Queen's University: Kingston, Ontario, 1995), p. 81.

[43] Gafarly, M., 'Tsentralnoaziatskiy soyuz prevraschayetsya v voyenny blok' [Central Asian Union transforms into a military bloc], *Nezavisimaya Gazeta*, 20 Dec. 1997; and Korbut, A., 'Novye ucheniya v Tsentralnoy Azii' [New manoeuvres in Central Asia], *Nezavisimaya Gazeta*, 2 Apr. 1998.

[44] Radio Tashkent (Tashkent), 21 Sep. 1998, in 'Uzbekistan: NATO partnership C. Asian exercises begin in Uzbekistan', Foreign Broadcast Information Service, *Daily Report–Central Eurasia: Military Affairs (FBIS-UMA)*, FBIS-UMA-98-264, 25 Sep. 1998.

[45] Chen Feng, 'The international strategic situation of 1997', *International Strategic Studies* (Beijing), no. 1 (1998), p. 5.

Kenneth Spencer Yalowitz or Turkish Deputy Chief of General Staff General Cevik Bir, Turkey and the USA were considering the possible deployment of a peacekeeping force in the Caucasus under the aegis of NATO.[46] One of the possible reasons for such an action would be to ensure the safety of oil routes from Azerbaijan across Georgia to the Black Sea coast or to Turkey.

These plans were welcomed in Azerbaijan which, judging by the statement made by its defence minister in Brussels in June, was prepared to host NATO military installations on its soil.[47]

In Georgia, too, there was a noticeable shift in favour of strengthening security cooperation with the West while existing security arrangements with Russia were either significantly reduced in scope or totally discontinued. Thus the Georgian Parliament continued to withhold ratification of the agreement with Russia signed in September 1995 'On the presence of Russian military bases in Georgia', which was the basis for the status of Russian troops in Georgia. There were mounting demands for these bases to be closed down and for Russian troops to be withdrawn from the country. In July 1998 the parliament passed a law under which Russian border guards deployed in the country were to hand over complete control of the borders to the Georgian forces within the next two years and to withdraw fully from Georgia.[48] This process started in August when Georgia took over from Russia responsibility for patrolling its sea borders.[49] Soon afterwards the Georgian Black Sea ports of Poti and Batumi were visited for the first time by ships of the US 6th Fleet.[50] In November two agreements were signed in Moscow by Georgia and Russia redefining the latter's diminishing role in helping to guard Georgia's borders. One of the two agreements defined the ongoing areas of cooperation, which no longer included protecting Georgia's maritime borders. The second dealt with the gradual transfer of the areas still being jointly guarded and of property currently owned by the Russian Federal Border Guard Service.[51] Finally, although Georgia repeatedly stated its dissatisfaction with the presence of Russian peacekeepers along the border between Abkhazia and the rest of Georgia, it stopped short of demanding their withdrawal, at least until arrangements were made to replace them with an alternative force.

Although, as some Georgian security analysts noted, there were many reasons for the cooling of Georgia's security relations with Russia, the main one seemed to be the oil factor. In the opinion of many Georgian politicians, especially those who did not regard Russia as an ally (even though both countries were CIS members and parties to the CIS Treaty on Collective Security) but rather as a major threat to Georgia's sovereignty, laying an oil pipeline

[46] *RFE/RL Newsline*, vol. 2, no. 130, part I (9 July 1998).

[47] Mukhin, V., 'Prichiny antirossiyskoy pozitsii ryada gosudarstv SNG' [Reasons for the anti-Russian stand of a number of CIS member states], *Nezavisimaya Gazeta*, 24 July 1998.

[48] *RFE/RL Newsline*, vol. 2, no. 138, part I (21 July 1998); and Zapivakhin, O., 'Tbilisi beryot pod kontrol svoyi granitsy' [Tbilisi takes control over its borders], *Krasnaya Zvezda*, 4 July 1998.

[49] Kopyev, A., 'Rossiyskikh pogranichnikov vynudili pokinut Poti' [Russian border guards forced to leave Poti], *Krasnaya Zvezda*, 8 Sep. 1998.

[50] *RFE/RL Newsline*, vol. 2, no. 176, part I (11 Sep. 1998).

[51] *RFE/RL Newsline*, vol. 2, no. 124, part I (5 Nov. 1998).

from Azerbaijan across Georgia as part of the east–west transport project would enhance Western interest in protecting Georgia's security and reducing its dependence on Russia in security affairs.[52]

The pro-Western shift in the security postures of Azerbaijan and Georgia was received with deep apprehension and suspicion in Armenia and Russia and helped to intensify their strategic cooperation. Among other things they established a regional air-defence command and control post in Armenia that facilitated the creation of a coordinated system for all Russian air-defence facilities deployed in the North Caucasus and Armenia and capable of receiving and processing information in the airspace between the Black and Caspian seas.[53] Armenia and Russia also agreed to step up their cooperation in patrolling the Armenian border with Turkey, as well as in training Armenian military personnel. A number of other bilateral agreements on military cooperation were signed during the visit of Russian Defence Minister Marshal Igor Sergeyev to Armenia in July 1998.[54]

Predictably, Azerbaijan responded negatively to this strengthening of Armenian–Russian military cooperation, accusing Russia of violating the 1990 Treaty on Conventional Armed Forces in Europe (the CFE Treaty) flank limits by putting more weapons into Armenia and the North Caucasus.[55] While no hard evidence was presented to substantiate this claim Azerbaijani President Heidar Aliyev, favouring closer cooperation with NATO in the context of the Armenian–Azerbaijani conflict, called on the alliance to make a 'serious effort' to prevent the 'militarization of Armenia' and even claimed that Russia was 'arming Armenia against . . . NATO'.[56] Rejecting these accusations, Armenia in turn claimed that it was Azerbaijan that was in violation of the treaty, exceeding its maximum limits in three categories of armaments for land forces.[57] The Russian Ministry of Defence came out in support of Armenia, stating at the end of July that the military balance between Armenia and Azerbaijan was heavily in favour of the latter and claiming that Azerbaijan exceeded Armenia in all major types of conventional land weapon.[58]

Regarding its own compliance with the CFE flank limits in the Transcaucasus, Russia continued to insist on their revision, justifying its stand by the fundamental changes in the geopolitical and strategic environment in the region after the disintegration of the Soviet Union. The Russian position on this issue hardened still further in 1998 in view of the increasing involvement

[52] Darchiashvili, D., *Georgia: The Search for State Security* (Center for International Security and Arms Control, Stanford University: Stanford, Calif., Dec. 1997), pp. 15–16.

[53] Shermatova, S., 'Is the Caspian threatened with militarization?', *Moscow News*, no. 15 (23–29 Apr. 1998).

[54] Falichev , O., 'Strategicheskoye partnyorstvo s pritselom na XXI vek' [Strategic partnership aimed at the 21st century], *Krasnaya Zvezda*, 17 July 1998.

[55] *RFE/RL Newsline*, vol. 2, no. 138, part I (21 July 1998); and vol. 2, no. 188, part I (29 Sep. 1998).

[56] ITAR-TASS (Moscow), 24 Oct. 1998, in 'Azerbaijan: Aliyev urges NATO to stop militarization of Armenia', FBIS-SOV-98-297, 27 Oct. 1998.

[57] *RFE/RL Newsline*, vol. 2, no. 150, part I (6 Aug. 1998).

[58] Pankov, Y., 'Tseli Rossii yasnye i odnoznachnye' [Russian aims are clear and unambiguous], *Krasnaya Zvezda*, 30 July 1998. For more detailed analysis of the compliance of Armenia, Azerbaijan and Russia with the CFE Treaty see chapter 14 in this volume.

of NATO members in Caspian regional affairs as well as of their perceived intentions of protecting their interests by coercive methods.

However, although developments in security affairs in the Caspian region in 1998 were certainly showing a dangerous tendency to transform the area into one of serious confrontation between different local and extra-regional countries, the possibility that the USA and/or NATO would play a direct military role in the defence of conflicting oil- and gas-related interests was regarded by some Western analysts with deep scepticism and as impractical and in fact counterproductive to Western interests.[59]

VI. Local conflicts

The political and security situation in the Caspian Basin continued to be destabilized by a number of partly or fully unresolved local conflicts in 1998. Although they had their own dynamics, some of these conflicts (in Abkhazia, Chechnya or Nagorno-Karabakh) became increasingly linked to the oil factor, since their settlement was regarded as a necessary condition for ensuring the security of both existing and planned oil and gas pipelines in the region. The interrelationship between the settlement of local conflicts and the resolution of the problem of transporting oil was another reason for the involvement of extra-regional countries in Caspian affairs.

The North Caucasus

The situation in and around *Chechnya* remained the single largest security concern in Russia. While Moscow continued to regard Chechnya as an integral part of the Russian Federation (while offering it the maximum possible degree of autonomy), President Aslan Maskhadov and other Chechen leaders repeatedly stated that the independence of Ichkeria (their preferred name for the Chechen Republic) was an indisputable reality and non-negotiable. However, the war-devastated Chechen economy and a severe shortage of domestic financial and investment resources to rebuild it forced Chechen leaders to search for massive outside economic assistance and to try in this connection to find some acceptable accommodation with Moscow.

Despite acute differences with the Russian Government and continuous security instability in Chechnya itself[60] and on its borders, the Grozny authorities were particularly careful to ensure the safety of the Baku–Novorossiysk pipeline. Although the Chechen leadership also tried to use the oil factor as

[59] Olcott, M. B., 'The Caspian's false promise', *Foreign Policy* (summer 1998), p. 111; and Jaffe, A. M. and Manning, R. A. 'The myth of the Caspian "great game": the real geopolitics of energy', *Survival*, vol. 40, no. 4 (winter 1998/99), p. 122.

[60] Continuous clashes in Chechnya between different armed groups were clear evidence of this internal instability. The largest was the fighting in Gudermes, the second largest city of Chechnya, in mid-July. One week later President Maskhadov himself barely escaped an attempt on his life staged in Grozny by his political opponents among radical Islamists. In Oct. the opposition led by field commanders Shamil Basaev, Salman Raduev and Khunkar-pasha Israpilov demanded Maskhadov's resignation. He responded by ordering the Prosecutor-General of Chechnya to open criminal proceedings against them on charges of attempting a state coup.

leverage in its political confrontation with the federal government, by threatening to retract its promise to ensure security of the pipeline,[61] Chechnya and Russia reached a new agreement on the transit of Azerbaijani oil in April. They also agreed to increase the amount of oil transported via the pipeline substantially (from 120 000 tons in 1997 to 1.5 million tons or more in 1998),[62] reflecting a rare community of business interests between Chechnya and Russia. This was possible because the revenues for the use of the pipeline constituted one of the very few stable sources of government income for Chechnya, while for Russia this continued to be the only realistic route for transporting Azerbaijani oil. Earlier Russian plans to lay another Caspian oil pipeline, to bypass Chechnya and run across Dagestan, came to be seriously undermined by the growing political and security instability in this North Caucasus republic.

The security situation in *Dagestan* was severely destabilized in 1998 by numerous abductions, killings and explosions, attributed primarily to Chechen radicals. Another source of political instability was the spread of the fundamentalist Wahhabi movement under anti-Russian slogans, the principal one being the creation of a united Islamic state consisting of Chechnya, Dagestan, Ingushetia, Kabardino-Balkaria and Karachai-Cherkessia.[63] The Wahhabi movement became a serious security threat in the region, especially in Dagestan, where its followers were engaged in anti-government activities under the guise of Muslim propaganda.

To prevent the security situation in the North Caucasus in general, and in Dagestan in particular, getting completely out of control, the Russian Government improved the protection of the state border through the high mountains of the Caucasus from the Caspian Sea to the Black Sea. Repairs and modernization of the existing engineering installations, radar stations and signalling and communications facilities were carried out, and border crossing points were fortified. These administrative and security steps failed to arrest the mounting wave of terrorism and separatism, however, and in spite of legal restrictions imposed on the Wahhabi movement in Dagestan[64] its members continued their illegal activities and periodically resorted to acts of violence. In August, residents of three villages in the Buinak district of Dagestan, most of whom were believed to be Wahhabis, declared 'an independent Islamic territory' and refused to acknowledge the jurisdiction of the republican authorities.

Instability in Dagestan developed still further after the establishment of a Congress of Chechen and Dagestani Peoples in April. It declared its ultimate objective to be the unification of Chechnya and Dagestan. Shamil Basaev,

[61] Maksakov, I., 'Moskva i Grozny dogovorilis' [Moscow and Grozny reached agreement], *Nezavisimaya Gazeta*, 29 Apr. 1998.

[62] Maksakov, I., 'Mashadov vnov ugrozhaet' [Maskhadov renews his threats], *Nezavisimaya Gazeta*, 10 Feb. 1998. In June the Chechen Government again threatened to halt shipments of oil through the Baku–Grozny–Novorossiysk pipeline, this time because Moscow failed to provide funds for its security in accordance with the Sep. 1997 agreement. Moscow's response to these demands was both quick and positive, which clearly demonstrated its interest in maintaining good relations with Grozny on this issue. *RFE/RL Newsline*, vol. 2, no. 114, part I (16 June 1998).

[63] *Inside Russia and the FSU*, vol. 6, no. 4 (15 Apr. 1998), p. 12.

[64] *RFE/RL Newsline*, vol. 1, no. 53, part I (17 Mar. 1998).

then acting Prime Minister of Chechnya, openly sided with the aims of the congress and became its chairman.[65] In May another group of Muslim radicals, followers of the Russian State Duma Deputy and Chairman of the Union of Muslims of Russia, Nadirshakh Khachilayev, used arms to seize a government building in Dagestan.[66] This was further proof of the highly unstable political and security situation in Dagestan. Recognizing this, for the first time in the history of post-Soviet Russian parliamentarism the Duma decided to strip Khachilayev of his immunity from prosecution, thus enabling the Russian Prosecutor-General's Office to open criminal proceedings against him.[67]

More serious proof of this instability was registered at the end of August, when the spiritual leader of Dagestan's Muslims, Mufti Said Mohammed Abubakayev, was assassinated. This criminal act was blamed on Islamic extremists. As a consequence of the assassination Dagestan was put literally on the brink of civil war.[68]

These events not only made Russian plans for a pipeline across Dagestan less and less viable, but also helped to enhance the role of Chechnya in transporting Azeri oil to Novorossiysk. Speaking at a Moscow press conference in November, Russian Fuel and Energy Minister Sergey Generalov finally dismissed plans for a bypass pipeline as purely political and stated that their implementation could undermine 'normal relations' with Chechnya.[69] For his part Maskhadov openly sided with Moscow in criticizing the Baku–Ceyhan pipeline project and stressed that he agreed with the Russian argument that the Baku–Novorossiysk route across Chechnya was the most economical.[70]

The Transcaucasus

In 1998 the oil factor also deeply overshadowed both domestic political life and foreign policy in *Georgia*. In anticipation of much-needed revenues from the transit of Caspian oil the government became particularly concerned about security threats presented to these plans by the lack of political stability in the country, allegedly instigated from abroad. The attempted assassination of Georgian President Eduard Shevardnadze on 9 February, the second in three years, organized by followers of the late President Zviad Gamsakhurdia, was therefore perceived by the Georgian Government and by Shevardnadze himself not so much as part of the domestic political struggle but as an attempt by political forces relying on outside support to undermine plans to transport oil across Georgia.[71]

[65] *RFE/RL Newsline*, vol. 2, no. 89, part I (12 May 1998).

[66] Maksakov, I., 'Gosudarstvenny perevorot mozhet stat realnostyu' [*Coup d'état* may become a reality], *Nezavisimaya Gazeta*, 22 May 1998.

[67] *RFE/RL Newsline*, vol. 1, no 185, part II (25 Sep. 1998).

[68] Maksakov, I. and Fatullaev, M., 'Dagestan balansiruet mezhdu mirom i voynoy' [Dagestan balances between peace and war], *Nezavisimaya Gazeta*, 25 Aug. 1998.

[69] *RFE/RL Newsline*, vol. 2, no. 222, part I (17 Nov. 1998).

[70] *RFE/RL Newsline*, vol. 2, no. 211, part I (2 Nov. 1998).

[71] 'Failed assassins seized: President Shevardnadze says he believes the group of attackers was trained abroad', *New Europe*, 22–28 Feb. 1998.

Russia's negative attitude to the idea of the east–west oil transport corridor was well known, and Russia was accused if not of direct involvement in the assassination attempt at least of failing to stop the activities of militant political opponents of Shevardnadze taking refuge on Russian territory. Fiery anti-Russian accusations were made in the parliament in this connection as well as demands that the Russian military bases in Georgia be closed down.[72]

An early resolution of its conflict with *Abkhazia* was considered by Georgia as absolutely essential for the security of an oil terminal in Supsa as well as of the Baku–Supsa oil pipeline, which, after reconstruction, would meet the Black Sea coast not far from the conflict zone. To achieve this goal the Georgian Government wanted the CIS peacekeeping forces stationed in the conflict zone and consisting of Russian servicemen to carry out Bosnia-type peace-enforcement functions. Speaking in February in the Georgian Parliament, Shevardnadze justified the need to resort to peace enforcement by the absence of any progress in resolution of the conflict by peaceful methods.[73] Russia, however, in whose opinion any such attempt would inevitably lead to new bloodshed, refused to support this proposal.

Georgia succeeded in obtaining approval for its other plan for resolution of the Abkhazia conflict at the April 1998 CIS summit meeting in Moscow, however, where the heads of 7 of the 11 CIS states expressed their agreement (by acclamation) with the main provisions of this plan. They envisaged: (*a*) the lifting of current economic sanctions against Abkhazia contingent on the successful repatriation to the Gali district of ethnic Georgians forced to flee their homes during the 1992–93 war between Abkhazia and Georgia; (*b*) the establishment of a joint Abkhaz–Georgian administration in Gali with Russian, UN and Organization for Security and Co-operation in Europe (OSCE) representation; and (*c*) the expansion of the safe zone controlled by peacekeeping forces from the Inguri River to the Ghalidza River.[74]

The implementation of this plan was put in doubt from the very beginning, however, since the Abkhaz authorities flatly refused to follow its provisions and threatened to use force to defend the current de facto independent status of Abkhazia. Another, and this time probably fatal, blow to the CIS-approved peace plan was delivered from within Georgia itself when, in the second half of May, Georgian extremists from the so-called White Legion attacked the Abkhaz militia in the Gali district. In the course of the hostilities, which lasted six days, many lives were lost on both sides of the conflict. Not only were the prospects for repatriation of ethnic Georgians who left the Gali district because of the 1992–93 war severely jeopardized, but another 30 000–40 000 Georgian residents of this district were forced to flee. The resulting situation was characterized by OSCE Chairman-in-Office Bronislaw Geremek as seri-

[72] This accusation was made among others by Irina Sarishvili, leader of the National Democratic Party of Georgia. Berulava, I., 'Krov v Tbilisi: Est li v ney sledy nefti?' [Blood in Tbilisi: Does it have traces of oil in it?], *Izvestiya*, 11 Feb. 1989.

[73] Strugovets, V., 'Kto zavtra vstanet na Inguri?' [Who will stand on the Inguri tomorrow?], *Krasnaya Zvezda*, 14 Mar. 1998.

[74] *RFE/RL Newsline*, vol. 2, no. 82, part I (29 Apr. 1998).

ously threatening UN-led efforts to achieve an overall solution of the Abkhazia–Georgia conflict and as posing a danger to the security of other regions of the Caucasus.[75] On 30 July 1998 the UN Security Council adopted a special resolution condemning the latest acts of violence and ethnic cleansing in Abkhazia and called on both sides to quickly resolve the conflict through negotiations.[76]

The Georgian authorities put the blame for these events on Russia. On 1 June, in a weekly radio address, Shevardnadze criticized the Russian peacekeeping force for failing to prevent additional Abkhaz forces from infiltrating the conflict zone.[77] Georgia perceived a clear linkage between Russia's passive reaction to the flare-up of hostilities in the Gali district and its negative attitude to the Baku–Supsa oil route. According to Peter Mamradze, Shevardnadze's chief of staff, 'the pipeline irritates forces in Russia and we think that has triggered all kinds of activities against Georgia'.[78] Georgia was not the only party to the conflict that criticized the Russian peacekeeping forces: Abkhaz leader Vladislav Ardzinba accused them of failing to implement their mandate and take effective measures to stop Georgian guerrilla activities.[79] However, neither the Abkhaz nor the Georgian side officially demanded the withdrawal of the peacekeepers from the conflict zone since it would almost certainly result in a further escalation of the conflict and, as a consequence, would severely undermine the safety of oil transit across Georgia.

The security of the Baku–Supsa pipeline, however, continued to be threatened not only by the unresolved conflict in Abkhazia but also by the overall political instability in Georgia. In October the situation in western Georgia was seriously aggravated following the mutiny of army units deployed in Kutaisi.[80] Although the insurrection was quickly put down by the loyal government troops all construction and restoration work on the oil pipeline had to be discontinued for some time, which would delay its completion.

In *Armenia* the beginning of 1998 was also marked by turbulence caused by the irreconcilable differences between then President Levon Ter-Petrosyan and his political opponents over the issue of *Nagorno-Karabakh*. These differences reached their climax when Ter-Petrosyan decided to support the 'phased approach' of the OSCE Minsk Group for the resolution of this long-standing conflict with Azerbaijan.[81] His opponents, led by Robert Kocharyan, at that time Armenia's prime minister and former president of the unrecognized

[75] *RFE/RL Newsline*, vol. 2, no. 102, part I (29 May 1998).

[76] UN Security Council Resolution 1187, 30 July 1998; and *RFE/RL Newsline*, vol. 2, no. 154, part I (12 Aug. 1998).

[77] *RFE/RL Newsline*, vol. 2, no. 104, part I (2 June 1998).

[78] Williams, S., 'Pipeline row sparked unrest, says Georgia', *Financial Times*, 29 May 1998.

[79] Interfax (Moscow), 27 May 1998, in 'Georgia: Abkhazia accuses Russian peacekeepers of ignoring mandate', FBIS-SOV-98-147, 27 May 1998.

[80] *RFE/RL Newsline,* vol. 2, no. 203, part I (20 Oct. 1998).

[81] The OSCE Minsk Group was set up in Mar. 1992 to monitor the situation in Nagorno-Karabakh; for the membership of the Minsk Group in 1998, see the glossary in this volume. The 'phased approach' proposal is described in Baranovsky, V., 'Russia: conflicts and peaceful settlement of disputes', *SIPRI Yearbook 1998: Armaments, Disarmament and International Security* (Oxford University Press: Oxford, 1998), pp. 132–33. If approved the proposal would eventually lead to a declaration of Nagorno-Karabakh autonomy within Azerbaijan.

republic of Nagorno-Karabakh, described the position of Ter-Petrosyan as a sell-out of national interests and forced his resignation.

In March Kocharyan won the heavily contested extraordinary presidential elections in the second round and became president of independent Armenia. The forced resignation of Ter-Petrosyan and Kocharyan's victory were received with considerable apprehension by the outside world, especially in neighbouring *Azerbaijan*, where these events were seen as a victory by the 'party of war' and as endangering the resolution of the Nagorno-Karabakh conflict. Indeed the hardened position of the new Armenian President and of his government on this conflict was formulated in a new policy which flatly rejected not only the 'phased approach' proposed by the OSCE Minsk Group but also the Lisbon Principles adopted by the OSCE summit meeting in 1996, which recognized Azerbaijan's territorial integrity in relation to the status of Nagorno-Karabakh.[82] Instead Armenia proposed a 'package approach' to the problem, which envisaged the resolution of all contentious issues within the framework of one document and direct unconditional talks between Baku and the leadership of Nagorno-Karabakh.[83] Elaborating further on this approach, Armenian Minister of Foreign Affairs Vardan Oskanyan said that Armenia was ready to resolve the conflict on the basis of three principles: (*a*) the rejection of the subordination of Nagorno-Karabakh to Azerbaijan; (*b*) the impossibility of Nagorno-Karabakh being an enclave; and (*c*) ensuring Nagorno-Karabakh's security and allowing it to have its own army.[84]

The increasingly complex problems of the Nagorno-Karabakh conflict as a result of these events were further exacerbated by the oil factor. The political changes in Armenia were interpreted in Baku as an attempt to destabilize the security situation in the Transcaucasus at a time when Azerbaijani and Western oil companies were reaching agreement on a southern oil export route to Ceyhan.[85] Indeed, without a settlement of the Nagorno-Karabakh conflict, the safety of the Baku–Ceyhan oil pipeline, regarded by the Azerbaijani, Turkish and US governments as a key element of an east–west transit corridor, could not be assured. The cost of the pipeline would also depend on when and how effectively this conflict was resolved. Since the shortest route from Baku to Ceyhan is across the territory of Nagorno-Karabakh and Armenia, an early and sustainable settlement of the Nagorno-Karabakh conflict was even more indispensable.

Taking all these factors into account, Azerbaijan was left with rather limited options for protecting its oil interests against the threats posed by the Nagorno-Karabakh imbroglio. One option was connected to a possible deployment of Turkish troops in Azerbaijan to ensure the safety of oil pipelines crossing its territory towards the south. According to information in the press this issue

[82] OSCE, Lisbon Document 1996, DOC.S/1/96, 3 Dec. 1996.

[83] Interview with Robert Kocharyan, *Izvestiya*, 8 Apr. 1998.

[84] Turan (Baku), 18 Sep. 1998, in 'Azerbaijan: Armenia foreign minister on Karabakh', FBIS-SOV-98-261, 21 Sep. 1998.

[85] 'Partiya mira v Armenii proigrala' [The party of peace in Armenia lost], *Kommersant Daily,* 5 Feb. 1998; and Gadzidze, A., 'Opaseniya Baku i nadezhdy Tbilisi' [Fears of Baku and hopes of Tbilisi], *Nezavisimaya Gazeta*, 6 Feb. 1998.

was discussed at a meeting of Azerbaijani President Aliyev and Turkish Chief of General Staff Hakki Karadai in Baku in April.[86]

The negative consequences of Turkish troop deployments in Azerbaijan could, however, far outweigh their possible advantages. Both Armenia and Russia would see them as a major security threat to their vital national interests and strengthen their political and military cooperation. The legal basis for such cooperation was established in August 1997 when Armenia and Russia signed a Treaty of Friendship, Co-operation and Mutual Assistance, which Aliyev termed 'a military alliance within the CIS'. Its provisions permitted Russia to step up arms transfers to Armenia, which could significantly alter the military balance in the area to the disadvantage of Azerbaijan.

It therefore seemed that continuing political dialogue in the framework of the OSCE-sponsored peace efforts remained a more realistic option for Azerbaijan in finding a solution to the Nagorno-Karabakh conflict and ensuring the safety of oil transit to the south. Indeed, Arkady Gukasyan, President of the Nagorno-Karabakh Republic, did not rule out agreement on an oil pipeline through Armenia and Nagorno-Karabakh 'if there is an appropriate resolution' of the Nagorno-Karabakh conflict.[87]

Despite the vital importance of such a pipeline for Azerbaijan's economy, Aliyev clearly had few options, especially before the presidential elections in Azerbaijan in October 1998, to propose any meaningful compromise on the status of Nagorno-Karabakh that would be acceptable to both Armenia and the republic. However, taking into account that recent changes in the Armenian position on Nagorno-Karabakh had for all practical purposes put an end to the phased approach advocated by the Minsk Group, he accepted the need to establish a direct dialogue with the Armenian leadership on a wide range of bilateral and regional issues. In this context Aliyev invited Kocharyan to attend an international conference on the TRACECA (Transport Corridor Europe–Caucasus–Asia) project in September in Baku.[88]

This bold step aimed at a normalization of relations with Armenia was welcomed, albeit cautiously, in both Yerevan and Stepanakert. Gukasyan welcomed Aliyev's initiative, describing it as a 'very serious step' in establishing a direct Armenian–Azerbaijani dialogue, but he also warned against excluding Nagorno-Karabakh from the peace process.[89] Kocharyan, while declining to attend the conference himself, sent to Baku a high-level delegation headed by Prime Minister Armen Darpinyan. The delegation signed a multilateral framework agreement on implementation of the TRACECA and separate technical agreements on rail and road transport and customs procedures. However, Darpinyan's proposal to route via Armenia a railway to connect Kars with Tbilisi and to construct a second rail link from the Georgian Black Sea ports of

[86] Milliyet (Istanbul), 21 Apr. 1998, in 'Azerbaijan: Turkish troops use in Caucasus said under discussion', FBIS-SOV-98-11, 23 Apr. 1998.

[87] Noyan Tapan (Yerevan), 26 May 1998, in 'Armenia: Karabakh head says N. Ireland could be example for NRK', FBIS-SOV-98-147, 27 May 1998.

[88] Alimov, G., 'Nezhdannoye predlozheniye Aliyeva Kocharyanu' [Aliyev's unexpected invitation to Kocharyan], *Izvestiya*, 5 Aug. 1998.

[89] *RFE/RL Newsline*, vol. 2, no. 153, part I (11 Aug. 1998).

Poti and Batumi via Armenia to Iran was flatly rejected by Turkish President Suleyman Demirel. Turkey indicated that these transport links could be considered only after the Nagorno-Karabakh conflict was resolved.[90]

VII. Conclusions

The political and security situation in the Caspian Basin in 1998 was strongly influenced by a conflict of interests over the vast oil and gas reserves there. The littoral countries became deeply involved in arguments over a legal regime for the Caspian Sea as well as over the demarcation of national economic zones and sectors. They were also drawn into debates over the problem of oil and gas transport routes from the Caspian Sea to the world market. This conflict of interests was further exacerbated by the growing involvement of the USA and a number of European and Asian countries.

In 1998 there was an increasing tendency towards militarization in the Caspian Basin. Realizing the dangerous consequences of this development for regional security, the littoral countries tried to defuse mounting interstate tensions in the region. A fundamental condition for preventing further escalation of these tensions could have been the achievement of a comprehensive agreement on the legal status of the Caspian Sea that was acceptable to all the littoral states. However, there was insufficient progress in this direction.

The continuing debates among the littoral states on the choice of oil and gas routes from the Caspian Basin reflected the deepening polarization of the positions taken by individual Caspian states. Azerbaijan, Kazakhstan and (to a lesser extent) Turkmenistan were opting for the US-supported routes via Georgia and Turkey that would bypass both Iran and Russia. The latter two countries considered these developments as detrimental to their national interests and joined forces in issuing strong protests against a trans-Caspian pipeline.

Finally, the security of oil and gas transport routes passing across or located close to zones of local conflicts (in Abkhazia, Chechnya and Nagorno-Karabakh) became increasingly linked to the resolution of these conflicts. Here again, there was no substantial progress. Moreover, the growing influence of radical and militant Islam in a number of Caspian littoral states and their neighbours threatened to further destabilize the security situation in the region.

[90] *RFE/RL Newsline*, vol. 2, no. 174, part I (9 Sep. 1998).

6. Europe: the institutionalized security process

ADAM DANIEL ROTFELD

I. Introduction

The process of adapting the European security organizations to the post-cold war environment made further progress in 1998. The three Protocols of Accession to the North Atlantic Treaty Organization (NATO), which had been signed with the Czech Republic, Hungary and Poland in December 1997, were ratified by the parliaments of the NATO members and the aspirant states.[1] This laid the legal foundation for the enlargement of NATO in March 1999, prior to the Washington NATO summit meeting held in commemoration of the 50th anniversary of the signing of the North Atlantic Treaty (the Washington Treaty). In March 1998 formal negotiations were opened with six candidates for membership of the European Union (EU). Qualitatively new tasks were entrusted to the Organization for Security and Co-operation in Europe (OSCE) as a result of developments in 1998 in the Kosovo conflict in the Federal Republic of Yugoslavia.

These and other decisions adopted during the year bore witness to the fact that the European multilateral security organizations are no longer based on a relationship between two adversarial alliances but rather on a common system of values among states. More importantly, none of these organizations is capable of achieving a monopoly on or taking the leading role in solving the problems of European security. Moreover, none is a 'single-issue' institution;[2] they are all engaged in managing a broad range of problems. It is also important to note that the organizations have more frequently revealed differences of interest between the major powers and various groups of states—between the United States and Europe as well as between Russia and the United States and its allies—than differences over the avowed political philosophy of collaboration, mutual reinforcement and complementarity. Nonetheless, scepticism has grown about the desirability of further enlarging NATO and of enlarging the European Union at all.

In 1998 the European security debate focused to a great extent on the future missions and mandates of the major security institutions—NATO, the EU, the Western European Union (WEU) and the OSCE—and their interrelationships as well as on the role of the great powers within these organizations. While the

[1] For a broader discussion of the protocols see Rotfeld, A. D., 'Europe: the transition to inclusive security', *SIPRI Yearbook 1998: Armaments, Disarmament and International Security* (Oxford University Press: Oxford, 1998), pp. 149–52.

[2] Rühle, M., 'Taking another look at NATO's role in European security', *NATO Review*, no. 4 (winter 1998), p. 21.

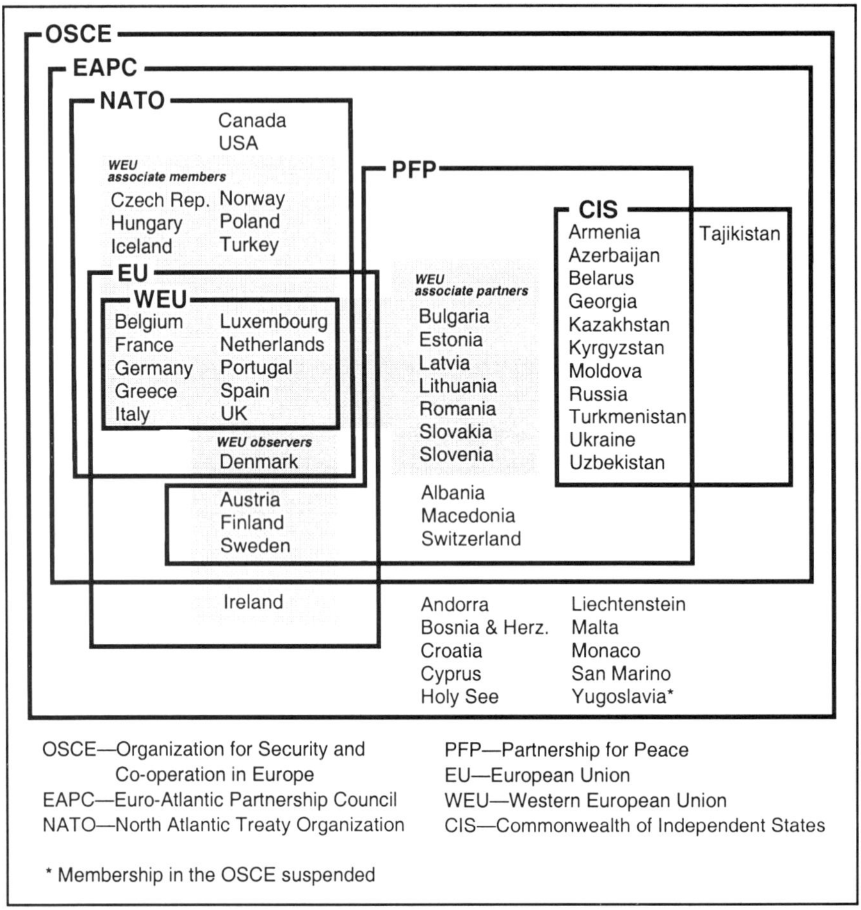

Figure 6.1. The overlapping membership of multilateral Euro-Atlantic security organizations, as of 1 April 1999

deliberations continued to deal mainly with their future tasks, mechanisms and procedures, the political context in which their activities take place is of paramount importance. Transatlantic relations, in particular the role of the USA in the new Europe, the shaping of a new political and economic order for Europe, and the events and changes in Russia and the other new states of the former Soviet Union are the key issues. In responding to the changes and other new challenges, NATO, the EU and the OSCE must undergo reform and recast their mutual relations.

Section II of this chapter examines transatlantic relations in 1998 and section III the new role of NATO. Section IV presents the developments in efforts to create a foreign and security policy within the European Union. Section V describes the new tasks and activities of the OSCE, and section VI presents the conclusions. Appendix 6A contains three documents on the European security issues discussed in this chapter.

II. Europe and the United States

In a speech delivered in Berlin on 13 May 1998, the 50th anniversary of the lifting of the blockade of the city, US President Bill Clinton enumerated the priorities of US policy towards Europe as follows:

> We seek a transatlantic partnership that is broad and open in scope, where the benefits and burdens are shared, where we seek a stable and peaceful future not only for ourselves, but for all the world. We begin with our common security of which NATO is the bedrock. . . .
>
> Yesterday's NATO guarded our borders against direct military invasion. Tomorrow's Alliance must continue to defend enlarged borders and defend against threats to our security from beyond them—the spread of weapons of mass destruction, ethnic violence, regional conflict. . . .
>
> Second, we must do more to promote prosperity throughout our community. . . .
>
> America will continue to support Europe's march toward integration. . . . We will continue to encourage your steps to enlarge the EU as well, eventually to embrace all central Europe and Turkey.
>
> Our third task is to strengthen the hand and extend the reach of democracy. . . .
>
> Our fourth and final task is strengthening our global cooperation.[3]

In the USA, the prevalent view is that NATO is based on the leadership and dominance of the United States. As expressed by the former director of the US National Security Agency, 'All NATO members informally acknowledge U.S. hegemony. Moreover, most NATO countries want Washington to play this role and would be disturbed if it did not continue to do so'.[4]

This view is shared to only a limited extent by the European NATO states. They are interested in a durable US presence in and commitment to Europe but only provided that transatlantic relations rest on a partnership, not on US hegemony. German analysts and officials, for example, have raised several questions. What are the US motives for emphasizing a global role for NATO? What are the European or German arguments in favour of broadening NATO's purpose to include the concept of 'globalization'? How should German foreign policy respond?[5]

From the US point of view, the 'vital interests' of the United States are more endangered in the Persian Gulf and the rest of the Middle East region, South Korea and the Taiwan Straits than in the Balkans. However, it was mainly the United States and its firm military action in the Balkan region—not that of the

[3] 'Remarks by the President to the people of Germany', Berlin, 13 May 1998, available in the Public Diplomacy Query (PDQ) database on the United States Information Agency Internet site, URL <http://pdq2.usia.gov>.

[4] 'The most important factor in NATO's success as a security alliance has been the dominance of U.S. power, military and economic.' Odom, W. E., 'Challenges facing an expanding NATO', *American Foreign Policy Interests* (National Committee on American Foreign Policy), vol. 20, no. 6 (Dec. 1998), p. 1.

[5] Kamp, K.-H., 'A global role for NATO?', *Washington Quarterly*, vol. 22, no. 1 (winter 1999), p. 8.

European NATO states—that resulted in 1998 in at least the temporary withdrawal of forces and the beginning of a search for peace.

The lack of action by Europe in various crisis situations has led US critics to 'castigate Europe for not contributing to regional and global order while demanding that Europeans shoulder more of the cost of leadership'.[6] According to European analysts, as in the period of the cold war, when European anti-Americanism damaged Western solidarity, 'American Eurobashing threatens to unravel transatlantic cooperation in the post-Cold War era'.[7] In their view, the USA expects Europe to make a larger contribution to the costs of US global engagement and strategic leadership while failing to respect European views and reservations.[8]

In summary, security developments in Europe and the political debate on the current and future role of the United States as the sole superpower show that Euro-Atlantic relations are determined by a US hegemonic posture, on the one hand, and by the forming of an anti-hegemonic posture by European states, on the other. The future of the North Atlantic Alliance depends on the extent to which Europe will be able to counterbalance the dominant position of the United States while accepting its leadership in protecting the vital security interests of the democratic community of states.

III. NATO: a new role and mission

In 1998 the fundamental role of NATO in the evolution of the politico-military integration of Europe was confirmed by the acceptance of the admission of three new members, the establishment of cooperative relations with Russia in the field of military security, the taking of military action to curb the armed conflicts in the Balkans, the facilitating of the peace process in Bosnia and Herzegovina, and the search for political solutions and a new status for Kosovo within the Federal Republic of Yugoslavia. NATO's role in the making of Europe's security system is determined by its transatlantic character, the military power of the United States, the combination of political and military functions, the cooperative attitude towards those European states that are not members of NATO and the capacity to make effective contributions to crisis management in the Euro-Atlantic area. Enlargement of the alliance is seen in Europe as an extension of the zone of stability.[9]

Risks and threats are prevalent in states both within and outside Europe which are not party to the 1949 North Atlantic Treaty. Against this background two concepts have emerged with regard to the future strategic role

[6] Wallace, W. and Zielonka, J., 'Misunderstanding Europe', *Foreign Affairs*, vol. 77, no. 6 (Nov./Dec. 1998), p. 65.

[7] Wallace and Zielonka (note 6), p. 66.

[8] 'The current approach, combining demands for greater burden-sharing with knee-jerk dismissals of European policies, risks alienating America's most important allies.' Wallace and Zielonka (note 6), p. 66.

[9] Bertram, C., 'Rozszerzanie znaczy stabilnosc' [Enlarging means stabilizing], *Rzeczpospolita*, 3 Dec. 1998, p. 6.

of NATO in Europe and the world at large. In the view of prominent US politicians, NATO's strategic goals should be as congruent as possible with US global priorities in different parts of the world, not only in Europe. Politicians and analysts in Europe, on the other hand, consider that 'any discussion of a potential global role for NATO is politically explosive'.[10] Indeed, the new US understanding of its strategic tenets—defence of common interests, going beyond common defence of members' territories—was not supported by all the NATO Allies.

Even before the decision to enlarge the alliance was taken, the 1990 London Declaration on a Transformed North Atlantic Alliance recommended that NATO initiate major reforms and reassess its tasks, especially in the light of the collapse of the bipolar system, and 'build new partnerships with all the nations of Europe'.[11]

In 1998 it was confirmed that the divisions between Europe and the USA stem from their different perspectives (global in the USA and regional in Europe) as well as their different understandings of NATO's role in the defence of 'vital interests'. The European NATO Allies cling to the traditional interpretation of the alliance's tasks, as formulated in Article 5 of the North Atlantic Treaty.[12] In the US understanding, a new mandate would include both defence of the NATO frontiers and a stand 'against threats to our security from beyond them'.[13] Specifically, it would include prevention of the proliferation of weapons of mass destruction, ethnic violence and regional conflicts; 'out-of-area' operations as a new mission for NATO forces; and engagement in efforts to resolve crises. It would also include a commitment 'to stand against intolerance and injustice as much as military aggression'.[14] The alliance's future-oriented agenda has to safeguard both common security interests and basic values in a new, often unpredictable security environment. The main challenge is to reinforce the transatlantic link and ensure a balance that allows the European NATO members to assume greater responsibility in the alliance.

The role of the United States in Europe as an integral element of security on the continent has not, however, been called into question. The USA still acts as a unique crisis manager—from its role in facilitating German unification to

[10] Kamp (note 5).

[11] The London Declaration is reproduced in Rotfeld, A. D. and Stützle, W., SIPRI, *Germany and Europe in Transition* (Oxford University Press: Oxford, 1991), pp. 150–52.

[12] In Article 5 of the North Atlantic Treaty, 'The Parties agree that an armed attack against one or more of them in Europe or North America shall be considered an attack against them all and consequently they agree that, if such an armed attack occurs, each of them, in exercise of the right of individual or collective self-defence recognized by Article 51 of the Charter of the United Nations will assist the Party or Parties so attacked by taking forthwith, individually and in concert with the other Parties, such action as it deems necessary, including the use of armed force, to restore and maintain the security of the North Atlantic area.

'Any such armed attack and all measures taken as a result thereof shall immediately be reported to the Security Council. Such measures shall be terminated when the Security Council has taken the measures necessary to restore and maintain international peace and security'. The North Atlantic Treaty, Washington, DC, 4 Apr. 1949.

[13] 'Remarks by the President . . .' (note 3).

[14] 'Remarks by the President . . .' (note 3).

resolving the conflict in Bosnia and Herzegovina and establishing under OSCE auspices the Kosovo Verification Mission (KVM). In addition, the 1999 NATO military intervention in Yugoslavia would have been unthinkable without the USA.

Transformation, adaptation and enlargement

On both sides of the Atlantic Ocean the belief has been expressed that NATO is and will remain the sole effective Euro-Atlantic security organization. Its internal transformation, adaptation to the new security environment and enlargement of its membership are its priority tasks. The fundamental objectives of NATO's internal adaptation, as officially defined, are 'to maintain the Alliance's military effectiveness . . . and its ability to react to a wide range of contingencies, to preserve the transatlantic link, and to develop the European Security and Defence Identity (ESDI) within the Alliance'. It was agreed to accelerate the work in this regard in order to enable the Council in Permanent Session 'to take a single and irreversible decision on the activation requests of all headquarters of the new NATO command structure by the beginning of March 1999'.[15]

European Security and Defence Identity

A European Security and Defence Identity would be an institutional expression of a strong Europe. In official documents, the USA has for several years supported this concept. In December 1998 US Secretary of State Madeleine Albright described one of the seven chief tasks of the alliance as 'to develop a European Security and Defence Identity, or ESDI, within the Alliance, which the United States has strongly endorsed'.[16] It is, however, a qualified support, with some reservations. Albright drew attention to this in the North Atlantic Council (NAC) in December 1998: 'Any initiative must avoid preempting Alliance decision-making by de-linking ESDI from NATO, avoid duplicating existing efforts, and avoid discriminating against non-EU members'.[17] This caveat was further developed by US Deputy Secretary of State Strobe Talbott. In response to the British–French initiative Saint-Malo initiative presented in December 1998 (see section IV) and developed by Prime Minister Tony Blair and Defence Secretary George Robertson at the March 1999 London conference 'NATO at Fifty', Talbott warned that ESDI carries with it both risks and costs: 'If ESDI is misconceived, misunderstood or mishandled, it could create the impression—which could eventually lead to the reality—that a new, European-only alliance is being born out of the old, trans-Atlantic one.

[15] Final Communiqué, Ministerial Meeting of the North Atlantic Council held at NATO Headquarters, Brussels, Press Release M-NAC-2(98)140, 8 Dec. 1998, URL <http://www.nato.int/docu/pr/1998/p981208e.htm>.

[16] Secretary of State Madeleine Albright, Statement to the North Atlantic Council, 8 Dec. 1998, URL <http://secretary.state.gov/www/statements/1998/981208.html>.

[17] Albright statement to North Atlantic Council (note 16).

If that were to happen, it would weaken, perhaps even break, those ties that I spoke of before—the ones that bind our security to yours'.[18] In his view, it is essential that ESDI does not take a form that discriminates against the USA or other NATO Allies which are not members of the EU—that is, Canada, the Czech Republic, Hungary, Iceland, Norway, Poland and Turkey. He noted that the principles and procedures of accommodating the ESDI in the NATO command structures, the division of roles and the planning capabilities were too complex to be decided before the 1999 Washington summit meeting.[19] They will remain open for further discussions, the first of which will take place in 1999 at the WEU ministerial meeting in Bremen and the EU Council meeting in Cologne.

Germany and NATO's nuclear policy

After the September 1998 election in Germany, won by a coalition of the Social Democrat and Green parties, the new German Foreign Minister, Joschka Fischer, signalled the need for an essential change in NATO's nuclear policy, namely, the adoption of a 'no-first-use' doctrine. The German parties had committed themselves to such a change in their coalition agreement. Not surprisingly, this evoked negative reactions from the US Administration. In effect, this issue dominated the agenda of Federal Defence Minister Rudolf Scharping's first visit to Washington, in November 1998. Following the talks, US Defense Secretary William Cohen stated: 'We discussed NATO's nuclear policy, and I made it clear that the United States opposes any changes in this policy because we believe that the current doctrine serves to preserve the peace and to enhance deterrence'.[20] The German response to this statement aimed at both appeasing the USA and leaving the question open. Scharping asserted that, globally, the German Government 'is following the vision of a nuclear weapons free world, but on the other side we are debating about NATO and its strategy'. For this reason, he continued, 'any conclusion must be drawn in consensus'. Therefore, Germany has 'no intention to take unilateral decisions which have an impact on the security of the alliance'.[21]

The change proposed by Germany was also received critically in Poland: unforeseen developments in Eastern Europe are seen by Polish security analysts as a potential threat to Poland's security. Poland therefore wants to maintain the 'nuclear umbrella', which envisages keeping various options open in the event of a 'worst-case scenario'.[22]

[18] 'Text: Talbott March 10 remarks on "A new NATO for a new era"', *USIS Washington File* (United States Information Service, US Embassy: Stockholm, 10 Mar. 1999), URL <http://www.usia.gov/current/news/topic/intrel/99031010.wpo.html?/products/washfile/newsitem.shtml>.

[19] Note 18.

[20] 'U.S., German defense officials on NATO nuclear policy', *USIA Washington File*, 24 Nov. 1998, available in the Public Diplomacy Query (PDQ) database on the United States Information Agency Internet site, URL <http://pdq2.usia.gov>.

[21] Note 20.

[22] Interventions at the Polish–German–American Forum for Security, Warsaw, 4 Dec. 1998, in *Polish German American Forum for Security 1998: Documentation* (Center for International Relations: Warsaw, forthcoming 1999).

A new Strategic Concept

In the US Senate debate on the accession to NATO of the Czech Republic, Hungary and Poland, enlargement was linked to the new NATO Strategic Concept and to the extent to which NATO should focus on new missions beyond those of collective defence.[23] The decision to prepare a new Strategic Concept had been taken at the 1997 Madrid NATO summit meeting, as reflected in paragraph 19 of the Madrid Declaration.[24] The new concept was expected to reaffirm NATO's commitment to collective defence and the trans-atlantic link. It was recommended that it should contain 'a full range of capabilities to enhance security and stability for countries in the Euro-Atlantic area in the 21st century, including through dialogue, cooperation and partnership and, where appropriate, non-Article 5 crisis response operations, such as that in Bosnia and Herzegovina, with the possible participation of partners'.[25] The decision was taken to complete the text of the concept before the Washington summit meeting for final approval by the NATO heads of state and government at the meeting.

Four points presented by US Secretary of State Albright at the December 1998 Brussels meeting of the North Atlantic Council summarized the US vision of a new NATO. According to Albright, the alliance should be strengthened by new members which are 'capable of collective defense; committed to meeting a wide range of threats to our shared interests and values; and acting in partnership with others to ensure stability, freedom and peace in and for the entire trans-Atlantic area'. She recognized that in the period of the cold war NATO members could easily identify 'an Article V threat to our territory and security'. The current and future threats, however, might come 'from a number of different sources, including from areas beyond NATO's immediate borders'. In this context, Albright mentioned 'a ballistic missile attack using a weapon of mass destruction from a rogue state'. In other words, out-of-area events—those beyond NATO's immediate borders—can affect vital NATO interests. The key task is to find 'the right balance between affirming the centrality of Article V collective defense missions and ensuring that the fundamental tasks of the Alliance are intimately related to the broader defense of our common interests'.[26]

Among the 'common interests' is the threat posed by weapons of mass destruction: the USA intends to increase information and intelligence sharing within NATO, accelerate the development of capabilities to deter and protect against potential use of these weapons and underscore the shared commitment to prevent proliferation. In her statement to the Luxembourg ministerial meeting of the North Atlantic Council on 28 May 1998, Albright proposed that

[23] Robell, J. P. and Sloan, S. R., *NATO: Senate Floor Consideration of the Accession of the Czech Republic, Hungary and Poland,* CRS Report for Congress 98-669 F (Congressional Research Service, Library of Congress: Washington, DC, 10 Aug. 1998).

[24] The 1997 Madrid Declaration on Euro-Atlantic Security and Cooperation is reproduced in *NATO Review*, no. 4 (July/Aug. 1997), Special insert, pp. 1–4.

[25] Final Communiqué (note 15), para. 5.

[26] Albright statement to North Atlantic Council (note 16).

NATO expand its efforts to include dealing with the proliferation of weapons of mass destruction, addressing the interoperability challenges across the Atlantic and promoting greater defence industrial cooperation 'in an age of shrinking defense budgets'.[27]

The opponents of NATO enlargement and a new alliance mandate questioned the proposed evolution of its mission. During the US Senate debate on enlargement, for example, Senator John Ashcroft introduced an amendment to the Senate Resolution on Ratification designed to prevent NATO from taking on missions which in his view would require an amendment of the Washington Treaty.[28] The amendment stipulated that the USA would oppose all NATO military operations unless 'the operation is intended for the purpose of collective self-defense in response to an armed attack on the territory of an Alliance member' or 'is in response to a threat to the territorial integrity, political independence, or security of a NATO member'.[29] Those against the amendment said it would undermine NATO's capability to defend its security interests.[30]

The Strategic Concept and NATO enlargement were seen as an interconnected issue. Senator Jeff Bingaman said, 'the Senate [is] being called upon to sign up to a policy of enlarging the alliance without a clear, coherent explanation of how expansion of NATO will serve NATO's strategic interests'. He proposed an amendment which would delay inviting additional countries until after NATO had approved a strategic concept.[31] Senator Joseph R. Biden, Jr, opposed the amendment, arguing that, if implemented, it could constitute a tool for those wishing to slow down or stop the process of enlargement. By refusing to agree to a new Strategic Concept, any NATO member could block the process of further NATO enlargement. The Bingaman Amendment was not adopted.[32]

The NATO Strategic Concept, as approved at the Washington summit meeting of 23–24 April 1999, stated that the security of the alliance is subject to

a wide variety of military and non-military risks which are multi-directional and often difficult to predict. These risks include uncertainty and instability in and around the Euro-Atlantic area and the possibility of regional crises at the periphery of the

[27] 'Statement at the North Atlantic Council, Luxembourg, 28 May 1998', URL <http://www.nato.int/usa/state/s980528a.htm>.

[28] 'I don't believe in treaty evolution any more than I believe in the evolution of the Constitution.' *Congressional Record*, 27 Apr. 1998, p. S3627, quoted in Robell and Sloan (note 23), p. CRS-3.

[29] Robell and Sloan (note 23), p. CRS-4.

[30] Prior to the vote on the Ashcroft Amendment, Senator Jon Kyl added to the Resolution of Ratification a statement of the Senate's 'understanding' of US policy towards NATO's Strategic Concept: 'the current resolution focuses too much on what NATO should not be and should not do. The resolution does not attempt to lay out a comprehensive set of principles to guide development of the strategic concept. . . . Our principal objective . . . is to ensure that NATO remains an arm of U.S. power and influence. . . . NATO . . . must be prepared to defend against a range of common threats to our vital interests.' *Congressional Record,* 28 Apr. 1998, p. S3659, quoted in Robell and Sloan (note 23), p. CRS-5. The Kyl Amendment 'tempered its recognition of the threats of ethnic or religious rivalries and historic disputes with a statement that only threats of this type occurring in the North Atlantic area should be within NATO's purview'. Robell and Sloan (note 23), p. CRS-5. The Senate approved the amendment by 90 votes to 9; it is reproduced in Robell and Sloan (note 23), appendix 2, pp. CRS-35–37.

[31] *Congressional Record,* 27 Apr. 1998, p. S3631, quoted in Robell and Sloan (note 23), p. CRS-5.

[32] Robell and Sloan (note 23), pp. CRS-5–6.

Alliance, which could evolve rapidly. . . . Ethnic and religious rivalries, territorial disputes, inadequate or failed efforts at reform, the abuse of human rights, and the dissolution of states can lead to local and even regional instability.[33]

The resulting tensions could lead to crises affecting Euro-Atlantic stability and security by spilling over into neighbouring countries. Alliance security interests can also be affected by other risks of a wider nature: the proliferation of nuclear, biological and chemical weapons and their means of delivery; the global spread of technology for the production of weapons, which may result in the greater availability of sophisticated military capabilities; the alliance's vulnerability owing to its reliance on information systems; acts of terrorism, sabotage and organized crime; the disruption of the flow of vital resources; and the uncontrolled movement of large numbers of people as a consequence of armed conflicts. All these security challenges and risks are seen by the alliance in both the Euro-Atlantic and the global contexts.

The admission of three new members

The US Resolution of Ratification of the accession to NATO of the Czech Republic, Hungary and Poland, as amended during the debate, was agreed by the Senate on 30 April 1998, after the parliaments of Canada, Denmark, Germany and Norway had ratified the three Protocols of Accession.[34]

On 29 January 1999 NATO Secretary General Javier Solana, having received the notifications of ratification of the accession protocols from all the NATO Allies, sent to the prime ministers of the Czech Republic, Hungary and Poland a letter inviting them to accept membership of the alliance.[35] This allowed the new members to participate in the final stage of elaboration of the new NATO Strategic Concept and to take part in the working out of a new NATO position in the negotiations with Russia on the adaptation of the 1990 Treaty on Conventional Armed Forces in Europe (the CFE Treaty) (see below).

[33] The Alliance's Strategic Concept, approved by the Heads of State and Government participating in the meeting of the North Atlantic Council in Washington D.C. on 23rd and 24th April 1999, Press communiqué, NAC-S(99)65, 24 Apr. 1999, para. 20, URL <http://nato50.gov/text/99042411.htm>. See also paragraphs 21–24.

[34] The 16 NATO members deposited their ratifications of the 3 Accession Protocols with the USA (depositary of the Washington Treaty) in 1998: Canada (4 Feb.), Denmark (17 Feb.), Norway (17 Mar.), Germany (24 Apr.), France (15 July), Luxembourg (24 July), Spain (29 July), Greece (31 July), the UK (17 Aug.), the USA (20 Aug.), Iceland (25 Aug.), Belgium (14 Sep.), Italy (23 Sep.), Turkey (3 Dec.), Portugal (3 Dec.) and the Netherlands (4 Dec.). Accession of the new member countries, NATO Fact Sheet, 1 Mar. 1999, Calendar of Ratification, URL <http://www.nato.int/docu/facts/access.htm>.

[35] The 2 months from the receipt of the notifications on conclusion of the ratification process (4 Dec. 1998) to the sending of the invitation letters (29 Jan. 1999) were meant to help the Czech Republic, Hungary and Poland meet the minimum conditions of membership defined by the alliance concerning, e.g., communications between the NATO command headquarters and governments of the allied governments, their air-defence systems, and legal and technical measures for protection of NATO classified data and information. Exposé of Janos Martonyi, Minister for Foreign Affairs of Hungary at the submission of the bill on the accession of the Republic of Hungary to NATO, 8 Feb. 1999, Hungarian Embassy in Stockholm.

On 17 February 1999 the Act on Accession of Poland to NATO was ratified by both chambers of the Polish Parliament; a similar decision had been taken a week earlier by the parliaments of the Czech Republic and Hungary. The Acts of Ratification of the North Atlantic Treaty were signed by Hungarian President Árpád Göncz on 10 February 1999 and by presidents Aleksander Kwasniewski of Poland and Vaclav Havel of the Czech Republic on 26 February.[36] Demonstrating their common goals, the foreign ministers of the three states agreed to hand jointly to the US Secretary of State their instruments of accession at a ceremony on 12 March 1999 in Independence, Missouri. The notification of the alliance members that the protocols had entered into force was the last formal act of the procedure leading to membership status.

Admission of these three Central and East European (CEE) states to NATO has a bearing on the strengthening of the US presence in Europe. According to observers in the USA and the new members, Poland's relations with the USA are of a 'special', 'intimate' character.[37] As Polish Defence Minister Janusz Onyszkiewicz said in his address to the US National Press Club on 27 January 1999, Poland also sees NATO 'as the basis for a strong U.S. presence in Europe, a presence that is essential for imparting a sense of security to Europe'.[38] Polish analysts believe that Poland's security interests compel it to support the presence of the United States in Europe and its policy of global engagement.[39] In a 1997 address at the ministerial meeting of the NATO Euro-Atlantic Partnership Council (EAPC), Polish Foreign Minister Bronislaw Geremek stressed not only Poland's national security interests but also the fact that 'NATO can make Europe safe for democracy. No other organization can replace the Alliance in this role'.[40] In 1998 he said that Poland wanted 'to join NATO because Article five gives the best protection of Polish territory and the sovereignty of the Polish state'.[41]

In the context of the new Euro-Atlantic relations, Hungarian Foreign Minister Janos Martonyi noted: 'The relationship stretching beyond the Atlantic Ocean continues to be of unchanged importance for Europe, which is gradually increasing its strength and unity'.[42] On 16 November 1998 Hungarians voted in a referendum to decide whether or not the country should join the North Atlantic Alliance. There had been widespread apathy in the population (voter turnout was only about 51 per cent), although 85 per cent of those vot-

[36] *Rzeczpospolita*, 27–28 Feb. 1999, pp. 1–4. The instrument of ratification submitted by Poland is reproduced in appendix 6A in this volume.

[37] 'Ties that bind: who helps the U.S. in times of trouble? Poland, of course. From NATO to economics: Warsaw swings firmly into Washington's orbit', *Wall Street Journal,* 8–9 Jan. 1999, pp. 1, 2, 10.

[38] Marshall, R., 'Poland's Onyszkiewicz sees US preserving NATO cohesion', *USIS Washington File*, 27 Jan. 1999.

[39] Nowak-Jezioranski, J., 'NATO: potrzebna nowa wizja' [NATO: a new vision is needed], *Rzeczpospolita*, 2 Feb. 1999, p. 8.

[40] Bronislaw Geremek Address at Accession Accords Signing Ceremony, Brussels, 16 Dec. 1997.

[41] Bronislaw Geremek, Interview for Polish Radio, 14 Apr. 1998.

[42] Martonyi (note 35); and Joó, R. (ed.), *Hungary: A Member of NATO* (Hungarian Ministry for Foreign Affairs: Budapest, 1999), pp. 13–27.

ing in the referendum and all the political parties represented in parliament approved NATO membership.

The situation in the Czech Republic was different. Opinion polls showed that only 54 per cent of Czechs favoured joining NATO (an increase over support in 1997, when it was below 50 per cent). As a US security analyst rightly predicted, one of the Czech Government's most difficult tasks was to 'sell' NATO to Czech citizens, since membership implied what were likely to be greater national obligations and resource requirements for defence.[43] One of the most enthusiastic promoters of Czech membership of NATO was President Havel. In his view, the enlargement of the alliance 'signifies the real and definitive end of the imposed division of Europe and the world, the real and definitive fall of the Iron Curtain and the real and definitive demise of the so-called Yalta arrangement'.[44]

For all three new members, membership of NATO means additional security guarantees for their external borders and the strengthening of their chances for democratic development. It also means a pro-US orientation in their foreign policy, including the readiness to become engaged globally, although this may lead them to a situation in which their security policy would be on a collision course with the concepts of security of some West European states.

NATO, Russia and adaptation of the CFE Treaty

The conflicting positions at the negotiations on the adaptation of the CFE Treaty reflected the tensions between the parties.[45] The general political philosophy of the 19 participating states (the 16 NATO members plus the then 3 candidates) was expressed in the NAC Statement on CFE, issued in Brussels on 8 December 1998, in which they confirmed their commitment to maintain only 'such military capabilities as are commensurate with our legitimate security needs'.[46] The need to adapt the CFE Treaty to the new politico-military environment is not called into question by any of the parties. Although the treaty was signed by 22 states, it was negotiated and agreed between two military blocs, the Warsaw Pact and NATO.

With the dissolution of the Warsaw Pact, the break-up of the USSR and the subsequent emergence of 15 new states, and the accession of three former Warsaw Pact members to NATO, the CFE Treaty regime is in need of not only formal revision but also adaptation to the new security environment. In this regard, a number of decisions have been adopted by NATO in order to

[43] Simon, J., *NATO Enlargement and Central Europe: A Study in Civil–Military Relations* (National Defence University, Institute for National Strategic Studies: Washington, DC, 1996), p. 309.

[44] Speech by Vaclav Havel, President of the Czech Republic, at the summit meeting in Washington, DC, 23 Apr. 1999, Embassy of the Czech Republic in Stockholm. See also Havel's contribution in *NATO Review*, Commemorative Edition, 50th Anniversary, Apr. 1999, p. 25.

[45] For a more detailed discussion of CFE Treaty adaptation see chapter 14 in this volume.

[46] The text of the Statement on CFE issued at the Ministerial Meeting of the North Atlantic Council with the Three Invited Countries held in Brussels on 8th December 1998, Adaptation of the Treaty on Conventional Armed Forces in Europe (CFE): Restraint and Flexibility, is reproduced in appendix 14C in this volume.

address Russia's concerns. On 14 March 1997 the NAC, under the chairmanship of NATO Secretary General Solana, issued the following Unilateral Statement: 'In the current and foreseeable security environment, the Alliance will carry out its collective defence and other missions by ensuring the necessary interoperability, integration and capability for reinforcement rather than additional permanent stationing of substantial combat forces'.[47] Together with the 1996 NATO declaration that it has 'no intention, no plan and no reason'[48] to station nuclear weapons in the new member states, this statement reaffirmed the NATO commitment to CFE Treaty adaptation.

Thus Russia's concerns about a possible new conventional weapon imbalance in Europe were taken seriously into account by NATO before or at least as soon as the CFE adaptation talks had begun. Improved transparency is probably more important for Russia than lower ceilings, for which it has been pressing.[49] The end of the bipolar world necessitates a departure from thinking in terms of a balance of power or equilibrium of forces. After the dissolution of the Warsaw Pact and the demise of the Soviet Union, the concept is no longer adequate to either the needs of or the capabilities for ensuring Russia's national security.

The elaboration of a new position by NATO and the new members was complicated by the fact that Russia wanted the territories of the former Warsaw Pact countries that have joined NATO to be given a special status within the adapted CFE regime that is different from that of the other alliance members. Such a solution, which Russia pressed to have adopted even before the new members joined NATO, was opposed by the states concerned, in particular Poland. The point is that, whatever Russia has demanded and whatever solutions might result from negotiations in 1999, Russia's intention in early 1999 was once again to hamper NATO enlargement and, more important, to undermine NATO's proclaimed 'open door' philosophy for the future.[50] Historically, Russia has had a consistent political strategy of trying to build a cordon sanitaire or buffer zone on its western borders. This policy has not been renounced, but only adapted and readapted to the new, changing circumstances.

An 'open door' policy without a second tranche?

From the US perspective, NATO enlargement is one part of a strategic policy 'aimed at stabilizing Europe and adapting NATO to deal with new threats on

[47] NATO Press Release (97)27, Brussels, 14 Mar. 1997.

[48] NATO Press Communiqué M-NAC-2(96)165, 10 Dec. 1996.

[49] Arbatov, A. G. and Hartelius, D., *Russia and the World: A New Deal. Policy Recommendations Based on the International Project: 'Russia's Total Security Environment'* (EastWest Institute: New York, 1999), p. 17.

[50] See also chapter 14 in this volume; and German Ministry for Foreign Affairs, *Zum Stand der KSE-Adaptierung* [On the status of CFE adaptation], (Ministry for Foreign Affairs: Bonn, 17 Apr. 1997).

Europe's periphery and beyond its borders'.[51] The political debate during the process of admitting new members has resulted in a specific dual strategy for further enlargement: to reaffirm that the door remains open to NATO membership, on the one hand, and to slow down the enlargement process so as not to alter the political and military character of the alliance, on the other hand. According to some US security analysts, 'The three prospective members are contributing to military missions on NATO's periphery. . . . they are producing more security than they consume'.[52]

In the context of further NATO enlargement, 12 European states are under consideration. Nine of these states (Romania, Slovenia and Slovakia; Albania, Bulgaria and Macedonia; and Estonia, Latvia and Lithuania) have declared that they wish to join the alliance. However, at the 35th International Conference on Security, held at Munich on 6–7 February 1999, the new German Chancellor, Gerhard Schröder, ruled out the possibility that an invitation to a new group of candidates would be issued at the Washington meeting.[53] Similarly, in the USA the view prevailed that at this stage further enlargement to the east could diminish the cohesion and effectiveness of the alliance. The opponents of further enlargement fear that '[s]wift movement to a larger alliance could alter the political and military character of NATO' and make consensus building and decision making significantly more difficult, thus eroding the effectiveness of the alliance. In effect, the nine countries which aspire to NATO membership would, if admitted, water down the alliance rather than enhance security.[54]

The opponents demand that the standards for and criteria of further enlargement should be subordinated to the strategic goals 'so that the door is kept open but new members are admitted only when this step makes strategic sense and furthers NATO security interests'.[55] New members would be admitted only when: (*a*) admission directly supports NATO interests, strategy and security goals; (*b*) NATO can effectively absorb and integrate new members and truly provide them with collective defence protection; (*c*) candidates can 'produce security for NATO, not just consume it'; (*d*) the cohesion of the alliance, its decision-making process and its military effectiveness in carrying out old and new missions are enhanced, not diminished; and (*e*) admission will meaningfully enhance Europe's stability rather than trigger instability.[56] Slow,

[51] Binendijk, H. and Kugler, R. L., 'NATO after the first tranche: a strategic rationale for enlargement', *Strategic Forum* (National Defense University, Institute for National Strategic Studies), no. 149 (Oct. 1998), p. 1.

[52] Binendijk and Kugler (note 51), p. 1.

[53] Rede von Bundeskanzler Gerhard Schröder anlässlich der Münchner Tagung für Sicherheitspolitik zum Thema: Deutsche Sicherheitspolitik an der Schwelle des 21. Jahrhunderts [Speech by Federal Chancellor Gerhard Schröder at the Munich Conference on German Security Policy on the Eve of the 21st century], 6 Feb. 1999. See also *Rzeczpospolita*, 8 Feb. 1999, p. 5.

[54] 'A significantly larger alliance might not produce a more stable Europe or even render new members secure'. Binendijk and Kugler (note 51), p. 2.

[55] Binendijk and Kugler (note 51), p. 2.

[56] Binendijk and Kugler (note 51), pp. 2–3.

selective and discriminating enlargement should give NATO time to integrate the first three new members.[57]

From this perspective, only three countries would be eligible in a second round of enlargement—the declared neutral or non-aligned states of Austria, Finland and Sweden. The paradox is that only in Austria, which under its State Treaty of 1955 had pledged under international law to observe eternal and permanent neutrality, is there a serious debate on joining NATO. The public exchanges of views on this matter in Finland and Sweden show that for their respective political leaders a substantial alteration of the security policies and early entry into NATO are not on the agenda.[58] Such an option might be considered only in a situation of extreme external threat; the likelihood of such a threat in the foreseeable future is smaller than it has ever been.

Sweden is not considering NATO membership but is concerned about increasing the security effectiveness of the EU. On 12 January 1999 the Swedish Defence Commission, a body for government consultations on defence policy with the political parties in parliament, presented its report *A Changing World—A Reformed Defence*. The report stated that Sweden 'remains militarily non-aligned, with the aim of retaining the possibility of neutrality in the event of a war in its vicinity. This position is fully compatible with far-reaching security cooperation with NATO'.[59] The international security of Sweden is mainly connected with a greater role for the Common Foreign and Security Policy of the European Union.

Of the nine countries pursuing NATO membership, Romania and Slovenia were mentioned as possible new candidates in the 1997 Madrid Declaration,[60] and Slovakia declared its wish to join after the September 1998 election. Three of the Balkan states—Albania, Bulgaria and Macedonia—claim NATO membership as their strategic goal. The three Baltic states—Estonia, Latvia and Lithuania—see entry into NATO as a guarantee of their independence and sovereignty. All these countries have different politico-military situations and are on different levels of system transformation and at various stages of development of a market economy. For various reasons none of them meets the criteria for membership.[61]

[57] A suggestion was made to extend the invitation to at least 1 country to 'make the point that the door is still open, even as the alliance takes time out to digest the admission of the three new members'. 'NATO enlargement: the next step', *American Foreign Policy Interests* (National Committee on American Foreign Policy), vol. 21, no. 1 (Feb. 1999), p. 17.

[58] E.g., Carl Bildt, former Swedish Prime Minister, and Max Jakobson, former Finnish representative to the United Nations, have contributed to the debate which began in Jan. 1999. It has produced no new significant arguments. 'Neutraliteten ett falskspel för folket' [Neutrality a deception of the people], *Dagens Nyheter* (Stockholm), 9 Jan. 1999, p. A6; and '"Vi kan inte alltid räkna med USA"' ['We cannot always count on the USA'], *Dagens Nyheter*, 10 Jan. 1999, p. A6. An interesting point is the declassified testimonies to the Commission on Neutrality revealed during the debate. They testify to Sweden's cooperation with NATO in the period of the cold war. As a result, Bildt noted, a bizarre situation occurred in which the West and Russia knew much more about the close relations between NATO and Sweden than the Swedish public itself.

[59] Swedish Ministry of Defence, Defence Commission, *A Changing World—A Reformed Defence*, Executive Summary of the Swedish Defence Commission's report, Stockholm, 19 Jan. 1999, p. 4.

[60] See also Rotfeld (note 1), p. 149; and note 15 in this chapter.

[61] In his presentation at the Third Annual Stockholm Conference on Baltic Sea Security and Cooperation on 19 Nov. 1998, Zbigniew Brzezinski said that 'considering all three Baltic States at once would

In this connection, various intermediate solutions are being considered, such as a NATO–Baltic charter, proposed by Zbigniew Brzezinski in his address to the Lithuanian Parliament on 18 November 1998, to be modelled on the 1997 NATO–Russia Founding Act and the 1997 NATO–Ukraine Charter.[62] A NATO–Baltic charter 'could be a positive development which would not prejudge automatically the question of whether the Baltic States will or will not be members of NATO'.[63] This policy takes into account Russia's position, opposing the admission of the Baltic states to the alliance,[64] on the one hand, and calls for an institutional framework for security cooperation between NATO and the Baltic states, on the other hand. This is close to a concept of establishing such mutual relations as Sweden pursues in its foreign policy.

IV. The European Union: a security and defence policy?

The European Union has made much greater progress in economic and social integration and in the standardization of industrial norms and legal regulations than in implementing the provisions of the 1992 Maastricht Treaty and the 1997 Amsterdam Treaty on a Common Foreign and Security Policy (CFSP). The EU was ineffective in controlling the development of events in the Balkan region after the 1991 break-up of Yugoslavia and helpless in the face of the wars in Bosnia and Herzegovina and Kosovo. Two missions by US Special Envoy Richard Holbrooke broke the impasses and led to the conclusion of the 1995 General Framework Agreement for Peace in Bosnia and Herzegovina (the Dayton Agreement) as well as at least the temporary withdrawal of substantial numbers of Serbian special forces from Kosovo and the establishment of contacts to introduce autonomy for the region in 1998.[65]

The conventional wisdom has been that the EU's role is to consolidate security and stability through aid, trade and cooperation, while NATO provides

be premature in terms of the objective criteria and might also be subject to excessive political complications externally'. He therefore suggested that at this stage only Lithuania and Slovenia be considered for membership. Brzezinski, Z., 'An inclusive system of Baltic regional cooperation and the U.S. national interest', eds J. P. Kruzich and A. W. E. Fahraeus, *The Baltic Sea Region: Building an Inclusive System of Security and Cooperation* (US Embassy: Stockholm, 1999), p. 12.

[62] The NATO–Russia Founding Act is reproduced in *SIPRI Yearbook 1998* (note 1), appendix 5A, pp. 168–73. For a discussion of the Founding Act and the NATO–Ukraine Charter see Rotfeld (note 1), pp. 143–46.

[63] Brzezinski (note 61), p. 12.

[64] At the 35th International Conference on Security, held at Munich on 6–7 Feb. 1999, Russian Deputy Foreign Minister Yevgeniy P. Gusarow stated that if NATO 'crosses the red line' and admits even one of the states that constituted the former Soviet Union, Russia will radically change its attitude towards NATO and will see no possibility of cooperation with the Alliance. 'Russland warnt vor Aufnahme ehemaliger Sowjetrepubliken' [Russia warns against admission of the former Soviet republics], *Frankfurter Allgemeine Zeitung*, 8 Feb. 1999 , p. 6.

[65] It should be noted that, while this is well known, it is less well known that the EU member states bear the main cost of the peace operations in Bosnia and Herzegovina and of implementation of the programme for building a civil society in the region. The EU also contributes to the Middle East peace process, particularly in humanitarian and economic aid for the Palestinian Authority, and to the prevention of conflicts in Africa and other regions of the world. Costy, A. and Gilbert, S., *Conflict Prevention and the European Union: Mapping the Actors, Instruments, and Institutions* (International Alert: London, 1998), p. 23, box 7, 'Regional frameworks for aid'.

territorial defence and power projection accompanied 'by its own stability-promoting programmes of enlargement, prospective enlargement and partnership and cooperation programmes'.[66] The two organizations are neither symmetrical nor similar.[67] Although the European Union is a supranational organization, with many attributes of a sovereign state, defence policy and military matters must be decided by individual member states.

In 1998 two issues concerning the EU drew attention: the future of European defence and enlargement of the Union.

The future of European defence

British Prime Minister Blair reopened the debate on European defence by presenting new ideas in a speech delivered at the informal European Union summit meeting held in Pörtschach, Austria, on 25 October 1998. The British message was that the EU ought 'to have a more united and influential voice, articulated with greater speed and coherence through the Common Foreign and Security Policy of the EU, and backed up when the need arises with effective and prompt military action'.[68] Blair was supported by Defence Secretary Robertson at the informal conference of EU defence ministers in Vienna in November 1998 and by Foreign Secretary Robin Cook at the WEU ministerial meetings in Rome the same month.[69] The British position can be summarized as: the EU should be given 'the ability both to decide and to act quickly and effectively, in order to achieve common goals'.[70]

This raises not so much the issue of the EU's future role as that of the very future of the WEU. Over 50 years after the signing of the 1948 Treaty of Economic, Social and Cultural Collaboration and Collective Self-Defence among Western European States (the Brussels Treaty),[71] the WEU is at a crossroads as to the role it should play in shaping a new European security system. In accordance with the decisions of the 1992 meeting of the WEU Council at Petersberg, Germany, and the June 1996 Berlin Ministerial Meeting of the North Atlantic Council, the WEU was viewed as a link between the EU and NATO, 'as the instrument for European-led crisis management operations, in

[66] Crowe, B. L. (Director General of the Common Security and Foreign Policy Directorate at the Council of the European Union), 'Roles of NATO and EU in transatlantic security', Presentation at the Workshop on NATO's Role in Shaping European Security, organized by the US Mission to the North Atlantic Treaty Organization, Brussels, 18 Sep. 1998.

[67] For more on the differences between the organizations see Rotfeld (note 1), pp. 157–60.

[68] 'The future of European defence, Speech by British Defence Secretary George Robertson to the WEU Assembly, Paris, 1 December 1998', Institute for Defense and Disarmament Studies, *Arms Control Reporter* (IDDS: Brookline, Mass.), sheet 402.D.141, Dec. 1998.

[69] Robertson, in *Arms Control Reporter* (note 68).

[70] Robertson, in *Arms Control Reporter* (note 68), sheets 402.D.141–42.

[71] Article IV of the 1948 Brussels Treaty, which later became Article V of the so-called modified Brussels Treaty, defined the following commitment: 'If any of the High Contracting Parties should be the object of an armed attack in Europe, the other High Contracting Parties will, in accordance with the provisions of Article 51 of the Charter of the United Nations, afford the Party so attacked all the military and other aid and assistance in their power'. The Brussels Treaty was modified by the 1954 Protocols (Paris Agreements on the Western European Union), which entered into force on 6 May 1955.

Europe or beyond'.[72] For various reasons these provisions have so far remained on paper.

In these circumstances, the UK proposed 'some fresh thinking' on the future direction of European defence. What is essential in the British reasoning is that defence should remain under the control of national governments and parliaments, on the one hand, and that neither the European Commission nor the European Parliament should play a direct role in defence matters, on the other hand. In other words, common European defence should remain intergovernmental, not become transnational, and defence decisions should continue to be arrived at by consensus among the European states.

The Treaty of Amsterdam recognized the central role of NATO for European defence. The search for new politico-military solutions aims at ensuring for Europe such a position in the world that it 'can speak with authority and act with decisiveness', while not undermining the transatlantic relationship.[73] The task is to implement political commitments to crisis management (the Petersberg tasks) within the new legal framework of the Amsterdam Treaty. In the British understanding, an important institutional step towards carrying out this programme will be the appointment of a High Representative for the CFSP 'with real standing and authority'. Shared political will is essential. However, to give credibility to political positions a European armed force is needed. This requires the member states to address the questions of investment, prioritization and restructuring of the European defence industries. It also implies an increase in spending on national forces and the development of combined military capabilities as well as an increase in the operational effectiveness of the existing European multinational forces.[74]

In this context, the extent to which the existing institutional arrangements satisfy the new requirements is also topical. In line with the 1992 Petersberg decisions, the WEU should 'support the EU in framing the defence aspects of the Common Foreign and Security Policy, and . . . the EU can avail itself of the WEU for operational purposes, particularly relating to the Petersberg tasks'. In the 1996 Berlin NAC decisions, 'NATO declared its readiness to provide assets and capabilities to the WEU for European-led operations'. The British Defence Secretary informed the WEU Assembly in Paris on 1 December 1998 that '[s]ome of our Partners have argued for some time for the wholesale merger of the Western European Union into the European Union. The United Kingdom resisted this proposal at Amsterdam. While we do not rule it out today, we recognize that it continues to present difficulties'.[75] Sev-

[72] *Western European Union: A European Journey* (WEU Secretariat-General: Brussels, 1998), p. 130.

[73] Robertson, in *Arms Control Reporter* (note 68), sheet 402.D.142.

[74] 'Within NATO, the European Allies with more than 60 percent of the population of the Alliance, and almost two-thirds of the Allies' armed forces personnel, provide only 40 per cent of the total defence spending. More importantly, the European allies account for less than a third of the total equipment spending, and around a sixth of the Research and Development spending. Furthermore, the key military assets required for the type of demanding peace support operation that we may face, in particular air assets, are overwhelmingly American. Had NATO aircraft undertaken air strikes to enforce the UN Security Council Resolutions on Kosovo, less than a third would have been European.' Robertson, in *Arms Control Reporter* (note 68), sheet 402.D.144.

[75] Robertson, in *Arms Control Reporter* (note 68), sheet 402.D.145.

eral variants of institutional relations were considered in the NATO–EU–WEU triangle, but no conclusive decision was reached. However, an understanding emerged that this issue should neither constitute an obstacle to nor hamper the new thinking about these matters.[76]

The first formal document that spelled out the new approach by France and the UK in this regard was the Joint Declaration on European Defence (the Saint-Malo Declaration) presented by President Jacques Chirac and Prime Minister Blair at their summit meeting held in Saint-Malo, France, on 3–4 December 1998.[77] The central goal of the document is to determine the role of the EU concerning European defence, taking into account EU–NATO relations. It is significant that the declaration made only a brief mention of the WEU. The essence of the declaration is to impart practical significance to Article V of the Amsterdam Treaty. To this end, 'the Union must have the capacity for autonomous action, backed up by credible military forces, the means to decide to use them, and a readiness to do so, in order to respond to international crises'.

According to the declaration, the European states will operate within the institutional framework of the EU. Three bodies were mentioned: the European Council, the General Affairs Council and meetings of defence ministers (the WEU was not included in this context). For the purposes of European defence, the EU must be given appropriate structures and capacity for analysis of situations, sources of intelligence and a capability for relevant strategic planning. It will also need to have 'recourse to suitable military means'.[78] In order to fulfil its new tasks, the EU needs to have strengthened armed forces 'that can react rapidly to the new risks, and which are supported by a strong and competitive European defence industry and technology'. Whether such tasks can be fulfilled remains an open question.

There are many indications that the construction of an EU 'fourth pillar' (in addition to the existing economic, political and judicial pillars, defence is seen as a fourth pillar) would mean a total incorporation of the WEU into the EU. Such a solution would aim at strengthening Europe militarily, thus making it a more attractive partner for the United States without weakening NATO. The proponents of this solution claim that 'Europe's current inability and unwillingness to assert its security interests is more damaging to the transatlantic relationship than a broad-shouldered Europe demanding to be considered in American calculations'.[79]

[76] The British Prime Minister stated: 'European defence is not about new institutional fixes. It is about new capabilities both military and diplomatic'. 'Speech by the Prime Minister, Tony Blair, NATO 50th Anniversary Conference, Royal United Services Institute, London, Monday, 8 March 1999', URL <http://www.fco.gov.uk/news/speechtext.asp?2094>.

[77] The text of the Joint Declaration on European Defence, adopted on 4 Dec. 1998, is reproduced in appendix 6A in this volume.

[78] The Joint Declaration explains that 'suitable military means' are 'European capabilities predesignated within NATO's European pillar or national or multinational European means outside the NATO framework'.

[79] Schake, K., Bloch-Lainé, A. and Grant, C., 'Building a European defence capability', *Survival*, vol. 41, no. 1 (spring 1999), p. 21.

To sum up, the Saint-Malo initiative determined the direction of the debate on future European defence policy and prompted the USA to cooperate in developing the ESDI within NATO. An open question is what the framework of European autonomy in the field of security and defence will be. As things stand now, the United States does not accept any solution which would limit its leadership within the alliance structures.

EU enlargement

On 31 March 1998 five CEE states—the Czech Republic, Estonia, Hungary, Poland and Slovenia—and Cyprus began separate negotiations on admission to the EU in the Accession Conferences. The main task of the first negotiation phase is to screen the national legislation of each candidate to find out whether and to what extent it is compatible with EU law. The 1997 Luxembourg meeting of the Council of the European Union invited the European Commission, among other things, to prepare regular reports on the progress made towards accession by each of the candidate countries.[80] The Commission set out to analyse whether reforms which had been announced had been carried out. The criteria, which were established at the 1993 Copenhagen Council meeting, require that each candidate state has stable institutions for guaranteeing democracy, the rule of law, human rights, and respect for and protection of minorities. In late 1998 the Commission 'drew the overall conclusion that all the candidate countries, except one, met the political criteria even if a number of them still had to make progress concerning the practice of democracy and protection of human rights and minorities'.[81] In the Commission's view, a common problem for all the candidate states is the inherent weakness of the judiciary, from the training of judges to procedural reform aimed at overcoming excessive delays in court cases. 'This is particularly serious in Poland, the Czech Republic, Slovenia and Estonia. For Slovakia, one of the main issues remains the independence of judges.' The Commission's report recommended that Slovakia and the other candidates strengthen the fight against corruption and, in some cases, the independence of radio and television.[82] Progress was noted in Latvia's protection of minority rights after the 1998 referendum on the citizenship law since it will facilitate the naturaliza-

[80] The 1997 Luxembourg meeting of the Council of the European Union concluded: 'The Commission will make regular reports to the Council, together with any necessary recommendation for opening bilateral intergovernmental conferences, reviewing the progress of each central and east European applicant state towards accession in the light of the Copenhagen criteria, in particular the rate at which it is adopting the Union acquis'. Cited in European Commission, Composite paper, Reports on progress towards accession by each of the candidate countries, 4 Nov. 1998, URL <http://europa.eu.int/comm/dg1a/enlarge/report_11_98_en/composite/index.htm>.

[81] European Commission (note 80). The Commission considered that only Slovakia (under the Meciar Government) did not satisfy the political conditions. The new Slovak Government introduced reforms which have improved this situation.

[82] 'In the specific case of Romania, the Government has continued to take measures, with Phare support, to improve the protection of the nearly 100,000 abandoned children in state orphanages.' European Commission (note 80).

tion of non-citizens and their stateless children.[83] It also welcomed the tangible improvement of the situation of the Hungarian minority in Romania.

In summary, the process of accession of the CEE countries has contributed to resolving, alleviating or preventing crises in relations between states of the region. This is a new, essential security dimension. It is difficult to assess the extent to which the NATO membership of the Czech Republic, Hungary and Poland will affect the integration process of Central Europe with the EU. In their endeavours to join the EU, the countries of the region referred to external threat as a significant motivating factor. Now, after the admission to NATO of the first three states from the region, this element may lose in importance in the EU context,[84] even though the undoing of the Yalta division was seen as one of the goals of joining the Union.[85] In the view of a Swedish analyst, the involvement of the Baltic states in the European Union enlargement process will increase their security in two specific ways:

> First, it will give a Western identity to these countries in a way which, in contrast to the enlargement of the North Atlantic Treaty Organization (NATO), is not contested in Russia, and is even seen by some Russians as being to their advantage. Second, by not following the border line of NATO enlargement, EU enlargement serves to soften what might otherwise be perceived as a new and rigid border between East and West.[86]

In its January 1999 report the Swedish Defence Commission stated that 'future enlargement of the European Union is of great importance in improving European security' and expressed 'its concern at emerging signs of a slow-down in that process'.[87] This statement should be seen in the broader context of the new security relationships between the EU and NATO.

In the view of some experts, the distinction between the NATO and non-NATO, including non-aligned, states is becoming increasingly blurred.[88] However, although enlargement of the EU would have a bearing on the security of the member states, particularly in the case of the admission of non-

[83] For Estonia, the report noted that 'it is regrettable that Parliament has not yet adopted amendments to the Citizenship law to allow stateless children to become citizens'. European Commission (note 80).

[84] Kolarska-Bobinska, L., *Completed Transformation: Integration into the European Union* (Institute of Public Affairs: Warsaw, 1999), p. 13.

[85] 'It is to be hoped that the Union member states realize that they also stand to gain from the fact that the entry of Poland and the other Central European candidate countries will put an end once and for all to the post-Yalta division in European history.' Parzymies, S., 'European Union member states and eastward enlargement', *Polish Quarterly of International Affairs*, no. 2 (spring 1998), p. 6.

[86] Herolf, G., 'Enlargement and flexibility—recurrent items on the agenda', ed. G. Herolf, *EU Enlargement and Flexibility* (Swedish Institute of International Affairs: Stockholm, 1998), p. 4.

[87] Swedish Ministry of Defence (note 59), p. 2. 'The Government attaches the highest priority to the enlargement of the EU. We must counteract the drawing of new dividing lines in Europe, both through a successful enlargement process and by strengthening EU cooperation with the European countries not included in the enlargement. It is a vital Swedish interest that the countries in our vicinity are incorporated into the new Europe.' Anna Lindh, Swedish Minister for Foreign Affairs, Statement of government policy in the parliamentary debate on foreign affairs, 10 Feb. 1999, p. 5.

[88] 'It is difficult to make a clear distinction between the international attitude of, say, NATO member Denmark and neutral Sweden, and it would be impossible, certainly for anyone who is not a national of either state, to explain any differences between the foreign policies of those two countries on the basis of their chosen international status.' Parmentier, G., 'Security and defence policy—the use of flexibility', ed. Herolf (note 86), p. 82.

NATO states, the alliance is still the main organization which European states aspire to join and is perceived as a centre of gravity for the organization of their national and international security.[89]

V. The OSCE: a new dimension of security cooperation

The OSCE pursued three main goals in 1998: (*a*) further evolution of the OSCE as a 'primary instrument for conflict prevention, crisis management and post-conflict rehabilitation';[90] (*b*) designing a framework for cooperation between international security institutions; and (*c*) the work on a Platform for Co-operative Security, proposed to be an essential element of the OSCE Document–Charter on European Security. The Chairman-in-Office (CIO), Bronislaw Geremek of Poland, defined five tasks for the OSCE under his chairmanship in 1998: (*a*) 'strengthening the existing interactions between the OSCE and other international organizations dealing with European security, as well as their complementarity and compatibility'; (*b*) making the early-warning system more effective; (*c*) periodically evaluating OSCE activities and the extent to which they are in line with decisions taken by the 1996 Lisbon Summit Meeting and the 1997 Copenhagen Ministerial Council meeting; (*d*) establishing a system of permanent consultations within the OSCE; and (*e*) adopting, as a standard practice for implementation of important tasks, the ad hoc appointment of high-ranking European personalities as representatives of the CIO.[91]

An instrument for democracy and conflict prevention

In 1998 US Government representatives repeatedly emphasized the significant role of the OSCE with the intention of giving it a new impetus in two areas: consolidation of democracy in the newly emerged states; and conflict prevention and management as well as post-conflict rehabilitation. President Clinton, in his May 1998 Berlin address, referred to the OSCE as an 'important tool' in strengthening the hand and extending the reach of democracy. 'Its broad membership projects a unity and moral authority unparalleled on the continent.'[92] He stressed that at the November 1999 Istanbul summit meeting 'we should encourage even greater engagement in the areas where democracy's roots are still fragile—in the Balkans, in Central Asia and the Caucasus—and we must develop practical new tools for the OSCE such as training police to support peacekeeping missions and dispatching democracy teams to build

[89] Højberg, A.-E., 'Enlargement and flexibility—security policy', ed. Herolf (note 86), p. 89.

[90] As defined in the Budapest Document 1994, Budapest Summit Declaration: Towards a Genuine Partnership in a New Era, para. 8. The text is reproduced in *SIPRI Yearbook 1995: Armaments, Disarmament and International Security* (Oxford University Press: Oxford, 1995), pp. 309–13.

[91] Address by Bronislaw Geremek, Minister for Foreign Affairs of Poland, OSCE Chairman-in-Office (Permanent Council, 15 Jan. 1998), OSCE document CIO.GAL/1/98, 15 Jan. 1998, pp. 2–3.

[92] 'Remarks by the President . . .' (note 3).

more open societies'.[93] Secretary of State Albright specified the role which, in the US view, the OSCE has to play in resolving 'the real world challenges we face in Europe': it should 'develop institutions that set standards of international behavior and that require their members to cooperate in upholding those standards'.[94]

The practical embodiment of these expectations was the OSCE involvement in Albania and in Kosovo (Yugoslavia). The OSCE has repeatedly condemned the excessive and indiscriminate use of force in police and military actions in Kosovo.[95] On 25 October the OSCE Permanent Council formally established the Kosovo Verification Mission for one year with the aim of deploying 2000 persons.[96] If its tasks are implemented in accordance with the mandate, it would be the most significant OSCE mission in the field.

The OSCE has continued to play a leading role in the international community's civilian stabilization efforts in Albania, Bosnia and Herzegovina, and the Former Yugoslav Republic of Macedonia. It took on the unprecedented task of deploying civilian police monitors in the Croatian Danube region (following the expiry of the mandate of the UN Police Support Group, UNPSG).

In early 1998 the OSCE's Advisory and Monitoring Group began operating in Belarus, and the role of the OSCE in Central Asia was enhanced: new centres were opened in Ashkhabad (Turkmenistan), Bishkek (Kyrgyzstan) and Almaty (Kazakhstan). The missions in Bosnia and Herzegovina, Croatia, Estonia, Georgia, Latvia, Moldova, Tajikistan and Ukraine successfully continued their activities, as did the Spillover Monitor Mission to Skopje, the OSCE Presence in Albania, the OSCE Assistance Group in Chechnya (the Russian Federation) and the OSCE Liaison Office in Central Asia.

In 1998 the High Commissioner on National Minorities (HCNM) increased the scope and intensity of his activities. In accordance with the concept endorsed by the OSCE Permanent Council in June 1997, the Office for Democratic Institutions and Human Rights (ODIHR) developed its activities in the observation and promotion of elections, in practical involvement in the promotion of human rights and democratic institutions, and in monitoring the implementation of commitments in the human dimension.

[93] 'Remarks by the President . . .' (note 3).

[94] 'Albright statement to OSCE Permanent Council', 3 Sep. 1998, available in the Public Diplomacy Query (PDQ) database on the United States Information Agency Internet site, URL <http://pdq2.usia.gov>.

[95] 'On 11 March [1998], the Permanent Council called on the Federal Republic of Yugoslavia to accept without preconditions an immediate return of the OSCE missions of long duration to Kosovo, Sanjak and Voivodina. . . . In July, exploratory talks between the OSCE and the FRY were initiated on the basis of a joint statement by Presidents Yeltsin and Milosevic, issued on 16 June 1998. . . . [The] OSCE Technical Assistance Mission was sent to the FRY, in mid-July. . . . Pursuant to UN Security Council Resolution 1160, the Chairman-in-Office has reported regularly to the UN Secretary-General on the situation in Kosovo.' *Annual Report 1998 on OSCE Activities* (1 December 1997–30 November 1998), OSCE Secretary General, Vienna, 1998, pp. 1–2.

[96] *Annual Report 1998* (note 95), pp. 2 and 26. See also chapter 2 and appendix 2A, table 2A, notes 121 and 123, in this volume.

The OSCE and other European security organizations

The new agenda for all European multilateral security structures, including the OSCE, should deal with three questions:

1. What should be done to make the existing OSCE tools and mechanisms of cooperation with other European and universal organizations more efficient?
2. How can the decision-making process be improved?
3. How may the implementation process be facilitated?

The Common Concept, adopted in December 1997 at the Copenhagen meeting of the OSCE Ministerial Council, declared that 'the goal is to strengthen the mutually-reinforcing nature of the relationship between those organizations and institutions concerned with the promotion of comprehensive security within the OSCE area'.[97]

An essential factor in the transformation and adaptation of many institutions to the new security environment is that structures, by their very nature, are static, while international security is a dynamic process. This leads to a paradoxical situation: the weaker the organizational structures, the easier it is to make changes. In other words, the OSCE's weaknesses are an asset in the current volatile situation. The OSCE's ability to take ad hoc decisions and its flexibility make it unique among the European security structures. However, in the longer run, the strength of an organization cannot be measured by its ad hoc activities; it should be measured by its constant and continuing efforts to resolve the questions falling under its mandate.

The OSCE's cooperation with NATO is central. In NATO's perception, it is still significant that for many years the Soviet Union, and later Russia, tried to exploit the opportunities of the process initiated in Helsinki in order to weaken NATO. Elements of that approach could be discerned in Russia's proposal to establish a hierarchical security architecture which in practice would subordinate all other security-related structures and organizations to the OSCE. In US political philosophy, no new institution likely to undermine the cohesion of the alliance should receive serious political support. However, with the process of NATO enlargement and the manifested interest of the CEE states in joining the EU and other Western institutions, the OSCE now enjoys the qualified support of the USA.

The next, and probably the most important, factor to be taken into account in defining the OSCE's role among other European security structures is that the mandates of all international organizations deal with the relations between states. The body of principles, norms and procedures of international law regulates inter-state relations. The new post-cold war challenge is that, without exception, all the conflicts in the OSCE area are of a domestic nature. Because the OSCE has a unique and specific character, and most of its commitments

[97] The Common Concept for the Development of Cooperation between Mutually-Reinforcing Institutions, OSCE document MC(6).DEC/5, 19 Dec. 1997.

are of a political rather than legal nature, its norms, procedures and institutions can be adjusted to the needs and challenges of the new security agenda.

It is noteworthy that a pragmatic approach has prevailed in OSCE practice. On the other hand, it is still unclear why such ambitious solutions as, for example, the Conciliation Commissions and the Arbitral Tribunal—which together constitute the Court of Conciliation and Arbitration under the 1992 Convention on Conciliation and Arbitration, elaborated along the lines of classic peaceful settlement of disputes initially within the Conference on Security and Co-operation in Europe (CSCE, now the OSCE)—do not play an appropriate role.

Many OSCE bodies, including the Chairman-in-Office and his Personal Representatives, various missions, the HCNM, the ODIHR and some other institutions, enjoy a wide range of competencies. They are not limited by the consensus rule in their activities. While it is true that consensus is required for agreeing on their mandates, this is an advantage rather than a shortcoming of the decision-making process because specific actions are thus politically legitimized by all members of the organization. In fact, the participating states have used their right to veto decisions in a responsible manner. In addition, because of the consensus rule, they have a more acute sense of being bound by and accountable for the decisions taken, even though the OSCE commitments are of a political rather than legal nature.

In order to enhance the effectiveness of the OSCE its cooperative approach, rather than a formalistic one, should continue to prevail. Politically significant OSCE decisions are inspired by the philosophy of inclusiveness rather than exclusiveness. As a rule, politically binding decisions are adopted by consensus at summit meetings and in the Ministerial Council and the Permanent Council. Operational decisions are the responsibility of the Chairman-in-Office, who should take them in consultation with the participating states. He could also delegate some of his competencies to his Personal Representatives. The roles of the Secretary General and the heads of other OSCE institutions (the ODIHR, the HCNM, the missions, etc.) are and should remain of an executive character.

Leadership is of key importance for any international or regional security structure. While leadership of multilateral organizations is identified with the existence of an organ like the Security Council of the United Nations, in the OSCE this function might be fulfilled by the existing Contact Group after modification of its mandate and composition. Although it was called into being for implementation of the Dayton Agreement, the Contact Group has become an important institution with competencies which extend beyond its original mandate (e.g., in the Kosovo conflict).

Cooperation between the OSCE and other security-related structures is institutionalized in different ways (e.g., in the High-Level Tripartite meetings of the OSCE, the Council of Europe and the UN, as well as in various agreements). However, NATO and the EU, the strongest integrated institutions, must both help to enforce the OSCE principles and confirm that they are bound by them.

In 1998 cooperation between the OSCE and other security-related organizations and institutions was conducted in two areas: (*a*) deepening relations and links with other structures; and (*b*) work undertaken in the field. In the first area, the OSCE concluded memoranda of understanding with several other institutions. The UN High Commissioner for Human Rights and the ODIHR signed an agreement on cooperation on 19 June and the Office of the UN High Commissioner for Refugees and the OSCE Secretariat signed a memorandum on 15 October. In-depth discussions between the OSCE and the Council of Europe continued. Both organizations, while acknowledging that they have different responsibilities, structures, working tools and methods, recognized their shared principles and objectives of promoting human rights and democracy in Europe. This calls for a clearer division of tasks to avoid duplication of work and improved cooperative relations between them.[98]

The other area of cooperation involves activities in the field. The OSCE Secretary General's report reviewed numerous cases of common efforts made with various UN bodies, the EU, the Council of Europe, and humanitarian and other organizations in Albania, Bosnia and Herzegovina, Croatia and Kosovo.[99]

The OSCE Security Model

The basis for the OSCE's work on the Security Model in 1998 was the 1997 Copenhagen Ministerial Council decision on Guidelines on an OSCE Document–Charter on European Security.[100] In accordance with the guidelines, two additional working groups were set up to deal with specific elements of the charter. The Security Model Committee also conducted talks on issues not covered by the working groups.

The negotiation on the final text of the Charter on European Security is difficult, partly because of the fundamental disagreements between Russia and the USA, and to a minor extent among key European states, on the respective roles of NATO and other international organizations, on the one hand, and the OSCE, on the other hand. Considerable progress was made on a number of issues in 1998, at both the conceptual and the practical levels. At the same time, significant differences of opinion on numerous questions emerged. In the view of the Polish CIO, the drafting process would be facilitated by adoption of the structure of the charter, based on the work done. Accordingly, the CIO presented an indicative and non-exhaustive table of contents of a future char-

[98] *Annual Report 1998* (note 95), p. 54. For suggestions for improving cooperation between different security organizations, see Rotfeld, A. D., 'Prescriptions for improving OSCE effectiveness in responding to the risks and challenges of the 21st century', eds V.-Y. Ghebali and D. Warner, *The OSCE and Preventive Diplomacy,* PSIO Occasional Paper no. 1 (Graduate Institute of International Studies: Geneva, 1999), pp. 51–70.

[99] *Annual Report 1998* (note 95), pp. 54–56.

[100] Decision no. 5, Guidelines on an OSCE Document–Charter on European Security, OSCE document MC(6).DEC/5, 19 Dec. 1997.

ter. He also prepared, in cooperation with the Troika (the past, present and next appointed CIOs), a comprehensive Basic Framework of the Charter on European Security.[101]

The CIO Progress Report for 1998 presented the status of negotiations on the following items: (*a*) new risks and challenges to security; (*b*) the politico-military aspects of security; (*c*) early warning, conflict prevention, crisis management and post-conflict rehabilitation, including the OSCE's role with regard to police operations; (*d*) assistance in adherence to and implementation of principles, norms and commitments; (*e*) jointly considered actions; (*f*) the human dimension; (*g*) economic and environmental issues; (*h*) the Platform for Co-operative Security, including the OSCE as a forum for the interaction of regional and subregional groupings and for peacekeeping (in the light of its overall role in conflict prevention); and (*i*) security and cooperation in adjacent areas.[102]

VI. Conclusions

The European security organizations will need to take creative and bold action if they are to implement the necessary reforms to be able to prepare for and address the security risks and challenges to Europe in the next century. In consolidating transatlantic relations and coordinating the action of these organizations, the United States must become a member of genuine partnerships rather than a hegemonic actor in NATO and the OSCE and in its relations with the EU and individual European states.

In 1998 the US–Russian relationship did not have a decisive influence on European security developments, as was the case in previous years. The development of relations with the EU is given a higher priority by Russia.[103] From the European perspective, this process is seen as Russia's comeback to its rightful place on the European scene.[104] However, for both West and Central Europe and Russia, the US security presence in Europe is essential.

The Euro-Atlantic and world communities must take into account the legitimate security interests of every state. Europe must also fully recognize the reality that the threats and conflicts of the end of the 20th century are mainly of a domestic nature—the most serious threats to security on the continent will come from sub-state and non-state actors and from the strong link today

[101] C-i-O Progress Report on the work in 1998 on a Document–Charter on European Security, OSCE document MC.GAL/3/98, 1 Dec. 1998, Annex 2.

[102] C-i-O Progress Report (note 101).

[103] Zhurkin, V. V., *Yevropeyskiy Soyuz: Vnyeshnyaya Politika, Bezopasnost, Oborona* [European Union: foreign policy, security, defence], (Russian Academy of Sciences, Institute of Europe: Moscow, 1998), p. 61. A joint study by the Institute of Europe of the Russian Academy of Sciences and the WEU Institute for Security Studies sketched 4 possible scenarios for the further development of Russia–EU relations. 'Whichever route is taken, the important thing is that a consensus exists on both sides that improvements are required.' Danilov, D. and De Spiegeleire, S., *From Decoupling to Recoupling: A New Security Relationship between Russia and Western Europe* (WEU Institute for Security Studies: Paris, 1998), p. 49.

[104] 'After a long interlude, a democratizing and liberalizing Russia is gradually reclaiming its rightful place within Europe.' Danilov and De Spiegeleire (note 103), p. 50.

between international security and the evolution of domestic affairs. Although steps have been taken to reform the European security structures, they are not adequately prepared to address domestic sources of instability and insecurity. The sine qua non for cooperative management of security in Europe is firm commitment to the norms and principles of the transatlantic community. These include the indivisibility of security, transparency, predictability, commitment to multilateral cooperation in confronting new security threats, and resolute joint action to prevent or resolve conflicts.

Despite its present economic, military and political weakness, Russia is still of primary importance in the shaping of the European security system. This is because of the size of the country, its predominant role among the former Soviet republics and the possible nuclearization of its defence policy. However, Russia's standing in European and world affairs will be determined by the success or failure of its internal transformation.

Neither internal transformation nor the best document, however, will work unless all states of the transatlantic community move beyond verbal declarations and adopt strategic decisions committing them firmly to multinational obligations to transform and adapt the existing European security institutions to the new needs and requirements. The implementation of such decisions will certainly enhance the effectiveness of the emerging cooperative European security system.

Appendix 6A. Documents on European security

OSLO MINISTERIAL DECLARATION

Adopted by the OSCE Ministerial Council at Oslo on 3 December 1998

I.

We have discussed the challenges to security in our region, the OSCE's contribution to meeting them and how this can be developed in future. We stress the need for the international community to develop co-ordinated responses to such challenges. 1998 has been an important year in this regard, including for the OSCE.

The crisis in Kosovo has come to the forefront of the OSCE's concerns and action. We urge the parties to stop all violence and to co-operate in the negotiation of a political settlement.

The Kosovo Verification Mission (KVM) is the largest and most difficult operation ever put into the field by the OSCE. It marks the international community's recognition of the Organization's developing potential and expertise to contribute to security. Success for the KVM requires not only the use of internal mechanisms for transparent consultations, but also effective co-operation with other intergovernmental bodies, as well as with non-governmental organizations; and it requires adequate allocation of resources by participating States.

This year the OSCE successfully supervised the general elections in Bosnia and Herzegovina. It will continue to further the gradual processes of transferring responsibility for democracy building to the authorities in this country.

The OSCE role in police monitoring in the Danubian region of Croatia marks a new and practical development of the OSCE's operational capabilities.

The OSCE will continue and strengthen its efforts directed at the resolution of conflicts in Georgia and Moldova, as well as the Nagorno-Karabakh conflict. It is necessary that the OSCE responds with equal energy and determination to all of its tasks.

We welcome the Memoranda of Understanding signed between the OSCE/Office for Democratic Institutions and Human Rights and the governments of Georgia, Armenia and Azerbaijan aimed at deepening the co-operation in the fields of democracy and human rights. We take note of the proposal of the Chairman-in-Office to open OSCE offices in the Republic of Armenia and the Republic of Azerbaijan.

We note with satisfaction the growing involvement of the OSCE in Central Asia and welcome the establishment of the OSCE Centres in Kazakhstan, Kyrgyzstan and Turkmenistan as a further expression of our commitment to promote stability and co-operation throughout the entire OSCE area. We also welcome the signature by the Chairman-in-Office of Memoranda of Understanding on co-operation between the OSCE/Office for Democratic Institutions and Human Rights and the governments of Kazakhstan and Kyrgyzstan.

We recognize that the expansion of OSCE operations requires further strengthening of operational capabilities of the OSCE, including its Secretariat, and appreciate that the Secretary General has taken initial steps towards this goal. We support an early finalization of an OSCE strategy for training, the object of which is to enhance the ability of the Organization to carry out its tasks.

II.

We have taken stock of the progress this year in the work on a Document–Charter on European Security. This has been achieved through focused, target-oriented negotiation. Emphasis has been on the practical development of OSCE instruments for action, including co-operation with other organizations and institutions. At both conceptual and practical level, there has been progress in the development of the OSCE Platform for Co-operative Security as an instrument enhancing European solidarity and partnership and one of the essential elements of a Document–Charter. Developments on the ground have enriched the discussion of the role of the OSCE in conflict settlement.

We urge rapid progress in the development of a Document–Charter.

III.

We conclude once again that the potential of the OSCE to contribute to security stems from its broad membership, its shared values, and its decision making based on transparency and consensus. We underline that respect for OSCE principles and implementation of OSCE commitments remain fundamental to security. Promoting compliance and reinforcing thereby democracy, the rule of law, respect for human rights and fundamental freedoms, including rights of persons belonging to national minorities, the development of free market economies and social progress, and alleviating the plight of refugees and displaced persons, require constant effort. Primary responsibility for achieving these goals lies with individual States, but much depends upon solidarity in the OSCE and a genuine partnership based on sovereign equality.

We stress the importance of sub-regional and bilateral co-operation to complement OSCE-wide activities in the promotion of solidarity and partnership.

This spirit of solidarity and partnership is essential to OSCE's capacity to respond to risks and challenges to security. This extends not only to partnership between States, but to co-operation among the different organizations and institutions to which those States belong. In this pragmatic, flexible and non-hierarchical co-operation the OSCE should continue to develop its own operational activities in areas in which it has proved its strength.

We recognize that the OSCE police operations are now an integral part of the Organization's efforts in early warning, conflict prevention, crisis management and post-conflict rehabilitation. International police operations can provide an important contribution to building a society based on the rule of law that can consolidate democracy and enhance respect for human rights and fundamental freedoms. The participating States will enhance the capacity of the OSCE with regard to police operations. To this end, close co-operation with the international organizations having relevant experience in conducting police operations, and in the first instance the United Nations, will be established.

IV.

We reaffirm our commitment to arms control as an important element of our common security.

We reaffirm the importance of the CFE Treaty as a cornerstone of European security. Full implementation of the Treaty and its adaptation to the changing security environment in Europe will be an essential contribution to our common and indivisible security. In this context, we take note of the report by the Chairman of the Joint Consultative Group. We welcome the commitment made by the States Parties to complete the adaptation process by the time of the OSCE Summit in 1999. This goal will require that outstanding key issues be resolved and drafting begun in the first months of next year. We welcome the mutual commitment by the States Parties to redouble their efforts to achieve this goal.

We take positive note of the report on the activities of the Forum for Security Co-operation (FSC). We declare the objective to complete the work on the review of the Vienna Document 1994 by the OSCE Summit in 1999. We welcome the increased attention given by the FSC to the regional dimension of security and confidence building measures, in accordance with the decisions of the Lisbon Summit and the Copenhagen Ministerial meeting.

We reaffirm the significance of the Open Skies Treaty and the necessity of its entry into force without delay.

We note with satisfaction that agreement was achieved on the mandate for negotiations on regional stability, as foreseen under Article V of Annex 1-B of the General Framework Agreement for Peace in Bosnia and Herzegovina.

V.

We reaffirm that strengthened security and co-operation in adjacent areas, in particular the Mediterranean, is important for stability in the OSCE region.

We welcome Jordan as a new Mediterranean Partner for Co-operation. We value the long-standing relationship with the Mediterranean Partners and their interest in the work of the OSCE. As mutual dialogue develops, improvements in mechanisms of co-operation to reinforce the principles and values of the OSCE could be considered. We support the work of the Mediterranean Contact Group in Vienna and encourage the Mediterranean Partners to continue to contribute to OSCE activities including through sending visitors to OSCE missions and guest observers to OSCE election monitoring operations.

The OSCE welcomes support for its activities from its Partners for Co-operation. We appreciate the contributions of Japan and the Republic of Korea to OSCE efforts. We thank Japan for its generous financial support for Bosnia and Herzegovina elections and in the context of Kosovo.

Source: OSCE document MC.DOC/1/98, 3 Dec. 1998, URL <http://www.osce.org/e/minf-l-e.htm>.

BRITISH–FRENCH JOINT DECLARATION ON EUROPEAN DEFENCE

Adopted at Saint-Malo, France, on 4 December 1998

The Heads of State and Government of France and the United Kingdom are agreed that:

1. The European Union needs to be in a position to play its full role on the international stage. This means making a reality of the Treaty of Amsterdam, which will provide the essential basis for action by the Union. It will be important to achieve full and rapid implementation of the Amsterdam provisions on CFSP. This includes the responsibility of the European Council to decide on the progressive framing of a common defence policy in the framework of CFSP. The Council must be able to take decisions on an intergovernmental basis, covering the whole range of activity set out in Title V of the Treaty of European Union.

2. To this end, the Union must have the capacity for autonomous action, backed up by credible military forces, the means to decide to use them, and a readiness to do so, in order to respond to international crises.

In pursuing our objective, the collective defence commitments to which member states subscribe (set out in Article 5 of the Washington Treaty, Article V of the Brussels Treaty) must be maintained. In strengthening the solidarity between the member states of the European Union, in order that Europe can make its voice heard in world affairs, while acting in conformity with our respective obligations in NATO, we are contributing to the vitality of a modernised Atlantic Alliance which is the foundation of the collective defence of its members.

Europeans will operate within the institutional framework of the European Union (European Council, General Affairs Council, and meetings of Defence Ministers).

The reinforcement of European solidarity must take into account the various positions of European states.

The different situations of countries in relation to NATO must be respected.

3. In order for the European Union to take decisions and approve military action where the Alliance as a whole is not engaged, the Union must be given appropriate structures and a capacity for analysis of situations, sources of intelligence, and a capability for relevant strategic planning, without unnecessary duplication, taking account of the existing assets of the WEU and the evolution of its relations with the EU. In this regard, the European Union will also need to have recourse to suitable military means (European capabilities pre-designated within NATO's European pillar or national or multinational European means outside the NATO framework).

4. Europe needs strengthened armed forces that can react rapidly to the new risks, and which are supported by a strong and competitive European defence industry and technology.

5. We are determined to unite in our efforts to enable the European Union to give concrete expression to these objectives.

Source: International Affairs and Defence Section of the British House of Commons Library.

ACT OF RATIFICATION OF THE NORTH ATLANTIC TREATY BY POLAND

Similar Acts of Ratification were submitted by the Czech Republic, Hungary and Poland

Submitted by the President of the Republic of Poland on 26 February 1999

On behalf of the Republic of Poland
PRESIDENT
of the Republic of Poland
makes it publicly known:

Whereas the North Atlantic Treaty was done at Washington on 4 April 1949

Having considered the aforesaid Treaty, I hereby declare on behalf of the Republic of Poland that:

– it has been acknowledged to be just as a whole and in each of the provisions therein contained,

– the Republic of Poland decides to accede

to the Treaty,

– the provisions of the aforesaid Treaty are ratified, accepted, confirmed and will be inviolably observed.

In witness whereof, the present Act is issued to which the Seal of the Republic of Poland has been affixed.

Done at Warsaw, this 26th Day of February, 1999

PRESIDENT
OF THE REPUBLIC OF POLAND
Aleksander Kwasniewski

CHAIRMAN OF THE COUNCIL OF MINISTERS
Jerzy Buzek

Source: Chancellery of the President of the Republic of Poland.

Part II. Military spending and armaments, 1998

7. Military expenditure

ELISABETH SKÖNS, AGNÈS COURADES ALLEBECK, EVAMARIA LOOSE-WEINTRAUB and PETTER STÅLENHEIM

I. Introduction

World military expenditure was still on a declining trend in 1998. The best estimates currently available indicate that it was reduced by one-third over the 10-year period 1989–98. Total financial resources devoted to military activities in 1998 amounted to roughly $745 billion.[1] This corresponds to 2.6 per cent of global gross national product (GNP) and $125 per capita.

The global trend in military expenditure of a one-third reduction in real terms during the 10-year period 1989–98 includes wide variation between regions, as shown in table 7.1. The sharpest reduction was in Central and Eastern Europe, the result entirely of developments in the Russian Federation. In Western Europe the 10-year reduction was only 14 per cent. Other regions which exhibited significant reductions of military expenditure are Africa and the Americas, with reductions of 25 and 30 per cent, respectively. In Asia and Oceania military expenditure has been growing continuously; this also applies to most individual countries in the region. Middle East military expenditure in the aftermath of the 1991 Persian Gulf War has been roughly constant and still takes a large share of economic resources there.

The reduction in 1998 was 3.5 per cent in real terms.[2] This was due primarily to the sharp reduction in Russian military expenditure, which fell dramatically in 1998, not because of government priorities but because of economic factors. Non-payment of funds budgeted and an inflation rate much higher than expected meant that actual military expenditure fell far short of that budgeted. Thus, while the budget for 1998 foresaw a reduction in military expenditure of 17 per cent in real terms, provisional figures for actual out-turn show the fall to have been as much as 55 per cent, from $24.9 billion in 1997 to $11.2 billion in 1998 (both figures in constant 1995 prices and at 1995 exchange rates).[3]

[1] This estimate in current dollars is derived from the figure of $696 billion in constant (1995) prices (table 7.1 and appendix 7A) by applying the US inflation rate between 1995 and 1998 (7.1% over 3 years).

[2] Military expenditure estimates for the most recent years are likely to change because the figures for these years are based on budgets adopted and actual expenditures often differ significantly from budget allocations. In addition, the deflators for the most recent year are estimates and therefore also subsequently revised. Thus, the SIPRI estimate for world military expenditures for 1997 has been revised from $704 billion in the *SIPRI Yearbook 1998* to $721 billion in the current volume.

[3] The exchange rate used for the Russian Federation is the purchasing power parity rate as estimated by the World Bank. The choice of method for conversion into dollars has a crucial impact on the international comparison of Russian military expenditure. Using the market exchange rate, Russian military expenditure in 1998 would be $4.9 billion at 1995 prices and exchange rates. Expressed in current prices,

Table 7.1. Regional military expenditure estimates, 1989–98

Figures are in US $b., at constant 1995 prices and exchange rates. Figures in italics are percentages. Figures do not always add up to totals because of the conventions of rounding.

Region[a]	1989	1990	1991	1992	1993	1994	1995	1996	1997	1998	% change 1989–98
Africa	12	11	10	10	10	10	9	9	9	[9]	*– 25*
North	3	2	3	3	3	3	3	3	3	4	*+ 29*
Sub-Saharan	9	9	8	7	7	6	6	6	6	[6]	*– 40*
Americas	406	385	338	358	342	325	310	293	295	283	*– 30*
North	385	369	325	342	325	307	289	273	271	260	*– 32*
Central	0.8	0.8	0.6	0.6	0.5	0.5	0.5	0.5	0.4	. .	*– 50*[b]
South	20	16	13	15	17	17	21	19	24	. .	*+ 18*[b]
Asia	104	106	109	115	117	117	121	126	130	131	*+ 27*
Central	. .	. .	. .	[1]	[1]	[1]	[1]	[1]	[1]	[1]	[*+ 9*]
East	92	95	98	103	103	104	107	112	115	116	*+ 25*
South	11	11	11	11	12	12	13	13	14	14	*+ 27*
Oceania	8	9	10	9	9	9	9	9	9	9	*+ 6*
Middle East	37	[46]	[64]	[45]	42	41	39	39	44	43	*+ 17*
Europe	483	447	. .	280	265	259	235	234	234	[220]	*– 55*
Central/East	[250]	[213]	. .	[59]	[52]	[51]	[36]	[34]	[35]	[21]	[*– 92*]
CIS	0	0	. .	[50]	[44]	[43]	[28]	[26]	[28]	[14]	[*– 76*][c]
West	232	234	231	221	213	208	199	201	199	199	– 14
World	**1 050**	**1 004**	**. .**	**817**	**785**	**762**	**723**	**709**	**721**	**[696]**	*– 34*
Change (%)	*– 1.8*	*– 4.3*	. .	. .	*– 3.9*	*– 2.9*	*– 5.1*	*– 1.9*	*1.7*	*– 3.5*	*– 4.5*

[a] Countries included in the geographical regions are listed in appendix 11A in this volume. Some countries are excluded because of lack of consistent time-series data. Africa excludes Angola, Congo (Brazzaville), Libya and Somalia; Asia excludes Afghanistan, Cambodia and Laos; Europe excludes Armenia and Yugoslavia; and the Middle East excludes Iraq and Qatar. World totals exclude all these countries.

[b] Change over the period 1989–97.

[c] Change over the period 1992–98.

Source: Appendix 7A, table 7A.1.

If Russia is subtracted from the world total, the decline in 1998 was only 1.6 per cent, that is, below the 10-year annual average decline of 4.5 per cent. Most of this decline took place in North America, primarily in the USA. Middle East military expenditure also declined in 1998, but this decline was preceded by an exceptionally high increase in 1997. In the other regions and subregions military expenditure did not decline in 1998 but stayed roughly constant (South Asia, Oceania and Western Europe) or even increased (North Africa and East Asia).

During the next few years world military expenditure is likely to begin growing again. The USA, which accounts for by far the greatest part of world

it translates into $11 billion at the exchange rate prevailing before the economic crisis but $3.5 billion at the rate prevailing at the end of 1998.

military expenditure (slightly more than one-third), is embarking on a six-year defence plan which represents a change into growth.

Chinese military expenditure is difficult to assess because of the lack of relevant information. There is broad consensus among China experts that the official defence budget does not cover all the military expenditure of China but there is disagreement as to the extent of the coverage and it is difficult to identify the expenditure which should be added. SIPRI has therefore commissioned a study on the problems involved in estimating Chinese military expenditure which constitutes appendix 7D. It presents the available information and uses it to construct a series of military expenditure estimates in local currency for China for the period 1989–98. These estimates are used as the new SIPRI series for military expenditure in China. This means that SIPRI's figures, which were previously based on the official Chinese figures, have been revised upwards by 60–85 per cent. The new estimates show that Chinese military expenditure amounted to 156 billion yuan in 1998, which corresponded to 1.9 per cent of gross domestic product (GDP) and, when converted to dollars at the market exchange rate, to $16.9 billion in constant 1995 dollars.

Military expenditure data involve a number of weaknesses which pose limits to their accuracy, reliability, consistency over time and international comparability, and estimates should therefore be used with caution. Limited transparency makes it difficult, and sometimes impossible, to know which items are covered in official defence expenditure figures. Sometimes it is known which items are excluded but not what they amount to, so that they cannot be added to the official figures. For some countries it is impossible to obtain any data. For this reason it has not been possible to make any regional military expenditure estimate for 1998 for Central and South America. There are also changes over time in national accounting practices, which may affect the coverage of the defence budget. The SIPRI data are adjusted to correct for such changes as far as possible in order to achieve consistency over time but this affects the accuracy for individual years.

The general problems involved in cross-country comparisons of economic data also apply to military expenditure. Conversion to a common currency unit by market exchange rates involves several sources of distortion. In theory, purchasing power parity (PPP) rates are more suitable for cross-country comparisons of the economic burden of military expenditure since PPPs are based on the comparative purchasing power of currencies on the domestic markets. In practice, however, PPPs are not yet sufficiently developed for all countries for this purpose. Therefore, for the SIPRI data, PPPs are used only for the countries in economic transition, for which the problem of using market exchange rates is considered particularly serious. Appendix 7C includes a description of PPPs and a table comparing military expenditures converted to dollars using PPPs and market exchange rates for a selection of countries.

Military expenditure data for Central Asia are particularly uncertain for several reasons: their coverage is not known, the costs of the military are not based on market prices, and there are wide margins of error for these countries' economic indicators, which are used in converting their military expenditure to dollars and estimating the economic burden. SIPRI provides data based on the official data available for these countries, although these can only constitute very rough indicators of actual military expenditure.

This chapter presents the trends in military expenditure by region. The basic data on military expenditure are provided in appendix 7A and the sources and methods used in compiling them in appendix 7C. Appendix 7B presents NATO data on expenditures for military equipment. Appendix 7D is the commissioned study on the military expenditure of China.

II. Africa

On 16 April 1998, UN Secretary-General Kofi Annan called for a reduction in the military expenditure of African countries.[4] He asked African countries to commit themselves to a zero-growth policy for defence budgets for a period of 10 years and to agree to reduce their purchases of arms and munitions to below 1.5 per cent of GDP. Although the report recognized the right of states to provide for their own defence, it stressed that resources had to be rechannelled from military purposes to economic development.

With some exceptions, data on the arms procurement expenditure of African countries are not available and it is not possible to make a comprehensive list of those whose arms and munitions purchases exceed 1.5 per cent of GDP. As far as total defence budgets are concerned, a zero-growth policy does not seem unrealistic, since Africa as a region has experienced a long-term reduction in military expenditure during the past decade. The main factors behind this trend are poor economic conditions, budget constraints and the process of demilitarization in Southern Africa and more specifically in South Africa. However, as illustrated by events in 1998, levels of military expenditure can increase suddenly if conflict arises and cannot be resolved by peaceful means.

Conflict-related increases of military expenditure

Developments in Africa illustrate the diversion of resources from economic development to military purposes as a consequence of armed conflict. There are three major components in the economic burden of military activities in addition to official military expenditures as monitored by SIPRI: (*a*) hidden government military expenditure; (*b*) the diversion of national resources to finance non-government military activities; and (*c*) the additional costs of war. Algeria and Angola experienced continuing civil wars, a border conflict between Ethiopia and Eritrea threatened to develop into full-scale war, and Central and Southern Africa experienced a process of regional remilitarization

[4] United Nations, The causes of conflict and the promotion of durable peace and sustainable development in Africa: report of the Secretary-General, UN document S/1998/318, 13 Apr. 1998, p. 6, URL <http://www.un.org/ecosocdev/geninfo/afrec/sgreport/report.htm>.

as a result of the violent conflict which emerged following the establishment of the new regime of Laurent-Désiré Kabila in the Democratic Republic of Congo (DRC), formerly Zaire.

Algeria has one of the highest levels of military expenditure in Africa. During the past decade (1989–98) it has tripled its military expenditure in real terms. This increase is clearly not motivated by external threats. Algerian security concerns are mainly focused on domestic affairs and the fight against the Front Islamique du Salut (FIS) and the Groupe Islamique Armé (GIA). Military expenditure increased most significantly after January 1992, when the election was interrupted, the FIS dissolved and a state of emergency imposed. In 1995 election confirmed and legitimized the mandate of President Liamine Zeroual. However, his relationship to the military leadership still remains unclear. As long as the internal conflict continues at the same level, military expenditure cannot be expected to fall. In 1998 Algeria's defence budget accounted for 15 per cent of total recurrent expenditures and 3.9 per cent of GDP, a significant increase from 1991, when these shares were 9 and 1.2 per cent, respectively.[5]

Angola's economy continues to be severely affected by military activities and the civil war. Official military expenditure is very high. During the period 1995–97 it represented 11–19 per cent of GDP. In addition, there are expenditures for military purposes outside the official defence budget. At least one-third and as much as one-half of government revenues and expenditures are reportedly not accounted for in the official state budget, partly in order to conceal the real size of military expenditure.[6] Estimates made by the International Monetary Fund (IMF), incorporated in the SIPRI series, indicate that the share of military expenditure in GDP was probably as high as 35 per cent in 1994. Second, additional resources are also diverted by non-government military activities: the rebel movement União Nacional para a Independência Total de Angola (UNITA) funds its war effort by smuggling diamonds mined in areas under its control, using for military purposes resources potentially usable for social purposes. The UN Security Council has therefore banned any international purchases of Angolan diamonds not sanctioned by the government.[7] Third, in addition to the cost of military activities over the years, there are the other costs of the war. The costs of damage and lost production were estimated in 1992 at $35–40 billion for the period 1975–91.[8] This does not account for the social and human costs of displaced populations and war-caused injuries. Angola has one of the highest estimated numbers of amputees per capita in the world.[9] Its level of military expenditure is expected to remain

[5] 'Budget général de l'Etat pour 1998', *Journal Officiel de la République*, no. 89 (31 Dec. 1997), p. 38, and Economist Intelligence Unit, *Country Profile 1990/91, Algeria* (Economist Intelligence Unit: London: 1991), p. 34.

[6] Economist Intelligence Unit, *Country Report Angola*, 3rd quarter 1998, p. 17.

[7] UN Security Council Resolution 1173, 12 June 1998, URL <http://www.un.org:80/plweb-cgi/>.

[8] Embassy of the Republic of Angola, London, 'Economic memorandum on the Republic of Angola', 1992, p. 6.

[9] Estimated at 1 per 356 of the population in 1997. United Nations, 'Country report: Angola', URL <http://www.un.org/Depts/Landmine/country/angola.htm>.

high because of continued security concerns. Exploiting the instability across Angola's northern border in the DRC, UNITA has been able to delay final implementation of the 1994 Lusaka Protocol. Tension rose during 1998 and observers feared a return to full-scale war.

The military expenditures of both Eritrea and Ethiopia have been slowly increasing since the mid-1990s. A border clash in May 1998 quickly developed into an open conflict. Several attempts at mediation failed. As a consequence, both governments decided to increase their military budgets further. In 1998 military expenditure rose by 8 per cent in real terms in Ethiopia. Figures for Eritrea were not available for 1997 and 1998. However, it is known that Eritrea has imported weapons[10] and mobilized its largest force ever, estimated at 200 000 excluding the militia.[11] It is also likely that this is one reason for the expected rise in Eritrea's budget deficit in 1998.[12] Remittances from expatriates, the country's main foreign-exchange earners, increased from $200 million in 1997 to $300 million in 1998. The increase is claimed to be assistance to the war effort.[13] Eritrea had just succeeded in reducing its budget deficit from 18 per cent of GDP in 1996 to 4.2 per cent in 1997.[14]

The overthrow of the Mobutu regime in former Zaire in 1997 was supported militarily by several neighbouring countries—Angola, Rwanda and Uganda—partly motivated by their interest in undermining the strength of their respective rebel movements which had found sanctuary inside the DRC. During 1998 a new internal conflict emerged in the DRC, rooted in the conflict which had led to Mobutu's overthrow Angola, Namibia and Zimbabwe have emerged as Kabila's strongest supporters. Rwanda and Uganda, having previously supported Kabila, now back the various Congolese opposition movements. The war has also drawn in countries to the north, such as Chad.

The Kabila Government is believed to have spent up to 50 per cent of total government expenditure on defence in 1998. Considering that an estimated 40 per cent of government revenue probably escaped into secret budget accounts, the military expenditure was probably even higher.[15] In addition Kabila leased strategic mineral resources and oilfields, disregarding contractual arrangements with international oil companies, to those who supported his regime, including Angola, Namibia and Zimbabwe.[16] This represents a diversion of national resources for military purposes beyond what appears in official military expenditure data.

[10] See chapter 11, section II in this volume.

[11] Economist Intelligence Unit, *Country Report Eritrea*, 4th quarter 1998, p. 25.

[12] This was acknowledged by a senior government financial expert quoted in a Reuters report from Asmara on 22 June 1998, stating that 'the deficit could rise slightly due to the need to defend ourselves from foreign aggression'. Cited in Economist Intelligence Unit, *Country Report Eritrea*, 3rd quarter 1998, p. 29.

[13] Economist Intelligence Unit, *Country Report Eritrea*, 3rd quarter 1998, p. 29.

[14] Economist Intelligence Unit, *Country Report Eritrea*, 4th quarter 1998, p. 11.

[15] Economist Intelligence Unit, *Country Report Democratic Republic of Congo*, 3rd quarter 1998, p. 29.

[16] Economist Intelligence Unit, *Country Report Democratic Republic of Congo*, 4th quarter 1998, p. 23.

The turmoil in the DRC had a clear impact on the level of military expenditure in other countries in the region. In some cases, following a period of reductions, defence budgets received extra allocations, either on the basis of interference in the conflict or on the grounds of increased security concern. Zimbabwe is reported to have spent $1.3 million a day to finance operations in the DRC and Namibia adopted a supplementary budget of $30 million in 1998 to cover its military and humanitarian operations in the DRC.[17]

Military expenditure reductions in South Africa

Between 1989 and 1998 South Africa experienced a transition to democracy, its first democratic, non-racial elections in April 1994, the formulation of a new defence policy (the 1996 White Paper on Defence) and the restructuring of the South African National Defence Force (SANDF).[18] During the same period South Africa reduced its military expenditure by 58 per cent in real terms, the share of military expenditure in GDP from 4.1 to 1.6 per cent, and its share in total government expenditure from 15.6 per cent in 1989 to around 5 per cent in 1998.[19] The South African Government has formally linked disarmament and development in the Reconstruction and Development Programme (RDP). There has been an increase in the share of total expenditure going to social services from 43 per cent in 1985 to 54 per cent in financial year (FY) 1998/99 and this share is projected to reach 55.5 per cent by 2001/02.[20]

The South African Defence Review completed in 1998 adhered to this goal by declaring its support for the 'national imperative of channelling the financial resources of the state to the RDP' in order to address poverty and socio-economic inequality. The Defence Review therefore recommended that military force levels be limited to those needed for an 'affordable peace-time force' and, in the absence of any foreseeable external military threat, that no wartime operations of the SANDF be provided for in the defence budget.[21]

However, there are indications that the reductions in the South African defence budget have come to an end because of the difficulties of combining a

[17] 'DRC allies meet to discuss cost of war', Johannesburg SAfm Radio Network, 21 Oct. 1998, in Foreign Broadcast Information Service, *Daily Report–Sub-Saharan Africa (FBIS-AFR)*, FBIS-AFR-98-294, 22 Oct. 1998; 'Namibian Finance Minister predicts economic "plunge"', SAPA, 23 Sep. 1998, in FBIS-AFR-98-266, 24 Sep. 1998; and 'Namibia: army spends $30 million on DR Congo operation', Namibian Broadcasting Corporation Network (Windhoek), 28 Oct. 1998, in FBIS-AFR-98-301, 30 Oct. 1998.

[18] For the development of South African military expenditure and arms production during the period 1989–97, see Batchelor, P. and Willett, S., SIPRI, *Disarmament and Defence Industrial Adjustment in South Africa* (Oxford University Press: Oxford, 1998).

[19] South African Department of Defence, 'Defence budget vote', *Bulletin of the Department of Defence*, no. 28/1998 (26 May 1998), URL <http://www.mil.za/Media/Bulletins/26may98.htm>.

[20] South African Government, 'Poverty and inequality in South Africa', Report prepared for the Office of the Executive Deputy President and the Inter-Ministerial Committee for Poverty and Inequality, 13 May 1998, p. 10, URL<http://www.gcis.gov.zas97is.vts?action=View&VdkVgwKey=>; and South African Department of Finance, 'Medium-term budget policy statement 98: the medium-term expenditure framework', URL<http://www.finance.gov.za/bo/mtbps_98/chap06.htm>, p. 3.

[21] South African Department of Defence, 'Key concepts underpinning the Defence Review', in 'South African defence review 1998', p. 4, URL<http://www.mil.za/Secretariat/Main%20 Review.htm>.

high share of personnel costs with the requirements for equipment modernization, as defined in the Defence Review.[22] Personnel costs still absorb 57 per cent of the 1998/99 defence budget, up from 39 per cent in 1995/96.[23] This is primarily the result of the integration process in the SANDF, which started in 1994 and was completed in 1998.[24] According to the Defence Review, the size of the SANDF, currently around 93 000 personnel including 20 000 civilians, is planned to be reduced to 70 000 by the year 2001.[25] The challenge is to respond to political demands for a force that is racially representative while retaining qualified personnel. The lower ranks of the SANDF are largely black and the senior ranks largely white.[26] The high proportion of the military budget allocated to personnel costs means a limited amount is available for weapon acquisitions, which have shrunk from 35 per cent of military expenditure in 1991 to less than 10 per cent in 1998.[27] The objective is a redistribution of military expenditure by the year 2001 to 40 per cent for personnel, 30 per cent for operations and maintenance and 30 per cent for arms procurement.[28]

In November 1998 the South African Government announced plans for major purchases of military equipment from a number of 'preferred suppliers', including Germany, Italy, Sweden and the UK. The cost of the equipment, which includes military aircraft, helicopters, naval ships and submarines, is estimated at 30 billion rand,[29] much higher than the original estimate presented in 1997 of 10 billion rand for the entire modernization programme for the SANDF.[30] Offsets, in the form of investment and counter-purchases, are set to play a major role in the modernization programme. While South Africa, according to its defence industrial participation policy from 1997, demanded 100 per cent offsets divided 50 : 50 between the defence and civil sectors, some of the European suppliers have offered offset rates of 200 per cent.[31]

In the face of public concerns and criticism from opposition politicians, the government has stated that the SANDF's modernization programme would be carried out 'without putting a strain on the budget and in a way that will bene-

[22] *South African Defence Review 1998* (note 21), chapter 8, option 1: Recommended growth: core force design, URL<http://www.mil.za/DoD/Secretariat/Defence%20 Review.htm>.

[23] *South African Defence Review 1998* (note 21), Conclusion, Table on budget allocation category, p. 4, URL<http://www.mil.za/DoD/Secretariat/Defence%20Review.htm>.

[24] Soldiers of Umkhonto we Sizwe (MK, 'Spear of the Nation'—the former armed wing of the African National Congress, ANC) and the Azanian People's Liberation Army (APLA—the armed branch of the Pan-Africanist Congress) were integrated into the SANDF.

[25] 'Defence budget vote' (note 19); and *South African Defence Review 1998* (note 21).

[26] Of the full-time force, 70% are black and 30% white, while 30% of officers are black. South African Department of Defence, 'Accelerating transformation, Address by the Minister of Defence, J. Modise MP, on the cccasion of the defence budget vote, National Assembly, 26 May 1998', URL<http://www.mil.za/DoD/Secretariat/address.htm>.

[27] South African Department of Defence, 'Accelerating transformation, Address by the Minister of Defence, Mr J. Modise MP, on the occasion of the defence budget vote, National Assembly, 26 May 1998', URL <http://www.mil.za/DoD/Secretariat/address.htm>.

[28] South African Department of Defence (note 22).

[29] 'Paper comments on country's R30 billion arms deal', *Johannesburg Beeld*, 20 Nov. 1998, in FBIS-AFR-98-324, 23 Nov. 1998.

[30] 'South Africa arms bidders move to final round', *Defense News*, 17–23 Aug. 1998, pp. 3–20.

[31] Campbell, K., 'South Africa's arms packages: the latest twists', *Military Technology*, no. 4 (1998), p. 12; 'South Africa arms bidders move to final round' (note 30), p. 3; and 'South African equipment decision by mid-year', *Jane's Defence Weekly*, 18 Feb. 1998, p. 3.

fit the economy' and estimated that the procurement package would generate investment in South Africa worth 110 billion rand over 17 years and create 65 000 jobs over seven years.[32] As 8 billion rand of the total cost of 30 billion rand will be financed outside the defence budget,[33] the remaining 22 billion rand will then have to be funded within the limits of the Medium-Term Expenditure Framework (MTEF). In order not to burden the defence budget before 2002, the government is seeking a three-year payment holiday from the armament suppliers.[34] According to the MTEF, defence and intelligence expenditure is projected to remain constant in real terms between FYs 1998/99 and 2001/02, thus falling from 7.5 per cent of total government expenditure (excluding interest payments) in 1997/98 to 6.6 per cent in 2000/01.[35] Although the defence budget adopted for 1999/2000 declined in real terms by nearly 3 per cent over the previous year, the Special Defence Account (SDA), which is used to fund armaments purchases, increased by 8 per cent in real terms.[36]

III. The Americas

The 30 per cent reduction in military expenditure in the Americas over the 10-year period 1989–98 is due primarily to the reduction in US military expenditure, which accounts for 92 per cent of the regional total. However, the declining trend has been even sharper in *Central America*, where regional military expenditure was halved over the nine years 1989–97. Since the beginning of the 1990s, great advances have been made in war termination, reduction of foreign military involvement, democratization and economic stabilization in the region as a whole. However, the cessation of hostilities and demilitarization of the conflicts is only the first stage in the transformation, and most of the region's economies have experienced only modest recoveries. Extreme economic inequalities, underemployment and rural landlessness remain. This, in combination with the natural disaster that swept the region in 1998, continues to threaten social peace.

Military expenditure in *South America* rose between 1991 and 1997, although estimates are uncertain because of rapid inflation and changes of currency in several countries. It rose in Argentina, Brazil and Colombia; Venezuela, however, has cut its military expenditure since 1993. The trend for 1998 is difficult to discern because of scarcity of data. Brazil, the largest spender in the region, increased its military expenditure by 40 per cent during

[32] South African Department of Defence, 'Benefits of the defence acquisition package', *Bulletin of the Department of Defence*, no. 90/1998 (26 Nov. 1998), URL<hhtp://www.mil.za/Media/Bulletins/26november98.htm>.

[33] Batchelor, P., 'Guns or butter? The SANDF's R30 billion weapons procurement package', *NGO Matters*, vol. 3, no. 11 (Nov. 1998).

[34] Batchelor, P., 'The 1999 defence budget: more money for arms?', *Sunday Independent* (Johannesburg), 21 Feb. 1999.

[35] South African Department of Finance (note 20), p. 3.

[36] Batchelor (note 34).

the two years 1997–98, much of the increase being for military pensions. Military expenditure in Argentina and Chile declined in 1998.

With all governments of the region in civilian hands, much remains to be done in reforming the armed forces. The costs of pay and pensions still seem to be disproportionately high. The Brazilian Army has been called on to play a more active role in opposing urban violence and drug-trafficking.[37] New duties for the armed forces in other countries in the region include support of the civil authorities in combating organized crime, in many cases drug-related, as well as natural resource protection and peacekeeping operations.

Positive developments in the security environment in the region may affect future military expenditure trends. Two territorial disputes were settled during 1998: between Argentina and Chile over the southern ice fields (Campos de Hielo Sur/Hielos Continentales)[38] and between Ecuador and Peru over the demarcation of a 50-mile strip of border in the Andes highland jungle.[39] Ecuador and Peru are now looking for international funding for a 10-year $3 billion border development plan. It envisages building roads between the two countries and jointly developing irrigation and oil and mineral resources. Ecuador has pledged to cut its armed forces considerably and turn a significant part of them into policemen, and the Peruvian President, Alberto Fujimori, has pledged cuts in arms procurement.[40]

Latin America is a region with little transparency in military expenditure. A reporting lag of two years or more for the majority of countries makes accurate estimates of military expenditure difficult. Disaggregated data are almost non-existent. Activities to improve the situation are encouraged within the Organization of American States (OAS), which at a regional conference in El Salvador in February 1998 adopted the Declaration of San Salvador on Confidence- and Security-Building Measures, which among other measures recommended 'studies for establishing a common methodology in order to facilitate the comparison of military expenditure in the region'.[41]

The United States

US military expenditure is returning to growth after a declining trend since 1987.[42] The FY 1999 budget represented an increase in real terms over the

[37] Economist Intelligence Unit, *Country Profile 1997/98 Brazil* (Economist Intelligence Unit: London: 1997), pp. 11–12.

[38] An accord was signed in Buenos Aires on 16 Dec. 1998. 'Argentina and Chile agree to settle their last territorial dispute' (Southern Cone Report), *Latin American Regional Reports,* vol. 10 (22 Dec. 1998), p. 1.

[39] The accord was signed in Brasilia on 26 Oct. 1998. 'Peace agreement with Ecuador', *Keesing's Record of World Events*, vol. 44, no. 10 (Oct. 1998), pp. 42547–68.

[40] 'Peru, Ecuador vow to end arms race', *Interavia Air Letter,* no. 14 176 (10 Feb. 1999), p. 5.

[41] Organization of American States Conference on Confidence-and Security-Building Measures (CSBMs), San Salvador, 25–27 Feb. 1998.

[42] The year in which the decline started differs depending on data source. SIPRI data, which are based on US data as reported to NATO, show a decline in real terms since 1987. According to official US data, 1987 was the peak year for outlays on national defence, while 1985 was the peak year for budget authority for national defence. Kosiak, S. M., Center for Strategic and Budgetary Assessments, *Analysis*

previous year, not in its original version, but as a result of the supplementary budget bill adopted in October 1998. The proposed defence budget for FY 2000 represented a slight decline over the previous year but included a long-term increase in military expenditure for the next six-year period, which was officially announced as the first increase in the US defence budget since the end of the cold war.

The defence budget for FY 1999

The budget for FY 1999 (beginning 1 October 1998) was presented in February 1998 but not adopted until late September 1998.[43] Only a few weeks later, in October 1998, a supplementary bill for FY 1999 was also adopted. The budget request for national defence[44] represented a reduction of 0.9 per cent in budget authority and 1.4 per cent in outlays (table 7.2).[45] The planned trend for total national defence for the five-year period 1999–2003 (the Future Years Defense Program, FYDP) was relatively constant up to and including FY 2002, ending with a slight increase in FY 2003 (table 7.2.).[46]

The size of the budget and the budget plan were to a significant extent determined by economic policy, in particular by the fiscal policy of reducing government debt in compliance with the balanced budget act of 1997, under which the federal budget is scheduled to come close to balance by FY 2002.[47]

Attempts by Congress to add funding which was not requested in the president's budget proposal were not successful to any great extent.[48] The budget as adopted in September 1998 included virtually unchanged budget authority for 'national defence', at $270.5 billion, while the Department of Defense (DOD)

of the Fiscal Year Defense Budget Request (Center for Strategic and Budgetary Asseessments: Washington, DC, Mar. 1998), tables 2 (budget authority) and 3 (outlays).

43 The FY 1999 defence appropriation bill was approved on 28 Sep. by the House and on 30 Sep. by the Senate. It covers almost the entire US national defence budget ($250.8 billion out of a total of $270.6 billion for FY 1999). The remainder is included in 5 other appropriations bills—for military construction, energy and water development, civil defence activities, the Departments of Commerce, Justice and State, and defence-related activities of the coastguard. The US federal budget process for defence is described in Daggett, S., *Appropriations for FY1999: Defense*, CRS Report for Congress (Library of Congress, Congressional Research Service: Washington, DC, updated 2 Oct. 1998).

44 The title 'National defense' includes Department of Defence (DOD) and defence items of other departments, primarily nuclear weapons of the Department of Energy (DOE).

45 'Budget authority' means the legal authority to obligate funds. The US congressional budget process includes a number of steps. The 'authorization' bill provides the general authorization for each programme and recommends its funding level. On this basis, the 'appropriation' bill decides the allocation of funds and grants the government 'budget authority' to enter into 'obligations' (binding procurement agreements with suppliers), which are later paid in 'outlays' (expenditure). Thus, authorizations, appropriations and budget authority have an impact on outlays in subsequent years, while outlays refer to expenditure in the given year.

46 US Department of Defense, *Annual Report of the Secretary of Defense to the President and the Congress, 1998* (US Government Printing Office: Washington, DC, 1998).

47 US Congressional Budget Office, *An Analysis of the President's Budgetary Proposals for Fiscal Year 1999* (US Government Printing Office: Washington, DC, Mar. 1998); and US Congressional Budget Office, *The Economic and Budget Outlook* (US Government Printing Office: Washington, DC, Sep. 1998).

48 The US Congress includes every year a substantial amount of funding which was not requested by the president, which is damaging when it fails to take account of future spending that it will generate. US Department of Defense, *Annual Report 1998* (note 46), p. 187.

Table 7.2. The US defence budget: budget authority and outlays, FYs 1985–2003

Figures are in US $b., in constant (FY 1999) prices. Figures in italics are percentages. Figures do not add up because of the conventions of rounding.

	Actual FY98	Request FY99	Planned FY00	FY01	FY02	FY03	% change FY85–98	% change FY98–03
Budget authority								
Personnel	71.7	70.8	68.8	67.7	67.1	66.7	*– 30*	*– 7.0*
O&M	96.1	94.8	93.8	93.6	93.2	93.1	*– 17*	*– 3.1*
Procurement	45.5	48.7	53.2	59.3	57.6	59.3	*– 67*	*+ 30.3*
RDT&E	37.2	36.1	33.3	31.8	31.7	31.9	*– 18*	*– 14.2*
Construction	5.2	4.3	4.8	4.2	3.5	3.7	*– 36*	*– 28.8*
Family housing	3.9	3.5	3.8	3.8	3.7	3.9	*– 6*	*± 0.0*
Total DOD	260.1	257.3	257.2	259.5	256.7	259.6	*– 38*	*– 0.2*
National defence	**273.0**	**270.6**	**270.0**	**271.6**	**268.7**	**271.6**	***– 36***	***– 0.5***
Annual change	*– 3.2*	*– 0.9*	*– 0.2*	*+ 0.6*	*– 1.1*	*+ 1.1*	. .	. .
Outlays								
National defence	269.4	265.5	263.0	258.3	254.9	264.6	*– 0.3*	*– 1.8*
Annual change	*– 4.4*	*– 1.4*	*– 0.9*	*– 1.8*	*– 1.3*	*+ 3.8*	–	. .
Share of total budget	*15.8*	*15.3*	*15.1*	*14.7*	*14.6*	*14.8*	–	. .
Share of GDP	*3.2*	*3.1*	*3.0*	*2.9*	*2.8*	*2.8*	–	. .

Notes: On budget authority and outlays, see note 45. For the definition of national defence, see note 44. DOD = Department of Defense.

Sources: Daggett, S. and Tyszkiewicz, M., *Defense Budget for FY 1999: Data Summary*, CRS Report 98-155 (Library of Congress, Congressional Research Service: Washington, DC, 23 Feb. 1998), using data from US Office of Management and Budget, *Historical Tables: Budget of the US Govt, FY 1999*, Feb. 1988; and Kosiak, S. M., Center for Strategic and Budgetary Assessments, *Analysis of the Fiscal Year Defense Budget Request* (Center for Strategic and Budgetary Assessments: Washington, DC, Mar. 1998), appendix tables 2, 3, 4 and 10.

received $250.5 billion, that is, $7 billion less than proposed in the original budget.

Budget breakdown

An important element in the process of military expenditure reductions is the distribution of cuts between services and between functions. The decline in US military expenditure has been achieved mainly through cuts in the size of the military forces and by slowing down the pace of weapon modernization. The sharpest cuts have been in arms procurement, which declined by 67 per cent in real terms between FY 1985 and FY 1998,[49] while personnel expenditure was cut by 30 per cent (table 7.2). According to the Quadrennial Defense Review,[50] the number of active-duty military personnel is planned to fall from 2.2 million in FY 1987 to 1.4 million by FY 2003.

[49] NATO data on the trend in US expenditure on military equipment show a much slower reduction: by 34% between 1989 and 1998 (see appendix 7B) and by 38% since 1986.

[50] US Department of Defense, *Report of the Quadrennial Defense Review* (DOD: Washington, DC, May 1997).

Table 7.3. The US FY 2000 defence budget: budget authority, FY 1999–2005

Figures are in US $b., in constant (FY 2000) prices. Figures in italics are percentages. Figures do not add up because of the conventions of rounding.

	Actual 1999	Request 2000	Planned 2001	2002	2003	2004	2005	% change 1999–2005
Personnel	73.6	73.7	73.8	73.3	73.2	73.1	73.2	*– 0.5*
O&M	99.8	103.5	101.1	99.7	99.8	100.3	100.4	*+ 0.6*
Procurement	49.8	53.0	60.8	60.2	63.1	64.2	68.2	*+ 36.9*
RDT&E	37.3	34.4	33.7	33.5	32.6	32.3	30.9	*– 17.2*
Construction	5.2	2.3	7.0	4.0	4.0	4.1	4.3	*– 17.3*
Family housing	3.7	3.1	3.7	3.5	3.5	3.6	3.5	*– 5.4*
Total DOD	**268.6**	**267.2**	**279.3**	**274.3**	**277.1**	**277.8**	**280.4**	***+ 4.4***
Annual change		*– 0.5*	*4.5*	*– 1.8*	*1.0*	*0.2*	*0.9*	
National defence	282.5	280.8	293.1	287.7	290.2	290.5	292.7	*+ 3.6*
Annual change		*– 0.6*	*4.4*	*– 1.8*	*0.9*	*0.1*	*0.8*	

Source: US Center for Strategic and Budgetary Assessments, 'President proposes modest near-term and major long-term plus-up for defense', 1 Feb. 1999, update compiled by S. Kosiak and E. Heeter.

The defence budget proposal for FY 1999 showed a profound change in trend for procurement expenditure: it was set to grow by 30 per cent in real terms between FY 1998 and FY 2003, while most other functions continued to show reductions in real terms (table 7.2). The supplementary budget for FY 1999, adopted in October 1998, included an unusually large amount for defence (a total of $8.3 billion[51]) and resulted in the first real increase in military expenditure in 12 years. The size of the increase was motivated mainly by the need to improve the deteriorating readiness of the armed forces. The structure of the supplementary allocations was unexpected, with roughly $1 billion for ballistic missile defence, about the same amount as for military readiness.

The defence budget for FY 2000

The defence budget requested for FY 2000, presented on 1 February 1999, was for $267.2 billion (in current prices) in budget authority ($260.8 billion in outlays) for the DOD and $280.8 billion for total national defence, including non-DOD military expenditure (primarily of the Department of Energy).[52] The proposed budget represented a nominal increase of 1.7 per cent for national defence over the previous year but a reduction of 0.6 per cent in real terms (table 7.3).[53] However, during the next five fiscal years there will be a change

[51] *Defense News*, 26 Oct.–1 Nov. 1998, p. 16.

[52] US Department of Defense, Office of the Assistant Secretary of Defense (Public Affairs), 'Department of Defense budget for FY 2000', Press release no. 032-99, Washington, DC, 1 Feb. 1999, URL <http://www.defenselink.mil/news>.

[53] US Center for Strategic and Budgetary Assessments, 'President proposes modest near-term and major long-term plus-up for defense', 1 Feb. 1999, update compiled by S. Kosiak and E. Heeter. The FY 2000 budget request was announced as an increase of $12.6 billion. However, this was in comparison

in trend from decline to growth. Proposed budget authority for national defence is planned to increase by 3.6 per cent in real terms between FY 1999 and FY 2005. This represents, in the words of the DOD, 'the first sustained long-term increase in defence funding since the end of the cold war'.[54]

The increase addresses a 'triad' of concerns: (*a*) pay and retirement of military personnel; (*b*) improving military readiness; and (*c*) modernization of military equipment.[55] It included provision for pay increases of 4.4 per cent, effective from 1 January 2000, major improvements in retirement benefits for military personnel, and significant increases for arms procurement for FY 2000 and the next five years—an increase of $53 billion in budget authority for FY 2000 (almost 7 per cent in real terms) and a further 15 per cent increase in FY 2001.[56] A major part of the additional funds will go to missile defence.

Missile defence

In January 1999 the US Secretary of Defense, William S. Cohen, announced a major expansion of US missile defence programmes. These are the National Missile Defence (NMD) programme for the protection of US territory against long-range missiles and the Theater Missile Defense (TMD) programme for the protection of US forces abroad and allied forces and nations against short- and intermediate-range missiles.[57] In recent years Congress has initiated legislation to promote missile defence programmes, but these have been vetoed by the president. The new announcement thus represented a shift in the priorities of the US Administration.

The FY 2000 budget request included an increase of $6.6 billion in funding for NMD compared with FY 1999 and funding will have increased threefold to $10.5 billion by FY 2005. This was motivated by the perception of the existence of 'a growing threat and that it will pose a danger not only to our troops overseas, but also to Americans here at home'.[58] In particular, reference was made to the test by North Korea on 31 August 1998 of a three-stage ballistic missile. The administration's policy has been the '3 plus 3' strategy: to develop NMD technology over a period of three years up to and including the year 2000 sufficiently to allow a system to be deployed three years later, by 2003, if a decision is made to do so. A deployment readiness review is scheduled for the summer of 2000 in order to assess the progress of the NMD programme for a deployment decision.

not with the previous year but with the planned allocation for FY 2000 under the defence plan of the previous year.

[54] 'Department of Defense Budget for FY 2000' (note 52).

[55] Garamone, J., 'New budget boosts pay, readiness, modernization', American Forces Press Service, 22 Jan. 1999, URL <http://www.defenselink.mil/news/>.

[56] 'Department of Defense Budget for FY 2000' (note 52).

[57] Daggett, S., and Shuey, R., *National Missile Defense: Status of the Debate*, CRS Report 97-862 F (Library of Congress, Congressional Research Service: Washington, DC, updated 18 Sep. 1998). On NMD and TMD, see also chapter 12, section VII, in this volume.

[58] US Department of Defense, 'Cohen announces plan to augment missile defense programs', DOD News release, 20 Jan. 1999, URL <http://www.defenselink.mil/news/>.

As regards TMD, the FY 2000 budget included funding for continued flight-testing of the Theater High-Altitude Area Defense (THAAD) programme and increased funding for the Navy Theater-Wide (NTW) programme in order to allow accelerated deployment from the dates currently planned of 2008 and 2010, respectively. In addition, the DOD plans include a proposal to restructure the Medium Extended Air Defense System (MEADS) programme in collaboration with German and Italian partners.

IV. Asia

Military expenditure in Asia has continued to grow after the end of the cold war when the trend has been declining in most other regions. In South Asia this is related to the conflict between India and Pakistan,[59] which was intensified during 1998 by the nuclear testing in both countries,[60] and to the civil war in Sri Lanka. While there are also long-term latent conflicts in East Asia—primarily on the Korean peninsula and between China and Taiwan—and these have influenced the trend in and level of East Asian military expenditure, the rapid economic growth in most East Asian countries has also been a determinant. The financial crisis in 1997 was therefore expected to have a strong impact on East Asian military expenditures.

Military expenditures in the countries of Central Asia are difficult to assess, since the coverage of their defence budgets is unknown and since all economic statistics are uncertain for these countries.

South Asia

India and Pakistan account for more than 90 per cent of military expenditure in the region. In India military expenditure has been on a rising trend since 1992, while in Pakistan the trend was rising until 1993 and has since declined somewhat. In both countries the economic burden of military activities, as measured by their share in GDP and in total government expenditure, is high but has not increased during the most recent 10-year period (table 7.4).

The series of nuclear tests carried out by India and Pakistan during May 1998 were followed by announcements in both countries of further increases in their military budgets. Both countries already divert significant economic resources to military purposes and a significant proportion of their populations lives in poverty.[61] The sanctions imposed by several countries which provide development assistance are likely to impose an additional burden—although

[59] See appendix 1D in this volume.

[60] See chapter 9 in this volume.

[61] India and Pakistan are both classified as countries with low human development according to the United Nations Development Programme (UNDP) human development index (HDI), which is a combined index of GDP per capita, life expectancy and education. Of 175 countries classified, India and Pakistan ranked 139 and 138, respectively. *Human Development Report 1998* (Oxford University Press: Oxford and New York, 1998), Indicators, table 1.

Table 7.4. South Asia: military expenditure, 1989–98

Figures are in US $b., at constant 1995 prices and exchange rates. Figures in italics are percentages.

	1989	1990	1991	1992	1993	1994	1995	1996	1997	1998	% change 1988–98
Military expenditure											
South Asia	11.3	11.4	11.2	11.2	12.2	12.1	12.6	12.9	13.7	14.3	*27*
India	7.8	7.6	7.1	6.8	7.7	7.8	8.0	8.2	9.1	9.8	*27*
Pakistan	3.0	3.1	3.4	3.6	3.6	3.4	3.4	3.6	3.4	3.3	*11*
Share of GDP											
India	*3.1*	*2.8*	*2.6*	*2.4*	*2.5*	*2.4*	*2.3*	*2.3*	*2.4*	*2.5*	
Pakistan	*6.6*	*6.8*	*6.8*	*6.7*	*6.8*	*6.2*	*5.8*	*5.8*	*5.3*	*4.9*	
Share of CGE											
India	*13.4*	*12.9*	*12.7*	*12.1*	*12.6*	*12.3*	*12.1*	*11.7*	..	*[13.0]*	
Pakistan	*24.5*	*26.8*	*27.0*	*25.5*	*25.0*	*23.8*	*23.9*	..	*[24.0]*	*[24.0]*	

CGE = central government expenditure.

Source: Appendix 7A and the SIPRI military expenditure database.

much less than originally forecast[62]—which also can be seen as the cost of military activities, although not included in the military expenditure measure.

India's defence budget for FY 1998/99 was presented on 1 June 1998, immediately after its series of nuclear tests. It had been raised compared to the level planned and this was motivated by the tests. It represented an increase of 14 per cent over the revised estimates for the previous year in cash terms, roughly 7 per cent in real terms. It also represented an increased economic burden in relation both to GDP and to the total government budget. Still, it was considered inadequate and Finance Minister Yashwant Sinha said in his budget speech that he would consider further increases during the course of the year.[63] The navy received a particular boost of 25 per cent, with additional funds promised in the supplementary budget,[64] and a major modernization programme for the navy was reported in August 1998, amounting to around $2.5 billion.[65] The costs of relocating the Western Fleet to a new base over the next 10-year period are estimated at a further $3.1 billion.[66] This is in the context of fears that India is running into a severe economic crisis, primarily

[62] US economic sanctions, which would be the most serious, have been estimated to cost India around $2.5 billion per year. 'Indian daily optimistic over US sanctions', *Calcutta Telegraph*, 22 June 1998, p. 8, in Foreign Broadcast Information Service, *Daily Report–Near East and South Asia (FBIS-NES)*, FBIS-NES-98-174, 23 June 1998. On the imposition of sanctions, see also chapter 15, section III, in this volume.

[63] 'Defence allocation pegged at 41 000 cr: up by 14 per cent', *Times of India*, 2 June 1998.

[64] Roy-Chaudhury, R., 'Indian naval expenditure in the 1990s', *Strategic Analysis*, vol. 22, no. 5 (Aug. 1998), pp. 675–90. This article provides an account of the trend in India's naval expenditure and its general context.

[65] 'Indian Navy moves forward on modernization program', *Defense News*, 17–23 Aug. 1998, p. 7.

[66] 'Indian Navy plans $3b relocation', *Jane's Defence Weekly*, 30 Sep. 1998, p. 19.

because of excessive government expenditure in a situation when one-half of government revenues is already spent on servicing earlier loans.[67]

The Pakistani budget for FY 1998/99, adopted on 25 June 1998, included an increase in the defence budget by 6 per cent compared to the previous year, or around 0.2 per cent in real terms. It meant an increased share in total government expenditure, which was cut significantly with the explicit purpose of counteracting the effects of economic sanctions following the nuclear testing. Pakistan is vulnerable to sanctions because of its weak economy. More than one-half of the total government budget and two-thirds of government current expenditure is devoted to defence and debt servicing, and the country depends to a great extent on foreign economic aid. The measures introduced in June to counter the adverse economic impact of sanctions included cutting government current expenditure by half and substituting imports with domestic production. The government is also seeking economic aid from Kuwait, Saudi Arabia and the United Arab Emirates.[68]

The sanctions initially announced on Pakistan included the suspension of $1.5 billion in new loans from the IMF, which had been approved in October 1997 for the period 1998–2000, loans from the World Bank of $1.5 billion, and US aid, loans and loan guarantees to the amount of $2.9 billion. By January 1999 the IMF and the World Bank had resumed their financial assistance and the Paris Club of creditor nations had approved the rescheduling of its $3.3 billion foreign debt in return for a Pakistani promise to sign the 1996 Comprehensive Nuclear Test-Ban Treaty before September 1999 and to halt production of fissile material.[69]

East Asia

Military expenditure in East Asia did not decline in 1998, as could have been expected after the financial crisis of 1997–98, but continued to increase, although at a slower rate. This increase was the result of the trends in military expenditure primarily in China,[70] but also in Singapore and Taiwan, which were not affected by the crisis to any great extent. In the five countries most severely affected by the financial crisis—Indonesia, South Korea, Malaysia, the Philippines and Thailand—combined military expenditure fell by almost 7 per cent in real terms in 1998 (table 7.5). Of these only the Philippines did not reduce its defence budget in 1998. Even so, these reductions were not as

[67] 'Dismal state of Indian economy viewed', *Calcutta Anandabazaar Patrike*, 12 Jan. 1999, p. 4 (in Bengali), in FBIS-NES-99-023, 23 Jan. 1999.

[68] 'Pakistan's economy too weak to stand many sanctions', *Financial Times*, 12 June 1998, p. 4.

[69] Islamabad Radio Pakistan Network (in English), 31 Jan. 1999, in 'Pakistan: growing world confidence on Pakistan's economy viewed', in FBIS-NES-99-032, 1 Feb 1999; and 'After getting the loan?' (editorial), *Karachi Jasarat*, 23 Jan. 1999, p. 4 (in Urdu), in FBIS-NES-99-027, 27 Jan. 1999. See also chapter 12, section II in this volume.

[70] See appendix 7D in this volume.

Table 7.5. East Asia: military expenditure, 1989–98

Figures in US$ are at constant 1995 prices and exchange rates. Figures in italics are percentages.

	1989	1990	1991	1992	1993	1994	1995	1996	1997	1998
East Asia ($b.)	**92.4**	**95.0**	**97.8**	**103**	**103**	**104**	**107**	**112**	**115**	**116**
Military expenditure ($m.)										
Indonesia	1 944	2 150	2 187	2 354	2 261	2 499	2 513	2 772	3 633	2 767
Korea, South	11 253	11 666	12 638	13 130	13 002	13 625	14 424	15 481	15 564	(15 042)
Malaysia	1 399	1 502	2 044	2 032	2 159	2 339	2 444	2 349	2 322	[2 000]
Philippines	1 158	938	854	861	969	1 026	1 187	1 158	[1 363]	[1 580]
Thailand	2 402	2 471	2 656	2 987	3 279	3 311	3 561	3 552	3 500	3 234
Total	**18 156**	**18 727**	**20 379**	**21 364**	**21 670**	**22 800**	**24 129**	**25 312**	**26 383**	**24 623**
Share of GDP										
Indonesia	*1.6*	*1.6*	*1.4*	*1.4*	*1.3*	*1.3*	*1.2*	*1.3*	*1.5*	*1.1*
Korea, S.	*4.0*	*3.7*	*3.7*	*3.6*	*3.4*	*3.3*	*3.2*	*3.2*	*3.1*	*(3.2)*
Malaysia	*2.7*	*2.6*	*3.3*	*3.0*	*3.0*	*2.9*	*2.8*	*2.4*	*2.2*	*[2.1]*
Philippines	*1.7*	*1.4*	*1.3*	*1.3*	*1.4*	*1.4*	*1.6*	*1.5*	*[1.6]*	*[1.9]*
Thailand	*2.4*	*2.2*	*2.2*	*2.3*	*2.3*	*2.2*	*2.1*	*2.0*	*2.0*	*2.0*
Share of CGE										
Indonesia	*8.1*	*8.2*	*8.5*	*7.8*	*7.8*	*8.3*	*8.5*	*8.6*	*9.4*	. .
Korea, South	*24.9*	*23.0*	*22.2*	*21.4*	*20.1*	*18.7*	*17.9*	*17.3*	*16.7*	. .
Malaysia	*9.3*	*8.7*	*11.4*	*10.5*	*11.6*	*12.2*	*12.5*	*11.1*	*11.1*	. .
Philippines	*9.6*	*7.0*	*6.6*	*6.6*	*7.8*	*7.8*	*8.9*	*8.0*	*[8.6]*	*[10.8]*
Thailand	*16.8*	*15.9*	*15.2*	*15.3*	*14.6*	*13.2*	*13.5*	*12.4*	*10.8*	. .
Military expenditure in local currency, current prices, calendar year										
Indonesia (b. rupiahs)	2 648	3 156	3 512	4 066	4 281	5 135	5 562	6 734	9 401	9 740
Korea, S. (b. won)	5 921	6 665	7 892	8 709	9 040	10 057	11 125	12 533	13 160	(13 800)
Malaysia (m. ringgits)	2 761	3 043	4 323	4 500	4 951	5 565	6 121	6 091	6 183	[5 700]
Philippines (b. pesos)	15.9	14.7	15.9	17.5	21.1	24.4	30.5	32.3	[39.9]	[50.9]
Thailand (b. baht)	44.8	48.8	55.5	65.0	73.7	78.3	89.0	94.0	97.8	98.5

Notes: CGE = central government expenditures as provided in International Monetary Fund, *Government Finance Statistics Yearbook* (annual) and for most countries updated in International Monetary Fund, *International Financial Statistics* (monthly).

Sources: Appendix 7A and the SIPRI military expenditure database.

heavy as had been expected and even reported,[71] and not as strong as the impact on employment, income distribution and poverty.[72]

The impact of the crisis on the East Asia countries' military expenditure, as expressed in local currency, in constant 1995 dollars or as a share of GDP, was relatively mild. There has not been a significant reduction in the economic burden of military expenditure. According to the preliminary estimates for 1998, the share of GDP spent on military activities declined only in Indonesia and Malaysia, stayed constant in Thailand and went up in South Korea and the Philippines. The effect on their arms imports because of the deterioration in exchange rates was much more significant.

The course of the purchasing power of the Philippine arms procurement programme is illustrative. In February 1995 the government authorized 331 billion pesos for a 15-year modernization programme for the armed forces. The dollar value of this programme was then $13.2 billion. By the end of 1998 it had been reduced to $8.5 billion.[73] In 1996 the modernization programme, as a result of economic constraints, was cut by one-half to 164.6 billion pesos, corresponding to $6.3 billion, but by the end of 1998 this had been reduced to $4.2 billion.[74] Thus, in terms of purchasing power, the arms imports programme has been cut by more than two-thirds.

The forced reductions in planned arms imports in all the countries affected have led to the cancellation and postponement of some planned or even decided arms imports, to concern about the altered balance of military strength in the region and to calls for increased defence budgets. Increases in expenditure have been decided in some of these countries. South Korea's defence budget for 1999 showed a slight decrease (by 0.36 per cent)[75] for the first time since the beginning of the Korean War 50 years ago, but in early 1999 the government announced a five-year defence plan under which military expenditure is set to increase at an average annual rate of 5–6 per cent between 1999 and 2004 in order to finance a major arms procurement programme, including a new surface-to-air missile system, attack helicopters, three destroyers and 60 fighter aircraft.[76] The reduction in Thailand's military expenditure continued in the budget for FY 1999 (starting 1 October 1998),[77]

[71] 'Regional defence budgets slashed', *Asia–Pacific Defence Reporter*, Apr./May 1998, pp. 12–14; and 'Asian military spending: a casualty of bad times', *International Herald Tribune*, 23 Oct. 1998, pp. 1, 4, predicting an 18% reduction in East Asia overall.

[72] Jong-Wha Lee and Changyong Rhee, *Social Impacts of the Asian Crisis: Policy Challenges and Lessons*, Human Development Report Occasional Paper no. 33, United Nations Development Programme (Oxford University Press: New York, Jan. 1999).

[73] See similar calculations in 'Philippines begins military modernization program', *Defense News*, 4–10 May 1998, p. 12.

[74] 'Currency woes force Philippines to rethink modernization plan', *Defense News*, 13–19 Oct. 1997; and 'Philippines may juggle modernization priorities', *Defense News*, 10–16 Aug. 1998, p. 4.

[75] 'South Korean budget proposal hits spending', *Jane's Defence Weekly*, 30 Sep. 1998, p. 6; and 'South Korea: ROK plans to freeze defense budget at this year's level', *Seoul Yonhap*, 27 Aug. 1998, in Foreign Broadcast Information Service, *Daily Report–East Asia (FBIS-EAS)*, FBIS-EAS-98-239, 27 Aug. 1998.

[76] 'More details on ROK's five-year defense plan, budget', *Korea Times*, 13 Feb. 1999, p. 1, in FBIS-EAS-1999-0212, 13 Feb. 1999; and 'Korea announces five-year defense program', 15 Feb. 1999, URL <http://defence-data.com/current/page 3766.htm>.

[77] The reduction was 4.4% in real terms. 'Thai budget cut', *Armed Forces Magazine*, July 1998.

but this will probably be the last year of cuts and the government has declared itself willing to provide supplementary allocations for defence during the year.[78] The Philippines' defence budget for 1998 increased by 19 per cent in real terms, according to its 1998 Defense Policy Paper, taking a larger share of GDP (1.9 per cent as compared with 1.6 per cent in 1997) and of central government expenditure (10.8 per cent in 1998 as compared with 8.6 per cent in 1997),[79] while the budget adopted for 1999 probably represents a fall in real terms (51.7 billion pesos were allocated for the Department of Defense).[80] Indonesia and Malaysia are the only countries which are not likely to increase their military expenditure in real terms in the near future.

Central Asia

The assessment of military expenditure in the five newly independent states of Kazakhstan, Kyrgyzstan, Tajikistan, Turkmenistan and Uzbekistan is a difficult matter. The coverage of their defence budgets is largely unknown and all economic statistics are uncertain for these countries. This section presents and discusses the available military expenditure estimates for the five countries.

Having inherited the military structures of the former Soviet Union, these states have large military entities not included under the budget head 'defence'. In most of them the border guard and the interior troops are not part of the ordinary military forces. In some this may be appropriate, but in most the equipment and training of the border guard and interior troops are such that they should be considered part of the military forces of the country. It is not always possible to assess whether different types of security forces in these countries should be defined as paramilitary forces, and thus included in military expenditure according to the SIPRI definition. Even when this can be done, it may not be possible to identify expenditures for these forces. It is not even clear whether they are domestically financed or paid for by Russia.[81] In some countries they are financed through the budget of the interior ministry rather than that of the defence ministry. Information about the financing of arms imports is even more scarce. For many of these countries it is not known if the cost of arms imports is included in their military expenditure.

The five states are all characterized by traditionalism, a strong leadership and state, collective rights and national consolidation. Although there are differences between them, their common cultural background and historical experience continue to play a significant role. By the autumn of 1995 all had

[78] 'Thai defence allowed to seek more budget for security', *Bangkok Post*, 2 Jan. 1999, in FBIS-EAS-99-005, 5 Jan. 1999.

[79] Philippines Department of National Defense, 'In defense of the Philippines: 1998 defense policy paper', Manila, 1998, p. 81.

[80] 'Estrada signs national budget for 1999', *Manila Bulletin* (Internet version in English), 31 Dec. 1998, in FBIS-EAS-98-365, 31 Dec. 1998.

[81] For an overview of bilateral agreements on military assistance between the Central Asian countries and Russia, see Jonson, L., *Russia and Central Asia: A New Web of Relations* (Royal Institute of International Affairs: London, 1998).

Table 7.6. Central Asia: military expenditure, 1995–98

Figures in italics are percentages. All figures are uncertain.

	1995	1996	1997	1998
Military expenditure (US $m.)[a]				
Kazakhstan	401	401	391	414
Kyrgyzstan	56	51	59	. .
Tajikistan	59	72	50	. .
Turkmenistan	148	143	216	255
Uzbekistan	294	369	. .	. .
Share of GDP				
Kazakhstan	*1.1*	*1.1*	*1.0*	*1.1*
Kyrgyzstan	*1.5*	*1.3*	*1.4*	. .
Tajikistan	*1.1*	*1.3*	*1.4*	. .
Turkmenistan	*1.4*	*2.1*	*4.6*	*4.5*
Uzbekistan	*1.1*	*1.2*	. .	. .
Share of government expenditure[b]				
Kazakhstan	*5.6*	*6.1*	*5.2*	*5.0*
Kyrgyzstan	*4.9*	*5.5*	7.3	. .
Tajikistan	*4.2*	*7.7*	*9.1*	. .
Turkmenistan	*10.0*	*12.5*	*15.6*	*16.1*
Uzbekistan	*2.9*	*3.1*	. .	. .
Military expenditure per capita (US $m.)[a]				
Kazakhstan	24	24	25	. .
Kyrgyzstan	12	11	13	. .
Tajikistan	10	12	8	. .
Turkmenistan	36	34	47	. .
Uzbekistan	13	16	. .	. .
Armed/paramilitary forces				
Kazakhstan	40 000	40 000	35 100	55 100
	34 500	34 500	34 500	34 500
Kyrgyzstan	7 000	7 000	12 200	12 200
	. .	5 000	5 000	5 000
Tajikistan	. .	. .	9 000	9 000
	. .	. .	1 200	1 200
Turkmenistan	11 000	18 000	18 000	19 000
	. .	. .	. .	. .
Uzbekistan	. .	. .	70 000	80 000
	. .	. .	16 000	18 000

[a] At constant 1995 prices and exchange rates, converted using PPP rates. See appendix 7C.

[b] Government expenditure is not uniformly defined for this table. The ratios are therefore not strictly comparable between countries. Data for Kazakhstan are for total government expenditure (including local government). For Tajikistan data are for central government only. For Turkmenistan data exclude the special state funds and capital investments of public enterprises.

Sources: International Monetary Fund, Staff Country Reports: *Republic of Kazakhstan,* no. 98/84 (Aug. 1998); *Kyrgyz Republic*, no. 98/8 (Jan. 1998); *Republic of Tajikistan,* no. 98/16 (Feb. 1998); *Turkmenistan,* no. 98/81 (Aug. 1998); and *Republic of Uzbekistan,* no. 98/116 (Oct. 1998), p. 88. Armed and paramilitary forces: International Institute for Strategic Studies, *The Military Balance* (Oxford University Press: Oxford, 1994/95–1998/99).

adopted new constitutions, all of a 'presidential' type, providing for almost dictatorial rule through top-heavy executive branches. None of these countries has created anything resembling the Western due process of law, is considered to meet international standards of election processes or has a functioning deliberative assembly protected by a true separation of powers. None of them has a legislative branch that is independently capable of establishing national budget priorities or an independent judiciary.

Since 1992 they have all created armed forces with varying capabilities to meet their particular needs, perceived threats, geopolitical position, economic situation, cadre resources, ethnic divisions and political sensitivities. Each has faced serious challenges. Although differing in size and power, they have many common problems, including transnational threats from drug smuggling, potential spillover from the war in Tajikistan, and fear of a politicized Islam and the spread of instability from Afghanistan.

Several kinds of uncertainty are involved in estimating their military expenditure. Most of these are associated with their relatively recent independence and simultaneous transition from a socialist to a capitalist economic system. There are still no functioning price mechanisms. Budget and national account systems are not fully developed, which means that not even data on total government expenditure and GDP are reliable. Systems for measuring inflation are not yet reliable and exchange rates do not allow international comparisons of public expenditure. These are all general problems associated with the economic statistics of these countries.[82] Additional problems include first of all the lack of data and lack of transparency. It has not been possible to obtain any data directly from these countries.[83] The data presented in table 7.6 are almost exclusively based on data published by the IMF, which is the only source for consistent time-series of government expenditure for these countries. These include a one-line item for 'defence', but its coverage is not known. The most problematic items are paramilitary forces and arms imports.

The 1998 central government budget for *Kazakhstan* included 20 billion tenge for defence ($414 million, in constant 1995 prices and exchange rates).[84] On the basis of the IMF statistics, however, it is not possible to discern whether expenditure on total law enforcement is included.[85] While the final assessment of the 1998 budget has yet to be made, evidence points to continuing difficulties in achieving planned revenue collection because of the fall in export prices for oil and metals, and thus difficulties in providing the ministries with the amounts allocated in the official budget. Such difficulties have affected the defence budget before.

[82] 'Global economic prospects and policies', *World Economic Outlook*, Oct. 1997, pp. 16–17.

[83] SIPRI has attempted to improve the availability of data by writing to their ministries of defence, foreign affairs and finance and the central banks. None has replied.

[84] International Monetary Fund, *Republic of Kazakhstan: Recent Economic Developments*, IMF Staff Country Report, no. 98/84 (IMF: Washington, DC, Aug. 1998), p. 24.

[85] Expenditure on total law enforcement includes the Committee for State Security, the Internal Troops, the Military Border Troops Institute and the State Technical Committee for Information (Protection of the President and Cabinet Ministers).

The military expenditure figure for *Kyrgyzstan* includes allocations to the defence ministry only: law enforcement expenditure is accounted for elsewhere in the central government budget.[86] A joint Kyrgyz–Russian border troop command was established in 1992, in which some 5000 Russian border guards are working for the host country but come under the Russian command structure. The agreement was renewed in March 1997.[87] Up to the end of 1998, Kyrgyzstan paid for 20 per cent of the costs of these forces and Russia the remaining 80 per cent.[88] As of January 1999, however, Russia stopped funding those border troops that are stationed on the Kyrgyz–Chinese border, and Kyrgyzstan took over the funding. A small Russian group will continue to serve as military advisers, paid for by Kyrgyzstan. In early 1993 the total strength of the armed forces was around 30 000. Financial considerations have been a major factor behind a severe cut in personnel, to about 12 200 by 1998, and there is little in the defence budget to pay for military development, since priority is given to paying for the border forces.

The official defence budget for *Tajikistan* in 1997 accounted for 9.1 per cent of planned government expenditure and 1.4 per cent of GDP. Allocations for law enforcement and the activities of judicial bodies accounted for up to 14.3 per cent.[89]

As in other former Soviet republics, *Turkmenistan's* army inherited a large amount of equipment, much of it at present not fully serviceable. For example, over half of Turkmenistan's 389 combat aircraft have been mothballed.[90] The 1998 defence budget amounted to 613 billion manats ($255 million in constant 1995 prices and at 1995 exchange rates) and accounted for around 4.5 per cent of GDP or 16 per cent of central government expenditure—roughly the same share as in 1997. This represented an increase of 3 per cent in real terms, mainly for salary increases for military personnel because of higher living costs caused by the ending of subsidies on milk and meat.[91] Since 1994 Turkmenistan has paid the entire cost of Russia's military personnel on its territory.[92] If all military-related spending were added to the official defence budget, the share of military expenditure in the central budget would rise considerably.

Uzbekistan, the first country in Central Asia to do so, submitted a report of its military expenditure to the United Nations in 1998. The reported data did not include expenditure for the forces on the Afghan and Tajik borders or

[86] International Monetary Fund, *Kyrgyz Republic: Recent Economic Developments*, IMF Staff Country Report, no. 98/8 (IMF: Washington, DC, Jan. 1998), table 21, pp. 111–12.

[87] 'Kyrgyz Republic: international relations and defence', Economist Intelligence Unit, *Country Profile 1997/98 Kyrgyz Republic* (Economist Intelligence Unit: London: 1997), p. 8.

[88] Smith, D. L., *Breaking Away from the Bear* (US Army War College Strategic Studies Institute: Carlisle, Pa., 1998), Aug. 1998, pp. 14–18.

[89] International Monetary Fund, *Tajikistan: Recent Economic Developments,* IMF Staff Country Report no. 98/16 (IMF: Washington, DC, Feb. 1998), p. 94.

[90] 'Turkmenistan: International relations and defence', Economist Intelligence Unit, *Country Profile 1997/98 Turkmenistan* (Economist Intelligence Unit: London: 1997), pp. 57–58.

[91] International Monetary Fund, *Turkmenistan: Recent Economic Developments,* IMF Staff Country Report no. 98/81 (IMF: Washington, DC, Aug. 1998), pp. 26, 30–31 and 99.

[92] Smith (note 88), pp. 30–32.

other paramilitary forces. The large Uzbek armed forces have inherited a sizeable amount of Soviet equipment and training facilities, for which Uzbekistan has experienced problems in securing spare parts and maintenance support. Plans to raise troop strength from the present 80 000 to around 100 000[93] will be difficult to realize and allocations of defence expenditure will continue to favour interior ministry troops.

V. The Middle East

The countries of the region all devote a comparatively high share of GNP to military expenditure. Official data show military expenditure ranging from 3 to 13 per cent of GDP in 1997—still probably an underestimate for most of these countries. Recurrent features of the region are the non-availability or unreliability of information on actual military expenditure and the widespread use of barter trade and undisclosed accounts for arms imports.

The decade 1989–98 saw 17 per cent growth in military expenditure in the region, including a sharp peak in 1991 caused by the Persian Gulf War.[94] Much of this growth was concentrated in 1997 and primarily in Saudi Arabia. The increase was the reflection of a high level of arms purchases, although, as in the cases of oil-for-arms transactions, arms procurement outlays are not always included in the defence budget.

Directly or indirectly, oil prices affect the level of military expenditure of oil-exporting countries which are heavily dependent on foreign exchange earnings to finance government expenditure.[95] Many are likely to face difficult budget decisions in the short and medium term if the oil price remains much below the 1997 level.[96] The world collapse in oil prices in 1998 could result in a reduction in military expenditure in the region, especially in Saudi Arabia.[97]

Israel's military expenditure rose by 14 per cent over the decade 1989–98. However, its share in GDP fell from 12 to 9 per cent over the same period as a result of favourable economic conditions. Israel relies on US grants to an annual value of $1.8 billion from the Foreign Military Financing (FMF) programme and $1.2 billion from United States Agency for International Development (USAID) Economic Support Funds (ESF).[98] US assistance is under review and a new bilateral aid accord starting in 2000 and to last 10 years is under discussion. Direct military aid is expected to increase to $2.4 billion a year while economic aid is to be gradually phased out.[99]

[93] International Institute for Strategic Studies, *The Military Balance 1998/99* (Oxford University Press: Oxford, 1998), p. 116.

[94] This excludes Iraq, for which data remain unavailable.

[95] According to the World Bank, 9 out of 14 countries in the Middle East rely on oil exports for more than 50% of their export earnings.

[96] The price of oil fell from $19 a barrel in 1997 to an estimated $13 a barrel in 1998. International Monetary Fund, 'Issues relating to growth and inflation in developing countries and countries in transition', *World Economic Outlook* (IMF: Washington, DC, Oct. 1998), p. 76.

[97] 'Saudi set to reduce weapons purchases', *Financial Times*, 25 Feb.1999, p. 7.

[98] US Agency for International Development, *Overseas Loans and Grants: Obligations and Loan Authorizations, July 1, 1945–Sept. 30, 1997* (USAID, Office of Budget: Washington, DC, 1998).

[99] 'Israeli–US talks focus on military aid boost', *Jane's Defence Weekly*, 6 May 1998, p. 5.

VI. Europe

The European region includes countries with very different conditions and trends. In 1998 Central and Eastern Europe including Russia accounted for 10 per cent of total European military expenditure, Western Europe accounting for the rest.

The trend in Central and Eastern Europe excluding the CIS countries has been falling dramatically since 1989, but in 1998 there was a slight increase of 1.3 per cent in real terms. Bulgaria and the three new NATO members—the Czech Republic, Hungary and Poland—all increased their military budgets in real terms in 1998, while the Slovak Republic and Romania reduced theirs. The Czech and Hungarian military budgets increased by 10 per cent each and Poland's by 2.3 per cent. Target levels for the share of military expenditure in GDP are estimated to be around 2 per cent by the year 2001 for the Czech Republic, 1.8 per cent for Hungary by 2001 and 2.4 per cent for Poland by 2002.[100] These increases are intended to support planned force reorganization and modernization of equipment, since NATO common-funded contributions will fund mainly the direct costs of NATO membership (primarily investment in infrastructure).[101] The Polish Government has estimated the direct cost to it of joining NATO at approximately $3 billion for the period 1998–2010, or about 5 per cent of the annual defence budget, while the indirect costs of integration (achieving interoperability with NATO armed forces) and of modernization of equipment are expected to be some $8.3 billion over 15 years.[102]

The Baltic states devote less of their resources to the military. In 1998 the share of military expenditure in GDP was 1.2 per cent in Estonia, 0.9 per cent in Latvia and 0.8 per cent in Lithuania.

It is difficult to assess the official figures for Bosnia-Herzegovina and Yugoslavia (Serbia and Montenegro). There is greater transparency in Croatia and Slovenia. Croatian military expenditure fell in 1996 and 1997 but in 1998 there was a slight increase of 2 per cent. The official defence budget for Croatia includes only activities of the Ministry of Defence, while several military functions come under the Ministry of the Interior.[103] Slovenia's military

[100] Interview with Vladimir Vetchy, Defence Minister of the Czech Republic, *Jane's Defence Weekly*, 30 Sep. 1998, p. 40; Wright, R., 'A new security blanket: accession to NATO will confirm that traditional threats have melted away', *Financial Times*, 7 Dec. 1998, p. 3; and Polish Ministry of National Defence, 'Report on Poland's integration with NATO', Feb. 1998, pp. 28–29.

[101] For a more detailed account of the candidates for NATO membership see, Sköns, E. *et al.*, 'Military expenditure and arms production', *SIPRI Yearbook 1998: Armaments, Disarmament and International Security* (Oxford University Press: Oxford, 1998), pp. 207–13.

[102] Polish Ministry of National Defence (note 100), p. 28.

[103] Before the break-up of the Socialist Federal Republic of Yugoslavia, federal laws and the constitution prohibited Croatia from establishing its own regular armed forces but in 1990 and especially in the first part of 1991 Croatian military units were organized as police forces, nominally under the Ministry of the Interior. In Sep. 1991 military units were also organized as the Croatian Armed Forces in the organizational framework of the Ministry of Defence and under a standard military chain of command. In 1991 the budget for the Ministry of the Interior was higher than that of the Ministry of Defence. In 1992–95 special and other police units, including police reserves, were deployed in all military operations in Croatia. In 1998 there were still military-organized and military-equipped special

expenditure has been roughly constant since 1995 but increased by 8 per cent in 1998, the share of procurement rising from 2.8 per cent in 1997 to 3.5 per cent in 1998.[104] Macedonia is building its own army. In 1998, for the first time since independence in 1992, it published a White Paper on defence.[105] About half of the 1998 defence budget went to personnel costs.

The Russian Federation[106]

The level of Russian military expenditure in 1998 was determined primarily by economic factors. The budget adopted for 1998 turned out to be unrealistic in many ways. Actual payments were much lower than approved allocations and inflation was higher than expected. Economic factors are likely to continue to have a great impact on the defence budget for 1999. The budget proposal for 1999 was the subject of much debate during December 1998 and early 1999 and it was clear that there would be a determined effort in 1999 to reverse the sharp fall in military expenditure.

The declining trend in Russian military expenditure since 1992[107] thus continued in 1998. The only exception to the trend was in 1997, when actual military expenditure increased by 6 per cent in real terms and by 0.3 percentage points of GDP, in spite of actual outlays being 21 per cent lower than the adopted budget (table 7.7).

The defence budget adopted for 1998

The federal budget law for 1998 was adopted in March 1998, three months after the beginning of the budget year.[108] It included 81.8 billion roubles for national defence, representing 16 per cent of total federal expenditure, 22 per cent of federal revenues, and 2.9 per cent of forecast GDP (table 7.7).

Compared with the 1997 budget for national defence (104.3 billion roubles), this was a sharp cut. Part of this decline was, however, the effect of changes in budget classifications between these two years, the main change being that the item 'pensions for military personnel' had been moved from the 'national defence' chapter to the 'social security' chapter of the budget. Allocations for military pensions amounted to 11 billion roubles in the 1998 budget. Thus, the comparable total for national defence amounted to 92.8 billion roubles in the budget adopted for 1998 (table 7.8). Adding other defence-related items, the total military budget decreased from 134 billion roubles in 1997 to 117 billion

police units (2408 policemen), commanded by a general (not a police rank). Information received from Prof. Ozren Zunek, University of Zagreb, Croatia, 15 Oct. 1998.

[104] SIPRI military expenditure database.

[105] Macedonia, Ministry of Defense, *White Paper of the Defense of the Republic of Macedonia* (Skopje, Aug. 1998), pp. 1–7 (in English).

[106] Prof. Julian Cooper of the University of Birmingham has provided invaluable assistance in the collection and analysis of data on the Russian Federation.

[107] Cooper, J. , 'The military expenditure of the USSR and the Russian Federation, 1987–97', *SIPRI Yearbook 1998* (note 101), appendix 6D.

[108] The budget was adopted by the State Duma on 4 Mar. and by the Federation Council on 12 Mar. and was signed into law by the president on 28 Mar. 1998.

Table 7.7. The Russian Federation: military expenditure, 1992–99

Figures in italics are percentages.

	National defence[a] (m. current roubles)	Total military expenditure[b] (m. current roubles)	Total military expenditure[b] (constant 1995 US $m.)[c]	GDP (m. current roubles)	National defence as % of GDP	Total military expenditure as % of GDP
1992	855	1 049	47.5	19 006	*4.5*	*5.5*
1993	7 213	9 037	41.9	171 510	*4.2*	*5.3*
1994	28 500	35 890	40.5	610 745	*4.7*	*5.9*
1995	49 600	63 220	25.7	1 585 026	*3.1*	*4.0*
1996	63 891	82 485	23.4	2 200 225	*2.9*	*3.7*
1997B	[104 318]	[133 562]	[31.7]	[2 725 000]	[*3.8*]	[*4.9*]
1997E	[75 500]	[101 500]	[24.1]	[2 675 000]	[*2.8*]	[*3.8*]
1997	79 692	105 034	24.9	2 602 270	*3.1*	*4.0*
1998B[d]	[81 765]	. .	. .	[2 840 000]	[*2.9*]	. .
1998B[e]	[92 765]	[117 025]	[27.2]	[2 840 000]	[*3.3*]	[*4.1*]
1998E[d]	[45 000]	. .	. .	[2 500 000]	[*1.8*]	. .
1998E[e]	[52 800]	[70 400]	[9.2]	[2 500 000]	[*2.1*]	[*2.8*]
1998[d]	[56 704]	. .	. .	[2 685 000]	[*2.1*]	. .
1998[e]	68 004	85 574	11.2	2 685 000	*2.5*	*3.2*
1999B[d]	[93 703]	. .	. .	[4 000 000]	[*2.3*]	. .
1999B[e]	[121 486]	[148 639]	[15.0]	[4 000 000]	[*3.0*]	[*3.7*]

Notes: Figures show actual expenditure if not indicated otherwise. The rouble was redenominated on 1 Jan. 1998 at the rate of 1 new rouble = 1000 old. All rouble figures are expressed in new roubles. B = budget as first adopted and signed into law; E = estimated out-turn.

[a] Military pensions are excluded from the budget chapter 'national defence' from 1998 onwards.

[b] Total military expenditure includes military pensions and military-related items under budget chapters such as paramilitary forces and military R&D.

[c] Constant dollar figures are in PPP terms with 1995 as the base year.

[d] Excluding military pensions.

[e] Including military pensions.

Sources: For 1992–1996, 1997B and 1997E: Cooper, J., 'The military expenditure of the USSR and the Russian Federation, 1987–97', *SIPRI Yearbook 1998: Armaments, Disarmament and International Security* (Oxford University Press: Oxford, 1998), appendix 6D, updated by personal communication, 7 Dec. 1998; for 1997 (final): URL <http://www.minfin.ru/isp/3.htm>; for 1998B: *Rossiyskaya Gazeta,* 31 Mar. 1998; for 1998: Ministry of Finance report on budget execution, URL <http://www.minfin.ru/isp/>; and for 1999B (budget as adopted 22 Feb. 1999): *Sobraniye Zakonodatelstva Rossiyskoy Federatsii,* no. 9 (1999), article 1093. PPP rate for 1995: *World Bank Atlas 1997* (World Bank: Washington, DC, 1997), p. 37.

roubles for 1998. Using the inflation forecast of only 5.7 per cent for 1998 in the budget, this was a reduction in real terms of 17 per cent in 1998.

In reality the reduction was sharper. While the budget may reflect government priorities, it has little relation to developments in the Russian economy. The actual out-turn for national defence in 1997 was 79.7 billion roubles—an

Table 7.8. The Russian defence budget for 1998

Figures are in m. current roubles.

	1997	1998
National defence		
Build-up and maintenance of the armed forces:		
Maintenance of the armed forces (personnel/O&M)	48 661	43 553
Military personnel	–	33 268
Central staff	–	319
Pensions	13 859	–
Development, procurement, operation and repairs		27 848
Procurement	20 963	15 148
R&D	11 575	10 800
Repairs and manufacturing	–	1 900
Construction	7 141	3 300
Military reform	. .	3 995
One-time retirement benefits		1 186
Housing	. .	2 100
Household benefits and transport	. .	709
Health care		256
Education and educational institutions		132
ROSTO	24	. .
Total build-up and maintenance for the armed forces		**79 403**
Military activities of the Ministry for Atomic Energy	2 095	2 095
Mobilization and extra military training		250
Total official 'national defence' head	**104 318**	**81 765**
Pensions for military personnel	–	11 000
Total national defence	**104 318**	**92 765**
Other military expenditure		
Paramilitary forces		
Interior troops	4 147	3 714
Border troops	5 765	–
Border services	–	3 943
State security agencies	–	6 969
Security services	6 930	–
Total paramilitary	16 842	14 626
International arms agreements	3 111	1 922
Military-related R&D[a]	(5 086)	(3 720)
Total other military expenditure	**29 244**	**24 260**
Total military expenditure	**(133 562)**	**(117 025)**

[a] Military R&D estimated as 40% of total expenditure on science.

Source: Rossiyskaya Gazeta, 31 Mar. 1998.

implementation rate of 75 per cent of budget. For 1998 implementation was significantly lower because of the political and economic crises during the year. They resulted in significant changes in federal government expenditure, partly because revenues were much lower than planned and partly because rapidly increasing debt interest payments squeezed out other kinds of federal government expenditure. This also had an impact on military expenditure.

The first downward revision came with the new government of Prime Minister Sergey Kiriyenko, which cut the budget for 'national defence' to 61 billion roubles. The succeeding government, of Prime Minister Yevgeny Primakov, made further reductions in expenditure for national defence. Actual military expenditure for 1998, at 85.6 billion roubles (table 7.7),[109] was 27 per cent less than budgeted. Furthermore, the 1998 rate of inflation was 84 per cent—much higher than the forecast.[110] On these estimates, Russian military expenditure was thus reduced by 55 per cent in real terms during 1998.

The 1999 defence budget

The draft budget for 1999 (as reported on 15 December 1998) provided for expenditure of 575 billion roubles and revenues of 474 billion roubles. The allocation to the 'national defence' budget head was 92.2 billion roubles, excluding military pensions.[111] All figures were based on planned GDP of 4000 billion roubles and an inflation rate of 30 per cent, which meant that allocations to national defence would represent 2.3 per cent of GDP and a real decline of 13 per cent over the amount budgeted for 1998 but a real increase of 25 per cent over actual expenditure for national defence in 1998.

The budget adopted on 22 February 1999[112] raised the allocation for national defence to 93.7 billion roubles. Adding to this the allocation for military pensions (13.4 billion) and additional allocations of 14.4 billion roubles[113] for national defence, financed by an increase of 1 per cent on personal income tax and other funds, including a 'task fund for the support of military reform', the total allocation for national defence was 121 billion roubles (table 7.7). If other military-related expenditure is added, the total military budget for 1999 amounted to 149 billion roubles—27 per cent higher than the 1998 budget in nominal terms, but roughly the same in real terms if the inflation forecast of 30 per cent for 1999 is applied. However, compared with actual military expenditure for 1998, the 1999 budget represents an increase of 74 per cent in nominal terms and one-third in real terms. It is clearly the goal of government policy to restore some of the sharp and unplanned cuts in its military expenditure which took place during 1998. Implementation of this policy will depend on how realistic the economic assumptions were on which the budget is based. Political and economic uncertainties make it difficult to predict the final outcome.

[109] Russian Ministry of Finance, 'Report on budget execution, Jan.–Sep. 1998', URL <http://www.minfin.ru/isp>.

[110] Interfax (Moscow), 'Interfax business report for 21 Jan. 99' (in English), in Foreign Broadcast Information Service, *Daily Report–Central Eurasia (FBIS-SOV)*, FBIS-SOV-99-020, 20 Jan. 1999.

[111] ITAR-TASS (Moscow), 15 Dec. 1998 (in English), in 'Russia: further items of draft budget expenditure reported', FBIS-SOV-98-349, 15 Dec. 1998.

[112] *Rossiyskaya Gazeta*, 25 Feb. 1999.

[113] The sum of 14.4 billion roubles was provided by the Russian Finance Minister, Mikhail Zadornov. *Krasnaya Zvezda*, 12 Mar. 1999, p. 1.

Western Europe

Military expenditure in Western Europe fell by 14 per cent in real terms over the 10-year period 1989–98 (table 7.1). The aggregate trend included wide variations between countries. The three major spenders, France, Germany and the UK, which together accounted for 58 per cent of the West European total in 1998, reduced their military expenditure by 12, 28 and 24 per cent, respectively, during this period, while Cyprus, Greece and Turkey moved in the opposite direction, increasing their military expenditure by 73, 24 and 74 per cent in real terms, respectively.[114] These three were also the only West European countries which spent more than 4 per cent of their GDP on defence in 1998. Given the escalation of tension over the Cyprus issue during 1998, there was concern about potential instability in the region.[115]

Most West European countries have reviewed the goals and instruments of their defence policy in the light of the new security environment after the cold war and increasing financial constraints. There is a general consensus that the military threat from a well-armed enemy on West European territory has diminished dramatically, at least for the foreseeable future. West European armed forces are increasingly involved in peacekeeping and other kinds of international operations. Combat readiness, deployability and interoperability are greatly emphasized in all defence reviews. The new NATO Strategic Concept, adopted at the Washington summit meeting of April 1999, will have an impact on the procurement plans of all European NATO member countries.

The reduction in military expenditure in Western Europe was concentrated on NATO member countries and on the first half of the 10-year period, mostly because of procurement cuts. Equipment expenditure by the European NATO members fell by 23 per cent in real terms over the 10-year period.[116] Since the mid-1990s their military expenditure has stabilized, which indicates that most countries had by then found the level of military expenditure which they consider appropriate for their post-cold war defence. In 1998 they broke the trend and increased their equipment expenditure by 11 per cent in real terms.

France cut its equipment expenditure in 1998 and announced further cuts of $3 billion by the year 2002.[117] This was due to its decision to phase out conscription by the year 2002. The cost of professionalization made it impossible to fulfil the defence programme for the period 1997–2015,[118] according to which procurement expenditure should remain stable. Spain and Italy have embarked on similar plans of full professionalization of their armies by 2003

[114] See appendix 7A, table 7A.3.

[115] For an analysis of the escalation of tensions with regard to Cyprus' potential arms purchases, see chapter 11 in this volume.

[116] This refers to NATO data and excludes France. See appendix 7B in this volume.

[117] 'Défense: professionnalisation et respect des engagements: un "recalage" par rapport à la programmation', *Le Monde*, 11 Sep. 1998, p. 6.

[118] France, Ministry of Defence, 'Une défense nouvelle 1997–2015', Feb. 1996. For an account of major planned changes in French defence policy, see George, P. *et al.*, 'Military expenditure', *SIPRI Yearbook 1997: Armaments, Disarmament and International Security* (Oxford University Press: Oxford, 1997), pp. 167–69.

and 2005, respectively.[119] British equipment expenditure increased by 12.5 per cent in real terms in 1998.[120] The future trend in the British defence budget, according to the 1998 Strategic Defence Review,[121] is a reduction of 4 per cent in real terms by FY 2001/02,[122] while procurement expenditure is planned to increase by another 5 per cent between FYs 1998/99 and 2001/02.[123] The German Government appointed a Defence Structures Commission in 1998 to review the tasks, structure and equipment of the Bundeswehr, to be completed before 2000. The German defence budget for 1998 gave priority to procurement with an increase of 17 per cent in real terms; that for 1999 was slightly reduced by 0.5 per cent to balance the overall budget.[124]

The Netherlands, which last undertook a defence review in 1993, cutting its forces by 50 per cent, in 1998 announced significant cuts in its military expenditure up to and including 2002[125] and further cuts were announced in January 1999 as a result of planned restructuring of the armed forces over the next decade, to be presented in a Defence White Paper in 2000. The basic principles, as outlined in January 1999,[126] included the redefinition of defence tasks into three main types: (*a*) territorial defence; (*b*) protection of the international rule of law, involving peacekeeping operations and, 'if there is sufficient international legal basis', operations involving the threat or use of force; and (*c*) support of civilian authorities disaster relief and peace-building. As regards implications for resource allocation, priority was given to the two latter tasks 'at the expense of the scale of the resources for defence against a large-scale attack on NATO territory'.[127]

Most non-NATO European countries did not reduce their military expenditure during the period 1989–98. Cyprus, Finland, Ireland and Malta experienced double-digit growth, while Austria and Sweden kept a roughly constant level of military expenditure. This will change in Sweden after the decision in February 1999 to cut its military expenditure in the range of an annual 10 per cent for the period 2002–2004.[128] With a 32 per cent decrease in real terms, Switzerland was the only non-aligned country in Western Europe to reduce its military expenditure significantly during the past decade.

[119] 'Italy moves towards all-volunteer forces', *Jane's Defence Weekly*, 10 Feb. 1999, p. 12; and 'Spain again will boost defense budget', *Defense News*, 26 Oct.–1 Nov. 1998, p. 20.

[120] See appendix 7B in this volume.

[121] British Ministry of Defence, *Strategic Defence Review* (Ministry of Defence: London, 1998).

[122] British House of Commons, Defence Committee, *Strategic Defence Review, Eighth Report, Session 1997798,* vol. 1 (Her Majesty's Stationery Office: London, 3 Sep. 1998), p. cliii (HC 138–I).

[123] *Strategic Defence Review* (note 122), p. clv.

[124] *Jane's Defence Weekly*, 27 Jan. 1999, p. 15.

[125] In 1998 the Netherlands Parliament adopted a cut of 375 million DFL ($195 million) or 2.7% for 1999 and mandated similar cuts up to and including 2002. 'Dutch plan military redesign', *Defense News,* 8 Feb. 1999, p. 4.

[126] Netherlands Ministry of Defence, 'Framework memorandum for the 2000 Defence White Paper', 25 Jan. 1999, unofficial translation, URL <http://www.MINDEF.NL/english/framework.htm>.

[127] Netherlands Ministry of Defence (note 126), chapter 6, 'Strategic discussion of the future of defence'.

[128] 'Försvarsuppgörelse med centern' [Defence agreement with the Centre], Pressmeddelande, Försvarsdepartementet, 3 Feb. 1999, URL <http://www.regeringen.se/galactica/service=irnews/owner =sys/action=obj_show?c_obj_id=>.

Appendix 7A. Tables of military expenditure

ELISABETH SKÖNS, AGNÈS COURADES ALLEBECK, EVAMARIA LOOSE-WEINTRAUB and PETTER STÅLENHEIM[1]

Sources and methods are explained in appendix 7C. Notes and explanations of the conventions used appear below table 7A.4. Data in this appendix should not be combined with those in previous SIPRI Yearbooks because of revision.[2]

Table 7A.1. Military expenditure by region, in constant US dollars, 1989–98

Figures are in US $b., at constant 1995 prices and exchange rates,[3] for calendar year. Figures do not always add up to totals because of the conventions of rounding.

	1989	1990	1991	1992	1993	1994	1995	1996	1997	1998
World total	**1 050**	**1 004**	. .	**817**	**785**	**762**	**723**	**709**	**721**	**[696]**
Geographical regions										
Africa	12.2	11.3	10.3	9.8	9.6	9.5	8.8	8.9	9.1	[9.2]
North Africa	2.8	2.4	2.5	2.7	2.9	3.4	3.1	3.2	3.4	3.6
Sub-Saharan Africa	9.4	9.0	7.8	7.1	6.7	6.2	5.7	5.7	5.6	[5.6]
Americas	406	385	338	358	342	325	310	293	295	[283]
North America	385	369	325	342	325	307	289	273	271	260
Central America	0.8	0.8	0.6	0.6	0.5	0.5	0.5	0.5	0.4	. .
South America	20.2	15.5	12.7	14.7	16.9	17.1	20.8	19.0	23.8	. .
Asia	104	106	109	115	117	117	121	126	130	131
Central Asia (CIS Asia)	0	0	0	[1.1]	[1.4]	[0.9]	[1.0]	[1.0]	[1.1]	[1.2]
East Asia	92.4	95.0	97.8	103	103	104	107	112	115	116
South Asia	11.3	11.4	11.2	11.2	12.2	12.1	12.6	12.9	13.7	14.3
Europe	483	447	. .	280	265	259	235	234	234	[220]
Central and Eastern Europe	[250]	[213]	. .	[59.2]	[52.0]	[51.4]	[36.4]	[33.6]	[35.1]	[21.3]
CIS Europe	0	0	. .	[49.5]	[43.7]	[43.4]	[28.2]	[25.7]	[27.5]	[13.6]
Western Europe	232	234	231	221	213	208	199	201	199	199
Middle East	37.0	[46.2]	[63.6]	[44.7]	42.1	41.2	38.6	38.5	43.5	43.3
Oceania	8.4	8.7	10.1	9.3	9.0	9.2	8.8	8.7	8.9	9.2

Organizations										
ASEAN	9.5	10.0	10.8	11.4	11.9	12.5	14.2	14.7	20.5	19.6
CIS	. .	. .	. .	[50.3]	[45.0]	[44.2]	[29.0]	[26.6]	[28.4]	[14.6]
EU	209	209	206	195	188	183	184	185	183	183
NATO	601	585	538	546	522	498	472	458	454	443
OECD	672	657	612	620	595	572	548	553	550	539
OPEC	26.4	34.1	50.4	31.5	30.9	29.2	26.7	26.5	33.1	31.6
OSCE	867	814	. .	622	590	566	524	507	505	[480]
Income group (GNP/cap. 1995)										
Low (≤ $765)	30.8	33.7	33.0	36.4	36.5	35.5	36.0	37.8	40.4	43.2
Middle ($766–$3100)	272	235	. .	82.6	78.2	79.3	64.0	62.2	66.1	[51.8]
Upper ($3101 –$9385)	58.6	54.0	64.7	55.6	57.9	56.1	57.5	55.8	65.0	63.1
High (≥ $9386)	689	681	640	642	613	591	566	553	549	538

Notes:

The country coverage of geographical regions and organizations in table 7A.1 are the same as those for the SIPRI arms transfer statistics (provided in appendix 11A) except for *East Asia:* Brunei, Cambodia, China, Indonesia, Japan, North Korea, South Korea, Laos, Malaysia, Myanmar, the Philippines, Singapore, Taiwan, Thailand, and Viet Nam; and *Oceania:* Australia, Fiji, New Zealand and Papua New Guinea. *OPEC (Organization of Petroleum-Exporting Countries)*: Algeria, Ecuador (–1992), Gabon (–1995), Indonesia, Iran, Iraq, Kuwait, Libya, Nigeria, Qatar, Saudi Arabia, United Arab Emirates and Venezuela.

The country coverage of income groups is based on figures of 1995 GNP per capita as calculated by the World Bank and presented in its *World Development Report 1997* (International Bank for Reconstruction and Development and Oxford University Press: Washington, DC and New York, June 1997).

Totals for geographical regions add up to the world total and subregion totals add up to regional totals. Totals for regions and income groups cover the same group of countries for all years, while totals for organizations cover only the member countries in the year given.

The world total and the totals for regions, organizations and income groups in table 7A.1 are estimates, based on data in table 7A.3. When military expenditure data for a country are missing for a few years, estimates are made, most often on the assumption that the rate of change in that country's military expenditure is the same as that for the subregion to which it belongs. When no estimates can be made, countries are excluded from the totals. The countries excluded from all totals in table 7A.1 are: Afghanistan, Angola, Armenia, Cambodia, Congo (Brazzaville), Iraq, Laos, Libya, Qatar, Somalia, the former Yugoslavia and Yugoslavia (Serbia and Montenegro).

Table 7A.2. Military expenditure by region and country, in local currency, 1989–98

Figures are in local currency, current prices.

State	Currency	1989	1990	1991	1992	1993	1994	1995	1996	1997	1998
Africa											
North Africa											
Algeria	m. dinars	6 500	[8 470]	10 439	[20 125]	29 810	46 800	58 847	79 519	101 126	112 248
Libya	m. dinars	. .	. .	. .	. .	. .	. .	. .	. .	. .	. .
Morocco	m. dirhams	11 264	8 816	10 002	10 488	11 071	13 557	13 245	12 602	. .	. .
Tunisia	m. dinars	269	287	315	319	347	364	326	343	369	398
Sub-Saharan											
Angola[4]	m./b./tr. kwanzas	58.0	52.0	102	438	7 204	| 231	2 754	| 128	[170]	389
Benin	m. francs	9 100	8 935	. .	. .	. .	. .	. .	. .	. .	. .
Botswana	m. pulas	208	291	348	376	450	457	460	467	596	824
Burkina Faso	m. francs	21 315	22 997	19 608	18 824	17 139	(16 730)	(18 330)	(18 900)	(22 400)	. .
Burundi	m. francs	6 014	6 782	7 760	8 121	8 579	10 126	11 010	14 630	20 019	[28 000]
Cameroon	m. francs	58 278	55 891	51 277	48 300	48 300	53 100	57 850	57 550	. .	[86 000]
Cape Verde	m. escudos	. .	. .	. .	. .	220	281	477	352	382	. .
Central Afr. Rep.	m. francs	. .	. .	6 093	6 137	5 421	5 935	6 496	6 239	. .	. .
Chad	m. francs	. .	. .	. .	. .	11 085	12 333	10 000	12 681	. .	. .
Congo	m. francs	. .	. .	. .	. .	. .	. .	. .	. .	. .	. .
Congo, Dem. Rep.[5]	th./m./b. new zaïres	9.0	14.0	235	| 33.0	1 258	10 816	| 122	. .	[28 916]	. .
Côte d'Ivoire	m. francs	41 368	39 199	40 671	41 503	42 088	46 677	. .	52 516	54 588	. .
Djibouti	m. francs	4 705	4 709	4 809	. .	. .	. .	7 204	6 092	. .	. .
Equatorial Guinea	m. francs	. .	. .	. .	. .	. .	1 321	1 721	. .	. .	. .
Eritrea[6]	m. birr	. .	. .	. .	. .	539	439	771	968	. .	. .
Ethiopia	m. birr	1 748	1 744	1 140	666	703	710	726	761	805	913
Gabon	m. francs	. .	. .	. .	. .	. .	. .	. .	. .	. .	8 952
Gambia	m. dalasis	20.7	27.3	34.9	31.2	23.3	22.2	30.1	40.9	. .	. .
Ghana	m. cedis	6 106	9 006	15 230	23 242	39 481	36 147	58 823	72 644	93 148	. .

Guinea	m. francs	. .	. .	54 100	50 200	42 000	44 800	. .	. .	. .	. .
Guinea-Bissau[7]	m. francs	123	. .	. .	. .	. .	400	615	770	. .	. .
Kenya	m. shillings	5 362	6 438	6 034	5 052	5 047	6 344	8 203	. .	. .	. .
Lesotho	m. maloti	59.3	62.5	62.4	60.1	62.4	81.9	95.1	107	138	. .
Liberia[8]	m. dollars	[27.4]	28.3	21.7	23.6	37.3	41.3	. .	. .	. .	. .
Madagascar	b. francs	48.5	56.7	63.7	68.9	72.4	84.6	116	201	. .	. .
Malawi	m. kwachas	62.9	66.3	66.5	90.9	118	151	225	317	328	. .
Mali	b. francs	14.7	14.2	. .	. .	. .	. .	. .	. .	. .	. .
Mauritania	m. ouguiyas	3 229	3 239	3 232	3 427	3 640	3 644	3 900	. .	. .	. .
Mauritius	m. rupees	96.5	137	165	178	190	213	234	233	. .	. .
Mozambique[9]	b. meticais	102	136	178	259	417	1 016	626	704	830	(1 040)
Namibia[10]	m. rand	. .	. .	309	355	229	202	248	286	386	436
Niger	m. francs	5 749	12 315	. .	. .	. .	. .	. .	. .	. .	. .
Nigeria	m. nairas	2 220	2 286	[3 554]	4 822	6 382	6 608	9 361	15 500	17 450	23 100
Rwanda	m. francs	3 336	7 964	13 184	11 863	12 900	5 700	14 700	. .	. .	. .
Senegal	m. francs	30 489	31 300	29 928	29 056	33 962	36 725	40 389	40 809	41 324	. .
Seychelles	m. rupees	73.6	79.2	87.6	105	67.1	60.1	55.2	52.4	51.0	. .
Sierra Leone	m. leones	577	1 369	4 792	10 081	13 244	15 546	18 898	(17 119)	(9 315)	. .
Somalia	m. shillings	4 200	. .	. .	. .	. .	. .	. .	. .	. .	. .
South Africa	m. rand	9 749	10 038	9 408	9 576	9 428	10 721	10 697	11 121	10 475	9 840
Sudan	m. pounds	3 050	4 420	7 420	13 750	29 500	49 900	80 600	208 200	. .	. .
Swaziland	m. emalangeni	21.6	34.7	41.7	56.4	73.1	86.3	98.3	117	111	. .
Tanzania	m. shillings	10 823	12 196	16 130	. .	. .	33 467	(46 393)	. .	. .	. .
Togo	m. francs	13 354	13 817	12 950	13 000	14 200	14 100	15 400	. .	. .	. .
Uganda	m./b. shillings	26 655	39 625	48 675	56 904	72 174	92 880	| 107	[121]	[130]	[195]
Zambia	m. kwachas	2 315	4 220	5 575	16 835	23 149	42 083	47 756	45 702	[55 100]	. .
Zimbabwe	m. dollars	803	954	1 116	1 269	1 439	1 826	2 214	2 742	3 393	3 613

State	Currency	1989	1990	1991	1992	1993	1994	1995	1996	1997	1998
Americas											
Central America											
Belize	th. dollars	8 711	9 538	9 466	10 584	12 261	15 799	16 106	15 932	18 790	. .
Costa Rica[11]	m. colones	1 870	1 973	2 310	2 651	3 449	4 424	7 901	12 485	14 379	. .
El Salvador	m. colones	926	975	1 011	975	888	829	849	843	850	. .
Guatemala	m. quetzals	368	502	661	785	869	1 008	(837)	(817)	(880)	(798)
Honduras	m. lempiras	247	276	252	280	263	(385)	445	530	548	. .
Nicaragua[12]	m. gold córdobas	[0.2]	[32.2]	211	211	224	232	242	269	260	. .
Panama	m. balboas	101	74.1	80.1	86.7	94.6	98.7	96.8	101	. .	. .
North America											
Canada[13]	m. dollars	12 854	13 473	12 830	13 111	13 293	13 008	12 457	11 511	10 801	10 044
Mexico	m. new pesos	1 964	2 665	3 661	4 530	5 445	7 554	7 860	11 034	13 281	14 220
USA[13]	m. dollars	304 085	306 170	280 292	305 141	297 637	288 059	278 856	271 417	276 324	269 763
South America											
Argentina[14]	m. pesos	[53.6]	[877]	[2 555]	[3 280]	[3 830]	4 021	4 361	4 136	4 016	3 962
Bolivia	m. bolivianos	225	357	440	473	537	569	612	682	760	. .
Brazil[14]	th./m. reais	(6.8)	(142)	(448)	7 018	| 188	4 108	10 008	9 994	(15 919)	(15 654)
Chile	b. pesos	[180]	[220]	[280]	330	370	408	492	514	583	481
Colombia	b. pesos	211	281	347	470	588	982	1 318	2 040	. .	. .
Ecuador	b. sucres	102	156	273	532	841	982	893	1 260	. .	. .
Guyana[15]	m. dollars	. .	142	227	453	562	759	801	780	[1 000]	. .
Paraguay	m./b. guaranies	57 340	79 883	| 137	154	167	[202]	[240]	[266]	. .	. .
Peru[12]	m. new soles	[2.0]	130	480	1 001	(1 390)	(1 778)	[1 878]	[2 000]	. .	. .
Uruguay	m. pesos	114	233	363	813	974	2 083	1 816	2 228	2 638	. .
Venezuela	m. bolivares	(32 404)	(45 379)	45 269	54 994	94 995	110 940	196 841	240 576	473 388	. .
Asia											
Central Asia											
Kazakhstan[16]	b. tenge	. .	. .	. .	. .	[0.3]	[3.8]	[10.8]	[15.0]	[17.2]	[20.0]

Kyrgyzstan[16]	m. soms	. .	. .	. .	. .	[38.3]	[105]	[237]	[291]	[425]	. .
Tajikistan[16]	m. roubles	. .	. .	. .	[2.6]	[243]	[347]	[713]	[3 977]	[7 240]	. .
Turkmenistan[16]	b. manats	. .	. .	. .	. .	. .	[1.5]	[15.1]	[158]	[440]	[613]
Uzbekistan[16]	m. soms	. .	. .	. .	[11.7]	[164]	[991]	[3 355]	[6 900]	. .	. .
East Asia											
Brunei[17]	m. dollars	363	419	424	410	378	400	405	420	[435]	. .
Cambodia	b. riels	. .	. .	. .	. .	[165]	[302]	302	298	305	(410)
China, P. R.[18]	b. yuan	[43.9]	[49.2]	[53.7]	[69.2]	[73.1]	[87.2]	[105]	[124]	[139]	[156]
Indonesia	b. rupiahs	2 648	3 156	3 512	4 066	4 281	5 135	5 652	6 734	9 401	9 740
Japan	b. yen	4 043	4 130	4 329	4 510	4 618	4 673	4 714	4 815	4 917	4 932
Korea, North	b. won	(4.1)	(4.3)	(4.5)	(4.6)	(4.7)	(4.8)	. .	. .	. .	. .
Korea, South	b. won	5 921	6 665	7 892	8 709	9 040	10 057	11 125	12 533	13 160	(13 800)
Laos	b. kip	. .	. .	. .	. .	. .	. .	87.6	. .	. .	. .
Malaysia	m. ringgits	2 761	3 043	4 323	4 500	4 951	5 565	6 121	6 091	6 183	[5 700]
Mongolia	m. tugriks	850	592	888	1 184	4 795	7 017	9 339	11 663	. .	. .
Myanmar	m. kyats	3 689	5 160	5 924	8 366	12 695	16 742	22 283	27 667	. .	. .
Philippines	m. pesos	15 907	14 707	15 898	17 462	21 132	24 401	30 510	32 269	[39 920]	[50 890]
Singapore	m. dollars	2 751	3 266	3 495	3 799	4 010	4 273	5 206	5 782	6 618	[7 161]
Taiwan	b. dollars	188	211	227	239	253	255	261	277	288	298
Thailand	m. baht	44 831	48 846	55 502	64 961	73 708	78 300	88 983	93 959	97 783	98 461
Viet Nam	b. dong	2 047	3 319	4 292	3 730	3 168	4 730	. .	. .	. .	. .
South Asia											
Afghanistan	m. afghanis	. .	. .	. .	. .	. .	. .	. .	. .	. .	. .
Bangladesh	m. taka	11 450	11 965	13 980	16 095	17 290	18 080	19 110	21 376	24 327	[24 926]
India	b. rupees	140	151	160	171	206	228	260	288	345	399
Nepal	m. rupees	834	988	1 114	1 320	1 607	1 801	1 939	2 064	2 274	2 526
Pakistan	m. rupees	50 961	58 122	69 683	81 604	90 610	97 001	108 459	124 875	133 407	139 380
Sri Lanka	m. rupees	4 073	6 736	10 317	12 876	15 413	19 415	35 186	38 117	37 062	(44 000)

State	Currency	1989	1990	1991	1992	1993	1994	1995	1996	1997	1998
Europe											
Albania	m. leks	[1 075]	[1 030]	[895]	2 368	3 837	4 412	4 922	4 401	4 928	[4 915]
Armenia[16]	b. dram	. .	. .	. .	1.3	17.9	. .	21.2	21.7	30.5	33.3
Austria	m. shillings	17 849	17 537	18 208	19 600	20 500	21 200	21 500	21 635	22 023	22 265
Azerbaijan[16]	b. manats	. .	. .	. .	0.8	7.9	85.6	248	305	353	. .
Belarus[16]	b. roubles	. .	. .	. .	1.5	17.7	365	1 723	2 231	5 051	6 448
Belgium	m. francs	152 917	155 205	157 919	132 819	129 602	131 955	131 156	131 334	131 859	134 146
Bosnia and Herz.[19]	m. marks	. .	. .	. .	. .	. .	(335)	(462)	(189)	(254)	(230)
Bulgaria	m. leva	1 605	1 615	4 434	5 748	8 113	12 920	21 840	37 853	374 525	487 506
Croatia[20]	m. kuna	. .	. .	. .	200	3 422	7 149	9 282	7 760	7 000	7 500
Cyprus	m. pounds	82.0	127	131	191	90.0	99.0	91.0	141	(200)	(205)
Czech Rep.[21]	m. korunas	. .	. .	. .	. .	[26 230]	27 008	22 275	30 509	30 214	36 877
Czechoslovakia[22]	m. korunas	43 784	41 900	43 037	48 503	. .	. .	. .	. .	. .	. .
Denmark	m. kroner	15 963	16 399	17 091	17 129	17 390	17 293	17 468	17 896	18 521	19 133
Estonia[23]	m. kroons	. .	. .	. .	68.0	174	327	629	653	811	854
Finland	m. markkaa	6 853	7 405	8 903	9 298	9 225	9 175	8 594	9 291	9 246	10 003
France	m. francs	225 331	231 911	240 936	238 874	241 199	246 469	238 432	237 375	242 357	239 578
Georgia[16]	th./m. lari	. .	. .	. .	3.5	200	| [40.0]	[55.0]	77.0	95.0	[101]
German DR[24]	m. marks	. .	. .	. .	. .	. .	. .	. .	. .	. .	. .
Germany[25]	m. marks	63 178	68 376	65 579	65 536	61 529	58 957	58 986	58 671	57 602	58 142
Greece	m./b. drachmas	503 032	612 344	693 846	835 458	932 995	| 1 053	1 171	1 343	1 511	1 725
Hungary	m. forints	47 763	52 367	53 999	61 216	67 492	67 996	76 937	85 954	96 814	122 502
Ireland	m. pounds	264	355	362	376	385	412	429	460	494	511
Italy	b. lire	27 342	28 007	30 191	30 813	32 364	32 835	31 561	36 170	38 701	40 089
Latvia[23]	m. lai	. .	. .	. .	. .	12.0	19.0	23.0	21.0	29.0	23.0
Lithuania[23]	m. lats	. .	. .	. .	. .	85.4	79.3	115	169	303	602
Luxembourg	m. francs	2 995	3 233	3 681	3 963	3 740	4 214	4 194	4 380	4 797	5 149
Macedonia[26]	m. denar	. .	. .	. .	. .	. .	. .	. .	5 223	4 163	4 359

Malta	th. liri	7 426	6 722	7 029	8 513	9 419	10 533	10 996	12 002	12 105	11 727
Moldova[16]	m. lei	. .	. .	. .	. .	9.7	36.7	60.0	70.7	(80.5)	60.0
Netherlands	m. guilders	13 571	13 513	13 548	13 900	13 103	12 990	12 864	13 199	13 345	13 425
Norway	m. kroner	20 248	21 251	21 313	23 638	22 528	24 019	22 224	22 813	23 010	24 114
Poland	m. zlotys	215	1 495	1 830	2 624	3 980	5 117	6 595	8 313	10 077	11 550
Portugal	m. escudos	229 344	267 299	305 643	341 904	352 504	360 811	403 478	401 165	418 585	428 752
Romania	b. lei	29.0	30.0	80.0	196	420	1 185	1 538	1 959	4 772	6 320
Russia[27]	m. roubles	[134]	[123]	. .	[1 049]	[9 037]	[35 890]	[63 220]	[82 485]	[105 034]	[85 600]
Slovak Rep.[21]	m. korunas	. .	. .	. .	. .	8 211	9 614	12 932	13 412	13 901	14 628
Slovenia[20]	m. tolars	. .	. .	. .	[22 870]	[26 100]	[30 650]	39 664	44 666	46 434	54 288
Spain	b. pesetas	923	923	947	928	1 055	995	1 079	1 091	1 123	1 108
Sweden	m. kronor	28 210	31 212	34 974	35 744	35 476	36 483	38 673	40 973	37 600	38 568
Switzerland	m. francs	5 431	5 947	6 104	6 014	5 524	5 723	5 011	4 782	4 634	4 637
Turkey	b./tr. liras	7 158	13 866	23 657	42 320	77 717	| 157	303	612	1 183	2 165
UK[13]	m. pounds	20 868	22 287	24 380	22 850	22 686	22 490	21 439	22 330	21 556	22 242
Ukraine[16]	th./m. hryvnias	. .	. .	. .	. .	7 949	| 337	1 665	2 833	3 428	3 712
Yugoslavia[28]	m. dinars	. .	. .	. .	. .	678	1 200	1 611	(4 210)	(7 593)	(6 550)
Yugoslavia (former)[29]	m. new dinars	6 113	5 180	. .	. .	. .	. .	. .	. .	. .	. .
Middle East											
Bahrain	m. dinars	74.0	81.0	89.0	95.0	94.0	96.0	103	[106]	[135]	. .
Egypt	m. pounds	3 352	3 855	4 646	5 265	5 723	6 142	6 682	7 164	7 557	8 026
Iran	b. rials	811	1 011	1 235	1 482	2 255	4 023	4 457	5 478	7 682	9 670
Iraq	m. dinars	. .	. .	. .	. .	. .	. .	. .	. .	. .	. .
Israel	m. new shekels	10 566	12 940	14 776	16 919	17 539	19 836	22 216	26 489	29 257	32 600
Jordan	m. dinars	252	255	270	273	300	348	387	417	444	469
Kuwait	m. dinars	610	2 585	3 674	1 852	900	979	1 102	(1 108)	[1 037]	[1 020]
Lebanon	b. pounds	. .	97.9	140	499	518	704	795	760	702	811
Oman	m. riyals	601	742	643	778	738	779	776	737	698	(698)
Qatar	m. dinars	. .	. .	. .	. .	. .	. .	. .	. .	. .	. .
Saudi Arabia	m. riyals	48 946	[50 000]	[100 000]	54 000	61 636	53 549	49 501	50 025	67 975	(65 000)

State	Currency	1989	1990	1991	1992	1993	1994	1995	1996	1997	1998
Syria	m. pounds	16 654	18 429	32 483	33 412	29 948	37 270	40 500	41 741	[38 313]	[39 500]
UAE[30]	m. dirhams	5 827	5 827	5 827	7 163	7 750	7 342	7 160	[7 400]	. .	. .
Yemen[31]	m. rials	. .	10 382	13 227	16 812	19 752	30 273	35 897	44 964	53 087	53 842
Oceania											
Australia	m. dollars	8 128	[9 164]	[10 012]	[10 062]	10 382	10 821	10 879	10 947	11 196	11 726
Fiji	m. dollars	43.1	45.2	47.9	45.9	49.4	49.3	48.8	51.2	. .	. .
New Zealand	m. dollars	[1 340]	[1 300]	1 210	1 097	1 050	1 015	1 004	1 023	1 159	1 239
Papua New Guinea	m. kina	45.6	65.6	50.1	56.5	67.1	54.3	. .	. .	. .	. .

Table 7A.3. Military expenditure by region and country, in constant US dollars, 1989–98

Figures are in US $m., at constant 1995 prices and exchange rates.[3]

State	1989	1990	1991	1992	1993	1994	1995	1996	1997	1998
Africa										
North Africa										
Algeria	542	[606]	593	[868]	1 067	1 298	1 235	1 371	1 650	1 733
Libya	. .	. .	. .	. .	. .	. .	. .	. .	. .	. .
Morocco	1 890	1 383	1 453	1 441	1 446	1 684	1 551	1 433	. .	. .
Tunisia	402	402	407	390	409	409	345	349	363	378
Sub-Saharan										
Angola[4]	. .	. .	. .	. .	. .	. .	1 001	1 107	[896]	. .
Benin	31.8	30.8	. .	. .	. .	. .	. .	. .	. .	. .
Botswana	151	190	204	189	198	182	166	153	180	229
Burkina Faso	57.5	62.6	52.0	51.0	46.2	(36.0)	(36.7)	(35.7)	(41.3)	. .
Burundi	42.9	45.3	47.5	48.8	47.0	48.3	44.1	46.3	48.3	[59.7]
Cameroon	176	167	153	144	149	121	116	110	. .	[159]
Cape Verde	. .	. .	. .	. .	3.1	3.9	6.2	4.3	4.6	. .
Central African Rep.	. .	. .	17.4	17.7	16.1	14.2	13.0	12.0	. .	. .
Chad	. .	. .	. .	. .	34.0	26.9	20.0	22.6	. .	. .
Congo	. .	. .	. .	. .	. .	. .	. .	. .	. .	. .
Congo, Dem. Rep.[5]	71.0	60.8	45.3	150	274	9.9	17.4	. .	[197]	. .
Côte d'Ivoire	128	123	125	122	121	107	. .	103	101	. .
Djibouti	36.8	34.1	32.6	. .	. .	. .	40.5	32.9	. .	. .
Equatorial Guinea	. .	. .	. .	. .	. .	3.0	3.4	. .	. .	. .
Eritrea[6]	. .	. .	. .	. .	98.5	76.6	123	141	. .	. .
Ethiopia	549	521	251	132	135	127	118	130	143	154
Gabon	. .	. .	. .	. .	. .	. .	. .	. .	. .	16.1
Gambia	3.3	3.9	4.6	3.8	2.7	2.5	3.1	4.2	. .	. .
Ghana	24.7	26.5	38.0	52.7	71.6	52.5	49.0	45.1	45.3	. .

State	1989	1990	1991	1992	1993	1994	1995	1996	1997	1998
Guinea	. .	. .	74.9	59.6	46.6	47.7	. .	. .	. .	. .
Guinea-Bissau[7]	3.9	. .	. .	. .	. .	2.1	2.2	1.8	. .	. .
Kenya	355	368	288	186	128	124	159	. .	. .	. .
Lesotho	33.7	31.8	27.0	22.2	20.4	24.7	26.2	26.9	32.6	. .
Liberia[8]	[27.4]	28.3	21.7	23.6	37.3	41.3	. .	. .	. .	. .
Madagascar	36.0	37.7	39.0	36.8	35.1	29.6	27.2	39.3	. .	. .
Malawi	18.8	17.7	15.8	17.6	19.1	18.1	14.7	15.1	14.2	. .
Mali	39.4	37.8	. .	. .	. .	. .	. .	. .	. .	. .
Mauritania	37.5	35.2	33.3	32.1	31.1	29.9	30.1	. .	. .	. .
Mauritius	8.9	11.1	12.5	12.9	12.4	13.0	13.4	12.6	. .	. .
Mozambique[9]	115	104	103	103	116	174	69.4	53.8	60.1	(75.3)
Namibia[10]	. .	. .	133	130	77.0	61.3	68.2	73.0	90.4	96.9
Niger	15.0	32.3	. .	. .	. .	. .	. .	. .	. .	. .
Nigeria	759	728	[1 001]	939	791	522	428	548	568	692
Rwanda	38.8	89.0	123	101	97.9	. .	56.1	. .	. .	. .
Senegal	85.3	87.3	85.0	82.6	97.0	79.3	80.9	79.5	79.1	. .
Seychelles	17.4	18.0	19.5	22.7	14.3	12.6	11.6	11.1	10.8	. .
Sierra Leone	10.3	11.6	20.1	25.5	27.4	25.9	25.0	(18.4)	(8.7)	. .
Somalia	. .	. .	. .	. .	. .	. .	. .	. .	. .	. .
South Africa	5 244	4 718	3 836	3 428	3 078	3 210	2 949	2 853	2 478	2 196
Sudan	308	270	203	173	184	145	139	154	. .	. .
Swaziland	12.1	17.6	19.1	23.9	26.4	27.3	27.1	28.7	25.6	. .
Tanzania	86.8	72.0	74.0	. .	. .	75.7	(80.7)	. .	. .	. .
Togo	43.0	44.1	41.2	40.8	44.5	32.7	30.9	. .	. .	. .
Uganda	90.6	101	96.9	74.4	88.9	104	110	[117]	[117]	[165]
Zambia	173	152	104	117	55.7	65.9	55.7	36.4	[35.2]	. .
Zimbabwe	365	369	350	280	249	259	256	261	273	223

Americas										
Central America										
Belize	5.0	5.3	5.2	5.7	6.5	8.1	8.1	7.5	8.7	. .
Costa Rica[11]	29.8	26.4	24.0	22.6	26.8	30.3	44.0	59.1	60.1	. .
El Salvador	241	204	185	161	123	104	97.0	87.7	84.6	. .
Guatemala	176	170	168	182	180	188	(144)	(127)	(125)	(106)
Honduras	81.9	74.1	50.5	51.6	43.8	(52.6)	47.0	45.2	38.9	. .
Nicaragua[12]	[111]	[229]	49.3	39.8	35.1	34.1	32.1	31.9	28.3	. .
Panama	108	78.5	83.7	89.1	96.7	99.6	96.8	99.9	. .	. .
North America										
Canada[13]	10 965	10 976	9 897	9 963	9 917	9 686	9 077	8 262	7 625	6 999
Mexico	869	932	1 043	1 118	1 225	1 589	1 224	1 279	1 276	1 185
USA[13]	373 618	356 994	313 647	331 280	313 784	296 188	278 856	263 727	262 159	251 836
South America										
Argentina[14]	[5 228]	[3 544]	[3 796]	[3 910]	[4 127]	4 156	4 362	4 127	3 987	3 886
Bolivia	96.4	131	133	127	133	131	127	126	135	. .
Brazil[14]	(9 220)	(6 360)	(4 005)	5 605	7 402	7 431	10 906	9 408	(14 015)	(13 125)
Chile	[1 097]	[1 059]	[1 105]	1 127	1 127	1 110	1 240	1 207	1 287	1 008
Colombia	908	936	887	946	965	1 301	1 444	1 858	. .	. .
Ecuador	308	317	373	471	514	471	348	395	. .	. .
Guyana[15]	. .	1.1	1.8	3.6	4.5	6.1	6.4	6.2	[8.0]	. .
Paraguay	93.0	93.8	129	126	116	[116]	[122]	[123]	. .	. .
Peru[12]	[1 243]	1 042	754	908	(848)	(877)	[834]	[796]	. .	. .
Uruguay	412	396	306	406	316	467	286	273	270	. .
Venezuela	(1 615)	(1 608)	1 195	1 104	1 382	1 003	1 113	681	893	. .
Asia										
Central Asia										
Kazakhstan[16]	. .	. .	. .	. .	[609]	[390]	[401]	[401]	[391]	[414]
Kyrgyzstan[16]	. .	. .	. .	. .	[45.8]	[38.1]	[56.4]	[51.4]	[59.4]	. .
Tajikistan[16]	. .	. .	. .	. .	[144]	[82.2]	[59.1]	[72.4]	[50.0]	. .
Turkmenistan[16]	. .	. .	. .	. .	. .	[167]	[148]	[143]	[216]	[255]

State	1989	1990	1991	1992	1993	1994	1995	1996	1997	1998
Uzbekistan[16]	. .	. .	. .	[133]	[431]	[189]	[294]	[369]	. .	. .
East Asia										
Brunei[17]	305	344	343	328	290	299	286	291	. .	. .
Cambodia	. .	. .	. .	. .	[70.9]	[125]	123	110	109	(130)
China, P. R.[18]	[9 900]	[10 800]	[11 400]	[13 800]	[12 700]	[12 200]	[12 500]	[13 700]	[14 900]	[16 900]
Indonesia	1 944	2 150	2 187	2 354	2 261	2 499	2 513	2 772	3 633	2 767
Japan	47 409	46 984	47 676	48 819	49 377	49 632	50 112	51 095	51 320	51 285
Korea, North	(1 871)	(1 988)	(2 058)	(2 112)	(2 162)	(2 220)	. .	. .	. .	. .
Korea, South	11 253	11 666	12 638	13 130	13 002	13 625	14 424	15 481	15 564	(15 042)
Laos	. .	. .	. .	. .	. .	. .	109	. .	. .	. .
Malaysia	1 399	1 502	2 044	2 032	2 159	2 339	2 444	2 349	2 322	[2 000]
Mongolia	. .	53.2	40.1	29.3	32.2	25.1	20.8	17.8	. .	. .
Myanmar	2 530	3 007	2 610	3 023	3 480	3 699	3 932	4 199	. .	. .
Philippines	1 158	938	854	861	969	1 026	1 187	1 158	[1 364]	[1 580]
Singapore	2 278	2 615	2 706	2 875	2 967	3 068	3 673	4 026	4 518	[4 803]
Taiwan	8 886	9 584	9 952	10 023	10 324	9 996	9 858	10 163	10 471	10 620
Thailand	2 402	2 471	2 656	2 987	3 279	3 311	3 561	3 552	3 500	3 234
Viet Nam	950	884	625	462	373	486	. .	. .	. .	. .
South Asia										
Afghanistan	. .	. .	. .	. .	. .	. .	. .	. .	. .	. .
Bangladesh	376	364	397	438	470	475	474	517	557	[526]
India	7 756	7 642	7 134	6 819	7 702	7 765	8 004	8 165	9 098	9 842
Nepal	29.5	32.3	31.5	31.9	36.1	37.3	37.4	36.4	38.9	. .
Pakistan	2 986	3 123	3 349	3 582	3 617	3 444	3 428	3 576	3 431	3 319
Sri Lanka	157	214	293	328	351	408	687	642	569	(609)
Europe										
Albania	[92.8]	[88.9]	[76.7]	62.4	54.6	51.3	53.1	42.1	35.4	[28.9]
Armenia[16]	. .	. .	. .	. .	. .	. .	. .	. .	. .	. .

Austria	2 146	2 041	2 051	2 121	2 141	2 151	2 133	2 108	2 118	2 118
Azerbaijan[16]	. .	. .	. .	611	490	302	171	175	195	. .
Belarus[16]	. .	. .	. .	671	615	545	318	270	373	311
Belgium	6 051	5 939	5 855	4 808	4 566	4 540	4 449	4 362	4 312	4 328
Bosnia and Herz.[19]	. .	. .	. .	. .	. .	(186)	(257)	(105)	(141)	(128)
Bulgaria	1 026	1 098	695	470	383	312	325	253	211	217
Croatia[20]	. .	. .	. .	1 305	1 410	1 421	1 775	1 422	1 232	1 257
Cyprus	239	354	348	476	214	225	201	303	(414)	. .
Czech Rep.[21]	. .	. .	. .	. .	[1 187]	1 110	839	1 056	965	1 061
Czechoslovakia[22]	2 683	2 334	2 398	2 702	. .	. .	. .	. .	. .	. .
Denmark	3 224	3 226	3 283	3 224	3 230	3 150	3 118	3 126	3 168	3 206
Estonia[23]	. .	. .	. .	21.4	28.9	36.7	54.9	46.3	52.0	49.8
Finland	1 854	1 887	2 180	2 219	2 155	2 120	1 968	2 114	2 078	2 213
France	52 099	51 851	52 198	50 527	49 979	50 233	47 768	46 596	47 037	45 978
Georgia[16]	. .	. .	. .	127	215	[273]	[143]	144	166	[166]
German DR[24]	. .	. .	. .	. .	. .	. .	. .	. .	. .	. .
Germany[25]	53 840	56 760	52 533	49 951	44 930	41 906	41 160	40 343	38 906	38 878
Greece	5 001	5 059	4 797	4 987	4 866	4 950	5 056	5 359	5 712	6 211
Hungary	1 511	1 284	987	910	819	694	612	554	527	580
Ireland	495	645	637	642	648	678	688	726	768	772
Italy	22 846	21 974	22 283	21 643	21 758	21 220	19 376	21 369	22 409	22 809
Latvia[23]	. .	. .	. .	. .	38.6	45.0	43.6	33.8	43.1	32.5
Lithuania[23]	. .	. .	. .	. .	51.3	27.7	28.8	33.9	55.8	104
Luxembourg	121	126	139	145	132	146	142	147	158	168
Macedonia[26]	. .	. .	. .	. .	. .	. .	. .	133	104	107
Malta	25.5	22.4	22.8	27.2	28.9	31.0	31.2	33.2	32.4	30.5
Moldova[16]	. .	. .	. .	. .	31.7	20.5	30.0	29.0	(29.7)	20.5
Netherlands	9 907	9 627	9 362	9 308	8 549	8 249	8 011	8 051	7 970	7 859
Norway	3 745	3 774	3 660	3 968	3 697	3 885	3 508	3 557	3 498	3 577
Poland	3 442	3 661	2 536	2 502	2 773	2 675	2 720	2 853	2 984	3 053
Portugal	2 435	2 503	2 569	2 639	2 547	2 486	2 670	2 573	2 629	2 622

State	1989	1990	1991	1992	1993	1994	1995	1996	1997	1998
Romania	1 411	1 401	1 362	1 072	647	771	756	694	664	546
Russia[27]	[240 000]	[203 000]	. .	[47 500]	[41 900]	[40 500]	[25 700]	[23 400]	[24 900]	[11 200]
Slovak Rep.[21]	. .	. .	. .	. .	344	356	435	426	417	410
Slovenia[20]	. .	. .	. .	[343]	[297]	[291]	335	344	327	354
Spain	10 164	9 517	9 224	8 529	9 275	8 347	8 652	8 451	8 529	8 241
Sweden	5 345	5 382	5 533	5 503	5 228	5 242	5 421	5 744	5 229	5 337
Switzerland	5 653	5 874	5 699	5 395	4 795	4 928	4 238	4 010	3 869	3 865
Turkey	4 552	5 502	5 655	5 948	6 578	6 442	6 609	7 402	7 704	7 920
UK[13]	42 645	41 583	42 954	38 828	37 962	36 712	33 841	34 404	32 201	32 320
Ukraine[16]	. .	. .	. .	. .	376	1 608	1 665	1 574	1 643	1 561
Yugoslavia[28]	. .	. .	. .	. .	251	444	597	(1 559)	(2 812)	(2 426)
Yugoslavia (former)[29]	. .	. .	. .	. .	. .	. .	. .	. .	. .	. .
Middle East										
Bahrain	212	230	251	268	259	262	274	[282]	[358]	. .
Egypt	2 205	2 171	2 185	2 178	2 113	2 096	1 971	1 971	1 988	2 043
Iran	1 754	2 030	2 118	2 022	2 539	3 444	2 550	2 431	2 910	2 985
Iraq	. .	. .	. .	. .	. .	. .	. .	. .	. .	. .
Israel	7 515	7 851	7 533	7 706	7 200	7 250	7 378	7 905	8 010	8 540
Jordan	514	448	439	426	454	508	552	559	578	587
Kuwait	2 574	9 928	12 933	6 555	3 172	3 367	3 693	(3 583)	[3 335]	[3 264]
Lebanon	. .	300	283	458	382	480	490	428	376	414
Oman	1 802	2 022	1 675	2 008	1 882	1 999	2 018	1 879	1 745	(1 753)
Qatar	. .	. .	. .	. .	. .	. .	. .	. .	. .	. .
Saudi Arabia	14 912	[14 913]	[28 433]	15 369	17 360	14 997	13 218	13 204	17 926	(17 142)
Syria	3 020	2 801	4 529	4 197	3 322	3 585	3 608	3 435	[3 094]	[3 155]
UAE[30]	2 279	2 149	1 905	2 231	2 300	2 096	1 950	[1 951]	. .	. .
Yemen[31]	. .	1 365	1 279	1 256	1 101	1 157	879	846	947	885

Oceania										
Australia	7 320	[7 692]	[9 125]	[8 446]	8 214	8 402	8 067	7 915	8 074	8 299
Fiji	40.1	38.9	38.7	35.3	36.1	35.8	34.7	35.3	. .	. .
New Zealand	[1 033]	[945]	858	770	727	691	659	656	735	775
Papua New Guinea	. .	. .	51.8	56.0	63.4	49.9	. .	. .	. .	. .

Table 7A.4. Military expenditure by region and country, as percentage of gross domestic product, 1989–97

State	1989	1990	1991	1992	1993	1994	1995	1996	1997
Africa									
North Africa									
Algeria	1.7	[1.5]	1.2	[1.9]	2.6	3.2	3.0	3.3	3.9
Libya	. .	. .	. .	. .	. .	. .	. .	. .	. .
Morocco	5.8	4.1	4.1	4.3	4.4	4.9	4.7	3.9	. .
Tunisia	2.8	2.7	2.6	2.3	2.4	2.3	1.9	1.8	1.8
Sub-Saharan									
Angola[4]	. .	5.8	6.8	12.0	25.6	35.2	18.9	15.1	[11.4]
Benin	1.9	1.8	. .	. .	. .	. .	. .	. .	. .
Botswana	3.2	3.9	4.2	4.1	4.0	3.6	3.1	2.6	3.0
Burkina Faso	2.9	3.0	2.4	2.3	2.0	(1.8)	(1.7)	(1.6)	(1.7)
Burundi	3.3	3.4	3.8	3.6	3.2	4.0	3.6	5.3	6.2
Cameroon	1.7	1.7	1.5	1.5	1.5	1.6	1.4	1.3	. .
Cape Verde	. .	. .	. .	. .	0.8	1.0	1.5	1.0	1.0
Central African Rep.	. .	. .	1.6	1.7	1.6	1.2	1.2	1.1	. .
Chad	. .	. .	. .	. .	3.8	2.7	2.0	2.2	. .
Congo	. .	. .	. .	. .	. .	. .	. .	. .	. .
Congo, Dem. Rep.[5]	0.8	0.6	0.5	1.9	4.7	. .	0.3	. .	. .
Côte d'Ivoire	1.4	1.5	1.4	1.4	1.4	1.1	. .	1.0	0.9
Djibouti	6.4	6.3	5.9	. .	. .	. .	8.3	7.1	. .
Equatorial Guinea	. .	. .	. .	. .	. .	2.0	2.1	. .	. .
Eritrea[6]	. .	. .	. .	. .	21.4	13.0	19.9	22.8	. .
Ethiopia	11.1	10.4	5.9	3.2	2.6	2.5	2.1	2.0	1.9
Gabon	. .	. .	. .	. .	. .	. .	. .	. .	. .
Gambia	1.1	1.2	1.3	1.1	0.9	0.8	. .	. .	. .
Ghana	0.4	0.4	0.6	0.8	1.1	0.7	0.8	0.7	0.7
Guinea	. .	. .	2.4	1.7	1.3	1.3	. .	. .	. .

Guinea-Bissau[7]	0.2	. .	. .	. .	. .	0.3	0.5	0.6	. .
Kenya	3.1	3.3	2.7	1.9	1.5	1.6	1.8	. .	. .
Lesotho	4.4	3.9	3.8	3.2	2.7	3.0	3.1	2.9	. .
Liberia[8]	[2.3]	. .	. .	. .	. .	. .	. .	. .	. .
Madagascar	1.2	1.2	1.3	1.2	1.1	0.9	0.9	1.2	. .
Malawi	1.5	1.3	1.1	1.4	1.3	1.5	1.0	0.9	0.8
Mali	2.3	2.1	. .	. .	. .	. .	. .	. .	. .
Mauritania	4.0	3.8	3.6	3.5	3.2	2.9	2.8	. .	. .
Mauritius	0.3	0.4	0.4	0.4	0.3	0.3	0.3	0.3	. .
Mozambique[9]	10.3	10.1	8.7	8.3	7.6	11.7	4.6	3.6	3.7
Namibia[10]	. .	. .	4.4	4.3	2.6	1.8	2.0	2.1	2.5
Niger	0.9	1.9	. .	. .	. .	. .	. .	. .	. .
Nigeria	1.0	0.9	[1.1]	0.9	0.9	0.7	0.5	0.5	0.6
Rwanda	1.8	3.7	5.5	4.4	4.5	3.5	4.2	. .	. .
Senegal	2.1	2.0	1.9	1.8	2.1	1.8	1.8	1.7	1.6
Seychelles	4.3	4.0	4.4	4.7	2.8	2.5	2.3	2.1	1.9
Sierra Leone	0.6	0.7	1.5	2.2	2.4	2.2	2.7	. .	. .
Somalia	. .	. .	. .	. .	. .	. .	. .	. .	. .
South Africa	4.1	3.6	3.0	2.8	2.5	2.5	2.2	2.0	1.8
Sudan	3.2	2.9	2.5	2.2	2.3	2.1	1.7	2.0	. .
Swaziland	1.2	1.6	1.7	1.9	1.8	2.2	2.3	2.2	1.9
Tanzania	1.7	1.5	1.5	. .	. .	1.5	(1.5)	. .	. .
Togo	3.1	3.1	3.1	2.9	4.0	2.6	2.4	. .	. .
Uganda	2.3	2.5	2.2	1.5	1.8	1.8	1.8	[1.8]	[1.7]
Zambia	4.2	3.7	2.6	3.0	1.6	1.9	1.6	1.2	[1.1]
Zimbabwe	4.6	4.5	3.8	3.7	3.4	3.3	3.3	3.2	3.2
Americas									
Central America									
Belize	1.2	1.2	1.1	1.1	1.2	1.4	1.4	1.3	1.5
Costa Rica[11]	0.4	0.4	0.3	0.3	0.3	0.3	0.5	0.7	0.6

State	1989	1990	1991	1992	1993	1994	1995	1996	1997
El Salvador	2.9	2.7	2.4	2.0	1.5	1.2	1.0	0.9	0.9
Guatemala	1.6	1.5	1.4	1.5	1.4	1.4	(1.0)	(0.9)	(0.8)
Honduras	2.4	2.2	1.5	1.5	1.2	(1.3)	1.2	1.1	0.9
Nicaragua[12]	[6.5]	[2.1]	2.8	2.3	2.0	1.9	1.7	1.6	1.4
Panama	2.1	1.4	1.4	1.3	1.3	1.3	1.2	1.2	. .
North America									
Canada[13]	2.0	2.0	1.9	1.9	1.9	1.7	1.6	1.4	1.3
Mexico	0.4	0.4	0.4	0.4	0.4	0.5	0.4	0.4	0.4
USA[13]	5.6	5.3	4.7	4.9	4.5	4.2	3.8	3.5	3.4
South America									
Argentina[14]	[1.7]	[1.3]	[1.4]	[1.4]	[1.5]	1.4	1.6	1.4	1.2
Bolivia	1.8	2.3	2.3	2.1	2.2	2.1	1.9	1.9	1.9
Brazil[14]	(1.7)	(1.3)	(0.7)	1.1	1.3	1.2	1.5	1.3	(1.8)
Chile	[2.4]	[2.4]	[2.3]	2.2	2.1	1.9	1.9	1.8	1.8
Colombia	1.4	1.4	1.3	1.4	1.3	1.7	1.8	2.3	. .
Ecuador	2.0	1.9	2.2	2.7	3.1	2.7	1.9	2.1	. .
Guyana[15]	. .	0.9	0.6	1.0	1.0	1.0	0.9	0.8	[0.9]
Paraguay	1.2	1.2	1.6	1.6	1.4	[1.4]	[1.4]	[1.4]	. .
Peru[12]	[1.9]	2.0	1.5	1.9	(1.7)	(1.6)	[1.4]	[1.3]	. .
Uruguay	2.4	2.4	1.8	2.3	1.8	2.5	1.6	1.5	1.4
Venezuela	(2.2)	(2.0)	1.5	1.3	1.7	1.3	1.4	0.8	1.1
Asia									
Central Asia									
Kazakhstan[16]	. .	. .	. .	. .	[1.0]	[0.9]	[1.1]	[1.1]	[1.0]
Kyrgyzstan[16]	. .	. .	. .	. .	[0.7]	[0.9]	[1.5]	[1.3]	[1.4]
Tajikistan[16]	. .	. .	. .	[0.4]	[3.9]	[2.0]	[1.1]	[1.3]	[1.4]
Turkmenistan[16]	. .	. .	. .	. .	. .	[1.1]	[1.4]	[2.1]	[4.6]
Uzbekistan[16]	. .	. .	. .	. .	[3.2]	[1.5]	[1.1]	[1.2]	. .

East Asia									
Brunei[17]	. .	. .	6.4	6.2	5.7	6.0	5.7	5.6	. .
Cambodia	. .	. .	. .	. .	[3.0]	[4.9]	4.2	3.6	3.3
China, P. R.[18]	[2.6]	[2.7]	[2.5]	[2.7]	[2.1]	[1.9]	[1.8]	[1.8]	[1.8]
Indonesia	1.6	1.6	1.4	1.4	1.3	1.3	1.2	1.3	1.5
Japan	1.0	1.0	0.9	1.0	1.0	1.0	1.0	1.0	1.0
Korea, North	. .	. .	. .	. .	. .	. .	. .	. .	. .
Korea, South	4.0	3.7	3.7	3.6	3.4	3.3	3.2	3.2	3.1
Laos	. .	. .	. .	. .	. .	. .	6.2	. .	. .
Malaysia	2.7	2.6	3.3	3.0	3.0	2.9	2.8	2.4	2.2
Mongolia	7.9	5.7	4.7	2.5	2.9	2.5	2.2	2.2	. .
Myanmar	3.0	3.4	3.2	3.4	3.5	3.5	3.7	3.5	. .
Philippines	1.7	1.4	1.3	1.3	1.4	1.4	1.6	1.5	[1.6]
Singapore	4.6	4.8	4.6	4.7	4.3	3.9	4.3	4.4	4.6
Taiwan	4.8	4.9	4.7	4.5	4.3	4.0	3.8	3.7	3.5
Thailand	2.4	2.2	2.2	2.3	2.3	2.2	2.1	2.0	2.0
Viet Nam	. .	8.7	6.1	3.4	2.3	2.8	. .	. .	. .
South Asia									
Afghanistan	. .	. .	. .	. .	. .	. .	. .	. .	. .
Bangladesh	1.6	1.4	1.5	1.7	1.7	1.5	1.5	1.5	1.5
India	3.1	2.8	2.6	2.4	2.5	2.4	2.3	2.3	2.4
Nepal	0.8	0.8	0.7	0.8	0.8	0.8	0.8	0.7	. .
Pakistan	6.6	6.8	6.8	6.7	6.8	6.2	5.8	5.8	5.3
Sri Lanka	1.6	2.1	2.8	3.0	3.1	3.4	5.3	5.0	4.2
Europe									
Albania	. .	. .	. .	4.4	3.1	2.3	2.2	1.6	1.4
Armenia[16]	. .	. .	. .	. .	2.1	. .	4.1	3.3	3.8
Austria	1.1	1.0	0.9	1.0	1.0	0.9	0.9	0.9	0.9
Azerbaijan[16]	. .	. .	. .	3.3	5.0	4.6	2.3	2.2	2.3
Belarus[16]	. .	. .	. .	1.6	1.8	2.0	1.4	1.2	1.4

State	1989	1990	1991	1992	1993	1994	1995	1996	1997
Belgium	2.5	2.4	2.3	1.8	1.7	1.7	1.6	1.6	1.5
Bosnia and Herz.[19]	. .	. .	. .	. .	. .	. .	. .	. .	. .
Bulgaria	. .	. .	3.3	2.9	2.7	2.5	2.5	2.2	2.2
Croatia[20]	. .	. .	. .	7.3	8.2	8.4	9.8	7.5	6.2
Cyprus	3.6	5.0	4.9	6.2	2.7	2.7	2.3	3.4	(4.6)
Czech Rep.[21]	. .	. .	. .	. .	[2.6]	2.4	1.7	2.0	1.8
Czechoslovakia[22]	. .	. .	. .	. .	. .	. .	. .	. .	. .
Denmark	2.1	2.1	2.0	1.9	1.9	1.8	1.7	1.7	1.7
Estonia[23]	. .	. .	. .	0.5	0.8	1.1	1.5	1.2	1.2
Finland	1.4	1.4	1.8	2.0	1.9	1.8	1.6	1.6	1.5
France	3.7	3.6	3.6	3.4	3.4	3.3	3.1	3.0	3.0
Georgia[16]	. .	. .	. .	. .	1.2	[2.9]	[1.5]	1.4	1.4
German DR[24]	. .	. .	. .	. .	. .	. .	. .	. .	. .
Germany[25]	2.8	2.8	2.3	2.1	2.0	1.8	1.7	1.7	1.6
Greece	4.6	4.7	4.3	4.5	4.4	4.4	4.4	4.5	4.6
Hungary	2.8	2.5	2.2	2.1	1.9	1.6	1.4	1.3	1.1
Ireland	1.0	1.3	1.3	1.2	1.2	1.2	1.1	1.1	1.0
Italy	2.3	2.1	2.1	2.1	2.1	2.0	1.8	1.9	2.0
Latvia[23]	. .	. .	. .	. .	0.8	0.9	1.0	0.7	0.9
Lithuania[23]	. .	. .	. .	. .	0.7	0.5	0.5	0.5	0.8
Luxembourg	1.1	1.1	0.9	0.9	0.8	0.9	0.8	0.8	0.8
Macedonia[26]	. .	. .	. .	. .	. .	. .	. .	3.3	2.5
Malta	1.1	0.9	0.9	1.0	1.0	1.0	1.0	1.0	0.9
Moldova[16]	. .	. .	. .	. .	0.5	0.8	0.9	0.9	(0.9)
Netherlands	2.8	2.6	2.5	2.5	2.3	2.1	2.0	2.0	1.9
Norway	3.0	2.9	2.8	3.0	2.7	2.8	2.4	2.2	2.1
Poland	1.8	2.7	2.3	2.3	2.6	2.4	2.3	2.3	2.3
Portugal	2.8	2.8	2.8	2.8	2.6	2.5	2.6	2.4	2.4
Romania	3.6	3.5	3.6	3.3	2.1	2.4	2.1	1.8	1.9

Russia[27]	[14.2]	[12.3]	. .	[5.5]	[5.3]	[5.9]	[4.0]	[3.7]	[4.0]
Slovak Rep.[21]	. .	. .	. .	. .	2.2	2.2	2.5	2.3	2.1
Slovenia[20]	. .	. .	. .	. .	[1.8]	[1.7]	1.8	1.7	1.6
Spain	2.0	1.8	1.7	1.6	1.7	1.5	1.5	1.5	1.4
Sweden	2.3	2.3	2.4	2.5	2.5	2.4	2.3	2.4	2.2
Switzerland	1.9	1.9	1.8	1.8	1.6	1.6	1.4	1.3	1.3
Turkey	3.3	3.5	3.7	3.7	3.8	3.9	3.8	4.3	4.1
UK[13]	4.0	4.0	4.2	3.8	3.6	3.4	3.0	3.0	2.7
Ukraine[16]	. .	. .	. .	. .	0.5	2.8	3.1	3.5	3.7
Yugoslavia[28]	. .	. .	. .	. .	. .	. .	3.8	. .	. .
Middle East									
Bahrain	5.4	5.4	5.3	5.3	5.0	4.8	5.0	[4.9]	[5.9]
Egypt	4.4	4.0	4.2	3.8	3.6	3.5	3.3	3.1	2.9
Iran	2.9	2.8	2.5	2.2	2.4	3.1	2.5	2.4	2.7
Iraq	. .	. .	. .	. .	. .	. .	. .	. .	. .
Israel	12.3	12.3	11.0	10.5	9.4	8.8	8.5	8.7	8.6
Jordan	10.6	9.6	9.5	7.8	7.9	8.3	8.3	8.1	8.2
Kuwait	8.5	48.5	117.3	31.8	12.4	13.3	13.9	(11.9)	[11.3]
Lebanon	. .	5.0	3.4	5.2	4.0	4.6	4.4	3.7	3.1
Oman	18.6	18.3	14.7	16.2	15.4	15.7	14.7	13.0	11.2
Qatar	. .	. .	. .	. .	. .	. .	. .	. .	. .
Saudi Arabia	15.7	[12.8]	[22.6]	11.7	13.9	11.9	10.5	9.8	13.1
Syria	8.0	6.9	10.4	9.0	7.2	7.4	7.3	6.2	[5.6]
UAE[30]	5.8	4.7	4.7	5.5	5.9	5.5	4.9	[4.5]	. .
Yemen[31]	. .	. .	9.1	9.2	9.0	11.3	8.0	6.9	7.2
Oceania									
Australia	2.3	[2.4]	[2.6]	[2.5]	2.5	2.4	2.3	2.2	2.1
Fiji	2.3	2.2	2.3	2.0	1.9	1.8	1.7	1.7	. .
New Zealand	[1.9]	[1.8]	1.7	1.5	1.3	1.2	1.1	1.1	1.2
Papua New Guinea	. .	. .	1.4	1.3	1.4	1.0	. .	. .	. .

Conventions:

( ) Uncertain figure.

[ ] SIPRI estimate.

Notes:

[1] Contributions of military expenditure data, estimates and advice are gratefully acknowledged from: Julian Cooper (CREES, University of Birmingham) for Russia and the newly independent states in Europe, Paul Dunne (Middlesex Business University, London), Ivan Hostnik (Centre for Strategic Studies, Slovenia) for Slovenia, Thomas Scheetz (Buenos Aires) for Argentina, Ron Smith (Birkbeck College, London), Shaoguang Wang (Yale University, New Haven) for China and Ozren Zunec (University of Zagreb) for Croatia.

[2] Military expenditure data from different volumes of the SIPRI Yearbook should not be linked together because of data revision between volumes. The SIPRI military expenditure database has undergone significant revision during 1997 and 1998. Some series of basic military expenditure data (in local currency) have been revised in order to improve consistency over time or because of shifting to a series which better conforms to the SIPRI definition. Other revisions are due to the transfer of the data to a computerized relational database system (Foxpro) in 1998. As part of this process, all economic data (deflators, exchange rates and gross domestic products) have been updated and reassessed, which has resulted in revisions in the series for military expenditures in constant dollars (table 7A.3) and as a share of GDP (table 7A.4) even when basic military expenditure data have not been revised.

Data in fiscal year are converted to calendar year. With the introduction of the new computerized database there has been a slight change in the method of calculating calendar year data (only full months are counted). This has resulted in a slight change in data for countries which have a fiscal year which does not start at the beginning of a month.

[3] Figures in constant dollars are converted by the market exchange rate for all countries except Armenia, Azerbaijan, Belarus, Georgia, Kazakhstan, Kyrgyzstan, Moldova, Russia, Tajikistan, Turkmenistan, Ukraine and Uzbekistan. For these countries conversion to dollars has been made using the purchasing power parity (PPP) rates as derived from GNP per capita data of the World Bank and the European Bank for Reconstruction and Development (EBRD).

[4] Figures for Angolan military expenditure are estimates made by the IMF. These are significantly higher than the recorded official expenditures.

[5] Formerly Zaire.

[6] Became independent from Ethiopia in May 1993. Figures for 1995 include expenditure for demobilization.

[7] Figures in local currency are in Communauté financière africaine (CFA) francs. In previous Yearbooks data are expressed in pesos. The peso was replaced in 1997 at the rate of 65 pesos per CFA franc.

[8] Figures in the table for constant dollars are at current prices and 1995 exchange rate.

[9] Figures include expenditure for the demobilization of government and RENAMO soldiers and the formation of a new unified army from 1994 onward.

[10] Became independent on 21 Mar. 1990.

[11] Figures are official figures from the Costa Rica Ministry for Internal Security expenditure. Figures in *SIPRI Yearbooks 1997* and *1998* covered total expenditure for public order and safety.

[12] This state has changed currency during the period. All figures have been converted to the most recent currency.

[13] Figures are for fiscal year rather than for calendar year.

[14] Figures are uncertain because of very rapid inflation and a change in the currency. All figures have been converted to the most recent currency.

[15] Figures in the table for constant dollars are at 1992 prices and exchange rate.

[16] Became independent after the disintegration of the Soviet Union in Dec. 1991. Dollar figures are converted using the PPP.

[17] Current expenditure on the Royal Brunei Armed Forces.

[18] Figures are for estimated total military expenditures. For sources and methods of the military expenditure figures for China in local currency and as a share of GDP, see appendix 7D in this volume. Dollar figures are converted using the market exchange rate.

[19] Declared its independence from the former Yugoslavia in Mar. 1992 and was recognized by the European Community and the USA on 7 Apr. 1992. The creation of a Federation of Bosnia and Herzegovina was announced in Mar. 1994. The local currency since Jan. 1998 is the convertible mark, set at 1 convertible mark = 1 Deutsche mark. Figures in the table for constant dollars are at current prices and the 1998 exchange rate for the Deutsche mark.

[20] Declared its independence from the former Yugoslavia in June 1991 and was recognized by the European Community in Jan. 1992 and by the United Nations in May 1992.

[21] Formed on 1 Jan. 1993 after the break-up of Czechoslovakia.

[22] Divided into the Czech Republic and the Republic of Slovakia on 1 Jan. 1993. Figures in the table for constant dollars are at current prices and 1990 exchange rate.

[23] Became independent in Sep. 1991.

[24] The German Democratic Republic ceased to exist in Oct. 1990 when it was unified with the Federal Republic of Germany (West Germany).

[25] Figures up to and including 1990 refer to the former Federal Republic of Germany (West Germany).

[26] Declared its independence from the former Yugoslavia in Nov. 1992 and was admitted to the United Nations in Apr. 1993.

[27] Figures up to and including 1991 are for the Soviet Union. The rouble was redenominated on 1 Jan. 1998 at the rate of 1 'new' rouble = 1000 old. The figures in local currency (table 7A.2) have been converted to 'new' roubles in this edition of the Yearbook. Dollar figures are converted using the PPP. For sources and methods of the military expenditure figures for the USSR and Russia, see Cooper, J., 'The military expenditure of the USSR and the Russian Federation, 1987–97', *SIPRI Yearbook 1998: Armaments, Disarmament and International Security* (Oxford University Press: Oxford, 1998), appendix 6D, pp. 243–59.

[28] Serbia and Montenegro announced the creation of the Federal Republic of Yugoslavia in Apr. 1992. Figures in the table for constant dollars are at current prices and 1995 exchange rate.

[29] Former Yugoslavia including Croatia, Macedonia and Slovenia has a separate entry up to and including the year 1991.

[30] Figures exclude local military expenditure by each of the 7 emirates that form the United Arab Emirates.

[31] The Republic of Yemen was formed in May 1990 by the merger of the People's Democratic Republic of Yemen (South Yemen) and the Yemen Arab Republic (North Yemen). Figures in the table for constant dollars are at current prices and 1990 exchange rate.

Source: SIPRI military expenditure database.

Appendix 7B. Tables of NATO military expenditure

Table 7B.1. NATO distribution of military expenditure by category, 1989–98

Figures are in US $m., at 1995 prices and exchange rates. Figures in italics are percentage changes from previous year.

State	Item	1989	1990	1991	1992	1993	1994	1995	1996	1997	1998
North America											
Canada	Personnel	5 252	5 488	4 889	4 972	4 730	4 979	4 339	3 792	3 241	3 653
	Person. change	*4.6*	*4.5*	*– 10.9*	*1.7*	*– 4.9*	*5.3*	*– 12.9*	*– 12.6*	*– 14.5*	*12.7*
	Equipment	2 018	1 866	1 791	1 853	1 904	1 685	1 679	1 289	984	952
	Equip. change	*– 9.2*	*– 7.5*	*– 4.0*	*3.4*	*2.7*	*– 11.5*	*– 0.4*	*– 23.2*	*– 23.7*	*– 3.2*
USA	Personnel	142 722	130 660	135 496	130 193	121 748	115 513	110 985	102 326	102 504	100 483
	Person. change	*0.5*	*– 8.5*	*3.7*	*– 3.9*	*– 6.5*	*– 5.1*	*– 3.9*	*– 7.8*	*0.2*	*– 2.0*
	Equipment	94 525	88 535	85 626	75 863	69 032	86 487	77 243	70 943	68 161	*62 455*
	Equip. change	*0.9*	*– 6.3*	*– 3.3*	*– 11.4*	*– 9.0*	*25.3*	*– 10.7*	*– 8.2*	*– 3.9*	*– 8.4*
Europe											
Belgium	Personnel	4 060	4 062	4 034	3 140	3 178	3 147	3 163	3 010	2 988	2 943
	Person. change	*3.7*	*0.0*	*– 0.7*	*– 22.2*	*1.2*	*– 1.0*	*0.5*	*– 4.8*	*– 0.7*	*– 1.5*
	Equipment	599	469	480	394	320	354	240	231	267	234
	Equip. change	*– 18.8*	*– 21.7*	*2.3*	*– 17.9*	*– 18.9*	*10.8*	*– 32.2*	*– 3.8*	*15.6*	*– 12.6*
Denmark	Personnel	1 928	1 884	1 878	1 828	1 835	1 849	1 886	1 867	1 863	1 885
	Person. change	*0.6*	*– 2.3*	*– 0.3*	*– 2.7*	*0.4*	*0.8*	*2.0*	*– 1.1*	*– 0.2*	*1.2*
	Equipment	422	481	519	574	472	501	390	391	434	468
	Equip. change	*– 11.2*	*13.8*	*7.9*	*10.6*	*– 17.8*	*6.2*	*– 22.2*	*0.3*	*11.1*	*7.8*
Germany	Personnel	27 512	29 572	29 734	29 271	26 689	25 479	25 354	25 053	24 394	23 871
	Person. change	*2.5*	*7.5*	*0.5*	*– 1.6*	*– 8.8*	*– 4.5*	*– 0.5*	*– 1.2*	*– 2.6*	*– 2.1*
	Equipment	10 230	10 047	8 195	6 643	4 987	4 568	4 692	4 478	4 202	4 899
	Equip. change	*– 1.9*	*– 1.8*	*– 18.4*	*– 18.9*	*– 24.9*	*– 8.4*	*2.7*	*– 4.6*	*– 6.2*	*16.6*

Greece	Personnel	3 076	3 243	3 089	3 062	3 027	3 119	3 201	3 280	3 553	3 751
	Person. change	*– 1.0*	*5.4*	*– 4.7*	*– 0.9*	*– 1.2*	*3.0*	*2.6*	*2.5*	*8.3*	*5.6*
	Equipment	1 095	1 083	974	1 167	1 202	1 208	1 001	1 131	1 108	1 279
	Equip. change	*– 12.0*	*– 1.2*	*– 10.1*	*19.8*	*3.0*	*0.5*	*– 17.1*	*12.9*	*– 2.0*	*15.5*
Italy	Personnel	13 410	13 536	14 284	13 787	13 686	13 921	13 059	14 787	16 896	16 628
	Person. change	*2.4*	*0.9*	*5.5*	*– 3.5*	*– 0.7*	*1.7*	*– 6.2*	*13.2*	*14.3*	*– 1.6*
	Equipment	4 683	3 845	3 632	3 246	3 742	3 289	2 906	3 056	2 532	2 897
	Equip. change	*0.8*	*– 17.9*	*– 5.5*	*– 10.6*	*15.3*	*– 12.1*	*– 11.6*	*5.1*	*– 17.1*	*14.4*
Luxembourg	Personnel	93	100	98	110	102	114	115	121	125	129
	Person. change	*– 5.4*	*7.4*	*– 2.1*	*12.0*	*– 7.1*	*11.6*	*1.0*	*5.0*	*3.0*	*3.6*
	Equipment	5	4	8	7	4	3	3	6	6	8
	Equip. change	*24.4*	*– 12.4*	*86.4*	*– 11.1*	*– 44.5*	*– 17.3*	*11.6*	*76.0*	*– 8.0*	*51.9*
Netherlands	Personnel	5 320	5 189	5 168	5 352	5 078	4 809	4 807	4 492	4 463	3 961
	Person. change	*– 0.1*	*– 2.5*	*– 0.4*	*3.6*	*– 5.1*	*– 5.3*	*– 0.0*	*– 6.5*	*– 0.7*	*– 11.3*
	Equipment	1 744	1 723	1 461	1 322	1 197	1 386	1 250	1 506	1 251	1 415
	Equip. change	*– 12.9*	*– 1.2*	*– 15.3*	*– 9.5*	*– 9.4*	*15.8*	*– 9.8*	*20.5*	*– 16.9*	*13.1*
Norway	Personnel	1 596	1 634	1 695	1 738	1 331	1 356	1 308	1 334	1 347	1 406
	Person. change	*– 4.0*	*2.4*	*3.7*	*2.5*	*– 23.4*	*1.9*	*– 3.5*	*1.9*	*1.0*	*4.4*
	Equipment	929	853	805	968	1 020	1 107	891	896	861	909
	Equip. change	*35.5*	*– 8.2*	*– 5.6*	*20.2*	*5.4*	*8.5*	*– 19.5*	*0.6*	*– 4.0*	*5.6*
Portugal	Personnel	1 739	1 830	1 924	2 125	2 032	1 956	2 077	2 076	2 103	2 092
	Person. change	*13.0*	*5.2*	*5.2*	*10.4*	*– 4.3*	*– 3.7*	*6.2*	*0.0*	*1.3*	*– 0.5*
	Equipment	290	258	218	58	183	104	158	162	216	210
	Equip. change	*18.9*	*– 11.0*	*– 15.3*	*– 73.4*	*215.8*	*– 43.1*	*50.9*	*2.9*	*33.0*	*– 2.7*
Spain	Personnel	5 824	5 901	5 968	5 928	5 778	5 526	5 684	5 687	5 638	5 686
	Person. change	*8.8*	*1.3*	*1.1*	*– 0.7*	*– 2.5*	*– 4.4*	*2.9*	*0.1*	*– 0.9*	*0.9*
	Equipment	1 860	1 209	1 190	930	1 252	1 018	1 177	1 132	1 160	997
	Equip. change	*– 8.5*	*– 35.0*	*– 1.6*	*– 21.9*	*34.7*	*– 18.7*	*15.5*	*– 3.8*	*2.4*	*– 14.0*

State	Item	1989	1990	1991	1992	1993	1994	1995	1996	1997	1998
Turkey	Personnel	2 098	2 657	2 743	2 897	3 585	3 285	3 364	3 420	3 729	3619
	Person. change	*49.8*	*26.6*	*3.2*	*5.6*	*23.8*	*– 8.4*	*2.4*	*1.7*	*9.0*	*– 2.9*
	Equipment	783	1 100	1 284	1 475	1 506	1 888	1 963	2 280	2 080	2 313
	Equip. change	*– 11.6*	*40.6*	*16.7*	*14.9*	*2.1*	*25.3*	*4.0*	*16.1*	*– 8.8*	*11.2*
UK	Personnel	16 845	16 800	18 041	17 007	16 513	15 199	14 146	13 865	12 687	12 249
	Person. change	*– 2.8*	*– 0.3*	*7.4*	*– 5.7*	*– 2.9*	*– 8.0*	*– 6.9*	*– 2.0*	*– 8.5*	*– 3.5*
	Equipment	9 382	7 443	8 333	7 028	9 870	9 141	7 445	8 223	8 018	9017
	Equip. change	*– 13.2*	*– 20.7*	*12.0*	*– 15.7*	*40.4*	*– 7.4*	*– 18.6*	*10.4*	*– 2.5*	*12.5*
NATO Europe	Personnel	83 500	86 408	88 655	86 243	82 835	79 759	78 166	78 992	79 786	78 222
	Person. change	*2.3*	*3.5*	*2.6*	*– 2.7*	*– 4.0*	*– 3.7*	*– 2.0*	*1.1*	*– 1.0*	*– 2.0*
	Equipment	32 021	28 515	27 098	23 812	25 756	24 567	22 116	23 491	22 135	24 645
	Equip. change	*– 6.4*	*– 10.9*	*– 5.0*	*– 12.1*	*8.2*	*– 4.6*	*– 10.0*	*6.2*	*– 5.8*	*11.3*
NATO total	Personnel	231 474	222 555	229 040	221 408	209 313	200 251	193 489	185 110	185 530	182 358
	Person. change	*1.3*	*– 3.9*	*2.9*	*– 3.3*	*– 5.5*	*– 4.3*	*– 3.4*	*– 4.3*	*– 0.2*	*– 1.7*
	Equipment	128 564	118 915	114 515	101 529	96 692	112 740	101 038	95 723	91 279	88 052
	Equip. change	*– 1.2*	*– 7.5*	*– 3.7*	*– 11.3*	*– 4.8*	*16.6*	*– 10.4*	*– 5.3*	*– 4.6*	*– 3.5*

Note: The NATO data show percentage shares; the dollar figures have been calculated using these percentages and the total expenditures shown in table 7A.3. NATO data on the distribution between the different expenditure categories include a fourth category—infrastructure—which is of minor importance and has been excluded. France does not return figures giving this breakdown to NATO. For data on French equipment expenditure for the period 1988–97, as presented in the French defence budget, the reader is referred to *SIPRI Yearbook 1998*, table 6B.2. The French Government has not released such data for the year 1998, so it was not possible to update this table for the *SIPRI Yearbook 1999*.

Sources: NATO, *Financial and Economic Data Relating to NATO Defence*, Press release (98)147, 17 Dec. 1998, URL <http://www.nato.int/docu/pr/1998/p98-147e.htm>, version current on 17 Dec. 1998; and NATO Press releases M-DPC-2(96)168 (17 Dec. 1996) and M-DPC-2(93)76 (8 Dec. 1993).

Appendix 7C. Sources and methods for military expenditure data*

This appendix provides only the most basic information.[1] The military expenditure tables in appendix 7A cover 162 countries for the 10-year period 1989–98. These data cannot be combined with the series for earlier years as published in previous SIPRI Yearbooks, since these are updated each year and the revisions can be extensive—not only are significant changes made in figures which were previously estimates, but entire series are revised when new and better sources come to light. As a result there is sometimes considerable variation between data sets for individual countries in different Yearbooks.

I. Purpose of the data

The main purpose of the data on military expenditures is to provide an easily identifiable measure of the scale of resources absorbed by the military. Military expenditure is an input measure which is not directly related to the output of military activities, such as military capability or military security. Long-term trends in military expenditure and sudden changes in trend may be signs of a change in military output, but such interpretations should be made with caution.

Military expenditure data as measured in constant dollars (table 7A.3) are an indicator of the trend in the volume of resources used for military activities with the purpose of allowing comparisons over time for individual countries and comparisons between countries. The share of gross domestic product (GDP—table 7A.4) is a rough indicator of the proportion of national resources used for military activities, and therefore of the economic burden imposed on the national economy.

II. Sources

The sources for military expenditure data are, in order of priority: (*a*) primary sources, that is, official data provided by national governments, either in their official publications or in response to questionnaires; (*b*) secondary sources which quote primary data; and (*c*) other secondary sources.

The first group consists of national budget documents, defence white papers and public finance statistics published by ministries of finance and of defence, central banks and national statistical offices. It also includes government responses to questionnaires about military expenditure sent out by SIPRI, the United Nations or the Organization for Security and Co-operation in Europe (OSCE).

The second group includes international statistics, such as those of NATO and the International Monetary Fund (IMF). Data for NATO countries are taken from NATO defence expenditure statistics as published in a number of NATO sources. Data for

[1] For an overview of the conceptual problems and sources of uncertainty involved in the compilation of military expenditure data, the reader is referred to Brzoska, M., 'World military expenditures', eds K. Hartley and T. Sandler, *Handbook of Defense Economics*, vol. 1 (Elsevier: Amsterdam, 1995).

* The section on purchasing power parity rates was written by Petter Stålenheim.

many developing countries are taken from the IMF's *Government Financial Statistics Yearbook*, which provides a defence line for most of its member countries. This group also includes publications of other organizations which provide proper references to the primary sources used. The three main sources in this category are the *Europa Yearbook* (Europa Publications Ltd, London), the *Country Reports* of the Economist Intelligence Unit (London), and *Länderberichte* (German Federal Statistical Office, Wiesbaden).[2]

The third group of sources consists of specialist journals and newspapers.

III. Methods

Definition of military expenditure

Although the lack of sufficiently detailed data makes it difficult to apply a common definition of military expenditure on a worldwide basis, SIPRI has adopted a definition, based on the NATO definition, as a guideline. Where possible, SIPRI military expenditure data include all current and capital expenditure on: (*a*) the armed forces, including peacekeeping forces; (*b*) defence ministries and other government agencies engaged in defence projects; (*c*) paramilitary forces, when judged to be trained and equipped for military operations; and (*d*) military space activities. Such expenditures should include: (*a*) military and civil personnel, including retirement pensions of military personnel and social services for personnel; (*b*) operations and maintenance; (*c*) procurement; (*d*) military research and development; and (*e*) military aid (in the military expenditure of the donor country). Excluded are civil defence and current expenditures for previous military activities, such as for veterans' benefits, demobilization, conversion and weapon destruction.

In practice it is not possible to apply this definition for all countries, since this would require much more detailed information than is available about what is included in military budgets and off-budget military expenditure items. In many cases SIPRI cannot make independent estimates but is confined to using the national data provided. Priority is then given to the choice of a uniform definition over time for each country to achieve consistency over time, rather than to adjusting the figures for single years according to a common definition. In cases where it is impossible to use the same source and definition for all years, the percentage change between years in the deviant source is applied to the existing series in order to make the trend as correct as possible. In the light of these difficulties, military expenditure data are not suitable for close comparison between individual countries and are more appropriately used for comparisons over time.

Calculations

The SIPRI military expenditure figures are presented on a calendar-year basis with a few exceptions. The exceptions are Canada, the UK and the USA, for which NATO statistics report data on a fiscal-year basis. Calendar-year data are calculated on the assumption of an even rate of expenditure throughout the fiscal year.

[2] *Länderberichte* ceased publication in 1995.

A difficult methodological problem is the reliability of national official data. As a general rule, SIPRI takes national data to be accurate until there is convincing information to the contrary. Where that is the case, estimates have to be made.

The deflator used for conversion from current to constant prices is the consumer price index (CPI) of the country concerned. This choice of deflator is connected to the purpose of the SIPRI data—that they should be an indicator of resource use on an opportunity cost basis.[3]

For most countries the conversion to dollars is done by use of the average market exchange rates (MERs). The exceptions are countries in transition whose economies are still so closed that MERs, which are based on price ratios in foreign transactions only, do not accurately reflect the price ratios of the entire economy. For these countries conversion to dollars is made by use of purchasing power parity (PPP) rates.

The ratio of military expenditure to GDP is calculated in domestic currency at current prices and for calendar years.

Table 7A.1 presents aggregate military expenditure data for geographical regions, organizations and economic groupings. The geographical regions and organizations have been harmonized with those used for the SIPRI arms transfers statistics (appendix 11A). The economic groupings are based on figures for 1995 gross national product (GNP) per capita as calculated by the World Bank and presented in its *World Development Report 1997*. For the purpose of calculating aggregate totals estimates have been made for the countries for which data are lacking for some years. These estimates are made on the assumption that the trend for these countries is the same as for the geographical region in which they are located.

Estimates and the use of brackets

Where accurate military expenditure data are not available, estimates are made as far as possible. SIPRI estimates are presented in square brackets in the tables and are often highly approximate. Estimates are made in two types of case: (*a*) when data are not available; and (*b*) when there is sufficient evidence that the data provided are unreliable. Estimates are always based on empirical evidence and never on assumptions, in order not to build in assumptions in the military expenditure statistics.

Round brackets are used when data are uncertain for other reasons, such as the reliability of the source or the economic context. Figures are more unreliable when inflation is rapid and unpredictable. Supplementary allocations made during the course of the year to cover losses in purchasing power often go unreported and recent military expenditure can appear to be falling in real terms when it is in fact increasing.

Data for the most recent years include two types of estimate which apply to all countries: (*a*) figures for the most recent years are for adopted budget, budget estimates or revised estimates, and are thus more often than not revised in subsequent years; and (*b*) the deflator used for the last year in the series is an estimate. Unless exceptional uncertainty is involved in these estimates, they are not bracketed.

Countries which require special studies for the preparation of a complete and reliable set of military expenditure tables include China, Russia and the member countries of the Commonwealth of Independent States (CIS). For this edition of the SIPRI Yearbook a special study was commissioned for China (appendix 7D).

[3] A military-specific deflator would be the more appropriate choice if the objective were to measure the purchasing power in terms of military personnel, goods and services.

Purchasing power parity rates

To make international comparisons of economic data, it is necessary to convert the data to a common unit. The unit most often used is a common reference currency, almost always the US dollar, and the exchange rate used is the annual average MER. However, the use of the MER does not always produce comparable economic data because it reflects only the relative prices in the sectors influenced by foreign exchange. For countries with a significant sector which is unaffected by foreign exchange, the use of purchasing power parity (PPP) rates is more relevant for producing internationally comparable economic indicators. For most of the developed countries the difference between PPP rates and MER is not very significant, but for countries in transition and developing countries the difference between the two can be as large as 5–10 times. Thus, conversion using PPP rates gives developing countries and countries in transition higher military expenditures than would conversion using MERs. This section describes the main issues involved in producing economic data which are suitable for international comparisons.

The limitations of using market exchange rates for international comparisons

Conceptually the intention of converting military expenditures to a reference currency is to relate the amount spent on military activities in one country to the amount of goods and services that could be bought for this amount in the country of reference.

The MER is the price that one currency commands in relation to another based on the demand for and supply of the currency on the market. The demand for the currency is determined by the value of direct and indirect trade and investment between two countries, which means that the MER is to a great extent determined by the world market prices for internationally traded goods. This is a problem for cross-country comparisons, since in most countries international trade and the economic activities depending on foreign exchange constitute only part of the economy. Another important part of the national economy consists of domestically produced goods and services that are not exposed to international competition, and thus not much affected by the price ratios in the external sector. While products that are traded on the world market and exposed to international competition tend to have almost the same prices all over the world, in all markets, the prices of non-traded goods are determined by the supply and demand on the domestic market and can be very different between countries, since in countries with low purchasing power the demand for traded and non-traded goods is lower than in countries with high purchasing power.

Purchasing power is determined by the relation between income (wages) and prices. As the price for internationally traded goods is an externally determined variable, wages have to be set according to productivity per working hour in the external sector. The prices in the domestic sector for non-traded goods are then set by the demand determined by the externally-decided wage level.

The price relationship between non-traded and traded goods can therefore differ quite significantly between countries. The ratio is the greater, the greater (*a*) the share of non-traded goods in the national economy and (*b*) the gap between the prices of non-traded and traded goods. Since the MER does not take the prices of non-traded goods into account, it does not reflect the price levels of the total economy and therefore does not reflect the relative purchasing powers of the currencies being compared. For countries with a large difference between the prices of traded and non-traded goods, the deviation between the real relative purchasing power and the market exchange rate can be very high. This effect is exacerbated by the fact that the market exchange rate also carries the market risk aversion, which raises the MER.

To improve international comparisons of economic data the United Nations International Comparison Project has developed an exchange rate which better reflects economic reality for domestic actors—the PPP rate.[4] PPP rates can be seen as an artificial exchange rate based on explicit price comparisons of a wider set of goods and services than those exposed to foreign trade. The most common way of constructing PPP rates is to compare the price of a common standardized basket of goods and services, weighted by the quantities of each of the items included, and to use the US dollar as a reference currency. This means that the PPP rate is the number of units of local currency that can buy as much goods in the domestic market as one US dollar can buy in the US market. The basket of goods and services used for the comparison can be designed to suit the conversion of specific economic data, or it can be structured to be representative of the entire economy according to the GDP.

The most relevant type of PPP rate for international comparisons of the opportunity costs of military expenditures is PPP rates based on GDP comparisons, the underlying question being what civilian goods and services could have been bought instead of the military goods and services, not in the international market alone but in the entire economy.

If, however, the purpose is rather to use military expenditure data in international comparisons of military capability, then it would be more appropriate to use military-specific PPP rates. Personnel costs, which account for more than half of the defence budgets in many countries, cannot be considered exposed to international competition. Similarly, operations and maintenance services and procurement are to a large extent supplied from a protected domestic market. PPP rates based on GDP or GNP comparisons are provided by the World Bank,[5] the European Bank for Reconstruction and Development (EBRD)[6] and the Organisation for Economic Co-operation and Development (OECD).[7]

The difference between market exchange rates and PPP rates

The effect of using PPP rates instead of MERs varies significantly between countries. Table 7C.1 shows that the difference between PPP rates and MERs is largest in developing countries and countries in transition. For these countries military expenditures (and any other type of expenditure) are substantially higher in PPP dollar terms than in MER dollar terms. The meaning of the higher level of military expenditures in PPP terms is that, if the economic resources allocated to military activities had been used instead for purchases in the civilian sphere, then it would have been possible to buy more than the MER dollar figures suggest.

[4] An extensive discussion over the methods used by the International Comparisons Project can be found in Kravis, I. B. *et al.*, *A System of International Comparison of Gross Product and Purchasing Power* (John Hopkins University Press: Baltimore, Md., 1975). The robustness of the ICP PPP rates is discussed in Kravis, I. B. and Lipsey, R. E., *The International Comparison Program: Current Status and Problems*, NBER Working Paper no. 3304 (National Bureau of Economic Research: Cambridge, 1990).

[5] Reported annually in *World Bank Atlas* (Communications Development Incorporated: Washington, DC and New York, with Grundy and Northedge, London). The World Bank uses the Atlas method for calculating GNP data and PPP data from the ICP.

[6] Reported annually in European Bank for Reconstruction and Development, *Transition Report*.

[7] OECD, *Main Economic Indicators*, Feb. 1998. URL <http://www.oecd.org/std/ppp1.pdf>.

Table 7C.1. Comparison of military expenditure by market exchange rates and purchasing power parity rates, selected countries, 1995

Rank[a] 1	Country[b] 2	MER (local curr./ US$) 3	PPP rate[c] (local curr./ US$) 4	Deviation index[d] (3/4) 5	Mil. exp. in MER terms US $m.[e] 6	Mil. exp. in PPP terms, $m.[f] 7
Developing countries						
1	Mozambique	9024	891.3	10.1	69.4	700
2	Ethiopia	6.158	1.369	4.5	118	530
3	Tanzania	574.8	107.8	5.3	80.7	430
4	Burundi	249.8	63.43	3.9	44.1	174
5	Malawi	15.28	3.464	4.4	14.7	65
6	Chad	499.2	128.4	3.9	20.0	78
7	Rwanda	262.2	87.4	3.0	56.1	168
8	Sierra Leone	755.2	234.4	3.2	25.0	81
9	Nepal	51.89	8.862	5.8	37.4	217
12	Madagascar	4 266	1 533	2.8	27.2	76
Countries in transition						
34	Georgia	1.288	0.385	3.3	42.7	143
47	Kyrgyzstan	10.822	4.20	2.6	21.9	56
55	Uzbekistan	27.80	11.40	2.4	120	294
62	Kazakhstan	60.95	26.9	2.3	177	401
71	Ukraine	1.473	1.000	1.5	1 130	1 665
77	Belarus	11 050	5 417	2.0	156	318
79	Latvia	0.530	0.360	1.5	43.6	64
88	Slovak Rep.	29.71	24.28	1.2	435	533
98	Czech Rep.	26.54	10.51	2.5	839	2 118
100	Hungary	125.7	80.78	1.6	612	952
Developed countries						
124	Belgium	29.48	33.63	0.88	4 449	3 900
125	France	4.992	5.931	0.84	47 768	40 196
126	Singapore	1.417	1.664	0.85	3 673	3 130
127	Austria	10.08	12.76	0.79	2 133	1 685
128	USA	1.000	1.000	1.000	278 856	278 856
129	Germany	1.433	1.964	0.73	41 160	30 030
130	Denmark	5.602	7.887	0.71	3 118	2 215
131	Norway	6.335	9.023	0.70	3 508	2 465
132	Japan	94.06	168.6	0.56	50 112	28 000
133	Switzerland	1.183	1.858	0.64	4 238	2 695

[a] GDP/capita rank according to World Bank data at URL <http://www.worldbank.org/data/databytopic/gnppc97.pdf>.

[b] The countries selected are the 10 countries with lowest GDP/capita, 10 randomly selected countries in transition and the 10 countries with the highest GDP/capita for which PPP data are available.

[c] GDP-based PPP rates, as developed by the UN International Comparison Project (ICP).

[d] The deviation index = MER/PPP. It is a measure of how much the PPP rate differs from MER. If the deviation index is > 1, then the military expenditure could have bought more civil products than indicated by the dollar figures converted by MER; if it is < 1 it would have bought less.

[e] Military expenditures converted to US$ by use of MERs.

[f] Military expenditures converted to US$ by use of PPP rates.

Sources: SIPRI military expenditure database; *World Bank Atlas 1997* (Communications Development Incorporated: Washington, DC and New York, with Grundy and Northedge: London, 1997), pp. 36–37; and European Bank for Reconstruction and Development, *Transition Report 1997*, pp. 215–39.

Although table 7C.1 suggests a rather strong correlation between per capita GDP and PPP rates deviation from MER, other factors also influence the deviation index. One of the most notable is the openness of the economy. As a closed economy is not very much involved in international trade and the internal market mostly comprises domestically produced and priced goods, the MER, if one exists, is not at all adequate as a converter for international comparison of economic measures. Some developing countries and countries in transition have rather closed economies, a fact that exacerbates the image of these countries as having low GDPs.

In developed countries long-standing national and international market competition has made the internal sector very small and productivity within it very similar to productivity in the external sector. Furthermore, items which in developing countries are to be seen as non-traded goods can in a developed economy, with its better infrastructure and more open economy, be considered as traded goods. As the table shows, the result is that prices in developed countries are very much the same as or higher than those in the reference country, the USA.

Appendix 7D. The military expenditure of China, 1989–98

SHAOGUANG WANG*

I. Introduction

It is an open secret that the official defence budget is just a part of the resources used to support the military establishment of China. Most analysts believe that China's published budget substantially understates its total expenditure on national defence, although there is no consensus as to where its 'hidden sources' of military financing lie and how large its actual defence spending really is. Estimates of China's total military expenditure vary widely, ranging from $20 billion to $140 billion.[1]

A major problem with any analysis of China's military expenditure is the veil of secrecy shrouding military allocations. Of course, the difficulty of gathering statistical data of sufficient reliability in this area is not peculiar to the case of China,[2] but the traditional preoccupation of Chinese leaders with secrecy makes them extremely reluctant to publish details of the country's military expenditure even in the crudest aggregated form. Until China published its first defence White Paper in 1995, the outside world had only known a single-line entry for defence in the annual state budget.[3] Neither the 1995 nor the 1998 White Paper reveals much about the country's total military expenditure.[4] For instance, defence expenditure outside the official defence budget was not mentioned at all.

However, the absence of systematic data on military expenditure does not mean that it is impossible to improve the accuracy of estimates. It is only necessary to look a little further to find a surprisingly large amount of material published in China on defence economics. Examples include professional newspapers, journals, books, and national and provincial statistical publications of various kinds.[5] Since they are prepared for a domestic audience and some are classified as 'for internal circulation only', it is reasonable to assume that these sources are relatively reliable. Although it is often necessary to search through dozens of such publications in order to find a few useful references, these sources nevertheless represent a gold mine from which many missing pieces of China's military expenditure puzzle can be found.

[1] International Institute for Strategic Studies, 'China's military expenditure', *The Military Balance 1995/96* (Oxford University Press: Oxford, 1996), p. 270.

[2] Herrera, R., *Statistics on Military Expenditure in Developing Countries: Concepts, Methodological Problems and Sources* (OECD: Paris, 1994), p. 23.

[3] The White Paper only provides a breakdown into 3 categories: salaries and living expenses; maintenance, construction and training; and R&D, procurement and transport.

[4] Chinese State Council, Information Office, 'Zhongguo di junbei kongzhi yu caijun' [China's arms control and disarmament], *Renmin Ribao* [People's daily], 17 Nov. 1995; and Chinese State Council, Information Office, *China's National Defense* (State Council, Information Office: Beijing, 1998) (in English).

[5] Examples are *Zhongguo Jungong Bao* [Chinese defence industry tribune], *Zhongguo Junzhuanmin Bao* [Chinese defence conversion tribune], *Junshi Jingji Yanjiu* [Research in defence economics], *Jundui Caiwu* [Military finance], and dozens of books on defence economics published since 1985.

* The author is grateful for comments received from Bates Gill, David Shambaugh, Michel Oksenberg and others.

Table 7D.1. Official Chinese central and local expenditures for defence, 1989–98

Figures are in b. current yuan.

Year	Central PLA	Local Militia	Central PAP	Local PAP
1989	24.908	0.239	2.291	0
1990	28.782	0.249	3.037	0
1991	32.749	0.282	3.221	0
1992	37.475	0.311	3.883	0
1993	42.248	0.332	5.000	0
1994	54.708	0.363	6.325	0
1995	63.270	0.402	7.386	0
1996	71.508	0.498	8.794	0.229
1997	[80.651]	[0.606]	[10.623]	[0.277]
1998	[90.990]	[0.720]	[12.833]	[0.334]

Notes: Figures in square brackets are estimates for 1997 and 1998 which are derived from the data on the previous years. The average growth rates in the previous three years are assumed to be the growth rates in these two years. PLA = People's Liberation Army. PAP = People's Armed Police.

Source: Chinese Ministry of Finance, *Zhongguo Caizheng Nianjian* [China public finance yearbook], various years.

This appendix attempts to tap these Chinese sources in the hope of clarifying certain key issues about Chinese military expenditure and, wherever possible, using concrete figures to replace guesstimates. The following three sections examine in turn the three major components of Chinese military expenditure. Section II considers the officially published defence budget; section III looks at defence-related items in the budgets of other government ministries; and section IV examines the extra-budgetary earnings of the People's Liberation Army (PLA). Section V uses the findings of these three sections to construct estimates of China's total military expenditure for the 10 years 1989–98.

II. China's official military budget

Before making any estimate, military expenditure must first be clearly defined. In this appendix, it is defined as the total amount spent for national defence purposes regardless of source of funding. The categorization of military expenditure suggested by SIPRI is adopted:[6] (*a*) pay and allowances of military personnel; (*b*) pensions of retired military personnel; (*c*) operations and maintenance (O&M); (*d*) procurement;

[6] There are of course other ways of defining military expenditure, such as those proposed by the International Monetary Fund (IMF), NATO, the United Nations and the US Department of Defense (DOD). For more information, see Sen, S., 'Military expenditure data for developing countries: methods and measurement', ed. G. Lamb, *Military Expenditure and Economic Development: A Symposium on Research Issues* (World Bank: Washington, DC, 1992); and Deger, S., *Military Expenditure in Third World Countries: The Economic Effects* (Routledge & Kegan Paul: London, 1986). The SIPRI definition is preferable for 3 reasons. First, it is in line with the general definition given above. Second, while it is fairly close to the IMF, NATO, UN and DOD categorizations, it is more comprehensive. Third, the SIPRI Yearbook provides more detailed statistics on national defence for more countries than any of the above organizations.

(*e*) military research and development (R&D); (*f*) construction; (*g*) military aid provided; (*h*) paramilitary forces; and (*i*) military space activities.

Using the SIPRI classification as a framework, the sources of each group of expenditure can be identified, starting with the categories in the official military budget and then adding the components of military expenditure that are not included in the official figures.

The 'China public finance yearbook' (*Zhongguo Caizheng Nianjian)* divides the official defence budget into two parts, central and local (table 7D.1). The 'local' part apparently covers the costs of maintaining the militia, because it is also referred to as 'militia operation funds' (*minbing shiyefei*).[7] The 'central' part of the budget covers 13 major categories of expenditure for the PLA, which are listed in table 7D.2.[8]

'Personnel' covers all those serving in the PLA, including all its defence forces, military service mobilization organs, administrative organs of military-run agriculture and sideline production, civilian employees of the PLA and active-service personnel in the reserve forces.[9]

In China, former officers and soldiers normally receive no money from the government after being demobilized except a one-off demobilization allowance. Former officers' new employers rather than the government budget pay their salaries and health and hospital expenses. Only a very small percentage of senior officers who have already passed retirement age when demobilized receive pensions, housing allowances and perhaps other kinds of benefit. The official defence budget bears all these expenses as well as the demobilization allowances.[10]

'Procurement' is an important category in the official defence budget. According to Chinese sources, the defence budget covers the following three broad categories of weapons and equipment: (*a*) space equipment, aircraft, missiles, nuclear warheads and bombs, ships and boats, tanks and armoured vehicles; (*b*) artillery, other ordnance and ground force arms; and (*c*) ammunition, electronics and communications, transport vehicles, reconnaissance equipment and logistic support.[11] This list includes all the items under the 'procurement' heading of the UN definition of military expenditure.[12]

[7] Chinese Ministry of Finance, *Zhongguo Caizheng Nianjian 1997* [China public finance yearbook] (China Public Economics Press: Beijing, 1997), p. 395.

[8] China's 'Ordinance on military budget categorization' (of which there have been many revisions) requires the PLA to adopt a detailed accounting matrix of military expenditure. Between 1986 and 1991 there were 11 broad categories subdivided into 59 items. In July 1991 China adopted a new system which breaks down the military budget into 13 broad categories and 61 items. *Zhongguo Junshi Caiwu Shiyong Daquan* [Complete reference book of Chinese military finance] (PLA Press: Beijing, 1993), p. 37; and Lu Zhuhao (ed.), *Zhongguo Junshi Jingfei Guanli* [Management of Chinese military expenditures] (PLA Press: Beijing, 1995), pp. 87–90. See also Ding, A. S., 'China's defense finance: content, process and administration', *China Quarterly*, no. 146 (1996).

[9] Chinese State Council (note 4), p. 26. See also the PLA's 'Wenzhi ganbu zanxing tiaoli' [Provisional regulations on civilian employees] cited in Luo Dejun *et al.*, *Da Guofang Lun* [On comprehensive national defence] (Hunan People's Press: Changsha, 1988), pp. 287–92.

[10] Hong Xuezhi, former Deputy Secretary-General of the Central Military Commission, once complained that those expenses constituted a heavy burden on the official defence budget. 'Hong Xuezhi's speech at the Symposium of Defense Economics', ed. Chinese Society of Defense Economics, *Guofang Jingjixue Lunwenji* [A collection of research papers on defence economics] (PLA Press: Beijing, 1986), p. 417. The situation is more or less the same today. *Zhongguo Junshi Caiwu Shiyong Daquan* (note 8); and Lu (note 8), pp. 359–413.

[11] You Qianzhi *et al.*, *Zhongguo Guofang Jingji Yunxing Fenxi* [A functional analysis of the Chinese defence economy] (Chinese Financial Economic Press: Beijing, 1991), p. 170; and Lu (note 8), p. 486.

[12] United Nations, Reduction of military budgets, UN document A/40/421, 1986.

Table 7D.2. Spending categories in the Chinese official defence budget

Personnel (*shenghuo fei*)	Pay and fringe benefits for PLA personnel; food, uniforms and other living expenses; pensions for retired senior officers; settlement allowances for demobilized officers and soldiers[a]
Maintenance (*gongwu fei*)	Power and other utilities; allowances for business trips; special allowances; other running expenses
Operations (*shiye fei*)	Intelligence; meteorological observation; topographic survey; provision and management of housing, medical and other services for PLA personnel; communications and transport; fuels and other basic materials; political work
Education and training (*jiaoyu xunlian fei*)	Military academies, training equipment and installations, operational costs of the military training establishment
Procurement (*zhuangbei gouzhi fei*)	Weapons and equipment from domestic suppliers; some imports
Procurement and maintenance of logistic equipment	Procurement and maintenance of logistic equipment
Maintenance of weapons and equipment (*zhuangbei weichi guanli fei*)	Spare parts, tools and auxiliary materials; repair and maintenance of weapons and equipment
Fuel (*youliao fei*)	Procurement and maintenance of fuel supplies
Construction (*jiben jianshe fei*)	Military buildings, facilities, civil air defence and other national defence works
Scientific research (*kexue yanjiu fei*)	Research in military science; military medical research; testing and evaluating weapons and equipment
War preparation and combat costs	Stockpiling strategic defence materials and combat costs
Miscellaneous (*qita jingfei*)	Foreign affairs; money rewards for captured enemy personnel; others
MAC reserve fund	Reserve fund of the Central Military Commission

[a] For a detailed discussion of what this category covers, see *Zhongguo Junshi Caiwu Shiyong Daquan* [Complete reference book of Chinese military finance] (PLA Press: Beijing, 1993), pp. 221–383; and Lu Zhuhao (ed.), *Zhongguo Junshi Jingfei Guanli* [Management of Chinese military expenditures] (PLA Press: Beijing, 1995), pp. 351–550.

Whereas there is little doubt that the official defence budget pays for procurement from domestic suppliers, it is not clear how the military accounts for purchases from foreign suppliers. According to China's 'Ordinance on military budget categorization', funding for arms imports is already included in the official defence budget,[13] but Western analysts generally suspect that major foreign weapon purchases may be funded, at least partially, through special appropriations outside the defence budget. The fact is that very little is known about this.

'Construction' covers ground force bases, naval bases, air bases, infrastructure for missile projects (*erpao gongcheng*), communication centres, scientific research centres, warehouses and depots, training bases, barracks, quarters for families of military personnel and shelters.[14]

[13] *Zhongguo Junshi Caiwu Shiyong Daquan* (note 8), pp. 312–13; and Lu (note 8), p. 486.

[14] *Zhongguo Junshi Caiwu Shiyong Daquan* (note 8), pp. 349–59; and Lu (note 8), pp. 519–29. See also Fan Gonggao, *Guofang Jingjixue* [Defence economics] (Fujian People's Press: Fuzhou, 1988), pp. 199–201.

The official defence budget does not cover the costs of R&D on new weapons and equipment. There is a distinction in Chinese usage between 'military research' (*junshi kexue yanjiu*) and 'defence research' (*guofang kexue yanjiu*). The former means primarily research in military science but also includes medical research for military purposes, the testing and evaluation of weapons and equipment, and research for minor improvements to weapons and equipment currently used by the PLA. In any case, 'military research' is done exclusively by PLA research institutes. 'Defence research' refers to all kinds of defence-related research carried out by research institutes that belong to other government agencies. The official defence budget funds only the former.[15] Section III discusses the latter.

III. Military expenditure in other budget categories

It is clear from the above that, except for a small portion spent on maintenance of the militia, the official defence budget is essentially the budget for the PLA.[16] Some important defence-related outlays are actually excluded from it and instead listed under other headings in the central and local government budgets. According to a recent internal publication, key defence-related items funded from other national and local government sources include the paramilitary People's Armed Police (PAP); some research, development, testing and evaluation (RDT&E) costs; and capital construction of defence projects.[17] To this list should be added some demobilization and military pension costs and subsidies to defence industries that help lower the cost of indigenous arms procurement for the armed forces. In addition, arms acquisitions from abroad are probably also financed by funds listed under other budget categories.

People's Armed Police

Established in 1983, the PAP's main functions are to maintain domestic order and protect the country's frontier.[18] It has a separate budget which is published in the 'China public finance yearbook'. The PAP is financed by both central and provincial governments.[19] However, as can be seen in table 7D.1, the 'China public finance yearbook' did not provide the breakdown between central and provincial until 1996.

Defence RDT&E

For much of the 1980s, government funding for defence RDT&E was declining. By 1990, government spending in this category was equivalent to less than one-tenth of the official defence budget.[20] The falling trend was probably reversed after the 1991

[15] *Zhongguo Junshi Caiwu Shiyong Daquan* (note 8), pp. 360–67; and Lu (note 8), pp. 529–37.

[16] It is often referred to as the 'expenses of the military' (*junfei*) in China.

[17] Li Yingcheng and Shi Xuzhong, 'Lun guofang jianshe hongguan xiaoyi pingjia di keguan jichu' [The basis for cost–benefit analysis of a defence build-up], *Jingji Yanjiu Cankao*, no. 1147 (21 Mar. 1998).

[18] Chinese State Council, Information Office (note 4), p. 16. For a detailed discussion of the PAP's functions, see Tai Ming Cheung, 'Guarding China's domestic front line: the People's Armed Police and China's stability', *China Quarterly*, no. 146 (1996).

[19] *Zhongguo Junshi Caiwu Shiyong Daquan* (note 8), pp. 424–53.

[20] Shaoguang Wang, 'Estimating China's defense expenditure: some evidence from Chinese sources', *China Quarterly*, no. 147 (1996), pp. 896–98. See also Arnett, E., 'Military technology: the case of

Persian Gulf War. The use of high-technology weapons in the war served as a wake-up call to the Chinese military leadership, reminding them how far China was behind in its armaments. Military technology may have received more attention since the Gulf War than before. However, analysts cannot agree on how much China is devoting to this sector.[21]

To arrive at a realistic estimate, it is necessary to know where defence RDT&E funds come from. According to well-informed Chinese military economists, defence RDT&E is financed from two sources: the general R&D fund and the 'new product promotion fund'.[22] The former is defined as 'all actual expenditure made for R&D (including basic research, applied research and experimental development)'.[23] It pays for both direct and indirect expenditure on R&D (including management expenses, administrative expenses and capital construction relating to R&D). The latter refers to 'the expenses appropriated from the government budget for scientific and technological expenditure, including new product development expenditure, expenditure for intermediate trial and subsidies for important scientific researches'.[24] Both sources include allocations for defence purposes, but of both the greater part is devoted to civilian programmes. The defence portion of the general R&D fund is called 'expenditure on research' (*yanzhi jingfei*) and its counterpart in the new product development fund 'expenditure on test, evaluation and prototypes' (*shizhi jingfei*).[25]

Since 1980, national defence has consistently ranked lowest in China's 'four modernizations' programmes (for industry, agriculture, science and defence). The Gulf War may have heightened China's interest in modern weaponry, but economic modernization is still the top priority. For this reason, it is assumed here that 10 per cent of the general R&D fund was spent on national defence for the three-year period 1989–91 and 15 per cent for the seven-year period 1992–98 (taking deliberately high estimates in order not to underestimate total military expenditure). Column 2 of table 7D.3 calculates China's defence-related R&D expenditure from 1989 to 1998. The defence-related test and evaluation (T&E) figures shown in column 3 are estimated by a similar method, although it is assumed that the defence portion of the new product development fund was higher (30 and 35 per cent for the periods before and after the Gulf War, respectively, again taking high estimates). This assumption is made because, ranging from two-thirds to three-quarters, the central share in this government expenditure is much higher than in almost all budget categories except national defence, the PAP and a few others, and there is no reason for the central government to monopolize the development of new 'products' unless a significant proportion of the products to be developed are defence-related. In particular, China's space and nuclear projects are probably covered by the 'new products' category.[26]

China', *SIPRI Yearbook 1995: Armaments, Disarmament and International Security* (Oxford University Press: Oxford, 1995), pp. 375–77.

[21] SIPRI itself has given 2 very different estimates. Bergstrand, B.-G. *et al.*, 'World military expenditure', *SIPRI Yearbook 1994* (Oxford University Press: Oxford, 1994), chapter 12, section V by D. Shambaugh; and Arnett (note 20).

[22] Li and Shi (note 17), pp. 19–20; and Jiang Baoqi and Zhang Shengwang, *Zhongguo Guofeng Jingji Fazhan Zhanlue Yanjiu* [A study of China's strategy of defence economic development] (National Defense University Press: Beijing, 1990), p. 50.

[23] China State Statistical Bureau, *Zhongguo Tongji Nianjian 1996* [China statistical yearbook] (China Statistical Publishing House: Beijing, 1996), p. 700.

[24] *Zhongguo Tongji Nianjian 1996* (note 23), p. 248.

[25] Li and Shi (note 17), pp. 19–20. See also *Zhongguo Junshi Caiwu Shiyong Daquan* (note 8), pp. 454–75; and Lu (note 8), pp. 315–20.

[26] *Zhongguo Junshi Caiwu Shiyong Daquan* (note 8), pp. 469–71; and Lu (note 8), pp. 556–59.

Table 7D.3. Estimated off-budget military expenditure of China, 1989–98

Figures are in b. current yuan.

Year 1	R&D[a] 2	T&E[b] 3	Construction[c] 4	Subsidies to demobilized personnel[d] 5	Subsidies to military production[e] 6	Commercial earnings[f] 7	Total 8
1989	1.000	1.740	1.927	1.443	4.990	2.515	13.6
1990	1.254	1.904	2.190	1.661	4.824	2.903	14.8
1991	1.423	2.200	2.238	1.721	4.253	3.303	15.1
1992	2.535	3.129	2.780	1.845	3.698	5.668	19.7
1993	2.940	3.730	2.960	2.078	3.481	6.387	21.6
1994	3.330	3.998	3.199	2.478	3.411	6.608	23.0
1995	4.290	4.761	3.946	2.911	3.218	7.640	26.8
1996	4.905	5.199	4.537	3.278	3.470	8.640	30.0
1997	[5.827]	[5.814]	[5.240]	[3.400]	[3.740]	[9.751]	[33.8]
1998	[6.922]	[6.502]	[6.052]	[3.600]	[4.033]	[11.040]	[38.1]

Notes: Figures in square brackets are estimates derived from data on the previous years, assuming the same average growth rates as in the previous 3 years. For 'subsidies' (col. 5), however, the growth rate in 1996 is used to estimate figures for 1997 and 1998.

[a] (General R&D) x 0.1 for 1989–91; (General R&D) x 0.15 for 1992–98.

[b] (New product test) x 0.3 for 1989–91; (New product test) x 0.35 for 1992–98. T&E = test and evaluation.

[c] (Capital investment) x 0.04 for 1989–91; (Capital investment) x 0.05 for 1992–98.

[d] 'Compensation expenditure' in the budget of the Ministry of Civil Affairs.

[e] (Subsidies to loss-making productive state-owned enterprises) x 1/3 x 1/2 for 1989–98.

[f] (Defence budget) x 0.10 for 1989–91; (Defence budget) x 0.15 for 1992–93; (Defence budget) x 0.12 for 1994–98.

Source: Chinese Ministry of Finance, *Zhongguo Caizheng Nianjian* [China public finance yearbook], various years.

Table 7D.3 seems to confirm the estimates made by Arnett and Gill and Kim: China's expenditure on defence-related RDT&E is in the region of $1–$1.5 billion.[27] It is very unlikely that actual expenditure is higher than this.

Construction

As pointed out in the preceding section, the official defence budget covers most, if not all, construction costs of military facilities directly controlled by the PLA. However, expenditure on other types of defence project, including research facilities and military production lines operated by civilian institutions, is listed under the budget category 'capital construction'.

In the first 30 years of the People's Republic, the defence-related share of capital construction averaged around 5 per cent.[28] After 1980, the government substantially

[27] Arnett (note 20); and Gill, B. and Taeho Kim, *China's Arms Acquisitions from Abroad: A Quest for 'Superb and Secret Weapons'*, SIPRI Research Report no. 11 (Oxford University Press: Oxford, 1995), pp. 100–101.

[28] Yang Yongliang, *Zhongguo Junshi Jingjixue Gailun* [An introduction to Chinese defence economics] (Chinese Economic Press: Beijing, 1987), pp. 148, 243. The defence-related share peaked in

reduced its budget allocations to defence construction projects.[29] Thus, it is reasonable to assume that the portion of capital construction expenditure allocated to defence projects was below 4 per cent for the period 1989–91. Even if China has decided to devote more resources to defence projects after the Gulf War, it certainly has not attached as much importance to national defence as it did before 1979. It is therefore unlikely that the defence-related share of capital construction is higher than 5 per cent. Column 4 of table 7D.3 reports the author's estimates of China's spending on defence construction projects.

Subsidies to demobilized military personnel and their dependants

The official defence budget pays for part of the pensions of retired military personnel and demobilization allowances, but not all. The Ministry of Civil Affairs (MCA) also has some responsibility for supporting former servicemen and their dependants. Within the MCA's budget, there is an item called 'compensation expenditure' (*fuxu zhichu*), which is designated to help mainly but not only veterans and their families.[30] In 1998, for instance, 490 000 'revolutionary martyrs'' dependants, 890 000 disabled army men and 2.54 million veterans living in the countryside received regular subsidies from the MCA.[31] A small part of this MCA budget is also used to help demobilized servicemen resettle. Column 5 of table 7D.3 shows compensation expenditure for the period 1989–98, assuming that it is spent entirely on former military personnel and their families.

Subsidies to military production

It is essential to distinguish two distinct categories of enterprise: (*a*) *jungong* enterprises, or those managed by ministries and corporations under the State Council; and (*b*) *jundui* enterprises, or those run by the PLA.[32] While *jungong* enterprises are frequently portrayed as being controlled by the PLA, this is in fact not the case. Each system has its own budget. The focus here is on *jungong* enterprises. *Jundui* enterprises are discussed in detail in the next section.

In the early 1980s, China's defence industry (aerospace, aeronautics, electronics, ordnance, nuclear and shipbuilding) comprised roughly 1000 large and medium-sized firms and over 200 research institutes, which altogether employed nearly 3 million staff and workers, including about 300 000 scientists, engineers and technicians.[33] Since then, because of a substantial fall in PLA procurement, this part of the state sector has been in serious decline. China's defence sector is now at best a small

1970 and 1971 at 17.2% and 12.5%, respectively. Jin Zhude and Chen Zaifang, 'Zhongguo guofang jingji de jige wenti' [Issues of China's defence economy], ed. Chinese Society of Defense Economics (note 10), p. 30.

[29] Sun Guangyun, 'Guanyu xianxing junping jiage di gaige wenti' [Issues concerning reform of the price system for military products], ed. Chinese Society of Defense Economics (note 10), pp. 258–59.

[30] *Zhongguo Tongji Nianjian 1996* (note 23), p. 246.

[31] New China News Agency, Beijing, 16 Nov. 1998.

[32] Fan (note 14), pp. 163–64.

[33] Jin Zhude and Guo Tiejun, 'Shilun zhenzhixin guofang' [On profit-making defence], ed. Beijing Society of Defense Economics, *Guofang Jingji Fazhan Zhanlue Lunwenji* [A collection of essays on the development of defence economics] (Beijing: PLA Press, 1987), p. 46; and China Academy of Military Science, *Weilai de Guofang Jianshe* [Future defence construction], vol. 1 (Military Science Press: Beijing, 1990), p. 177.

player in the national economy. Its asset value accounts for only about 4 per cent of the state industrial total.[34] In terms of output value and employment, its shares are even smaller.[35]

To cope with the difficulties arising from declining procurement orders, China's defence industry has been undergoing conversion since the early 1980s.[36] By the early 1990s, civilian production constituted 80 per cent of total output value of the defence industries. In some sectors such as electronics, the civilian share of total production was nearly 100 per cent.[37] Overall, more than 40 per cent of defence producers had converted completely to civilian production, no longer producing any defence goods, and another 40 per cent were engaged in both military and civilian production. Only around 10 per cent produced solely for the military market.[38]

Conversion, however, is a very painful process. Currently, most defence enterprises are in trouble.[39] Profits generated from civilian production fall far short of covering losses from their military operations.[40] Thus, government subsidies are necessary to keep the defence sector afloat.

Data on state subsidies for loss-making productive enterprises in general are available. Given that the defence sector constitutes only a very small part of China's industry, it is highly unlikely that more than one-third of such subsidies goes to the defence sector alone. Even if one-third does go to the defence sector, a large portion of these funds (perhaps 50 per cent) must have been allocated to facilitating military conversion—the sector's central task since the early 1980s. Such costs should not be considered as defence-related expenditure. On the basis of these two assumptions, column 6 of table 7D.3 provides the estimates of state subsidies used to underwrite the production of weaponry. It is assumed that the share of state subsidies to military production did not increase after the Gulf War in 1991 because since the early 1980s China has adopted a guideline for its domestic arms production, 'more research and development but less production' (*duokaifa, shaoshengchan*).[41] In other words, even

[34] It amounted to only 1.38% of total state assets. *Zhongguo Caizheng Nianjian 1997* (note 7), pp. 583–85.

[35] Feng-Cheng Fu and Chi-Keung Li, 'An economic analysis', eds J. Brommelhorster and J. Frankenstein, *Mixed Motives, Uncertain Outcomes: Defense Conversion in China* (Lynne Rienner: Boulder, Colo., 1997), pp. 61–62.

[36] SIPRI once praised China as 'the first country in the world which made "swords into ploughshares" an operational and effective concept'. Deger, S. and Sen, S., 'World military expenditure', *SIPRI Yearbook 1992: World Armaments and Disarmament* (Oxford University Press: Oxford, 1992), p. 249.

[37] Li Yintao, 'Guofang keji gongye junzhuangming fazhan jieduan yanjiu' [Research on the phases of conversion in defence science and technology industry], *Junshi Jingji Yanjiu*, no. 2 (1996), pp. 20–22. See also Gurtov, M., 'Swords into market shares: China's conversion of military industry to civilian production', *China Quarterly* (June 1993), p. 214; and Folta, P. H., *From Swords to Plowshares? Defense Industry Reform in the PRC* (Westview Press: Boulder, Colo., 1992).

[38] *Jane's Defence Weekly*, 19 Feb. 1994, p. 31. See also Ball, N., 'Adjusting to reductions in military expenditure and defense procurement', eds G. Lamb and V. Kallab, *Military Expenditure and Economic Development: A Symposium on Research Issues* (World Bank: Washington, DC, 1992), p. 72.

[39] Frankenstein, J., 'Perspectives on China's defense industries', Asia Research Center, Copenhagen Business School, 1998, unpublished. It was reported in 1994 that the ordnance industry was the biggest money-loser, while the situation in the aeronautics and astronautics industry was only slightly better. China News Agency, 1 Dec. 1994.

[40] Zhang Yanzhong, 'Guofang gongye zouxiang shichang jingji ruogan wenti de sikao' [Thoughts on issues concerning how to integrate defence industries into the market economy], *Zhongguo Jungong Bao*, 5 July 1994, p. 3.

[41] Chinese Country Study Group, 'China', ed. R. P. Singh, SIPRI, *Arms Procurement Decision Making*, vol. I (Oxford University Press: Oxford, 1998), pp. 8–47. See also Jiang Luming, 'Guo fangfei di biandong qushi jiqi zhanlue xianzhe' [Changing trend of defence expenditure and strategic choice], *Junshi Jingji Yanjiu*, no. 1 (1995), pp. 41–46; and Zhao Surong, 'Jiaqiang guofang keji yuyan touru di

if spending on RDT&E has increased, new weapon systems are not necessarily built and deployed. 'Very little evidence exists that the Chinese government will invest heavily in modernizing the defence industrial plant.'[42]

Special appropriations for arms imports

China meets most of its weapon requirements from domestic production. Dependence on foreign arms suppliers is considered a political handicap: China has learned from its experience in dealing with the former Soviet Union in the 1950s and the USA in the 1980s that 'in the eventuality of a crisis, China could become subject to foreign political influence or embargo'.[43]

Despite its desire for self-reliance, however, China is clearly aware of the need to import arms. Otherwise it would not be possible to accelerate military modernization. Since the mid-1970s, China has shown great interest in purchasing weapons and weapon technologies from the advanced countries but before the 1990s, while it did a good deal of 'window shopping', its actual arms imports were modest even compared with those of some of its much smaller neighbours.[44] This could probably be attributed to cutbacks in China's overall defence expenditure during this period. After the Gulf War, China speeded up its arms acquisitions from Russia.[45] The total costs of its purchases from Russia since 1990 are estimated to be equivalent to *c.* $10 billion.[46] However, according to some analysts, 'the actual cash outlay is perhaps one-third to one-half less as early purchases were covered in part by barter, and some deals have not been completed'.[47]

Where does the PLA get funds to pay for arms imports? One Chinese source claims that the money is already included in the procurement element of the official defence budget,[48] while Western analysts generally suspect that arms imports are funded through special appropriations. Assuming that most spending on foreign purchases lies outside the defence budget, it is possible that additional allocations come from the budget category 'other expenditures',[49] but details of this category are not specified. For this reason the value of China's arms imports can only be estimated from Western sources. This is an unsatisfactory method since the arms trade data in these sources do not reflect actual payments but are estimated values of weapons delivered. Estimates for Chinese arms trade values as shown in table 7D.4, are derived from the time-series data of the US Arms Control and Disarmament Agency (ACDA).[50]

biyaoxing' [On the importance of strengthening budget input in defence science and tchnology], *Junshi Jingji Yanjiu*, no. 6 (1995), pp. 20–21.

[42] Frankenstein, J. and Gill, B., 'Current and future challenges facing Chinese defense industries', *China Quarterly*, no. 146 (1996), p. 421.

[43] Chinese Country Study Group (note 41), p. 33.

[44] Gill and Kim (note 27), pp. 34–47.

[45] Gill and Kim (note 27), pp. 48–70.

[46] Gill, B., 'Chinese defense procurement spending: determining Chinese military intentions and capabilities', Paper presented at the Conference on the People's Liberation Army, Wye Conference Center, Md., Sep. 1997, p. 8.

[47] Gill (note 46).

[48] *Zhongguo Junshi Caiwu Shiyong Daquan* (note 8), pp. 312–13; and Lu (note 8), p. 486. See also Fan (note 14), pp. 296–98.

[49] It may not be a coincidence that the size of the 'others' category in the central budget almost quadrupled between 1992 and 1996. Chinese Ministry of Finance, *Zhongguo Caizheng Nianjian* [China public finance yearbook], various years.

[50] US Arms Control and Disarmament Agency (ACDA), *World Military Expenditure and Arms Transfers 1997* (US Government Printing Office: Washington, DC, 1997). ACDA data cover a broader category of weapons than SIPRI data.

IV. Military expenditure deriving from extra-budgetary sources

'The overriding financial fact in the development of the PLA throughout the Deng period has been inadequate funding.'[51] Most of the expenditures discussed in the above section are beyond the direct control of the PLA. To compensate for the PLA's budget shortfalls, beginning from 1985, the central leadership gave it the go-ahead to engage in various kinds of business activities, ranging from hotels to pager services. Revenues generated by such activities are generally referred to in China as extra-budgetary earnings of the PLA, which do not appear in the state budget at all.[52] Some of these revenues are used for defence purposes.

The PLA has two main sources of extra-budgetary revenue—its domestic commercial activities and earnings from arms exports.

Earnings from domestic business activities

The PLA has a long tradition of participation in not-for-profit economic activities, but it was not until 1985 that it was given permission to engage in for-profit commercial activities. Expanded involvement in economic activities soon bore fruit. By 1987, the total turnover and profits of PLA-affiliated enterprises had reached 9.59 billion and 2.41 billion yuan (equivalent to 11.5 per cent of the published defence budget), respectively.[53] While such extra-budgetary incomes certainly helped improve the army's financial situation, the negative effects of involvement in commerce also became evident before long. In 1989, the central government was compelled to take measures curtailing the military's business activities. The PLA then began to withdraw from the commercial front.

However, the process of retreat was disrupted by Deng Xiaoping's visit to southern China at the beginning of 1992, which was followed by two years of 'high-speed, free-wheeling growth for the military–business complex'.[54] Total profits from military business operations reportedly reached 5 billion yuan (equivalent to 13.3 per cent of the published defence budget) in 1992[55] and 6 billion yuan (equivalent to 14.2 per cent of the published defence budget) in 1993.[56] The military's enthusiasm for money making again quickly gave rise to serious problems, including increasing corruption, worsening civil–military relations, poor discipline and morale, falling levels of professionalism, widening gaps between coastal and inland units, and so on. Alarmed by these trends, the central leadership launched another rectification campaign at the end of 1993. Combat units were banned from running businesses except farming and

[51] Joffe, E., 'The PLA and the economy: The effects of involvement', Paper presented at the IISS/CAPS Conference on Chinese Economic Reform: the Impact on Security Policy, Hong Kong, 8–10 July 1994, p. 12.

[52] Fan (note 14), pp. 296–98; and Sun Bolin, 'Guofangfei zhiding de xincelue' [A new strategy in drawing up the defence budget], ed. Beijing Society of Defense Economics (note 33), pp. 350–52.

[53] Fu and Li (note 35), p. 54.

[54] Tai Ming Cheung, 'The Chinese Army's new marching orders: winning on the economic battlefield', eds Brommelhorster and Frankenstein (note 35), p. 183.

[55] Tai Ming Cheung (note 54), p. 194.

[56] Tai Ming Cheung (note 54, p. 195) reported 6 billion yuan. Ka Po Ng suggested that the annual profit in 1993 was 5 billion yuan. Ka Po Ng, 'China defense budgeting: structure and dynamics', eds Lo Chi-kin, S. Pepper and Tsui Kai-yuen, *China Review 1995* (Chinese University Press: Hong Kong, 1995), pp. 9, 18.

sideline production. Their enterprises were closed, transferred to higher-level military units, or handed over to local governments. This time the order was more rigorously enforced. By the beginning of 1995, according to a Chinese report, 40 per cent of PLA business entities had already been closed down,[57] leading to a levelling off of the PLA's commercial earnings. The PLA's profits from economic activities in 1997, for instance, were reportedly around 4–6 billion yuan (at most equivalent to 7.4 per cent of the published defence budget).[58]

In July 1998, President Jiang Zemin issued an order removing the PLA and the PAP from business altogether.[59] By early December 1998, the PLA and PAP units in seven provinces (Beijing, Shanghai, Jiangsu, Guangdong, Guangxi, Hainan and Jiangxi) had completely withdrawn from commercial activities. Except for Jiangxi, these were the provinces where military enterprises had been most flourishing. A total of 580 enterprises with gross assets of 8–9 billion yuan were handed over to local governments.[60] The total value of military business assets in the country was estimated at around 50 billion yuan, or 1–1.5 per cent of the total assets of state-owned enterprises. The central government has promised to compensate the military in the defence budget for its lost business revenues.

On the basis of the above it is assumed that total profits from the PLA's domestic commercial activities were equivalent to 10 per cent of the published defence budget from 1989 to 1991, 15 per cent for the two years 1992–93, and 12 per cent in the five years 1994–98. This is the basis of the figures in column 7 of table 7D.3. It is highly unlikely that such incomes have contributed to the PLA's coffers by anything more than 15 per cent of official budget allocations to the PLA. In fact, internal Chinese publications insist that it has rarely exceeded 10 per cent.[61]

Where did the money go? The bulk of it was used to make up the PLA's budget shortfalls, and particularly to subsidize soldiers' living expenses.[62] However, a large proportion was either reinvested in new commercial ventures or wasted in conspicuous consumption by those directly involved in business dealings.[63] Worse still, some of the income was simply siphoned off by corrupt officers.[64]

Since not all profits from the PLA's commercial activities were used for military purposes, it is not appropriate to count them all as such. However, in order not to underestimate China's military expenditure, it is assumed here that all profits were spent on defence goods.

[57] Tai Ming Cheung (note 54), p. 184.

[58] Tai Ming Cheung, 'The Chinese Army's conversion to supplement defense budgets', *Bonn International Center for Conversion Bulletin*, no. 8 (July 1998). Many of these PLA businesses were losing money. Hu Xiaochun, Huang Guoan and Li Yongdao, 'Junban qiyc kuisun di yuanying ji duice' [Losses in military enterprises: casuses and solutions], *Junshi Jingji Yanjiu*, no. 9 (1996), pp. 11–13.

[59] New China News Agency, Beijing, 28 July 1998.

[60] New China News Agency, Beijing, various reports in late Nov. and early Dec. 1998.

[61] Wang Qinming and Wang Wenhua, 'Lun Jiang Zemin tongzhi guanyu jundui chi huangliang di sixiang' [On Comrade Jiang Zeming's idea of supporting the army by central budgetary allocations], *Junshi Jingji Yanjiu*, no. 10 (1996), p. 58.

[62] *Zhongguo Junshi Caiwu Shiyong Daquan* (note 8), pp. 476–86.

[63] Wang Junying, 'Wujia shangzhang dui junfei he shiyong di yingxiang' [Impact of inflation on the distribution and use of military expenditure], *Junshi Jingji Yanjiu*, no. 4 (1994), p. 40.

[64] Interview with a high-level official, Beijing, 10 June 1994.

Table 7D.4. Chinese arms imports and exports, 1989–98

Figures are in current prices.

Year	Imports (US $m.)	Imports (b. yuan)[c]	Exports (US $m.)	PLA's share of exports[b] (US $m.)	PLA's share of export earnings[a] (US $m.)	(b. yuan)[c]
1	2	3	4	5	6	7
1989	500	1.9	2 700	1 350	270	1.0
1990	300	1.4	2 000	1 000	200	1.0
1991	300	1.6	1 400	700	140	0.7
1992	1 300	7.2	1 100	550	110	0.6
1993	575	3.3	1 100	550	110	0.6
1994	260	2.2	725	363	73	0.6
1995	725	6.1	625	313	63	0.5
1996	[1 500]	12.5	584	292	58	0.5
1997	[1 500]	12.5	260	130	26	0.2
1998	[1 500]	12.5	120	70	12	0.1

Notes. Figures are for deliveries, not payment.

[a] Author's estimates of PLA's export earnings as 20% of PLA export revenues.

[b] Author's estimates of PLA's export revenues as 50% of total exports.

[c] Converted using official exchange rates.

Source: US Arms Control and Disarmament Agency (ACDA), *World Military Expenditure and Arms Transfers 1997* (US Government Printing Office: Washington, DC, 1997).

Arms exports

Earnings from overseas arms sales have been said to be another main source of extra-budgetary revenue for the PLA. However, their role should not be exaggerated, for three reasons.

First, China's arms exports have suffered substantial declines since their peak year of 1988. According to ACDA estimates, they fell from $3.75 billion in 1988 to $0.58 billion in 1996.[65] In 1997, China's arms exports dipped by 55 per cent and 1998 saw a drop of similar magnitude, according to SIPRI.[66] Similar declines are given by ACDA (see table 7D.4). Second, it is important to distinguish the PLA's arms sales from those conducted by the defence industrial corporations. Most Chinese arms sales agents are affiliated with the defence industrial corporations rather than with the PLA. Only arms sales by PLA companies would benefit the PLA. Such sales account for less than half of China's total.[67] Third, in order to estimate earnings realized, the cost of development and manufacture should be deducted from the total revenues from arms sales.[68] During the period under discussion (1989–98), most if not all PLA arms exports were supplied by the defence industries, rather than coming from its own inventories. A large portion of its gross income must therefore

[65] *World Military Expenditure and Arms Transfers 1997* (note 50), p. 265.

[66] See chapter 11, table 11.1 in this volume. SIPRI data refer to major weapon systems only.

[67] Interview by the author with a well-informed former employee of NORINCO, Mar. 1995.

[68] Frankenstein, J., 'The People's Republic of China: arms production, industrial strategy and problems of history', ed. H. Wulf, SIPRI, *Arms Industry Limited* (Oxford University Press: Oxford, 1993), p. 311.

be paid back to producers. It is highly unlikely that the PLA's net earnings exceeded 20 per cent of the income from its arms exports.[69]

Estimates of the PLA's earnings (or profits) from arms exports are shown in table 7D.4. They are based on ACDA estimates of values of Chinese arms export deliveries as an approximation of arms export revenues. If the assumptions above are correct, then the earnings from arms sales added little to the military coffers—so little that they were almost negligible (see columns 5 and 6 of table 7D.4).

How does the PLA spend its profits from arms sales? Some argue that China's arms imports are largely financed by such earnings. Table 7D.4 makes it clear that this is not possible: the values of imports are many times higher than the PLA's earnings from arms exports. Since there is no information about the outlets for such earnings, it is assumed here that they are used for unspecified military purposes.

V. China's total military expenditure

Table 7D.5 provides figures on China's official defence budget and total military expenditure, the latter being calculated from the data presented in tables 7D.1, 7D3 and 7D.4. Comparing the two time-series, it appears that total military expenditure has consistently been about 1.7–1.8 times the official defence budget. In current prices, it seems to have undergone double-digit increases every year since 1989. However, China experienced relatively high inflation between 1992 and 1995. While total military expenditure rose by 51.8 per cent over these four years, commodity prices went up 66.6 per cent during the same period. China's total military expenditure therefore actually decreased in real terms.

Since nominal figures give no proper indication of the real trend, the nominal time-series data must be deflated by a suitable price index to make them reflect variations in China's total military expenditure over time in real terms. In principle, the best method would be to derive a series of military price deflators which could then be used to show the real change in terms of the expenditure mix of the armed forces. Unfortunately, no such deflator series is available in China. This study, therefore, uses the overall consumer price index as a deflator to convert the nominal military expenditure series into constant prices.

In 1989 constant prices, China's total military expenditure increased by 73.1 per cent for the whole period 1989–98. The increases occurred mainly in two sub-periods—1989–92 and 1996–98—while the period 1992–95 witnessed downslides rather than upsurges.

This study makes no attempt to provide estimates of Chinese military expenditure in US dollars. The use of market exchange rates for international comparison can lead to enormous distortions in comparing defence efforts, and purchasing power parities (PPPs) are not used for the purposes of this appendix. The construction of a PPP requires detailed military expenditure data at a sufficiently disaggregated level, and in the study of China's military expenditure it is information that is in short supply.[70] In the absence of an explicit military PPP, 'short-cut' methods can be used instead,

[69] The author is grateful to Bates Gill for drawing his attention to this point.

[70] The PPP is defined as 'the number of units of a country's currency required to buy the quantity of goods and services that can be bought in the US with one US dollar'. The PPP is believed to be able to provide a better measure for comparing volume indices of output, since it supposedly reflects the relative purchasing power of domestic currency and the dollar. Whynes, D. K., *The Economics of Third World Military Expenditure* (Macmillan: London, 1979), pp. 49–50. See also appendix 7C in this volume.

Table 7D.5. China's military burden, 1989–98

	Military expenditure					
Year	Official (b. yuan, current prices)[b]	Official (b. yuan, constant 1989 prices)	Total[a] (b. yuan, current prices)	Total[a] (b. yuan, constant 1995 prices)[c]	Military exp./GDP: Official (%)	Military exp./GDP: Total (%)
1	2	3	4	5	6	7
1989	25.147	25.147	43.9	82.9	*1.5*	*2.6*
1990	29.031	28.153	49.3	90.1	*1.6*	*2.7*
1991	33.031	30.980	53.7	95.1	*1.5*	*2.5*
1992	37.786	33.315	69.2	115.1	*1.4*	*2.7*
1993	42.580	32.731	73.1	106.1	*1.2*	*2.1*
1994	55.071	34.117	87.2	102.0	*1.2*	*1.9*
1995	63.672	33.687	104.5	104.5	*1.1*	*1.8*
1996	72.006	35.906	124.0	114.4	*1.1*	*1.8*
1997	81.257	39.415	138.7	124.5	*1.1*	*1.8*
1998	91.710	44.045	155.6	141.1	*1.1*	*1.9*

[a] Total military expenditure = official + PAP (table 7D.1) + off-budget military expenditure (table 7D.3) + arms imports + PLA earnings from arms exports (table 7D.4).
[b] PLA + militia (see table 7D.1).
[c] Deflated using the domestic consumer price index (CPI).

Sources: Calculated from the data in tables 7D.1, 7D.3 and 7D.4. CPI and GDP data: International Monetary Fund, *International Financial Statistics*, monthly as provided in China Statistical Bureau, *Statistical Yearbook of China.*

namely, converting military expenditure by gross domestic product (GDP) parity or government expenditure PPP. However, no time-series on either is available in the case of China. At best there are only some rough estimates of the $PPP yuan value for a few specific years and they vary considerably, ranging from 3 to 9 times the exchange-rate conversion.[71] There is no consensus among economists as to which of them is most realistic. Thus, the PPP-adjusted estimates of Chinese military expenditure would be extremely sensitive to the choice of PPP yuan/$ rate.[72] In fact, much of the variance in estimating Chinese military expenditure in the West is attributable precisely to differing PPPs.[73]

Given the difficulty of making a judgment as to which PPP yuan/$ rate is most appropriate, this study makes no estimate of Chinese military expenditure in dollar terms. An estimate can be derived from the basic data provided here if wished. However, if what is at issue is international comparison of the defence burden, no conversion seems to be necessary. The share of military expenditure in GDP can serve as a very good indication of the military burden.[74] Whether converting military

[71] Waller, D., 'Estimating non-transparent military expenditures: the case of China (PRC)', *Defense and Peace Economics*, vol. 8 (1997), pp. 236–39.
[72] Sen (note 6), pp. 10–11.
[73] Waller (note 71).
[74] It is also a common practice to compare shares of military expenditure in total government expenditure. However, this is not done here because the ratio of total government expenditure to GDP has been unusually small in China. While in most countries this share ranges from 25% to 45%, it has fluc-

expenditure at the GDP-wide PPP, by exchange rates or making no conversion at all, the military expenditure/GDP ratio stays the same.

In the 10-year period 1989–98, China's economy was booming with GDP growing at an average annual rate of 9.4 per cent. The country could have afforded a military expenditure that kept pace with the general economy, had it chosen to do so. That did not happen. Rather, the share of total military expenditure in GDP was falling from 1992 to 1995, while it remained more or less unchanged for the other two sub-periods of 1989–92 and 1995–98. By 1998, the share was 0.7 percentage points lower than it had been in 1989. China currently spends less than 2 per cent of GDP on national defence as compared with 3.5 per cent in Taiwan, 2.4 per cent in India, 3.2 per cent in South Korea. 4.0 per cent in Russia and 3.4 per cent in the United States.[75]

VI. Conclusions

Given Chinese leaders' obsession with secrecy, analysis of Chinese real military expenditure is not an easy task. There are three essential steps: clearly defining the concept of military expenditure; ascertaining what items are already covered by the official defence budget; and identifying the possible sources of other defence outlets. On the basis of such an analytical framework, the general conclusions are:

1. China's total military expenditure has consistently been about 1.7–1.8 times its official defence budget (comparing columns 2 and 4 of table 7D.5).
2. The resources available to the Chinese military have increased by about 75 per cent since 1989 (see column 5 of table 7D.5).
3. As a share of GDP, Chinese military expenditure has steadily declined (see column 7 of table 7D.5) over the 10-year period 1989–98.
4. China's defence burden is modest. The military expenditure/GDP ratio is lower than those of all major powers and its neighbouring countries, with the exception of Japan.

Since the late 1980s voices within the PLA have advocated that the Chinese Government should change the way it allocates resources to national defence.[76] More specifically, two changes have been proposed. First, all sources of funding for military expenditure should be incorporated into the official defence budget. Second, the overall defence budget should be fixed at a certain percentage of GDP (2 or 3 per cent).[77] It is not clear whether or when the government will accept these proposals. However, recent visitors to Beijing have received the impression that the PLA will in future receive a fixed percentage of GDP and, although figures given to these visitors were not consistent, all were below 2 per cent.[78] It is unlikely that China's overall military expenditure will exceed 2.5 per cent of GDP for the foreseeable future.

tuated between 11% and 12% in China in recent years. Shaoguang Wang, 'China's 1994 fiscal reform: an initial assessment', *Asian Survey*, vol. 37, no. 9 (Sep. 1997), p. 810.

[75] See appendix 7A, table 7A.4 in this volume.

[76] See, e.g., Jiang and Zhang (note 22).

[77] Chen Changshou, Zhang Zhicheng and Dai Zhongyi, 'Guofangfei zhenzhang jizhi lun' [Growth mechanism of military expenditure], *Junshi Jingji Yanjiu*, no. 8 (1994), pp. 44–47; Fang Jizha *et al.*, 'Lun zhongguo guofangfei guanli fazhihua' [On the regulation of the management of military expenditure], *Junshi Jingji Yanjiu*, no. 8 (1995), pp. 34–42; Li and Shi (note 17), pp. 22–23; and Wang Qinming and Wang Wenhua (note 51), p. 58.

[78] Personal communication from Bates Gill and David Shambaugh following a visit to senior officials in the newly established General Logistics Department in late 1998.

8. Military research and development

ERIC ARNETT

I. Introduction

Annual expenditure on military research and development (R&D) by the world's governments has fallen to about $60 billion,[1] of which $38 billion is accounted for by the USA, $49 billion by NATO and $53 billion by the Organisation for Economic Co-operation and Development (OECD) countries. With the US decision to begin increasing military R&D investment in fiscal year (FY) 1999, a downward trend appears to have come to an end. Initial, mainly short-term increases were already observable before 1998 in some major investors, as seen in table 8.2. As has long been the case, the main area of emphasis for most of the states spending most heavily on R&D is combat aircraft and related weapons, with Israel and the USA also funding missile defence heavily (table 8.3 shows US funding).[2] The other most notable events in 1998 were:

1. India redoubled its struggle to develop arms indigenously after a new government took power and technology transfer was disrupted in response to the nuclear tests.
2. Three Asian countries—Iran, North Korea and Pakistan—tested ballistic missiles with estimated ranges greater than 1000 km, each for the first time.
3. Israel initiated new projects in air and missile defence which signal an increase in military technology efforts after a decade of reductions.
4. After cutting its military R&D budget by 20 per cent in 1998, Japan decided to join the US Navy Theater-Wide missile-defence programme following years of study.
5. China restructured the development and procurement of arms.

[1] This figure is expressed in 1995 dollars derived from the sum of the best publicly known estimates for most recent years and 1% of military expenditure in states where no figure for military R&D is publicly known. It is accurate to 1 significant digit. The estimate of China's expenditure is elaborated in Arnett, E., 'Military technology: the case of China', *SIPRI Yearbook 1995: Armaments, Disarmament and International Security* (Oxford University Press: Oxford, 1995), pp. 375–77. The estimate that China spends of the order of $1 billion to 1 significant digit means that it spends between $0.5 and $1.5 billion, but no more precise estimate is possible. This range corresponds roughly to $2–7 billion in purchasing power.

[2] In China and Russia, nuclear delivery systems appear to receive greater emphasis, as discussed in Arnett, E., 'Military research and development', *SIPRI Yearbook 1997: Armaments, Disarmament and International Security* (Oxford University Press: Oxford, 1997), pp. 219, 221. In 1998, funding for the Russian nuclear forces was given special legal protection up to and including 2010. Korotchenko, I., [Funding of strategic nuclear forces will be guaranteed by law], *Nezavisimoye Voyennoye Obozreniye*, 6–12 Nov. 1998, pp. 1, 3 (in Russian), in Foreign Broadcast Information Service, *Daily Report–Central Asia: Military Affairs [FBIS-UMA)*, FBIS-UMA-98-313, 10 Nov. 1998. See also chapters 4 and 13 in this volume. In France, strategic R&D (which includes nuclear and space systems) increased significantly in the 1998 budget at the expense of aircraft, as discussed below. As seen in section IV, Iran apparently favours ballistic missiles over other projects.

Table 8.1. Official figures for government military R&D expenditure[a]

Country	Local currency, current prices	(1995 US $m.) Exch. rate	(1995 US $m.) PPP[b]	Year	Source
Nuclear weapon states party to the 1968 Non-Proliferation Treaty (NPT)					
USA (m. dollars)	39 000	38 000	38 000	1997	OECD
France (b. francs)	24	4 600	4 000	1997	OECD
UK (b. pounds)	2.2	3 300	3 400	1997	OECD
Russia (tr. roubles)	7.44	970	1 900	1997	UN
China[c]	. .	1 000	. .	1994	PRC Govt
Non-nuclear weapon states party to the NPT and states not party to the NPT					
Germany (m. D. marks)	3 000	2 100	1 600	1997	OECD
Japan (b. yen)	170	1 800	1 100	1997	OECD
India (b. rupees)	[24]	630	2 600	1997	Indian Govt
Spain (b. pesetas)	79	600	650	1997	OECD
Sweden (b. kronor)	4.1	570	450	1996	OECD
South Korea (b. won)	430	510	660	1997	ROK Govt
Taiwan (b. T. dollars)	8.9	350	. .	1994	ROC Govt
Brazil (m. reais)	390	340	510	1997	UN
Italy (b. lire)	480	300	320	1995	OECD
Australia (m. A. dollars)	220	170	190	1994	OECD
South Africa (m. rand)	572	150	240	1996	RSA Govt
Canada (m. C. dollars)	170	120	120	1996	OECD
Ukraine (b. karbonavets)	416	120	180	1994	UN
Switzerland (m. francs)	117	100	68	1995	UN
Netherlands (m. guilders)	170	100	87	1996	OECD
Norway (m. kroner)	460	69	54	1997	OECD
Poland (m. zlotys)	179	53	100	1997	UN

[a] Includes only states spending more than $50 million on military R&D and making figures available. Estimates for Iran and Israel are discussed in section IV of the text. Figures are for the year indicated only.

[b] PPP = Purchasing power parity.

[c] Figures for China are accurate to only 1 significant digit.

Sources: OECD Main Science and Technology Indicators no. 1 (1998) and no. 2 (1998); UN documents A/51/209, 24 July 1996, A/52/310, 25 Aug. 1997, and A/53/218, 4 Aug. 1998; Arnett (note 1); Wu Fangming and Wu Xizhi, 'On dealing correctly with the relations of our defence establishment to our economic construction', *National Defence*, 15 Feb. 1996, pp. 4–6 (in Chinese), in Foreign Broadcast Information Service, *Daily Reports–China (FBIS-CHI)*, FBIS-CHI-96-203, 15 Feb. 1996; India, Department of Science and Technology, *Research and Development Statistics* (various publishers, various years); Republic of Korea, Ministry of National Defense, *Defense White Paper* (Ministry of National Defense: Seoul, various years); Republic of China, *National Defense Report, 1993–94* (Ministry of National Defense: Taipei, 1994); and Cilliers, J., 'Defence research and development in South Africa', *African Security Review*, vol. 5, no. 5 (1996), p. 42.

6. The UK completed its Strategic Defence Review.

7. Spain continued a programme of increases in funding for military R&D that could bring about a 1999 level almost six times higher than that of 1996.

8. France cancelled military R&D programmes for the first time since the end of the cold war, although these were mainly minor efforts.

Table 8.2. Government expenditure on military R&D in select countries, 1986–97
Figures are in US $m., at 1995 constant prices and exchange rates.

Country	1986	1989	1992	1993	1994	1995	1996	1997	1992–96
USA	51 000	51 000	44 000	43 000	39 000	37 000	37 000	38 000	200 000
France	6 200	7 100	6 800	6 200	6 000	5 200	5 000	4 600	29 200
UK	5 400	4 100	3 500	3 800	3 300	3 300	3 400	3 300	17 300
Germany[a]	2 300	3 100	2 400	1 900	1 900	2 000	2 200	2 100	10 400
Japan	[820]	1 100	1 400	1 500	1 500	1 600	1 800	1 800	7 800
Italy	540	750	600	620	590	[560]	[680]	. .	3 500
Sweden	660	680	690	650	500	570	570	. .	2 980
India	340	410	380	470	510	[540]	[490]	[630]	2 390
South Korea	120	170	340	390	400	440	460	510	2 030
Spain	75	460	410	340	280	300	310	600	1 640

[a] Figures for 1986 and 1989 are for the Federal Republic of Germany (West Germany) only.

Sources: *OECD Main Science and Technology Indicators*, no. 1 (1998), no. 2 (1998), no. 2 (1995), no. 1 (1990) and 1981–87; India, Department of Science and Technology, *Research and Development Statistics* (various publishers, various years); Republic of Korea, Ministry of National Defense, *Defense White Paper* (Ministry of National Defense: Seoul, various years).

After a note on sources and methods in section II, this chapter examines the impact of India's elections on its R&D efforts (in section III) not directly related to the May 1998 nuclear tests (which are discussed in chapter 9 in this volume); Iran's missile test and Israel's related increase in military R&D (section IV); and Japanese and Chinese military R&D policies (in sections V and VI). Section VII discusses military R&D in NATO Europe, which has increased its emphasis on aerospace since the end of the cold war and continues to encounter obstacles in efforts to coordinate requirements in the hope that a common technological and production base can be created and duplication reduced. Recent decisions show Britain and France emphasizing forces for military intervention outside NATO's area of responsibility, in which Germany has less interest. Italy and Spain are devoting significant resources to cooperative projects without having much say in the underlying military requirements.

II. Sources of information

As discussed more comprehensively in the *SIPRI Yearbook 1996*,[3] publicly available information on military R&D has improved since the early 1980s but is still quite limited. The most complete information is available from certain national governments, in particular that of the USA. Data from any one state, however, are not easily compared with those from another. Often only R&D undertaken by the defence ministry is counted, neglecting other projects of

[3] Arnett, E., 'Military research and development', *SIPRI Yearbook 1996: Armaments, Disarmament and International Security* (Oxford University Press: Oxford, 1996), pp. 387–88.

Table 8.3. Appropriations for major US R&D programmes, 1999

Figures are in current US $m.

Programme	R&D budget	Service or agency
Aircraft and associated weapons		
F-22 Raptor fighter	1 575	Air Force
Joint Strike Fighter	471	Navy
RAH-66 Comanche attack helicopter	368	Army
Tomahawk sea-launched cruise missile	265	Navy
Helicopter development	262	Navy
Endurance unpiloted aerial vehicles	189	Air Force
Joint Air-to-Surface Stand-off Missile (JASSM)	178	Air Force, Navy
C-17 transport aircraft	119	Air Force
Land-attack technology	106	Navy
E-8A JSTARS surveillance aircraft	102	Air Force
Sub-total	**3 635**	
Missile defence		
National Missile Defense	950	BMDO
Space Based Infrared (SBIR) satellite	542	Air Force
Theater High-Altitude Area Defense (THAAD)	445	BMDO
Navy Theater-Wide (Upper Tier)	338	BMDO
Airborne Laser (ABL)	267	Air Force
Joint theatre missile defence	208	BMDO
Sub-total	**2 750**	
Other or unknown		
Evolved Expendable space Launch Vehicle (EELV)	260	Air Force
New SSN attack submarine	236	Navy
Brilliant Anti-armour Technology (BAT) submunition	129	Army
Marine Corps assault vehicles	105	Navy
Total	**7 115**	

Notes: Includes only those programmes allocated more than $100 million. Does not include Department of Energy nuclear programmes (nuclear weapons and naval reactors). JSTARS = Joint Surveillance and Target Attack Radar, BMDO = Ballistic Missile Defense Organization.

Sources: US Congress, House of Representatives, *Conference Report on Department of Defense Appropriations Act, 1999* (US Government Printing Office: Washington, DC, 1998).

military importance. The largest set of comparable data on military R&D comes from the OECD, which compiles a survey of national budgets to produce aggregate figures for total civil and military R&D investment in member states.[4]

Although considerable effort was put into making the data submitted to the UN register of military expenditure comparable, it is difficult to know how governments derive the figures they submit; practice varies over time, and some do not disaggregate military R&D. Moreover, although the UN register still enjoys unanimous support in the First Committee of the UN General

[4] Definitions and methods are described in Organisation for Economic Co-operation and Development, *Frascati Manual 1993* (OECD: Paris, 1993).

Assembly, only 64 states have submitted R&D data in any year since the register was started in 1980; 18 of these (mainly African and Latin American states) have only ever filed a nil report and only 32 have given figures for any year since 1993. Among the largest investors in military R&D, China, India, Iran, South Africa and South Korea have never filed a return, although India has given figures to UNESCO for its *Statistical Yearbook*.[5]

This chapter uses OECD figures where possible, falling back when necessary on UN or Organization for Security and Co-operation in Europe (OSCE) submissions and other national data, in that order of preference. Even so, precise estimates of military R&D funding in Iran and Israel are not possible; it appears that both are among the 20 largest investors, each spending more than $200 million. R&D undertaken independently by firms in the expectation that it will be recouped during procurement is not included, although it may constitute more than half of all military R&D investment in some cases, such as that of Japan (see section V).

In general, this chapter seeks to evaluate and compare the results of R&D programmes rather than the opportunity cost to governments of the relevant expenditures and human resources (the concern of chapter 7 of the *SIPRI Yearbook*). Nevertheless, current figures are deflated using the local consumer price index and converted to US dollars at the 1995 exchange rate in order to facilitate comparisons between figures in the two chapters. Purchasing power parity (PPP) conversions are usually preferable for comparing R&D figures, but are difficult to derive for military goods and technology services. For the sake of comparison, PPP conversions are given in table 8.1. They are based on R&D prices for OECD member states and on prices in the economy at large for other states.[6]

III. India

A new government led by the Bharatiya Janata Party (BJP, or Indian People's Party) came to power in India in March 1998 promising that the country's first ever Strategic Defence Review would be conducted by a National Security Council (NSC), which was formed in November 1998. The BJP's election manifesto on security policy made specific references to technology projects: '. . . views with concern the inadequate pace of defence research and development despite abundant talent in DRDO [Defence Research and Development Organisation]. Inadequate budgetary support is a major reason for this. The inordinate delays in the LCA [Light Combat Aircraft], nuclear submarine and guided missiles, and other programmes are matters of particular concern'. The manifesto specifically promised to 'expedite the development of the Agni series of ballistic missiles with a view to increasing their range and accuracy'.[7]

[5] United Nations Educational, Scientific and Cultural Organization, *Statistical Yearbook* (UNESCO: Paris, various years).

[6] On the use of PPPs in assessing military expenditure, see appendix 7C in this volume.

[7] Bharatiya Janata Party, *On Nation's Security and Foreign Policy* (BJP: New Delhi, 1998). Previous governments had promised to double the DRDO's budget by 2000, but initially had not made the required increases, as seen in table 8.2. Arnett (note 2), pp. 222–25.

In the first BJP budget the DRDO was given 30 per cent real growth, and its authority over the Department of Atomic Energy's activities related to nuclear weapons, for which budget figures are not publicly known, was increased. On-budget funding of military R&D rose to an estimated 30 billion rupees, the equivalent of $820 million in foreign exchange or $3.4 billion using purchasing power equivalents.[8] On the other hand, the nuclear tests authorized by the BJP and conducted in May 1998 disrupted the DRDO's relationships with foreign technology suppliers, setting back several projects for 'indigenous' weapon systems.[9] The DRDO Director-General, A. P. J. Abdul Kalam, acknowledged that the domestic component of Indian equipment has actually decreased since the DRDO launched its latest indigenization drive in 1995.[10] His previous exaggerated claims of self-reliance in military technology may have led the BJP leadership to underestimate the impact of sanctions, imposed following India's nuclear tests, on conventional military modernization. By the end of 1998, he was stressing international cooperation on military technology with India's remaining partners, France, Israel, and primarily Russia:[11] 'India has to graduate to design, development and production of newer aerospace systems through international partnerships . . . Our strategy for technological growth is to go for co-development'.

The Light Combat Aircraft

The LCA project had to be fundamentally restructured in 1998 after continuing problems and the withdrawal of US involvement after the nuclear tests in May.[12] The first flight of the LCA, already postponed from 1996, has now been put off until July 1999 at the earliest.[13] Flight-testing of the avionics on

[8] The DRDO is budgeted to receive 24.7 billion rupees in fiscal year 1998/99 and 27.9 billion rupees in 1999/2000, a further 20% increase. Actual Indian military R&D funding is generally 20% higher because of R&D funded by the armed forces from their budgets. India, Ministry of Defence, *Annual Report* (Thomson Publishers: New Delhi, 1998); and India, Department of Science and Technology, *Research and Development Statistics* (various publishers, various years). The budget of the Department of Atomic Energy's nuclear weapon programme is unknown, nor is it known whether the DRDO receives additional funds for nuclear activities.

[9] See chapter 9 in this volume.

[10] 'The 1995 plan for the DRDO projected that the defence sector should achieve 70% indigenization [by 2005] with the rest made up through imported components. However the trend is just the opposite', he said. 'Dr Kalam urges defence scientists to strive harder', *Deccan Herald*, 10 Aug. 1998. Defence Minister George Fernandes put the current value of foreign content in Indian equipment at 50 billion rupees, even before the $8 billion arms contract with Russia of 1998. *Deccan Herald*, 24 Sep. 1998, in Foreign Broadcast Information Service, *Daily Report–Arms Control (FBIS-TAC)*, FBIS-TAC-98-267, 25 Sep. 1998.

[11] Reuters, 'Agni in full production', 8 Dec. 1998.

[12] US involvement with the LCA project began in Oct. 1988. Sharma, P., 'India, US pact on LCA', *Hindustan Times*, 22 Oct. 1988. US interest in military technology cooperation with India dates to Caspar Weinberger's tenure as US Secretary of Defense. Talks about cooperation on a light combat aircraft began in 1982, before the LCA project had begun. 'India', *Defense and Foreign Affairs*, Jan./Feb. 1983, p. 13.

[13] The project was postponed by 2 years after the nuclear tests, but Defence Minister Fernandes later said that the prototype might fly by July 1999. 'Sanctions will not affect the Arjun and LCA: Defence Minister', *Deccan Herald*, 10 July 1998; Bedi, R., 'Sanctions stall first flight test of Indian LCA', *Jane's Defence Weekly*, 8 July 1998, p. 15; *Asian Age*, 23 June 1998, p. 2; and 'Russia to play major role in LCA project', *Asian Age*, 21 June 1998. The LCA project is described more completely in Arnett, E.,

US aircraft in the USA by Lockheed Martin stopped immediately upon news of the nuclear tests and Indian participants were sent home.[14] Problems with the development of an indigenous engine suggest that the LCA would have had to continue to rely on US-made General Electric engines.[15] Several minor components, including generators, pumps and valves, will now have to be copied from US-supplied equipment on the prototype for local production, presumably without US assistance.[16]

Even before the withdrawal of US cooperation, there were suggestions that the first flight would be put back until the year 2000 or later.[17] Furthermore, successfully flying the prototypes assembled with US cooperation does not necessarily mean that the project can continue. Body panels are now made in Italy, and even if fabrication begins in India carbon fibres will have to be imported.[18] No funds have yet been allocated for a serial production facility.[19] Jasjit Singh, a retired air commodore involved in setting up the NSC, has said that the LCA will probably not enter service in meaningful numbers until 2010.[20] Ironically, since the LCA was originally intended to provide an alternative to reliance on arms supplied by the Soviet Union, Russia is likely to become the primary cooperation partner if the project is not cancelled.

The nuclear submarine and the Sagarika missile

New information was made available in 1998 regarding the Advanced Technology Vessel (ATV) project for a nuclear-propelled submarine and an associated missile, the Sagarika. So far the ATV consists primarily of a prototype naval reactor which is too large to go to sea. An unnamed source at the

'Military technology: the case of India', *SIPRI Yearbook 1994* (Oxford University Press: Oxford, 1994), pp. 349–50.

[14] Jaideep, V. G., 'LCA scientists sent back by US', *Asian Age*, 25 May 1998; and Krishnaprasad, S., 'US sanctions may delay LCA project', *Times of India*, 27 May 1998. Indian equipment in the USA was not returned. 'US refuse to release LCA gear', *Asian Age*, 18 Aug. 1998.

[15] The Indian Kaveri engine is being tested in Russia, suggesting that a Russian supplier might fill the gap left by General Electric, requiring the sort of redesign that led to the failure of India's only previous indigenous fighter, the HF-24 Marut, which was developed in the 1960s. Paramanand, B., 'Sanctions may delay LCA programme to take off', *Economic Times*, 14 May 1998.

[16] LCA Project Director Kota Harinarayana, referred to in David, S., 'Grounded again', *India Today*, 12 Sep. 1998.

[17] Gupta, S., 'Foreign tie-ups for LCA under study', *Hindustan Times*, 5 Aug. 1998; Chengappa, B. M., 'LCA unlikely to fly this year', *Indian Express*, 17 Apr. 1998; and 'First flight of LCA is still a few years away', *Times of India*, 25 Apr. 1998. Testing of the flight-control system in the USA was scheduled for completion in 2000. Krishnaprasad (note 14). Engineers working on the LCA have tried in vain to gain authority to fly the LCA without completing the testing. Jaideep, V. G., 'Scientists look for shortcut to keep LCA project alive', *Asian Age*, 30 May 1998.

[18] Composite skins have thus far been made by Alenia. Hindustan Aircraft Ltd completed construction of an autoclave for curing composite skins in 1998. 'Milestone in hi-tech', *The Hindu*, 8 Aug. 1998; Raj, N. G., *The Hindu*, 1 Dec. 1995, p. 2; and Ahmedullah, M., 'India aims for the sky', *Military Technology*, Feb. 1996, p. 46. Of the LCA's components, 70% are generally believed to be imported. Arnett (note 13), p. 349.

[19] The production line is expected to cost 16 billion rupees. David (note 16).

[20] Singh, J., 'Defence: budgeting for security needs', *Frontline*, 18–31 July 1998. Abdul Kalam claims that the LCA can enter service as early as 2003 and that at least 200 will be in service by 2010. Production of the LCA will cost 300 billion rupees, he has said, and represent 20% of all Indian arms production. 'IAF will induct LCA by 2003: Kalam', *The Hindu*, 20 Aug. 1998.

Bhabha Atomic Research Centre said in an interview that the prototype of a smaller version 'will take at least five years to build' after progress was slowed by conflicts over technical requirements between the Indian Navy and the Department of Atomic Energy (DAE).[21] DRDO officials said in 1995 that the ATV would require another 25 billion rupees in R&D funding.[22] Since the reactor has not been designed yet, much less the hull, reports that the ATV resembles existing French, German or Russian designs appear to be premature. There is no sign that the navy's leadership is changing its reluctance to pursue the project. The 30-year Submarine Plan released in 1998 emphasizes conventional submarines.[23] Indeed, the navy's decision, approved by the government in 1998, to move ahead with a 120 billion-rupee aircraft-carrier project suggests that its priorities are elsewhere.[24]

DRDO sources have confirmed that the Sagarika missile is associated with the ATV, which will be the only vessel configured to carry and launch it.[25] The Sagarika project was begun in 1992 with a budget of 1 billion rupees as part of a new initiative under the DRDO's Integrated Guided Missile Development Programme (IGMDP).[26] It has been described as a 'multiple-stage ramjet-powered strategic weapon', suggesting it would be armed with a nuclear warhead.[27] Other sources have said that the ATV requires a missile with a range of 1000 km.[28]

The Sagarika project was made public in 1994, when the DRDO requested a 100 per cent increase in its budget. The DRDO also promised to develop the Astra air-to-air missile, the Koral supersonic anti-ship missile, the Prakash surface-to-air missile for shooting down airborne warning and control aircraft, and the Surya intercontinental ballistic missile, as well as a naval version of the Prithvi ballistic missile called Dhanush, indigenous smart bombs and anti-tank sub-munitions. Of the missiles developed under the rubric of the IGMDP since 1983, only the Prithvi short-range ballistic missile has entered low-rate production, while the Nag anti-tank missile and the Akash and Trishul air-defence missiles are struggling in testing.

[21] Koch, A. R., 'Nuclear-powered submarines: India's strategic trump card', *Jane's Intelligence Review*, June 1998, p. 35. The DAE has been working on a naval reactor since 1976.

[22] Of this amount, $285 million (*c.* 1 billion rupees) had reportedly been spent by mid-1996. Kumar, D., 'Submarine's n-power plant getting ready', *Times of India*, 29 Dec. 1995; 'Indigenous n-sub's energy plant to be land tested soon', *Economic Times*, 10 Mar. 1996; and Mann P., 'Subcontinent poised for nuke deployment', *Aviation Week & Space Technology*, 3 Aug. 1998, p. 25. Report says that between 12 and 20 billion rupees had been spent by 1998. Rai, R. B., 'The price of going nuclear', *The Pioneer*, 3 Aug. 1998, p. 9; and Gupta, S., 'Nuclear submarine programme languishing', *Hindustan Times*, 28 Oct. 1998.

[23] Singh, M., 'Navy plan to beef up submarine fleet left high and dry in ministry', *Indian Express*, 5 Sep. 1998. India spent 450 million rupees on a facility to build 2 German submarines in the 1980s, but it has largely been idle since then and many of the skilled workers trained there have reportedly emigrated to Australia to build Swedish submarines under licence.

[24] 'Decks cleared for India's home-made naval aircraft carrier', *Indian Express*, 18 July 1998.

[25] Koch (note 21), p. 35. The Chief of Naval Staff, Vishnu Bhagwat, professed no knowledge of the Sagarika in Dec. 1998. 'Prithvi naval version to be test fired on Jan. 26', *Deccan Herald*, 1 Dec. 1998.

[26] 'India models SLBM after Prithvi missile', *Defense News*, 25–31 July 1994, p. 15.

[27] An unnamed DRDO scientist, quoted in Srikath, B. R., 'India begins work on new generation of missiles and nuclear submarines', *Asian Age*, 15 Aug. 1994.

[28] Kumar, D., 'Submarine's n-power plant getting ready', *Times of India*, 29 Dec. 1995.

The Agni ballistic missile

The Agni ballistic missile has become a cause célèbre among Indian nationalists, largely because of the tenacity with which the US Government has opposed it. As a result, the BJP specifically promised to pursue the development of the Agni in its 1998 election manifesto despite the armed forces' lack of interest. Since the May nuclear tests, the Agni has garnered interest as a possible nuclear delivery system, despite the government's position that China, the only plausible target for the Agni, is only a 'potential adversary', not an immediate nuclear threat.[29]

Much of this interest presupposes that the Agni will be able to reach targets 5000 km away. The longest range achieved in a test so far, in 1994, is 1450 km.[30] The DRDO requested an additional 500 million rupees for five more tests in 1996 and 1997.[31] Upon the BJP's forming a coalition government, the request was increased to 6 billion rupees for a redesign to produce a missile capable of reaching 2200 km.[32] Although a DRDO statement claims that the design used in the 1994 test can attain that range, the redesign will feature solid-fuel engines.[33] Jasjit Singh, the retired air commodore who advises the government, said in June 1998 that 'at least 24 more tests' would be necessary 'before adequate operational reliability could be ensured'.[34] He stated in 1998 that an additional prototype had been produced in 1997,[35] but it was not tested in 1998. Then Prime Minister Atal Bihari Vajpayee promised the parliament in December that Agni test flights would continue.[36]

IV. Iran, Israel and ballistic missile defence

On 22 July 1998, Iran tested the Shahab 3, a missile that may be capable of reaching Israel.[37] An Iranian Foreign Ministry official stated in April 1995 that

[29] See chapter 9 in this volume.

[30] The 1989 test missile reached 750 km. The 1992 test failed after 5 delays. The 1994 test missile apparently reached 1450 km after a delay, although initial estimates were 'around 1000 km'. The missile was extensively redesigned each time. 'India ready for lift-off on Agni missile production', *Jane's Defence Weekly*, 25 Feb. 1998, p. 17; and Joshi, M., 'Missile program on hold', *Asia–Pacific Defence Reporter*, Apr./May 1994, p. 20. These tests may have been at reduced payloads. Warrier, H. K., 'Is it cash crunch crippling defence projects?', *The Pioneer*, 24 Mar. 1996. The Agni is discussed at greater length in Arnett (note 13), pp. 360–62.

[31] Raghuvanshi, V., 'India's DRDO awaits approval for Agni flight tests', *Defense News*, 26 Aug.–1 Sep. 1996, p. 14.

[32] Including between 4 and 6 more tests Raghuvanshi, V. and Opall-Rome, B., 'India's new Agni raises missile race stakes', *Defense News*, 11–17 May 1998, p. 4; and Dixit, A., 'A new government in New Delhi', *Asia–Pacific Defence Reporter*, Apr./May 1998, p. 10.

[33] 'India ready' (note 30); and 'India to revive "Agni" project', *The Hindu*, 31 July 1997.

[34] Chanda, N. *et al.*, 'Security: the race is on', *Far East Economic Review*, 11 June 1998, p. 20. Singh had said previously that 36 tests over 10 years would be necessary. Srikanth, B. R., 'Preparations for Agni test belie capping reports', *Asian Age*, 30 Dec. 1996.

[35] Singh, J., 'Defence: budgeting for security needs', *Frontline*, 18–31 July 1998.

[36] Mohan, C. R., 'PM rejects demands to limit nuclear capabilities', *The Hindu*, 16 Dec. 1998, p. 1.

[37] The missile was destroyed by 2 explosions after flying 50 km in 100 seconds. Fulghum, D. A., 'Slipup spoils coverage of Iranian missile test', *Aviation Week & Space Technology*, 3 Aug. 1998, p. 24; and Alon, G., 'Netanyahu warns Iran: "Israel will defend itself"', *Ha'aretz*, 5 Aug. 1998.

Iran had no interest in such a weapon,[38] but Iran's medium-range ballistic missile programme was apparently reinvigorated later that year.[39] The 1998 launch may have tested only the engine of the Shahab 3, which Iranian officials acknowledge is based on technology from North Korea.[40] If so, not all the technological hurdles involved in the missile's development, including re-entry and guidance, have necessarily been cleared. Indeed, there is reason to believe that the test was largely political in its intent.[41]

It is not known how much Iran invests in military R&D, but Defence Minister Ali Shamkani revealed in 1998 that $600 million had been spent on the Shahab 3.[42] Shamkani further remarked, 'Certainly we will work on the development of the Shahab 4 and 5, but this does not mean we will start tomorrow'.[43] Iran has an extensive ballistic missile and rocket manufacturing base, but most of its other military technology projects involve extending the service life of imported weapons in the inventory. There are also suspicions that Iran is developing non-conventional weapons despite being a party to the 1968 Non-Proliferation Treaty (NPT), the 1993 Chemical Weapons Convention and the 1972 Biological and Toxin Weapons Convention.[44]

Even before the Iranian test—indeed before it was publicly known that Iran had reinvigorated its missile programme—Israel had been investing heavily in missile defences. Israeli investment in military R&D is probably about $300 million per year, of which on average $50 million goes to missile defence.[45] Although some of the systems in development might be useful against Syrian short-range missiles, Israeli Government officials have stated that Iran is the

[38] Arnett, E., 'Beyond threat perception: assessing military capacity and reducing the risk of war in southern Asia', ed. E. Arnett, SIPRI, *Military Capacity and the Risk of War: China, India, Pakistan and Iran* (Oxford University Press: Oxford, 1997), p. 5.

[39] 'Iran successfully tests medium-range missile', *Tehran Times*, 26 July 1998. By 1995, Iran's efforts to buy conventional weapons abroad had faltered under US pressure on suppliers, perhaps freeing resources for the missile programme. The alleged military nuclear programme may also have been reduced or abandoned in 1995, according to one report. Fitchett, J., 'Ousting Iranian, Russia signalled US on arms', *International Herald Tribune*, 9 Dec. 1997, p. 4. A controversy in 1995 over Iran's civil nuclear programme raised fears of preventive war, which Iran has sought to deter. Arnett, E., 'Reassurance versus deterrence: opportunities to expand Iranian participation in confidence-building measures', *Security Dialogue* (Oslo), vol. 29, no 4 (Dec. 1998).

[40] Schiff, Z., 'After the Iranian test', *Ha'aretz*, 29 July 1998, p. B1; and Finnegan, P. and Rodan, S., 'Israelis scale back Iran missile estimate', *Defense News*, 2–8 Feb. 1998, p. 8.

[41] A Shahab 3 was exhibited during a 25 Sep. military parade, accompanied by anti-Israel and anti-US slogans. Blanche, E., 'Israel mulls strike on Iran', *Jane's Defence Weekly*, 7 Oct. 1998, p. 27.

[42] 'Iran successfully tests medium-range missile', *Tehran Times*, 26 July 1998. Shamkani, who had previously articulated a policy of non-offensive defence, also said that Iran would not use the missile unless attacked. Blanche, E., 'Shahab 3 launch success spurs Israeli response', *Jane's Defence Weekly*, 12 Aug. 1998, p. 18.

[43] Associated Press, 'Iran to develop new missile', 26 Sep. 1998. Shamkani did not specify what requirements the Shahab 4 and 5 would be designed to meet. Later he said, 'In Iran's defence strategy, there is no need at present for ballistic missiles' despite the perceived threat from Israel and the USA. Dareini, A. A., '"Shahab-3 has created regional security balance, confidence" Shamkani says', *Kayhan International*, 25 Oct. 1998 (in English), in Foreign Broadcast Information Service, *Daily Report–Near East and South Asia (FBIS-NES)*, FBIS-NES-98-312, 25 Oct. 1998.

[44] Arnett (note 39). See also chapter 14 in this volume.

[45] The $300 million estimate is meant to imply that Israel spends between $250 and $350 million on military R&D, a figure that is about the same in terms of foreign exchange or purchasing power parity (PPP).

main state of concern.[46] Indeed, the Israeli Arrow missile-defence system, which will be deployed beginning in late 1999,[47] is designed to defend against missiles launched from the direction of Iran or Iraq, allowing it to use relatively unsophisticated searching and tracking technologies. Israel is also spending roughly $200 million annually on a new project to maintain air supremacy over and above the official R&D budget, which was about $60 million in 1994.[48]

The July test and subsequent Iranian statements officially confirmed for the first time reports that Iran was developing ballistic missiles with a range greater than 1000 km. The Shahab 3 test, along with Pakistan's test of the 1500-km Ghauri/Hatf V and North Korea's attempt to launch a satellite with a three-stage booster,[49] called into question the proposition that states capable of fielding shorter-range ballistic missiles might still have difficulties with missiles of range greater than 1000 km or so, which leave and re-enter the atmosphere during their flight trajectories.[50] Although a few test flights of such missiles by India, Iran, North Korea and Pakistan are not conclusive,[51] developments in 1998 reinforced the decision of the US Administration, under pressure from the Republican-led Congress, to raise the priority of ballistic-missile defence systems like Navy Theater-Wide and Space-Based Laser which attack missiles in flight outside the atmosphere and are therefore useful only against missiles with ranges greater than about 1000 km.[52] At $4 billion, or 9 per cent of the US military R&D budget, missile defence is the second priority after combat aircraft and associated weapons—a higher priority than nuclear weapons.[53]

[46] Opall-Rome, B., 'Netanyahu orders Israel defense budget hike', *Defense News*, 17–23 Aug. 1998, p. 3.

[47] Ettinger, A., *Ma'ariv*, 9 Oct. 1998, pp. 10–12 (in Hebrew), in FBIS-NES-98-284, 14 Oct. 1998. In this article, Ilan Biran, Director-General of the Israeli Defense Ministry, summarized Israel's missile-defence effort. In addition to the Arrow, Israel has spent $30 million on a drone that can launch interceptors at ballistic missiles shortly after they are launched, and may spend an additional $200 million on the project. Biran says that the Nautilus airborne laser, which will cost $150–200 million each, could be deployed in late 1999 if the USA provides enough money—an estimate at odds with the relatively early stage at which the equivalent US project remains. So far the Nautilus has cost $90 million, of which the USA has provided $60 million. The US airborne laser programme is discussed in Fulghum, D. A., 'Airborne laser aimed at new defense roles', *Aviation Week & Space Technology*, 5 Oct. 1998, p. 111.

[48] Opall-Rome, B., 'Israelis broaden missile defense role for laser', *Defense News*, 6–12 July 1998, p. 3; and Arnett (note 2), p. 213. Israel's military R&D budget is divided into a main fund and special projects, which often are much greater than the central budget. In addition to the special projects discussed in the text, Israel invested more than $1 billion in the Lavi fighter aircraft in the 1980s, for example.

[49] US Department of Defense, *News Briefing*, 15 Sep. 1998.

[50] Karp, A., SIPRI, *Ballistic Missile Proliferation: the Politics and Technics* (Oxford University Press: Oxford, 1996), pp. 21, 110–34.

[51] India's Agni has been tested 3 times at reduced range and payload with mixed results. See above. North Korea's Ro-dong 1 has been tested once. Pakistan's Ghauri has been tested once. See chapter 9 in this volume.

[52] For a summary of ballistic-missile defence projects and the missiles against which they might be effective, see Arnett, E., 'Military research and development', *SIPRI Yearbook 1998: Armaments, Disarmament and International Security* (Oxford University Press: Oxford, 1998), p. 280. For a more detailed and recent summary of US programmes, see Pike, J., 'Ballistic missile defense: is the US "rushing to failure"?', *Arms Control Today*, Apr. 1998, pp. 10–13.

[53] This figure includes about $1 billion added to the budget at the last minute by the Congress. Total military R&D in the FY 1999 budget act comes to $41.8 billion, 3.8% more than requested by the

V. Japan

After interrupting its steady 20-year, 700 per cent increase in military R&D funding in 1997, Japan decreased its military R&D expenditure by 20 per cent to 128 billion yen in an overall defence budget that embodies an increase of just 0.6 per cent for 1998.[54] The most important new system under development is the Chu-SAM medium-range surface-to-air missile begun in 1996, which accounts for 24 billion yen (about $200 million). Development of the FI-X—the preliminary designation for the successor to the F-2—continued, with 6 billion yen going to engine development. An additional 3 billion yen was appropriated to solve problems with the F-2, most of them associated with the locally developed wing, one of the few components not carried over from the original US F-16, from which the F-2 is derived.[55] The most significant new project is the short-range AAM-5 air-to-air missile, which received 900 million yen 1998, its first year of full-scale development.[56]

Despite strong public reaction to North Korea's launching of a three-stage rocket over Japan on 31 August 1998 after five years without a long-range missile test, Japan continued to stall US efforts to involve it in missile-defence development efforts. A decision had been promised for June 1998, but none was announced. Instead, 19 million yen were earmarked for further study of the need for missile defences.[57] Japanese officials had previously expressed scepticism about the purported threat of North Korean missiles to Japan and expressed a belief in the possibility that North Korea will have ceased to exist by the time more advanced defences can be deployed (at least 10 years from now in the case of the US Navy Theater-Wide system).[58] Japan's current

Defense Department and 3.5% more than the 1998 budget. American Association for the Advancement of Science, *A Preview Report for Congressional Action on Research and Development in the FY 1999 Budget* (AAAS: Washington, DC, 1998). With the exception of this special addition to the 1999 budget and a small increase in 1997, US military R&D funding has been decreasing since the end of the cold war. This trend looks unlikely to continue after the FY 2000 budget request.

[54] Japan, Defense Agency, *Defense of Japan* (Japan Times: Tokyo, 1998). Actual funding of military R&D may be twice this figure, since independent funding of military R&D may equal or exceed government funding, with firms reimbursed during procurement. Chinworth, M. W., *Financing Japan's Defense Build-up* (Massachusetts Institute of Technology, Center for International Studies: Cambridge, Mass., 1992), p. 4; Samuels, R., J., *'Rich Nation, Strong Army': National Security and the Technological Transformation of Japan* (Cornell University Press: Ithaca, NY, 1994), p. 192; and Green, M. J., *Arming Japan: Defense Production, Alliance Politics, and the Postwar Search for Autonomy* (Columbia University Press: New York, 1995), p. 16.

[55] The F-2's problems are summarized in Sekigawa, E., 'F-2 tests delayed for wing repairs', *Aviation Week & Space Technology*, 12 Oct. 1998, p. 31. See also Arnett (note 2) for a summary of the F-2 and Japanese military R&D since 1976.

[56] *Tokyo Asagumo*, 16 Apr. 1998 (in Japanese), in Foreign Broadcast Information Service, *Daily Report–East Asia (FBIS–EAS)*, -EAS-98-162, 15 June 1998.

[57] Usui, N., 'N. Korea missile test may force JDA budget plan review', *Defense News*, 21–27 Sep. 1998, p. 33. Some 560 million yen (about $4 million) had been spent over the 4 previous years (1994–97), the period during which the USA had been pressing Japan to join.

[58] Kyodo (Tokyo), 19 Mar. 1998 (in English), in FBIS-EAS-98-077, 20 Mar. 1998; and Taoka, S., 'Pitfalls of participating in theater missile defense initiative', *AERA* (Tokyo), 10 Aug. 1998, pp. 58–59 (in Japanese), in FBIS-EAS-98-277, 6 Oct. 1998. Japan would only be involved in the 2nd generation of Navy Theater-Wide, called Block II, and therefore would not receive interceptors sooner, even if the main US programme is accelerated. Holzer, R., 'Theater Wide proponents seek quicker deployment', *Defense News*, 16–22 Nov. 1998, p. 34.

Patriot forces, which have been upgraded to the latest Patriot Advanced Capability PAC-2 standard, are thought to be capable of handling the 500-km Hwasong 6 (Scud C) currently deployed by North Korea.[59]

After the North Korean rocket launch, the Japan Defense Agency requested 963 million yen for FY 1999 and 20–30 billion yen over the next five years for R&D on missile defence, most of which will go to Navy Theater-Wide. Total costs to Japan could reach 1 trillion yen.[60] This reaction to the political shock of the launch may not be sustained through to deployment. Japanese opponents of greater cooperation on more capable missile defences have already tried to divert interest from co-development of interceptor systems with the USA to indigenous development of a missile warning satellite[61] and signalled concerns over Japanese contributions of technology to US missile-defence systems.[62] The latter fear may stem in part from the possibility that Japanese technology from the Chu-SAM will be lost to US firms. Other issues include total cost, technological risk, and the increasingly frank complaints from China about Japan's possible strategic intentions. Despite these concerns, the government funded the FY 1999 missile-defence request in full in December and approved a plan to launch four satellites by April 2003.

VI. China

China fundamentally restructured its arms development and procurement organizations beginning in March 1998.[63] Military R&D activities at dedicated institutes will be coordinated by a newly created organization initially known in English as the General Armaments Department (GAD), an organ of the People's Liberation Army (PLA). The PLA will set requirements for systems to be developed indigenously through the GAD and may have to pay something like market price for the results, rather than receiving them essentially gratis as in the past. The Commission on Science, Technology and Industry for National Defense (COSTIND), which used to be responsible for military

[59] *Tokyo Shimbun*, 3 Sep. 1998, p. 1 (in Japanese), in FBIS-EAS-98-248, 9 Sep. 1998. Reports that North Korean was already deploying the longer-range Ro-dong, based on US satellite imagery, were debated in Japan in Jan. 1999. Kyodo (Tokyo), 4 Jan. 1999 (in English), in FBIS-EAS-99-004, 4 Jan. 1999; and Kyodo (Tokyo), 5 Jan. 1999 (in English), in FBIS-EAS-99-005, 5 Jan. 1999.

[60] Kyodo (Tokyo), 23 Oct. 1998 (in English), in FBIS-EAS-98-296, 23 Oct. 1998. In comparison, the USA will spend $310 million on Navy Theater-Wide in 1999. Japan's contribution is therefore less than 4%. US Navy officials say the Block II variant in which Japan would be involved would cost $700 million (about 100 billion yen) for R&D. Holzer (note 58).

[61] Suganama, K., 'The North Korean missile starts a heated "air-defense debate"', *Tokyo Shimbun*, 7 Sep. 1998, p. 2 (in Japanese), in FBIS-EAS-98-253, 14 Sep. 1998; 'Concern over introduction of reconnaissance satellite', *Mainichi Shimbun*, 10 Sep. 1998, p. 5 (in Japanese), in FBIS-EAS-98-254, 14 Sep. 1998; and 'If the Japanese Government considers discussing a multi-purpose satellite', *Tokyo Shimbun*, 16 Sep. 1998, p. 4 (in Japanese), in FBIS-EAS-98-261, 21 Sep. 1998. Initial funding for 4 satellites is 10 billion yen and total costs could reach 150 billion yen. Saegusa, A., 'Japan split over US aid for spy satellites', *Nature*, 3 Dec. 1998, p. 401.

[62] Kyodo (Tokyo), 22 Oct. 1998 (in English), in FBIS-EAS-98-295, 23 Oct. 1998.

[63] The following passage is based on interviews with Chinese officials conducted in Oct. 1998. See also Pomfret, J., 'Chinese army out of business', *Washington Post*, 23 Nov. 1998, p. A20, reprinted as 'How China plans to rein in army', *International Herald Tribune*, 24 Nov. 1998, p. 7; and Gilley, B., 'Stand-down order', *Far East Economic Review*, 10 Sep. 1998.

R&D, is now bureaucratically independent of the PLA. About half of COSTIND's former staff will move to the GAD, including all those in the PLA chain of command. After the reorganization, COSTIND's responsibilities will include military and civilian production, arms imports and the negotiation of arms control agreements.

Although several decisions remained to be made at the end of 1998, the implications of this restructuring could be significant. The immediate goal was apparently to get the PLA out of business, including military and civilian production, as part of President Jiang Zemin's effort to reduce the potentially distracting, if not corrupting, influence of commerce on the military. While limiting the possibilities of distraction and the opportunities for corruption may contribute to a more professional armed force, a decision in future to make the PLA pay more for lower-quality domestically produced arms would give them a greater incentive to import, a tendency that was already strong. If COSTIND is responsible for such 'make versus buy' decisions, as the new chief Liu Jibin claimed in November 1998, there may be a renewed bias in favour of indigenous production, which is likely to mean less capable systems. The GAD may terminate a number of redundant R&D programmes. If it does, it is not clear whether the efforts involved in those projects will then be continued independently or whether the resources freed will be reinvested in other military projects or on the civilian side.

VII. Western Europe

Western Europe, here comprising NATO Europe and Sweden,[64] features the most active military technology base outside the USA, with combined military R&D expenditure of roughly $11 billion annually. This is less than one-third of US annual investment. European efforts are highly segmented and duplicative, despite efforts to centralize procurement, and France, the most ambitious investor in European NATO, spends less than one-seventh of what the USA does.[65] The gap between European and US technology suggests that US arms will enjoy even greater superiority, but also raises the prospect that US and NATO arms will not work well together in future coalition operations.[66]

Aerospace research dominates military R&D spending, claiming 39 per cent of non-strategic R&D in France,[67] 37 per cent of all military R&D in the UK, 53 per cent in Germany, and 67 per cent in Italy.[68] Between 1990 and 1993, Spain devoted 81 per cent of its military R&D budget to the Eurofighter pro-

[64] Sweden is broadening its cooperation with European partners. Arnett (note 3).

[65] Furthermore, investment by Western Europe amounts to only about $10 billion in terms of purchasing power.

[66] For trends in the arms export market, see chapter 11 in this volume.

[67] This figure is for 1998. France spent 58% of its military R&D budget on 'strategic' programmes that year, including nuclear delivery systems and military space, both of which have a major aerospace component. E.g., the M 51 strategic missile is one of France's biggest R&D projects. In 1997, France spent 49% of military R&D funds on strategic programmes and 42% of the remainder on other aerospace. UN documents A/52/310, 25 Aug. 1997, pp. 31-32; and A/53/218, 4 Aug. 1998, pp. 41–43.

[68] Figures from 1996, 1997 and 1996, respectively. UN document A/53/218 (note 67), pp. 44–46, 50–52, 92–96.

ject while independently committing additional funds to its indigenous light attack aircraft, the F-A/A-X.[69] In 1997 the Eurofighter still laid claim to 62 per cent of Spanish military R&D.[70] Aerospace has been least affected by the major cuts in military R&D funding since the cold war, growing from 18 to 40 per cent of the British military R&D budget between 1990 and 1995, for example.[71]

If there is agreement in Western Europe that aerospace is important, there is something less than consensus on the assumptions that should inform military planning and therefore military R&D priorities. With new parties taking over several important governments after elections in the last two years, assumptions are being re-evaluated. Most fundamentally, the question whether West European militaries can focus on homeland defence in a relatively peaceful and democratic corner of the world, and thereby realize a greater peace dividend, is running into renewed interest in military intervention in conflicts elsewhere, whether south-eastern Europe (traditionally within NATO's operational area and Europe's sphere of interest) or the Persian Gulf (traditionally outside NATO's operational area).

This section considers the military R&D programmes of the UK, Germany, Spain and France. It will be seen that collaborative military R&D has recently had as many failures as successes and that military requirements are, if anything, diverging.

The United Kingdom

Decisions about R&D priorities made by the Labour Government will have significant effects on the forces that the UK will operate in the future. Britain has been reducing its military R&D investment steadily since before the end of the cold war. In 1996, the funding level was 58 per cent of what it had been in 1983.[72] Between 1990 and 1995, funding of land and naval systems fell sharply.[73]

The most significant conclusion of the 1998 Strategic Defence Review (SDR)[74] was that the Navy's 20 000-tonne aircraft-carriers, developed to operate anti-submarine forces in concert with French and US carriers during the cold war, should be replaced by 30 000- to 40 000-tonne carriers capable of launching and recovering twice as many aircraft as part of an intervention force that would not necessarily involve the USA. The primary candidate for

[69] Spain, Ministerio de Defensa, *Memoria de la IV Legislatura*, 1989–93 [Proceedings of the fourth parliament, 1989–93]; and *OECD Main Science and Technology Indicators*, no. 1 (1998).

[70] Spain, Ministerio de Economia y Hacienda, *Presupuestos Generales del Estado 1997* [General allocations of the State 1997] (Madrid, 1997).

[71] British cuts began in the mid-1980s, before the end of the cold war, as is seen in Arnett (note 52), p. 269.

[72] Arnett (note 52), p. 269.

[73] Between 1993 and 1996, funding of land systems fell from £247 million to £61 million in current figures, 13% to 4% of the declining R&D budget in 1993 and 1996, respectively, while funding for naval systems fell from £548 million (29%) to £242 million (16%). UN documents A/50/277, 20 July 1995, pp. 87–89; and A/53/218 (note 67).

[74] British Ministry of Defence, *Strategic Defence Review* (Ministry of Defence: London, 1998).

use on these carriers is the US Joint Strike Fighter, to which the UK has already committed $200 million for R&D, about 2 or 3 per cent of the total. A variant of the Eurofighter will also be considered. The navy as a whole is structurally switching its role from alliance defence to out-of-area intervention. Smaller warships are increasingly seen as land-attack missile launchers rather than task force escorts.[75]

The SDR also emphasized other new technologies for strike. It contains a commitment to developing the Astute Class attack submarine, which will be armed with US-supplied Tomahawk land-attack cruise missiles, and new strike aircraft, including the possibility of 'stand-off missiles or unmanned aircraft'. All existing attack submarines will now be armed with Tomahawks as well. The number of nuclear warheads deployed with the Trident force, which is no longer under development, will be reduced, and the SDR emphasizes that they have a 'sub-strategic' role.[76]

The SDR was reserved about European cooperation programmes: 'We may need to be selective about the technologies we develop nationally or on a European basis, and be prepared to use US technologies in other areas'.[77] It emphasized that cooperation should be pursued with 'all allies'.[78] In this vein, the UK will buy four C-17 transport aircraft from the USA as a hedge against problems with the European effort to develop a Future Large Aircraft (FLA).[79] No firm commitment to the FLA was made, only a promise to 'seek to ensure that there are realistic European options to be considered'. British interest in two European programmes, the Horizon frigate and the Multi-Role Armoured Vehicle, was reiterated, but a pall was cast over European partnerships by Britain's withdrawal from Trimilsatcom, a £1 billion communications satellite being developed jointly with France and Germany, which British officials said would not be ready in time for their needs after France moved to extend its development time.[80]

Britain remained unconvinced that ballistic-missile defences were necessary. 'Technologies in this area are changing rapidly, and it would, at this stage, be premature to decide on acquiring such a capability'.[81]

Although the SDR has been criticized for missing a unique opportunity for the ruling Labour Party to cut military expenditure more dramatically on the basis of less grandiose planning assumptions, it appears likely that military R&D funding will continue to fall as Britain leaves the nuclear weapon business and depends more on the USA for aerospace partnership.[82] Furthermore, the SDR, like the US Quadrennial Defense Review in 1997, is based on

[75] Scott, R., 'Frigate reshaped for land attack', *Jane's Defence Weekly*, 28 Oct. 1998, p. 3.
[76] See appendix 12A in this volume.
[77] *Strategic Defence Review* (note 74).
[78] *Strategic Defence Review* (note 74).
[79] Britain had already ordered 55 C-130J transport aircraft from the USA in 1996.
[80] Barrie, D., 'UK bails out of trination satellite project', *Defense News*, 17–23 Aug. 1998, pp. 1, 19.
[81] *Strategic Defence Review* (note 74). See also Arnett (note 2), p. 218; and Arnett (note 52), pp. 281–82.
[82] Lewis, P., 'United Kingdom', ed. E. Arnett, SIPRI, *Nuclear Weapons after the Comprehensive Test Ban: Implications for Modernization and Proliferation* (Oxford University Press: Oxford, 1996).

assumptions about future funding that may not be realized when required.[83] If the option of intervening without US cooperation is undertaken seriously, costs will be particularly high since NATO forces generally rely on US surveillance capabilities when operating out of the traditional operational area.

Germany

After increases during the cold war, by 1993 Germany had reduced its military R&D budget to about 15 per cent higher than its 1983 level. In 1997, it returned to the 1993 level after two years of slightly higher spending.[84] German military R&D funding is expected to remain roughly constant in current Deutschmarks, implying a slight reduction in real terms, over the five-year period 1997–2001, during which R&D for the Eurofighter will be completed.[85]

The Christian Democrat Government which left power in 1998 had previously paid lip-service to European cooperation on defence technology but not funded its commitments adequately, leading to considerable uncertainty and hard feelings as other partners, both other governments and German firms, were left to pick up the bill. In particular a 30 per cent cut in German funding of military R&D between 1990 and 1993 appears to have been inconsistent with its commitments to the Eurofighter, the FLA and various satellite projects.

Unlike the UK, where the election of a centrist Labour Government led to a stronger embrace of the idea of military intervention in conflicts not directly threatening the homeland as the organizing principle of defence planning, Germany after the 1998 election, which brought the Socialist Democratic Party to power with support from the Greens, seems likely to remain reluctant to embroil itself in regional conflicts and therefore unwilling to shoulder a heavier defence burden or harmonize its arms requirements with those of Britain and France. (France also continues to plan for intervention.) The decision between intervention forces and forces more suited to defence of the homeland will drive the conclusions of the new government's defence review, which is likely be reflected in the FY 2000 budget.[86] The prospect, then, is one of more rather than fewer problems for German collaboration in military R&D.

[83] *Strategic Defence Review* (note 74). 'We need to solve the problems of undermanning and additional overstretch which comes from over-commitment'. On the Quadrennial Defense Review, see Arnett (note 52), pp. 276–78.

[84] Arnett (note 52), pp. 269–70.

[85] Eurofighter R&D accounted for DM 645 million—23% of all military R&D funding—in 1997. Montgomery, J., 'Shoehorning defence into the German budget', *International Security Review 1998* (Royal United Services Institute: London, 1998), pp. 184–86.

[86] Barrie, D. and Hoschouer, J., 'Bundeswehr review looms', *Defense News*, 10–16 Aug. 1998, pp. 1, 19.

Spain

After five years of declining or roughly steady spending on military R&D, Spain increased funding again in 1997. Having built up its military technology base in the 1980s with a nearly eight-fold increase between 1983 and 1991, Spain withdrew from several major international programmes when it was realized that too many commitments had been made.[87] Funding fell by more than 40 per cent in the three years that followed but has since more than doubled, and in 1997 stood at a level 17 per cent higher than the peak in 1991.

The increases, which include a nearly 50 per cent rise in 1997 alone, can be attributed to the increasing burden of the Eurofighter project, which arrives at the same time as conscription is being abolished, pushing personnel costs up. Spain must now complete its share of development and begin production, but is less well prepared than the other project partners. To catch up, the government made an additional Ptas 25 billion allocation to the Ministry of Industry over and above the Ptas 24 billion allocated to the Ministry of Defence for the Eurofighter in 1997.[88] Similar preparations are under way on a smaller scale for the F100 frigate, which will be equipped with the US Aegis radar, Spain having withdrawn from comparable European programmes.

Military R&D is expected to continue its dramatic increases to a level almost three times the 1997 level (in current pesetas) for 1999.[89] Generous budgets have encouraged new investments, and Spain is rejoining the French-led Helios 2 satellite project after quitting in 1995. Spain will assume between 3 and 6 per cent of the $2 billion project.[90]

France

In the latest of a series of defence reviews, France announced its first post-cold war arms programme cancellations in April 1998. Although the Rubicon was thereby crossed, the programmes cancelled were of minor military and fiscal importance. The implications for international cooperation were more interesting.

Most significantly, France withdrew from the $2.4 billion German-led Horus radar satellite. France's share in Horus was 40 per cent, but the programme was of much less interest to France than the French-led Helios 2

[87] Arnett (note 3).

[88] *Presupuestos Generales del Estado 1997* (note 70); and Hélène Dernis, OECD, personal communication, 14 Aug. 1998. The Spanish Government apparently does not agree with the OECD that funds spent on preparing for Eurofighter production count as military R&D, since their figures submitted to the UN do not reflect an increase. The R&D expenditure for 1997 given is Ptas 36.12 billion. UN document A/53/218, 4 Aug. 1998, pp. 83–85. Future funding of the Eurofighter, the F100 frigate and the Leopard tank—totalling Ptas 141 billion per year for 2006–2009—is summarized in González, M., 'Defensa tiene comprometidas compras de armamento por casi dos billones de pesetas' [Defence has promised arms purchases for almost 2 trillion pesetas], *El País*, 3 Sep. 1998, p. 13.

[89] Cátedra UNESCO sobre Paz y Derechos Humanos de la UAB, *Los Presupestos de Investigación Armamentista para 1999 Superan a los Recursos Destinados a Investigación Civil* [Funds for armament research for 1999 exceed those destined for civil research] (Autonomous University of Barcelona: Bellaterra, 21 Dec. 1998).

[90] 'Spain to take a small stake in Helios 2', *Defense News*, 19–25 Oct. 1998, p. 2.

optical satellite, from which Germany had withdrawn. Two other cooperative programmes were scrapped: the Trigat-LR long-range anti-tank missile (five years behind schedule after Britain and Spain withdrew) and the MILAS anti-submarine missile.[91] In addition, four all-French programmes were terminated: the IZ (Interdiction Zone) variant of the Apache air-launched cruise missile (ALCM); a new torpedo; a new anti-tank missile; and a space-surveillance radar. More advanced ALCMs are already under development in France and elsewhere in Europe, and the Apache IZ was originally intended to attract German interest rather than to serve any French need.[92] Indeed, France retains duplicative excess research capacity in a number of missile fields.[93] Finally, the French decision to extend the service life of an existing communications satellite and 'review' the schedule for developing Trimilsatcom led directly to Britain's decision to drop the project, as mentioned above.

On the other hand, the 1998 review accelerates the development of the M 51 strategic submarine-launched ballistic missile by two years. With FY 1999 funding of 1.4 billion francs, the M 51 is among France's biggest R&D projects. The year also saw France launching a new 25 billion-franc project to develop a new attack submarine, the SMAF (Sous-Marin d'Attaque Futur, or Barracuda), the largest new programme started since the end of the cold war.[94] With military R&D funding having fallen in 1997 to the level typical of the years before the big increases of the 1980s, it is difficult to believe that so many major projects can be seen through to a satisfactory conclusion.[95]

VIII. Conclusions

As has been the case for several years, the USA continues to dominate the development of military technology. Its determined pursuit of new capabilities ensures that the gap between it and other states, hostile and friendly alike, will yawn wider still. Any consolation others might have taken in the emergence of the spin-on phenomenon, in which technology is taken from the civilian sector for military uses, comes up against the fact that the USA retains important advantages in civilian technology and appears to be more effective in harnessing spin-on than other states pursuing advanced military technology, even

[91] Even these cuts were equivocal, with the Defence Ministry expressing interest in Trigat later in the year. Lewis, J. A. C., 'Budget boost for French defence spending', *Jane's Defence Weekly*, 16 Sep. 1998, p. 4. In any case, the previous agreement prevents France from withdrawing fully until investment in production facilities begins. Tanguy, J.-M., 'France's programme review', *Military Technology*, June 1998, p. 99.

[92] Tanguy (note 91), p. 99.

[93] French firms are involved in developing 19 missile and drone programmes, not including the strategic M 51. Langereux, P., 'Aérospatiale-Matra, second missilier mondial' [Aérospatiale-Matra: the world's number two missile builder], *Air et Cosmos*, 28 Aug. 1998, p. 20.

[94] 'Defense Ministry launches its new nuclear attack submarine plan', *Les Echos*, 6 Oct. 1998, p. 11 (in French), in Foreign Broadcast Information Service, *Daily Report–Western Europe (FBIS–WEU)*, FBIS-WEU-98-279, 7 Oct. 1998.

[95] The 1997 level shown in table 8.2 is roughly equal to the budget in 1979. In 1980, after a decade of constant funding, French military R&D funding rose to a level almost 50% higher for the following 7 years, before increasing a further 25% for 3 years and dropping rapidly after 1990.

as it continues its investment in military-specific technologies, which are by no means rendered irrelevant.

While US dominance in the development of military technology was still apparent in 1998, the year saw evidence of new political consequences. Most obviously, its technological advantage makes the USA the most attractive partner for technology sharing among states that still conceptualize their security in military and technological terms, even if ideological preferences might make them ambivalent. This is why even champions of European military cooperation find themselves dropping European projects and taking up with the USA. It also accounts for India's pursuit of aerospace self-reliance by way of US firms, which now will have to be abandoned because of the nuclear tests.

Events in 1998 pointed up more starkly than before the central issues of military technology in the post-cold war era. For the industrialized states on close terms with the USA, the issue is whether to compete with or complement US technological advantages. Further, these states must decide how far they are willing to invest to participate in using military force for missions other than homeland defence, and whether technology for defending the homeland must be indigenously designed and produced. For US partners in Europe, the issue is whether military intervention should be the basis of military planning, as Britain and France have apparently accepted. If it should not, the question arises whether states like Germany, Italy, Spain and Sweden should invest in projects that are mainly suited to military intervention rather than redirecting or reducing their military technology bases. In the Pacific, conflict scenarios of military intervention from a US perspective are homeland defence from a Japanese or South Korean perspective. The issue is not whether capabilities are needed so much as whether they need be developed indigenously. This is the central concern of the US–Japanese discussion of missile defence.

Viewed from the other end of the missile's trajectory, the problem is whether military action from the advanced industrialized states can be deterred. Ballistic missiles are popular with states that fear they may be on the receiving end of US and allied military power precisely because they still cannot be defended against reliably. What states like Iran, Iraq and North Korea, which include deterring US attack among their highest defence planning concerns, must take into consideration is whether a missile force can actually deter the use of force in plausible conflict scenarios. Given the investment that Iran and North Korea are making in missiles, the judgement for now appears to be that it can. It remains to be seen whether the funds devoted to these projects, which can destroy confidence as well as deter conflict, will produce systems that contribute meaningfully to their security or simply signal desperation in the face of US technological accomplishment.

9. Nuclear tests by India and Pakistan

ERIC ARNETT

I. Introduction

At 3.45 p.m. local time on 11 May 1998, Indian scientists conducted three nuclear test explosions, violating a global norm that had been observed since July 1996, when China conducted its last nuclear test. The tests culminated more than two decades of research and more than two years of secretive preparations and scientists' pleas for authorization from the government. The tests were finally made possible by the formation of a government led by the Bharatiya Janata Party (BJP, Indian People's Party), which had made 'exercising the nuclear option' one of its campaign themes. The first three Indian test explosions were followed by two more on 13 May and six Pakistani test explosions two weeks later: five on 28 May and one on 30 May.

This chapter summarizes the publicly available technical information related to the tests (section II) and the reasons why they were carried out (section III). It then goes on to consider the possible military implications of the tests (section IV).[1] The conclusions are presented in section V.

The immediate cause of the Indian tests was the formation of a government led by the BJP, which was willing to authorize the tests that the nuclear establishment had been hoping to carry out since late 1995. The Indian tests created an opportunity for Pakistani scientists to gain authorization for their own tests. Despite the apparent personal reluctance of Pakistani Prime Minister Nawaz Sharif, the public and media outcry for tests and the military's growing fascination with nuclear deterrence as a means to compensate for inferiority in conventional weapons made it unlikely that Pakistan would not leap through the window of opportunity opened by India.

Although the tests came almost eight years after both countries apparently achieved the ability to deliver nuclear bombs by aircraft,[2] they are nonetheless significant in their own right and will have a variety of implications. Militarily, the main effect of the tests was that on military technology transfer

[1] This chapter discusses only the implications of the tests related to Indian military programmes and the possibility that India and Pakistan will expand their nuclear capabilities. The implications of the tests for nuclear arms control are discussed in chapter 12, their technical characteristics are presented in greater detail in appendix 12B and the international response to the tests is discussed in chapter 15.

[2] The decision to pursue the option of acquiring nuclear weapons, the decision to acquire nuclear weapons and the decision to test nuclear weapons are 3 separate phenomena that are often confused, especially in the case of India and Pakistan. Former Pakistani Chief of Army Staff General Mirza Aslam Beg said in 1998 that the ability to deliver nuclear weapons by aircraft was achieved in late 1990, several months after the Kashmir crisis of the previous spring. Rashid, A. and Sidhva, S., 'Might and menace', *Far Eastern Economic Review*, 4 June 1998, p. 34. India reportedly decided to acquire deliverable nuclear weapons in 1988 and achieved that end in 1990. Chengappa, R., 'The bomb makers', *India Today*, 22 June 1998.

from the USA to India, which was immediately cut off. As a result, the foreign dependence of India's 'indigenous' military research and development (R&D) programmes has been revealed. These programmes will have to be restructured or abandoned, leaving India more dependent on other arms suppliers.[3]

No clear decision to expand their nuclear capabilities has yet been made by either government. There are encouraging signs that India will limit the size of its arsenal and may not change the nature of its deployment immediately. With a policy of not using nuclear weapons first, India seeks mainly to deter Pakistani first use of nuclear weapons and preserve an option to respond appropriately if relations with China deteriorate. The situation in Pakistan is less clear, but the indications are that the military continues to exaggerate the value of nuclear deterrence and may move more decisively towards deployments of a provocative sort. The threat to use nuclear weapons first is central to Pakistani strategic thinking and has long been associated in military planners' minds with deterring a conventional military response to provocations in Kashmir short of war, for example, incitement and material support to local insurgents and infiltration of Mujahideen (guerrilla fighters) trained elsewhere.[4]

II. Technical information related to the tests

Relatively little technical information about the tests had been made public by the end of 1998. India and Pakistan both revealed the expected yields of their test devices and stated that those yields had been achieved, although there are suspicions that not all of the tests were successful.[5] No additional information from either state has been made public. Indian officials have specifically said that additional information will not be released, as it was after the Indian test in 1974, which was officially carried out for peaceful purposes. Most of the information about the Pakistani tests in public discussions originates from Abdul Qadeer Khan, who was instrumental in launching Pakistan's uranium enrichment project but is not necessarily well informed about the current activities of the Pakistan Atomic Energy Commission (PAEC).[6]

India

In announcing the first three explosions on 11 May, Prime Minister Atal Bihari Vajpayee described them as comprising 'a fission device, a low-yield device and a thermonuclear device'. The two additional explosions two days

[3] See also chapter 8 in this volume.

[4] The Kashmir conflict is discussed in appendix 1B in this volume

[5] Scientists at the Bhabha Atomic Research Center (BARC) later wrote that the 'upper estimate' based on local seismic measurements was 60 kt—the expected yield—for the first 3 explosions combined. The mean estimate of the actual yield would be lower. Sikka, S. K. and Kakodkar, A., 'Some preliminary results of May 11–13, 1998 nuclear detonations at Pokhran', *BARC Newsletter*, no. 172 (May 1998), reproduced in *Strategic Digest*, July 1998. The discrepancies in yield estimates that have fuelled suspicions are discussed in appendix 12B.

[6] Khan and his laboratory 'had nothing to do with the blasts', according to Samar Mubarak Mand, the PAEC Member (Technical) who led the test team. Abbas, Z., 'Sibling rivalry', *The Herald* (Karachi) July 1998.

later were of low-yield devices modified after the preliminary data from the first low-yield test had been examined. The three low-yield devices were of different configurations and each had a yield below 1 kiloton.[7] The initial yield estimates given by India were based only on seismological measurements and were expected to be calibrated against radiochemical analyses after samples could be extracted from the test site.[8] A. P. J. Abdul Kalam, the Science Adviser to the Defence Minister, said four months later that the yield estimates had not been revised.[9] Roughly 20 more cores had reportedly been produced between 1974 and 1998, and enough weapon-grade plutonium separated for another 10 or so. This gives India the wherewithal to deploy 30 nuclear weapons on fairly short notice. The fissile pits of India's five test devices reportedly weighed 5–10 kilograms each, making possible a rough estimate of how much fissile material has been consumed in the production of Indian nuclear weapons.[10]

Pakistan

There is some confusion about how many test explosions were conducted by Pakistan, estimated to have had enough weapon-grade uranium for 15–25 weapons before the tests. The confusion stems in part from A. Q. Khan's statement that Pakistan had not intended to carry out the first five explosions simultaneously on 28 May and had planned two for 30 May.[11] The following week, Karl Inderfurth, the US Assistant Secretary of State responsible for South Asia, was asked how many tests India and Pakistan had conducted. 'Less than they say', he replied.[12] In response, A. Q. Khan asserted that Pakistan had more fissile material than observers had previously believed. He said that Pakistan had continued to produce highly enriched uranium despite the Benazir Bhutto Government's 1991 freeze on production of weapon-grade uranium and implied that Pakistan had used less than one-third of its stock for the tests.[13]

[7] Subramanian, T. S., 'We got everything we wanted', *Frontline*, vol. 15, no. 12 (6–19 June 1998). A kiloton is the equivalent explosive power of 1000 tons of TNT.

[8] Subramanian, T. S., 'India must become strong', *Frontline*, vol. 15, no. 11 (23 May–5 June 1998). In addition to standard seismological instruments, Indian scientists used the controversial CORRTEX (continuous reflectometry and radius time experiment) technique. Sikka and Kakodkar (note 5); and Bhatt, A., 'Pokhran blasts tested new ideas: BARC chief', *The Hindu*, 20 May 1998. CORRTEX, the focus of controversy during negotiations on the verification of the 1974 Threshold Test Ban Treaty in the 1980s, is discussed in Din, A. M., 'Means of nuclear test ban verification other than seismological', eds J. Goldblat and D. Cox, SIPRI, *Nuclear Weapon Tests: Prohibition or Limitation?* (Oxford University Press: Oxford, 1988), pp. 243–44.

[9] Press Trust of India, 'If there is CTBT, there also are loopholes: Kalam', *Indian Express*, 22 Sep. 1998.

[10] Chengappa (note 2); and Hibbs, M., 'India made about 25 cores for nuclear weapons stockpile', *Nucleonics Week*, 11 June 1998, p. 15.

[11] Hashmi, F., 'Mass-scale production of Ghauri begins', *Dawn* (Karachi), 1 June 1998.

[12] Kumar, P., 'No place for India and Pakistan in NPT', *Asian Age*, 5 June 1998.

[13] Iqbal, A., 'Mass production of Ghauri missile begins: Qadeer', *The News* (Islamabad), 1 June 1998. Pakistan is also developing the means to produce nuclear weapons from plutonium, but these are not yet near fruition.

III. Reasons for the tests

India and Pakistan conducted their nuclear tests for very different reasons. Authorization for India's tests was sought by the scientific establishment for reasons that may not have had much military relevance. The BJP was unusual among India's political parties in its eagerness to test and deploy nuclear capabilities and authorized the tests as a political statement to gain public support and differentiate itself from its competitors. In contrast, Pakistan's political establishment is much more uniform in its enthusiasm for nuclear deterrence, as is the military, but both had been cowed from testing by the threat of sanctions. India's tests provided a chance for Pakistan to test with less risk of consequences. Prime Minister Nawaz's apparent personal reluctance to test reinforced the perception on the part of some Western observers in the wake of the tests that Pakistan was less blameworthy.[14]

India

Despite much speculation after the Indian tests about their possible military implications, they seem to have been conducted mainly as a scientific experiment and authorized in 1998 for political rather than security reasons.

Scientific reasons

Indian scientists had been requesting authorization to test since late 1995 at least. The nuclear establishment apparently feared that the extension of the 1968 Non-Proliferation Treaty, the then-imminent conclusion of the 1996 Comprehensive Nuclear Test-Ban Treaty (CTBT) and tightening export controls would effectively close India's nuclear option, which was perceived as a necessary hedge against the possibility that relations with China might deteriorate, even if far in the future.[15] During a brief period in 1996 when the BJP tried but failed to form a government, the party leadership authorized tests that were never conducted before being dismissed.[16] No other government had been willing to authorize tests despite national opposition to the CTBT.

Military, nuclear and space R&D have dominated Indian science since major investments in science were begun in the mid-1960s (see table 9.1).[17] Indeed, the fraction of India's publicly known national R&D funding devoted to military R&D was greater in 1996 than in any state other than the USA.[18]

[14] See, e.g., 'A turn off the nuclear road', *Washington Post*, 31 Aug 1998, p. 20, reprinted as 'A choice for Pakistan', *International Herald Tribune*, 1 Sep. 1998, p. 8.

[15] Deshingkar, G., 'India', ed. E. Arnett, SIPRI, *Nuclear Weapons after the Comprehensive Test Ban: Implications for Modernization and Proliferation* (Oxford University Press: Oxford, 1996). The latent threat from China and the option were linked in part because a capability perceived to be adequate for deterrence of Pakistani first use was already in place. See below.

[16] Joshi, M., 'Nuclear shock wave', *India Today*, 25 May 1998.

[17] Government of India, Department of Science and Technology, *Research and Development Statistics 1994/95* (The Offsetters: New Delhi, 1996).

[18] Arnett, E., 'Military research and development', *SIPRI Yearbook 1998: Armaments, Disarmament and International Security* (Oxford University Press: Oxford, 1998), p. 274.

Table 9.1. Expenditure on research and development by the Indian Government, fiscal years 1965/66–1994/95

Figures are in billion current rupees and US $m. at 1995 prices and exchange rates.

Fiscal Year	Defence[a] (A) Rs	Defence[a] (A) $	DAE[b] (B) Rs	DAE[b] (B) $	DOS[c] (C) Rs	DOS[c] (C) $	Total[d] (D) Rs	Total[d] (D) $	(A+B+C)/D (%)
1965/66	0.12	41	0.20	69	. .	. .	0.52	180	*50*
1970/71	0.22	55	0.29	73	. .	. .	0.89	220	*55*
1975/76	0.52	75	0.54	78	0.37	53	2.24	320	*64*
1980/81	0.93	110	0.73	86	0.56	66	4.38	520	*51*
1981/82	1.21	130	0.88	92	0.75	79	5.47	570	*52*
1982/83	1.50	150	1.16	110	0.97	94	7.37	720	*49*
1983/84	1.97	170	1.43	120	1.10	95	8.32	720	*54*
1984/85	3.13	250	1.82	150	1.83	150	11.50	920	*59*
1985/86	3.94	300	1.43	110	2.13	160	13.35	1 000	*56*
1986/87	4.92	340	1.61	110	3.10	220	15.33	1 100	*63*
1987/88	6.33	410	1.79	110	3.66	230	18.08	1 200	*65*
1988/89	6.80	400	2.10	120	4.22	250	20.47	1 200	*64*
1989/90	7.36	410	2.50	140	3.99	220	22.07	1 200	*63*
1990/91	7.99	410	2.76	140	3.86	200	23.13	1 200	*63*
1991/92	8.39	370	3.06	140	4.60	200	25.55	1 100	*63*
1992/93	9.54	380	3.11	120	4.99	200	27.55	1 100	*64*
1993/94	12.45	470	3.76	140	6.95	260	35.33	1 300	*66*
1994/95	14.93	510	4.18	140	7.57	260	39.32	1 300	*68*

[a] Defence includes R&D conducted by the DRDO and the armed services.

[b] Department of Atomic Energy.

[c] Department of Space.

[d] Total government expenditure on R&D.

Source: Government of India, Department of Science and Technology, *Research and Development Statistics* (various years).

While most of these funds are not spent on nuclear weapons and delivery systems—indeed, funding of nuclear weapons apparently does not appear in official budget statistics—they give an indication of the bureaucratic power enjoyed by the Big Science establishment associated with the nuclear weapon programme. Their clout was sufficient to reverse India's position in favour of the CTBT within two years, largely because of closer cooperation between the Defence Research and Development Organisation (DRDO) and the Department of Atomic Energy (DAE), which feared for its future if the option of testing was foreclosed.[19]

Although the DRDO and the DAE succeeded in convincing public opinion and a series of governments that the CTBT was incompatible with Indian security, they were not successful in gaining authorization to test before 1998. The DAE sought such authorization to confirm the performance of advanced

[19] Deshingkar, G., 'Indian politics and arms control: recent reversals and new reasons for optimism', ed. E. Arnett, *Nuclear Weapons and Arms Control in South Asia after the Test Ban*, SIPRI Research Report No. 14 (Oxford University Press: Oxford, 1998).

designs developed after the 1974 test and to produce data for computer models.[20]

Political reasons

After the 1998 national elections, the BJP was asked to form a government. Having failed at the task in 1996, the party leadership was desperate to succeed. Even with a very inclusive approach, however, they were not able to produce a majority government, and they were forced to govern with support from parties outside their governing coalition.[21] As a result, the BJP-led government is doubly weak, needing to compromise and pass out favours to its coalition partners while wooing support from outside. The predictable result was paralysis, a state of affairs complicated by the political weaknesses and corruption problems of regional parties in the BJP's coalition.

Previously, some observers had predicted that the BJP would have to moderate its stance on the nuclear issue in order to govern a weak coalition with outside support.[22] The BJP leadership instead took a very different approach from the moment they were asked to form the government. On the assumption that nuclear tests and their commitment to indigenous military technology would strengthen their political support and make other initiatives possible, they immediately told Ministry of Defence Science Adviser Abdul Kalam and Atomic Energy Commission Chairman R. Chidambaram to prepare for nuclear tests at the earliest possible date.

Military reasons

Military considerations were less important. Military and nuclear experts had previously stated that tests were not necessary for the credibility of India's nuclear capability, which is intended mainly to deter Pakistani first use.[23] India already had warheads and delivery systems appropriate for use against China or Pakistan, as was acknowledged by an unnamed official in the Prime Minister's Office after the tests.[24] On 20 March 1998, upon taking up his post as Defence Minister, George Fernandes said, 'I don't think we need to test at this point'. He said that a decision about testing would await the completion of a

[20] Doordarshan Television, Interview with R. Chidambaram, 23 May 1998. Between the 1974 and 1998 tests, scientists had undertaken 'simulation, design, verification, and . . . many laboratory experiments', according to Abdul Kalam. Subramanian, T. S., 'A man and his mission: interview with A. P. J. Abdul Kalam', *Frontline*, vol. 15, no. 19 (12–25 Sep. 1998). See also Sikka and Kakodkar (note 5).

[21] Such an arrangement may be inescapable for the foreseeable future in India. Deshingkar (note 19).

[22] This is the main theme of Deshingkar (note 19).

[23] K. Sundarji, the former Chief of Army Staff, advocated signing the CTBT since in his judgement India did not need additional tests after 1974, even for a large arsenal deployed against China. Sundarji, K., 'The CTBT debate: choice before India', *Indian Express*, 4 Dec. 1995, p. 8. G. Balachandran, who is well connected in the Defence Ministry, wrote that a decision against testing 'will not in any way worsen India's security'. Balachandran, G., 'CTBT and Indian security', *Times of India*, 3 Sep. 1996. Raja Ramanna, the scientist responsible for the 1974 test, is cited as saying no more tests were needed. 'No need for further tests', *Statesman*, 28 Oct. 1996. An unnamed 'senior scientist working with the Atomic Energy Commission' is cited to this effect in Sawhney, P., 'Arjun, in its present form, is nothing more than a showpiece', *Asian Age*, 1 Feb. 1996, p. 13.

[24] Burns, J. F., 'India's line in the sand: "minimum" nuclear deterrent against China', *International Herald Tribune*, 8 July 1998, p. 4.

strategic defence review, which in turn would await the formation of the National Security Council, which came about only in November 1998.[25]

Nevertheless, there was a perceived need to respond after Pakistan tested the Ghauri ballistic missile on 6 April. Some Indian observers had not thought Pakistan capable of deploying a 1500-km missile, and there was a new feeling of vulnerability after the Ghauri test. Previously, only potential targets within a few hundred kilometres of the border were thought to be vulnerable. In this context, the nuclear tests could be seen as a way of reassuring public opinion after the surprise of the Ghauri test and a reminder to Pakistan that India has a nuclear deterrent.

Pakistan

In contrast to its Indian counterparts, Pakistan's political elite is less abashed about the need for nuclear deterrence. Military fears that the Pakistani nuclear capability was not taken seriously in India combined with a feeling of growing military inferiority after being abandoned by the USA after the cold war to create an imperative to test that was resisted before May 1998 only because of the threat of sanctions. The Indian tests created a situation in which the Pakistani leadership saw an even greater need to test and a possible opening to justify the test as a response that was both politically and strategically understandable.

Military reasons

By 1998 the Pakistani military had grown very sensitive to the decline in its conventional military capabilities after US cooperation was virtually stopped by sanctions in 1990. Between 1990 and 1995 (some US military equipment that had been paid for in the 1980s was released under a 'one-time waiver' in 1996) Pakistan became more dependent on Chinese arms, which are far from the 'state of the art', while every major arms supplier (except China) was involved in cooperation with India.[26] In addition to major weapon systems (see table 9.2), a number of inexpensive but militarily significant components and command and control technologies were ordered by or delivered to India, including laser-guided bombs, artillery-spotting radars, and reportedly an airborne warning and control system (AWACS) aircraft.[27]

[25] 'N-tests ruled out', *Times of India*, 21 Mar. 1998.

[26] In 1995 Bruce O. Riedel, the US Deputy Assistant Secretary of Defense for Near Eastern and South Asian Affairs, told Congress, 'US–Indian defense ties are better now than at any time in the past 30 years'. US House of Representatives, Committee on International Relations, *US Interests in South Asia* (US Government Printing Office: Washington, DC, 1997), p. 96.

[27] Laser-guided bombs and related technology were delivered by France, Israel, Russia, the UK and the USA beginning in the early 1990s. Although inexpensive, these pose a direct threat to Pakistan's main nuclear delivery systems. Arnett, E., 'Conventional arms transfers and nuclear stability in South Asia', in Arnett (note 19), pp. 79–81. Artillery-spotting radars were delivered from the USA in 1998. A Russo-Israeli AWAC system is apparently being developed for India. Opall-Rome, B., 'Israel, US lock horns over transfers to India', *Defense News*, 2–8 Nov. 1998, pp. 3, 19.

Table 9.2. Indian and Pakistani imports of major conventional weapons, 1960–97

Figures are in SIPRI trend-indicator values expressed in US $m. at constant 1990 prices; figures in brackets are percentages.

Year	1960–65		1966–71		1972–77		1978–83		1984–89		1990–95		1996		1997	
To Pakistan:																
China	108	*(20)*	532	*(35)*	683	*(42)*	1 776	*(46)*	1 491	*(38)*	1 906	*(57)*	118	*(16)*	41	*(7)*
USA	402	*(75)*	7	*(0.5)*	105	*(7)*	805	*(21)*	2 008	*(51)*	217	*(6)*	291	*(40)*	43	*(8)*
France	0	*(0)*	519	*(34)*	575	*(36)*	881	*(23)*	55	*(1)*	38	*(1)*	84	*(12)*	76	*(13)*
UK	16	*(3)*	40	*(3)*	57	*(4)*	223	*(6)*	148	*(4)*	532	*(16)*	0	*(0)*	0	*(0)*
Other	8	*(1)*	423	*(28)*[a]	189	*(12)*	150	*(4)*	233	*(6)*	670	*(20)*	151	*(32)*[b]	412	*(72)*[c]
Total	**534**	***(100)***	**1 521**	***(100)***	**1 609**	***(100)***	**3 835**	***(100)***	**3 935**	***(100)***	**3 363**	***(100)***	**644**	***(100)***	**572**	***(100)***
To India:																
USSR/Russia	1 635	*(46)*	4 121	*(68)*	6 363	*(75)*	8 338	*(82)*	15 683	*(76)*	5 402	*(72)*	970	*(79)*	876	*(74)*
UK	1 611	*(45)*	1 025	*(17)*	1 190	*(14)*	1 532	*(15)*	1 603	*(8)*	615	*(8)*	33	*(3)*	62	*(5)*
France	124	*(3)*	137	*(2)*	138	*(2)*	158	*(2)*	2 207	*(11)*	320	*(4)*	6	*(0.5)*	0	*(0)*
Germany	0	*(0)*	212	*(4)*	165	*(2)*	0	*(0)*	401	*(2)*	399	*(5)*	52	*(4)*	11	*(1)*
Other	175	*(5)*[d]	547	*(9)*	576	*(7)*	183	*(2)*	803	*(4)*	731	*(10)*[e]	169	*(14)*	236	*(20)*
Total	**3 545**	***(100)***	**6 042**	***(100)***	**8 432**	***(100)***	**10 211**	***(100)***	**20 697**	***(100)***	**7 467**	***(100)***	**1 230**	***(100)***	**1 185**	***(100)***

[a] Includes $229 million worth of deliveries from the USSR.

[b] Includes $86 million worth of deliveries from Russia (for transport helicopters) and $64 million from Italy.

[c] Includes $399 million worth of deliveries from Ukraine.

[d] Includes $96 million worth of deliveries from the USA.

[e] Includes $18 million worth of deliveries from the USA in 1992.

Source: SIPRI arms transfers database.

Pakistan's loss of its arms suppliers to India, and especially the loss of arms imports from the USA, has led to a feeling of abandonment and resentment. As Asghar Khan, a retired air marshall, said in March 1998, 'We have neither support from our friends, nor have any military equipment, or new aircraft'.[28] Mohammad Sarwar Cheema, Chairman of the National Assembly's Standing Committee for Defence Affairs, agreed: 'The order in conventional arms . . . has now been disturbed to a great extent'.[29]

The feeling of abandonment reinvigorated the military's interest in nuclear deterrence of conventional war. Pakistani officials have been making statements intended to signal that their nuclear capability should make India reluctant to use conventional force. The utility of nuclear weapons as a deterrent to conventional war was specifically cited by Prime Minister Nawaz when he sought to explain his decision to authorize Pakistan's tests: 'These weapons are to deter aggression, whether nuclear or conventional'.[30] A similar view was put forward more completely by Asad Durrani, former director of Inter-Services Intelligence (and as such responsible for Pakistani support to the Kashmir insurgency) and former director of the National Defence College: 'Our deterrence is already working. . . . Our aim is to prevent war, also a conventional one. . . . The effectiveness of our deterrent lies in a known or a perceived capability, and in the notion that we might have a desperate propensity to use it.'[31]

Durrani specifically links Pakistan's interest in using nuclear weapons first in the early stages of a war to its inferiority in conventional weapons: 'Because of its known deficiencies in the conventional forces, [Pakistan is] likely to pull the nuclear trigger. . . . In view of the upgraded potential that India should now be assumed to possess, we must be prepared to unleash our potential before it could be seriously impaired.'[32]

Before the 1998 tests, Indian officials had spoken and written about their doubts that Pakistan had really mastered the technology of uranium enrichment, as claimed by Pakistani officials. P. K. Iyengar said in 1994 that he doubted 'there is any proof that Pakistan has this capability' to make nuclear weapons.[33] Raja Ramanna elaborated: 'From our experience in using centrifuges to enrich uranium we know that these are difficult to maintain. And

[28] 'No chance of India–Pakistan nuclear war', *Dawn*, 22 Mar. 1998.

[29] *The News* (Islamabad), 7 June 1998, in 'Pakistan: Pakistani Army not to have nuclear weapons', Foreign Broadcast Information Service, *Daily Report–Arms Control (FBIS-TAC)*, FBIS-TAC-98-159, 9 June 1998.

[30] Radio Pakistan (Islamabad), 28 May 1998, in 'Pakistan: Sharif reassures world on n-tests', Foreign Broadcast Information Service, *Daily Report–Near East and South Asia (FBIS-NES)*, FBIS-NES-98-148, 29 May 1998.

[31] Durrani, A., 'Our friend, the enemy', *The News*, 11 June 1998. Then President Ghulam Ishaq Khan, the civilian political leader who has taken the greatest interest in Pakistan's nuclear planning, confirmed in 1990, 'In the event of war with India, Pakistan would use nuclear weapons at an early stage'. McDonald, H., 'Destroyer of worlds', *Far East Economic Review*, 30 Apr. 1992, p. 24.

[32] Durrani, A., 'Pakistan's nuclear card', *Defence Journal*, June 1998. See also the view of Lt Gen. Talat Masood (ret.): 'If conventional strength, particularly the air arm and surveillance networks, continues to decrease . . . then the nuclear capability can be neutralized by pre-emptive conventional surgical strikes'. Masood, T., 'Evolving a correct nuclear posture', *Dawn*, 21 Aug. 1998.

[33] Prabhu, R., 'US targeting Indian high-tech capability: P. K. Iyengar', *Indian Express*, 12 May 1994.

given the state of their industrial capability, it is apparent that Pakistan's plant is working nowhere to the capacity planned . . . In the past, Pakistan got plenty of mileage by making tall claims. But that is now turning into paper mileage'.[34]

This scientific scepticism may have been a factor in Indian military planning. Before the 1998 tests, the Indian military may not have 'believe[d] that Pakistan has a viable deterrent', according to P. R. Chari, former Additional Secretary of Defence, the second-ranking civilian responsible for the Indian Air Force.[35] Former Chief of Army Staff General V. N. Sharma shared this view: 'I don't see any threat of nuclear capacity or capability in Pakistan'.[36]

Viewed from Pakistan, the Indian military's belief that Pakistan's nuclear capability was a bluff appeared to be responsible for India continuing to emphasize its option to wage conventional war in response to Pakistani provocations in Kashmir. Just before India's nuclear tests, retired Lieutenant General V. K. Nayar told the Indian press that the army could even intentionally prolong a conventional war to achieve unspecified strategic objectives.[37]

The Pakistani military therefore saw nuclear tests as indispensable for making credible their nuclear deterrent, on which they based their claim to be able to keep the nation secure. Furthermore, Pakistani planners have seen nuclear deterrence as a guarantor of their freedom to pursue measures short of war in Kashmir.[38] Former ISI Director Durrani links Pakistan's nuclear deterrent and Kashmir most explicitly when he claims that Pakistan would 'use our nuclear capabilities when our national objectives are threatened, for example, a major crackdown on [the] freedom movement in Kashmir'.[39]

Political reasons

Despite pressure from the military and the opportunity opened by the Indian tests, Nawaz was apparently reluctant to authorize them. On 19 May, a week after the Indian tests, he said, 'Why we are not testing this capability is because of the fact I want to show the world that Pakistan is a responsible country. . . . If India is doing it out of sheer madness, we do not have to blindly follow suit'.[40] With constitutional reforms passed in 1997, Nawaz was in a stronger position vis-à-vis the Army than any of his predecessors since the *coup d'état* that brought General Mohammad Zia ul-Haq to power in 1977. He could not be dismissed and, with Benazir Bhutto in legal trouble but still

[34] Ramanna, R., 'We have enough plutonium', *India Today*, 15 Sep. 1994, p. 53.

[35] Chari, P. R., *Indo-Pak Nuclear Standoff: The Role of the United States* (Manohar: New Delhi, 1995), pp. 112–15, 127; and Chari, P. R., 'Pakistan's bomb: a strategy of deterrence crafted on make believe', *Indian Express*, 28 Aug. 1994.

[36] Sharma, V. N., 'It's all bluff and bluster', *Economic Times*, 18 May 1993.

[37] *Asian Age*, 2 May 1998, p. 2.

[38] So reports Stephen P. Cohen after interviews in 1980. Cohen, S. P., *The Pakistan Army* (University of California Press: London, 1984), p. 153. A new edition was published in 1998 by Oxford University Press, Karachi.

[39] Durrani, A., *Pakistan's Security and the Nuclear Option* (Institute for Policy Studies: Islamabad, 1995), p. 92.

[40] Shaikh, S., 'Pakistan not to sit back if India attacks, declares Nawaz', *The News*, 20 May 1998.

Table 9.3. Expenditure on atomic energy research by the Pakistani Government, fiscal years 1979/80–1995/96

Figures are in m. current rupees and US $m. at 1995 prices and exchange rates.

	Atomic energy research expenditure	
Fiscal years	Rs	$
1979/80	124	10
1980/81	125	9
1981/82	135	8
1982/83	140	8
1983/84	197	11
1984/85	278	22
1985/86	278	21
1987/88	376	26
1988/89	390	25
1989/90	404	24
1991/92	480	23
1992/93	539	24
1994/95	945	34
1995/96	969	31

Source: Government of Pakistan, Finance Division, *Demand for Grants and Appropriations* (various years).

leading the opposition, there was no alternative outside his party, the Pakistan Muslim League–Nawaz.

Opinion polls showed that the electorate supported testing, a view that was driven home to Nawaz in a meeting with newspaper editors on 21 May.[41] In announcing his decision to the world, he exclaimed, 'Oh, God! What step are my people asking me to take?'[42]

Scientific reasons

As in the case of India, there were no doubt those in the Pakistani nuclear establishment who wanted to verify the performance of the nuclear devices they had designed. As seen in table 9.3, Pakistan dramatically increased its on-budget investment in nuclear technology in the mid-1980s (although the extent to which this reflects investment in nuclear weapons is unexplained in government reports), and so there was less time to conduct simulations and experiments without nuclear yield. Pakistan's nuclear establishment as a whole is also much smaller than India's, offering fewer opportunities to share expertise with those involved in civilian applications. That said, Pakistan may not see a need for thermonuclear or low-yield devices, which have been developed and tested by India.[43]

[41] Husain, F., *The Nation* (Islamabad), 22 May 1998.
[42] Radio Pakistan (note 30).
[43] 'Pakistan can make hydrogen bomb: Qadeer', *The News*, 2 Nov. 1998.

IV. Military implications

The 1998 nuclear tests have had immediate military effects. Some of these may be less significant than expected in the days immediately following the tests, while others may still be underestimated. The two central questions are whether India and Pakistan will expand their nuclear capabilities and what approach India will take to compensate for the loss of military technology partners.

Expanded weaponization?

Both India and Pakistan expressed their determination to press ahead with the weaponization and deployment of their nuclear capabilities after the tests, although the precise meaning of these terms in a context in which both already have nuclear bombs that can be delivered by aircraft is not clear. In India, there has been a vigorous public discussion. It appears that the nuclear weapons will remain in the custody of the Ministry of Defence rather than the armed forces and additional systems will not necessarily be deployed in the immediate future. In Pakistan, there are fewer public indications of the course to be followed, but there is evidence of a crisis mentality in which nuclear weapons and their delivery systems, especially ballistic missiles, might soon be deployed in provocative ways.

India

For now, India's nuclear capability is apparently intended to dissuade Pakistan from using nuclear weapons first while preserving India's option to use conventional forces in response to, say, an increase in Pakistani support to Kashmiri insurgents.[44] As Army Chief of Staff V. P. Malik put it after the tests, Indian nuclear weapons are perceived as a deterrent to Pakistan's 'fuelling more insurgency in [Indian] territory'.[45] In principle, relatively few nuclear weapons would be needed for this posture. Defence Minister Fernandes said after the tests that the nuclear arsenal would not cost more than Rs 200 billion, about $5 billion at market exchange rates or $20 billion in purchasing power parity terms.[46] Prime Minister Vajpayee, having said in June 1998 that India's

[44] Indian officials were quick to articulate a no-first-use position after the tests, even as they reiterated their willingness to use military force. See, e.g., the remarks of Home Minister Advani in 'Pakistan to roll back anti-India policy', *Times of India*, 19 May 1998. See also 'India declares moratorium on nuclear testing', *The Hindu*, 22 May 1998. Prime Minister Vajpayee has also said that India's nuclear arsenal 'should prevent the use of these weapons'. Cooper, K. J., 'Leader says India has a "credible" deterrent', *Washington Post*, 17 June 1998, p. A21.

[45] 'Nukes keep Pakistan away, says Indian army chief', *Dawn*, 30 Nov. 1998. On 10 Feb. 1999 Malik reiterated, 'Having crossed the nuclear threshold does not mean conventional war is out. Nuclear deterrence only restricts all-out war employing weapons of mass destruction'. '"Excerpt" of Indian Army Chief V. P. Malik's address at Maharshi Dayanand University', *Pioneer* (New Delhi), 13 Feb. 1999, p. 9.

[46] '5 Pak tests doubtful: George', *Asian Age*, 1 June 1998; and 'Tests are nowhere near India's: Fernandes', *Times of India*, 1 June 1998.

deterrent was credible, emphasized in a December speech that the size of the arsenal should be the minimum for credible deterrence.[47]

There are public indications of how Vajpayee could reach the conclusion that India does not need any more nuclear weapons for the time being. Retired Air Commodore Jasjit Singh, an adviser to Vajpayee in the matter of creating a national security council, wrote after the tests that India should develop a triad of roughly three dozen air-, land- and sea-based weapons over 15–20 years, reserving the decision to deploy them until its security situation demanded this. Tactical nuclear weapons would not be necessary. The air force would 'retain' the primary responsibility for nuclear delivery, with 5000-km ballistic missiles and sea-based weapons being deployed later if necessary.[48] Defence Minister Fernandes said that a viable nuclear command and control system is already 'in position', a claim that reflects the air force's long experience with the means to prepare strike missions and measures the Indian armed forces have taken since the 1980s to be able to operate after the use of nuclear weapons.[49] Other retired military leaders who have gone on the record appear to agree that India does not need more than 30–50 weapons for the foreseeable future, has no need to put nuclear warheads on the short-range Prithvi ballistic missile and should keep costs to a minimum.[50]

Pakistan

Since Pakistan's ability to produce nuclear weapons was made clear publicly in 1990, it has generally been assumed that they could be delivered by aircraft.[51] Since Pakistan fears losing air superiority to India relatively early in a war—a loss that would make its air bases vulnerable to heavier and more accurate bombardment from the air—and seeks the flexibility to use nuclear weapons first against military targets, short-range ballistic missiles (SRBMs) have a definite military appeal.[52] Pakistan received SRBMs from China in the early 1990s.[53] A. Q. Khan has stated that the May 1998 tests included warheads for SRBMs as well as air-dropped weapons and longer-range missiles[54] but that thermonuclear weapons are not needed for Pakistan's deterrence con-

[47] Mohan, C. R., 'PM rejects demands to limit nuclear capabilities', *The Hindu*, 16 Dec. 1998, p. 1.

[48] Singh, J., 'A nuclear strategy for India', ed. J. Singh, *Nuclear India* (Knowledge World: New Delhi, 1998), pp. 314–24; and Singh, J., 'Defence: budgeting for security needs', *Frontline*, 18–31 July 1998; and Singh's remarks in Cooper, K. J., 'Nuclear dilemmas: vital issues face India as a nuclear power', *Washington Post*, 25 May 1998, p. A1. As stated above, India already has the ability to deploy 30 warheads on short notice. Until now, its nuclear warheads have been in the custody of the Department of Atomic Energy.

[49] Aneja, A., 'No headway in CTBT talks: Fernandes', *The Hindu*, 9 Dec. 1998, p. 1.

[50] See, e.g., the views of retired generals K. Sundarji and V. N. Sharma in Chengappa, R. and Joshi, M., 'Future fire', *India Today*, 25 May 1998, p. 33.

[51] Rashid and Sidhva (note 2).

[52] Arnett (note 27).

[53] Arnett, E., 'Military research and development in southern Asia: limited capabilities despite impressive resources', ed. E. Arnett, SIPRI, *Military Capacity and the Risk of War: China, India, Pakistan and Iran* (Oxford University Press: Oxford, 1997), pp. 268–71. The first deliveries may have been as early as 1988.

[54] Iqbal, A., 'Pakistan can explode H-bomb: A. Q. Khan', *The News*, 30 May 1998; and Karniol, R., 'Vital aid?', *Jane's Defence Weekly*, 4 Nov. 1998, p. 21.

cept.[55] He further affirmed that Pakistan already has adequate command and control of its nuclear capabilities,[56] although it is not clear that this would be the case if the arsenal expanded or had to withstand sustained conventional bombardment.

Pakistan has also sought to develop or acquire longer-range ballistic missiles. The Hatf III project for a 600-km range ballistic missile was launched in 1987.[57] On 6 April 1998 Pakistan flight-tested a new, longer-range missile designated Hatf V or Ghauri, which had been under development since 1993, when Nawaz returned to power. The nominal range given for the missile is 1500 km with a payload of 700 kg, but the range demonstrated in the test was 1100 km.[58] Unnamed US officials said that a 'handful' of Ghauris and other weapons had been purchased from North Korea in 1997.[59]

A. Q. Khan suggested that a decision to test weapons without deploying them was a distinction without a difference: 'We can deploy [nuclear weapons] within days'.[60] Nevertheless, Foreign Secretary Shamshad Ahmed said, 'We do not wish to engage in a nuclear arms race and do not want to embark on a weaponisation programme or one that involves deployment of nuclear warheads on our missiles'.[61]

The effect of withdrawing military cooperation on India's military power

Among the international responses to India's tests,[62] the USA stopped its technical cooperation with Indian military projects.[63] Although the projects being pursued by the DRDO were funded in part to make India less vulnerable to disruptions in relationships with unreliable suppliers, most of the major projects were discovered to be dependent on foreign cooperation. US firms were supplying technology to the Light Combat Aircraft (LCA), the Advanced Light Helicopter (ALH) and Bharat Electronics Ltd, which is involved in DRDO-designed missiles.[64] These projects will have to be taken up by French, Israeli and Russian suppliers or replaced by importing complete systems.[65]

55 *The News* (note 43).

56 'No pressure to roll back N-programme, says Qadeer', *Dawn*, 25 Nov. 1998.

57 'Hataf-III is superior to Prithvi: Beg', *The Muslim*, 5 July 1997. It is not clear whether this is the same missile as the solid-fuel Shaheen developed by the PAEC. The designations Hatf I and Hatf II refer to Pakistan's SRBMs.

58 Koch, A. R. and Sidhu, W. P. S., 'South Asia goes ballistic, then nuclear', *Jane's Intelligence Review*, June 1998, p. 36.

59 Smith, R. J., 'A feared scenario around the corner', *Washington Post*, 14 May 1998, p. A29.

60 Hussain, Z., 'Interview, A. Q. Khan', *Newsline*, June 1998.

61 Sehbai, S., 'Pakistan reassessing position on CTBT', *Dawn*, 1 July 1998.

62 See chapter 15 in this volume.

63 As seen in table 9.2 Pakistan had already been cut off from US and British arms. Pakistan's military technology and production bases are much less extensive than India's and rely on cooperation with China. They are therefore not as vulnerable to Western sanctions. They are also much less transparent and therefore cannot be examined in detail here.

64 For a discussion of the LCA and Agni missile, see chapter 8 in this volume.

65 As seen in table 9.2, Russia is India's primary arms supplier. France is supplying India with avionics for its Russian Su-30 attack aircraft. Israeli firms have supplied India with smart-bomb technology and technical assistance with the T-80 Fast Attack Craft, and one is supplying the radar for an AWACS—although US sanctions have disrupted this deal. Laskar, R. H., 'Navy built vessel with Israeli help', *Asian Age*, 24 June 1998. All 3 states are involved in a project to upgrade 125 MiG-21s as an

After the tests India and Russia negotiated a new 10-year arms supply arrangement, worth at least $8 billion.[66]

Although the BJP-led government increased India's military R&D budget by 30 per cent,[67] it is unlikely that more money alone would have allowed India to deploy the vast array of systems said to be in development, even if technology transfer had not been interrupted by the tests. Since economic liberalization began in the early 1990s, government organizations like the DRDO are seen as undesirable and unprofitable employers, in good measure because of their inability to bring major system designs to fruition. These problems will be all the worse if the USA is successful in encouraging other suppliers to join them in embargoing India.[68]

On the other hand, India's military capability would probably increase if the disruption of technology transfer to its ostensibly indigenous programmes led to the purchase of superior systems from abroad. Major systems will have to be imported in any case because of delays created by the US embargo, but the increases in military R&D funding make it difficult to pay for imported weapons. Since India sees nuclear weapons as preserving the option of waging conventional war, acquisition of conventional weapons is unlikely to be forgone completely for the sake of expanding nuclear capability. As a result, India has an incentive to keep its nuclear force limited and save funds for advanced conventional systems.

V. Conclusions

While the 1998 nuclear tests may have focused international attention on the problems of war and nuclear risk in South Asia, they may have served more as a reminder or warning of related problems than as a cause of instability in themselves. The greatest risk of nuclear war in South Asia arises from Pakistan's long-standing strategy of using nuclear weapons to deter conventional war through the threat of early first use, even as it tries to use this deterrent to preserve its freedom of action in Kashmir. As long as Indian military planners believe that their own nuclear capability will deter Pakistani first use and therefore leave them the option of launching a punitive conventional war, the risk of nuclear escalation is not only real but also stems directly from the perfectly logical designs of the states involved. It is not necessary to postulate an accident or an officer prepared to use nuclear

interim measure while the LCA is developed or an alternative is sought. Laskar, R. H., *Asian Age*, 14 Oct. 1998, p. 2.

[66] 'Pact with Russia on defence needs', *The Pioneer*, 23 June 1998.

[67] See chapter 8 in this volume.

[68] The Brownback Amendment (India–Pakistan Relief Act) to the budget act passed and signed into law in Oct. 1998 allows US President Bill Clinton to waive sanctions for up to 12 months but does not apply to military technology, which will remain under embargo. France has made clear its intention to expand arms exports to India. Mohan, C. R., 'PM sees change in world perception of n.-policy', *The Hindu*, 2 Oct. 1998. Personal requests from Clinton to Russian President Boris Yeltsin and Israeli Prime Minister Benjamin Netanyahu to join the military technology embargo were rebuffed, as was a request from the US Government to the French Government. Israel did freeze the sale of surveillance drones destined for ballistic missile units of the Indian Army.

weapons without proper authorization to envision nuclear war in South Asia. All that is required is for the Indian and Pakistani militaries to do what the public record strongly suggests they intend to do in a crisis.

10. Arms production

ELISABETH SKÖNS and REINHILDE WEIDACHER

I. Introduction

The structure of world arms production is highly concentrated. Only a few countries maintain significant military industrial capabilities. The exact volume and distribution of global arms production are unknown because there is little transparency in the production of weapons. Rough estimates of national arms production, based on data from governments and defence industry associations, show that in 1996 the 10 largest arms-producing countries worldwide accounted for almost 90 per cent of world arms production, estimated to be in the range of $195–205 billion at current prices and exchange rates. The United States accounted for almost half of the world total, while the next two countries in size, France and the UK, accounted for 10 per cent each and the three next—Germany, Japan and Russia—for roughly 4 per cent each. The changes in the global arms industry which have taken place since 1996 have probably reinforced this concentration.

The declining trend in arms production since the late 1980s appears to have come to a halt. This assessment is based on arms sales data for the 100 largest arms-producing companies in the Organisation for Economic Co-operation and Development (OECD) and developing countries except China. Since 1994 there has been a slight increase in real terms in the combined arms sales of the top 100 companies in these countries which, at $156 billion in 1997 (table 10.1), represent more than three-quarters of world arms production.

Two major arms-producing countries are not included in these statistics—China and Russia. There are no official data on Chinese arms production. The Russian Government provides some statistics, although not on the volume of output but only on trends, as an index. These show that Russian production of military equipment increased by 5 per cent in real terms in 1998. This was the first increase after a period of steep decline since 1991, which by 1997 had brought the level of Russian arms production to less than one-tenth of what it was in 1991.

During 1998 restructuring of the arms industries continued in most parts of the world, including the United States, most West European countries and several smaller arms-producing countries. In Russia the financial crisis placed further constraints on the implementation of the government restructuring programme for the arms industry as presented in 1997. The concentration process in the USA appears to have peaked in 1998, having accelerated during a five-year period of government-supported mergers and acquisitions. Between 1990 and 1998 four huge arms-producing companies absorbed more than 20 other major defence firms. Further concentration among the four was blocked in July 1998 when anti-trust concerns in the US Department of Defense (DOD) led to its refusing the planned merger between two of the four, Lockheed Martin and Northrop Grumman. West European arms-producing companies are heading towards cross-border integration in Europe and, at the same time, it is clear that European integration does not preclude transatlantic military industrial links.

The internationalization of military production tends to reduce national government control over arms production. Political control over production of military equipment will therefore increasingly require agreements on a multilateral level.

This chapter analyses trends and developments in the world arms industry on the basis of available data and information. These are of different kinds. Section II is based on arms sales data up to and including 1997 from the SIPRI arms industry database and focuses on the top 100 arms-producing companies in the OECD and developing countries, but also takes into account developments in 1998. Russian arms-producing enterprises are not included in the SIPRI database, since no arms sales data are provided on the enterprise level in Russia. Section III summarizes recent developments in the Russian arms industry, including Russian official data on total national arms production. Section IV analyses recent developments in the restructuring of the arms industry in the USA and Western Europe. Section V presents and discusses new SIPRI estimates of national arms production and the global distribution of military production.

II. The SIPRI top 100

After a period of declining arms sales in real terms in 1990–94, the combined arms sales of the 100 largest arms-producing companies in the OECD and developing countries (except China)[1] have been increasing slightly since 1994. Comparing the top 100 companies in each year, combined arms sales increased slightly in 1995 and remained relatively constant in real terms in 1996 and 1997.[2]

The process of military industrial concentration, which continued during 1997, is reflected in the increasing gap in arms sales between the smaller and the larger companies. Taking the average arms sales of the five smallest of the top 100 companies and comparing them with the five largest, this ratio increased from 1 : 34 in 1996 to 1 : 45 in 1997. This is the effect of a rapid increase in the size of the largest companies because of their acquisitions. At the same time new and by definition smaller companies enter the list, replac-

[1] For a list of member countries in the OECD and the coverage of developing countries, see appendix 11A in this volume.

[2] This trend applies to a shifting group of companies because the companies in the top 100 group change over the years. If the comparison is made instead only for the companies which were among the top 100 in 1997, there was a nominal increase of 9% in 1997 over 1996 ($143 billion). The increase in constant dollars was roughly the same because, for the group of top 100 companies, the fluctuations in exchange rates during 1997 tended on average to outweigh inflation.

Table 10.1. Regional/national shares of arms sales[a] for the top 100 arms-producing companies in the OECD and in the developing countries in 1997[b]

Number of companies, 1997	Region/ country	Percentage of total arms sales 1996	1997	Arms sales 1997 (US $b.)
41	USA	*52.7*	*55.7*	86.8
37	*West European OECD*	***37.8***	***35.6***	**55.7**
12	UK	*14.2*	*15.0*	23.4
11	France	*13.9*	*11.9*	18.5
6	Germany	*4.6*	*4.0*	6.2
2	Italy	*2.4*	*2.2*	3.5
3	Sweden	*1.5*	*1.2*	1.9
2	Switzerland	*0.8*	*0.7*	1.2
1	Spain	*0.4*	*0.6*	1.0
11	*Other OECD*	***5.9***	***5.0***	**7.9**
8	Japan[c]	*5.1*	*4.3*	6.7
2	Australia	*0.5*	*0.5*	0.8
1	Turkey	*0.3*	*0.2*	0.4
11	*Non-OECD countries*	***3.6***	***3.5***	**5.7**
6	Israel	*2.0*	*1.9*	3.0
3	India	*0.9*	*0.9*	1.5
1	Singapore	*0.4*	*0.4*	0.7
1	South Africa	*0.3*	*0.3*	0.5
		100.0	***100.0***	**156.1**

[a] Arms sales include sales for domestic procurement and exports.

[b] China, South Korea and Taiwan are not included because of lack of data. For a list of member countries in the OECD and the coverage of developing countries, see appendix 11A.

[c] For Japanese companies data are for new military contracts rather than arms sales.

Source: Appendix 10A.

ing companies which have been acquired and those which have sold off their military production. The arms sales of the company ranked 100 in 1996 were valued at $290 million; in 1997 they were $250 million.

US and West European companies account for the overwhelming share of total sales—around 56 and 36 per cent, respectively. The share of the 41 US companies increased by 3 percentage points over 1996, while the share of the 37 West European companies fell by 2.2 percentage points. This reflects the more rapid rate of concentration in the US arms industry, where a number of mergers and acquisitions resulted in a sharp increase in the arms sales of the US companies on the list, by 13 per cent in real terms, while the West European companies' sales increased by only 7 per cent.[3]

Other OECD countries had 11 companies on the top 100 list with combined arms sales of roughly $8 billion in 1997, representing 5 per cent of the total. The decline in their share as compared to 1996 is mainly due to the deterior-

[3] In nominal terms (current dollars) the difference was even greater—a 15% rise for US companies compared with a 3% rise for West European companies.

ating exchange rate of the Japanese yen against the dollar.[4] Eleven companies in four non-OECD countries had combined arms sales of $5.7 billion in 1997, accounting for 3.5 per cent of the total. The number of companies in non-OECD countries has increased by three compared to the top 100 list for 1996 as presented in the *SIPRI Yearbook 1998*. These three are Singapore Technologies, the largest arms-producing company in Singapore, for which no data were available in previous years; Bharat Electronics, India, which increased its arms sales in 1997; and El-Op, Israel, included as smaller companies join the top 100.

State-owned Singapore Technologies (ST) has more than doubled its arms sales since 1994,[5] the result mainly of upgrade programmes for fighter aircraft and the development and production of naval vessels. The first prototype of an indigenous infantry fighting vehicle was completed in 1997. Also in 1997 the company combined its major arms-producing subsidiaries—ST Aerospace, ST Automotive, ST Electronics and ST Marine—into the newly established ST Engineering with more than 50 per cent of its sales in arms production. Only the production of ordnance and ammunition remained a separate group in ST, Chartered Industries of Singapore.

Other OECD and non-OECD companies and countries would be on the list if data were available, and therefore have a greater share in world arms production than the SIPRI list suggests. Apart from the obvious cases of China, Russia and other countries in transition which are outside the coverage of the SIPRI arms industry database, these include South Korea and Taiwan. For companies in these countries it has not been possible to obtain sufficient information to include them in the top 100 list for 1997. However, available information about their production programmes and arms sales in previous years indicates that at least three companies in South Korea and two in Taiwan would rank among the top 100 if data were provided.

The South Korean companies are the large private and diversified conglomerates (*chaebols*) Daewoo, Hyundai and Samsung, which in 1995 had arms sales in the range of $400–1160 million.[6] A far-reaching restructuring process was initiated in 1998. Problems of excessive debt accumulation and corruption within the *chaebols* were uncovered as a result of the Asian financial crisis. In 1998 the five largest *chaebols* agreed to a government plan to sell off unprofitable units, increase management transparency and merge units according to core competencies.[7] Although the restructuring is not specifically aimed at military production, it involves the major arms-producing companies, including the aerospace divisions of Daewoo, Hyundai and Samsung, which are to

[4] The trend in Japanese arms sales is very different when measured in yen than in US dollars. The total arms sales of the 8 Japanese companies in table 10.1 show a fall by 9% in current dollars (from $7.4 billion in 1996) but remained virtually unchanged in constant dollars.

[5] Arms sales data for ST in 1994 are provided by Dr Lee Boon Yang, Minister of Defence of Singapore, in an interview in *Asian Defence Journal*, no. 7 (1995), p. 7.

[6] Sköns, E., Weidacher, R. and the SIPRI Arms Industry Network, 'The 100 largest arms-producing companies, 1996', *SIPRI Yearbook 1998: Armaments, Disarmament and International Security* (Oxford University Press: Oxford, 1998), appendix 6E, pp. 260–66.

[7] Opall-Rome, B., 'S. Korea begins sweeping restructuring of conglomerates', *Defense News*, 11 Jan. 1999, p. 4.

be merged into a new aerospace company, Korean Aerospace Industries (KAI), in early 1999. The plan permits foreign companies to acquire equity shares in the new companies, including those involved in arms production.[8]

The Taiwanese companies which would rank among the top 100 if data were made available are the Aerospace Industrial Development Corporation (AIDC), whose arms sales are likely to decrease after the end of the Indigenous Defensive Fighter programme at the end of 1999, and the China Shipbuilding Corporation (CSBC). These are government enterprises under the control of the Ministry of Economic Affairs, but there are plans to privatize them in 2000 and 2001. A third state-owned arms-producing company, Taiwan Machinery Manufacturing Corporation, was privatized in 1998.[9]

III. Russia

The sharp reduction in Russian arms production since 1991 was halted in 1998.

During the period 1991–97 there was a massive decline in the military output of Russian defence enterprises and organizations. According to statistics of the Ministry of the Economy, the level of military production in 1997 was only 8.8 per cent of what it had been in 1991 (table 10.2). Most of this decline took place in 1992 as a result of the economic reforms implemented in that year.[10] Since then the average rate of decline has been roughly 30 per cent per year. In 1998 there was an increase in military output—by 5 per cent—for the first time since the break-up of the Soviet Union. Total output of the Russian defence industry (including civilian production) continued to fall in 1998 but at a slower rate. This slowdown in the decline was the result of a continued increase in the missile and space sectors and a change to growth in the aircraft, radio and shipbuilding sectors.[11] The return to growth in a few industrial sectors in 1997 and 1998 can, however, not outweigh the state of overall dissolution of the Russian arms industry throughout the 1990s.

The dramatic decline in domestic procurement is exacerbated by the practice of debt financing of procurement and research and development (R&D) contracts by the state.[12] The accumulated debt of the Defence Ministry to the

[8] 'Big chaebols trying to induce foreign companies' equity participation', *Joong Ang Ilbo* (Seoul), 8 Oct. 1998, URL <http://english.joongang.co.kr/>. In Apr. 1998 the government decided to allow foreign mergers and acquisitions in the arms industry if national security was not challenged. 'ROK to allow foreign hostile take-overs of defence firms', *Seoul Yonhap in English*, 5 Apr. 1998, in Foreign Broadcast Information Service, *Daily Report–East Asia (FBIS–EAS)*, FBIS-EAS-98095, 5 Apr. 1998.

[9] Taiwan Ministry of Economic Affairs, *Introduction to the Commission of National Corporations* (Ministry of Economic Affairs: Taipei, 1997).

[10] For an overview of the decline in Russian arms production in the period 1991–96, see Sköns, E. and Cooper, J., 'Arms production', *SIPRI Yearbook 1997: Armaments, Disarmament and International Security* (Oxford University Press: Oxford, 1997), pp. 254–58.

[11] Teleinformatsionnaya Sem (TS-VPK), URL <http://www.vpk.ru:8082/www-vpk/vpk/reports/q/1998/11/index.htm>.

[12] Military procurement orders are issued before the start of the calendar year and therefore before the necessary funds have been appropriated. Denezhkina, E., 'Russian defence firms and the external market', ed. I. Anthony, SIPRI, *Russia and the Arms Trade* (Oxford University Press: Oxford, 1998), pp. 124–25.

Table 10.2. Output of the Russian arms industry, 1991–98

Index: 1991 = 100 (constant prices).

	1991	1992	1993	1994	1995	1996	1997	1998
Military	100.0	49.5	32.5	19.9	16.6	12.8	8.8	9.2
Civilian	100.0	99.6	85.6	52.6	41.3	29.1	. .	. .
Total	**100.0**	**80.4**	**64.6**	**39.2**	**31.2**	**22.7**	**19.0**	**18.5**

Note: This table covers enterprises previously belonging to the Ministry of the Defence Industry (Minoboronprom). After the abolition of this ministry in 1997, the Ministry of the Economy assumed responsibility for the defence industrial enterprises and organizations. It provides monthly reports on the output of the arms industry, some published on the Internet. Figures are available only in index form. They are based on production (not sales) in constant roubles, deflated by the use of specific price indices for military and civilian products.

Source: Based on Teleinformatsionnaya Sem (TS-VPK), URL <http://www.vpk.gov.ru>, version current on 9 Feb. 1999 (subsequently changed to http://ts.vpk.gov.ru).

arms industry was estimated at around 20 billion roubles in 1997, around 25 per cent of which was for unpaid wages.[13] Underfunding of military procurement and R&D in 1997 was significantly worse than underfunding of military expenditure generally: funds were allocated for less than 20 per cent of planned procurement and R&D contracts.[14] Whether this changes in the longer term will depend largely on whether reform of the armed forces releases funds.[15]

Export dependence increased throughout the 1990s as a result of the dramatic decline of the domestic market. According to official Russian estimates, exports account for up to two-thirds of military production.[16] They are the most important source of hard-currency income for arms-producing companies and for some enterprises play a role far greater than the more limited addition to domestic demand which exports normally represent for Western companies. After a sharp decline in the early 1990s, according to the state arms export company, Rosvooruzheniye, the value of military exports

[13] This figure excludes debts to arms-producing companies incurred by the Ministry of Internal Affairs, the Federal Security Service, the Federal Government Communication and Information Agency, and other departments. Shulunov, A., 'If the defence sector goes on the attack . . .', *Ekonomika i Zhizn,* 25 July 1998, p. 6, in Foreign Broadcast Information Service, *Daily Report–Central Eurasia (FBIS–SOV),* FBIS-SOV-98-217, 5 Aug. 1998.

[14] Sokut, S., 'New tailor assigned to patch defence industry's threadbare coat', *Nezavisimoye Voyennoye Obozreniye,* 31 July–6 Aug. 1998, pp. 1, 6, in FBIS-SOV-98-233, 21 Aug. 1998.

[15] See chapter 4 in this volume. The 'Concept for military organizational development in the Russian Federation in the period through 2005' drafted by the Armed Forces General Staff establishes that during the period of restructuring in 1998–2000 normal supplies should be provided, while in 2001–2005 the industry should embark on accelerated weapon modernization. Urinson, Yu. (former Russian Minister for the Economy), 'The command has been given: get the defence sector back on its feet. On the restructuring and conversion of the defence industry', *Rossiyskaya Gazeta,* 30 Dec. 1997, p. 5, in Foreign Broadcast Information Service, *Daily Report–Central Asia: Military Affairs (FBIS–UMA),* FBIS-UMA-98-008, 8 Jan. 1998.

[16] Interview with First Deputy Prime Minister Yuriy Maslyukov, *Krasnaya Zvezda,* 1 Dec. 1998.

increased to more than $3 billion in 1995 and 1996 but declined in 1997 to $2.5 billion and was forecast to have declined further by the end of 1998.[17]

The decline in the military market was not compensated for by an increase in civilian sales. On the contrary, the civilian sales of the defence industry were also falling—by over 70 per cent in the period 1991–96 (table 10.2). No data have been provided on the civilian output of the defence industry in 1997 and 1998. However, since total defence industry output fell in 1998 while its military component rose slightly, civilian output must have continued to fall. Federal conversion programmes were adopted for 1992–95 and 1995–97, but were largely underfunded. Actual appropriations for conversion accounted for only 25 per cent of funds budgeted in 1995 and in 1996 for a minute 11 per cent; in 1997 no funds at all were actually appropriated.[18] Instead, the main source of funding for investment in conversion was industry and banks.[19]

Institutional framework

In 1997 a programme was drafted for a dramatic restructuring of the Russian arms industry. The Federal Programme for Restructuring and Conversion of the Defence Industry for the years 1998–2000 was prepared in late 1997 by the Ministry of the Economy, which assumed responsibility for the defence industries in 1997.[20] This draft programme included plans for a significant reduction of the number of arms-producing enterprises, from around 1700 to 670 by the year 2000 and by a further 35 enterprises by 2005. This reduction was to be achieved through the rationalization of arms production, primarily through vertical integration within industrial sectors and a limited number of horizontal mergers.[21] The programme also included funding and support for conversion to civil production. A Government Commission for the Financial Improvement of the Defence Industry Organizations was established in February 1998 to facilitate implementation of the programme.[22] In March 1998 a Federal Law on Defence Industry Conversion was adopted by the State Duma.[23] The cost of the programme over the period 1998–2000 was estimated

[17] Perera, J., 'Rosvooruzhenie exposed', *Jane's Intelligence Pointer*, Nov. 1998, p. 4. According to SIPRI arms transfer data, the value of Russian exports of major weapons was roughly constant in 1998. See chapter 11 in this volume. The same chapter has a discussion of the reliability of official Russian data on arms exports.

[18] Urinson (note 15).

[19] Bonn International Center for Conversion (BICC), *Conversion Survey 1998: Global Disarmament, Defence Industry Consolidation and Conversion* (Oxford University Press: Oxford, 1998), p. 110.

[20] The responsibility for the management of the defence industries was with the Ministry of Industry in 1991–92, with the Committee on the Defence Industry in 1992–93, with the State Committee on the Defence Industry in 1993–96, and with the Ministry of the Defence Industry in 1996–97, and has been with the Ministry of Economics since 1997.

[21] Saradzhyan, S., 'Russian firms to form radar conglomerate', *Defence News*, 24–30 Aug. 1998, p. 16; and Saradzhyan, S., 'Official offers radical Russian industry restructuring plan', *Defence News*, 16–22 Nov. 1998, p. 24.

[22] 'On the formation of a government commission on the financial improvement of defence industry organizations', Decree no. 191, 15 Feb. 1998, *Rossiyskaya Gazeta*, 3 Mar. 1998, p. 6, FBIS-SOV-98-070, 11 Mar. 1998.

[23] 'On conversion of the defence industry in the Russian Federation', Law of the Russian Federation adopted by the State Duma on 20 Mar. 1998, ratified by the Federation Council on 1 Apr. 1998 and

at around 25.5 billion roubles (in 1998 prices), of which around half was to be allocated from the federal budget.[24]

The draft programme was formulated before the culmination of the Russian financial and economic crisis in August 1998. The crisis exacerbated long-standing budget constraints which will probably reduce the possibilities of implementing the programme. The devaluation of the rouble may have an economic impact on the arms industry in two ways: it may contribute to increase exports in the short term, but it will also reduce the real value of state indebtedness to the arms industry.[25]

Within the government of Prime Minister Yevgeny Primakov, which came to power in the aftermath of the financial crisis, the minister responsible for economic and industrial policy, First Deputy Prime Minister Yuriy Maslyukov, has shown a strong interest in the defence industry.[26] In October 1998 the government created a new Commission on Military and Technical Cooperation with Foreign States, chaired by Maslyukov, with the task of overseeing Russian arms sales abroad.[27] The organization of Russian arms exports are largely centralized under Rosvooruzheniye, allowing for a high degree of control. A more decentralized approach giving individual arms-producing companies greater autonomy has been advocated by the industry in order to avoid the bureaucratic hurdles of a centralized system.[28] However, no major changes to the system had been introduced by the new government by January 1999.

IV. Restructuring in the USA and Western Europe

The USA

The decline in the demand for military equipment has been very sharp in the USA, much sharper than in Europe. Department of Defense (DOD) outlays for procurement of military equipment decreased by 58 per cent over fiscal years (FYs) 1987–97, while outlays for research, development, testing and evaluation (RDT&E) fell by around 22 per cent over the same period.[29] This trend will change from FY 1998 onward: planned procurement expenditure for the period FYs 1999–2005 will increase by 37 per cent in real terms.[30]

signed by the President of the Russian Federation on 13 Apr. 1998, No. 60-FZ. For the text, see *Rossiyskaya Gazeta,* 15 Apr. 1998, p. 4, in FBIS-SOV-98-118, 28 Apr. 1998.

[24] Urinson (note 15).

[25] Saradzyhan, S., 'Russian defence industry enjoys temporary boost from ruble crisis', *Defense News,* 14–20 Sep. 1998, p. 38.

[26] Harter, S., *Die Russische Rüstungsindustrie: Eine Bestandaufnahme,* Aktuelle Analysen (Bundes-institut für ostwissenschaftliche und internationale Studien, Cologne, 19 Oct. 1998).

[27] 'Issues of RF military–technical cooperation with foreign states', Edict no. 1488, 7 Dec. 1998, *Rossiyskaya Gazeta,* 15 Dec. 1998, p. 4, in FBIS-UMA-99-004, 4 Jan. 1999.

[28] For a discussion of the Russian arms export system, see Denezhkina (note 12), pp. 133–35.

[29] US Office of Management and Budget, URL <http://www.access.gpo.gov/su_docs/budget/index.html>. These are the official US Government expenditure figures. NATO data on US expenditure on military equipment show a less rapid decline. See appendix 7B in this volume.

[30] See chapter 7, table 7.3 in this volume.

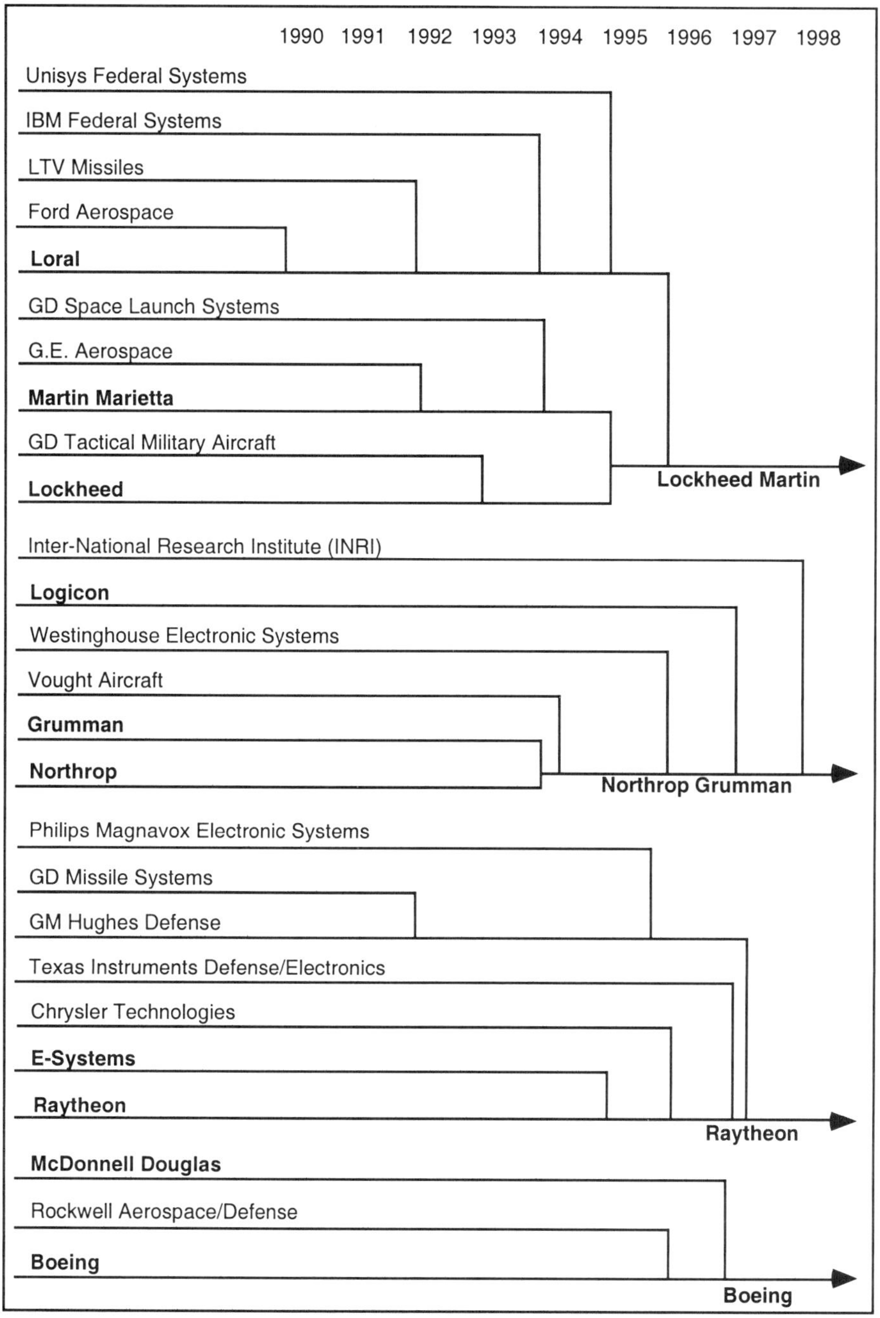

Figure 10.1. US aerospace industry consolidation

Note: Companies in bold are parent companies.

Source: adapted from *Aviation Week & Space Technology*, 16 Mar. 1998, p. 25.

Table 10.3. US companies whose arms sales changed the most, 1993–97

Figures are in US $m., current prices. Figures in italics are percentages.

		Arms sales			Arms sales share (%)		
Company	Sector, 1997	1993	1997	Change	1993	1997	Change
Companies with the largest increase in arms sales[a]							
Boeing	Ac El Mi	3 800	14 500	10 700	15	32	*17*
Lockheed Martin[b]	Ac El Mi	10 070	18 500	8 430	77	66	*– 11*
Northrop Grumman[c]	Ac El Mi SA/O	4 480	7 210	2 730	89	79	*– 10*
TRW	Comp (El MV)	2 790	3 800	1 010	35	35	*0*
General Dynamics	MV Sh	3 000	3 650	650	94	90	*– 4*
Tracor	Comp (Ac El Mi)	320	930	610	46	74	*28*
General Motors	El Eng Mi	6 900	7 450	550	5	4	*– 1*
Companies with the largest fall in arms sales[a]							
Rockwell Internat.	El Mi	3 350	540	– 2 810	31	7	*– 24*
Texas Instruments	El	1 840	810	– 1 030	22	8	*– 14*
General Electric	Eng	2 400	1 500	– 900	4	2	*– 2*
United Technol.	El Eng	4 200	3 310	– 890	20	13	*– 7*
Textron	Ac El Eng MV	1 600	1 000	– 600	18	9	*– 9*
GTE	El	1 100	730	– 370	6	3	*– 3*
Gencorp	El Eng	850	520	330	45	33	*– 12*

[a] This table includes the 7 US companies in the top 100 list for 1997 whose arms sales increased and decreased the most (in absolute value, not percentage) between 1993 and 1997.

[b] Lockheed Martin in 1997 is compared to Lockheed in 1993.

[c] Northrop Grumman in 1997 is compared to Northrop in 1993.

Source: SIPRI arms industry database.

Restructuring in the US arms industry has resulted in major changes among the largest arms-producing companies. Some have expanded their arms sales to unprecedented levels; others have sold off their military production or been acquired by other companies (table 10.3). The four largest arms-producing companies in 1998 are the end-product of a process of mergers and acquisitions during the period since 1990, involving the absorption of at least 22 large companies (figure 10.1).

The number of large-scale mergers and acquisitions seems to have passed its peak among the top US prime contractors, while among subcontractors it has led to increased pressure for economies of scale and scope.[31] The planned merger between Lockheed Martin and Northrop Grumman was abandoned in July 1998 because of anti-trust concerns on the part of the DOD and the Justice Department, which argued that the merger would have seriously reduced competition in military electronics and in particular in electronic warfare, airborne early-warning radar, and naval and undersea warfare.[32] The

[31] Advantages derived from 2nd- and 3rd-tier concentration are discussed in 'L-3: a model for second tier consolidation', *Jane's Defence Industry*, Oct. 1998, pp. 3–4.

[32] US Department of Defense, 'Department of Defense completes review and says it opposes proposed merger of Lockheed Martin–Northrop Grumman', News Release no. 125-98 (703)695-0192 (media), 23 Mar. 1998.

merger would have created a horizontally and vertically integrated aerospace company with a total turnover of around $37 billion, of which up to 70 per cent would have been arms production.

Among smaller arms-producing companies there were continued mergers and acquisition activities during 1997 and 1998. At the level of second- and third-tier companies acquisitions are also enhanced by the divestiture of competing business units by large military contractors in order to elude anti-trust concerns (Raytheon) or in order to focus on their core business areas (Lockheed Martin).

The impact of restructuring on employment, costs and competition

Restructuring and downsizing have resulted in continued employment cuts. The DOD forecast that defence-related industrial employment would fall from around 2.7 million in 1993 to around 2.1 million by the end of 1998, or by around 22 per cent.[33] There will be further cuts in the near future. During 1998 there were several announcements of lay-offs in arms production, including 14 000 by Raytheon as a result of the closure of 20 plants, 10 500 by Northrop Grumman (4300 resulting from the completion of production of B-2 bombers) and up to 2500 in missiles and space at Lockheed Martin.

The process of concentration has been supported by the DOD with the aim of achieving savings in weapon costs through rationalization of production. Since 1993 the DOD has therefore provided the opportunity for companies to write off their restructuring costs against military contracts. During the period 1993–97 the DOD share of certified restructuring costs for seven major mergers and acquisitions was $765 million, with the forecast that this would result in DOD savings in weapon acquisitions of more than $4 billion over five years.[34] Such savings are, however, difficult to identify. In a 1998 review, the US General Accounting Office concluded that estimating savings derived from industry restructuring is inherently difficult, and DOD estimates of savings include some which may not be directly related to restructuring. Moreover, the impact of the estimated savings from restructuring on the DOD's budget requirements has been limited.[35]

Savings in weapon costs through rationalization measures must be weighed against the negative effect of tendencies to monopolistic pricing. The overall impact on competition in arms production is still not possible to assess. One possible negative impact is that the dominant market position of single arms producers may increase their strength in relation to the DOD.[36] It is clear that the dominant position of top arms-producing companies among DOD prime

[33] US General Accounting Office (GAO), *Defence Industry Restructuring: Updated Cost and Savings Information,* Report to Congressional Committees, GAO/NSIAD-98-156, Apr. 1998, pp. 6–7.

[34] Cohen, S. W., Secretary of Defense, 'Industrial capabilities and international programs', *Annual Report to the President and the Congress, 1998* (US Government Printing Office: Washington, DC, 1998), p. 180.

[35] US General Accounting Office (note 33), pp. 9–11.

[36] Hartung, W. D., *Military–Industrial Complex Revisited: How Weapons Makers are Shaping US Foreign and Military Policies* (Interhemispheric Resource Center: Albequerque, and Institute for Policy Studies: Washington, DC, Nov. 1998), URL <http://www.foreignpolicy-infocus.org/papers/micr>.

contractors has increased: the five companies receiving the largest DOD prime contract awards accounted for 29.9 per cent of total contract awards in FY 1998 as compared to 21.6 per cent in FY 1990, and the single company receiving the largest award accounted for 10 per cent in FY 1998 as compared to 6.3 per cent in FY 1990.[37]

The rate of concentration varies between sectors. The reduction in the number of prime contractors in the period 1990–98 has been strongest in tactical missiles, fixed-wing aircraft and space launch vehicles. Sectors with a relatively high number of prime contractors by early 1998 included shipbuilding, satellites and military vehicles.[38] In shipbuilding this may change as a result of a merger in late 1998 and another merger proposed in early 1999, which would reduce the number of prime contractors from five to three.[39]

In an effort to maintain competition between merged or acquired units within the same company, artificial techniques have been adopted, including the establishment of 'firewalls' and the selling off of competing business units.[40] Agreed standards in the design of weapon systems, or open systems architecture, also aim to help a wider range of subsystem suppliers to participate in the production process. The reduction in the numbers of military contractors to a few large ones will increase the need for monitoring and regulation of arms production.[41]

Western Europe

While the process of concentration of the West European arms industry has been relatively slow during most of the 1990s, because it was difficult to achieve cross-border integration, there were many indications during 1998 that the industry is headed towards greater European integration and that this is increasingly supported by most governments. The trend towards international company formations continued in aerospace and electronics and is

[37] US Department of Defense, Directorate for Information Operations and Reports, *100 Companies Receiving the Largest Dollar Volume of Prime Contract Awards, Fiscal Year 1998* (US Government Printing Office: Washington, DC, 1999); and *100 Companies Receiving the Largest Dollar Volume of Prime Contract Awards, Fiscal Year 1990* (US Government Printing Office: Washington, DC, 1991).

[38] US General Accounting Office (GAO), *Defence Industry Consolidation: Competitive Effects of Mergers and Acquisitions*, Testimony Before the Subcommittee on Acquisition and Technology, Committee on Armed Services, US Senate, GAO/NSIAD-98-112, 4 Mar. 1998.

[39] General Dynamics, owner of Bath Iron Works, acquired NASSCO, and the proposed merger was between Newport News and Avondale Industries. The 3rd US naval shipbuilding contractor is Litton.

[40] Firewalls are 'arrangements created by a company to limit or prevent the exchange of competition sensitive information among parts of the company'. US General Accounting Office (GAO), *Defence Industry: Consolidation and Options for Preserving Competition*, Report to Congressional Committees, GAO/NSIAD-98-141, Apr. 1998.

[41] Eric Pages, Vice-President for Policy and Programs, Business Executives for National Security (BENS), calls for tighter regulation and guaranteed subsidies for 'defence-unique firms'. Pages, E., 'The new defence monopolies: Is the Pentagon ready to treat US defence conglomerates like privately owned arsenals?', *Armed Forces Journal*, July 1998, pp. 26–28. According to others, the consolidated US arms industry can and should be allowed to be fully integrated in the wider national industrial base, mainly through the deregulation of military-specific acquisition rules and standards. Center for Strategic and International Studies (CSIS), Senior Policy Panel on the US Defense Industrial Base, *Defence Restructuring and the Future of the US Defense Industrial Base*, Mar. 1998, URL <http://www.csis.org/html/dib report.html>.

also beginning to speed up in military vehicles and ordnance and ammunition; moves towards the formation of transnational defence companies were more determined; several steps were taken towards the privatization and concentration of the French arms industry, partly removing the main obstacles to European integration; and the governments of the major arms-producing countries became more active in calling for an integrated European arms industry. It also became increasingly clear during 1998 that European industrial integration does not preclude closer transatlantic military industrial links. On the contrary, British interest in transatlantic links appears rather to have been reinforced by the slow rate of progress in West European integration.

Although European integration is likely to move faster during the next few years, this cannot be expected to be a smooth process. The French position is still rather different from the British and German as regards the concrete measures required, and negotiations between companies and governments to assure a fair distribution of costs and benefits will be complicated. However, European companies and governments feel that time is running out and will be hard pressed to come to some crucial decisions during 1999.

Employment in arms production in France, Germany and the United Kingdom (the major West European arms-producing countries) fell by roughly 29 per cent, 64 per cent and 27 per cent, respectively, in the period 1990–97,[42] and further job cuts were announced in 1998.

Continued internationalization

Cross-border activities continued during 1997 and 1998 through mergers and acquisitions and the formation of new joint ventures and consortia (table 10.4). While much of the debate centred around the discussion about creating a Europe-wide aerospace and defence company, there were also substantial activities in other areas, in particular in military electronics. The high content of electronics in all weapon systems and the increasing interdependence between military and civilian development and production make military electronics the most dynamic arms industrial sector. Merger and acquisition activities among West European military electronics companies mainly assumed the form of takeovers of military electronic companies by platform producers as a means to increase systems integration capabilities, the largest and most recent being the proposed merger of the military electronics branch of GEC with British Aerospace (BAe).[43]

[42] In 1997 total employment in arms production (direct and indirect) amounted to 250 000 in France, 100 000 in Germany and 320 000 in the UK. (The UK figure is 'employment dependent on equipment expenditures'.) Lewis, J. A. C., 'Three French unions join in battle against '98 cuts', *Jane's Defence Weekly,* 27 Aug. 1997, p. 19; Bundesverband der Deutschen Luft-, Raum- und Ausrüstungsindustrie (BDLI), in *German Brief,* 9 Jan. 1998, p. 10; and British Ministry of Defence, *UK Defence Statistics 1998* (Government Statistical Office: Norwich, 1998), p. 17.

[43] The merger is subject to approval by anti-trust authorities in the UK and the European Commission and may also be subject to approval by US anti-trust authorities given the large share of US businesses in GEC.

Table 10.4. Cross-border joint ventures in the West European arms industry, January 1998–January 1999

Company (parent company), country (share)	Joint venture company,[a] activities	Comments
Aircraft		
British Aerospace, UK (50%) Dassault Aviation, France (50%)	*European Aerosystems* Research on fighter aircraft	Formed Sep. 1998
Agusta (Finmeccanica), Italy GKN Westland (GKN), UK	Helicopters	Under discussion. MOU Apr. 1998
Missiles		
Bofors (Celsius), Sweden (33%) LFK (DASA), Germany (67%)	*Taurus Systems* Missiles	Announced Aug. 1998
Space		
DASA, Germany GEC, UK Largardère, France	Space	Agreed Dec. 1998; 11 000 employees. $3 b. total sales. Plans to include Finmeccanica, Italy
Electronics		
Racal Electronics, UK (50%) Thomson-CSF, France (50%)	*MBN Limited* Communication systems	Agreed Sep. 1998
Alenia Difesa, Italy (50%) GEC-Marconi, UK (50%)	*Alenia Marconi Systems* Ground, naval, missile systems, air traffic control systems	Formed Dec. 1998; 9500 employees $1.7 b. total sales
Shipbuilding		
DCN, France (50%) Kockums (Celsius), Sweden (50%)	Research on future submarines	Announced Aug. 1998
Ammunition		
Rheinmetall, Germany (51%) Swiss Munitions Enterprise, Switzerland (49%)	*Nitrochemie* Ammunition	Established Jan. 1998 500 + 200 employees $68 m. + $30 m. total sales
Celsius, Sweden (27.5%) Patria, Finland (27.5%) Raufoss, Norway (27.5%)	*Nammo* Ammunition	Formed Oct. 1998 1400 employees $210 m. total sales
Military vehicles		
GIAT Industries, France GKN, UK Krauss Maffei (Mannesmann), Germany Wegmann, Germany	*Armoured Technology* Multirole armoured vehicle MRAV/VBT/GTK	Under discussion
GIAT Industries, France Vickers, UK	Land systems; only design, development and sales	MOU Jan. 1999

[a] Names of joint venture companies are given in italics where known.

MOU = memorandum of understanding.

Source: SIPRI arms industry files.

European production of military vehicles has remained fragmented, even on the national level. According to one count, there were 37 producers of military vehicles and artillery systems in Western Europe in 1998.[44] In the SIPRI database there were three armoured vehicle manufacturers in France (GIAT, Panhard and Renault) in 1998, four in Germany (Henschel, Krauss-Maffei, Rheinmetall and Wegmann) and three in the UK (Alvis, GKN and Vickers).[45] Counts are difficult to make and depend on the definition of vehicle used, but they do indicate the structure of the industry. However, during 1997 and 1998 there was also significantly more concentration in this sector, which is forecast to be strongly influenced by the changing demand for military vehicles.

The ordnance and ammunition sector is undergoing significant changes which pass relatively unnoticed because companies are comparatively small, often entirely focused on military production, and not, as in the case of most other military production, part of large companies that also engage in civilian production. This sector is strongly affected by declining domestic demand and competition from low-cost production in Israel, Portugal and South Africa.

Towards a European Aerospace and Defence Company

The debate about cross-border integration in Western Europe in 1998 was most advanced in the aerospace sector and centred around the negotiations for the formation of a European Aerospace and Defence Company (EADC). In March 1998 the partner companies in Airbus Industrie (Aérospatiale, BAe, CASA and Daimler-Chrysler)[46] agreed in principle to the formation of a unified EADC, which in addition to existing Airbus activities would include military aircraft, helicopters, missiles and space activities. The agreement left unresolved the issues of the inclusion of regional aircraft, satellites and ballistic missile production, as well as the ownership structure and the timetable for a future merger.

In July 1998 negotiations were extended to include the aerospace companies of Italy (Finmeccanica) and Sweden (Saab). The six governments involved (France, Germany, Italy, Spain, Sweden and the UK) together called on their main aerospace companies to produce a draft of the shareholder structure and process of integration of a future EADC. Although their industry ministers agreed that governments should have no direct influence on the management of a future EADC, they agreed that the company should remain a European enterprise and not divest itself of defence-related assets without government approval. Moreover, they recognized the need for appropriate export assis-

[44] Barre, D. and Hoschouer, J., 'Armor may not yield to Europe consolidation', *Defense News*, 31 Aug.–6 Sep. 1998, pp. 10, 20.

[45] In Nov. 1998 the military vehicle business of GKN merged with Alvis.

[46] Airbus Industrie was established in 1970 as a Groupement d'Intérêt Économique (GIE)—a company which makes no profits or losses in its own right. The distribution of shares among the partner companies was as follows by the end of 1998: Aérospatiale 37.9%, Daimler-Chrysler Aerospace 37.9%, British Aerospace 20% and CASA 4.2%. The transformation from a GIE into a unified European company was in 1998 further delayed to mid- or late 1999.

Table 10.5. Partner companies in Airbus Industrie and other potential partners in a European Aerospace and Defence Company (EADC), December 1998

Company, country, share in Airbus	Arms sales 1997 (US $m.)	Ownership structure	Sector
Partner companies in Airbus			
BAe, UK (20%)	10 410	90.7% individuals	Fighter, transport and patrol aircraft; missiles; space; electronics; land systems
DASA, Germany (37.9%)	2 820	Subsid. of Daimler-Chrysler Benz (Germany/USA)	Fighter and transport aircraft; helicopters; missiles; space; electronics; engines
Aérospatiale, France (37.9%)	1 990	100% state[a]	Transport and patrol aircraft; helicopters; missiles
CASA, Spain (4.2%)	350	Subsidiary of SEPI state holding co.[b]	Fighter and transport aircraft; space
Other potential partner companies in EADC			
Finmeccanica, Italy	2 410	Subsidiary of IRI, state holding co.[b]	Fighter and transport aircraft; helicopters; missiles; space; electronics; land systems
Dassault Aviation, France	1 870	49.9% Dassault Industries, 46% Aérospatiale[c]	Fighter aircraft
Saab, Sweden	670	20% Investor (36% votes) 35% BAe (35% votes) 45% individuals	Fighter aircraft; missiles

[a] Aérospatiale is to be merged with Matra Haute Technologies. See table 10.6.
[b] The government is planning the privatization of the company.
[c] A merger between Dassault Aviation and a future Aérospatiale/MHT is under discussion.

Source: SIPRI arms industry database, SIPRI arms industry files.

tance to a future EADC.[47] In their November 1998 response, the companies agreed to include satellite and regional aircraft production in a future EADC. They also agreed that the company management should be free from interference by national governments, except for 'the protection of 'specific strategic interests', such as French ballistic missile activities.[48] They did not, however, reach agreement on the distribution of shares in a unified company. The ownership and military programmes of the partner companies in Airbus and potential partner companies in EADC are summarized in table 10.5.

The pace of integration is largely dependent on developments within the mainly state-owned French arms industry because Germany and the UK have made private ownership a fundamental requirement for their participation in an EADC and view state ownership as a likely obstacle to the necessary indus-

[47] Joint Declaration by the Ministers of France, Germany, Spain, Sweden and the United Kingdom on the European Restructuring of the Aerospace and Defence Industry, Paris, 9 July 1998.

[48] Neu, J. P., 'Manufacturers' consensus on European aeronautical and defence grouping', *Les Echos,* 17 Nov. 1998, p. 10, in Foreign Broadcast Information Service, *Daily Report–West Europe (FBIS-WEU)*, FBIS-WEU-98-321, 17 Nov. 1998.

trial restructuring after unification. The prospects for a balanced partnership in a future EADC changed, first when BAe and DASA in the autumn of 1998 began negotiations for a bilateral merger ahead of a joint agreement on the EADC, and more so in January 1999 when GEC agreed to merge its military electronics and naval shipbuilding business, Marconi Electronics Systems, with BAe.[49] This was a serious setback for the EADC concept.

Restructuring in France

Pressure has been increasing on the French Government to begin privatization and a fundamental restructuring of its arms industry, as first announced by President Jacques Chirac in February 1996. The reasons have been threefold: (*a*) to reduce the economic burden of French arms production; (*b*) to improve competitiveness in export markets; and (*c*) in recent years perhaps the most important factor, to avoid being left out of the process of European military industrial integration.

In mid-1998, after more than two years of discussion, the long-awaited process of national restructuring began to unfold, with several major decisions by the French Government: (*a*) to privatize its largest defence company, Thomson-CSF, which was followed by an agreement with Dassault Industrie for the transfer of its subsidiary, Dassault Électronique, in return for a 6 per cent share in Thomson-CSF; (*b*) to transfer its 46 per cent ownership in Dassault Aviation to Aérospatiale; and (*c*) to partly privatize Aérospatiale by merging it with Matra Haute Technologies (subsidiary of the private company Lagardère). This was followed by a series of agreements in December 1998 between the companies involved in the restructuring, setting out their respective responsibilities in the areas of avionics, missile systems and satellites. First, Aérospatiale sold off its 50 per cent share in Sextant Avionique to Thomson-CSF. Second, both Aérospatiale and Thomson-CSF will continue missile production. Third, in view of its planned merger with Matra Haute Technologies, Aérospatiale is not required to withdraw from the satellite business (table 10.6).[50]

Since the agreement on the partial privatization of Thomson-CSF in October 1997, the French Government has taken significant steps towards the privatization of its state-owned arms-producing companies. Privatization has, however, been only partial and the government continues to determine the pace of restructuring and of international integration.

[49] 'GEC deal with BAe creates aerospace giant', Press Association, 19 Jan. 1999, URL <http://www.pa.press.net/news/extra/city_bae.html>.

[50] 'Joint press release by Aérospatiale, Alcatel, Lagardère and Thomson-CSF: Agreement in avionics, missile systems and satellites', 9 Dec. 1998, URL <http://www.thomson-csf.com/anglais/actualite/communiques/courants/comm981209a.html>.

Table 10.6. Restructuring of the French arms industry, 1998

Company	Status	Ownership structure	Sector	Previously included in company
Thomson-CSF (new)	Implemented Sep. 1998	40% Thomson (state) 32.9% stock market 15.8% Alcatel Alsthom 5.8% Dassault Industrie 3.9% Aérospatiale 1.5% employees	Electronics, missiles	Aérospatiale, Alcatel, Dassault Electronique, Sextant Avionique (100%), Thomson CSF (33.3% of Eurosam)
Alcatel Space	Implemented July 1998	51% Alcatel Alsthom 49% Thomson-CSF	Space	Aérospatiale, Alcatel, Thomson-CSF
Aérospatiale/ Matra Haute Technologies (MHT)[a]	Agreed 15 Feb. 1999	47% state 33% Lagardère 20% stock market	Missiles, heli-copters, patrol aircraft, transport aircraft, space	Aérospatiale (33.3% of Euromissile, 33.3% of Eurosam), MHT (50% of Matra BAe Dynamics), Aérospatiale (70% of Eurocopter), MHT (51% of Matra Marconi Space)
Dassault Aviation[a]	Decided 15 May 1998	50% Dassault Industries 46% Aérospatiale	Fighter aircraft	Dassault Aviation

[a] A merger of the military production of Dassault Aviation with a future Aérospatiale/MHT was under discussion.

Source: SIPRI arms industry files.

Government initiatives

Throughout the 1990s European arms industry restructuring has been largely industry-led. Governments have tried to forge agreements on procurement and arms exports through international agreements and multilateral organizations but have failed to achieve much progress. Industry has tested the limits of existing rules on foreign ownership, competition and technology transfers and the European Commission has presented a series of initiatives[51] to remove obstacles to industrial integration by the application of European Union rules—on the award of public contracts, export controls, standardization, state aid and competition—to the military sector as well, which would mean that Article 223 of the Treaty of Rome would have to be annulled.[52]

[51] European Commission, 'The challenges facing the European defence-related industry: contribution for action at European level', COM (96) 10 final (the 'Bangemann report'), 25 Jan. 1996; and 'Implementing European Union strategy on defence-related industries', COM (97) 583 final, 12 Nov. 1997.

[52] Article 223 states that any member state 'may take such measures as it considers necessary for the protection of the essential interests of its security which are connected with the production of or trade in arms, munitions and war material'.

Two events during 1998 indicate that there was a slight change towards a stronger government role in the integration of the West European arms industry. First, in July 1998 the defence ministers of the six major West European arms-producing countries (France, Germany, Italy, Spain, Sweden and the UK) reached agreement on principles for a 'cooperative framework to facilitate the restructuring of the European arms industry' and on the adoption of specific arrangements required for their 'effective application' before the end of 1999.[53] The most important of these referred to the establishment of a Transnational Defence Company (TDC), in the first place in aerospace, and included principles for: (*a*) the security of supply of military equipment for countries which would have to abandon domestic production; (*b*) the facilitation of exports between the participants in defence articles and services; (*c*) security provisions for classified information in a TDC; (*d*) sharing of the costs and benefits of military research and technology; and (*e*) the harmonization of rules on disclosure and use of technical information, and military requirements.

The second event was the signing in September 1998 of a treaty by which the Organisme Conjoint de Coöpération en Matière d'Armement (OCCAR), a joint armaments cooperation organization, was given the legal authority to autonomously manage collaborative projects and issue procurement orders to industry.[54] By the end of 1998, OCCAR was responsible for the management of four collaborative programmes (the Tiger helicopter and the Hot, Milan and Roland missiles), while four additional programmes were being discussed. OCCAR was founded in November 1996, primarily because of difficulties in reaching agreement on a future European Armaments Agency (EAA). Its member countries are the four largest of the 13 members of the Western European Union (WEU)—France, Germany, Italy and the UK. It is open to new members, but becoming a member is a complicated process.

A renewed effort to revive the momentum for an EAA was made within the WEU during 1998. A report by the WEU Defence Committee in November 1998, the Colvin Report,[55] recommended the establishment of an EAA within a WEU framework, with OCCAR to be granted the status of a WEU subsidiary body in order to allow all WEU countries to participate in the longer term.[56] The report acknowledged, however, that no decision could be reached before the three remaining disagreements were resolved: on *juste retour*; on the pooling of industrial and technological capabilities; and on the autonomy of the EAA.

[53] *Measures to Facilitate the Restructuring of European Defence Industry,* Letter of Intent between the defence ministers of France, Germany, Italy, Spain, Sweden and the United Kingdom, London, 6 July 1998.

[54] 'European defence ministers sign new arms procurement organization treaty', 9 Sep. 1998, *UK Ministry of Defence News*, URL <http://www.mod.uk/news/prs/225_98.htm>.

[55] 'European armaments restructuring and the role of WEU', Report submitted on behalf of the Defence Committee by Mr Colvin, Rapporteur, Assembly of Western European Union, WEU document 1623, 9 Nov. 1998.

[56] 'European defence ministers sign new arms procurement organization treaty' (note 53), p. 4.

Transatlantic military industrial links

The rapid rate of military industrial concentration in the United States and the efforts in Western Europe to combine military technological and industrial resources gave rise to debate during 1997 and 1998 about a possible future transatlantic divide in arms procurement and the development of two military industrial 'fortresses'. There are, however, strong interests on both sides of the Atlantic in resisting this: (*a*) the strong traditional links between US and British, and to a lesser extent between US and German and Italian, companies, strengthened by the delay in French privatization;[57] (*b*) the interests of US companies in avoiding the development of a 'fortress Europe';[58] and (*c*) the requirement for interoperability in the equipment of NATO member countries. Continued concentration on both sides of the Atlantic is thus concurrent with a process of wider internationalization of arms production.

While previously the predominant form for transatlantic military industrial ties was government armaments collaboration projects, with European companies often in a subordinate position, in 1998 the debate extended to company integration. The major British and German arms-producing companies were involved in merger and acquisition activities and plans with companies in the USA. The German Daimler Benz, parent company of Daimler-Benz Aerospace, merged with the US company Chrysler,[59] and the British GEC purchased the US military electronics company Tracor in 1998.[60] BAe, GEC and Daimler-Chrysler Aerospace showed interest in acquiring units left over from the proposed (but never implemented) Northrop Grumman–Lockheed Martin merger and continued their interest in US arms-producing companies after the merger agreement had been withdrawn.[61]

The acquisition of Tracor by GEC gained swift approval by the Committee on Foreign Investment in the United States (CFIUS).[62] The US industry was, however, awaiting the formulation of a clear political framework.[63] In response to the intense debate in the industry on transatlantic mergers and acquisitions, and in particular to the European interest in acquiring US arms-producing companies, the US Government initiated a policy review. In 1998 Defense Secretary William Cohen formed two special panels to consider the impact of the internationalization of the arms industry on technology and

[57] 'Cohen, Robertson discuss defence industry rationalisation', *Defence Systems Daily,* 20 Nov. 1998, URL <http://defence-data.com/current/page3281.htm>.

[58] A view expressed by the Chief Executive Officer of Lockheed Martin. Nicoll, A., 'Lockheed chief warns of risks of a "fortress Europe"', *Financial Times,* 30 Oct. 1998, p. 5.

[59] Chrysler had sold off its military business in 1995.

[60] The takeover was agreed in Apr. 1998 for a price of £833 million, or $1.4 billion. *Air Forces Monthly,* June 1998, p. 2. Tracor had arms sales of more than $900 million in 1997.

[61] 'Northrop open to European alliance', *Financial Times,* 8 Sep. 1998, p. 23; 'DASA targets foreign acquisitions', *Air Letter,* 27 May 1998, p. 1; and Gow, D., 'GEC aims to buy into US arms sector', *The Guardian,* 3 July 1998, p. 18.

[62] The CFIUS had in 1992 opposed the Thomson-CSF takeover bid for LTV Corporation. Finnegan, P., 'US officials give quick nod to GEC's buy of Tracor Inc.', *Defense News,* 15–21 June 1998, p. 8.

[63] Hitchens, T. and Barrie, D., 'Defense executives are sceptical about transatlantic firms: Pentagon resistance stymieing effort', *Defense News,* 21–27 Sep. 1998, p. 12.

security: one on globalization and security under the aegis of the Defense Science Board and led by Jacques Gansler; and one on the globalization of business and industry under the Defense Policy Board and led by Deputy Secretary of Defense John Hamre. The first panel addressed in particular the implications for US security of the increasing reliance on foreign subcontractors and on civilian components, and of foreign ownership of US arms-producing companies, while the second was concerned with the general commercial and economic impact of globalization.

The new US interest in setting up a clear political framework derived not only from the industry's need to anticipate political responses to its activities but also from the government's need to monitor and regulate the process, in particular to guarantee security of supply and to control the transfer of technology. The concentration of arms production, particularly internationally, may result in a shift of leverage from government to industry through reduced competition and diminished possibilities of regulation.[64] The internationalization of arms production therefore increases the need for political control.

V. The global structure of arms production

The restructuring which has taken place in the arms industries of most countries since the late 1980s is likely to have brought about major changes in the volume and structure of world arms production. It is clear that the reduction in arms production in most countries must have resulted in cuts in global arms production. It is also likely that the global distribution of arms production has changed considerably because the rate of reduction has varied greatly between countries. There is, however, not much information available about the extent and nature of these changes. This section presents the scarce information which it has been possible to compile.

Many countries do not provide any information at all on national arms production. Those which do provide data provide approximate figures and use different definitions of what is included in arms production. Since military equipment is not a separate category in industrial and trade statistics, there are no detailed or precise statistics available in any country. Any presentation of national, regional and global arms production therefore has to resort to estimates.

There are two types of estimates of national arms production, depending on method of calculation, one based on the sum of arms sales by arms-producing companies in the country, the other based on government expenditure on arms procurement and military R&D plus arms exports and minus arms imports. The estimates provided by governments are of both types. The second type of data is often also provided by national defence industry associations. Although there is always a difference between the two types, it is not big enough to

[64] Markusen, A., *Should We Welcome a Transnational Defense Industry?* (Council on Foreign Relations: New York, Oct. 1998), p. 2.

Table 10.7. Arms production 1996: the 10 largest arms-producing countries excluding China

Figures are in US $b., current prices. Figures in italics are percentages.

Country	Arms production estimates based on Procurement data[a]	Company data[b]	Arms prod. as share of world total	Arms exports[c] as share of production
USA	95	. .	*46–49*	Medium
UK	20	. .	*10*	Very high
France	20.5	19	*9–10*	High
Japan	9	. .	*4–5*	Low
Germany	. .	8	*4*	Medium
Russia	7–9	. .	*3–4*	Very high
Italy	3.5	4	*2*	Medium
Canada	. .	3.8	*2*	High
South Korea	. .	3.7	*2*	Low
Israel	. .	3.5	*2*	Very high
Total of 10	**170–180**	**170–180**	***80–90***	
Total world	**195–205**	**195–205**	***100***	

[a] Data are for government expenditures on arms procurement and military R&D plus arms exports minus arms imports.

[b] Data are for the sum of arms sales in the national arms industry as provided by national government organizations or defence industry associations. In a few cases data are SIPRI estimates for aggregate arms sales by companies within the country.

[c] Data on arms exports are from reports by governments and defence industry associations. Export share categories: low, 0–9%; medium, 10–19%; high, 20–39%; very high, ≥ 40%.

Sources:

USA: Procurement: US Office of Management and Budget, *The Budget of the United States Government: Historical Tables* (annual). Exports: US DOD, Directorate for Information Operations and Reports (DIOR), *Foreign Military Sales, Foreign Military Construction Sales and Military Assistance Facts, as of 30 Sep. 1996.*

UK: British Ministry of Defence, *UK Defence Statistics* (Government Statistical Service: London 1997); and Society of British Aerospace Companies (SBAC), URL <http:www.sbac.co.uk/infeb98c.htm>.

France: Assemblée Nationale, *Rapport fait au nom de la commission des finances, de l'économie générale et du plan sur la projet de loi de finances pour 1998 (n° 230),* annexe 40, 9 Oct. 1997, p. 75 (for procurement and R&D), and pp. 173–175 (for arms sales).

Japan: Japan Defense Agency, *Defense of Japan, 1996* (JDA: Tokyo, 1996), p. 300. Imports from the USA: US DOD, DIOR, *Foreign Military Sales, Foreign Military Construction Sales and Military Assistance Facts, as of 30 Sep. 1996*, pp. 16–17, and pp. 56–57.

Germany: Production: SIPRI arms industry database. Arms sales data are for 1995. Exports: German Ministry of the Economy, as reported in *SIPRI Yearbook 1998: Armaments, Disarmament and International Security* (Oxford University Press, Oxford 1998), table 8.5.

Russia: Cooper, J., 'The military expenditure of the USSR and the Russian Federation, 1987–97', *SIPRI Yearbook 1998,* p. 250. Rouble figures are converted to dollars by the use of a 1996 PPP of 3.6 roubles = $1. Exports: *SIPRI Yearbook 1998*, p. 308.

Italy: Procurement: Italian Ministero della Difesa, *Nota aggiuntiva allo stato di previsione per la difesa*, 1997. Arms sales: SIPRI estimate based on company data. Exports and imports:

Camera dei Deputati, *Relazione sulle operazioni autorizzate e svolte per il controllo dell'esportazione, importazione e transito dei materiali di armamento nonchè dell'esportazione e del transito dei prodotti ad alta technologia,* 1997, pp. 12–13.

Canada: Grover, B., *Canadian Defence Industry 1997: A Statistical Overview of the Canadian Defence Industry* (Canadian Defence Preparedness Association: Ottawa, 3 Nov. 1997), 2nd edn.

Israel: SIPRI arms industry database.

South Korea: South Korean Ministry of National Defense, *Defense White Paper, 1997–1998* (Ministry of National Defense: Seoul, 1998), p. 183.

affect a general illustration of the trends in and structure of worldwide military production.

These qualifications having been made, estimates of national arms production in 1996 in the 10 largest arms-producing countries are provided in table 10.7. This table excludes China for lack of sufficient information. If the share of arms procurement in total Chinese military expenditure is within the range of 15–30 per cent as it is in other major arms-producing countries, the value of Chinese arms production amounted to $2.25–4.50 billion in 1996.[65] However, since there is no firm basis for this assumption, this estimate is not used here.

The aggregate value of arms production in these 10 largest arms-producing countries (excluding China) is estimated at around $170–180 billion in 1996. The next 10 countries in size have annual arms production of $1 billion or more but less than $3 billion. These countries are Australia, China, India, the Netherlands, South Africa, Spain, Sweden, Switzerland, Taiwan and Turkey. Another 15 countries have annual arms production in the range of $200–$999 million. The majority of these are in Western Europe—Austria, Belgium, Denmark, Finland, Greece, Norway and Portugal. Their combined arms sales are estimated at around $2.5 billion in 1996. This group also includes countries in Central and Eastern Europe (the Czech Republic and Poland), Asia (North Korea, Pakistan and Singapore), the Middle East (Egypt and Iran) and South America (Brazil). In Africa only South Africa has a significant arms industry. On the basis of these rough estimates of arms production for the 35 largest arms-producing countries in the world, global arms production in 1996 is estimated at roughly $200 billion (± $5 billion) (in current prices).

These estimates point to a very strong concentration of world arms production. The 10 largest arms-producing countries worldwide accounted for close to 90 per cent of estimated world arms production in 1996 and the three largest arms-producing countries for around two-thirds.

The structure of world arms production has been altered by the changes which have taken place during the past 10-year period of military industrial restructuring and downsizing. This can be inferred from the differences

[65] Estimates of Chinese military expenditure and its components are provided in appendix 7D in this volume. Chinese military expenditure in 1996 is estimated as 124 billion yuan at current prices, which at the market exchange rate of 8.3 yuan to the dollar translates into around $15 billion, giving arms procurement of $2.25–4.50 billion, while expenditure for military RDT&E, estimated at roughly $1.2 billion (10 billion yuan) and net imports of $1.0 billion balance each other out.

Table 10.8. National arms production in the six major arms-producing countries, change 1990–96

Index: 1990 = 100 (constant prices).

Country	1990	1996
Russia[a]	100	10
Germany[b]	100	45
USA	100	60
France	100	70
Japan	100	90
United Kingdom	100	90

[a] Data are for the six-year period 1991–96.

[b] Data are for the six-year period 1990–95. (1990 includes former West Germany only.)

Source: Table 10.7 and SIPRI arms industry files. For Russia: table 10.2.

between countries in their rate of downsizing of arms production. The differences between the six major arms-producing countries during the period 1990–96 are shown in table 10.8. However, it is difficult to assess the scale of the changes worldwide.

Some tentative indications are provided by a comparison of national shares in world arms production with those made for the mid-1980s by Keith Krause.[66] These are not strictly comparable to those in table 10.7, the main difference being the absence of China, ranked as number five by Krause with estimated arms production of $5–10 billion. In the following comparison, China is excluded from Krause's figures to make them comparable with those in table 10.7. The degree of concentration found by Krause for the mid-1980s was in broad terms roughly similar to what it was in the mid-1990s: the 10 largest arms-producing countries accounted for 86–94 per cent of world arms production and the two largest for 65–73 per cent. However, there were differences in the structure of the industry and the composition was significantly different. In the mid-1980s the USA and the Soviet Union were by far the largest arms producers, accounting for roughly one-third each of world arms production, which was estimated to amount to around $260–290 billion. In 1996 the combined world share of the USA and Russia was around 50 per cent, with Russia accounting for only 4 per cent. Russian arms production cannot be compared to that of the mid-1980s Soviet Union, but the greater part of the facilities for arms production and military R&D in the Soviet Union was located on the territory of the current Russian Federation—75 and 90 per cent, respectively.[67]

This decline in the Russian share of arms production has resulted in increased shares for US and major West European producers, in spite of the

[66] Krause, K., *Arms and the State: Patterns of Military Production and Trade* (Cambridge University Press: Cambridge, 1992), pp. 93–97.

[67] Cooper, J., *Conversion of the Former Soviet Defence Industry* (Royal Institute of International Affairs: London, 1993), p. 5.

reductions in their actual output. Thus, in the mid-1980s, the next four countries in size apart from China—France, the UK, Germany and Japan—had much smaller shares than in 1996, ranging from 2–7 per cent, and together accounted for only 17 per cent of the world total, compared to approximately 30 per cent in 1996. In the mid-1980s there was one country in Central and Eastern Europe—Poland—among the 10 largest arms-producing countries. In 1996 the top 10 included two industrializing countries outside Europe—Israel and South Korea—which in the mid-1980s accounted for very small shares of the world total: 0.7 and 0.2 per cent, respectively.[68]

Most of the largest 10 arms-producing countries in table 10.7 are net exporters of weapons. These are the USA, Russia, France, Germany, Italy and the UK. Of the other countries in the table, Canada, Israel and South Korea import more weapons than they export while Japan is prohibited by its constitution from exporting military equipment. The degree of dependence on exports in total military production varies considerably. Only Japan and South Korea were dependent on exports for less than 10 per cent of total sales in 1996. The USA, which accounts for almost half of estimated total arms production in the world, has a huge domestic market, but exports still take a medium share in production, a proportion comparable to that in Germany or Italy. France and the UK have strongly supported the maintenance of national arms production capabilities through the promotion of exports. In 1996 their export dependence was approximately 30 and 45 per cent, respectively. Three countries were dependent on exports for 40 per cent or more of the national total—Israel, Russia and the UK.

[68] According to Krause, India was among the 10 largest arms-producing countries in the mid-1980s. However, this was probably the result of a different method of estimation, since according to recent estimates it is not likely that the level of India's arms production was so high in the mid-1980s.

Appendix 10A. The 100 largest arms-producing companies, 1997

ELISABETH SKÖNS, REINHILDE WEIDACHER and the SIPRI ARMS INDUSTRY NETWORK*

Table 10A contains information on the 100 largest arms-producing companies in the OECD and the developing countries ranked by their arms sales in 1997.[1] Companies with the designation *S* in the column for rank in 1996 are subsidiaries; their arms sales are included in the figure in column 6 for the holding company. Subsidiaries are listed in the position in which they would appear if they were independent companies. In order to facilitate comparison with data for the previous year, the rank order and arms sales figures for 1996 are also given. Where new data for 1996 have become available, this information is included in the table; thus the 1996 rank order and the arms sales figures for some companies which appeared in table 6E in the *SIPRI Yearbook 1998* have been revised.

Sources and methods

Sources of data. The data in the table are based on the following sources: company reports, a questionnaire sent to over 400 companies, and corporation news published in the business sections of newspapers, military journals and on the Internet. Company archives, marketing reports, government publication of prime contracts and country surveys were also consulted. In many cases exact figures on arms sales were not available, mainly because companies often do not report their arms sales or lump them together with other activities. Estimates were therefore made.

Definitions. Data on total sales, profits and employment are for the entire company, not for the arms-producing sector alone. Profit data are after taxes in all cases when the company provides such data. Employment data are either a year-end or a yearly average figure as reported by the company. Data are reported on the fiscal year basis reported by the company in its annual report.

Key to abbreviations in column 5. A = artillery, Ac = aircraft, El = electronics, Eng = engines, Mi = missiles, MV = military vehicles, SA/O = small arms/ordnance, Sh = ships, and Oth = other. Comp ( ) = components of the product within the parentheses. It is used only for companies which do not produce any final systems.

[1] For the membership of the Organisation for Economic Co-operation and Development, see the glossary in this volume. For countries in the developing world, see appendix 11A in this volume.

* Participants in the SIPRI Arms Industry Network: Dipankar Banerjee, Institute for Peace and Conflict Studies (New Delhi); Peter Batchelor, Centre for Conflict Resolution (Cape Town); Paul Dunne, Middlesex Business University (London); Ken Epps, Project Ploughshares Canada (Ontario); Jean-Paul Hébert, CIRPES (Paris); Peter Hug (Bern); Christos Kollias, School of Business and Economics (Larissa); Luc Mampaey, Groupe de Recherche et d'Information sur la Paix et la Sécurité, GRIP (Brussels); Lesley McCulloch, Australia National University (Canberra); Arcadi Oliveres, Centre d'Estudis sobre la Pau i el Desarmament (Barcelona); Ton van Oosterhout, TNO (Den Haag); and Reuven Pedatzur, The Galili Center for Strategy and National Security (Ramat Efal).

Table 10A. The 100 largest arms-producing companies in the OECD and developing countries, 1997

Figures in columns 6, 7, 8 and 10 are in US $m.[a] Figures in italics are percentages.

1	2	3	4	5	6	7	8	9	10	11
Rank[b]					Arms sales		Total sales	Col. 6 as	Profit	Employment
1997	1996	Company[c]	Country	Sector[d]	1997	1996	1997	% of col. 8	1997	1997
1	1	Lockheed Martin	USA	Ac El Mi	18 500	18 010	28 069	*66*	1 300	180 000
2	9	Boeing[e]	USA	Ac El Mi	14 500	4 000	45 800	*32*	– 178	239 000
3	3	British Aerospace, BAe	UK	A Ac El Mi SA/O	10 410	8 340	13 996	*74*	264	43 400
4	5	General Motors, GM[f]	USA	El Eng Mi	7 450	6 660	178 174	*4*	6 698	. .
5	4	Northrop Grumman[g]	USA	Ac El Mi SA/O	7 210	6 700	9 153	*79*	407	52 000
S	S	Hughes Electronics (GM)[f]	USA	El Mi	7 100	6 340	17 726	*40*	1 159	. .
6	6	GEC	UK	El Sh	6 030	5 530	18 180	*33*	1 109	71 960
7	8	Raytheon[h]	USA	El Mi	4 600	4 030	13 673	*34*	527	119 150
8	7	Thomson	France	El Mi SA/O	4 220	4 570	. .	. .	. .	. .
S	S	Thomson-CSF (Thomson)	France	El Mi SA/O	4 220	4 540	6 602	*64*	364	44 840
9	13	TRW	USA	Comp (El MV)	3 800	3 360	10 831	*35*	– 49	79 700
10	14	General Dynamics[i]	USA	MV Sh	3 650	3 310	4 062	*90*	316	29 000
11	15	Litton	USA	El Sh	3 470	3 220	4 176	*83*	162	31 500
12	11	United Technologies	USA	El Eng	3 310	3 380	24 713	*13*	1 072	180 100
13	10	DCN[j]	France	Sh	3 040	3 470	3 099	*98*	. .	19 280
14	12	Daimler Benz	FRG	Ac El Eng MV Mi	2 840	3 360	71 536	*4*	4 638	300 070
S	S	Daimler-Benz Aerospace, DASA, (Daimler Benz)	FRG	Ac El Eng Mi	2 820	3 330	8 815	*32*	4	43 520
15	17	IRI	Italy	A Ac El MV Mi SA/O Sh	2 680	2 540	22 232	*12*	2 868	126 930
S	S	Finmeccanica (IRI)	Italy	A Ac El MV Mi SA/O	2 410	2 290	8 973	*27*	– 1 325	61 240

1	2	3	4	5	6	7	8	9	10	11
Rank					Arms sales					
1997	1996	Company	Country	Industry	1997	1996	Total sales 1997	Col. 6 as % of col. 8	Profit 1997	Employment 1997
16	16	Mitsubishi Heavy Industries[k]	Japan	Ac MV Mi Sh	2 250	3 030	25 590	*9*	501	. .
17	21	Rolls Royce	UK	Eng	2 130	2 010	7 098	*30*	452	42 600
18	18	Aérospatiale Groupe	France	Ac Mi	1 990	2 310	9 645	*21*	244	37 090
19	29	Dassault Aviation Groupe	France	Ac	1 870	1 230	3 606	*52*	225	12 580
20	24	Newport News	USA	Sh	1 600	1 730	1 707	*94*	– 48	18 400
21	20	Alcatel Alsthom	France	El	1 590	2 070	31 845	*5*	799	189 550
S	S	Matra BAe Dynamics (Matra HT/BAe, UK)	France	Mi	1 540	1 580	1 540	*100*	. .	6 000
22	22	General Electric	USA	Eng	1 500	1 800	90 840	*2*	8 203	276 000
23	28	Allied Signal	USA	Ac El	1 350	1 260	14 472	*9*	1 170	70 500
24	33	Lagardère	France	El Mi Oth	1 320	1 190	11 291	*12*	236	46 230
S	S	Matra HT (Lagardère)	France	El Mi Oth	1 320	1 190	3 547	*37*	362	19 400
25	62	Rheinmetall[l]	FRG	A El MV SA/O	1 310	540	3 783	*35*	104	28 510
26	25	CEA	France	Oth	1 250	1 510	3 156	*40*	– 33	16 280
27	44	Kawasaki Heavy Industries[k]	Japan	Ac Eng Mi Sh	1 210	910	10 722	*11*	153	26 100
28	32	GKN	UK	Ac MV	1 150	1 200	5 540	*21*	462	32 680
29	27	GIAT Industries	France	A MV SA/O	1 120	1 340	1 148	*98*	– 488	10 900
30	36	Israel Aircraft Industries	Israel	Ac El Mi	1 100	1 030	1 690	*65*	24	14 000
31	38	ITT Industries	USA	El	1 100	1 010	8 777	*13*	108	. .
32	S	United Defense[m]	USA	MV	1 070	1 020	1 257	*85*	33	. .
33	30	Mitsubishi Electric[k]	Japan	El Mi	1 060	1 210	. .	. .	. .	. .
34	63	SEPI[n]	Spain	Ac El Oth	1 010	540	9 835	*10*	2 828	49 190
35	31	Celsius	Sweden	A El SA/O Sh	1 000	1 200	1 525	*65*	27	10 940
36	39	Textron	USA	Ac El Eng MV	1 000	1 000	10 544	*9*	558	64 000
37	45	Tracor	USA	Comp (Ac El Mi)	930	850	1 266	*74*	34	10 740

S	S	Matra BAe Dynamics France (Matra BAe Dynamics)	France	Mi	930	830	930	*100*	10	. .
38	43	SNECMA Groupe	France	Eng	910	910	3 950	*23*	128	20 260
39	40	Alliant Tech Systems	USA	SA/O	910	940	1 076	*84*	68	6 550
40	35	Siemens[o]	FRG	El	870	1 060	61 663	*1*	1 504	386 000
S	S	Royal Ordnance (BAe)	UK	A SA/O	820	. .	820	*100*	. .	4 000
41	41	FIAT	Italy	Eng MV SA/O	810	920	52 569	*2*	1 419	239 460
42	23	Texas Instruments[h]	USA	El	810	1 770	10 562	*8*	1 805	. .
S	S	Eurocopter Group (Aérospatiale/DASA, FRG)	France	Ac	770	960	1 705	*45*	4	8 500
43	49	Harris	USA	El	760	690	3 797	*20*	208	29 000
44	48	GTE	USA	El	730	690	23 260	*3*	2 794	114 000
45	57	Ordnance Factories	India	A SA/O	720	620	838	*86*	. .	. .
46	52	Hunting	UK	Oth	720	640	2 157	*34*	29	12 590
47	–	Singapore Technologies, ST	Singap.	A El Eng MV Mi SA/O	690	. .	3 620	*19*	– 231	22 400
48	58	Saab	Sweden	Ac El Mi	670	580	1 136	*59*	– 496	8 110
49	72	Eidgenössische Rüstungsb.	Switzerl.	A Ac Eng SA/O	640	460	740	*87*	– 138	4 430
50	47	SAGEM Groupe	France	El	630	690	2 871	*22*	120	13 920
51	55	BDM International[p]	USA	El Oth	630	630	1 000	*63*	. .	9 000
52	65	NEC[k]	Japan	El	620	530	40 508	*2*	341	152 450
S	S	Rheinmetall Ind. (Rheinmetall)	FRG	A El MV SA/O	600	540	600	*100*	20	3 460
53	60	Racal Electronics	UK	El	590	550	1 874	*31*	– 358	12 910
54	61	Ceridian[i]	USA	El	590	550	1 664	*35*	472	8 000
55	64	Vickers	UK	Eng MV SA/O	560	540	1 960	*28*	– 4	. .
56	59	Dassault Electronique	France	El	550	570	842	*65*	22	3 970
57	50	Ishikawajima-Harima[k]	Japan	Eng Sh	550	660	9 003	*6*	129	. .
58	–	L-3 Communications[q]	USA	El	550	0	704	*78*	16	. .
S	–	Singapore Technologies Engineering, STE (ST)	Singap.	Ac El Eng Sh	550	0	995	*55*	87	7 500
59	19	Rockwell International	USA	El Mi	540	2 200	7 762	*7*	644	45 000
S	S	SAGEM (SAGEM Groupe)	France	El	540	600	1 926	*28*	84	8 250

1	2	3	4	5	6	7	8	9	10	11
Rank					Arms sales		Total sales	Col. 6 as	Profit	Employment
1997	1996	Company	Country	Industry	1997	1996	1997	% of col. 8	1997	1997
60	54	Oerlikon-Bührle	Switzerl.	A Ac El Mi SA/O	520	630	2 700	*19*	52	14 830
61	70	Gencorp	USA	El Eng	520	470	1 568	*33*	137	9 460
62	56	Diehl	FRG	SA/O	510	620	1 746	*29*	. .	12 900
63	84	Babcock International Group, BI	UK	Sh Oth	510	370	931	*55*	– 14	7 720
S	S	Babcock Rosyth Defence (BI)	UK	Sh Oth	510	370	510	*100*	. .	. .
64	68	Avondale Industries	USA	Sh	510	480	614	*83*	27	5 500
S	S	Saab Military Aircraft (Saab)	Sweden	Ac	510	380	587	*87*	. .	3 880
65	71	Rafael	Israel	SA/O Oth	500	460	520	*96*	– 30	3 970
S	S	MTU (DASA)	FRG	Eng	500	540	1 709	*29*	. .	6 020
66	78	Honeywell	USA	El Mi	490	440	8 028	*6*	471	57 500
67	74	Hindustan Aeronautics	India	Ac Mi	470	450	498	*94*	30	33 970
68	75	Denel	S. Africa	A Ac El MV Mi SA/O	460	450	689	*66*	– 83	13 700
S	S	Bofors (Celsius)	Sweden	A MV SA/O	460	550	536	*85*	3	4 020
69	46	Lucent Technologies[i]	USA	El	450	750	26 360	*2*	1 507	. .
S	S	FIAT Aviazione (FIAT)	Italy	Eng SA/O	450	490	1 367	*33*	. .	6 390
70	93	Mannesmann	FRG	MV	420	320	22 545	*2*	352	120 860
S	S	Bazan (SEPI)[n]	Spain	El Eng Sh	420	390	487	*87*	– 85	7 350
71	87	Smiths Industries	UK	El	410	360	1 763	*23*	216	13 300
S	S	LFK (DASA)	FRG	Mi	410	590	410	*100*	– 11	1 230
72	–	Tenix	Australia	Sp	400	. .	446	*90*	. .	2 400
73	77	Koor Industries	Israel	A El	400	440	3 655	*11*	141	21 500
74	67	Toshiba[k]	Japan	El Mi	400	480	44 467	*1*	60	186 000
75	–	Stewart & Stevenson	USA	MV	400	200	1 115	*36*	52	. .
S	S	Tadiran (Koor Industries)	Israel	El	400	380	1 113	*36*	62	7 480
76	83	AM General Corporation	USA	MV	390	390	468	*83*	– 10	1 390
77	82	EDS	USA	El	380	400	15 236	*2*	731	. .

78	80	Mitre	USA	Oth	380	410	487	*77*	. .	. .
79	95	Elbit Systems	Israel	El	370	310	370	*100*	22	1 760
80	66	Dyncorp	USA	Comp (Ac)	370	530	1 146	*32*	7	16 100
81	88	EG&G	USA	Comp (El Oth)	370	360	1 461	*25*	34	. .
S	S	Agusta (Finmeccanica)	Italy	Ac	370	430	556	*67*	. .	5 230
82	90	ADI	Australia	El SA/O Sh	360	330	465	*78*	32	3 470
83	85	Israel Military Industries/TAAS	Israel	A MV SA/O	360	360	512	*70*	14	4 040
84	86	MKEK	Turkey	SA/O	360	360	720	*50*	12	10 770
S	S	Matra Marconi Space (Matra HT/GEC,UK)	France	Oth	360	. .	1 450	*25*	54	4 750
S	S	GM Canada (GM, USA)	Canada	Eng.	350	320	24 736	*1*	. .	. .
S	S	Hollandse Signaalapparaten (Thomson-CSF, France)	Netherl.	El	350	420	355	*99*	26	3 010
S	S	CASA (SEPI)[n]	Spain	Ac	350	380	823	*42*	44	7 700
85	73	Allegheny Teledyne	USA	El Eng Mi	340	460	3 745	*9*	298	22 000
86	–	Cobham	UK	Comp (Ac El)	320	260	529	*60*	58	4 260
S	S	Sextant Avionique (Thomson-CSF)	France	El	320	340	806	*40*	. .	6 120
87	–	Marine United[k]	Japan	Comp (Sh)	310	. .	. .	. .	. .	. .
88	–	BFGoodrich[r]	USA	Comp (Ac)	300	220	3 373	*9*	178	16 840
S	S	Marconi (GEC, UK)	Italy	El	300	. .	996	*30*	. .	7 120
89	–	Devonport Management	UK	Sh	290	260	360	*80*	3	3 840
90	–	Oshkosh Truck	USA	MV	290	250	683	*42*	10	. .
91	51	Preussag	FRG	Sh	280	650	15 373	*2*	229	62 600
S	S	HDW (Preussag)	FRG	Sh	280	650	623	*45*	. .	3 440
92	–	Komatsu[k]	Japan	MV SA/O	280	270	8 994	*3*	157	26 870
93	100	Motorola	USA	El	280	290	29 794	*1*	1 180	150 000
94	–	Primex Technologies	USA	SA/O	280	280	491	*58*	11	2 680
S	S	Fincantieri Gruppo (IRI)	Italy	Sh	280	220	2 323	*12*	6	9 430
95	–	Sundstrand	USA	Ac Oth	270	240	1 752	*15*	183	. .
S	S	Singapore Aerospace (STE)	Singap.	Ac El Eng	270	240	454	*59*	42	. .

1	2	3	4	5	6	7	8	9	10	11
Rank					Arms sales		Total sales	Col. 6 as	Profit	Employment
1997	1996	Company	Country	Industry	1997	1996	1997	% of col. 8	1997	1997
96	–	Bharat Electronics	India	El	260	210	347	*75*	15	16 000
97	–	Ericsson	Sweden	El	260	328	21 970	*1*	1 564	100 770
S	S	Ericsson Microwave (Ericsson)	Sweden	El	260	328	642	*40*	71	3 670
98	99	Sema Group	UK	Oth	260	290	1 851	*14*	72	16 260
99	–	Kaman	USA	Ac El	260	250	1 043	*25*	71	4 320
S	S	Computing Devices Canada (Ceridian, USA)	Canada	El	260	260	296	*87*	23	1 200
S	S	IVECO (FIAT)	Italy	MV	260	320	4 210	*6*	. .	17 800
100	–	Federman	Israel	El	250	260	. .	. .	. .	. .
S	S	El-Op (Federman)	Israel	El Oth	250	260	296	*84*	. .	1 900

[a] The period average of market exchange rates of the International Monetary Fund's *International Financial Statistics* is used for conversion to US dollars.

[b] Rank designations in the column for 1996 may not correspond to those given in table 6E in the *SIPRI Yearbook 1998* because of subsequent revision. A dash (–) in this column indicates either that the company did not produce arms in 1996, or that it did not exist as it was structured in 1996, in which case there is a zero (0) in column 7, or that it did not rank among the 100 top companies in 1996. Companies with the designation S in the column for rank are subsidiaries.

[c] Names in brackets are names of parent companies.

[d] A key to abbreviations in column 5 is provided on p. 412.

[e] Boeing merged with McDonnell Douglas Corporation in Aug. 1997. Boeing data for 1997 include data for MDC for the entire year.

[f] General Motors arms sales data are Hughes Electronics arms sales plus military sales of its Canadian subsidiary. Hughes Electronics, the major arms-producing subsidiary of General Motors, spun off its military business, Hughes Defense, in Dec. 1997 and it was subsequently acquired by Raytheon.

[g] Northrop Grumman merged with Logicon in Aug. 1997. Northrop Grumman data for 1997 include data for Logicon for the entire year.

[h] Raytheon data for 1997 include data for Texas Instruments' Defence Systems and Electronics business (which it acquired in July 1997) for 6 months, and Hughes Defense (which it acquired in Dec. 1997) for 2 weeks.

[i] General Dynamics acquired defence units from Lockheed Martin in Jan. 1997 (Defence Systems and Armaments Systems); from Lucent Technologies in Oct. 1997 (the Advanced Technology Systems); and from Ceridian in Dec. 1997 (Computer Devices International). The latter 2 have been integrated within General Dynamics Information Systems in 1998.

[j] Data for 1997 are estimates.

[k] For Japanese companies, data in the arms sales column represent new military contracts rather than arms sales.

[l] Rheinmetall took control of STN Atlas Elektronik in 1997.

[m] In Oct. 1997 FMC Corp. and Harsco Corp. sold their co-owned subsidiary United Defense to the Carlyle Group. United Defense is here listed as an independent company as the Carlyle Group is an investment company.

[n] Sociedad Estatal de Participaciones Industrial (SEPI) took control of the arms-producing companies Bazan and Santa Barbara in Sep. 1997, when their parent company Agencia Industrial del Estado (AIE) was dissolved.

[o] Siemens sold off its defence units in Apr. 1998 to British Aerospace (Siemens Plessey Electronics Systems Australia and Siemens Plessey Systems) and to Daimler Benz Aerospace (Siemens Unterschleisshei). The transactions were announced in Oct. 1997.

[p] BDM International data are estimates. BDM International was acquired by TRW in Dec. 1997.

[q] L-3 Communications was spun off from Lockheed Martin in Apr. 1997.

[r] BFGoodrich acquired Rohr in Dec. 1997. BFGoodrich data for 1997 include data for Rohr for the entire year.

11. Transfers of major conventional weapons

BJÖRN HAGELIN, PIETER D. WEZEMAN and
SIEMON T. WEZEMAN

I. Introduction

Since annual variations in global transfers of major conventional weapons are often the result of a few large deliveries and tend to overemphasize peaks and troughs, a better understanding of the main trends can be achieved by studying average values over several years.[1] The SIPRI arms transfers project identifies such trends using the SIPRI trend indicator.[2]

The five-year moving average curve in figure 11.1 reflects three distinct phases since 1984: (*a*) the last years of the cold war (1984–88) during which the level of arms transfers was relatively high; (*b*) a transitional period of steep decline between 1989 and 1994; and (*c*) from 1995 to the present day when the level of arms transfers has been fairly stable and much lower than in the late 1980s. The level in 1998 ($21.9 billion at constant 1990 prices) was not much higher than that in 1994 ($20 billion), the lowest level since 1970.[3]

Section II of this chapter surveys the dominant trends among the major suppliers and recipients of major conventional weapons and presents some of the developments in arms transfers policy in 1998. The global reduction in arms transfers in 1998 is primarily the result of procurement decisions made several years ago, rather than an effect of the financial crisis which began in Asia in 1997. There were only minor changes in the ranking of the top major suppliers in 1994–98 compared with 1993–97. On the recipient side, Asia and the Middle East showed reductions in their imports of 27 and 18 per cent respectively, that is, much smaller than the reductions of around 50 per cent in the Americas and Africa. Western Europe was the only region with an increase in imports between 1997 and 1998.

Greece and Turkey are both major arms recipients and both are pursuing military modernization programmes. The decision by Cyprus to acquire a

[1] Five-year moving averages are calculated as a more stable measure of the trend in arms transfers than the often erratic year-to-year figures.

[2] The SIPRI data on arms transfers refer to actual deliveries of major conventional weapons. To permit comparison between the data on such deliveries of different weapons and identification of general trends, SIPRI uses a *trend-indicator value*. The SIPRI values are therefore only an indicator of the volume of international arms transfers and not of the actual financial values of such transfers. Thus they are not comparable to economic statistics such as gross domestic product or export/import figures. The method used in calculating the trend-indicator value is described in appendix 11C. A more extensive description of the methodology used, including a list of sources, is available on the SIPRI Internet website URL <http://www.sipri.se/projects/armstrade/atmethods.html>.

[3] The figures for years before 1998 differ from those given in previous SIPRI Yearbooks. The SIPRI database on arms transfers is constantly updated as new data become available, and the trend-indicator values are revised each year. For this reason it is advisable for readers who require time-series data for periods before the years covered in this Yearbook to contact SIPRI.

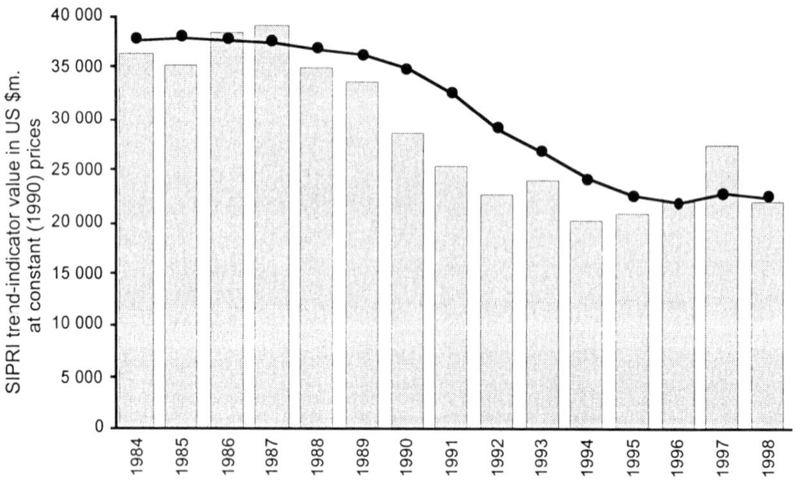

Figure 11.1. The trend in transfers of major conventional weapons, 1984–98

Note: The histogram shows annual totals and the curve denotes the five-year moving average. Five-year averages are plotted at the last year of each five-year period.

long-range air defence system from Russia resulted in a political crisis in the relations between these countries in 1998, putting a spotlight on tensions in this region. The dynamics of this crisis are described in section III.

International arms embargoes in force at any time since 1994 and a general discussion on the effectiveness of arms embargoes are presented in section IV.

An encouraging development in 1998 was the adoption by European Union (EU) member states of a common Code of Conduct for Arms Exports. Although the code is basically a restatement of the Common Criteria of 1991 and 1992, it provides a more institutionalized framework for cooperation. Section V describes the aims and implications of the code.

Section VI examines the transparency of arms transfer data in government publications and of the reports to the UN Register of Conventional Arms (UNROCA) for the calendar year 1997. Although there are still few countries which regularly make available detailed information at the national level about their overall arms exports, the level of detail has improved in recent years. In 1998 the UNROCA included data on holdings of weapons and procurement from national production for the first time.

SIPRI has conducted research on the transfers of major conventional weapons since the 1960s. During the 1990s, in particular, another aspect of the arms trade has received increasing attention on the international political agenda, namely the trade in light weapons. Appendix 11E summarizes efforts to control the trade in such weapons.

II. Main developments in 1998

The suppliers of major conventional weapons

The USA remains the largest supplier of major conventional weapons, a position which it has held since 1991. In 1998 it accounted for 56 per cent of global arms transfers. In 1994–98 Taiwan, Saudi Arabia and Egypt were the main recipients of US conventional weapons (see table 11.2). Existing orders indicate that the USA will remain the major supplier for at least the next 10 years,[4] even when compared to all the *EU* member states combined. In 1998 the combined deliveries of major arms from all EU member states to non-member states were less than 50 per cent of total US transfers (see appendix 11.A).

France, whose arms exports have increased steadily since 1994, accounted for 17 per cent of global major arms deliveries in 1998 and passed the UK in the ranking for the period 1994–98. French deliveries to Taiwan and the United Arab Emirates (UAE) in 1998 remained at approximately the same level as in 1997. While the last items of two major programmes for frigates and combat aircraft were delivered to Taiwan in 1998, major new orders were received from the UAE. Together with outstanding deliveries to Saudi Arabia and Pakistan this means that France is likely to retain a high position for at least the next few years.

After increasing levels between 1994 and 1997, deliveries by *the UK* decreased by almost 80 per cent between 1997 and 1998, giving it a mere 3 per cent share of global major arms transfers in 1998. The main reason is the drastic drop in orders for combat aircraft, which have made up the bulk of the UK's arms exports in recent years. In 1998 the last Tornado IDS aircraft were delivered to Saudi Arabia, its major recipient, in accordance with a contract from 1993.

Russia retained second position in 1994–98 with India and China remaining its largest recipients. However, its level of arms transfers has declined since 1996 and fell by almost 60 per cent between 1997 and 1998.[5] Although existing orders—mainly ships and combat aircraft for India and China—will serve to increase the level of Russian arms transfers in the coming years, Russian sources have admitted for the first time that without major new investments in military technologies the country's military exports are likely to diminish even further.[6] In the case of the Su-30MKI combat aircraft for India, a major part of

[4] The US Department of Defense reportedly signed deals for $8.5 billion in new arms transfers with just over 100 countries in fiscal year 1998. Ruppe, D., 'Pentagon inked $8.5 billion in fiscal-1998 arms-export deals', *Defense Week*, 16 Nov. 1998.

[5] An investigation into the activities of the state export agency Rosvooruzheniye revealed a major discrepancy between the official and the real figures for Russian arms sales. Novichkov, N., 'Russian arms sales are inflated, says audit', *Jane's Defence Weekly,* 7 Oct. 1998, p. 31.

[6] Novichkov, N., 'Russia may exhaust potential in technologies trade in 5 yrs', *Jane's Defence Weekly,* 18 Nov. 1998, p. 22. See also Wezeman, S. T. and Wezeman, P. D., 'Transfers of major conventional weapons', *SIPRI Yearbook 1998: Armaments, Disarmament and International Security* (Oxford University Press, Oxford: 1998), p. 296.

Table 11.1. The 31 leading suppliers of major conventional weapons, 1994–98

The list includes countries/non-state actors with aggregate exports of $100 million or more for 1994–98. The countries are ranked according to the 1994–98 aggregate exports. Figures are trend-indicator values expressed in US $m. at constant (1990) prices.

Suppliers and rank 1994–98		1993–97[a]	1994	1995	1996	1997	1998	1994–98
1	USA	1	9 844	9 580	9 712	12 404	12 342	53 882
2	Russia	2	1 155	3 271	3 602	2 956	1 276	12 260
3	France	5	756	806	1 924	3 284	3 815	10 585
4	UK	3	1 494	1 708	1 800	3 238	673	8 913
5	Germany	4	2 637	1 425	1 399	686	1 064	7 211
6	China	6	731	849	751	338	157	2 826
7	Netherlands	7	495	378	414	551	506	2 344
8	Italy	8	306	330	366	442	298	1 742
9	Ukraine	10	189	192	195	516	449	1 541
10	Canada	9	365	436	239	137	217	1 394
11	Spain	11	275	111	99	637	221	1 343
12	Israel	12	115	206	257	292	147	1 017
13	Czech Rep.	13	378	188	132	30	16	744
14	Belarus	14	8	24	129	516	16	693
15	Belgium	16	20	296	144	89	51	600
16	Sweden	17	63	180	155	51	136	585
17	Moldova	15	165	–	–	392	–	557
18	Poland	20	131	184	65	20	1	401
19	Australia	19	24	22	15	318	3	382
20	Switzerland	18	70	75	122	62	35	364
21	Norway	21	186	54	9	56	2	307
22	Denmark	22	230	–	3	–	–	233
23	Slovakia	23	28	85	48	44	–	205
24	Uzbekistan	63	–	–	–	–	170	170
25	Brazil	25	38	40	28	28	–	134
26	Singapore	31	11	2	–	75	41	129
27	Korea, North	24	48	48	22	–	–	118
28	Indonesia	33	25	38	–	–	52	115
29	Qatar	26	51	15	–	44	–	110
30	Korea, South	29	8	25	20	27	30	110
31	Greece	35	–	–	30	52	18	100
	Others[b]		226	298	303	131	209	1 167
	Total		**20 073**	**20 861**	**21 984**	**27 416**	**21 944**	**112 278**

[a] The rank order for suppliers in 1993–97 differs from that published in the *SIPRI Yearbook 1998* (p. 294) because of the subsequent revision of figures for these years.

[b] Includes at least 34 countries (some identified imports from unidentified suppliers) with aggregate 1994–98 exports of less than $100 million.

Note: The SIPRI data on arms transfers refer to actual deliveries of major conventional weapons. To permit comparison between the data on such deliveries of different weapons and identification of general trends, SIPRI uses a *trend-indicator value*. The SIPRI values are therefore only an indicator of the volume of international arms transfers and not of the actual financial values of such transfers. Thus they are not comparable to economic statistics such as gross domestic product or export/import figures. Figures may not add up because of rounding.

Source: SIPRI arms transfers database.

the development costs has been paid for by India.[7]

Investments in future military technology also constitute a problem for countries with a traditionally strong defence industry such as China, the Czech Republic, Poland and Slovakia. All these suppliers show unstable or decreasing trends in their levels of arms transfers over the past five years (table 11.1).[8] Despite its mainly increasing export trend in the past five years, Ukraine will face the same problem. Suppliers which cannot sustain and invest in new military technologies will find it difficult to remain on the market.

The recipients of major conventional weapons

Since 1995 *Asia* has had the largest regional share of global arms imports, accounting for over 40 per cent (see appendix 11A, table 11A.1). In 1998 countries in *North-East Asia*—primarily Japan, South Korea and Taiwan—received 74 per cent of Asian imports. Taiwan passed Saudi Arabia as the number one recipient for the past five-year period (table 11.3). The relatively high levels of imports in North-East Asia were in contrast to greatly reduced import levels between 1997 and 1998 mainly in *South-East Asia*, for example, in Malaysia and Thailand (over 90 per cent), and Indonesia (over 50 per cent). In these and some other countries the financial crisis may explain part of the reductions.[9] However, although South-East Asia's global share dropped from 10 to 6 per cent between 1997 and 1998, the reduction is not significant in global terms. This puts into question suggestions that the crisis may have profound consequences on the global trend. *South Asia's* global share of arms imports fell from 7 to 5 per cent between 1997 and 1998. This reflects a drop in India's imports by more than 60 per cent. However, existing Indian orders indicate that this decline will only be temporary (see appendix 11B). Despite its ambition to increase self-reliance in arms procurement to 70 per cent by 2005,[10] India is likely to remain dependent on foreign support for complete systems and critical technologies for the foreseeable future.

At the same time military tensions remain in Asia. Continued anxiety over existing or possible nuclear programmes in India, Pakistan and North Korea may stimulate demands for delivery systems such as missiles and combat aircraft, which in turn could influence procurement decisions for counter-systems in other countries. This was illustrated by debates in Japan, South Korea and

[7] Arnett, E., 'Military research and development', *SIPRI Yearbook 1998* (note 6), p. 272.

[8] Russia and France may be willing to strengthen political–military relations with China in order to secure a military market but also to counterbalance the position of the USA. 'France and India contemplate strategic alliance', *Defence Systems Daily*, Global Intelligence Update, 15 Jan. 1999, URL <http://defence-data.com/current/page3588.htm>; and 'China–Russia relations at the turn of the century', *Beijing Review*, 14–20 Dec. 1998, pp. 6–8.

[9] Simon, S. W., *The Economic Crisis and ASEAN States' Security* (Strategic Studies Institute, US Army War College: Carlisle, Pa., Oct. 1998).

[10] 'India reviews indigenous defence production', *Defence Systems Daily*, 11 Dec. 1998, URL <http://defence-data.com/current/page3403.htm>; and Singh, R. P., 'India', ed. R. P. Singh, SIPRI, *Arms Procurement Decision Making*, vol. 1 (Oxford University Press: Oxford, 1998), p. 49.

Table 11.2. The leading recipients of major conventional weapons from the six major suppliers, 1994–98

The list includes countries/non-state actors with aggregate imports of $500 million or more for 1994–98 from at least one of the major suppliers. Figures are trend-indicator values expressed in US $m. at constant (1990) prices.

	Suppliers							
Recipients	USA	Russia	France	UK	Germany	China	Others	**Total**
Africa	**233**	**653**	**320**	**52**	**10**	**109**	**871**	**2 248**
Asia	**19 520**	**7 487**	**5 878**	**2 327**	**1 917**	**2 009**	**5 177**	**44 315**
China	–	2 116	110	10	–	. .	356	**2 592**
India	–	2 745	95	223	224	–	862	**4 149**
Indonesia	6	–	35	510	1 115	–	47	**1 713**
Japan	3 965	–	–	66	10	–	52	**4 093**
Kazakhstan	–	547	–	–	–	–	–	**547**
Korea, South	4 098	196	170	1	540	–	166	**5 171**
Malaysia	532	695	40	992	–	–	376	**2 635**
Myanmar	–	86	–	–	–	604	–	**690**
Pakistan	371	86	140	355	–	528	1 136	**2 616**
Singapore	1 022	35	95	20	–	–	593	**1 765**
Taiwan	8 098	–	5 154	–	–	–	59	**13 311**
Thailand	1 277	–	40	8	22	746	1 039	**3 132**
Viet Nam	–	724	–	–	–	–	63	**787**
Others	151	257	–	142	6	131	428	**1 115**
Americas	**1 801**	**499**	**342**	**1 816**	**649**	–	**3 953**	**9 060**
Brazil	192	12	64	848	256	–	224	**1 596**
Canada	553	–	72	76	39	–	152	**892**
USA	. .	–	30	779	4	–	1 707	**2 520**
Others	1 056	487	176	113	350	–	1 870	**4 052**
Europe	**14 167**	**2 458**	**1 540**	**699**	**4 488**	**19**	**3 312**	**26 683**
Germany	860	–	27	–	. .	–	99	**986**
Greece	2 371	542	53	36	1 138	–	614	**4 754**
Finland	1 580	225	80	45	77	–	18	**2 025**
Italy	694	–	5	368	48	–	–	**1 115**
Spain	1 541	–	185	40	150	–	198	**2 114**
Sweden	34	–	42	–	618	–	34	**728**
Switzerland	1 255	–	–	5	–	–	–	**1 260**
Turkey	3 459	147	420	70	2 018	–	501	**6 615**
Others	2 372	1 544	728	135	439	19	1 848	**7 085**
Middle East	**17 631**	**1 165**	**2 493**	**4 012**	**19**	**690**	**2 714**	**28 724**
Egypt	5 287	148	–	–	10	–	437	**5 882**
Iran	–	271	–	–	–	578	327	**1 176**
Israel	2 391	–	39	–	–	–	–	**2 430**
Kuwait	1 834	198	214	706	–	–	55	**3 007**
Oman	53	–	131	634	–	–	80	**898**
Qatar	–	–	686	307	–	–	36	**1 029**
Saudi Arabia	6 867	–	36	2 016	–	–	829	**9 748**
UAE	425	539	1 369	348	4	–	582	**3 267**
Others	774	9	18	–	5	112	368	**1 286**
Oceania	**531**	–	**11**	**5**	**90**	–	**564**	**1 201**
UN[a]	–	–	–	–	**37**	–	**11**	**48**
Total	**53 883**	**12 263**	**10 584**	**8 911**	**7 210**	**2 827**	**16 602**	**112 278**

[a] The UN is included as a non-state actor and not as a combination of all member states.

Note: The SIPRI data on arms transfers refer to actual deliveries of major conventional weapons. To permit comparison between the data on such deliveries of different weapons and identification of general trends, SIPRI uses a *trend-indicator value*. The SIPRI values are therefore only an indicator of the volume of international arms transfers and not of the actual financial values of such transfers. Thus they are not comparable to economic statistics such as gross domestic product or export/import figures. Figures may not add up because of rounding.

Source: SIPRI arms transfers database.

Taiwan about ballistic missile defence systems in reaction to North Korean and Chinese ballistic missile tests.[11] Reports that China has modernized its missile arsenal which is targeted at Taiwan may further stimulate arms procurement in the region.[12]

Europe accounted for approximately 28 per cent of global arms imports in 1998. Countries in Western Europe accounted for 98 per cent of the European share. With the exception of Turkey and Greece, which are discussed in section III, few countries placed major import orders. No decisions were taken in 1998 to go ahead with previously discussed major procurement orders in Central and East European countries, mainly because of a lack of funds. The Czech Republic, Hungary and Poland were anticipating NATO membership in 1999 and the possible consequences with regard to harmonization of their arms inventories.

Since 1994, the *Middle East* has held roughly the same average share of the global market as Europe. In 1998 its share was 24 per cent. While Saudi Arabia lost its leading position to Taiwan on the list of importers in 1994–98, the UAE and Israel moved up and Egypt retained its fourth position. All these recipients showed reduced levels of imports in 1998 with the exception of Israel, which recorded an enormous increase compared with 1997. This is mainly the result of the delivery of 16 F-15I fighter aircraft from the USA.

Africa and Latin America together account for less than 4 per cent of global arms imports. *Africa's* share is less than 1 per cent.[13] In 1998 Sub-Saharan Africa accounted for virtually all arms imports to Africa. During 1998 orders for major weapons were placed by both Eritrea and Ethiopia, including those for advanced combat aircraft (MiG-29s and Su-27s). South Africa also made some major arms procurement decisions but these are not likely to have an effect on Africa's ranking in the foreseeable future.[14] There has been no

[11] Elizabeth Becker claims that the sensitivities are so acute that the US Administration has twice delayed sending Congress a classified report on a proposed missile system to defend Japan, South Korea, and Taiwan and the US troops stationed in the region. Becker, E., 'Missile defense: US weighs risk to Chinese ties', *International Herald Tribune*, 23–24 Jan. 1999, p. 2.

[12] 'Pentagon denies that China increased missiles aimed at Taiwan', *International Herald Tribune*, 13–14 Feb. 1999, p. 3.

[13] For an account of arms transfers to African countries in conflict see Wezeman and Wezeman (note 6), pp. 302–305.

[14] South Africa's planned acquisitions will be spread out over several years between 2002 and 2014. 'Acquisition timescales set', *Jane's Defence Weekly*, 16 Dec. 1998, p. 15; and 'South Africa announces $5.8 billion arms procurement deal', *Defence Systems Daily*, Defence & Aerospace News, 19 Nov. 1998, URL <http://defence-data.com/current/page3271.htm>.

Table 11.3. The 72 leading recipients of major conventional weapons, 1994–98

The list includes countries/non-state actors with aggregate imports of $100 million or more for 1994–98. The countries are ranked according to the 1994–98 aggregate imports. Figures are trend-indicator values expressed in US $m. at constant (1990) prices.

Recipients and rank order								
1994–98		1993–97[a]	1994	1995	1996	1997	1998	1994–98
1	Taiwan	2	731	1 162	1 451	5 311	4 656	13 311
2	Saudi Arabia	1	1 298	1 249	1 961	3 292	1 948	9 748
3	Turkey	3	1 386	1 327	1 132	1 394	1 376	6 615
4	Egypt	4	1 926	1 645	940	931	440	5 882
5	Korea, South	5	642	1 553	1 589	731	656	5 171
6	Greece	7	1 172	943	241	832	1 566	4 754
7	India	8	497	932	988	1 266	466	4 149
8	Japan	6	678	948	624	662	1 181	4 093
9	UAE	11	629	442	600	840	756	3 267
10	Thailand	12	758	628	555	1 128	63	3 132
11	Kuwait	10	49	974	1 338	418	228	3 007
12	Malaysia	15	453	1 143	200	780	59	2 635
13	Pakistan	14	683	242	552	614	525	2 616
14	China	9	112	427	1 115	834	104	2 592
15	USA	13	711	459	431	696	223	2 520
16	Israel	20	796	229	73	46	1 285	2 429
17	Spain	18	646	395	441	230	402	2 114
18	Finland	19	196	162	581	439	647	2 025
19	Singapore	26	187	232	538	123	685	1 765
20	Indonesia	21	600	359	547	141	66	1 713
21	Brazil	23	236	236	491	437	196	1 596
22	Switzerland	31	114	106	199	400	441	1 260
23	Chile	25	151	537	223	194	103	1 208
24	Iran	16	348	243	537	24	24	1 176
25	Italy	24	131	187	241	552	4	1 115
26	Qatar	36	14	15	58	553	389	1 029
27	Germany	17	596	130	110	18	132	986
28	Oman	30	201	175	347	158	17	898
29	Canada	27	432	177	164	86	33	892
30	Peru	29	142	97	182	469	–	890
31	UK	44	38	93	216	88	362	797
32	Viet Nam	37	–	277	246	96	168	787
33	Australia	28	302	71	149	24	189	735
34	Mexico	40	65	65	63	230	306	729
35	Sweden	35	252	84	47	258	87	728
36	Norway	34	57	102	200	186	170	715
37	Netherlands	38	140	47	187	99	242	715
38	Myanmar	32	–	223	93	243	131	690
39	Kazakhstan	39	–	162	219	166	–	547
40	Algeria	41	161	332	5	29	–	527
41	Argentina	47	148	85	44	98	110	485
42	Armenia	45	310	51	106	–	–	467
43	Portugal	33	431	15	3	14	–	463
44	Denmark	49	66	129	53	74	141	463
45	Austria	54	56	37	14	169	177	453

Recipients and rank order 1994–98		1993–97	1994	1995	1996	1997	1998	1994–98
46	France	55	3	41	30	160	210	444
47	Colombia	50	39	87	39	160	119	444
48	New Zealand	46	16	4	18	349	17	404
49	Morocco	43	129	40	89	143	–	401
50	Cyprus	48	61	29	177	110	18	395
51	Bahrain	51	14	26	225	74	9	348
52	Jordan	64	–	24	43	104	164	335
53	Hungary	22	4	67	125	72	58	326
54	Sri Lanka	50	56	60	158	42	40	356
55	Slovakia	41	35	252	35	–	–	322
56	Poland	58	6	154	114	–	–	274
57	Philippines	56	109	32	30	54	47	272
58	Bangladesh	57	89	126	4	24	–	243
59	Yemen/ Southern rebels[b]	62	196	–	–	–	–	196
60	Angola	63	96	1	10	3	84	194
61	Croatia	60	57	86	2	37	–	182
62	Tunisia	64	21	58	60	40	1	180
63	Belgium	59	64	28	2	34	34	162
64	Bulgaria	65	1	–	51	77	16	145
66	Yemen	67	–	142	–	–	–	142
67	Syria	53	63	43	21	–	–	127
68	Lebanon	66	13	59	27	6	17	122
69	Eritrea	75	16	1	30	48	27	122
70	Romania	73	43	1	35	12	20	111
71	Cambodia	72	64	–	34	6	4	108
72	South Africa	68	19	38	51	20	–	128
	Others[c]		334	342	398	512	241	1 827
	Total		**20 073**	**20 861**	**21 984**	**27 416**	**21 944**	**112 278**

[a] The rank order for recipients in 1993–97 differs from that published in the *SIPRI Yearbook 1998* (pp. 300–301) because of the subsequent revision of figures for these years.

[b] Southern rebels refers to those forces in Yemen which, in 1994, tried to re-establish an independent South Yemen.

[c] Includes 65 countries and 6 non-state actors (the UN, the Palestinian Autonomous Authority and 4 rebel groups) with aggregate 1994–98 imports of less than $100 million.

Note: The SIPRI data on arms transfers refer to actual deliveries of major conventional weapons. To permit comparison between the data on such deliveries of different weapons and identification of general trends, SIPRI uses a *trend-indicator value*. The SIPRI values are therefore only an indicator of the volume of international arms transfers and not of the actual financial values of such transfers. Thus they are not comparable to economic statistics such as gross domestic product or export/import figures. Figures may not add up because of rounding.

Source: SIPRI arms transfers database.

regional arms 'surge' in *Latin America* after the 1997 relaxation of President Jimmy Carter's restrictive US export policy. Of the deliveries made in 1998, most were of surplus *matériel* and orders for new arms remained few. In late 1998 Peru decided to suspend military orders following a peace agreement in

October with Ecuador,[15] and Chile postponed its procurement of fighter aircraft. The financial crisis in Brazil, a major recipient in the region, will delay major orders by this country.

Developments in arms transfer policy in 1998

Although the post-cold war trend of declining arms production has come to a halt,[16] many defence industries, supported by the respective governments, are still seeking ways to survive the effects of cuts in military spending and reduced domestic demand for military equipment. One way is to share costs and exchange technology through military industrial cooperation, which is, in itself, a form of military transfer. A regional initiative by six European governments to facilitate the restructuring of the European defence industry by supporting the creation of a Transnational Defence Company (TDC) is the July 1998 Letter of Intent.[17] Although not legally binding, the Letter of Intent stipulates that the participating countries will accept mutual interdependence and seek to simplify the supply of military equipment to each other not only in peacetime but also in times of crisis and war.

Another result of reduced domestic demand for military equipment is an increased pressure to export. Against the background of tough global and regional competition, industrial and political ambitions to finance the development of new weapons and certain arms production capacities by way of arms exports[18] may lead to different national interpretations of export limitations and technology transfers to the possible detriment of arms control.[19] This was illustrated in 1998 by the differing national reactions to India's and Pakistan's nuclear tests. While the USA imposed sanctions on both countries, its example was not followed by other major suppliers. Another case was the attempt by the US Administration to prevent the British Government from

[15] 'Peace accord leaves Peru's procurement plans uncertain', *World Aerospace & Defense Intelligence*, 20 Nov. 1998, p. 8.

[16] See chapter 10 in this volume.

[17] *Measures to Facilitate the Restructuring of European Defence Industry*, Letter of Intent between the defence ministers of France, Germany, Italy, Spain, Sweden and the United Kingdom, London, 6 July 1998. See also chapter 10, section IV in this volume.

[18] It was reported in late 1998 that the US Defense Security Cooperation Agency at the Department of Defense is strengthening its arms export adviser organizations in countries previously closed to US defence personnel, such as the former Soviet Union and South Africa. Ruppe, D., 'US arms advisors chase new markets', *Defense Week*, 2 Nov. 1998, URL <http://www.kingpublishing.com/indx-df.html>; and 'Aerospace in Central and Eastern Europe', *Jane's Defence Industry*, vol. 15, no. 6 (Oct. 1998), p. 4. In an attempt to encourage potential buyers to 'buy British', the members of the National Military Industries Council (comprising the major defence companies and the Ministry of Defence) in 1998 joined together to develop a Customer Support Code of Practice. British Ministry of Defence, Press Release, *New Code Puts UK Defence Industry Support First in the World*, URL <http://www.mod.uk/news/prs/222_98.htm>, 7 Sep. 1998. According to the *MOD Performance Report 1997/98* (The Stationery Office: London, 1998), p. 33, British defence export orders increased in 1997/98 by around 10%.

[19] For fear of putting major arms export deals at risk, both politicians and suppliers may oppose the extension, creation of all-inclusive, or even implementation of national arms embargoes or sanctions. Part of the dilemma is reflected in Helms, J., 'What sanctions epidemic?', *Foreign Affairs*, vol. 78, no. 1 (Jan./Feb. 1999), pp. 2–8.

approving the sale of the Black Shahine air-to-ground missile to the UAE,[20] arguing that its range exceeded the 300 km stipulated in the Missile Technology Control Regime (MTCR). The UK rejected this argument and the deal was approved in late 1998.

Intensified competition has also led to an increasing tendency among suppliers to agree to high compensations to offset the buyer's costs. This is illustrated, for instance, in the negotiations of contracts for the modernization of the South African defence forces. South Africa's aim is that the estimated 30 billion rand ($5 billion) cost of acquiring corvettes, submarines, helicopters, jet trainers and combat aircraft during the next 15 years will be compensated by direct investments, exports and local sales worth 110 billion rand ($18 billion) from the bidders over the next 17 years and the creation of 65 000 jobs over the next 7 years.[21] The willingness of suppliers to agree to investments even before deals have been concluded and sometimes totalling more than the cost of a purchase is likely to mean that anticipated economic and technological benefits will become an increasingly important consideration for the recipients. Financial arrangements may also mean that some of the economic risks are shifted from the buyer to the supplier. In 1998, for example, it emerged that British taxpayers would have to cover the costs of Hawk fighter/trainer aircraft to Indonesia after the Indonesian Government admitted it could not keep up payments on debts endorsed by the British Government.[22]

III. Arms transfer dynamics and the Cyprus crisis

In 1998 the planned delivery of a Russian air defence system to Cyprus became the centre of a new crisis in the relations between Cyprus and Greece on one side and Turkey on the other.[23] The deal is interesting because it spotlights arms transfers to two of the world's top arms importers—Turkey and Greece. It also shows how an arms transfer deal which is not very large or offensive in nature can increase tension to a level at which the use of force is considered. The wealth of information available on this deal makes it possible to use it as an illustration of some of the main elements of arms transfer dynamics, including supplier competition and the use of arms transfers as an instrument of foreign policy.

[20] Barrie, D. and Opall-Rome, B., 'Britain will allow UAE Black Shahine sale', *Defense News*, 26 Oct.–1 Nov. 1998, p. 3.

[21] Batchelor, P., 'Guns or butter? The SANDF's R30 billion weapons procurement package', *NGO Matters*, vol. 3, no. 11 (Nov. 1998); Roos, J. G., 'Beyond South Africa's arms deal', *Armed Forces Journal International*, Feb. 1999, p. 24; and Engelbrecht, L., 'South African arms negotiation team starts work', *Defence Systems Daily*, URL <http://defence-data.com/current/page 3568.htm>.

[22] Amrams, F., 'Britain to meet £25m jets bill', *The Independent*, 26 Sep. 1998, p. 2.

[23] Long-term tensions between Greece and Turkey centre on the division since 1974 of Cyprus into a Greek Cypriot and a Turkish Cypriot area and on territorial claims in the Aegean Sea. Settlement talks have been held for the reunification of the island, so far without success. Bahcheli, T., Couloumbis, T. A. and Carley, P., *Greek–Turkish Relations and US Foreign Policy: Cyprus, the Aegean and Regional Stability*, Peaceworks, no. 17 (United States Institute of Peace: Washington, DC, Aug. 1997).

Table 11.4. Suppliers of major conventional weapons to Cyprus, Greece and Turkey, 1994–98

Figures are trend-indicator values expressed in US $m. at constant (1990) prices.

Supplier	Cyprus	Greece	Turkey
Austria	–	45	–
Canada	5	–	–
France	61	53	420
Greece	100	–	–
Germany	–	1 220	1 715
Italy	–	7	95
Netherlands	–	460	16
Norway	–	102	–
Russia	229	542	147
UK	–	36	51
USA	–	2 371	3 400
Total	**395**	**4 837**	**6 222**

Note: The SIPRI data on arms transfers refer to actual deliveries of major conventional weapons. To permit comparison between the data on such deliveries of different weapons and identification of general trends, SIPRI uses a *trend-indicator value*. The SIPRI values are therefore only an indicator of the volume of international arms transfers and not of the actual financial values of such transfers. Thus they are not comparable to economic statistics such as gross domestic product or export/import figures.

Source: SIPRI arms transfers database.

Table 11.4 shows the volume of deliveries of major conventional weapons to the three main actors in the conflict and illustrates the arms recipient–supplier relationships. Although Turkey and to a lesser extent Greece have built up arms industries they are still mainly dependent on imports and take third and sixth positions respectively in 1994–98 in the table of major arms recipients (see table 11.3). As both have major arms procurement programmes, it is likely that they will remain among the leading recipients for some years.[24]

The two rivals acquire their weapons from the same suppliers—mainly the USA and other NATO countries. These countries supply arms for commercial reasons and as a NATO aid commitment in the form of large numbers of surplus weapons. The tense relations between the two recipients are rarely taken into account. Russia has entered the market for what seem mainly to be commercial reasons.

In the case of Turkey arms transfers are used as an instrument of foreign policy by both suppliers and recipients. A number of suppliers have enforced long- and short-term arms embargoes on Turkey, partially or completely halting arms deals in reaction to Turkish actions in the war against Kurdish rebel groups. Recent examples are related to an ongoing Turkish procurement com-

[24] See appendix 11B for details on orders and deliveries. Enginsoy, U., 'Turkish budget anticipates arms-buying program', *Defense News*, 26 Oct.–1 Nov. 1998, p. 32; and 'Greek arms deals in the pipeline', *Jane's International Defense Review*, Nov. 1998, p. 10.

petition for combat helicopters. The US State Department granted licences to US companies to market their entries in the contest under the clear stipulation that Turkey would have to improve its human rights record before an actual sale could take place. Furthermore, in late 1998 the German Government blocked the display in Turkey of the French–German entry to the competition.[25]

Turkey in turn has tried to use its position as a potential customer to coerce supplier states to change their attitude to Turkey. In early 1998 arms negotiations with France came to a temporary standstill after the French National Assembly recognized the killing of 1.5 million Armenians in Turkey during World War I as genocide.[26] Although Turkey was reported to have announced in mid-1998 that its arms procurement policy would in future be shaped more by military than by foreign policy considerations, in November Italian firms were suspended from the competition for large Turkish weapon orders as a reaction to Italy's refusal to extradite the leader of the Kurdish Workers' Party (PKK).[27]

Despite the erratic relationships with arms suppliers, embargoes on both the supplier and recipient side have always been short-lived and deliveries of arms have not been much affected. Probably because of its difficult relations with suppliers, Turkey has diversified its sources of arms supply in recent years. It significantly developed its relations with Israel in 1996 through a major order for arms, and in 1993–96 it received weapon deliveries from Russia, which is now competing for major new orders.[28]

Greece has enjoyed a more stable relationship with its arms suppliers. Nevertheless, in 1998 Greece diversified its sources of arms supply beyond the NATO countries when it received Russian air defence systems.

Despite its conflict with Turkey and the Turkish occupation of northern Cyprus since 1974, Cyprus did not embark on a serious armament programme until the mid-1980s. Even then its land forces received only small supplies of arms while its air force and navy remain very small. Greece has supplied some weapons but its main contribution to the Cypriot defence is a defence pact, according to which Greece will provide military support in case of crisis.[29] The most important supplier in 1985–94 was France, which supplied, *inter alia*, tanks and a missile coastal defence system. Since 1995 the leading supplier has been Russia, which has delivered advanced T-80U tanks and armoured vehicles.

Although these arms transfers to Cyprus have been an issue of concern to Turkey, it was the Cypriot order for one SA-10d/S-300PMU-1 surface-to-air

[25] 'Tiger order delayed, pulled out from Turkey', *Air Letter*, 23 Dec. 1998, p. 4; and 'Turkey keeps option open in attack copter contest', *Defense News*, 7–13 Sep. 1998.

[26] Jack, A., 'French arms deals threatened', *Financial Times*, 11 June 1998, p. 6.

[27] Enginsoy, U., 'Turkey freezes deals with Italy in Kurdish protest', *Defense News*, 23–29 Nov. 1998, p. 6.

[28] SIPRI arms transfers database; and 'The Turkish–Israeli affair', *The Economist*, 19 Sep. 1998, pp. 55–56.

[29] Boyne, S., 'Moves to settle the Cypriot problem', *Jane's Intelligence Review*, vol. 7, no. 9 (Sep. 1995), pp. 403–406.

missile (SAM) system from Russia in January 1997 that caused a crisis in their relations. The SA-10 is a modern long-range air defence system that can intercept aircraft at a range of up to 150 km.[30] Its procurement would mean a major leap in capability as Cyprus' air defence at present is very limited. Besides being a reaction to the regular overflights by Turkish fighter aircraft in Cypriot airspace, the motive for the procurement of the SA-10 was to protect the Paphos airfield, which was constructed to enable Greek aircraft to operate from Cyprus.[31] Cyprus also hoped to use the order as a diplomatic tool to attract international attention and to break the deadlock in reunification talks.

Turkey reacted to the order for the SA-10 with outrage, claiming that, with its long range, the system is offensive and threatens the airspace of Turkey and northern Cyprus.[32] However, it is very unlikely that Cyprus would want to target aircraft in Turkish airspace as such long-distance engagements would carry the considerable risk of hitting wrongly identified aircraft, such as non-Turkish or civilian aircraft. Turkey's anger is better explained by threat perceptions of encirclement by Greece and a fear of losing military supremacy in the region, especially since the opening of the Paphos airbase on Cyprus. It appears to have been fuelled by domestic political considerations: a tough stance against Cyprus finds favour with widespread pro-Turkish Cypriot sentiments.[33]

Turkey repeatedly stated that it would do everything in its power to prevent the delivery and it refused to accept anything less than cancellation of the order.[34] It threatened to attack the SA-10 if it were deployed and in 1998 it searched two ships passing the Bosporus strait for SA-10 components.[35] It also made it clear to Russia that Russian arms producers would be ruled out as potential suppliers for planned large arms orders if the delivery to Cyprus went ahead.[36]

On the whole, Turkey's threat was taken seriously and few countries were prepared to support Cyprus in this matter. Arguing that the deal would be destabilizing, the USA, EU member states and UN Secretary-General Kofi Annan criticized the Cypriot move, pressured Cyprus not to proceed with the deployment and tried to find diplomatic solutions to the problem.[37] The USA also tried to convince Russia that delivery was irresponsible.[38]

[30] Here the NATO designation SA-10 is used although the system is often referred to by its Russian designation S-300. Cullen, T. and Foss, C. F. (eds), *Jane's Land-Based Air Defence 1997–98* (Jane's Information Group: Coulsdon, 1997), p. 137.

[31] 'Cyprus: Mikhailidhis says missiles only "deterrent"', Cyprus News Agency (Nicosia), 6 Jan. 1997, in Foreign Broadcast Information Service, *Daily Report–West Europe (FBIS-WEU)*, FBIS-WEU-97-004; and 'Cyprus orders S-300', *Military Technology*, Feb. 1997, p. 56.

[32] 'Greeks feel Turkish ire over Cyprus arms', *Financial Times*, 12 Jan. 1997, p. 2.

[33] Nuttal, C., 'Turks pose new threats over Cyprus', *The Guardian*, 11 Jan. 1997.

[34] 'Turkey urges Cyprus to abandon missile order', *Air Letter*, 18 Sep. 1998, p. 5.

[35] 'Turkey threatens Cyprus attack', *Financial Times*, 10 Jan. 1997, p. 2; and 'Turks powerless to stop missile shipments', *Air Letter*, 23 Sep. 1998, p. 5.

[36] 'Turkey flexes purchasing muscle to halt S-300 delivery to Cyprus', *Defense News*, 4–10 May 1998, p. 24.

[37] 'Cyprus missile contract', Press statement by Nicholas Burns, US Department of State Office of the spokesman press statement, 6 Jan. 1997, URL <http://secretary.state.gov/www/briefings/statements/

Russia was unwilling to accept interference by the USA and the EU in what it considered a legitimate commercial deal.[39] Russia's position seemed mainly to be based on commercial considerations and a wish to show defiance to Western pressure. In October the Russian State Duma issued a statement proclaiming that objections to the SA-10 deployment were a 'propaganda campaign' aimed at undermining Russian arms exports.[40] While, on the one hand, Russia expressed a willingness to cancel the order if Cyprus' demands for headway in the flagging peace process were met, it was also reported that, if Cyprus were to postpone the delivery of the SA-10, it would be charged storage costs.[41] Russia's position towards Turkey was ambiguous. On the one hand it stuck to the deal and even offered to protect the SA-10 delivery against a possible Turkish attack by using Russian Navy ships for transport, but on the other hand some officials in Russia said they would consider a cancellation of the order if Turkey were to grant part of its major planned arms procurement orders to Russia.[42]

Initially Greece backed the Cypriot order and made it clear that Turkish military action against the SA-10 would be considered a cause for war, underlining its support by using the Paphos airbase in an exercise with fighter aircraft.[43] From mid-1998, however, anxious to avoid hostilities and in response to pressure from the USA and the EU, Greece softened its position and tried first to persuade Cyprus to change its order to a short-range air defence system and, in late 1998, to agree to place the SA-10 on Crete.[44]

In December, after having delayed delivery twice in 1998, Cyprus finally accepted the Greek offer to place the SA-10 on Crete.[45] However, a final solution was not reached since Turkey remained opposed to delivery in any form to any place.[46]

970106/htm>; 'Turkey flexes purchasing muscle to halt S-300 delivery to Cyprus', *Defense News*, 4–10 May 1998, p. 24; and 'Annan hopes Cyprus will not deploy S-300s', *Air Letter*, 12 May 1998, p. 5.

[38] 'Russia to press ahead on Cyprus missiles', *International Herald Tribune*, 29 Apr. 1998, p. 1; and Regular report from the Commission on progress towards accession: Cyprus, 4 Nov. 1998, URL <http://www.europa.eu.int/comm/dg1a/enlarge/report_11_98_en/cyprus/120.htm>.

[39] 'Cyprus: Russian ambassador criticizes US stand on S-300', Cyprus News Agency (Nicosia), 4 Dec. 1998, in FBIS-WEU-98-338.

[40] 'Russia: Duma supports Russian cooperation with Cyprus', Interfax (Moscow), 16 Oct. 1998, in Foreign Broadcast Information Service, *Daily Report–Central Eurasia (FBIS-SOV)*, FBIS-SOV-98-289.

[41] 'Russia: spokesman clarifies comments on Cyprus missile deal', ITAR-TASS, 3 July 1998, in FBIS-SOV-98-184; and 'Missile delay to cost USD 1 mln per month, MP', *New Europe*, 8–14 Nov. 1998, p. 29.

[42] 'Russian battle group to deliver S-300s to Cyprus', *Jane's Defence Weekly*, 22 July 1998, p. 4; 'Turkey: diplomat: Russia will stop missile delivery if it wins bid', Anatolia (Ankara), 13 June 1998, in Foreign Broadcast Information Service, *Daily Report–Arms Control (FBIS-TAC)*, FBIS-TAC-98-164. Both in the UK and USA hidden Russian motives were suspected. One suspicion was that with the SA10 deal Russia was trying to add to the strains between NATO allies Greece and Turkey. Gordon, R., 'Russia to press ahead on Cyprus missiles', *International Herald Tribune*, 29 Apr. 1998, p. 1.

[43] 'Greece backs Cypriot missile plan', *Air Letter*, 8 Sep. 1998, p. 5; and 'Turkey, Greece edge closer to Cyprus clash', *Defense News*, 22–28 June 1998, p. 3.

[44] 'Athens loses taste for Cypriot missile row', *The Guardian*, 3 Aug. 1998, p. 7; and 'Greece seeks to pull Cyprus out of S-300 missile question', *New Europe*, 29 Nov.–5 Dec. 1998, p. 28.

[45] Fitchett, J., 'Deployment of missiles is scrapped by Cyprus', *International Herald Tribune*, 30 Dec. 1998, p. 1.

[46] Press conference by Foreign Minister Ismail Cem on the S-300s issue, Turkish Ministry of Foreign Affairs, 30 Dec. 1998, URL <http://.mfa.gov.tr/default.asp?param=/GRUPH/release/1998/320.htm>.

The Cypriot Government had to balance its military and foreign policies and national political considerations. Cypriot President Glafkos Clerides stated repeatedly that the deployment of the SA-10 would be suspended if progress were made in the Cyprus dispute resulting in an eventual demilitarization of the island.[47] These hopes to use the SA-10 deal as a diplomatic lever proved a misjudgement and in the end international pressure caused Cyprus to step back. One of the main reasons for this was the negative impact of the purchase on Cypriot negotiations for accession to the EU. The decision not to deploy the SA-10 entailed great political risks for both the Cypriot and the Greek governments as the general mood in both countries was that the order was legitimate and non-deployment meant losing to Turkey. Cypriot ministers resigned in reaction to the decision not to deploy the SA-10 on Cyprus and in a heated national debate President Clerides was strongly criticized.[48]

While intervention by the USA and EU states helped to prevent the SA-10 crisis from escalating into an armed conflict it is not surprising that the general feeling in Cyprus is that the solution was unjust. The USA and the EU showed little willingness to depart from commercial interests and deep-rooted alliance thinking in order to reach a solution. The logic of defining the Cypriot order for an air defence system as destabilizing—which it became as a result of Turkish reactions—is undermined by deliveries of large quantities of more offensive weapons to the other actors in the conflict.

IV. International embargoes on arms transfers

In 1998 the total number of countries under international arms embargoes was 20. Table 11.5 lists all the countries subject to partial or complete embargo on arms transfers, military services or other military-related transfers at any time during 1994–98.

The UN arms embargo on Sierra Leone, which was first implemented in October 1997 after a coup by the military and former rebels displaced President Ahmed Tejan Kabbah, was lifted on 5 June 1998 after foreign intervention had restored Kabbah to power. However, the ousted junta remained a major threat, so in the same resolution a new embargo directed only against the rebel junta forces was imposed.[49]

Between 1991 and 1996, as part of the efforts to contain and solve the conflicts related to the break-up of Yugoslavia in 1991 and 1992, a UN arms embargo was imposed on the entire region of the former Yugoslavia. On

[47] 'Cyprus not yet committed to delaying S-300 deployment', *New Europe*, 30 Aug.–5 Sep. 1998, p. 29; and Kambas, M., 'Cyprus denies scrapping missile delivery plans', *New Europe*, 13–19 Dec. 1998, p. 29.

[48] 'Cyprus ministers quit over cancelled missiles', *Financial Times*, 5 Jan. 1999, p. 3; and 'Cyprus missiles decision under attack', *Financial Times*, 13 Dec. 1998, p. 2.

[49] UN Security Council Resolution 1171, 5 June 1998.

Table 11.5. International arms embargoes in effect, 1994–98

Target	Entry into force	Lifted	Legal basis	Organization
Afghanistan[a]	22 Oct. 1996	–	UNSCR 1076	UN
Afghanistan[a,b]	17 Dec. 1996	–	–	EU
Angola (UNITA)	15 Sep. 1993	–	UNSCR 864	UN
Armenia[c]	28 Feb. 1992	–	–	OSCE
Azerbaijan[c]	28 Feb. 1992	–	–	OSCE
Bosnia and Herzegovina	1991	–	–	EU
Burundi	Aug. 1996	–	–	Neighbours[d]
China	27 June 1989	–	–	EU
Croatia	1991	–	–	EU
Haiti	30 Sep. 1991	15 Oct. 1994	–	OAS
Haiti[e]	13 Oct. 1993	15 Oct. 1994	UNSCR 841	UN
Iraq	6 Aug. 1990	–	UNSCR 661	UN
Iraq	4 Aug. 1990	–	–	EU
Liberia[f]	19 Nov. 1992	–	UNSCR 788	UN
Libya	27 Jan. 1986	–	–	EU
Libya	31 Mar. 1992	–	UNSCR 748	UN
Myanmar[b]	29 July 1991[g]	–	–	EU
Nigeria	24 Apr. 1996	?	–	Commonwealth
Nigeria[b]	20 Nov. 1995	–	–	EU
Rwanda	17 May 1994	16 Aug. 1995[h]	UNSCR 918	UN
Rwanda (rebels)[i]	16 Aug. 1998	–	UNSCR 1011	UN
Sierra Leone	8 Oct. 1997	5 June 1998	UNSCR 1132	UN
Sierra Leone (rebels)[j]	5 June 1998	–	UNSCR 1171	UN
Sierra Leone	8 Dec. 1997	–	–	EU
Slovenia	1991	10 Aug. 1998	–	EU
Somalia	23 Jan. 1992	–	UNSCR 733	UN
South Africa[k]	Nov. 1977	24 May 1994	UNSCR 418	UN
Sudan[b]	15 Mar. 1994	–	–	EU
Yugoslavia	25 Sep. 1991	1 Oct. 1996	UNSCR 713	UN
Yugoslavia (S & M)	31 Mar. 1998	–	UNSCR 1160	UN
Yugoslavia	1991	–	–	EU
Zaire/Congo, Dem Rep[b]	7 Apr. 1993	–	–	EU

[a] Voluntary (non-mandatory) embargo.

[b] Does not apply to deliveries under existing contracts.

[c] Embargo on deliveries to forces engaged in combat in the Nagorno-Karabakh area.

[d] Congo (Dem. Rep. of), Ethiopia, Kenya, Rwanda, Tanzania and Uganda.

[e] Originally imposed in June 1993, but temporarily suspended until Oct. 1993.

[f] Does not apply to deliveries to ECOMOG forces in Liberia.

[g] A 'decision to refuse the sale of any military equipment' was made by the EU General Affairs Council on 29 July 1991. On 28 Oct. a decision confirming the embargo (96/635/CFSP) was made by the EU Council of Ministers for Foreign Affairs.

[h] The arms embargo was suspended on this date and formally ended on 1 Sep. 1996.

[i] Does not apply to deliveries to government forces in Rwanda. Embargo on equipment for persons in neighbouring states if the equipment is for use in Rwanda.

[j] Does not apply to deliveries to government or ECOMOG forces in Sierra Leone.

[k] A voluntary arms embargo commenced in Aug. 1963 UN (UNSCR 181) and a voluntary embargo on arms imports from South Africa in Dec. 1985 (UNSCR 558).

Sources: SIPRI arms transfers archives.

31 March 1998 the UN imposed a mandatory arms embargo on Yugoslavia (Serbia and Montenegro) as a result of Serb actions in Kosovo.[50] While EU embargoes on other successor states to the former Yugoslavia have continued to remain in force since 1991, the embargo on Slovenia was lifted in August 1998 because of improved stability.

Although embargoes are undeniably a strong political signal of disfavour, their effectiveness is questionable. While many embargoes have been enforced on states engaged in internal wars, they do not seem to have had much influence on the level of violence or to have led to an end to the fighting.[51]

Enforcement has been another problem. In practically all cases of embargo, including mandatory UN embargoes, reports have emerged of illegal arms transfers. While these reports are often difficult to verify, more direct and circumstantial evidence of breaches of embargoes emerged during 1998, including new information about possible deliveries of weapons and other military equipment to South Africa during the UN embargo of 1977–94.[52] Some of the evidence is circumstantial in that the number of certain types of equipment (combat aircraft, helicopters) that have been acknowledged to be in service today is much higher than the number of such equipment known to have been transferred before the embargo was imposed.[53] Other evidence is more direct, including statements from former South African officials that South Africa received French deliveries of helicopters in kit form in the 1980s.[54]

Fresh evidence also emerged of some large-scale breaches of the UN embargoes on Yugoslavia and its successor states.[55] Direct evidence came in the case of Croatia where there has even been official acknowledgement of the transfer of Mi-24 combat helicopters, even though the official version claims these were 'ambulance helicopters'.[56] In 1991–95, 6500 tons of weapons and ammunition were delivered from Argentina to Croatia. The ongoing investigation of this case in Argentina reads like a classic spy story and has revealed

[50] UN Security Council Resolution 1160, 31 Mar. 1998. See also chapter 2 in this volume.

[51] Anthony, I. *et al.*, 'Arms production and arms trade', *SIPRI Yearbook 1994* (Oxford University Press: Oxford, 1994), pp. 493–502.

[52] South Africa was under embargo for decades, but still managed to maintain the most powerful and best equipped armed forces in Sub-Saharan Africa, even emerging from the embargo era with a highly advanced military industry. For a discussion of the embargo and the ways in which South Africa dealt with it, see Landgren, S., SIPRI, *Embargo Disimplemented* (Oxford University Press: Oxford, 1989); and Bachelor, P. and Willett, S., SIPRI, *Disarmament and Defence Industrial Adjustment in South Africa* (Oxford University Press: Oxford, 1998).

[53] The number of Cheetah combat aircraft acknowledged to have been produced is 69. The Cheetah is an upgrade of existing Mirage-3 aircraft, but the number of such aircraft known to have been delivered in the 1960s and 1970s is no more than 58. Several reports have implicated Israel as supplier of their Mirage-5 derivative, the Kfir. Carroll, I., *World Air Forces Directory 1998–99* (Mach III Plus: Stevenage, 1998), p. 156.

[54] 'Former S. African minister enters helicopter row', Reuters, 24 Apr. 1998.

[55] For an overview of reports on breaches of the embargo since 1991, see Berghezan, G., *Ex-Yougoslavie: L'embargo sur les armes et le réarmement actuel* [Ex-Yugoslavia: the arms embargo and current rearmament] (GRIP: Brussels, 1997).

[56] 'Croatia quietly builds air force despite embargo', *World Aerospace & Defense Intelligence*, 3 Mar. 1995, p. 6; and 'Croatie, une force aérienne sous controle' [Croatia, an air force under control], *Air & Cosmos/Aviation International*, 12 May 1995, p. 32.

some of the ways in which such 'impossible' transfers are made possible.[57] The effectiveness of the NATO/Western European Union sea blockade in enforcing the UN embargo will clearly be questioned if the weapons and ammunition have actually reached Croatia.

In a very different case the UK allowed weapons to be transferred to Sierra Leone just days after the UN Security Council had agreed on an arms embargo. One official British line of argument was that while the UN embargo was agreed upon British legislation for its implementation was not yet in force. Another claimed that information that the British company Sandline International planned to transfer weapons to Sierra Leone's ousted president had failed to reach the Minister of Foreign Affairs after mistakes in the processing of the information.[58]

V. The EU Code of Conduct

On 25 May 1998 the EU members adopted a common Code of Conduct for Arms Exports outlining general principles and guidelines for future exports of military equipment.[59] Together with the French Government the UK, which took over presidency of the EU for six months in January 1998, produced a first draft for discussion within the Council of Ministers' Group for Cooperation in the Field of Armaments and the Harmonisation of European Export Policies (COARM) in February 1998. The early cooperation with France was clearly calculated to minimize possible French opposition. In recent years France has proved to be opposed to any European coordination of conventional arms export controls that could 'force' it to give up some of its, by European standards, liberal arms export policies.

Between February and May 1998 four drafts were discussed. Leaked copies of the first draft drew heavy fire from non-governmental organizations (NGOs) since some of the proposed criteria and the preamble suggested that the code would contain even weaker constraints than the EU Common Criteria for arms exports from 1991 and 1992.[60] The discussions of the drafts revealed deep divisions among EU members about the weight of such a document. Agreement proved impossible at the civil servant level, largely because France

[57] 'Arms and the men', *The Economist*, 12 Sep. 1998, p. 60; 'Illegal arms sales test for Menem', *The Independent*, 27 Oct. 1998, p. 15; 'US denies knew of Argentine arms sales to Croatia', Reuters, 7 Oct. 1998; and 'Argentina's Menem backs ministers in arms scandal', Reuters, 9 Sep. 1998.

[58] 'British ministers cleared in arms-to-Africa affair', Reuters, 27 July 1998.

[59] The complete text is included as appendix 11D in this volume. In early Aug. 1998 Bulgaria, Cyprus, the Czech Republic, Estonia, Hungary, Iceland, Latvia, Lithuania, Norway, Poland, Romania, Slovakia and Slovenia also committed themselves to follow the EU Code of Conduct. *Arms Trade News*, Aug./Sep. 1998, p. 3. See also appendix 11E, section III in this volume.

[60] Clegg, E. and McKenzie, A., 'Developing a common approach? The EU Code of Conduct on Arms Exports', *Bulletin of Arms Control*, no. 32 (Dec. 1998), p. 23. For the text of the EU Common Criteria see URL <http://www.sipri.se/projects/expcon/eu_criteria.htm>. See also *SIPRI Yearbook 1992: World Armaments and Disarmament* (Oxford University Press: Oxford, 1992), pp. 295–97 and *SIPRI Yearbook 1993: World Armaments and Disarmament* (Oxford University Press: Oxford, 1993), pp. 461–62 for a discussion of these criteria.

refused to accept a restrictive code. The final text was decided at a meeting of the European foreign ministers in Brussels on 25 May 1998.

Although the final version of the code is not much more than a restatement of the Common Criteria agreed upon in 1991 and 1992, there are a couple of distinctions. The most obvious is that the code asks EU members to notify each other of refusals to export. A second distinction is that it is clearly intended as a first step in a process towards the creation of common export regulations. In addition to eight criteria for arms exports, there are several 'operative provisions' for further development of the code. The most important of these is that all EU members will provide an annual report on their arms exports and on the national implementation of the code. These reports will be discussed at an annual meeting within the framework of the EU Common Foreign and Security Policy (CFSP). During these meetings the development of the code will also be on the agenda, thereby creating an institutionalized process of review and discussion instead of ad hoc initiatives. The code also specifically mentions the need for a 'common list of military equipment' to which it would apply.

However, as it stands now the code is no more than a first small step towards what should result in common EU arms export legislation, or at least an alignment of the national legislations and policies of the member states. Since it was adopted as a Council Declaration, the code is merely a political not a legally binding document. Furthermore, most of the criteria and operative provisions are, as in the earlier Common Criteria, worded in such a vague way that they are open to almost any interpretation by national governments, which in the end still have absolute control over their export policies.

While a number of gaps are directly addressed in the operative provisions, other problems will have to be negotiated at the annual meetings or elsewhere. The issue of what to do if one EU country wants to grant an export licence to a country for which another EU country has already refused permission has been one of the most contentious areas of negotiation and remains unresolved. The code also fails to address the problem of 'after-delivery controls' through the verification of end-user certificates and controls of the actual use of delivered equipment or the issue of licences for production of equipment developed in an EU state but produced elsewhere.

Transparency

Since a number of governments of EU member states seem to embrace the view of transparency as necessary for developing a responsible arms export policy it is disappointing that there are no provisions for parliamentary oversight or public scrutiny in the Code of Conduct. The code mentions neither public reports nor the need to develop common standards for annual reports on arms exports. The only explicit mention of transparency is a general statement that, with a view to achieving greater transparency, the exchange of relevant information between EU members should be strengthened.

During the drafting of the code a number of NGOs called for greater transparency and accountability. They also recommended that member states should report annually to their national parliaments all arms exports denied or granted, and provide parliament or a parliamentary committee in advance with a list of all sensitive export licences applied for, including information about cases in which similar licence applications have been denied by other member states.[61] Although, in an early draft of the code, the British Government proposed the inclusion of references to public accountability this was opposed mainly by France, which blocked the inclusion of a provision on annual publication by all EU countries of full and detailed reports on arms exports.[62]

Outside the code's framework, the existing national reports of EU member states give only limited possibilities to assess the implementation of the code at a national level. The most common form of reports on arms exports among EU states—reporting their monetary value—is mainly useful for assessments of the economic aspects of arms exports, and only to a very limited extent for assessment of military aspects. The code, on the other hand, mainly focuses on military implications of exports, either directly for the use of weapons in aggression or human rights violations or for the behaviour of recipients and the possibility of punishing recipients by not supplying arms.[63] The economic value of military equipment gives no real indication of the relevance of the equipment for human rights violations, internal repression, provoking or prolonging armed conflicts or external aggression. The export of an expensive radar network may have a much less negative impact than the export of a batch of cheap armoured vehicles or rifles. Especially in cases where the equipment is second-hand or is exported to a less developed region, the monetary value is no real indication of its military value in the local context.

The available public reports on arms exports from EU member states include cases of exports to countries which do not seem to fulfil all the criteria of the Code of Conduct.[64] However, the current data do not reveal whether the equipment in question is intended for purposes which conflict with the criteria or whether it is considered to be of strategic value but not specifically for military use. The categories given in the existing reports are mostly of a generic type such as 'aerospace' or 'explosives' and do not distinguish between separate items. 'Aerospace' can include anything from combat aircraft to transport aircraft with civil applications. For example, while deliveries of combat aircraft might be considered destabilizing to regional security, the delivery of

[61] Clegg, L., 'Proposals for an effective EU Code of Conduct on the Arms Trade', Saferworld, in consultation with Amnesty International, BASIC and Oxfam, 1998.

[62] 'French threat to European arms sales code', *The Independent,* 25 May 1998, p. 8; and 'Cook's code on arms sales faces unfriendly fire', *The Independent,* 30 Apr. 1998, p. 10.

[63] One criterion of the 8 mentions economic aspects and stresses the need to take into account relative levels of military and social expenditure of the recipient countries in arms export decisions.

[64] For example, in its 1997 annual report on arms exports Sweden reported values for deliveries to Pakistan and India—countries in conflict—and to Indonesia, which has a questionable human rights record. In the same year the Netherlands reported values for deliveries to Algeria which is involved in internal conflict and to China which is under an EU arms embargo.

similarly valued transport aircraft might be essential in providing transport of civilian necessities to remote regions.

VI. National and international transparency in arms transfers

Official national data on arms exports

Government statistics on the value of arms exports are presented in table 11.6. SIPRI records and disseminates official data on the value of arms exports for four reasons: (*a*) to make such information more accessible; (*b*) to highlight the lack of complete government data; (*c*) to underline the fact that data from different countries are only comparable to a limited extent; and (*d*) as the statistics present real values (in contrast to the SIPRI trend-indicator values), to provide a rough indication of the financial scale of arms exports.

The data are from official national documents, official statements or official replies to SIPRI's requests for information. Using the SIPRI estimates of deliveries of major conventional weapons as a baseline, the countries providing statistics together accounted for an estimated 98 per cent of total arms exports in 1998.

Readers are cautioned in using these data in analysis. The table is not comprehensive and there are other countries, such as China and Israel, whose exports would be larger than those of some countries listed in the table. Furthermore, arms export definitions are not consistent from country to country, and not all countries explain their export statistics fully.[65]

The problem of inconsistency is illustrated in Spain, where the value given by the Ministry of the Economy differs radically from a three-year average provided by the Ministry of Defence, which is more than five times higher.[66] An analysis of the Italian arms exports report has led to the conclusion that the Italian data for 1997 were miscalculated and should probably be 1487 billion lire instead of 2165 billion lire, although this has not yet been officially confirmed.[67]

In 1998 confusion and political problems in Russia led once more to seemingly conflicting claims. Yevgeniy Ananyev, director of the Russian arms export organization Rosvooruzheniye, denied claims by his predecessor that Russia had earned $3.5 billion from arms sales in 1996. Ananyev said that the figure was just over $2 billion and that the remaining arms had been sent abroad to pay off debts. He, in turn, was accused by the Russian General Control Department (GKU) of overestimating expected arms sales figures for

[65] For a more detailed assessment of official arms export data, see *SIPRI Yearbook 1998* (note 6), pp. 306–11.

[66] The Spanish Ministry of Defence gives Ptas 82 810 million as an average for the period 1993–95 while the report to the parliament by the Ministry of Economics gives an average of Ptas 14 582 million. Spanish Ministry of Defence, Secretaria de Estado de la Defensa, Direccion General de Armamento y Material, *La Industria Espanola de Defensa, 1996* [The Spanish defence industry, 1996], p. 9.

[67] *Rapporto informativo dell'osservatorio sul commercio delle armi e sull'applicazione della legge 185/90*, OSCAR report 15 (IRES: Florence, May/June 1998), p. 2.

1998. While Ananyev estimated sales of $2–3 billion, the GKU expected the figure to fall to well below $2 billion.[68]

This year for the first time official data on arms exports were received from Slovenia. There are also data on aggregated arms exports from India and Taiwan and on French, Italian, Swedish and British export orders (as opposed to deliveries) which have not previously been reported in the SIPRI Yearbook.

Developments in national transparency in 1998

Effective parliamentary oversight of arms exports is rare and the countries which regularly make available detailed information on their overall arms exports remain the exception rather than the rule. In recent years, however, the issue of arms export transparency has received increased attention, which has led to improved reporting in a number of countries.[69]

Although table 11.6 only includes aggregate arms export data, some of the contributing countries publish more comprehensive reports that show the value of military equipment exported to individual countries. In 1998 Australia, Canada, Finland, Italy, the Netherlands, Spain, Sweden, Switzerland and the USA published such reports. Germany plans to follow their example in the near future and the UK submitted its report in early 1999 (see below). Transparency has also improved through the increased availability of arms export reports on the Internet.[70]

The Netherlands Government published its first comprehensive report on arms transfers in the autumn of 1998, including values for arms export licences by country and by category. Instead of specifying values of delivered military equipment, as was originally intended, the report includes the values of licences granted, which were considered more useful to parliamentarians since they give an insight into planned deliveries rather than information after the fact.[71] Unlike the Swedish and Italian governments, the Netherlands Government did not publish both data on licences and actual deliveries.

The Spanish Government's first annual report to parliament on arms exports was published in February 1998 for the period 1991–96, and it was followed in July by a report on 1997 deliveries of defence *matériel.*

The British Government published its first annual report on arms exports in March 1999.[72] The report is relatively complete with details of licences

[68] For a discussion of reports on the value of Russian arms exports, see Anthony, I., 'Economic dimensions of Soviet and Russian arms exports', ed. I. Anthony, SIPRI, *Russia and the Arms Trade* (Oxford University Press: Oxford, 1998), p. 72; Perera, J, 'Rosvooruzheniye exposed', *Jane's Intelligence Review Pointer*, Nov. 1998, p. 4; and Novichkov (note 5).

[69] See, e.g., Carlman, Å., *Arms Trade from the EU: Secrecy vs Transparency* (Svenska freds- och skiljedomsföreningen: Stockholm, 1998).

[70] SIPRI collects hyperlinks to websites containing official arms export data at URL <http://www.sipri.se/projects/armstrade/atlinks.html>.

[71] Netherlands Ministry of Economic Affairs, *Jaarrapport Nederlands wapenexportbeleid 1997* [The Netherlands' arms export policy in 1997], Tweede Kamer, Kamerstuk 22054, nr. 39, Oct. 1998.

[72] British Foreign and Commonwealth Office, 'Annual report on arms exports', 25 Mar. 1999, URL <http://www.fco.gov.uk/text_only/newstext.asp?2163>.

Table 11.6. Official data on arms exports, 1993–97

Country	Currency unit (current prices)	1993	1994	1995	1996	1997	1997 (US $m.)	Explanation of data
Australia[a]	m. A. dollars	67.3	28.4	39.2	435.2	19	12	Value of shipments of military goods (fiscal years)
Belgium[b]	m. B. francs	11 684	11 403	8 230	8 180	7 460	241	Value of licences for arms exports
Brazil[c]	m. US dollars	. .	2.6	12.4	8.7	26	26	Value of arms exports
Canada[d]	m. C. dollars	335.9	497.4	447.3	464.8	304.3	220	Shipments of military goods, excluding exports to the USA
Czech Rep.[e]	m. US dollars	167	194	154	117	182	182	Value of arms exports
Finland[f]	m. F. marks	62	61	132	69	81.5	16	Value of exports of defence *matériel*
France[g]	m. francs	14 600	11 600	10 900	18 600	. .	. .	Value of exports of defence equipment
	m. francs	20 600	16 800	19 000	29 400	43 300	7 419	Value of deliveries of defence equipment and associated services
	m. francs	38 900	31 700	33 500	19 400	30 200	5 174	Value of export orders for defence equipment and associated services
Germany[h]	m. D. marks	2 577	2 131	1 982	1 006	1 384	798	Value of exports of weapons of war
India[i]	m. rupees	. .	. .	960	1 430	1 860	51	Value of exports by defence public-sector undertakings and ordnance factories (fiscal years)
Italy[j]	b. lire	1 080	920	1 230	1 196	2 165	1 271	Value of deliveries of military equipment
Netherlands[k]	m. guilders	1 475	1 006	1 029	922	2 438	1 250	Value of export licences for military goods
Norway[l]	m. kronor	. .	. .	. .	985	1 060	150	Value of actual deliveries of defence *matériel*
Portugal[m]	m. escudos	3 944	3 430	6 803	4 157	3 205	18	Value of exports of defence materials, equipment and technology
Russia[n]	m. US dollars	2 500	1 700	3 100	3 500	2 500	2 500	Value of exports of military equipment
Slovakia[o]	m. koruna	2 257	3 320	2 452	2 214	1 273	38	Value of exports of military production
Slovenia[p]	m. tolar	3 360	2 730	966	2 290	726	5	Value of exports of defence equipment
South Afr.[q]	m. rand	. .	. .	855	517	1 324.9	288	Value of export permits issued
Spain[r]	m. pesetas	17 867	9 478	16 400	19 473	95 128	650	Value of exports of defence *matériel* (excl. dual-use equipment)
Sweden[s]	m. kronor	2 863	3 181	3 313	3 087	3 101	406	Value of actual deliveries of military equipment; changes in the coverage of data occurred in 1992–93
Switzerland[t]	m. S. francs	260.2	221	141.2	232.9	294.3	203	Value of exports of war *matériel*
Taiwan[u]	m. NT dollars	. .	. .	. .	. .	25 500	(929.6)	Value of military sales in 2-year periods

UK	m. pounds[v]	. .	. .	. .	. .	3 359.6	5 502	Value of deliveries of defence equipment
	m. pounds[w]	1 914	1 798	2 076	3 402	4 598	7 481	Value of deliveries of defence equipment
	m. pounds[w]	2 969	2 946	4 723	. .	. .	. .	Value of deliveries of defence equipment and items where the official commodity classifications do not distinguish between military and civil aerospace equipment
	m. pounds[w]	7 074	4 608	4 970	5 080	5 540	9 072	Value of export orders for defence equipment
Ukraine[x]	m. US dollars	. .	. .	. .	. .	600	600	Value of arms exports
USA[y]	m. dollars	11 314	9 468	11 940	11 574	19 233	19 233	Value of deliveries of defence articles and services through the US Government (foreign military sales) in fiscal years
	m. dollars	3 808	3 339	2 773	1 082	1 921	1 921	Value of military and certain dual-use equipment transfers from US commercial suppliers in fiscal years
	m. dollars	31 109	13 292	8 950	10 300	8 778	8 778	Value of agreements on sales of defence articles and services through the US Government (foreign military sales) in fiscal years

. . = no data available or received

[a] Australian Department of Defence, Industry and Procurement Infrastructure Division, *Annual Report: Exports of Defence and Strategic Goods from Australia, 1997/98*, June 1999.

[b] Belgian Ministry of Foreign Affairs, *Rapport van de regering aan het parlement over de toepassing van de wet van 5 augustus 1991 betreffende de in-, de uit-, en de doorvoer van wapens, munitie, en speciaal voor militair gebruik dienstig materieel en de daaraan verbonden technologie, 1 januari 1997 tot 31 december 1997* [Government report to parliament on the implementation of the law of 5 Aug. 1991 on the import, export and passage of weapons, ammunition and *matériel* for military use and related technology, 1 Jan.–31 Dec. 1997], 1998.

[c] Information received from the Brazilian Embassy, Stockholm, 24 Nov. 1997.

[d] Canadian Department of Foreign Affairs and International Trade, Exports Controls Division, Export and Import Controls Bureau, *Annual Report: Export of Military Goods from Canada, 1997*, Nov. 1998.

[e] *Hospodarske Noviny*, 15 Apr. 1998, data confirmed by the Embassy of the Czech Republic, Stockholm.

[f] Information received from the Finnish Ministry of Defence, Helsinki, 18 Dec. 1998.

[g] Assemblée Nationale, *Rapport fait au nom de la commission des finances, de l'économie générale et du plan sur le projet de loi de finances pour 1998* [Report for the Commission on Finance, General Economy and Planning on the 1998 draft budget bill], annexe nr 40, Défense, 9 Oct. 1997, p. 174; and 'Big rise in orders for French arms', *Financial Times*, 26 June 1998.

[h] Information received from the German Ministry of Economics, Bonn, 30 Oct. 1998.

[i] Indian Ministry of Defence, *Annual Report 1997/98*; and *International Air Letter*, 14 July 1998, p. 4.

[j] Camera dei Deputati, *Relazione sulle operazioni autorizzate e svolte per il controllo dell'esportazione, importazione e transito dei materiali di armamento nonchè dell'esportazione e del transito dei prodotti ad alta technologia (anno 1997)*, 30 Mar. 1998.

[k] Netherlands Ministry of Economic Affairs, *Jaarrapport Nederlands wapenexportbeleid 1997* [The Netherlands' arms export policy in 1997], Tweede Kamer, Kamerstuk 22054, nr. 39, Oct. 1998.

[l] Norwegian Ministry of Foreign Affairs, *Eksport av forsvarsmateriell frå Noreg 1997* [Arms exports from Norway in 1997], St meld nr 43 (1997/98), May 1998.

[m] Portuguese Ministry of Defence, *Anuario Estatistico da Defesa Nacional 1997* [Annual national defence statistics, 1997], Oct. 1998, p. 103.

[n] 'Tumultuous year unsettles Russian arms sales', *Defense News*, 20–26 July 1998, p. 26; and 'Rising sales bring hard currency into Russia', *Jane's Defence Weekly*, 13 May 1998, p. 18. Values reported by the official Russian arms marketing agency, Rosvooruzheniye.

[o] Information received from the Ministry of the Economy, Republic of Slovakia.

[p] Information received from the Ministry of Foreign Affairs, Republic of Slovenia.

[q] Website of the National Conventional Arms Control Committee, Republic of South Africa, URL <http://www.mil.za/ncacc.htm>.

[r] Spanish Ministry of Economy and Agriculture, *Exportaciones realizadas de material de defensa y de doble uso en 1997, por países de destino* [Exports of military and dual-use equipment in 1997, by country of destination], 30 July 1998.

[s] Swedish Ministry for Foreign Affairs, *Redogörelse för den svenska krigsmaterielexporten år 1997* [Swedish Exports of Military Equipment in 1997], Regeringens skrivelse 1997/98:147, 7 May 1998.

[t] Eidgenössisches Militärdepartement Information, 'Ausfuhr von Kriegsmaterial 1997' [Exports of defence *matériel* 1997], Pressemitteilung, 5 Feb. 1998.

[u] Chinese Ministry of National Defense, Taipei, *1998 National Defense Report*, Apr. 1998.

[v] British Foreign and Commonwealth Office, *Annual Report on Arms Exports*, 25 Mar. 1999, URL <http://www.fco.gov.uk/text_only/news/ newstext.asp?2163&>.

[w] Government Statistical Service, *UK Defence Statistics*, 1998 edn. The 2 British Government sources used in this table give different figures under the same heading 'Value of deliveries of defence equipment'.

[x] 'Ukraine increased military equipment exports last year 2.3 fold', Interfax, Moscow, 23 Apr. 1998, in Foreign Broadcast Information Service, *Daily Report–Central Eurasia*, FBIS-SOV-98-113, 23 Apr. 1998.

[y] *Foreign Military Sales, Foreign Military Construction Sales and Military Assistance Facts, as of September 30, 1997*, Deputy for Financial Management Comptroller, Department of Defense Security Assistance Agency, Washington, DC.

Sources: The table is based on government publications, official statements and information received on request from governments. Comments are worded as closely as possible to details in the documents cited. Sources refer to the last year reported here. For earlier years see earlier SIPRI Yearbooks. The 1997 US $ series is calculated with average 1997 exchange rates. SIPRI collects hyperlinks to websites containing official arms export data at URL <http://www.sipri.se/projects/armstrade/atlinks.html>.

granted and total values of arms exports per recipient. The report was planned for publication in 1998 but was delayed owing to difficulties in compiling one set of data derived from the available but inconsistent data from the Department of Trade and Industry (DTI), the Ministry of Defence (MOD) Defence Export Services Organization (DESO) and Customs and Excise. Furthermore, while the publication of a more specific account of equipment covered by licences granted was acceptable to all parties, the British Government's desire to publish details of actual exports met with resistance. The attempts of the Foreign Office to achieve greater transparency were reportedly blocked by the DTI and the MOD, which were concerned that more openness would harm companies' competitiveness and that it would make their own work more cumbersome.[73]

In the coalition treaty between the parties that formed the new German Government in October 1998 it was announced that an annual arms export report would be submitted to parliament.[74] The new government also announced that it was working towards the inclusion in the European Code of Conduct of a demand for transparency from possible recipient countries. This would probably require the recipient countries to report their imports to the UNROCA.

In 1998 the US Government once again published a 'Section 655' report, containing much greater detail on the quantities and types of weapons exported than reports from any other country.[75]

The UN Register of Conventional Arms

On 2 September 1998 the UN Secretary-General released the sixth annual report of information received from governments on their arms imports and/or exports for calendar year 1997.[76] By that time, 91 countries, and the Cook Islands and Niue, had responded in some way to the request for information.[77] As of 21 March 1999, this number had increased to 97 countries.[78]

Since the previous report, released in August 1997, a number of changes have been introduced. The 'deadline' for reporting has been moved from

[73] *Arms Trade Bulletin* (Saferworld, London), no. 10 (5 Nov. 1998); and Nicoll, A., 'Accounting for arms exports delayed', *Financial Times*, 12 Nov. 1998, p. 10.

[74] SPD, *Der Koalitionsvertrag, Aufbruch und Erneuerung Deutschlands Weg ins 21. Jahrhundert* [The coalition treaty, departure and renewal as Germany enters the 21st century], Bonn, 20 Oct. 1998, URL <http//www.spd.de/politik/koalition/uebers.html>.

[75] US Department of State and US Department of Defense, Foreign Military Assistance Act Report to Congress, *Authorized US Commercial Exports, Military Assistance and Foreign Military Sales and Military Imports, Fiscal Year 1997*, Washington, DC, Sep. 1998.

[76] UN document A/53/334, 2 Sep. 1998.

[77] This does not include the 18 countries and Palestine for which, as members of the Arab League, Saudi Arabia submitted a *note verbale* reiterating the sentiments of the Arab League's *note verbale* in 1997, which expressed support for the idea of the UNROCA but at the same time disagreed with the present structure. The Arab League members were therefore unwilling to provide the information requested. Reply by Saudia Arabia dated 17 June 1998, as included in UN document A/53/334, 2 Sep. 1998, pp. 109–10. See also the reply by Mauritania dated 2 Sep. 1997, as included in UN document A/52/312, 28 Aug. 1997, pp. 71–72. Only 3 Arab League members, Jordan, Libya and Qatar, reported on actual arms imports and/or exports.

[78] For a full list of participating countries and their reports see the official UN Register of Conventional Arms, URL <http://domino.un.org/REGISTER.NSF>.

30 April to 31 May as a reaction to the fact that very few countries managed to provide the requested data before 30 April.[79] Another significant change is the inclusion of data from a large number of governments on holdings of weapons and procurement from national production. Although several governments have provided such data in previous years, these were not reproduced in the actual UN report. Their inclusion must be seen as a step towards development of the UNROCA into a tool for identification of possibly destabilizing accumulations of weapons, as was the original goal of the register. As such it should cover not merely transfers of systems that could be destabilizing in an international context, but also all procurement of such systems.[80]

Less successful was a request in a General Assembly resolution from December 1997 for countries to provide 'nil' reports on arms imports and/or exports if appropriate, rather than not replying at all as had seemed to be the practice in earlier years.[81] Despite this call, the number of states that submitted reports did not increase significantly. The same resolution also stressed the possibility of giving information on, for example, the designation of the weapon in the 'Remarks' column of the standardized reporting form. The 1998 report is clearly an improvement on the five earlier reports, largely because the USA for the first time used the 'Remarks' column to give the designation of the weapons transferred. It hereby follows the example it set in providing such details in a substantive national report published for the first time in 1997.[82] In earlier reports the USA only gave data on the recipient and the number of items delivered in each UNROCA category.[83] Since the USA is the biggest exporter and especially since many of the US reports on exports did not match the reports from the recipients, part of the basic goal of the UNROCA was not fulfilled. While this problem still exists, it is now easier to determine why these differences occur.

There was, however, one major disappointing development in 1998, namely that China, one of the leading exporters of weapons, refused to provide data to the UNROCA in protest against the inclusion of data on arms transfers to Taiwan.[84] In 1996 the USA, which in publicly available sources is identified, together with France, as the only supplier to Taiwan of weapons which fall into the categories of equipment which are to be registered, started to report its deliveries to Taiwan as a footnote to the standardized format of reporting.[85]

[79] In 1997 only 33 countries reported before the deadline of 30 Apr. 1997. In 1998, 55 countries reported before the new deadline of 31 May 1998.

[80] UN General Assembly Resolution 46/36 L, 9 Dec. 1991.

[81] UN General Assembly Resolution 52/38 R, 9 Dec. 1997.

[82] US Department of State (note 75).

[83] The categories of equipment which are to be registered in the UNROCA are: battle tanks; armoured combat vehicles; large-calibre artillery systems; combat aircraft; attack helicopters; warships; and missiles and missile launchers.

[84] Taiwan is the only country not requested by the UN Secretary-General to provide data (despite requests for data from other non-members such as Switzerland and the Holy See).

[85] France, known to have delivered combat aircraft and warships in 1997, did not, however, include exports to Taiwan in its report to the UNROCA.

China protested from the start, and according to an official Chinese statement this finally 'forced' it not to participate from 1998.[86]

The geographical pattern of participation in 1998 was similar to that of previous years. Participation is high among states that are members of international organizations in which confidence-building measures are an important point on the agenda. Nearly all Organization for Security and Co-operation in Europe (OSCE) participating states, and Organization of American States (OAS), Association of South-East Asian Nations (ASEAN) and ASEAN Regional Forum (ARF) members reported. On the other hand participation was again extremely low in the Middle East and Africa. One surprise was the participation of Jordan and Qatar, both of which for the first time submitted reports on arms imports, and apparently did not follow the line of the other Arab League states as outlined in a *note verbale* to the UN.[87] Israel was the only other Middle Eastern country that had responded by the time the Secretary-General's report was released. Iran, which has consistently submitted data after the annual report, had not submitted a return to the register by April 1999.

The number of countries reporting consistently to the UNROCA seems to have stabilized. Nearly all countries identified by SIPRI from open sources as exporters of weapons which fall into the UNROCA categories of equipment have reported since 1992. However, of the importers, many Middle Eastern countries have never reported despite having been identified in open sources and in UNROCA exporters' reports as major recipients. A few relatively small importers, mainly in Africa, have also never reported.

Discrepancies between the information submitted by exporting and importing states for their bilateral transfers in the same year are still common. The discrepancies make the data in the register difficult to interpret.[88] However, in 1998 there were far fewer cases of this kind than in earlier years, and some of the discrepancies are even noted in the respective exporter and importer submissions. While Argentina, for example, reports importing 36 A-4AR combat aircraft from the USA, the USA only reports exporting 13 A-4 and TA-4 combat aircraft but gives a possible explanation by noting that Argentinian and US definitions of 'transfer' differ. In other cases, such as the report by Belarus of delivery of 18 Su-25 combat aircraft to Peru, an explanation has to be found outside the UNROCA. These aircraft are not reported by Peru, possibly because Peru does not regard them as real deliveries since it does not yet operate them.

[86] Deen, T., 'China withdraws from register in protest', *Jane's Defence Weekly*, 18 Nov. 1998, p. 6.

[87] See note 77.

[88] The problem of discrepancies led some government experts to suggest the creation of a consultative mechanism whereby the UN Secretariat could question member states about the contents of their annual returns with a view to harmonizing the information presented by exporters and importers. However, there was no consensus to support this idea. See also Laurence, E. J., Wezeman, S. T. and Wulf, H., *Arms Watch: SIPRI Report on the First Year of the UN Register of Conventional Arms*, SIPRI Research Report no. 6 (Oxford University Press: Oxford, 1993).

Appendix 11A. The volume of transfers of major conventional weapons, 1989–98

BJÖRN HAGELIN, PIETER D. WEZEMAN and SIEMON T. WEZEMAN

Table 11A.1. Volume of imports of major conventional weapons

Figures are SIPRI trend-indicator values expressed in US $m. at constant (1990) prices. Regional and group figures include transfers between countries/non-state actors in the same region or organization, unless otherwise noted.

	1989	1990	1991	1992	1993	1994	1995	1996	1997	1998
World total	33 518	28 690	25 476	22 470	23 817	20 073	20 861	21 984	27 416	21 944
Developing world	18 980	17 536	14 787	10 783	13 100	11 969	14 457	16 008	20 130	14 164
Industrialized world	14 538	11 154	10 689	11 687	10 712	8 066	6 397	5 976	7 287	7 777
Africa	1 431	1 249	1 250	404	288	570	596	404	464	214
North	1 083	623	1 019	92	127	311	430	154	211	1
Sub-Saharan	348	626	231	312	161	259	166	250	253	213
Americas	1 907	1 544	2 455	1 731	1 480	1 927	1 761	1 707	2 472	1 193
North	536	519	1 409	1 082	1 059	1 208	701	658	1 012	561
Central	243	316	152	6	6	–	7	6	12	4
South	1 128	709	894	642	414	718	1 053	1 043	1 448	628
Asia	12 185	9 889	7 783	5 723	6 308	5 693	8 536	8 962	12 224	8 900
Central	. .	. .	. .	–	–	24	162	219	166	–
North-East	3 668	3 341	3 289	3 516	4 038	2 173	4 121	4 781	7 539	6 597
South-East	1 001	1 214	1 079	752	912	2 171	2 894	2 260	2 605	1 273
South	7 518	5 335	3 415	1 457	1 357	1 325	1 360	1 702	1 913	1 031
Europe	11 497	8 945	7 507	8 657	7 762	5 964	4 605	4 548	5 414	6 152
Western	6 142	5 211	6 603	8 184	6 225	5 456	3 855	3 879	5 065	6 021
Central and Eastern	5 356	3 735	904	474	1 537	509	750	668	350	131
Middle East	5 571	6 656	6 237	5 559	7 502	5 549	5 263	6 190	6 447	5 276
Oceania	926	406	243	397	474	334	92	173	396	206
UN	–	–	–	–	4	37	8	–	–	3
Rebel groups	53	9	29	1	1	197	2	12	1	–
Unknown	–	–	–	–	4	37	9	–	–	3
ASEAN	820	871	906	696	607	2 107	2 670	2 133	2 599	1 268
CSCE/OSCE	11 995	9 434	8 897	9 719	8 698	7 130	5 402	5 311	6 284	6 392
CIS	1 558	909	85	101	60	360	238	325	242	3
CIS Europe	. .	. .	. .	101	60	336	238	325	242	3
EU	4 384	3 473	5 075	5 814	3 434	3 333	2 290	2 171	2 969	4 016
EU from non-EU	3 168	2 920	3 798	4 608	2 310	2 078	2 498	2 205	3 215	4 969
GCC	2 698	3 691	2 145	2 492	4 280	2 205	2 881	4 529	5 335	3 347
NATO	6 203	5 180	7 425	8 436	6 475	5 873	4 071	3 456	4 464	4 902
P5	2 263	1 459	2 656	3 066	2 024	864	1 040	1 792	1 776	901
OECD	9 183	7 419	9 786	11 202	9 175	7 534	5 549	6 888	7 804	8 665
WEU	3 998	3 356	4 915	5 777	3 403	3 221	1 879	1 475	2 027	2 960

Note: Tables 11A.1 and 11A.2 show the volume of arms transfers for different geographical regions and subregions, selected groups of countries, rebel groups and international organizations. Countries/rebel groups can belong to only one region. As many countries are included in more than one group or organization, totals cannot be derived from these figures. Countries are included in the values for the different international organizations from the year of joining. Figures may not necessarily add up because of conventions of rounding. The following countries/rebel groups are included in each group.

Table 11A.2. Volume of exports of major conventional weapons

Figures are SIPRI trend-indicator values expressed in US $m. at constant (1990) prices. Regional and group figures include transfers between countries/non-state actors in the same region or organization, unless otherwise noted.

	1989	1990	1991	1992	1993	1994	1995	1996	1997	1998
World total	33 518	28 690	25 476	22 470	23 817	20 073	20 861	21 984	27 416	21 944
Developing world	1 746	1 461	1 335	1 243	1 768	1 089	1 290	1 240	869	588
Industrialized world	31 769	27 229	24 141	21 227	22 048	18 926	19 570	20 733	26 524	21 356
Africa	4	55	38	94	54	10	18	32	10	29
North	–	39	–	–	–	–	–	–	–	–
Sub-Saharan	4	16	38	94	54	10	18	32	10	29
Americas	9 535	8 992	10 973	13 180	12 643	10 253	10 059	10 050	12 568	12 561
North	9 493	8 913	10 879	13 032	12 571	10 210	10 016	9 951	12 540	12 555
Central	2	8	2	87	30	–	–	21	–	–
South	40	72	92	60	41	43	43	78	28	2
Asia	1 424	1 231	1 092	859	1 394	844	1 065	815	448	492
Central	. .	. .	. .	–	–	–	86	9	6	171
North-East	1 331	1 132	1 088	851	1 363	803	938	806	373	228
South-East	94	4	1	8	27	36	40	–	75	93
South	1	94	3	1	3	4	3	1	–	–
Europe	22 255	18 172	13 171	8 174	9 431	8 674	9 431	10 789	13 663	8 623
Western	7 380	6 519	6 435	4 997	5 314	6 559	5 389	6 521	9 153	6 867
Central and Eastern	14 875	11 652	6 737	3 178	4 117	2 115	4 044	4 268	4 511	1 758
Middle East	275	96	119	154	263	209	265	271	385	235
Oceania	22	144	84	8	30	26	22	15	318	3
UN	–	–	–	–	–	–	–	–	–	–
Rebel groups	–	–	2	1	–	–	–	–	–	–
Unknown	3	–	–	–	1	58	1	11	23	–
ASEAN	46	4	1	8	27	36	40	–	75	93
CSCE/OSCE	31 747	27 084	24 023	21 207	22 002	18 884	19 532	20 749	26 203	21 353
CIS	12 915	10 411	5 674	2 865	3 643	1 517	3 659	3 935	4 380	1 912
CIS Europe	. .	. .	. .	2 865	3 643	1 517	3 573	3 926	4 380	1 741
EU	6 759	5 861	5 665	4 428	4 992	6 212	5 259	6 348	9 034	6 822
EU to non-EU	5 543	5 305	4 389	3 225	3 868	4 957	4 466	5 710	8 045	5 898
GCC	–	2	–	–	49	52	42	4	82	88
NATO	16 338	14 802	16 708	17 465	17 661	16 608	15 122	16 140	21 575	19 211
P5	28 311	23 967	19 862	1 836	19 494	13 983	16 216	17 790	22 220	18 266
OECD	16 895	15 577	17 405	18 050	17 931	16 811	15 441	16 665	22 094	19 472
WEU	6 758	5 757	5 656	4 428	4 844	5 983	5 054	6 176	9 979	6 646

Developing world: Afghanistan, Algeria, Angola, Argentina, Bahamas, Bahrain, Bangladesh, Barbados, Belize, Benin, Bhutan, Bolivia, Botswana, Brazil, Brunei, Burkina Faso, Burundi, Cambodia, Cameroon, Cape Verde, Central African Republic, Chad, Chile, China, Colombia, Comoros, Congo (Brazzaville), Congo (Dem. Rep.), Costa Rica, Côte d'Ivoire, Cuba, Cyprus, Djibouti, Dominica, Dominican Republic, Ecuador, Egypt, El Salvador, Equatorial Guinea, Eritrea, Ethiopia, Fiji, Gabon, Gambia, Ghana, Grenada, Guatemala, Guinea, Guinea-Bissau, Guyana, Haiti, Honduras, India, Indonesia, Iran, Iraq, Israel, Jamaica, Jordan, Kenya, Kiribati, North Korea, South Korea, Kuwait, Laos,

Lebanon, Lesotho, Liberia, Libya, Madagascar, Malawi, Malaysia, Maldives, Mali, Marshall Islands, Mauritania, Mauritius, Mexico, Micronesia, Mongolia, Morocco, Mozambique, Myanmar, Namibia, Nepal, Nicaragua, Niger, Nigeria, Oman, Pakistan, Palau, Palestinian Autonomous Authority, Panama, Papua New Guinea, Paraguay, Peru, Philippines, Qatar, Rwanda, St Vincent & the Grenadines, Samoa, Sao Tomé and Principe, Saudi Arabia, Senegal, Seychelles, Sierra Leone, Singapore, Solomon Islands, Somalia, South Africa, Sri Lanka, Sudan, Suriname, Swaziland, Syria, Taiwan, Tanzania, Thailand, Togo, Tonga, Trinidad & Tobago, Tunisia, Tuvalu, Uganda, United Arab Emirates, Uruguay, Vanuatu, Venezuela, Viet Nam, North Yemen (–1990), South Yemen (–1990), Yemen (1991–), Zambia, Zimbabwe

Industrialized world: Albania, Armenia (1992–), Australia, Austria, Azerbaijan (1992–), Belarus (1992–), Belgium, Bosnia and Herzegovina (1992–), Bulgaria, Canada, Croatia (1992–), Czechoslovakia (–1992), Czech Republic (1993–), Denmark, Estonia (1991–), Finland, France, Georgia (1992–), German DR (–1990), Germany, Greece, Hungary, Iceland, Ireland, Italy, Japan, Kazakhstan (1992–), Kyrgyzstan (1992–), Latvia (1991–), Liechtenstein, Lithuania (1991–), Luxembourg, Macedonia (1992–), Malta, Moldova (1992–), Monaco, Netherlands, New Zealand, Norway, Poland, Portugal, Romania, Russia (1992–), Slovakia (1993–), Slovenia (1992–), Spain, Sweden, Switzerland, Tajikistan (1992–), Turkey, Turkmenistan (1992–), UK, Ukraine (1992–), USA, USSR (–1991), Uzbekistan (1992–), Yugoslavia (–1991), Yugoslavia (Serbia and Montenegro) (1992–)

Africa: Algeria, Angola, Benin, Botswana, Burkina Faso, Burundi, Cameroon, Cape Verde, Central African Republic, Chad, Comoros, Congo (Brazzaville), Congo (Dem. Rep.), Côte d'Ivoire, Djibouti, Equatorial Guinea, Eritrea, Ethiopia, Gabon, Gambia, Ghana, Guinea, Guinea-Bissau, Kenya, Lesotho, Liberia, Libya, Madagascar, Malawi, Mali, Mauritania, Mauritius, Morocco, Mozambique, Namibia, Niger, Nigeria, Rwanda, Sao Tomé and Principe, Senegal, Seychelles, Sierra Leone, Somalia, South Africa, Sudan, Swaziland, Tanzania, Togo, Tunisia, Uganda, Zambia, Zimbabwe

North Africa: Algeria, Libya, Morocco, Tunisia

Sub-Saharan Africa: Angola, Benin, Botswana, Burkina Faso, Burundi, Cameroon, Cape Verde, Central African Republic, Chad, Comoros, Congo (Brazzaville), Congo (Dem. Rep.), Côte d'Ivoire, Djibouti, Equatorial Guinea, Eritrea, Ethiopia, Gabon, Gambia, Ghana, Guinea, Guinea-Bissau, Kenya, Lesotho, Liberia, Madagascar, Malawi, Mali, Mauritania, Mauritius, Mozambique, Namibia, Niger, Nigeria, Rwanda, Sao Tome and Principe, Senegal, Seychelles, Sierra Leone, Somalia, South Africa, Sudan, Swaziland, Tanzania, Togo, Uganda, Zambia, Zimbabwe

Americas: Argentina, Bahamas, Barbados, Belize, Bolivia, Brazil, Canada, Chile, Colombia, Costa Rica, Cuba, Dominica, Dominican Republic, Ecuador, El Salvador, Grenada, Guatemala, Guyana, Haiti, Honduras, Jamaica, Mexico, Nicaragua, Panama, Paraguay, Peru, St Vincent & the Grenadines, Suriname, Trinidad & Tobago, Uruguay, USA, Venezuela

North America: Canada, Mexico, USA

Central America: Bahamas, Barbados, Belize, Costa Rica, Cuba, Dominica, Dominican Republic, El Salvador, Grenada, Guatemala, Haiti, Honduras, Jamaica, Nicaragua, Panama, St Vincent & the Grenadines, Trinidad & Tobago

South America: Argentina, Bolivia, Brazil, Chile, Colombia, Ecuador, Guyana, Paraguay, Peru, Suriname, Uruguay, Venezuela

Asia: Afghanistan, Bangladesh, Bhutan, Brunei, Cambodia, China, India, Indonesia, Japan, Kazakhstan (1992–), North Korea, South Korea, Kyrgyzstan (1992–), Laos, Malaysia, Maldives, Mongolia, Myanmar (Burma), Nepal, Pakistan, Philippines, Singapore, Sri Lanka, Taiwan, Tajikistan (1992–), Thailand, Turkmenistan (1992–), Uzbekistan (1992–), Viet Nam

Central Asia: Kazakhstan (1992–), Kyrgyzstan (1992–), Tajikistan (1992–), Turkmenistan (1992–), Uzbekistan (1992–)

North-East Asia: China, Japan, North Korea, South Korea, Taiwan

South-East Asia: Brunei, Cambodia, Indonesia, Laos, Malaysia, Myanmar, Philippines, Singapore, Thailand, Viet Nam

South Asia: Bangladesh, Bhutan, India, Maldives, Nepal, Pakistan, Sri Lanka

Europe: Albania, Armenia (1992–), Austria, Azerbaijan (1992–), Belarus (1992–), Belgium, Bosnia and Herzegovina (1992–), Bulgaria, Croatia (1992–), Cyprus, Czechoslovakia (–1992), Czech Republic (1993–), Denmark, Estonia (1991–), Finland, France, Georgia (1992–), German DR (–1990), Germany, Greece, Hungary, Iceland, Ireland, Italy, Latvia (1991–), Liechtenstein, Lithuania (1991–), Luxembourg, Macedonia (1992–), Malta, Moldova (1992–), Monaco, Netherlands, Norway, Poland, Portugal, Romania, Russia (1992–), Slovakia (1993–), Slovenia (1992–), Spain, Sweden, Switzerland, Turkey, UK, Ukraine (1992–), USSR (–1991), Yugoslavia (–1991), Yugoslavia (Serbia and Montenegro) (1992–)

Western Europe: Austria, Belgium, Cyprus, Denmark, Finland, France, Germany, Greece, Iceland, Ireland, Italy, Liechtenstein, Luxembourg, Malta, Monaco, Netherlands, Norway, Portugal, Spain, Sweden, Switzerland, Turkey, UK

Central and Eastern Europe: Albania, Armenia (1992–), Azerbaijan (1992–), Belarus (1992–), Bosnia and Herzegovina (1992–), Bulgaria, Croatia (1992–), Czechoslovakia (–1992), Czech Republic (1993–), Estonia (1991–), Georgia (1992–), German DR (–1990), Hungary, Latvia (1991–), Lithuania (1991–), Macedonia (1992–), Moldova (1992–), Poland, Romania, Russia (1992–), Slovakia (1993–), Slovenia (1992–), Ukraine (1992–), USSR (–1991), Yugoslavia (–1991), Yugoslavia (Serbia and Montenegro) (1992–)

Middle East: Bahrain, Egypt, Iran, Iraq, Israel, Jordan, Kuwait, Lebanon, Oman, Palestinian Autonomous Authority, Qatar, Saudi Arabia, Syria, United Arab Emirates, North Yemen (–1990), South Yemen (–1990),Yemen (1991–)

Oceania: Australia, Fiji, Kiribati, Marshall Islands, Micronesia, New Zealand, Palau, Papua New Guinea, Samoa, Solomon Islands, Tonga, Tuvalu, Vanuatu

UN: UN as a non-state actor, not as a combination of all member states

Rebel groups (only those rebel groups which had imports/exports in the period 1989–98 are listed): Farabundo Marti National Liberation Front (FMLN, El Salvador), Hizbollah (Lebanon), Kurdish Workers' Party (PKK, Turkey), Lebanese Forces (LF, Lebanon), Liberation Tigers of Tamil Eelam (LTTE, Sri Lanka), Mujahideen (Afghanistan), South Lebanese Army (SLA, Lebanon), Southern Rebels (Yemen), Union for the Total Independence of Angola (UNITA, Angola)

Association of South-East Asian Nations (ASEAN): Brunei, Indonesia, Laos (1997–), Malaysia, Myanmar (Burma) (1997–), Philippines, Singapore, Thailand, Viet Nam (1995–)

Conference on Security and Co-operation in Europe (CSCE)/Organization for Security and Co-operation in Europe (OSCE): Albania (1991–), Andorra, Armenia (1992–), Austria, Azerbaijan (1992–), Belarus (1992–), Belgium, Bosnia and Herzegovina (1992–), Bulgaria, Canada, Croatia (1992–), Cyprus, Czechoslovakia (–1992), Czech Republic (1993–), Denmark, Estonia (1991–), Finland, France, Georgia (1992–), German DR (–1990), Germany, Greece, Holy See, Hungary, Iceland, Ireland, Italy, Kazakhstan (1992–), Kyrgyzstan (1992–), Latvia (1991–), Liechtenstein, Lithuania (1991–), Luxembourg, Macedonia (1995–), Malta, Moldova (1992–), Monaco, Netherlands, Norway, Poland, Portugal, Romania, Russia (1992–), San Marino, Slovakia (1992–), Slovenia (1992–), Spain, Sweden, Switzerland, Tajikistan (1992–), Turkey, Turkmenistan (1992–), UK, Ukraine (1992–), USA, USSR (–1992), Uzbekistan (1992–), Yugoslavia (–1991), Yugoslavia (Serbia and Montenegro, suspended since 1992)

Commonwealth of Independent States (CIS): Armenia, Azerbaijan, Belarus, Georgia (1993–), Kazakhstan, Kyrgyzstan, Moldova, Russia, Tajikistan, Turkmenistan, Ukraine, Uzbekistan

Commonwealth of Independent States (CIS) Europe: Armenia, Azerbaijan, Belarus, Georgia (1993–), Moldova, Russia, Ukraine

European Union (EU): Austria (1995–), Belgium, Denmark, Finland (1995–), France, Germany, Greece, Ireland, Italy, Luxembourg, Netherlands, Portugal, Spain, Sweden (1995–), UK

GCC (Gulf Co-operation Council): Bahrain, Kuwait, Oman, Qatar, Saudi Arabia, United Arab Emirates

NATO: Belgium, Canada, Denmark, France, Germany, Greece, Iceland, Italy, Luxembourg, Netherlands, Norway, Portugal, Spain, Turkey, UK, USA

P5: (5 Permanent members of the UN Security Council) China, France, Russia (1992–)/USSR (–1992), UK, USA

Organisation for Economic Co-operation and Development (OECD): Australia, Austria, Belgium, Canada, Czech Rep. (1995–), Denmark, Finland, France, Germany, Greece, Hungary (1996–), Iceland, Ireland, Italy, Japan, South Korea (1996–), Luxembourg, Mexico (1994–), Netherlands, New Zealand, Norway, Poland (1996–), Portugal, Spain, Sweden, Switzerland, Turkey, UK, USA

Western European Union (WEU): Belgium, France, Germany, Greece, Italy, Luxembourg, Netherlands, Portugal, Spain, UK

Appendix 11B. Register of the transfers and licensed production of major conventional weapons, 1998

BJÖRN HAGELIN, PIETER D. WEZEMAN and SIEMON T. WEZEMAN

This register lists major weapons on order or under delivery, or for which the licence was bought and production was under way or completed during 1998. 'Year(s) of deliveries' includes aggregates of all deliveries and licensed production since the beginning of the contract. Sources and methods for the data collection are explained in appendix 11C. Conventions, abbreviations and acronyms are explained at the end of this appendix. Entries are alphabetical, by recipient, supplier and licenser. 'Deal worth' values in the comments refer to real monetary values as reported in sources and not to SIPRI trend-indicator values.

Recipient/ supplier (S) or licenser (L)	No. ordered	Weapon designation	Weapon description	Year of order/ licence	Year(s) of deliveries	No. delivered/ produced	Comments
Algeria							
S: Russia	6	SS-N-25 ShShMS	ShShM system	1998		. .	Probably for refit of 3 Koni Class frigates and 3 Nanuchka Class corvettes
	(96)	SS-N-25/X-35 Uran	ShShM	1998		. .	Probably for 3 refitted Koni Class frigates and 3 refitted Nanuchka Class corvettes
L: UK	3	Kebir Class	Patrol craft	(1990)		. .	Algerian designation El Yadekh Class
Angola							
S: Russia	(6)	MiG-23ML Flogger-G	Fighter aircraft	1998	1998	(6)	Ex-Russian Air Force
	(6)	Su-22 Fitter-J	FGA aircraft	1998	1998	(6)	Ex-Russian Air Force

Argentina							
S: Italy	20	Palmaria 155mm turret	Turret	(1983)	1996–98	(20)	Turret for TAMSE VCA-155 self-propelled gun; delivered to Argentina; status of TAMSE VCA-155 uncertain
USA	36	A-4M Skyhawk-2	FGA aircraft	1994	1997–98	(8)	Ex-US Marines; deal worth $282 m; incl 9 refurbished before delivery and 27 refurbished in Argentina with US-supplied kits; Argentine designation A-4AR Fightinghawk; incl 4 refurbished to TA-4AR trainer version
	16	Bell-205/UH-1H	Helicopter	1996	1997–98	(16)	Ex-US Army; EDA aid; incl 8 for Navy
	6	P-3B Orion	ASW/MP aircraft	1996	1998	(6)	Ex-US Navy; for Navy; EDA aid; 1 or 2 more delivered for spares only
L: Germany	(120)	TAM	Main battle tank	1994	1994–98	(120)	
Australia							
S: Canada	47	Piranha 8x8	APC	1998		. .	Incl 5 ambulance, 18 radar reconnaissance and 11 fitter version; Australian designation ASLAV-PC/A/S/F; assembled in Australia
	16	Piranha/LAV(C)	APC/CP	1998		. .	Australian designation ASLAV-C; assembled in Australia
	5	Piranha/LAV(R)	ARV	1998		. .	Australian designation ASLAV-R; assembled in Australia
	82	Piranha/LAV-25	IFV	1998		. .	Australian designation ASLAV-25; assembled in Australia
Norway	(60)	Penguin Mk-2-7	Air-to-ship missile	1998		. .	Deal worth $48 m; for SH-2G helicopters; for Navy
Sweden	8	9LV	Fire control radar	(1991)	1996–98	(2)	For 8 MEKO-200ANZ Type (Anzac Class) frigates
	8	Sea Giraffe-150	Surveillance radar	1991	1996–98	(2)	For 8 MEKO-200ANZ Type (Anzac Class) frigates
UK	12	Hawk-100	FGA/trainer aircraft	1997		. .	Deal worth $640 m incl 21 licensed production
	(420)	ASRAAM	Air-to-air missile	1998		. .	For F/A-18 FGA aircraft; deal worth A$100 m
USA	12	C-130J-30 Hercules	Transport aircraft	1995		. .	Deal worth $670 m; option on 24 more
	2	CH-47D Chinook	Helicopter	1998		. .	Deal worth $45 m
	3	P-3B Orion	ASW/MP aircraft	1994	1995–98	3	Ex-US Navy; modified in Australia to TAP-3 for training; 1 more delivered for spares only

Recipient/ supplier (S) or licenser (L)	No. ordered	Weapon designation	Weapon description	Year of order/ licence	Year(s) of deliveries	No. delivered/ produced	Comments
	11	SH-2G Super Seasprite	ASW helicopter	1997		. .	Ex-US Navy SH-2Fs rebuilt to SH-2G; for Navy; US export designation SH-2G(A); deal worth $600 m incl Penguin Mk-2-7 missiles
	8	127mm/54 Mk-45	Naval gun	(1989)	1994–98	(4)	For 8 MEKO-200ANZ Type (Anzac Class) frigates
	8	AN/SPS-49	Surveillance radar	1993	1996–98	(2)	For 8 MEKO-200ANZ Type (Anzac Class) frigates
	8	Mk-41	ShAM system	(1991)	1996–98	(2)	For 8 MEKO-200ANZ Type (Anzac Class) frigates
	(48)	RIM-7P Seasparrow	ShAM	(1991)	1996–98	(24)	For 4 MEKO-200ANZ Type (Anzac Class) frigates
	(192)	RIM-7PTC ESSM	ShAM	(1998)		. .	For 4 MEKO-200ANZ Type (Anzac Class) frigates; final contract not yet signed
	6	Mk-41	ShAM system	(1998)		. .	For refit of 6 Adelaide (Perry) Class frigates
	(288)	RIM-7PTC ESSM	ShAM	(1998)		. .	For 6 refitted Adelaide (Perry) Class frigates; final contract not yet signed
	. .	AIM-120B AMRAAM	Air-to-air missile	(1998)		. .	Final contract not yet signed
	51	Popeye-1	ASM	1998		. .	For F-111C/G bomber aircraft; deal worth $90 m
	12	RGM-84A/C Harpoon	ShShM	1995	1998	(12)	Deal worth $38 m incl 21 training missiles
	4	AN/TPS-117	Surveillance radar	1998		. .	Deal worth $68 m; assembled in Australia
L: Germany	8	MEKO-200ANZ Type	Frigate	1989	1996–98	2	Australian designation Anzac Class; more produced for export
Italy	6	Gaeta Class	MCM ship	1994		. .	Australian designation Huon Class
Sweden	6	Type-471	Submarine	1987	1996–98	3	Deal worth $2.8 b; Australian designation Collins Class; option on 2 more
UK	21	Hawk-100	FGA/trainer aircraft	1997		. .	Deal worth $640 m incl 12 delivered direct
Austria							
S: France	22	RAC	Surveillance radar	1995	1997–98	(15)	Deal worth $129 m (offsets $344 m) incl Mistral missiles
Germany	(552)	HOT-3	Anti-tank missile	1996	1998	(552)	For 69 RJPz-1 tank destroyers
Netherlands	114	Leopard-2	Main battle tank	1996	1997–98	114	Ex-Dutch Army; deal worth $236 m
Norway	1	Bell-212/UH-1N	Helicopter	1998	1998	1	Second-hand

Sweden	(1 700)	RBS-56 Bill-2	Anti-tank missile	1996	1998	(100)	Austrian designation PAL-2000
USA	54	M-109A5 155mm	Self-propelled gun	1995	1997–98	(54)	Austrian designation M-109A5Ö; deal worth $48.6 m
	20	AIM-9P Sidewinder	Air-to-air missile	1992	1998	(20)	For S-35Ö fighter aircraft
Bahamas							
S: USA	2	Bahamas Class	Patrol craft	1997		. .	
Bahrain							
S: Netherlands	35	M-113C&R	Recce vehicle	1997	1997–98	(35)	Ex-Dutch Army
USA	10	Bell-209/AH-1E	Combat helicopter	1995	1997–98	(6)	Ex-US Army
	(8)	F-16C Fighting Falcon	FGA aircraft	1998		. .	Incl F-16D trainer version; option on more
Bangladesh							
S: Korea, South	(1)	Daewoo 2300t Type	Frigate	1998		. .	
Belgium							
S: Singapore	2	A-310-200	Transport aircraft	1997	1997–98	2	Deal worth $36 m; second-hand
Sweden	1	KBV-171 Class	Patrol craft	1998	1998	1	Ex-Swedish Coast Guard; deal worth $1.2 m
USA	72	AIM-120B AMRAAM	Air-to-air missile	1995	1998	(20)	For F-16A/B-MLU FGA aircraft
L: Austria	54	Pandur	APC	1997	1998	(10)	Incl 5 APC/CP, 4 ARV and 4 ambulance version; deal worth $42 m (offsets 100%)
Bosnia and Herzegovina							
S: USA	15	Bell-205/UH-1H	Helicopter	1996	1998	15	Ex-US Army; Train and Equip Program aid; incl 2 UH-1V version
Botswana							
S: Austria	(20)	SK-105A1 Kurassier	Tank destroyer (G)	1997	1998	(10)	Option on 20 more
Brazil							
S: Belgium	87	Leopard-1A1	Main battle tank	1995	1997–98	(87)	Ex-Belgian Army
France	5	F-406 Caravan-2	Light transport ac	1998		. .	Deal worth $25.6 m; incl 1 for maritime patrol

Recipient/ supplier (S) or licenser (L)	No. ordered	Weapon designation	Weapon description	Year of order/ licence	Year(s) of deliveries	No. delivered/ produced	Comments
	(4)	Mirage-3E	Fighter aircraft	1996	1997	2	Ex-French Air Force; probably incl 2 Mirage-3D trainer version; no. ordered could be 2
Germany	2	Grajau Class	Patrol craft	(1996)		. .	
Italy	13	Orion RTN-30X	Fire control radar	1995		. .	For refit of 6 Niteroi Class frigates; deal worth $111.5 m incl 7 RAN-20S radars and 6 Albatros ShAM systems
	7	RAN-20S	Surveillance radar	1995		. .	For refit of 6 Niteroi Class frigates; deal worth $111.5 m incl 13 RTN-30X radars and 6 Albatros ShAM systems
	6	Albatros Mk-2	ShAM system	1995		. .	For refit of 6 Niteroi Class frigates; deal worth $111.5 m incl 13 RTN-30X and 7 RAN-20S radars
	(144)	Aspide Mk-1	ShAM	1996		. .	For 6 refitted Niteroi Class frigates; deal worth $48.5 m
Kuwait	23	A-4K Skyhawk-2	FGA aircraft	1998	1998	23	Ex-Kuwaiti Air Force; for Navy; incl 3 TA-4K trainer version; deal worth $83 m incl weapons; Brazilian designation AF-1 and AF-1A
	(100)	AIM-9H Sidewinder	Air-to-air missile	1998	1998	(100)	Ex-Kuwaiti Air Force; for Navy A-4M/TA-4K FGA aircraft
Sweden	5	Erieye	AEW radar	(1994)		. .	Deal worth $143 m; for 5 ERJ-145SA AEW aircraft
UK	4	River Class	Minesweeper	1997	1998	4	Ex-UK Navy; Brazilian designation Do Valle Class; minesweeping gear removed before transfer; mainly for use as buoy tenders, and survey and training ships
USA	6	AN/TPS-34	Surveillance radar	1997		. .	For SIVAM air surveillance network; US export designation TPS-B-34
L: Germany	1	SNAC-1	Submarine	1995		. .	Brazilian designation Tikuna Class
	3	Type-209/1400	Submarine	1984	1994–96	2	Brazilian designation Tupi Class
Singapore	2	Grajau Class	Patrol craft	1996	1998	1	

Brunei							
S: France	3	MM-38/40 ShShMS	ShShM system	(1997)		. .	For 3 Yarrow-95m Type frigates
	(48)	MM-40 Exocet	ShShM	(1997)		. .	For 3 Yarrow-95m Type frigates
	. .	Mistral	Portable SAM	1998		. .	Deal worth $30 m
Indonesia	(3)	CN-235-110	Transport aircraft	1995		. .	
Netherlands	3	Goalkeeper	CIWS	(1997)		. .	For 3 Yarrow-95m Type frigates
UK	3	Yarrow-95m Type	Frigate	(1997)		. .	
	3	Seawolf GWS-26	ShAM system	(1997)		. .	On 3 Yarrow-95m Type frigates
	3	AWS-9	Surveillance radar	(1997)		. .	On 3 Yarrow-95m Type frigates
	3	ST-1802SW	Fire control radar	(1997)		. .	On 3 Yarrow-95m Type frigates; part of Seawolf ShAM system
	(96)	Seawolf VL	ShAM	(1997)		. .	On 3 Yarrow-95m Type frigates
USA	4	S-70A/UH-60L	Helicopter	1995	1996–98	4	US export designation S-70A-14
Cambodia							
S: Czech Republic	6	L-39Z Albatros	Jet trainer aircraft	(1994)	1997–98	(5)	Ex-Czech Air Force; deal worth $3.6 m incl refurbishment and training in Israel
Cameroon							
S: South Africa	4	MB-326K Impala-2	Ground attack ac	1996	1998	4	Ex-South African Air Force
Canada							
S: Germany	121	Leopard-1A5 turret	Turret	(1996)	1997–98	(121)	Ex-FRG Army; deal worth $105 m; for refurbishment of 114 Canadian Leopard-1 tanks; 2 more delivered for spares only
Italy	15	EH-101-500	Helicopter	1998		. .	Deal worth $404 m (offsets 110%); for SAR; Canadian designation AW-520 Cormorant
UK	18	Hawk-100	FGA/trainer aircraft	1997		. .	Deal worth $574 m; for civilian company for training of pilots from Canadian and other NATO air forces under NATO Flying Training in Canada (NFTC) programme; option on 7 or 8 more; UK export designation Hawk Mk-115
	4	Upholder Class	Submarine	1998		. .	Lease in exchange for UK use of Canadian bases for training for 8 years

Recipient/ supplier (S) or licenser (L)	No. ordered	Weapon designation	Weapon description	Year of order/ licence	Year(s) of deliveries	No. delivered/ produced	Comments
USA	24	PC-9/T-6A Texan-2	Trainer aircraft	1997		. .	For civilian company for training of pilots from Canadian and other NATO air forces under NATO Flying Training in Canada (NFTC) programme; US export designation T-6A-1
L: Switzerland	240	Piranha-3 8x8	IFV	1997	1998	(50)	Deal worth $358 m; Canadian designation Kodiak
	120	Piranha-3 8x8	IFV	1998		. .	Deal worth $163 m; Canadian designation Kodiak
	203	Piranha/LAV-25	IFV	1993	1996–98	(203)	Deal worth $367 m; Canadian designation Coyote
USA	100	Bell-412	Helicopter	1992	1994–98	(100)	Deal worth $505.5 m; Canadian designation CH-146 Griffon
Chile							
S: France	10	AMX-30D	ARV	1996	1998	(10)	Ex-French Army
	1	Scorpene Class	Submarine	1997		. .	Deal worth $400 m incl 1 from Spain
Germany	4	Combattante-2 Type	FAC(M)	1996	1997–98	4	Ex-FRG Navy; Chilean designation Riquelme Class; German designation Tiger Class or Type-148; 1 or 2 more delivered for spares only
	4	TRS-3050 Triton-G	Surveillance radar	1996	1997–98	4	On 4 ex-FRG Navy Combattante-2 Type FAC
	6	Castor-2B	Fire control radar	1996	1997–98	4	On 4 ex-FRG Navy Combattante-2 Type FAC; for use with 76mm and 40mm guns
	4	MM-38/40 ShShMS	ShShM system	1996	1997–98	4	On 4 ex-FRG Navy Combattante-2 Type FAC
Israel	2	Phalcon	AEW&C aircraft	(1989)	1995	1	Chilean designation Condor
Italy	128	M-113A2	APC	(1996)	1997–98	(24)	Ex-Italian Army
Netherlands	200	Leopard-1V	Main battle tank	1998	1998	14	Ex-Dutch Army; refurbished before delivery; deal worth DFL 90 m
South Africa	24	M-71 155mm	Towed gun	1998	1998	24	Ex-South African Army; deal worth $2.5 m; for coast defence
Spain	1	Scorpene Class	Submarine	1997		. .	Deal worth $400 m incl 1 from France
UK	. .	Rayo	MRL	1995	1998	1	Assembled in Chile; ammunition produced in Chile

USA	8	Cessna-208 Caravan-1	Light transport ac	(1997)	1998	(8)	For Army
	1	S-70A/UH-60L	Helicopter	1998	1998	1	Deal worth $10 m; option on more
L: Switzerland	(120)	Piranha 8x8D	APC	(1991)	1994–98	(75)	No. ordered could be 100
China							
S: France	(6)	DRBV-15 Sea Tiger	Surveillance radar	1986	1987–96	4	For 2 Luhu Class (Type-052) and 2 Luhai Class, and refit of 2 Luda-1 Class (Type-051) destroyers; probably assembled in China
	(6)	Castor-2B	Fire control radar	(1986)	1994–96	(4)	For 2 Luhu Class (Type-052) and 2 Luhai Class, and refit of 2 Luda-1 Class (Type-051) destroyers; probably assembled in China
	(6)	Crotale Naval EDIR	ShAM system	1986	1994–96	(4)	For 2 Luhu Class (Type-052) and 2 Luhai Class, and refit of 2 Luda-1 Class (Type-051) destroyers; probably assembled in China; Chinese designation HQ-7
	(144)	R-440N Crotale	ShAM	1986	1990–96	(100)	For 2 Luhu Class (Type-052) and 2 Luhai Class, and refit of 2 Luda-1 Class (Type-051) destroyers; possibly assembled in China; US/NATO designation of Chinese Crotale CSA-4
Israel	(2)	EL/M-2075 Phalcon	AEW radar	(1997)		. .	For modification of 1 Il-76 transport aircraft delivered from Uzbekistan to AEW&C aircraft; option on 3 to 6 more
Russia	(8)	Ka-27PL Helix-A	ASW helicopter	1998		. .	Incl 4 Ka-28PS SAR version
	2	Sovremenny Class	Destroyer	1996		. .	Originally ordered for Soviet/Russian Navy, but cancelled before completion
	4	AK-130 130mm	Naval gun	1996		. .	On 2 Sovremenny Class destroyers
	6	Palm Fond	Surveillance radar	1996		. .	On 2 Sovremenny Class destroyers
	2	Top Plate	Surveillance radar	1996		. .	On 2 Sovremenny Class destroyers
	4	Bass Tilt	Fire control radar	1996		. .	On 2 Sovremenny Class destroyers; for use with AK-630 30mm guns
	12	Front Dome	Fire control radar	1996		. .	On 2 Sovremenny Class destroyers; for use with SA-N-7 ShAMs

Recipient/ supplier (S) or licenser (L)	No. ordered	Weapon designation	Weapon description	Year of order/ licence	Year(s) of deliveries	No. delivered/ produced	Comments
	2	Kite Screech	Fire control radar	1996		. .	On 2 Sovremenny Class destroyers; for use with AK-130 130mm guns
	4	SA-N-7 ShAMS/Shtil	ShAM system	1996		. .	On 2 Sovremenny Class destroyers
	(132)	SA-N-7 Gadfly/Smerch	ShAM	1996		. .	For 2 Sovremenny Class destroyers; designation could be SA-N-17 Grizzly
	2	SS-N-22 ShShMS	ShShM system	1996		. .	On 2 Sovremenny Class destroyers
	(50)	SS-N-22 Sunburn/P-80	ShShM	1998		. .	For 2 Sovremenny Class destroyers
	2	Kilo Class/Type-636E	Submarine	1993	1997	1	
UK	2	Jetstream-41MPA	MP aircraft	1997	1998	2	For use by Hong Kong Government Flying Service
	(6)	Searchwater	AEW radar	1996		. .	Deal worth $62 m; for use on Y-8 MP aircraft or possibly SA-341/Z-8 helicopter
Uzbekistan	(1)	Il-76M Candid-B	Transport aircraft	(1997)		. .	Probably second-hand; possibly refurbished in Russia before delivery; for modification to AEW&C aircraft in Israel; option on more
L: France	. .	AS-350B Ecureuil	Helicopter	(1992)	1994–97	(4)	Chinese designation Z-11
	. .	AS-365N Dauphin-2	Helicopter	1988	1992–98	(12)	Chinese designation Z-9A-100 Haitun; more produced for civilian customers
	. .	SA-321H Super Frelon	Helicopter	(1981)	1989–97	(13)	Chinese designation Z-8; for Navy
Israel	. .	Python-3	Air-to-air missile	1990	1990–98	(7 274)	Chinese designation PL-8
Russia	(200)	Su-27SK Flanker-B	FGA aircraft	1996	1998	(1)	Incl some only assembled in China; Chinese designation J-11
Colombia							
S: Germany	6	Do-328-100	Transport aircraft	1996	1996–98	6	For military airline SATENA
	1	Lüneburg Class	Depot ship	(1998)	1998	1	Ex-FRG Navy; Colombian designation Cartagena de Indias Class
Spain	3	CN-235-100	Transport aircraft	1997	1998	(3)	Deal worth $55 m
	2	Lazaga Class	Patrol craft	1997	1998	(2)	Ex-Spanish Navy; deal worth $137 m; refitted before delivery

USA	(12)	Bell-205/UH-1H	Helicopter	(1997)	1997–98	(12)	Ex-US Army; aid for Police anti-narcotics operations
Cyprus							
S: Greece	(84)	4K-7FA-G-127	APC	(1995)	1996–8	(84)	Greek designation Leonidas-2
	(50)	AMX-30B2	Main battle tank	(1993)	1996–98	(50)	Ex-Greek Army; refurbished before delivery
Italy	. .	Aspide Mk-1	SAM	(1997)		. .	Status uncertain
Russia	(41)	T-80U	Main battle tank	(1998)		. .	Deal worth $160 m
	(1)	SA-10d/S-300PMU-1	SAM system	1997		. .	Deal worth $420 m incl missiles; to be based in Greece (on Crete)
	(96)	SA-10 Grumble/5V55R	SAM	1997		. .	Deal worth $420 m incl 1 SA-10d/S-300PMU-1 SAM system; to be based in Greece (on Crete)
Denmark							
S: Canada	1	Challenger-604	Transport aircraft	1997	1998	1	For MP, SAR and VIP transport; lease
	(3)	Challenger-604	Transport aircraft	1998		. .	For MP, SAR and VIP transport; option on 2 more
France	8	RAC	Surveillance radar	1996	1997–98	(8)	Deal worth $35 m
Germany	51	Leopard-2A4	Main battle tank	1997		. .	Ex-FRG Army; deal worth $91 m
	3	TRS-3D	Surveillance radar	1993	1998	3	For refit of 3 Niels Juel Class corvettes
Italy	1	RAT-31SL	Surveillance radar	1995	1998	(1)	
Norway	8	Arthur	Tracking radar	1997		. .	Deal worth $40 m
Switzerland	2	Piranha-3 8x8	APC	1998		. .	Option on 20 more; for evaluation; for use with peacekeeping forces
USA	(8)	M-270 MLRS 227mm	MRL	1996	1998	(8)	
	. .	AIM-120A AMRAAM	Air-to-air missile	1994	1997–98	(84)	For F-16A/B-MLU FGA aircraft; option on more
	4	Mk-48	ShAM system	1993	1998	(4)	Deal worth $20 m; option on more; for 4 Flyvefisken Class (Stanflex-300 Type) patrol craft/MCM ships
	(36)	RIM-7M Seasparrow	ShAM	(1994)	1998	(36)	For 4 Flyvefisken Class (Stanflex-300 Type) patrol craft/MCM ships
Ecuador							
S: Israel	2	Kfir C2	FGA aircraft	1998		. .	Ex-Israeli Air Force; refurbished before delivery; deal worth $60 m incl refurbishment of some 10 Kfir C2 in Ecuadorean service
USA	2	Bell-412EP Sentinel	ASW helicopter	(1996)	1998	1	For Navy

Recipient/ supplier (S) or licenser (L)	No. ordered	Weapon designation	Weapon description	Year of order/ licence	Year(s) of deliveries	No. delivered/ produced	Comments
Egypt							
S: USA	4	CH-47D Chinook	Helicopter	1998		. .	FMS deal worth $104 m
	21	F-16C Fighting Falcon	FGA aircraft	1996		. .	Aid
	2	Gulfstream-4	Transport aircraft	1996	1997–98	(2)	Deal worth $80 m; for VIP transport
	10	SH-2G Super Seasprite	ASW helicopter	1994	1998	10	Ex-US Navy SH-2F rebuilt to SH-2G; US export designation SH-2G(E); option on 10 more
	24	M-109/SP-122 122mm	Self-propelled gun	1996	1997–98	(24)	Deal worth $28 m; FMF aid
	50	M-88A2 Hercules	ARV	1997		. .	FMS deal worth $197.9 m; assembled in Egypt
	1	Perry Class	Frigate	1998	1998	1	Ex-US Navy; Egyptian designation Mubarak Class
	1	Phalanx Mk-15	CIWS	1998	1998	1	On 1 ex-US Perry Class frigate
	1	AN/SPS-49	Surveillance radar	1998	1998	1	On 1 ex-US Perry Class frigate
	1	AN/SPS-55	Surveillance radar	1998	1998	1	On 1 ex-US Perry Class frigate
	1	AN/SPG-60 STIR	Fire control radar	1998	1998	1	On 1 ex-US Perry Class frigate; for use with Standard ShAM
	1	WM-28	Fire control radar	1998	1998	1	On 1 ex-US Perry Class frigate; for use with 76mm gun
	1	Mk-13	ShAM system	1998	1998	1	On 1 ex-US Perry Class frigate
	(54)	RIM-66B Standard-1MR	ShAM	(1998)		. .	For 1 Perry (Mubarak) Class frigate
	1	Perry Class	Frigate	1998		. .	Ex-US Navy; Egyptian designation Mubarak Class
	1	Phalanx Mk-15	CIWS	1998		. .	On 1 ex-US Perry Class frigate
	1	AN/SPS-49	Surveillance radar	1998		. .	On 1 ex-US Perry Class frigate
	1	AN/SPS-55	Surveillance radar	1998		. .	On 1 ex-US Perry Class frigate
	1	AN/SPG-60 STIR	Fire control radar	1998		. .	On 1 ex-US Perry Class frigate; for use with Standard ShAM
	1	WM-28	Fire control radar	1998		. .	On 1 ex-US Perry Class frigate; for use with 76mm gun
	1	Mk-13	ShAM system	1998		. .	On 1 ex-US Perry Class frigate
	927	AGM-114K Hellfire	Anti-tank missile	1996	1998	(463)	Deal worth $45 m; for AH-64A helicopters
	(2 372)	BGM-71D TOW-2	Anti-tank missile	1996		. .	Deal worth $59 m

	8	I-HAWK SAMS	SAM system	(1996)	1998	(1)	Ex-US Army; EDA aid; refurbished for $206 m before delivery
	180	MIM-23B HAWK	SAM	1996		. .	Ex-US Army
	42	RGM-84A/C Harpoon	ShShM	1998		. .	
L: Germany	. .	Fahd	APC	1978	1986–98	(627)	Developed for production in Egypt; more produced for export
USA	31	M-1A1 Abrams	Main battle tank	1996	1997–98	(31)	
	. .	AIM-9P Sidewinder	Air-to-air missile	(1988)	1989–98	(4 150)	
El Salvador							
S: Chile	5	T-35 Pillan	Trainer aircraft	1997	1998	5	Ex-Chilean Air Force; refurbished before delivery
USA	2	MD-520N	Helicopter	(1997)	1998	2	For Policia Nacional Civil
Eritrea							
S: Russia	(5)	MiG-29 Fulcrum-A	Fighter aircraft	1998	1998	(2)	Probably ex-Russian Air Force; no. ordered could be up to 10
Estonia							
S: Finland	19	M-61/37 105mm	Towed gun	1997	1997–98	(19)	Ex-Finnish Army; gift
France	(1)	Rasit-E	Battlefield radar	1996	1998	(1)	
Sweden	8	RBS-56 Bill	Anti-tank missile	1997	1998	(2)	Ex-Swedish Army; loan; deal also incl 2 launchers; for use with BaltBat joint Baltic peacekeeing unit
Ethiopia							
S: Bulgaria	(40)	T-55M	Main battle tank	(1998)		. .	Ex-Bulgarian Army
Czech Republic	(4)	L-39C Albatros	Jet trainer aircraft	(1997)		. .	
Russia	. .	Mi-24D Hind-D	Combat helicopter	1998	1998	(2)	Ex-Russian Air Force
	. .	Mi-8T Hip-C	Helicopter	1998		. .	Ex-Russian Air Force
	(4)	Su-27 Flanker-B	Fighter aircraft	1998	1998	(2)	Ex-Russian Air Force; no. ordered could be up to 12

Recipient/ supplier (S) or licenser (L)	No. ordered	Weapon designation	Weapon description	Year of order/ licence	Year(s) of deliveries	No. delivered/ produced	Comments
Finland							
S: France	(510)	Mistral	Portable SAM	1989	1990–98	(510)	For Navy; for Sako (modified SADRAL) SAM system on 1 Rauma-2, 4 refitted Helsinki and 4 Rauma Class FAC, and 2 Hameenma and 1 refitted Pohjanmaa Class minelayers
USA	57	F/A-18C Hornet	FGA aircraft	1992	1996–98	(31)	Assembled in Finland
	(384)	AIM-120A AMRAAM	Air-to-air missile	1992	1996–98	(200)	For 64 F/A-18C/D FGA aircraft
	480	AIM-9S Sidewinder	Air-to-air missile	1992	1996–98	(300)	For 64 F/A-18C/D FGA aircraft
France							
S: Spain	7	CN-235-100	Transport aircraft	1996	1998	3	Deal worth $90 m (offsets 100%, incl Spanish order for 15 AS-552UL helicopters)
USA	2	E-2C Hawkeye	AEW&C aircraft	1995	1998	1	For Navy (offsets incl French production of components)
	5	KC-135A Stratotanker	Tanker aircraft	1994	1997–98	(5)	Ex-US Air Force; deal worth $220 m; refurbished to KC-135R before delivery
Georgia							
S: Turkey	1	AB-25 Class	Patrol craft	1998	1998	1	Ex-Turkish Navy
Germany							
S: France	13	AS-365N Dauphin-2	Helicopter	1997		. .	For Border Guard; option on 2 more
	3	AS-532U2 Cougar-2	Helicopter	(1997)	1998	3	For VIP transport
Netherlands	4	APAR	Surveillance radar	(1997)		. .	For 4 Sachsen Class (Type-124) frigates
	4	SMART-L	Surveillance radar	(1997)		. .	For 4 Sachsen Class (Type-124) frigates
Sweden	10	HARD	Surveillance radar	1998		. .	For ASRAD SAM systems
UK	7	Super Lynx	ASW helicopter	1996		. .	Deal worth $154 m; UK export designation Lynx Mk-88A; for Navy
USA	4	Mk-41	ShAM system	1997		. .	Deal worth $87 m; for 4 Sachsen Class (F-124 Type) frigates

	21	Roland SAMS	SAM system	1998	1998	21	Ex-US Air Force; originally owned by USA but manned by Germany
	(78)	AGM-88A HARM	Anti-radar missile	(1995)	1997–98	(78)	
	96	AIM-120A AMRAAM	Air-to-air missile	1991	1995–98	96	For refurbished F-4F FGA aircraft; deal worth $53.6 m
	320	AIM-120B AMRAAM	Air-to-air missile	1995		. .	For refurbished F-4F FGA aircraft; deal worth $170 m
L: USA	4 500	FIM-92A Stinger	Portable SAM	1986	1993–98	(3 300)	German designation Fliegerfaust-2; more produced for export
Greece							
S: Brazil	4	EMB-145	Transport aircraft	(1998)		. .	For modification to AEW&C aircraft in Sweden; deal worth $575 m incl 4 Erieye radars; final contract not yet signed
France	11	Crotale NG SAMS	SAM system	1998		. .	Incl 2 for Navy; incl offsets
	(176)	VT-1	SAM	1998		. .	For 11 Crotale NG SAM systems
Germany	(170)	Leopard-1A5	Main battle tank	1997		. .	Ex-FRG Army; offsets for Greek order for modernization of F-4E FGA aircraft in Germany; no. ordered could be 171
	5	TRS-3050 Triton-G	Surveillance radar	(1986)	1994–96	(2)	For 5 Jason Class landing ships; probably ex-FRG Navy; refurbished before delivery
	5	TRS-3220 Pollux	Fire control radar	(1986)	1994–96	(2)	For 5 Jason Class landing ships; probably ex-FRG Navy; refurbished before delivery
	(1 250)	FIM-92A Stinger	Portable SAM	1986	1993–98	(780)	
Netherlands	4	DA-08	Surveillance radar	(1989)	1992–98	(3)	For 4 MEKO-200HN Type (Hydra Class) frigates
	4	MW-08	Surveillance radar	(1989)	1992–98	(3)	For 4 MEKO-200HN Type (Hydra Class) frigates
	8	STIR	Fire control radar	1989	1992–98	(6)	For 4 MEKO-200HN Type (Hydra Class) frigates; for use with 127mm guns and Seasparrow ShAM system
Russia	(16)	BTR-60P	APC	1998	1998	(16)	For use with 64 SA-8b AAV(M)s
	21	SA-15/Tor-M1	AAV(M)	1998		. .	Final contract not yet signed
	(336)	SA-15 Gauntlet/9M330	SAM	1998		. .	For 21 SA-15 SAM systems; final contract not yet signed
	(64)	SA-8b/9K33-AK	AAV(M)	1998	1998	(64)	Ex-Russian Army
	(16)	Thin Skin	Surveillance radar	1998	1998	(16)	For use with 16 SA-8b AAV(M)s; designation uncertain

Recipient/ supplier (S) or licenser (L)	No. ordered	Weapon designation	Weapon description	Year of order/ licence	Year(s) of deliveries	No. delivered/ produced	Comments
	(1 050)	SA-8b Gecko/9M33M	SAM	1998	1998	(1 050)	For 64 SA-8b SAM systems
Sweden	4	Erieye	AEW radar	(1998)		. .	For modification of 4 EMB-145 transport aircraft delivered from Brazil to AEW&C aircraft; deal worth $575 m incl aircraft; final contract not yet signed
USA	7	CH-47D Chinook	Helicopter	1997		. .	Deal worth $376 m
	40	F-16C Fighting Falcon	FGA aircraft	1993	1997–98	40	'Peace Xenia' programme worth $1.8 b; incl 8 F-16D FGA/trainer version
	52	AGM-88B HARM	Anti-radar missile	1994	1998	(52)	FMS deal worth $27 m; for F-16C/D FGA aircraft
	50	AIM-120B AMRAAM	Air-to-air missile	1996		. .	For F-16C/D FGA aircraft; deal worth $90 m incl 84 AGM-88B missiles
	84	AGM-88B HARM	Anti-radar missile	1996	1998	(84)	FMS deal worth $90 m incl 50 AIM-120B missiles
	100	AIM-120A AMRAAM	Air-to-air missile	(1995)		. .	Deal worth $70 m
	45	PC-9/T-6A Texan-2	Trainer aircraft	1998		. .	Deal worth $200 m
	2	S-70B/SH-60B Seahawk	ASW helicopter	1997		. .	For Navy; US export designation S-70B-6 Aegean Hawk
	12	M-109A5 155mm	Self-propelled gun	1997	1998	(6)	Option on 12 more
	18	M-270 MLRS 227mm	MRL	1998		. .	Part of FMS deal worth $245 m incl 81 MGM-140A ATACMS SSMs, 11 M-577 APC/CPs, ammunition, trucks and radios
	40	MGM-140A ATACMS	SSM	1996	1998	(20)	For use with M-270 MLRS MLR
	(2)	AN/TPQ-37	Tracking radar	1996		. .	
	4	Patriot SAMS	SAM system	1998		. .	Option on 2 more
	. .	MIM-104 PAC-2	SAM	1998		. .	
	4	127mm/54 Mk-45	Naval gun	(1989)	1992–98	(3)	For 4 MEKO-200HN Type (Hydra Class) frigates
	4	Mk-48	ShAM system	1988	1992–98	(3)	For 4 MEKO-200HN Type (Hydra Class) frigates
	(96)	RIM-7M Seasparrow	ShAM	(1988)	1992–98	(72)	For 4 MEKO-200HN Type (Hydra Class) frigates
	8	Phalanx Mk-15	CIWS	1988	1992–98	(6)	For 4 MEKO-200HN Type (Hydra Class) frigates
	4	RGM-84 ShShMS	ShShM system	1989	1992–98	(3)	For 4 MEKO-200HN Type (Hydra Class) frigates
	248	AGM-114K Hellfire	Anti-tank missile	1998		. .	FMS deal worth $24 m; for AH-64A helicopters
	914	BGM-71C I-TOW	Anti-tank missile	(1996)	1997–98	(914)	

	(32)	UGM-84A Sub Harpoon	SuShM	(1989)	1993–97	(24)	For 4 refitted Type-209 (Glavkos Class) submarines
L: Austria	(344)	4K-7FA-G-127	APC	1987	1988–98	(344)	Greek designation Leonidas-2; more produced for export
	57	4K-7FA-G-127	APC	1997	1997–98	(57)	Deal worth $57.7 m; incl some IFV and tank destroyer version
Denmark	4	Osprey-55 Type	Patrol craft	1998		. .	Greek designation Pirpolitis Class or Hellenic-56 Type
Germany	3	MEKO-200HN Type	Frigate	1988	1996–98	2	Deal worth $1.2 b incl 1 delivered direct (offsets $250 m); partly financed by Germany 'Rüstungssonderhilfe' aid programme and USA; Greek designation Hydra Class
Guatemala							
S: Chile	(5)	T-35 Pillan	Trainer aircraft	(1998)	1998	5	Ex-Chilean Air Force; refurbished before delivery
Hungary							
S: France	180	Mistral	Portable SAM	1997	1998	(180)	Deal worth $100 m incl SHORAR-2D radars, ATLAS launchers and trucks
Italy	(1)	SHORAR-2D	Surveillance radar	1997	1998	(1)	Deal worth $100 m incl Mistral missiles, ATLAS launchers and trucks; sold through France
Russia	97	BTR-80	APC	1995		. .	Payment for Russian debt to Hungary
	(435)	BTR-80	APC	1994	1996–98	(435)	Payment for Russian debt to Hungary
India							
S: Italy	(6)	Seaguard TMX	Fire control radar	1993	1998	(2)	For 3 Brahmaputra Class (Project-16A Type) frigates; for use with AK-630 30mm CIWS
Netherlands	3	LW-08	Surveillance radar	(1989)	1998	(1)	For 3 Brahmaputra Class (Project-16A Type) frigates; incl assembly in India; Indian designation RALW
	6	ZW-06	Surveillance radar	(1989)	1998	(2)	For 3 Brahmaputra Class (Project-16A Type) frigates
	3	LW-08	Surveillance radar	(1996)	1997	(1)	For 3 Delhi Class (Project-15 Type) destroyers; incl assembly in India; Indian designation RALW or RAWL-2
	6	ZW-06	Surveillance radar	1990	1997	(2)	For 3 Delhi Class (Project-15 Type) destroyers; incl assembly in India; Indian designation Rashmi

Recipient/ supplier (S) or licenser (L)	No. ordered	Weapon designation	Weapon description	Year of order/ licence	Year(s) of deliveries	No. delivered/ produced	Comments
Poland	1	TS-11 Iskra	Jet trainer aircraft	(1998)	1998	1	Ex-Polish Air Force
Russia/USSR	3	Ka-31 Helix	AEW helicopter	(1997)		. .	For Navy; deal worth $29 m
	40	Su-30MK Flanker	FGA aircraft	1996	1997	8	Deal worth $1.55 b; incl 32 Su-30MKI version; option on licensed production of 120 more
	10	Su-30MK Flanker	FGA aircraft	1998		. .	
	(360)	AA-10c Alamo/R-27RE	Air-to-air missile	1996	1997	(60)	For Su-30MK/MKI FGA aircraft
	(720)	AA-11 Archer/R-73	Air-to-air missile	(1996)	1997	(144)	For Su-30MK/MKI FGA aircraft
	. .	AA-12 Adder/R-77	Air-to-air missile	(1996)		. .	For 125 MiG-21bis fighter aircraft upgraded to MiG-21-93 and possibly also for MiG-29 fighter aircraft
	(12)	2S6M Tunguska	AAV(G/M)	(1996)	1997–98	(12)	No. ordered could be up to 50
	(192)	SA-19 Grison	SAM	(1996)	1997–98	(192)	For 12 2S6 AAV(G/M)s
	(300)	T-90	Main battle tank	(1998)		. .	Deal worth $750 m; probably incl assembly or licensed production of 200 in India
	2	Kilo Class/Type-877E	Submarine	1997	1997	1	Incl 1 originally built for Russian Navy, but sold to India before completion; Indian designation Sindhughosh Class
	3	Krivak-4 Class	Frigate	1997		. .	
	3	AK-100 100mm L/59	Naval gun	(1997)		. .	On 3 Krivak-4 Class frigates
	3	Top Plate	Surveillance radar	1997		. .	On 3 Krivak-4 Class frigates; designation uncertain
	3	Kite Screech	Fire control radar	1997		. .	On 3 Krivak-4 frigates; for use with AK-100 100 gun
	3	SS-N-25 ShShMS	ShShM system	(1997)		. .	On 3 Krivak-4 Type frigates
	3	Garpun	Fire control radar	1997		. .	On 3 Krivak-4 Class frigates; for use with SS-N-25 ShShM system
	3	SA-N-9 ShAMS	ShAM system	(1997)		. .	On 3 Krivak-4 Class frigates; status uncertain
	. .	SA-N-9 Tor-M	ShAM	(1997)		. .	For 3 Krivak-4 Class frigates; status uncertain
	. .	Cross Sword	Fire control radar	(1997)		. .	For 3 Krivak-4 Class frigates; for use with SA-N-9 ShAM system; status uncertain
	3	Head Net-C	Surveillance radar	1989	1998	(1)	For 3 Brahmaputra Class (Project-16A Type) frigates
	3	SS-N-25 ShShMS	ShShM system	1993	1998	(1)	For 3 Brahmaputra Class (Project-16A Type) frigates

	3	Garpun	Fire control radar	(1993)	1998	(1)	For 3 Brahmaputra Class (Project-16A Type) frigates; for use with SS-N-25 ShShM system
	3	SA-N-4/ZIF-22	ShAM system	(1989)	1998	(1)	For 3 Brahmaputra Class (Project-16A Type) frigates
	(90)	SA-N-4 Gecko/Osa-M	ShAM	(1989)	1998	(20)	For 3 Brahmaputra Class (Project-16A Type) frigates
	3	AK-100 100mm L/59	Naval gun	(1986)	1997	(1)	For 3 Delhi Class (Project-15 Type) destroyers
	3	Kite Screech	Fire control radar	(1986)	1997	(1)	For 3 Delhi Class (Project-15 Type) destroyers; for use with AK-100 100mm gun
	6	Bass Tilt	Fire control radar	(1986)	1997	(2)	For 3 Delhi Class (Project-15 Type) destroyers; for use with AK-650 30mm guns
	(216)	SA-N-7 Gadfly/Smerch	ShAM	(1986)	1997	(72)	For 3 Delhi Class (Project-15 Type) destroyers
	6	SA-N-7 ShAMS/Shtil	ShAM system	(1986)	1997	(2)	For 3 Delhi Class (Project-15 Type) destroyers
	18	Front Dome	Fire control radar	(1986)	1997	(6)	For 3 Delhi Class (Project-15 Type) destroyers; for use with SA-N-7 ShAM system
	3	SS-N-25 ShShMS	ShShM system	1992	1997	(1)	For 3 Delhi Class (Project-15 Type) destroyers
	(98)	SS-N-25/X-35 Uran	ShShM	1992	1997	(32)	For 3 Delhi Class (Project-15 Type) destroyers
	3	Garpun	Fire control radar	(1993)	1997	(1)	For 3 Delhi Class (Project-15 Type) destroyers; for use with SS-N-25 ShShMs
	8	Cross Dome	Surveillance radar	(1983)	1989–98	(5)	For 8 Khukri Class (Project-25/25A Type) corvettes
	8	Plank Shave	Surveillance radar	(1983)	1989–98	(5)	For 8 Khukri Class (Project-25/25A Type) corvettes
	8	Bass Tilt	Fire control radar	1983	1989–98	(5)	For 8 Khukri Class (Project-25/25A Type) corvettes; for use with 76mm gun and AK-630 30mm CIWS
	(320)	SA-N-5 Grail/Strela-2M	ShAM	(1983)	1989–98	(200)	For 8 Khukri Class (Project-25/25A Type) corvettes
	4	SS-N-25 ShShMS	ShShM system	(1996)	1998	(1)	For last 4 Khukri Class (Project-25A Type) corvettes
	(64)	SS-N-25/X-35 Uran	ShShM	(1996)	1998	(16)	For last 4 Khukri Class (Project-25A Type) corvettes
Singapore	3	Tara Bai Class	Patrol craft	1995	1997–98	3	For Coast Guard
UK	2	Harrier T-Mk-4	FGA/trainer aircraft	1996		. .	Ex-UK Navy; refurbished to Harrier T-Mk-60 before delivery; for Navy
	1	Magar Class	Landing ship	(1996)		. .	
Ukraine	(180)	AA-10a Alamo/R-27R	Air-to-air missile	(1996)	1997	(80)	For Su-30MK/MKI FGA aircraft; designation uncertain
	(180)	AA-10b Alamo/R-27T	Air-to-air missile	(1996)	1997	(24)	For Su-30MK/MKI FGA aircraft; designation uncertain

Recipient/ supplier (S) or licenser (L)	No. ordered	Weapon designation	Weapon description	Year of order/ licence	Year(s) of deliveries	No. delivered/ produced	Comments
Uzbekistan	(2)	Il-78M Midas	Tanker aircraft	1997	1998	(2)	Sold via Russia; no. ordered could be up to 6; possibly incl ex-Russian Air Force
L: Germany	33	Do-228-200MP	MP aircraft	1983	1989–98	(20)	For Coast Guard
	(15)	Do-228-200MP	MP aircraft	(1989)	1991–98	(11)	For Navy
	1	Aditya Class	Support ship	1987		. .	Designed for production in India; option on 1 more
Korea, South	3	Samar Class	OPV	1991	1996–98	3	For Coast Guard
Netherlands	212	Flycatcher	Fire control radar	(1987)	1988–98	(202)	Indian designation PIW-519
UK	15	Jaguar International	FGA aircraft	1993	1995–98	(14)	Indian designation Shamsher
	(17)	Jaguar International	FGA aircraft	1998		. .	No. ordered could be 18; Indian designation Shamsher
Indonesia							
S: France	(120)	Mistral	Portable SAM	1996	1997–98	(120)	For 6 refitted Van Speyk (Ahmad Yani) Class frigates; deal also incl SIMBAD launchers
UK	16	Hawk-200	FGA aircraft	1993	1996–98	(16)	UK export designation Hawk Mk-209
	16	Hawk-200	FGA aircraft	1996		. .	Deal worth $266 m; UK export designation Hawk Mk-209
	(45)	Scorpion-90	Light tank	1997	1997	(25)	Deal worth $134 m
	(91)	Stormer	APC	1995	1996–98	(38)	Incl 2 APC/CPs, some bridgelayer and ambulance version
	(14)	Tactica	APC	(1997)	1997–98	(14)	Incl APC/CP, explosive disposal and water cannon armed version; for police; no. delivered could be 34
L: France	16	AS-332B Super Puma	Helicopter	1997		. .	
Germany	. .	Bo-105CB	Helicopter	1976	1978–91	(45)	For Army, Navy and Police
	4	PB-57 Type	Patrol craft	1993		. .	Indonesian designation Singa Class
Spain	6	C-212-200MPA Aviocar	MP aircraft	1996		. .	For Navy
USA	1	Bell-412	Helicopter	1996		. .	Deal worth $4.2 m; for Navy

Iran							
S: China	(10)	C-801/802 ShShMS	ShShM system	(1995)	1996	(5)	For refit of 10 Kaman Class (Combattante-2 Type) FAC
	(3)	C-801/802 ShShMS	ShShM system	(1995)	1996–97	(2)	For 3 refitted Alvand Class (Vosper Mk-5 Type) frigates
	(80)	C-802/CSS-N-8 Saccade	ShShM	(1995)	1996	(40)	For 10 refitted Kaman Class (Combattante-2 Type) FAC; Iranian designation Tondar
USSR	(200)	T-72	Main battle tank	1989	1993–96	122	
Ukraine	(12)	An-74TK Coaler-C	Transport aircraft	(1997)		. .	
L: Korea, North	(100)	M-1985 240mm	MRL	(1987)	1988–98	(100)	Iranian designation Fadjr-3
Russia	. .	T-72S1	Main battle tank	(1996)	1997–98	(20)	
Ireland							
S: UK	(12)	L-118 105mm	Towed gun	(1997)	1998	(12)	
	1	Mod. Guardian Class	OPV	1997		. .	
Israel							
S: France	(7)	AS-565SA Panther	ASW helicopter	1994	1996–98	(7)	Ordered through USA; partly financed by USA; Israeli designation Atalef; for Navy
Germany	2	Dolphin Class	Submarine	1991		. .	Deal worth $570 m; financed by Germany
	1	Dolphin Class	Submarine	1994		. .	Deal worth $300 m; 50% financed by Germany
USA	21	F-15I Strike Eagle	Fighter/bomber ac	1994	1998	(16)	Deal worth $1.76 b (offsets $1 b); financed by USA; Israeli designation Ra'am
	4	F-15I Strike Eagle	Fighter/bomber ac	1995		. .	Israeli designation Ra'am
	15	S-70A/UH-60L	Helicopter	1997	1998	15	Deal worth $110 m
	(8)	Super King Air-200	Light transport ac	1997		. .	Israeli designation Zufut
	42	M-270 MLRS 227mm	MRL	1995	1995–98	(42)	FMS deal worth $108 m incl 1500 rockets
	36	M-48 Chaparral	AAV(M)	1996	1998	(12)	Ex-US Army; EDA aid
	500	MIM-72C Chaparral	SAM	1996		. .	Ex-US Army; EDA aid
Italy							
S: USA	18	C-130J Hercules-2	Transport aircraft	1997		. .	

Recipient/ supplier (S) or licenser (L)	No. ordered	Weapon designation	Weapon description	Year of order/ licence	Year(s) of deliveries	No. delivered/ produced	Comments
	233	AIM-120B AMRAAM	Air-to-air missile	1997		. .	Deal worth $116 m; for Navy; for AV-8B+ FGA aircraft
	735	FIM-92A Stinger	Portable SAM	1998		. .	FMS deal worth $110 m
L: France	(23 000)	Milan-2	Anti-tank missile	1984	1985–98	(23 000)	
Germany	2	Type-212	Submarine	1996		. .	Option on 2 more
USA	77	Bell-412SP/AB-412SP	Helicopter	1980	1983–98	(77)	Incl 18 for Army, 34 for Police and 25 for Coast Guard; more produced for export and civilian customers; incl Bell-412HP and Bell-412EP versions
Japan							
S: Italy	4	127mm/54	Naval gun	(1988)	1993–96	(3)	For 4 Kongo Class destroyers
USA	11	BAe-125/RH-800	Transport aircraft	1995	1997–98	(7)	For SAR; 'H-X' programme; Japanese designation U-125A
	10	Beechjet-400T	Light transport ac	1992	1994–96	9	For training; Japanese designation T-400; 'TC-X' programme
	2	Boeing-767/AWACS	AEW&C aircraft	1993	1998	2	Deal worth $840 m; Japanese designation E-767
	2	Boeing-767/AWACS	AEW&C aircraft	1994		. .	Deal worth $773 m; Japanese designation E-767
	(9)	Gulfstream-4	Transport aircraft	1994	1996–98	(4)	Japanese designation U-4
	2	Super King Air-350	Light transport ac	1997		. .	For Army; Japanese designation LR-2
	(72)	M-270 MLRS 227mm	MRL	1993	1994–98	(45)	
	40	AIM-120B AMRAAM	Air-to-air missile	(1998)		. .	Deal worth $22 m
	12	AN/SPG-62	Fire control radar	(1988)	1993–96	(9)	For 4 Kongo Class destroyers; part of Standard ShAM system
	4	AN/SPY-1D	Surveillance radar	1988	1993–96	(3)	Part of Aegis air defence system for 4 Kongo Class destroyers
	8	Phalanx Mk-15	CIWS	1988	1993–96	(6)	For 4 Kongo Class destroyers
	4	RGM-84 ShShMS	ShShM system	1993	1993–96	(3)	For 4 Kongo Class destroyers
	4	Mk-32 Mod-2	ShAM System	(1988)	1993–96	(3)	For 4 Kongo Class destroyers
	4	Mk-41	ShAM system	(1988)	1993–96	(3)	For 4 Kongo Class destroyers

	9	Mk-32 Mod-2	ShAM System	(1993)	1996–97	(2)	For 9 Murasame Class frigates
	9	Mk-48	ShAM system	(1993)	1996–97	(2)	For 9 Murasame Class frigates
	18	Phalanx Mk-15	CIWS	(1993)	1996–97	(4)	For 9 Murasame Class frigates
	11	RGM-84A/C Harpoon	ShShM	1995	1997–98	(11)	
	5	RIM-66M Standard-2	ShAM	1998		. .	
	57	RIM-66M Standard-2	ShAM	1995	1997–98	(57)	
	. .	RIM-7M Seasparrow	ShAM	1993	1996–97	(32)	Deal worth $13.4 m
L: France	. .	MO-120-RT-61 120mm	Mortar	1992	1993–98	(270)	
Germany	. .	FH-70 155mm	Towed gun	(1982)	1984–98	(445)	
USA	(89)	Bell-209/AH-1S	Combat helicopter	1982	1984–98	(87)	For Army
	53	CH-47D Chinook	Helicopter	1986	1988–98	(50)	Incl for Army; Japanese designation CH-47J and CH-47JA
	3	EP-3C Orion	ELINT aircraft	1992	1995–98	3	For Navy
	(44)	F-15DJ Eagle	FGA/trainer aircraft	1978	1988–98	(29)	
	(169)	F-15J Eagle	FGA aircraft	1978	1982–98	(155)	
	209	Hughes-500/OH-6D	Helicopter	1977	1978–98	(208)	Incl 193 for Army and 16 for Navy
	53	S-70/UH-60J Blackhawk	Helicopter	1988	1991–98	(34)	Incl 18 for Navy and 15 for Army
	82	S-70B/SH-60J Seahawk	ASW helicopter	1988	1991–98	(63)	For Navy
	3	UP-3D Orion	EW aircraft	1994	1997–98	2	For Navy
	(1 330)	AIM-7M Sparrow	Air-to-air missile	1990	1990–98	(1 330)	Deal worth $477 m
	(10 000)	BGM-71C I-TOW	Anti-tank missile	(1983)	1985–98	(10 000)	
	(980)	MIM-104 Patriot	SAM	1986	1989–98	(980)	
Jordan							
S: USA	16	F-16A Fighting Falcon	FGA aircraft	1996	1997–98	16	Ex-US Air Force; lease; 'Peace Falcon' deal worth $220 m; refurbished before delivery; incl 4 F-16B trainer version
	(96)	AIM-7M Sparrow	Air-to-air missile	1998		. .	Aid; for 16 F-16A/B FGA aircraft
	. .	AIM-9M Sidewinder	Air-to-air missile	(1998)		. .	Aid, for 16 F-16A/B FGA aircraft
Kazakhstan							
S: Russia	(38)	Su-27SK Flanker-B	FGA aircraft	(1995)	1996–97	(10)	Ex-Russian Air Force; payment for Russian debt to Kazakhstan

Recipient/ supplier (S) or licenser (L)	No. ordered	Weapon designation	Weapon description	Year of order/ licence	Year(s) of deliveries	No. delivered/ produced	Comments
	1	SA-10c/S-300PMU	SAM system	(1998)		. .	Probably ex-Russian Army
	. .	SA-10 Grumble/5V55R	SAM	(1998)		. .	For 1 SA-10c SAM system
Korea, North							
L: USSR	. .	AT-4 spigot	Anti-tank missile	(1987)	1991–98	(800)	
Korea, South							
S: France	5	F-406 Caravan-2	Light transport ac	1997	1998	1	Deal worth $24 m; for Navy; for use as target tugs
	(50)	Crotale NG SAMS	SAM system	(1989)		. .	Korean designation Pegasus; for use with Korean developed missiles; mounted on Korean K-200 APC
	(1 294)	Mistral	Portable SAM	(1997)	1998	(400)	Deal worth $300 m
Germany	12	Bo-105CB	Helicopter	1997		. .	Assembled in South Korea; for Army
Indonesia	8	CN-235-220	Transport aircraft	1997		. .	Deal worth $143 m (offsets incl Korean deliveries of vehicles and other military equipment to Indonesia)
Israel	(101)	Harpy	Anti-radar missile	1997	1998	(50)	
Italy	3	127mm/54	Naval gun	(1993)	1996–97	2	For 3 Okpo Class (KDX-2000 or KDX-1 Type) frigates
Netherlands	2	Goalkeeper	CIWS	(1991)	1998	(2)	For 1 Okpo Class (KDX-2000 or KDX-1 Type) frigate
	4	Goalkeeper	CIWS	1995		. .	For 2 Okpo Class (KDX-2000 or KDX-1 Type) frigates
Russia	(33)	BMP-3	IFV	1995	1996–98	(33)	Part of payment for Russian $210 m debt to South Korea; incl for Marines; no. ordered could be up to 70
	(528)	AT-10 Bastion/9M117	Anti-tank missile	1995	1996–98	(528)	For BMP-3 IFVs
UK	13	Super Lynx	ASW helicopter	1997		. .	For Navy; deal worth $328 m incl Sea Skua missiles and upgrade of 11 South Korean Navy Super Lynx helicopters
USA	8	RH-800XP	Reconnaissance ac	1996		. .	Deal worth $461 m; incl 4 RH-800SIG SIGINT aircraft

	29	M-270 MLRS 227mm	MRL	1996	1998	(1)	Deal worth $624 m incl 1626 rockets, 111 ATACMS SSMs, 14 M-577A2 APC/CPs, 4 M-88A1 ARVs and 54 light trucks
	111	MGM-140A ATACMS	SSM	1997		. .	Deal worth $624 m incl 29 M-270 MRLR MRLs, 1626 MLRS rockets, 14 M-577A2 APC/CPs, 4 M-88A1 ARVs and 54 light trucks
	14	M-577A2	APC/CP	1996		. .	Deal worth $624 m incl 29 M-270 MRLR MRLs, 1626 MLRS rockets, 111 ATACMS SSMs, 4 M-88A1 ARVs and 54 light trucks
	4	M-88A1	ARV	1996	1998	(4)	Deal worth $624 m incl 29 M-270 MRLR MRLs, 1626 MLRS rockets, 111 ATACMS SSMs, 14 M-577A2 APC/CPs and 54 light trucks
	3	AN/SPS-49	Surveillance radar	1994	1998	(1)	For 3 Okpo Class (KDX-2000 or KDX-1 Type) frigates
	3	RGM-84 ShShMS	ShShM system	(1992)	1998	(1)	For 3 Okpo Class (KDX-2000 or KDX-1 Type) frigates
	1	Mk-48	ShAM system	1997		. .	For 1 Okpo Class (KDX-2000 or KDX-1 Type) frigate
	(45)	RIM-7P Seasparrow	ShAM	1992	1998	(24)	For Okpo Class (KDX-2000 or KDX-1 Type) frigates; FMS deal worth $19 m
	3	Mk-41	ShAM system	(1997)		. .	For 3 KDX-2 Class destroyers
	(132)	AGM-88A HARM	Anti-radar missile	1995	1997–98	(132)	For F-16C/D FGA aircraft
	100	Popeye-1	ASM	1997		. .	Deal worth $125 m incl modification of 30 F-4E FGA aircraft
	(46)	RGM-84A/C Harpoon	ShShM	1996	1997–98	(46)	Incl some UGM-84A SuShM version
L: Germany	3	Type-209/1200	Submarine	1994	1998	1	Deal worth $510 m; Korean designation Chang Bogo Class
Netherlands	3	MW-08	Surveillance radar	1994	1998	(1)	For 3 Okpo Class (KDX-2000 or KDX-1 Type) frigates
	6	STIR	Fire control radar	(1992)	1998	(2)	For 3 Okpo Class (KDX-2000 or KDX-1 Type) frigates; for use with Seasparrow and 127mm gun
USA	72	F-16C Fighting Falcon	FGA aircraft	1991	1997–98	(37)	Deal worth $2.52 b incl 48 delivered direct; incl some F-16D trainer version
	57	S-70A/UH-60P	Helicopter	(1994)	1995–98	(47)	

Recipient/ supplier (S) or licenser (L)	No. ordered	Weapon designation	Weapon description	Year of order/ licence	Year(s) of deliveries	No. delivered/ produced	Comments
	. .	K-1A1/Type-88	Main battle tank	(1994)	1996–97	(3)	Incl 3 prototypes
	57	LVTP-7A1	APC	1995	1997–98	(14)	Incl ARV and APC/CP versions; deal worth $91 m; for Marines
	. .	M-167 Vulcan	AAA system	(1986)	1986–98	(210)	Incl some fitted on KIFV APC chassis
Kuwait							
S: Australia	22	S-600 APC	APC	1997	1997–98	22	For National Guard; deal worth $12 m
China	18	PZL-45 155mm	Self-propelled gun	1998		. .	Deal worth $186.5 m
France	8	P-37BRL Type	FAC(M)	1995	1998	4	'Garoh' deal worth $475 m; Kuwaiti designation Um Almaradim Class
	8	MRR-3D	Surveillance radar	1995	1998	4	On 8 P-37BRL Type FAC
	1	TRS-22XX	Surveillance radar	1995	1998	1	Deal worth $54 m
UK	(80)	Sea Skua SL	ShShM	1997		. .	For 8 PB-37BRL Type FAC; deal worth $89 m
USA	16	AH-64D Apache	Combat helicopter	1997		. .	Deal worth $800 m incl 384 AGM-114K missiles; status uncertain
	70	Pandur	APC	1996	1998	(70)	Incl IFV, APC/CP, APC/mortar carrier, ARV, ambulance and armoured car versions; option on 200 more
	384	AGM-114K Hellfire	Anti-tank missile	1997		. .	Deal worth $800 m incl 16 AH-64D Longbow helicopters
Laos							
S: Russia	12	Mi-17 Hip-H	Helicopter	1997	1997–98	(8)	
Latvia							
S: Sweden	8	RBS-56 Bill	Anti-tank missile	1997	1998	(8)	Ex-Swedish Army; loan; deal incl also 2 launchers; for use with BaltBat joint Baltic peacekeeing unit

Lebanon							
S: USA	16	Bell-205/UH-1H	Helicopter	1996	1998	(16)	Ex-US Army; aid
Lithuania							
S: Czech Republic	2	L-39ZO Albatros	Jet trainer aircraft	1998	1998	2	Deal worth $2 m
Germany	3	Mi-8TV Hip-F	Helicopter	1998	1998	3	Ex-FRG Air Force; originally former GDR equipment; aid
Sweden	8	RBS-56 Bill	Anti-tank missile	1997	1998	(8)	Ex-Swedish Army; loan; deal incl also 2 launchers; for use with BaltBat joint Baltic peacekeeing unit
Macedonia							
S: Germany	60	BTR-70	APC	1998	1998	60	Former GDR equipment; gift
Italy	. .	M-113A1	APC	1998		. .	Ex-Italian Army; aid
Kazakhstan	12	BTR-80	APC	1998	1998	12	Ex-Kazakh Army; first armoured vehicles for Macedonia
Turkey	20	F-5A Freedom Fighter	FGA aircraft	1998		. .	Ex-Turkish Air Force; aid; possibly refurbished before delivery; first combat aircraft for Macedonia
USA	36	M-101A1 105mm	Towed gun	1998	1998	18	Ex-US Army; incl 18 aid
Malaysia							
S: France	2	MM-38/40 ShShMS	ShShM system	(1992)		. .	For 2 Lekiu Class frigates
Indonesia	6	CN-235-220	Transport aircraft	1995	1998	(4)	Option on 12 more; deal worth $102 m; (offsets incl Indonesian order for 20 MD-3-160 trainer aircraft and 500 cars); delivery postponed from 1997 to 1998
Italy	2	Assad Class	Corvette	1997		. .	Originally built for Iraq but embargoed; Malaysian designation Laksamana Class
	2	RAN-12L/X	Surveillance radar	1997		. .	On 2 Assad Class corvettes
	4	RTN-10X	Fire control radar	1997		. .	On 2 Assad Class corvettes; for use with Albatros ShAM system and 76mm and 40mm guns
	2	Albatros Mk-2	ShAM system	1997		. .	On 2 Assad Class corvettes
	(12)	Aspide Mk-1	ShAM	(1997)		. .	For 2 Assad Class corvettes
	2	Otomat/Teseo	ShShM system	1997		. .	On 2 Assad Class corvettes
	(24)	Otomat Mk-2	ShShM	(1997)		. .	For 2 Assad Class corvettes
Netherlands	2	DA-08	Surveillance radar	1992		. .	For 2 Lekiu Class frigates

Recipient/ supplier (S) or licenser (L)	No. ordered	Weapon designation	Weapon description	Year of order/ licence	Year(s) of deliveries	No. delivered/ produced	Comments
Russia	(96)	AA-12 Adder/R-77	Air-to-air missile	(1997)		. .	For 16 MiG-29S FGA aircraft
Sweden	2	Sea Giraffe-150	Surveillance radar	1992		. .	For 2 Lekiu Class frigates
UK	32	Seawolf VL	ShAM	1993		. .	For 2 Lekiu Class frigates
	2	Lekiu Class	Frigate	1992		. .	Deal worth $600 m incl training; delivery postponed from 1996 after problems with software for combat system
USA	2	S-70A/UH-60L	Helicopter	1996	1997–98	2	For VIP transport
L: Germany	(6)	MEKO-A-100 Type	OPV	1998		. .	Deal worth $1.34 b; 'New Generation Patrol Vehicle' programme
Malta							
S: UK	1	BN-2B Islander	Light transport ac	1998	1998	1	Second-hand; refurbished before delivery
Mexico							
S: Russia	12	Mi-8T Hip-C	Helicopter	1997	1997–98	(12)	Deal worth $15 m; for Navy
USA	2	Knox Class	Frigate	1997	1998	2	Ex-US Navy; refitted before delivery; 1 more transferred for spares only
	2	127mm/54 Mk-42/9	Naval gun	1997	1998	2	On 2 ex-US Knox Class frigates
	2	Phalanx Mk-15	CIWS	1997	1998	2	On 2 ex-US Knox Class frigates
	2	AN/SPS-40B	Surveillance radar	1997	1998	2	On 2 ex-US Knox Class frigates
	2	AN/SPS-53	Surveillance radar	1997	1998	2	On 2 ex-US Knox Class frigates; for use with Mk-42/9 127mm gun
	2	AN/SPS-67	Surveillance radar	1997	1998	2	On 2 ex-US Knox Class frigates; designation uncertain
Morocco							
S: France	2	Floreal Class	Frigate	1998		. .	Deal worth $180 m
Myanmar							
S: China	24	A-5C Fantan	FGA aircraft	(1992)	1997–98	(24)	

	(144)	PL-2B	Air-to-air missile	1992	1998	(144)	For 24 A-5C FGA aircraft; status uncertain
	10	F-7M Airguard	Fighter aircraft	(1993)		. .	
	2	FT-7	Fighter/trainer ac	(1993)		. .	
	(72)	PL-2B	Air-to-air missile	1993		. .	For 12 F-7M/FT-7 fighter aircraft
Namibia							
S: South Africa	24	5.5in Gun Mk-3	Towed gun	1998	1998	24	Ex-South African Army; gift; South African designation G-2
Netherlands							
S: Finland	90	XA-188	APC	1997	1998	(20)	Deal worth $82 m (offsets 100%); incl 20 for Marines
Germany	(726)	FIM-92A Stinger	Portable SAM	1986	1993–98	(726)	
	874	FIM-92C Stinger	Portable SAM	(1992)	1998	(200)	
Italy	2	127mm/54	Naval gun	1996		. .	For 2 LCF Type frigates; option on 2 more; ex-Canadian Navy guns sold back to producer and refurbished before delivery
USA	30	AH-64D Apache	Combat helicopter	1995	1998	(4)	Deal worth $686 m (offsets $873 m)
	605	AGM-114K Hellfire	Anti-tank missile	1995	1996	(50)	For AH-64D helicopters; deal worth $127 m
	6	CH-47D Chinook	Helicopter	1993	1998	4	
	2	Mk-41	ShAM system	(1996)		. .	Deal worth $54 m; for 2 LCF Type frigates
	36	AGM-65G Maverick	ASM	1997		. .	Deal worth $6 m; not incl some as short-term lease from USA before delivery started
	200	AIM-120A AMRAAM	Air-to-air missile	1995	1998	(200)	For F-16A/B-MLU FGA aircraft
	16	RIM-66M Standard-2	ShAM	(1998)		. .	FMS deal worth $24 m incl 8 training missiles; for LCF type frigates
New Zealand							
S: Australia	2	MEKO-200ANZ Type	Frigate	1989	1997	1	Deal worth $554.7 m; New Zealand designation Te Kaha Class; option on 2 more not used
France	23	Mistral	Portable SAM	1996	1997–98	(23)	Deal worth $16 m incl 12 MANPADS launchers, 2 radars and 7 thermal sights
Sweden	2	9LV	Fire control radar	1991	1997	1	For 2 MEKO-200ANZ Type (Te Kaha Class) frigates; for use with Seasparrow ShAM system and 127mm gun

Recipient/ supplier (S) or licenser (L)	No. ordered	Weapon designation	Weapon description	Year of order/ licence	Year(s) of deliveries	No. delivered/ produced	Comments
	2	Sea Giraffe-150	Surveillance radar	1991	1997	1	For 2 MEKO-200ANZ Type (Te Kaha Class) frigates
USA	26	F-16A Fighting Falcon	FGA aircraft	1998		. .	Incl 13 F-16B fighter/trainer version; deal worth $200 m; 10 lease with option to buy; 2 more F-16B for spares only
	4	SH-2F Seasprite	ASW helicopter	1997	1997–98	4	Ex-US Navy; for use until delivery of SH-2G version and then probably for spares only
	4	SH-2G Super Seasprite	ASW helicopter	1997		. .	For Navy; deal worth $185 m (offsets 36%); option on 2 more; US export designation SH-2G(NZ)
	3	Super King Air-200	Light transport ac	(1998)	1998	3	Second-hand; operated by civilian company for training and transport
	2	127mm/54 Mk-45	Naval gun	(1989)	1997	(1)	For 2 MEKO-200ANZ Type (Te Kaha Class) frigates
	2	AN/SPS-49	Surveillance radar	(1993)	1997	1	For 2 MEKO-200ANZ Type (Te Kaha Class) frigates
	2	Mk-41	ShAM system	1992	1997	1	For 2 MEKO-200ANZ Type (Te Kaha Class) frigates
	(24)	RIM-7P Seasparrow	ShAM	(1991)	1997	(12)	For 2 MEKO-200ANZ Type (Te Kaha Class) frigates
Norway							
S: France	7 200	Eryx	Anti-tank missile	1993	1995–98	(7 200)	Deal worth $115 m incl 424 launchers; option on more (offsets incl production of components)
Germany	9	Leopard-1/BL	ABL	1995	1998	(5)	Ex-FRG Army Leopard-1 tanks modified to ABL before delivery
Sweden	104	CV-9030	IFV	1994	1996–98	(32)	Deal worth $241 m (offsets $184 m); option on more
	12	Arthur	Tracking radar	1997		. .	Deal worth $85 m
UK	5	AWS-9	Surveillance radar	1994	1997–98	(5)	Deal worth $29 m; incl 4 for refit of 4 Oslo Class frigates and 1 for training
USA	12	M-270 MLRS 227mm	MRL	1995	1997–98	12	Deal worth $199 m incl 360 rockets and practice rockets
	24	AN/TPQ-36A Firefinder	Artillery radar	1994	1995–98	(24)	For Norwegian Advanced Surface-to-Air Missile System (NASAMS)
	. .	AIM-120A AMRAAM	SAM	1994	1995–97	210	Deal worth $106 m; for NASAMS

	. .	AGM-114A Hellfire	Anti-tank missile	1996	1996	(4)	For coast defence; deal worth $36 m (offsets 100%); assembled in Sweden; Norwegian designation N-HSDS
	500	AIM-120A AMRAAM	Air-to-air missile	1996	1998	(100)	For F-16A/B-MLU FGA aircraft; deal worth $150 m
	. .	BGM-71F TOW-2A	Anti-tank missile	1996		. .	Deal worth $46 m (offsets 100%)
Oman							
S: France	51	VBL	Recce vehicle	1996	1997–98	51	
UK	1	Jaguar-S	FGA aircraft	1994	1998	1	Ex-UK Air Force; refurbished before delivery
	20	Challenger-2	Main battle tank	1997		. .	Deal worth $172 m
	80	Piranha 8x8	APC	1994	1995–98	(80)	Deal worth $138 m; incl ARV, APC/CP, 81mm APC/mortar carrier, ambulance and artillery observation versions; option on 46 more
Pakistan							
S: Belarus	(1 920)	AT-11 Sniper/9M119	Anti-tank missile	1996	1997–98	(1 400)	For 320 T-80UD tanks
China	. .	K-8 Karakorum-8	Jet trainer aircraft	1987	1994	6	Incl some assembled in Pakistan; some components produced in Pakistan; status of planned licensed production uncertain
	4	Type-347G	Fire control radar	(1996)	1997	(1)	For 4 Jalalat-2 Class FAC; for use with Type-76A 37mm guns
	4	C-801/802 ShShMS	ShShM system	(1996)	1997	(1)	For 4 Jalalat-2 Class FAC
	(32)	C-802/CSS-N-8 Saccade	ShShM	(1996)	1997	8	For 4 Jalalat-2 Class FAC
France	6	Mirage-3D	Fighter/trainer ac	1996	1998	6	Ex-French Air Force; refurbished before delivery; ‘Blue Flash-6’ programme worth $120 m incl 34 Mirage-5 FGA aircraft
	34	Mirage-5	FGA aircraft	1996	1998	2	Ex-French Air Force; refurbished before delivery; ‘Blue Flash-6’ programme worth $120 m incl 6 Mirage-3D fighter/trainer aircraft
	2	Agosta-90B Type	Submarine	1994		. .	Incl 1 assembled in Pakistan; deal worth $750 m incl 1 licensed production; deal also incl additional $200 m modernization of Karachi Shipyard to build submarines

Recipient/ supplier (S) or licenser (L)	No. ordered	Weapon designation	Weapon description	Year of order/ licence	Year(s) of deliveries	No. delivered/ produced	Comments
	(60)	SM-39 Exocet	SuShM	1994		. .	Deal worth $100 m; for 3 Agosta-90B Type submarines
Netherlands	(4)	DA-08	Surveillance radar	1994	1997–98	(4)	For refit of 4 Tariq (Amazon) Class frigates
Sweden	. .	RBS-70	Portable SAM	(1985)	1988–98	(160)	Assembled in Pakistan
Ukraine	320	T-80UD	Main battle tank	1996	1997–98	215	Deal worth $550 m; incl 50 taken from Ukrainian Army inventory
L: China	. .	Hongjian-8	Anti-tank missile	1989	1990–98	(1 300)	Pakistani designation Baktar Shikan
	. .	QW-1 Vanguard	Portable SAM	(1993)	1994–98	(375)	Pakistani designation Anza-2
France	1	Agosta-90B Type	Submarine	1994		. .	Deal worth $750 m incl 2 delivered direct
	1	Eridan Class	MCM ship	1992	1998	1	Pakistani designation Munsif Class
Sweden	. .	Supporter	Trainer aircraft	1974	1981–98	(137)	Pakistani designation Mushshak; for Army and Air Force; more produced for export
USA	755	M-113A2	APC	1989	1991–98	(725)	Assembled in Pakistan from kits delivered between 1989 and 1991
Paraguay							
S: Taiwan	12	F-5E Tiger-2	FGA aircraft	1997	1998	12	Ex-Taiwanese Air Force; incl 2 F-5F trainer version; gift
Peru							
S: Russia	3	MiG-29S Fulcrum-C	FGA aircraft	1998		. .	Deal worth $117.4 m incl spare parts and support for 18 MiG-29s delivered from Belarus
Philippines							
S: Australia	3	Transfield-56m Type	Patrol craft	1997		. .	For Coast Guard; partly financed by Australia
Korea, South	10	F-5A Freedom Fighter	FGA aircraft	(1997)	1998	10	Ex-South Korean Air Force; gift
USA	2	C-130B Hercules	Transport aircraft	(1995)	1998	2	Ex-US Air Force; refurbished before delivery; EDA aid
	5	Cessna-172/T-41	Trainer/light ac	(1997)	1998	5	Second-hand

Portugal							
S: UK	21	L-119 105mm	Towed gun	1997		. .	
USA	20	F-16A Fighting Falcon	FGA aircraft	1998		. .	Ex-US Air Force; refurbished before delivery; incl 4 F-16B trainer version; 5 more delivered for spares only; 'Peace Atlantis-2' programme worth $268 m
Qatar							
S: France	12	Mirage-2000-5	FGA aircraft	1994	1997–98	(9)	Deal worth $1.25 b; French export designation Mirage-2000-5EDA; incl 3 Mirage-2000DDA trainer version
	. .	Apache-A	ASM	1994		. .	For Mirage-2000-5 FGA aircraft
	(144)	MICA-EM	Air-to-air missile	1994	1997–98	(108)	Deal worth $280 m incl R-550 missiles; for 12 Mirage 2000-5 FGA aircraft
	(144)	R-550 Magic-2	Air-to-air missile	1994	1997–98	(108)	Deal worth $280 m incl MICA-EM missiles; for 12 Mirage 2000-5 FGA aircraft
	10	AMX-30B	Main battle tank	(1997)	1998	10	Ex-French Army; gift
UK	4	Piranha 8x8	APC	1996	1997–98	4	Incl 2 APC/CP and 2 ARV version; option on more
	36	Piranha 8x8 AGV-90	Armoured car	1996	1998	(24)	Option on more
	. .	Starburst	Portable SAM	1996	1998	(50)	
Romania							
S: France	(200)	R-550 Magic-2	Air-to-air missile	1996		. .	For MiG-21, MiG-23 and MiG-29 fighter aircraft; may incl assembly or licensed production in Romania
Germany	(36)	Gepard	AAV(G)	(1997)		. .	Ex-FRG Army; refurbished before delivery; gift worth DM80 m; 7 more for spares only
Israel	(960)	NT-D Spike	Anti-tank missile	(1998)		. .	For 24 modified SA-330 (IAR-330) helicopters; designation uncertain
	(1 000)	Python-3	Air-to-air missile	(1997)	1998	(20)	For 110 MiG-21 fighter aircraft modified to MiG-21 Lancer and for IAR-99 trainer aircraft
USA	5	AN/FPS-117	Surveillance radar	1995	1998	(3)	Deal worth $82 m
Saudi Arabia							
S: Canada	1 117	Piranha/LAV-25	IFV	1990	1994–98	(874)	Deal worth $700 m; incl 111 LAV-TOW tank destroyers, 130 LAV-90 armoured cars, 73 LAV-120

Recipient/ supplier (S) or licenser (L)	No. ordered	Weapon designation	Weapon description	Year of order/ licence	Year(s) of deliveries	No. delivered/ produced	Comments
							APC/mortar carriers and 449 other version; for National Guard
France	12	AS-532U2 Cougar-2	Helicopter	1996	1998	(4)	For SAR
	2	La Fayette Class	Frigate	1994		. .	Deal worth $3.42 b incl other weapons, construction of a naval base and training (offsets 35%); French export designation F-3000S Type
	2	100mm Compact	Naval gun	1994		. .	On 2 La Fayette Class frigates
	2	DRBV-26C Jupiter-2	Surveillance radar	1994		. .	On 2 La Fayette Class frigates
	2	Arabel	Fire control radar	(1994)		. .	On 2 La Fayette Class frigates
	2	Castor-2J	Fire control radar	1994		. .	On 2 La Fayette Class frigates
	2	Crotale Naval EDIR	ShAM system	1994		. .	On 2 La Fayette Class frigates
	(72)	VT-1	ShAM	(1994)		. .	For 2 La Fayette Class frigates; for use with Crotale ShAM system
	2	EuroSAAM VLS	ShAM system	(1994)		. .	On 2 La Fayette Class frigates
	2	MM-38/40 ShShMS	ShShM system	1994		. .	On 2 La Fayette Class frigates
	(32)	MM-40 Exocet	ShShM	1994		. .	For 2 La Fayette Class frigates
	1	La Fayette Class	Frigate	1997		. .	French export designation F-3000S Type
	1	100mm Compact	Naval gun	1997		. .	On 1 La Fayette Class frigate
	1	DRBV-26C Jupiter-2	Surveillance radar	1997		. .	On 1 La Fayette Class frigate
	1	Arabel	Fire control radar	1997		. .	On 1 La Fayette Class frigate
	1	Castor-2J	Fire control radar	(1997)		. .	On 1 La Fayette Class frigate
	1	Crotale Naval EDIR	ShAM system	(1997)		. .	On 1 La Fayette Class frigate
	1	EuroSAAM VLS	ShAM system	1997		. .	On 1 La Fayette Class frigate
	1	MM-38/40 ShShMS	ShShM system	(1997)		. .	On 1 La Fayette Class frigate
	(16)	MM-40 Exocet	ShShM	(1997)		. .	For 1 La Fayette Class frigate
	(36)	VT-1	ShAM	(1997)		. .	For 1 La Fayette Class frigate; for use with Crotale ShAM system
	48	ASTER-15	ShAM	(1997)		. .	For 3 La Fayette Class frigates
UK	48	Tornado IDS	FGA aircraft	1993	1996–98	48	Part of ‘Al Yamamah-2’ deal; incl 6 reconnaissance version

	73	AMS 120mm	Mortar	1996	1996–98	(40)	Deal worth $57 m incl ammunition; for 73 LAV-25 APC/mortar carriers
USA	72	F-15S Strike Eagle	Fighter/bomber ac	1992	1995–98	(55)	Deal worth $9 b incl AGM-65D/G, AIM-7M and AIM-9S missiles
	900	AGM-65D Maverick	ASM	1992	1995–98	(650)	For 72 F-15S fighter/bomber aircraft; incl AGM-65G version
	300	AIM-7M Sparrow	Air-to-air missile	1992	1995–98	(240)	For 72 F-15S fighter/bomber aircraft
Singapore							
S: Israel	12	EL/M-2228	Fire control radar	(1993)	1996–98	(12)	For 12 Fearless Class patrol craft/FAC
	. .	Python-4	Air-to-air missile	(1997)	1997–98	(60)	For F-5E and F-16 FGA aircraft
Russia	350	SA-16 Gimlet/Igla-1	Portable SAM	1997	1998	(350)	Deal also incl 30 launchers; option on 500 more
Sweden	3	Sjöormen Class	Submarine	1997		. .	Ex-Swedish Navy; refitted before delivery; Singaporean designation Challenger Class
UK	18	FV-180 CET	AEV	1995	1996–98	(18)	
USA	18	F-16C Fighting Falcon	FGA aircraft	1994	1998	18	Incl 10 F-16D version; 'Peace Carven-2' deal worth $890 m incl 50 AIM-7M and 36 AIM-9S missiles
	50	AIM-7M Sparrow	Air-to-air missile	1994	1997–98	(50)	Deal worth $890 m incl 18 F-16C/D FGA aircraft and 36 AIM-9S missiles
	36	AIM-9S Sidewinder	Air-to-air missile	1994	1998	(36)	Deal worth $890 m incl 18 F-16C/D FGA aircraft and 50 AIM-7M missiles
	12	F-16C Fighting Falcon	FGA aircraft	(1997)		. .	Deal worth $350 m; incl 6 F-16D trainer version
	4	KC-135A Stratotanker	Tanker aircraft	1997		. .	Ex-US Air Force; deal worth $280 m incl refurbishment to KC-135R before delivery
	24	AGM-84A/C Harpoon	Air-to-ship missile	1996	1997–98	(24)	Deal worth $39 m; for Fokker-50 ASW/MP aircraft
Slovakia							
S: France	2	AS-350B Ecureuil	Helicopter	1997		. .	Assembled in Slovakia; status uncertain
	(5)	AS-532U2 Cougar-2	Helicopter	1997		. .	Assembled in Slovakia; status uncertain
Russia	1	SA-10d/S-300PMU-1	SAM system	(1998)		. .	Part of payment of Russian debts to Slovakia
	. .	SA-10 Grumble/5V55R	SAM	(1998)		. .	Part of payment of Russian debts to Slovakia
Slovenia							
S: Switzerland	2	PC-6B Turbo Porter	Light transport ac	1997	1998	2	

Recipient/ supplier (S) or licenser (L)	No. ordered	Weapon designation	Weapon description	Year of order/ licence	Year(s) of deliveries	No. delivered/ produced	Comments
L: Austria	(70)	Pandur	APC	(1998)	1998	(5)	Slovenian designation Valuk
South Africa							
S: France	. .	Mistral	Portable SAM	(1998)		. .	For Rooivalk combat helicopter; final contract not yet signed
Germany	4	MEKO-160 Type	Frigate	(1998)		. .	Deal worth $1 b (offsets 110 to 250%); final contract not yet signed
	3	Type-209/1400	Submarine	(1998)		. .	Deal worth $881 m (offsets $542 m); final contract not yet signed
Italy	40	A-109 Hirundo	Helicopter	(1998)		. .	Deal worth $373 m (incl offsets); final contract not yet signed
Sweden	28	JAS-39 Gripen	FGA aircraft	(1998)		. .	Deal worth $1.8 b (incl offsets); incl some JAS-39B trainer version; final contract not yet signed
UK	24	Hawk-100	FGA/trainer aircraft	(1998)		. .	Deal worth $797 m (incl offsets); final contract not yet signed
	4	Super Lynx	ASW helicopter	(1998)		. .	Deal worth $133 m (incl offsets); final contract not yet signed
USA	2	C-130B Hercules	Transport aircraft	1995		. .	Ex-US Air Force; gift; refurbished in UK before delivery
Spain							
S: France	15	AS-532U2 Cougar-2	Helicopter	1997	1998	(8)	Deal worth $205 m (offsets 100%)
Germany	16	Buffel	APC	1998		. .	Spanish designation Leopard-2A5E; deal worth Ptas 338 b (offsets 80%) incl 219 Leopard-2A5+ tanks
Italy	1	RAN-30X	Surveillance radar	(1993)		. .	For use with Meroka CIWS on 1 LPD Type AALS
	2	Spada-2000	SAM system	(1996)	1998	1	For Air Force
	(51)	Aspide-2000	SAM	(1996)	1997–98	(27)	For use with Spada-2000 SAM system
UK	56	L-118 105mm	Towed gun	1995	1996–98	(56)	Deal worth $63 m incl ammunition
USA	24	F/A-18A Hornet	FGA aircraft	1995	1995–98	(24)	Ex-US Navy; option on 6 more; deal worth $288 m; refurbished before delivery; Spanish designation C.15

	4	127mm/54 Mk-45	Naval gun	(1998)		. .	For 4 F-100 Class frigates
	4	AN/SPY-1F	Surveillance radar	1996		. .	Deal worth $750 m; part of AEGIS air defence system for 4 F-100 Class frigates
	2	AN/VPS-2 Modified	Fire control radar	(1993)		. .	For 2 Meroka CIWS on 1 LPD Type AALS
	4	Mk-41	ShAM system	(1997)		. .	For 4 F-100 Class frigates
	(200)	AIM-120A AMRAAM	Air-to-air missile	(1996)		. .	
	100	AIM-7P Sparrow	Air-to-air missile	1997		. .	For F-18A/B FGA aircraft
	(384)	RIM-7PTC ESSM	ShAM	(1997)		. .	For 4 F-100 Class frigates
L: Germany	219	Leopard-2A5+	Main battle tank	1998		. .	Spanish designation Leopard-2A5E; deal worth Ptas338 b (offsets 80%) incl 16 Buffel ARVs
UK	4	Sandown/CME Type	MCM ship	1993	1998	1	Deal worth $381 m
USA	(2 000)	BGM-71F TOW-2A	Anti-tank missile	1987	1995–98	(2 000)	Deal incl also 200 launchers
Sri Lanka							
S: China	3	Shanghai Class	Patrol craft	(1996)	1998	3	Sri Lankan designation Rana Class
Russia	3	Mi-24P Hind-F	Combat helicopter	(1998)	1998	3	Ex-Russian Army; deal worth $7.95 m; refurbished before delivery; ordered specifically for use against LTTE rebels
UK	3	C-130K Hercules	Transport aircraft	(1998)		. .	Ex-UK Air Force; possibly refurbished before delivery
Sri Lanka/LTTE							
S: Unknown	1	Cessna-150	Trainer/light ac	(1998)	1998	1	Designation uncertain
	1	R44	Helicopter	(1998)	1998	1	Possibly second-hand
Suriname							
S: Spain	1	C-212-400 Aviocar	Transport aircraft	1998	1998	1	
	1	C-212-400 Patrullero	MP aircraft	1998	1998	1	
Sweden							
S: France	. .	TRS-2620 Gerfaut	Surveillance radar	1993	1997–98	(30)	Deal worth $17.7 m; for CV-90 AAV(G)s
Germany	(31)	BLG-60	ABL	(1994)	1998	(31)	Former GDR equipment; possibly refurbished in Germany or in other country before delivery
	29	Leopard-2A5	Main battle tank	1994	1996–98	29	Prior to licensed production; assembled in Sweden

Recipient/ supplier (S) or licenser (L)	No. ordered	Weapon designation	Weapon description	Year of order/ licence	Year(s) of deliveries	No. delivered/ produced	Comments
	610	MT-LB	APC	1993	1994–98	610	Former GDR equipment; refurbished before delivery incl to ARV and tank destroyer; incl 60 MT-LBu (ACRV) APC/CPs; deal worth $10.3 m (not incl refurbishment) incl 215 MT-LB and 228 2S1 SP gun chassis for spares only; Swedish designation Pbv-401 (APC), Bgbv-4102 (ARV) and Pbv-4020 (APC/CP)
South Africa	(2)	Mamba Mk-2	APC	1998	1998	(2)	For use by Swedish UN forces in Western Sahara
Switzerland	3	Piranha-3 10x10	APC/CP	1996	1997–98	3	
	5	Piranha-3 10x10	APC/CP	1998	1998	(1)	Option on more
USA	100	AIM-120A AMRAAM	Air-to-air missile	1994		. .	Deal worth $190 m (offsets 100%); for JAS-39 FGA aircraft
L: Germany	91	Leopard-2A5+	Main battle tank	1994	1998	(20)	Deal worth $770 m incl 160 ex-FRG Army Leopard-2 tanks (offsets 120%); option on 90 more; Swedish designation Strv-122
Switzerland							
S: France	12	AS-532UC Cougar-1	Helicopter	1998		. .	Deal worth $208 m; incl 10 assembled in Switzerland
	. .	Master-A	Surveillance radar	1998		. .	Part of Florako air surveillance network
USA	34	F/A-18C/D Hornet	FGA aircraft	1993	1996–98	(21)	Deal worth $2.3 b; incl 8 F/A-18D trainer version; incl assembly of 32 in Switzerland
	150	AIM-120A AMRAAM	Air-to-air missile	(1993)	1997–98	(134)	For 34 F/A-18C/D FGA aircraft
	12 000	BGM-71D TOW-2	Anti-tank missile	(1985)	1988–98	(10 950)	Deal worth $209 m incl 400 launchers and night vision sights; assembled in Switzerland
Taiwan							
S: Canada	30	Bell-206B JetRanger-3	Helicopter	1997	1998	(22)	For training as TH-67 Creek
France	60	Mirage-2000-5	FGA aircraft	1992	1997–98	60	Deal worth $2.6 b (offsets 10%); French export designation Mirage-2000-5Ei; incl 12 Mirage-2000-

							5Di trainer version; option on 40 more; 'Flying Dragon' programme
	(960)	MICA-EM	Air-to-air missile	(1992)	1996–98	(960)	Deal worth $1.2 b incl 400 R-550 missiles; for 60 Mirage-2000-5 FGA aircraft
	(480)	R-550 Magic-2	Air-to-air missile	1992	1997–98	(480)	Deal worth $1.2 b incl 960 MICA-EM missiles; for 60 Mirage-2000-5 FGA aircraft
	6	La Fayette Class	Frigate	1991	1996–98	6	Deal worth $2.8 b; Taiwanese designation Kang Ding Class; 'Kwang Hua-2' project
	12	Castor-2C	Fire control radar	1995	1996–98	12	On 6 La Fayette (Kang Ding) Class frigates; for use with 76mm and 40mm guns
	6	DRBV-26C Jupiter-2	Surveillance radar	1995	1996–98	6	On 6 La Fayette (Kang Ding) Class frigates
	6	TRS-3050 Triton-G	Surveillance radar	1995	1996–98	6	On 6 La Fayette (Kang Ding) Class frigates
USA	13	Bell-206/OH-58D(I)	Combat helicopter	(1997)		. .	FMS deal worth $172 m incl ammunition
	9	Bell-209/AH-1W	Combat helicopter	1997	1998	(9)	FMS deal worth $479 incl option on 12 more
	4	C-130H Hercules	Transport aircraft	1996	1997–98	(4)	Deal worth $200 m
	9	CH-47D Chinook	Helicopter	1998		. .	Deal worth $486 m
	150	F-16A-MLU	FGA aircraft	1992	1997–98	(120)	Deal worth $5.8 b incl 600 AIM-7M and 900 AIM-9S missiles; incl 30 F-16B-MLU trainer version
	600	AIM-7M Sparrow	Air-to-air missile	1992	1997–98	(496)	Deal worth $5.8 b incl 150 F-16A/B FGA aircraft and 900 AIM-9S missiles
	900	AIM-9S Sidewinder	Air-to-air missile	1992	1997–98	(720)	Deal worth $5.8 b incl 150 F-16A/B FGA aircraft and 600 AIM-7M missiles
	11	S-70B/SH-60B Seahawk	ASW helicopter	1997		. .	For Navy; US export designation S-70C(M)-2 Thunderhawk
	4	S-70C	Helicopter	(1997)	1998	4	For SAR; US export designation S-70C-6 Super Blue Hawk
	28	M-109A5 155mm	Self-propelled gun	(1996)	1998	28	
	160	M-60A3 Patton-2	Main battle tank	(1994)	1995–98	(160)	Ex-US Army; deal worth $91 m; refurbished before delivery
	. .	AN/FPS-117	Surveillance radar	1992		. .	
	7	Phalanx Mk-15	CIWS	1991	1993–98	(7)	For 7 Perry (Cheng Kung) Class frigates
	7	AN/SPG-60 STIR	Fire control radar	(1989)	1993–98	(7)	For 7 Perry (Cheng Kung) Class frigates; for use with Standard ShAM system
	7	AN/SPS-49	Surveillance radar	(1989)	1993–98	(7)	For 7 Perry (Cheng Kung) Class frigates

Recipient/ supplier (S) or licenser (L)	No. ordered	Weapon designation	Weapon description	Year of order/ licence	Year(s) of deliveries	No. delivered/ produced	Comments
	7	WM-28	Fire control radar	(1989)	1993–98	(7)	For 7 Perry (Cheng Kung) Class frigates
	7	Mk-13	ShAM system	1989	1993–98	(7)	For 7 Perry (Cheng Kung) Class frigates
	(323)	RIM-66B Standard-1MR	ShAM	(1994)	1994–98	(323)	For Perry (Cheng Kung) Class frigates
	6	Phalanx Mk-15	CIWS	1995	1996–98	(6)	Deal worth $75 m incl 6 Mk-75 76mm guns and ammunition; for 6 La Fayette (Kang Ding) Class frigates
	1 786	BGM-71D TOW-2	Anti-tank missile	1997		. .	Deal worth $80 m
	1 299	FIM-92A Stinger	Portable SAM	1997		. .	Deal worth $200 m incl 79 Avenger AAV(M)s, 50 man-portable launchers and training
	728	FIM-92A Stinger	Portable SAM	1998		. .	FMS deal worth $180 m incl 61 launchers
L: USA	12	Jiin Chiang Class	OPV	(1992)	1994	1	Designed for Taiwanese production; 'Kwang Hua-3' project
	7	Perry Class	Frigate	1989	1993–98	7	Taiwanese designation Cheng Kung Class; 'Kwang Hua-1' project; 1 more cancelled for financial reasons
Thailand							
S: Canada	20	Bell-212	Helicopter	1993	1997–98	(10)	Deal worth $130 m
Italy	2	Gaeta Class	MCM ship	1996		. .	Deal worth $120 m; Thai designation Lat Ya Class
Switzerland	16	PC-9	Trainer aircraft	(1997)	1998	(5)	
	(18)	GHN-45 155mm	Towed gun	1997	1998	(18)	
USA	3	AN/FPS-130X	Surveillance radar	1995	1998	1	
	(2)	AGM-84D Harpoon	Air-to-ship missile	1996	1998	2	For F/A-18 FGA aircraft; order cancelled after 2 delivered
L: Australia	3	LCU-50m Type	Landing craft		1997	. .	Thai designation Man Nok Class
UK	3	Khamronsin Class	OPV	1997		. .	Supplier uncertain

Tunisia							
S: USA	2	White Sumac Class	Cargo ship	1998	1998	2	Ex-US Coast Guard; gift
Turkey							
S: France	2	AS-532UL Cougar-1	Helicopter	1997		. .	Deal worth $430 m incl 28 licensed production; incl 1 for Army and 1 AS-532AL version for SAR
	5	Circe Class	MCM ship	1997	1998	3	Ex-French Navy; refitted before delivery; deal worth $50 m; Turkish designation Edincuk Class
Germany	197	RATAC-S	Battlefield radar	1992	1995–98	(150)	Incl assembly in Turkey; Turkish designation Askarad
	4 800	FIM-92A Stinger	Portable SAM	1986	1993–98	(3 400)	
	1	Kilic Class	FAC(M)	1993	1998	1	Deal worth $250 m incl 2 licensed production
	1	MEKO-200T-2 Type	Frigate	1994	1998	1	Deal worth $525 m incl licensed production of 1 (incl DM 150 m financed by German aid); Turkish designation Barbaros Class
	4	Type-209/1400	Submarine	1998		. .	Turkish designation Preveze Class; deal worth $556 m
Israel	(50)	Popeye-1	ASM	1998		. .	For F-4E-2000 FGA aircraft
Italy	5	Bell-412SP/AB-412SP	Helicopter	1998		. .	Deal worth $52 m; for SAR; for Coast Guard; status uncertain after Italian refusal to extradite PKK leader to Turkey
	4	Seaguard	CIWS	(1994)	1998	2	For 2 MEKO-200T-2 Type (Barbaros Class) frigates; for use with Sea Zenith 25mm CIWS
Netherlands	3	MW-08	Surveillance radar	1995	1998	1	For 3 Kilic Class FAC
	3	STING	Fire control radar	1995	1998	1	For 3 Kilic Class FAC; for use with 76mm and 35mm guns
	4	STIR	Fire control radar	(1994)	1998	2	For 2 MEKO-200T-2 Type (Barbaros Class) frigates; for use with Seasparrow VLS ShAM system and 127mm gun
Spain	9	CN-235-100	Transport aircraft	(1998)		. .	Incl 6 for Navy and 3 for Coast Guard; modified to maritime patrol aircraft in Turkey; deal worth $108 m
UK	2	AWS-6 Dolphin	Surveillance radar	(1994)	1998	1	For 2 MEKO-200T-2 Type (Barbaros Class) frigates
	2	AWS-9	Surveillance radar	(1994)	1998	1	For 2 MEKO-200T-2 Type (Barbaros Class) frigates
USA	7	KC-135A Stratotanker	Tanker aircraft	1994	1997–98	7	Ex-US Air Force; refurbished to KC-135R before delivery

Recipient/ supplier (S) or licenser (L)	No. ordered	Weapon designation	Weapon description	Year of order/ licence	Year(s) of deliveries	No. delivered/ produced	Comments
	50	S-70A/UH-60L	Helicopter	(1998)		. .	Originally ordered 1992, but deal suspended 1994–98 for financial reasons and as reaction to US policy towards Turkish actions against Kurds
	8	S-70B/SH-60B Seahawk	ASW helicopter	1998		. .	For Navy; US export designation S-70B-28
	3	Perry Class	Frigate	1998		. .	Ex-US Navy
	3	Phalanx Mk-15	CIWS	1998		. .	On 3 ex-US Perry Class frigates
	3	WM-28	Fire control radar	1998		. .	On 3 ex-US Perry Class frigates
	3	AN/SPG-60 STIR	Fire control radar	1998		. .	On 3 ex-US Perry Class frigates
	3	AN/SPS-49	Surveillance radar	1998		. .	On 3 ex-US Perry Class frigates
	3	AN/SPS-55	Surveillance radar	1998		. .	On 3 ex-US Perry Class frigates
	3	Mk-13	ShAM system	1998		. .	On 3 ex-US Perry Class frigates
	(40)	RIM-7P Seasparrow	ShAM	(1994)	1996–98	(25)	For 2 MEKO-200T-2 Type (Barbaros Class) frigates
	2	127mm/54 Mk-45	Naval gun	(1994)	1998	1	For 2 MEKO-200T-2 Type (Barbaros Class) frigates
	2	Mk-41	ShAM system	1994	1997–98	2	For 2 MEKO-200T-2 Type (Barbaros Class) frigates
	2	RGM-84 ShShMS	ShShM system	(1992)	1998	1	For 2 MEKO-200T-2 Type (Barbaros Class) frigates
	16	RGM-84A/C Harpoon	ShShM	1995		. .	Deal worth $15.3 m; for 1 MEKO-200T-2 Type (Barbaros Class) frigate
	3	RGM-84 ShShMS	ShShM system	1993	1998	(1)	For 3 Kilic Class FAC
	. .	AGM-114A Hellfire	Anti-tank missile	(1997)		. .	For S-70B/SH-60B helicopters; for Navy
	138	AIM-120A AMRAAM	Air-to-air missile	(1993)	1997–98	(138)	For F-16C/D FGA aircraft
	500	AIM-9S Sidewinder	Air-to-air missile	1994	1998	(200)	Deal worth $55 m incl 30 training missiles
	72	MGM-140A ATACMS	SSM	(1996)	1998	(72)	FMS deal worth $47.9 m
	(48)	RGM-84A/C Harpoon	ShShM	1993	1998	(16)	For 3 Kilic Class FAC
	(24)	UGM-84A Sub Harpoon	SuShM	(1993)	1997	(3)	For 4 Type-209/1400 (Preveze Class) submarines
L: France	28	AS532UL Cougar-1	Helicopter	1997		. .	Deal worth $430 m incl 20 delivered direct; incl 9 for Army and 19 AS-532AL version for SAR
Germany	2	Kilic Class	FAC(M)	1993		. .	Deal worth $250 m incl 1 delivered direct

	1	MEKO-200T-2 Type	Frigate	1994		. .	Deal worth $525 m incl 1 delivered direct (incl DM 150 m financed by German aid); Turkish designation Barbaros Class
	2	Type-209/1400	Submarine	1993	1998	1	Turkish designation Preveze Class
Spain	50	CN-235-100	Transport aircraft	1991	1992–98	(50)	Deal worth $550 m incl 2 delivered direct
UK	. .	Shorland S-55	APC	(1990)	1994–98	(50)	For Gendarmerie
USA	40	F-16C Fighting Falcon	FGA aircraft	1992	1996–98	(40)	Deal worth $2.8 b; first part of 'Peace Onyx-2' deal
	40	F-16C Fighting Falcon	FGA aircraft	1994	1998	(15)	Deal worth $1.8 b; second part of 'Peace Onyx-2' deal
	650	AIFV	IFV	1988	1990–98	(298)	Deal worth $1.08 b incl 830 APC, 48 tank destroyer and 170 APC/mortar carrier version (offsets $705 m)
United Arab Emirates							
S: France	(7)	AS-565SA Panther	ASW helicopter	1995	1998	(4)	For Abu Dhabi; deal worth $230 m incl AS-15TT missiles; no. ordered may be 6
	2	AS-565SA Panther	ASW helicopter	1997		. .	For Dubai; deal worth $30 m incl 5 SA-342K helicopters
	30	Mirage-2000-9	FGA aircraft	1998		. .	Deal worth $3.4 b incl upgrade of 33 UAE Air Force Mirage-2000 to Mirage-2000-9; incl 11 Mirage-2000DAD trainer version; incl 12 ex-French Air Force Mirage-2000 rebuilt to Mirage-2000-9
	5	SA-342K Gazelle	Helicopter	1997		. .	For Dubai; deal worth $30 m incl 2 AS-565SA helicopters
	390	Leclerc	Main battle tank	1993	1994–98	(221)	Deal worth $4.6 b incl 46 Leclerc ARVs (offsets 60%); incl 2 Leclerc Driver Training Tank version
	46	Leclerc DNG	ARV	1993	1997–98	(25)	Deal worth $4.6 b incl 390 Leclerc tanks (offsets 60%)
	(56)	AS-15TT	Air-to-ship missile	(1997)		. .	Deal worth $230 m incl 7 AS-565SA helicopters
	. .	MICA-EM	Air-to-air missile	1998		. .	For 30 new Mirage-2000-9 and 33 Mirage-2000 modified to Mirage-2000-9
Indonesia	4	CN-235MPA	MP aircraft	1998		. .	Deal worth $150 m
Netherlands	87	M-109A3 155mm	Self-propelled gun	1995	1997–98	(50)	Ex-Dutch Army; refurbished before delivery for $33 m; for Abu Dhabi
	2	Kortenaer Class	Frigate	1996	1997–98	2	Ex-Dutch Navy; refitted before delivery; deal worth $320 m incl training; UAE designation Abu Dhabi Class

Recipient/ supplier (S) or licenser (L)	No. ordered	Weapon designation	Weapon description	Year of order/ licence	Year(s) of deliveries	No. delivered/ produced	Comments
	2	Goalkeeper	CIWS	1996	1997–98	2	For refit of 2 Kortenaer Class frigates
	2	LW-08	Surveillance radar	1996	1997–98	2	On 2 ex-Dutch Kortenaer Class frigates
	2	STIR	Fire control radar	1996	1997–98	2	On 2 ex-Dutch Kortenaer Class frigates; for use with Seasparrow ShAM system
	10	Scout	Surveillance radar	1996	1997–98	(2)	For refit of 2 Kortenaer Class Frigates and 8 other ships
	2	WM-25	Fire control radar	1996	1997–98	2	On 2 ex-Dutch Kortenaer Class frigates; for use with 76mm gun
	2	Mk-29	ShAM system	1996	1997–98	2	On 2 ex-Dutch Kortenaer Class frigates
	2	RGM-84 ShShMS	ShShM system	1996	1997–98	2	On 2 ex-Dutch Kortenaer Class frigates
Russia	6	BM-9A52/BM-23	MRL	1996	1998	(6)	
	. .	BMP-3	IFV	(1994)	1994–98	(280)	For Dubai
Sweden	6	Sea Giraffe-50	Surveillance radar	(1994)	1996–98	(6)	For refit of 6 TNC-45 Type (Ban Yas Class) FAC
Turkey	128	AIFV-APC	APC	1997	1998	(10)	For Dubai; incl 75 artillery support/logitic version; deal worth $75 m incl 8 ARV version
	8	AIFV-ARV	ARV	1997		. .	For Dubai; deal worth $75 m incl 128 AIFV-APC version
UK	. .	Black Shahine	ASM	1998		. .	For Mirage-2000-9 FGA aircraft
USA	80	F-16C Block-60	FGA aircraft	1998		. .	Incl 40 F-16D Block-60 trainer version; deal worth $5 b; final contract not yet signed
	636	AGM-114A Hellfire	Anti-tank missile	1996		. .	For AH-64A helicopters
	24	RGM-84A/C Harpoon	ShShM	1998		. .	For 2 Kortenaer (Abu Dhabi) Class frigates; FMS deal
	72	RIM-7M Seasparrow	ShAM	1997		. .	Deal worth $27 m; for 2 Kortenaer (Abu Dhabi) Class frigates
UK							
S: France	38	AS-350B Ecureuil	Helicopter	1996	1997–98	(38)	Operated by civilian company for UK armed forces pilot training
Germany	85	G-115D	Trainer aircraft	1998		. .	Deal worth $28 m incl option on 15 more; for civilian company for training of UK pilots

	Italy	2	4-Runner Class	Cargo ship	(1998)	1998	(2)	Leased from civilian owner; UK designation Sea Chieftain Class; for use with Joint Rapid Deployment Force
	Netherlands	2	Goalkeeper	CIWS	(1996)		. .	For 2 Albion Class AALS
	USA	8	AH-64D Apache	Combat helicopter	1995		. .	Deal worth \$3.95 b (offsets 100%) incl 59 licensed production and 980 AGM-114 missiles; UK designation WAH-64D
		25	C-130J-30 Hercules	Transport aircraft	1994	1998	(2)	Deal worth \$1.56 b (offsets 100%); UK designation Hercules C-Mk-4; option on 5 more
		6	CH-47D Chinook	Helicopter	1995	1997–98	6	Deal worth \$365 m incl 8 MH-47E version; UK designation Chinook HC-Mk-2
		8	MH-47E Chinook	Helicopter	1995	1998	(1)	Deal worth \$365 m incl 6 CH-47D version; UK designation Chinook HC-Mk-3
		980	AGM-114 Longbow	Anti-tank missile	1995		. .	Deal worth \$3.95 m incl 67 AH-64D helicopters; assembled in UK
		65	BGM-109 T-LAM	SLCM	1995	1997–98	(18)	Deal worth \$142 m; for 7 Swiftsure and Trafalgar Class submarines
L:	USA	59	AH-64D Apache	Combat helicopter	1995		. .	Deal worth \$3.95 b (offsets 100%) incl 8 delivered direct and 980 AGM-114 missiles; UK designation WAH-64D
USA								
S:	Canada	17	Piranha 8x8	APC	1995	1997–98	(17)	Chassis for LAV-AD AAV(G/M); for Marines
	France	. .	Box Mortar 120mm	Mortar	1997		. .	For Marines
	Israel	50	Popeye-1	ASM	1996	1997–98	(50)	Deal worth \$39 m; US designation AGM-142A Have Nap
		1 700	Popeye-1/AGM-142	ASM	1998		. .	
	South Africa	(9)	Husky	AMV	(1997)	1998	(6)	Part of 'Chubby' mine-clearing system; deal worth \$14 m incl Meerkat AMVs
		(9)	Meerkat	AMV	(1997)	1998	6	Part of 'Chubby' mine-clearing system; deal worth \$14 m incl Husky AMVs
	UK	8	UFH 155mm	Towed gun	1997		. .	US designation XM-777

Recipient/ supplier (S) or licenser (L)	No. ordered	Weapon designation	Weapon description	Year of order/ licence	Year(s) of deliveries	No. delivered/ produced	Comments
L: Italy	12	Osprey Class	MCM ship	1986	1993–98	11	
Switzerland	(711)	PC-9/T-6A Texan-2	Trainer aircraft	1995		. .	Incl 339 for Navy; 'JPATS' programme worth $7 b; US designation Beech Mk-2 or T-6A Texan-2
UK	172	Hawk/T-45A Goshawk	Jet trainer aircraft	1981	1988–98	(101)	For Navy; US designation T-45A Goshawk; 'VTXTS' or 'T-45TS' programme; incl 2 prototypes
	(723)	UFH 155mm	Towed gun	(1997)		. .	Incl 450 for Marines; US designation M-777
	1	Cyclone Class	Patrol craft	1997		. .	Deal worth $23.2 m
Uganda							
S: Bulgaria	(40)	T-55M	Main battle tank	(1998)		. .	Ex-Bulgarian Army
South Africa	(1)	Husky	AMV	(1997)	1998	(1)	Part of 'Chubby' mine-clearing system
	(1)	Meerkat	AMV	(1997)	1998	(1)	Part of 'Chubby' mine-clearing system
Ukraine	90	T-55M	Main battle tank	(1998)	1998	62	Ex-Ukranian Army
United Nations							
S: South Africa	. .	RG-31 Nyala	APC	1998	1998	(10)	For UN peacekeeping, monitoring and humanitarian operations
	27	RG-32 Scout	APC	1998	1998	(10)	For UN peacekeeping, monitoring and humanitarian operations
Uruguay							
S: UK	5	Wessex HC-Mk-2	Helicopter	1997	1998	5	Ex-UK Air Force
USA	10	Cessna-U206	Light aircraft	(1998)	1998	10	
Venezuela							
S: Canada	4	Bell-412EP	Helicopter	1997		. .	For SAR
Italy	8	MB-339FD	Jet trainer aircraft	1998		. .	Deal worth $110 m; 16 to be ordered later; order not yet signed
	12	SF-260E/F	Trainer aircraft	1998		. .	Deal worth $12 m
Netherlands	2	Reporter	Surveillance radar	1997		. .	

Poland	(6)	M-28 Skytruck	Light transport ac	(1997)		. .	For National Guard; deal worth $20 m
Spain	3	C-212-400 Patrullero	MP aircraft	1997	1998	3	For Navy
Sweden	4	Giraffe-AD	Surveillance radar	1998		. .	
Viet Nam							
S: Russia	(6)	Su-27UBK Flanker-C	FGA/trainer aircraft	(1996)	1997–98	6	
	2	Bass Tilt	Fire control radar	1996		. .	For 2 BPS-500 Type FAC; for use with 76mm and AK-630 30mm guns
	2	Cross Dome	Surveillance radar	1996		. .	For 2 BPS-500 Type FAC
	2	SS-N-25 ShShMS	ShShM system	1996		. .	For 2 BPS-500 Type FAC
	(16)	SS-N-25/X-35 Uran	ShShM	1996		. .	For 2 BPS-500 Type FAC
	(48)	SA-N-5 Grail/Strela-2M	ShAM	(1996)		. .	For 2 BPS-500 Type FAC; designation uncertain
L: Russia	2	BPS-500 Type	FAC(M)	1996		. .	
Zimbabwe							
S: Italy	6	SF-260E/F	Trainer aircraft	1997	1998	6	Deal worth $2.6 m

Abbreviations and acronyms

ac	Aircraft
AAA	Anti-aircraft artillery
AALS	Amphibious assault landing ship
AAV	Anti-aircraft vehicle
ABL	Armoured bridge layer
ACRV	Armoured command and reconnaissance vehicle
AEV	Armoured engineer vehicle
AEW	Airborne early-warning
AEW&C	Airborne early-warning and control
AIFV	Armoured infantry fighting vehicle
AMV	Anti-mine vehicle
APC	Armoured personnel carrier
APC/CP	Armoured personnel carrier/command post
ARV	Armoured recovery vehicle
ASM	Air-to-surface missile
ASW	Anti-submarine warfare
CIWS	Close-in weapon system
EDA	Excess Defense Articles
ELINT	Electronic intelligence
EW	Electronic warfare
FAC	Fast attack craft
FGA	Fighter/ground attack
FMF	Foreign Military Funding
FMS	Foreign Military Sales
FRG	Federal Republic of Germany
(G)	Gun-armed
GDR	German Democratic Republic
IFV	Infantry fighting vehicle
incl	Including/includes
LTTE	Liberation Tigers of Tamil Eelam
(M)	Missile-armed
MCM	Mine countermeasures
MP	Maritime patrol
MRL	Multiple rocket launcher
OPV	Offshore patrol vessel
Recce	Reconaissance
SAM	Surface-to-air missile
SAR	Search and rescue
ShAM	Ship-to-air missile
ShShM	Ship-to-ship missile
SIGINT	Signals intelligence
SLCM	Submarine-launched cruise missile
SSM	Surface-to-surface missile
SuShM	Submarine-to-ship missile
VIP	Very important person
VLS	Vertical launch system

Conventions

. .	Data not available or not applicable
( )	Uncertain data or SIPRI estimate
m	million (10^6)
b	billion (10^9)

Appendix 11C. Sources and methods[1]

I. The SIPRI sources

The sources for the data presented in the arms transfer registers are of a wide variety: newspapers; periodicals and journals; books, monographs and annual reference works; and official national and international documents. The common criterion for all these sources is that they are open—published and available to the general public.

Published information cannot provide a comprehensive picture because not all arms transfers are fully reported in the open literature. Published reports provide partial information, and substantial disagreement among reports is common. Therefore, the exercise of judgement and the making of estimates are important elements in compiling the SIPRI arms transfers database. Order dates, delivery dates and exact numbers of weapons ordered and delivered may not always be known and are sometimes estimated—particularly with respect to missiles. It is common for reports of arms deals involving large platforms—ships, aircraft and armoured vehicles—to ignore missile armaments. Unless there is explicit evidence that platforms were disarmed or altered before delivery, it is assumed that a weapon fit specified in one of the major reference works is carried. As new data become available continually, the SIPRI arms transfers database is constantly updated.

II. Selection criteria

SIPRI arms transfer data cover six categories of major conventional weapons or systems. The statistics presented refer to the transfer of systems in these six categories only. The categories are defined as:

1. Aircraft: all fixed-wing aircraft and helicopters, with the exception of microlight aircraft and powered and unpowered gliders.
2. Armoured vehicles: all vehicles with integral armour protection, including all types of tank, tank destroyer, armoured car, armoured personnel carrier, armoured support vehicle and infantry combat vehicle.
3. Artillery: multiple rocket launchers; naval, fixed and towed guns, howitzers and mortars, with a calibre equal to or above 100-mm; as well as all armoured self-propelled guns, regardless of calibre.
4. Guidance and radar systems: all land- and ship-based surveillance and fire-control radars, and all non-portable land- and ship-based launch and guidance systems for missiles covered in the SIPRI 'missile' category.
5. Missiles: all powered, guided missiles with explosive conventional warheads. Unguided rockets, guided but unpowered shells and bombs, free-fall aerial munitions, anti-submarine rockets, drones and unmanned air vehicles (UAV) and all torpedoes are excluded.
6. Ships: all ships with a standard tonnage of 100 tonnes or more, and all ships armed with artillery of 100-mm calibre or more, torpedoes or guided missiles.

[1] A more extensive description of the SIPRI Arms Transfers Project methodology, including a list of sources used and examples of calculations, is available on the SIPRI Internet website, URL <http://www.sipri.se/projects/armstrade/atmethods.html>.

The registers and statistics do not include transfers of small arms, trucks, towed or naval artillery under 100-mm calibre, ammunition, support items, services and components or component technology. Publicly available information is inadequate to track these items satisfactorily on a global scale.

To be included in the SIPRI arms transfers registers, items must be destined for the armed forces, paramilitary forces or intelligence agencies of another country and they must be transferred voluntarily by the supplier. This excludes captured weapons and weapons obtained through defectors. Arms supplied to rebel forces in an armed conflict are included as deliveries to the individual rebel forces.[2] Arms supplied for technical or arms procurement evaluation purposes only, or to companies, are not included.

In cases where it has not been possible to identify a supplier or recipient with an acceptable degree of certainty, deliveries are identified as coming from 'unknown' suppliers or going to 'unknown' recipients.

III. The SIPRI trend-indicator value

The SIPRI valuation system is not comparable to official economic statistics such as gross domestic product, public expenditure and export/import figures. The monetary values assigned do not correspond to the actual prices paid, which vary considerably depending on different pricing methods, the length of production runs and the terms involved in individual transactions. For instance, a deal may or may not cover spare parts, training, support equipment, compensation, offset arrangements for the local industries in the buying country, and so on. Furthermore, using only actual sales prices—even assuming that the information were available for all deals, which it is not—would exclude military aid and grants, and the total flow of arms would therefore not be measured. In the SIPRI register of the transfers and licensed production of major conventional weapons (appendix 11B), however, actual contract values are given when available and verifiable. These values are included in order to give an indication of the financial scope of the respective deal.

The SIPRI system for valuation of arms transfers is designed as a *trend-measuring device*, to permit the measurement of changes in the total flow of major weapons and its geographical pattern. Expressing the valuation in trend-indicator values, in which similar weapons have similar prices, reflects both the quantity and quality of the weapons transferred. Values are based only on *actual deliveries* during the year/years covered in the relevant tables and figures.

Production under licence is included in the arms transfers statistics in such a way as to reflect the import share embodied in the weapon. In reality, this share is normally high in the beginning, gradually decreasing over time. SIPRI has attempted to estimate an average import share for each weapon produced under licence.

[2] This differs from previous SIPRI Yearbooks, in which deliveries to rebel forces were included in the imports of the country where the rebels operated.

Appendix 11D. The European Union Code of Conduct for Arms Exports

Adopted in Luxembourg on 8 June 1998

The Council of the European Union,

Building on the Common Criteria agreed at the Luxembourg and Lisbon European Councils in 1991 and 1992,

Recognising the special responsibility of arms exporting states,

Determined to set high common standards which should be regarded as the minimum for the management of, and restraint in, conventional arms transfers by all EU Member States, and to strengthen the exchange of relevant information with a view to achieving greater transparency,

Determined to prevent the export of equipment which might be used for internal repression or international aggression, or contribute to regional instability,

Wishing within the framework of the CFSP to reinforce their cooperation and to promote their convergence in the field of conventional arms exports,

Noting complementary measures taken by the EU against illicit transfers, in the form of the EU Programme for Preventing and Combating Illicit Trafficking in Conventional Arms,

Acknowledging the wish of EU Member States to maintain a defence industry as part of their industrial base as well as their defence effort,

Recognising that states have a right to transfer the means of self-defence, consistent with the right of self-defence recognised by the UN Charter,

Have adopted the following Code of Conduct and operative provisions:

CRITERION ONE

Respect for the international commitments of EU member states, in particular the sanctions decreed by the UN Security Council and those decreed by the Community, agreements on non-proliferation and other subjects, as well as other international obligations

An export licence should be refused if approval would be inconsistent with, inter alia:

a. the international obligations of member states and their commitments to enforce UN, OSCE and EU arms embargoes;

b. the international obligations of member states under the Nuclear Non-Proliferation Treaty, the Biological and Toxin Weapons Convention and the Chemical Weapons Convention;

c. their commitments in the frameworks of the Australia Group, the Missile Technology Control Regime, the Nuclear Suppliers Group and the Wassenaar Arrangement;

d. their commitment not to export any form of anti-personnel landmine.

CRITERION TWO

The respect of human rights in the country of final destination

Having assessed the recipient country's attitude towards relevant principles established by international human rights instruments, Member States will:

a. not issue an export licence if there is a clear risk that the proposed export might be used for internal repression;

b. exercise special caution and vigilance in issuing licences, on a case-by-case basis and taking account of the nature of the equipment, to countries where serious violations of human rights have been established by the competent bodies of the UN, the Council of Europe or by the EU.

For these purposes, equipment which might be used for internal repression will include, inter alia, equipment where there is evidence of the use of this or similar equipment for internal repression by the proposed end-user, or where there is reason to believe that the equipment will be diverted from its stated end-use or end-user and used for internal repression. In line with operative paragraph 1 of this Code, the nature of the equipment will be considered carefully, particularly if it is intended for internal security purposes. Internal repression includes, inter alia, torture and other cruel, inhuman and degrading treatment or punishment, summary or arbitrary executions, disappearances, arbitrary detentions and other major violations of human rights and fundamental freedoms as set out in relevant international human rights instruments, including the Universal Declaration on Human Rights and the International Covenant on Civil and Political Rights.

CRITERION THREE

The internal situation in the country of final destination, as a function of the existence of tensions or armed conflicts

Member States will not allow exports which would provoke or prolong armed conflicts or aggravate existing tensions or conflicts in the country of final destination.

CRITERION FOUR

Preservation of regional peace, security and stability

Member States will not issue an export licence if there is a clear risk that the intended recipient would use the proposed export aggressively against another country or to assert by force a territorial claim.

When considering these risks, EU Member States will take into account inter alia;

a. the existence or likelihood of armed conflict between the recipient and another country;

b. a claim against the territory of a neighbouring country which the recipient has in the past tried or threatened to pursue by means of force;

c. whether the equipment would be likely to be used other than for the legitimate national security and defence of the recipient;

d. the need not to affect adversely regional stability in any significant way.

CRITERION FIVE

The national security of the member states and of territories whose external relations are the responsibility of a Member State, as well as that of friendly and allied countries

Member States will take into account:

a. the potential effect of the proposed export on their defence and security interests and those of friends, allies and other member states, while recognising that this factor cannot affect consideration of the criteria on respect of human rights and on regional peace, security and stability;

b. the risk of use of the goods concerned against their forces or those of friends, allies or other member states;

c. the risk of reverse engineering or unintended technology transfer.

CRITERION SIX

The behaviour of the buyer country with regard to the international community, as regards in particular to its attitude to terrorism, the nature of its alliances and respect for international law

Member States will take into account inter alia the record of the buyer country with regard to:

a. its support or encouragement of terrorism and international organised crime;

b. its compliance with its international commitments, in particular on the non-use of force, including under international humanitarian law applicable to international and non-international conflicts;

c. its commitment to non-proliferation and other areas of arms control and disarmament, in particular the signature, ratification and implementation of relevant arms control and disarmament conventions referred to in sub-paragraph b) of Criterion One.

CRITERION SEVEN

The existence of a risk that the equipment will be diverted within the buyer country or re-exported under undesirable conditions

In assessing the impact of the proposed export on the importing country and the risk that exported goods might be diverted to an undesirable end-user, the following will be considered:

a. the legitimate defence and domestic security interests of the recipient country, including any involvement in UN or other peace-keeping activity;

b. the technical capability of the recipient country to use the equipment;

c. the capability of the recipient country to exert effective export controls;

d. the risk of the arms being re-exported or diverted to terrorist organisations (anti-terrorist equipment would need particularly careful consideration in this context).

CRITERION EIGHT

The compatibility of the arms exports with the technical and economic capacity of the recipient country, taking into account the desirability that states should achieve their legitimate needs of security and defence with the least diversion for armaments of human and economic resources

Member States will take into account, in the light of information from relevant sources such as UNDP, World Bank, IMF and OECD reports, whether the proposed export would seriously hamper the sustainable development of the recipient country. They will consider in this context the recipient country's relative levels of military and social expenditure, taking into account also any EU or bilateral aid.

OPERATIVE PROVISIONS

1. Each EU Member State will assess export licence applications for military equipment made to it on a case-by-case basis against the provisions of the Code of Conduct.

2. This Code will not infringe on the right of Member States to operate more restrictive national policies.

3. EU Member States will circulate through diplomatic channels details of licences refused in accordance with the Code of Conduct for military equipment together with an explanation of why the licence has been refused. The details to be notified are set out in the form of a draft pro-forma at Annex A. Before any Member State grants a licence which has been denied by another Member State or States for an essentially identical transaction within the last three years, it will first consult the Member State or States which issued the denial(s). If following consultations, the Member State nevertheless decides to grant a licence, it will notify the Member State or States issuing the denial(s), giving a detailed explanation of its reasoning.

The decision to transfer or deny the transfer of any item of military equipment will remain at the national discretion of each Member State. A denial of a licence is understood to take place when the member state has refused to authorise the actual sale or physical export of the item of military equipment concerned, where a sale would otherwise have come about, or the conclusion of the relevant contract. For these purposes, a notifiable denial may, in accordance with national procedures, include denial of permission to start negotiations or a negative response to a formal initial enquiry about a specific order.

4. EU Member States will keep such denials and consultations confidential and not use them for commercial advantage.

5. EU Member States will work for the early adoption of a common list of military equipment covered by the Code, based on similar national and international lists. Until then, the Code will operate on the basis of national control lists incorporating where appropriate elements from relevant international lists.

6. The criteria in this Code and the consultation procedure provided for by paragraph 2 of the operative provisions will also apply to dual-use goods as specified in Annex 1 of Council Decision 94/942/CFSP as amended, where there are grounds for believing that the end-user of such goods will be the armed forces or internal security forces or similar entities in the recipient country.

7. In order to maximise the efficiency of this Code, EU Member States will work within the framework of the CFSP to reinforce their cooperation and to promote their convergence in the field of conventional arms exports.

8. Each EU Member State will circulate to other EU Partners in confidence an annual report on its defence exports and on its implementation of the Code. These reports will be discussed at an annual meeting held within the framework of the CFSP. The meeting will also review the operation of the Code, identify any improvements which need to be made and submit to the Council a consolidated report, based on contributions from Member States.

9. EU Member States will, as appropriate, assess jointly through the CFSP framework the situation of potential or actual recipients of arms exports from EU Member States, in the light of the principles and criteria of the Code of Conduct.

10. It is recognised that Member States, where appropriate, may also take into account the effect of proposed exports on their economic, social, commercial and industrial interests, but that these factors will not affect the application of the above criteria.

11. EU Member States will use their best endeavours to encourage other arms exporting states to subscribe to the principles of this Code of Conduct.

12. This Code of Conduct and the operative provisions will replace any previous elaboration of the 1991 and 1992 Common Criteria.

. . .

Source: Conference on Disarmament document CD/1544, 19 June 1998.

Appendix 11E. Efforts to control the international trade in light weapons

BERNARD ADAM*

I. Introduction

Since the mid-1990s and particularly since 1997, the widespread availability of light weapons[1] and the consequences of their use have become a growing concern for public opinion and among certain political circles. Public opinion has become more and more aware that human tragedies are made worse in weapons-ridden countries; private and public actors in development cooperation have become fully aware that their efforts are wrecked by the resort to arms; and political leaders have been faced with the implementation of peacekeeping operations that have failed for the most part because of the proliferation of light weapons.

Compared with major conventional weapons, light weapons are easier to purchase, cheap, easily transported and if necessary hidden, not quickly outdated and easy to use. They can be used by child soldiers and by a large range of actors from terrorist groups to ordinary citizens defending themselves. Their widespread availability makes conflict more lethal; leads to increased human suffering, the violation of human rights and humanitarian law, and internal destabilization; weakens efforts to establish democratic structures; ruins development efforts; and increases international insecurity.[2] It furthers the development of a 'culture of violence'. During 1999 the success of the International Campaign to Ban Landmines (ICBL) convinced a number of non-government organizations (NGOs) and governments that the worldwide accumulation of light weapons could be tackled in the same way as the landmines issue.

[1] 'Light weapons' is here used as a general term referring to conventional weapons of a calibre less than 100 mm and suitable ammunition and explosives. The UN defines light weapons as heavy machine-guns, hand-held and mounted grenade launchers, portable anti-aircraft guns, portable anti-tank guns, recoilless rifles, portable launchers of anti-tank missile and rocket systems, portable launchers of anti-aircraft missile systems and mortars of calibre < 100 mm. It defines 'small arms' as revolvers, self-loading pistols, rifles, carbines, sub-machine-guns, assault rifles and light machine-guns. United Nations, General and complete disarmament: small arms, note by the Secretary-General, UN document A/52/298, 5 Nov. 1997, pp. 11–12.

[2] Renner, M., *Small Arms, Big Impact: The Next Challenge of Disarmament*, Paper no. 37 (Worldwatch Institute: Washington, Oct. 1997); International Committee of the Red Cross, *Arms Availability and Violations of International Humanitarian Law and the Deterioration of the Situation of Civilians in Armed Conflicts* (Norwegian Red Cross: Oslo, 1998); Laurance, E., *Light Weapons and Intrastate Conflict, Early Warning Factors and Preventive Action* (Carnegie Corporation of New York: Washington, DC, July 1998); Berghezan, G., Adam, B. *et al.*, *Armes légères, clés pour une meilleure compréhension* [Light weapons, keys for a better understanding], Special Issue (GRIP: Brussels, 1998); Bonn International Center for Conversion (BICC), *The New Field of Micro-Disarmament*, Brief 7 (BICC: Bonn, Sep. 1996); BICC, *Reasonable Measures*, Brief no. 11 (BICC: Bonn, Aug. 1998); and Greene, O., *Tackling Light Weapons Proliferation: Issues and Priorities for the EU* (Saferworld: London, Apr. 1997).

* Georges Berghezan, Ilhan Berkoll and Alain Reisenfeld provided assistance in the research for this appendix and it was translated from French by Caroline Pailhe.

There have been numerous attempts to estimate the number of light weapons manufactured and in circulation in the world.[3] Light weapons essentially flow through two channels. On the one hand, newly manufactured weapons are mainly produced in and exported from the industrialized countries. On the other hand, countries in conflict and those in post-conflict regions have large weapon stockpiles now useless for their own needs but still in circulation. These countries are mainly situated in the 'south', but 'northern' countries (like the former USSR) have also had excess arms stockpiles since the end of the cold war.

Restraining the diffusion of light weapons thus requires better control over (*a*) newly manufactured weapons, (*b*) existing stockpiles and (*c*) transfers of both. Control over production is in theory implemented by national authorities but it is an indirect control essentially on exports by private companies. As far as stockpiles are concerned, several efforts have been undertaken in post-conflict countries where programmes of weapon collection and sometimes destruction have been implemented more or less successfully. Examples are Cambodia, Mozambique, Somalia and El Salvador.

The control of light weapons broadly requires two kinds of action. First of all, illicit arms trafficking must be confronted. There is broad consensus among political leaders for further curbing this traffic as part of a more general fight against terrorism and banditry. Unfortunately, in contrast, there is no extensive agreement on strengthening the criteria for legal arms transfers. In the absence of any genuine international regulation, they remain the responsibility of individual states.

A total prohibition of light weapons is unlikely. Only illicit transfers and the illegal use of licit transfers must be totally banned. A major difficulty is therefore determining precisely what is licit and what is not.

The following sections focus on the many initiatives taken at various levels to address directly or indirectly the question of the transfer and accumulation of light weapons.

II. International initiatives

Former UN Secretary-General Boutros Boutros-Ghali was one of the first officials to pay special attention to the problems of light weapons proliferation. In the aftermath of the UN peacekeeping operations in the early 1990s, he highlighted the importance of 'micro-disarmament' (called later 'practical disarmament'), namely, the collection of light weapons.[4] As far as arms control is concerned, he observed that 'progress

[3] See, e.g., Isenberg, D., 'Small arms, deadly results', *Defense Monitor*, vol. 2, no. 1 (8 Jan. 1997); Hart Ezell, V., *Report on International Small Arms Production and Proliferation* (Institute for Research on Small Arms in International Security: Alexandria, Va., Mar. 1995), p. 9, cited in United Nations, General and complete disarmament: small arms, note by the Secretary-General, UN document A/52/298, 27 Aug. 1997, p. 14; Renner (note 2), pp. 19–21; Klare, M., 'The new arms race: light weapons and international security', *Current History* (Philadelphia), Apr. 1997, p. 176; and figures collected by Berkol, I. (GRIP associate researcher) in Gander, T. J. (ed.), *Jane's Infantry Weapons 1998–99*, 24th edn (Jane's Information Group: Coulsdon, 1998), pp. 773–83.

[4] United Nations, Supplement to *An Agenda for Peace*, UN document A/50/60–S/1995/1, 3 Jan. 1995, para. 61. On the lessons drawn from light weapons collection and destruction during UN peacekeeping operations, see United Nations Institute for Disarmament Research (UNIDIR), *Managing Arms in Peace Processes: The Issues*, document 96/46 (UNIDIR: Geneva, 1996). Several UN General Assembly resolutions focus on 'practical disarmament measures', in particular, UN General Assembly Resolution 51/45 N, 10 Dec. 1996; and UN General Assembly Resolution 52/38 G, 9 Dec. 1997, both proposed by Japan and Germany.

since 1992 in the area of weapons of mass destruction and major weapons systems must be followed by parallel progress in conventional arms, particularly with respect to light weapons'.

The UN Panel of Governmental Experts on Small Arms

The first major initiative within the UN framework was the report of the Panel of Governmental Experts on Small Arms whose mandate was, among other things, to examine 'ways and means to prevent and reduce the excessive and destabilizing accumulation and transfer of small arms and light weapons'. Set up under General Assembly Resolution 50/70B of 12 December 1995 (proposed by Japan), the panel was formed in April 1996 by the appointment of 16 experts and held three sessions in New York and one in Tokyo. There were also three regional workshops to which 72 other experts were invited. The report was sent to the Secretary-General on 7 August 1997.[5]

The report of the panel considers the causes of the'excessive and destabilizing' accumulation of light weapons. It notes that 'there are no globally agreed norms and standards to determine the excessive or destabilizing levels of this class of weapons'. The UN experts propose as criteria that weapons accumulation can be excessive and destabilizing: (*a*) 'when a state, whether supplier or recipient, does not exercise restraint in the production, transfer and acquisition of such weapons beyond those needed for legitimate national and collective defence and internal security'; (*b*) when a state, whether a supplier or recipient, cannot exercise effective control to prevent the illegitimate acquisition, transfer, transit or circulation of such weapons'; and (*c*) 'when the use of such weapons manifests itself in armed conflict, in crime, such as arms and drug trafficking, or other actions contrary to the norms of national or international laws'. It notes that as a general rule the transfer of such weapons to regions of tension and conflict 'is characterized by a lack of transparency'.

The report ends with a series of 22 recommendations, among them: (*a*) the adoption of an integrated approach to security and development; (*b*) the collection and destruction of weapons in the illegal possession of civilians, including within the framework of post-conflict peace agreements; (*c*) the strengthening of information exchange and international cooperation in combating arms trafficking; (*d*) the implementation by all states of the Guidelines for International Arms Transfers adopted by the Disarmament Commission in 1996;[6] (*e*) restraint by all states in the transfer of surplus light weapons, these surpluses being ideally completely destroyed; (*f*) the adoption of regional or subregional moratoriums on the transfer and manufacture of light weapons; (*g*) an international conference to be organized by the UN on the illicit arms trade; (*h*) a study of the establishment of a reliable system for marking weapons from the time of their manufacture; (*i*) study of the establishment of a database of authorized manufacturers and dealers; and (*j*) a study of the specific problem of ammunition.

[5] United Nations, General and complete disarmament: small arms, note by the Secretary-General, UN document A/52/298, 27 Aug. 1997.

[6] United Nations, Report of the Disarmament Commission, General Assembly, Official Records, 51st Session, Supplement no. 42, UN document A/51/42, Annex 1, 22 May 1996. For the text of the 1991 Guidelines for Conventional Arms Transfers, see Anthony, I. (ed.), SIPRI, *Russia and the Arms Trade* (Oxford University Press: Oxford, 1998), appendix 1, p. 233.

The discussions among panel members were sometimes controversial and the report was a consensus report. According to the Canadian expert to the panel, 'The most controversial issues stemmed from the supply and demand factors. Many of the non-western panel members saw the issue as more of a supply factor while the western side saw it as at least 50 per cent demand'.[7]

Following this report, the General Assembly adopted on 9 December 1997 a resolution[8] subscribing globally to the panel of Experts' recommendations but endorsing only 2 of the 22 recommendations. These concerned the initiation of a study on ammunition and the preparation of an international conference on the illicit arms trade. The study on ammunition began in early 1998 by the setting up of a questionnaire in June 1998 to all member states. In July 1998, the Swiss Government was reported to have offered to host in 2000 the international conference on the illicit arms trade in Geneva.[9] The resolution also asks the Secretary-General to produce a new report with a new group of experts and to make further recommendations to the 54th session of the General Assembly in 1999.[10] In April 1998 the Secretary-General nominated 23 experts to constitute this second group. The five permanent members of the UN Security Council (China, France, Russia, the UK and the USA) are part of it, in contrast to the first group of experts on which of the five only Russia and the USA were represented. The membership of China is likely to complicate even more the achievement of a consensus, considering its well-known reticence about any proposal aimed at improving arms transfers control. This second group of experts met in May 1998 in New York and in September 1998 in Tokyo.

On 14 August 1998 the Secretary-General announced the establishment within the Department for Disarmament Affairs of a body called Coordinating Action on Small Arms (CASA) in charge of harmonizing all action undertaken on light weapons within the UN system.[11]

On 4 December 1998 the General Assembly adopted two more resolutions on light weapon transfers. The first formally endorsed the project for an international conference on the illicit arms trade in 2001 at the latest and requests the Secretary-General to launch a study on the feasibility of limiting the production of and trade in light weapons to producers and dealers authorized by states.[12] The second requested the Secretary-General to hold broadly based consultations on the reality of illicit trafficking in light weapons, on possible measures to combat it and on the role to be played by the UN in collecting and disseminating information on the issue.[13]

[7] Cited in Goldring, N. J., British–American Security Information Council, *After Discord, Consensus on UN Small Arms Report*, BASIC Reports no. 59 (BASIC: Washington, DC, 25 Aug. 1997), p. 1.

[8] UN General Assembly Resolution 52/38 J, 'Small arms', 9 Dec. 1997.

[9] United Nations, General and complete disarmament: assistance to states for curbing the illicit traffic in small arms and collecting them, Report of the Secretary-General, UN document A/53/207, 31 July 1998, p. 5.

[10] On 9 Dec. 1997, besides Resolution A/RES/52/38 J, the UN General Assembly adopted 2 additional resolutions on light weapons collection: UN General Assembly Resolution 52/38 C, 'Assistance to states for curbing the illicit traffic in small arms and collecting them'; and UN General Assembly Resolution 52/38 G, 'Consolidation of peace through practical disarmament measures', 9 Dec. 1997.

[11] United Nations, Department for Disarmament Affairs, 'Department for Disarmament Affairs designated UN focal point to coordinate action on small arms within UN system', Press Release DC/2611, 14 Aug. 1998; and Wurst, J., British–American Security Information Council, *UN Lobbies for Coordination on Small Arms*, BASIC Reports no. 65 (BASIC: Washington, DC, 14 Aug. 1998), pp. 5–7.

[12] UN General Assembly Resolution 53/77 E, 'Small arms', 4 Dec. 1998.

[13] UN General Assembly Resolution 53/77 T, 'Illicit traffic in small arms', 4 Dec. 1998. On 4 Dec. 1998, 2 additional resolutions were adopted by the General Assembly on light weapons collection: UN General Assembly Resolution 53/77 B, 'Assistance to states for curbing the illicit traffic in small arms

Guidelines for international arms transfers

On 7 May 1996 the Disarmament Commission of the General Assembly, after three years of discussion, finally agreed on Guidelines for International Arms Transfers in the Context of General Assembly Resolution 46/36H of 6 December 1991.[14] These guidelines include the need for transparency in arms transfers and highlight states' responsibility in exercising restraint over arms production, procurement and transfers. They urge states to seek to ensure effective control of the excessive accumulation of light weapons in order to prevent illicit trafficking. Unfortunately, they concentrate mainly on illicit trafficking and are silent on possible criteria for licit transfers.[15]

The UN Security Council and light weapons in Africa

On 7 September 1995, the Security Council established an International Commission of Inquiry on arms transfers to the former government of Rwanda and its militia.[16] The commission's investigation took place between October 1995 and October 1996 and resulted in four reports.[17] On 9 April 1998, the Security Council reactivated the commission,[18] which submitted two more reports in the same year.[19]

The armaments on which the investigation focused were mostly light weapons. Several recommendations were formulated, including a proposal to establish in Central Africa a moratorium on the transfer and manufacture of light weapons similar to that implemented in West Africa (discussed below), the standardization of end-use certificates, the establishment of an effective system of arms marking and identifying, and the identification of arms brokers. The commission declared its agreement with most recommendations formulated by the Panel of Governmental Experts on Small Arms. It did valuable work, but the time and means at its disposal were regrettably insufficient. In the light of the disastrous situation in the region, analysts urge the creation of a permanent commission of inquiry on arms flows in Central Africa.

A report of the Secretary-General on 13 April 1998 on 'The causes of conflict and the promotion of durable peace and sustainable development in Africa'[20] underlines the urgent need to stop light weapons proliferation in the region and formulates

and collecting them'; and UN General Assembly Resolution 53/77 M, 'Consolidation of peace through practical disarmament measures'.

[14] See note 6.

[15] On 28 Apr. 1998, the Disarmament Commission of the General Assembly adopted 'Guidelines on conventional arms control/limitation and disarmament, with particular emphasis on consolidation of peace in the context of General Assembly Resolution 51/45 N'. These guidelines mainly concern practical disarmament measures but also express the need for stricter criteria on light weapons transfers.

[16] UN Security Council Resolution 1013, 7 Sep. 1995.

[17] United Nations, Letter dated 26 January 1996 from the Secretary-General addressed to the President of the Security Council, UN document S/1996/67 and Corr.1, 29 Jan. 1996; Letter dated 13 March 1996 from the Secretary-General addressed to the President of the Security Council, UN document S/1996/195, 14 Mar. 1996; Letter dated 1 November 1997 from the Secretary-General addressed to the President of the Security Council, UN document S/1997/1010, 24 Dec. 1997; and Letter dated 22 January 1998 from the Secretary-General addressed to the President of the Security Council, UN document S/1998/63, 26 Jan. 1998.

[18] UN Security Council Resolution 1161, 9 Apr. 1998.

[19] United Nations, Letter dated 18 August 1998 from the Secretary-General addressed to the President of the Security Council, UN document S/1998/777, 19 Aug. 1998; and Letter dated 18 November 1998 from the Secretary-General addressed to the President of the Security Council, UN document S/1998/1096, 18 Nov. 1998.

[20] United Nations, Report of the Secretary-General on the situation in Africa, UN document S/1998/318, 13 Apr. 1998.

several recommendations with respect to conventional weapons in general—the encouragement of African countries to report to the UN Register of Conventional Arms and to create subregional registers of conventional arms; restraint on the part of arms-exporting countries; and the public identification of international arms dealers. Following this report, the Security Council adopted a resolution aimed at strengthening arms embargoes[21] and a second focusing on light weapons and arms trafficking.[22] The Security Council notes that 'commercial and political motives play an unduly important role in the illicit transfer and accumulation of small arms in Africa' and subscribes to all the recommendations formulated by the Secretary-General. In particular it stresses the collection and sharing of information on the nature and general scope of the illicit arms trade with and in Africa.

Transparency in light weapons transfers

During the discussions within the Group of Government Experts on the review of the UN Register, which took place in 1997 and ended with a consensus report,[23] the question whether to include light weapons in the scope of the register was deliberated but finally rejected. Only seven categories of major conventional weapons are covered by the UN Register. Some states were clearly unwilling to include light weapons. There was also some overlap between the mandates of the two groups of government experts working on light weapons and on the register: each assuming that the other would look into transparency issues, neither broached the question properly.[24] Considering the limited results of the UN Register review, some analysts propose the creation of regional registers, particularly in Africa.[25]

III. Regional initiatives

The European Union

On 26 June 1997, on the impulsion of the Dutch presidency, the Council of the EU adopted a Programme for Preventing and Combating Illicit Trafficking in Conventional Arms.[26] Considering the excessive accumulation of conventional weapons and arms trafficking to be detrimental to the internal security of states and to respect for human rights, the programme primarily aims to coordinate the individual efforts of the 15 member states in this matter. Indeed, as far as arms transfers and the fight against arms trafficking are concerned, the national competence of the EU member states still remains the ultimate safeguard.

The EU programme provides a framework in three main areas: (*a*) it seeks to strengthen cooperation between the bodies in charge of combating illicit trafficking and encourages information exchange within the EU; (*b*) it aims to help other coun-

[21] UN Security Council Resolution 1196, 16 Sep. 1998.
[22] UN Security Council Resolution 1209, 19 Nov. 1998.
[23] United Nations, General Assembly, General and complete disarmament: transparency in armaments, Report on the continuing operation of the United Nations Register of Conventional Arms and its further development, UN document A/52/316, 29 Aug. 1997.
[24] Goldring (note 7), p. 2.
[25] Meek, S., 'Developing a regional register of conventional arms: an option for Africa ?', *Africa Security Review*, vol. 6, no. 4 (1997), pp. 49–55.
[26] Council of the European Union, 'EU programme for preventing and combating illicit trafficking in conventional arms', A Council Declaration, 9057/97, 26 June 1997.

tries strengthen their legal systems for effective regulation and monitoring of arms transfers; and (*c*) it allows for assistance to post-conflict countries in weapons collection, buy-back and destruction programmes. Even if the programme broadly addresses the question of conventional weapons, particular emphasis is placed on light weapons trafficking.

This programme is undoubtedly a step forward in the fight against the proliferation of light weapons and of conventional weapons generally since it resolutely subscribes to the perspective of conflict prevention and of the close connection between security and development. In contrast to the Organization of American States (OAS) convention (which is discussed below), the EU programme does not confine itself to the issue of firearms in connection with criminal activities but encompasses the whole problem of conventional weapons used for military as well as civilian purposes.

The criticisms of the programme are threefold. First, it is only a statement of intent (in contrast to the OAS convention which is legally binding), requiring political will from each of the 15 member states if it is to be implemented. Second, the demand factor is emphasized in comparison with the supply side. Third, the programme does not tackle one of the basic causes of trafficking within the EU, namely the lack of harmonization between the 15 member states' arms transfers policies and regulations.

In June 1998, as established by the programme, a first annual report pointed out the various initiatives taken in implementing the programme.[27] In February 1998, the European Conference on Trafficking in Arms identified the actions to be carried out. In May 1998, the EU supported a seminar in South Africa organized by two NGOs (Saferworld, UK, and the Institute for Security Studies, South Africa) to concentrate efforts to combat arms trafficking in southern Africa.

On 25 May 1998, following the initiative of the British presidency, the Council of the European Union adopted a Code of Conduct on Arms Exports that concerns conventional armaments generally, including light weapons.[28] Its adoption is the result of a campaign led by a coalition of 600 NGOs whose project dates back to 1994.[29] Although less ambitious than the initial NGO project, the code represents an essential first step towards harmonization of the 15 member states' policies and regulations on arms transfers. Many states were in favour of a more binding code but France put a brake on its partners, which had to resign themselves to a compromise text in order to reach unanimity.

The Code builds on the eight common criteria for arms exports adopted in 1991 and 1992 and provides for a consultation mechanism between member states. Four main criticisms can be made: (*a*) it is a statement of intent and is not legally binding; (*b*) some criteria, including those relevant to human rights, are not sufficiently explicit; (*c*) restraint in arms transfers remains a national decision that cannot be countered by any partner; and (*d*) transparency is lacking since information exchange remains confidential.

On 17 December 1998, now on the initiative of the German presidency, the Council of the EU adopted a Joint Action to 'combat and contribute to ending the destabilizing accumulation and spread of small arms'.[30] Since a Joint Action is a bind-

[27] Council of the European Union, internal document, unpublished paper.

[28] See chapter 11, section V in this volume. The text is published as appendix 11D in this volume.

[29] Under the initiative of a British NGO coalition, the UK Working Group on Arms, now made up of Amnesty International (UK), BASIC, Christian Aid, International Alert, Oxfam (UK), Save the Children and Saferworld.

[30] Council of the European Union, 'Joint Action 1999/34/CFSP', *Official Journal of the European Communities*, L 9/1, 15 Jan. 1999.

ing intergovernmental agreement this text is legally more important than the Programme for Preventing Illicit Trafficking or the Code of Conduct on Arms Exports. The Joint Action will: (*a*) attempt to build a consensus on a programme of action aimed at preventing light weapons proliferation and including a certain restraint on the part of importing countries in accordance with appropriate criteria; and (*b*) contribute to post-conflict weapons collection, destruction and security reform programmes. Like the Programme on Preventing Illicit Trafficking, it emphasizes the 'demand' factor in developing countries. A further step has nevertheless been taken aimed at curbing EU arms exports in accordance with the Code of Conduct as well as with further criteria still to be defined.

The Organization of American States

On 13 November 1997, following an initiative led by Mexico since 1996, 29 member states of the OAS signed in Washington an Inter-American Convention Against the Illicit Manufacturing of and Trafficking in Firearms, Ammunition, Explosives, and Other Related Materials.[31] The 30-article convention determines a series of control mechanisms, legal requirements and cooperation procedures. The Mexican proposal was strongly supported by Brazil, Canada, El Salvador, Uruguay and the USA and adopted after only one year of discussions because of its simple, uncontroversial and more or less binding objectives. It is considered an excellent regional model.[32]

Although the main purpose was to combat drugs trafficking, the convention provides a basis for the fight against the excessive accumulation of firearms in general ('military' as well as 'civilian'). Nevertheless, its scope is narrow. First, it does not affect national legislation related to firearms of a domestic nature. This is the result of lobbying by the US National Rifle Association, which actively opposes the limitation of arms sales by US citizens. This restriction might prevent the convention from meeting its objectives, since the main problem is the laxity of the US domestic gun laws. According to Brazilian diplomats, 99 per cent of the weapons seized in one particular anti-drug operation had come through illegal channels from the USA.[33] Second, the convention is designed to combat crime, not for conflict prevention or to support development. Third, no weapon destruction is provided for after seizure.

In parallel with the OAS convention, the Inter-American Drug Abuse Control Commission (CISAD) developed Model Regulations for the Control of the International Movement of Firearms, Their Parts and Components and Ammunition which propose concrete measures for a harmonized import/export system to combat firearms trafficking.

Initiatives in Africa

In March 1996, in cooperation with the UN, Mali implemented a light weapons collection and destruction programme within the framework of a peace agreement

[31] Organization of American States, General Assembly Resolution, OAS document OEA/Ser.P, AG/RES. 1 (XXIV-E/97), 13 Nov. 1997, also reproduced in Conference on Disarmament document CD/1488, 22 Jan. 1998.

[32] O'Callaghan, G., British–American Security Information Council, *Combating Illicit Light Weapons Trafficking: Developments and Opportunities*, BASIC Report 98.1 (BASIC: Washington, DC, Jan. 1998), pp. 11–13.

[33] O'Callaghan (note 32), p. 11.

with Tuareg opposition groups. Following this operation, President Alpha Oumar Konaré of Mali took the initiative to propose to West African countries an agreement aimed at combating the proliferation of light weapons in the region. This brought about, on 31 October 1998, the adoption by the heads of state and government of the 16 member states of the Economic Community of West African States (ECOWAS)[34] of a Declaration of a Moratorium on Importation, Exportation and Manufacture of Light Weapons in West Africa.[35] This moratorium came into force on 1 November 1998 for a renewable period of three years. An operational structure called the Programme for Coordination and Assistance for Security and Development (PCASED) is designed to control and supervise the moratorium and to establish a database, a sub-regional register on light weapons and training programmes for the forces of law and order in the signatory countries. The PCASED is financed by the UN Development Programme (UNDP) and supported by the UN Department of Political Affairs (DPA) and the United Nations Institute for Disarmament Research (UNIDIR).

Norwegian efforts must be highlighted, in particular the Norwegian Initiative on Small Arms Transfers (NISAT)[36] which convened on 1–2 April 1998 in Oslo, with the support of the UNDP, a multilateral consultation gathering representatives from 13 West African countries and 23 member states of the WTO to facilitate the moratorium process.[37] This agreement undoubtedly represents a model that can be extended to other regions in Asia or Latin America.

In southern Africa, with the encouragement of South Africa, intensive discussions on the improvement of controls on arms flows have been taking place since 1995 and above all since 1997 within the Southern African Development Community (SADC)[38] in the Interstate Defence and Security Committee (ISDC), composed of ministers concerned with defence and internal security issues. One of its tasks is to facilitate cooperation and information exchange in combating arms trafficking. Another regional organization established in 1995, the Southern African Regional Police Chiefs Cooperation Organization (SARPCCO), brings together the police chiefs of the SADC member states and aims to improve the fight against crime, including illicit arms trafficking. Although no negotiated agreement between the SADC member states exists on the question of arms transfers, discussions are developing and a Southern Africa Regional Action Programme on Light Arms and Illicit Arms Trafficking is likely to be adopted in the near future. Until then, close bilateral cooperation is already operational between South Africa and Mozambique, which on January 1995 signed a cross-border cooperation agreement and led several joint operations to counter arms trafficking (as part of 'Operation Rachel') during which several thousand light weapons and several million rounds of ammunition were seized and destroyed.

[34] Benin, Burkina Faso, Cape Verde, Côte d'Ivoire, Gambia, Ghana, Guinea, Guinea-Bissau, Liberia, Mali, Mauritania, Niger, Nigeria, Senegal, Sierra Leone and Togo.

[35] Economic Community of West African States, Declaration of a Moratorium on Importation, Exportation and Manufacture of Light Weapons in West Africa, 21st Ordinary Session of the Authority of Heads of State and Government, Abuja, 30–31 Oct. 1998.

[36] NISAT was launched in Dec. 1997 with financial support by the Norwegian Ministry of Foreign Affairs. NISAT includes 2 NGOs, the Norwegian Red Cross and the Norwegian Church Aid, as well as 2 research institutes, the International Peace Research Institute, Oslo (PRIO) and the Norwegian Institute of International Affairs.

[37] Lodgaard, S. and Rønnfeld, C. F. (eds), *A Moratorium on Light Weapons in West Africa* (Norwegian Initiative on Small Arms Transfers and Norwegian Institute of International Affairs: Oslo, 1998).

[38] Formerly the Southern African Development Co-ordination Conference (SADCC) founded in 1979 and renamed in 1992. On the SADC and its membership, see the Glossary.

The Council of Ministers of the Organization of African Unity (OAU) which met on 4–7 June 1998 in Ouagadougou, Burkina Faso, following a South African initiative, adopted a resolution highlighting the importance for the OAU of coordinating African countries' efforts to find solutions to the problems posed by light weapons proliferation. During this meeting, the OAU decided to collect information from member states on the extent of the problem and on possible measures to tackle it.[39]

IV. National and other initiatives

International and regional initiatives were facilitated by various national actions often associating NGO and government representatives. Broadly speaking, the countries most active in the field are, among the industrialized countries, Canada, Japan, Norway, Switzerland and five EU countries—Belgium, Germany, the Netherlands, Sweden and the UK. Among the developing countries, three African states clearly stand out—Mali, Mozambique and South Africa.

In July 1998, Canada presented a proposal for an International Convention to Stop Transfers of Arms and Light Weapons to Non-State Actors, aimed at prohibiting official arms transfers to actors other than government-controlled military and police organizations and law enforcement agencies.[40] On 13–14 July 1998 the Norwegian Government convened 20 other states in Oslo in order to draw up possible guidelines of a common policy.[41] Although promising, these elements are a rather weak compromise since some countries were not willing to push the Canadian proposals forward. On 12–13 October 1998 an international conference in Brussels on Sustainable Disarmament for Sustainable Development attended by officials from 98 countries and 100 NGOs included in its concluding text (the Brussels Call for Action), aimed at the adoption of an international programme for a better-integrated approach, calls for improving the fight against arms trafficking and for restricting arms transfers from the importing countries.[42]

Besides official initiatives, several actions developed from civil society. Since May 1997 the former President of Costa Rica, Oscar Arias Sánchez, has proposed with other Nobel Peace Prize laureates an International Code of Conduct on Arms Transfers aimed at restraining and better controlling conventional arms transfers.[43] In December 1997, Professor Edward Laurance from the Monterey Institute of International Studies proposed a Convention on the Prevention of the Indiscriminate and Unlawful Use of Light Weapons.[44] On 14 October 1998, 200 NGO representatives

[39] Organization of African Unity, Council of Ministers, Decision CM/Dec. 432 (LXVIII), 4–7 June 1998.

[40] Canadian Government, The Canadian Government's Proposal for an International Convention to Stop Transfers of Arms and Light Weapons to Non-States Actors, non-paper, July 1998.

[41] The 21 participating countries were: Belgium, Brazil, Burkina Faso, Canada, Colombia, France, Germany, Indonesia, Japan, Mali, Mexico, Mozambique, the Netherlands, Norway, Philippines, South Africa, Sweden, Switzerland, the UK, the USA and Zimbabwe. At the end of the meeting, the 21 'like-minded states' adopted an International Agenda on Small Arms and Light Weapons: Elements of a Common Understanding.

[42] Belgian Secretary of State for Development Cooperation, Brussels Call for Action, 12 and 13 Oct. 1998 conference on Sustainable Disarmament for Sustainable Development, URL <http://www.grip.org/bdg/g1644.pdf>.

[43] Arias Foundation for Peace and Human Progress, International Code of Conduct on Arms Transfers, May 1997, URL <http://www.arias.or.cr/fundarias/cpr/code2-span.shtml>.

[44] Laurance, E., 'Proposed Convention on the Prevention of the Indiscriminate and Unlawful Use of Light Weapons', Monterey Institute of International Studies, presented to the Ottawa Process Forum, Ottawa, 5 Dec. 1997, URL <http://prepcom.org/low/pc2/pc2d1.htlm>.

around the world met in Brussels to establish an International Action Network on Small Arms (IANSA) to coordinate their actions in an international campaign.[45]

V. Conclusions

Light weapons proliferation and its destabilizing consequences have become a widespread concern among diplomats and political leaders but official actions lack coordination. They either result from the willingness of like-minded states encouraged by NGOs and public opinion (as in the EU) or address the specific problems of particular regions (as on the American continent or in Africa). Time and a strong political will are still necessary if tangible results are to be achieved beyond the current mere statements of intent. Following the example of the ICBL, an international campaign will be launched in 1999 by IANSA to reinforce the diplomatic and political efforts undertaken by a dozen countries on this complex problem.

Some of the initiatives have broad official consensus and are therefore likely to develop quickly. They involve practical disarmament measures in post-conflict or weapons-ridden regions and measures to combat arms trafficking connected to terrorism, banditry and drug trafficking. In contrast, individual states, particularly industrialized countries, are less inclined to limit their legal transfers through the adoption of stricter criteria even if restrictions must clearly be applied to the supply as well as the demand side.

Restraints on arms transfers come up against two main problems. On the one hand, many industrial circles still have important financial interests in the defence industry. On the other hand, internationally recognized standards on the legitimate and legal possession of armaments are difficult to define. In a domestic perspective, private firearms ownership has to be better regulated. At the national and international levels, the threshold of armaments beyond which demand is considered incommensurate with self-defence and security requirements must be settled. On the supply side, the next steps will probably involve transparency in transfers by including light weapons in the UN Register, creating regional registers and, in the long run, an international system of marking (through a universal system of producer identification) and tracing (through a database) light weapons. These are the future measures for pushing this particular form of arms control ahead.

[45] The 14 Oct. 1998 NGO meeting on IANSA was hosted by Amnesty International, BASIC, GRIP, International Alert, Oxfam, Pax Christi and Saferworld.

Part III. Non-proliferation, arms control and disarmament, 1998

12. Nuclear arms control and non-proliferation

SHANNON KILE

I. Introduction

Efforts to advance the nuclear arms control and non-proliferation agenda encountered a number of setbacks in 1998. The nuclear explosions carried out by India and Pakistan violated the emergent global norm against nuclear testing. Taking place shortly after the second meeting of the Preparatory Committee for the year 2000 Review Conference of the 1968 Non-Proliferation Treaty (NPT) had ended without substantive results, the tests raised renewed concern about the nuclear non-proliferation regime, of which the NPT forms the principal legal foundation. As the year ended, another nuclear non-proliferation initiative, the 1994 US–North Korea Agreed Framework, appeared to be collapsing because of new doubts about North Korea's compliance with its NPT commitments.

The nuclear arms reduction process made little progress during the year. The centrepiece of US–Russian nuclear arms control endeavours, the 1993 Treaty on Further Reduction and Limitation of Strategic Offensive Arms (START II Treaty), was not ratified by the Russian Federal Assembly (Parliament). The controversies over ballistic missile defences and the future of the 1972 Anti-Ballistic Missile Treaty (the ABM Treaty) jeopardized support for deeper reductions in strategic nuclear forces.

There were some positive developments during the year. The Indian and Pakistani prime ministers both indicated that they were willing to consider signing the 1996 Comprehensive Nuclear Test-Ban Treaty (CTBT), thereby potentially removing major obstacles to the treaty's entry into force. The Conference on Disarmament (CD) finally managed to form a committee to negotiate a global Fissile Material Treaty (FMT) banning the production of fissile material for use in nuclear explosives, although this decision had been made possible only by postponing or papering over key outstanding issues. Paradoxically, the nuclear tests facilitated these positive developments by creating circumstances in which India and Pakistan felt compelled to adopt more cooperative approaches to the CTBT and the FMT.

This chapter reviews the principal developments in nuclear arms control and non-proliferation in 1998. Section II describes the international reactions to the Indian and Pakistani nuclear tests and assesses their implications for the NPT regime. Section III describes developments related to the CTBT, focusing on possible changes in the Indian and Pakistani positions on the treaty, while section IV examines the CD decision to open negotiations on the FMT. Section V gives an account of the other regional and global initiatives to curb the proliferation of nuclear weapons, highlighting the US–North Korean

Agreed Framework. Section VI examines US–Russian nuclear arms control efforts, concentrating on the long-running controversy in the State Duma (the lower house of the Russian Federal Assembly) over ratification of the START II Treaty. Section VII examines the continuing controversies over ballistic missile defences and the future of the ABM Treaty, and section VIII presents the conclusions.

Appendix 12A provides data on the nuclear forces of the five NPT-defined nuclear weapon states and appendix 12B data on the Indian and Pakistani nuclear explosions and information on other issues related to nuclear testing.

II. The Indian and Pakistani nuclear tests

On 11 and 13 May 1998 India carried out a series of five nuclear explosions. Pakistan conducted its own series of five nuclear explosions on 28 May and carried out a sixth test on 30 May.[1] Following the completion of their respective series of tests, both states declared unilateral moratoria on further testing.

In announcing the tests, government spokesmen in both New Delhi and Islamabad emphasized that the explosions violated no legal commitments undertaken by the two states within the framework of international treaties. Neither state had signed the CTBT and neither was a party to the NPT. The strident tone of the Indian Government in defending its decision to carry out the nuclear tests in part reflected the fact that in India the NPT is widely viewed as 'legitimizing the possession in eternity of nuclear weapons by the five nuclear weapon states'.[2] A key question was how the international community should respond to actions taken by states which violate important norms and principles enshrined in multilateral arms control treaties to which they are not parties.

International reactions

Although prior to the tests India and Pakistan (along with Israel) were characterized as 'threshold' nuclear weapon states and widely believed to possess nuclear weapon capabilities, the overt demonstration of these capabilities came as a surprise for the international community.[3] The tests were condemned by many countries for undermining global efforts to halt the spread of nuclear weapons. They also heightened international concern that potentially catastrophic hostilities would break out between India and Pakistan. The bellicose rhetoric from both capitals that accompanied the announcements of the explosions gave a visible nuclear dimension to the territorial conflict over

[1] For further details see appendix 12B in this volume. See also chapters 9 and 15.

[2] Press release, Ministry of External Affairs, External Publicity Division, New Delhi, 15 May 1998. For a discussion of the political and military motivations underlying the Indian and Pakistani decisions to carry out nuclear tests, see chapter 9 in this volume.

[3] India detonated a 'nuclear explosive device' at its Pokhran site in 1974.

Kashmir.[4] It was also feared that the tests heralded a destabilizing nuclear arms race in South Asia with the two long-time rivals poised to weaponize their nuclear capabilities and deploy ballistic missiles capable of delivering nuclear warheads. More broadly, the tests created a new sense of unease about what might lie ahead in the Middle East and North-East Asia, two regions of acute non-proliferation concern.

The Indian and Pakistani actions gave rise to international appeals for both states to take steps to reduce tensions and advance nuclear non-proliferation and disarmament undertakings. On 6 June 1998 the UN Security Council adopted Resolution 1172, expressing its 'grave concern about the negative effects of the nuclear tests conducted by India and Pakistan'. The resolution called on them to: (*a*) immediately undertake to halt all nuclear tests and adhere to the CTBT; (*b*) refrain from deploying nuclear weapons; (*c*) cease further production of fissile material for use in nuclear weapons and contribute constructively to the negotiations in the CD on an FMT; and (*d*) confirm their policies of not exporting technology that could contribute to weapons of mass of destruction or missiles capable of delivering them. It also called on the two states to resume a dialogue aimed at reducing tension, building confidence and encouraging the peaceful resolution of their differences.[5]

There was a strong consensus in international bodies and elsewhere against amending the NPT in order to allow India and Pakistan to join it with the status of nuclear weapon states.[6] The UN Security Council resolution rejected the claim made by Indian Prime Minister Atal Bihari Vajpayee that India had become a nuclear weapon state and must be legally recognized as such.[7] It declared that in accordance with the NPT India and Pakistan cannot have the status of nuclear weapon states.[8] This statement echoed one contained in a communiqué issued two days earlier by the foreign ministers of the five permanent members of the Security Council (the P5).[9] It reinforced a statement issued by 47 states at the CD which, in addition to refusing to legally recognize India and Pakistan as nuclear weapon states, had appealed to both coun-

[4] Buchan, D., 'Tension on the roof of the world', *Financial Times*, 16–17 May 1998, p. 7; Reuters, 'Pakistan, Indian tests boost nuclear war fears', 28 May 1998; Smith, R. J., 'In a "qualitatively different" Kashmir, miscalculation is feared', *International Herald Tribune,* 6–7 June 1998, p. 7; and Erlanger, S., 'The new cold war in South Asia?', *International Herald Tribune*, 13 July 1998, p. 4. See appendix 1B in this volume for an account of the Kashmir conflict.

[5] UN Security Council Resolution 1172, 6 June 1998.

[6] As defined in Article IX of the NPT, only states that manufactured and exploded a nuclear weapon or other nuclear explosive device prior to 1 Jan. 1967 are recognized as nuclear weapon states. By this definition, China, France, Russia, the UK and the USA are nuclear weapon states. The text of the NPT is reproduced in Müller, H., Fischer, D. and Kötter, W., SIPRI, *Nuclear Non-proliferation and Global Order* (Oxford University Press: Oxford, 1994), appendix A, pp. 210–13.

[7] After the nuclear tests, Vajpayee asserted that 'India is now a nuclear weapon state. This is a reality that cannot be denied. It is not a conferment that we seek; nor is it a status for others to grant'. Statement of Prime Minister Shri Atal Bihari Vajpayee in Parliament, 27 May 1998, text reproduced in United Newspapers of India (UNI) press service, 'PM's statement on N-tests in parliament', *Hindustan Times*, 28 May 1998, URL <http://www.hindustantimes.com/ht/nonfram/280598/ detnat01.htm>.

[8] UN Security Council Resolution 1172 (note 5).

[9] Joint Communiqué on the nuclear tests in South Asia, issued by the Foreign Ministers of China, France, the Russian Federation, the United Kingdom of Great Britain and Northern Ireland, and the United States of America, UN press release S/1998/473, 4 June 1998.

tries to renounce their nuclear weapon programmes and to accede 'without delay' to the NPT as non-nuclear weapon states.[10]

Sanctions against India and Pakistan[11]

Despite the widespread condemnation of the nuclear tests, there was little support from international bodies, such as the UN and the European Union (EU), or from national capitals for the imposition of economic sanctions against India and Pakistan. The UK joined with France in expressing scepticism about the efficacy of sanctions in response to the tests.[12] China and Russia condemned the tests but refused to support sanctions.[13] However, in the USA, the Clinton Administration announced the imposition of comprehensive economic sanctions against the two South Asian neighbours, as required by Section 102 of the 1994 Arms Export Control Act (called the Glenn Amendment after its legislative sponsor, Senator John H. Glenn).[14] Some states, such as Denmark, Japan and Sweden, suspended or curtailed development assistance programmes to the region, while the USA spearheaded an embargo campaign to deny military technology to India. The USA subsequently moved to ease its application of economic sanctions and export controls in conjunction with its bilateral discussions with India and Pakistan on non-proliferation issues.

Talks on reducing nuclear dangers in South Asia

The demonstrations by India and Pakistan of their nuclear weapon capabilities prompted the Clinton Administration to launch high-level 'nuclear dialogues' with them.[15] The talks were aimed at accommodating India and Pakistan within the global nuclear non-proliferation regime. According to US officials, the immediate objectives were to discuss steps that could be taken to reduce nuclear weapon-related dangers and to lower tensions in the region while advancing non-proliferation measures.[16] These steps included signing the

[10] 'Statement read by Amb. Clive Pearson, New Zealand, Special session of the Conference on Disarmament', 2 June 1998, text reproduced by the Acronym Institute, London, URL <http://www.gn.apc.org/acronym/spint2.htm>.

[11] For a more comprehensive discussion of the imposition of sanctions and export controls on India and Pakistan and of their use as non-proliferation instruments, see chapter 15 in this volume.

[12] Friedman, A., 'A summit bid to head off nuclear race', *International Herald Tribune*, 16–17 May 1998, pp. 1, 5.

[13] 'China not to impose economic sanctions against India', *Indian Express,* 20 May 1998, URL <http://www.expressindia.com/news/13800031.htm>; and ITAR-TASS (Moscow), 2 June 1998, 'Primakov: Russia to oppose India, Pakistan sanctions', in Foreign Broadcast Information Service, *Daily Report–Central Eurasia* (*FBIS-SOV*), FBIS-SOV-98-153, 2 June 1998.

[14] While supporting sanctions in principle, US Administration officials complained that the rigid terms of the legislation had unintended negative consequences and hindered the ability of the USA to effectively engage India and Pakistan on nuclear issues of common interest. Statement by Karl Inderfurth, Assistant Secretary of State for South Asian Affairs, before the International Committee, Subcommittee on Near Eastern and South Asian Affairs, US House of Representatives, 18 June 1998.

[15] Diamond, H., 'India, Pakistan respond to arms control initiatives', *Arms Control Today*, vol. 28, no. 5 (June/July 1998), p. 24.

[16] Transcript of remarks of Karl Inderfurth, Assistant Secretary of State for South Asian Affairs, 'Dialogue', WorldNet television service of the US Information Agency, 11 Dec. 1998, *European Wash-*

CTBT, halting the production of fissile material, exercising restraint in the development and deployment of ballistic missiles and associated warheads, and tightening export controls on sensitive nuclear and ballistic missile technology. US officials also urged the two states to resume their bilateral dialogue on Kashmir and other outstanding security issues.[17]

The discussions appeared to make some headway in the autumn of 1998. The Indian and Pakistani governments signalled a new willingness to consider adhering to the CTBT and did not block the establishment of the CD committee to negotiate a Fissile Material Treaty. They also committed themselves to strengthening controls on the export of nuclear and ballistic missile technology; this issue had emerged as a focus of the US–Pakistani discussions.[18] For its part, the USA moved to ease certain economic sanctions imposed under the Glenn Amendment and showed greater flexibility on export controls.[19]

However, the year ended with differences remaining over key issues. US efforts to persuade India and Pakistan to adopt 'strategic restraint measures', including limitations on the development and deployment of ballistic missiles and the forward basing of aircraft capable of carrying nuclear weapons, were unsuccessful. Indian Prime Minister Vajpayee rejected the 'unreasonable' US demands that India limit its nuclear capabilities.[20] He declared that India would not restrict its weapon research and development (R&D) programmes in response to outside pressure and was committed to moving ahead with the flight-testing of an advanced version of the Agni medium-range ballistic missile as well as with the development of other delivery vehicles. He also rejected US requests that India divulge details about its fissile material stocks and deployment locations. Vajpayee noted, however, that India would not embark on an open-ended nuclear weapon programme. Its nuclear doctrine would be based on twin pillars: pledging not to use nuclear weapons first in a conflict; and building a minimum but credible nuclear deterrent.[21]

The latter position met with some understanding from the top US official in the talks. According to US Deputy Secretary of State Strobe Talbott, in the 'near to medium term' the USA was prepared to accept 'responsible' minimum nuclear deterrent postures, provided they were defined at the 'lowest possible levels' consistent with Indian and Pakistani security requirements.[22]

ington File (United States Information Service, US Embassy: Stockholm, 15 Dec. 1998), URL <http://www.usis.usemb.se/wireless/500/eur507.htm>.

[17] 'US diplomacy in South Asia: a progress report', Address delivered by Strobe Talbott, Deputy Secretary of State, at the Brookings Institution, Washington, DC, 12 Nov. 1998, URL <http://www.brook.edu/pa/transcripts/19981112a.htm>.

[18] 'Ongoing US non-proliferation engagement with India and Pakistan', *Disarmament Diplomacy*, no. 32 (Nov. 1998), p. 53.

[19] Indian officials have complained, however, that the easing of US sanctions has favoured Pakistan. Mohan, C., 'Indo-US nuclear dialogue', *The Hindu*, 12 Nov. 1998, URL <http://www.webpage.com/hindu/daily/981112/05/05122523.htm>.

[20] Quoted in Mohan, C., 'PM rejects demands to limit nuclear capabilities', *The Hindu*, 16 Dec. 1998, URL <http://www.hinduonline.com/hindu/daily/981216/01/01160001.htm>.

[21] Mohan (note 20); and Phadnis, U., 'Core elements of India's N-stance', *Dawn,* 12 Aug. 1998, URL <http://dawn.com/daily/19980812/top16.htm>.

[22] Talbott (note 17).

He added, however, that the USA remained committed to its long-term goal of achieving universal adherence to the NPT and was not willing to accord to India and Pakistan any sort of intermediate nuclear status. Talbott warned that 'unless and until they disavow nuclear weapons and accept safeguards on all their nuclear activities, they will continue to forfeit the full recognition and benefits that accrue to members in good standing of the NPT', including access to civil nuclear technology.[23]

Indo-Pakistani nuclear discussions

Senior Indian and Pakistani ministers met in October for separate bilateral talks on confidence-building measures to reduce nuclear weapon-related tensions between the two states.[24] These measures included an agreement proposed by India on the early exchange of information on ballistic missile test flights as well as procedures designed to avert the accidental or unauthorized use of nuclear weapons.[25] The talks adjourned with no substantive achievements but with an agreement to resume discussions in early 1999.

The NPT regime after the nuclear tests

Contrary to initial fears, the Indian and Pakistani tests did not lead other states suspected of harbouring nuclear weapon ambitions to follow suit. There was no evidence that the tests had shifted perceptions of the political and military utility of nuclear weapons or had altered the structure of proliferation incentives in regional trouble spots such as the Middle East and North-East Asia. There were also no additional allegations of states violating their commitments under the NPT, other than those connected with the three non-nuclear weapon state parties (Iran, Iraq and North Korea) whose NPT compliance record had already come under close scrutiny.

However, the Indian and Pakistani decisions to openly cross the nuclear threshold dealt a setback to hopes that the NPT regime would achieve universal adherence and legitimacy. Indian leaders and opinion makers, especially those within Hindu nationalist groups such as Vajpayee's Bharatiya Janata Party (BJP), have long been outspoken critics of the NPT and its discrimination between nuclear and non-nuclear weapon states. In recent years the treaty has been denounced in India as being tantamount to 'nuclear apartheid' because it allegedly perpetuates this discriminatory status quo by not requiring a time-bound framework for disarmament by the nuclear weapon states.[26] The

[23] Talbott (note 17).

[24] In 1988 India and Pakistan signed the Agreement on the Prohibition of Attack against Nuclear Installations and Facilities, in which each side pledged not to attack the other's nuclear facilities. The agreement entered into force in 1991 and involves an annual exchange of lists of nuclear facilities.

[25] 'India and Pakistan discuss CBMs', *Disarmament Diplomacy*, no. 31 (Oct. 1998), p. 56. Pakistan had earlier rejected Indian calls for a no-first-use agreement.

[26] See, e.g., Singh, J., 'Against nuclear apartheid', *Foreign Affairs*, vol. 77, no. 5 (Sep./Oct. 1998), pp. 41–52. Indian critics complain that, especially after the decision in 1995 to indefinitely extend the duration of the NPT, the nuclear weapon states have shown little inclination to fulfil their commitment

Indian and Pakistani tests marked a clear break in a positive trend: states such as Argentina, Brazil and South Africa have recently given up their nuclear weapon programmes—or, in the case of South Africa, actually dismantled a clandestine nuclear arsenal—and joined the NPT as non-nuclear weapon states.[27]

Of perhaps greater significance for the future effectiveness of the NPT regime, as well as for the broader system of rules and constraints designed to prevent the spread of weapon-usable fissile material and bomb-making technology, was the fact that the international community's reaction to the tests was confined largely to statements of condemnation and regret that quickly subsided. There was little willingness among most states and international institutions to impose punitive measures or take other concrete steps that would translate from words into deeds their commitment to halting nuclear proliferation. The 'business as usual' response from the international community has led to a concern that while support for the non-proliferation norm enshrined in the NPT is nearly universal it is not particularly robust.

III. The Comprehensive Nuclear Test-Ban Treaty

The entry into force of the CTBT continued to be hampered in 1998 by the requirement set out in Article XIV that it must first be ratified by the 44 states members of the CD with nuclear power or research reactors on their territories, as listed in Annexe 2 of the treaty.[28] This requirement has proved to be problematic because several of these 44 states have been reluctant or unwilling for various reasons to sign and ratify the treaty.[29]

Efforts to bring the treaty into force did make some progress over the course of the year. On 6 April 1998 France and the UK jointly deposited their instruments of ratification and became the first of the five NPT-defined nuclear weapon states to ratify the treaty.[30] As of 1 January 1999 the CTBT had been ratified by 26 states and signed but not ratified by 151 states.[31]

under Article VI of the treaty to 'pursue negotiations in good faith on effective measures relating to the cessation of the nuclear arms race at an early date'.

[27] Beginning with the first NPT Review Conference, in 1975, there has been a steady increase in the number of parties to the treaty. As of 1 Jan. 1999, 4 UN member states had not ratified the NPT: Cuba, India, Israel and Pakistan. Pakistan has in the past indicated that it would accede to the treaty if India did. On 13 July 1998 Brazil ratified the NPT. 'Secretary-General commends Brazil for its loyal support of United Nations, resolve to meet domestic challenges', UN press release SG/SM/6637, 13 July 1998. For the list of parties to the NPT see annexe A in this volume.

[28] This requirement, which was the source of considerable controversy during the CTBT negotiations, reflected the view that the treaty must capture a certain minimum set of nuclear weapon-capable states to be effective in promoting non-proliferation objectives. Arnett, E., 'The Comprehensive Nuclear Test-Ban Treaty', *SIPRI Yearbook 1997: Armaments, Disarmament and International Security* (Oxford University Press: Oxford, 1997), p. 405. The 44 states are listed in annexe A in this volume.

[29] Of the 44 states, India, North Korea and Pakistan had not signed the treaty at the end of 1998; 34 of the states had signed but not ratified the treaty, including China, Israel, Russia and the USA. See annexe A in this volume.

[30] 'France and United Kingdom jointly ratify CTBT', Press release, Preparatory Commission for the Comprehensive Nuclear Test-Ban Treaty Organization (CTBTO) Provisional Technical Secretariat, Vienna, 6 Apr. 1998.

[31] For the list of states which have signed or ratified the CTBT see annexe A in this volume.

Changes in the positions of India and Pakistan?

India's opposition to the CTBT has been a key stumbling block in bringing the treaty into force. India had reversed its previous support for the CTBT during the negotiating endgame in the CD, seeking to undo hard-won compromises and ultimately vetoing the treaty's adoption by that body in August 1996.[32] This reversal reflected the success of the Indian nuclear research establishment and its allies in arguing that the country should keep open its option to develop nuclear weapons, which some treaty critics claimed India would not be able to do if it joined a global ban on testing.[33] Indian opponents of the CTBT also denounced it as representing 'the NPT through the back door'; they complained that the treaty was a discriminatory measure that was far from comprehensive since it did not prohibit the nuclear weapon laboratories of the nuclear weapon states from carrying out subcritical tests and other types of research that could enable these states to develop new types of nuclear weapons and to maintain existing weapons *in perpetuum*.[34] Finally, Indian officials denounced the inclusion of India in the list of 44 states whose ratification is necessary for the CTBT's entry into force. They vowed to resist international pressure to sign and ratify the treaty, complaining that it contains language which implicitly threatens India with sanctions if it fails to ratify it.[35]

Following the completion of the nuclear tests, the Vajpayee Government began to edge away from its uncompromising rejection of the accord. In an effort to defuse international criticism, it announced that India would 'consider adhering to some of the undertakings in the CTBT'.[36] The Indian Prime Minister later indicated that his government would consider transforming its May 1998 unilateral moratorium on nuclear tests into a 'formal obligation' if this were linked to a number of unspecified 'reciprocal activities'.[37] He noted that in imposing this moratorium on further testing India had already accepted the basic obligation of the CTBT.[38] Significantly, in response to the

[32] The CTBT was adopted in the UN General Assembly by a vote of 158 to 3 on 10 Sep. 1996, after the draft text had been forwarded there from the CD. For a summary of developments leading up to the CTBT's adoption by the General Assembly see Arnett (note 28), pp. 403–407.

[33] Deshingkar, G., 'Indian politics and arms control: recent reversals and new reasons for optimism', ed. E. Arnett, *Nuclear Weapons and Arms Control in South Asia after the Test Ban*, SIPRI Research Report no. 14 (Oxford University Press: Oxford, 1998), pp. 29–32. This argument was motivated in part by fears that the nuclear establishment would collapse without the option of testing.

[34] See also section IV of appendix 12B in this volume.

[35] If the CTBT has not entered into force 3 years after the date of the anniversary of its opening for signature (Sep. 1999), the treaty provides in Article XIV for the states which have deposited their instruments of ratification to convene an annual review conference to consider measures 'consistent with international law' to facilitate bringing it into force.

[36] Press release, Ministry of External Affairs, External Publicity Division, New Delhi, 11 May 1998; and 'India will not sign the CTBT unconditionally: PM', *The Hindu*, 15 May 1998, URL <http://www.the-hindu.com/1998/05/15/front.htm#Story1>.

[37] 'PM declares nuclear moratorium', *Hindustan Times*, 22 May 1998, URL <http://www.hindustantimes.com/ht/nonfram/220598/detfro01.htm>.

[38] Speech by Prime Minister Atal Bihari Vajpayee to the UN General Assembly, 24 Sep. 1998, text reproduced by the Acronym Institute in *Disarmament Diplomacy*, no. 30 (Sep. 1998), pp. 14–15; Bhushan, B., 'India ready to sign CTBT: PM', *Hindustan Times*, 25 Sep. 1998, URL <http://www.hindustantimes.com/nonfram/250998/detfro01.htm>; and Goshko, J., 'India ready to sign nuclear treaty ban', *Washington Post*, 25 Sep. 1998, p. A30.

widespread criticism of Indian demands for wholesale changes to the treaty text, Vajpayee said that India would no longer insist that the CTBT be amended to include language committing the five nuclear weapon states to a time-bound framework for nuclear disarmament.[39] Comments from other Indian officials suggested that the Vajpayee Government sought to use the prospect of India's signing the treaty as a bargaining chip in its bid to persuade the USA to at least tacitly recognize India's status as a nuclear weapon state and to lift the economic sanctions it imposed after the tests. It also sought an easing of restrictions on high-technology exports to India and an end to the international prohibition on civil nuclear commerce with the country.[40]

The government of Pakistani Prime Minister Nawaz Sharif also appeared to be reconsidering its position on the CTBT after Pakistan had conducted its nuclear tests. The treaty has been a contentious domestic political issue in Pakistan, where it enjoys little support. The previous government, led by Prime Minister Benazir Bhutto, had given its cautious backing to the treaty, attempting to deflect opposition charges that it was betraying the country's vital interests while at the same time not provoking an international backlash by openly opposing the test ban. It officially supported the CTBT in international forums but made Pakistan's signature contingent on India signing it first.[41]

Seeking to improve relations with the USA and other key international actors, the Sharif Government showed signs of adopting a more flexible approach to the treaty.[42] In the summer of 1998 Foreign Minister Gohar Ayub Khan told reporters that, while Pakistan would not necessarily sign the CTBT even if India did so, it also did not rule out signing the accord before India.[43] In a speech to the UN General Assembly on 23 September 1998, Sharif announced that Pakistan would sign and ratify the CTBT before the conference of parties provided for under Article XIV, scheduled to take place in September 1999. He emphasized, however, that Pakistan would only adhere to the treaty if India did so as well and would oppose any attempts at the 1999 conference to amend the treaty so that it could enter into force without the adherence of all the 44 states listed in Annexe 2. Sharif also linked Pakistan's signing of the treaty to a lifting of the 'discriminatory sanctions' imposed after

[39] Burns, J., 'India's line in the sand: "minimum" nuclear deterrent against China', *International Herald Tribune*, 8 July 1998, p. 4; and Katyal, K., 'CTBT: changed realities', *The Hindu*, 21 July 1998, URL <http://www.hinduonline. com/hindu/daily/980721/05/05212523.htm>.

[40] Dugger, C., 'India and Pakistan ask of test ban treaty: "what's in it for us"', *International Herald Tribune,* 1 Oct. 1998, p. 6.

[41] Ahmed, S., 'Public opinion, democratic governance and the making of Pakistani nuclear policy', ed. Arnett (note 33), pp. 66–67.

[42] Sehbai, S., 'Pakistan reassessing position on CTBT', *Dawn*, 1 July 1998, URL <http://www.dawn.com/daily/19980701/top1.htm>.

[43] 'CTBT signing not linked to Indian decision: Gohar', *Dawn*, 15 July 1998, URL <http://www.dawn.com/daily/19980715/top1.htm>. A Pakistani proposal to discuss a regional test ban with India was dismissed by government officials in New Delhi.

its nuclear tests, stating that 'Pakistan's adherence to the treaty will take place only in conditions free from coercion or pressure'.[44]

The announcements by India and Pakistan were received cautiously by the USA. The Clinton Administration welcomed their more conciliatory approaches to the CTBT but deemed them to be insufficient to warrant lifting sanctions in the absence of 'substantial progress' towards implementing the measures outlined in UN Security Council Resolution 1172.[45] Senior US officials were particularly concerned about offering any quid pro quo that would seem to reward the nuclear tests, for example, allowing India to purchase advanced technology from US suppliers.[46] The cautious US response was also motivated by the evident lack of consensus on joining the CTBT within the fractious BJP-led governing coalition in India.[47]

Ratification prospects in the US Senate

The CTBT had in September 1997 been sent by President Bill Clinton to the Senate for its advice and consent. Ratification by the USA is widely considered to be crucial to the treaty's prospects of being ratified by other countries, including India.[48] However, the CTBT remained stalled in the Senate Foreign Relations Committee.[49] Opponents of US ratification of the treaty have argued that a permanent halt to testing would undermine the safety and reliability of the USA's nuclear arsenal. They have also claimed that compliance with the test ban cannot be verified with sufficient confidence, and the Indian and Pakistani nuclear tests did little to allay this concern. Treaty critics pointed to the poor performance of the International Monitoring System (IMS) being established by the Comprehensive Nuclear Test-Ban Treaty Organization (CTBTO), especially in detecting the low-yield Indian nuclear explosions of 13 May.[50] The tests also led some key Republican senators to argue that the test ban had been made irrelevant.[51]

[44] UN General Assembly, 53rd session, Official Records A/53/PV.12, 23 Sep. 1998; and Taylor, P., 'Pakistan to sign nuclear test ban, talk to India', Reuters, 23 Sep. 1998, URL <http:dailynews.yahoo.com/headlines/ts/story.html?s=v/nm/19980923/ts/nuclear_3.html>.

[45] Remarks of James Rubin, State Department spokesman, US Department of State Daily Briefing, 25 Sep. 1998, *European Washington File* (United States Information Service, US Embassy: Stockholm, 28 Sep. 1998), URL <http://www.usis.usemb.se/wireless/100/eur102.htm>.

[46] Padgaonkar, D., 'US lukewarm to India, Pakistan offer on CTBT', *Times of India*, 26 Sep. 1998, URL <http://www.timesofindia.com/today/26home2.htm>.

[47] 'Inching towards CTBT', *Times of India*, 10 Sep. 1998, URL <http://www.timesofindia.com/today/10edit1.htm>; and 'Consensus needed for signing the CTBT', *Deccan Herald*, 12 Sep. 1998, URL <http://www.deccanherald.com/deccanherald/sept12/ctbt.htm>.

[48] Indian officials have indicated that India will not sign the CTBT until it has been ratified by the USA. Mahorta, J., 'India wants US to ratify the CTBT before signing', *Indian Express*, 25 Oct. 1998.

[49] The committee chairman, Senator Jesse Helms, has stated that the CTBT has a low legislative priority and will not be considered by his committee until after it deals with a set of amendments to the ABM Treaty signed in 1997 (which the Clinton Administration has stated that it will not transmit to the Senate until after the Russian Duma ratifies the START II Treaty) and with the Kyoto Protocol on global climate change.

[50] Broad, W., 'Blasts expose problems of verification', *International Herald Tribune*, 16–17 May 1998, p. 5. However, 2 analysts pointed out that the IMS was incomplete at the time of the explosions. They also noted that India and Pakistan, both non-signatories of the CTBT, had not contributed the geophysical calibration data that would have permitted better detection and identification of seismic events on the Indian subcontinent. Findlay, T. and Clark, R., 'The Indian and Pakistani tests: did verification

In a preliminary test of support for the treaty, the Senate voted on 1 September 1998 to approve the USA's $29 million contribution to the 1999 budget of the CTBTO. The narrow margin of the vote was seen as a sign that the treaty enjoyed only lukewarm support, although ratification of the test ban treaty was set as the highest arms control priority of the Clinton Administration.[52]

IV. A ban on the production of fissile material

On 11 August 1998 the CD decided to establish an ad hoc committee to negotiate a Fissile Material Treaty that would ban the production of fissile material for nuclear weapons.[53] The decision came more than three years after the CD had adopted a mandate to 'negotiate a non-discriminatory, multilateral and effectively verifiable treaty banning the production of fissile material for nuclear weapons or other nuclear explosive devices'.[54] The lengthy delay was the result of the inability of the CD, which operates on the consensus principle, to bridge key differences left unresolved by the so-called 'Shannon mandate'.[55] Against the background of the CD's conspicuous inactivity in taking up other disarmament issues, this stalemate had contributed to the widespread sense in recent years that the CD was in crisis.

There had been two main obstacles to forming an ad hoc committee to open negotiations on the convention. The first was the Indian-led demand that the FMT negotiations be placed in the context of a time-bound framework for general nuclear disarmament. This demand gained support from the Group of 21 (G-21) non-aligned states in the CD[56] but was rejected by France, Russia, the UK and the USA, which have consistently refused to consider establishing an ad hoc committee on nuclear disarmament. The second obstacle was the insistence of Egypt, Pakistan and other states that the ban should go beyond mandating a cut-off of fissile material production and also place existing stockpiles of fissile material under international safeguards. This proposal generated strong opposition from the P5 states, which have large inventories of fissile material for military purposes, and from India and other states. These states argued that the mandate should apply only to the future production of fissile material.

fail?', Verification Technology and Information Centre (VERTIC), *Trust and Verify*, no. 80 (May 1998), pp. 1–4.

[51] Cerniello, C., 'South Asian nuclear tests cloud prospects for CTBT ratification', *Arms Control Today*, vol. 28, no. 4 (May 1998), pp. 24, 27.

[52] Lippman, T., 'Senate vote bodes ill for nuclear treaty', *International Herald Tribune*, 4 Sep. 1998, p. 6.

[53] Decision on the establishment of an ad hoc committee under item 1 of the agenda entitled 'Cessation of the nuclear arms race and nuclear disarmament', Conference on Disarmament document CD/1547, 12 Aug. 1998. The CD also voted on 26 Mar. 1999 to establish an ad hoc committee to negotiate a legally binding negative security assurances convention.

[54] Conference on Disarmament document CD/1299, 24 Mar. 1995.

[55] The Mar. 1995 mandate is named after Canadian Ambassador Gerald Shannon, who was appointed Special Coordinator by the CD.

[56] See the glossary in this volume for the member states of the Group of 21.

In the aftermath of the 1998 nuclear tests, progress was made towards resolving the impasse in the CD. India signalled that it would no longer insist on a linkage between an FMT and a time-bound framework for nuclear disarmament.[57] To accommodate the G-21 demand that the treaty should be a 'nuclear disarmament measure and not just a non-proliferation measure', the P5 agreed to establish the ad hoc committee under item 1 of the CD agenda ('Cessation of the nuclear arms race and nuclear disarmament'). The CD presidency pledged that it would 'continue to pursue intensive consultations' with respect to this agenda item.[58]

The decision to establish an ad hoc committee on the basis of the Shannon mandate did not settle the issue of existing fissile material stocks, which delegates decided not to take up until the negotiations were under way. The P5 states and India reiterated their views that under the Shannon mandate existing stockpiles fell outside the purview of the proposed FMT. By contrast, delegations from the non-aligned states other than India continued to argue that the treaty would be effective only if it applied to stockpiles as well as future production. Pakistan, in particular, expressed concern that the treaty would freeze the imbalance in the size of the Indian and Pakistani fissile material stockpiles to its disadvantage. In the Middle East, where Israel's ambiguous nuclear weapon status has complicated nuclear non-proliferation and disarmament measures, Egypt and other Arab states insisted that all stocks of weapon-usable fissile materials would have to be declared and be subject to inspection and inventory under international supervision and control.

The decision to establish an ad hoc committee brought to the fore another likely sticking point in the upcoming negotiations: the issue of verification. The main question is the degree to which the verification regime of the FMT should 'converge' with that of the NPT, that is, impose NPT verification safeguards on the non-NPT states as well as the NPT-defined nuclear weapon states. Some analysts have argued that in the absence of such convergence the FMT would be considered discriminatory; moreover, the negotiation of deeper cuts in nuclear arsenals and their eventual abolition might actually be impeded.[59] However, the states with nuclear weapon capabilities which are not parties to the NPT (i.e., India, Pakistan and Israel) have shown no interest in permitting intrusive verification in connection with an FMT. Similarly, the P5 states have been reluctant to consider accepting intrusive verification of adherence to a norm which they are already observing.[60]

[57] Johnson, R., 'CD dominated by tests and calls for nuclear disarmament and fissile material cut-off', Geneva Update no. 41, *Disarmament Diplomacy*, no. 28 (June 1998), p. 14.

[58] Presidential statement, Ambassador Mykola Maimeskul, Conference on Disarmament document CD/1548, 11 Aug. 1998.

[59] Albright, D., Berkhout, F. and Walker, W., SIPRI, *Plutonium and Highly Enriched Uranium 1995: World Inventories, Capabilities and Policies* (Oxford University Press: Oxford, 1995).

[60] The USA has suggested that the verification regime be placed under the auspices of the IAEA, which would routinely monitor all enrichment and reprocessing facilities, as well as so-called 'downstream facilities' (those that use, process or store newly produced material) when such material is present; the regime would cover all newly produced fissile material. Remarks of John Holum, Under Secretary of State for Arms Control and International Security Affairs, to the opening session of the Conference on Disarmament, 21 Jan. 1999, *European Washington File* (United States Information Ser-

V. Other developments

The NPT Preparatory Committee

The second meeting of the Preparatory Committee (PrepCom) for the year 2000 Non-Proliferation Treaty Review Conference took place in Geneva on 27 April–8 May 1998 and was attended by 97 states parties to the NPT.[61] The outcome of the meeting was a considerable disappointment for proponents of a strengthened review of implementation of the NPT. It adjourned without taking decisions on any substantive or procedural issues, other than on the dates and chairmanship for the 1999 PrepCom meeting.

One obstacle to progress at the meeting was the dispute over procedure for the presentation of official background documentation for the 2000 Review Conference and over which documents should be allowed. Fourteen Arab states, supported by the Non-Aligned Movement (NAM),[62] asked the PrepCom to allow documentation on the 1995 Middle East Resolution.[63] The USA rejected the request, arguing that documents introduced in the PrepComs must address articles of the NPT and questioning whether the Middle East Resolution was an integral part of the package of three decisions taken at the NPT Review and Extension Conference.[64] In doing so, it challenged the view held by the Arab and many non-aligned states that the resolution was as valid and binding as the decision to extend indefinitely the duration of the NPT.[65]

The meagre results of the meeting highlighted the continuing division between the nuclear 'haves' and 'have nots' over the role of the PrepCom in the review process, its principles and objectives, and the procedures governing its activities. Several non-nuclear weapon states sought to give the PrepCom a

vice, US Embassy: Stockholm, 21 Jan. 1999), URL <http://www.usis.usemb.se/wireless/400/eur409.htm>.

[61] The 1995 NPT Review and Extension Conference had sought to strengthen the review process by requiring that PrepCom meetings be held in each of the 3 years leading up to the 5-yearly Review Conferences. The purpose of the PrepCom meetings is to 'consider principles, objectives and ways in order to promote the full implementation of the Treaty, as well as its universality, and to make recommendations thereon to the Review Conference'. 'Strengthening the review process for the treaty', New York, 11 May 1995, NPT/CONF.1995/32 (Part I), reproduced in *SIPRI Yearbook 1996: Armaments, Disarmament and International Security* (Oxford University Press: Oxford, 1996), appendix 13A, pp. 590–91.

[62] The NAM members are listed in the glossary in this volume, under the Conference on Disarmament.

[63] The Resolution on the Middle East was sponsored by the USA (along with Russia and the UK) at the 1995 NPT Review and Extension Conference. It amended a resolution sponsored by Arab states calling on Israel to accede to the treaty 'without delay'; these states had threatened to withhold their support for indefinitely extending the NPT unless such a document was included in the package of decisions. As approved, the resolution did not specifically name Israel but called *inter alia* for the universality of the NPT and the implementation of comprehensive IAEA safeguards by all states in the region. Resolution on the Middle East, reported in the Final Document of the Review and Extension Conference of the Parties to the Treaty on the Non-Proliferation of Nuclear Weapons as NPT/CONF.1995/32/RES.1, 11 May 1995.

[64] The 3 decision documents, which were adopted simultaneously and without a vote on 11 May 1995, involved: making the NPT of indefinite duration; strengthening the process for reviewing the implementation of the treaty; and establishing a set of detailed 'yardsticks' for evaluating implementation. Simpson, J., 'The nuclear non-proliferation regime after the NPT Review and Extension Conference', *SIPRI Yearbook 1996* (note 61), pp. 563–68.

[65] Johnson, R., *Reviewing the Non-Proliferation Treaty: Problems and Processes*, ACRONYM Report no. 12 (Acronym Institute: London, Sep. 1998), pp. 9, 34–36.

more substantive role in the review process, particularly with regard to implementation of the nuclear disarmament commitments contained in the NPT and the programme of action outlined in the Principles and Objectives adopted at the 1995 NPT Review and Extension Conference.[66] They also proposed expanding the role of the PrepCom Chairman's report in presenting collective views on important NPT-related issues requiring prompt attention.[67] These proposals failed because of the opposition from the nuclear weapon states, which in the view of many of the participants acted increasingly *en bloc* to prevent the forging of a consensus.[68] The nuclear weapon states sought to limit the role of the PrepCom to compiling a list of proposals to be taken up at the 2000 Review Conference and to deciding on the procedural arrangements for that conference. They showed little interest in allowing the PrepComs to move in the direction of becoming 'mini-review conferences', arguing that the meetings should remain preparatory in nature.

This division reflected the rival interpretations among the states parties of the meaning and aims of the strengthened review process and, indeed, of the NPT. For many of the non-nuclear weapon states, the treaty is an instrument for promoting steps towards complete nuclear disarmament. By contrast, the nuclear weapon states tend to see it more as an instrument for capping the number of states with nuclear arsenals. Evaluating the results of the second PrepCom, some observers warned that the nuclear weapon states have become complacent since the indefinite extension of the NPT in 1995 and show little interest in upholding their end of the NPT 'bargain'; this complacency threatens to erode international support for the treaty regime and for broader nuclear non-proliferation efforts.[69]

The US–North Korean Agreed Framework

The 1994 US–North Korean Agreed Framework was the product of intense high-level diplomatic bargaining to resolve the crisis arising from North Korea's non-compliance with its NPT obligations to allow International Atomic Energy Agency (IAEA) inspection of its nuclear programme.[70] North

[66] NPT/CONF.2000/PC.II/12 and 17 (South Africa). The Principles and Objectives are grouped under 7 headings: universality; non-proliferation; nuclear disarmament; nuclear weapon-free zones; security assurances; safeguards; and peaceful uses of nuclear energy. 'Decision on principles and objectives for nuclear non-proliferation and disarmament', New York, 11 May 1995, NPT/CONF.1995/32/DEC.2, reproduced in *SIPRI Yearbook 1996* (note 61), appendix 13A, pp. 591–93.

[67] NPT/CONF.2000/PC.II/34 (Canada).

[68] Rauf, T., 'The 1998 NPT PrepCom: farewell to the strengthened review process?', *Disarmament Diplomacy*, no. 26 (May 1998), p. 3.

[69] Johnson (note 65), pp. 16–17. Concern that the international community was lapsing into complacency with regard to its previous commitments to work towards nuclear disarmament prompted 8 nations to issue a Joint Declaration urging a new nuclear disarmament agenda. The declaration, which was adopted by the UN First Committee, called for a 'clear commitment to the speedy, final and total elimination' of nuclear weapons by the states possessing them. 'A nuclear-weapons-free world: the need for a new agenda', Joint Declaration by the Ministers for Foreign Affairs of Brazil, Egypt, Ireland, Mexico, New Zealand, Slovenia, South Africa and Sweden, 9 June 1998.

[70] For more detail about the Agreed Framework see Goodby, J., Kile, S. and Müller, H., 'Nuclear arms control', *SIPRI Yearbook 1995: Armaments, Disarmament and International Security* (Oxford University Press: Oxford, 1995), pp. 653–54.

Korea's behaviour had raised suspicions, particularly in the USA, that it was illicitly diverting separated plutonium from a research reactor for use in the manufacture of nuclear weapons.

Under the accord, North Korea has halted the operation of the 5-megawatt electric (MW(e)) research reactor and plutonium reprocessing plant at Yongbyon and has frozen construction work on two larger reactors (a 50-MW reactor at Yongbyon and a 200-MW reactor at Taechon).[71] In return the USA has organized, in cooperation with Japan and South Korea, an international consortium—the Korean Peninsula Energy Development Organization (KEDO)—which is responsible for providing North Korea with two 1000-MW light-water reactors (LWRs).[72] The reactors are scheduled to be completed by the end of the year 2003.[73] The lion's share of the estimated $4.6 billion cost of the LWR project is to be covered by a $3.2 billion contribution from South Korea, with Japan contributing $1 billion; the EU has also agreed to contribute to the project. The USA has assumed the main responsibility for underwriting the costs of compensatory oil supplies (500 000 tonnes of heavy fuel oil per annum) to North Korea until the new reactors are in operation.

Implementation of the Agreed Framework came to a halt during 1998 against the background of rising political tensions in the region. North Korea's unexpected test flight of a ballistic missile on 31 August provoked Japan to temporarily suspend its participation in the accord's activities; the three-stage missile—which North Korea claimed had carried a small satellite into orbit—had crossed over the main Japanese island of Honshu before landing in the northern Pacific Ocean.[74] There was also a series of North Korean naval incursions into South Korean waters which led to armed clashes and heightened suspicions about Pyongyang's intentions.[75]

Despite signs of progress in early 1998, the USA and North Korea became embroiled in a number of disputes related to implementation of the accord. The difficulties experienced by the USA in honouring its obligation to provide

[71] The 5-MW reactor was thought to be capable of producing *c.* 7 kg of plutonium per year; the 2 reactors under construction were expected to yield another 200 kg of plutonium annually. US General Accounting Office, *Nuclear Nonproliferation: Implications of the US/North Korean Agreement on Nuclear Issues* (GAO/RCED/NSIAD-97-8), Oct. 1996, p. 3. North Korea is believed to have produced enough plutonium to manufacture several nuclear weapons before freezing its nuclear programme under the terms of the 1994 accord.

[72] The LWRs are considered to pose less of a nuclear weapon proliferation risk since fuel rods from LWRs—unlike those from the graphite-moderated reactor at Yongbyon—do not require reprocessing.

[73] Work will be halted upon completion of the first reactor containment building pending the satisfactory conclusion of an IAEA special inspection to clarify how North Korea disposed of its spent reactor fuel. Once North Korea is deemed to be in compliance with its full-scope IAEA safeguards agreement, the work on the LWRs will resume; North Korea will then proceed with phased dismantling of its nuclear plants and related facilities.

[74] Kirk, D., 'North Korea test-fires a missile off Japan's north', *International Herald Tribune*, 1 Sep. 1998, pp. 1, 4; and Myers, S. L., 'Tokyo and Seoul outraged by North's missile test', *International Herald Tribune*, 2 Sep. 1998, p. 4. According to US officials, the missile did not place a satellite into orbit.

[75] Kristof, N., 'North Korean raider washes up in South', *International Herald Tribune*, 13 July 1998, p. 4; and Yoon, J., 'South Korea sinks North Korean vessel after firefight', Reuters, 18 Dec. 1998, URL <http://dailynews.yahoo.com/headlines/ts/story.html?s=v/19981218/ts/korea_7.html>.

fuel oil to compensate for the interim loss of nuclear power generation led the North Korean Government to complain repeatedly that Washington was not fulfilling its end of the bargain. The North Korean Government also noted that KEDO was behind in its preparations to build the new LWR reactors.[76] In May, North Korean Foreign Minister Kim Yong Nam announced that North Korea had suspended the canning of spent fuel rods from the Yongbon reactor and had opened the previously sealed plant there 'to conduct maintenance'; it would resume cooperation once the USA had a chance to 'catch up' on its commitments.[77] US officials conceded that the fuel oil delivery programme had experienced financial difficulties but expressed confidence that the 500 000 tonnes of oil would be delivered as promised by the end of KEDO's fiscal year, in October.[78] At the same time, they complained that North Korea was breaking its pledge to allow US inspectors to account for and oversee the storage of plutonium-bearing spent fuel at Yongbyon.[79]

A more serious dispute arose in August over allegations that North Korea was building an underground nuclear weapon-related facility at Kumchang-ri, approximately 50 kilometres north-west of its nuclear plant at Yongbyon.[80] US officials pressed North Korea for access to the complex in order to 'clarify the nature of the suspect construction'.[81] They subsequently warned that failure to resolve suspicions about the site, which was revealed in satellite surveillance photographs, could call into question the viability of the Agreed Framework.[82] However, in the light of South Korean concerns about provoking the North, US officials were careful to note that they lacked 'conclusive evidence' about the purpose of the construction site.[83] For its part, North Korea denied allegations that it was building a nuclear weapon-related facility. A Foreign Ministry spokesman indicated that North Korea was willing to grant US and IAEA inspectors one-time access to the site provided it was suitably compensated for the 'grave insult' to North Korean sovereignty

[76] 'US should take practical steps as soon as possible', Press statement issued by the Korean Central News Agency, Democratic People's Republic of Korea, 8 May 1998, URL <http://www.kcna.co.jp/calendar/frame.htm>.

[77] Rosenthal, E., 'In a taunt at US, North Korea suspends nuclear freeze agreement', *International Herald Tribune*, 14 May 1998, p. 5.

[78] Reuters, 'US short of cash for Pyongyang oil', *International Herald Tribune*, 8 July 1998, p. 8; and Transcript of remarks by Kenneth Bacon, Defense Department spokesman, US Department of Defense Daily Briefing, 18 Aug. 1998, *European Washington File* (United States Information Service, US Embassy: Stockholm, 18 Aug. 1998), URL <http://www.usis.usemb.se/wireless/200/eur201.htm>.

[79] Diamond, H., 'N. Korea warns on nuclear freeze, halts DOE cleanup at Yongbyon', *Arms Control Today*, vol. 28, no. 4 (May 1998), p. 35.

[80] Priest, D., 'US warns North Korea on underground project', *International Herald Tribune,* 27 Aug. 1998, p. 4; and Pomfret, J., 'US team reports Korean starvation', *International Herald Tribune*, 20 Aug. 1998, p. 4.

[81] 'US–DPRK talks', Press statement, US Department of State, 10 Sep. 1998, reproduced in 'US statement on North Korea talks', *Disarmament Diplomacy*, no. 30 (Sep. 1998), pp. 45–46.

[82] Morse, J., 'Underground site threatens US–North Korea pact', *European Washington File* (United States Information Service, US Embassy: Stockholm, 10 Nov. 1998), URL <http://www.usis.usemb.se/wireless/200/eur03.htm>; and Transcript of press conference remarks by Ambassador Charles Kartman, US Special Envoy for the Korean Peace Talks, 19 Nov. 1998, *European Washington File* (United States Information Service, US Embassy: Stockholm, 19 Nov. 1998), URL <http://www.usis.usemb.se/wireless/400/eur412.htm>.

[83] Kirk, D., 'Clinton raises heat on North Korea', *International Herald Tribune,* 23 Nov. 1998, pp. 1, 6.

Table 12.1. START I aggregate numbers of strategic nuclear delivery vehicles and accountable warheads, 1 July 1998[a]

Category	Russia	Ukraine[b]	Ex-Soviet total[c]	USA	Final limits 5 Dec. 2001[d]
Strategic nuclear delivery vehicles	1 478	99	1 577	1 482	1 600
Total treaty-accountable warheads	6 674	866	7 540	7 982	6 000
ICBM and SLBM warheads	6 110	514	6 624	6 227	4 900

ICBM = intercontinental ballistic missile; SLBM = submarine-launched ballistic missile.

[a] The numbers given in this table are in accordance with the START I Treaty counting rules and include delivery vehicles which have been deactivated; the estimates of the number of operational systems in figure 12.1 and appendix 12A are smaller.

[b] The transfer of strategic nuclear warheads from Ukraine to Russia was completed in May 1996. The warheads remain START-accountable until their associated delivery vehicles have been eliminated in accordance with procedures specified in the treaty.

[c] Belarus and Kazakhstan have completed the elimination of the former Soviet ICBMs and bombers based on their territories.

[d] These ceilings applied equally to the USA and the Soviet Union as the signatories of the START I Treaty. Of the former Soviet parties, only Russia will retain strategic nuclear forces at the end of the START I implementation period.

Source: START I Treaty Memorandum of Understanding, 1 July 1998.

entailed by the inspection; without such compensation, it would consider scrapping the accord altogether over US demands for unconditional and repeated access.[84] US State Department officials rejected North Korea's reported demand for $300 million to allow the inspection.[85] The year ended with intensive bilateral diplomatic discussions under way to prevent the Agreed Framework from collapsing.

VI. US–Russian nuclear arms control

Implementation of the START I Treaty

The Treaty on the Reduction and Limitation of Strategic Offensive Arms (START I Treaty) was signed by the Soviet Union and the United States in 1991 and entered into force in 1994. The obligations of the Soviet Union were assumed by Russia as its legal successor state and later by Belarus, Kazakhstan and Ukraine, the other former Soviet republics with strategic nuclear weapons based on their territories. Under the treaty, the USA and the former

[84] 'Foreign Ministry spokesman on Pyongyang negotiation about underground facility', Press statement issued by the Korean Central News Agency, Democratic People's Republic of Korea, 24 Nov. 1998, URL <http://www.kcna.co.jp/calendar/frame.htm>.

[85] Tarrant, B., 'N. Korea rattles sabre as US envoy begins tour', Reuters, 7 Dec. 1998, URL <http://dailynews.yahoo.com/headlines/ts/story.html?s=v/nm/19981207/ts/korea_4.html>. North Korea reportedly dropped the demand for payment, suggesting instead that it would allow US inspectors access if Washington agreed to provide more food aid. Sanger, D., 'North Korea warns of new missile shot', *International Herald Tribune*, 28 Dec. 1998, p. 5.

Soviet parties undertake to make phased reductions in their strategic offensive nuclear forces, with the final limits on strategic nuclear delivery vehicles (SNDVs) and accountable warheads to be reached by December 2001 (see table 12.1). The treaty also places limits on inventories of mobile and heavy intercontinental ballistic missiles (ICBMs) and on aggregate ballistic missile throw-weight. Belarus, Kazakhstan and Ukraine committed themselves as parties to the treaty to eliminate all the nuclear weapons based on their territories, leaving Russia as the sole nuclear weapon successor state of the USSR. In 1998 implementation of the treaty continued to proceed ahead of the interim reduction deadlines.

The START II Treaty

The START II Treaty was signed by Russia and the United States on 3 January 1993. It was ratified by the US Senate in January 1996 but has encountered significant opposition in the Russian Duma.[86] Under the terms of START II, the two signatories undertake to reduce the number of their deployed strategic nuclear warheads to no more than 3500 each.[87] This ceiling represents about one-third of the size of the deployed Soviet and US strategic nuclear forces before the signing of the START I Treaty in 1991. In addition to lowering nuclear force levels, the treaty bans all land-based ICBMs carrying multiple independently targetable re-entry vehicles (MIRVs). This ban would herald a major advance in nuclear arms control in that it would rid the Russian and US strategic nuclear arsenals of what many experts consider to be their most destabilizing weapons.

In 1997 Russia and the USA signed a Protocol to the START II Treaty extending the deadlines by which the START II reductions must be completed. Under the original terms of the treaty, their strategic nuclear forces would be reduced in two phases, to be completed by 1 January 2003. The START II Protocol, which must be ratified by the legislatures of both countries, extends the final reduction deadline by five years to 31 December 2007; it also extends the interim reduction deadline from 5 December 2001 (i.e., seven years after the entry into force of the START I Treaty) to 31 December 2004.[88] By giving Russia additional years over which to spread the costs connected with the safe elimination of large numbers of missiles and destruction or conversion of their launch silos, the proposed changes are intended to ease

[86] For a description of the US Senate's ratification conditions and a discussion of Russian concerns about START II see Kile, S., 'Nuclear arms control', *SIPRI Yearbook 1997* (note 28), pp. 371, 374–77.

[87] The treaty also places limits on the number of warheads deployed on SLBMs and contains counting rules different from those in START I for determining the weapon loadings of heavy bombers. For a description of the provisions of the START II Treaty see Lockwood, D., 'Nuclear arms control', *SIPRI Yearbook 1993: World Armaments and Disarmament* (Oxford University Press: Oxford, 1993), pp. 554–59.

[88] Accompanying the Protocol was an exchange of letters between the Russian and US foreign ministers committing the 2 sides to deactivate by 31 Dec. 2003 all missiles slated for elimination, either by removing their re-entry vehicles or by taking 'other jointly agreed steps'. For a fuller description of the START II Protocol see Kile, S., 'Nuclear arms control', *SIPRI Yearbook 1998: Armaments, Disarmament and International Security* (Oxford University Press: Oxford, 1998), pp. 410–11.

the financial burden of implementing the reductions; this had been a key Russian concern about the treaty. The extension also means that the scheduled decommissioning of the ageing MIRVed ICBMs which constitute the backbone of the Russian Strategic Rocket Forces will now more or less coincide with the end of the service lives of these missiles.

Russian ratification proceedings

In 1998 the Duma again failed to bring up START II for a ratification vote.[89] The treaty had appeared to be set to win that body's reluctant consent, only to be side-tracked at the end of the year by international developments unrelated to the accord that unleashed a wave of anti-US sentiment among Russian parliamentarians. During the autumn legislative session, a new draft ratification bill was drawn up by representatives from the four committees in the Duma (Defence, Geopolitics, International Affairs and Security) responsible for overseeing consideration of START II.[90] This bill was drafted as an alternative to one which had been transmitted to the Duma by President Boris Yeltsin in April.[91] Opposed by the communist deputies and their nationalist allies who controlled the lower chamber, the earlier bill had been shelved during the bitter battle over Yeltsin's appointment of Sergey Kiriyenko as the country's new prime minister.[92]

The new bill contained a number of conditions for ratification and reservations. These were related to the negotiation of a follow-on START III agreement, the preservation of the ABM Treaty and the non-deployment of nuclear weapons on the territory of new NATO member states.[93] It also stipulated that the executive branch must elaborate a treaty-compatible plan for strategic nuclear force modernization that would ensure both the maintenance of a robust nuclear deterrence posture and stable funding of that plan.[94] These latter

[89] According to the 1993 Russian Constitution, treaty ratification requires a simple majority vote in both the lower (Duma) and the upper (Federation Council) chambers of parliament. It is believed that the Federation Council will probably follow the decision taken by the Duma with regard to START II ratification.

[90] Interfax (Moscow), 12 Nov. 1998, in 'Russian Duma considering new law on START II ratification', FBIS-SOV-98-316, 12 Nov. 1998.

[91] Along with START II, Yeltsin also submitted for the Duma's approval the package of strategic arms control agreements signed by Russia and the USA in 1997, including the START II Protocol and several agreements related to the ABM Treaty. Cerniello, C., 'Yeltsin submits START II, ABM–TMD agreements to Duma', *Arms Control Today*, vol. 28, no. 3 (Apr. 1998), p. 24.

[92] Interfax (Moscow), 20 May 1998, in 'Yeltsin to discuss START II at meeting of "four"', FBIS-SOV-98-140, 20 May 1998; 'Russian domestic concerns stall START', Non-Proliferation Project of the Carnegie Endowment for International Peace, *Proliferation Brief*, vol. 1, no. 6 (7 June 1998); and Hoffman, D., 'Opponents in Duma reaffirm hard line against arms pact', *International Herald Tribune*, 19 May 1998, p. 6.

[93] Federal bill on ratification of the Treaty between the Russian Federation and the United States of America on Further Reduction and Limitation of Strategic Offensive Arms, Dec. 1998, draft text reproduced by the Centre for Policy Studies in Russia (PIR), Moscow, URL <http://www.pircenter.org/acl/messages/55.htm>.

[94] First Deputy Prime Minister Yuriy Maslyukov outlined Russia's strategic force modernization priorities as follows: deploying 35–40 Topol-M ICBMs (known also by its NATO designation, SS-27) beginning in the year 2000; constructing 7 Yuriy Dolgorukiy Class ballistic missile submarines, to enter service by the year 2010; and improving the strategic forces' command, control and communications

conditions were crucial for gaining the backing of deputies concerned that the treaty reductions would dangerously undermine Russia's nuclear strength at a time when its conventional military capabilities were considerably diminished. They were supported by a draft law drawn up by the Duma Defence Committee setting out investment priorities and 'inviolable' funding levels for Russia's strategic nuclear forces through the year 2010.[95]

The new draft law was submitted to the executive branch for its consideration in early December.[96] Treaty proponents in parliament expressed optimism that Yeltsin would support the ratification law's reservations and conditions, which had been drafted in consultation with the foreign and defence ministries;[97] the text was expected to be officially transmitted to the Duma for a floor vote in the second half of December. However, the bombing attacks launched against Iraq by US and British military forces in mid-December prompted Duma leaders to again halt action on the treaty.[98] According to the Speaker of the Duma, Gennady Seleznev, the bombing campaign 'raised a serious obstacle on the path to ratification of START II'.[99] Other parliamentary leaders indicated that no further discussion of the treaty would take place until the spring 1999 session.

Despite the unexpected postponement of action on the treaty, the prospects for START II ratification clearly had brightened over the course of 1998. Several factors contributed to boosting its chances for gaining the Duma's approval. First, the package of treaty amendments and related measures that had been agreed by Russia and the USA the previous year went a considerable way towards addressing the main concerns about START II's allegedly inequitable impact on Russia's nuclear force structure and defence budget.[100] Second, the new government, headed by Yevgeny Primakov (former foreign minister), began to push vigorously for the Duma to approve START II; Primakov had been one of the treaty's most consistent champions and his views commanded wide respect in parliament. Third, treaty opponents among the communist and nationalist factions began to adopt more flexible positions in the light of the growing realization that a rapid downsizing of the Russian strategic nuclear forces was unavoidable because of the chronic investment

systems as well as their early-warning capabilities. Cited in 'Russian minister calls for nuclear modernization, deep reductions', *Disarmament Diplomacy*, no. 31 (Oct. 1998), pp. 55–56.

[95] Korotchenko, I., 'Funding of strategic nuclear forces will be guaranteed by law: Russian strategic nuclear forces will be free from short-term political considerations', *Nezavisimoye Voyennoye Obozreniye*, 6–12 Nov. 1998, p. 3, in 'Draft law on strategic forces outlined', Foreign Broadcast Information Service, *Daily Report–Central Eurasia: Military Affairs (FBIS-UMA)*, FBIS-UMA-98-313, 9 Nov. 1998.

[96] ITAR-TASS (Moscow), 3 Dec. 1998, in 'Russian Duma committees revise START II ratification bill', FBIS-SOV-98-337, 3 Dec. 1998.

[97] Interfax (Moscow), 19 Nov. 1998, in 'Duma member: time "right" for law on START II ratification', FBIS-SOV-98-323, 19 Nov. 1998.

[98] Associated Press, 'Russia puts off debate on START II', *Washington Post*, 22 Dec. 1998, Internet edition, URL <http://www.search.washingtonpost.com/wp-srv/WAPO/19981222/V000457-122298-idx.html>.

[99] Quoted in Hoffman, D., 'Russian Parliament delays work on START II Treaty', *Washington Post*, 23 Dec. 1998, Internet edition, URL <http://www.search.washingtonpost.com/wp-srv/WPlate/1998-12/23/0321-122398-idx.html>.

[100] Kile (note 88), pp. 409–11, 414–16.

shortfalls. The expert hearings on START II convened in the spring and early summer of 1998 served to impress upon deputies that Russian nuclear force levels were set to decline well below the START II limits during the first decade of the new century, regardless of whether or not the treaty entered into force. Senior Russian military officials dismissed as 'unrealistic' calls from some parliamentarians for heavy investments to be made in the manufacture of new multiple-warhead missiles.[101]

The growing awareness that Russia's strategic nuclear force levels would decline sharply early in the next century reinforced a key argument made by treaty proponents, namely, that START II ratification was necessary in order to preserve an approximate numerical balance between the Russian and US strategic nuclear forces.[102] They pointed out that the USA was obligated under the terms of START II to make significant reductions in the number of its deployed strategic nuclear warheads, including those carried by the bomber and submarine forces in which it enjoyed a comparative technological advantage. In the absence of the treaty, the USA could maintain its strategic forces at the START I ceiling of 6000 deployed warheads—a level which would considerably exceed that of Russia's forces in the next decade.[103]

Furthermore, proponents of ratification noted that START II's entry into force would pave the way for the negotiation of a follow-on START III accord—for which Clinton and Yeltsin had agreed an outline at their 1997 summit meeting in Helsinki—mandating cuts by both states to a total of 2000–2500 strategic nuclear warheads each.[104] The idea of making these deeper bilateral reductions became an increasingly attractive one in the Duma, even among some arms control sceptics, since it held out the prospect of requiring the USA to make reductions to the force levels that Russia can afford to sustain as it eliminates ICBMs, ballistic missile submarines and heavy bombers reaching the end of their service lives.[105] In urging his

[101] Col-Gen. Vladimir Yakovlev, Commander-in-Chief of the Strategic Rocket Forces, quoted by ITAR-TASS (Moscow), 12 May 1998, in 'Russian strategic commander says no alternative to START II', FBIS-SOV-98-132, 12 May 1998.

[102] Arbatov, A. and Romashkin, P., 'There is no alternative to START II ratification: Russia needs the next treaty, START III', *Nezavisimoye Voyennoye Obozreniye*, no. 7 (20–26 Feb. 1998), p. 6, in 'Arbatov, Romashkin favor START II ratification', FBIS-SOV-98-089, 30 Mar. 1998; and Interfax (Moscow), 19 Mar. 1998, in 'Russian general: START II "hostage to political ambitions"', FBIS-SOV-98-078, 19 Mar. 1998.

[103] In an effort to gain leverage over the Duma's treaty deliberations, Congress has prohibited the Department of Defense from reducing US strategic forces below START I levels prior to the entry into force of START II. However, as a cost-saving measure Pentagon officials reportedly have recommended cuts in the US nuclear arsenal even if the Duma does not ratify START II. Myers, S. L., 'Cost-conscious Pentagon supports unilateral cuts in US nuclear arsenal', *International Herald Tribune*, 24 Nov. 1998, p. 4.

[104] The Clinton Administration has stated that, while it is prepared to begin negotiations on a START III accord, it will not do so until the Duma has ratified START II.

[105] However, Russian military planners and defence experts increasingly see Russia as being unable to maintain strategic force levels near the START III ceilings agreed by Clinton and Yeltsin; a force consisting of 1000–1500 deployed nuclear warheads in the year 2008 is often cited in Russia as a more realistic figure. Korbut, A., 'The generals debate: they suspect the proponents of the unification of the nuclear forces of blind imitation of the United States', *Nezavisimoye Voyennoye Obozreniye*, no. 44 (20–26 Nov. 1998), p. 3, in 'Russia: impact of unified command on START 2 viewed', FBIS-SOV-98-331, 27 Nov. 1998; and Interfax (Moscow), 23 Nov. 1998, in 'Russian expert calls for ratification of START II Treaty', FBIS-SOV-98-327, 23 Nov. 1998.

colleagues to advance the START arms reduction process, the chairman of the Duma's International Affairs Committee declared that he agreed 'with Communists who put forward the slogan "No" to the disarmament of Russia but would add one word: "No" to the *unilateral* disarmament of Russia'.[106]

Cooperative strategic warning

At a summit meeting held in Moscow on 1–2 September 1998, presidents Clinton and Yeltsin announced that they had reached agreement on several modest arms control measures.[107] Potentially the most significant of these was an agreement on a cooperative bilateral initiative regarding the exchange of early-warning information on missile launches.[108] This initiative had been advocated by US defence officials and experts concerned about the deterioration of Russia's strategic early-warning and nuclear command and control systems. The overriding goal of the initiative is to reduce the risk of a false missile attack warning and to prevent the launching of a retaliatory attack in response to such a warning. It would involve the continuous exchange of information on worldwide launches of ballistic missiles and space vehicles derived from the early-warning systems of both sides, and include the possible establishment of a joint centre for the exchange of missile launch data that would be independent of national command centres. In addition, the two presidents pledged to examine the possibility of establishing a multilateral ballistic missile pre-launch notification regime in which other states could participate.[109]

VII. The ABM Treaty and ballistic missile defence

The debate over ballistic missile defence (BMD) and the future of the ABM Treaty continued to complicate US–Russian nuclear arms reduction efforts and to generate partisan controversy in Washington.[110] Statements from

[106] Vladimir Lukin, quoted by Interfax (Moscow), 28 May 1998, in 'Duma deputy: Duma unlikely to ratify START II before fall', FBIS-SOV-98-148, 28 May 1998 (emphasis added).

[107] Reuters, 'Moscow summit yields 2 agreements on arms', *International Herald Tribune*, 2 Sep. 1998, p. 8.

[108] 'Joint statement on the exchange of information on missile launches and early warning', *European Washington File* (United States Information Service, US Embassy: Stockholm, 2 Sep. 1998), URL <http://www.usis.usemb.se/ wireless/300/eur308.htm>; and Interfax (Moscow), 2 Sep. 1998, in 'Russia, US to exchange information on missile launches', FBIS-SOV-98-245, 2 Sep. 1998.

[109] The 2 presidents also signed an agreement committing Russia and the USA to remove 50 tonnes of plutonium from old nuclear warheads and to dispose of it so that it cannot be recycled for use in fabricating new weapons. 'Plutonium disposition', White House Fact Sheet, 2 Sep. 1998, *European Washington File* (United States Information Service, US Embassy: Stockholm, 2 Sep. 1998), URL <http://www.usis.usemb.se/ wireless/300/eur315.htm>.

[110] The ABM Treaty was signed by the USA and the USSR on 26 May 1972 and entered into force in Oct. of that year. Amended in a protocol in 1974, the treaty obligates the parties not to undertake to build nationwide defences against strategic ballistic missile attack and sharply limits the development and deployment of permitted missile defences. Among other provisions, it prohibits the parties from giving air defence missiles, radars or launchers the technical ability to counter strategic ballistic missiles and from testing them in a strategic ABM mode. For the text of the ABM Treaty; the Agreed Statements, Common Understandings and Unilateral Statements; and the 1974 Protocol, see Stützle, W., Jasani, B.

the US Administration indicating that it was prepared to seek changes in the ABM Treaty in connection with the possible deployment of a limited national missile defence (NMD) system led to sharp warnings from Moscow that the moves would spell the end of nuclear arms control cooperation. In addition, the year witnessed a continuation of the dispute between Republicans in Congress and the Clinton Administration over whether the ABM Treaty was still in force.

The ABM Treaty and US national missile defences

In January 1999 US Secretary of Defense William Cohen announced that the Clinton Administration would seek funding for work on deploying a limited NMD system.[111] The administration would request an additional $6.6 billion in NMD funding up to and including fiscal year (FY) 2005; this amount would come on top of the nearly $4 billion already budgeted for NMD R&D programmes over this period.[112] According to Cohen, the proposed system was intended to provide a limited defence of the 50 US states 'against a long-range missile threat posed by rogue nations'.[113] He noted that in the spring of 1998 a special commission headed by former Defense Secretary Donald Rumsfeld had presented a 'sobering' report on the rapidly changing and unpredictable nature of the threats posed by medium- and long-range ballistic missiles to US troops deployed overseas and potentially to US territory. Cohen also cited North Korea's launch on 31 August 1998 of a three-stage ballistic missile as evidence that the USA 'will face a rogue missile threat to our homeland against which we will have to defend the American people'.[114] He stressed, however, that a decision to deploy a limited NMD system would not be made until June 2000, when a Deployment Readiness Review will assess the programme's technical feasibility.

The Clinton Administration's decision to move ahead more vigorously in laying the groundwork for a limited NMD system was made against the background of renewed efforts in Congress to require the Pentagon to deploy an NMD shield. While it represented a shift in administration priorities—prompting some critics of the decision to denounce it as a partisan ploy to preempt the Republican legislative agenda—it did not represent a fundamental change in the direction of US missile defence policy. The USA had been committed since 1997 under the so-called '3+3' formula to pursue a technology development programme for a limited NMD system which could be deployed within three years of a decision to do so, with an initial decision

and Cowen, R., SIPRI, *The ABM Treaty: To Defend or Not to Defend?* (Oxford University Press: Oxford, 1987), pp. 207–13.

[111] See also chapter 7, section III, in this volume.

[112] 'Cohen announces plan to augment missile defense programs', US Department of Defense News Release no. 018-99, Office of the Assistant Secretary of Defense (Public Affairs), 20 Jan. 1999. The additional funds will also be used to accelerate key 'upper tier' theatre missile defence programmes.

[113] Transcript of remarks by William S. Cohen, Secretary of Defense, US Department of Defense News Briefing, Office of the Assistant Secretary of Defense (Public Affairs), 20 Jan. 1999.

[114] Transcript of Cohen news briefing remarks (note 113).

about deployment to take place in the year 2000. However, in order to reduce technical risks and avoid the accusations of 'rushing to failure' that have surrounded the development of theatre missile defences (TMD), the administration now proposed to delay the target date for deploying an NMD system to the year 2005.[115]

Cohen acknowledged that a US decision to deploy a limited NMD system might require modifications to the ABM Treaty. These changes, the nature of which had yet to be determined, would be the subject of negotiations with the other parties to the treaty. He noted that the treaty had been amended before and saw 'no reason' why it could not be amended again. He added that the ABM Treaty 'also provides, of course, for the right of withdrawal with six months notice if a party concludes that it is in its supreme national interests' to do so.[116]

Senior administration officials rejected subsequent press accounts that Cohen had threatened a US withdrawal from the ABM Treaty, emphasizing that the USA supported efforts to 'strengthen the treaty and enhance its viability and effectiveness'.[117] Following discussions in late January 1999 with Russian Foreign Minister Igor Ivanov, US Secretary of State Madeleine Albright reaffirmed the USA's commitment to preserving the treaty as the 'cornerstone of strategic stability'. She noted, however, that there are 'new threats in the world that frankly both countries need to consider'.[118] Her comments echoed those of John Holum, Director of the US Arms Control and Disarmament Agency, who told reporters that the ABM Treaty is 'a flexible, living document that should be susceptible to modification as the international environment changes'. He said that the USA would seek to adjust the treaty in order to permit the deployment of an NMD system designed to respond to the threat of a few warheads but which 'would not interfere with the basic purpose of the treaty'.[119] This latter distinction has been criticized by some arms control advocates, however, who point out that the 'basic purpose' of the treaty is to prevent the deployment of national missile defences.[120]

[115] Gilbert, D., 'Cohen announces national missile defence plan', American Forces Press Service, 21 Jan. 1999, URL <http://www.defenselink.mil/news/Jan1999/n01211999_9901213.html>.

[116] Transcript of Cohen news briefing remarks (note 113).

[117] Robert Bell, Senior Director for Defense and Arms Control Policy, National Security Council, quoted in Ross, W., 'US developing limited missile defense against rogue state threat', US Information Agency, *European Washington File* (United States Information Service, US Embassy: Stockholm, 21 Jan. 1999), URL <http://www.usis.usemb.se/wireless/400/eur03.htm>.

[118] Transcript of press conference remarks of Secretary of State Madeleine Albright and Foreign Minister Igor Ivanov, Moscow, 26 Jan. 1999, Office of the Spokesman, US Department of State, *European Washington File* (United States Information Service, US Embassy: Stockholm, 26 Jan. 1999), URL <http://www.usis.usemb.se/wireless/500/eur510.htm>; and ITAR-TASS (Moscow), 26 Jan. 1999, in 'Albright reassures Ivanov on deployment of new ABM system', FBIS-SOV-99-026, 26 Jan. 1999.

[119] Transcript of press conference remarks of John Holum, Under Secretary of State for Arms Control and International Security Affairs, at the Conference on Disarmament, Geneva, 21 Jan. 1999, Office of the Spokesman, US Department of State, *European Washington File* (United States Information Service, US Embassy: Stockholm, 22 Jan 1999), URL <http://www.usis.usemb.se/wireless/500/eur510.htm>.

[120] This distinction is also problematic for technical reasons: the sensors needed for a limited national ballistic missile defence system also provide the foundation for a much more extensive BMD deployment. Dyakov, A. *et al.*, 'ABM Treaty is still assessed as the basis of strategic stability, but agreements signed recently in New York practically destroy it', *Nezavisimoye Voyennoye Obozreniye* (Moscow), 3–9 Oct. 1997, pp. 1, 6, in FBIS-SOV-97-307, 3 Nov. 1997.

Russian officials rejected the idea of making any changes to the ABM Treaty to permit the deployment of an NMD system.[121] Some Russian political analysts predicted that the news that the USA was contemplating unspecified changes in the ABM Treaty could prove to be the death knell for START II in the Duma.[122] Particular concern was expressed by defence ministry officials in Moscow that even a limited US NMD system would have considerable inherent capabilities against the dwindling Russian ICBM force, thereby undermining the stabilizing logic of mutual assured destruction embodied in the ABM Treaty. Dismissing as 'slyness' US assertions that such a defence was needed in response to threats posed by rogue states, some of them cautioned that Russia would be compelled to take appropriate countermeasures to assure a robust strategic nuclear retaliatory capability, such as placing multiple warheads on its new single-warhead Topol-M (SS-27) ICBM.[123] The negative reaction in Moscow made clear that the future of the ABM Treaty is likely to become an even more contentious issue on the nuclear arms control agenda. While the Clinton Administration has expressed interest in adapting the treaty to permit the deployment of missile defences in response to what it perceives to be emerging threats, officials in Moscow continue to view the treaty primarily from the perspective of maintaining the US–Russian strategic nuclear balance.

In addition, US moves towards developing an NMD system are likely to have ramifications for nuclear force developments beyond the USA's arms control relationship with Russia. Some analysts have warned that China may feel compelled to respond to new US missile defences with compensatory measures, which presumably would involve the further expansion and modernization of its strategic nuclear forces.[124] These measures, which might require a resumption of nuclear testing, would undermine the emergent norm against nuclear force modernization and set back efforts within the global non-proliferation regime to cap 'vertical proliferation' among the nuclear weapon states'.

Other ABM Treaty controversies

The US–Russian dispute over amending the ABM Treaty to permit limited national missile defences also seemed likely to complicate the fate of a 1997 deal on the permissibility of advanced-capability TMD under the ABM Treaty. Russia and the USA had signed a series of Agreed Statements setting

[121] Williams, D., 'Russia rejects any changes in ABM Treaty', *International Herald Tribune*, 23–24 Jan. 1999, p. 2.

[122] Hoffman, D., 'US plan threatens Moscow arms pact', *International Herald Tribune*, 22 Jan. 1999, pp. 1, 5.

[123] Interfax (Moscow), 25 Jan. 1999, in 'Russian Defense Ministry sources on revision of ABM Treaty', FBIS-UMA-99-025, 25 Jan. 1999.

[124] Becker, E., 'Missile defense: US weighs risk to Chinese ties', *International Herald Tribune*, 23–24 Jan. 1999, p. 2; Lamson, J. and Bowen, W., '"One arrow, three stars": China's MIRV programme, Part One', *Jane's Intelligence Review*, vol. 9, no. 5 (May 1997), p. 18; and Shen, D., 'China', ed. E. Arnett, *Nuclear Weapons After the Comprehensive Test Ban: Implications for Modernization and Proliferation*, SIPRI Research Report no. 8 (Oxford University Press: Oxford, 1996), p. 26.

out technical parameters to clarify the demarcation line between strategic and theatre (non-strategic) missile defences, thereby resolving a protracted dispute over the issue.[125] However, in 1998 the terms of the agreement came under fire from some Republicans in Congress for allegedly hindering the development of effective missile defences to protect the population of the USA as well as US troops and allies overseas. At the same time, they elicited criticism in Russia for imposing no meaningful constraints on new US TMD systems and effectively eviscerating the ABM Treaty. As a result, the politically charged demarcation agreement, which must be ratified by the legislatures of all five signatory states (Belarus, Kazakhstan, Russia, Ukraine and the USA), faced considerable scepticism in the Russian Duma and outright hostility in the US Senate.

In the USA there was also a sharpening of the dispute between Republicans in Congress and the Clinton Administration over whether the ABM Treaty remained in force. The dispute had arisen in connection with the signing in 1997 of a set of agreements making the ABM Treaty a multilateral accord. The agreements included a Memorandum of Understanding on Succession (MOUS) signed by the foreign ministers of Belarus, Kazakhstan, Russia, Ukraine and the USA, pursuant to which the four former Soviet republics collectively assumed the rights and obligations of the USSR under the ABM Treaty.[126] However, in October 1998 Senate Majority Leader Trent Lott and six other Republican senators sent a letter to President Clinton stating that in their view 'the ABM Treaty has lapsed and is of no force and effect unless the Senate approves the Memorandum of Understanding [on Succession], or some similar agreement to revive the treaty'.[127] A similar claim had been made in an earlier letter sent to Clinton by Republican leaders in the House and Senate.[128] The Clinton Administration rejected this view, arguing that while the Senate's failure to approve the MOUS would leave succession arrangements unsettled, the ABM Treaty would clearly remain in force.[129]

The year ended with Clinton continuing to withhold submission of the demarcation and ABM Treaty succession agreements to the Senate for its

[125] TMD systems occupy a 'grey zone' and are not formally subject to the restrictions of the ABM Treaty, which limits only strategic ABM systems. However, the demarcation between strategic and theatre ballistic missiles is not clearly defined and the technical characteristics of defences against them overlap considerably. For a description of the Agreed Statements and related documents see Kile (note 88), pp. 420–23.

[126] At the fifth review meeting of the ABM Treaty, held on 13 Oct. 1998, representatives of all 5 states signed a follow-on agreement related to CBMs, including data exchanges and notifications connected with certain theatre missile defence systems, agreed upon the previous year. ITAR-TASS (Moscow), 14 Nov. 1998, in 'START II ratification of strategic importance for Russia', Foreign Broadcast Information Service, *Daily Report–Arms Control* (*FBIS-TAC*), FBIS-TAC-98-318, 14 Nov. 1998; and 'Missile defence developments', *Disarmament Diplomacy*, no. 31 (Oct. 1998), pp. 56–57.

[127] Letter to President Bill Clinton signed by Senators Coverdale, Craig, Helms, Kyl, Mack, Nickles and Smith, 5 Oct. 1998, quoted in 'Missile defence developments', *Disarmament Diplomacy*, no. 31 (Oct. 1998), pp. 56–57.

[128] Letter to President Bill Clinton signed by Representative Benjamin Gilman and Senator Jesse Helms, 21 May 1998, quoted in Cerniello, C., 'Administration, Congress continue debate over membership, future of ABM Treaty', *Arms Control Today*, vol. 28, no. 4 (May 1998), p. 36.

[129] Cerniello (note 128).

advice and consent pending the Duma's ratification of START II.[130] It was clear, however, that the partisan dispute on Capitol Hill over ballistic missile defences and the future of the ABM Treaty meant that the agreements faced a difficult struggle to win the approval of that body. In this regard, they represented a potential 'show stopper' that could halt the entry into force of the START II Treaty. The Duma's draft ratification bill stipulated that exchange of the START II instruments of ratification can take place only after the US Senate ratifies the 1997 demarcation agreement and reaffirms the USA's commitment to adhere to the ABM Treaty.[131]

VIII. Conclusions

In 1998 concerns about the vitality of the NPT regime and broader international efforts to curb the proliferation of nuclear weapons moved to the top of the nuclear arms control and disarmament agenda. Although the nuclear tests carried out by India and Pakistan did not pose a direct challenge to the NPT, since neither state is a party to the treaty, they underscored the fact that the treaty regime did not enjoy universal legitimacy. The Indian and Pakistani demonstrations of their widely suspected nuclear weapon capabilities also gave new urgency to the question how the international community should respond to the possession of nuclear weapons by states which are not parties to the NPT. Despite widespread international condemnation of the tests, there was little willingness in most capitals to take measures aimed at forcing India and Pakistan to abandon their nuclear weapon programmes and to join the NPT as non-nuclear weapon states. The US-led efforts to draw the two states into legally binding arrangements, such as the CTBT and the FMT, that complement the NPT in promoting important non-proliferation objectives yielded few concrete results.

The year also witnessed the re-emergence of concerns about the ability of the NPT regime to deal effectively with suspicions of non-compliance by parties to the treaty. There was renewed concern that North Korea, whose record of compliance with its NPT commitments was already under close scrutiny, was engaged in a clandestine nuclear weapon development programme. There was also a breakdown of the UN inspection system in Iraq designed to oversee the elimination of Iraqi programmes to acquire nuclear and other weapons of mass destruction.[132] Together with the 1998 nuclear tests, these crises contributed to a growing sense that the NPT was under siege from within and without by an unprecedented series of challenges which threatened to overwhelm the treaty regime.

Overall, the year 1998 was a largely disappointing one for nuclear arms control efforts. The CTBT did not enter into force. The negotiations in the CD

[130] Burgess, L., 'Republicans see cracks in missile defence resistance', *Defense News*, vol. 13, no. 37 (14–20 Sep. 1998), p. 36.

[131] Federal bill on ratification of the Treaty between the Russian Federation and the United States of America on Further Reduction and Limitation of Strategic Offensive Arms (note 93).

[132] See chapters 3 and 13 in this volume.

on a global ban on the production of fissile material for nuclear explosives faced considerable obstacles. The START II Treaty remained stalled in the Duma, thereby blocking progress towards deeper reductions in the still sizeable US and Russian nuclear arsenals in the framework of a START III accord. This also blocked progress towards important new arms control initiatives, most notably the establishment of a warhead dismantling and transparency regime which could 'lock in' nuclear force reductions and make them irreversible. In addition, the controversies over US BMD programmes and the future of the ABM Treaty threatened to reverse the progress made in recent years in reducing strategic nuclear arsenals. As the year ended, it was clear that a renewed and sustained commitment to advancing the post-cold war nuclear arms control and disarmament agenda was required from the international community, especially from the nuclear weapon states, if the dangers arising from nuclear weapons are to be eventually eliminated.

Appendix 12A. Tables of nuclear forces

ROBERT S. NORRIS and WILLIAM M. ARKIN

Nearly 10 years after the end of the cold war, Russia and the United States continue to deploy large numbers of strategic nuclear delivery vehicles and associated warheads, despite the reductions made by both countries within the framework of the 1991 Treaty on the Reduction and Limitation of Strategic Offensive Arms (START I Treaty). The number of deployed Russian strategic nuclear warheads is set to decline sharply over the next decade because of shortfalls in planned investments to replace current systems as they reach the end of their service lives. Tables 12A.1 and 12A.2 show the composition of the US and Russian operational strategic nuclear forces, with notes about developments in 1998.

The nuclear arsenals of the three other declared nuclear weapon states—the United Kingdom, France and China—are considerably smaller than those of Russia and the USA; data are presented in tables 12A.3, 12A.4 and 12A.5, respectively. In 1998 the British Government announced the results of its Strategic Defence Review, which sets out the future composition of the UK's nuclear forces. China is modernizing its nuclear forces, but its plans for the size and composition of these forces are unknown.

The figures contained in the tables are estimates based on public information but contain some uncertainties, as reflected in the notes. The acronyms which appear in the tables are defined in the list at the front of this volume.

Table 12A.1. US strategic nuclear forces, January 1999

Type	Designation	No. deployed	Year first deployed	Range (km)[a]	Warheads x yield	Warheads
Bombers						
B-52H[b]	Stratofortress	71/44	1961	16 000	ALCM 5–150 kt	400
					ACM 5–150 kt	400
B-2[c]	Spirit	21/9	1994	11 000	Bombs, various	950
Total		**92/53**				**1 750**
ICBMs						
LGM-30G[d]	Minuteman III					
	Mk-12	200	1970	13 000	3 x 170 kt	600
	Mk-12A	300	1979	13 000	3 x 335 kt	900
LGM-118A	MX/Peacekeeper	50	1986	11 000	10 x 300 kt	500
Total		**550**				**2 000**
SLBMs						
UGM-96A[e]	Trident I (C-4)	192	1979	7 400	8 x 100 kt	1 536
UGM-133A[f]	Trident II (D-5)					
	Mk-4	192	1992	7 400	8 x 100 kt	1 536
	Mk-5	48	1990	7 400	8 x 475 kt	384
Total		**432**				**3 456**

[a] Range for aircraft indicates combat radius, without in-flight refuelling.

[b] B-52Hs can carry up to 20 air-launched cruise missiles (ALCMs)/advanced cruise missiles (ACMs) each. Because of a shrinking bomber force, only about 400 ALCMs and 400 ACMs

Table 12A.1 *Notes, contd*

are deployed, with over 900 other ALCMs in reserve. The Nuclear Posture Review (NPR) released on 22 Sep. 1994 recommended retaining 66 B-52Hs. The Air Force has since recommended retaining 71. The B-52Hs have been consolidated at 2 bases, the 2nd Bomb Wing at Barksdale Air Force Base (AFB), Louisiana, and the 5th Bomb Wing at Minot AFB, North Dakota. The first figure in the *No. deployed* column is the total number of B-52Hs in the inventory, including those for training, test and backup; the second figure is the operational number available for nuclear and conventional missions.

Under the START II Treaty the B-1Bs will not be counted as nuclear weapon carriers. The USA has completed a reorientation of its B-1Bs to conventional missions. By the end of 1997 all B-1Bs were out of the strategic war plan altogether and are not included in the table. Of the original 100 B-1Bs, 6 have crashed: 1 in 1987, 2 in 1988, 1 in 1992, 1 on 19 Sep. 1997 and the most recent on 18 Feb. 1998.

[c] The first B-2 bomber was delivered to the 509th Bombardment Wing at Whiteman AFB, Missouri on 17 Dec. 1993. The wing has 2 squadrons, the 393rd and the 325th. The first squadron, the 393rd, was declared operational on 1 Apr. 1997. The second squadron was activated on 8 Jan. 1998.

The B-2 is configured to carry various combinations of nuclear and conventional munitions. The first 16 bombers were produced as Block 10 versions, able to carry the B83 nuclear bomb (and the Mk 84 conventional bomb). These were followed by 3 production Block 20 versions, able to carry the B61 nuclear bomb. Finally, the last 2 bombers were production Block 30 versions (able to carry both types of nuclear bomb and an assortment of conventional bombs, munitions and missiles). Earlier Block 10 and Block 20 aircraft are being upgraded to Block 30 standards at the Northrop Grumman factory in Palmdale, California. In the year 2000 the upgrades will be completed and there will be 21 Block 30 B-2s. The first figure in the *No. deployed* column is the total number of B-2s delivered to Whiteman; the second figure is an approximate number of those available for nuclear and conventional missions.

[d] The 500 Minuteman IIIs have been consolidated from 4 bases to 3. The last Minuteman III missile, deployed at Grand Forks AFB, North Dakota, was removed from its silo on 3 June 1998 for transfer to Malmstrom AFB, Montana, or to Hill AFB, Utah, to be used as spares. There are 200 Minuteman IIIs at Malmstrom and 150 each at Minot AFB, North Dakota, and F. E. Warren AFB, Wyoming.

To comply with the ban on multiple independently targetable re-entry vehicles (MIRVs) when the START II Treaty enters into force, each of the 500 Minuteman III missiles will have the number of warheads reduced from 3 to 1. Currently, 300 missiles have the higher-yield W78 warhead and 200 have the W62 warhead. Several de-MIRVing options are possible. One would be to place a single W87 warhead on each Minuteman III. Five hundred W87s will be removed from the 50 MX missiles when they are retired. The W87 warhead has the preferred safety features, including insensitive high explosive (IHE), fire-resistant pit (FRP) and the enhanced nuclear detonation system (ENDS), whereas the W78 has only ENDS. A drawback is the difficulty of putting multiple warheads back on the missiles if the force is reconstituted. A second option is to use a single W78 on each missile. The third and perhaps preferred option would be to put W78s on a portion of the force, e.g., 150 of the 500 missiles, and W87s on the rest. This option uses the newer warhead and permits easier re-MIRVing. Previously, the downloading was to have been accomplished within 7 years of the entry into force of START I, i.e., by 5 Dec. 2001. Under the 1997 START II Protocol it does not have to be completed until the end of 2007.

Silo destruction has been completed in accordance with the START I Treaty Protocol on Conversion or Elimination at Ellsworth AFB, South Dakota, and Whiteman AFB, 2 bases that once deployed Minuteman II intercontinental ballistic missiles (ICBMs). Thus far none of the 150 silos that once housed the Minuteman IIIs and the 15 missile alert facilities (sometimes called launch control centres) at Grand Forks has been blown up.

A 3-part programme to upgrade the Minuteman missiles continues: (*a*) the missile alert facilities (i.e., launch control centres) have been updated with Rapid Execution and Combat Targeting (REACT) consoles; (*b*) improvements to the missile's guidance system are being conducted by Boeing Autonetics and will continue until 2002—these measures will eventually increase the accuracy of the Minuteman III to near that of the current MX, a circular error probable (CEP) of 100 metres; and (*c*) the first and second stages are being 'repoured', incorporating the latest solid-propellant and bonding technologies, and the third stage will be either refurbished or rebuilt.

In Mar. 1997 Presidents Clinton and Yeltsin, at a summit meeting in Helsinki, agreed to adjust some of the timetables regarding elimination and deactivation. On 26 Sep. 1997 Russia and the USA signed a Protocol extending the START II implementation period by 5 years, from the beginning of 2003 to the end of 2007. However, all missiles which would be eliminated to meet the START II limits will still have to be deactivated by the end of 2003 through the removal of warheads or through some other jointly agreed method.

[e] The W76 warheads from the Trident I missiles have been fitted on Trident II submarines home-ported at Kings Bay, Georgia, and are supplemented by 400 W88 warheads, the number built before the nuclear weapon complex ceased production in 1990.

[f] Eighteen Ohio Class submarines constitute the SSBN (nuclear-powered ballistic-missile submarine) fleet. The first 8 submarines of the class carry the Trident I (C-4) submarine-launched ballistic missile (SLBM); the final 10 are equipped with the Trident II (D-5) SLBM.

The 1994 NPR recommended completing construction of 18 Ohio Class SSBNs (nuclear-powered ballistic-missile submarines) and then retiring 4 older SSBNs. The Navy has chosen the submarines that will be upgraded and those that will be retired. The 4 newest Trident I-equipped SSBNs based in the Pacific at Bangor, Washington, will be backfitted to fire Trident II missiles. In order of their upgrade they are: *Alaska* (732) and *Nevada* (733)—during 2000–2001—followed by *Jackson* (730) and *Alabama* (731)—during 2004–2005. The 4 older submarines (*Ohio, Michigan, Florida* and *Georgia*) will be retired, at the rate of 2 each in 2002 and 2003. A possibility would be to convert 2 or all 4 of the submarines to carry cruise missiles and also be used for special operations missions. Conversion is permitted but is a more costly and extensive process since the submarine's missile launch tubes must be removed. Modification leaves the tubes empty but must be agreed by both sides. START I contained an Agreed Statement allowing for 2 US special-purpose Poseidon submarines. If the Navy wanted to replace those 2 Poseidons with 2 Trident submarines, this would have to be agreed upon in a future treaty. Given those complexities and the cost involved, it is unlikely that this option will be pursued.

The Navy continues to purchase Trident II SLBMs. In the fiscal year (FY) 1999 Pentagon budget, 5 missiles were purchased. The NPR called for backfitting 4 Trident I-equipped SSBNs with Trident IIs, increasing the number of missiles to be procured from 390 to 434, at an extra cost of $2.2 billion. Twenty-eight additional missiles were bought for the research and development programme. The total cost of the programme is now $27.5 billion, or $60 million per missile. Through FY 1999 over $24 billion has been authorized. Some have questioned the need to continue to buy more missiles if the future force under START III is going to be smaller than 14 SSBNs. E.g., a force of 10 submarines requires 347 missiles and would result in significant savings.

The Bangor base will have to undergo some adaptation to support the Trident II and a 10-year, $5 billion programme is scheduled to begin in 2000. The backfitting of the 4 SSBNs will take place from FY 2000 to FY 2005. Eventually, 2 or 3 submarines will be shifted from Kings Bay to Bangor to balance the 14-submarine fleet. To comply with START II warhead limits the Navy will have to download its SLBMs, retire additional SSBNs or do both. Under the new timetable set out in the START II Protocol, SLBMs can have no more than 2160 warheads by the end of 2004 and no more than 1750 warheads by the end of 2007. If there is a START III treaty with limits of 2000–2500 deployed strategic warheads, the SSBN portion would probably account for *c.* one-half. This would mean a fleet of 10–12 submarines, depen-

Table 12A.1 *Notes, contd*

ding on the number of warheads per SLBM. Some speculate that with an SSBN fleet of a dozen or fewer submarines the Bangor base could be closed, although war planners object because China would not be adequately targeted.

Although the START counting rules attribute 8 warheads per Trident, the actual loading of a submarine will normally be less than the full complement of 192 warheads per boat. A missile's range can be extended by carrying fewer warheads. Some SLBMs may have 5 or 6 warheads, while others have 7 or 8. It is the Single Integrated Operational Plan (SIOP) that ultimately determines how an SSBN will be loaded, where the SLBMs will be launched from, and which targets the warheads are aimed at.

While much has changed, some things have not. The practice of maintaining 2 crews for each SSBN remains unchanged. In 1999, at any given time, 9 or 10 US SSBNs are on patrol in the Atlantic and Pacific oceans, a rate equal to that at the height of the cold war. Roughly one-half the number of those on patrol (2 or 3 in each ocean) are on 'hard' alert, i.e., within range of their targets. The remaining patrolling SSBNs are in transit to or from their launch-point.

Sources: Cohen, W. S., Secretary of Defense, *Annual Report to the President and the Congress,* 1999, pp. 67–75; Cohen, W. S., Secretary of Defense, *Annual Report to the President and the Congress*, Apr. 1997, pp. 207–11; START I Treaty Memoranda of Understanding, 1 Sep. 1990, 5 Dec. 1994, 1 July 1995, 1 Jan. 1996, 1 July 1996, 1 Jan. 1997, 1 July 1997, 1 Jan. 1998 and 1 July 1998; US Senate Committee on Foreign Relations, START II Treaty, Executive Report 104-10, 15 Dec. 1995; Air Force Public Affairs, personal communications; and Natural Resources Defense Council (NRDC), 'Nuclear notebook', *Bulletin of the Atomic Scientists,* various issues.

Table 12A.2. Russian strategic nuclear forces, January 1999

Type	NATO designation	No. deployed	Year first deployed	Range (km)[a]	Warheads x yield	Warheads
Bombers						
Tu-95M[b]	Bear-H6	29	1984	12 800	6 x AS-15A ALCMs, bombs	174
Tu-95M[b]	Bear-H16	35	1984	12 800	16 x AS-15A ALCMs, bombs	560
Tu-160[c]	Blackjack	6	1987	11 000	12 x AS-15B ALCMs or AS-16 SRAMs, bombs	72
Total		**70**				**806**
ICBMs[d]						
SS-18[e]	Satan	180	1979	11 000	10 x 550/750 kt	1 800
SS-19[f]	Stiletto	160	1980	10 000	6 x 550 kt	960
SS-24 M1/M2[g]	Scalpel	36/10	1987	10 000	10 x 550 kt	460
SS-25[h]	Sickle	360	1985	10 500	1 x 550 kt	360
SS-27[i]	. .	10	1997	10 500	1 x 550 kt	10
Total		**756**				**3 590**
SLBMs[i]						
SS-N-18 M1	Stingray	176	1978	6 500	3 x 500 kt	528
SS-N-20[j]	Sturgeon	60	1983	8 300	10 x 200 kt	600
SS-N-23	Skiff	112	1986	9 000	4 x 100 kt	448
Total		**348**				**1 576**

[a] Range for aircraft indicates combat radius, without in-flight refuelling.

[b] According to the 1 July 1998 START I Memorandum of Understanding, the Bear bombers are deployed as follows: Bear H16s—19 at Mozdok (Russia), 16 at Ukrainka (Russia), and 14 at Uzin (Ukraine); Bear H6s—2 at Mozdok, 27 at Ukrainka and 3 at Uzin. The 40 Bear-H bombers (27 Bear H6s and 13 Bear-H16s) that were based in Kazakhstan were withdrawn to Russia, including some 370 AS-15 ALCM warheads. The 17 Bear bombers in Ukraine, at Uzin, are poorly maintained and are not considered operational. Seven additional Bear bombers at Uzin are in storage.

[c] Nineteen Blackjack bombers are based in Ukraine at Priluki; the remaining 6 are in Russia at Engels AFB near Saratov. The Blackjacks at Priluki are poorly maintained and are not considered operational. An agreement announced on 24 Nov. 1995 that called for Ukraine to eventually return the 19 Blackjack and 25 Bear bombers and more than 300 cruise missiles to Russia collapsed in the spring and summer of 1997. Ukraine plans to dismantle the Blackjacks.

[d] Deactivation and retirement of ICBMs and their launchers proceed through at least 4 stages. In step 1, an ICBM is removed from alert status by electrical and mechanical procedures. Next, warheads are removed from the missile. In step 3 the missile is withdrawn from the silo. Finally, to comply with START-specified elimination procedures, the silo is blown up and eventually filled in. The number of missiles and warheads will vary depending upon which step the analyst chooses to feature.

[e] In the Sep. 1990 START I Treaty Memorandum of Understanding, the Soviet Union declared 104 SS-18s in Kazakhstan (at Derzhavinsk and Zhangiz-Tobe) and 204 in Russia (30 at Aleysk, 64 at Dombarosvki, 46 at Kartaly and 64 at Uzhur). All the SS-18s in Kazakhstan and 24 in Russia are considered to be non-operational, leaving 180 in Russia. Beginning in Apr. 1995 the first SS-18 silos in Kazakhstan were blown up. By mid-1997 all 104 had been destroyed. Under the START I Treaty Russia is permitted to retain 154 SS-18s. If the START II Treaty is fully implemented, all SS-18 missiles will be destroyed, but Russia may convert up to 90 SS-18 silos for deployment of single-warhead ICBMs.

[f] In the Sep. 1990 START I Treaty Memorandum of Understanding, the Soviet Union declared 130 SS-19s in Ukraine and 170 in Russia. A Nov. 1995 agreement included the sale of 32 SS-19s, once deployed in Ukraine, back to Russia. Some SS-19s in Russia are being withdrawn from service. Under START II Russia may keep up to 105 SS-19s downloaded to a single warhead.

[g] Of the original 56 silo-based SS-24 M2s, 46 were in Ukraine at Pervomaysk and 10 are in Russia at Tatishchevo. At the beginning of 1999 only the 10 in Russia were considered operational. All 36 rail-based SS-24 M1s are in Russia—at Bershet, Kostroma and Krasnoyarsk.

[h] By 27 Nov. 1996 the last remaining SS-25 missiles in Belarus and their warheads had been shipped back to Russia. The new variant of the SS-25 is called the Topol-M by the Russians and designated the SS-27 by NATO. It is assembled at Votkinsk in Russia and is the only Russian strategic weapon system still in production. Flight-testing began on 20 Dec. 1994. On 22 Oct. 1998 a Topol-M ICBM exploded after being launched from the Plesetsk test site. It was the fifth test launch and was intended to fly across Russia to a target on the Kamchatka Peninsula. The sixth test, on 8 Dec. 1998, was successful. Two silo-based SS-27s were put on 'trial service' in Dec. 1997 in south-western Russia's Saratov region in Tatishchevo. On 27 Dec. 1998, according to the Russian Government, the 104th Regiment, under the Taman Missile Division, had 10 missiles that were operational. The silos formerly housed SS-19 missiles.

[i] An ambitious Topol-M (SS-27) production schedule was announced by General Vladimir Yakovlev, Commander in Chief of the Strategic Rocket Forces. He said that 20–30 SS-27s a year were planned to be made operational over the next 3 years and 30–40 a year for the 3 years after that. If this schedule is adhered to by the end of 2001, there could be 70–100 missiles and, by the end of 2004, 160–220. A more realistic rate, given the limited resources, is 10–15 missiles per year, with perhaps some 60–80 fielded by 2005.

Table 12A.2 *Notes, contd*

[j] Nearly two-thirds of the SSBN fleet has been withdrawn from operational service. The table assumes that all the Yankee Is, Delta Is and Delta IIs and 3 Delta IIIs and 3 Typhoons have been withdrawn from operational service, leaving 21 operational SSBNs of 3 classes (11 Delta IIIs, 7 Delta IVs and 3 Typhoons). According to Russian Vice-Admiral Viktor Topilin, 2 Typhoons are 'unfit for combat'; hence they are not included in the table of operational forces. A third Typhoon was withdrawn during 1998 and the entire class may be retired. Operational SSBNs are based on the Kola Peninsula (at Nerpichya and Yagelnaya) and at Rybachi (15 km south-west of Petropavlovsk) on the Kamchatka Peninsula. The patrol rates of the Russian SSBNs has been reduced significantly since the end of the cold war. Currently, it was reported that 1 submarine in the Atlantic and 1 in the Pacific are on patrol, with at least another in each fleet on pier-side alert. Reportedly, for a 3-month period from May through June 1998 there were no SSBNs on patrol because of concerns over safety. The keel of the first of the new Borey Class SSBNs, the *Yuriy Dolgorukiy*, was laid in Nov. 1996. Construction has been intermittent and was suspended altogether during 1998. Chief of the Navy Admiral Kuroyedov announced that the submarine was being redesigned, not an auspicious sign. It is unlikely that any Borey Class SSBNs will join the fleet over the next 5 years. Despite the rhetoric about maintaining a sea-based leg of the triad, the future of the Russian SSBN force remains very much in doubt.

Sources: START I Treaty Memoranda of Understanding, 1 Sep. 1990, 5 Dec. 1994, 1 July 1995, 1 Jan. 1996, 1 July 1996, 1 Jan. 1997, 1 July 1997, 1 Jan. 1998 and 1 July 1998; International Institute for Strategic Studies (IISS), *The Military Balance 1998/99* (Oxford University Press: Oxford, 1998); Natural Resources Defense Council (NRDC), 'Nuclear notebook', *Bulletin of the Atomic Scientists,* various issues; Podvig, P. L. (ed.), *Strategicheskoye yadernoye vooruzheniye Rossii* [Russian strategic nuclear weapons], (IzdAT: Moscow, 1998); and Wilkening, D. A., *The Evolution of Russia's Strategic Nuclear Force* (Stanford University, Center for International Security and Cooperation: Stanford, Calif., 1998).

Table 12A.3. British nuclear forces, January 1999[a]

Type	Designation	No. deployed	Year first deployed	Range (km)	Warheads x yield	Warheads in stockpile
SSBNs/SLBMs[b]						
D-5	Trident II	48	1994	7 400	1–3 x 100 kt	185[c]

[a] In July 1998 the results of the Strategic Defence Review (SDR), undertaken by the Labour Government, were announced. The decisions with regard to British nuclear forces were:

1. Only 1 submarine will be on patrol at any time carrying a reduced load of 48 warheads—half the Conservative Government's announced ceiling of 96.

2. The submarine on patrol will be at a reduced alert state and will carry out a range of secondary tasks; its missiles will be detargeted, and after notice the SSBN will be capable of firing its missiles within several days, rather than within several minutes, as during the cold war.

3. There will be fewer than 200 operationally available warheads, a one-third reduction from the Conservative Government's plans.

4. The number of Trident D-5 missiles already purchased or ordered was reduced from 65 to 58.

As a result of these decisions the total explosive power of the operationally available weapons will be reduced by over 70% compared to the eventual future force. The explosive power of each Trident submarine will be one-third less than that of the 4 Chevaline-armed Polaris submarines, the last of which was retired in 1996.

The Royal Air Force operated 8 squadrons of dual-capable Tornado GR.1/1A aircraft. At the end of Mar. 1998, with the withdrawal of the last remaining WE177 bombs from operational service, the Tornadoes ended their nuclear role, terminating a 4-decade long history of RAF aircraft carrying nuclear weapons. By the end of Aug. 1998 the remaining WE177 bombs had been dismantled. The *c.* 40 Tornadoes currently at RAF Bruggen in Germany will be reassigned to RAF Lossiemouth and RAF Marham in the UK by the end of 2001, and the base at Bruggen will be closed.

[b] The first submarine of the new Trident class, HMS *Vanguard*, went on its first patrol in Dec. 1994. The second submarine, *Victorious*, entered service in Dec. 1995. The third submarine, *Vigilant*, was launched in Oct. 1995 and entered service in the autumn of 1998. The fourth and final boat of the class, *Vengeance*, was launched on 19 Sep. 1998, with service entry scheduled for late 2000 or early 2001. The current estimated cost of the Trident submarine programme is $18.8 billion.

Each Vanguard Class SSBN carries 16 US-produced Trident II D-5 SLBMs. In the SDR the Labour Government announced that 58 missiles would be purchased from the USA instead of 65. There are no specifically US or British Trident II missiles. There is a pool of SLBMs at Strategic Weapons Facility Atlantic at the Kings Bay Submarine Base, Georgia. The UK has title to 58 SLBMs but does not actually own them. A missile that is deployed on a US SSBN may at a later date be deployed on a British one, or vice versa.

[c] Several factors go into the calculation of the number of warheads that will be in the future British stockpile. It is assumed that the UK will only produce enough warheads for 3 boatloads of missiles, a practice it followed with Polaris. As was stated in the SDR, there will be 'fewer than 200 operationally available warheads' with no more than 48 warheads per boat. If all 4 boats were fully loaded (MIRV x 3) that would total 192 warheads. The government also stated that it will be the practice that normally only 1 SSBN will be on patrol, with the other 3 in various states of readiness. A further consideration is the 'sub-strategic mission'. A Ministry of Defence official described it as follows: 'A sub-strategic strike would be the limited and highly selective use of nuclear weapons in a manner that fell demonstrably short of a strategic strike, but with a sufficient level of violence to convince an aggressor who had already miscalculated our resolve and attacked us that he should halt his aggression and withdraw or face the prospect of a devastating strategic strike'. Omand, D., 'Nuclear deterrence in a changing world: the view from a UK perspective', *RUSI Journal,* June 1996, pp. 15–22.

The sub-strategic mission has begun with *Victorious* and 'will become fully robust when *Vigilant* enters service', according to the 1996 White Paper. If this has remained the policy then some Trident II SLBMs already have a single warhead and are assigned targets once covered by WE177 gravity bombs. E.g., when the *Vigilant* is on patrol, 10, 12 or 14 of its SLBMs may carry up to 3 warheads per missile, while the other 2, 4 or 6 missiles may be armed with just 1 warhead. There is some flexibility in the choice of yield of the Trident warhead. (Choosing to detonate only the unboosted primary could produce a yield of 1 kt or less. Choosing to detonate the boosted primary could produce a yield of a few kilotons.) With these 2 missions an SSBN would have approximately 36–44 warheads on board during its patrol.

This table assumes that the future British stockpile for the SSBN fleet will be around 160 warheads. With an additional 15% for spares the total stockpile is estimated to be *c.* 185 warheads. At any given time the sole SSBN on patrol would carry about 40 warheads. The second and third SSBNs could put to sea fairly rapidly, with similar loadings, while the fourth may take longer because of its cycle of overhaul and maintenance.

Sources: Norris, R. S., Burrows, A.S. and Fieldhouse, R. W., *Nuclear Weapons Databook Vol. V: British, French, and Chinese Nuclear Weapons* (Westview: Boulder, Colo., 1994), p. 9; Secretary of State for Defence, *Strategic Defence Review* (Ministry of Defence: London, July 1998); Ministry of Defence Press Releases; and Natural Resources Defense Council (NRDC), 'Nuclear notebook', *Bulletin of the Atomic Scientists,* Nov./Dec. 1996, pp. 64–67.

Table 12A.4. French nuclear forces, January 1999[a]

Type	No. deployed	Year first deployed	Range (km)[b]	Warheads x yield	Warheads in stockpile
Land-based aircraft[c]					
Mirage 2000N/ASMP	45	1988	2 750	1 x 300 kt ASMP	60
Carrier-based aircraft					
Super Étendard[d]	24	1978	650	1 x 300 kt ASMP	20
SLBMs[e]					
M4A/B	48	1985	6 000	6 x 150 kt	288
M45	16	1996	6 000	6 x 100 kt	96

[a] On 22 and 23 Feb. 1996 President Jacques Chirac announced several reforms for the French armed forces for the period 1997–2002. The decisions in the nuclear area were a combination of the withdrawal of several obsolete systems with a commitment to modernize those that remain.

After officials considered numerous plans to replace the silo-based S3D IRBM during President François Mitterrand's tenure, President Chirac announced that the missile would be retired and that there would be no replacement. On 16 Sep. 1996 all 18 missiles on the Plateau d'Albion were deactivated and the silos and complex have since then been dismantled.

In July 1996, after 32 years of service, the Mirage IVP was converted from its nuclear role and retired. Five Mirage IVPs will be retained for reconnaissance missions at Istres. The other aircraft will be put into storage at Châteaudun.

[b] Range for aircraft assumes combat mission, without refuelling, and does not include the 90- to 350-km range of the Air-Sol Moyenne Portée (ASMP) air-to-surface missile.

[c] Three squadrons of Mirage 2000Ns have now assumed a 'strategic' role, in addition to their 'pre-strategic' one. A fourth Mirage 2000N squadron at Nancy—now conventional—is scheduled to be replaced with Mirage 2000Ds. Those aircraft may be modified to carry the ASMP and be distributed to the 3 2000N squadrons at Luxeuil and Istres, along with the Mirage IVP's ASMP missiles. It is estimated that *c.* 80 were produced for ASMP missiles. The number of missiles built was probably closer to 100. In a Feb. 1996 speech, President Chirac said that a longer-range ASMP (500 km as opposed to 300 km, sometimes called the 'ASMP Plus') will be developed for service entry in about a decade.

The Rafale is planned to be the multi-purpose Navy and Air Force fighter/bomber for the 21st century. Its roles include conventional ground attack, air defence, air superiority and nuclear delivery of the ASMP and/or ASMP Plus. The carrier-based Navy version will be introduced first, with the Air Force Rafale D attaining a nuclear strike role in *c.* 2005. The Air Force still plans to buy a total of 234 Rafales.

[d] France built 2 aircraft-carriers, 1 of which entered service in 1961 (*Clemenceau*) and the other in 1963 (*Foch*). Both were modified to handle the AN 52 nuclear gravity bomb with Super Étendard aircraft. The *Clemenceau* was modified in 1979 and the *Foch* in 1981. The AN 52 was retired in July 1991. Only the *Foch* was modified to 'handle and store' the replacement ASMP, and *c.* 20 were allocated for 2 squadrons—*c.* 24 Super Étendard aircraft. The *Clemenceau* was never modified to 'handle and store' the ASMP. The 32 780-ton aircraft-carrier was decommissioned in Sep. 1997. The new 40 600-ton aircraft-carrier, *Charles de Gaulle*, is scheduled to enter service in Dec. 2000, 4 years behind schedule, at a cost of well over $3 billion. At that time the *Foch* will be laid up and decommissioned. The *Charles de Gaulle* will have a single squadron of Super Étendards (with presumably about 10 ASMPs) until the Rafale M is introduced in 2002. At about that time a second carrier may be ordered. The Navy plans to purchase a total of 60 Rafale Ms, of which the first 16 will perform an air-to-air role. Missions for subsequent aircraft may include the ASMP and/or the ASMP Plus.

[e] The lead SSBN, *Le Triomphant*, was rolled out from its construction shed in Cherbourg on 13 July 1993. It entered service in Sep. 1996 armed with the M45 SLBM and new TN 75 warheads. The second SSBN, *Le Téméraire*, is scheduled to enter service in mid-1999. The schedule for the third, *Le Vigilant*, has slipped and it will not be ready until 2001. The service date for the fourth SSBN is *c.* 2005. It is estimated that there will eventually be 288 warheads for the fleet of 4 new Triomphant Class SSBNs, because only enough missiles and warheads will be purchased for 3 boats. This loading is the case today, with 5 submarines in the fleet—only 4 sets of M4 SLBMs were procured. President Chirac announced on 23 Feb. 1996 that the fourth submarine would be built and that a new SLBM, known as the M51, will replace the M45. The service entry date has been advanced to 2008 instead of 2010.

Sources: Norris, R. S., Burrows, A. S. and Fieldhouse, R. W., *Nuclear Weapons Databook Vol. V: British, French, and Chinese Nuclear Weapons* (Westview: Boulder, Colo., 1994), p. 10; and *Air Actualités; Le Magazine de l'Armée de l'Air*, Address by M. Jacques Chirac, President of the Republic, at the École Militaire, Paris, 23 Feb. 1996.

Table 12A.5. Chinese nuclear forces, January 1999

Type	NATO designation	No. deployed	Year first deployed	Range (km)[a]	Warheads x yield	Warheads in stockpile
Aircraft[a]						
H-6	B-6	120	1965	3 100	1–3 bombs	120
Q-5	A-5	30	1970	400	1 x bomb	30
Land-based missiles[b]						
DF-3A	CSS-2	40	1971	2 800	1 x 3.3 Mt	40
DF-4	CSS-3	20	1980	4 750	1 x 3.3 Mt	20
DF-5A	CSS-4	20	1981	13 000+	1 x 4–5 Mt	20
DF-21A	CSS-6	48	1985–86	1 800	1 x 200–300 kt	48
SLBMs[c]						
Julang-1	CSS-N-3	12	1986	1 700	1 x 200–300 kt	12
Julang-2	CSS-N-4	0	Late 1990s	8 000	1 x 200–300 kt	?
Tactical weapons						
Artillery/ADMs, Short-range missiles					Low kt	120

[a] All figures for bomber aircraft are for nuclear-configured versions only. Hundreds of aircraft are also deployed in non-nuclear versions. The Hong-5 has been retired and the Hong-7 will not have a nuclear role. Aircraft range is equivalent to combat radius. Assumes 150 bombs for the force, with yields estimated between 10 kt and 3 Mt.

[b] China defines missile ranges as follows: short-range, <1000 km; medium-range, 1000–3000 km; long-range, 3000–8000 km; and intercontinental range, >8000 km. The nuclear capability of the medium-range M-9 is unconfirmed and not included. China is also developing 2 other ICBMs: the DF-31, with a range of 8000 km and carrying one 200- to 300-kt warhead, may be deployed in the late 1990s; and the DF-41, with a range of 12 000 km, is scheduled for deployment around 2010 and may be MIRVed if China develops that capability.

Sources: Norris, R. S., Burrows, A. S. and Fieldhouse, R. W., *Nuclear Weapons Databook Vol. V: British, French, and Chinese Nuclear Weapons* (Westview: Boulder, Colo., 1994), p. 11; Lewis, J. W. and Hua, D., 'China's ballistic missile programs: technologies, strategies, goals', *International Security*, vol. 17, no. 2 (fall 1992), pp. 5–40; Allen, K. W., Krumel, G. and Pollack, J. D., *China's Air Force Enters the 21st Century* (Rand: Santa Monica, Calif.,1995); International Institute for Strategic Studies (IISS), *The Military Balance 1998/99* (Oxford University Press: Oxford, 1998); and Natural Resources Defense Council (NRDC), 'Nuclear notebook', *Bulletin of the Atomic Scientists*, Nov./Dec. 1996, pp. 64–67.

Appendix 12B. Nuclear explosions, 1945–98

RAGNHILD FERM

I. Introduction

In May 1998 nuclear tests were carried out by India and Pakistan. Since the signing of the Comprehensive Nuclear Test-Ban Treaty (CTBT) on 24 September 1996 none of the declared nuclear weapon states[1] has conducted any nuclear explosions.

II. The 1998 Indian and Pakistani tests

On 11 May the Indian Prime Minister announced that on the same day India had conducted three underground nuclear explosions.[2] The explosions, code-named Shakti 1, 2 and 3, were carried out at the Pokhran test site, *c.* 530 km south-west of New Delhi in the Rajasthan desert, the same location as was used for the 1974 Indian nuclear explosion. According to the Indian Department of Energy the explosions included a 43-kiloton thermonuclear device, a 12-kt fission device and a 0.2-kt fission device.[3] Scientists at the Bhaba Atomic Research Center (BARC), using regional seismological systems and the CORRTEX technique,[4] estimated that the explosions had yields of 45 kt, 15 kt and 0.2 kt, respectively. They reported that the yield of the thermonuclear device was deliberately low to avoid damage to villages in the neighbourhood.[5] The nuclear devices were detonated within a fraction of a second of each other. The two major explosions were carried out in two shafts, drilled about 1 km apart. According to some reports, the third and smallest device was exploded in a shaft 2.2 km away.[6] Other sources report that the low-yield device was detonated in the same shaft as one of the large ones.[7]

Experts have compared the seismological data of the explosions with those of the Indian test in 1974, for which a body wave magnitude of 5.0 or 5.1 on the Richter scale was estimated by Indian scientists to correspond to a yield of 10–12 kt. The

[1] According to the 1968 Non-Proliferation Treaty (NPT), Article IX, 3: 'a nuclear-weapon State is one which has manufactured and exploded a weapon or other nuclear explosive device prior to 1 January, 1967'. By this definition China, France, Russia, the UK and the USA are nuclear weapon states, but not India or Pakistan.

[2] Press statement issued in New Delhi on 11 May, Conference on Disarmament document CD 1504, 12 May 1998. The nuclear tests by India and Pakistan are also examined in chapter 9 in this volume.

[3] The joint statement by R. Chidambaram, Chairman, Atomic Energy Commission and A. P. J. Abdul Kalam, Head of the Defence Research and Development Organization, on the Indian nuclear tests, 17 May 1998, is reproduced in Institute for Defense and Disarmament Studies, *Arms Control Reporter* (IDDS: Brookline, Mass.), sheets 454.D.9–10, 1998.

[4] CORRTEX = continuous reflectometry for radius versus time experiments. The CORRTEX system is a technique for measuring the velocity of an explosion's shock wave. See Ferm, R., 'Nuclear explosions', *SIPRI Yearbook 1989: World Armaments and Disarmament* (Oxford University Press: Oxford, 1989), pp. 52–53.

[5] Sikka, S. K. and Kakodkar, A., 'Some preliminary results of May 11–13, 1998 nuclear detonations at Pokhran', *BARC Newsletter*, no. 172 (May 1998), reproduced in *Strategic Digest*, vol. 28, no. 7 (July 1998), pp. 1085–86.

[6] Bagla, P., 'Size of Indian blasts still disputed', *Science*, vol. 281, no. 5385 (25 Sep. 1998), p. 1939.

[7] van der Vink, G. *et al.*, 'False accusations, undetected tests and implications for the CTB Treaty', *Arms Control Today*, vol. 28, no. 4 (May 1998), pp. 7–13; and van Moyland, S. and Clark, R., 'The paper trail', *Bulletin of the Atomic Scientists*, vol. 54, no. 4 (July/Aug. 1998), pp. 26–29.

11 May explosions, supposedly conducted in the same geological environment, were registered by 62 stations and estimated to have had a body wave magnitude of 5.2–5.3. This could hardly correspond to the yields announced by the Indian authorities. The experts rather suggested a combined yield of not more than 25 kt. It is therefore considered very doubtful that the announced thermonuclear device worked properly.[8]

On 13 May two more simultaneous explosions occurred at the Pokhran test site, with announced yields of 0.2 and 0.6 kt.[9]

No signals were recorded by seismological stations outside India for the 13 May explosions. The International Monitoring System (IMS), now being set up to verify the CTBT after its entry into force, does not yet have stations in India or Pakistan, but there are other stations in the area, not part of the IMS, that could have provided data. For example, the US–Pakistani Nilore station in Pakistan, 750 km from the Indian test site, recorded no seismic signal corresponding to these explosions. It has been suggested that the announced explosions could have been two subcritical experiments fuelled by chemical explosions (see section IV).[10]

In response to the Indian tests Pakistan announced that it had exploded five nuclear devices on 28 May and one on 30 May.[11] The 28 May explosions were carried out at the Ras Koh test range in the Chagai Mountains in Baluchistan, near the Afghan border. The explosions were conducted simultaneously. Pakistani nuclear scientists reported that the yield of the largest explosion was 30–35 kt, the other four explosions were of low yield and the aggregate yield of the explosions was 40–45 kt.[12] Transmission of data from the Nilore station stopped two hours before the event, but other seismological stations in the region recorded the explosions. According to these stations the body wave magnitude was 4.6, which in this region indicates an explosion with a yield of about 10 kt.[13]

According to international seismic data the 30 May test was conducted *c.* 100 km south-west of the first test, in the Kharan desert. Its yield was announced to be 15–18 kt, but averaging the reports from more than 50 non-Pakistani seismological stations indicated a body wave magnitude of 4.3, corresponding to a yield of 2–8 kt.[14] Two tests were actually planned for 30 May, but as the results of the explosions of 28 May were considered sufficient only one was conducted.[15]

There are discrepancies between the announced yields of the Indian and Pakistani tests and the recorded seismic signals.[16] One explanation for this is that the Indian and

[8] Goppi Rethinaraj, T. S. and Moorty, D. N., 'Nuclear politics in South Asia', *Jane's Intelligence Review: Special Report*, no. 20 (Dec. 1998), pp. 20–22.

[9] Press statement issued in New Delhi on 13 May, Conference on Disarmament document CD/1504/Add.1, 13 May 1998.

[10] Marshall, E., 'Did test ban watchdog fail to bark?', *Science*, vol. 280, no. 5372 (26 June 1998), pp. 2038–40.

[11] Statement made by the Prime Minister Muhammad Nawaz Sharif (28 May 1998), Conference on Disarmament document CD/1518, 2 June 1998; and Statement by the Foreign Secretary on 30 May 1998, Conference of Disarmament document CD/519, 2 June 1998.

[12] Wallace, T. C., 'The May 1998 India and Pakistan nuclear tests', *Seismological Research Letters*, vol. 69, no. 5 (Sep./Oct. 1998), pp. 386–93.

[13] van der Vink (note 7)

[14] 'NRDC nuclear notebook: Known nuclear tests worldwide, 1945–98', *Bulletin of the Atomic Scientists*, vol. 54, no. 6 (Nov./Dec. 1998), pp. 65–67.

[15] Albright, D., 'The shots heard 'round the world', *Bulletin of the Atomic Scientists*, vol. 54, no. 4 (July/Aug. 1998), pp. 20–25.

[16] Wallace (note 12), pp. 386–93; and Barker, B. *et al.*, 'Monitoring nuclear tests', *Science,* vol. 281, no. 5385 (25 Sep. 1998), pp. 1967–68.

Pakistani authorities, perhaps for political reasons, did not announce the true yields of the tests. Neither India nor Pakistan has provided any additional information about the tests. They may have exaggerated the yields on purpose or announced the expected yields, even if the explosions did not work as well as planned. Another explanation is that the environment of the tests may have weakened the signals.

The fact that not all the announced explosions were detected raised questions about the CTBT verification capabilities, especially among those critical of the treaty.[17] None of the IMS seismological, radionuclide, hydroacoustic or infrasound systems called for by the CTBT[18] is yet complete, but the seismological network is the most developed. When fully operational it will include 50 primary stations continuously transmitting data and 120 auxiliary stations which transmit data upon request by the International Data Centre (IDC) in Vienna. Most scientists agree that the seismological system in fact worked well and will work even better in the area if or when India and Pakistan decide to adhere to the CTBT and provide seismic stations on their territories for the international monitoring network. The IMS provided effective and timely data for the 11, 28 and 30 May tests, and even though there was high background noise from a large earthquake that occurred in Afghanistan 30 minutes before the 30 May test the explosion was not screened out. One conclusion is that the contradictory reports from the events just illustrate that different kinds of monitoring are needed, as seismic data alone may not be enough to tell whether small or muffled events are natural or not.

Both Indian and Pakistani authorities gave assurances that all the tests were fully contained and that they did not leak into the atmosphere. However, based upon US laboratories' examination of air samples collected by high-flying aircraft US intelligence reports indicated that low levels of plutonium were present in the air after the 30 May test. The results of the analysis of the samples were included in a classified report.[19]

Satellite monitoring is not included in the CTBT verification machinery, but according to Article IV.5 states parties are free to use and exchange information obtained by national technical means of verification. Suspicious activities such as drilling and digging in certain areas may indicate preparations for nuclear testing. In late 1995 US intelligence agencies detected preparations for testing at the Pokhran test site[20] and confronted the Indian Government with this information. The planned tests were cancelled at that time, but the Bharatiya Janata Party (BJP) Government quietly resumed work on the test programme after coming to power in March 1998. This time the preparations were better concealed and much of the work had already been done in 1995. Consequently, its nature was not recognized by intelligence analysts, who operated on the assumption that there would be no major change to the nuclear status quo in south Asia. Even though the preparations for the Pakistani tests took only seven to eight days, they were still detected by US intelligence.[21]

[17] van der Vink (note 7).

[18] Article IV, para. B.16 of the CTBT. The text of the 1996 Comprehensive Nuclear Test-Ban Treaty is reproduced in *SIPRI Yearbook 1997: Armaments, Disarmament and International Security* (Oxford University Press: Oxford, 1997), pp. 414–31.

[19] Priest, D., 'US labs at odds on whether Pakistani blast used plutonium', *Washington Post*, 17 Jan. 1999.

[20] Gupta, V. and Pabian, F., 'Investigating the allegations of Indian nuclear test preparations in the Rajasthan desert', *Science & Global Security*, vol. 6 (1997), pp. 101–88.

[21] Albright (note 15).

III. Environmental consequences of nuclear explosions

In 1993–98 International Atomic Energy Agency (IAEA) missions assessed the radiological situation at three former nuclear test sites: the Bikini Atoll in the Marshall Islands, where the USA conducted nuclear tests in 1946–58; the Semipalatinsk area, in north-eastern Kazakhstan, where the Soviet Union conducted tests in 1949–89; and the Mururoa and Fangataufa atolls in French Polynesia, which were the sites for the French tests in 1966–1996.

Twenty-three tests were conducted on and around the Bikini Atoll, all atmospheric or carried out on the surface of the ground. A number of radiological surveys have since been carried out on the atoll to investigate whether it would be safe for the inhabitants who were evacuated before the USA started its series of tests in the area to return. As a result, 139 Bikini islanders moved back in the beginning of the 1970s, but they remained unconvinced of the safety of their environment. After additional radiological data had been evaluated, the 139 people were relocated to other atolls. Further studies continued the evaluation of the radiological situation, and in 1997 the IAEA sent an environmental monitoring team to the atoll to conduct environmental measurements and sampling to assess the reliability of the data collected by previous studies. The earlier data were verified and it was recommended that the Bikini Atoll should not be permanently resettled under the present radiological conditions.[22]

At the request of the Government of Kazakhstan the IAEA undertook three missions to the former test site in Semipalatinsk, in 1993, 1994 and 1998. Of the 456 nuclear tests conducted at this test site, 116 were conducted in the atmosphere. Radiological data from the area were collected to evaluate the present and potential future doses to residents. In compliance with a UN General Assembly Resolution of December 1997,[23] the third mission also examined the humanitarian situation in the area. The results of the investigations indicated elevated residual radioactivity levels in areas where surface tests were performed and where a few underground tests leaked to the atmosphere. Remedial measures are considered necessary for these areas, but because of budgetary constraints it is suggested that the most appropriate action would be to restrict access to these areas.[24]

A study of the radiological situation at Mururoa and Fangataufa, two inhabited atolls in French Polynesia, was released by the IAEA in May 1998.[25] France conducted 193 nuclear weapon tests on and around these atolls—46 in the atmosphere and 147 underground. In 1995 France had requested the IAEA to undertake a study to assess the radiological situation after the cessation of testing at the atolls and to evaluate the expected future consequences. It was found that there were still low concentrations of radioactive material in the accessible environment of the atolls. The sediments in the lagoons contained several kilograms of residual plutonium, and elevated levels of caesium-137 remained in small areas of the atolls. However, the study concluded that the radiological significance of the findings was limited. The residual radioactive material was not expected to have any health effects that could be

[22] Stegnar, P., 'Review at Bikini Atoll. Assessing radiological conditions at Bikini Atoll and the prospects for resettlement', *IAEA Bulletin*, vol. 40, no. 4 (1998), pp. 15–17.

[23] UN General Assembly Resolution 52/169M, 16 Dec. 1997.

[24] IAEA, Radiological Assessment Reports Series, *Radiological Conditions at the Semipalatinsk Test Site, Kazakhstan: Preliminary Assessment and Recommendations for Further Study* (IAEA: Vienna, 1998).

[25] IAEA, Radiological Assessment Reports Series, *The Radiological Situation at the Atolls of Mururoa and Fangataufa: Main Report* (IAEA: Vienna, 1998).

medically diagnosed in an individual or epidemiologically discerned in a group of people. The study also assessed the implications of the residual radioactivity for the local biota and concluded that they would not be affected. It was suggested that an environmental monitoring programme might be useful to reassure the public about environmental safety.[26]

IV. Announced subcritical experiments

During the CTBT negotiations it was understood by all states that so-called subcritical experiments would continue even after the treaty was signed. Subcritical experiments use conventional high explosives to create high pressures on nuclear weapon material, but the material is not allowed to become subcritical with fast neutrons. Before it signed the treaty the USA declared its intention to continue conducting these experiments to gather data for improved computer simulations of nuclear performance, to ensure that its nuclear stockpile did not deteriorate and to maintain the skills of the relevant experts should the CTBT fail and nuclear weapon test explosions resume. US subcritical tests are conducted underground at the Nevada Test Site. Since they do not produce seismic signals, they are not detected by seismological stations.

The USA conducted two subcritical experiments in 1997 and three in 1998. All these events were announced by the US Department of Energy (DOE). On each occasion protests were raised by activist groups claiming that, although subcritical tests are not explicitly forbidden by the CTBT,[27] they violate the spirit and aims of the treaty because they may contribute to the improvement of weapon designs. However, others argue that at least one critical explosion is needed to certify the reliability of a nuclear weapon design.

The Russian Ministry of Atomic Energy (Minatom) has declared that Russia has been carrying out subcritical tests (hydrodynamic experiments) since 1995 at its test site on Novaya Zemlya. Between 14 September and 13 December 1998 five subcritical tests were conducted there.[28] Individual experiments have not been announced.[29]

[26] France formally disbanded its agency responsible for nuclear testing on 23 June 1998, and closed its test site in Polynesia on 31 July, becoming the first declared nuclear weapon state to close a nuclear test site.

[27] The CTBT, in its Preamble, only recognizes that 'the cessation of all nuclear weapon test explosions and all other nuclear explosions, by constraining the development and qualitative improvement of nuclear weapons and ending the development of advanced new types of nuclear weapons constitutes an effective measure of nuclear disarmament and non-proliferation in all its aspects.' CTBT (note 18).

[28] Associated Press, 'Russia admits to five subcritical nuclear tests', 24 Dec. 1998.

[29] Romanenkova, V., ITAR-TASS (Moscow), 25 Sep. 1998, in 'Russia: Minister denies preparations for nuclear explosions', Foreign Broadcast Information Service, *Daily Report–Central Eurasia (FBIS-SOV)*, FBIS-SOV-98-268, 28 Sep. 1998; and Yurkin, A., ITAR-TASS (Moscow), 25 Dec. 1998, in 'Russia: Russian nuclear ministry comments on Novaya Zemlya tests', Foreign Broadcast Information Service, *Daily Report–Arms Control (FBIS-TAC)*, FBIS-TAC-98-359, 30 Dec. 1998.

V. About the tables

The tables in this appendix list all nuclear explosions, including nuclear tests conducted in nuclear weapon test programmes, explosions carried out for peaceful purposes and the two nuclear bombs dropped on Hiroshima and Nagasaki in August 1945. The totals also include French, Soviet and US experiments (not British) conducted for safety purposes, irrespective of the yield and irrespective of whether or not they caused a nuclear explosion.[30] The tables do not include subcritical experiments.

Simultaneous detonations, sometimes called salvo explosions, were carried out both by the USA (from 1963) and the Soviet Union (from 1965), mainly for economic reasons.[31] Twenty per cent of the Soviet and 6 per cent of the US tests were salvo experiments. In defining a nuclear test for its tables SIPRI uses the definition of the 1990 Protocol to the 1974 Threshold Test Ban Treaty (TTBT), which states that a test is either a single nuclear explosion conducted at a test site 'or two or more nuclear explosions conducted at a test site within an area delineated by a circle having a diameter of two kilometers and conducted within a total period of time of 0.1 second'.[32] That definition has also been used by the DOE and the Russian Minatom.[33] For the Indian detonations on 11 May the precise data to determine whether they should be counted as one or two tests, according to the TTBT definition, are not yet available. On the basis of available information one test is listed. The explosions announced by India on 13 May are also counted as one test, as are Pakistan's five explosions on 28 May.

[30] In a safety experiment, or a safety trial, more or less fully developed nuclear devices are subject to simulated accident conditions. The nuclear weapon core is destroyed by conventional explosives with no or very small releases of fission energy. Safety experiments were carried out in the atmosphere and underground.

[31] On 2 occasions the USSR conducted simultaneous tests including as many as 8 devices: on 23 Aug. 1975 and on 24 Oct. 1990 (the last Soviet test).

[32] The 1990 Protocol to the1974 Treaty between the USA and the USSR on the Limitation of Underground Nuclear Weapon Tests (Threshold Test Ban Treaty, TTBT), Section I, para. 2. The relevant excerpts from the Protocol are reproduced in *SIPRI Yearbook 1991: World Armaments and Disarmament* (Oxford University Press: Oxford, 1991), p. 547. For peaceful nuclear explosions SIPRI uses for its tables the definition of the 1976 Treaty between the USA and the USSR on Underground Nuclear Explosions for Peaceful Purposes (Peaceful Nuclear Explosions Treaty, PNET). It defines an explosion (Article II.a) as 'any individual or group underground nuclear explosion for peaceful purposes' and a 'group explosion' (Article II.c) as 'two or more individual explosions for which the time interval between successive individual explosions does not exceed five seconds and for which the emplacement points of all explosives can be interconnected by straight line segments, each of which joins two emplacement points and each of which does not exceed 40 kilometres'. For the text of the PNET see Goldblat, J., SIPRI, *Agreements for Arms Control: A Critical Survey* (Taylor & Francis: London, 1982), pp. 218–27.

[33] Ministry of the Russian Federation for Atomic Energy and Ministry of Defense of the Russian Federation, *USSR Nuclear Weapons Tests and Peaceful Nuclear Explosions, 1949 through 1990* (Russian Federal Nuclear Center–All-Russian Research Institute of Experimental Physics (VNIIEF): Sarov, 1996).

Table 12B.1. Nuclear explosions in 1998

Date	Origin time (GMT)	Latitude (degrees)	Longitude (degrees)	Region	Body wave magnitude[a]
India					
11 May	10.13.44.2	27.07 N	71.76 E	Pokhran	5.3
13 May	06.51	27.078 N	71.719 E	Pokhran	
Pakistan					
28 May	10.16.17.6	28.90 N	64.89 E	Chagai	5.1
30 May	06.54.57.1	28.49 N	63.78 E	Kharan	5.0

[a] Body wave magnitude (m_b) indicates the size of the event. In order to be able to give a reasonably correct estimate of the yield it is necessary to have detailed information, e.g., on the geological conditions of the area where the test is conducted. Giving the m_b figure in this table is therefore an unambiguous way of listing the size of an explosion. Location and m_b data for the tests were provided by the Swedish National Defence Research Establishment (FOA).

Table 12B.2. Estimated number of nuclear explosions, 1945–98

a = atmospheric (or in a few cases under water); u = underground.

	USA[a]		USSR/Russia		UK[a]		France		China		India		Pakistan		
Year	a	u	a	u	a	u	a	u	a	u	a	u	a	u	Total
1945	3	–	–	–	–	–	–	–	–	–	–	–	–	–	**3**
1946	2[b]	–	–	–	–	–	–	–	–	–	–	–	–	–	**2**
1947	–	–	–	–	–	–	–	–	–	–	–	–	–	–	–
1948	3	–	–	–	–	–	–	–	–	–	–	–	–	–	**3**
1949	–	–	1	–	–	–	–	–	–	–	–	–	–	–	**1**
1950	–	–	–	–	–	–	–	–	–	–	–	–	–	–	–
1951	15	1	2	–	–	–	–	–	–	–	–	–	–	–	**18**
1952	10	–	–	–	1	–	–	–	–	–	–	–	–	–	**11**
1953	11	–	5	–	2	–	–	–	–	–	–	–	–	–	**18**
1954	6	–	10	–	–	–	–	–	–	–	–	–	–	–	**16**
1955	17[b]	1	6[b]	–	–	–	–	–	–	–	–	–	–	–	**24**
1956	18	–	9	–	6	–	–	–	–	–	–	–	–	–	**33**
1957	27	5	16[b]	–	7	–	–	–	–	–	–	–	–	–	**55**
1958	62[c]	15	34	–	5	–	–	–	–	–	–	–	–	–	**116**
1959	–	–	–	–	–	–	–	–	–	–	–	–	–	–	–[d]
1960	–	–	–	–	–	–	3	–	–	–	–	–	–	–	**3**[d]
1961	–	10	58[b]	1	–	–	1	1	–	–	–	–	–	–	**71**[d]
1962	39[b]	57	78	1	–	2	–	1	–	–	–	–	–	–	**178**
1963[e]	4	43	–	–	–	–	–	3	–	–	–	–	–	–	**50**
1964	–	45	–	9	–	2	–	3	1	–	–	–	–	–	**60**
1965	–	38	–	14	–	1	–	4	1	–	–	–	–	–	**58**
1966	–	48	–	18	–	–	6	1	3	–	–	–	–	–	**76**
1967	–	42	–	17	–	–	3	–	2	–	–	–	–	–	**64**
1968	–	56	–	17	–	–	5	–	1	–	–	–	–	–	**79**
1969	–	46	–	19	–	–	–	–	1	1	–	–	–	–	**67**

Year	USA[a]		USSR/Russia		UK[a]		France		China		India		Pakistan		Total
	a	u	a	u	a	u	a	u	a	u	a	u	a	u	
1970	–	39	–	16	–	–	8	–	1	–	–	–	–	–	**64**
1971	–	24	–	23	–	–	5	–	1	–	–	–	–	–	**53**
1972	–	27	–	24	–	–	4	–	2	–	–	–	–	–	**57**
1973	–	24	–	17	–	–	6	–	1	–	–	–	–	–	**48**
1974	–	22	–	21	–	1	9	–	1	–	–	1	–	–	**55**
1975	–	22	–	19	–	–	–	2	–	1	–	–	–	–	**44**
1976	–	20	–	21	–	1	–	5	3	1	–	–	–	–	**51**
1977	–	20	–	24	–	–	–	9	1	–	–	–	–	–	**54**
1978	–	19	–	31	–	2	–	11	2	1	–	–	–	–	**66**
1979	–	15	–	31	–	1	–	10	1	–	–	–	–	–	**58**
1980	–	14	–	24	–	3	–	12	1	–	–	–	–	–	**54**
1981	–	16	–	21	–	1	–	12	–	–	–	–	–	–	**50**
1982	–	18	–	19	–	1	–	10	–	1	–	–	–	–	**49**
1983	–	18	–	25	–	1	–	9	–	2	–	–	–	–	**55**
1984	–	18	–	27	–	2	–	8	–	2	–	–	–	–	**57**
1985	–	17	–	10	–	1	–	8	–	–	–	–	–	–	**36**[f]
1986	–	14	–	–	–	1	–	8	–	–	–	–	–	–	**23**[f]
1987	–	14	–	23	–	1	–	8	–	1	–	–	–	–	**47**[f]
1988	–	15	–	16	–	–	–	8	–	1	–	–	–	–	**40**
1989	–	11	–	7	–	1	–	9	–	–	–	–	–	–	**28**
1990	–	8	–	1	–	1	–	6	–	2	–	–	–	–	**18**
1991	–	7	–	–	–	1	–	6	–	–	–	–	–	–	**14**
1992	–	6	–	–	–	–	–	–	–	2	–	–	–	–	**8**[g]
1993	–	–	–	–	–	–	–	–	–	1	–	–	–	–	**1**[g]
1994	–	–	–	–	–	–	–	–	–	2	–	–	–	–	**2**[g]
1995	–	–	–	–	–	–	–	5	–	2	–	–	–	–	**7**[g]
1996	–	–	–	–	–	–	–	1	–	2	–	–	–	–	**3**
1997	–	–	–	–	–	–	–	–	–	–	–	–	–	–	**0**
1998	–	–	–	–	–	–	–	–	–	–	–	2	–	2	**4**
Subtotal	217	815	219	496	21	24	50	160	23	22	–	3	–	2	2 052
Total	**1 032**		**715**		**45**		**210**		**45**		**3**		**2**		**2 052**

[a] All British tests from 1962 were conducted jointly with the USA at the Nevada Test Site, so the number of US tests is actually higher than indicated here. The British Labour Government observed a unilateral moratorium on testing in 1965–74.

[b] One of these tests was carried out under water.

[c] Two of these tests were carried out under water.

[d] The UK, the USA and the USSR observed a moratorium on testing in the period Nov. 1958–Sep. 1961.

[e] On 5 Aug. 1963 the USA, the USSR and the UK signed the Partial Test Ban Treaty (PTBT), prohibiting nuclear explosions in the atmosphere, in outer space and under water.

[f] The USSR observed a unilateral moratorium on testing in the period Aug. 1985–Feb. 1987.

[g] The USSR observed a moratorium on testing from Jan. 1991 and the USA from Oct. 1992; France observed a moratorium in the period Apr. 1992–Sep. 1995.

Sources for tables 12B.1–12B.2

Swedish National Defence Research Establishment (FOA), various estimates, including information from the prototype International Data Center (IDC); Reports from the Australian

Seismological Centre, Australian Geological Survey Organisation, Canberra; US Department of Energy (DOE), *United States Nuclear Tests: July 1945 through September 1992* (DOE: Washington, DC, 1994); Norris, R. S., Burrows, A. S. and Fieldhouse, R. W., 'British, French and Chinese nuclear weapons', *Nuclear Weapons Databook, Vol. V* (Natural Resources Defense Council [NRDC]: Washington, DC, 1994); Direction des centres d'experimentations nucléaires [DIRCEN] and Commissariat à l'Energie Atomique [CEA], *Assessment of French Nuclear Testing* (DIRCEN and CEA: Paris, 1998); Ministry of the Russian Federation for Atomic Energy and Ministry of Defense of the Russian Federation, *USSR Nuclear Weapons Tests and Peaceful Nuclear Explosions, 1949 through 1990* (Russian Federal Nuclear Center–All-Russian Research Institute of Experimental Physics (VNIIEF): Sarov, 1996); and 'NRDC nuclear notebook: Known nuclear tests worldwide, 1945–98', *Bulletin of the Atomic Scientists,* vol. 54, no. 6 (Nov./Dec. 1998).

13. Chemical and biological weapon developments and arms control

JEAN PASCAL ZANDERS, ELISABETH M. FRENCH and NATALIE PAUWELS

I. Introduction

The 1993 Chemical Weapons Convention (CWC) seems well on track to becoming a strong, near-universal disarmament treaty. States parties must overcome many technical problems and on some issues face a steep learning curve. Nevertheless, provided the political will is present and the willingness to cooperate remains, the CWC will achieve its most important disarmament goals. Destruction of chemical weapons (CW) and former CW-related facilities is under way. However, Russia's persistent economic, social and political difficulties continue to raise questions about its ability to destroy the world's largest declared CW stockpile.

The experience of the first 20 months after entry into force of the CWC should generate confidence that a protocol to strengthen the 1972 Biological and Toxin Weapons Convention (BTWC) regime is feasible. Although political momentum to support the protocol is building, a workable and credible consensus between security and economic matters remains to be achieved between the governments of the parties to the BTWC and their biotechnological industries. Progress in the negotiations was therefore modest and the conclusion of such a document is not expected before 2000.[1]

Despite progress in efforts to implement the CWC and strengthen the BTWC regime, the proliferation of chemical and biological weapons (CBW) continued to be a cause of concern. Major policy programmes to prevent or reverse CBW proliferation as well as measures to counter terrorist use of CBW are being implemented. In a year of rapidly escalating crises Iraq suspended the activities of the inspectors of the United Nations Special Commission on Iraq (UNSCOM). By the end of 1998 the continued existence of UNSCOM in its current form was in doubt in view of the deep divisions within the United Nations Security Council.

Section II of this chapter deals with the implementation of the CWC, the efforts to destroy CW in Russia and the United States, and the programmes of several parties to the CWC to dispose of old and abandoned chemical weapons. The negotiations to strengthen the BTWC disarmament regime are discussed in section III. Sections IV and V deal with CBW proliferation concerns and UNSCOM's activities in Iraq, respectively. Section VI deals with

[1] A brief summary of both conventions and lists of parties are given in annexe A in this volume. Full texts are available at the SIPRI CBW Project web site, URL <http://www.sipri.se/cbw>.

the issue of chemical and biological terrorism. Section VII presents the conclusions. Appendix 13A discusses the benefits and threats of developments in biotechnology and genetic engineering.

II. Chemical weapon disarmament

Implementing the CWC

The CWC entered into force on 29 April 1997. By 31 December 1998, 121 states had become parties and an additional 48 states had signed the convention.[2] Twenty-three members of the United Nations have neither signed nor ratified the CWC.[3] None of the countries of greatest concern in Asia or the Middle East moved to join the treaty.[4] Africa remains the most under-represented continent. As of January 1999, 90 parties had submitted their initial declarations and 85 parties had also informed the Organisation for the Prohibition of Chemical Weapons (OPCW) in The Hague of their National Authority.[5] OPCW inspectors have completed 384 inspections in 28 countries since entry into force of the CWC.[6] In November 1998 the Third Conference of States Parties (CSP) was held in The Hague.

In 1998 several representatives of non-governmental organizations criticized the slow pace at which the CWC provisions are being implemented.[7] Several parties failed to meet one or more of the many deadlines in the CWC, especially those for the submission of initial declarations and other required notifications. Other parties provided the OPCW with partial or incomplete information.[8] However, the delays can often be accounted for by the complexity of the convention, the relatively short time-frames of many provisions, the unfamiliarity of some parties with its provisions and difficulty in obtaining the required information from the industry and other relevant bodies of a party. The Technical Secretariat (TS) of the OPCW has implemented a programme

[2] Botswana, Burundi, Cyprus, Gambia, Indonesia, Lithuania, Malawi, Mauritania, Panama, Senegal, Tanzania, Ukraine and Viet Nam became parties in 1998.

[3] Andorra, Angola, Antigua and Barbuda, Barbados, Belize, Egypt, Eritrea, Iraq, Kiribati, Korea (North), Lebanon, Libya, Mozambique, Palau, Sao Tome and Principe, Solomon Islands, Somalia, Sudan, Syria, Tonga, Tuvalu, Vanuatu, and Yugoslavia (Serbia and Montenegro).

[4] The reasons certain Middle Eastern countries are reluctant to sign or ratify the CWC are discussed in Zanders, J. P. and French, E. M., 'Article XI of the Chemical Weapons Convention: between irrelevance and indispensability', *Contemporary Security Policy*, vol. 20, no. 1 (Apr. 1999), pp. 72–74.

[5] 'News in Brief', *OPCW Synthesis*, no. 1 (1999), p. 10.

[6] As of 11 Jan. 1999, these comprise 9 inspections of abandoned CW sites, 82 inspections of CW destruction facilities, 95 inspections of CW production facilities, 57 inspections of CW storage facilities, 19 inspections of old CW sites, 37 inspections of Schedule 1 facilities, 72 inspections of Schedule 2 facilities and 13 inspections of Schedule 3 facilities. 'An inspection team at work', *OPCW Synthesis* (note 5), p. 9.

[7] Kelle, A., 'Assessing the first year of the Chemical Weapons Convention', *Nonproliferation Review*, vol. 5, no. 3 (spring/summer 1998), pp. 27–35; Leklem, E. J., 'At one year, CWC progress tempered by limited transparency', *Arms Control Today*, vol. 28, no. 3 (Apr. 1998), pp. 27–28; Smithson, A. E., *Rudderless: The Chemical Weapons Convention at 1 1/2*, report no. 25 (Henry L. Stimson Center: Washington, DC, Sep. 1998); and Kelle, A., 'Business as usual in implementing the CWC? Not quite yet!', *Disarmament Diplomacy*, no. 32 (Nov. 1998), pp. 8–12.

[8] Note by the Director-General: status of initial declarations and notifications, OPCW Conference of the States Parties document C-III/DG.11, 13 Nov. 1998.

to help parties prepare their submissions and, in many cases, views the missing of these deadlines as a technical problem that can be resolved in the near future.[9]

Also of concern is the non-payment or partial payment of the assessed contributions to the OPCW,[10] which can seriously hamper the inspections and other activities of the TS, and the difficulties in reaching agreement on certain practical issues of implementation. One example is the request by some parties for access to the notebooks and other data recorded by inspectors. This may seriously affect the unbiased and independent nature of the inspection records since during the subsequent debriefing session the inspectors may come under intense pressure to delete some information. The CWC is ambiguous on the matter of whether the inspected state may have access to the inspectors' data. It states that the papers, correspondence and records of inspection teams enjoy diplomatic immunity,[11] but it also permits a party to receive copies, at its request, of the information and data gathered about its facilities and requires the inspection team to provide the inspected party with a preliminary report of its findings.[12] Although custom in international law would dictate that the issue be resolved in the spirit of the CWC—upholding the inviolability of the notebooks—the Executive Council (EC) of the OPCW requested the Director-General to instruct inspection team leaders to provide copies of the content of the notebooks at the end of an inspection if requested by the inspected state.[13]

The question of the transfer of saxitoxin, a powerful neurotoxin produced by certain dinoflagellates, was also the subject of complex discussions. Saxitoxin is listed in Schedule 1 of the CWC, which means that it can only be produced in limited quantities for certain specified uses, including medical and pharmaceutical purposes.[14] It causes paralytic shellfish poisoning in humans. It is used in extremely small quantities (5 micrograms) in kits for medical and diagnostic tests and for research purposes. Only Canada and the USA are known to produce saxitoxin (less than a total of 10 grams per year), although milligram quantities are transferred from Canada to the United Kingdom for tritiation and then re-exported for physiological research.[15] The CWC's notification requirements for the transfer of Schedule 1 chemicals cause delays in the delivery of the medical kits to a state party (or restocking them) at short

[9] Gee, J. (Deputy Director-General, OPCW), 'Implementing the CWC: the first year', *The Arena*, no. 8 (Chemical and Biological Arms Control Institute: Alexandria, Va., July 1998), pp. 3, 6.

[10] As of 6 Nov., 50 of the then 119 parties had paid their contributions in full; an additional 21 parties had paid partially; and the remaining 48 parties had not paid. Report by the Director-General: status of assessed contributions as of 6 November 1998, OPCW Conference of the States Parties document C-III/DG.10, 13 Nov. 1998.

[11] CWC, Verification Annex Part II, para. 11 (a).

[12] CWC, Verification Annex Part II, paras 50, 60.

[13] Feakes, D., 'Developments in the Organisation for the Prohibition of Chemical Weapons', *CBW Conventions Bulletin*, no. 39 (Mar. 98), p. 15; and Smithson (note 7), pp. 30–32.

[14] CWC, Verification Annex Part VI, para. 2. The production, withdrawal from CW stocks or transfer of Schedule 1 chemicals is limited to an annual aggregate amount of 1 tonne.

[15] Sutherland, R., 'Saxitoxin and the Chemical Weapons Convention', Paper presented to the OPCW Seminar on Saxitoxin, The Hague, 23–24 Sep. 1998, p. 3.

notice; non-parties are not allowed to purchase the kits.[16] Moreover, Schedule 1 chemicals cannot be retransferred to a third state party, which poses problems for the export of tritiated saxitoxin from the UK.[17] A seminar on saxitoxin was organized in The Hague on 23–24 September 1998, and the issue was also raised at the first meeting of the Scientific Advisory Board of the OPCW. Based on these reports, on 9 October the EC took an interim decision of limited duration (270 days) on the transfer (but not retransfer) of saxitoxin.[18] A definitive solution, however, requires amendment of the CWC, and Canada has submitted proposals to that effect.[19]

Although other problems exist, notable progress was made on the model facility agreements for Schedule 1 and Schedule 2 facilities, which will facilitate a more standardized inspection of these installations.[20] In addition, end-user certificates for transfer of Schedule 2 and 3 chemicals to non-parties must be issued by the competent government authority of the non-party rather than by the recipient trader or trading house.[21] Implementation of the CWC may prove to be politically more arduous and technically more challenging than the negotiators anticipated, but a relatively strong disarmament regime is nonetheless emerging.

In the USA domestic legislation for implementing the CWC was not signed into law until 28 October 1998.[22] Consequently, the US Government was unable to collect the required industry declarations for submission to the OPCW. This, in turn, prevented OPCW inspections of US industry facilities. Furthermore, the USA could not declare its National Authority; at the end of 1998 implementation policies were still causing practical problems for the US chemical industry.[23] The delays led to severe criticism by OPCW Director-General José M. Bustani and by several European states that have undergone a

[16] Both parties involved in the transfer of a Schedule 1 chemical must notify the TS 30 days prior to the transaction and each party must make detailed annual declarations regarding transfers during the previous year. CWC, Verification Annex part VI, paras 5 and 6. Canada noted that an additional delay of at least 10 days must be taken into account to obtain an export licence from the National Authority. Sutherland (note 15), p. 2.

[17] CWC, Verification Annex, part VI, para. 4.

[18] 'Saxitoxin: the notification dimension of access', note accompanying Proposal for a change pursuant to paragraphs 4 and 5 of Article XV of the Convention, to address Part VI of the Annex on Implementation and Verification, Section B, paragraph 5, submitted by Canada, 13 Nov. 1998, para. 6, document distributed at the Seminar on Saxitoxin, The Hague, 23–24 Sep. 1998.

[19] Proposal for a change . . . (note 18); and Proposal for a change pursuant to paragraphs 4 and 5 of Article XV of the Convention, to address Part VI of the Annex on Implementation and Verification, Section B, paragraph 4, submitted by Canada jointly with the United Kingdom of Great Britain and Northern Ireland, 13 Nov. 1998, document distributed at the Seminar on Saxitoxin, The Hague, 23–24 Sep. 1998.

[20] Decision: model facility agreement for Schedule 1 facilities, OPCW Executive Council document EC-XII/DEC.1, 9 Oct. 1998; and Decision: model facility agreement for Schedule 2 plant sites, OPCW Executive Council document EC-XI/DEC.4, 4 Sep. 1998. The decisions were approved at the 3rd CSP.

[21] Decision: paragraph 32 of part VII and paragraph 26 of Part VIII of the Verification Annex of the Convention, OPCW Executive Council document EC-IX/DEC.11, 24 Apr. 1998. The decision was approved at the 3rd CSP.

[22] Earle, R., 'United States implementation legislation', *OPCW Synthesis*, no. 1/99, p. 3. The legislation is S. 610 incorporated as Division I of the FY 1999 Omnibus Appropriations Act (H.R. 4328, P.L. 105-277).

[23] Ember, L., 'Getting to regulations', *Chemical and Engineering News*, vol. 77, no. 3 (18 Jan. 1999), p. 41.

disproportionate number of industry inspections, which is claimed to place their companies at a competitive disadvantage.[24] As a consequence, some European states parties to the CWC have been involved in 'interminable arguments over the minutiae of the draft programme and budget' for 1999, which has affected the work of the EC and the TS.[25] The US Senate ratified the CWC in April 1997 and attached 28 conditions, many of which are reflected in the domestic legislation. The president was authorized to refuse a challenge inspection on grounds of national security interests, and the removal of samples collected at US facilities on US territory for analysis was prohibited.[26] These conditions may set dangerous precedents for other nations, and serious concern about their impact on the strength of the disarmament regime was expressed by US supporters of the CWC, the OPCW and several states parties.[27]

Despite Russia's continuing economic and political difficulties and the significant devaluation of the rouble on 17 August,[28] the country remained formally committed to the CWC and the destruction of its CW arsenal. Russia supplied the OPCW with its initial declarations on 3 January 1998.[29] The initial inspections of all 24 declared CW production and 7 storage facilities were completed by August.[30] The internal problems nevertheless caused certain groups to question Russia's membership in the CWC. The Chairman of the Ecology Committee of the Duma, Tamara Zlotnikova, declared that it would be cheaper for Russia to preserve its CW stockpiles than to destroy them. She stated that ratification of the CWC was a mistake and noted that the Ecology Committee intended to make a motion for Russia's withdrawal from the CWC at the next plenary meeting of the Duma.[31] The Federal Government, however, adopted a resolution to accept proposals for changes in the implementation plan of the federal laws concerning ratification of the CWC and the destruction of chemical weapons.[32] Responsibility for CW issues and their destruction has been the task of the Committee on Conventional Problems of Chemical and Biological Weapons under President Boris Yeltsin. However, the resignation

[24] Statement by the Director-General to the Conference of the States Parties at its Third Session, OPCW Conference of the States Parties document C-III/DG.12, 16 Nov. 1998, p. 4; and Statement by Ambassador Alexander Christiani (Austria) on behalf of the European Union to the Third Conference of the States Parties, document distributed at the 3rd CSP, 16 Nov. 1998.

[25] Statement by the Director-General . . . (note 24);

[26] Earle (note 22).

[27] Statement by the Director-General . . . (note 24), pp. 2–3.

[28] See chapter 4 in this volume.

[29] Statement of the Delegation of the Russian Federation to the Third Conference of the States Parties, document distributed at the 3rd CSP.

[30] Statement of José M. Bustani, Director-General of the OPCW to the United Nations First Committee (Disarmament and International Security), 19 Oct. 1998, document distributed at the 3rd CSP.

[31] Kaliadin, A., 'Voprosi sobliudeniya Rossiei Konventsii o zapreshchenii khimicheskogo oruzhiya v usloviyax nedofinansirovaniya' [Issues of Russian compliance with the Chemical Weapons Convention without sufficient funding], Presentation to SIPRI Research Staff Collegium, 3 Dec. 1998; Ermolin, V., 'Khimicheskiye arsenali Rossii ostayutsiya netronutimi' [Russia's chemical arsenals remain untouched], *Izvestiya*, 22 Oct. 1998, p. 2; and Felgengauer, P., 'Chemical weapons will have to be liquidated already by another president', OPCW in the press: Nov. 1997–Nov. 1998, cited in *Segodnya*, 30 Oct. 1998.

[32] Resolution of the Government of the Russian Federation no. 673, 20 June 1998, *Rossiyskaya Gazeta*, 9 July 1998, p. 3; and '30 June', *CBW Conventions Bulletin*, no. 41 (Sep. 1998), p. 33.

on 29 December of its chairman, Pavel Syutkin, caused uncertainty about the future direction of the committee.[33]

In 1998 there continued to be calls in certain quarters in India and Pakistan for withdrawal from the CWC, in part because of fear that inspections might reveal secret information about the respective nuclear programmes. The military in India expressed concern over their lack of involvement in the way India declared its CW stockpile and vowed that in future they would play a greater role in the development of national security policy.[34] The Pakistani Parliament was bypassed when Pakistan ratified the CWC, which contributed to its constitutional crisis. Some alarmist reports claimed that India was not a party to the convention, that Pakistan's nuclear installations would be inspected by scores of OPCW inspectors or that India has a large contingent on the OPCW inspectorate.[35]

In the Middle East, arguably the region of greatest concern regarding CBW proliferation, no new states joined the CWC. Partly as a consequence of the faltering peace process and the internal instability of the government of Israeli Prime Minister Benjamin Netanyahu, the CWC (which Israel signed in 1993) was not ratified by Israel. The security questions involved in ratifying the CWC started an internal debate on the role of CW in Israel's deterrence posture. The CWC will prohibit the import by Israel of some key chemical compounds for its chemical industry from states parties as of April 2000. Opponents of ratification argued that the impact of this is overestimated and that trade restrictions are unlikely to be imposed.[36] At the Third Conference of the States Parties Iran submitted its declarations to the Technical Secretariat and admitted to an offensive CW production programme for deterrence purposes during the final years of the 1980–88 Iraq–Iran War. It claimed that after the end of the war the decision to acquire CW was reversed and the programme terminated.[37] The statement suggests that Iran did not use CW during the Iraq–Iran War. It is also understood that the Iranian declarations only include facilities and sites, not CW munitions.[38]

[33] ITAR-TASS World Service (Moscow), 29 Dec. 1998, in 'Russia: President Yeltsin relieves chief of CBW committee', Foreign Broadcast Information Service, *Daily Report–Arms Control (FBIS-TAC)*, FBIS-TAC-98-363, 30 Dec. 1998. No public statements were made concerning Syutkin's resignation; however, some political analysts believe the reason to be internal difficulties within the CW disarmament programme and the inability of the Russian Government to adequately fund CW demilitarization.

[34] Bedi, R., 'Eyes on Asia', *Jane's Defence Weekly*, vol. 29, no. 22 (3 June 1998), p. 43.

[35] '4 January', *CBW Conventions Bulletin*, no. 39 (Mar. 1998), p. 33; and Shahid, R., 'US attacks on Iraq and disclosure of Pakistan's signatures on CWC', *Pakistan* (Islamabad), 24 Dec. 1998, p. 10, in 'Pakistan: Paper slams Pakistan's signing of CWC', FBIS-TAC-98-361, 30 Dec. 1998.

[36] Steinberg, G., *The Chemical Weapons Convention in the Middle East: Israeli Ratification Dilemmas and Options*, MIT Security Studies Program seminar report (Center for International Studies, Massachusetts Institute of Technology: Cambridge, Mass., 9 Feb. 1998).

[37] Statement by Ambassador Mohammad R. Alborzi to the Third Conference of the States Parties, 16–20 Nov. 1998, document distributed at the 3rd CSP.

[38] According to information provided by a representative of Iran to the OPCW at the Third CSP, Iran destroyed its CW before the conclusion of the CWC negotiations in 1992.

Destruction of chemical weapons and related facilities

The United States

The United States possesses the world's second largest declared CW stockpile.[39] In 1998 CW destruction continued at the two operational disposal facilities, the Johnston Atoll Chemical Agent Disposal System (JACADS) and the Tooele Chemical Agent Disposal Facility (TOCDF). At JACADS a milestone was reached with the destruction of all sarin (1514 agent tons) at the site. It is to be closed in 2000.[40] As of January 1999, 2270 tonnes of chemical agent had been destroyed through incineration at the TOCDF.[41] Closure of the facility is scheduled for 2004.[42]

Construction work continued at the Umatilla Chemical Depot and completion is scheduled by April 2000.[43] Construction also progressed at the Anniston Chemical Agent Disposal Facility, and operations are slated to begin in 2001.[44] Construction of the Pine Bluff Chemical Disposal Facility was delayed pending approval from the Arkansas Department of Pollution Control and Ecology.[45]

The US CW destruction methods are high-temperature incineration and chemical neutralization. In addition to JACADS and TOCDF, incineration is also planned to be used at five other CW stockpile locations: Anniston, Blue Grass, Pine Bluff, Pueblo and Umatilla. Neutralization facilities are planned

[39] The CW stockpile, which originally totalled 31 495 agent tons, is stored at 9 locations: Anniston, Alabama; Blue Grass, Kentucky; Edgewood, Maryland; Newport, Indiana; Pine Bluff, Arkansas; Pueblo, Colorado; Tooele, Utah; Umatilla, Oregon, and Johnston Island in the Pacific Ocean.

Overall responsibility for the disposal of CW lies with the Program Manager for Chemical Demilitarization (PMCD). In Nov. 1998 the newly created US Army Soldier and Biological Chemical Command (SBCCOM) was assigned the main responsibility for the safe and secure storage of CW at the 8 US stockpile sites in the continental USA. Additional responsibilities include the remediation (soil detoxfication) of the Rocky Mountain Arsenal and the management of a DOD programme for Assembled Chemical Weapons Assessment, which attempts to find alternative solutions for destroying CW. SBCCOM was formed through the merger of 2 Materiel Commands, the US Army Chemical and Biological Defense Command (CBDCOM) and the US Army Soldier Systems Command (SSCOM). SBCCOM, 'About us fact sheet', URL <http://www.cbdcom.apgea.army.mil/sbccom/au_fs.html> and Tischbin, M., PMCD Outreach and Information Office, Aberdeen Proving Ground, Md., Private communication with E. M. French, 12 Mar. 1999.

[40] Chemical Stockpile Disposal Project, 'Chemical stockpile disposal milestone: the end of GB at JACADS', URL <http://www-pmcd.apgea.army.mil/text/CSDP/IP/FS/EndGB/index.html>.

[41] Chemical Stockpile Disposal Project, 'Tooele Chemical Agent Disposal Facility', 21 Jan. 1999, URL <http://www-pmcd.apgea.army.mil/text/CSDP/SL/DCD/index.html>; and *CBW Conventions Bulletin*, no. 42 (Dec. 1998), p. 30.

[42] Chemical Stockpile Disposal Project, 'Tooele Chemical Agent Disposal Facility' (note 41); and 'Five million pounds of GB nerve agent destroyed', URL <http://www-pmcd.apgea.army.mil/text/CSDP/IP/PR/1999/199901/19990/OSA/index.html>.

[43] Chemical Stockpile Disposal Project, 'Chemical weapons at Umatilla', URL <http://www-pmcd.apgea.army.mil/text/CSDP/IP/FS/CWUmatilla/index.html/>.

[44] Anniston stores sarin and VX in rockets, projectiles, land mines and bulk containers and distilled mustard in projectiles, mortars and bulk containers. Chemical Stockpile Disposal Project, 'Anniston Chemical Agent Disposal Facility', URL <http://www-pmcd.apgea.army.mil/text/CSDP/SL/ANCA/disposal.html>.

[45] Chemical Stockpile Disposal Project, 'Pine Bluff Chemical Agent Disposal Facility', URL <http://www-pmcd.apgea.army.mil/text/CSDP/SL/PBCA/index.html>.

for the stockpiles at Edgewood, and Newport.[46] At the Edgewood facility, distilled mustard will be mixed with hot water; at the Newport Chemical Depot, VX will be neutralized with sodium hydroxide.[47]

The army began the Alternative Technologies and Approaches Project to investigate technologies other than incineration for the destruction of bulk chemical warfare agents in 1994.[48] At the start of 1997, the Department of Defense (DOD) authorized the Program Manager for Chemical Demilitarization (PMCD) to pilot test the neutralization process at the Newport and Edgewood facilities. In late September 1998, the US Army announced a Record of Decision to pilot test neutralization followed by bio-treatment as the method of destruction for the mustard stockpile at Edgewood.[49] In addition, the Assembled Chemical Weapon Assessment Program examines technologies for the destruction of chemical munitions with assembled explosive components stored at the Blue Grass Chemical Activity and the Pueblo Chemical Depot.[50] In general, the evaluation of alternative technologies will extend the length of the original CW destruction schedule by an estimated five to seven years, but it will not affect the 2007 deadline set by the CWC. It will certainly have an impact on the cost of destruction, but a precise estimate is not possible at this time.[51]

Progress has also been achieved in the Non-Stockpile Materiel Program. As of November 1998, over 142 000 of the 201 728 M687 155-mm binary chemical shells at Umatilla and Tooele had been recycled. Demilitarization of other binary chemical munitions at Pine Bluff has not yet commenced.[52]

[46] Chemical Stockpile Disposal Project, 'A brief history of the Chemical Stockpile Disposal Program' URL <http://www-pmcd.apgea.army.mil/text/CSDP/IP/FS/History/index.html>

[47] Chemical Stockpile Disposal Project, 'How will chemical weapons be destroyed?', URL <http://www-pmcd.apgea.army.mil/text/CSDP/IP/FS/CWdestruction/index.html>.

[48] Citizen concern over the incineration process prompted the army to implement the Alternative Technologies and Approaches Project (ATAP) in 1994. Citizen involvement has continued to be an integral part of the destruction process in the USA. Citizens' Advisory Commissions were established at the stockpile locations in order to channel communication and information among local communities, state agencies and the army. Williams, C., 'US citizen stakeholders demand an end to chemical incineration; fund safe alternatives to destroy stockpile', 1998 International Chemical Weapons Demilitarisation Conference, Bournemouth, UK, 23–25 June 1998.

[49] ATAP Information Products, *Press Release*, no. 98-09, 29 Sep. 1998, URL <http://www-pmcd.apgea.army.mil/text/ATAP/IP/PR/1998/199809/19980929/index.html>. On 2 Oct. 1998 the US Army awarded the contract for the Aberdeen Chemical Agent Disposal Facility (ABCDF), which will destroy the mustard agent stockpile stored at the Edgewood site, to Bechtel National, Inc. The $306 million contract is for the design completion; construction; equipment procurement and installation, systemization; operation; and closure of the facility. ATAP Information Products Press Release, 'Army awards Aberdeen Chemical Agent Disposal Facility contract', URL <http://www-pmcd.apgea.army.mil/text/ATAP/IP/PR/1998/199810/19981002/index/html>.

[50] CSDP Information Products, 'Disposal program overview', URL <http://www-pmcd.apgea.army.mil/text/CSDP/IP/FS/overview/index.html>.

[51] CSDP Information Products, 'Factors impacting schedule and cost of the Chemical and Stockpile Disposal Program', URL <http://www-pmcd.apgea.army.mil/text/CSDP/IP/FS/Schedule&Cost/index.html>.

[52] '2 November', *CBW Conventions Bulletin*, no. 42 (Dec. 1998), p. 41.

The Russian Federation

Preparations and planning for the Russian CW destruction facilities continued in 1998 despite economic, social and political problems. The cost of destruction of the Russian CW stockpile, which contains approximately 40 000 agent tonnes, is estimated at $5.7 billion, or 34354.3 million roubles.[53] In 1998 only 5 per cent of the budgeted amount for CW destruction was actually provided. Timely destruction of the CW stockpile will be difficult, even with additional outside assistance.[54]

According to the CWC time lines, Russia should have destroyed 110 tonnes of CW agents in 1998, and 310 tonnes were forecast for 1999.[55] However, by the end of 1998, destruction of the agents had not yet begun. General Stanislav Petrov, commander of the Radiation, Chemical and Biological Defence Forces, expressed concern about the destruction time-frames. He stated that Russia lacks the necessary financial base to destroy its CW stockpile within the 10-year limit set in the CWC and suggested that it will need an additional 5 years. However, Lieutenant General Valery Kapashin, the director of the Russian chemical demilitarization programme, estimated that Russia may be able to accomplish its goals within an additional 2 years.[56]

In January the Russian Ministry of Defence placed an order worth 45 million roubles (approximately $7.26 million) with the Volga Machine and Building Works in order to construct a CW demilitarization plant at Gorny in Saratov oblast.[57] Acting on a proposal from the Ministry of Defence, the Federal Government issued a decree outlining the creation of a training centre for specialists involved in CW destruction. The facility is to be located at Chapayevsk, the site of the first Russian destruction installation, which did not become operational because of local opposition. Residents continue to suspect that the facility may be used for destruction purposes.[58] The foundation stone for the proposed CW destruction facility at Shchuchye was laid on 25 September. Assistance from the US Cooperative Threat Reduction (CTR) programme has been essential to the progress achieved in Shchuchye. It is now estimated that

[53] 'Problemi Rossii v realizatsii Konventsii po zapreshchenii khimicheskogo oruzhiya' [Russian problems in implementation of the Chemical Weapons Convention], Obshchestvennii Forum, Rossisskii Zeleni Krest (Green Cross Russia Public Forum), 4 Nov. 1998; Kaliadin (note 31). In May 1998 the cost of destruction of CW in Russia was estimated at $3.64 billion. '18 May', *CBW Conventions Bulletin*, no. 40 (June 1998), p. 37.

[54] SIPRI seminar with Duma member Alexei Arbatov, Stockholm, Sweden, 26 Nov. 1998.

[55] *Parlamentskaya Gazeta*, 26 Aug. 1998; and *Trud*, 1 Sep. 1998, cited in '30 June' (note 32).

[56] 'Russia needs aid to destroy chemical weapons', Radio Free Europe/Radio Liberty, *RFE/RL Newsline*, vol. 2 (19 May 1998); and Interfax (Moscow), 23 June 1998, in 'Russia: general warns of delay in destroying chemical weapons', Foreign Broadcast Information Service, *Daily Report–Central Eurasia (FBIS-SOV)*, FBIS-SOV-98-174, 25 June 1998. The 10-year period is to be counted from the entry into force of the CWC on 29 April 1997, not from the date the CWC enters into force for a particular country. In exceptional circumstances an extension of up to 5 years may be granted.

[57] Radio Rossii Network (Moscow), 19 Jan. 1998, in 'Russia: Volga gets contract for rigs to destroy chemical weapons', FBIS-TAC-98-019, 21 Jan. 1998.

[58] Decree of the Government of the Russian Federation, no. 171, 10 Feb. 1998, Moscow, *Rossiyskaya Gazeta*, 3 Mar. 1998; '10 February', *CBW Conventions Bulletin*, no. 40 (June 1998), p. 20; and Mikhailova, O., 'Chapayevsk: farewell to arms', *Trud*, 1 Sep. 1998, p. 2.

the entire CW demilitarization process at this site, from pre-design requirements to complete destruction of the weapons, will take 10 years.[59]

Destruction of two CW production facilities began in 1998 with US assistance. The Russian Government accepted $2.2 million in assistance to dismantle certain equipment and parts of buildings at the former CW production plant in Volgograd. Conversion of former CW production facilities remains a contentious issue. Russia successfully converted one former production facility for V agents, Khimprom Cheboksary in Chuvashia. The plant currently manufactures some 300 different chemical products for civilian consumers.[60] OPCW inspectors began their second stage of inspections at the facility in July 1998.[61]

Foreign assistance in 1998 for CW destruction was received from Germany, the Netherlands, Sweden and the USA and may in future also be provided by France, Italy, Norway and the UK.[62] Of the total amount of $464 million for fiscal year (FY) 1999, $88.4 million is designated for the Russian chemical demilitarization programme. In December 1998 the Netherlands and Russia signed a cooperation agreement. The Netherlands Government earmarked 10 million guilders (*c.* $5 million) to develop and deliver technology and equipment to build and operate a CW destruction facility near Kambarka. A maximum of 15 million guilders (*c.* $7.5 million) can be appropriated for future follow-on projects.[63] German assistance amounted to approximately DM 25.5 million worth ($14.25 million) of equipment.[64] Italy is reportedly planning to give $8 million for the creation of a social infrastructure (gas and water pipelines) and renovation of the regional hospital in Kizner, Udmurt Republic, one of the CW stockpile locations.[65] However, Russia has experienced difficulty in managing the assistance money offered, which may affect the willingness of donor states to contribute to the CW demilitarization programmes in future.[66]

Another former Soviet CW production facility, in Nukus, Uzbekistan, was also slated to be destroyed. The dismantling process was intended to be carried

[59] 'Rehabilitation of the territory first, the CWD facility thereafter', *Novy Mir Kurgan*, 12 Aug. 1998. The USA appropriated $382 million in CTR funds for FY 1998 and $464 million for FY1999.

[60] 'Khimprom Cheboksary: a turnaround story', *Capital Markets Report*, 4 Sep. 1998.

[61] 'News in brief', *Rossiyskaya Gazeta*, 23 July 1998, p. 2.

[62] On 25–27 Feb. a delegation from the Russian Defence Ministry met with the British Ministry of Defence to discuss CW destruction cooperation between the 2 countries. Bazhenov, S., ITAR-TASS World Service (Moscow), 25 Feb. 1998, in 'Russia: biological protection chief commences visit to UK', Foreign Broadcast Information Service, *Daily Report–Central Eurasia: Military Affairs (FBIS-UMA)*, FBIS-UMA-98-056, 3 Mar. 1998.

[63] 'Hulp Nederland bij opruimen wapens Rusland' [Help Netherlands with disposal weapons Russia], *De Limburger*, 21 Dec. 1998; and 'Foreign Ministry Press Briefing December 24, 1998', Federal Information Systems Corporation, Official Kremlin International News Broadcast, 24 Dec. 1998.

[64] '16 May', *CBW Conventions Bulletin*, no. 4 (June 1998), p. 37. EU Technical Assistance for the Commonwealth of Independent States (Tacis) funding for 2 Russian chemical demilitarization projects totals 5 million ECU.

[65] Bronshtein, B., 'Zelenii Krest: ozabochen khimicheskim oruzhuyem' [Green Cross: concerned about chemical weapons], *Izvestiya*, 30 May 1998, p. 2.

[66] Statement by Ambassador Alexander Christiani (note 24).

out by private corporations and is to be supported by US CTR funds for FY1999.[67]

Japan

Japan declared the facility where the religious sect Aum Shinrikyo manufactured the sarin used in its March 1995 attack in the Tokyo underground as a CW production plant. On 4 September 1998 the Executive Council of the OPCW approved combined destruction and verification plans, and Japan immediately began destruction operations. In December OPCW inspectors ensured that the factory had been completely destroyed and that no risks remain for the population.[68]

Old chemical weapons

According to figures from the French Ministry of Defence, France annually recovers 30–50 tonnes of old chemical weapons (OCW) along the World War I front line. The amount represents 10 per cent of all unearthed munitions. An additional 3–5 per cent comprises smoke, flare and incendiary devices. The current stockpile of chemical munitions consists of 146 tonnes or about 14 800 pieces of ammunition, located at three sites: Arras (112 tonnes), Laon (23 tonnes) and Metz (11 tonnes).[69] From these figures it is clear that France must have recently disposed of its entire stockpile of World War I chemical munitions. Until 1990 France destroyed such munitions near Le Crotoy in the Somme estuary.[70]

In 1997 France initiated the SECOIA programme[71] under the responsibility of the department for armaments, Délégation générale pour l'armement (DGA), of the Ministry of Defence. By November 1997, three competitors for

[67] Russian Federation Directive, no. 1817, 27 Dec. 1997, *Rossiyskaya Gazeta* (Moscow), 18 Feb. 1998, p. 6, in 'Russia: US aid to destroy Volgograd CW facility accepted', FBIS-TAC-98-049, 21 Feb. 1998; 'Sole source chemdemil tender withdrawn by US defense agency', *Post-Soviet Nuclear & Defense Monitor*, vol. 5 no. 1 (16 Jan. 1998), pp. 1–2; '18 October', *CBW Conventions Bulletin*, no. 42 (Dec. 1998), p. 38; 'Review of US assistance programs to Russia, Ukraine and the new independent states', Hearing before the Committee on International Relations House of Representatives, 105th Congress, 2nd session, 26 Mar. 1998 (US Government Printing Office: Washington, DC, 1998), pp. 125–29, 155–58; and National Defense Authorization Act for FY 1999, Public Law 105-261, H.R. 3616, reproduced in Thomas, US Congress on the Internet, 'Bill summary & status for the 105th Congress', URL <http://thomas.loc.gov/cgi-bin/bdquery/z?d105:h.r.03616:>.

[68] OPCW, 'OPCW team to verify destruction of religious sect "nerve gas factory" in Japan', OPCW *Press Release*, no. 034/98 (9 Dec. 1998); and *Kyodo* (Tokyo), 10 Dec. 1998, in 'Japan: international chemical weapons inspectors visit Aum site', FBIS-TAC-98-344, 14 Dec. 1998.

[69] d'Espagne, B., 'Status and treatment of old chemical weapons in France', 1998 International Chemical Weapons Demilitarisation Conference (note 48).

[70] The chemical munitions were placed in a large pit together with some explosives and covered with sand. At high tide the conventional charges were detonated. Under the combined weight of the covering sand and water an uncontrolled, high-temperature incineration process occurred, which destroyed the munitions. Vander Mast, A. (Sr Cpt), Private communication with J. P. Zanders, Bournemouth, 23 June 1998. France is also reported to have destroyed its CW shortly before signing the CWC in Jan. 1993. 'The desperate efforts to block the road to doomsday', *The Economist*, 6 June 1998, p. 22.

[71] Site d'élimination de chargement d'objets identifiés anciens; officially translated as: Site for elimination of oldest identified loaded objects.

the destruction project had been short-listed. In June 1998 they were informed of the contract specifications on the basis of which they must submit their final proposals. According to the timetable, one remaining competitor would begin the final conceptualization in September 1999. Construction of the facility will start in December 2000. Testing is envisaged for April 2002, and the facility should be fully operational by October 2002. Its processing capacity is specified to be 100 tonnes of CW per year (50–60 pieces of ammunition per day), so that the existing stockpile can be eliminated in 4–5 years.[72] The total cost is estimated at 300 million French francs.[73]

Belgium, like France, recovers large amounts of toxic munitions from World War I each year. A dismantling installation at Poelkapelle was completed in 1996. The re-identification of 'problem' munitions started in April 1998,[74] and the first dismantling tests with live munitions began in May. The installation is expected to be fully operational in 1999. The stockpile as of 31 December 1998 is 324.7 tonnes (26 722 projectiles). Each year an average of 17 tonnes (*c.* 1500 items) is added to the stockpile. The dismantling facility can theoretically process 3600 items per year, so the stockpile is expected to decrease annually by approximately 2100 projectiles. After 13 years, the stockpile (current OCW plus subsequently recovered munitions) should be destroyed.[75]

Abandoned chemical weapons

Under the CWC Japan has assumed full responsibility for the chemical munitions abandoned by it in China after World War II and will provide experts and all the financial, technical and other resources needed to destroy the abandoned chemical weapons (ACW). It will also construct the necessary destruction facilities. Based on data supplied by the Chinese authorities, 19 sites with an estimated total of 678 729 ACW have been identified.[76] The sites are scattered over a wide area in north-east China. They contain canisters, drums with bulk agent and shells of different calibres. The single largest location is in the Haerbaling area of Dunhua city, Jilin Province, with an estimated 674 000 pieces of ammunition in three burial sites.[77]

[72] d'Espagne (note 69).

[73] Isnard, J., 'La France va construire une usine de destruction d'armes chimiques' [France will construct a plant for the destruction of chemical weapons], *Le Monde*, 12 Feb. 1998.

[74] Problem munitions include all recovered World War I projectiles which cannot be positively identified as non-toxic on the basis of their external characteristics. During the re-identification process munitions are X-rayed to determine their content.

[75] Vander Mast, A. (Sr Cpt), 'The dismantling of chemical WW1 ammunition at Poelkapelle', 1998 International Chemical Weapons Demilitarisation Conference (note 48); and Vander Mast, A. (Sr Cpt), Letter to J. P. Zanders, 8 Jan. 1999.

[76] According to Seigi Hinata of the ACW Destruction Project in China, the Chinese authorities, who had previously estimated that nearly 2 million CW had been abandoned, now accept the figure of nearly 700 000 based on a 1996 joint Sino-Japanese survey. Hinata, S., Response in question and answer session, 1998 International Chemical Weapons Demilitarisation Conference (note 48). However, a 1998 briefing document for Chinese national representatives stated that 1.8 million ACW have been found at 20 locations in 11 provinces. Document supplied by Gong Chunsen, First Secretary, Chinese Delegation to the OPCW, the Hague, the Netherlands.

[77] Hinata, S., 'ACW destruction project in China', 1998 International Chemical Weapons Demilitarisation Conference (note 48).

The Japanese Government established a technology study group composed of Japanese experts to decide on the most appropriate destruction technology and to solicit technology proposals from companies worldwide. However, in November the Japanese authorities announced that the disposal plant would not be ready before 2003, thereby missing the original deadline of 2000 for commencing destruction operations by at least three years. In addition, it was said that Japan might fail to complete the destruction operation in China by 2007 and would have to make a request to the OPCW for an extension of the deadline.[78] The principal reason for the delays cited was bureaucratic inertia: by November 1998 the Japanese Government had not yet determined which ministry or agency should be in charge and thus request the budget.[79] Meanwhile, Japan continues to hold consultations with China regarding the plant's location, environmental standards, the technology to be used and the actual destruction operations.

The Ukrainian Government again asked Russia to disclose whether at any time during the history of the Soviet Union chemical weapons were buried or dumped on the territory of Ukraine.[80]

III. Biological weapon disarmament

Developments in biotechnology and genetic engineering, Russia's admission that the USSR conducted illicit biological weapon (BW) activities and the discovery of a substantial offensive BW programme in Iraq have heightened BW threat perceptions and highlighted the lack of adequate verification procedures and compliance mechanisms in the BTWC.[81] The CWC demonstrates that the international community can accept stringent verification and compliance measures. The 1994 BTWC Special Conference established the Ad Hoc Group (AHG) and mandated it to consider verification mechanisms and other measures to strengthen the BTWC.

The AHG is currently negotiating a draft protocol to the BTWC. It met four times in 1998.[82] Having decided at the January session to refrain from reviewing the entire rolling text on every occasion, the focus of most meetings was on the most substantive issues: visits, facility investigations and field investigations, the configuration of a future BTWC organization and Article X of the convention (corresponding to Article VII of the draft protocol) on cooperation

[78] JIJI Press Newswire (Tokyo) via Reuters, 'Business briefing: Japan may miss deadline for removing chemical arms in China', 6 Nov. 1998.

[79] Kyodo News Service, 'Japan immobile on chemical weapons disposal in China', 23 Nov. 1998.

[80] Since 1994 Ukraine has been formally requesting Russia to provide information concerning the dumping or burying of CW on its territory, but even after 3 bilateral consultations a substantive formal reply had not been received. Statement of the Ukrainian Deputy Foreign Minister Kostyantyn Gryshchenko at the Second Conference of States Parties, 2 Dec. 1997. Statement at 1998 International Chemical Weapons Demilitarisation Conference (note 48).

[81] See appendix 13A in this volume.

[82] The 9th, 10th, 11th and 12th sessions were held on 5–23 Jan., 9–13 Mar., 22 June–10 July and 14 Sep.–9 Oct., respectively.

and exchanges for peaceful purposes.[83] Three revised versions of the rolling text were presented in 1998; the most recent, the sixth version, is the lengthiest.[84] Entire sections remain enclosed in square brackets, reflecting the divergence of views and preferences of the delegations. As in previous years, Friends of the Chair (FoC) were appointed to assist the AHG chairman on particular issues.

Substantial problems related to the definition of fundamental terms in Article II of the draft protocol remain, not least because some parties fear that the introduction of definitions could lead to restrictions in the scope of the BTWC. Regarding verification procedures, four types of non-challenge visit (random, clarification, request and voluntary) are now listed. The category 'ambiguity-related visits' was removed from the rolling text. Reservations continued to be expressed about the utility of such visits, since the apparent ease of clandestine production of BW in a commercial biotechnology facility renders the potential for non-challenge visits to uncover illicit activities poor. The pharmaceutical and biotechnology industries strongly endorsed the view that such visits pose a risk to confidential information. The opposing view holds that such visits would encourage parties to provide accurate declarations and promote transparency while potentially deterring would-be violators.[85]

Provisions for ensuring the confidentiality of information related to civil and military activities and facilities during visits and investigations also received consideration under Article IV, which establishes a regime for ensuring 'effective protection against unauthorized disclosure' (for which the Director-General of a future BTWC organization would have 'the primary responsibility'), and under Annex E, which describes the proposed regime in detail.[86] Confidentiality is important to all parties and their national industries. However, there are disagreements regarding the extent to which such provisions should be spelled out in the body of the protocol text and how much of the detailed procedures should be left for development during a Preparatory Committee (PrepCom) and by the future organization.[87]

In all four sessions the AHG paid particular attention to Annex D on investigations,[88] but consensus was not reached on many issues (e.g., the circumstances in which an investigation would be initiated, or the procedures to be followed during an investigation). Three possible types of investigation remain in brackets: (*a*) field investigations, which would cover alleged use of BW; (*b*) facility investigations, intended to cover activities prohibited under Article I of the BTWC; and (*c*) investigations into illegal transfers, as defined

[83] 'Biological Weapons Convention chronology 1998, 5–23 January', Institute for Defense and Disarmament Studies, *Arms Control Reporter* (IDDS: Brookline, Mass.), sheets 701.B.185–86, Apr. 1998.

[84] Procedural Report of the Ad Hoc Group of the States Parties to the Convention on the Prohibition of the Development, Production and Stockpiling of Bacteriological (Biological) and Toxin Weapons and on Their Destruction, Ad Hoc Group document BWC/AD HOC GROUP/43, 15 Oct. 1998.

[85] Ad Hoc Group document BWC/AD HOC GROUP/43 (note 84), part I, annex I, p.46, fns 26, 27.

[86] Ad Hoc Group document BWC/AD HOC GROUP/43 (note 84), part I, annex I, pp. 83, 209–220.

[87] Ad Hoc Group document BWC/AD HOC GROUP/43 (note 84), part I, annex I, p.209, fn. 116.

[88] The investigations proposed in the draft protocol are similar in concept to challenge inspections under the CWC.

under Article III of the BTWC. On the issue of procedures for requesting an investigation, the FoC on Compliance Measures proposed 'to include the possibility of following the models of both the CWC and CTBT [Comprehensive Nuclear Test-Ban Treaty], requiring the submission of investigation requests simultaneously to the Executive Council and to the Director-General'.[89] Some concerns remain to be addressed. For instance, the issue of unnatural outbreaks of disease more directly affects states located in regions that are prone to such outbreaks, since they may be the targets of a disproportionate number of investigations.[90]

The pharmaceutical and biotechnology industries continued to object to elements of the rolling text, notably visits. Several states in which industry representatives have played an active role in influencing governmental positions in the negotiations have indicated that they would seek to cooperate more closely with national industries on sensitive issues.

Many countries have expressed their political support for the future protocol and committed themselves to honour its provisions. On 9 March 1998 the European Union (EU) adopted a common position 'with a view to concluding the substantive negotiations by the end of 1998, so that the Protocol can be adopted by a Special Conference of States Parties early in 1999'.[91] It called for the enhancement of contacts between EU member governments, the European Commission and industry 'with the aim of furthering understanding between representatives of European industry and those involved in the negotiations in the Ad Hoc Group'.[92] This initiative was also endorsed by the countries of Central and Eastern Europe associated to the EU, Cyprus and the European Free Trade Association (EFTA) members of the European Economic Area, which in a separate declaration stated that they would 'ensure that their national policies conform to that Common Position'.[93] Joint statements were also issued by the USA and China (27 June), the USA and Russia (2 September), the Non-Aligned Movement (3 September) and the G8 (the G7 plus Russia) foreign ministers following their pre-summit meeting on 8–9 May,[94]

[89] Working Paper submitted by the Friend of the Chair on Compliance Measures, Ad Hoc Group document BWC/AD HOC GROUP/WP.267, 26 Feb. 1998. p. 6. The CWC contains the so-called red-light and the CTBT the green-light procedure. Under the red-light procedure an inspection would go ahead unless a majority voted against it; under the green-light procedure initiation of a challenge inspection would require a majority vote. For further discussion, see Klotz, L. C. and Sims, M. C., 'The BWC: challenge investigation voting procedures', *CBW Conventions Bulletin*, no. 41 (Sep. 1998), pp. 1, 3.

[90] E.g., Group of NAM and Other Countries, Investigations: exclusion of all natural outbreaks of disease, Ad Hoc Group document BWC/AD HOC GROUP/4/WP.262.

[91] Working paper submitted by the United Kingdom of Great Britain and Northern Ireland on behalf of the European Union, Ad Hoc Group document BWC/AD HOC GROUP/WP.272, 9 Mar. 1998, article 2, para. 1.

[92] Ad Hoc Group document BWC/AD HOC GROUP/WP.272 (note 91), article 3, para. 4; and Williams, F., 'UK bid to speed germ war talks,' *Financial Times*, 10 Mar. 1998, p. 4.

[93] Declaration by the associated countries of Central and Eastern Europe, the associated country Cyprus and the EFTA countries members of the European Economic Area on progress towards a legally binding protocol to strengthen compliance with the Biological and Toxin Weapons Convention (BTWC) and the intensification of work in the Ad Hoc Group to that end, Brussels, 6 Mar. 1998.

[94] United States Information Service, 'US–China joint statement on biological weapons,' *Washington File*, URL <http://www.fas.org/nuke/control/bwc/news/98070201_epo.html>; and '8–9 May', *CBW Conventions Bulletin*, no. 41 (Sep. 1998), p. 21.

among others. A Ministerial Meeting (convened by Australia) held in New York resulted in a declaration, co-sponsored by 57 countries, restating their commitment to 'sustaining high level political support for the negotiations' and calling for the convening of another high-level meeting in 1999 in order to lend further support to the work of the AHG.[95] It appears that the protocol will not be finalized before 2000, since many key issues remain unresolved.

IV. Chemical and biological weapon proliferation concerns

Concerns about the proliferation of chemical and biological weapons are two-fold. On the one hand, more states in conflict zones are assessed (especially by the USA) to be acquiring CBW. On the other hand, states with existing CBW armament programmes are seen to be improving their capabilities in terms of the quality of the chemical and biological warfare agents and their means of delivery.

As a consequence of the grouping together of several categories of weapons, it is difficult to isolate the CBW threat assessment. In the only known statement in 1998 by a US Government official in which the figure did not encompass nuclear weapons, Deputy Secretary of Defense John J. Hamre noted that 'At least two dozen nations already possess chemical and biological weapons or have active development programs to build them'.[96] One US intelligence estimate in 1998 assessed that 'around 30 countries possess, once possessed but no longer maintain, or are possibly pursuing CW capabilities', approximately one-half of which are party to the CWC.[97] The statement, however, is of little use as it can encompass programmes as far back as World War I.

Concerns continue to be expressed about certain Chinese and Russian exports of dual-use technologies, which might be diverted for offensive CBW programmes, despite statements by officials that new export control regulations are being established or existing ones strengthened. As a consequence of the economic and social collapse of Russia, fear has increased that Russian scientists and technicians may seek employment abroad or that criminal organizations may start trafficking in critical dual-use technologies. Russian

[95] Working paper submitted by Argentina *et al.*, Ad Hoc Group document BWC/AD HOC GROUP/WP.296, 10 July 1998; Working paper submitted by Australia, Declaration of the informal ministerial meeting on the negotiation towards conclusion of the protocol to strengthen the Biological Weapons Convention, Ad Hoc Group document BWC/AD HOC GROUP/WP.324, 9 Oct. 1998; and Radio Australia (Melbourne), 24 Sep. 1998, 'Australia: Australia welcomes stronger Biological Weapons Convention', Foreign Broadcast Information Service, *Daily Report–East Asia* (*FBIS-EAS*), FBIS-EAS-98-267, 28 Sep. 1998.

[96] The 22 June 1998 statement by Hamre at the NATO Workshop in Vienna is reproduced in US Department of Defense, 'Hamre: counterproliferation efforts must include defense against cyberattacks, WMD', *Defense Viewpoint*, vol. 13, no. 44, URL <http://www.defenselink.mil/speeches/1998/s19980622-depsecdef.html>.

[97] Written replies by the Central Intelligence Agency to questions by Richard C. Shelby, Chairman, Select Committee on Intelligence, US Senate, *Current and Projected National Security Threats to the United States*, Hearing before the Select Committee on Intelligence, US Senate, 105th Congress, 2nd session (US Government Printing Office: Washington, DC, 1998), p. 143.

organized crime does not yet appear to be involved in trafficking in CBW-related materials.[98]

The strike against an alleged CW factory in Sudan

On 20 August 1998, as part of Operation Infinite Reach, 13 US Tomahawk cruise missiles demolished the al-Shifa Pharmaceutical Industries factory in Sudan in response to the bombings of the US embassies in Kenya and Tanzania on 7 August. US officials blamed the embassy bombings on a world-wide terrorist network, the Jihad Islamic Front Against Jews and Crusaders, led and funded by the Saudi millionaire Usama bin Ladin.[99] The plant, located in Khartoum North, was said to be part of the Sudanese military industrial complex to which bin Ladin had made financial contributions and to be making precursors for the nerve agent VX.[100] The US assessment that the terrorist organization was seeking to acquire CW was one of the four reasons cited by President Bill Clinton for ordering the attack.[101]

Part of the justification was the certainty that the al-Shifa plant was not producing any commercial products[102] but rather a penultimate precursor to the manufacturing of VX, which was claimed to be not included in any of the three schedules in the CWC.[103] However, later it became clear that the precursor in question was O-ethyl methylphosphonothioic acid (EMPTA), a chemical on Schedule 2B of the CWC.[104]

Soon after the attack the US assertions about the pharmaceutical plant and bin Ladin's connections to it proved inaccurate. British, Italian, Jordanian and US consultants or engineers involved in the construction or maintenance of the al-Shifa plant stated that they had never seen any signs of CW production.[105] By the end of August, US officials justified the strike on the grounds that Iraq was involved in the production of VX in Sudan. They claimed that Iraq had

[98] Written replies by the Federal Bureau of Investigation to questions by Richard C. Shelby, *Current and Projected National Security Threats to the United States* (note 97), p. 157.

[99] Other simultaneous strikes were directed against 6 training bases in Afghanistan used by bin Ladin's terrorist network.

[100] Department of Defense, 'Response by US Secretary of Defense William S. Cohen to questions by journalists', *News Briefing*, 20 Aug. 1998, URL <http://www.defenselink.mil/news/Aug1998/t08201998_t820brfg.html>; and Loeb, V. and Graham, B., 'US fleshes out the intelligence that led it to target Sudan plant', *International Herald Tribune*, 2 Sep. 1998, p. 2.

[101] White House, 'Statement by the President', 20 Aug. 1998, URL <http://www. state.gov/www/regions/africa/strike_clinton980820.html>.

[102] 'Background briefing', 20 Aug. 1998, URL <http://www.defenselink.mil/news/Aug1998/x08201998_x820bomb.html>. US officials at the UN, however, had approved the sale of medicine produced at al-Shifa in Jan. 1998. Barletta, M., 'Chemical weapons in the Sudan: allegations and evidence', *Nonproliferation Review*, vol. 6, no. 1 (fall 1998), p. 118.

[103] Response by National Security Advisor Sandy Berger, in White House, 'Press briefing, on US strikes in Sudan and Afghanistan', 20 Aug. 1998, URL <http://secretary.state.gov/www/statements/1998/980820.html>.

[104] EMPTA might be used in limited quantities for legitimate purposes (e.g., fungicides, pesticides and anti-microbial agents).

[105] Loeb, V., 'Justification for attack in Sudan still disputed', *International Herald Tribune*, 27 Aug. 1998, p. 6; and Barletta (note 102), p. 119.

used the EMPTA-based technique to develop its stockpiles in the 1980s.[106] However, the Iraqi connection did not feature systematically in official statements. The traces of the precursor chemical were said to have been found in a soil sample taken outside the factory months before the strike. A single soil sample without multiple control samples from the same area does not constitute proof that the compound had been produced at the al-Shifa plant; the traces could also have been the consequence of, for example, a spill or effluent deposits. Late in September the claim was made that US agents had penetrated the plant and taken the sample from a discharge pipe.[107]

The US refusal to allow an independent UN investigation team to examine the al-Shifa plant undermined the credibility of the claim that the factory was involved in the production of chemical warfare agents.

Russian BW proliferation concerns

Russia continues to be accused of maintaining illicit domestic BW programmes and assisting similar programmes abroad.[108] A Russian press article alleged that the anthrax released in Sverdlovsk in 1979 had been altered in order to have the greatest possible effect on adult men.[109] Another source suggested that the Centre for Military and Technical Problems of Anti-Bacteriological Defence, the successor to Compound 19 at Sverdlovsk, has plans to resume the offensive production of anthrax.[110]

Dr Ken Alibek, former First Deputy Director of Biopreparat in the USSR and currently Program Manager for Battelle Memorial Institute in the USA, testified in May before the Joint Economic Committee of the US Congress that the Soviet programme had become the most sophisticated BW programme in the world and that it continued to expand even after the signing of the BTWC in 1972. Alibek alleged that the Soviet BW programme was effective in developing BW agents for which no prevention or cure exists, such as strains of plague. He echoed concerns that Russia has not opened up the Soviet military BW facilities to international inspection. In particular, military laboratories at Kirov, Sergeyev Posad (formerly Zagorsk), Strizi and Yekaterinburg (formerly Sverdlovsk) are suspected of harbouring components of BW research.[111]

[106] Crossette, B. *et al.*, 'Iraq tied to chemical plant in Sudan', *International Herald Tribune*, 26 Aug. 1998, p. 8.

[107] 'Making a case', *Newsweek*, no. 39 (25 Sep. 1998), p. 5.

[108] Arms Control and Disarmament Agency, 'Adherence to and compliance with arms control agreements', 1998, URL <http://www.acda.gov/reports/annual/comp97.htm>; 'The threatening shadow of Russian biological weapons', *World Reporter*, 4 Aug. 1998; and Fyodorov, L., 'Death from the test tube', *New Times*, Sep. 1998, pp. 22–36.

[109] Fyodorov (note 108); and Miller, J. and Broad, W. J., 'Germ weapons: in Soviet past or in the new Russia's future?', *New York Times*, 28 Dec. 1998, URL <http://www.nytimes.com/library/world/europe/122898-germ-warfare.html>.

[110] Yevtushenko, A. and Avdeyev, S., 'Sverdlovsk was infected with anthrax: nineteen years ago the Soviet Army used a bacteriological weapon against its own people', *Komsomolskaya Pravda* (Moscow), 30 Apr. 1998, pp. 4–5, in 'Russia: further on 1979 Sverdlovsk anthrax release', FBIS-SOV-98-159, 9 June 1998.

[111] Biopreparat is alleged to have been the civilian branch of the Soviet BW programme. According to Alibek, Biopreparat comprised over 50% of the BW programme's personnel and facilities. He was

Through the CTR programme the United States attempts to defuse the BW threat from the former Soviet Union. The former Soviet BW facility in Stepnogorsk, Kazakhstan, is being dismantled with US assistance. It was used to produce weapons for an offensive biological warfare programme, including production of resistant strains of anthrax.[112] The dismantlement contract is between the US Defense Special Weapons Agency and JSC Biomedpreparat and the National Centre on Biotechnology of Kazakhstan. Work is expected to be completed by July 2000.[113]

There have been continuing allegations that Russia is involved in BW-relevant transfers to Iran and other Middle Eastern countries.[114] In February 1998 the Russian Foreign Ministry and Russian Defence Minister Igor Sergeyev rejected reports of Russian Government approval of the sale of fermentation equipment to Iraq which could also be used to produce BW agents.[115] Russia nevertheless tried to prevent proliferation with new legislation. In January then Prime Minister Viktor Chernomyrdin issued a directive which prohibits Russians from engaging in foreign economic activities concerning goods and services potentially applicable for nuclear, biological and chemical (NBC) weapons or missile delivery systems.[116] In May the Russian Federal Currency and Export Control Service issued a procedural explanation of the functioning of the export control system created by the federal directive.

South Africa's CBW programmes

Following preliminary investigations in 1996 and 1997, the Truth and Reconciliation Commission (TRC) started its in-depth investigation of South Africa's CBW programme in February 1998. The TRC held public hearings in June and July 1998 and published its main findings in its Final Report to President Nelson Mandela in October.[117] The focus of the research, however, had to be restricted considerably because of the breadth of the matter and serious time constraints. While the report noted the investigations into anthrax,

apparently responsible for 32 000 employees and 40 facilities. Statement by Dr Kenneth Alibek before the Joint Economic Committee, US Congress, 20 May 1998, URL <http://www.house.gov/jec/hearings/intell/alibek.htm>.

[112] '30 June' (note 32).

[113] '30 June' (note 32).

[114] Jahanbagloo, J. and Mendenhall, P., 'Russian denies Iranian germ link', MSNBC, 4 Jan. 1999, URL <http://www.msnbc.com:80/news/228551.asp>; and Miller, J. and Broad, W. J., 'Iranians, bioweapons in mind, lure needy ex-Soviet scientists', *New York Times*, 8 Dec. 1998, URL <http://search.nytimes.com/>,

[115] Rohde, D., 'A possible Russian link to Iraq arms buildup', *New York Times*, 12 Feb. 1998, URL <http://search.nytimes.com/>; Smith, R. J., 'Did Moscow try to skirt sanctions?', *Moscow Times*, 13 Feb. 1998, URL <http://www.moscowtimes.ru/archive/issues/1998/Feb/13/story2.html>; Smith, R. J., 'Russian firms discussed factory sale with Iraqis', *Moscow Times*, 19 Feb. 1998, URL <http://www.moscowtimes.ru/archive/issues/1998/Feb/19/story4.html>; and 'Russia denies allegations in "Washington Post"', *RFE/RL Newsline*, 12 Feb. 1998, URL <http://search.rferl.org/newsline/1998/02/120298.html>.

[116] Russia: stricter export controls imposed on goods usable in arms production, Russian Federation Government Directive, no. 57, *Rossiyskaya Gazeta* (Moscow), 18 Feb. 1998, p. 1, in 'Russia: Chernomyrdin decree on dual-use goods export controls', FBIS-TAC-98-048, 21 Feb. 1998.

[117] Truth and Reconciliation Commission, *Final Report*, presented to President Mandela on 29 Oct. 1998, vol. 2, ch. 6, URL <http://www.truth.org.za/final/2chap6c.htm>.

botulism, chemical poisoning, cholera and drugs for crowd control (which were later sold for profit), as well as the development of poisons and lethal micro-organisms for use against individuals,[118] many details of Project Coast, the South African CBW programme, remain undisclosed.[119] An important part of the section of the report on the CBW programme deals with its institutional and structural aspects.

Project Coast was overseen by a management committee, which included the chief of the South African Defence Force (SADF), the chief of staff finances, the head of counter-intelligence, the chief of staff intelligence, the surgeon general, who acted as project leader, and the project officer, Dr Wouter Basson. Once the front companies, which developed and manufactured the chemical and biological devices and then sold them to the SADF, had been established the management committee met once a year to approve the project's budget or in cases of emergency. Basson, the central figure in South Africa's CBW programme who also headed the army's 7th Medical Battalion,[120] apparently reported to the surgeon general and the head of Special Forces, and to various other authorities, including the Minister of Defence, the chief of the SADF and the Minister of Police, as needed. The TRC was unable to clarify the role of the surgeon general as project leader or to determine the exact responsibility of the members of the management committee.[121]

Officially, the CBW programme was claimed to be defensive and designed to acquire the necessary expertise to be able to react to external chemical or biological warfare threats and to have a retaliatory capability available. The TRC has uncovered many indications of research and development related to an offensive chemical and biological warfare capability. The programme included, among others, the development of weapons for covert assassinations by poisoning, the manipulation of fertility and animal experimentation on chimpanzees and baboons. A number of drugs, including dagga, ecstasy, LSD and Mandrax, were manufactured as part of the CBW programme. According to testimony, extracts of dagga, LSD and Mandrax were to be charged in grenades in an attempt to subdue rioters. Some of the substances were also reportedly used during interrogation of prisoners.[122] In another scheme, Roodeplaat Research laboratories was said to have tried to develop a bacter-

[118] These included anthrax in cigarettes, botulinum in milk and paraoxon in whiskey, many of which were developed at Roodeplaat Research Laboratories, a front company, whose head researcher was Dr André Immelman. Several of the items may have been used by operatives of the Civil Cooperation Bureau. Immelman's affidavit provided the TRC with insight into the development of these assassination tools. Truth and Reconciliation Commission (note 117), paras 18–19.

[119] Officially, the government does not want to provide potential proliferators with details of the programmes. A key figure in the programme, Dr Wouter Basson, still faces criminal charges. The TRC was consequently unable to cross-examine him thoroughly and had limited access to documentary evidence so as not to prejudice his trial. Project Coast is discussed in Zanders, J. P. and Hart, J., 'Chemical and biological weapon developments and arms control', *SIPRI Yearbook 1998: Armaments, Disarmament and International Security* (Oxford University Press: Oxford, 1998), p. 478.

[120] The role of the 7th Medical Battalion is described in the 1992 Steyn Report. Zanders and Hart (note 119), p. 478.

[121] Truth and Reconciliation Commission (note 117), paras 36–39.

[122] SAPA, 'Use of drugs by former security forces quizzed by TRC', reports from SAPA, 11 June 1998, URL <http://www.truth.org.za/sapa/9806/s980611a.htm>.

ium, which acted selectively on the basis of pigmentation, that would render infertile only Black people in order to curb their birth rate. Although it was claimed that progress was made, no tests were made on humans.[123]

Despite the international sanctions against the apartheid regime, countries shared information on CBW matters with the SADF. They included Germany, Israel, Taiwan and the USA; there was also a manifest link with Belgian nationals and companies. The TRC report does not state whether the foreign involvement concerned offensive or defensive aspects of CBW research. It concluded that, although the role of foreign governments in supporting the South African CBW programme is not entirely clear, the programme would not have been possible without some level of foreign assistance. The TRC hearings revealed little about CBW for military operations in war.[124]

The 1992 El Al aircraft crash in Amsterdam

Israel has long been presumed to be engaged in offensive CBW programmes. However, little concrete information has been available about the extent of these programmes or whether they were offensive or defensive. It was revealed in September 1998 that the El Al Boeing 747-200F aircraft, which crashed into an apartment complex in Amsterdam on 4 October 1992, was carrying about 190 litres (*c.* 240 kg) of diethyl methylphosphonate (DMMP) in 10 plastic drums destined for the Israel Institute for Biological Research in Nes Ziona, south of Tel Aviv.[125] The chemical was described in the shipping documents as an inflammable liquid. The amount of the chemical suffices for the manufacture of a maximum of 270 kg of sarin. Two other ingredients for the production of sarin, hydrogen fluoride and isopropanol were also on board in smaller quantities.

Israeli authorities said that the chemical was intended for the testing of gas masks and filter systems for collective shelters. Nevertheless, the shipment represented a large quantity. Annual consumption of sarin for scientific research in European laboratories rarely exceeds several hundred grams, and one German research programme used only a few kilograms annually.[126] Although the Israel Institute for Biological Research (IIBR) had been sus-

[123] Lovell, J., 'Apartheid sought to sterilize blacks–witness', Reuters via Yahoo News, 11 June 1998, URL <http://dailynews.yahoo.com>.

[124] Truth and Reconciliation Commission (note 117), paras 31, 32, 34.

[125] van den Berg, H. and Knip, K., 'Grondstof gifgas in Boeing El Al' [Ingredient poison gas in Boeing El Al], *NRC Handelsblad* (Rotterdam), 30 Sep. 1998, pp. 1, 3; and Knip, K., 'El Al-zending genoeg voor 270 kilo Zenuwgas sarin' [El Al shipment enough for 270 kg of nerve agent sarin], *NRC Handelsblad* (Rotterdam), 30 Sep. 1998, p. 3. As early as the 1960s researchers working at the Israel Institute for Biological Research in Ness Ziona published papers on CBW-related topics, including one which ostensibly dealt with the synthesis of V-agents. SIPRI, *Chemical and Biological Warfare*, vol. 2, *CB Weapons Today* (Almqvist & Wiksell: Stockholm, 1973), p. 242. IIBR also conducts legitimate research in CBW defence and protection and commercializes some of its products. Information about IIBR is available at URL <http://www.iibr.gov.il/>.

[126] van den Berg and Knip (note 125), p. 1.

pected of being involved in the production of CW, this was the first indication that it was consuming precursor chemicals in considerable quantities.[127]

In February 1999 the Netherlands Parliament began public hearings into the nature of the cargo of the aircraft and the involvement of the Netherlands in arms shipments to Israel.

The Cuban biological warfare allegation

On 30 June 1997 Cuba submitted a request to Russia, one of the three co-depositaries of the BTWC, to convene a formal consultative meeting to investigate an alleged US attack with the insect pest *thrips palmi* in October 1996. The parties to the BTWC were unable to resolve the issue in August 1997 and mandated British Ambassador Ian Soutar to investigate and report on the allegation before the end of 1997.[128] His report, delivered on 15 December 1997, concluded that 'due inter alia to the technical complexity of the subject and to passage of time, it has not proved possible to reach a definitive conclusion with regard to the concerns raised by the Government of Cuba'.[129] Comments from 12 parties to the BTWC are annexed to the report.[130] Some countries stated that upon further examination they could not establish a causal link between the outbreak of *thrips palmi* in Cuba in December 1996 and the overflight of a US aircraft two months earlier. Other countries stated that they were unable to draw any definitive conclusions in view of the technical complexity and lack of additional information. Further investigation of the Cuban allegation was suggested by China, North Korea and Viet Nam but the suggestion was not taken up. The investigation was conducted according to Article V of the BTWC and the consultative process established by the Third Review Conference. The report noted that there was general agreement that throughout the process these requirements had 'been fulfilled in an impartial and transparent manner'.

V. UNSCOM developments

UNSCOM was created by the UN Security Council to uncover the full extent of Iraq's CBW and missile programmes after the defeat of Iraq in the 1991 Persian Gulf War.[131] UNSCOM is further mandated to ensure the destruction

[127] DMMP has legitimate commercial use as a flame retardant in building materials. It can also be used as a nerve-agent simulant for outdoor testing. In the 1980s the US Army ceased to use it in open-air tests because it had been determined to be a mild carcinogen and a potent renal toxin. Cole, L. C., *The Eleventh Plague* (W. H. Freeman and Co.: New York, 1997), pp. 61–64.

[128] The allegation and investigative procedure are described in Zanders and Hart (note 119), pp. 479–80.

[129] Letter from Ambassador S. I. Soutar, United Kingdom Permanent Representation to the Conference on Disarmament, to All States Parties to the Biological and Toxin Weapons Convention, Geneva, 15 Dec. 1997.

[130] The 12 were Australia, Canada, China, Cuba, Denmark, Germany, Hungary, Japan, Korea (North), the Netherlands, New Zealand and Viet Nam.

[131] The International Atomic Energy Agency (IAEA) is responsible for uncovering and dismantling Iraq's nuclear weapon programme with the assistance and cooperation of UNSCOM. UNSCOM is also discussed in chapters 3 and 15 in this volume.

of Iraq's stockpiles, production facilities and other related installations, and to establish a long-term monitoring programme to prevent Iraq from acquiring new non-conventional weapon capabilities.

In 1997 there was a marked increase of incidents between UNSCOM inspectors and Iraqi officials. (The UNSCOM missions are listed in table 13.1.) In December a major crisis erupted when Iraq refused the inspectors access to several facilities, including the presidential sites.[132]

The crisis over the presidential sites was defused by UN Secretary-General Kofi Annan's Memorandum of Understanding (MOU) with the Iraqi leadership on 23 February, whereby the UNSCOM inspectors were to have immediate, unconditional and unrestricted access in conformity with UN resolutions. UNSCOM pledged to respect the legitimate concerns of Iraq relating to national security, sovereignty and dignity. At the presidential sites the inspectors were to be accompanied by diplomats 'friendly' to Iraq and experts who would ensure that Iraq's national sovereignty and dignity were respected. The MOU stated that 'the United Nations and the government of Iraq agree to improve cooperation and efficiency, effectiveness and transparency of work, so as to enable UNSCOM to report to the Council expeditiously under paragraph 22 of Resolution 687 (1991)', which deals with the lifting of sanctions.[133] On 2 March the Security Council endorsed the document (Resolution 1154).[134] UN Under-Secretary-General for Disarmament Affairs Jayantha Dhanapala was appointed special commissioner as an interlocutor in the Iraq–UNSCOM dispute.

The MOU averted the use of military force, but the agreement was flawed. Iraq would have had ample time to remove whatever components of its illegal armament programmes it may have hidden in the presidential sites,[135] and the principle of unannounced and surprise inspections at these locations was lost as the arrival of senior diplomats would give Iraq an early warning. The MOU also accorded Iraq a number of rights which were not part of Resolution 687. The MOU ended the principle of the unconditional implementation of Resolution 687 and created room for compromise solutions. In the following months Iraq repeatedly invoked these rights to justify its refusal to cooperate

[132] Zanders and Hart (note 119), pp. 481–85; and SIPRI, 'Iraq: the UNSCOM experience', *Fact Sheet*, Oct. 1998, available at URL <http://www.sipri.se/pubs/Factsheet/unscom.html>. On 12 Jan. 1998 Iraq blocked Concealment Investigation Mission UNSCOM 227 on grounds that its composition was unbalanced (the team comprised 1 Australian, 5 British, 1 Russian and 9 US nationals.) 'Iraq blasts composition of UN arms team', Reuters via Fox News, 11 Jan. 1998, URL <http://www.foxnews.com/news/wires2/0111/n_rt_0111_67.sml>; and Aita, J., 'UN Secretary-General Annan urges Iraq not to ban American', *Washington File* (United States Information Service, US Embassy: Stockholm, 12 Jan. 1998), URL <http://www.usis.usemb.se/wireless/100/eur123.htm>.

[133] Memorandum of Understanding between the United Nations and the Republic of Iraq, 23 Feb. 1998, URL <http://www.un.org/NewLinks/uniraq.htm>.

[134] UN Security Council Resolution 1154, 2 Mar. 1998.

[135] Following the visits to the presidential sites, Charles Duelfer, Deputy Executive Chairman of UNSCOM, reported that 'it was clearly apparent that all sites had undergone extensive evacuation'. Report of the Special Group established for entries into Iraqi presidential sites, appendix III, 'Initial entry to the presidential sites: summary report of the Head of Team', para. 11, UN document S/1998/326, 15 Apr. 1998.

Table 13.1. UNSCOM inspections, October 1997–December 1998

Type of inspection/date	Team
Biological	
14 Oct.–12 Nov. 1997	BG 11
6–15 Dec. 1997	BW 57/UNSCOM 212
22 Nov. 1997–5 Jan. 1998	BG 12
6 Jan.–2 Feb. 1998	BG 13
5–19 Jan. 1998	BW 60/UNSCOM 215
9–14 Jan. 1998	BW 58/UNSCOM 213
17–29 Jan. 1998.	BW 61/UNSCOM 222
1 Jan.–15 Feb. 1998	BW 62/UNSCOM 223
3 Feb.–3 Apr. 1998	BG 14
12–25 Mar. 1998	BW 64/UNSCOM 225
4 Apr.–30 June 1998	BG 15
19 Apr.–2 May 1998	BW 63/UNSCOM 224
11–25 May 1998	BW 65/UNSCOM 226
19 May–2 June 1998	BW 59/UNSCOM 214
28 May–11 June 1998	BW 66/UNSCOM 230
1 July–3 Oct. 1998	BG 16
1–6 July 1998	BW 67/UNSCOM 231
14–23 July 1998	BW 68/UNSCOM 244
17–24 July 1998	BW 69/UNSCOM 250
1–6 Dec. 1998	BW 70/UNSCOM 253
3–10 Dec. 1998	BW 74/UNSCOM 261
6–10 Dec. 1998	BW 73/UNSCOM 260
10–14 Dec. 1998	BW 72/UNSCOM 256
4 Oct.–15 Dec. 1998	BG 17
Chemical	
14 Oct. 1997–28 Jan. 1998	CG 12
18–23 Oct. 1997	CBW+M 1/UNSCOM 211
29 Jan.–14 Apr. 1998	CG 13
4–10 Feb. 1998	CW 44/UNSCOM 221
14–20 Mar. 1998	CW 45/UNSCOM 229
9–15 Apr. 1998	CW 46/UNSCOM 238
15 Apr.–4 July 1998	CG 14
26 Apr.–2 May 1998	CW 47/UNSCOM 239
29 May–11 June 1998	CW 48/UNSCOM 210
12–16 July 1998	CW 49/UNSCOM 246
15 July–25 Oct. 1998	CG 15
27–31 July 1998	CW 50/UNSCOM 248
26 Oct.–15 Dec. 1998	CG 16
24–31 Aug. 1998	CW 51/UNSCOM 251
22–30 Nov. 1998	CW 52/UNSCOM 257
Ballistic missile	
6–16 Oct. 1997	MG 14A
15 Oct. 1997–14 Jan. 1998	MG 15
10–19 Dec. 1997	BM 64/UNSCOM 220
11–21 Dec. 1997	MG 15A
27 Dec. 1997–1 Jan. 1998	MG 15B
15 Jan.–3 Apr. 1998	MG 16

Type of inspection/date	Team
14–22 Mar. 1998	BM 65/UNSCOM 228
9 Mar.–present (currently suspended)	BM 66/UNSCOM 240
22–30 Mar. 1998	BM 63/UNSCOM 241
4 Apr.–17 July 1998	MG 17
19–30 Apr. 1998	MG 17A
19–24 Apr. 1998	BM 66A/UNSCOM 240A
24–26 Apr. 1998	BM 66B/UNSCOM 240B
18 May–18 June 1998	BM 66C/UNSCOM 240C
18–24 June 1998	BM 66D/UNSCOM 240D
18 June–1 July 1998	BM 68/UNSCOM 247
16 July–21 Sep. 1998	MG 18
13–21 July 1998	BM 62/UNSCOM 232
22 July–4 Aug. 1998	BM 67/UNSCOM 242
27–31 July 1998	BM 69/UNSCOM 252
3–15 Dec. 1998	BM 70/UNSCOM 259
22 Sep.–15 Dec. 1998	MG 19
Export/import	
6 Oct. 1997–15 Jan. 1998	EG–8
16 Jan.–16 Mar. 1998	EG–9
17 Mar.–31 May 1998	EG–10
1 June–30 Aug. 1998	EG–11
13 July–3 Aug. 1998	EXIM 4/UNSCOM 249
31 Aug.–15 Dec. 1998	EG–12
Concealment investigation missions	
18–24 Dec. 1997	CIM 9/UNSCOM 218
11–17 Jan. 1998	CIM 10/UNSCOM 227
5–12 Mar. 1998	CIM 10B/UNSCOM 227B
20–23 May 1998	CIM 11/UNSCOM 233
28 Apr.–1 May 1998	CIM 12/UNSCOM 245
6–14 Dec. 1998	CIM 15/UNSCOM 258
Special missions to Baghdad	
12–16 Dec. 1997	Executive Chairman's visit
19–21 Jan. 1998	Executive Chairman's visit
22–26 Mar. 1998	Executive Chairman's visit
11–15 June 1998	Executive Chairman's visit
2–4 Aug. 1998	Executive Chairman's visit
Technical evaluation meetings	
1–6 Feb. 1998	Missile warhead TEM
2–6 Feb. 1998	VX TEM
20–27 Mar. 1998	BW TEM
Presidential site missions	
25 Mar.–4 Apr. 1998	PSV 1/UNSCOM 243

BG = Biological Monitoring Group, BM = ballistic missiles, BW = biological weapons, CBW = chemical and biological weapons, CIM = Concealment Investigation Mission, CG = Chemical Monitoring Group, CW = chemical weapons, EG = Export/Import Monitoring Group, EXIM = Export/import, M = Missile, MG = Missile Monitoring Group, PSV = Presidential Site Visit, TEM = Technical Evaluation Meetings.

Source: Information provided by UNSCOM spokesman.

with UNSCOM. The lifting of sanctions, in particular, became the focal point of Iraq's intransigence on inspections. Iraq viewed Annan as the guarantor of the agreement,[136] placing him in the awkward position of balancing the UNSCOM reports of non-compliance with the newly granted rights. Consequently, each time Iraq created a new crisis the search for a compromise further eroded UNSCOM's authority. In the shifting political environment the UNSCOM reports looked increasingly uncompromising.

Meanwhile the technical evaluation meetings, called for by Iraq to determine whether it had indeed destroyed its prohibited weapons and terminated the relevant armament programmes, concluded that many questions about the VX and missile programmes remained unanswered.[137] Another technical evaluation meeting on biological weapons determined that it had no confidence in the veracity of the full, final and complete disclosure. Between the summers of 1997 and 1998, groups of international experts outside UNSCOM found Iraq's declarations to be defective on four occasions.[138]

A series of serious events soon brought UNSCOM's activities to a halt, despite work by UNSCOM Executive Chairman Richard Butler on a so-called road map—a list of priority tasks that need to be completed to give a final account of Iraq's proscribed weapon programmes and capabilities—to enable lifting the sanctions. In late June information was made public that Iraq had apparently loaded missile warheads with VX. In July Colonel Gabrielle Kraatz, a German and the new head of the UNSCOM BW group, obtained a document at the headquarters of the Iraqi Air Force which listed the chemical and biological missile warheads and munitions and detailed their consumption during the Persian Gulf War. On the basis of that document UNSCOM would have been able to determine how many chemical and biological munitions still remain unaccounted for. After a four-hour stand-off between Kraatz and members of the Iraqi military, UNSCOM and Iraq sealed the document and transferred it to the National Monitoring Centre, the Iraqi national authority for disarmament affairs. Iraq has since steadfastly refused to hand over the document, arguing that it pertained to the Iraq–Iran War and that the UN Security Council resolutions only refer to documents on the Persian Gulf War (which is incorrect).[139]

[136] Omaar, R., 'Iraq's diplomatic gains', *Middle East International*, no. 569 (27 Feb. 1998), p. 4; and Hiro, D., 'Iraq and the US: Saddam wins the first round', *Middle East International*, no. 570 (13 Mar. 1998), p. 18.

[137] Report on the technical evaluation meeting on chemical warfare agent VX, 12 Feb. 1998; and Report of the Special Commission's team to the technical evaluation meeting on proscribed missile warheads (Baghdad, 1–6 Feb. 1998), UN document S/1998/176, 27 Feb. 1998.

[138] Report of the Executive Chairman on the activities of the Special Commission established by the Secretary-General pursuant to paragraph 9 (b) (i) of Resolution 687 (1991), UN document S/1998/332, 16 Apr. 1998, para. 65; and Report of the Executive Chairman on the activities of the Special Commission established by the Secretary-General pursuant to paragraph 9 (b) (i) of Resolution 687 (1991), UN document S/1998/920, 6 Oct. 1998, para. 31.

[139] Interview with Dutch UNSCOM inspector Koos Ooms, who participated in the 3 Aug. meeting in Baghdad. Stein, M., '"Iraakse leiders zijn boeven, tuig van de richel"' [Iraqi leaders are bandits, scum of the earth], *NRC Handelsblad* (Rotterdam), 18 Aug. 1998, p. 6. The continued refusal to hand over this document, despite a Security Council request to do so, was one of the main reasons why, in Dec. 1998,

Such incidents were presented by the Iraqi leadership as further evidence that the sanctions would never be lifted. On 3 August, during Butler's visit to Baghdad, Deputy Prime Minister Tariq Aziz demanded that UNSCOM certify that Iraq had revealed all details of its non-conventional weapon programmes and refused to provide any further answers to UNSCOM questions. The meeting was cut short. Two days later Iraq announced that UNSCOM inspectors could no longer carry out challenge inspections. Routine monitoring work, pursuant to UN Security Council Resolution 715, could continue, although the inspectors were permitted to monitor only those sites that Iraq allowed them to visit.[140] UNSCOM's position became extremely complicated. It was revealed that US Secretary of State Madeleine Albright had repeatedly pressured Butler to rescind planned challenge inspections.[141] This apparent lack of willingness by the USA to uphold the UN Security Council resolutions on the disarmament of Iraq led to the resignation of Scott Ritter, an experienced UNSCOM inspector, on 26 August.[142] The August crisis also demonstrated that in the absence of US-led initiatives the three critics of the British and US attitude towards Iraq (China, France and Russia) cannot or will not initiate measures to restore the authority of the Security Council in the face of gross violations of its resolutions.[143]

Emboldened by the vacuum left by the Security Council, Iraq made new demands such as the restructuring of UNSCOM and the relocation of the UNSCOM headquarters to Geneva from New York. On 9 September the Security Council suspended its regular sanctions reviews.[144] Resolution 1194 also held out the prospect of a comprehensive review of Iraq's compliance after it had resumed full cooperation with UNSCOM and International Atomic Energy Agency (IAEA) inspectors. This 'carrot', however, raised the question of how much evidence UNSCOM should disclose to demonstrate Iraq's failure to fulfil its obligations. UNSCOM feared that with this knowledge Iraq might conceal or destroy further evidence of its prohibited programmes. A spokesperson for the UN Secretary-General indicated that such evidence would also have to be placed before the Security Council.[145] A proposal for a comprehensive review by Kofi Annan was rejected by Tariq Aziz during a meeting in New York on 28 September. Discussions continued, but on

Butler submitted a negative report to the Security Council. Letter from Richard Butler, Executive Chairman of UNSCOM to Kofi A. Annan, Secretary-General of the United Nations, 15 Dec. 1998.

[140] Diamond, H., 'Ambassador Richard Butler: keeping Iraq's disarmament on track', *Arms Control Today*, vol. 28, no. 6 (Aug./Sep. 1998), p. 3. As part of its mandate to inspect and oversee the destruction of Iraq's CBW and ballistic missiles UNSCOM can organize surprise visits to any location. UNSCOM's second priority is monitoring of previously inspected installations in order to ensure that Iraq does not rebuild its prohibited capabilities once UNSCOM has certified that they have been destroyed.

[141] Gellman, B., 'US repeatedly blocked UN inspections in Iraq', *International Herald Tribune*, 28 Aug. 1998, p. 2.

[142] Miller, J., 'Inspector quits, calling Iraq searches a "farce"', *International Herald Tribune*, 28 Aug. 1998, pp. 1, 4.

[143] Both France and Russia would benefit from an end to the sanctions as Iraq owes them $5 billion and $7 billion, respectively. In addition, both countries expect sizeable contracts to rebuild Iraq's civilian, industrial and military infrastructure. China is wary of US global hegemonic policies.

[144] UN Security Council Resolution 1194, 9 Sep. 1998.

[145] Williams, I., 'Iraq must comply', *Middle East International*, no. 585 (16 Oct. 1998), p. 12.

31 October, just after the Security Council had stated its terms for the comprehensive review, the Iraqi leadership announced the suspension of all UNSCOM activities, including those by the monitors who had been able to continue their work from 5 August to 31 October, although 'at a less than satisfactory level'.[146]

In November the crisis over the expulsion of the UNSCOM inspectors and monitors escalated rapidly and both the UK and the USA were poised to launch air strikes at targets in Iraq. Despite formal assurances by Iraq on 14 November that full cooperation would be given to the Security Council, which averted the air strikes, the UNSCOM report covering the period 17 November–15 December detailed many obstructions and new forms of restrictions which the UNSCOM inspectors and monitors encountered upon their return.[147] This lack of cooperation led to the swift initiation of US and British air strikes. Iraq has since suspended all cooperation with UNSCOM. Butler was strongly criticized by China, France and Russia for submitting the negative report. Russia, however, has maintained a campaign of calling for his resignation or dismissal on grounds of being untrustworthy and biased on an almost daily basis. By the end of 1998 Russia had emerged as the leading supporter of the Iraqi cause to lift the sanctions.

UNSCOM needs to be maintained in order to disarm Iraq, but its role and function have become hostage to the increasingly personalized conflict between UNSCOM's two main supporters, the UK and the USA, and Iraqi President Saddam Hussein. The coupling between the sanctions and the UNSCOM inspection regime has also become problematic. On the one hand, the UNSCOM mandate is open-ended. As Iraq displays no willingness to cooperate in the disarmament regime established under Resolution 687 and the international community does not trust Iraq to comply with its provisions in the future, grounds for suspicion that Iraq has not completely abandoned its non-conventional weapon programmes will remain. UNSCOM can therefore never issue the 'clean bill of health' that Iraq seeks. On the other hand, Iraq's defiance of the UN Security Council will continue to grow because Iraq feels that the sanctions will remain in place no matter what measures of compliance it undertakes. In its view, the UK and the USA seek to overthrow the regime in Baghdad, and UNSCOM is a tool to maintain the sanctions and justify military intervention. Thus far all 15 of the members of the UN Security Council have agreed on the fundamental principle of disarming Iraq but have differed on the method to achieve that objective. If the removal of Saddam Hussein becomes a stated goal, the Security Council members can be expected to become sharply divided over the fundamental goal.

[146] UN document S/1998/920 (note 138), para. 67.
[147] Letter from Richard Butler (note 139).

VI. Countering CBW terrorism

Since the March 1995 attack with the nerve agent sarin in the Tokyo underground system by the religious sect Aum Shinrikyo the perception of the threat posed by terrorism with CBW has risen steeply. Consequently, countermeasures are being taken on the international and national levels.

International cooperative efforts against CBW terrorism

Several efforts towards international cooperation in combating terrorism have been launched. Following a US initiative within the G7 and the Russian Federation in July 1996 the UN General Assembly adopted the text of the International Convention for the Suppression of Terrorist Bombings on 9 January 1998.[148] Attacks fall within the scope of the convention if they are carried out with an 'explosive or other lethal device'.[149] These include not only conventional explosives or other incendiary devices, but also toxic chemicals, biological agents or toxins or similar substances, and radiation or radioactive material.[150] This is the first time that chemical and biological weapons are explicitly mentioned in an international counter-terrorism agreement. While the CWC and the BTWC require parties to criminalize certain conduct by their nationals or people and bodies on their territory, the Terrorist Bombing Convention provides for broad international law enforcement cooperation in specified circumstances.[151]

President Clinton's address to the UN General Assembly on 21 September 1998 was devoted entirely to the issue of terrorism as a world problem and the vulnerability of any nation to chemical, biological and other kinds of attacks.[152] At the ministerial meeting of the North Atlantic Council (NAC) on 8 December, the United States proposed creating a new NATO Centre for Weapons of Mass Destruction. It would be a clearing house for increased intelligence sharing to produce more unified threat assessments about certain states and non-state actors, such as terrorist organizations. Some states have voiced reluctance, not least because the plan, in conjunction with proposals of alliance collaboration to deter and defend against proliferation, appears to move beyond NATO's traditional role of collective defence of the territory of member states.[153] The United States also reached an understanding with the

[148] *International Legal Materials*, vol. 37, no. 2 (Mar. 1998), pp. 249–260. As of 7 Jan. 1999, 1 country, Uzbekistan, had ratified the convention and 39 states had signed it: Algeria, Argentina, Austria, Belgium, Burundi, Canada, Comoros, Costa Rica, Côte d'Ivoire, Cyprus, Czech Republic, Finland, France, Germany, Greece, Iceland, Ireland, Italy, Japan, Lithuania, Luxembourg, Macedonia (Former Yugoslav Republic of), Monaco, the Netherlands, Norway, Panama, Philippines, Romania, Russia, Slovakia, Slovenia, Spain, Sri Lanka, Sweden, Togo, the UK, the USA, Uruguay and Venezuela.

[149] International Convention for the Suppression of Terrorist Bombings, article 2, para. 1.

[150] International Convention for the Suppression of Terrorist Bombings, article 1, para. 3.

[151] Witten, S. M., 'The International Convention for the Suppression of Terrorist Bombings', *American Journal of International Law*, vol. 92, no. 4 (Oct. 1998), p. 777, fn. 20.

[152] White House, 'Remarks by the President to the opening session of the 53rd United Nations General Assembly', 21 Sep. 1998, URL <http://www.pub.whitehouse.gov/uri-res/I2R?urn:pdi://oma.eop.gov.us/1998/9/22/2.text.1>.

[153] Erlanger, S., 'US urging allies to refocus NATO', *International Herald Tribune*, 7 Dec. 1998, p. 1.

EU on shared objectives, consultation and information exchanges, and the need for further cooperation to combat terrorism.[154]

The US counter-terrorism programme

The United States, which has suffered a spate of bloody terrorist attacks domestically and against installations abroad, invests heavily in domestic preparedness programmes.[155] In recent years the number of investigations by the Federal Bureau of Investigation (FBI) into the use or threatened use of NBC-related materials has increased significantly.

The US policy on terrorism is based on four pillars: reduction of vulnerability to terrorism, deterrence of terrorist acts before they occur, response to terrorist acts if they occur and consequence management of such acts, and addressing the threat posed by NBC materials or weapons.[156] A distinction is made between domestic acts of terrorism and terrorist acts against US targets abroad. In the former case, the FBI has been designated as the lead agency for countering terrorism. In the latter case, the Department of State coordinates counter-terrorism policy and operations abroad.[157] In addition, the DOD spearheads activities to enhance domestic preparedness for responding to and managing the consequences of terrorist use of non-conventional weapons. The US Army Soldier and Biological Chemical Command (SBCCOM) leads the Domestic Preparedness Program.[158] The training programme is being implemented in the 120 largest US cities, which were selected on the sole criterion of city population. By 31 December 1998 one-third of these cities should have received the training, and the entire programme is expected to be completed by FY 2001.[159]

[154] United States Information Service, 'US–EU declaration on counterterrorism', *Washington File*, 18 May 1998, URL <http://www.usia.gov/current/news/topic/intrel/98051808.wpo.html?/products/washfile/newsitem.shtml>.

[155] Presidential Decision Directive (PDD) 39 of 21 June 1995 laid out the first steps to address the threat posed by CW and BW terrorism. In the event of an incident of domestic terrorism, crisis management is to be led by the FBI and crisis management by the Federal Emergency Management Agency (FEMA). The Nunn–Lugar–Domenici Domestic Preparedness Program was established by the Defense Against Weapons of Mass Destruction Act, contained in the National Defense Authorization Act for FY 1997, Public Law P.L. 104-201, 23 Sep. 1996, Title XIV. The programme seeks to enhance the capability of the federal government to prevent and respond to terrorist incidents and provide support to improve the capabilities of state and local agencies to respond to such incidents.

[156] Prepared statement of Louis J. Freeh, Director, Federal Bureau of Investigation, *Counterterrorism*, Hearing before the Committee on Appropriations, United States Senate, 105th Congress, 1st session (US Government Printing Office: Washington, DC, 1998), p. 12.

[157] Prepared statement of Madeleine Albright, Secretary of State, *Counterterrorism* (note 156), p. 31.

[158] 'Fact sheet', US Army Soldier and Biological Chemical Command (SBCCOM), updated 3 Feb. 1999, URL <http://www.sbccom.apgea.army.mil/sbccom/au_fs.html>. Initially, the Chemical and Biological Defense Command was tasked by the Secretary of the Army to implement the Domestic Preparedness Program through the Army Director of Military Support. The Director of Military Support and CBDCOM designed a training programme to enhance the knowledge and capability of local fire, law enforcement and medical personnel and hazardous materials technicians. In November 1998 CDBCOM merged with another Army Materiel Command, SSCOM, into SBCCOM.

[159] General Accounting Office, *Combating Terrorism: Opportunities to Improve Domestic Preparedness Program Focus and Efficiency*, GAO/NSIAD-99-3 (US General Accounting Office: Washington, DC, Nov. 1998), p. 4. The document includes detailed descriptions of the programme and lists the cities involved.

Meanwhile efforts are under way to coordinate the policies and activities of federal agencies, bureaux and offices involved in combating terrorism, which numbered over 40 in 1997,[160] as well as those of the federal, state and local authorities. The Conference Committee Report accompanying the 1998 Appropriations Act for the departments of Commerce, Justice and State, the Judiciary and related agencies directs the attorney-general to develop a 5-year interdepartmental counter-terrorism and technology crime plan by 31 December 1998 to serve as a baseline strategy for coordination of national policy and operational capabilities to combat terrorism.[161] Presidential Decision Directive 62 of 22 May 1998 updated the national policy to enhance capabilities to prevent and respond to terrorist events involving non-conventional weapons.[162]

VII. Conclusions

Progress has been made in the development of strong CBW disarmament regimes. The treaty-building process of the CWC has advanced steadily. Outstanding issues are gradually being resolved, although some issues still require political solutions by the states parties. Of continuing concern, however, are the major delays in the inspections of the US industry facilities and the fact that Russia, the holder of the world's largest CW stockpile, still has not begun destroying its chemical weapons. Several issues remain to be resolved, but given sufficient political will they should not be insurmountable. Negotiations to add a protocol to the BTWC, which will include verification provisions, are proceeding at a slower pace than initially hoped for. Work still remains to be done to strike a balance between industry and security interests. Most observers nevertheless still anticipate the conclusion of the negotiations before the Fifth Review Conference of the BTWC in 2001.

Proliferation of CBW remains a major concern and many Western states are in the process of implementing policies to counter such a threat. Chemical or biological terrorism poses governments with risks that are difficult to gauge, because of the uncertainties regarding the types of agent to be used, and the timing and location of an eventual strike. The UNSCOM experience in Iraq further demonstrates the difficulties in reversing CBW proliferation in the face of determined efforts to maintain a major CBW armament programme.

[160] General Accounting Office, *Combating Terrorism: Federal Agencies' Efforts to Implement National Policy and Strategy*, GAO/NSIAD-97-254 (US General Accounting Office: Washington, DC, Sep. 1997), pp. 33–34.

[161] Prepared statement of Attorney-General Janet Reno, *Counterterrorism: Evaluating the 5-Year Plan*, Hearing before a Subcommittee of the Committee on Appropriations, United States Senate, 105th Congress, 1st session (US Government Printing Office: Washington, DC, 1998), p. 9.

[162] White House, 'Combating terrorism: Presidential Decision Directive 62', *Fact Sheet*, 22 May 1998, URL <http:www.pub.whitehouse.gov/uri-res/I2R?urn:pdi://oma.eop.gov.us/1998/5/22/7.text.1>. PDD 62 is a classified document.

Appendix 13A. Benefits and threats of developments in biotechnology and genetic engineering

MALCOLM DANDO*

I. Introduction

As concerns about the proliferation and possible use of biological weapons (BW) have increased during the 1990s[1] more attention has been given to the history of the development of this form of weaponry in the offensive biological warfare programmes of states of international significance over the past century.[2] It is clear that soon after scientists such as Louis Pasteur and Robert Koch had established, in the last decades of the 19th century, that specific micro-organisms cause specific diseases in humans, animals and plants, attempts were made to sabotage valuable draught animal stocks through the use of biological weapons by both sides in World War I.[3] Subsequently, the developments in the science of aerobiology and in production capabilities for antibiotics were significant elements in the major US offensive programme of the mid-20th century, and the developing understanding of virology and the advent of genetic engineering were important in the Soviet programme in the latter decades of the cold war.[4] While current capabilities in genetic engineering could continue to be applied in today's offensive BW programmes, the question arises as to what kinds of weapon might be possible in the future as a result of ongoing developments in biotechnology.[5]

Concerns over the near-term development of new weapons have been voiced recently.[6] Moreover, both national and international medical associations have warned that future scientific and technological advances could be misused for such purposes.[7]

[1] E.g., Miller, J. and Broad, W. J., 'Clinton sees threat of germ terrorism', *International Herald Tribune*, 23–24 Jan. 1999, pp. 1, 3; and Leitenberg, M., 'Biological weapons: a reawakened concern', *The World & I* (Washington, DC), Jan. 1999, pp. 289–305.

[2] Dando, M. R., 'The impact of the development of modern biology and medicine on the evolution of offensive biological warfare programmes in the 20th century', *Defense Analysis*, vol. 15, no. 1 (1999), pp. 43–62.

[3] Redmond, C. *et al.*, 'Deadly relic of the Great War', *Nature*, vol. 393 (25 June 1998), pp. 747–48.

[4] Dando (note 2).

[5] This question was the subject of analysis in Bartfai, T., Lundin, S. J. and Rybeck, B., 'Benefits and threats of developments in biotechnology and genetic engineering', *SIPRI Yearbook 1993: World Armaments and Disarmament* (Oxford University Press: Oxford, 1993), pp. 293–305.

[6] E.g., Starr, B., 'Cohen warns of new terrors beyond CW', *Jane's Defence Weekly*, 4 June 1997, p. 27; and Starr, B. and Evers, S., 'Interview: US Secretary of Defense, William Cohen', *Jane's Defence Weekly*, 13 Aug. 1997, p. 32.

[7] British Medical Association, *Biotechnology, Weapons and Humanity* (Harwood Academic: London, 1999); and World Medical Association, 'Statement: weapons and their relation to life and health', Paper presented at the 48th World Medical Association General Assembly, Somerset West, South Africa, 20–26 Oct. 1996.

* The work reported here is supported by a research fellowship from the United States Institute of Peace.

This appendix updates the 1993 SIPRI contribution[8] and reconsiders its central concern about the possible development of BW targeted at the genetic characteristics of specific ethnic or racial groups, in the light of scientific and technological developments in 1993–98. This concern is also set within a broader consideration of related scientific, technological and industrial developments.

II. Advances in scientific knowledge and genome mapping

The modern world has been shaped by a series of technological revolutions: steam power, electricity, internal combustion engines and oil-based chemicals, and electronic computers and microelectronics.[9] There can be little doubt that the early stages of a profound new revolution in biotechnology are already having major effects on the pharmaceutical and agricultural industries worldwide.[10] Rifkin, for example, has argued that the growing scientific understanding of genetics is at the centre of at least seven strands of technological and social forces that will produce a new 'operational matrix' underpinning a rapid and fundamental transformation of the current way of life.[11] In his view, 'The Biotech Century brings with it a new resource base, a new set of transforming technologies, new forms of commercial protection to spur commerce, a global trading market to seed the Earth with an artificial second Genesis' and, he continues, a supporting conceptual framework: 'an emerging eugenics science, a new supporting sociology, a new communications tool to organize and manage economic activity at the genetic level, and a new cosmological narrative to accompany the journey'. The whole of this vision need not be accepted in order to see that '[g]enomics has substantial government support, massive corporate investment, powerful enabling technologies, and short-term cash-generating potential'.[12] It is clear that the massive worldwide chemical industry is reorienting itself to take advantage of these new opportunities and that enormous scientific and technological developments are inevitable.[13] An indicator of the rate of change is that the US Patent and Trademark Office received patent requests for 4000 nucleic acid sequences in 1991 and 500 000 in 1996.[14] The developments in genome mapping must be understood in this context.

There can be no doubt that the Human Genome Project (HGP) is the single most important project in biology and medicine today. Although this is an international collaborative effort, it is centred in the USA, where it is sponsored by the National Human Genome Research Institute. In a major US review of 1998 it was announced that all the major goals of the 1994–98 five-year plan had been achieved, and a new plan was presented for 1999–2003 in which human DNA sequencing is the central objective. According to the review, 'An ambitious schedule has been set to complete the full sequence by the end of 2003, 2 years ahead of previous projections. In the course of completing the sequence, a "working draft" of the human sequence will be

[8] Bartfai, Lundin and Rybeck (note 5).

[9] Freeman, C., 'Technological revolutions: historical analogies', eds M. Fransman *et al.*, *The Biotechnology Revolution* (Blackwell: Oxford, 1995), pp. 7–24.

[10] Sharp, M., 'Applications of biotechnology: an overview', eds Fransman *et al.* (note 9), pp. 163–73.

[11] Rifkin, J. T., *The Biotech Century: The Coming Age of Genetic Commerce* (Victor Gollancz: London, 1998).

[12] Enriques, J., 'Genomics and the world's economy', *Science*, vol. 281 (14 Aug. 1998), pp. 925–26.

[13] Service, R. F., 'Chemical industry rushes towards greener pastures', *Science*, vol. 282 (23 Oct. 1998), pp. 608–10.

[14] Enriques (note 12), p. 925.

produced by the end of 2001'.[15] When the review was released a physical map of 30 000 human genes—approximately one-half of the estimated total—was published by an international group of researchers.[16]

The goals of the US Human Genome Project[17] are particularly significant in light of the concern over the possible development of weapons targeted at the specific genetic characteristics of different ethnic groups. It has been argued that 'if investigations provide sufficient data on ethnic genetic differences between population groups, it may be possible to use such data to target suitable micro-organisms to attack known receptor sites for which differences exist at cell membrane level or even to target DNA sequences inside cells by viral vectors'.[18] Clearly, there are differences between ethnic groups in gene expression because otherwise physical distinctions could not be recognized. Thus targeting of the different products of gene expression (e.g., in cell membrane receptor sites) might be feasible. However, as gene sequences constitute a very small proportion of the total DNA in the human genome, a wider range of possibilities might arise if DNA itself could be targeted. This could open up for potential attack not just the gene sequences, but also gene control systems and the vast stretches of DNA which have no currently known function. In order to develop ethnic-specific genetic weapons it would be necessary to know the differences between the genetics of different ethnic groups, have a working knowledge of genome function and be able to target specific functions in specific genomes with particular vectors.[19] Developments in vector technology (gene therapy) are discussed below. What is noticeable about the aspirations for the US HGP in the forthcoming period are two new goals: determination of *human sequence variation* and *functional analysis* of the operation of the whole genome (table 13A.1). These are of direct relevance to the first two steps necessary to produce ethnic-specific genetic weapons.

The reason why human sequence variation is important can be seen in current discussions of the future of medicine. Currently, doctors treat symptoms which may derive from diverse pathophysiological mechanisms with drugs which may be metabolized in very different ways—both a result of individual differences in genetics. Therefore, although the medical profession is interested in the HGP's sequencing of the whole human genome by 2003, more importantly to them, 'as many as 100 000 single nucleotide polymorphisms are likely to be detected over the same timeframe' and thus, 'This set of polymorphisms is likely to provide a handle on many of the important genetic determinants of disease susceptibility and response to therapy that exist in the population'.[20] Single nucleotide polymorphisms (SNPs, single base-pair differences in DNA) are the most common polymorphism in the human genome and are abundant and widespread across the genome. The goal of mapping 100 000 SNPs is likely to be achieved, but the potential downside of such knowledge is obvious. A sub-goal of the HGP, for example, is stated to be 'e) Create public resources of DNA

[15] Collins, F. S. *et al.*, 'New goals for the US Human Genome Project: 1998–2003', *Science*, vol. 282 (23 Oct. 1998), pp. 682–89.

[16] Deloukas, P. *et al.*, 'A physical map of 30,000 human genes', *Science*, vol. 282 (23 Oct. 1998), pp. 744–46.

[17] Collins *et al.* (note 15).

[18] Bartfai, Lundin and Rybeck (note 5), p. 304.

[19] Bartfai, Lundin and Rybeck (note 5).

[20] Bell, J., 'The human genome', eds M. Marinker and M. Peckham, *Clinical Futures* (British Medical Journal Books: London, 1998), pp. 20–42.

Table 13A.1. Some goals of the Human Genome Project (HGP) for 1998–2003

Area	Goals
Genetic map	Completed
Physical map	Completed
DNA sequence	One-third finished by end 2001, working draft of rest by end 2001, completed by 2003
Sequencing technology	Integrate and further low-cost automation
Human sequence variation[a]	100 000 mapped single nucleotide polymorphisms, develop technology
Gene identification	Full-length cDNAs
Functional analysis[a]	Develop genomic-scale technologies
Model organisms' complete DNA sequences	*Escherichia coli*, published Sep. 1997; yeast, released Apr. 1996; *Caenorhabditis elegans*, completed Dec. 1998; *Drosophila*, to be completed 2002; mouse, to be completed 2005

[a] New goal.

Source: Collins, F. S. *et al.*, 'New goals for the US Human Genome Project: 1998–2003', *Science*, vol. 282 (23 Oct. 1998), pp. 683.

samples and cell lines' and within that sub-goal it is argued that to 'maximize discovery of common variants in all human populations, a resource is needed that includes individuals whose ancestors derive from diverse geographic areas'.[21] As is apparent in the following discussion, that means specifying the variations found in different ethnic groups.

For the medical practitioner or biologist the structure of the human genome is of little value without a knowledge of how it operates as a system. The study of the operation of the whole genome is termed functional genomics.[22] There are already, on the basis of the discovery of the genomic structure of simpler organisms, impressive examples of what will become available for human genomics in the next century.[23] Furthermore, the regulation of the function of genes may turn out to be relatively straightforward to understand and model.[24] It should also be noted that dramatic progress is now being made in the understanding of plant genomes.[25]

Finally, while the HGP will continue to include work on ethical, legal and social implications (ELSI),[26] even detailed and informed discussions of these topics rarely mention the possible misuse of genomics in biological warfare.[27]

[21] Collins *et al.* (note 15), p. 686.

[22] Lander, E. S., 'The new genomics: global views of biology', *Science*, vol. 274 (25 Oct. 1996), pp. 536–39.

[23] Chu, S. *et al.*, 'The transcription program of sporulation in budding yeast', *Science*, vol. 282 (23 Oct. 1998), pp. 699–705.

[24] Wray, G. A., 'Promoter logic', *Science*, vol. 279 (20 Mar. 1998), pp. 1871–72; and Chiou-Hwa, Y., Bolouri, H. and Davidson, E. H., 'Genomic *cis*-regulatory logic: experimental and computational analysis of a sea urchin gene', *Science*, vol. 279 (20 Mar. 1998), pp. 1896–1902.

[25] Gale, M. D. and Devos, K. M., 'Plant comparative genetics after 10 years', *Science*, vol. 282 (23 Oct. 1998), pp. 656–58.

[26] Collins *et al.* (note 15), pp. 687–88.

[27] Greely, H. T., 'Legal, ethical and social issues in human genome research', *Annual Review of Anthropology*, vol. 27 (1998), pp. 473–502.

III. Biotechnology

Heterologous gene expression, genetically engineered organisms, protein engineering and human monoclonal antibodies remain important topics,[28] but of particular interest are the improvements in detection and identification technologies since the 1991 Persian Gulf War. The deficiencies in detection and protection measures available to Coalition forces at that time and the increasing perception that biological weapons may be used in future wars have led to considerable efforts in some NATO countries to develop better technologies.[29] Yet despite this increased military expenditure it is clear that the dominant developments are taking place in the civil sphere.

The commercial potential inherent in being able to identify SNPs and thus to link differences to diseases and treatment strategies is fuelling a race to find fast and sensitive methods of screening large numbers of DNA samples.[30] It has proved possible to modify the lithographic production techniques used to make computer chips in order to make arrays of DNA chips. The arrays are made by starting with a silicon surface coated with linker molecules that bind the four DNA building blocks—adenine, cytosine, guanine and thymidine. The linker molecules are initially coated with a photosensitive blocker compound. Light is then used to expose certain areas of the linker molecules, and the chip is incubated with one of the bases. The blocker is then reapplied and the process is repeated. In just 32 cycles it is possible to build an array of 65 000 different oligonucleotides, each eight base pairs long. This array of oligonucleotides is capable of binding to complementary stretches of DNA and therefore of acting as a sensor. Researchers can isolate RNA molecules (which are evidence of gene expression in tissues), convert them to DNA and tag this DNA with a fluorescent marker. By floating the tagged DNA across the array of oligonucleotides and, by means of a laser to excite fluorescence, checking the strands that bind, the sequence of the tagged DNA, and thus the expressed RNA, can be determined from the positions of the known oligonucleotides on the array.

The idea for this DNA chip technology was first published in 1991. Today, the originator's company, Affymetrix, has commercial products to test for mutations, for example, in the human immunodeficiency virus (HIV) genome and in the p53 tumour-suppressor gene which is thought to be implicated in 50 per cent of all human cancers. Surveys by financial houses suggest an immediate market of some $1 billion per annum and numerous ways in which technology and applications could develop. Many now believe that such DNA chips—capable of holding hundreds of thousands of immobilized DNA fragments and thus tracking huge numbers of gene expressions at the same time—will replace the current silicon chips as the important chips of the 21st century.[31] The use of such DNA arrays on chips opens up the possibility of examining the functions of cellular genomes. As the director of the US National Institutes of Health is reported to have commented at the end of 1998, 'we will [eventu-

[28] Bartfai, Lundin and Rybeck (note 5), pp. 295–98.

[29] Roberts, B. and Pearson, G. S., 'Bursting the biological bubble: how prepared are we for biowar?', *Jane's International Defence Review*, Apr. 1998, pp. 21–24; Beal, C., 'Facing the invisible enemy', *Jane's Defence Weekly*, 4 Nov. 1998, pp. 23–26; and Hewish, M., 'On alert against bio agents', *Jane's International Defence Review*, Nov. 1998, pp. 53–57.

[30] Pennisi, E., 'Sifting through and making sense of genome sequences', *Science*, vol. 280 (12 June 1998), pp. 1692–93.

[31] Service, R. F., 'Microchip arrays put DNA on the spot', *Science*, vol. 282 (16 Oct. 1998), pp. 396–98.

ally] be looking at the totality of gene behaviour in individual cells, even [in] whole organisms'.[32]

IV. Medical and health improvements

It is difficult to overestimate the enthusiasm in the medical community for the wide range of therapeutic opportunities that will open up in the coming age of molecular medicine.[33] This is clearly seen as an objectively manipulatable technology based on a mechanistic scientific understanding of functional genomics. This section concentrates on advances in gene therapy, but to ignore the broader background would be to seriously misunderstand current developments and future possibilities.

The reasons for medical interest in gene therapy are understandable. A common disease such as cystic fibrosis is caused by a single defective gene.[34] Correction of the deficiency by the addition of a normal gene could effect a cure. Many cancers are caused by a series of single mutations in genes that control cell growth.[35] Correction of one of these mutations could halt the unregulated cellular proliferation. Medical success in dealing with genetic defects is not a totally new phenomenon. Phenylketonuria (PKU), for example, resulting from abnormality of the gene for the liver enzyme phenylalanine hydroxylase (PAH), which is involved in the metabolism of the amino acid phenylalanine, was described in the 1930s. Defects in the gene occur in many populations and particularly in Caucasian groups. It is possible, however, to test for the abnormality at birth and, by controlling diet, to restrict phenylalanine intake in sufferers, and thus avoid the mental retardation which results from the faulty metabolism caused by the defective gene.[36]

The question is whether gene therapy—the attempt to effect changes at the level of the gene rather than to deal with the consequences of the operation of a defective gene as in the case of PKU—will live up to the early hopes of the medical community.[37] Clearly, there are ways in which DNA can be introduced into cells by physical means, and viruses themselves have evolved to enter and take over the cellular machinery of the cell, but the problem is one of altering the function of the cell in a controlled manner in order to achieve the desired change.[38] Recent reviews suggest a period of consolidation but in tandem with steady advance towards a usable technol-

[32] Pennisi, E., 'DNA chips give new view of classic test', *Science*, vol. 283 (1 Jan. 1999), pp. 17–18.

[33] E.g., Leder, M. D. *et al.*, *Introduction to Molecular Medicine* (Scientific American Inc.: New York, 1994); Bradley, J. *et al.*, *Lecture Notes on Molecular Medicine* (Blackwell Science: Oxford, 1995); Mauik, S. and Patel, S. D., *Molecular Biotechnology: Therapeutic Applications and Strategies* (Wiley-Liss: New York, 1997); and Sudbery, P., *Human Molecular Genetics* (Longman: London, 1998).

[34] E.g., Welsh, M. J. and Smith, A. E., 'Cystic fibrosis', *Scientific American*, Dec. 1995, pp. 36–43; and Wagner, J. A. and Gardner, P., 'Toward cystic fibrosis gene therapy', *Annual Review of Medicine*, vol. 48 (1997), pp. 203–16.

[35] Weinberg, R. A., 'How cancer arises', *Scientific American: Special Issue on Cancer*, Sep. 1996, pp. 32–40.

[36] E.g., Polednak, A. P., *Racial and Ethnic Differences in Disease* (Oxford University Press,: Oxford, 1989); and Scriver, C. R. *et al.*, 'The phenylalanine hydroxylase locus: a marker for the history of phenyulketonuria and human genetic diversity', ed. K. M. Weiss, *Variation in the Human Genome* (John Wiley and Sons: Chichester, 1996), pp. 73–96.

[37] E.g., Miller, A. D., 'Human gene therapy comes of age', *Nature*, vol. 357 (11 June 1992), pp. 455–60; and Friedmann, T., 'A brief history of gene therapy', *Nature Genetics*, vol. 2 (Oct. 1992), pp. 93–98.

[38] E.,g., Weatherall, D. J., 'Scope and limitations of gene therapy', eds A. M. L. Lever and P. Goodfellow, *Gene Therapy*, *British Medical Bulletin*, vol. 51, no. 1 (Jan. 1995), pp. 1–11; and Smith, A. E., 'Viral victors in gene therapy', *Annual Review of Microbiology*, vol. 49 (1995), pp. 807–38.

Table 13A.2. US clinical trials of gene therapy, as of early 1998

Target/type	Number	Percentage
Disease targets for therapeutic clinical protocols		
Cancer	138	*69.0*
Genetic diseases	33	*16.5*
Cystic fibrosis	16	. .
Other diseases (mostly monogenic)	17	. .
Acquired immunodeficiency syndrome (AIDS)	23	*11.5*
Other	6	*3.0*
Total	**200**	***100.0***
Vectors employed for therapeutic clinical protocols		
Viral	. .	*80*
Retroviral	. .	*60*
Adenoviral	. .	*10*
Other	. .	*10*
Non-viral	. .	*20*

Source: French Andersen, W., 'Human gene therapy', *Nature*, vol. 392, supp. (30 Apr. 1998), p. 28.

ogy.[39] This viewpoint is reinforced by the flood of detailed scientific papers in the literature (*Human Gene Therapy*, a journal now in its ninth volume, carried well over 200 articles in 1998) and by the steady accumulation of clinical trials (table 13A.2) now involving over 3000 people.[40]

The general advantages and disadvantages of the various vector systems are well known. RNA retroviruses, which are used in the majority of current clinical protocols (table 13A.2), can carry out gene transfer to many cell types and integrate stably into the host genome. The problems involve getting efficient delivery to target cells, the inability to infect non-dividing cells, sustaining long-term expression of the inserted gene, and manufacturing the vector virus in a cost-effective manner. DNA adenoviruses can also transfer genes to a wide range of cell types including non-dividing cells and can be manufactured in large quantities. On the other hand, they do not integrate stably into the host cell genome and therefore require repeated administration, when their tendency to provoke strong immune responses can cause problems.

While the technical problems involved in using the different types of viral vector can be addressed (e.g., better understanding of the structure of the proteins involved in the initial docking of retroviruses[41] should eventually allow more specific targeting of the desired cell types) there is reason to believe that, eventually, non-viral vectors

[39] French Andersen, W., 'Human gene therapy', *Nature*, vol. 392, supp. (30 Apr. 1998), pp. 25–30; Kay, M. A. *et al.*, 'Gene therapy', *Proceedings of the National Academy of Sciences*, vol. 94 (Nov. 1997), pp. 12744–46; Verma, M. and Somia, N., 'Gene therapy—promises, problems and prospects', *Nature*, vol. 389 (18 Sep. 1997), pp. 239–42; Blau, H. and Khavari, P., 'Gene therapy: progress, problems, prospects', *Nature Medicine*, vol. 3 (June 1997), pp. 612–13; and Friedmann, T., 'Overcoming the obstacles to gene therapy', *Scientific American: Special Report: Making Gene Therapy Work* (June 1995), pp. 96–102.

[40] French Andersen (note 39), p. 28.

[41] Fass, D. *et al.*, 'Structure of a murine leukemia virus receptor-binding glycoprotein at 2.0 Ångström resolution', *Science*, vol. 277 (12 Sep. 1997), pp. 1662–66.

will become more important.[42] These may become much easier to manufacture and will be inherently safer than modified natural organisms. Additionally, great progress is likely to be made in the use of anti-sense oligonucleotides and ribozymes to modulate gene expression.[43] The scale and pace of change in this technology are best illustrated by reference to specific examples.

In the one phase III clinical trial of gene therapy in the USA in early 1998 Genetic Therapy Inc./Novartis targeted a malignant brain tumour, glioblastoma multiforma.[44] A mouse producer cell line was injected into the tumour mass. The mouse cells produced the retroviral vector (G1TkSvNa) which had been modified to carry the herpes simplex thymidine kinase (HSTk) gene. Since the retrovirus only attacks dividing cells and the only dividing cells would be those of the tumour and its blood supply vasculature, these should be the only cells infected by the retroviruses produced by the mouse cells. The viral HSTk can, as human thymidine kinase cannot, add a phosphate group to a non-phosphorylated nucleoside. Thus when an abnormal nucleoside, in the drug ganciclovir, is subsequently given to patients only cells expressing the HSTk gene should be able to phosphorylate the drug, add it into their DNA synthesis system and hence be killed. Not only cells infected with the virus are affected; 'bystander' effects (e.g., transmission of the toxic ganciclovir triphosphate across gap junctions to other cells) also operate to achieve reductions in tumours. The phase III trial included 40 centres in North America and Europe and 250 patients in total.

Another approach is targeted at the p53 tumour suppressor gene which is found to be faulty in over 50 per cent of cancers. It is known that two sets of genes are crucially involved in triggering cancer. Normally, these genes control the life cycle of the cell: '[p]roto-oncogenes encourage cell growth, whereas tumour suppressor genes inhibit it. . . . When mutated, proto-oncogenes can become carcinogenic oncogenes that drive excessive multiplication. . . . Tumour suppressor genes, in contrast, contribute to cancer when they are inactivated by mutations'.[45] Fortunately, for a cancer to develop mutations must occur in a number of different genes in order to disrupt a cell's complex growth and division regulatory mechanism.

When p53 functions correctly it prevents the cell from duplicating damaged DNA or foreign DNA (e.g., that of an adenovirus). In order to get the cell to replicate viral DNA an adenovirus has to prevent the p53 protein (derived from the p53 gene) from operating. The E1B region of an adenovirus genome codes, among others, for the protein which binds to, and thus prevents the operation of, the p53 protein. It follows that if the E1B region is removed from an adenovirus genome, the adenovirus will not be able to replicate in a cell with a normal, functional p53 gene. However, if the p53 gene of the cell is not functioning, as in many cancers, the adenovirus lacking the E1B region will still be able to replicate and thus kill the cell. Moreover, if injected into a tumour, the adenoviruses released from the killed cell should go on to successfully attack other tumour cells which will also lack the functional p53 gene.[46]

[42] E.g., Schofield, J. P. and Caskey, C. T., 'Non-viral approaches to gene therapy', eds Lever and Goodfellow (note 38), pp. 56–71; and Langer, R., 'Drug delivery and targeting', *Nature*, vol. 392, supp. (30 Apr. 1998), pp. 5–10.

[43] E.g., Rozsi, J. J., 'Therapeutic antisense and ribozymes', eds Lever and Goodfellow (note 38), pp. 217–25; and Kleiner, K., 'Antisense starts making sense', *New Scientist*, 1 Aug. 1998, p. 12.

[44] E.g., French Andersen (note 39); and Ram, Z. *et al.*, 'Gene therapy of malignant brain tumours by intratumoral implantation of retroviral vector-producing cells', *Nature Medicine*, vol. 3, no. 12 (Dec. 1997), pp. 1354–61.

[45] Weinberg (note 35), p. 33.

[46] E.g., Pennisi, E., 'Will a twist of viral fate lead to a new cancer treatment?', *Science*, vol. 274 (18 Oct. 1996), pp. 342–43; Bischoff, J. R. *et al.*, 'An adenovirus mutant that replicates selectively in

While the mechanisms may be complex,[47] in clinical trials with patients whose head and neck cancers have not responded to other treatments use of ONYX-015, a gene-attenuated adenovirus, has achieved excellent results particularly in combination with chemotherapy.[48] In 2 of the first 10 people treated with both therapies tumours disappeared within a month and in 7 more there was a 50 per cent shrinkage of the tumour. It seems that this approach can also be generalized to use other viruses and other parts of the cellular control mechanism.[49]

The general picture as described in one recent review is that 'in the not too distant future, gene therapy will become as routine a practice as heart transplants are today'.[50]

V. Genomic diversity and DNA fingerprinting

It has long been known that different ethnic groups vary in the incidence among them of congenital diseases and obviously genetically determined characteristics such as blood groups.[51] However, before the flood of new data on the actual nucleotide sequences of genes became available, understanding was constrained by a model which suggested that a single normal 'wild-type' gene recurrently mutated back and forth with a single mutant-type gene that caused the visible disease. As information has accumulated, for example on the cystic fibrosis gene[52] and the phenylalanine hydroxylase gene,[53] the true situation has been seen to be far more complex. Most genes have been found to occur in many different alleles caused by different changes in the nucleotide sequence. Moreover, these changes remain in the chromosome and, as most people throughout history have remained close to home, such mutations tend to characterize local populations and to be added to by newer local mutations. As noted by Weiss, 'most mutations, especially recent mutations, have in the course of human history tended to be (and remain) geographically localized. The younger the mutation the more localized. Only older mutations, often those existing at the origin of our species, are found dispersed across several continents'.[54] It follows therefore that, as more detailed information on gene sequences becomes available, it should be expected that markers, or at least small sets of markers, will be discovered that will distinguish between different groups. Such information is likely to become available

p53-deficient human tumor cells', *Science*, vol. 274 (18 Oct. 1996), pp. 373–76; Lowe, S. W., 'Progress of the smart bomb cancer virus', *Nature Medicine*, vol. 3, no. 6 (June 1997), pp. 606–08; and Heise, G. *et al.*, 'ONYX-015, an E1B gene-attenuated adenovirus, causes tumor-specific cytolysis and antitumoral efficacy that can be augmented by standard chemotherapeutic agents', *Nature Medicine*, vol. 3, no. 6 (June 1997), pp. 639–45.

[47] Lane, D. P., 'Killing tumor cells with viruses—a question of specificity', *Nature Medicine*, vol. 4, no. 9 (Sep. 1998), pp. 1012–13; and Hall, A. R. *et al.*, 'p53-dependent cell death/apoptosis is required for a productive adenovirus infection', *Nature Medicine*, vol. 4, no. 9 (Sep. 1998), pp. 1068–72.

[48] Barinaga, M., 'From bench top to bedside', *Science*, vol. 278 (7 Nov. 1997), pp. 1036–39; and Pennisi, E., 'Training viruses to attack cancer cells', *Science*, vol. 282 (13 Nov. 1998), pp. 1244–46.

[49] Pennisi (note 48); and Coffey, M. C. *et al.*, 'Reovirus therapy of tumors with activated Ras pathway', *Science*, vol. 282 (13 Nov. 1998), pp. 1332–34.

[50] Verma and Somia (note 39), p. 242.

[51] E.g., British Medical Association (note 7); and Polednak (note 36).

[52] Bertranpetit, J. and Calafell, F., 'Genetic and geographical variability in cystic fibrosis: evolutionary considerations', ed. K. M. Weiss, *Variation in the Human Genome* (John Wiley and Sons: Chichester, 1996), pp. 97–118.

[53] Scriver (note 36); and Kleimann, S. *et al.*, 'Origins of hyperphenylalaninemia in Israel', *European Journal of Human Genetics*, vol. 2 (1994), pp. 24–34.

[54] Weiss, K. M., 'Is there a paradigm shift in genetics? Lessons from the study of human diseases', *Molecular Phylogenetics and Evolution*, vol. 5, no. 1 (Feb. 1996), pp. 259–65.

not only through the efforts of the HGP and drug companies,[55] but also through those of anthropologists and forensic scientists,[56] despite the difficulties scientists have experienced in starting an organized Human Genome Diversity Project.[57]

The work of anthropologists is of particular relevance here. It is clear that almost all of our primate relatives have recognizable subspecies whereas humans do not.[58] From the fossil record a range of hominid species can be seen to have died out over the past 5 million years.[59] Modern *Homo sapiens* probably originated approximately 120 000 years ago and appears to be quite distinct from Neanderthal man who died out some 30 000 years ago.[60] *Homo sapiens*, although remaining a single species, has spread progressively across the globe in ways that are well known in a general way.[61] Much current work is concerned with analysing the details and consequences of these human migrations.[62]

Anthropologists, of course, have long had an interest in the origins and evolution of the species, but modern genetics has given them a much enhanced capacity to analyse such issues.[63] There is also clearly an overlap between their interests and those of the medical/pharmaceutical community in discovering the links between genes and diseases. This is most easily done if rather homogeneous, long-isolated populations can be studied since gene-to-disease links are more easily established in such populations than in heterogeneous groups where other factors are likely to obscure relationships. In order to find gene-to-disease links there is also a need to have markers spaced evenly across all human chromosomes so that the particular regions connected with particular diseases in affected individuals can be determined. The HGP objective to use single nucleotide polymorphisms for that purpose is discussed above. Another

[55] E.g., Shields, P. G., 'Pharmacogenetics: detecting sensitive populations', *Environmental Health Perspectives*, vol. 102, supp. 11 (Dec. 1994), pp. 81–87; Brower, V., 'From human rights to the human genome—stopping biopiracy', *Nature Medicine*, vol. 3, no. 10 (Oct. 1997), p. 1056; Doll, J. J., 'The patenting of DNA', *Science*, vol. 280 (1 May 1998), pp. 689–90; Garte, S., 'The role of ethnicity in cancer susceptibility gene polymorphisms: the example of CYP1A1', *Carcinogenesis*, vol. 19, no. 8 (1998), pp. 1329–32; and Beutler, E. *et al.*, 'Racial variation in the UDP-glucouronosyltransferase 1 (UGT1A1) promoter: a balanced polymorphism for regulation of bilirubin metabolism', *Proceedings of the National Academy of Sciences USA*, vol. 95 (July 1998), pp. 8170–74.

[56] National Research Council, *The Evaluation of Forensic DNA Evidence: An Update* (National Academy Press: Washington, DC, 1996).

[57] Friedlander, J., 'Genes, people, and property: introduction to a special issue', *Cultural Survival Quarterly*, summer 1996, pp. 22–24; and Marshall, E., 'DNA studies challenge the meaning of race', *Science*, vol. 282 (23 Oct. 1998), pp. 654–55.

[58] Ruvolo, M., 'Genetic diversity in hominoid primates', *Annual Review of Anthropology*, vol. 26 (1997), pp. 515–40.

[59] Foley, J., 'Hominid species', Talk.Origins Archive, URL <http://www.talkorigins.org/faqs/homs/species.html>.

[60] Krings, M. *et al.*, 'Neandertal DNA sequences and the origin of modern humans', *Cell*, vol. 90 (11 July 1997), pp. 19–30.

[61] Cavalli-Sforza, L. L. *et al.*, *The History and Geography of Human Genes* (Princeton University Press: Princeton, N.J., 1994); and Cavalli-Sforza, L. L. and Cavalli-Sforza, F., *The Great Human Diasporas* (Addison-Wesley: New York, 1995).

[62] E.g., Chu, J. Y. *et al.*, 'Genetic relationship of populations in China', *Proceedings of the National Academy of Sciences USA*, vol. 95 (Sep. 1998), pp. 11763–68; Chikhi, L. *et al.*, 'Clines of nuclear DNA markers suggest a largely neolithic ancestry of the European gene pool', *Proceedings of the National Academy of Sciences USA*, vol. 95 (July 1998), pp. 9053–58; Gibbons, A., 'The peopling of the Americas', *Science*, vol. 274 (4 Oct. 1996), pp. 31–33; Morell, V., 'Genes may link ancient Eurasians, Native Americans', *Science*, vol. 280 (24 Apr. 1998), p. 520; and Murray-McIntosh, R. O. *et al.*, 'Testing migration patterns and estimating founding population size in Polynesia by using human mt DNA sequences', *Proceedings of the National Academy of Sciences USA*, vol. 95 (July 1998), pp. 9047–52.

[63] Weiss, K. M., 'Coming to terms with human variation', *Annual Review of Anthropology*, vol. 27 (1998), pp. 273–300.

useful type of marker is micro-satellites—tandem repeats of the same short sequence of 2–4 base pairs.

While there remains debate among anthropologists about many of the details of recent human evolution, certain points are clear. First, a 'variety of genetic data have been examined at the population level with a consistent result: Sub-Saharan African populations tend to be the most genetically distant, and non-African regional populations tend to be more similar to one another than any are to Africa'.[64] This pattern, consistent with the rapid expansion of part of an African population out of the continent, has been found for mitochondrial DNA (mt DNA, maternal inheritance), Y chromosomes (paternal inheritance), *Alu* insertion polymorphisms and micro-satellite DNA as well as classic genetic markers. Second, according to the same author, 'roughly 10–15% of total genetic variation is between groups and 85–90% is within groups'. This finding, which would again be consistent with the rapid expansion of a previously small population during the middle or early upper Pleistocene,[65] has been found for classic genetic markers, nuclear DNA restriction site polymorphisms, micro-satellite DNA and *Alu* insertion polymorphisms. Different estimates based on some micro-satellite loci and mt DNA may reflect higher mutation rates at these sites.[66]

Despite the low level of genetic variability between different human groups, given the nature of variation in human DNA discussed above, it should nevertheless be sufficient for the genetic identification of different groups. Moreover, because of the lower rate of male migration the non-recombining part of the Y chromosome (paternally inherited) appears to exhibit much greater between-group variation: 'Y chromosome variants tend to be more localized geographically than those of mt DNA and the autosomes. The fraction of variation within human populations for Y chromosome single nucleotide polymorphisms is 35.5% versus 80–85% for the autosomes and mtDNA'.[67] Certainly there appear to be a number of obviously localized Y chromosome polymorphisms.[68]

With the accumulation of new data on DNA sequences the probability of finding differences at the total DNA level between races increases dramatically.[69] As one recent report concluded, '[w]e have demonstrated that it is possible to identify a panel of dimorphic and micro-satellite genetic markers that will allow confident EAE [ethnic-affiliation estimation] in African Americans, European Americans, and

[64] Relethford, J. H., 'Genetics of modern human origins and diversity', *Annual Review of Anthropology*, vol. 27 (1998), pp. 1–23.

[65] Harpending, H. C. *et al.*, 'Genetic traces of ancient demography', *Proceedings of the National Academy of Sciences USA*, vol. 95 (Feb. 1998), pp. 1961–67.

[66] Relethford (note 64).

[67] Seielstad, M. T. *et al.*, 'Genetic evidence for a higher female migration rate in humans', *Nature Genetics*, vol. 20 (Nov. 1998), pp. 278–80.

[68] Underhill, P. A. *et al.*, 'Detection of numerous Y chromosome biallelic polymorphisms by denaturing high-performance liquid chromatography', *Genome Research*, vol. 7 (1997), pp. 996–1005.

[69] E.g., Wang, D. G. *et al.*, 'Large-scale identification, mapping, and genotyping of single-nucleotide polymorphisms in the human genome', *Science*, vol. 280 (15 May 1998), pp. 1077–82; Barbujane, G. *et al.*, 'An apportionment of human DNA diversity', *Proceedings of the National Academy of Sciences USA*, vol. 94 (Apr. 1997), pp. 4516–19; Gill, P. and Evett, I., 'Population genetics of short tandem repeat (STR) loci', ed. B. S. Weir, *Human Identification: The Use of DNA Markers* (Kluwer Academic Publishers: Dordrecht, The Netherlands, 1995); Deka, R. *et al.*, 'Population genetics of dinucleotide $(dC–dA)_n \cdot (dG–dT)_n$ polymorphisms in world populations', *American Journal of Human Genetics*, vol. 56 (1995), pp. 461–74; and Bowcock, A. M. *et al.*, 'High resolution of human evolutionary trees with polymorphic microsatellites', *Nature*, vol. 368 (31 Mar. 1984), pp. 455–57.

Hispanic Americans'.[70] It argued, furthermore, that '[s]imilar sets of markers could be developed for the identification of other populations common in the United States, such as Chinese Americans, Native Americans, and Polynesian Americans'. There is little reason to doubt that such levels of discrimination will rapidly become available worldwide.

VI. The possible use of biotechnology for political and weapon purposes

There is increasing awareness of the threat faced by both the developed and the developing world from new and emerging diseases.[71] The potential use of biological weapons is part of that threat. Clearly, the classic agents,[72] such as anthrax, weaponized in the mid-20th century US programme, present the greatest current threat because they would not have to be extensively tested again today. However, in the view of the US Department of Defense (DOD) in 1997, advances in biotechnology and genetic engineering could confer the ability to modify current agents and tailor them in various ways (table 13A.3).[73] Capabilities to modify, for example, the immunogenic properties of anthrax for medical purposes certainly exist today.[74]

Three examples of potential misuse of modern biotechnology and genetic engineering have previously been considered: the enhancement of bacterial and viral virulence, heterologous gene expression and protein engineering of toxins, and genetic weapons.[75] The background to consideration of these examples, it must be emphasized, is the further rapid development of microbial genomics. The previous studies of viral genomes underlie current capabilities for investigating new outbreaks of disease (e.g., of deadly influenza) quickly[76] and for making broad comparisons and generalizations about viral virulence.[77] The major change in recent years, however, has been an explosion of information on the much larger bacterial pathogen genomes: '[i]n the past three years, the genome sequences of seven pathogenic bacterial species have been published and, in the near future, the complete sequence information of the genomes of a further 30 bacterial pathogens is likely to become available'.[78] Such an avalanche of new data cannot fail to profoundly affect capabilities to deal with indi-

[70] Shriver, M. D. *et al.*, 'Ethnic-affiliation estimation by use of population-specific DNA markers', *American Journal of Human Genetics*, vol. 60 (1997), pp. 957–64.

[71] Brundtland, G. H., 'Reaching out for world health', editorial, *Science*, vol. 280 (26 June 1998), p. 2027; Barrett, R. *et al.*, 'Emerging and re-emerging infectious diseases: the third epidemiologic transition', *Annual Review of Anthropology*, vol. 27 (1998), pp. 247–71; and Spratt, B. G., 'Preface' [to a special issue on resurgent/emergent infectious diseases], *British Medical Bulletin*, vol. 54, no. 3 (1998), pp. 521–23.

[72] Franz, D. *et al.*, 'Clinical recognition and management of patients exposed to biological warfare agents', *Journal of the American Medical Association*, vol. 278, no. 5 (6 Aug. 1997), pp. 399–411.

[73] Cohen, S., 'Proliferation: threat and response, technical annex', US Department of Defense, URL <http://www.defenselink.mil/pubs/prolif97/annex.html>.

[74] Pomerontsev, A. P. *et al.*, 'Expression of cereolysine AB genes in *Bacillus anthracis* vaccine strain ensures protection against experimental hemolytic anthrax infection', *Vaccine*, vol. 15, no. 17/18 (1997), pp. 1846–50.

[75] Bartfai, Lundin and Rybeck (note 5), pp. 300–304.

[76] Vogel, G., 'Sequence offers clues to deadly flu', *Science*, vol. 279 (16 Jan. 1998), p. 324; and Subbarao, K. *et al.*, 'Characterisation of an avian influenza A (H5N1) virus isolated from a child with a fatal respiratory illness', *Science*, vol. 279 (16 Jan. 1998), pp. 393–96.

[77] Balter, M., 'Viruses have many ways to be unwelcome guests', *Science*, vol. 280 (10 Apr. 1998), pp. 204–05.

[78] Frosch, M. *et al.*, 'Genomics in infectious diseases: approaching the pathogens', *Trends in Microbiology*, vol. 6 (9 Sep. 1998), pp. 346–47.

vidual pathogens and the view of the microbial world and of pathogenicity in general.[79] Capabilities for misuse of bacterial pathogens can hardly be unaffected by such large-scale scientific change. The technique of DNA shuffling might, for example, allow the rapid directed evolution of enhanced biological agent capabilities.[80] Toxins, which are clearly being reassessed as a potential threat,[81] are undoubtedly also now much better understood at the molecular level.[82] It is clear that it was possible, for example, to modify the antibiotic resistance of agents using classic genetic techniques, but it was difficult to alter just one characteristic without altering others in such a way as to decrease the utility of the agent. The impact of genetic engineering has been to allow much more precise changes to be made. According to the DOD,[83] '[a]dvances in biotechnology, genetic engineering, and related scientific fields provide increasing potential to control more of these factors, possibly leading to the ability to use biological warfare agents as tactical battlefield weapons'.

Standard US sources suggest that four military concepts of use need to be considered for biological weapons: superpower vs. superpower, state vs. state, state vs. factional element or vice-versa, and terrorist use.[84] The era in which a superpower might consider it necessary to amass huge quantities of biological weapons has passed.[85] However, in state vs. state or state vs. factional element scenarios there could clearly be an advantage in having the capability to 'tailor' agents, for example, to interrupt the provision of supplies to an intervention force by attacking naval and merchant seamen with BW modified for that specific purpose.[86] These trends reinforce the seriousness of the current threats pointed out by the DOD. In the longer term, over the early decades of the next century, the unregulated growth and spread of the new biotechnology capabilities could open up a wide range of new potential threats. It is not difficult, for example, to see how advances in understanding the immune system or bioregulatory peptides[87] might be misused in new weapon systems.

In regard to genetic weapons targeted at specific ethnic groups, the British contribution to the background paper on scientific and technological developments for the Fourth Review Conference of the 1972 Biological and Toxin Weapons Convention (BTWC) stated:

[79] E.g., Balter, M., 'Molecular methods fire up the hunt for emerging pathogens', *Science*, vol. 282 (9 Oct. 1998), pp. 219–21; Andersson, S. G. E. *et al.*, 'The genome sequence of *Rickettsia prowazekii* and the origin of mitochondria', *Nature*, vol. 396 (12 Nov. 1998), pp. 133–40; Pennisi, E., 'Genome data shake tree of life', *Science*, vol. 280 (1 May 1998), pp. 672–74; Doolittle, R. F., 'Microbial genomes opened up', *Nature*, vol. 392 (26 Mar. 1998), pp. 339–42; Strauss, E. J. and Falkow, S., 'Microbial pathogenesis: genomics and beyond', *Science*, vol. 276 (2 May 1997), pp. 707–12; and Moxon, E. R., 'Whole genome sequencing of pathogens: a new era in microbiology', *Trends in Microbiology*, vol. 3, no. 9 (Sep. 1995), pp. 335–37.

[80] Crameri, A. *et al.*, 'DNA shuffling of a family of genes from diverse species accelerates directed evolution', *Nature*, vol. 391 (15 Jan. 1998), pp. 288–91.

[81] Hamilton, M. G., 'Toxins: the emerging threat', *ASA Newsletter*, 98-3 (26 June 1998), pp. 1, 20–28.

[82] E.g., Coffield, J. A. *et al.*, 'Clostridial neurotoxins in the age of molecular medicine', *Trends in Microbiology*, vol. 2, no. 3 (Mar. 1994), pp. 67–69; and Michie, C. A. and Cohen, J., 'The clinical significance of T-cell superantigens', *Trends in Microbiology*, vol. 6, no. 2 (Feb. 1998), pp. 61–65.

[83] Cohen (note 73).

[84] Spertzel, R. O. *et al.*, *Biological Weapons Proliferation: Technical Report*, Defense Nuclear Agency, Alexandria, Va., DNA-MIPR-90-715, Apr. 1994.

[85] Steinbrunner, J. D., 'Biological weapons: a plague upon all houses', *Foreign Policy*, winter 1997/98, pp. 85–96.

[86] Dando (note 2).

[87] Dando, M. R., *A New Form of Warfare: The Rise of Non-Lethal Weapons* (Brassey's: London, 1996).

Table 13A.3. US Department of Defense view of the potential impact of biotechnology and genetic engineering

Potential types of novel biological agents (micro-organisms) that could be produced
Benign micro-organisms, genetically altered to produce a toxin, venom or bioregulator
Micro-organisms resistant to antibiotics, standard vaccines and therapeutics
Micro-organisms with enhanced aerosol and environmental stability
Immunologically altered micro-organisms able to defeat standard identification, detection and diagnostic methods
Combinations of the above four types with improved delivery systems

Source: Cohen, S., 'Proliferation: threat and response, technical annex', US Department of Defense, URL <http://www.defenselink.mil/pubs/prolif97/annex.html>.

It is predicted that the human genome will be sequenced by the year 2005. The information is expected to lead to radical new treatments for a broad range of human diseases. . . . It cannot be ruled out that information from such genetic research could be considered for the design of weapons targeted against specific ethnic or racial groups. However, it is far from clear that the development of such weapons will ever be anything more than a theoretical possibility . . .[88]

The use of biological weapons against a specific ethnic group need not necessarily involve a direct attack on their genomes. An attack could be as crude as the dropping of a toxin on a target population or the use of a biological agent against which friendly troops had previously been vaccinated. However, if a technically sophisticated attack on the specific genetic characteristics of a particular ethnic group were to be successful it would clearly be necessary to have a good knowledge of the structure and function of the human genome and detailed knowledge of the genetic differences between different ethnic groups, knowledge which appears likely to be increasingly available. It would also be necessary to know how to target the genetic differences in order to produce a damaging effect. That capability does not seem to be available today. Nevertheless, while producing such malign outcomes is far from the intent of the practitioners of medical gene therapy, usable technological capabilities do seem to have advanced significantly since 1993. It appears probable that such advances will continue at an increasing rate as success breeds success. In particular, it seems likely that the understanding of how to insert viral agents[89] will increase, especially when set in the general context of the growing knowledge of how other important mobile genetic elements operate in mammalian genomes.[90] Thus while the British assessment would appear to be a correct description of the current situation, the gap between theoretical possibility and practical reality seems to be closing steadily. Significant new successes in the applications of gene therapy, in particular, should be carefully

[88] United Kingdom, Background paper on new scientific and technological developments relevant to the convention on the prohibition of the development, production and stockpiling of bacteriological (biological) and toxin weapons and on their destruction, Fourth Review Conference of the Parties to the Convention on the Prohibition of the Development, Production and Stockpiling of Bacteriological (Biological) and Toxin Weapons and on their Destruction, BTWC Fourth Review Conference document BWC/CONF.IV/4, 30 Oct. 1996, p. 10.

[89] Smith (note 38).

[90] Sheratt, D. J. (ed.), *Mobile Genetic Elements* (Oxford University Press: Oxford, 1995).

monitored and assessed. While it can be hoped that ethnically specific weapons will never become a reality, it would be foolish to imagine that they are an impossibility or that incredibly precise targeting might not become possible. Moreover, crude capabilities for indiscriminate insertion of deleterious genes in a non-specific manner could arise before precise targeting was possible. It would certainly be unwise to suppose that our species is morally strong enough at present to refuse to consider the use of such capabilities if they became available to parties involved in desperate internecine conflicts. Moreover, in such situations parties might be willing to accept relatively imprecise targeting which did some damage to their own community as long as it did much more harm to their enemies.

VII. Conclusions

It has to be emphasized that the scientific and medical advances centred on the Human Genome Project discussed here could bring great benefits to humanity.[91] As the Final Declaration of the 1996 Fourth Review Conference of the BTWC stated, in regard to Article X (on peaceful cooperation):

> The Conference once more emphasises the increasing importance of the provisions of Article X, especially in the light of recent scientific and technological developments in the field of biotechnology, bacteriological (biological) agents and toxins with peaceful applications, which have vastly increased the potential for cooperation between States to help promote economic and social development, and scientific and technological progress . . .[92]

The BTWC does not, of course, restrain the beneficial research designed to achieve the kinds of medical advances described above. What the parties undertake in Article I of the convention is, 'never in any circumstances to develop, produce, stockpile or otherwise acquire or retain . . . [m]icrobial or other biological agents, or toxins whatever their origin or method of production, of types and in quantities that have no justification for prophylactic, protective or other peaceful purposes'. The Final Declaration of the Fourth Review Conference of the BTWC therefore also stated, in regard to the scope of the convention as set out in Article I:

> The Conference, conscious of apprehensions arising from relevant scientific and technological developments, *inter alia*, in the fields of microbiology, biotechnology, molecular biology, genetic engineering, and any applications resulting from genome studies, and the possibilities of their use for purposes inconsistent with the objectives and the provisions of the Convention, reaffirms that the undertakings given by the States Parties in Article I [apply] to all such developments.[93]

It is to be hoped that the papers on technical developments prepared for the Fifth Review Conference of the BTWC in 2001 by the states parties will give proper atten-

[91] Dando, M. R., 'Biotechnology in a peaceful world economy', eds E. Geissler, L. Gazso and E. Buder, *Conversion of Former BTW Facilities*, NATO Science Series (Kluwer Academic Publishers: Dordrecht, The Netherlands, 1998), pp. 25–44.

[92] United Nations, Final Document, Fourth Review Conference of the Parties to the Convention on the Prohibition of the Development, Production and Stockpiling of Bacteriological (Biological) and Toxin Weapons and on their Destruction, BTWC Fourth Review Conference document BWC/CONF.IV/9, 6 Dec. 1996, p. 15.

[93] United Nations, Final Document (note 92).

tion to the potential misuse of science discussed here. The biotechnology revolution will cause enormous social changes for humanity and require major revisions of ethical and moral codes. Part of that revision will have to be a reinforcement of the norm which promotes the peaceful use of the new biotechnology capabilities but prevents their misuse in offensive BW programmes.

In that regard, the urgent necessity now is for the verification protocol to the BTWC, currently being negotiated in Geneva, to be completed so that parties to the convention can be seen to be living up to their undertakings. All the current indications are that an effective and efficient protocol could be agreed before the Fifth Review Conference in 2001 and that this would considerably strengthen the prohibitions embodied in the convention.[94] In order to achieve agreement, however, a much greater knowledge of these issues and support for strengthening the convention will be required from the relevant scientific and technological communities around the world. The pace of scientific and technological change in genomics and its applications is such that any delay in agreeing a verification protocol entails a risk that a situation will arise in which parties have increasing concerns, because of the absence of a protocol regime that builds confidence that states parties are indeed in compliance with the BTWC, that these advances are being misused for a whole new range of biological weapons, including perhaps genetic weapons targeted against ethnic groups in genocidal wars.

[94] Detailed accounts and summaries of the negotiations are available at the joint SIPRI/Bradford Department of Peace Studies Internet site at URL <http://www.brad.ac.uk/acad/sbtwc>.

14. Conventional arms control

ZDZISLAW LACHOWSKI

I. Introduction

Neither the expected watershed in the advance of conventional arms control in Europe nor the planned revisions of the Vienna Document 1994 of the Negotiations on Confidence- and Security-Building Measures in Europe were achieved in 1998. Instead a November 1999 deadline was set for the adaptation of the 1990 Treaty on Conventional Armed Forces in Europe (the CFE Treaty[1]) and the review of the Vienna Document. It was not until early 1999 that noticeable headway was made towards drafting an adapted CFE Treaty. The entry into force of the 1992 Open Skies Treaty remained stalemated.

On the regional plane, successful compliance was reported with the 1996 Agreement on Sub-Regional Arms Control (the Florence Agreement)[2] by the parties to the conflict in the former Yugoslavia and with the 1996 Agreement on Confidence- and Security-Building Measures in Bosnia and Herzegovina,[3] in contrast to the mixed record of implementation of the civilian provisions of the 1995 General Framework Agreement for Bosnia and Herzegovina (the Dayton Agreement). Efforts to get negotiations under way on a regional security process for the Balkans have resulted in an agreement on the mandate for negotiations on regional stabilization.

Outside Europe progress in conventional arms control-related measures was only noted in the Asia–Pacific region and Latin America. Elsewhere the situation either remained unchanged or had worsened, as in South Asia.

This chapter describes the major issues and developments relating to conventional arms control in 1998.[4] Section II deals with critical aspects of CFE Treaty implementation and the CFE Treaty adaptation negotiations, and section III covers regional arms control efforts in Europe. The status of implementation of the Open Skies Treaty is briefly reviewed in section IV. Section V reviews conventional arms control-related developments outside Europe, and the conclusions are presented in section VI. Appendix 14A examines developments in the field of European confidence- and security-building measures (CSBMs) and the implementation of and debate on those

[1] The CFE Treaty and Protocols are reproduced in Koulik, S. and Kokoski, R., SIPRI, *Conventional Arms Control: Perspectives on Verification* (Oxford University Press: Oxford, 1994), pp. 211–76.

[2] The text of the Florence Agreement is reproduced in *SIPRI Yearbook 1997: Armaments, Disarmament and International Security* (Oxford University Press: Oxford, 1997), pp. 517–24.

[3] Established according to the General Framework Agreement for Peace in Bosnia and Herzegovina, Annex 1-B, Agreement on Regional Stabilization, Article II, Confidence- and Security-Building Measures in Bosnia and Herzegovina. For the text of the Agreement on Confidence- and Security-Building Measures in Bosnia and Herzegovina, see URL <http://www.yale.edu/lawweb/avalon/intdip/bosnia/day menu.htm>.

[4] Issues of transparency in conventional arms procurement are dealt with in chapter 11 in this volume.

agreed in the Vienna Document 1994.[5] Anti-personnel mines are addressed in appendix 14B. The 8 December 1998 North Atlantic Council Statement on CFE is reproduced in appendix 14C.

II. Conventional arms control in Europe: the CFE Treaty

The 1990 CFE Treaty set equal ceilings within its Atlantic-to-the-Urals (ATTU) application zone on the major categories of heavy conventional armaments and equipment of the groups of states parties, originally the NATO and the Warsaw Treaty Organization (WTO) states. There are now 30 individual parties.[6] The main reduction of excess treaty-limited equipment (TLE) was carried out in three phases from 1993 to 1995. By 1 January 1998, some 51 300 pieces of conventional armaments and equipment within the ATTU area had been scrapped or converted to civilian use by the states parties, with many parties reducing their holdings to lower levels than required. By May 1998, Russia had notified the destruction or conversion of a further 11 808 items (75 per cent of its total liability of 15 755 items—see table 14.1) inherited from the former Soviet Union outside the ATTU area, and more than 3000 intrusive on-site inspections had taken place since 1993. Data on CFE ceilings and holdings in the treaty application zone as of 1 January 1998 are presented in table 14.2.

Treaty operation and implementation issues

The Joint Consultative Group (JCG), the body established to monitor implementation, resolve issues arising from implementation and consider measures to enhance the viability and effectiveness of the CFE Treaty, focused on the challenge of adapting the treaty to Europe's new security environment. At the same time it continued to scrutinize the operation and implementation of the treaty in 1998.

In June Russia and Slovakia signed an agreement on the redivision of their respective treaty entitlements of combat aircraft and attack helicopters. Under the agreement, Russia provided Slovakia with the right to possess an additional 15 helicopters (the Russian-made 'Black Shark' Ka-50) in place of 15 fighter aircraft from Slovakia's quota.[7]

The JCG subworking group on the CFE Treaty Protocol on Existing Types of Conventional Armaments and Equipment continued its updating work with regard to the removal and addition of specific items from the Protocol.[8]

[5] The Vienna Document 1994 is reproduced in *SIPRI Yearbook 1995: Armaments, Disarmament and International Security* (Oxford University Press: Oxford, 1995), pp. 799–820.

[6] A list of states parties to the CFE Treaty is given in annexe A in this volume. For discussion of conventional arms control in Europe before 1998, see the relevant chapters in previous SIPRI Yearbooks.

[7] TASR (Bratislava), in 'Slovakia: More on Slovak–Russian arms quota division agreement', 27 June 1998, Foreign Broadcast Information Service, *Daily Report-Eastern Europe (FBIS—EEU)*, FBIS-EEU-98-180, 30 June 1998.

[8] For the text of the protocol see Koulik and Kokoski (note 1), pp. 225–32.

Table 14.1. Destruction or conversion of Russian conventional armaments and equipment beyond the Urals to civilian use, valid as of May 1998

Numbers in parentheses are percentages of liabilities reduced.

Area	Tanks	ACVs[a]	Artillery	Total
Liabilities				
Beyond the Urals	6 000	1 500	7 000	**14 500**
Naval infantry/ coastal defence	331	488	436	**1 255**
Reductions				
Beyond the Urals	3 247 (*54.1*)	2 160 (*144.0*)	5 146 (*73.5*)	**10 553 (*72.8*)**
Naval infantry/ coastal defence	331 (*100.0*)	488 (*100.0*)	436 (*100.0*)	**1 255 (*100.0*)**

[a] Armoured combat vehicles.

Source: Joint Consultative Group, Group on Treaty Operation and Implementation, Joint Consultative Group document, JCG.TOI/15/98, Vienna, 21 July 1998.

Although the treaty adaptation process had begun in early 1997, several parties had still not met or fully complied with all of their original treaty commitments by the end of 1998. Most of the compliance issues that were reported in 1997 continued to be of concern.[9] The eight CFE states parties that were formerly Soviet republics had made little or no progress towards fulfilling their collective obligation to declare and complete TLE reductions equal to those the Soviet Union would have been obliged to complete (the shortfall is 1970 TLE items). Progress was made in the JCG in developing measures to tackle the problem of unaccounted for and uncontrolled TLE, however, and a reconnaissance visit by British experts to Moldova led to agreement on the necessary arrangements for an on-site visit concerning this type of equipment.

Russia stayed within its maximum entitlements (maximum national levels for holdings, MNLHs), but the following concerns remained: (*a*) as of 1 January 1998, the total of 605 TLE items decommissioned and awaiting export exceeded the treaty limit of 250; (*b*) the improper designation by Russia of armoured personnel carriers (APCs) as ambulances was not resolved by the end of 1998 (the number of 'ambulances', if counted as armoured combat vehicles—ACVs—would exceed the flank limit of 4379); (*c*) Russian forces were stationed on the territory of other states parties (Georgia, Moldova) without their consent and TLE had been handed over to Armenia;[10] and (*d*) Russia continued to refuse to report MT-LBU armoured personnel carrier

[9] Lachowski, Z., 'Conventional arms control', *SIPRI Yearbook 1998: Armaments, Disarmament and International Security* (Oxford University Press: Oxford, 1998), pp. 502–504.

[10] Russia claims that the CFE Treaty does not limit or control exports of conventional arms but merely 'sets limits of availability'. Russian Foreign Ministry spokesman Vladimir Rakhmanin advised that the issue of transfers to Armenia should be referred to the trilateral Russian–Azerbaijani–Armenian commission and stated that Russia had reached an agreement (as yet unratified) with Moldova on the temporary deployment of Russian forces in Moldova. Interfax (Moscow), in 'Russia: Moscow rejects US charges of departure from CFE Treaty', 7 July 1998, Foreign Broadcast Information Service, *Daily Report—Central Eurasia (FBIS–SOV)*, FBIS-SOV-98-188, 7 July 1998.

Table 14.2. CFE ceilings and holdings, as of 1 January 1998

	Tanks		ACVs		Artillery		Aircraft		Helicopters	
State[a]	Ceilings	Holdings	Ceilings	Holdings	Ceilings	Holdings	Ceilings	Holdings	Ceilings	Holdings
Armenia	220	102	220	218	285	225	100	6	50	7
Azerbaijan	220	270	220	557	285	301	100	48	50	15
Belarus	1 800	2 320	2 600	2 984	1 615	1 533	294	335	80	79
Belgium	334	155	1 099	539	320	243	232	137	4	46
Bulgaria	1 475	1 475	2 000	1 985	1 750	1 744	235	234	67	43
Canada	77	0	263	0	32	0	90	0	13	0
Czech Republic	957	948	1 367	1 238	767	767	230	122	50	36
Denmark	353	343	336	286	553	503	106	74	12	12
France	1 306	1 210	3 820	3 672	1 292	1 107	800	619	396	303
Georgia	220	79	220	111	285	107	100	7	50	3
Germany	4 069	3 135	3 281	2 500	2 852	2 445	900	532	293	204
Greece	1 735	1 735	2 498	2 306	1 920	1 887	650	503	30	20
Hungary	835	835	1 700	1 316	840	840	180	138	108	59
Italy	1 348	1 247	3 339	2 924	1 955	1 758	650	531	142	134
Moldova	210	0	210	209	250	154	50	0	50	0
Netherlands	743	667	1 080	624	607	405	230	180	50	12
Norway	170	170	275	165	491	216	100	73	24	0
Poland	1 730	1 727	2 150	1 440	1 610	1 580	460	306	130	105
Portugal	300	187	430	354	450	340	160	101	26	0
Romania	1 375	1 373	2 100	2 095	1 475	1 435	430	362	120	16
Russia[b]	6 400	5 559	11 480	9 841	6 415	5 999	3 416	2 868	890	805
Slovakia	478	478	683	683	383	382	115	113	25	19
Spain	794	688	1 588	1 187	1 310	1 154	310	198	90	28
Turkey	2 795	2 542	3 120	2 529	3 523	2 839	750	388	103	26
Ukraine[b]	4 030	4 014	5 050	4 502	4 040	3 749	1 090	966	330	290
UK	1 015	505	3 176	2 449	636	431	900	550	384	271
USA	4 006	927	5 152	1 809	2 742	497	784	218	404	138

[a] Iceland, Kazakhstan and Luxembourg have no TLE in the application zone. [b] TLE belonging to the Black Sea Fleet is not reported.

Source: Joint Consultative Group, Group on Treaty Operation and Implementation, JCG.TOI/15/98, Vienna, 21 July 1998.

Table 14.3. Reductions of TLE belonging to naval infantry and coastal defence forces required by the legally binding Soviet pledge of 14 June 1991, as of May 1998

Numbers in parentheses indicate the percentage of liabilities reduced.

State/area	Tanks	ACVs[a]	Artillery	**Total**
Liabilities of				
Russia				
Outside ATTU area	331	488	436	**1 255**
Inside ATTU area	331	488	436	**1 255**
Ukraine/Russia	158/113	369/380	152/56	**679/549**
Sub-total in ATTU area	602	1 237	644	**2 483**
Total	**933**	**1 725**	**1 080**	**3 738**
Reductions by				
Russia				
Outside ATTU area	331	488	436	**1 255**
Inside ATTU area	331	488	436	**1 255**
Ukraine[b]/Russia	0	0	0	**0**
Sub-total in ATTU area	331 (*55.0*)	488 (*39.5*)	436 (*67.7*)	**1 255 (*50.5*)**
Total	**662 (*71.0*)**	**976 (*56.6*)**	**872 (*80.7*)**	**2 510 (*67.2*)**

[a] Armoured combat vehicles.

[b] As the overall number of artillery pieces belonging to Ukraine is lower than its maximum national level for holdings, the Ukrainian reduction norm amounts to zero.

Source: Consolidated matrix on the basis of data available as of 1 May 1998, Joint Consultative Group, Vienna, 21 July 1998.

look-alikes, which are accountable under the Protocol on Existing Types of Conventional Armaments and Equipment.

With two-thirds of their liabilities reduced by 1995, compliance by Russia and Ukraine has since remained deadlocked. They share an unfulfilled obligation to carry out naval infantry/coastal defence-related reductions equal to those specified in the USSR's legal commitment of 14 June 1991 (see table 14.3). Some progress has been made, however. Russia and Ukraine agreed on the division of the assets of the former Soviet Black Sea Fleet on 28 May 1997.[11] In spite of the Ukrainian Parliament's vote on 14 January 1998 against the ratification of that agreement, on 17 March Ukraine announced that it had corrected its temporary deployment (106 tanks, 241 ACVs and 72 artillery pieces) by getting rid of 132 ACVs and 24 artillery pieces. This enabled the Russian deployments on Ukrainian territory to be accommodated under the agreement on the Black Sea Fleet assets.

[11] The Russian–Ukrainian agreement envisaged that Russian naval infantry units would be 'temporarily stationed on Ukrainian territory', and that their equipment would not exceed 132 ACVs and 24 artillery pieces. These amounts complied with the CFE flank limits. Institute for Defense and Disarmament Studies, *Arms Control Reporter* (IDDS: Brookline, Mass.), sheet 407.B.568, 1997. The resolution of the issue of the Black Sea Fleet is examined in Baranovsky, V., 'Russia: conflicts and peaceful settlement of disputes', *SIPRI Yearbook 1998* (note 9), pp. 118–19.

Concerns remained over the quantities of equipment Belarus, Bulgaria,[12] Hungary and Ukraine had declared to be temporarily in the ATTU zone while awaiting export. Belarus gave rise to particular concern since it had used TLE declared as awaiting export as a stock for replacing and modernizing its armaments.[13]

Armenia and Azerbaijan continued to exceed their maximum levels of TLE in one or more categories.[14] Neither state has ever declared a proper reduction obligation or carried out the reductions required by the treaty, and they continued to accuse each other of exceeding their CFE weapon ceilings.[15] Armenian armed forces and TLE remained on the territory of Azerbaijan (Nagorno-Karabakh) without Azerbaijani consent.

Russia failed to declare a unit and its TLE and notified excessive numbers of decommissioned TLE as temporarily in the area of application awaiting disposal. In addition, Ukrainian data of 1 January 1998 showed Ukraine to have exceeded limits on equipment in active units in the expanded central zone (CFE Treaty sub-zone IV.3). Belarus and Russia failed to comply with treaty provisions on on-site inspections: both states improperly denied full access to one or more sites, while Russia also restricted in-country inspection time on one or more occasions.[16]

Slow progress at the negotiations

Reports at the end of 1997 indicated slow progress at the CFE Treaty adaptation negotiations and they drew to a standstill in the first half of 1998. The stalemate stemmed from several obstacles. Russia's demands, especially those for a ban on the stationing of foreign forces and the elimination of the flank regime, and its marked opposition to various solutions proposed in the JCG certainly presented major obstacles. However, controversies and the lack of common standpoints among NATO states on certain negotiated issues also impinged on progress. In drawing up its new Strategic Concept to be adopted at the NATO Washington summit meeting in April 1999, the alliance also faced a crucial dilemma regarding the kind of priorities to be adopted in building the future conventional arms control regime and, in the broader context, security in Europe: to maximize NATO's effectiveness and flexibility, on the one hand, or to overcome its lingering fears about Russia's future conduct and develop its positions within a broader cooperative security approach that ref-

[12] In Apr. 1998 a Bulgarian newspaper reported that Bulgaria was offering 200 T-55 tanks for sale. 'Army sells 200 old tanks', *Trud* (Sofia), 21 Apr. 1998, p. 2, in 'Bulgaria: Bulgarian defense minister offers to sell 200 "old tanks"', FBIS-EEU-98-11, 21 Apr. 1998.

[13] Belarus declared *c.* 300 tanks as awaiting export and then exchanged *c.* 150 of these with tanks in active units. *Arms Control Today*, June/July 1998, p. 30.

[14] At the beginning of 1998 Azerbaijan still exceeded its maximum national levels in all 3 ground categories (by 316 items) and Armenia exceeded its maximum national levels in 1 subcategory, AIFVs/HACVs (168 vs the limit of 135). The Armenian data delivered to the JCG did not indicate that any Russian deliveries of TLE had taken place since 1993. Lachowski (note 9), pp. 503–504.

[15] Lachowski (note 9), pp. 503–504; and *Arms Control Reporter*, sheets 407.B.591–2, 1998.

[16] *ACDA 1997 Annual Report*, chapter VII, Adherence to and Compliance with Arms Control Agreements (Arms Control and Disarmament Agency: Washington, DC, 1998), URL<http://www.acda.gov/reports/annual/chpt7.htm>.

lects a desire for good relations in Europe, on the other. The US position has been characterized to a large degree by the former attitude, while France and Germany have offered various suggestions and solutions seeking to meet Russian concerns halfway. At the tactical level, NATO was slowing down the negotiations in 1998 to see whether and how Russia was meeting its flank commitments to be implemented by the May 1999 deadline. The resulting impasse in negotiations led Russia, seriously concerned about the military consequences of NATO enlargement, to complain about the distinct gulf between the underlying principle of treaty adaptation (a retreat from the bloc approach) and the need to deal with the sluggish alliance.[17] Other participants have also actively sought to promote their views and interests.

The main NATO proposals submitted in June 1998 concerning mechanisms for temporary deployments, transits of TLE and revisions to territorial ceilings were initially found 'quite one-sided' by Moscow.[18] It was not until early October that the Russian chief delegate came up with a number of suggestions aimed at a 'reasonable compromise'.[19] The stalemate, however, made it unlikely that the negotiation would be concluded by the end of 1998. In the autumn, the April 1999 date for NATO enlargement or even the November 1999 Organization for Security and Co-operation in Europe (OSCE) summit meeting were mentioned as informal deadlines for completing the adaptation talks. A follow-up agreement to the partial framework agreement on 'certain basic elements' for treaty adaptation,[20] approved by the JCG on 23 July 1997, was expected to be prepared for the OSCE 7th Ministerial Council Meeting in Oslo in December 1998. To this end, working groups consisting of heads of delegations from states parties were established.[21]

CFE Treaty issues were also addressed at the NATO–Russia Permanent Joint Council meetings in the spring and autumn. On 3 September in Moscow, the US and Russian presidents stressed the importance of accelerating the pace of negotiations and completing the adaptation of the CFE Treaty while fully complying with the existing CFE Treaty obligations until the adapted treaty takes effect. Both sides resolved to seek to make 'significant progress' by the Oslo ministerial meeting.[22] This, however, proved impossible. At the Oslo meeting on 2–3 December, the states parties to the CFE Treaty agreed to set the November 1999 OSCE summit meeting in Istanbul as the new deadline for completing the negotiations and pledged to 'redouble' their efforts to achieve

[17] Statement by A. V. Grouchko, Head of the Delegation of the Russian Federation, for questions of military security and arms control to the JCG, Joint Consultative Group document JCG.DEL/20/98, Vienna, 13 May 1998.

[18] See note 10.

[19] Statement by the Head of the Delegation of the Russian Federation, A.V. Grouchko, in the JCG, Joint Consultative Group document JCG.DEL/45/98, 6 Oct. 1998.

[20] The Decision of the Joint Consultative Group Concerning Certain Basic Elements for Treaty Adaptation, Vienna, 23 July 1997, is reproduced in *SIPRI Yearbook 1998* (note 9), pp. 541–43.

[21] *Arms Control Reporter*, sheets 407.B.591–2, 1998.

[22] 'Joint statement on common security challenges at threshold of the 21st century', *Disarmament Defence,* 2 Sep. 1998; and 'Albright statement to OSCE Permanent Council', 3 Sep. 1998, available in the Public Diplomacy Query (PDQ) database on the United States Information Agency Internet site, URL <http://pdq2.usia.gov>.

this goal.[23] Russia, supported by France and Germany, strove in Oslo for a de facto deadline for 'resolving key issues of the adaptation' by the NATO Washington summit meeting in April 1999, but this was rejected by the three then NATO candidate countries—the Czech Republic, Hungary and Poland. Nevertheless a consensus was reached to speed up the CFE adaptation talks in Vienna in the first months of 1999. A week later, on 8 December, NATO, joined by the three states about to become members, issued the 'Statement on CFE'[24] setting a framework for its negotiating position in the run-up to the signature of an adapted treaty at the Istanbul summit meeting.

On 2 January 1999, the Russian Foreign Ministry issued a statement urging 'decisive progress' at the adaptation talks before the formal enlargement of the Atlantic Alliance.[25] The rationale for this was that the inclusion of the three new members would destabilize the equilibrium underlying the current CFE Treaty regime.

The next round of negotiations began on 21 January 1999, with the aim of intensifying efforts towards prompt and tangible progress. The fact that NATO air intervention in Yugoslavia did not prevent Russia from reaching agreement on CFE Treaty adaptation emphasized the standing of this negotiation. In early March Russia and NATO made several concessions which facilitated a compromise by the states parties on several issues regarding lower national and territorial ceilings on armed forces, flank arrangements and stronger verification measures, documented in the JCG decision of 30 March 1999.[26] This also set the stage for finalizing the adaptation agreement.

The following issues were outstanding in 1998: (*a*) national ceilings (NCs) and territorial ceilings (TCs); (*b*) revision of TCs; (*c*) temporary deployments in excess of TCs; (*d*) transit of TLE; (*e*) the flank issue; (*f*) stationing of troops; (*g*) the stability zone; and (*h*) verification and data exchanges.

National and territorial ceilings

The system of national and territorial ceilings is intended to replace the group (bloc) structure of the cold war period. Following NATO's 26 June 1997 statements of intent to cut back collectively its weapon entitlements by some 10 000 items, and the adoption of the July 1997 'basic elements' decision, on 2 December 1997 individual NATO states offered 'illustrative' pledges to make further reductions in their own arsenals (see table 14.4). Their condition was that a satisfactory adaptation of the treaty be agreed and that these pledges

[23] OSCE, Oslo Ministerial Declaration, OSCE document MC(7).JOUR/2, Agenda item 9, Annex 1, 2 Dec. 1998, URL <http://www.osceprag.cz/news/mc07ej01.htm>.

[24] The text of the Statement on CFE issued at the Ministerial Meeting of the North Atlantic Council with the Three Invited Countries held in Brussels on 8th December 1998, Adaptation of the Treaty on Conventional Armed Forces in Europe (CFE): Restraint and Flexibility, NAC Press Release M-NAC-D-2 (98) 141, 8 Dec. 1998, is reproduced in appendix 14C.

[25] Statement made by a representative of the Ministry of Foreign Affairs of the Russian Federation concerning adaptation of the Treaty on Conventional Armed Forces in Europe, Conference on Disarmament document CD/1560, 6 Jan. 1999.

[26] Decision of the Joint Consultative Group on CFE Treaty Adaptation, Joint Consultative Group document JCG.DD/4/99, 30 Mar. 1999.

Table 14.4. NATO's illustrative ceilings for ground TLE, December 1997

	Battle tanks			ACVs			Artillery		
State[a]	MNLH	NC	TC	MNLH	NC	TC	MNLH	NC	TC
Belgium	334	300	544	1 099	989	1 505	320	288	497
Canada[b]	77	77	. .	263	263	. .	38	32	. .
Denmark	353	335	353	336	336	336	503	446	503
France	1 306	1 226	1 306	3 820	3 700	3 820	1 292	1 192	1 292
Germany	4 069	3 644	4 904	3 281	3 281	6 772	2 445	2 255	3 407
Greece	1 735	1 735	1 735	2 498	2 498	2 498	1 920	1 920	1 920
Italy	1 348	1 267	1 723	3 339	3 172	3 972	1 955	1 818	2 199
Luxembourg	0	0	143	0	0	174	0	0	47
Netherlands	743	669	958	1 080	972	1 328	607	546	712
Norway[c]	170	170	170	275	275	275	491	491	557
Portugal	300	300	300	430	430	430	450	450	450
Spain	891	750	891	2 047	1 588	2 047	1 370	1 276	1 370
Turkey	2 795	2 795	2 795	3 120	3 120	3 120	3 523	3 523	3 523
UK	887	843	843	3 176	3 017	3 029	614	583	583
USA[b]	4 006	1 812	. .	5 125	3 037	. .	2 242	1 553	. .
Total	**19 014**	**15 923**	**16 665**	**29 889**	**26 678**	**29 306**	**17 770**	**16 373**	**17 060**

Notes: ACV = armoured combat vehicle; MNLH = maximum national level for holdings; NC = national ceiling; TC = territorial ceiling.

[a] Iceland has no weapon limits in the ATTU area.

[b] No territory in the ATTU area.

[c] Norway's TC on ACVs could be 282 after an ongoing reallocation process is completed.

Source: JCG data cited in Institute for Defense and Disarmament Studies, *Arms Control Reporter* (IDDS: Brookline, Mass.), sheets 407.B.579–581, 1997.

find reciprocity from other partners. Several former WTO states also declared their own 'illustrative' limits on their holdings. Russia stated that its national ceilings under the adapted treaty will not exceed its maximum national levels for holdings and that it 'does not rule out' the possibility of reducing its NCs in certain TLE categories, making this dependent mainly on NATO refraining from substantial stationing of combat forces on the territories of the new members. It promised to define its territorial ceilings once other parties' positions on the key aspects of treaty adaptation were clarified.[27] In the autumn of 1998, the Russian delegation to the JCG expressed satisfaction with the way in which the national ceilings for tanks and artillery pieces were being defined in the adapted treaty. The attitudes of other states parties to the other three TLE categories—ACVs, aircraft and helicopters—however, were said to be a matter of 'great concern' to Russia.[28] Russia continued to resist the proposal concerning designated permanent storage sites (DPSS).[29]

[27] Statement by the Delegation of the Russian Federation, Joint Consultative Group document JCG.DEL/4/98, 10 Feb. 1998.

[28] Statement by the Head of the Delegation of the Russian Federation (note 19).

[29] NATO has proposed that states either retain their stored equipment entitlements or eliminate four-fifths of it and include the remainder in active units.

Table 14.5. Projected and adjusted levels for the territorial ceilings of the Czech Republic, Hungary, Poland and Slovakia, as of 30 March 1999

State	Tanks	ACVs[a]	Artillery	**Total**
Projected territorial ceilings				
Czech Republic	957	1 367	767	**3 091**
Hungary	835	1 700	840	**3 375**
Poland	1 730	2 150	1 610	**5 490**
Slovakia	478	683	383	**1 544**
Total	**4 000**	**5 900**	**3 600**	**13 500**
Adjusted territorial ceilings[b]				
Czech Republic	795	1 252	657	**2 704**
Hungary	710	1 560	750	**3 020**
Poland	1 577	1 780	1 370	**4 727**
Slovakia	323	643	383	**1 349**
Total	**3 405**	**5 235**	**3 160**	**11 800**
Difference	**– 595**	**– 665**	**– 440**	**– 1 700**

[a] Armoured combat vehicles.

[b] The adjustments will take place no later than the end of 2002 for the Czech Republic and Hungary, and no later than the end of 2003 for Slovakia and Poland.

Source: Decision of the Joint Consultative Group on CFE Treaty Adaptation, Joint Consultative Group document JCG.DD/4/99, 30 Mar. 1999, chart 2.

The future system of national and territorial ceilings will be more constraining than the existing CFE Treaty's structure of limits on the TLE that may be located in large regional zones. In the JCG decision of 30 March it is agreed that any upward revision of the national ceiling of one state party should be compensated by a corresponding reduction in the NCs on the same TLE category of one or more other states parties. It is proposed that prior notification should be made 90 days before the revision becomes effective and that it should be registered appropriately. Between five-yearly review conferences national ceilings may be revised by a total amount of 20 per cent of the codified national ceilings, or 150 tanks, 250 ACVs and 100 artillery pieces, whichever is lower. The amount available for upward revision 'will be no less than 40 tanks, 60 ACVs, 20 artillery pieces'. Upward revisions of NCs in excess of permitted levels will be subject to a consensus decision by all states parties.[30]

For a long time there was no commonly accepted concept of or scope for territorial ceilings either among the CFE states parties or within NATO. Like national ceilings, territorial ceilings will be codified as binding limits in a protocol and will be subject to regular review. Most states parties do not have foreign troops stationed on their territory, and their TCs are likely to be equal to the related NCs. NATO has stated that it 'sees adjustment of Territorial Ceilings as a procedure to address long-term shifts in security needs, and not

[30] JCG (note 26).

as a means to achieve tactical flexibility'.[31] Some NATO states, however, would like TCs not to overly restrict the alliance's military flexibility. Notwithstanding their earlier assurance that their total future aggregate national ceilings for ground TLE will be 'significantly' lower under the adapted treaty than their current group ceiling,[32] a number of NATO countries (such as Belgium, Italy, the Netherlands and Norway) demanded territorial ceilings higher than their current national entitlements in individual or all ground categories, and some members did not plan to lower their TCs below their current national entitlements at all. While this was not against the letter of the negotiating mandate, it contradicted the avowed intention of making substantial cuts. Although the three NATO candidates grudgingly accepted the stability zone requirement regarding TCs, they suspected that this (let alone Russia's pressure on Poland, for example, to lower its current MNLH) puts them in a 'second-class' category among the alliance members. Russia promoted the idea of 'one NC, one TC for each state', thus ignoring the security concerns voiced by several of its neighbours. It had modified its earlier insistence on including aircraft under TCs and was ready to reduce the territorial limitations to four, instead of the called-for five, TLE categories—the three ground categories and attack helicopters.

In its January 1999 statement Russia demanded that the Czech Republic, Hungary and Poland include their entitlements in and adjust them to NATO's current aggregate weapon quota,[33] pointing out that Russia's security would otherwise be jeopardized and its right to carry out inspections on the territories of the new members, as well as on the territories of the other members of the alliance, would be infringed. Consequently, Russia declared that it reserves the right to convene an extraordinary conference of all the states parties to examine the exceptional circumstances. NATO retorted that no artificial linkage should be established between enlargement and the CFE Treaty.[34] Russia's pressure for substantial reductions by the enlarged alliance resulted in NATO's early 1999 suggestions to its candidates that they might reduce their national ceilings, for example by 300 tanks 'for a country such as Poland'.[35]

Under the 30 March 1999 decision on treaty adaptation, the Czech Republic, Hungary, Poland and Slovakia agreed to lower their territorial limits by a total of 1700 TLE by 2002/2003, thus limiting the number of foreign troops to be deployed on their territories (see table 14.5).

[31] NAC Statement on CFE (note 24), para. 8.

[32] Compare NATO's Proposal on Basic Elements for Adaptation of the CFE Treaty, Joint Consultative Group document JCG.PRO(4)/2/97, Vienna, 20 Feb. 1997.

[33] In early 1998 NATO's TLE was some 22 200 items below its aggregate entitlement of almost 76 000. It had declared that it would cut its aggregate entitlements by *c.* 10%. Moreover, it had planned to reduce 80% of its stored weapons and unallocated active entitlements (8100 TLE items). Since the candidate states' entitlements are some 13 100 items, the enlarged NATO would have an excess of some 6000 TLE items.

[34] *Atlantic News*, no. 3071 (8 Jan. 1999), p. 2.

[35] *Frankfurter Allgemeine Zeitung*, 25 Jan. 1999, p. 6.

Revision of territorial ceilings

It was generally assumed that territorial ceilings would be at least equal to[36] and more rigid (through various restrictions) than national ceilings, which would limit the flexibility of the latter. Canada and the USA, with no territorial ceilings in the area of application, will distribute their entitlements among various territorial units with the consent of the host states. In the face of these and other constraints, the alliance came forward with ideas for flexibilities aimed at enabling it to retain more room for military manoeuvre. This would include mechanisms to adjust both kinds of ceiling, the ability to use head-rooms within the three ground force categories to accommodate the presence of TLE from any state party, and provisions for temporarily exceeding territorial ceilings in specific circumstances (missions in support of peace, military training exercises and temporary deployments).

One concern was how to create mechanisms for revising or reallocating the ceilings once they are in force, ensuring that such revisions do not lead to destabilizing accumulations of forces. Various proposals and suggestions, ranging from extreme to moderate, have been put forward in this regard: (*a*) to make each change dependent on all participants' agreement; (*b*) to restrict the number of states with whom an exchange can be made (e.g., neighbouring states); (*c*) to restrict the scope of the revision (to a certain percentage of a territorial limit or to a certain TLE level); (*d*) to offer the right for states to raise questions about the intended revision; and (*e*) to call an extraordinary conference if the response has not satisfied those concerned. A temporary freeze on some TCs in order to reinforce stability in a given region was also proposed.

On 22 June 1998 the NATO states proposed that, within a five-year period, a state party may unilaterally revise its territorial ceiling upwards by a total of 150 tanks, 250 ACVs and 100 artillery pieces, or by 20 per cent of the territorial ceiling, whichever is lower.[37] An upward revision would be preceded or accompanied by a commensurate reduction in the TC(s) of another state or states. Upward revisions of territorial ceilings in excess of the above-mentioned levels would require consensus of the states parties, and the levels would be addressed during review conferences. A state party might also unilaterally reduce its territorial ceiling, provided it is not lower than its national ceiling (such a revision might contribute to excessive concentrations elsewhere). Any changes would be notified 90 days in advance.

In response, Russia announced in October that it would not object to changes in national and territorial ceilings within strictly defined limits.[38] In March 1999 Russia accepted the parameters for upward revision of NCs and TCs.

[36] TCs are to be the sum of up-to-date MNLHs of the host states in the 3 ground categories, taking into account decisions reached in relation to DPSS provisions, plus the entitlements of the stationing states, who have first secured the explicit consent of the host states.

[37] NATO's Proposal on Certain CFE Treaty Mechanisms, Joint Consultative Group document JCG.DEL/28/98, Vienna, 22 June 1998. The JCG decision of 30 Mar. 1990, while adopting NATO proposals, stipulated that the 'amount available for upward revision will be no less than 40 tanks, 60 ACVs, 20 artillery pieces'. JCG (note 26).

[38] Statement by the Head of the Delegation of the Russian Federation (note 19).

Temporary deployments in excess of territorial ceilings

Revising TCs upwards is one of the ways of providing military flexibility under the adapted treaty. Its disadvantage is that under specific circumstances it requires the consent of another state or states, resulting in a cumbersome and slow process. Temporary deployments[39] are a more expedient alternative, especially in crisis situations or other security contingencies. The point is, however, that they should not have a destabilizing effect. Exemptions for notified military training exercises or UN/OSCE-mandated missions in support of peace are generally not contested. Parameters for force levels and the duration of UN/OSCE-mandated missions will be guided by the mandate. As far as notified exercises are concerned, prior notification 42 days in advance and a duration not exceeding 42 days are envisaged. Attempts to circumvent the 42-day limit (by holding a series of exercises) will also be prevented. In no case will an exercise cause a national ceiling to be exceeded; nor will it cause a territorial ceiling to be exceeded by more than the temporary deployment/ exceptional temporary deployment level.

Defining exemptions for other temporary deployments proved a contentious issue. Italy, Spain, the UK and the USA, as well as the Central European NATO candidates, pressed for generous room for manoeuvre for considerable temporary force deployments (a 'preventive deployment' of up to two divisions[40]) in excess of TCs (with the exception of territories of the 12 states in the flank zone). This provoked resistance and calls for rethinking from France, Germany and the Netherlands (as well as Russia and the other flank states), which pointed to the excessively military-oriented nature and potentially counterproductive political and arms control effects of such a solution. These states did not want too strong a force deployed near Russia's borders, fearing that it might prove destabilizing and provoke Russia (and its partners—Belarus and Ukraine) to take similar countermeasures or even eventually withdraw from the CFE Treaty adaptation negotiations and the regime itself. Germany proposed, in this context, to make use of temporary flank deployment provisions providing for a deployment of up to 153 tanks, 241 ACVs and 140 artillery pieces in one flank country.[41] Russia declared that it would be

[39] The time limit for a temporary deployment has not yet been specified. NATO has stated that temporary deployment provisions are not intended and will not be used for the purpose of permanent stationing of combat forces. In the context of the flank area, the USA has pointed out that such deployments should be measured 'in days, weeks, at most, several months, but not years'. Lachowski (note 9), p. 506.

[40] Within NATO, various requirements have been laid down. The UK went the furthest: it originally wanted a temporary deployment of up to 4 divisions; NATO's first draft Study on Flexibility Requirements of 18 Nov. 1997 suggested that in an emergency an additional 3 divisions could be sent, e.g., to Poland. *Arms Control Reporter*, sheet 407.B.576, 1997. Later, the USA proposed a preventive deployment of up to 2 divisions—*c.* 460 tanks, 770 ACVs and 325 artillery pieces—in 1 country. Poland was opting for greater freedom in hosting temporary deployments of foreign forces on its territory—up to 500 tanks or 1000 ACVs. Polish Defence Minister Janusz Onyszkiewicz's interview 'Assistance from the first moment', *Rzeczpospolita* (Warsaw), 22 June 1998, p. 6, in 'Poland: defense minister views NATO, Russia, CFE', Foreign Broadcast Information Service, *Daily Report–Arms Control (FBIS-TAC)*, FBIS-TAC-98-174, 23 June 1998. Eventually, the 3 candidate countries (the Czech Republic, Hungary and Poland) supported the NATO proposal of 22 June 1998.

[41] Germany argued, e.g., that hypothetically the Polish forces, reinforced by 2 NATO divisions, would risk facing Russian, Belorussian and Ukrainian forces reinforced by an additional 6 divisions. See 'Zum

ready to accept deployment of, at a maximum, three light (Bundeswehr-type) brigades on the territories of the new NATO members, provided that no more than one brigade was stationed in each of the countries, plus one temporarily deployed (for less than 42 days).[42]

Another problem was the response to potential risks posed by conflicts outside Europe which would require higher temporary deployments. Here Spain, the UK and the USA, as well as the NATO military staff, opted for substantial 'preventive deployments' (up to two divisions). Germany was in favour of an equivalent of one division.[43]

Eventually, NATO's June proposal[44] provided for two kinds of temporary deployment in excess of TCs: (*a*) a 'basic' deployment up to the equivalent of a brigade (up to 153 tanks, 241 ACVs and 140 artillery pieces); and (*b*) for 'exceptional circumstances' (such as a threat from outside the ATTU area), a deployment in each state party outside the Article V area of up to three brigades, or two divisions (i.e., 459 tanks, 723 ACVs and 420 artillery pieces). In no case would temporary deployment/exceptional temporary deployment cause any national ceilings to be exceeded. Both kinds of deployment would be subject to specific enhanced transparency and verification measures. Prior to implementing the temporary deployment/exceptional temporary deployment provision, states would be required to exercise restraint by fully using any available headroom. Explanatory reports to the JCG and regular updates are envisaged.

In an exceptional situation, a conference of states parties would be convened for up to 48 hours, no later than 7 days after the notification of a temporary deployment in excess of one brigade, at which the states concerned would explain the nature of the circumstances. The proposal did not foresee circumstances, in the current and foreseeable environment, requiring deployments on the territory of any state party in excess of the TLE levels proposed for exceptional temporary deployments. NATO stated that such deployments would not be frequent or routine; nor would they be directed against any specific country.[45]

Responding to this proposal, Russia expressed its willingness to use the NATO figures for basic temporary deployments. It promised to consider the possibility of using headrooms for temporary deployments within the same parameters—consequently, a single country could temporarily deploy up to 306 tanks, 482 ACVs and 280 artillery pieces (including the equivalent of one

Stand der KSE-Adaptierung' [On the state of the CFE adaptation], a report published on 17 Apr. 1998 by the German Federal Foreign Ministry, URL <http://www.auswaertiges-amt.de/3_auspol/6/3-6-3b.html>. The text was removed from this site when Germany agreed to NATO's June proposal (note 37).

[42] Statement by the Head of the Delegation of the Russian Federation, A.V. Groushko in the JCG, Joint Consultative Group document JCG.DEL/38/97, Vienna, 15 Dec. 1997. A light Bundeswehr brigade has 106 tanks, 120 ACVs and 34 artillery pieces.

[43] Schmidt, H.-J., 'Die Anpassung des KSE-Vertrages: Konventionelle Rüstungskontrolle zwischen Bündnisverteidigung und kooperativer Sicherheit' [Adaptation of the CFE Treaty: conventional arms control between allied defence and cooperative security], Hessische Stiftung Friedens- und Konflikt-Forschung, *HSFK-Report*, no. 1 (1998), p. 27.

[44] NATO's proposal (note 37).

[45] NAC Statement on CFE (note 24), para. 11.

brigade filling a headroom). At the same time, Russia called for other precise measures to avoid accumulation of the temporary deployment entitlements, for example, in combination with other flexibilities or within a single region. It also found it possible to consider exceptional temporary deployments subject to the consensus of all participating states.[46] Here, Russia's main concern was to limit the aggregate TLE that might be deployed in its vicinity (particularly in Poland) as a result of both territorial ceilings and temporary deployments. In the longer perspective Russia also seeks to address the challenge of possible further NATO enlargement (for example, the admission of the Baltic states).

These concerns were addressed in NATO's Statement on CFE, in which the alliance pledged to exercise restraint with regard to temporary deployments. It declared that exceptional temporary deployments will be accompanied by 'appropriate political measures' within the OSCE, through which the nature of the exceptional circumstances having given rise to any such deployment might be explained. Furthermore the Alliance assured that its use of treaty flexibilities will not result in TLE in excess of a territorial ceiling by more than the amount permitted for an exceptional temporary deployment.[47] Eventually, in March 1999, Russia 'took note of' the state's right to receive up to two divisions (three brigades) on its territory in exceptional circumstances.[48]

Adapting the transit provision

Seeking greater flexibility for the movement of equipment under the adapted treaty, in December 1997 the USA suggested exempting TLE in 'internal' transit across territorial boundaries in the ATTU area, in addition to Article III 'external' constraints.[49] France and Germany opposed exempting TLE transited in unlimited numbers within the area of application from territorial levels for up to 42 days in individual states, as proposed by the USA. While in favour of maintaining the relevant part of Article III, France and Germany considered that such 'internal' exceptions should apply only to such warranted cases as exercises, temporary exceeding of territorial ceilings and transfers of troops when they move across the territory of third CFE states. They were prepared to agree to extend the time of transit to 14 days.[50]

According to NATO's June proposal, armaments and equipment would be exempt from the territorial ceilings of transited states parties under a number of specific conditions: (*a*) the host state gives its express consent; (*b*) national ceilings are not exceeded; (*c*) there is no numerical limit for TLE in transit to a destination outside the application zone; (*d*) the amount of TLE in transit within the area of application is no greater than the amount permitted under

[46] Statement by the Head of the Delegation of the Russian Federation (note 19).
[47] NAC Statement on CFE (note 24), para. 11.
[48] *Rzeczpospolita*, 9 Mar. 1999, p. 6
[49] Article III, para 1(G) of the CFE Treaty provides that TLE in transit through the area of application from and to a location outside the ATTU area for no longer than a total of 7 days is not to be counted against the treaty's numerical limitations. Transferring, e.g., US equipment through the territories of its allies would, under the terms of the adapted treaty, raise problems of exceeding the TCs of the states concerned.
[50] Schmidt (note 43), pp. 35–36.

the treaty for the territory of final destination; (*e*) for the equipment in transit associated with a UN or OSCE peace mission the treaty does not specify a limit (the force size will be consistent with the mandate); (*f*) the entire transit takes no longer than 42 days; and (*g*) the TLE in transit does not remain in any single territorial unit longer than 21 days.[51] All these conditions were included in the March 1999 JCG decision and were supplemented with additional provisions: (*a*) if TLE in transit remains in a state party longer than 21 days, it will be thereafter considered a temporary deployment; (*b*) transits will not be used as a substitute for temporary deployments or military exercises; and (*c*) TLE in transit will be subject to appropriate transparency measures (to be developed).[52]

The flank issue

Because of its separate special status (specific limitations on ground forces, territorial constraints and additional verification measures) and divergent views about how it should be accommodated in the new conventional arms control regime, the flank issue remains most controversial. With regard to the area defined under Article V of the CFE Treaty, the 1997 partial framework agreement on 'certain basic elements' for treaty adaptation required that its substance be 'maintained but reconciled' with the structure of the adapted treaty. During 1998 several principles were developed concerning: (*a*) the abolition of all elements referring to the bloc structure; (*b*) restraint in setting TCs; (*c*) temporary deployment provisions; and (*d*) restrictions on the possibility of revising TCs upwards. Controversies remained, however, as to the numerical implications of the flank issue.[53]

Russia and NATO adopted contradictory standpoints on this issue. As in previous years, in 1998 Russia continued to press for a change in the flank regime, which it would prefer to see omitted from the adapted treaty. Russia considered itself to be the state most discriminated against because of the number and rigidity of the limitations applied to its territory as compared with the status of and the various proposed flexibilities for the states parties outside the flank zone.[54] It had therefore demanded equal treatment and proposed that its legally binding obligations regarding restraint in the flank zone be replaced by commitments of a political nature. Moscow's line of reasoning, as presented in the Russian delegation's statement of 20 January and subsequent documents, proceeded from the assumption of 'one national level for each participating State and one territorial level for each participating State having territory in the area of application'.[55] By applying a national/territorial ceiling system to

[51] NATO's Proposal (note 37).

[52] JCG Decision (note 26).

[53] OSCE, Letter from the Chairman of the Joint Consultative Group to the Minister for Foreign Affairs of Poland, Chairman of the Seventh Meeting of the OSCE Ministerial Council, MC(7).JOUR/2, Agenda item 11, Annex 5, 2 Dec. 1998, URL <http://www.osceprag.cz/news/mc07ej04x.htm>.

[54] As things stood, Russia was facing 8 different limitations: NCs and TCs; the former and new flank limitations; and 4 upper limits on ACVs in the areas excluded from the former flank.

[55] Statement by the delegation of the Russian Federation to the Joint Consultative Group, Joint Consultative Group document JCG.JOUR/287, Vienna, 20 Jan. 1998.

states parties in the Article V area, the elements of flank discrimination might either be made simpler or taken away altogether. Evidently seeking to downgrade the 1996 Flank Document[56] (by calling into question its legally binding character and depicting it as a temporary solution), Russia insisted on 'rationalizing' the complex rules of TLE deployment in the Leningrad and North Caucasus military districts (MDs) with the formula 'new numbers in the old geography'. According to this formula, Russia was willing to retain as valid only the aggregate sublimits for the ground TLE (1800 tanks, 3700 ACVs and 2400 artillery pieces, to be reached by 31 May 1999). A new system of national and territorial ceilings, claimed the Russian delegation, would be sufficient to head off any destabilizing accumulation of forces, thus making redundant separate sublimits on TLE in the former and new flank areas as well as additional verification measures, as agreed under the 1996 Flank Document. The Russian TLE stationed in Armenia, Georgia, Moldova and the Ukrainian Crimea would be excluded from the flank limitations and limited by Russia's national ceiling and the TCs notified by the host countries. In return, Russia would be prepared, 'outside the framework of the Treaty', to show restraint in the deployment of its TLE in certain parts of its territory and to offer 'appropriate assurances' to that effect.[57]

Furthermore, Russia suggested that two large bases for the maintenance and repair of weapons and equipment in the St Petersburg region and in Kushchevskaya in the North Caucasus region (where considerable amounts of equipment have already accumulated) should not be counted against the CFE Treaty limits while 'non-combat-worthy' equipment is there for repair and upgrading.[58] Enhanced transparency measures would be given 'the broadest possible application' at the bases. This proposal was reiterated and developed on 23 March in a confidential memorandum to the JCG in Vienna, its main rationale being the impracticality and cost of transporting ageing equipment to and from Russia's repair sites in Siberia.[59] A US-led multinational expert team visited the repair facilities in Kushchevskaya and St Petersburg and produced a comprehensive report to help resolve the issues of accumulation of equipment there.[60]

NATO (joined by its three candidates) sought further clarification of the Russian proposal, and other flank states (Bulgaria and Romania) requested that the substance of the Russian position be explained. To compound the

[56] CFE, Final Document of the First Conference to Review the Operation of the Treaty on Conventional Armed Forces in Europe and the Concluding Act of the Negotiation on Personnel Strength, Vienna, 15–31 May 1996, CFE-TRC/DG.2 Rev. 5, 31 May 1996, Annex A: Document Agreed Among the States Parties to the Treaty on Conventional Armed Forces in Europe of 19 November 1990 (the Flank Document). Excerpts from the Flank Document are reproduced in *SIPRI Yearbook 1997* (note 2), pp. 512–17.

[57] Statement by the delegation of the Russian Federation to the Joint Consultative Group (note 55).

[58] Under Article III of the CFE Treaty a state party can, in accordance with strict rules, temporarily exempt its equipment from the numerical limitations in the following cases: (*a*) manufacture of new equipment; (*b*) R&D; (*c*) historical collections; (*d*) awaiting disposal after decommissioning; (*e*) export and re-export; (*f*) internal security needs; and (*g*) transit movements. This proposal supposes another exception.

[59] *Defense News*, 11–17 May 1998, pp. 3, 28.

[60] OSCE (note 53).

problem, Russia's progress in reducing and redistributing its holdings in the former and present flank areas, especially in the Caucasus, in its run-up to the deadline of 31 May 1999 has been reported as unsatisfactory over the past two years. Several states parties have accordingly expressed their concern.

The NATO response reiterated the view that the substance of the flank regime (numerical limitations on ground TLE, geographical areas, inherent flexibilities, temporary deployment provisions, and additional information and verification arrangements) can be reconciled with the structure of the adapted treaty only through the application of the system of national and territorial ceilings to the states parties' territories in the flank zone.[61] A certain amount of flexibility was envisaged with regard to the format or the ways and means of maintaining and integrating the substance of the regime. The alliance stated that the reconciliation of the flank regime with the structure of the adapted treaty should: conform to the 'basic elements' decision; form an integral part of treaty adaptation; retain the legally binding character of the flank obligations; not compromise the security interests of any state party or lead to less stability and predictability than in the rest of the ATTU area; ensure that the flank countries enjoy a political status equal to that of other states parties; and enable the opening of the adapted treaty to accession by other states.

NATO's proposal would apply the flank limitations under the adapted treaty to the areas currently defined in Article V of the CFE Treaty as modified by the Flank Document. The territorial ceilings of the 12 states parties with territory in the flank zone[62] would not exceed their updated CFE Treaty maximum national levels for holdings as of the date of signature of the adapted treaty; an additional unilateral lowering of the TCs resulting from this procedure would be possible, but these could not be lower than the related NCs. In addition to national and territorial ceilings for the 12 flank states, Russia and Ukraine will continue to have one sublimit each, subordinate to their TCs, applied to the Leningrad and North Caucasus MDs (Russia) and the former Odessa MD (Ukraine). The upper limits established for the areas removed from the flank area and the overall limitations for Russia in the former flank zone will also be maintained. In no case will the NC of a state party be exceeded as a result of a temporary deployment, and a TC or sublimit may not be exceeded temporarily by more than 153 tanks, 241 ACVs or 140 artillery pieces in the flank area.

The flank regime is evidently in need of streamlining. Its complex system of limitations calls for non-discriminatory, more suitable and simpler solutions acceptable both to Russia and the other states concerned. Russia has declared its willingness to show flexibility in the flank question but failed to give details. Another problem compounding the situation is that some other countries (Bulgaria and Romania) are seeking to leave the flank regime in their efforts to join NATO.

[61] NATO's Proposal on the Substance of the Flank Regime and Its Reconciliation with the Structure of the Adapted Treaty, Joint Consultative Group document JCG.DEL/15/98, Vienna, 31 Mar. 1998.

[62] Armenia, Azerbaijan, Bulgaria, Georgia, Greece, Iceland, Moldova, Norway, Romania, Russia, Turkey and Ukraine.

The March 1999 decision set out a number of 'principles and modalities' to guide the 'maintenance and reconciliation' of the substance of the modified Article V provisions in the adapted Treaty. The principles included: (*a*) the legally binding character of the provisions; (*b*) preventing a build-up of forces; (*c*) initial TCs will equal initial NCs/up-to-date maximum national levels for holdings; (*d*) upward revision of the relevant TCs and sublimits only through transfers among the flank states; (*e*) brigade-level temporary deployments, and (*f*) an enhanced regime of verification and information exchange. The modalities prescribed: (*a*) single sublimits for Russia and Ukraine; (*b*) subordination of Russian forces in other countries to general rules regarding NCs, TCs and temporary deployments; and (*c*) the desirability of an early solution to the reduction of Russian forces in Georgia and of the withdrawal of Russian forces from Moldova. To satisfy Russia's concerns and demands, NATO (and Turkey in particular) has once more conceded to Russia having more ACVs—up to 2140 (formerly 1380 including 800 in storage)—in its redefined flank zone.

Stationing of troops

Russia's position on a ban on permanent stationing of foreign TLE where it was not deployed before 17 November 1995 has not changed very much since early 1997. NATO maintains that it needs flexibility to conduct its missions and to ensure equal status for its new members. Faced with NATO's unswerving determination not to yield on the issue, Russia proposed in the autumn that NATO members should not be permitted to deploy combat aircraft or attack helicopters on a permanent basis in the ATTU area beyond the limits of the territories of the current '16', which would be accompanied by corresponding transparency measures.[63] In response, in the 8 December 'Statement on CFE', the '16+3' states reiterated the declaration of 14 March 1997[64] that NATO will refrain from additional permanent stationing of substantial combat forces, with the clarification that this covers substantial *ground and air* combat forces. The statement went on to assert that this does not relate to headquarters or other military support activities needed to meet the Alliance's military requirements for reinforcement, interoperability or integration. NATO also promised increased transparency with regard to its defence plans and programmes in the context of any future stationing.[65]

The stability zone

The problem remains of restrictions in the Central European stability zone proposed by NATO in February 1997.[66] According to the NATO 'basic elements' proposal, the national and territorial ceilings would be the same for

[63] Statement by the Head of the Delegation of the Russian Federation (note 19).
[64] The North Atlantic Council declaration of 14 March 1997 (NATO Press Release 97 (27)) is quoted in *SIPRI Yearbook 1998* (note 9), p. 511.
[65] NAC Statement on CFE (note 24), para. 12.
[66] NATO's Proposal (note 32). For more on the stability zone see Lachowski (note 9), pp. 509–10.

each country in the zone and states would provide additional information on stationed forces and temporary deployments on their territory as well as accept additional inspection quotas. Russia's official position on the stability zone was that it was 'absolutely unjustified' in view of NATO enlargement and its consequences for Russia's military security. Russia's clinging to the position 'one national level for each state, and one territorial level for each state having territory in the area of application', thus rejecting the establishment of additional numerical sublimits for the Kaliningrad region (like those for the flank zone), hampered progress on this issue. This has further contributed to strengthening Polish scepticism about this issue[67] and magnified the fears of the three Baltic states, which remain outside the CFE Treaty regime. In the autumn of 1998, however, Russia hinted that if 'adequate solutions' are found to the issue of temporary deployments, particularly in the context of Central European stability, Russia will be willing to show restraint in the Kaliningrad region.[68]

The three new NATO members were clearly unenthusiastic about placing themselves in a 'second-class' category of alliance membership and treaty status with the various limitations and constraints stemming from the stability zone concept. In this context, Russian pressure has led to a suggestion that the states parties concerned (the Article V states plus others—de facto, the Central European states) abstain, on the basis of treaty provisions or specific commitments, from making use of the treaty provisions on exceptional temporary deployments. Poland was against linking the Central European zone and the flank areas[69] and, were such a zone to be established, considered that it should include at least one 'old' NATO member state (preferably Germany).[70] In a goodwill gesture, the German delegation stated in March 1999 that Germany will not make use of the mechanism for upward revision of TCs,[71] as all the other Central European states concerned (except Russia) have agreed to do.

The Polish determination led Russia to make some concessions. It has declared its intention to make reductions in its aggregate weapon limits and, importantly, to 'freeze' its holdings in the Kaliningrad oblast[72] (and the Pskov oblast adjacent to the Baltic states). Belarus also gave up its earlier insistence

[67] Onyszkiewicz (note 40); and Wagrowska, M., 'Goscie z duzym bagazem' [Guests with heavy luggage], *Rzeczpospolita*, 10 July 1998, p. 7, in 'Poland: CFE talks, new NATO members security seen', FBIS-EEU-98-201, 20 July 1998. Under the adapted treaty devoid of territorial constraints, Russia might locate all its armed forces in the region.

[68] Statement by the Head of the Delegation of the Russian Federation (note 19).

[69] Russia has reportedly offered to reduce heavy equipment in its flank in order to have Norway and Turkey bring pressure to bear on Poland to make concessions with regard to the Russian demands. *Rzeczpospolita*, 22 Jan. 1999, p. 5.

[70] US Secretary of State Madeleine Albright is reported to have promised Polish Foreign Minister Bronislaw Geremek on 5 Dec. 1998 in Brussels that the USA will not consent to an adapted CFE Treaty that fails to accord Poland the same privileges as those to be enjoyed by each of the '16'. In return, Poland supported the US stance on the change of the Alliance's strategy, including its independence from UN Security Council decisions. *Rzeczpospolita*, 10 Dec. 1998, p. 6.

[71] Erklärung der deutschen Delegation in der KSE-Gemeinsamen Beratungsgruppe am 30. März 1999 [Declaration of the German delegation to the CFE Joint Consultative Group, 30 Mar. 1999], Joint Consultative Group document JCG.DEL/23/99, 30 Mar. 1999.

[72] The Russian TLE holdings in the Kaliningrad region are now as follows: 829 tanks, 866 ACVs, 341 artillery pieces, 100 aircraft and 35 helicopters.

on letting its holdings exceed the current MNLH by 20 per cent. In return, Poland agreed to lower its territorial ceilings over the next three to four years and undertook not to revise them upwards while reserving for itself the right to immediate and full access to exceptional temporary deployments.[73]

Verification and data exchanges

Overshadowed by other substantial political issues the technical and political problems of enhanced verification and data exchange have so far only been discussed in general terms at the treaty adaptation talks. The states parties have already agreed to increase passive quotas of on-site inspections, introduce specific transparency and verification measures for military exercises and temporary deployments, and maintain the obligations of Russia and Ukraine under the Flank Document regarding supplementary passive declared site inspections. States are considering ways to strengthen, streamline and make more efficient and cost-effective the regime of national and multinational inspections (central coordination of national and international inspections, avoidance of duplication, non-counting of at least part of the conducted multinational inspection against the national quotas of every participant, reduction of the costs, calculating future inspection quotas according to the number of weapons rather than the object-of-verification system, and so on). There are plans to establish a new centre within the OSCE (within the Forum for Security Co-operation, FSC) to handle verification and data exchanges. Such a data registration and assessment centre could lower costs, enhance the effectiveness of information exchanges and improve access to them. In this context, a Verification Coordination Centre would probably be integrated in the FSC.[74]

III. Regional arms control in Europe

The only regional arms control arrangement now operating below the pan-European level is the 1996 Florence Agreement on Sub-Regional Arms Control, signed by Bosnia and Herzegovina and its two entities (the Muslim–Croat Federation of Bosnia and Herzegovina and the Republika Srpska), Croatia and Yugoslavia (Serbia and Montenegro).[75]

In 1998 the implementation of the civilian provisions of the Dayton Agreement showed mixed results compared with the more successful implementation of the arms control provisions. The Bosnia Peace Implementation Council, meeting in Madrid on 15–16 December 1998, affirmed that military stability had been maintained throughout Bosnia and Herzegovina and that the entity armed forces (those of the Muslim–Croat Federation of Bosnia and

[73] Statement by the delegation of Poland to the Joint Consultative Group, Joint Consultative Group document JCG.DEL/24/99, 30 Mar. 1999.

[74] Schmidt (note 43), p. 36. The prospects for such a centre did not look promising in early 1999.

[75] For the purpose of this section, 'regional' in the OSCE context refers to areas beneath the continental/OSCE level. Regional CSBMs, including the 1996 Agreement on Confidence- and Security-Building Measures in Bosnia and Herzegovina, are discussed in appendix 14A in this volume. The text of the Florence Agreement is reproduced in *SIPRI Yearbook 1997* (note 2), pp. 517–24.

Herzegovina and the Bosnian Serb Republika Srpska), having met in full their obligations with regard to equipment limited by the Florence Agreement, continued to comply with the military provisions of the Dayton Agreement.[76] The irony is that the successful implementation of the Florence Agreement was accompanied by the armed conflict in Kosovo.

Despite the success of the arms control process, several shortcomings and deficiencies remained, including: (*a*) hesitation and delays in developing cooperation and confidence between the entity armed forces; (*b*) the destabilizing factor of the existence of two, in practice three (Muslim, Croatian and Serb), armies in Bosnia and Herzegovina; (*c*) the lack of a common security policy leading progressively to a state dimension of defence, requiring, among others, a strengthening of the Standing Committee on Military Matters established by the Presidency of Bosnia and Herzegovina; (*d*) the increasing divergence in doctrine and training between the entity armed forces; and (*e*) insufficient security cooperation. The latter concerned the lack of transparent, publicly accountable external assistance to the entity armed forces; the high levels of defence expenditure; and the lack of defence revenues and expenditures in both the Federation of Bosnia and Herzegovina and the Republika Srpska. The Peace Implementation Council warned that, in the event of the entities concerned not meeting the requirement of full transparency in these areas, it will review the overall provision of assistance provided to them. The Council declared that, in cooperation with the NATO-led Stabilization Force (SFOR), the OSCE, and armed forces and entity and state governments, it would work to maintain military stability, increase cooperation and confidence between entity armed forces, nurture stronger joint defence mechanisms and remove the military from inappropriate involvement in the political process.[77]

In the spring of 1998, the USA suspended its weapon deliveries under the Train and Equip Program to Croatia, accusing the latter of obstructing the Federation, not integrating some HVO (Croatian) military units into the Federation's Joint Command and not accepting its common insignia, ranks and symbols. Denying these accusations, the Croatian officials complained that the practices of training, financing and distributing weapons, and the fact that the training takes place mostly in Islamic countries, benefit the Bosnian–Muslim component of the Federation Army and discriminate against the Croatian component. On 4 June, the US Department of State decided to suspend the military assistance programme to Bosnia until the Federation's Defence Ministry bans the flying of former Bosnian–Muslim and Croat flags in military installations.[78]

[76] Reinforcing Peace in Bosnia and Herzegovina—The Way Ahead. The Peace Implementation Agenda. Annex to the Declaration issued by the Peace Implementation Council, Chapter VII, Madrid, 16 Dec. 1998.

[77] Declaration of the Peace Implementation Council, Madrid, 16 Dec. 1998.

[78] 'Americans imposed sanctions on HVO', *Vecernji List* (Zagreb), 11 May 1998, in 'Bosnia and Herzegovina: Klein confirms suspension of equipment for HVO', FBIS-EEU-98-132, 12 May 1998; and *Atlantic News*, no. 3017 (10 June 1998), p. 4.

Implementation of the Florence Agreement

Under the Florence Agreement, more than 6600 items of heavy equipment have been scrapped or converted. An additional 250 heavy weapons were destroyed after the end of the reduction period (i.e., since November 1997). Nearly all the 180 inspections had been characterized by transparency and cooperation. The inspections revealed no major discrepancies with the information exchanged. The notification and inspection regimes have been consolidated with the OSCE assistance to the parties.

The first conference to review implementation was held in Vienna on 15–19 June 1998 and chaired by the Personal Representative of the OSCE Chairman-in-Office (CIO), General Carlo Jean. The parties agreed on measures to improve the level of implementation, and appropriate instructions were given to the Sub-Regional Consultative Commission (SRCC).[79]

A programme of action for 1999 and beyond was set out.[80] Weapon holdings will be monitored. The chairmanship of the SRCC will be transferred from the Personal Representative of the Chairman-in-Office to the five parties to the Florence Agreement as from the beginning of 1999. The OSCE will continue, in 1999 and beyond, to provide assistance to the parties in assuming the SRCC chairmanship, planning and evaluation of the inspections, inspecting and evaluation teams, training for inspectors and the improvement of data exchange.[81] A workshop will be held to standardize notifications of relevant data and of inspections. Inspections of undeclared sites (challenge inspections) will take place, for the first time, in 1999. Software for the verification centres will be made homogeneous, and a common interpretation of weapons in historical collections, something which has caused frequent misunderstandings, will be sought.

As a long-term objective the OSCE plans to reduce the excessive exemptions of the armaments ceilings under the agreement, for instance in the field of decommissioning, with a view to reducing weapon levels and combat readiness.

Negotiations under Article V of the Agreement on Regional Stabilization

The go-ahead for consultations under Article V of the Agreement on Regional Stabilization[82] was given by the December 1997 Copenhagen OSCE Ministerial Council meeting. The events in the Balkan region in 1998 and early

[79] Implementation Review Conference on Article IV (Annex 1-B) of Dayton accords a success, OSCE, Press Release no. 38/98, Vienna, 19 June 1998.

[80] Status of 1999 Programs for the Implementation of the Vienna (CSBMs) and Florence (Sub-Regional Arms Control) Agreements. General Carlo Jean (Italian Army), Personal Representative of the OSCE Chairman-in-Office for Articles II and IV, Oslo, Norway, 2 Dec. 1998, OSCE document MC.GAL/5/98, 2 Dec. 1998.

[81] *OSCE Newsletter*, vol. 5, no. 10 (Oct. 1998).

[82] Annex 1-B of the Dayton Peace Agreement (note 3), Article V, Regional Arms Control Agreement. For the Copenhagen premises for the Article V negotiations see Lachowski (note 9), p. 521.

1999, notably in Kosovo,[83] provided further evidence of the need for regional stabilization in south-eastern Europe.

In spite of expectations that the Article V consultations would start the process of creating a regional balance by the summer of 1998, it was not until the autumn that consensus was reached on a number of important items specifying how negotiations should be conducted. Although the preliminary discussions, according to observers, were contingent on the satisfactory implementation of Articles II and IV, the volatile situation in the Balkans and the unfinished business of CFE Treaty adaptation have also affected the pace of the consultations.

On 28 October, the CIO Special Representative for Article V negotiations, Ambassador Henry Jacolin, reported to the Permanent Council that a general understanding had been developed on what should be contained in the agreement. It had been agreed that the region will remain undefined, as 20 states from both within and outside the region have indicated their willingness to be involved in the process.[84] One challenge, according to Ambassador Jacolin, is to achieve 'a synthesis between the dialectic of balancing regional concerns with the indivisible nature of security'. Another challenge is to balance the interests of states within the region with those outside states which have an interest in the region's security.[85]

Work on the mandate of the Article V negotiations was concluded on 27 November. The talks were to begin in mid-January 1999, but were postponed because of the situation in Kosovo and the Rambouillet negotiations.

IV. The Open Skies Treaty

The entry into force of the 1992 Open Skies Treaty remained deadlocked by the failure of Belarus, Russia and Ukraine to ratify this international confidence-building instrument. No progress had been made towards ratification by these three countries by the end of 1998. In March 1998 the Ukrainian Supreme Council failed for the third time to pass the draft law on the ratification of the treaty (the earlier votes were held in January and September 1996). Many Ukrainian deputies voiced their concern that ratification might lead to a deterioration in Ukrainian–Russian relations and that participation in the treaty might become an (undesirable) engine for integration with NATO.[86]

On 12 June 1998 Georgia ratified the treaty, raising the number of ratifications to 23.[87]

As in previous years, signatories actively continued a programme of reciprocal overflights of Germany, Italy, Norway, Russia, Slovakia, the UK and

[83] The Kosovo conflict is described in appendix 1C in this volume.

[84] These are the 5 former Yugoslav republics plus Albania, Austria, Bulgaria, France, Germany, Greece, Hungary, Italy, the Netherlands, Romania, Russia, Spain, Turkey, the UK and the USA.

[85] *OSCE Newsletter*, vol. 5, no. 10 (Oct. 1998).

[86] Hryshchenko, K. (Deputy Foreign Minister of Ukraine), 'The road to the Open Skies', *Holos Ukrayiny* (Kiev), 31 July 1998, in 'Ukraine: Minister on Open Skies Treaty', FBIS-SOV-98-224, 12 Aug. 1998.

[87] Georgia's instrument of ratification was deposited on 31 Aug. 1998. For the status of the 1992 Open Skies Treaty and the conditions for its entry into force, see annexe A in this volume.

Ukraine. Ten joint trial overflights took place in 1998,[88] and another 20 were scheduled for 1999.

V. Conventional arms control endeavours outside Europe

In 1998 conventional arms control endeavours outside the OSCE area continued to be limited for the most part to various types of confidence-building measures and activities rather than developing towards disarmament or arms reduction. In such regions as the Middle East, South Asia and North-East Asia, the most heavily armed and conflict-prone regions in the world, competitive strategic interests and domestic political pressures precluded cooperative security or arms control approaches. In Africa, a promising development was the 16-nation Economic Community of West African States (ECOWAS) three-year arms production and transfer moratorium which entered into force on 1 November 1998; now the challenge is to have its 'soft', that is, non-verifiable, arms control commitments respected.[89] In Asia–Pacific and Latin America there were some developments in the cooperative security- and confidence-enhancing process.

Asia–Pacific

South-East Asia was the most visible in its efforts to maintain and develop a regular confidence-building dialogue which aspires to combine talks on political and security-related developments in the region, defence policies, non-proliferation and arms control, including various voluntary confidence-building steps and measures.

The ASEAN Regional Forum

The political and security dialogue conducted within the Association of South-East Asian Nations (ASEAN) Regional Forum (ARF) covers both military and defence-related measures and non-military issues, which have a significant impact on regional security.[90] Non-mandatory confidence-building measures (CBMs) as discussed and implemented within the ARF differ from European CSBMs in the terms and scope of the talks, the range of measures, the degree of institutionalization and enforcement, the nature of the challenges they address and the variety of participants. It is a flexible and regular step-by-step process characterized by a host of various types of annual meetings and with a steadily growing record of accomplishments.[91] It is intended that the ARF

[88] For the list of joint flights, see *Arms Control Reporter*, sheet 840.B.39, 1998.

[89] The moratorium was signed on 31 Oct. 1998. See also appendix 11E in this volume.

[90] Members of ASEAN and ARF are listed in the glossary in this volume.

[91] The CBMs as agreed at the ARF meetings in 1994–97 are:

1. Substantive CBMs (implemented): (*a*) continue and develop exchanges on security perceptions on a sub-regional and regional basis; (*b*) increase exchanges among national defence colleges and to this end convene meetings of the heads of national defence colleges; (*c*) convene an intersessional meeting on the role of defence authorities in disaster relief; and (*d*) exchange information on a voluntary basis on ongoing observer participation in and notification of military exercises.

should develop from incremental confidence building through preventive diplomacy to playing an active role in resolving conflicts, which may create the premises for an agreement. Two meetings of the Intersessional Support Group on CBMs (ISG on CBMs) are usually held between the annual meetings of the ARF. In the intersessional year 1997–98 the ISG, co-chaired by Australia and Brunei, met in Brunei on 4–6 November 1997 and in Sydney on 4–6 March 1998. Its mandate was extended for the next ISG on CBMs meetings in 1998–99, co-chaired by Thailand and the USA, and meetings were held in Honolulu (4–6 November 1998) and Bangkok (3–5 March 1999).

In accordance with the ARF's broadly conceived notion of comprehensive security, the participants seek to focus on defence-related CBMs, while also addressing a wide spectrum of non-military measures. At the Brunei and Sydney meetings, two new topics were addressed: (*a*) exploring the overlap between CBMs and preventive diplomacy; and (*b*) maritime issues (maritime safety, law and order at sea, and protection and preservation of the marine environment). These issues were further discussed in Honolulu (with a focus on CBMs and maritime cooperation) and Bangkok (CBMs/preventive diplomacy).

There is a belief among the participants that 'while good progress has been made in implementing a number of agreed CBMs, there is still considerable scope to develop and deepen cooperation on confidence building measures among ARF members'.[92] In the field of implementation of the agreed CBMs there were a number of security-related activities in 1997–98:

1. The first ARF meeting of heads of national defence colleges was held (7–8 October 1997 in Manila).
2. A range of regional (through meetings of the ISG Senior Officials and ARF Ministers), subregional (e.g., through Northeast Asia Cooperation Dialogue and ASEAN meetings) and bilateral exchanges on regional security perceptions were developed.
3. The number of high-level defence contacts expanded rapidly, including representation in the ISG on CBMs.

2. Substantive CBMs (partially implemented): (*a*) develop bilateral exchanges on security perceptions; (*b*) increase high-level defence contacts and military exchanges/training; (*c*) submit to the ARF or ARF Senior Officials Meetings an annual defence policy statement on a voluntary basis; (*d*) publish defence white papers or similar papers on a voluntary basis; (*e*) full participation in the UN Register on Conventional Arms (UNROCA); (*f*) circulate submissions to UNROCA simultaneously to other ARF participants on a voluntary basis; (*g*) sign and ratify global non-proliferation and disarmament regimes; (*h*) exchange views on the contents of annual defence policy or defence white papers; and (*i*) exchange views on defence conversion programmes on a voluntary basis.

3. Organizational CBMs (implemented): (*a*) complete and update a list of ARF contact points; and (*b*) circulate compilation of papers submitted to ISG on CBMs.

4. Organizational CBMs (partially implemented): (*a*) submit papers on defence contacts and other defence exchange programmes to the ARF Senior Officials Meetings; and (*b*) increase defence participation in ARF intersessional activities.

ARF (ASEAN), 'Distillation of Agreed CBMs from ARF 1-4. ARF5 Chairman's Statement, Annex E: Matrices & Tables, Attachment, 27 July 1998', URL <http://www.dfat.gov.au/arf/Matrix_Att.html>.

[92] 'Co-Chairmen's Summary Report of the Meetings of the ARF Intersessional Support Group on Confidence Building Measures held in Bandar Seri Begawan, Brunei Darussalam on 4–6 Nov. 1997 and in Sydney, Australia on 4–6 Mar. 1998', URL <http://www.dfat.gov.au/arf/arf5_C.html>.

4. ARF member participation in the UN Register of Conventional Arms was very high and members started to circulate their returns to each other.[93]

5. Several ARF members had voluntarily submitted annual defence policy statements and there had been 'very good progress' in the voluntary development of defence White Papers.

6. A number of ARF members invited observers to and provided notification of selected uni-, bi- and multilateral exercises on a voluntary and case-by-case basis.

Information on agreed CBMs was produced during the intersessional year 1997–98 in the form of a set of matrices and tables presenting: (*a*) a summary of agreed CBMs; (*b*) information on defence policy statements and publication of Defence White Papers and similar papers; (*c*) bilateral regional security dialogues; (*d*) high-level defence contacts; (*e*) defence training/exchanges since 1995; and (*f*) participation in global arms control and disarmament regimes, showing the degree of CBM implementation.[94] The Fifth Meeting of the ASEAN Regional Forum in Manila agreed on 27 July 1998 that these matrices and tables will be updated on an annual basis.[95]

As far as new CBMs are concerned, the ISG recommended two baskets of measures. They range from military-related measures to media support for the activities of the ARF, a counter-narcotics project and a contest among ARF riflemen. Basket I consists of CBMs recommended for consideration and implementation in the near future (over the next two intersessional years); and the second contains CBMs likely to need more time to be implemented. Basket I includes: (*a*) encouraging ARF members to exchange visits of naval vessels on a voluntary basis; (*b*) multilateral exchanges and cooperation in military logistics and academic research (e.g., in military medicine and law); (*c*) compilation of lists and contact points on CBMs; (*d*) training or a seminar for ARF foreign affairs and defence officials; (*e*) a seminar on the production of defence White Papers or other defence policy documents; and (*f*) encouraging visits to military establishments. Basket 2 envisages such security-related measures as ARF liaison with other regional forums and preventing and combating illicit trafficking in conventional small arms.[96]

Other developments in Asia

In other parts of Asia, several events seemed to demonstrate the awareness that arms control, confidence-building and risk-reduction steps might alleviate tensions and improve the political climate, but there were no major actions of consequence. The nuclear developments in South Asia effectively froze the difficult dialogue on CBMs between India and Pakistan, although it apparently

93 See chapter 11 in this volume for more on the UN Register of Conventional Arms.

94 ARF (ASEAN Regional Forum), Implementation of ARF agreed CBMs, URL <http://www.dfat.gov.au/arf/arfhomeMatrix.html

95 ARF (ASEAN Regional Forum), Chairman's Statement, The Fifth Meeting of the ASEAN Regional Forum, Manila, 27 July 1998, URL <http://www.dfat.gov.au/arf/arf5.html>.

96 ARF, List of new ARF CBMs, ARF document ISG/CBMs/1997-98/Meeting2/Doc5/Rev2., URL < http://www.dfat.gov.au/arf/arf5_F.html>.

did not affect the generally smooth management of border CBMs between India and China. In North-East Asia, the harsh economic crisis and famine in North Korea have reportedly affected the US and the South Korean assessment of the communist regime's military strength, which might result in US 'troop restructuring' or arms reduction initiatives in a subcommittee on tension reduction of the Geneva Four-Party (China, North Korea, South Korea and the USA) Peace Talks that was set up in January 1999.[97]

On 3 July 1998 China, Kazakhstan, Kyrgyzstan, Russia and Tajikistan reaffirmed CBMs at a summit meeting in Almaty, Kazakhstan. The parties agreed to troop reductions along their common borders. They also agreed to the 1997 proposal by Kazakhstan to convene a conference on 'interaction and confidence-building in Asia', although neither a timetable nor a list of participants was specified. This initiative is said to have stemmed from Kazakhstan's interest in holding an Asian security forum, paralleling the ARF.[98]

At the ARF, on 27 July 1998 the then Russian Foreign Minister, Yevgeny Primakov, presented a series of maritime CBMs to be applied in the Asia–Pacific region: (*a*) exchange of information on the purpose of naval activities, structure of forces, time-frame and areas of the activities, and level of command; (*b*) notification of large-scale exercises and movements of naval forces; (*c*) invitation of observers to naval exercises; (*d*) joint exercises on search and rescue at sea and assistance to victims of natural disasters; (*e*) the mutual renunciation of exercises and manoeuvres in sea straits, fishing zones and the airspace above them; and (*f*) multilateral agreements on preventing incidents at sea beyond territorial waters, based on the existing system of relevant bilateral agreements between leading naval powers.[99]

In the autumn, Russian Defence Minister Igor Sergeyev paid an official visit to Beijing where, in a good-neighbourly spirit, he stated that 'nearly 300 divisions and regiments' in military districts bordering China were disbanded or reduced in strength in 1998, and that the Trans-Baikal and Siberian MDs would be replaced before the end of the year by a new Siberian military district headquartered in Chita. Indirectly criticizing NATO, Sergeyev praised China as 'faithfully honouring' its security and CBM commitments and recommended that the Sino-Russian cooperation serve as a model for 'other regions, in particular Europe'. He also reiterated Primakov's proposal concerning naval CBMs for the Asia–Pacific region.[100]

[97] See, e.g., Nam Mun-hi, 'Hidden meaning of the US message that the ROK must reduce its arms first', *Sisa Journal* (Seoul), 2 Apr. 1998 in 'South Korea: US view on ROK arms reduction', Foreign Broadcast Information Service, *Daily Report East Asia (FBIS–EAS)*, FBIS-EAS-98-094, 4 Apr. 1998; and Pae Myong-pok, 'It is possible to discuss US troop reduction', *Chungang Ilbo* (Seoul), Internet version, 25 Oct. 1998, in 'South Korea: Official on possibility of discussing US troop reduction', FBIS-EAS-98-301, 28 Oct. 1998.

[98] *Arms Control Reporter*, sheet 850.B.451, 1998. For more on the 1996 Shanghai Agreement on confidence building in the military sphere see Jing-dong Yuan, 'Sino-Russian confidence-building measures: a preliminary analysis', *Asian Perspectives*, vol. 22 (spring 1998), pp. 73–108; and Lachowski, Z., 'Conventional arms control', *SIPRI Yearbook 1997* (note 2), p. 494

[99] Opening statement by H. E. Yevgeniy M. Primakov, Minister of Foreign Affairs, Russia, Fifth ARF, Manila, 27 July 1998, URL <http://www.dfat.gov.au/arf/5opstat4.html>.

[100] Interfax (Moscow), 21 Oct. 1998, in 'Russia: Sergeyev: Russia reducing troop numbers along PRC border', Foreign Broadcast Information Service, *Daily Report–Central Eurasia: Military Affairs (FBIS-*

Latin America

Since the early 1990s the Organization of American States (OAS) has pursued a dialogue aimed at strengthening military-to-military relations and reducing rivalries and tensions in the region. In 1995 a Committee on Hemispheric Security, the first regional forum for arms control, non-proliferation and security issues, was established. Despite fears that the US decision of 1997 to lift the 20-year ban on arms sales to the region would result in a renewed arms race in Latin America, the region which accounts for the lowest per capita military spending in comparison with other parts of the world, this was not the case in 1998.

As a follow-up to the 1995 OAS Declaration of Santiago on Confidence- and Security-Building Measures,[101] which contained a programme of action for the Western Hemisphere and called for each country gradually to adopt agreements on the prior notification of military exercises, participation in the UN Register of Conventional Arms and reporting to the UN on military expenditures, promotion of exchanges regarding defence policies and doctrines and the invitation of foreign observers to military exercises, another OAS conference was held on 25–27 February 1998 in San Salvador, El Salvador. Gathering 27 states of the region, the conference issued the Declaration of San Salvador on Confidence- and Security-Building Measures, complementing the 1995 Santiago Declaration. Along with measures designed to promote broadly conceived, non-military confidence-building endeavours (such as parliamentary exchanges, diplomatic training, border cooperation, small island states' special security concerns of an economic, financial and environmental nature, a cooperation programme regarding maritime transport of nuclear and other waste, and so on), the OAS governments agreed: (*a*) to encourage studies on a common methodology in order to facilitate the comparison of military expenditures in the region, taking into account the UN reporting system; (*b*) to improve and broaden the information submitted by the member states to the UN Register of Conventional Arms; and (*c*) to continue consultations and exchange of ideas to advance the limitation and control of conventional weapons in the region.

Participating states, which included more Central American and Caribbean countries than the Santiago Conference, recommended several steps to strengthen the OAS Committee on Hemispheric Security. In an attempt to institutionalize the CSBM dialogue there was a call for an annual meeting of experts at the OAS, an inter-parliamentary meeting and the inclusion of CBM topics in the Inter-American Service Chiefs meetings.[102]

UMA), FBIS-UMA-98-294, 21 Oct. 1998; and Radio Rossii Network (Moscow), 22 Oct. 1998, in 'Russia: Russia's Sergeyev suggests confidence-building measures', FBIS-SOV-98-295, 22 Oct. 1998.

[101] The text of the OAS Declaration of Santiago on Confidence- and Security-Building Measures, 10 Nov. 1995 is reproduced on the Henry L Stimson Center website on the Internet, URL <http://www.stimson.org/cbm/la/oasdeclr.htm>.

[102] On the Declaration of San Salvador on Confidence- and Security-Building Measures see US Arms Control and Disarmament Agency, (ACDA) Factsheet, Organization of American States Conference on Confidence- and Security-Building Measures (CSBMs), 25–27 Feb. 1998, San Salvador, El Salvador, URL <http://www.acda.gov/factshee/secbldg/oas.htm>.

VI. Conclusions

The stalemate that prevailed in conventional and other arms control processes in 1998 led some analysts to announce once again that arms control had reached a dead end or lost momentum altogether. In the context of conventional arms control, however, such an assessment is unfounded.

The primary challenge for European military security is to turn the symmetrical balance-of-forces system into an asymmetrical non-threatening arms control regime built on a cooperative basis. While the controversy in the CFE Treaty adaptation talks between the United States and some of its allies and Russia stalemated the negotiation, a more detailed outline of the future agreement was emerging in Vienna: (*a*) the further elaboration of the principles of the arms control regime; (*b*) flexibility mechanisms regarding the revision of national and territorial ceilings, temporary deployments and transits, as well as principles and modalities of maintaining and reconciling the flank provisions with the new treaty; (*d*) enhancing the verification regime; and (*e*) the creation of the stability zone in Central Europe. NATO has also addressed a number of political gestures to Russia, such as its unilateral declarations on non-deployment of nuclear weapons or substantial conventional weaponry on the territory of its new members and the engagement in an active political dialogue in the Permanent Joint Council under the NATO–Russia Founding Act.

The reasons for the impasse lie both in the European security environment and in the domestic policies of Russia and the USA. Internationally, 1998 bore witness to the progress in NATO's enlargement process, the continued weakening of Russia's economic, political and military status and the concomitant hardening of its negotiating position. In the domestic context, the USA evidently sought a middle way between the cooperative approach of the Administration and the conservative opponents of arms control in Congress and the Pentagon. Russia, in turn, faced with a plethora of grave internal problems, is still in the throes of identifying its security interests. It feels at a growing disadvantage as NATO approaches its borders, on the one hand, and is nudged to accept allegedly discriminatory Western arms control proposals, on the other. It has therefore sought to counter successive NATO proposals. The only clear Russian interest in conventional arms control seems to be limitation of the military implications of NATO enlargement and forging some semblance of a new balance of forces in Europe. Russia thus strove to transform the prospective members of NATO into a kind of grey zone, in conventional arms terms, between itself and the '16'. In turn, the candidate NATO states strove to preclude provisions that would make them 'second-class' participants of the adapted CFE regime. The flank problem proved to be another sticking point here, in which Russia sought to remove various constraints concerning weapon deployments. All this demonstrated that many states parties to the CFE Treaty have not yet forged their concepts as to what should be the role, place and functions of conventional arms control and, in the case of

Russia's western partners, to what extent they should take account of the security interests and concerns pronounced by Moscow.

An interesting phenomenon is that a more active role is increasingly played in the CFE talks by Western countries other than the USA, especially by Germany. At the beginning of 1999, the central issues vigorously addressed by the states parties in Vienna were flank limitations and the Central European stability zone. The March 1999 compromise was welcomed by all the CFE states parties as satisfactory and helping to smooth the road to the OSCE Istanbul summit meeting target date for adopting the adapted CFE Treaty.

On the regional level within Europe the successful implementation of the Florence Agreement remained an encouraging sign in spite of the mixed record of the implementation of the civilian aspects of the Dayton Agreement and the development of events in and around Yugoslavia. However, the fact that the success of the military provisions was neither translated into beneficial effects in other fields nor capable of curbing the raging conflict in nearby Kosovo appears to demonstrate the inadequacy of classic arms control solutions in handling situations of a new type. A mandate was agreed for the planned negotiation under Article V of the Agreement on Regional Stabilization, but the developments in Kosovo in 1999 prevented it from getting underway.

Developments outside Europe show a mixed record. The evolution in arms control dialogues in South-East Asia and Latin America shows that premises for sustained cooperative developments are better in regions which either enjoy a higher degree of security or lack major incentives to engage in an arms race. On the other hand, the nuclear stalemate in South Asia may lead to some sort of confrontational rather than cooperative conventional arms control in order to overcome the potentially disastrous security dilemma between the actors in the region.

Appendix 14A. Confidence- and security-building measures in Europe

ZDZISLAW LACHOWSKI and PIA KRONESTEDT

I. Introduction

The Organization for Security and Co-operation in Europe (OSCE) continued the implementation of and work on confidence- and security-building measures (CSBMs) on the pan-European and regional levels in 1998. As in the previous year, the 1998 Annual Implementation Assessment Meeting (AIAM) aimed at improving the Vienna Document 1994 of the Negotiations on Confidence- and Security-Building Measures and adapting it to the new security environment in Europe. The OSCE Forum for Security Co-operation (FSC) put forward a number of amendments with the aim of modernizing the Vienna Document in order to enhance transparency, predictability and cooperation. These efforts are reported in section II. The 1996 Agreement on Confidence- and Security-Building Measures in Bosnia and Herzegovina continued to operate successfully in 1998. This agreement and other regional CSBMs are examined in section III. Section IV reports on the third FSC Seminar on Defence Policies and Military Doctrines, held in January 1998, and the conclusions are reported in section V.

II. Vienna Document CSBMs

The Annual Implementation Assessment Meeting

The FSC held its eighth Annual Implementation Assessment Meeting on 2–4 March 1998 to assess the current status of implementation of the provisions of the Vienna Document 1994 and to discuss ways of improving the implementation record. Particular attention was given to enhancing the role of existing crisis prevention and conflict management measures.

Six ad hoc working groups met to modernize the Vienna Document, answer questions put by OSCE participating states and ensure information exchange among them. They made proposals within the framework set by the FSC in previous years to adapt the document to the European security situation and addressed eight broad topics.[1]

1. *Annual exchange of military information*. Participating states were generally in compliance with the requirements for exchange of military information. Some shortcomings were noted, particularly in relation to the timeliness of the information exchange, and small discrepancies were identified in the actual data exchanged. A need was felt for a follow-up mechanism to remind the participating states of their obligations under the Vienna Document. Various measures were discussed with the aim of increasing transparency. The working groups re-examined: (*a*) the relevance of

[1] OSCE Forum for Security Co-operation, 1998 Annual Implementation Assessment Meeting, Vienna, 2–4 March 1998, FSC.AIAM/49/98, 11 Mar. 1998. For background information on the proposals, see Lachowski, Z. and Henrichon, P., 'Confidence- and security-building measures in Europe', *SIPRI Yearbook 1998: Armaments, Disarmament and International Security* (Oxford University Press: Oxford 1998), appendix 12A, pp. 531–32.

the annual exchange, for instance with regard to lowering the notification thresholds and shortening the time period for notifying planned increases in personnel strength; (*b*) the possibility of including information on paramilitary forces in the information exchange; and (*c*) broadening the information on units to cover non-combat units. The possibility of combining the annual exchange and the Global Exchange of Military Information (GEMI) was recalled.

2. *Defence planning.* It was pointed out that many participating states had not provided any information on defence planning and that the quality of the information submitted was unsatisfactory. Suggestions were made for improving the quality and clarity of this information, for example, by establishing qualitative criteria for its analysis and by creating appropriate forms to facilitate replies.

3. *Military activities.* The existing provisions, including thresholds for notification and observation, were discussed. It was suggested that the costs of hosting an observation be distributed among the states involved. Concern was voiced that only about 50 per cent of the participating states submit annual calendars and information concerning constraining provisions. As well as the traditional issue of lowering thresholds, the debate covered such items as definitions and multinational activities (e.g., the NATO-led Stabilization Force, SFOR). Some group members expressed the view that the issue of lower thresholds should be addressed mainly in a regional context. It was suggested that the scope of notification, and hence of observation, be enlarged to cover 'military activities' instead of only 'exercises'. The question of paramilitary forces was seen as particularly important in this regard, and it was suggested that the term 'military significance' be redefined to cover situations which imply a risk of regional destabilization.

4. *Compliance and verification.* Once more the rapid exhaustion of evaluation quotas at the beginning of the year was a matter of concern. The problems of increasing the number of quotas, converting inspection quotas into evaluation quotas, spreading them over the calendar year, modifying the basis for their calculation, regional agreements on additional evaluation visits, and so on, were discussed. Introducing multinational evaluations and inspections was viewed by several participating states as an appropriate way of increasing the number of states involved, enhancing the significance of the Vienna Document, and compensating to some extent for the inadequate quota for evaluations. There was also a suggestion that quotas be coordinated through the OSCE Conflict Prevention Centre (CPC), but the fact of national responsibility for implementation makes this difficult. Increases in the size of evaluation teams were found inappropriate and unduly expensive.

5. *Contacts.* A wide range of contacts between the military forces of the participating states had been made by the beginning of 1998, and this was expected to continue. A few suggestions were made, for example, by Germany, that the CPC receive and distribute information on all visits to air bases in advance, and by Switzerland, that guests to planned contacts be selected on the basis of their knowledge of the kind of event taking place, local issues in the host country and linguistic abilities.

6. *Risk reduction.* The focus was on 'unusual military activities'. While the absence of any registered recourse to this measure in 1997 was taken as a clear sign of an improved security situation in the area of application, some room for improvement was indicated.

7. *Communications*. The essential role of the OSCE Communications Network in implementing the provisions of the Vienna Document was emphasized. Although participating states were sceptical about an early involvement of experts in the

process of adapting the Vienna Document in the field of communications, it was recognized that timely input of expert knowledge and experience would be required.

8. *Other agreed measures.* The participants discussed the norm- and standard-setting measures (the Code of Conduct on Politico-Military Aspects of Security, GEMI, principles governing arms transfers, principles governing non-proliferation and stabilizing measures for localized crisis situations) and several proposals and suggestions were presented, such as making the implementation of various measures more effective and comprehensive, extending the scope of measures to the proliferation of small arms and light weapons, illicit arms trafficking, and so on. Later in the year, the FSC approved the questionnaire on implementation of the Code of Conduct that participating states will answer on an annual basis. The first information exchange under this arrangement took place on 15 April 1999. The CPC will keep a record of this information for discussion at a special session of the appropriate FSC working group.[2]

The participating states also considered the prospects for the existing forms of regional security and the possibilities for including regional measures in the modernized Vienna Document. It was suggested that the OSCE develop a list of measures for use on a regional basis, allowing the participating states to decide whether they wish to apply the measures within their own regions. Several states considered that if regional measures were included in the document they should be complementary to and not in competition with the pan-European CSBMs.

Improving the Vienna Document 1994

On 16 September 1998 a 'rolling text' of the draft revised Vienna Document was presented by the coordinator of the FSC Ad Hoc Working Group on Vienna Document Revision, and there appeared to be agreement that the proposals therein could serve as the basis for further negotiation (which does not mean they will all be included in the new document). The suggestions were based on previous discussions held in 1997 and 1998 within the FSC and at the AIAMs.[3] The text suggested some editorial changes (including the incorporation of footnotes into the text, incorporation of FSC decisions and rearrangement of the annexes to the document) and included a series of new annexes with further proposals for amendment.

The major changes proposed included: (*a*) information on certain geographical areas located in the zone of application and designated as major ground combat training areas for routine training of military forces; (*b*) annual information on new or substantially improved military infrastructure, subject to evaluation; (*c*) multinational inspections to provide clarification on military activities giving rise to concern; (*d*) visits to new or improved military airfields and visits to naval bases; (*e*) annual plans for contacts; (*f*) lowering of notification and observation thresholds and inclusion of new parameters in constraints; (*g*) inclusion of provisions on naval activities in prior notifications, observation and calendars (Russia); (*h*) notification of the largest military activity, arrival or concentration of forces if no notifiable military activity, arrival or concentration takes place (see table 14A.1); (*i*) notification of non-

[2] FSC, Letter of the Chairman of the Forum for Security Co-operation to the Minister of Foreign Affairs of Poland, Chairman of the Seventh Ministerial Council of the OSCE, FSC.DEL/275/98, 25 Nov. 1998.

[3] On discussions in previous years, see Lachowski, Z., 'Confidence- and security-building measures in Europe', *SIPRI Yearbook 1997: Armaments, Disarmament and International Security* (Oxford University Press: Oxford, 1997), pp. 503–505; and Lachowski and Henrichon (note 1), pp. 533–35.

Table 14A.1. Existing and proposed notification and observation thresholds for and constraints on military activities

CSBM	Vienna Document 1994[a]	Vienna Document proposals 1998[b]
Notification	9000 troops, 250 tanks, 500 ACVs or 250 self-propelled and towed artillery pieces, mortars and multiple-rocket launchers (100-mm calibre and above); 3000 troops in amphibious or heliborne landings or parachute drops (obligatory, 42 days in advance; area: Europe plus the Central Asian republics). Air force included in notification if at least 200 sorties by aircraft, excl. helicopters, are flown	Thresholds as Vienna Document 1994,[c] with 2 amendments: (*a*) if no activity reaches troop, tank, ACV or artillery thresholds the largest military activity, in terms of total numbers of reportable major weapon systems and equipment involved, will be notified where the minimum notifiable level will be no less than battalion level; and (*b*) if an amphibious or heliborne landing or parachute assault does not reach the threshold of 3000 troops, the largest military activity in terms of troops involved will be notified
		Non-routine concentrations of military forces will be notified whenever they take place outside a major ground combat training area and involve at least 5000 troops or 150 tanks, 250 ACVs or 150 self-propelled and towed artillery pieces, mortars and multiple rocket launchers (100-mm calibre and above). Obligatory notification of such concentration no later than 7 days after its commencement
Observation	13 000 troops, 300 tanks, 500 ACVs or 250 artillery pieces, mortars and multiple rocket launchers (100 mm and above); 3500 troops in airborne or heliborne landings or parachute drops	As in Vienna Document 1994[d]
Constraints	Max. 1 activity >40 000 troops, 900 tanks or 2000 ACVs within 3 calendar years	Max. 1 activity >40 000 troops, 900 tanks, 2000 ACVs or 900 artillery pieces within 3 calendar years
	Max. 6 activities with 13 000–40 000 troops, 300–900 tanks or 500–2000 ACVs within 1 calendar year. Only 3 such activities may exceed 25 000 troops, 400 tanks or 800 ACVs each	Max. 6 activities with 13 000–40 000 troops, 300–900 tanks, 500–2000 ACVs or 300–900 artillery pieces within 1 calendar year. Only 3 such activities may exceed 25 000 troops, 400 tanks, 800 ACVs or 400 artillery pieces each
	Max. 3 simultaneous activities of >13 000 troops, 300 tanks or 500 ACVs each	Max. 3 simultaneous activities >13 000 troops, 300 tanks, 500 ACVs or 300 artillery pieces each
	Information due 15 Nov. each year on military activities >40 000 troops or 900 tanks planned for 2nd subsequent calendar year	Information due 15 Nov. each year on military activities >40 000 troops, 900 tanks, 2000 ACVs or 900 artillery pieces planned for 2nd subsequent calendar year
	No activities of >40 000 troops, 900 tanks or 2000 ACVs unless com municated as above and incl. in annual calendar by 15 Nov. each year	No activities of >40 000 troops, 900 tanks, 2000 ACVs or 900 artillery pieces unless communicated as above and incl. in annual calendar by 15 Nov. each year

[a] As amended by FSC decisions: FSC.DEC/7/96, 13 Nov. 1996 and FSC.DEC/7/97, 9 Apr. 1997.

[b] Based on Draft of Vienna Document [1998] of the Negotiations on Confidence and Security-Building Measures, FSC.VD/31/98, 16 Sep. 1998.

[c] France, Germany and Poland have proposed lowering thresholds to 5000 troops, 150 tanks, 250 ACVs and 150 artillery pieces. Russia has also proposed the following thresholds for naval activities in water areas adjacent to Europe: 20 combat ships (each of 1500 displacement tons), incl. support ships and vessels, or 10 combat ships (5000 d. tons) or 80 naval combat aircraft, including carrier-based. In the case of an arrival or concentration of naval forces, the thresholds would be: 10 combat ships (1500 d. tons) or 5 combat ships (5000 d. tons) or 30 naval combat aircraft.

[d] Ukraine has proposed thresholds of 9000 troops, 250 tanks and 3000 troops in airborne and heliborne landings or parachute drops.

Table 14A.2. Calendar of planned notifiable military activities in 1999, exchanged by 18 December 1998

States	Dates/Start window	Type/Name of activity	Area	Level of command	No. of troops	Type of forces or equipment	No./type of divs	Comments
1a. Canada, Denmark, France, Germany, Netherlands, Norway, UK, USA	16 Feb.–3 Mar.	FTX Battle Griffin 99	Norway	COMNORTH, COMJTFNON	22 070	Ground and air forces	. .	FTX for national and reinforcing forces in deployment, integration, employment and redeployment. Phases: (I) 16–25 Feb. combat enhancement and force integration; and (II) 26 Feb.–3 Mar. FTX
1b. Norway, USA	7–12 Mar.	FTX/Livex Battle Griffin 99	Central Norway	CINCNW	5 800	Amphibious forces	. .	. .
2. France, Germany, Greece, Italy, Netherlands, Spain, Turkey, UK, USA	1–30 Apr.	Destined Glory 99	Southern Spain	COMSTRIKE-FORSOUTH	*c.* 3 000	Amphibious forces	. .	. .
3. France, Germany, Greece, Italy, Netherlands, Spain, Turkey, UK, USA	1 Sep.–30 Oct.	Dynamic Mix 99	. .	COMSTRIKE-FORSOUTH	*c.* 3 000	Amphibious forces	. .	. .
Additional activities held in 1998								
1. France, Italy, Malta, Turkey[a]	. .	Canale 98	. .	. .	13 000	Ground and naval forces	. .	Control of merchant shipping, peace support and humanitarian assistance. Observers invited from Algeria, Cyprus, Jordan, Morocco, Palestine
2. Denmark, Germany, Netherlands[a]	7–28 Oct. 1998	FTX Cold Grouse 98	Zealand Group of Islands	COMBALTAP	9 475	Ground and air forces	. .	Exercise reception, deployment and support of multinational reaction forces

CINCNW = Commander-in-Chief Allied Forces North Western Europe; COMBALTAP = Commander Allied Forces Baltic Approaches; COMJTFNON = Commander Joint Task Force Northern Norway; COMNORTH = Commander Northern Europe; COMSTRIKEFORSOUTH = Commander Striking and Support Forces Southern Europe; divs = divisions; FTX = field training exercise; Livex = live exercise.

[a] Supplementary information on military activities in 1998.

routine concentrations of military forces (see table 14A.1); and (*j*) regional CSBMs (see below).

Because of the scope and complexity of some of the proposals, the FSC stated that it needed more time to complete the review.[4] Its goal was to conclude the modernization of the document by the OSCE Istanbul summit meeting in November 1999.

The implementation record for 1998

The only change in the planned notifiable military activities for 1998 was that in the date for the 'Strong Resolve 98' field training exercise (FTX).[5] 'Canale 98' and 'Cold Grouse 98' were also notified and carried out in 1998. SIPRI has been informed of four notifiable military activities for 1999 (see table 14A.2).

By 19 December 1998 a total of 49 inspections had been requested in 27 countries and 48 had been conducted in 27 countries. Seventy-one evaluation visits had also been requested and 69 such visits had been carried out.

Several non-notifiable military activities were notified to the OSCE and conducted in 1998. They included 'Baltic Challenge 98' (Klaipeda area), a peace support exercise conducted within the context of the Partnership for Peace (PFP) to develop a common understanding of peacekeeping operations and to improve interoperability; 'Cooperative Best Effort 98' (Krivolak, Bulgaria), a peacekeeping and peace operations training exercise; 'Co-operation Adventure Exchange 98' (Slovenia), a UN-mandated and NATO-led warning, activation, deployment and redeployment exercise; and the 'Filippos 98' (Central and Eastern Macedonia) exercise conducted by Greece. France and the UK also notified their respective SFOR contingents for 1998.

During 1998 regional CSBMs were applied during the 'Filippos 98', 'FTX Paramenion 98' and 'Vertes 98' exercises. Bulgaria was invited by Greece to the 'Filippos 98' and 'FTX Paramenion' exercises, according to their bilateral Athens Document of 1993. Romania and the Slovakia were invited to the Hungarian 'Vertes 98' exercise in accordance with the relevant bilateral agreements.

III. Regional CSBMs

A catalogue of possible regional CSBMs is set out in an annex to the draft revised Vienna Document to promote security and stability in the OSCE area.[6] The idea is that interested states may select appropriate measures and, if necessary, adapt them to regional needs. The participating states intend to emphasize the growing importance of the regional dimension of security as a response to new regional challenges and to promote new opportunities for regional cooperation. With the notable exception of the 1996 Agreement on Confidence- and Security-Building Measures in Bosnia and Herzegovina, CSBMs had hitherto been designed mainly for the entire OSCE area. The FSC has opened up prospects for tailoring CSBMs to regional needs. Selection of these measures will emphasize flexibility and the preferences of the states involved. The aim is: (*a*) to strengthen security and stability in the entire region; (*b*) to avoid isolating individual states in terms of security; and (*c*) to include all affected or interested states in talks and negotiations.

[4] FSC (note 2).

[5] The notified dates were 16–21 Mar., but the exercise took place on 14–21 Mar. FSC, Quarterly CPC Survey on CSBM Information Exchanged, FSC.GAL/13/99, 1 Feb. 1999.

[6] Draft of Vienna Document [1998] of the Negotiations on Confidence and Security-Building Measures, Chapter XIII, FSC.VD/31/98, 16 Sep. 1998.

A wide range of proposed measures address potential refinements to the provisions of the Vienna Document at the regional level as well as new CSBMs tailored to regional and local needs and cooperation between neighbouring states.

Confidence-building measures in the Aegean Sea region

In 1998 the tensions between Greece and Turkey in the Aegean Sea region continued, but at the same time efforts were made within NATO to make progress on confidence-building measures (CBMs). On 4 June 1998 NATO Secretary General Javier Solana announced that the permanent representatives of both states had informed him of their intentions to implement the agreed CBMs fully.[7] The CBMs are based on the Athens Memorandum of Understanding of 27 May 1988 and the Istanbul Guidelines for the Prevention of Accidents and Incidents on the High Seas and International Airspace of 8 September 1988, signed by Foreign Minister Karolos Papoulias of Greece and Foreign Minister Mesut Yilmaz of Turkey. Under the two CBM accords both sides were to aim to reduce tensions and avoid dangerous incidents in the Aegean region, including avoiding any harassment or interventions in international waters and airspace, refraining from the use of long-term exercises, the implementation of a moratorium on military exercises during the summer months, and taking the international rules, regulations and procedures as a basis for activities on the open sea and in international airspace.[8]

In the June statement the two sides declared their willingness where necessary to clarify and where possible to strengthen and complement the CBMs. The opportunities presented by the emerging NATO air command and control system (ACCS) for greater mutual exchange of information and coordination were also explored.

Public reactions to the declaration in both countries were careful, with the Greek response sounding more hopeful.[9] Rising tensions later in the year over Cyprus, including the planned deployment of S-300 anti-aircraft missiles on the Greek part of the island, and later on Crete, and violations of Cypriot airspace by Turkish aircraft have, however, hampered progress in following up on the June declaration. In early 1999 some cautious optimism was expressed that CBMs could progress at and after the NATO summit meeting in April.[10]

[7] Statement by the Secretary General on Confidence Building Measures between Greece and Turkey, NATO Press Release (98)74, 5 June 1998.

[8] The Greek–Turkish CBMs provide for: (*a*) avoiding interference with smooth shipping and air traffic; (*b*) avoiding isolating certain areas; (*c*) not blocking exercise areas for long periods of time; (*d*) not holding exercises during the peak tourist periods and main national and religious holidays; (*e*) due communication through diplomatic channels when required; (*f*) naval units refraining from acts of harassment of each other while operating in the high seas; (*g*) maintaining a position that does not hamper the smooth conduct of ships of the other party under surveillance during firing operations and other military activities; and (*h*) utmost caution by pilots when flying in proximity of aircraft of the other party and not manoeuvring or reacting in a manner that would be hazardous to the safety of the flight and/or affect the conduct of the mission of the aircraft. Memorandum of Understanding between Greece and Turkey, Athens, 27 May 1988; and Guidelines for the Prevention of Accidents and Incidents on the High Seas and International Airspace, Istanbul, 8 Sep. 1988.

[9] See, e.g., 'And a positive development', *I Kathimerini* (Athens), 5 June 1998, p. 3, in 'Greece: Greek daily describes agreement on CBMs as positive', Foreign Broadcast Information Service, *Daily Report–West Europe (FBIS-WEU)*, FBIS-WEU-98-156, 5 June 1998; and 'Better than nothing', *Milliyet* (Istanbul), 6 June 1998, in 'Turkey: NATO efforts on Greece–Turkey accord welcome', FBIS-WEU-98-157, 6 June 1998.

[10] 'Optimism of . . . trust', *Ta Nea* (Athens), 4 Feb. 1999, p, 7, in 'NATO said optimistic about Greek–Turkish relations', FBIS-WEU-99 [document no. not available], 4 Feb. 1999.

Implementation of the Agreement on CSBMs in Bosnia and Herzegovina

The Agreement on Confidence- and Security-Building Measures in Bosnia and Herzegovina of 26 January 1996 (negotiated under Article II of Annex 1-B of the 1995 General Framework Agreement for Peace in Bosnia and Herzegovina, the Dayton Agreement) outlines a set of measures to enhance mutual confidence and reduce the risk of conflict in the country.[11] The parties to the agreement are Bosnia and Herzegovina and its two entities: the Federation of Bosnia and Herzegovina and the Republika Srpska.

The first conference to review the implementation of the CSBM agreement was held in Vienna on 16–20 February 1998. Delegations from Bosnia and Herzegovina and its two entities took part under the chairmanship of the Personal Representative of the OSCE Chairman-in Office (CIO), General Carlo Jean. The conference took several decisions to update the existing agreement, and some other decisions were deferred to working groups. The conduct of the parties to the agreement was found 'very constructive and open' by the Personal Representative. A second review meeting was planned for February–March 1999 to assess the results and to define a programme for future Joint Consultative Commission examination.[12]

There were no major implementation problems in 1998 despite the turbulent political environment. Cooperation between the parties regarding visits, inspections, meetings and so on proceeded with openness and goodwill. Visits and military contacts between the two entities increased and there was a remarkable improvement in the quality of data exchanges and notifications. Visits to weapon manufacturing facilities began and a related protocol was approved for these visits. An experiment with challenge inspections (on 'specified sites') was conducted successfully with the support of Germany and the UK by means of training and practice exercises, and further challenge inspections will be carried out in 1999. As far as provisions on notifiable military activities are concerned, a voluntary limitation on military training exercises was accepted by the parties for 1999. Coordination of the entities' activities with the Office of the High Representative (OHR) and SFOR has improved.

Two general difficulties in achieving better implementation of the agreement were identified. The first related to the decision-making process of the joint institutions of Bosnia and Herzegovina, in which no progress was made on: (*a*) the composition of the delegation; (*b*) the Bosnia and Herzegovina inspection teams; or (*c*) the establishment of a verification centre (to be located initially in the Verification Operations Section of the Department for Regional Stabilization, OSCE Mission in Bosnia and Herzegovina). The second factor was related to a complete activation of the Military Liaison Missions between the defence staffs of the two entities. The latter problem was solved, and a memorandum of understanding was reached between the chiefs of defence staff.

Two seminars were organized in 1998: one on aerial observation, with a practical demonstration, and one on civil–military cooperation in the event of natural disasters

[11] The following review is based on the Status of Implementation of Article II and IV, Annex 1-B, General Framework Agreement for Peace in Bosnia and Herzegovina and Outlines of 1999 Planning, Vienna, CIO.GAL/70/98, 29 Oct. 1998; and Statutes of 1999 Programs for the Implementation of the Vienna (CSBMs) and Florence (Sub-Regional Arms Control) Agreements, Gen. Carlo Jean (Italian Army), Personal Representative of the OSCE Chairman-in-Office for Articles II and IV, Oslo, Norway, doc. MC.GAL/5/98, 2 Dec. 1998.

[12] OSCE, 'Review meeting measures progress in implementation of confidence- and security-building measures in Bosnia and Herzegovina', Press Release, no. 12/98 (undated). For information about the agreement in 1997, see Lachowski and Henrichon (note 1), pp. 536–38.

with the aim of developing a common doctrine for Bosnia and Herzegovina and field manuals for the entity armed forces. In May 1999 these common regulations will be tested in a field training exercise or command post exercise (CPX) involving SFOR, the OHR and the OSCE Mission. A seminar on democratic control of security policy and armed forces was planned for January 1999 with the aim of: (*a*) establishing or consolidating joint institutions, particularly the Standing Committee on Military Matters (SCMM) and a law on parliamentary control; (*b*) starting a debate on common security concepts of Bosnia and Herzegovina and its preparations for integration into international security systems; and (*c*) establishing a transparent financial planning and budgeting system. A network of independent security experts linked to similar institutions in OSCE countries was created at the universities of Bosnia and Herzegovina.

As far as the future efforts of the OSCE are concerned, they aim at developing contacts in the entity armed forces at subordinate levels (corps, brigade, etc.), improving data exchanges and transparency, and coordination of training with the assistance of OSCE countries. Better coordination of international efforts and a division of labour between the organizations involved in order to avoid overlapping, a congestion of initiatives in some periods, and so on, is envisaged. Reinforcement of the joint institutions of Bosnia and Herzegovina, extending the Military Liaison Mission tasks from the defence staffs of the entities to subordinate levels and supporting the network of security institutions and independent experts in the universities of Bosnia and Herzegovina, will also be pursued. In mid-January 1999 the Joint Consultative Commission was to seek to define a detailed programme in the field of military contacts, common training and military cooperation.

The Baltic Sea region

The sweeping CBM initiatives taken in the autumn of 1997 by Russia fell flat chiefly because of the unacceptable conditions attached, which aimed to deny the Baltic states future entry into NATO. Instead, a careful, step-by-step process of confidence building seems to be developing. On 21 April 1998 the foreign ministers of Finland and Sweden, Tarja Halonen and Lena Hjelm-Wallén, respectively, launched a new initiative for deeper security cooperation in the region of the Baltic Sea at a meeting with the Nordic foreign ministers. The main aims of the proposal were: (*a*) an increase of the voluntary military inspections carried out among the states in the Baltic Sea region in addition to the quotas of inspections envisaged in the Vienna Document 1998; (*b*) more efficient cooperation in the areas of crime prevention, border protection, search-and-rescue capabilities and the safety of civil and military traffic; (*c*) expanded training in peacekeeping activities; and (*d*) regional and deeper cooperation within the framework of the Euro-Atlantic Partnership Council.[13] Finland and Sweden also declared their intention of going beyond the mandatory provisions of the Vienna Document 1994 and raising their respective passive quotas for evaluation visits unilaterally by one visit each and for inspections by one inspection each. This offer was made to each of the neighbouring countries in the region (Denmark, Estonia, Germany, Latvia, Lithuania, Norway, Poland and Russia). Russia welcomed the initiative as a step towards furthering the dialogue on CBM endeavours.

[13] *OSCE Review*, vol. 6, no. 1 (1998).

IV. Seminar on Defence Policies and Military Doctrines

At the initiative of the Russian Federation the FSC held the third Seminar on Defence Policies and Military Doctrines in Vienna on 26–28 January 1998.[14] It was attended by over 350 representatives of the armed forces of the 54 OSCE states, and the heads of delegations included over 30 chiefs of staff. Representatives of NATO, the Commonwealth of Independent States and the Western European Union also attended. The purpose of the seminar was to exchange views on military issues related to European security and thereby promote openness and build confidence among the military forces of the OSCE states.[15] The discussion at the seminar was organized around three broad topics: (*a*) evolution of the European security environment and its influence on defence policies and military doctrines; (*b*) defence policies and international aspects of military doctrines; and (*c*) reform and restructuring of the armed forces. Many participants acknowledged that in order to adapt to the new risks and challenges in the OSCE area internal reform of the military was necessary, and that common security interests needed to be further defined as regional and intra-state conflicts are increasingly of concern to all the OSCE countries. Ideas were shared on restructuring and adapting armed forces to the security environment anticipated for the 21st century, the use of armed forces in crisis management and peacekeeping, and ways to enhance transparency in the development of defence policy and military doctrine.[16]

The participants acknowledged that Europe-wide military cooperation has been successfully developing and that the new security challenges and risks should be tackled jointly. The seminar confirmed that the threat of large-scale war with offensive defence policies has subsided and that the primary risks and threats lie elsewhere, mainly at the regional levels and below. Cooperative security, democratic control over the military, flexibility and openness in the pursuit of reassurance among the participants are the major elements of what one speaker called the 'era of partnership'.[17] The armed forces are now seen to be faced with new tasks. Their main objectives shifted from defence of national territory towards managing the threats that may endanger international security. Political control of military operations is much greater and more precise than in the past. The self-protection of the expeditionary forces has become a major and unavoidable priority. (Two different cases proved this: the 1991 Persian Gulf War and the 1994–96 conflict in Chechnya, in which the high casualties affected domestic political support and made the Russian Government seek a negotiated compromise). The most significant change in the shaping of military doctrines is political, and here the seminar found that there is no threat that will create enduring alliances between states.[18] Instead like-minded states will form case-by-case coalitions when deciding which regional crises deserve attention and response.

[14] For discussion of the first and second Military Doctrine Seminars, see Krohn, A., 'The Vienna Military Doctrine Seminar', *SIPRI Yearbook 1991: World Armaments and Disarmament* (Oxford University Press: Oxford, 1991), pp. 501–11; and Lachowski, Z., 'The Vienna Second Seminar on Military Doctrine', *SIPRI Yearbook 1992: World Armaments and Disarmament* (Oxford University Press: Oxford, 1992), pp. 496–505.

[15] OSCE, Press Release, no. 08/98 (28 Jan. 1998).

[16] FSC (note 2).

[17] OSCE (note 15).

[18] Evolution of Defence Policies and Military Doctrines, Seminar of Defence Policies and Military Doctrines 26–28 January 1998, Preliminary Draft (distributed at the request of the Italian delegation), 11 Jan. 1998, FSC.MD.DEL/18/98, 26 Jan. 1998.

At the same time, there is still a realization that the world is facing a spectrum of uncertainties. Three factors of particular interest were mentioned as challenging the international community: (*a*) the difficult and turbulent nature of democratic transition; (*b*) the expansion of worldwide economic markets, information systems, transportation systems and communication technologies (globalization), which bring nations together, but at the same time give rise to a number of growing transnational concerns (terrorism, organized crime, refugees, migrations, etc.); and (*c*) the lingering mistrust of the bipolar era.[19] Other new threats were identified that require defence policies in which military, political and economic measures are combined, such as the proliferation of weapons of mass destruction, terrorism, the fragmentation of nation-states, ethnic or extreme religious fundamentalist movements, international crime and the emergence of new 'rogue' states, and so on.[20] These threats create new scenarios which the armed forces must confront by shifting the objective from the defence of national territory towards the multidisciplinary functions—including management of crises and prevention or reduction of risks, peace support operations, peace enforcement and policing.

V. Conclusions

Although the OSCE participating states made headway in their efforts to modernize the Vienna Document 1994 and adapt it to the new security situation in Europe during 1998, the goal of having the final text agreed and adopted by the end of the year was not realized. The proposed adaptations will enhance the opportunities for transparency, predictability and cooperation. The proposal for a regional section in the draft document points to a shift of focus in ideas about the promotion of security in Europe. The pan-European CSBMs will encompass all participating states while further cooperation in the field of CSBMs will be strongly promoted at regional and local levels between neighbouring states. In this way the revised Vienna Document will emphasize deeper security cooperation adapted to regional differences. Furthermore, the use of the document as an important basis for the continued implementation of CSBMs at the regional and sub-regional level is highlighted by the meetings and seminars that took place during 1998, including the meeting of Nordic foreign ministers on the Baltic Sea region in April.

In Bosnia and Herzegovina, the implementation of CSBMs is proceeding smoothly under international surveillance. The Kosovo conflict,[21] however, constitutes a caveat demonstrating the fragility of arrangements between conflicting parties with a poor history of reconciliation and reconstruction in other fields.

The third Seminar on Defence Policies and Military Doctrines helped identify new risks and challenges as well as new tasks and directions for adapting the military doctrine and defence policies to the current and future security environment. It demonstrated the usefulness and confidence-enhancing effect of convening such meetings to discuss and clear up uncertainties in an environment marked by a degree of uncertainty and unpredictability.

[19] Executive Summary, Remarks by General Henry H. Shelton, Chairman of the Joint Chiefs of Staff, USA, to be delivered Jan. 26, 1998, at the Military Doctrine Seminar, FSC.MD.DEL/7/98, 20 Jan. 1998.

[20] Note 18.

[21] See also appendix 1C in this volume.

Appendix 14B. The ban on anti-personnel mines

ZDZISLAW LACHOWSKI

I. Introduction

The 1997 Convention on the Prohibition of the Use, Stockpiling, Production and Transfer of Anti-Personnel Mines and on their Destruction (the APM Convention) entered into force on 1 March 1999.[1]

Crowning the first stage of the 'Ottawa Process' of 1996–97,[2] the APM Convention is a hybrid agreement combining disarmament with humanitarian law. It aims at the elimination of all anti-personnel mines (APMs).[3] While the military utility of these weapons in interstate conflicts has been increasingly questioned they are still used extensively along international borders and in intra-state conflicts. It is estimated that 10–11 million stockpiled landmines have been destroyed since the convention was opened for signature in December 1997.[4] The main producers and exporters of landmines, China, India, Pakistan, Russia and the USA, as well as many user countries involved in conflicts around the world, have not signed the convention, however. It is also weakened by the absence of strong monitoring and enforcement provisions.

The 1996 amended Protocol II[5] of the 1981 Convention on Prohibitions or Restrictions on the Use of Certain Conventional Weapons which May be Deemed to be Excessively Injurious or to Have Indiscriminate Effects (the CCW Convention), restricting or prohibiting the use of 'mines, booby traps and other devices', entered into force on 3 December 1998.[6]

Efforts in the Conference on Disarmament (CD) to highlight the issue of landmines, and especially to negotiate a permanent ban on their transfer, produced a

[1] The text of the convention is reproduced in *SIPRI Yearbook 1998: Armaments, Disarmament and International Security* (Oxford University Press: Oxford, 1998), pp. 567–74. For details of the convention and a list of states parties and signatories, see annexe A in this volume.

[2] The Ottawa Process is the initiative launched by the Canadian Government in 1996 and led by the International Campaign to Ban Landmines. Lachowski, Z., 'Conventional arms control', *SIPRI Yearbook 1997: Armaments, Disarmament and International Security* (Oxford University Press: Oxford, 1997), pp. 498–99.

[3] 'Landmine' is the broad term commonly used for this type of weapon. The convention defines a mine as 'a munition designed to be . . . exploded by the presence, proximity or contact of a person or vehicle' (Article 2), and an APM as 'a mine designed to be exploded by the presence, proximity or contact of a person and that will incapacitate, injure or kill one or more persons'. Only APMs are prohibited by the convention, which does not cover anti-tank, other anti-vehicle mines or anti-ship mines at sea or in inland waterways.

[4] International Campaign to Ban Landmines, the Advocacy Project, *On the Record,* special issue on landmines, vol. 4 (20 Dec. 1998), URL <http://www.icbl.org/prelease/1998/dec21.html>.

[5] The text of the amended Protocol II is reproduced in *SIPRI Yearbook 1998* (note 1), pp. 559–67.

[6] For details of the convention and its protocols and lists of states parties and signatories, see annexe A in this volume. On 30 Jan. 1998 the 20th ratification (by Hungary) of Protocol IV to the CCW Convention (prohibiting the use and transfer of blinding laser weapons in armed conflict) also enabled this protocol to enter into force on 30 July 1998. On the origins and an assessment of Protocol IV see Goldblat, J., 'Land-mines and blinding laser weapons: the Inhumane Weapons Convention Review Conference', *SIPRI Yearbook 1996: Armaments, Disarmament and International Security* (Oxford University Press: Oxford, 1996), pp. 761–63.

stalemate in 1998, underscoring the political, institutional and programme crisis of this body.

The status of implementation of the convention and amended protocol are reviewed in sections II and III. The efforts of the CD are examined in section IV, and demining activities in 1998 are described in section V, which also presents new estimates of the numbers of landmines deployed worldwide. The conclusions are presented in section VI.

II. The APM Convention

The APM Convention entered into force relatively quickly, with the required 40 ratifications being achieved in just nine months. On 18 September 1998 Burkina Faso became the 40th state to ratify the convention and, in accordance with Article 17, it entered into force on 1 March 1999.

As of 1 May 1999, 135 states had signed the convention, 77 of which had ratified it.[7] The signatories included all the states of the Western Hemisphere except the USA and Cuba, all the NATO nations except the USA and Turkey, all the EU member states except Finland, 42 African countries and 23 states in the Asia–Pacific region (their regional distribution is indicated in table 14B). Of the former Soviet republics, Turkmenistan had both signed and ratified the convention, and Lithuania, Moldova and Ukraine had signed it. Belarus, China, Cuba, Egypt, India, Iran, Libya, Pakistan, Russia, Sri Lanka, Syria and the USA either are opposed to or claim to be unable to accede to the convention, but Belarus, China, Egypt, Pakistan and Russia have declared or extended unilateral moratoriums on the export of landmines.

The problem of US landmines stored on the territories of other NATO countries came to the fore in 1998. There was strong domestic and international grassroots pressure on Germany, Greece, Italy, Japan, Norway, Spain and the UK to ban the stockpiling of anti-personnel mines.[8]

In May 1998 the USA indicated its willingness to join the APM Convention in the future. The shift in policy was spelled out in a letter of 15 May from National Security Adviser Sandy Berger to Senator Patrick Leahy, a leading advocate of the ban on landmines.[9] This step was seen as a quid pro quo move by the Clinton Administration designed to prevent Senator Leahy, sponsor of the one-year moratorium on US use of landmines, declared in 1996 and scheduled to start in February 1999, from opposing its repeal.[10] The new US commitment included the following undertakings:

1. The USA will destroy all its 'dumb' APMs (without self-destruction or self-deactivation mechanisms) by 1999, except those in South Korea.

[7] States parties to and signatories of the convention are listed in annexe A in this volume.

[8] Fitchett, J., 'US and European allies split on use of land mines on NATO soil', *International Herald Tribune*, 5 Feb. 1998, p. 5; and International Campaign to Ban Landmines (ICBL), Press Release, 17 Sep. 1998.

[9] Myers, S. L., 'Clinton agrees to land-mine ban, but not yet', *New York Times*, 22 May 1998, p. A3.

[10] US Secretary of Defense William Cohen and the Chairman of the Joint Chiefs of Staff, Gen. Henry Shelton, had earlier expressed their 'grave and substantial' concerns about the moratorium and, in a letter to the Chairman of the Senate Armed Services Committee, Senator Strom Thurmond, asked for the power to waive it. On 25 June 1998 the US Senate authorized the President to waive the moratorium. Institute for Defense and Disarmament Studies, *Arms Control Reporter* (IDDS: Brookline, Mass.), sheets 708.B.41–42, 1998.

Table 14B. The status of the APM Convention, as of 29 April 1999

Region	Signed but not ratified	Signed and ratified	Unable to sign/ opposed	Unknown/ undecided	**Total**
Africa	25	17	2	9	**53**
Asia–Pacific	10	13	6	29	**58**
Americas	11	22	2	0	**35**
Europe	12	25	2	5	**44**
Total	**58**	**77**	**12**	**43**	**190**

Source: Based on International Campaign to Ban Landmines, 'Ratification updates', 29 Apr. 1999, URL <http://www.icbl.org>

2. It will cease using landmines outside South Korea by 2003 and pursue the objective of having alternatives for South Korea by 2006, including 'smart' landmines (with self-destruction or self-deactivation mechanisms).

3. It will search for alternatives to its mixed anti-tank systems[11] by: (*a*) actively exploring the use of APM alternatives in place of the self-destructing anti-personnel sub-munitions currently used; and (*b*) exploring the development of other technologies and/or operational concepts that offer alternatives that would enable the USA to eliminate its mixed systems entirely.

4. It will sign the convention by 2006 if efforts to identify and field suitable alternative technologies to US landmines and mixed anti-tank systems succeed.[12]

To compensate for the absence of a traditional verification mechanism in the APM Convention, with financial support from the Canadian Government the International Campaign to Ban Landmines (ICBL) established a civilian society-based monitoring network, called Landmine Monitor, to measure progress in compliance with the APM and CCW conventions and monitor other aspects of the 'global landmine crisis'. This global reporting network, for which an independent database is being developed, works in cooperation with governments and in parallel to the conventions. At the ICBL conference in Dublin on 14–18 September 1998, the Landmine Monitor prepared the outline of its first annual report on all aspects of implementation of the APM Convention, to be based on country reports from all states in the world and thematic reports on global landmine use, production and export, stockpiles, international legal activities, demining, mine awareness and survivor assistance.[13] The

[11] Unlike European armies that protect anti-tank mines by linking booby traps to the mines, the US mixed anti-tank systems consist of explosives not attached to the main mine. They are therefore considered to be APMs.

[12] Associated Press, 'Clinton may sign land mine treaty', 22 May 1998; and *Disarmament Diplomacy*, no. 26 (May 1998), p. 60.

[13] To guide research for the country reports the Landmine Monitor Core Group circulated a 'wish-list' of questions which the ICBL would like to see answered comprehensively in order better to address the needs of mine-affected communities. These concerned: (*a*) banning landmines—the APM Convention; other mine treaties (CCW Amended Protocol II, the position of the CD); production; transfer, stockpiling and destruction; use; (*b*) humanitarian mine action—funding; mine clearance—survey/assessment; mine awareness education; mine clearance; reconstruction and development of cleared areas; and (*c*) mine action: landmine casualties; provision of victim/survivor assistance. List of questions indicating desired contents of country reports, attached to letter received by SIPRI from the Landmine Monitor, 29 Sep. 1998.

report was presented to the first conference of states parties, in Maputo, Mozambique, on 3–7 May 1999.[14]

III. Amended Protocol II

The 1996 amended Protocol II of the CCW Convention supplemented the original protocol of 1981 with a number of provisions concerning its applicability, the detectability of all APMs, a ban on the transfer of prohibited mines, responsibility for mine clearance, and so on.

On 3 June 1998 Lithuania became the 20th state to ratify the protocol, allowing it to enter into force on 3 December.[15] The Clinton Administration had sent the amended Protocol II to the Senate for ratification in January 1997, but in 1998 it was still pending before the Senate Foreign Relations Committee. The Administration strove unsuccessfully to persuade the Senate Committee to take up the issue and ratify the protocol. This would enable US participation in an annual conference of states parties to the protocol, to be held soon after its entry into force.[16] On 27 June in Beijing President Bill Clinton and President Jiang Zemin issued the Sino-US Presidential Joint Statement on Anti-Personnel Landmines,[17] in which they agreed to work towards early ratification of amended Protocol II and to urge others to ratify it. China did so on 4 November 1998. Eleven EU countries plus Argentina, Australia, Canada, Japan and South Africa are among the countries that have deposited their instruments of ratification.

On 4 December 1998 the UN General Assembly requested the Secretary-General to convene in 1999 the first annual conference of states, in accordance with Article 13 of amended Protocol II.[18]

IV. The Conference on Disarmament

As in 1997,[19] the Conference on Disarmament remained virtually in limbo in 1998 (it established one ad hoc committee to discuss negative security assurances and another to start negotiations on a Fissile Material Treaty[20]). On 19 January the USA reaffirmed that it would seek to negotiate a ban on the transfer of APMs at the CD,[21] and later, together with Russia, proposed that the special coordinator for landmines be reappointed.

Because APMs did not feature as a separate item on the CD agenda in 1998, there was widespread scepticism regarding the chances of starting negotiations on this issue. It was only on 23 March, at the end of the first plenary session, that the Conference agreed to appoint a number of special coordinators, including a special coordinator on anti-personnel mines (under agenda item 6, 'Comprehensive programme of disarmament'). The post was again filled by John Campbell, Australian Ambassador

[14] International Campaign to Ban Landmines, Landmine Monitor, *Landmine Monitor Report 1999: Towards a Mine-Free World*, 1999.

[15] By 1 Jan. 1999, 29 states had ratified the protocol. These are listed in annexe A in this volume.

[16] *Arms Control Reporter*, sheet 708.B.42, 1998.

[17] For the text of the Joint Statement on Anti-Personnel Landmines, see URL <http://hsnc.scnu.edu.cn/corner/landmine.htm>.

[18] UN General Assembly Resolution 53/81, 8 Dec. 1998.

[19] On developments in the CD in 1997, see Lachowski, Z., 'The ban on anti-personnel mines', in *SIPRI Yearbook 1998* (note 1), pp. 547–58.

[20] See also chapter 12 in this volume.

[21] Reuters, 'Clinton seeks export ban on landmines', 20 Jan. 1998.

to the CD. On 26 March the CD adopted a programme of work, but 'for discussions rather than negotiation'.[22]

In June Campbell stated that 'there is a prospect that the Conference may be willing' to establish an ad hoc committee on landmines and that the decision would be accompanied by a 'statement of understanding'.[23] Later he had to admit that he was unable to put forward a proposal that would enjoy the full support of all CD members. While China and two of the CD regional groups (the Western group and the Eastern group) supported his proposals, the Group of 21 (G-21) still required time to consider them.[24] Campbell found it to be 'less a matter of crafting the right language and more a question of winning the necessary political will to take a decision'. Striking a more positive note, he drew attention to the fact that the positions on landmines of several major countries that produce and use APMs have become more flexible and cooperative. He also pointed out that a ban on transfers that included major producers and users would 'add considerably to a global solution' and 'bring Ottawa Convention non-signatories some way towards the norm established by that Convention rather than run the risk of being permanently alienated from it'. The special coordinator stressed that landmines now being laid, or which will be laid in the future, were and would continue to be chiefly supplied by non-state entities and argued that it is essential to address the problem from both the supply and demand sides.[25]

Canada, APM Convention signatories and some Western delegations opposed the CD talks going beyond a ban on transfers. Canadian delegate Mark Moher strongly warned against supporting any search for a more elaborate international instrument or the creation of a bureaucracy or verification regime liable to undermine that of the APM Convention.[26] Some delegates suggested that the proposed ban be considered at the meeting of the parties to the amended Protocol II, to be held in late 1999, or at the CCW Review Conference in 2001 rather than in the CD.

V. Demining

In 1998 the United Nations continued its demining activities which have been a concern of the UN General Assembly since 1993.

Since October 1997, the United Nations Mine Action Service (UNMAS) of the Department of Peace-keeping Operations of the UN Secretariat has served as the operational body for all UN mine-related issues and activities. All member states, non-governmental organizations (NGOs) and other entities are encouraged to coordinate their demining activities with the service and with the local UN authorities responsible for mine action in the field. UNMAS activities consist of four complementary components: (*a*) mine awareness and risk-reduction education; (*b*) minefield survey, mapping, marking and clearance; (*c*) assistance to victims, including rehabilitation and reintegration; and (*d*) advocacy to stigmatize the use of landmines

[22] Johnson, R., 'Geneva update no. 42', *Disarmament Diplomacy*, no. 29 (Aug./Sep. 1998), p. 20.

[23] Conference on Disarmament, Final record of the 799th plenary meeting, Conference on Disarmament document CD/PV.799, 25 June 1998, p. 20 (Mr Campbell, Australia).

[24] The Group of 21 was originally a group of 21 non-aligned CD member states. It now comprises 30 states.

[25] Conference on Disarmament, Final record of the 805th plenary meeting, Conference on Disarmament document CD/PV.805, 27 Aug. 1998, pp. 6–8 (Mr Campbell, Australia).

[26] Conference on Disarmament, Final record of the 799th plenary meeting, Conference on Disarmament document CD/PV.799, 25 June 1998, p. 11 (Mr Moher, Canada). The ICBL strongly opposes negotiating a ban on APM transfers at the CD.

and support a total ban on APMs.[27] In a policy paper the UN set out the guiding principles, responsibilities, coordination mechanisms and guidelines for resource mobilization, providing a basis for mine action.[28] UNMAS centres in Afghanistan, Angola, Bosnia and Herzegovina, Cambodia, Croatia, Iraq, Laos and Mozambique are the focal points for fully-fledged programmes including mine clearance, training, awareness activities and assistance to victims.

By October 1998, 37 states, 5 international organizations and many individuals had contributed a total of $43.2 million and pledged almost a further $6.3 million to the UN Voluntary Trust Fund for Assistance in Mine Clearance.[29] The major donors include the European Union and individual countries—Denmark, Japan, Norway, Switzerland, the UK and the USA. At present, 30 countries receive some level of United Nations technical assistance, ranging from awareness programmes to assessment missions. In February 1998 the World Bank pledged loans of $30 million for demining in Croatia and $3.75 million for Bosnia and Herzegovina.[30]

Numerous countries, NGOs and charities are engaged in intensive demining activities around the world. The USA, which has destroyed more than 3.3 million of its stockpiled 'dumb' landmines since 1996, provides considerable support to APM removal. Since 1993 it has spent over $236 million; it planned to commit another $82 million for global humanitarian demining in 1998 and has pledged to seek a further increase of this amount, to around $110 million in 1999. The USA is currently assisting 23 mine-infested countries, and removal of landmines from the ground is already under way in 14 of these countries. On 20–22 May 1998, the Washington Conference on Global Humanitarian Demining, convened in accordance with the US 2010 Global Humanitarian Demining Initiative announced in 1997, addressed international coordination of the removal of landmines and identified those areas which require improved focus and greater effort. The meeting helped clarify the relationship between the UN and the other key parties in mine-action technology. The USA and the European Commission agreed to coordinate their efforts in three areas identified by the UN: (*a*) the creation of internationally accepted standards to describe the types of mine-action technology; (*b*) the identification of a worldwide network of test and evaluation facilities to assess mine-action technology and aid in the creation of new or improved systems; and (*c*) the development of international technology demonstration projects.[31]

Despite pessimistic forecasts in previous years, international, governmental and private efforts have already led to some progress in removing landmines in various parts of the world. Namibia has become virtually mine-free thanks to international assistance. Rwanda is reported to have removed nearly one-quarter of its landmines. Nicaragua is also rapidly moving towards the goal of becoming landmine-free early in the next decade; had it not been for Hurricane Mitch in October 1998, it could have been expected that Central America would be declared free of landmines by the end of 2000. Landmine removal has reduced mine casualty rates in Afghanistan and

[27] UN, Assistance in mine clearance, Report of the Secretary-General, UN document A/53/496, 14 Oct. 1998.

[28] UN, Mine action and effective coordination: United Nations policy in assistance in mine clearance, Report of the Secretary-General, UN document A/S3/496, 14 Oct. 1998 , annex II, pp. 31–38.

[29] UN (note 27), annex I, p. 29.

[30] *Arms Control Reporter*, sheet 708.B.40, 1998.

[31] US Department of State, Bureau of Political-Military Affairs, *Hidden Killers 1998: The Global Landmine Crisis* (Office of Humanitarian Demining Programs: Washington, DC, Sep. 1998), URL <http://www.state.gov/www/global/arms/rpt_9809_demine_toc.html>. (Previous editions of this report were published in 1993 and 1994.)

Cambodia by two-thirds, but the renewed conflict in Angola has reversed the progress made by the landmine-clearing efforts.[32] In 1998 and the early months of 1999, the Yugoslav Army was reported to be laying landmines in Kosovo and along the borders with Albania and Macedonia to prevent aid reaching Kosovo and impede the movement of guerrillas and arms transfers.[33]

Progress has been made in the development of mine-clearing techniques and technologies. In Afghanistan, Angola, Bosnia and Herzegovina, Cambodia and Mozambique specially trained dogs have been extensively used to detect landmines. Particularly in the early phases of clearing a minefield they have proved more effective than mechanical mine detectors. Under the 2010 Demining Initiative, the USA is currently conducting research into designing a synthetic 'dog's nose' which could 'sniff out' landmines. The US Defence Department reported that it had developed 26 demining innovations and adapted commercial equipment and established technologies in 1997 and was examining another 25 concepts for equipment for clearance and detection of mines. In Norway, Sweden, Turkey, the UK and other countries various types of blast-proof mechanical equipment to destroy mines are being developed and offered for use in the developing countries.

In April the Geneva International Centre for Humanitarian Demining, a think-tank financed by the Swiss Ministry of Defence ($1.675 million for 1999), was established mainly to strengthen the coordinating role of UNMAS. In December, as part of its $100 million commitment to the worldwide mine action effort, Canada opened the new Centre for Mine Action Technologies, earmarking $11 million to develop new demining equipment.[34]

Mine clearance has encountered a number of problems. Demining groups complain that more resources go to the bureaucracy of demining, to research and development, and even to defence institutions than to actual demining. Financing is provided on a short-term basis which makes it difficult to plan for the longer term. Finally, money put into national mine action programmes does not necessarily go to demining.[35]

Estimates of the numbers of landmines

For many years the United Nations and various NGOs have published estimates of the numbers of mines deployed worldwide, indicating the enormity of the challenge facing the world community. However, it has also been pointed out that exaggerated numbers, often deliberately inflated by anti-mine campaigners to generate worldwide public support for a ban, have risked portraying the landmine issue as too big a problem to solve and thus contributed to a sense of hopelessness. Official landmine data have been criticized by independent sources which claim that the numbers are lower than originally estimated.[36]

[32] *Hidden Killers 1998* (note 31).

[33] The Macedonian Ministry of Defence and UN representatives in Skopje confirmed in Apr. 1999 that new mines were being laid on the Kosovo and Albanian borders. In Aug. 1998 a UN mission to Kosovo also confirmed reports from the ICRC and NGOs that Serb forces were using mines, particularly in the Junik region, and that there had been civilian casualties. 'Mines: a threat (menace) against refugees in Kosovo', Handicap International Press Release, 13 Apr. 1999, URL <http://www.icbl.org/prelease/1999/apr13.html>.

[34] 'Mineclearing center to promote new gear', *Defense News*, 14–20 Dec. 1998, p. 18.

[35] ICBL (note 4).

[36] Lachowski, Z., 'The ban on anti-personnel mines', in *SIPRI Yearbook 1998* (note 1), p. 545, footnote 3.

In a report published in February 1998 the UN Department of Humanitarian Affairs indicated that it would take years, rather than decades, to meet the challenges of the landmine crisis.[37]

The US Department of State presented new, 'realistic' data concerning landmines laid worldwide in its September report.[38] The new estimates are based on a systematic survey of US embassies around the world, international organizations, NGOs and other sources. They range from 60–70 million (the conservative estimate) to 45–50 million (the radical estimate) APMs scattered in at least 70 countries, in contrast to generally accepted figures of 80–110 million. The 12 most mine-infested countries (Afghanistan, Angola, Bosnia and Herzegovina, Cambodia, Croatia, Eritrea, Iraq (Kurdistan), Mozambique, Namibia, Nicaragua, Somalia and Sudan) profiled in the report account for almost 50 per cent of the world's landmines. Earlier UN estimates are revised drastically in the US report. For example, the earlier estimate of 10 million landmines in Afghanistan is revised to 5–7 million. The Hazardous Area Life-Support Organization (HALO) even estimates 620 000.[39] While the UN originally estimated that there were 10–15 million APMs in Angola the number is now said in the US report to be closer to 6 million; HALO placed the estimate at less than 0.5 million in 1997. For Mozambique the UN estimate of 3 million is revised in the US report to 1 million (the HALO estimate is 250 000–300 000). Kurdistan (Iraq) remains the most mine-affected region, however, with over 10 million mines, including 8 million APMs, buried in the ground. Another finding of the US report is that the rate of laying landmines is now well below the level of 2.5 million per year assumed by the UN, and that most probably more landmines are being removed from the ground than are being laid. UN mine-clearance experts have contested the former statement, however.[40]

VI. Conclusions

In 1998 the Ottawa Process maintained the momentum of the preceding year towards the goal of a total ban on landmines. The Landmine Monitor got off to a promising start with the aim of reporting on all activities related to the implementation of a ban. The numbers of states signing and ratifying the APM Convention rose significantly, although none of its major opponents had signed the convention: the USA promised to sign by 2006 on condition that suitable alternatives to APMs are developed.

The entry into force of the amended Protocol II (along with that of Protocol IV) of the CCW Convention strengthened efforts to eliminate inhumane weapons and constitutes a further step towards prohibiting the use of APMs.

Once more in 1998 the CD failed to address the issue of landmine transfers, and the prospects for a breakthrough in 1999 remain bleak.

[37] United Nations, Press Release IHA/646, PKO/67, 11 Feb. 1998; and UN Department of Humanitarian Affairs Study Report: The Development of Indigenous Mine Action Capacities, URL <http://www.un.org/Depts/Landmine/Reports/study/study.htm>.

[38] *Hidden Killers 1998* (note 31).

[39] Cited in *Hidden Killers 1998* (note 31). Established in 1988, the HALO Trust is a non-political British-registered charity that specializes in the removal of the debris of war. It concentrates on the humanitarian problem of immediate mine clearance so that other emergency and rehabilitation programmes can commence.

[40] *Arms Control Reporter*, sheet 708.B.46, 1998.

Appendix 14C. North Atlantic Council statement on CFE

ADAPTATION OF THE TREATY ON CONVENTIONAL ARMED FORCES IN EUROPE (CFE): RESTRAINT AND FLEXIBILITY

Ministerial Meeting of the North Atlantic Council with the Three Invited Countries held in Brussels

8 December 1998

The North Atlantic Council and the Representatives of the Czech Republic, the Republic of Hungary and the Republic of Poland stated on behalf of the 19 Governments represented the following:

1. The CFE Treaty will continue to be a cornerstone of European security. The States Parties have an historic opportunity and responsibility to adapt this legally-binding document to meet new security realities and ensure the Treaty's long-term effectiveness.

2. We, the North Atlantic Council, the Czech Republic, Hungary and Poland are committed to seek early and balanced progress on all outstanding Adaptation issues. Our objective is the signature of an Adapted Treaty by Heads of State and Government at the next OSCE Summit in 1999. We call on all other States Parties to contribute actively to realizing this goal.

3. Consistent with this objective, we reaffirm our commitment to maintain only such military capabilities as are commensurate with our legitimate security needs, taking into account our obligations under international law. We have no intention of using the adaptation Negotiations to secure narrow political or military advantages. CFE Treaty Adaptation should enhance the security of all States in Europe, whether or not they are members of a political military Alliance.

4. In Vienna, we have put forward a comprehensive series of detailed proposals dealing with all aspects of adaptation. These are designed to ensure continued predictability and transparency as well as a greater degree of stability in the European military environment and a further lowering of holdings of Treaty Limited Equipment among the CFE States Parties, consistent with the requirement of conflict prevention and crisis management.

5. In the context of a suitably adapted and legally binding CFE Treaty whose provisions meet our security needs, including our requirements for flexibility, we will continue to exercise restraint in relation to the levels and deployments of our conventional armed forces in all parts of the Treaty's Area of Application. This statement sets out how we would use the proposed mechanisms of an Adapted Treaty:

– Our military posture would reflect our common determination that, in the current and foreseeable security environment, we will carry out our collective defence and other missions by ensuring the necessary interoperability, integration, and capability for reinforcement rather than by additional permanent stationing of substantial ground or air combat forces.

– There would be significant reductions in permitted levels of Treaty Limited Equipment for many of us.

– Consistent with our previous proposals and in the context of comparable restraint from others in the region, many of us in and around Central Europe would not increase our Territorial Ceilings—the total levels of tanks, artillery and ACVs permitted on a permanent basis on our territories.

– Moreover, any temporary presence of Treaty Limited Equipment on our territories would be directly governed by the relevant legally-binding provisions of the Adapted Treaty.

– We and all our Treaty Partners would undertake broad and unprecedented transparency and predictability in our military activities.

– We would continue to pursue opportunities for cooperative efforts, not just among ourselves but with our partners, in crisis management and conflict prevention.

– We expect all other CFE States Parties to exercise comparable restraint, and working together as partners, to strengthen this new pattern of cooperative security in Europe as we continue our work on the complex task of adapting the CFE Treaty to better meet new security challenges.

On Ceilings and Holdings

6. An important goal of CFE Treaty Adaptation should be a significant lowering in the total amount of Treaty Limited Equipment (TLE) permitted in the Treaty's Area of Application. States Parties have already agreed to replace the bloc-to-bloc structure of the original Treaty with a new system of limitations based on National Ceilings (NCs) and Territorial Ceilings (TCs). This system will be more constraining than the Treaty's current structure of limits on the amount of equipment that may be located in large geographic zones.

7. Many of us have already indicated in Vienna the intention to accept limits on national equipment entitlements that are more restrictive than under the current Treaty. This was an early signal of the restraint with which we are determined to approach the adaptation process. Some Allies, in the context of a satisfactory Treaty package, are prepared to consider further reductions where possible.

8. The system of Territorial Ceilings itself ensures strict limits on deployments across national boundaries. Our proposals make clear that we see adjustment of Territorial Ceilings as a procedure to address long-term shifts in security needs, and not as a means to achieve tactical flexibility. Consistent with that approach we have proposed that all adjustments to Territorial Ceilings above a specified equipment level be agreed by consensus of the Treaty Parties. We reaffirm our proposed 'specific stabilising measures' which, inter alia, would require certain States Parties to set their Territorial Ceilings no higher than current maximum national levels for holdings and not revise them upward. In this context, some other nations may be prepared, in the framework of a satisfactory Treaty package, to renounce the flexibility of adjustment of ceilings, also subject to review at a specified time.

Stationing

9. On 14 March 1997 the North Atlantic Council stated that: 'In the current and foreseeable security environment, the Alliance will carry out its collective defence and other missions by ensuring the necessary interoperability, integration, and capability for reinforcement rather than by additional permanent stationing of substantial combat forces'. The governments of the 16 members of the Alliance reaffirm and the governments of the Czech Republic, the Republic of Hungary and the Republic of Poland associate themselves with this Statement, in its entirety.

10. This Statement covers ground and air combat forces. It does not relate to headquarters or other military support activities needed to meet our military requirements for reinforcement, interoperability or integration. We will provide further evidence of our intentions as to any future stationing through increased transparency with regard to our defence plans and programmes.

Treaty Mechanisms

11. The long-term nature of the Treaty, the fundamentally constraining function of the system of National and Territorial Ceilings, the existence of security uncertainties, and the difficulty of predicting the future, all make it important that States Parties can manage crises within the framework of the Adapted Treaty. The proposed System of Temporary Deployments above TCs is designed to meet this need. In fulfillment of our commitment to restraint, we will make use of the Temporary Deployment provisions of an Adapted Treaty only in a manner consistent with strengthening overall and regional stability in Europe. Any such deployment used for crisis management purposes should have a stabilising effect. Its size, structure and composition will be geared to the crisis situation underlying its immediate tasks. While reserving the right under an Adapted Treaty to use fully such flexibilities as Exceptional Temporary Deployments above and headroom below Territorial Ceilings, in order to meet future contingencies, in the current and foreseeable security environment, we do not expect circumstances requiring deployments on the Territory of any State Party in excess of the TLE levels we have proposed for Exceptional Temporary Deployments. In addition, we will seek to prevent any potentially threatening broader or concurrent build-up of conventional forces. We expect other States Parties to exercise similar restraint. To this end, we declare:

– It is not, and will not be, our policy to use Temporary Deployment provisions for the purpose of permanent stationing of combat forces.

– Without prejudice to the national right to use headroom under TCs, we will exercise restraint with regard to the levels of any equipment temporarily deployed. We undertake to use fully any headroom, where available, prior to any implementation of the Treaty's Temporary Deployment right to exceed TCs. This will have the effect of minimizing the actual amount of any equipment temporarily in excess of the TC.

– Similarly, our use of Exceptional Temporary Deployment (ETD) provisions under an adapted Treaty will not be routine. In the current and foreseeable security environment, we do not envisage circumstances requiring frequent resort to ETDs. Nor do we see the concept of such deployments as directed against any specific country.

– Because such an occurrence would be unusual, it will be accompanied by appropriate political measures, within the OSCE, through which the nature of the exceptional circumstances having given rise to any ETD might be explained. We have proposed that the Adapted Treaty include significantly enhanced opportunities for transparency and verification in connection with any such deployment.

– We will ensure that our use of Treaty flexibilities does not result in TLE in excess of a Territorial Ceiling by more than the amount permitted for an ETD.

12. Increased transparency will be essential in providing the basis for our approach to the above issues and should provide greater opportunities to monitor compliance to match the spirit of openness prevalent in Europe today. We are also taking parallel action in Vienna to provide greater transparency concerning new or substantially improved military infrastructure and, more broadly, militarily significant activities and developments.

Source: NAC Press Release M-NAC-D-2(98)141, 8 Dec. 1998, URL <http://www.nato.int/docu/pr/1998/p98-141e.htm>.

15. Non-cooperative responses to proliferation: multilateral dimensions

IAN ANTHONY and ELISABETH M. FRENCH*

I. Introduction

In spite of the strong legal and political norms against their further proliferation, it has long been strongly suspected that new states have acquired nuclear, chemical and biological weapons (NBC).[1] In regard of ballistic or cruise missiles, similar legal and political norms are lacking except in cases where such missiles are acquired as delivery systems for prohibited weapons.[2]

The primary objective of policy for the great majority of states with regard to NBC weapons is to ensure the elimination of existing weapons and to prevent new weapons from being developed and produced.[3] Ideally, this would be achieved through a verifiable commitment by governments for NBC disarmament. Recent events have raised awareness of the continued need for a comprehensive disarmament agenda but also highlighted (*a*) that no comprehensive framework is yet in place, and (*b*) that there are significant barriers to creating such a framework.

Throughout 1998 disputes over the implementation of United Nations Security Council resolutions intended to eliminate Iraq's NBC weapon programmes, among other things, led to three separate crises in which the use of force was threatened. At the end of 1998 the United Nations Special Commission on Iraq (UNSCOM) was unable to confirm that Iraq's chemical, biological and missile programmes had been eliminated.[4] In May 1998 there was confirmation of the nuclear weapon programmes in India and Pakistan when these states conducted a series of nuclear explosions. In August 1998 the United States responded militarily when a state (Sudan) was thought to be assisting a non-state armed group to acquire chemical weapons (CW) for use against the USA.[5]

[1] I.e., states other than those that have themselves acknowledged possession of such weapons.

[2] Weapons, equipment or means of delivery designed to use biological agents or toxins for hostile purposes or in armed conflict are included as part of the definition of a biological weapon in Article I of the Biological and Toxin Weapons Convention. Missile delivery systems for chemical warfare agents form part of the definition of a chemical weapon contained in Article II of the Chemical Weapons Convention.

[3] Cooperative approaches to NBC disarmament and non-proliferation and the impact of the nuclear tests by India and Pakistan on those processes are reported on in chapters 9 (implications of the tests for the nuclear capabilities of India and Pakistan) and 12 (implications for nuclear arms control and non-proliferation) and appendix 12B (their technical characteristics) of this volume.

[4] UNSCOM is discussed in chapters 3 and 13 in this volume.

[5] The allegation and the US response to it are described in chapter 13 in this volume.

* Gabriella Schittek assisted with the collection of data for this chapter.

Thus, while there is widespread agreement that disarmament and non-proliferation are desirable objectives, the decisions by Iraq not to comply with its obligations under the terms of the ceasefire agreed in 1991 and the nuclear tests conducted by India and Pakistan raise the question how to respond to proliferation.

This chapter examines the global, multilateral and national responses to selected proliferation events in 1998 with a focus on whether and how far these responses include the threat or actual use of force, sanctions or technology denial. The review is not a comprehensive survey of allegations related to potential NBC weapon programmes of concern.[6] The emphasis is placed on those proliferation events which were the main focus of attention from the international community. In another case, the violations of North Korea's commitments under the 1968 Treaty on the Non-Proliferation of Nuclear Weapons (NPT), coercive measures were considered during 1994. However, the current approach towards North Korea's nuclear programme is not based on sanctions.[7]

A categorization of non-cooperative responses to proliferation events

There were several responses to proliferation events. Those that took place within the framework of existing disarmament and non-proliferation treaties are considered elsewhere in this volume. While some of those treaties include provisions for responding to non-compliance—Article XII of the 1993 Chemical Weapons Convention (CWC) and Article V of the 1996 Comprehensive Nuclear Test-Ban Treaty (CTBT)—whether the treaty provisions will be adequate to manage a specific case of non-compliance has not been tested.[8] Under the 1972 Biological and Toxin Weapons Convention (BTWC) any party to it may lodge a complaint with the UN Security Council if it believes that any other party is acting in breach of its obligations under the convention.

Since the existing enforcement provisions in treaties are formulated in general terms which need interpretation and since not all treaties contain such provisions, the UN Security Council is likely to be involved in handling serious cases of non-compliance.[9]

An additional question remains how to respond to actions that challenge the norms and principles underpinning the treaty regimes taken by states that are not parties to those treaties. It could be added that for some governments preventing NBC weapon proliferation has such a high priority that, if evidence

[6] Alleged use or proliferation of biological and chemical weapons is discussed in chapter 13 in this volume.

[7] They are described in chapter 12 in this volume.

[8] Neither the NPT nor the BTWC contain provisions on how to respond in cases of non-compliance—although a process is under way to add compliance and verification mechanisms to the BTWC. The initiative to achieve a protocol to strengthen the BTWC is discussed in chapter 13 in this volume. It should also be pointed out that the CTBT has not yet entered into force. The CTBT is discussed in chapter 12 in this volume.

[9] The exception may be in the case of alleged breaches of the CWC, which might in theory be handled internally within the framework of the treaty regime.

exists of an active weapon programme in a state that is party to an existing treaty, actions for dealing with non-compliance may be considered an inadequate response in the face of the threat posed to international security.

While historically states have taken unilateral military action to deny other states certain military capabilities, in the 1990s multilateral responses to proliferation have become possible.[10] Whereas the cold war would have made such approaches difficult if not impossible, in January 1992 the UN Security Council (at its only meeting conducted at the level of heads of state and government) stated that the proliferation of weapons of mass destruction (WMD) constitutes a threat to international peace and security.[11] This was repeated in two statements from the Security Council President (on 14 May and 29 May 1998) and also contained in Security Council Resolution 1172 of 6 June 1998.[12]

The 1992 statement by the Security Council and its subsequent reaffirmation following the nuclear tests by India and Pakistan are potentially very important. Once the Security Council has determined the existence of a threat to the peace it may decide on measures to be taken in accordance with Articles 41 and 42 of the UN Charter in order to maintain or restore international peace and security.

Under Article 41 of the Charter, the Security Council may decide to impose economic sanctions and call upon the members of the United Nations to apply these measures. Under Article 42 of the Charter the Security Council may, if it considers that sanctions would be inadequate, 'take such action by air, sea or land forces as may be necessary to maintain or restore international peace and security. Such action may include demonstrations, blockade, and other operations by air, sea or land forces of Members of the United Nations'.

In future, multilateral responses to proliferation may not be confined to the UN Security Council. In 1994, at their meeting in Istanbul, NATO defence ministers agreed on a Policy Framework on Proliferation of Weapons of Mass Destruction in which they stated that the proliferation of NBC weapons and their means of delivery 'can pose a direct military risk to the member States of the Alliance and to their forces'.[13] The document acknowledged that, in spite of the best efforts of the international community, proliferation might occur.

[10] E.g., in 1981 Israel made a pre-emptive attack on the Osiraq nuclear facility in Iraq, arguing that this was a defensive action given the risk that Iraq would engage in genocide if equipped with nuclear weapons. Som, V., 'The Israeli raid on Osiraq: an analysis', *Indian Defence Review*, vol. 3 (Dec. 1997), pp. 65–69.

[11] The responsibility of the Security Council in the maintenance of international peace and security, Note by the President of the Security Council, UN document S/23500, 31 Jan. 1992.

[12] Statement by the President of the Security Council, 14 May 1998, UN document S/PRST/1998/12; Statement by the President of the Security Council, 14 May 1998, UN document S/PRST/1998/12; and UN Security Council Resolution 1172, 6 June 1998. Whereas the acronym NBC describes a technical characteristic of specific weapon categories, the acronym WMD describes the effect of use of weapon categories. It is sometimes disputed that chemical weapons have the capacity to cause mass destruction. Except in cases where there is a direct quotation from a document, the term NBC weapons is used in this chapter.

[13] 'Alliance Policy Framework on Proliferation of Weapons of Mass Destruction', NATO Press Release M-NAC-1(94)45, 9 June 1994. This document and other NATO statements are available at URL <http://www.sipri.se/projects/expcon/other_documents.htm>.

Consequently it was felt that the alliance must address the military capabilities needed 'to discourage WMD proliferation and use, and if necessary, to protect NATO territory, populations and forces'.

By December 1998 members of the alliance agreed to evaluate their defence posture to ensure that they could 'succeed in the full range of missions that they might have to face despite the threat of use, or actual use, of chemical or biological weapons'.[14] Statements by Javier Solana, the Secretary General of NATO, made clear that responding to NBC proliferation formed part of the NATO Strategic Concept being prepared at the end of 1998. However, it was unclear whether this response would be confined to defending against the possible use of NBC weapons against the territory or forces of allies, or whether the concept would take in other types of response to proliferation.[15]

A range of instruments have been considered to exert pressure on states believed to be acquiring NBC weapons. In February 1998 military pressure from a group of states led by the USA played a part in resolving the crisis over UNSCOM inspections in Iraq. Although this coalition of states made it clear that they would prefer not to use force, the steps necessary to permit that option were taken.[16]

Apart from military pressure it is also possible to deny a state believed to have an active NBC weapon programme access to something that it desires but lacks—such as finance or technology.

The impact and effectiveness of economic sanctions as an instrument of policy have recently been the subject of extensive analysis, reflecting their increased use after the end of the cold war.[17] Sanctions have been applied since the mid-1990s for a wide range of reasons including conflict resolution, promotion of democracy and human rights.[18] However, with some important

[14] Final Communiqué from the North Atlantic Council in Defence Ministers Session, 17 Dec. 1998, Press Communiqué M-NAC-D(98)152, Brussels, 17 Dec. 1998.

[15] At the meeting of NATO foreign ministers in Dec. 1998 US Secretary of State Madeleine Albright stated her view that the alliance 'needs to view the WMD issue not only in a defense context, but also as a political challenge that requires a more comprehensive response'. US Department of State, Secretary of State Madeleine K. Albright, 'Statement to the North Atlantic Council', Office of the Spokesman, Brussels, 8 Dec. 1998, URL <http://secretary.state.gov/www/statements/1998/981208.html>.

[16] 'We have always stressed that we want to explore all diplomatic avenues before any military action is taken . . . Any diplomatic initiative that can achieve our objectives is one that we would support. Let us be clear about those objectives though; the objective must be effective inspection by UNSCOM that stops Saddam Hussein acquiring chemical and biological weapons. If there is a prospect that a visit by Kofi Annan can secure that then we would support his visit.' Extract from a 16 Feb. 1998 doorstep interview by the British Foreign Secretary Robin Cook. Foreign & Commonwealth Office, London, 'Cook's comments on Iraq', URL <http://www.fco.gov.uk/text_only/news/newstext.asp?262>.

[17] Pape, R. A., 'Why economic sanctions do not work', *International Security*, vol. 22, no. 2 (fall 1997); Elliott, K. A., 'The sanctions glass: half full or completely empty?', *International Security*, vol. 23, no. 1 (summer 1998); Baldwin, D. A., 'Evaluating economic sanctions', *International Security*, vol. 23, no. 2 (fall 1998); and Szasz, P., 'The law of economic sanctions', eds M. Schmitt and L. Green, *The Law of Armed Conflict Into the Next Millennium* (Naval War College: Newport, R.I., 1998).

[18] For surveys see *Sanctions: Do They Work?*, a special issue of the *Bulletin of Atomic Scientists*, Nov. 1993; Hendrickson, D. C., 'The democratist crusade: intervention, economic sanctions and engagement', *World Policy Journal*, vol. 11, no. 4 (winter 1994/95); Conlon, P., 'The UN's questionable sanctions practices', *Aussenpolitik*, vol. 46, no. 4 (1995); and 'The costs and benefits of economic sanctions', *Structures of World Order: Proceedings of the 89th Meeting of the American Society of International Law*, New York, 5–8 Apr. 1995.

exceptions, notably Iraq, they have not been applied as an instrument of non-proliferation.

Once the Security Council has identified an act of aggression or a threat to international peace or security, international sanctions may be applied under Article 41 of the UN Charter, which states that: 'The Security Council may decide what measures not involving the use of armed force are to be employed to give effect to its decisions, and it may call upon the members of the United Nations to apply such measures. These may include complete or partial interruption of economic relations and of rail, sea, air, postal, telegraphic, radio, and other means of communication, and the severance of diplomatic relations'.

In 1998 the readiness of some states to use sanctions was reaffirmed when the five permanent members (P5) of the Security Council met in the wake of the nuclear tests by India and Pakistan. However, that meeting also underlined that the P5 could not agree on a set of measures beyond an expression of regret and condemnation of the tests and a call for both India and Pakistan to join existing cooperative arms control and disarmament processes.

Apart from military pressure and sanctions, another instrument which is used to interrupt weapon programmes of concern are export controls applied by those suppliers with industrial and technological capacities that could contribute to the development of NBC weapons.

Some multilateral responses based on export and import controls depend on cooperation among states. The parties to the CWC cooperate to manage national export and import controls in ways that should prevent legitimate trade from contributing to illegal weapon programmes. Cooperation of this kind is outside the direct scope of this chapter—although the success of cooperative exercises will certainly have an indirect impact on the perceived need for approaches that do not depend on cooperation.[19]

Export controls applied to civilian technologies that have potential applications in NBC weapons are different from economic sanctions. Export controls are not applied in order to modify the behaviour of the target state through coercion. Instead, they seek to prevent transfers which contribute to programmes of concern and do not exclude other forms of trade.[20] The authorities of the exporter are responsible for ensuring that civilian technologies are not to be used for an unauthorized end-use or transferred to an unauthorized end-user. In gaining this assurance the cooperation of importers is welcome. However, export controls do not depend on the cooperation of importers and they exist to meet the foreign and security policy requirements of exporters.

This chapter surveys events in 1998 in three areas: the use of force to eliminate possession, economic sanctions and non-proliferation export controls.

[19] See chapter 13 in this volume.

[20] In some cases it can be argued that export controls have the same effect as sanctions. E.g., the demand for full-scope International Atomic Energy Agency (IAEA) safeguards as a condition for the supply of controlled items by members of the Nuclear Suppliers Group (NSG) means that 3 countries—India, Israel and Pakistan—may not buy civilian items (e.g., light-water nuclear power reactors) from NSG-participating states.

II. Iraq: sanctions and use of force as instruments of disarmament and non-proliferation

Evaluating the use of coercive measures to eliminate Iraq's programmes to develop NBC weapons and related delivery systems is complicated by the fact that disarmament and non-proliferation are only one part of a series of unresolved problems between Iraq and the United Nations. A web of interlocking UN Security Council resolutions provide the framework for coercive actions against Iraq, but these resolutions address a wide range of issues other than disarmament and non-proliferation.[21] Although Iraq has committed itself to comply with these resolutions, it did not do so spontaneously but as a condition of ending the military operations of Desert Storm.[22]

Similarly, the actions taken against Iraq—including sanctions and the use of force—do not have a single objective. As well as ensuring that Iraq does not have and will not develop NBC weapons and related missile delivery systems, these actions are also intended to confirm that the United Nations has the will and capacity to implement its decisions and to ensure that Iraq will not in future represent a serious threat to international peace and security.[23]

The objectives of the military operations undertaken in December 1998 by the US and British armed forces were to diminish and degrade Iraqi President Saddam Hussein's military capability. Attacks focused on air defence systems, the command and control system for the Iraqi armed forces, missile production capability, and systems which could be used for chemical and biological warfare. In addition, the special Republican Guard organization—considered to be the elite of the Iraqi armed forces and involved in the NBC weapon programme—was a target for attacks.[24]

Economic sanctions against Iraq may be grouped into two sanctions regimes. The first has its origins in the Iraqi invasion of Kuwait, which had its basis in financial and territorial issues.[25] Diplomatic attempts to resolve these issues were ineffective, and on 2 August 1990 Iraqi troops invaded Kuwait.[26]

In response to requests from Kuwait and the USA, the Security Council convened shortly after the invasion and, acting under Chapter VII, Articles 39 and 40 of the UN Charter, adopted Resolution 660 which condemned the Iraqi

[21] Leurdijk, D. A. and Siekmann, R. C. R., 'The threat or use of force in a unipolar world: the Iraq crisis of winter 1997–98', *International Peacekeeping*, Jan.–Apr. 1998, pp. 63–76.

[22] SIPRI, 'Iraq: the UNSCOM experience', *Fact Sheet*, Oct. 1998, available at URL <http://www.sipri.se/pubs/Factsheet/unscom.html>.

[23] Foreign & Commonwealth Office, London, 'Vigilance vindicated by results: Foreign Secretary's article in "The Times"', 25 Feb. 1998, URL <http://www.fco.gov.uk/text_only/news/newstext.asp?238&printVersion=yes>.

[24] The objectives of Operation Desert Fox were detailed by Prime Minister Tony Blair at a press conference in London on 20 Dec. 1998. Foreign & Commonwealth Office, London, 'Assessment of Operation Desert Fox and forward strategy', URL <http://www.fco.gov.uk/news/newstext.asp?1860>.

[25] Iraq claimed that Kuwait had illegally extracted $2.4 billion of crude oil from its Rumala oilfield, that Kuwait and other OPEC countries were ignoring oil export quotas and depriving Iraq of a fair market share, and that Kuwait's possession of the Warba, Bubiyan and Failaka islands in the Persian Gulf was illegal and hindered Iraq's access to the Gulf.

[26] Boutros-Ghali, B., *The United Nations and the Iraq–Kuwait Conflict 1990–1996* (United Nations: New York, 1996), pp. 14–15.

invasion of Kuwait, demanded the immediate withdrawal of all Iraqi forces, and called upon Iraq and Kuwait to begin intensive negotiations to resolve their differences immediately.[27] Despite continued opposition from other nations in the region and around the globe, Iraq did not withdraw from Kuwait. In order to put pressure on Iraq, the Security Council adopted Resolution 661 on 6 August 1990 which imposed full and mandatory sanctions against Iraq.[28] Only humanitarian assistance such as foodstuffs and medical supplies was permitted to be imported by Iraq. This resolution also established the UN Security Council Sanctions Committee, comprised of all 15 Security Council members, which was mandated to oversee the sanctions measures imposed against Iraq. Significantly, Resolution 661 also cited the terms of Article 51 of the UN Charter in 'Affirming the inherent right of individual or collective self-defence, in response to the armed attack by Iraq against Kuwait.'[29]

Several other resolutions are also important in establishing elements of the first sanctions regime against Iraq.

Resolution 665 of 25 August 1990 called on member states with maritime forces in the region to halt all inward and outward shipping to ensure strict compliance with sanctions.[30] Resolution 666 called upon the Sanctions Committee to evaluate the need for humanitarian assistance to Iraq.[31] The Security Council requested the Sanctions Committee to formulate a response to states asking for economic assistance because of the implementation of sanctions against Iraq in Resolution 669.[32] Resolution 670 reaffirmed the obligation for strict compliance with the sanctions against Iraq and confirmed that the sanctions were in effect for all types of transport, including aircraft.[33]

[27] UN Security Council Resolution 660, 2 Aug. 1990. Chapter VII of the UN Charter concerns 'Action with respect to threats to the peace, breaches of the peace, and acts of aggression'. Article 39 of the Charter states that: 'The Security Council shall determine the existence of any threat to the peace, breach of the peace, or act of aggression and shall make recommendations, or decide what measure shall be taken in accordance with Articles 41 and 42, to maintain or restore international peace and security'.

Article 40 of the UN Charter states that: 'In order to prevent an aggravation of the situation, the Security Council may, before making the recommendations or deciding upon the measures provided for in Article 39, call upon the parties concerned to comply with such provisional measures as it deems desirable. Such provisional measures shall be without prejudice to the rights, claims, or position of the parties concerned. The Security Council shall duly take account of failure to comply with such provisional measures'.

[28] UN Security Council Resolution 661, 6 Aug. 1990.

[29] Chapter VII, Article 51 of the UN Charter states that: 'Nothing in the present Charter shall impair the inherent right of individual or collective self-defence if an armed attack occurs against a Member of the United Nations, until the Security Council has taken measures necessary to maintain international peace and security. Measures taken by Members in the exercise of this right of self-defence shall be immediately reported to the Security Council and shall not in any way affect the authority and responsibility of the Security Council under the present Charter to take at any time such actions as it deems necessary in order to maintain or restore international peace and security.' The Security Council has never lifted or modified Resolution 661 and as a result, the UK and the USA have argued that they have the authority under Article 51 to take such actions as they deem necessary to restore international peace and security.

[30] UN Security Council Resolution 665, 25 Aug. 1990.

[31] UN Security Council Resolution 666, 13 Sep. 1990.

[32] UN Security Council Resolution 669, 24 Sep. 1990.

[33] UN Security Council Resolution 670, 25 Sep. 1990.

Resolution 678 of 29 November 1990 demanded Iraqi compliance with Resolution 660 and all subsequent resolutions and authorized member states 'to use all necessary means to uphold and implement Resolution 660 and all subsequent resolutions and to restore international peace and security in the area' if Iraq did not withdraw from Kuwait before 15 January 1991.[34]

Iraq did not remove its troops from Kuwait by the 15 January 1991 deadline. As a consequence, military action by the international coalition began against Iraq on 17 January 1991. The offensive against Iraq continued until Kuwait was liberated on 27 February 1991. Throughout this time the first economic sanctions regime—instituted in order to pressure Iraq to withdraw from Kuwait—had remained in place. The liberation of Kuwait and the end of the military offensive did not signify the end of the sanctions, however. The first sanctions regime gave way to its successor upon the adoption of the ceasefire.

Sanctions related to disarmament and non-proliferation

The ceasefire resolution, Resolution 687, adopted on 3 April 1991, determined that the full trade embargo (other than medicine and health supplies) against Iraq would remain in force pending Iraqi compliance with the terms imposed under the resolution.[35] These terms included a comprehensive set of measures that Iraq was to undertake to ensure elimination of its NBC weapons and related missile delivery systems.

In this second sanctions regime the embargo was directed to continue, with a review every 60 days 'in the light of the policies and practices of the Government of Iraq, including the implementation of all relevant resolutions of the Council, for the purpose of determining whether to reduce or lift the prohibitions referred to therein'.[36] Under paragraph 22, the Security Council determined that the sanctions would continue until Iraq had complied with paragraphs 8–13 of the resolution. These paragraphs pertain specifically to the destruction, removal or rendering harmless, under international supervision, of all chemical and biological weapons (CBW), all stocks of agents, all related subsystems and components, and all related research, development, support and manufacturing facilities, as well as all ballistic missiles with a range greater than 150 km and related major parts and repair and production facilities. Iraq was also required to declare all locations, amounts and types of the above items within 15 days of the adoption of Resolution 687 and to agree to urgent, on-site inspections.

Paragraph 9 of the resolution provided for the creation of UNSCOM, mandated to implement immediate on-site inspections of Iraq's chemical, biological and missile capabilities, on the basis both of Iraq's own declarations and of the designation of the Special Commission itself. Iraq was also ordered

[34] UN Security Council Resolution 678, 29 Nov. 1990.

[35] UN Security Council Resolution 687, 3 Apr. 1991. Paragraph 20 states the prohibitions against the sale or supply to Iraq of commodities or products and prohibitions against financial transactions contained in Resolution 661, shall not apply to foodstuffs or materials and supplies for essential civilian needs.

[36] UN Security Council Resolution 687 (note 35), para. 21.

to yield possession of all items specified in paragraph 8 to UNSCOM in order that it may destroy, remove or render them harmless. This was to include items at locations designated by UNSCOM and the destruction by Iraq of all missile capabilities under UNSCOM's supervision. Furthermore, Iraq was ordered to unconditionally agree not to use, develop, construct or acquire any of the items specified in paragraphs 8 and 9 as well as to consult with UNSCOM as regards future monitoring and verification of Iraq's compliance with the terms of these paragraphs. Iraq was also ordered not to acquire or develop nuclear weapons or capabilities, to reaffirm its obligations under the NPT. Iraq was obliged to declare its nuclear material, equipment and sub-systems to the International Atomic Energy Agency (IAEA) and to be subject to the inspection and verification activities of the IAEA.

However, the scope of Resolution 687 is not confined to disarmament and non-proliferation issues as it requires Iraq's compliance concerning arrangements for the demarcation of the Iraq–Kuwait border and the establishment of a fund for compensating loss and damage sustained by Kuwait in the invasion by Iraq. Thus, the scope of the second sanctions regime goes further than did the first.

A partial lifting of the prohibition on the purchase of oil from Iraq by UN member states has been permitted for humanitarian purposes.[37] In order to ensure that this partial lifting was not exploited to undermine the purpose of the sanctions, Resolution 715 of 11 October 1991 requested the Sanctions Committee, in cooperation with UNSCOM and the Secretary-General of the United Nations, to develop an export control mechanism to monitor sales of potential dual-use commodities by other countries to Iraq.[38]

By the start of 1998 Iraq had not fully complied with the terms of Resolution 687, specifically in the area of chemical and biological weapons and agents, but continued to demand suspension of the sanctions against it. UNSCOM inspectors were not able to freely inspect all possible sites and could not confirm that all CBW and stocks of agents and related research and development had been destroyed, removed or rendered harmless. A particular issue of contention between UNSCOM and Iraq was the inspection of eight presidential sites, to which inspectors were repeatedly denied access. The issue of access to presidential sites precipitated a crisis in relations between the UN Security Council and Iraq which lasted between December 1997 and February 1998 and which included the threat of use of force against Iraq to secure compliance with existing resolutions. This crisis was resolved short of the use of force through a Memorandum of Understanding (MOU) between the United Nations and Iraq agreed between Secretary-General Kofi Annan and the Government of Iraq.[39]

[37] The terms of Resolution 712, which would have allowed Iraq to export certain quantities of oil in order to purchase humanitarian supplies, were refused by Iraq. The resolution would have required that all of Iraq's export contracts and imports and distribution of humanitarian goods be subject to UN monitoring. UN Security Council Resolution 712, 19 Sep. 1991.

[38] UN Security Council Resolution 715, 11 Oct. 1991, para. 7.

[39] Under the terms of the MOU Iraq reconfirmed its acceptance of the terms of all relevant resolutions of the Security Council, including resolutions 687 and 715. Iraq also promised compliance with

As a result of the inability to declare Iraq free from CBW, the economic sanctions against Iraq remained in place. In spite of diplomatic tensions and the possibility of military action, humanitarian assistance to Iraqi civilians was increased.[40]

During a 3 August visit to Iraq the Executive Chairman of UNSCOM, Richard Butler, was told by Deputy Prime Minister of Iraq Tariq Aziz to inform the Security Council that Iraq's obligations under section C of Resolution 687 had been fulfilled. When Butler responded that this was not possible, Aziz suspended the meeting. Two days later Iraq announced that it was halting cooperation with UNSCOM and the IAEA pending a termination of the oil embargo, a first step in full removal of the sanctions, as well as a reorganization of UNSCOM and transfer of its headquarters to either Geneva or Vienna. If these demands were met, Iraq would permit monitoring as outlined under Resolution 715.[41] The President of the Security Council deemed Iraq's actions unacceptable, and sanctions continue.

Iraq continued to hinder UNSCOM's monitoring activities and on 9 September 1998, in Resolution 1194, the Security Council decided not to conduct its 60-day sanctions reviews until Iraq rescinded its 5 August decision to halt cooperation with UNSCOM.[42]

This Iraqi decision was the proximate cause for the military operations (known as Operation Desert Fox) undertaken by the UK and the USA on 17–20 December 1998.

After the military action against Iraq, Trade Minister Mohammed Mehdi Saleh confirmed that Iraq refused the continuation of the Oil-for-Food assistance programme and demanded the lifting of sanctions—although the United Nations reported that it had not received official word from Iraq concerning such intentions.[43]

China, France and Russia continued to press for a far-reaching review of the approach towards securing Iraqi compliance with existing resolutions—including considering the lifting of sanctions against Iraq or their modification—while Saudi Arabia was said to be preparing an initiative to lessen the sanctions against Iraq in early 1999.[44]

UNSCOM and the IAEA. The MOU also noted that the lifting of sanctions was 'of paramount importance' to the people and Government of Iraq. The sanctions cannot be lifted until the Security Council determines that Iraq has fulfilled all of its obligations under the relevant Security Council resolutions, including Resolution 687. United Nations–Iraq Memorandum of Understanding, UN document S/1998/166, 23 Feb. 1998. UNSCOM's activities in 1998 are discussed in chapter 13 in this volume.

[40] The provisions of the Oil-for-Food Programme, established after 1995, were increased and in June 1998 states were authorized to export to Iraq parts and equipment to increase the export of petroleum and petroleum products. UN Security Council Resolution 1153, 20 Feb. 1998; and UN Security Council Resolution 1175, 19 June 1998.

[41] United Nations Special Commission, 'UNSCOM: a chronology of main events', URL <http://www.un.org/Depts/unscom/chronology.htm>.

[42] UN Security Council Resolution 1194, 8 Sep. 1998.

[43] Meixler, L., 'Iraq says it won't extend oil-for-food program', Associated Press, URL <http://foxnews.com/news/international/1228/i_ap_1228_10.sml>; and Reuters, 'UN not told of any halt in Iraq oil-for-food plan', URL <http://dailynews.yahoo.com/headlines/ts/story.html?s=v/nm/19981227/ts/iraqun_1.html>.

[44] Reuters, 'Saudi proposes easing of Iraqi sanctions—papers', URL <http://dailynews.yahoo.com/headlines/ts/story.html?s=v/nm/19990110/ts/sanctions_1.html>.

The military action against Iraq may lead to the demise of UNSCOM in its original form, but in consideration of the UN resolutions Iraqi compliance on several levels must be complete and unconditional in order for the prohibitions against the import of Iraqi commodities to be lifted. While it is now generally agreed that the nuclear part of the disarmament work has been completed to the degree that could reasonably be asked, by contrast, UNSCOM is convinced that some biological and chemical weapon-related materials remain in Iraq. Should the economic sanctions imposed against Iraq be at an end, it will be thanks to international pressure, not as a result of UN assurances that Iraqi biological and chemical weapon capabilities have been destroyed, removed or rendered harmless.

III. International response to nuclear tests by India and Pakistan

Much discussion and analysis have been devoted to the question of how the international community would respond if a state crossed the 'threshold' between non-nuclear weapon state status and possession of a nuclear weapon.[45] A certain ambivalence exists regarding how far events in 1998 shed light on this question. If it is argued that India and Pakistan, although not parties to the NPT, violated not only a norm against nuclear testing but also a norm against nuclear proliferation this would be an indirect recognition of Indian and Pakistani nuclear-weapon status. However, most states have withheld legal recognition arguing that to do otherwise would undermine the existing nuclear non-proliferation regime, particularly the NPT. According to this view, India and Pakistan have not crossed the threshold to nuclear-weapon status since this can only be conferred by the international community (through a revision of the NPT) and not claimed unilaterally.[46]

Events in 1998 were certainly significant, but their importance should not be exaggerated. While India and Pakistan presented the tests as a watershed, it can be argued that they actually crossed the nuclear threshold before 1998—India in 1974 and Pakistan around 1986—and that recent tests confirmed their nuclear status.[47]

Consequently, this section is confined to the international response to the violation of the norm against nuclear testing rather than nuclear proliferation.

The five permanent members of the UN Security Council met on 4 June to consider their response to the tests. The response included a condemnation of the tests and outlined positive measures that the P5 were prepared to support

[45] Article IX, para. 3 of the NPT defines a 'nuclear-weapon state' as 'one which has manufactured and exploded a nuclear weapon or other nuclear explosive device prior to 1 January, 1967'.

[46] The legal definition of a nuclear weapon state and a more political definition can coexist. E.g., for many years China was not recognized as a nuclear weapon state because it remained outside the NPT. At the same time, the existence of Chinese nuclear weapons was taken into account by states in conducting their international relations. See also chapter 12, section II in this volume.

[47] This issue is discussed further in chapter 9 in this volume.

to promote reconciliation and cooperation between India and Pakistan. The statement contained no mention of coercive measures or sanctions.[48]

US Secretary of State Madeleine Albright said that the P5 met 'because as the permanent members of the Security Council, we have an obligation to respond to what is clearly a threat to international peace and security'.[49] Moreover, in the same statement Albright made it clear that as part of this response 'a number of nations, including the United States, will maintain sanctions against India and Pakistan until this situation is resolved. The United States will also insist that no nation that disregards international norms become a permanent member of the UN Security Council'.

Asked what the P5 would do if nuclear weapons were deployed, Albright replied:

> we have set forth a very unified and united message about what we are calling on India and Pakistan to do in order to have them stop testing and try to avert an arms race, and sign up to the CTBT and refrain from deploying missiles and stop production of fissile materials. . . . I think we want to see how this message is received. It is, I think, a strong message from the permanent members of the Security Council, delivered loud and clear. . . . Should they [India and Pakistan] take additional steps, I think there are other ways that the international community can deal with this.[50]

The meaning of the word 'deployed' has not been clarified. In Indian statements it appears to mean introduced into the armed forces, meaning that in theory missiles might be built and stored without technically being deployed. Whether the United States accepts this definition is not clear.[51]

As noted above, the UN Security Council responded to the tests by India and Pakistan with agreed statements issued by the president and a resolution that were part of the widespread condemnation of the tests. While Resolution 1172 demanded that India and Pakistan refrain from further tests, it did not impose sanctions or any other measures that could be seen as punitive or specify measures that would be taken in case this demand was ignored.

The presidency of the European Union (EU) was held by the UK at the time that the tests took place. The UK issued a statement on 25 May.[52] According to that statement, the EU 'will take all necessary measures should India not accede to and move to ratify the relevant international non-proliferation agreements in particular the Comprehensive Test Ban Treaty'. Member states

[48] The agreed statement of 4 June 1998 by the P5 is available at Foreign & Commonwealth Office, London, 'Nuclear tests in South Asia', URL <http://www.fco.gov.uk/news/newstext.asp?1099>.

[49] US Department of State, Secretary of State Madeleine K. Albright, 'Statement at the P-5 foreign ministers meeting on South Asia', UN Offices Geneva, 4 June 1998, URL <http://secretary.state.gov/www/statements/1998/980604a.html>.

[50] US Department of State, Secretary of State Madeleine K. Albright, 'Press conference on the crisis in South Asia', Palais des Nations, Geneva, 4 June 1998, URL <http://secretary.state.gov/www/statements/1998/980604.html>.

[51] The USA and India have conducted a series of bilateral discussions in 1998 covering at least 4 issue areas: Indian membership of the CTBT, the prospects for a Fissile Material Treaty, Indian nuclear and nuclear-related export controls, and India's defence posture (including the role of nuclear weapons in it). Mohan, C. R., 'PM rejects demands to limit nuclear capabilities', *The Hindu* (Internet edn), 16 Dec. 1998, URL <http://www.webpage.com/hindu/today/01/01160001.htm>.

[52] 'Statement of the European Union on nuclear tests in India', *EU Bulletin*, 5-1998 (May 1998).

agreed to work for a delay in the consideration of loans to India before the World Bank and other financial institutions and asked the Commission of the European Communities 'to consider in its review of the General System of Preferences (GSP) the implications of the nuclear tests and India's progress in acceding to international nonproliferation agreements for India's continued eligibility for GSP preferences'.

The EU member states followed through on this statement and on 26 May the World Bank postponed consideration of three World Bank and one International Finance Corporation loans to India then before the Board of Governors. The value of these loans (which were not cancelled although consideration of them was indefinitely postponed) was roughly $850 million.[53] With proposals before other financial institutions, loans to India worth approximately $1.2 billion in total were delayed.

Subsequently, on 29 May the EU released a further statement after the tests conducted by Pakistan. In this statement the EU again agreed to 'take all necessary measures should Pakistan not accede to and move to ratify the relevant international non-proliferation agreements in particular the Comprehensive Test Ban Treaty'.[54]

While the EU statements left open the possibility of additional future measures should India and/or Pakistan conduct further tests, there was no agreement on a common action. This reflected the divergent national views on how to respond to the tests in an area (Common Foreign and Security Policy) where there is no obligation on member states to form a common view.

The issue of how cooperation against proliferation should be conducted was part of the discussion of a new transatlantic political agenda in 1998. In this area the EU member states all object to the use of the US national laws to affect matters considered to be sovereign decisions in individual EU countries. Speaking at the end of the British Presidency of the European Union, Prime Minister Tony Blair noted that 'We in Europe have always taken very seriously the fight to curb terrorism and the spread of weapons of mass destruction. But the US sanctions laws made our cooperation on these issues more, rather than less difficult'.[55] As trade falls within the competence of the EU, there are also instruments to pursue this common policy at a community level.

Following a year of negotiation between the European Commission and US authorities an agreement was reached in June 1998 related to European concerns about the impact of the 1996 Helms–Burton Act and Iran–Libya Sanctions Act.[56] The USA committed itself to issue waivers for EU companies under the two acts and to resist future attempts by Congress to push through

[53] World Bank, 'Loans to India postponed', *Press Release*, no. 98/1778/SAS, 26 May 1998.

[54] 'Statement of the European Union on nuclear tests in Pakistan', *EU Bulletin*, 5-1998 (May 1998).

[55] Prime Minister Tony Blair, statement after the EU/US summit meeting in London, 18 May 1998, Foreign & Commonwealth Office, London, 'US sanctions laws', URL <http://www.fco.gov.uk/news/newstext.asp?979>.

[56] The Helms–Burton Act, which is directed towards Cuba, is not in any way related to non-proliferation. The Iran–Libya Sanctions Act is.

similar legislation.[57] This would make it more difficult for the Congress to use domestic legislation to influence the approach of EU member states towards economic sanctions on India and Pakistan.

In addition to the UN and EU activities, the eight countries that meet annually to discuss political issues of mutual concern in the 'G8' process (the G7 plus Russia) issued a condemnation of the Indian nuclear tests at their summit meeting in Birmingham, UK (which took place before the nuclear tests by Pakistan).

The G8 is not an executive body but an informal meeting. The eight agreed that each should work to persuade the Indian Government to modify its policy using whichever method each country believed to be the most effective. The G8 also made a commitment to enhance cooperation on export controls designed to deny any kind of assistance to programmes for NBC weapons and their means of delivery.[58] The G8 states established a Senior Officials Task Force which met on an ad hoc basis in 1998 to consider responses to the nuclear tests, including economic sanctions. The G8 states invited senior officials from Argentina, Australia, Brazil, China and Ukraine to attend these meetings in 1998 and, in February 1999, also invited South Korea to join the group.[59]

The NATO–Russia Permanent Joint Council, meeting in Luxembourg in May 1998, also issued a condemnation of the nuclear tests by India and Pakistan. However, no sanctions against either India or Pakistan were agreed in the framework of NATO.[60]

Economic sanctions

The failure by the UN Security Council to include economic sanctions in Resolution 1172 may reflect both legal and political factors. The main political factor is the difference of view among the P5 about the effectiveness of sanctions. On 12 May 1998, then Russian Foreign Minister Yevgeny Primakov stated that 'we are very apprehensive about sanctions. Sanctions are, if you like, extreme measures that are not always productive . . . I do not think that we will support sanctions against India'.[61] Similarly, expert observers con-

[57] The EU in effect made progress on developing the Transatlantic Economic Partnership (an EU–US trade initiative sought by the USA) conditional on obtaining relief for European companies from the impact of US sanctions legislation.

[58] Documentation from the summit is available at 'Britain welcomes the summit of world leaders', URL <http://birmingham.g8summit.gov.uk>. The 8 participants are Canada, France, Germany, Italy, Japan, Russia, the UK and the USA.

[59] Ministry of Foreign Affairs, Japan, 'The Third Meeting of the Senior Officials Task Force on Nuclear Tests by the Republic of India and the Islamic Republic of Pakistan', Press Conference by the Press Secretary, 5 Feb. 1999, URL <http://www.mofa.go.jp/announce/1999/2/205.html>.

[60] North Atlantic Treaty Organization, 'Statement on the nuclear tests of Pakistan and India', NATO–Russia Permanent Joint Council Meeting at Ministerial Level, Luxembourg, 28 May 1998, URL <http://www.nato.int/docu/pr/1998/p980529e.htm>.

[61] Interview with Yevgeny Primakov by Svetlana Sorokina, NTV (Moscow), 12 May 1998, in 'Russia: Russia's Primakov interviewed on India, Iran', Foreign Broadcast Information Service, *Daily Report–Central Eurasia* (*FBIS-SOV*), FBIS-SOV-98-132, 14 May 1998. This view commands support across a wide political spectrum in Russia. Vladimir Lukin, leader of the Yabloko Party in the State

sidered it unlikely that China would ever support economic sanctions as a response to the nuclear tests in spite of the tensions in bilateral relations with India.[62]

It could be argued that there is not a sufficient legal basis for sanctions against India and Pakistan because if international sanctions are to be justified they must be imposed 'to induce compliance with some international obligation that the target state has failed to observe. Collective sanctions for essentially punitive purposes have no accepted place in international law'.[63] Sanctions against a state such as Iraq or North Korea—which have violated norms and agreements freely entered into—would be different in kind from sanctions against India and Pakistan, neither of which is a member of the international nuclear non-proliferation regime.

As the UN has no mechanism for implementing Security Council decisions, international sanctions are always given expression through national actions by UN members. Although in the case of India and Pakistan no international sanctions were agreed, some countries—notably the USA—have imposed sanctions as a response to the nuclear tests. The unilateral use of sanctions has aroused considerable controversy since the mid-1990s.[64]

Some states have put forward the view that unilateral sanctions 'are contrary to international law, the UN Charter and the norms and principles governing peaceful relations among states'.[65] Specifically, these measures are said to contravene General Assembly Resolution 2625 of 1970 by which 'no State may use or encourage the use of unilateral economic, political or any other type of measure to coerce another State in order to obtain from it the subordination of the exercise of its sovereign rights'.[66] However, in 1997 a UN expert group provided a list of cases where sanctions might be justified which included measures adopted 'in response to a clear violation of universally accepted norms, standards, or obligations, provided these States are not seeking advantages for themselves but are seeking an international community interest'.[67] The legitimacy of individual sanctions against India and Pakistan would then turn on a judgement about whether nuclear non-proliferation was a universally accepted norm in conditions where neither India nor Pakistan is a signatory to the main legal non-proliferation instruments.

Duma, said during a visit to New Delhi: 'Moscow will never resort to any sanctions against or pressure on Delhi and neither will it call the future of our bilateral relations in question'. Kotov, L., ITAR-TASS World Service (Moscow), 16 Sep. 1998, in 'Russia: Russian MPs, Iranian leaders discuss international issues', FBIS-SOV-98-259, 17 Sep. 1998.

[62] Ye Zhengija quoted in 'China not to impose economic sanctions against India', *Indian Express* (electronic edn), 20 May 1998, URL <http://www.expressindia.com/news/13800031.htm>.

[63] Szasz (note 17), p. 456.

[64] See also chapter 12 in this volume.

[65] This statement was made by the Ministers of Foreign Affairs and Heads of Delegation of the non-aligned countries at a meeting which occurred after India had conducted 2 sets of tests. Communiqué of the Ministerial Meeting of the Coordinating Bureau of the Movement of Non-Aligned Countries, Cartagena de Indias, Colombia, 19–20 May 1998, UN document A/52/970, 26 June 1998.

[66] UN General Assembly Resolution 2625, 24 Oct. 1970, is reproduced in *Yearbook of the United Nations, 1970*, vol. 24 (UN Office of Public Information: New York, 1970), pp. 788–92.

[67] United Nations, Report of the Secretary-General on Macroeconomic policy questions: trade and development, Economic measures as a means of political and economic coercion against developing countries, UN document A/52/459, 14 Oct. 1997, p. 22.

National responses

The failure to agree common policies within international bodies such as the UN and the EU was reflected in the divergent national policies adopted towards India and Pakistan.

The United States imposed a series of economic sanctions on India and Pakistan including ending assistance under the Foreign Assistance Act of 1961 (except for humanitarian assistance), ending military sales and financing, and denying other US financial aid. These measures were introduced with immediate effect. The changes to US export controls are considered further below. The main economic sanctions introduced consisted of the following measures: denial of any credit, credit guarantees, or other financial assistance by any part of the US Government; opposition to the extension of any loan for financial or technical assistance by any international financial institution; and prohibition of US banks from making any loan or providing any credit to the Government of India, except for the purposes of purchasing food or other agricultural commodities. In addition, the Board of Directors of the Export–Import Bank may not give approval to guarantee, insure, or extend credit, or participate in the extension of credit, in support of US exports to India.

These sanctions were required by a US law (section 102 of the Arms Export Control Act, AECA, also known as the Glenn Amendment) within which the administration has very little discretion to waive provisions depending on the specific context in which the law is invoked.[68] Moreover, as the law contains no provisions for lifting sanctions this would require separate legislation.

The Clinton Administration made no secret of its lack of enthusiasm for the Glenn Amendment and worked to introduce changes to allow the president greater flexibility in applying the law without codifying specific steps required from India and Pakistan as conditions to obtain relief from sanctions.

The Clinton Administration did not oppose the use of sanctions in principle but argued that they should be 'properly designed and implemented as part of a coherent strategy'. Under these conditions, sanctions could be 'a valuable tool for advancing American interests and defending US values'.[69]

In the specific case of Indian and Pakistani nuclear testing, however, economic sanctions were not considered useful although the USA is India's largest trade and investment partner. Recent changes in India's economic policy have been welcomed by the United States and sanctions were considered unhelpful at a time when Washington was calling on the Indian Government to renew its commitment to reform.

The Asian economic crisis subsequently made the timing of economic sanctions seem particularly perverse. From 1999 to 2001, $115–130 billion worth

[68] The Glenn Amendment was a response to a feeling in Congress that the State Department was interpreting the AECA vis-à-vis Pakistan in ways that were inconsistent with the intention of Congress. Specifically, the State Department was approving licences for certain defence articles and services to Pakistan which Congress believed should be denied. Consequently, the Glenn Amendment limited the discretion of the State Department.

[69] 'Economic sanctions', statement before the Senate Task Force on Sanctions by Stuart Eizenstat, Under Secretary of State for Economic, Business and Agricultural Affairs, 8 Sep. 1998.

of private investment is needed in India for planned infrastructure projects according to the World Bank—a significant increase in investment over current levels. There was concern that sanctions might raise concerns among private institutions (not prohibited from investing in or lending to India) already closely watching Indian reactions to the economic crisis.[70]

Mandated US economic sanctions had a smaller relative impact on Pakistan because most types of economic relations had already been scaled back in previous years, either in response to proliferation concerns or because Pakistan had failed to meet economic benchmarks. However, Pakistan was vulnerable to US actions in international financial institutions.

Some members of Congress also regarded economic sanctions as inappropriate.[71] In October 1998 the Congress passed the Omnibus Appropriations Act which included a section amending US sanctions law.[72] Under this act the president was allowed to waive certain sanctions up until October 1999, and on 1 December 1998 President Bill Clinton granted waivers permitting US loans and investments in the two nations and the use of foreign assistance funds for international military training and education programmes as well as allowing US participation in the International Monetary Fund (IMF) programme of economic measures agreed with Pakistan.[73]

Some governments were ambivalent about sanctions against India and Pakistan. The position of the British Government was summarized in the House of Lords:

> We are concerned that in both India and Pakistan the consequences of any renewed arms race may divert scarce resources from vital productive development and their efforts to reduce poverty and to improve their education provision. I can give my noble friend the assurance, at least in part, not necessarily that there will be no sanctions of any economic nature against either country, but that we shall do everything we can to sustain the diplomatic effort. We are enormously conscious of the importance of trying to sustain aid programmes which help the poorest people in those countries.[74]

After the nuclear tests were conducted there was a widespread reluctance to impose economic sanctions against India and Pakistan. Nevertheless, some

[70] E.g., sanctions might make private financing less likely once loan guarantees issued by the Export–Import Bank were halted. World Bank, 'Government of India, private sector to exchange views on private investment in India's infrastructure', *News Release* no. 99/1984/SAS, Conference on Private Investment in Infrastructure in India, Paris, 2–3 Nov. 1998, URL <http://www.worldbank.org/html/extdr/extme/1984.htm>; and 'Statement by the Hon. Yashwant Sinha, Governor of the Fund and the Bank for India', *Press Release* no. 34, 1998 Joint Annual Discussion between the International Monetary Fund and World Bank Group, Washington DC, 6–8 Oct. 1998.

[71] E.g., in July 1998 a bill was introduced in the House of Representatives to amend the Arms Export Control Act to give the president some flexibility in applying sanctions. No action was taken on this bill. India–Pakistan Sanctions Flexibility Act, H. R. 4209, 14 July 1998.

[72] The specific provision within the Appropriations Act is known as the India–Pakistan Relief Act of 1998, sometimes referred to as the Brownback Amendment.

[73] United States Information Agency, *Presidential Determination on India and Pakistan*, PD no. 99-7 (White House, Office of the Press Secretary: Washington, DC, 1 Dec. 1998), URL <http://www.usia.gov/regional/nea/sasia/docs/doc82.htm.>.

[74] Baroness Symons of Vernham Dean, British House of Lords, *Hansard*, 1 June 1998, col. 62.

governments did introduce economic sanctions against India and Pakistan even though they had no legal obligation to do so.

After India undertook its second set of tests the Government of Japan decided to suspend yen-loans for new projects to India and to 'cautiously examine' loans extended to India by international financial institutions. After Pakistan proceeded with tests Japan decided that grant aid for new projects should be frozen (except for emergency and humanitarian aid), suspended yen-loans to Pakistan and decided to 'cautiously examine' loan programmes to Pakistan by international financial institutions.[75] In November 1998 Japan was maintaining its sanctions.[76]

After India and Pakistan carried out nuclear tests Australia suspended all non-humanitarian economic assistance to India (worth approximately $12.5 million). Australia continued its economic assistance programmes with Pakistan, all of which were considered to be humanitarian in character.[77]

Canada cancelled talks on the scope of development assistance to India for 1999, which were scheduled to begin shortly after the tests took place. Non-humanitarian development assistance to India was stopped, and Canada opposed non-humanitarian loans to India from the World Bank. Moreover, after India's first test, Canada offered to divert assistance withdrawn from India to development assistance programmes in Pakistan if Pakistan refrained from testing.[78] However, a programme for humanitarian development assistance for 1999 and onwards was subsequently put in place for both countries, and Canada's response to both India and Pakistan vis-à-vis the use of development assistance is based on 'encouraging policy actions and reforms in support of stability, equity and growth' rather than on sanctions.[79]

Some European countries also took limited actions in linking levels of economic assistance to India and Pakistan directly to the conduct of nuclear tests. Germany cancelled its discussions with India and Pakistan of new programmes for economic development assistance and rescinded the remaining development aid resources agreed for 1998 (worth DM315 million in the case

[75] Ministry of Foreign Affairs of Japan, 'Comments by the Chief Cabinet Secretary on measures in response to the second nuclear testing conducted by India', 14 May 1998, URL <http://www2.nttca.com:8010/infomofa/announce/announce/1998/5/0312-09.html>; and Ministry of Foreign Affairs of Japan, 'Comments by the Chief Cabinet Secretary on measures in response to nuclear testing conducted by Pakistan', 29 May 1998, URL <http://www2.nttca.com:8010/infomofa/announce/announce/1998/5/p_measure.html>.

[76] Ministry of Foreign Affairs of Japan, 'Response of the Government of Japan to recent announcements by the Government of the United States concerning sanctions against the Republic of India and the Islamic Republic of Pakistan', 10 Nov. 1998, URL <http://www.mofa.go.jp/announce/press/1998/11/1110.html>.

[77] Statements by Australian Ministry for Foreign Affairs on 14 May (related to India) and 29 May 1998 (related to Pakistan), reproduced in *Australian Foreign Affairs and Trade Record*, June 1998, p. 28.

[78] Department of Foreign Affairs and International Trade, Canada, 'Notes for a statement by the Honourable Lloyd Axworthy, Minister of Foreign Affairs, to the Standing Committee on Foreign Affairs and International Trade "India's nuclear testing: implications for nuclear disarmament and the nuclear non-proliferation regime"', Ottawa, Ontario, 26 May 1998, URL <http://www.dfait-maeci.gc.ca/english/news/statements/98_state/98_040e.htm>.

[79] Canadian International Development Agency (CIDA), 'Country policy framework: India', URL <http://www.acdi-cida.gc.ca>.

of India and DM80 million in the case of Pakistan).[80] Sweden cancelled a newly reached three-year agreement with India on economic cooperation for development worth approximately $1.2 billion. The Swedish International Development Agency (SIDA) was tasked to develop a proposal for a new agreement focused narrowly on the alleviation of poverty and with a reduced volume of financing.[81]

Export controls and India and Pakistan

As noted above, export controls are not sanctions—although they can be used as one instrument to enforce sanctions. Export controls allow a choice to be made about whether or not to allow any given export of a controlled item to take place.

It is widely accepted that there should not be a free market in any type of military technology. If military technology were distributed only according to the ability to pay for it this would pose a serious security risk. By extension, states have an obligation to place controls on access to technologies developed on their territory.[82] While all states should develop a system that allows them to control exports of military technology and civil technology with military applications, there is no general agreement on how those controls should be applied.

In the early 1990s there was discussion among governments that had cooperated in the Coordinating Committee on Multilateral Export Controls (COCOM) about whether and how export controls might be used after the cold war. By 1998 most states that participated in multilateral discussions appeared to support the view that export controls should focus on weapon programmes of concern. Export controls should not be targeted on a state or group of states. Individual countries are not named and the phrase 'rogue states' does not appear in the documents of any export regime. Neither, according to this view, should controls target behaviour that is not related to the proliferation of weapons.[83]

This diversity was underlined in the responses to the nuclear tests by India and Pakistan. No international organization or informal regime imposed or agreed an embargo on supplies of arms or other controlled items to India or

[80] Bundesministerium für wirtschaftliche Zusammenarbeit, 'Bundesminister Spranger sagt Regierungsverhandlungen mit Indien ab' [Federal minister Spranger reneges on governmental negotiations with India] , Ministry for Economic Development Cooperation, *Press Statement*, 12 May 1998, URL <http://www.bmz.de/.bin/lay/presse/archiv/pm98051201.html>; and Bundesministerium für wirtschaftliche Zusammenarbeit, 'Atomtests in Pakistan: Spranger sagt entwicklungspolitische Konsultationen ab' [Atomic tests in Pakistan: Spranger reneges on development policy consultations] , Ministry for Economic Development Cooperation, *Press Statement*, 28 May 1998, <http://www.bmz.de/.bin/lay/presse/archiv/pm98052801.html>.

[81] Swedish Ministry for Foreign Affairs, 'Sverige säger upp samarbetsavtalet med Indien' [Sweden cancels cooperation agreement with India], *Press Statement*, 13 May 1998.

[82] Some states have gone beyond this to apply controls to activities of their citizens even if those activities take place abroad.

[83] The discussion is summarized in Anthony, I. *et al.*, 'Multilateral weapon-related export control measures', *SIPRI Yearbook 1995: Armaments, Disarmament and International Security* (Oxford University Press: Oxford, 1995).

Pakistan. The Zangger Committee issued a statement condemning the nuclear tests in October 1998. However, as far as is known the committee did not modify its guidelines for nuclear exports in response to the tests.

At their meeting in Geneva the five permanent members of the UN Security Council 'confirmed their respective existing policies to prevent the export of equipment, materials or technology that could in any way assist programmes in India or Pakistan for nuclear weapons or ballistic missiles capable of delivering such weapons'.[84] The P5 did not make any commitment to modify their national policies and, as noted below, there are significant differences in the national interpretation of their obligations.

In Resolution 1172 the Security Council encouraged all states 'to prevent the export of equipment, materials or technology that could in any way assist programmes in India or Pakistan for nuclear weapons or for ballistic missiles capable of delivering such weapons' and welcomed 'national policies adopted and declared in this respect'.[85]

National responses

Although no mandatory arms embargo has been imposed, the nuclear tests of India and Pakistan have had an impact on the export control practices of some states.

As noted above, once the President of *the United States* had made a determination that a nuclear explosive device had been detonated by a non-nuclear weapon state the US response was conditioned by the terms of the Arms Export Control Act. The president made this determination on 13 May for India and on 30 May for Pakistan.

In both cases, sales of defence articles, defence services, and design and construction services were terminated and all licences for the export of any item on the US Munitions List were revoked. This included all types of licence for manufacture, technical assistance and distribution of any kind. As a result, cooperation was terminated with immediate effect.[86]

The termination of defence sales and the revocation of munitions export licences also applied to retransfers of items of US origin to India or Pakistan by foreign end-users. According to the Arms Export Control Act, written approval from the Office of Defense Trade Controls within the State Department is required before the authorized end-user of a defence article can

[84] Foreign & Commonwealth Office, London, 'Nuclear tests in South Asia', 4 June 1998, URL <http://www.fco.gov.uk/news/newstext.asp?1099>.

[85] UN Security Council Resolution 1172 (note 12).

[86] *Federal Register*, vol. 63 no. 97 (20 May 1998), p. 27781; and *Federal Register*, vol. 63 no. 116 (17 June 1998), p. 33122. The impact of changes in the US export controls on cooperative projects is discussed in chapter 9 in this volume. The US Munitions List is the part of the secondary regulations (known as the International Traffic in Arms Regulations or ITAR) that defines which defence articles and services are subject to licensing. The list is divided into 16 sections which include all categories of military equipment: aircraft and related articles; amphibious and related articles; vessels of war and special naval equipment; chemical agents; components, accessories, attachments, parts, software and systems associated with end-items; firearms; forgings, castings and machined bodies; military explosives and propellants; and military fuel thickeners. The final category in the list consists of the entire equipment and technology annex defined by the Missile Technology Control Regime.

re-export or retransfer that article. A non-transfer and use certificate is a condition of granting a licence for defence articles, including manufacturing licences and technical data, and this certificate is binding on the foreign end-user. If the foreign end-user is not a government agency (e.g., if the transfer is to an overseas manufacturer) the State Department may also insist on a guarantee from the government of the end-user that the end-use of the licensed article will be verified. Violation of these provisions can lead to the original licence being revoked and/or the imposition of sanctions.

As a result, it may be that countries and companies outside the United States are in effect barred from making transfers to India and Pakistan because the products contain technologies or items that are subject to US law.

The Arms Export Control Act is not the only element of US export control law. The Bureau of Export Administration (BXA) within the Commerce Department is responsible for implementing controls on exports of civilian articles and services with potential military applications. These controls are currently exercised under executive orders issued by the president using the authority of the International Emergency Economic Powers Act. This is because the Congress has not been able to agree a new text of the Export Administration Act which provided the legal authority for export controls on civilian items with military applications until it expired in 1994.[87] The items subject to control are identified in a Commodity Control List (CCL). In addition, the United States operates a 'catch-all' which states that a licence is required for any transaction if the exporter knows or has reason to believe that the end-user is involved in a nuclear or missile-related activity. In November 1998, the BXA named 40 Indian and 46 Pakistani end-users believed to be involved in nuclear, missile or military programmes. Subsequently, under the catch-all provision, a licence was required for any transfer of any articles or services (whether or not on a control list) to these entities.

Russia is India's single most important partner in nuclear and military–technical cooperation and the approach to cooperation with India in the military sphere and as regards civilian technologies with military applications has a central bearing on Indian capabilities. It is not thought that Russia plays any role in either the design or the material base of India's nuclear weapon programme.[88] The preferred position of Russia, and before that the Soviet Union, has been that neither India nor Pakistan develop nuclear weapons. Russia and India have a range of nuclear cooperation projects including in the areas of research and power generation.

The development of Russia's system to control exports of technologies that may be used to develop or produce NBC weapons has been a subject of con-

[87] Since 1994 the US Congress has tried to agree a new text of the Export Administration Act on 3 occasions without success. It has not been possible to balance the concerns of those wishing to reduce the burden of controls on exporters with the concerns of those who see proliferation risks as paramount.

[88] The possible exception being transfers of technology from India's programme to develop space-launch vehicles, with which Russia has cooperated, to missile programmes that might lead to the development of a delivery system for Indian nuclear weapons. See the section on 'The Missile Technology Control Regime' in appendix 15A in this volume. It is also possible that the MiG-27 and Su-30 fighter aircraft may be nuclear-capable.

siderable external interest since the dissolution of the Soviet Union. Developing effective nuclear export controls has been given the highest priority and, as noted above, civil nuclear cooperation probably plays a minimal if any part in India's nuclear weapon programme.[89] Although in 1998 there were calls for modifications to Russian controls over nuclear materials and to Russian export controls, these discussions were not related to developments in India.[90]

In the area of conventional armaments the nuclear tests did not lead to a reduction in cooperation between Russia and India. On the contrary, events in 1998 underlined Russia's desire to deepen military–technical cooperation. During a visit to India Defence Minister Igor Sergeyev stated that 'our countries face the task of building up the volume of cooperation potential, which will be promoted by a long-term Russian–Indian cooperation programme in military relations (which is now being drafted) up to the year 2010'.[91] During the visit to New Delhi of Russian Deputy Foreign Minister Grigoriy Karasin this programme was said to be near completion and it was hoped that this would be one of the documents signed during the Russia–India summit meeting on 23 December 1998. Karasin underlined that, although Russia and India take different views on the issue of nuclear weapon proliferation, this would not prevent deepening of cooperation between the two countries.[92]

As *China* is Pakistan's single most important partner in nuclear and military–technical cooperation, the Chinese approach to cooperation with Pakistan in the military sphere and as regards civilian technologies with military applications has a central bearing on Pakistani capabilities. In contrast to the case of Russia–India relations, it has often been suggested that China has played an important role in the development of the Pakistani nuclear weapon capability. In India it is believed that Pakistan has received 'substantive assistance' from China in terms of nuclear weapon-related know-how and materials as well as transfers of missiles and missile-related technology that can contribute to a Pakistani nuclear weapon delivery system.[93] The US Government has also reached similar conclusions with the Director of the Central Intelligence Agency identifying China as 'the primary source of nuclear-related equipment and technology' to Pakistan. Similarly, it has also been claimed that Pakistan had received M-11 missiles from China in the early 1990s and technical assistance in developing its own missiles.[94]

[89] Bertsch, G. and Grillot, S. (eds), *Arms on the Market: Reducing the Risk of Proliferation in the Former Soviet Union* (Routledge: New York, 1998).

[90] See the discussion in the section 'The Missile Technology Control Regime' in appendix 15A in this volume.

[91] Kotov, L., ITAR-TASS (Moscow), 19 Oct. 1998, in 'Russia: Sergeyev praises Russian–Indian defense cooperation', FBIS-SOV-98-292, 21 Oct. 1998.

[92] Kotov, L., ITAR-TASS (Moscow), 3 Nov. 1998, in 'Russia: Russia's Karasin hold talks in Delhi', FBIS-SOV-98-307, 5 Nov. 1998.

[93] Singh, J., 'India, Europe and non-proliferation: Pokharan II and after', *IDSA Journal* (electronic version), Nov. 1998, URL <http://www.idsa-india.org/an-nov8-1.html>; and Banerjee, D., 'South Asian nuclear and missile environment', *Asian Defence Journal*, Nov. 1998, pp. 6–9.

[94] See chapter 9 of this volume. An overview of Sino-Pakistani nuclear and missile cooperation is available at the Center for Nonproliferation Studies, Monterey Institute of International Studies, 'Indian and Pakistani nuclear tests', URL <http://cns.miis.edu/research/india/chinatoc.htm>.

This assistance is said to have occurred in 1980–96 and in response the United States raised non-proliferation issues to the highest level in its bilateral dialogue with China in 1996–97. In this period China first pledged not to provide assistance to unsafeguarded nuclear facilities. Subsequently, China introduced new national export control regulations for nuclear materials and joined the discussion of nuclear export controls in the Zangger Committee.[95]

As a result, the impact of the Pakistani nuclear tests on its relations with China were of great interest. Speaking in June the US National Security Adviser said that the Chinese Government has 'indicated and, in fact, complied with a commitment not to provide assistance to unsafeguarded nuclear facilities—i.e. Pakistan'.[96] Speaking after the visit to China of President Clinton, Secretary of State Albright said that the Chinese had 'made clear this time that they would not be involved in missile transfers to Pakistan. They had hinted at various parts of that, but I think that this statement did go beyond that in making it clearer'.[97]

The United Kingdom, a significant arms supplier to India, responded to the tests with changes that were narrowly focused on nuclear-related exports. Foreign Office Minister Tony Lloyd announced that 'all export licence applications for items listed on the Nuclear Suppliers Group (NSG) Dual-Use List will be denied to nuclear and nuclear-related end-users in India and Pakistan, as will all other goods to these end-users which could contribute to the Indian and Pakistani nuclear programmes'.[98] The Anglo-French Jaguar fighter aircraft is often named as one of the most likely delivery platforms for Indian nuclear weapons. As far as is known, no changes were introduced regarding licensing of controlled items other than nuclear and nuclear-related dual-use items.

France has historically been and still remains a significant arms supplier to both India and Pakistan. As far as is known, the nuclear tests in 1998 did not lead to any changes in French export control policy.

In the past, *Germany* has had significant cooperation with India in the area of arms transfers and defence industrial cooperation. The main current programme involves a framework agreement to construct two additional Type-1500 submarines for the Indian Navy (in addition to four in service in India). However, implementation of this agreement depends on the appropriation of funds by India.[99] In 1998 German authorities decided that in applying arms export controls to India and Pakistan what was described as a highly restrictive policy would be further intensified.[100]

Other European countries that are or have recently been suppliers of arms to India and/or Pakistan also introduced changes in policy. In *Sweden* the

[95] Anthony, I. and Zanders, J. P., 'Multilateral security-related export controls', *SIPRI Yearbook 1998: Armaments, Disarmament and International Security* (Oxford University Press: Oxford, 1998), pp. 382–84

[96] White House press briefing by National Security Adviser Sandy Berger, 17 June 1998, URL <http://www.pub.whitehouse.gov/uri-res/I2R?urn:pdi://oma.eop.gov.us/1998/6/19/7.text.1>.

[97] US Department of State, Secretary of State Madeleine K. Albright, 'Press briefing', Beijing, 28 June 1998, URL <http://secretary.state.gov/www/statements/1998/980628a.html>.

[98] 'Nuclear industry', British House of Commons, *Hansard*, 10 July 1998, col. 688.

[99] *Jane's Fighting Ships, 1998–99* (Jane's Information Group: Coulsdon, Surrey, 1998), p. 291.

[100] German Foreign Ministry, Private communication with Ian Anthony, 19 Nov. 1998.

responsible minister stated that granting approval for licences to conduct new exports to India was 'completely out of the question'.[101] In *Switzerland* the Federal Council decided to deny any licences for war material to India and Pakistan, although this decision did not affect transfers of spare parts for licences granted before the tests.[102]

Following the tests, *Australia* suspended all defence relations with India and Pakistan, including training and advisory programmes.[103] *Canada* banned all military exports to India and Pakistan.[104]

After the establishment of full diplomatic relations in 1992 some observers have described an emerging range of contacts between Israel and India, including in the military field.[105] Immediately after the tests a visit to India by Israeli Chief of Staff Lieutenant General Amnon Lipkin-Shahak planned for June 1998 was cancelled. However, according to a close observer of the bilateral relationship there has been no evidence to suggest that emerging military cooperation between India and Israel will be interrupted.[106] Israel may face difficulties with the US policy of preventing re-export or retransfer of items supplied under licence.

IV. Conclusions

The decisions by Iraq not to comply with its obligations under the terms of the ceasefire agreed in 1991 and the nuclear tests conducted by India and Pakistan raised an important question: In conditions where achieving comprehensive disarmament through a multilateral treaty is not an available option, how should states respond to the reality of proliferation?

To state a preference for disarmament is not a policy so much as a statement of a desirable state of affairs. A policy would require the elaboration of steps and measures to reach this objective. However, in spite of sustained application of very severe economic sanctions and the use of force the United Nations was unable to give an assurance at the end of 1998 that Iraq had in fact eliminated its NBC weapons along with the delivery systems for them.

With regard to Iraq, while all of the permanent members of the UN Security Council made statements underlining the view that Security Council resolutions should be implemented in full, there were widespread differences of view about how this could be achieved.

[101] 'Svar i riksdagen av Leif Pagrotsky om vapenexport till Indien' [Response in Parliament by Leif Pagrotsky on arms exports to India], Department of Industry and Trade Press Statement, Stockholm, 19 May 1998.

[102] Swiss Federal Office for Foreign Economic Affairs, Private communication with Ian Anthony, 17 Nov. 1998.

[103] Statements by Australian Ministry for Foreign Affairs (note 77).

[104] Department of Foreign Affairs and International Trade, Canada, 'Axworthy condemns Pakistan's nuclear weapons tests and announces sanctions', Press release no. 136, 28 May 1998, URL <http://www.dfait-maeci.gc.ca/english/news/press_releases/>.

[105] Kumaraswamy, P. R., *India and Israel: Evolving Strategic Partnership*, Security and Policy Studies no. 40 (Begin–Sadat Center for Strategic Studies: Bar Ilan University, Sep. 1998).

[106] Kumaraswamy, P. R., Private communication with Ian Anthony, 22 Nov. 1998.

China, France and Russia—while expressing concern or outright opposition to the coercive approach taken by the UK and the USA—offered no practical alternative beyond the hope that diplomacy would succeed. In particular, during the two pre-December 1998 crises (in which force was not used) none of these three countries was able to define a diplomatic approach that would succeed in enforcing existing resolutions.

It remained unclear at the end of 1998 how far the UK and the USA were prepared to go in attempting to coerce Iraq into full compliance with UN resolutions. While a far-reaching assessment of how to achieve Iraqi compliance with UN resolutions was called for, existing arrangements could only be modified with the consent of all the permanent members of the Security Council, including the UK and the USA.

In the case of India and Pakistan, there is little evidence that coercive measures (whether the use of force or sanctions) were seen as central instruments to prevent the development of nuclear weapon arsenals. Although some economic sanctions were introduced, the preferred approach appeared to be a combination of diplomacy (intended to persuade India and Pakistan to join cooperative arms control and disarmament processes) along with enhanced export controls (intended to make weapon development as difficult and costly as possible for India and Pakistan).

Appendix 15A. Multilateral weapon and technology export controls

IAN ANTHONY and JEAN PASCAL ZANDERS

I. Introduction

This appendix describes identified changes in the membership, control lists, guidelines and procedures of five multilateral export control regimes. The regimes are the Nuclear Suppliers Group (NSG), the Zangger Committee, the Australia Group (AG), the Missile Technology Control Regime (MTCR) and the Wassenaar Arrangement on Export Controls for Conventional Arms and Dual-Use Goods and Technology (WA). In 1998 there were changes to the membership of the NSG and the MTCR and changes in the control lists used by the Wassenaar Arrangement. Table 15A.1 lists the members of these regimes.

II. The Nuclear Suppliers Group and the Zangger Committee

The Nuclear Suppliers Group is an informal group of states which seeks to ensure that exports of nuclear and nuclear-related dual-use items do not contribute to nuclear explosive or unsafeguarded nuclear activities. In 1998, 35 states were members of the NSG, with Latvia participating for the first time.

The annual plenary meeting of the NSG took place in Edinburgh, Scotland, on 30 March–2 April 1998. Coming before the nuclear tests in India and Pakistan, the meeting mainly addressed three issues: procedures for information exchange among the members, efforts to promote transparency and openness in NSG activities, and possible new members.

This reflects the impact of recent changes in the nuclear non-proliferation regime for the work of the NSG. Although there is no direct connection between the 1968 Treaty on the Non-Proliferation of Nuclear Weapons (NPT) and the NSG, the 1995 NPT Review and Extension Conference, in particular the decision on principles and objectives at that conference, has had an impact on the activities of the group. As the NSG has become more open in recent years its activities are being discussed by a wider range of states and non-state actors.[1]

The second issue taken up by the NSG is that of possible new members. Five countries—Belarus, China, Cyprus, Kazakhstan and Turkey—have expressed an interest in learning more about the NSG or in participating. A consensus is required among the existing membership before new states may participate. In addition to a demon-

[1] E.g., 1 principle adopted in 1995 was that full-scope safeguards should be a condition of any new supply arrangement while others enhanced the role of the International Atomic Energy Agency (IAEA) in verifying and assuring compliance with safeguards agreements and the role of the IAEA in dealing with cases of non-compliance. In 1992 the NSG participants adopted a standard by which a recipient must accept IAEA full-scope safeguards as a condition of supply for source and special fissionable materials. The 1995 decisions were considered by some to raise questions about the relationship between the NSG and the activities of the IAEA, the presentation of NSG activities in the NPT review process and even the continued need for the NSG.

Table 15A. Membership of multilateral weapon and technology export control regimes, as of 1 January 1999

State	Zangger Committee[a] 1974	NSG[b] 1978	Australia Group[a] 1985	MTCR[c] 1987	Wassenaar Arrangement 1996
Argentina	x	x	x	x	x
Australia	x	x	x	x	x
Austria	x	x	x	x	x
Belgium	x	x	x	x	x
Brazil		x		x	
Bulgaria	x	x			x
Canada	x	x	x	x	x
China	x				
Czech Republic	x	x	x	x[d]	x
Denmark	x	x	x	x	x
Finland	x	x	x	x	x
France	x	x	x	x	x
Germany	x	x	x	x	x
Greece	x	x	x	x	x
Hungary	x	x	x	x	x
Iceland			x	x	
Ireland	x	x	x	x	x
Italy	x	x	x	x	x
Japan	x	x	x	x	x
Korea, South	x	x	x		x
Latvia		x[d]			
Luxembourg	x	x	x	x	x
Netherlands	x	x	x	x	x
New Zealand		x	x	x	x
Norway	x	x	x	x	x
Poland	x	x	x	x[d]	x
Portugal	x	x	x	x	x
Romania	x	x	x		x
Russia	x	x		x	x
Slovakia	x	x	x		x
South Africa	x	x		x	
Spain	x	x	x	x	x
Sweden	x	x	x	x	x
Switzerland	x	x	x	x	x
Turkey				x	x
UK	x	x	x	x	x
Ukraine	x	x		x[d]	x
USA	x	x	x	x	x
Total	**33**	**35**	**30**	**32**	**33**

Note: The years in the column headings indicate when the export control regime was formally established, although the groups may have met on an informal basis before then.

[a] The European Commission is represented in this regime as an observer.

[b] The Nuclear Suppliers Group. The European Commission is represented in this regime as an observer.

[c] The Missile Technology Control Regime.

[d] This state became a member of the regime in 1998.

strated commitment to nuclear non-proliferation, new members must have in place national policies and procedures that allow them to implement commitments undertaken in the framework of the NSG.

The Zangger Committee, also known as the Nuclear Exporters Committee, developed out of the perceived need among a group of nuclear suppliers to clarify their obligations under Article III.2 of the NPT. Under this article parties may not provide source or special fissionable material, or equipment, or material especially designed or prepared for the processing, use or production of special fissionable material to any non-nuclear weapon state for peaceful purposes, unless the source or special fissionable material shall be subject to safeguards. The purpose of the Zangger Committee was to define how this commitment should be interpreted by nuclear suppliers. The agreement reached was that items identified on an agreed list (known as the Trigger List) would be exported only if the material in question was subject to safeguards under an agreement with the International Atomic Energy Agency (IAEA).

In 1998, 33 states participated in the Zangger Committee, which meets twice a year. At the time of the first 1998 meeting, in May, Pakistan was conducting nuclear tests and the implications were discussed by the group. At the October meeting the Zangger Committee produced an agreed statement condemning the tests by India and Pakistan.

The Zangger Committee considered but did not introduce changes to the Trigger List in 1998. These changes would consist of adding technologies used to convert nuclear facilities previously used for military purposes to the Trigger List. The consequence of this change would be that exports of such technologies would be conditional on a safeguards agreement between the recipient and the IAEA.

III. The Australia Group

The Australia Group is an informal group of states whose objective is to limit the transfer of chemical precursors, equipment used in the production of chemical and biological weapons (CBW), and biological warfare agents. The participating states have agreed to apply decisions taken collectively through their national export control systems. Created in 1985, the original objective of the AG was to prevent chemical weapon (CW) proliferation while the negotiations to complete the 1993 Chemical Weapons Convention (CWC) were being undertaken. Subsequently, it has also acted to prevent biological weapon (BW) proliferation during the process of developing improved measures to ensure compliance with the 1972 Biological and Toxin Weapons Convention (BTWC).[2]

The most recent annual meeting of the Australia Group was held in Paris on 9–15 October 1998. As in 1997, 30 states attended and the European Commission

[2] The history, structure and procedures of the AG are discussed in greater detail in Anthony, I. and Zanders, J. P., 'Multilateral security-related export controls', *SIPRI Yearbook 1998: Armaments, Disarmament and International Security* (Oxford University Press: Oxford, 1998), pp. 386–94.

participated as an observer.[3] No changes were made to the Australia Group's so-called warning lists.[4]

Following the 1995 sarin attack in the Tokyo underground, the Australia Group began in-depth political-level discussions of CBW proliferation and terrorism. At the behest of the USA, the participants at the 1998 plenary session shared information on the legal and regulatory efforts each member had taken to counter this threat.[5]

Conscious of the continuing criticism by some developing countries that no CBW-related export control arrangement should exist in addition to the BTWC and the CWC, the AG countries stressed in their media release that universal adherence to and compliance with the two treaties would be the most effective way to rid the world of CBW. They added that their consultations complemented and were consistent with the purposes of these conventions. The discussions on the national export licensing measures and procedures of each of the participating countries aimed to prevent the inadvertent contribution to CBW programmes, on the one hand, and to ensure that the trade in chemical precursors, biological agents and dual-use equipment for legitimate purposes is not inhibited, on the other hand. The AG participants remained prepared to assist other countries in implementing similar export control measures on a national basis and will continue to give briefings and regional seminars on export licensing practices for countries not participating in the Australia Group.[6]

IV. The Missile Technology Control Regime

The MTCR is an informal and voluntary process in which countries that share the goal of non-proliferation of unmanned delivery systems for weapons of mass destruction and seek to coordinate national export licensing efforts aimed at preventing their proliferation cooperate. Participating states have agreed a set of guidelines to be applied in making their national decisions whether or not to export an agreed set of equipment and technology.

In 1998 three new members—the Czech Republic, Poland and Ukraine—participated in MTCR meetings for the first time, bringing the membership to 32.[7] All three of these states have sought to participate in the regime for a number of years, including bringing their national export controls in line with the MTCR Guidelines and the Equipment and Technology Annex.[8] Until 1998 there was no consensus within the

[3] On 19 Dec. 1998, the Government of Cyprus announced that it had taken the decision to join the AG and that it had appointed a ministerial committee to draw up legal amendments and regulations for controlling certain substances passing through Cyprus. 'Cyprus to join in struggle against chemical weapons', *Xinhua* (Nicosia), CNN Custom News (19 Dec. 1998), URL <http://customnews.cnn.com/>.

[4] The AG export control warning lists include CW precursors; dual-use chemical manufacturing facilities and equipment, and related technology; biological agents; animal pathogens; dual-use biological equipment; and plant pathogens. The lists are available at URL <http://www.sipri.se/cbw/esearch/AG-mainpage.html>.

[5] Letter from the President to the Speaker of the House of Representatives and the President of the Senate, 12 Nov. 1998, URL <http://www.pub.whitehouse.gov/uri-res/I2R?urn:pdi://oma.eop.gov.us/1998/11/16/9.text.1>.

[6] Australia Group Meeting, 9–15 Oct. 1998, Media release, Australia Group document Doc AG/Oct/Press/Chair/21.

[7] Two countries, China and Israel, apply the MTCR Guidelines to their national exports without participating in the regime.

[8] The Equipment and Technology Annex of the MTCR is a restricted document. However, it is known to be divided into 2 categories of items. Category I, considered most sensitive and to which the greatest restrictions apply, consists of complete systems and specially designed production facilities for these systems along with complete subsystems usable in these systems and production facilities and pro-

regime about their admission to meetings and the decision to admit the Czech Republic and Poland does not seem related to any modification in their approach to missile proliferation. Rather, it seems linked to their impending membership of NATO and the anomaly that would be created by leaving members of the alliance outside the MTCR.

The issue of how to avoid missile proliferation while stimulating international cooperation in civilian aerospace programmes has become increasingly important with the growing commercial value of satellite-launch services and the civil space industry in general. This issue played an important role in the accession of Ukraine to the MTCR.

Cooperation to prevent missile proliferation has been one issue taken up in the bilateral Ukrainian–US Cooperation Commission (also known as the Kuchma–Gore Commission) which was initiated in 1997. The commission has discussed how to create conditions in which US–Ukrainian aerospace industry cooperation can take place while providing safeguards against missile proliferation.[9]

This issue was also central to China's relations with the MTCR in 1998. During preparations for the visit of President Bill Clinton to China in 1998, the USA raised the issue of Chinese membership of MTCR in the context of the impact on US national export controls. John Holum, the acting Under-Secretary for Arms Control and International Security Affairs, noted that if a US company is to launch a satellite on a Chinese rocket, that requires both an export licence and a technology security plan to avoid transfers of technology to Chinese military programmes. According to Holum, consideration of the licence could be expedited if China were to join the MTCR—although membership of MTCR would not lead to transfers of technology, only to a more rapid consideration of the application.[10]

The extent to which the MTCR is able to impact those missile programmes of most concern to the participating states is something of an open question. In its 1998 plenary meeting in Budapest the main discussions between participating states concerned missile programmes in China, India, Iran, Iraq, North Korea and Pakistan.[11] None of these states is a member of the MTCR.

North Korean programmes to develop and produce missiles as well as foreign sales of missiles and missile technologies by North Korea attracted widespread attention in 1998. North Korea was identified by Japan as the main source of technology for the Pakistani Ghauri missile, a surface-to-surface missile which was tested to a range of 1100 km in April 1998.[12] The Indian Ministry of Defence has claimed that China is the main supplier of the technology for Ghauri.[13] Pakistan claims to have developed and produced this missile indigenously.

duction equipment for the subsystems. Category II consists of a range of materials, components and equipment which can be of use in missile programmes.

[9] United States Information Agency, 'Transcript: remarks of Albright and Udovenko in Kiev', 9 Mar. 1998, URL <http://pdq2.usia.gov>.

[10] US Department of State, 'Special briefing on trip to China', 9 Apr. 1998, URL <http://www.state.gov/www.policy_remarks/1998/980409_holum_china.html>.

[11] MTI (Budapest), 9 Oct. 1998, in 'Hungary: Gyarmati briefs press on MTCR conference in Budapest', Foreign Broadcast Information Service, *Daily Report–East Europe* (*FBIS-EEU*), FBIS-EEU-98-285, 14 Oct. 1998.

[12] Japan's Foreign Minister Masahiko Komura stated that Japan has 'reliable information that the missile used in the launch was imported from North Korea'. Harney, A. and Farhan Bokhari, 'Pakistan fired N. Korean missile', *Financial Times* (Internet edn), 25 Sep. 1998; and chapter 9 in this volume.

[13] Institute for Defense and Disarmament Studies, *Arms Control Reporter* (IDDS: Brookline, Mass.), sheet 706.B.252–56, Apr. 1998.

In June 1998 North Korea officially acknowledged its missile exports, although without confirming which missiles are exported or to which countries.[14] The official news agency released the statement that North Korea will continue developing, testing and deploying missiles and will export these missiles to obtain foreign exchange.[15] In August and September 1998 North Korea and the USA held the third round of bilateral talks on missile-related issues, apparently without any change in North Korean policy although further talks will be held at an unspecified date.[16]

Although Russia is a member of the MTCR the question of Russian contributions to Iran's ballistic missile programme, raised in 1997, has mainly been discussed bilaterally with the United States and bilaterally with Israel.[17] Andrey Kokoshin, at that time Secretary of the Russian Security Council, visited Israel in August 1998. He reassured the Israeli Government that Russia had no intention of assisting missile proliferation in Iran and discussed cooperation between Russia and Israel—both in following up allegations of illegal transfers and expanding scientific and economic cooperation between the two countries.[18]

In July 1998 US Secretary of State Madeleine Albright handed over to the Russian Government the evidence gathered by the United States of participation by Russian entities in the Iranian missile programme. The documents mentioned 11 entities and organizations which were said to have provided support of some kind.[19]

Russian dual-use export controls are managed by the Government Commission on Export Control chaired by the Minister of Economy. In July 1998 the results of an inquiry into allegations of illegal exports of missile technologies by the commission led to further special investigations of nine enterprises and institutions where there appeared to be a case to answer.[20] The nine Russian entities were named and the United States in turn introduced restrictions on cooperation with them by US firms.[21]

The nine entities were: Glavkosmos, the INOR Scientific Production Centre, the Grafit State Scientific Research Institute, the Polyus Scientific Research Institute, the Tikhomirov Instrument Building State Research Institute, the Komintern Plant, the MOSO Company, Europalas 2000 Company and the Baltic State Technical University. It is alleged that cooperation between some of these Russian entities and partners in Tajikistan and Azerbaijan in fact provided a front for cooperation with Iran. However, according to investigations by the Russian Federal Security Service the Azerbaijani case (involving Europalas 2000) did not involve the export of metals

[14] North Korea has acknowledged exporting Scud-B and Scud-C missiles, both missiles with a shorter range than the Ghauri, and has not officially acknowledged supporting Pakistan's missile programme.

[15] Sang-Hun Choe, 'North Korea admits selling missiles', Associated Press, 16 June 1998, URL <http://wire.ap.org/APnews>; and Choson Ilbo (Seoul), 17 June 1998, in 'South Korea: Paper on intention behind DPRK admitting missile expert', in Foreign Broadcast Information Service, *Daily Report–Arms Control* (*FBIS-TAC*), FBIS-TAC-98-169, 19 June 1998.

[16] US Department of State, 'US–DPRK missile talks', Press statement by James P. Rubin, 2 Oct. 1998, URL <http://secretary.state.gov/www/briefings/statements/1998/ps981002.html>.

[17] Allegations of Russian–Iranian missile-related cooperation are discussed in Anthony and Zanders (note 2), pp. 397–98.

[18] Kuzmin, O., ITAR-TASS (Moscow), 11 Aug. 1998, in 'Russia: Kokoshin winds up three-day visit to Israel', FBIS-SOV-98-223, 13 Aug. 1998.

[19] Extracts from these primary documents were later published in Eggert, C., 'Meteor dlya ayatoll' [Meteor for the Ayatollah], *Izvestiya*, 22 Oct. 1998, p. 5.

[20] The national laws and procedures for controlling exports of dual-use technologies are different from those for conventional arms, although both were modified in 1998.

[21] Information on the 9 is compiled at Monterey Institute of International Studies, 'Institutions suspected by the Russian Government of violating export control legislation', URL <http://cns.miis.edu/research/summit/9firms.htm>.

subject to controls but rather stainless steel, although the export may have violated other customs laws and foreign exchange regulations.[22]

Following the investigations the Russian offices of an Iranian industrial group, Sanam, were closed and a group of Iranian students at the Baltic State Technical University (who were employees of Sanam) were sent home.

Non-proliferation issues are one part of a complex set of internal changes taking place in Russia. In 1998 changes were under way in Russia's export control procedures for missiles and missile-related technologies, in the organization of the government missile and space organizations and in the missile and space-launch vehicle production industry.

Within the Russian Defence Council and Security Council there have been active discussions of the future of Russia's space establishment and industry (both military and civilian), which has been described by President Boris Yeltsin as a central element of military reform.[23]

In the military sphere, the military space forces and missile defence forces are being merged into a unified branch of the armed forces responsible for intelligence gathering, communications, combat command and control, missile early warning and tracking as well as operation of strategic missile forces. In the civil sphere, Russia intends to participate in the development of a new global communications infrastructure partly based on satellites. In this effort the Russian Space Agency (RSA) plays a central role of coordination. Both the military and civilian effort rest on largely the same industrial base.

In 1998 the Russian Ministry of Economy transferred control of the main joint-stock companies engaged in developing and producing equipment to the RSA in order to permit the agency to implement a unified state policy for the missile and space industry. The RSA is also to implement a unified state policy in the development and production of strategic missile technology. Finally, the RSA was also instructed, in cooperation with the Ministry of Defence, to utilize strategic missiles withdrawn from service as space-launch vehicles.[24]

The civilian elements of the overall programme depend on cooperation with foreign partners, notably those in the USA.[25] This cooperation is dependent on the US Government being assured that technology provided for civilian commercial purposes will not be diverted either in to the Russian military programmes or to unauthorized foreign end-users.

[22] The investigation was conducted in cooperation with Azeri customs officers and underlined the potential importance of cooperation within the Commonwealth of Independent States. Interfax (Moscow), 22 Apr. 1998, in 'Azerbaijan: Azeri customs seize Iran-bound missile materials', FBIS-SOV-98-112, 28 Apr. 1998; and 'Transcription by A. Yelizarov of remarks by Major General Aleksandr Zdanovich, chief of the Federal Security Service [FSB] Public Relations Center', *Rossiyskaya Gazeta* (Moscow), 1 July 1998, p. 8, in 'Russia: FSB aide denies dual-use export charges', FBIS-SOV-98-182, 6 July 1998.

[23] In Jan. 1998 Yeltsin said that 'Space activity is of enormous importance in safeguarding national security and strengthening the country's defensive might and its economic, scientific and social development'. Anokhin, P., 'Kremlin's space directive: Russia determines fate of key sector on which country's security and future depend', *Rossiyskiye Vesti*, 21 Jan. 1998, pp. 1, 2, in 'Russia: Yeltsin on space issues at Defense Council', FBIS-SOV-98-021, 23 Jan. 1998. See chapter 4 in this volume.

[24] The implementing legislation for these changes is contained in Presidential decree no. 54, 'On the implementation of state policy in the sphere of the missile and space industry', 20 Jan. 1998; and Russian Federation Government decree no. 440, 'On measures to fulfil Russian Presidential decree no. 54', 12 May 1998.

[25] The US–Russian joint venture company Lockheed–Khrunichev–Energiya, which jointly develops and manufactures the Proton space-launch vehicle, is perhaps the best example.

In 1998 Russia and the USA formed a Joint Commission to Monitor Exports of Nuclear and Missile Technologies.[26] In the wake of the firing by North Korea of a rocket Russia and the United States also agreed to exchange information on missile launches and early-warning procedures. An ad hoc group of experts was to examine the idea of a multilateral missile launch early-warning regime open to other nations.[27]

Russia also undertook an internal programme intended to provide enterprises and companies with information and assistance to establish internal procedures that would allow them to prevent unauthorized foreign transfers of controlled items.[28]

V. The Wassenaar Arrangement on Export Controls for Conventional Arms and Dual-Use Goods and Technology

The Wassenaar Arrangement is an informal grouping of states in which participants exchange information and views on transfers of items contained on agreed lists of munitions and dual-use items, respectively—although there is nothing to exclude participating states from raising other issues. The participating states hope that information exchange and discussion will, by promoting transparency and greater responsibility, prevent destabilizing accumulations of conventional arms and sensitive dual-use technologies. Participating states in the WA use the information gathered through their multilateral discussions when making their national decisions on whether to approve or deny any given request to export a controlled item.

In the public statement following their plenary meeting in December 1998 the participating states underlined the increasing amount of information exchanged in the framework of the Wassenaar Arrangement.[29] During 1998 the participating states considered how to elaborate the meaning of the expression 'destabilising accumulation of conventional arms' for the particular purposes of implementing national export controls. At the meeting in December a document was adopted which contained what were described as 'elements for objective analysis and advice concerning potentially destabilising accumulations of conventional weapons'.[30]

The document identified a series of questions that national authorities might address in the process of deciding whether or not to permit a given transfer. The questions were grouped into six sets under the following headings: Assessment of Motivations of the State under Study; Regional Balance of Forces and the General Situation in the Region; Political/Economic Standing/Status of the State; Operational Capability; Acquisition of Military Technology; and Other Factors.

While the paper released by the Wassenaar Arrangement is not considered exhaustive, it would in some cases require a thorough analysis of the strategic environment into which conventional arms may be introduced before an export licence was

[26] ITAR-TASS (Moscow), 24 July 1998, in 'Russia: Russian Prime Minister, Gore issue joint statement', FBIS-SOV-98-205, 27 July 1998.

[27] These efforts are discussed in chapter 12 in this volume.

[28] 'Procedural guide for establishment of intraorganizational export control at enterprise', *Rossiyskaya Gazeta* (Moscow), 15 May 1998, in 'Russia: "methodological guide" for export control', FBIS-SOV-98-139, 21 May 1998.

[29] Wassenaar Arrangement on Export Controls for Conventional Arms and Dual-Use Goods and Technology, Public Statement, Vienna, 3 Dec. 1998.

[30] Elements for objective analysis and advice concerning potentially destabilising accumulations of conventional weapons, non-binding paper approved by the Wassenaar Arrangement, 3 Dec. 1998. It is available at URL <http://www.wassenaar.org> or URL <http://www.sipri.se/projects/expcon/expcon.htm>.

approved. For medium-sized and small states this is likely to increase the value of information exchanged in the framework of the WA as they may not have sufficient resources to conduct such an exhaustive analysis on a purely national basis. As such, the paper would seem to be a solid foundation for further development of the Wassenaar Arrangement.

At the meeting changes were also introduced to the control lists to eliminate coverage of commonly available civil telecommunications equipment and to update controls on encryption technologies to reflect the development and availability of commercial encryption products.

The Wassenaar Arrangement seeks to complement and reinforce other processes and initiatives without duplication. Reference was made in the public statement to processes intended to address the negative impact that transfers of small arms and light weapons may have.[31]

[31] Control of the trade in light weapons is discussed in appendix 11E in this volume.

Annexes

Annexe A. Arms control and disarmament agreements

Annexe B. Chronology 1998

Annexe A. Arms control and disarmament agreements

RAGNHILD FERM

Notes

1. The agreements are listed in the order of the date on which they were opened for signature (multilateral agreements) or signed (bilateral agreements); the date on which they entered into force and the depositary for multilateral treaties are also given. Information is as of 1 January 1999 unless otherwise indicated. Where confirmed information on entry into force or new parties became available in early 1999, this information is also given in notes.

2. The main source of information is the lists of signatories and parties provided by the depositaries of the treaties.

3. For a few major treaties, the substantive parts of the most important reservations, declarations and/or interpretive statements made in connection with a state's signature, ratification, accession or succession are given in footnotes below the list of parties.

4. The Russian Federation, constituted in 1991 as an independent state, has confirmed the continuity of international obligations assumed by the Soviet Union. The other former Soviet republics which were constituted in 1991 as independent sovereign states have subsequently signed, ratified or acceded to agreements in order to become signatories/parties.

5. Czechoslovakia split into two states, the Czech Republic and Slovakia, in 1993. Both states have succeeded to all the agreements listed in this annexe to which Czechoslovakia was a party.

6. The Socialist Federal Republic of Yugoslavia split into several states in 1991–92. The international legal status of what remains of the former Yugoslavia—the Federal Republic of Yugoslavia (FRY)—is ambiguous, but since it considers that it is the same entity 'Yugoslavia' is given as a party to those agreements which it has signed or ratified. (The former Yugoslav republics of Bosnia and Herzegovina, Croatia, Macedonia and Slovenia have succeeded, as independent states, to several agreements.)

7. Taiwan, while not recognized as a sovereign state by some nations, is given as a party to those agreements which it has ratified.

8. Unless otherwise stated, the multilateral agreements listed in this annexe are open to all states for signature, ratification, accession or succession.

9. A complete list of UN member states, with the year in which they became members, appears in the glossary at the front of this volume. Not all the states listed in this annexe are UN members.

Protocol for the Prohibition of the Use in War of Asphyxiating, Poisonous or Other Gases, and of Bacteriological Methods of Warfare (Geneva Protocol)

Opened for signature at Geneva on 17 June 1925; entered into force on 8 February 1928; depositary French Government.

The protocol declares that the parties agree to be bound by the prohibition on the use in war of these weapons.

Parties (132): Afghanistan, Albania, Algeria,[1] Angola,[1] Antigua and Barbuda, Argentina, Australia, Austria, Bahrain,[1] Bangladesh,[1] Barbados, Belarus, Belgium, Benin, Bhutan, Bolivia, Brazil, Bulgaria, Burkina Faso, Cambodia, Cameroon, Canada,[4] Cape Verde, Central African Republic, Chile, China,[1] Côte d'Ivoire, Cuba, Cyprus, Czech Republic, Denmark, Dominican Republic, Ecuador, Egypt, Equatorial Guinea, Estonia, Ethiopia, Fiji,[1] Finland, France, Gambia, Germany, Ghana, Greece, Grenada, Guatemala, Guinea-Bissau, Holy See, Hungary, Iceland, India, Indonesia, Iran, Iraq,[1] Ireland, Israel,[2] Italy, Jamaica, Japan, Jordan,[3] Kenya, Korea (North),[1] Korea (South),[1] Kuwait,[1] Laos, Latvia, Lebanon, Lesotho, Liberia, Libya,[1] Liechtenstein, Lithuania, Luxembourg, Madagascar, Malawi, Malaysia, Maldives, Malta, Mauritius, Mexico, Monaco, Mongolia, Morocco, Nepal, Netherlands, New Zealand, Nicaragua, Niger, Nigeria,[1] Norway, Pakistan, Panama, Papua New Guinea,[1] Paraguay, Peru, Philippines, Poland, Portugal,[1] Qatar, Romania, Russia,[4] Rwanda, Saint Kitts (Christopher) and Nevis, Saint Lucia, Saudi Arabia, Senegal, Sierra Leone, Slovakia, Solomon Islands, South Africa, Spain, Sri Lanka, Sudan, Swaziland, Sweden, Switzerland, Syria, Tanzania, Thailand, Togo, Tonga, Trinidad and Tobago, Tunisia, Turkey, Uganda, UK,[4] Uruguay, USA,[4] Venezuela, Viet Nam,[1] Yemen, Yugoslavia

[1] The protocol is binding on this state only as regards states which have signed and ratified or acceded to it. The protocol will cease to be binding on this state in regard to any enemy state whose armed forces or whose allies fail to respect the prohibitions laid down in it.

[2] The protocol is binding on Israel only as regards states which have signed and ratified or acceded to it. The protocol shall cease to be binding on Israel in regard to any enemy state whose armed forces, or the armed forces of whose allies, or the regular or irregular forces, or groups or individuals operating from its territory, fail to respect the prohibitions which are the object of the protocol.

[3] Jordan undertakes to respect the obligations contained in the protocol with regard to states which have undertaken similar commitments. It is not bound by the protocol as regards states whose armed forces, regular or irregular, do not respect the provisions of the protocol.

[4] The protocol shall cease to be binding on this state with respect to use in war of asphyxiating, poisonous or other gases, and of all analogous liquids, materials or devices, in regard to any enemy state if such state or any of its allies fails to respect the prohibitions laid down in the protocol.

Signed but not ratified: El Salvador

Treaty for Collaboration in Economic, Social and Cultural Matters and for Collective Self-defence among Western European states (Brussels Treaty)

Opened for signature at Brussels on 17 March 1948; entered into force on 25 August 1948; depositary Belgian Government.

The treaty provides for close cooperation of the parties in the military, economic and political fields.

Parties (7): *Original parties:* Belgium, France, Luxembourg, Netherlands, UK. Germany and Italy acceded through the 1954 Protocols.

See also the Protocols of 1954.

Convention on the Prevention and Punishment of the Crime of Genocide (Genocide Convention)

Adopted at Paris by the UN General Assembly on 9 December 1948; entered into force on 12 January 1951; depositary UN Secretary-General.

Under the convention any commission of acts intended to destroy, in whole or in part, a national, ethnic, racial or religious group as such is declared to be a crime punishable under international law.

Parties (128): Afghanistan, Albania,* Algeria,* Antigua and Barbuda, Argentina,* Armenia, Australia, Austria, Azerbaijan, Bahamas, Bahrain,* Bangladesh, Barbados, Belarus,* Belgium, Belize, Bosnia and Herzegovina, Brazil, Bulgaria,* Burkina Faso, Burundi, Cambodia, Canada, Chile, China,* Colombia, Congo (Democratic Republic of), Costa Rica, Côte d'Ivoire, Croatia, Cuba, Cyprus, Czech Republic, Denmark, Ecuador, Egypt, El Salvador, Estonia, Ethiopia, Fiji, Finland,* France, Gabon, Gambia, Georgia, Germany, Ghana, Greece, Guatemala, Haiti, Honduras, Hungary,* Iceland, India,* Iran, Iraq, Ireland, Israel, Italy, Jamaica, Jordan, Kazakhstan, Korea (North), Korea (South), Kuwait, Kyrgyzstan, Laos, Latvia, Lebanon, Lesotho, Liberia, Libya, Liechtenstein, Lithuania, Luxembourg, Macedonia (Former Yugoslav Republic of), Malaysia,* Maldives, Mali, Mexico, Moldova, Monaco, Mongolia,* Morocco,* Mozambique, Myanmar (Burma),* Namibia, Nepal, Netherlands, New Zealand, Nicaragua, Norway, Pakistan, Panama, Papua New Guinea, Peru, Philippines,* Poland,* Romania,* Russia,* Rwanda,* Saint Vincent and the Grenadines, Saudi Arabia, Senegal, Seychelles, Singapore,* Slovakia, Slovenia, South Africa, Spain,* Sri Lanka, Sweden, Syria, Tanzania, Togo, Tonga, Tunisia, Turkey, Uganda, UK, Ukraine,* Uruguay, USA,* Venezuela,* Viet Nam,* Yemen,* Yugoslavia, Zimbabwe

*With reservation and/or declaration upon ratification, accession or succession.

Signed but not ratified: Bolivia, Dominican Republic, Paraguay

Geneva Convention IV Relative to the Protection of Civilian Persons in Time of War

Opened for signature at Geneva on 12 August 1949; entered into force on 21 October 1950; depositary Swiss Federal Council.

The convention establishes rules for the protection of civilians in areas covered by war and on occupied territories.

Parties (188): Afghanistan, Albania,* Algeria, Andorra, Angola,* Antigua and Barbuda, Argentina, Armenia, Australia,* Austria, Azerbaijan, Bahamas, Bahrain, Bangladesh, Barbados,* Belarus,* Belgium, Belize, Benin, Bhutan, Bolivia, Bosnia and Herzegovina, Botswana, Brazil, Brunei, Bulgaria,* Burkina Faso, Burundi, Cambodia, Cameroon, Canada, Cape Verde, Central African Republic, Chad, Chile, China,* Colombia, Comoros, Congo (Brazzaville), Congo (Democratic Republic of), Costa Rica, Côte d'Ivoire, Croatia, Cuba, Cyprus, Czech Republic,* Denmark, Djibouti, Dominica, Dominican Republic, Ecuador, Egypt, El Salvador, Equatorial Guinea, Estonia, Ethiopia, Fiji, Finland, France, Gabon, Gambia, Georgia, Germany,* Ghana, Greece, Grenada, Guatemala, Guinea, Guinea-Bissau,* Guyana, Haiti, Holy See, Honduras, Hungary,* Iceland, India, Indonesia, Iran,* Iraq, Ireland, Israel,* Italy, Jamaica, Japan, Jordan, Kazakhstan, Kenya, Kiribati, Korea (North),* Korea (South),* Kuwait,* Kyrgyzstan, Laos, Latvia, Lebanon, Lesotho, Liberia, Libya, Liechtenstein, Lithuania, Luxembourg, Macedonia (Former Yugoslav Republic of),* Madagascar, Malawi, Malaysia, Maldives, Mali, Malta, Mauritania, Mauritius, Mexico, Micronesia, Moldova, Monaco, Mongolia, Morocco, Mozambique, Myanmar (Burma), Namibia, Nepal, Netherlands, New Zealand, Nicaragua, Niger, Nigeria, Norway, Oman, Pakistan,* Palau, Panama, Papua

New Guinea, Paraguay, Peru, Philippines, Poland,* Portugal,* Qatar, Romania,* Russia,* Rwanda, Saint Kitts (Christopher) and Nevis, Saint Lucia, Saint Vincent and the Grenadines, Samoa (Western), San Marino, Sao Tome and Principe, Saudi Arabia, Senegal, Seychelles, Sierra Leone, Singapore,* Slovakia,* Slovenia, Solomon Islands, Somalia, South Africa, Spain, Sri Lanka, Sudan, Suriname,* Swaziland, Sweden, Switzerland, Syria, Tajikistan, Tanzania, Thailand, Togo, Tonga, Trinidad and Tobago, Tunisia, Turkey, Turkmenistan, Tuvalu, Uganda, UK, Ukraine,* United Arab Emirates, Uruguay,* USA,* Uzbekistan, Vanuatu, Venezuela, Viet Nam,* Yemen,* Yugoslavia,* Zambia, Zimbabwe

* With reservation and/or declaration upon ratification, accession or succession.

Note: Kenya acceded to the conventions on 23 February 1999.

In 1989 the Palestine Liberation Organization (PLO) informed the depositary that it had decided to adhere to the four Geneva Conventions and the two Protocols of 1977.

See also Protocols I and II of 1977.

Protocols to the 1948 Brussels Treaty (Paris Agreements on the Western European Union)

Opened for signature at Paris on 23 October 1954; entered into force on 6 May 1955; depositary Belgian Government.

The three protocols modify the 1948 Brussels Treaty, allowing the Federal Republic of Germany and Italy to become parties in return for controls over German armaments and force levels (annulled, except for weapons of mass destruction, in 1984). The Protocols to the Brussels Treaty are regarded as having created the Western European Union (WEU). *Members of the WEU:* Belgium, France, Germany, Greece, Italy, Luxembourg, Netherlands, Portugal, Spain, UK.

Antarctic Treaty

Opened for signature at Washington, DC, on 1 December 1959; entered into force on 23 June 1961; depositary US Government.

Declares the Antarctic an area to be used exclusively for peaceful purposes. Prohibits any measure of a military nature in the Antarctic, such as the establishment of military bases and fortifications, and the carrying out of military manoeuvres or the testing of any type of weapon. The treaty bans any nuclear explosion as well as the disposal of radioactive waste material in Antarctica.

In accordance with Article IX, consultative meetings are convened at regular intervals to exchange information and hold consultations on matters pertaining to Antarctica, as well as to recommend to the governments measures in furtherance of the principles and objectives of the treaty.

The treaty is subject to ratification by the signatories and is open for accession by UN members or by other states invited to accede with the consent of all the parties entitled to participate in the consultative meetings provided for in Article IX.

Parties (43): Argentina,† Australia,† Austria, Belgium,† Brazil,† Bulgaria, Canada, Chile,† China,† Colombia, Cuba, Czech Republic, Denmark, Ecuador,† Finland,† France,† Germany,† Greece, Guatemala, Hungary, India,† Italy,† Japan,† Korea (North), Korea (South),† Netherlands,† New Zealand,† Norway,† Papua New Guinea, Peru,† Poland,† Romania,* Russia,† Slovakia, South Africa,† Spain,† Sweden,† Switzerland, Turkey, UK,† Ukraine, Uruguay,*† USA†

* With reservation and/or declaration upon ratification, accession or succession.

† Party entitled to participate in the consultative meetings.

The Protocol on Environmental Protection to the Antarctic Treaty (**Madrid Protocol**) was signed on 4 October 1991 and entered into force on 14 January 1998.

Treaty Banning Nuclear Weapon Tests in the Atmosphere, in Outer Space and Under Water (Partial Test Ban Treaty, PTBT)

Opened for signature at Moscow on 5 August 1963; entered into force on 10 October 1963; depositaries British, US and Russian governments.

Prohibits the carrying out of any nuclear weapon test explosion or any other nuclear explosion: (*a*) in the atmosphere, beyond its limits, including outer space, or under water, including territorial waters or high seas; and (*b*) in any other environment if such explosion causes radioactive debris to be present outside the territorial limits of the state under whose jurisdiction or control the explosion is conducted.

Parties (125): Afghanistan, Antigua and Barbuda, Argentina, Armenia, Australia, Austria, Bahamas, Bangladesh, Belarus, Belgium, Benin, Bhutan, Bolivia, Botswana, Brazil, Bulgaria, Bosnia and Herzegovina, Canada, Cape Verde, Central African Republic, Chad, Chile, Colombia, Congo (Democratic Republic of), Costa Rica, Côte d'Ivoire, Croatia, Cyprus, Czech Republic, Denmark, Dominican Republic, Ecuador, Egypt, El Salvador, Equatorial Guinea, Fiji, Finland, Gabon, Gambia, Germany, Ghana, Greece, Guatemala, Guinea-Bissau, Honduras, Hungary, Iceland, India, Indonesia, Iran, Iraq, Ireland, Israel, Italy, Jamaica, Japan, Jordan, Kenya, Korea (South), Kuwait, Laos, Lebanon, Liberia, Libya, Luxembourg, Madagascar, Malawi, Malaysia, Malta, Mauritania, Mauritius, Mexico, Mongolia, Morocco, Myanmar (Burma), Nepal, Netherlands, New Zealand, Nicaragua, Niger, Nigeria, Norway, Pakistan, Panama, Papua New Guinea, Peru, Philippines, Poland, Romania, Russia, Rwanda, Samoa (Western), San Marino, Senegal, Seychelles, Sierra Leone, Singapore, Slovakia, Slovenia, South Africa, Spain, Sri Lanka, Sudan, Suriname, Swaziland, Sweden, Switzerland, Syria, Taiwan, Tanzania, Thailand, Togo, Tonga, Trinidad and Tobago, Tunisia, Turkey, Uganda, UK, Ukraine, Uruguay, USA, Venezuela, Yemen, Yugoslavia, Zambia

Signed but not ratified: Algeria, Burkina Faso, Burundi, Cameroon, Ethiopia, Haiti, Mali, Paraguay, Portugal, Somalia

Treaty on Principles Governing the Activities of States in the Exploration and Use of Outer Space, Including the Moon and Other Celestial Bodies (Outer Space Treaty)

Opened for signature at London, Moscow and Washington, DC, on 27 January 1967; entered into force on 10 October 1967; depositaries British, Russian and US governments.

Prohibits the placing into orbit around the earth of any objects carrying nuclear weapons or any other kinds of weapons of mass destruction, the installation of such weapons on celestial bodies, or the stationing of them in outer space in any other manner. The establishment of military bases, installations and fortifications, the testing of any type of weapons and the conduct of military manoeuvres on celestial bodies are also forbidden.

Parties (96): Afghanistan, Algeria, Antigua and Barbuda, Argentina, Australia, Austria, Bahamas, Bangladesh, Barbados, Belarus, Belgium, Benin, Brazil,* Bulgaria, Burkina Faso, Canada, Chile, China, Cuba, Cyprus, Czech Republic, Denmark, Dominican Republic, Ecuador, Egypt, El Salvador, Equatorial Guinea, Fiji, Finland, France, Germany, Greece, Guinea-Bissau, Hungary, Iceland, India, Iraq, Ireland, Israel, Italy, Jamaica, Japan, Kazakhstan, Kenya, Korea (South), Kuwait, Laos, Lebanon, Libya, Madagascar,* Mali, Mauritius, Mexico, Mongolia, Morocco, Myanmar (Burma), Nepal, Netherlands, New Zealand, Niger, Nigeria, Norway, Pakistan, Papua New Guinea, Peru, Poland, Portugal, Romania, Russia, San Marino, Saudi Arabia, Seychelles, Sierra Leone, Singapore, Slovakia, South Africa, Spain, Sri Lanka, Sweden, Switzerland, Syria, Taiwan, Thailand, Togo, Tonga, Tunisia, Turkey, Uganda, UK, Ukraine, Uruguay, USA, Venezuela, Viet Nam, Yemen, Zambia

* With reservation and/or declaration upon ratification, accession or succession.

Signed but not ratified: Bolivia, Botswana, Burundi, Cameroon, Central African Republic, Colombia, Congo (Democratic Republic of), Ethiopia, Gambia, Ghana, Guyana, Haiti, Holy See, Honduras, Indonesia, Iran, Jordan, Lesotho, Luxembourg, Malaysia, Nicaragua, Panama, Philippines, Rwanda, Somalia, Trinidad and Tobago, Yugoslavia

Treaty for the Prohibition of Nuclear Weapons in Latin America and the Caribbean (Treaty of Tlatelolco)

Opened for signature at Mexico, Distrito Federal, on 14 February 1967; entered into force on 22 April 1968. The treaty was amended in 1990, 1991 and 1992; depositary Mexican Government.

Prohibits the testing, use, manufacture, production or acquisition by any means, as well as the receipt, storage, installation, deployment and any form of possession of any nuclear weapons by Latin American and Caribbean countries.

The parties should conclude agreements with the IAEA for the application of safeguards to their nuclear activities. The IAEA has the exclusive power to carry out special inspections.

The treaty is open for signature by all the independent states of the region.

Under *Additional Protocol I* states with territories within the zone (France, the Netherlands, the UK and the USA) undertake to apply the statute of military denuclearization to these territories.

Under *Additional Protocol II* the recognized nuclear weapon states (China, France, Russia (at the time of signing, the USSR), the UK and the USA) undertake to respect the statute of military denuclearization of Latin America and not to contribute to acts involving a violation of the treaty, nor to use or threaten to use nuclear weapons against the parties to the treaty.

Parties to the original treaty (32): Antigua and Barbuda, Argentina, Bahamas, Barbados, Belize, Bolivia, Brazil, Chile, Colombia, Costa Rica, Dominica, Dominican Republic, Ecuador, El Salvador, Grenada, Guatemala, Guyana, Haiti, Honduras, Jamaica, Mexico, Nicaragua, Panama, Paraguay, Peru, Saint Kitts (Christopher) and Nevis, Saint Lucia, Saint Vincent and the Grenadines, Suriname, Trinidad and Tobago, Uruguay, Venezuela

Parties to the amended treaty (12): Argentina, Barbados, Brazil, Chile, Guyana, Jamaica, Mexico, Paraguay, Peru, Suriname, Uruguay and Venezuela. (Note that some countries have ratified only certain amendments.)

Parties to Additional Protocol I: France,[1] Netherlands, UK,[2] USA[3]

Parties to Additional Protocol II: China,[4] France,[5] Russia,[6] UK,[2] USA[7]

Signed but not ratified: Cuba

[1] France declared that Protocol I shall not apply to transit across French territories situated within the zone of the treaty, and destined for other French territories. The protocol shall not limit the participation of the populations of the French territories in the activities mentioned in Article 1 of the treaty, and in efforts connected with the national defence of France. France does not consider the zone described in the

treaty as established in accordance with international law; it cannot, therefore, agree that the treaty should apply to that zone.

[2] When signing and ratifying Protocols I and II, the UK made the following declarations of understanding: The signing and ratification by the UK could not be regarded as affecting in any way the legal status of any territory for the international relations of which the UK is responsible, lying within the limits of the geographical zone established by the treaty. Should any party to the treaty carry out any act of aggression with the support of a nuclear weapon state, the UK would be free to reconsider the extent to which it could be regarded as bound by the provisions of Protocol II.

[3] The USA ratified Protocol I with the following understandings: The provisions of the treaty do not affect the exclusive power and legal competence under international law of a state adhering to this Protocol to grant or deny transit and transport privileges to its own or any other vessels or aircraft irrespective of cargo or armaments; the provisions do not affect rights under international law of a state adhering to this protocol regarding the exercise of the freedom of the seas, or regarding passage through or over waters subject to the sovereignty of a state. The declarations attached by the USA to its ratification of Protocol II apply also to Protocol I.

[4] China declared that it will never send its means of transportation and delivery carrying nuclear weapons to cross the territory, territorial sea or airspace of Latin American countries.

[5] France stated that it interprets the undertaking contained in Article 3 of Protocol II to mean that it presents no obstacle to the full exercise of the right of self-defence enshrined in Article 51 of the UN Charter; it takes note of the interpretation by the Preparatory Commission for the Denuclearization of Latin America according to which the treaty does not apply to transit, the granting or denying of which lies within the exclusive competence of each state party in accordance with international law. In 1974, France made a supplementary statement to the effect that it was prepared to consider its obligations under Protocol II as applying not only to the signatories of the treaty, but also to the territories for which the statute of denuclearization was in force in conformity with Protocol I.

[6] The USSR signed and ratified Protocol II with the following statement:

The USSR proceeds from the assumption that the effect of Article 1 of the treaty extends to any nuclear explosive device and that, accordingly, the carrying out by any party of nuclear explosions for peaceful purposes would be a violation of its obligations under Article 1 and would be incompatible with its non-nuclear weapon status. For states parties to the treaty, a solution to the problem of peaceful nuclear explosions can be found in accordance with the provisions of Article V of the NPT and within the framework of the international procedures of the IAEA. The USSR declares that authorizing the transit of nuclear weapons in any form would be contrary to the objectives of the treaty.

Any actions undertaken by a state or states parties to the treaty which are not compatible with their non-nuclear weapon status, and also the commission by one or more states parties to the treaty of an act of aggression with the support of a state which is in possession of nuclear weapons or together with such a state, will be regarded by the USSR as incompatible with the obligations of those countries under the treaty. In such cases the USSR reserves the right to reconsider its obligations under Protocol II. It further reserves the right to reconsider its attitude to this protocol in the event of any actions on the part of other states possessing nuclear weapons which are incompatible with their obligations under the said protocol.

[7] The USA signed and ratified Protocol II with the following declarations and understandings: Each of the parties retains exclusive power and legal competence, to grant or deny non-parties transit and transport privileges. As regards the undertaking not to use or threaten to use nuclear weapons against the parties, the USA would consider that an armed attack by a party, in which it was assisted by a nuclear weapon state, would be incompatible with the treaty.

Treaty on the Non-proliferation of Nuclear Weapons (Non-Proliferation Treaty, NPT)

Opened for signature at London, Moscow and Washington, DC, on 1 July 1968; entered into force on 5 March 1970; depositaries British, Russian and US governments.

Prohibits the transfer by nuclear weapon states (defined in the treaty as those which have manufactured and exploded a nuclear weapon or other nuclear explosive device prior to 1 January 1967) to any recipient whatsoever, of nuclear weapons or other nuclear explosive devices or of control over them, as well as the assistance, encouragement or inducement of any non-nuclear weapon state to manufacture or otherwise acquire such weapons or devices. Prohibits the receipt by non-nuclear weapon states from any transferor whatsoever, as well as the manufacture or other acquisition by those states, of nuclear weapons or other nuclear explosive devices.

The parties undertake to facilitate the exchange of equipment, materials and scientific and technological information for the peaceful uses of nuclear energy and to ensure that potential benefits from peaceful applications of nuclear explosions will be made available to non-nuclear weapon parties to the treaty. They also undertake to pursue negotiations in good faith on effective measures relating to cessation of the nuclear arms race at an early date and to nuclear disarmament, and on a treaty on general and complete disarmament.

Non-nuclear weapon states undertake to conclude safeguard agreements with the International Atomic Energy Agency (IAEA) with a view to preventing diversion of nuclear energy from peaceful uses to nuclear weapons or other nuclear explosive devices. A Model Protocol, additional to the agreements and strengthening the measures, was approved in 1997; Additional Safeguards Protocols are signed by states individually with the IAEA.

A Review and Extension Conference, convened in 1995 in accordance with the treaty, decided that the treaty should remain in force indefinitely.

Parties (188): Afghanistan,[†] Albania, Algeria,[†] Andorra, Angola, Antigua and Barbuda, Argentina,[†] Armenia,[†] Australia,[†] Austria,[†] Azerbaijan, Bahamas,[†] Bahrain, Bangladesh,[†] Barbados,[†] Belarus,[†] Belgium,[†] Belize,[†] Benin, Bhutan,[†] Bolivia,[†] Bosnia and Herzegovina, Botswana, Brazil, Brunei,[†] Bulgaria,[†] Burkina Faso, Burundi, Cambodia, Cameroon, Canada,[†] Cape Verde, Central African Republic, Chad, Chile, China, Colombia, Comoros, Congo (Brazzaville), Congo (Democratic Republic of),[†] Costa Rica,[†] Côte d'Ivoire,[†] Croatia,[†] Cyprus,[†] Czech Republic,[†] Denmark,[†] Djibouti, Dominica,[†] Dominican Republic,[†] Ecuador,[†] Egypt,[†] El Salvador,[†] Equatorial Guinea, Eritrea, Estonia,[†] Ethiopia,[†] Fiji,[†] Finland,[†] France,[†] Gabon, Gambia,[†] Georgia, Germany,[†] Ghana,[†] Greece,[†] Grenada,[†] Guatemala,[†] Guinea, Guinea-Bissau, Guyana,[†] Haiti, Holy See,[†] Honduras,[†] Hungary,[†] Iceland,[†] Indonesia,[†] Iran,[†] Iraq,[†] Ireland,[†] Italy,[†] Jamaica,[†] Japan,[†] Jordan,[†] Kazakhstan,[†] Kenya, Kiribati,[†] Korea (North),[†] Korea (South),[†] Kuwait, Kyrgyzstan, Laos, Latvia,[†] Lebanon,[†] Lesotho,[†] Liberia, Libya,[†] Liechtenstein,[†] Lithuania,[†] Luxembourg,[†] Macedonia (Former Yugoslav Republic of), Madagascar,[†] Malawi,[†] Malaysia,[†] Maldives,[†] Mali, Malta,[†] Marshall Islands, Mauritania, Mauritius,[†] Mexico,[†] Micronesia, Moldova, Monaco,[†] Mongolia,[†] Morocco,[†] Mozambique, Myanmar (Burma),[†] Namibia,[†] Nauru,[†] Nepal,[†] Netherlands,[†] New Zealand,[†] Nicaragua,[†] Niger, Nigeria,[†] Norway,[†] Oman, Palau, Panama, Papua New Guinea,[†] Paraguay,[†] Peru,[†] Philippines,[†] Poland,[†] Portugal,[†] Qatar, Romania,[†] Russia,[†] Rwanda, Saint Kitts (Christopher) and Nevis,[†] Saint Lucia,[†] Saint Vincent and the Grenadines,[†] Samoa (Western),[†] San Marino,[†] Sao Tome and Principe, Saudi Arabia, Senegal,[†] Seychelles, Sierra Leone, Singapore,[†] Slovakia,[†] Slovenia,[†] Solomon Islands,[†] Somalia, South Africa,[†] Spain,[†] Sri Lanka,[†] Sudan,[†] Suriname,[†] Swaziland,[†] Sweden,[†] Switzerland,[†] Syria,[†] Taiwan, Tajikistan, Tanzania, Thailand,[†] Togo, Tonga,[†] Trinidad and Tobago,[†] Tunisia,[†] Turkey,[†] Turkmenistan, Tuvalu,[†] Uganda, UK,[†] Ukraine,[†] United Arab Emirates, Uruguay,[†] USA,[†] Uzbekistan, Vanuatu, Venezuela,[†] Viet Nam,[†] Yemen, Yugoslavia,[†] Zambia,[†] Zimbabwe[†]

[†] Party with safeguards agreements in force with the International Atomic Energy Agency (IAEA), as required by the treaty, or concluded by a nuclear weapon state on a voluntary basis.

Additional Safeguards Protocols have been signed by 36 states and Euratom; they are in force for 5 of these states: Australia, Holy See, Jordan, New Zealand and Uzbekistan. Taiwan, although not an IAEA member, has agreed to the application of the measures contained in the protocols.

Treaty on the Prohibition of the Emplacement of Nuclear Weapons and other Weapons of Mass Destruction on the Seabed and the Ocean Floor and in the Subsoil thereof (Seabed Treaty)

Opened for signature at London, Moscow and Washington, DC, on 11 February 1971; entered into force on 18 May 1972; depositaries British, Russian and US governments.

Prohibits implanting or emplacing on the seabed and the ocean floor and in the subsoil thereof beyond the outer limit of a 12-mile seabed zone any nuclear weapons or any other types of weapons of mass destruction as well as structures, launching installations or any other facilities specifically designed for storing, testing or using such weapons.

Parties (94): Afghanistan, Algeria, Antigua and Barbuda, Argentina,[1] Australia, Austria, Bahamas, Belarus, Belgium, Benin, Bosnia and Herzegovina, Botswana, Brazil,[2] Bulgaria, Canada,[3] Cape Verde, Central African Republic, China, Congo (Brazzaville), Côte d'Ivoire, Croatia, Cuba, Cyprus, Czech Republic, Denmark, Dominican Republic, Equatorial Guinea, Ethiopia, Finland, Germany, Ghana, Greece, Guatemala, Guinea-Bissau, Hungary, Iceland, India,[4] Iran, Iraq, Ireland, Italy,[5] Jamaica, Japan, Jordan, Korea (South), Laos, Latvia, Lesotho, Libya, Liechtenstein, Luxembourg, Malaysia, Malta, Mauritius, Mexico,[6] Mongolia, Morocco, Nepal, Netherlands, New Zealand, Nicaragua, Niger, Norway, Panama, Philippines, Poland, Portugal, Qatar, Romania, Russia, Rwanda, Sao Tome and Principe, Saudi Arabia, Seychelles, Singapore, Slovakia, Slovenia, Solomon Islands, South Africa, Spain, Swaziland, Sweden, Switzerland, Taiwan, Togo, Tunisia, Turkey,[7] UK, Ukraine, USA, Viet Nam,[8] Yemen, Yugoslavia,[9] Zambia

Signed but not ratified: Bolivia, Burundi, Cambodia, Cameroon, Colombia, Costa Rica, Gambia, Guinea, Honduras, Lebanon, Liberia, Madagascar, Mali, Myanmar (Burma), Paraguay, Senegal, Sierra Leone, Sudan, Tanzania, Uruguay

[1] Argentina precludes any possibility of strengthening, through this treaty, certain positions concerning continental shelves to the detriment of others based on different criteria.

[2] Brazil stated that nothing in the treaty shall be interpreted as prejudicing in any way the sovereign rights of Brazil in the area of the sea, the seabed and the subsoil thereof adjacent to its coasts. It is the understanding of Brazil that the word 'observation', as it appears in para. 1 of Article III of the treaty, refers only to observation that is incidental to the normal course of navigation in accordance with international law.

[3] Canada declared that Article I, para. 1, cannot be interpreted as indicating that any state has a right to implant or emplace any weapons not prohibited under Article I, para. 1, on the seabed and ocean floor, and in the subsoil thereof, beyond the limits of national jurisdiction, or as constituting any limitation on the principle that this area of the seabed and ocean floor and the subsoil thereof shall be reserved for exclusively peaceful purposes. Articles I, II and III cannot be interpreted as indicating that any state but the coastal state has any right to implant or emplace any weapon not prohibited under Article I, para. 1 on the continental shelf, or the subsoil thereof, appertaining to that coastal state, beyond the outer limit of the seabed zone referred to in Article I and defined in Article II. Article III cannot be interpreted as indicating any restrictions or limitation upon the rights of the coastal state, consistent with its exclusive sovereign rights with respect to the continental shelf, to verify, inspect or effect the removal of any weapon, structure, installation, facility or device implanted or emplaced on the continental shelf, or the subsoil thereof, appertaining to that coastal state, beyond the outer limit of the seabed zone referred to in Article I and defined in Article II.

[4] The accession by India is based on its position that it has full and exclusive rights over the continental shelf adjoining its territory and beyond its territorial waters and the subsoil thereof. There cannot, therefore, be any restriction on, or limitation of, the sovereign right of India as a coastal state to verify, inspect, remove or destroy any weapon, device, structure, installation or facility, which might be implanted or emplaced on or beneath its continental shelf by any other country, or to take such other steps as may be considered necessary to safeguard its security.

[5] Italy stated, *inter alia*, that in the case of agreements on further measures in the field of disarmament to prevent an arms race on the seabed and ocean floor and in their subsoil, the question of the delimita-

tion of the area within which these measures would find application shall have to be examined and solved in each instance in accordance with the nature of the measures to be adopted.

[6] Mexico declared that the treaty cannot be interpreted to mean that a state has the right to emplace weapons of mass destruction, or arms or military equipment of any type, on the continental shelf of Mexico. It reserves the right to verify, inspect, remove or destroy any weapon, structure, installation, device or equipment placed on its continental shelf, including nuclear weapons or other weapons of mass destruction.

[7] Turkey declared that the provisions of Article II cannot be used by a state party in support of claims other than those related to disarmament. Hence, Article II cannot be interpreted as establishing a link with the UN Convention on the Law of the Sea. Furthermore, no provision of the Seabed Treaty confers on parties the right to militarize zones which have been demilitarized by other international instruments. Nor can it be interpreted as conferring on either the coastal states or other states the right to emplace nuclear weapons or other weapons of mass destruction on the continental shelf of a demilitarized territory.

[8] Viet Nam stated that no provision of the treaty should be interpreted in a way that would contradict the rights of the coastal states with regard to their continental shelf, including the right to take measures to ensure their security.

[9] In 1974, the Ambassador of Yugoslavia transmitted to the US Secretary of State a note stating that in the view of the Yugoslav Government, Article III, para. 1, of the treaty should be interpreted in such a way that a state exercising its right under this article shall be obliged to notify in advance the coastal state, in so far as its observations are to be carried out 'within the stretch of the sea extending above the continental shelf of the said state'. The USA objected to the Yugoslav reservation, which it considers incompatible with the object and purpose of the treaty.

Convention on the Prohibition of the Development, Production and Stockpiling of Bacteriological (Biological) and Toxin Weapons and on their Destruction (Biological and Toxin Weapons Convention, BTWC)

Opened for signature at London, Moscow and Washington, DC, on 10 April 1972; entered into force on 26 March 1975; depositaries British, Russian and US governments.

Prohibits the development, production, stockpiling or acquisition by other means or retention of microbial or other biological agents, or toxins whatever their origin or method of production, of types and in quantities that have no justification of prophylactic, protective or other peaceful purposes, as well as weapons, equipment or means of delivery designed to use such agents or toxins for hostile purposes or in armed conflict. The destruction of the agents, toxins, weapons, equipment and means of delivery in the possession of the parties, or their diversion to peaceful purposes, should be effected not later than nine months after the entry into force of the convention. According to a mandate from the 1996 BTWC Review Conference, verification and other measures to strengthen the convention are being discussed and considered in an Ad Hoc Group.

Parties (142): Afghanistan, Albania, Argentina, Armenia, Australia, Austria, Bahamas, Bahrain, Bangladesh, Barbados, Belarus, Belgium, Belize, Benin, Bhutan, Bolivia, Bosnia and Herzegovina, Botswana, Brazil, Brunei, Bulgaria, Burkina Faso, Cambodia, Canada, Cape Verde, Chile, China, Colombia, Congo (Brazzaville), Congo (Democratic Republic of), Costa Rica, Croatia, Cuba, Cyprus, Czech Republic, Denmark, Dominica, Dominican Republic, Ecuador, El Salvador, Equatorial Guinea, Estonia, Ethiopia, Fiji, Finland, France, Gambia, Georgia, Germany, Ghana, Greece, Grenada, Guatemala, Guinea-Bissau, Honduras, Hungary, Iceland, India,* Indonesia, Iran, Iraq, Ireland,* Italy, Jamaica, Japan, Jordan, Kenya, Korea (North), Korea (South), Kuwait, Laos, Latvia, Lebanon, Lesotho, Libya, Liechtenstein, Lithuania, Luxembourg, Macedonia (Former Yugoslav Republic of), Malaysia, Maldives, Malta, Mauritius, Mexico,* Mongolia, Netherlands, New Zealand, Nicaragua, Niger, Nigeria, Norway, Oman, Pakistan, Panama, Papua New Guinea, Paraguay, Peru, Philippines, Poland, Portugal, Qatar, Romania, Russia, Rwanda, Saint Kitts (Christopher) and Nevis, Saint Lucia,

San Marino, Sao Tome and Principe, Saudi Arabia, Senegal, Seychelles, Sierra Leone, Singapore, Slovakia, Slovenia, Solomon Islands, South Africa, Spain, Sri Lanka, Suriname, Swaziland, Sweden, Switzerland,* Taiwan, Thailand, Togo, Tonga, Tunisia, Turkey, Turkmenistan, Uganda, UK, Ukraine, Uruguay, USA, Uzbekistan, Vanuatu, Venezuela, Viet Nam, Yemen, Yugoslavia, Zimbabwe

* With reservation and/or declaration upon ratification, accession or succession.

Signed but not ratified: Burundi, Central African Republic, Côte d'Ivoire, Egypt, Gabon, Guyana, Haiti, Liberia, Madagascar, Malawi, Mali, Morocco, Myanmar (Burma), Nepal, Somalia, Syria, Tanzania, United Arab Emirates

Treaty on the Limitation of Anti-Ballistic Missile systems (ABM Treaty)

Signed by the USA and the USSR at Moscow on 26 May 1972; entered into force on 3 October 1972.

The treaty obligates the parties not to build nationwide defences against ballistic missile attack and limits the development and deployment of permitted strategic missile defences. It prohibits the parties from giving air defence missiles, radars or launchers the technical ability to counter strategic ballistic missiles and from testing them in a strategic ABM mode.

A *Protocol* to the ABM Treaty, introducing further numerical restrictions on permitted ballistic missile defences, was signed in 1974.

In September 1997 a Memorandum of Understanding (MOU) was signed in which Belarus, Kazakhstan, Russia and Ukraine would assume the obligations of the former USSR regarding the treaty. Russia and the USA also signed a set of Agreed Statements specifying the technical parameters for distinguishing between strategic missile defences which are not permitted by the treaty and non-strategic or theatre missile defences which are permitted under the treaty. The MOU and Agreed Statements must be ratified by the legislatures of all five states.

Treaty on the Limitation of Underground Nuclear Weapon Tests (Threshold Test Ban Treaty, TTBT)

Signed by the USA and the USSR at Moscow on 3 July 1974; entered into force on 11 December 1990.

The parties undertake not to carry out any individual underground nuclear weapon test having a yield exceeding 150 kilotons.

Treaty on Underground Nuclear Explosions for Peaceful Purposes (Peaceful Nuclear Explosions Treaty, PNET)

Signed by the USA and the USSR at Moscow and Washington, DC, on 28 May 1976; entered into force on 11 December 1990.

The parties undertake not to carry out any underground nuclear explosion for peaceful purposes having a yield exceeding 150 kilotons or any group explosion having an aggregate yield exceeding 150 kilotons.

Convention on the Prohibition of Military or Any Other Hostile Use of Environmental Modification Techniques (Enmod Convention)

Opened for signature at Geneva on 18 May 1977; entered into force on 5 October 1978; depositary UN Secretary-General.

Prohibits military or any other hostile use of environmental modification techniques having widespread, long-lasting or severe effects as the means of destruction, damage or injury to states party to the convention. The term 'environmental modification techniques' refers to any technique for changing—through the deliberate manipulation of natural processes—the dynamics, composition or structure of the earth, including its biota, lithosphere, hydrosphere and atmosphere, or of outer space. The understandings reached during the negotiations, but not written into the convention, define the terms 'widespread', 'long-lasting' and 'severe'.

Parties (64): Afghanistan, Algeria, Antigua and Barbuda, Argentina, Australia, Austria, Bangladesh, Belarus, Belgium, Benin, Brazil, Bulgaria, Canada, Cape Verde, Chile, Costa Rica, Cuba, Cyprus, Czech Republic, Denmark, Dominica, Egypt, Finland, Germany, Ghana, Greece, Guatemala, Hungary, India, Ireland, Italy, Japan, Korea (North), Korea (South),* Kuwait, Laos, Malawi, Mauritius, Mongolia, Netherlands,* New Zealand, Niger, Norway, Pakistan, Papua New Guinea, Poland, Romania, Russia, Saint Lucia, Sao Tome and Principe, Slovakia, Solomon Islands, Spain, Sri Lanka, Sweden, Switzerland, Tunisia, UK, Ukraine, Uruguay, USA, Uzbekistan, Viet Nam, Yemen

* With reservation and/or declaration upon ratification, accession or succession.

Signed but not ratified: Bolivia, Congo (Democratic Republic of), Ethiopia, Holy See, Iceland, Iran, Iraq, Lebanon, Liberia, Luxembourg, Morocco, Nicaragua, Portugal, Sierra Leone, Syria, Turkey, Uganda

Protocol I Additional to the 1949 Geneva Conventions, and Relating to the Protection of Victims of International Armed Conflict, and Protocol II Additional to the 1949 Geneva Conventions, and Relating to the Protection of Victims of Non-International Armed Conflicts

Opened for signature at Bern on 12 December 1977; entered into force on 7 December 1978; depositary Swiss Federal Council.

The protocols confirm that the right of the parties to international or non-international armed conflicts to choose methods or means of warfare is not unlimited and that it is prohibited to use weapons or means of warfare which cause superfluous injury or unnecessary suffering.

Parties to Protocol I (152) and Protocol II (145): Albania, Algeria,* Angola,[1]* Antigua and Barbuda, Argentina,* Armenia, Australia,* Austria,* Bahamas, Bahrain, Bangladesh, Barbados, Belarus, Belgium,* Belize, Benin, Bolivia, Bosnia and Herzegovina, Botswana, Brazil, Brunei, Bulgaria, Burkina Faso, Burundi, Cambodia, Cameroon, Canada,* Cape Verde, Central African Republic, Chad, Chile, China,* Colombia, Comoros, Congo (Brazzaville), Congo (Democratic Republic of),[1] Costa Rica, Côte d'Ivoire, Croatia, Cuba,[1] Cyprus, Czech Republic, Denmark,* Djibouti, Dominica, Dominican Republic, Ecuador, Egypt,* El Salvador, Equatorial Guinea, Estonia, Ethiopia, Finland,* France,[2] Gabon, Gambia, Georgia,

Germany,* Ghana, Greece, Grenada,[3] Guatemala, Guinea, Guinea-Bissau, Guyana, Holy See,* Honduras, Hungary, Iceland,* Italy,* Jamaica, Jordan, Kazakhstan, Korea (North),[1] Korea (South),* Kuwait, Kyrgyzstan, Laos, Latvia, Lebanon, Lesotho, Liberia, Libya, Liechtenstein,* Luxembourg, Macedonia (Former Yugoslav Republic of), Madagascar, Malawi, Maldives, Mali, Malta,* Mauritania, Mauritius, Mexico,[1] Micronesia, Moldova, Mongolia, Mozambique,[1] Namibia, Netherlands,* New Zealand,* Niger, Nigeria, Norway, Oman,* Palau, Panama, Paraguay, Peru, Philippines,[2] Poland, Portugal, Qatar,*[1] Romania, Russia,* Rwanda, Saint Kitts (Christopher) and Nevis, Saint Lucia, Saint Vincent and the Grenadines, Samoa (Western), San Marino, Sao Tome and Principe, Saudi Arabia,[1]* Senegal, Seychelles, Sierra Leone, Slovakia, Slovenia, Solomon Islands, South Africa, Spain,* Suriname, Swaziland, Sweden,* Switzerland,* Syria,*[1] Tajikistan, Tanzania, Togo, Tunisia, Turkmenistan, Uganda, UK, Ukraine, United Arab Emirates,* Uruguay, Uzbekistan, Vanuatu, Venezuela,[1] Viet Nam,[1] Yemen, Yugoslavia,* Zambia, Zimbabwe

Note: Kenya acceded to the protocols on 23 February 1999.

In 1989 the Palestine Liberation Organization (PLO) informed the depositary that it had decided to adhere to the four Geneva Conventions and the two Protocols.

* With reservation and/or declaration upon ratification, accession or succession.

[1] Party only to Protocol I.

[2] Party only to Protocol II.

[3] In accordance with the provisions of the protocols, they enter into force for a party 6 months after the deposit of its instrument of ratification or accession. This state ratified or acceded to the protocols in the second half of 1998 and the protocols entered into force for that state in 1999.

Convention on the Physical Protection of Nuclear Material

Opened for signature at Vienna and New York on 3 March 1980; entered into force on 8 February 1987; Depositary, IAEA Director General.

The convention obliges the parties to protect nuclear material for peaceful purposes during transport across their territory or on ships or aircraft under their jurisdiction.

Parties (58): Antigua and Barbuda, Argentina,* Armenia, Australia, Austria, Belarus, Belgium,† Bosnia and Herzegovina, Brazil, Bulgaria, Canada, Chile, China,* Croatia, Cuba, Cyprus, Czech Republic, Denmark,† Ecuador, Estonia, Euratom,*† Finland, France,*† Germany,† Greece,† Guatemala, Hungary, Indonesia,* Ireland,† Italy,*† Japan, Korea (South),* Lebanon, Liechtenstein, Lithuania, Luxembourg,† Macedonia (Former Yugoslav Republic of), Mexico, Moldova, Monaco, Mongolia,* Netherlands,*† Norway, Paraguay, Peru,* Philippines, Poland,* Portugal, Romania, Russia,* Slovakia, Slovenia, Spain,*† Sweden, Switzerland, Tajikistan, Tunisia, Turkey,* UK,† Ukraine, USA, Uzbekistan, Yugoslavia

* With reservation and/or declaration upon ratification, accession or succession.

† Belgium, Denmark, France, Germany, Greece, Ireland, Italy, Luxembourg, Netherlands, Spain and the UK signed as Euratom member states.

Signed but not ratified: Dominican Republic, Haiti, Israel, Morocco, Niger, Panama, South Africa

Convention on Prohibitions or Restrictions on the Use of Certain Conventional Weapons which may be Deemed to be Excessively Injurious or to have Indiscriminate Effects (CCW Convention, or 'Inhumane Weapons' Convention)

The Convention, with the three original protocols, was opened for signature at New York on 10 April 1981; entered into force on 2 December 1983; depositary UN Secretary-General.

The convention is an 'umbrella treaty', under which specific agreements can be concluded in the form of protocols.

Protocol I prohibits the use of weapons intended to injure by fragments which are not detectable in the human body by X-rays.

Protocol II prohibits or restricts the use of mines, booby-traps and other devices; amendments were adopted on 3 May 1996. The amended Protocol II, reinforcing the constraints regarding landmines, entered into force on 3 December 1998.

Protocol III restricts the use of incendiary weapons.

Protocol IV, adopted in 1995, prohibits the employment of laser weapons specifically designed to cause permanent blindness to unenhanced vision. Protocol IV entered into force on 30 July 1998.

Parties (72): Argentina,* Australia, Austria, Belarus, Belgium, Benin,[1] Bosnia and Herzegovina, Brazil, Bulgaria, Cambodia, Canada, Cape Verde, China, Croatia, Cuba, Cyprus,* Czech Republic, Denmark, Djibouti, Ecuador, Finland, France,*[2] Georgia, Germany, Greece, Guatemala, Holy See, Hungary, India, Ireland, Israel,[2] Italy, Japan, Jordan,[1] Laos, Latvia, Liechtenstein, Lithuania,[1] Luxembourg, Macedonia (Former Yugoslav Republic of), Malta, Mauritius, Mexico, Monaco,[3] Mongolia, Netherlands,* New Zealand, Niger, Norway, Pakistan, Panama, Peru,[1] Philippines, Poland, Portugal, Romania, Russia, Slovakia, Slovenia, South Africa, Spain, Sweden, Switzerland, Togo, Tunisia, Uganda, UK, Ukraine, Uruguay, USA,[2] Uzbekistan, Yugoslavia

* With reservation and/or declaration upon ratification, accession or succession.

[1] Party only to Protocols I and III.
[2] Party only to Protocols I and II.
[3] Party only to Protocol I.

Parties to the amended Protocol II (29): Argentina, Australia, Austria, Bulgaria, Cambodia, Canada, Cape Verde, China, Costa Rica, Czech Republic, Denmark, Finland, France, Germany, Hungary, Ireland, Japan, Liechtenstein, Lithuania, Monaco, New Zealand, Norway, Peru, Philippines, South Africa, Spain, Sweden, Switzerland, Uruguay

Parties to Protocol IV (34): Argentina, Australia, Austria, Bulgaria, Cambodia, Canada, Cape Verde, China, Costa Rica, Czech Republic, Denmark, Finland, France, Germany, Greece, Holy See, Hungary, Ireland, Japan, Latvia, Liechtenstein, Lithuania, Mexico, New Zealand, Norway, Panama, Peru, Philippines, South Africa, Spain, Sweden, Switzerland, Uruguay, Uzbekistan

Note: In the period 1 January–1 April 1999, Belgium, Greece, Italy, the Netherlands, Pakistan, Portugal and the UK became parties to the amended Protocol II; and Belgium, Italy, Netherlands and the UK became parties to Protocol IV.

Signed but not ratified: Afghanistan, Egypt, Iceland, Morocco, Nicaragua, Nigeria, Sierra Leone, Sudan, Turkey, Viet Nam

South Pacific Nuclear Free Zone Treaty (Treaty of Rarotonga)

Opened for signature at Rarotonga, Cook Islands, on 6 August 1985; entered into force on 11 December 1986; depositary Director of the South Pacific Bureau for Economic Co-operation.

Prohibits the manufacture or acquisition by other means of any nuclear explosive device, as well as possession or control over such device by the parties anywhere inside or outside the zone area described in an annex. The parties also undertake not to supply nuclear material or equipment, unless subject to IAEA safeguards, and to prevent in their territories the stationing as well as the testing of any nuclear explosive device and undertake not to dump, and to prevent the dumping of, radioactive wastes and other radioactive matter at sea anywhere within the zone. Each party remains free to allow visits, as well as transit, by foreign ships and aircraft.

The treaty is open for signature by the members of the South Pacific Forum.

Under *Protocol 1* France, the UK and the USA undertake to apply the treaty prohibitions relating to the manufacture, stationing and testing of nuclear explosive devices in the territories situated within the zone, for which they are internationally responsible.

Under *Protocol 2* China, France, Russia, the UK and the USA undertake not to use or threaten to use a nuclear explosive device against the parties to the treaty or against any territory within the zone for which a party to Protocol 1 is internationally responsible.

Under *Protocol 3* China, France, the UK, the USA and Russia undertake not to test any nuclear explosive device anywhere within the zone.

Parties (12): Australia, Cook Islands, Fiji, Kiribati, Nauru, New Zealand, Niue, Papua New Guinea, Samoa (Western), Solomon Islands, Tuvalu, Vanuatu

Signed but not ratified: Tonga

Party to Protocol 1: France, UK; **signed but not ratified:** USA

Parties to Protocol 2: China, France,[1] Russia, UK[2]; **signed but not ratified:** USA

Parties to Protocol 3: China, France, Russia, UK; **signed but not ratified:** USA

[1] France declared that the negative security guarantees set out in Protocol 2 are the same as the CD declaration of 6 Apr. 1995 which were referred to in the UN Security Council Resolution 984 of 11 Apr. 1995.

[2] The UK declared that nothing in the treaty affects the rights under international law with regard to transit of the zone or visits to ports and airfields within the zone by ships and aircraft. The UK will not be bound by the undertakings in Protocol 2 in case of an invasion or any other attack on the UK, its territories, its armed forces or its allies, carried out or sustained by a party to the treaty in association or alliance with a nuclear weapon state or if a party violates its non-proliferation obligations under the treaty.

Treaty on the Elimination of Intermediate-Range and Shorter-Range Missiles (INF Treaty)

Signed by the USA and the USSR at Washington, DC, on 8 December 1987; entered into force on 1 June 1988.

The treaty obliged the parties to destroy all land-based missiles with a range of 500–5500 km (intermediate-range, 1000–5500 km; and shorter-range, 500–1000 km) and their launchers by 1 June 1991. The treaty was implemented by the two parties before this date.

Treaty on Conventional Armed Forces in Europe (CFE Treaty)

Opened for signature at Vienna on 19 November 1990; entered into force on 9 November 1992; depositary Netherlands Government.

The treaty sets ceilings on five categories of treaty-limited equipment (battle tanks, armoured combat vehicles, heavy artillery, combat aircraft and attack helicopters) in an area stretching from the Atlantic Ocean to the Ural Mountains (the Atlantic-to-the-Urals, ATTU, zone).

The treaty was negotiated and signed by the member states of the Warsaw Treaty Organization (WTO) and NATO within the framework of the Conference on Security and Co-operation in Europe (from 1 January 1995 the Organization for Security and Co-operation in Europe, OSCE).

The **1992 Tashkent Agreement**, signed by the former Soviet republics, with the exception of the Baltic states, with territories within the ATTU zone, set out the division of the former Soviet CFE obligations and entitlements.

All the states which have ratified the CFE Treaty signed, at Oslo in 1992, the Final Document of the Extraordinary Conference of the States Parties to the CFE Treaty (**Oslo Document**), introducing necessary modifications because of the emergence of new states as a consequence of the breakup of the USSR.

The first Review Conference of the CFE Treaty, held in 1996, adopted a **Flank Document** which reorganized the flank areas geographically and numerically, allowing Russia and Ukraine to deploy more treaty-limited equipment along their borders.

In 1997 negotiations were opened to adapt the treaty to the new security environment in Europe. The **Decisions of the Joint Consultative Group concerning treaty adaptation** of 23 July 1997 and 30 March 1999 mapped out the course of negotiations towards an adapated CFE Treaty

Parties (30): Armenia, Azerbaijan, Belarus, Belgium, Bulgaria, Canada, Czech Republic, Denmark, France, Georgia, Germany, Greece, Hungary, Iceland, Italy, Kazakhstan, Luxembourg, Moldova, Netherlands, Norway, Poland, Portugal, Romania, Russia, Slovakia, Spain, Turkey, UK, Ukraine, USA

The Concluding Act of the Negotiation on Personnel Strength of Conventional Armed Forces in Europe (CFE-1A Agreement)

Opened for signature by the parties to the CFE Treaty at Helsinki on 10 July 1992; entered into force simultaneously with the CFE Treaty; depositary Netherlands Government

The agreement limits the personnel of the conventional land-based armed forces within the ATTU zone.

Vienna Documents 1990, 1992 and 1994 on Confidence- and Security-Building Measures

The Vienna Documents were adopted by all members of the Conference on Security and Co-operation in Europe (from 1 January 1995 the Organization for Security and Co-operation in Europe). The Vienna Document 1994 was adopted at Vienna on 28 November 1994.

The **Vienna Document 1990** on confidence- and security-building measures (CSBMs) repeats many of the provisions in the 1986 Stockholm Document on CSBMs and Disarmament in Europe and expands several others. It establishes a communications network and a risk reduction mechanism. The **Vienna Document 1992** on CSBMs builds on the Vienna Document 1990 and supplements its provisions with new mechanisms and constraining provisions. The **Vienna Document 1994** on CSBMs amends and expands the previous Vienna Documents. In 1995–97 several amendments to the Vienna Document 1994 were adopted.

Treaty on the Reduction and Limitation of Strategic Offensive Arms (START I Treaty)

Signed by the USA and the USSR at Moscow on 31 July 1991; entered into force on 5 December 1994.

The treaty requires the USA and Russia to make phased reductions in their offensive strategic nuclear forces over a seven-year period. It sets numerical limits on deployed strategic nuclear delivery vehicles (SNDVs)—ICBMs, SLBMs and heavy bombers—and the nuclear warheads they carry. In the 1992 Protocol to Facilitate the Implementation of the START Treaty (**Lisbon Protocol**), Belarus, Kazakhstan and Ukraine also assumed the obligations of the former USSR under the treaty. They pledged to eliminate all the former Soviet strategic weapons on their territories within the seven-year reduction period and to join the NPT as non-nuclear weapon states in the shortest possible time.

Treaty on Open Skies

Opened for signature at Helsinki on 24 March 1992; not in force as of 1 January 1999; depositaries Canadian and Hungarian governments.

The treaty obliges the parties to submit their territories to short-notice unarmed surveillance flights. The area of application stretches from Vancouver, Canada, eastwards to Vladivostok, Russia.

The treaty was negotiated between the member states of the Warsaw Treaty Organization (WTO) and NATO. It is open for signature by the NATO states and the former WTO members, including the new states of the former Soviet Union. For six months after entry into force of the treaty, any other OSCE member state may apply for accession. The treaty will enter into force 60 days after the deposit of 20 instruments of ratification, including those of the depositaries (Canada and Hungary), and all the signatories with more than eight 'passive quotas' (i.e., flights which the state is obliged to accept); that is, Belarus, Canada, France, Germany, Italy, Russia, Turkey, the UK, Ukraine and the USA.

23 ratifications deposited: Belgium, Bulgaria, Canada, Czech Republic, Denmark, France, Georgia, Germany, Greece, Hungary, Iceland, Italy, Luxembourg, Netherlands, Norway, Poland, Portugal, Romania, Slovakia, Spain, Turkey, UK, USA

Signed but not ratified: Belarus, Kyrgyzstan, Russia, Ukraine

Treaty on Further Reduction and Limitation of Strategic Offensive Arms (START II Treaty)

Signed by the USA and Russia at Moscow on 3 January 1993; not in force as of 1 January 1999.

The treaty requires the USA and Russia to eliminate their MIRVed ICBMs and sharply reduce the number of their deployed strategic nuclear warheads to no more than 3000–3500 each (of which no more than 1750 may be deployed on SLBMs) by 1 January 2003 or no later than 31 December 2000 if the USA and Russia reach a formal agreement committing the USA to help finance the elimination of strategic nuclear weapons in Russia.

On 26 September 1997 the two parties signed a *Protocol* to the treaty providing for the extension until the end of 2007 of the period of implementation of the treaty.

Convention on the Prohibition of the Development, Production, Stockpiling and Use of Chemical Weapons and on their Destruction (Chemical Weapons Convention, CWC)

Opened for signature at Paris on 13 January 1993; entered into force on 29 April 1997; depositary UN Secretary-General.

The convention prohibits both the use of chemical weapons (also prohibited by the 1925 Geneva Protocol) and the development, production, acquisition, transfer and stockpiling of chemical weapons. Each party undertakes to destroy its chemical weapons and production facilities within 10 years after the treaty enters into force.

Parties (121): Albania, Algeria, Argentina, Armenia, Australia, Austria, Bahrain, Bangladesh, Belarus, Belgium, Benin, Bolivia, Bosnia and Herzegovina, Botswana, Brazil, Brunei, Bulgaria, Burkina Faso, Burundi, Cameroon, Canada, Chile, China, Cook Islands, Costa Rica, Côte d'Ivoire, Croatia, Cuba, Cyprus, Czech Republic, Denmark, Ecuador, El Salvador, Equatorial Guinea, Ethiopia, Fiji, Finland, France, Gambia, Georgia, Germany, Ghana, Greece, Guinea, Guyana, Hungary, Iceland, India, Indonesia, Iran, Ireland, Italy, Japan, Jordan, Kenya, Korea (South), Kuwait, Laos, Latvia, Lesotho, Lithuania, Luxembourg, Macedonia (Former Yugoslav Republic of), Malawi, Maldives, Mali, Malta, Mauritania, Mauritius, Mexico, Moldova, Monaco, Mongolia, Morocco, Namibia, Nepal, Netherlands, New Zealand, Niger, Norway, Oman, Pakistan, Panama, Papua New Guinea, Paraguay, Peru, Philippines, Poland, Portugal, Qatar, Romania, Russia, Saint Lucia, Saudi Arabia, Senegal, Seychelles, Singapore, Slovakia, Slovenia, South Africa, Spain, Sri Lanka, Suriname, Swaziland, Sweden, Switzerland, Tajikistan, Tanzania, Togo, Trinidad and Tobago, Tunisia, Turkey, Turkmenistan, UK, Ukraine, Uruguay, USA, Uzbekistan, Venezuela, Viet Nam, Zimbabwe

Signed but not ratified: Afghanistan, Azerbaijan, Bahamas, Bhutan, Cambodia, Cape Verde, Central African Republic, Chad, Colombia, Comoros, Congo (Brazzaville), Congo (Democratic Republic of), Djibouti, Dominica, Dominican Republic, Estonia, Gabon, Grenada, Guatemala, Guinea-Bissau, Haiti, Holy See, Honduras, Israel, Jamaica, Kazakhstan, Kyrgyzstan, Liberia, Liechtenstein, Madagascar, Malaysia, Marshall Islands, Micronesia, Myanmar (Burma), Nauru, Nicaragua, Nigeria, Rwanda, Saint Kitts (Christopher) and Nevis, Saint Vincent and the Grenadines, Samoa (Western), San Marino, Sierra Leone, Thailand, Uganda, United Arab Emirates, Yemen, Zambia

Treaty on the Southeast Asia Nuclear Weapon-Free Zone (Treaty of Bangkok)

Opened for signature at Bangkok on 15 December 1995; entered into force on 27 March 1997; depositary Government of Thailand.

Prohibits the development, manufacture, acquisition or testing of nuclear weapons inside or outside the zone area as well as the stationing and transport of nuclear weapons in or through the zone. Each state party may decide for itself whether to allow visits and transit by foreign ships and aircraft. The parties undertake not to dump at sea or discharge into the atmosphere anywhere within the zone any radioactive material or wastes or dispose of radioactive material on land. The parties should conclude an agreement with the IAEA for the application of full-scope safeguards to their peaceful nuclear activities.

The zone includes not only the territories but also the continental shelves and exclusive economic zones of the states parties.

The treaty is open for signature by all the states in South-East Asia: Brunei, Cambodia, Indonesia, Laos, Malaysia, Myanmar (Burma), the Philippines, Singapore, Thailand and Viet Nam.

Under a *Protocol* to the treaty China, France, Russia, the UK and the USA are to undertake not to use or threaten to use nuclear weapons against any state party to the treaty. They should further undertake not to use nuclear weapons within the Southeast Asia nuclear weapon-free zone. The protocol will enter into force for each state party on the date of its deposit of the instrument of ratification.

Parties (9): Brunei, Cambodia, Indonesia, Laos, Malaysia, Myanmar (Burma), Singapore, Thailand, Viet Nam

Signed but not ratified: Philippines

Protocol: no signatures, no ratifications

African Nuclear-Weapon-Free Zone Treaty (Treaty of Pelindaba)

Opened for signature at Cairo on 11 April 1996; not in force as of 1 January 1999; depositary Secretary-General of the OAU.

Prohibits the research, development, manufacture and acquisition of nuclear explosive devices and the testing or stationing of any nuclear explosive device. Each party remains free to allow visits, as well as transit by foreign ships and aircraft. The treaty also prohibits any attack against nuclear installations. The parties undertake not to dump or permit the dumping of radioactive wastes and other radioactive matter anywhere within the zone. The parties should conclude an agreement with the IAEA for the application of comprehensive safeguards to their peaceful nuclear activities.

'African nuclear-weapon-free zone' means the territory of the continent of Africa, island states members of the OAU and all islands considered by the OAU to be part of Africa.

The treaty is open for signature by all the states of Africa. It will enter into force upon the 28th ratification.

Under *Protocol I* China, France, Russia, the UK and the USA are to undertake not to use or threaten to use a nuclear explosive device against the parties to the Treaty.

Under *Protocol II* China, France, Russia, the UK and the USA are to undertake not to test nuclear explosive devices anywhere within the zone.

Under *Protocol III* states with territories within the zone for which they are internationally responsible are to undertake to observe certain provisions of the treaty with respect to these territories. This protocol is open for signature by France and Spain.

The protocols will enter into force simultaneously with the treaty for those protocol signatories that have deposited their instruments of ratification.

8 ratifications deposited: Algeria, Burkina Faso, Gambia, Mauritania, Mauritius, South Africa, Tanzania, Zimbabwe

Signed but not ratified: Angola, Benin, Botswana, Burundi, Cameroon, Cape Verde, Central African Republic, Chad, Comoros, Congo (Brazzaville), Congo (Democratic Republic of), Côte d'Ivoire, Djibouti, Egypt, Eritrea, Ethiopia, Gabon, Ghana, Guinea, Guinea-Bissau, Kenya, Lesotho, Liberia, Libya, Malawi, Mali, Morocco, Mozambique, Namibia, Niger, Nigeria, Rwanda, Sao Tome and Principe, Senegal, Seychelles, Sierra Leone, Sudan, Swaziland, Togo, Tunisia, Uganda, Zambia

Protocol I ratification: China, France[1]; **signed but not ratified:** Russia,[2] UK,[3] USA

Protocol II ratification: China, France; **signed but not ratified:** Russia,[2] UK,[3] USA

Protocol III ratification: France

[1] When signing Protocol I France stated that the commitment expressed in Article I of the Protocol is equivalent to the negative security guarantee that France has given to non-nuclear states parties to the Non-proliferation Treaty, confirmed in a CD statement of 6 Apr. 1995 and in UN Security Council Resolution 984 of 11 Apr. 1995.

[2] The Russian Government declared that as long as a military base is located on the Chagos archipelago islands it cannot meet the requirements put forward by the treaty for the nuclear weapon-free territories and it considers itself not to be bound by the obligations in respect of these territories. As regards Article 1 of Protocol I Russia interprets it as meaning that it will not use nuclear weapons against a state which is a party to the treaty except in cases of invasion of or any other armed attack on Russia.

[3] The British Government declared that it does not accept the inclusion of the British Indian Ocean Territory within the African nuclear weapon-free zone without its consent and it does not accept any legal obligation in respect of that territory by its adherence to Protocols I and II. The UK will not be bound by Protocol I in case of an invasion of or any other attack on the UK, its dependent territories, its armed forces or its allies or carried out or sustained by a party to the treaty in association or in alliance with a nuclear weapon state.

Agreement on Sub-Regional Arms Control (Florence Agreement)

Signed at Florence on 14 June 1996; entered into force upon signature.

The agreement was negotiated under the auspices of the OSCE in accordance with the mandate in the 1995 General Framework Agreement for Peace in Bosnia and Herzegovina (Dayton Agreement). It sets numerical ceilings on armaments of the former warring parties: Bosnia and Herzegovina and its two entities, Croatia and Yugoslavia (Serbia and Montenegro). Five categories of heavy conventional weapons are included: battle tanks, armoured combat vehicles, heavy artillery (75 mm and above), combat aircraft and attack helicopters. The reductions were completed by 31 October 1997. It is confirmed that 6580 weapon items were destroyed by that date.

Parties (5): Bosnia and Herzegovina and its two entities—the Federation of Bosnia and Herzegovina and the Republika Srpska—Croatia, Yugoslavia (Serbia and Montenegro)

Comprehensive Nuclear Test-Ban Treaty (CTBT)

Opened for signature at New York on 24 September 1996; not in force as of 1 January 1999; depositary UN Secretary-General.

Prohibits the carrying out of any nuclear weapon test explosion or any other nuclear explosion, and urges each party to prevent any such nuclear explosion at any place under its jurisdiction or control and refrain from causing, encouraging, or in any way participating in the carrying out of any nuclear weapon test explosion or any other nuclear explosion.

The treaty will enter into force 180 days after the date of the deposit of the instrument of ratification of the 44 states listed in an annexe to the treaty but in no case earlier than two years after its opening for signature. All the 44 states possess nuclear power reactors and/or nuclear research reactors.

The 44 states whose ratification is required for entry into force are Algeria, Argentina, Australia, Austria, Bangladesh, Belgium, Brazil, Bulgaria, Canada, Chile, China, Colombia, Congo (Democratic Republic of), Egypt, Finland, France, Germany, Hungary, India, Indonesia, Iran, Israel, Italy, Japan, Korea (North), Korea (South), Mexico, Netherlands, Norway, Pakistan, Peru, Poland, Romania, Russia, Slovakia, South Africa, Spain, Sweden, Switzerland, Turkey, UK, Ukraine, USA and Viet Nam.

26 ratifications deposited: Argentina, Australia, Austria, Brazil, Canada, Czech Republic, Denmark, El Salvador, Fiji, France, Germany, Grenada, Japan, Jordan, Micronesia, Monaco, Mongolia, Peru, Qatar, Slovakia, Spain, Sweden, Tajikistan, Turkmenistan, UK, Uzbekistan

Signed but not ratified: Albania, Algeria, Andorra, Angola, Antigua and Barbuda, Armenia, Azerbaijan, Bahrain, Bangladesh, Belarus, Belgium, Benin, Bolivia, Bosnia and Herzegovina, Brunei, Burkina Faso, Burundi, Cambodia, Cape Verde, Chad, Chile, China, Colombia, Comoros, Congo (Brazzaville), Congo (Democratic Republic of), Cook Islands, Costa Rica, Côte d'Ivoire, Croatia, Cyprus, Djibouti, Dominican Republic, Ecuador, Egypt, Equatorial Guinea, Estonia, Ethiopia, Finland, Gabon, Georgia, Ghana, Greece, Guinea, Guinea-Bissau, Haiti, Holy See, Honduras, Hungary, Iceland, Indonesia, Iran, Ireland, Israel, Italy, Jamaica, Kazakhstan, Kenya, Korea (South), Kuwait, Kyrgyzstan, Laos, Latvia, Lesotho, Liberia, Liechtenstein, Lithuania, Luxembourg, Macedonia (Former Yugoslav Republic of) Madagascar, Malawi, Malaysia, Maldives, Mali, Malta, Marshall Islands, Mauritania, Mexico, Moldova, Morocco, Mozambique, Myanmar (Burma), Namibia, Nepal, Netherlands, New Zealand, Nicaragua, Niger, Norway, Panama, Papua New Guinea, Paraguay, Philippines, Poland, Portugal, Romania, Russia, Saint Lucia, Samoa (Western), San Marino, Sao Tome and Principe, Senegal, Seychelles, Slovenia, Solomon Islands, South Africa, Sri Lanka, Suriname, Swaziland, Switzerland, Thailand, Togo, Tunisia, Turkey, Uganda, Ukraine, United Arab Emirates, Uruguay, USA, Vanuatu, Venezuela, Viet Nam, Yemen, Zambia

Note: Azerbaijan, Finland, Greece, Italy, Netherlands, New Zealand, Panama and South Africa ratified the treaty between 1 January and 1 May 1999.

Joint Statement on Parameters on Future Reductions in Nuclear Forces

Signed by the USA and Russia at Helsinki on 21 March 1997.

In the Joint Statement the two sides agree that once the 1993 START II Treaty enters into force negotiations on a START III treaty will begin. START III will include lower aggregate levels of 2000–2500 nuclear warheads for each side.

Convention on the Prohibition of the Use, Stockpiling, Production and Transfer of Anti-Personnel Mines and on their Destruction (APM Convention)

Opened for signature at Ottawa on 3–4 December 1997 and at the UN Headquarters, New York, on 5 December 1997; entered into force on 1 March 1999; depositary UN Secretary-General.

The convention prohibits anti-personnel mines, which are defined as mines designed to be exploded by the presence, proximity or contact of a person and which will incapacitate, injure or kill one or more persons.

Each party undertakes to destroy all its stockpiled anti-personnel mines as soon as possible but not later that four years after the entry into force of the convention for that state party. Each party also undertakes to destroy all anti-personnel mines in mined areas under its jurisdiction or control not later than 10 years after the entry into force of the convention for that state party.

Parties as of 1 May 1999 (77): Andorra, Australia, Austria, Bahamas, Barbados, Belgium, Belize, Benin, Bolivia, Bosnia and Herzegovina, Bulgaria, Burkina Faso, Canada, Costa Rica, Croatia, Denmark, Djibouti, Dominica, Ecuador, El Salvador, Equatorial Guinea, Fiji, France, Germany, Grenada, Guatemala, Guinea, Holy See, Honduras, Hungary, Ireland, Italy, Jamaica, Japan, Jordan, Lesotho, Macedonia (Former Yugoslav Republic of), Malawi, Malaysia, Mali, Mauritius, Mexico, Monaco, Mozambique, Namibia, Netherlands, New Zealand, Nicaragua, Niger, Niue, Norway, Panama, Paraguay, Peru, Portugal, Qatar, Saint Kitts (Christopher) and Nevis, Saint Lucia, Samoa (Western), San Marino, Senegal, Slovakia, Slovenia, Solomon Islands, South Africa, Spain, Swaziland, Sweden, Switzerland, Thailand, Trinidad and Tobago, Turkmenistan, Uganda, UK, Venezuela, Yemen, Zimbabwe

Signed but not ratified: Albania, Algeria, Angola, Antigua and Barbuda, Argentina, Bangladesh, Botswana, Brazil, Brunei, Burundi, Cambodia, Cameroon, Cape Verde, Chad, Chile, Colombia, Cook Island, Côte d'Ivoire, Cyprus, Czech Republic, Dominican Republic, Ethiopia, Gabon, Gambia, Ghana, Greece, Guinea-Bissau, Guyana, Haiti, Iceland, Indonesia, Kenya, Liechtenstein, Lithuania, Luxembourg, Madagascar, Maldives, Malta, Marshall Islands, Mauritania, Moldova, Philippines, Poland, Romania, Rwanda, Saint Vincent and the Grenadines, Sao Tome and Principe, Seychelles, Sierra Leone, Sudan, Suriname, Tanzania, Togo, Tunisia, Ukraine, Uruguay, Vanuatu, Zambia

Annexe B. Chronology 1998

RAGNHILD FERM

For the convenience of the reader, key words are given in the right-hand column, opposite each entry; they refer to the subject-areas covered in the entry. The dates given in the left-hand column are those applying at the location when the events occurred (time changes may mean that they were reported elsewhere as occurring on different dates). Definitions of the acronyms can be found on page xvi.

11 Jan.	Iraq refuses to cooperate with the UN Special Commission on Iraq (UNSCOM) in allowing UNSCOM inspectors entry into some Iraqi sites, claiming that the team is dominated by US nationals.	Iraq/UN
16 Jan.	The presidents of the USA, Estonia, Latvia and Lithuania sign, in Washington, DC, a Charter of Partnership in which the four states declare that their shared goal is the full integration of the Baltic states into the European and transatlantic political, economic and defence institutions.	USA/Baltic states
19 Jan.	An agreement establishing a consultation mechanism to strengthen military maritime safety is signed in Beijing by US Defense Secretary Cohen and Chinese Defence Minister General Chi Haotian. The agreement was worked out during the visit of Chinese President Jiang Zemin to the USA in October 1997 and is designed to help avoid incidents at sea and provide for a dialogue between naval officers.	USA/China
22 Jan.	Russian Prime Minister Chernomyrdin issues a directive which prohibits Russians from engaging in foreign economic activities concerning goods and services potentially applicable for nuclear, biological and chemical weapons or missile delivery systems.	Russia; Weapons of mass destruction
23 Jan.	The UN Security Council rejects as unacceptable Iraq's refusal to allow UNSCOM inspections.	UN/Iraq
12–13 Feb.	Nigerian troops of the Economic Community of West African States Monitoring Group (ECOMOG) capture the centre of the capital of Sierra Leone (Freetown) to restore the elected civilian government which was overthrown in a coup in May 1997 by the Armed Forces Revolutionary Council (AFRC).	Sierra Leone; Nigeria; ECOWAS; UN
20 Feb.	The UN Security Council unanimously adopts Resolution 1153, expanding the 'oil-for-food' programme for Iraq.	UN/Iraq

23 Feb.	UN Secretary-General Annan and Iraqi Deputy Prime Minister Aziz sign, in Baghdad, a Memorandum of Understanding in which Iraq reaffirms its acceptance of all relevant UN Security Council resolutions and reiterates its undertaking to cooperate fully with UNSCOM and the IAEA and to allow their inspectors immediate, unconditional and unrestricted access to all sites. The UN reiterates the commitment of all member states to respect the sovereignty and territorial integrity of Iraq. The MOU is endorsed on 2 Mar. by the UN Security Council in Resolution 1154, which is adopted unanimously.	UN/Iraq
25–27 Feb.	As a follow-up to the Nov. 1995 Declaration of Santiago on Confidence- and Security-Building Measures (CSBMs) by the Organization of American States (OAS), a regional OAS conference on CSBMs is held in San Salvador. A final declaration is adopted, including the recommendation of a common methodology for facilitating the comparison of military expenditures in the region and the improvement of the information submitted by the member states to the UN Register of Conventional Arms.	OAS; CSBM; Military expenditure; Conventional arms
26 Feb.	France's dismantling of its land-based nuclear ballistic missiles at Plateau d'Albion is completed.	France; Nuclear weapons
27 Mar.	The UN Security Council unanimously adopts Resolution 1159, dispatching the United Nations Mission in the Central African Republic (MINURCA), with up to 1350 military personnel, effective from 15 Apr.	UN; Central African Rep.
30 Mar.	The negotiations for accession of 11 new states to the European Union are opened at London. More detailed membership negotiations are initiated with Cyprus, the Czech Republic, Estonia, Hungary, Poland and Slovenia.	EU
31 Mar.	The UN Security Council adopts Resolution 1160 by a vote of 14 to 0 (China abstains from voting), deciding that all states shall prevent the sale or supply to the Federal Republic of Yugoslavia (Serbia and Montenegro), including Kosovo, of arms and related *matériel* of all types, such as weapons, ammunition, and military vehicles and equipment, and shall prevent arming and training for terrorist activities there.	UN; Kosovo/ Yugoslavia
31 Mar.	In line with earlier decisions by the British Government, the last remaining aircraft-carried free-fall nuclear bombs (one-fourth of the British nuclear force) are withdrawn.	UK; Nuclear weapons
10 Apr.	Ending 30 years of conflict, the Northern Ireland Peace Agreement (Good Friday Agreement) is signed in Belfast by British Prime Minister Blair, Irish Prime Minister Ahern and representatives of eight political parties, including Sinn Féin.	Northern Ireland

6 May	Representatives of the Government of Sudan and the Sudan People's Liberation Army (SPLA), meeting in Nairobi under the chairmanship of Kenya's Foreign Minister, sign an agreement to hold an internationally supervised referendum on self-determination for the south.	Sudan
6 May	Russian President Yeltsin and Uzbek President Karimov sign, in Moscow, an agreement on resisting the advance of Islamic fundamentalism in Afghanistan, Tajikistan and Central Asia in general. Tajikistan becomes a party to the agreement shortly thereafter.	Russia; Uzbekistan; Tajikistan; Afghanistan
11 May	Indian Prime Minister Vajpayee announces that India has on the same day conducted three underground nuclear explosions at the Pokhran test range in the Rajasthan desert, 560 km south-west of New Delhi. On 13 May two more nuclear explosions are announced to have been conducted at the same site on the same day.	India; Nuclear tests
12 May	Eritrean troops occupy the Yirga Triangle, an area in Ethiopia claimed by Eritrea. The hostilities, including bombing, spread to other border areas.	Eritrea/ Ethiopia
21 May	Indian Prime Minister Vajpayee declares that India will observe a moratorium on nuclear tests.	India; Nuclear tests
21 May	Following months of rioting and protests against the government, Indonesian President Suharto resigns after 32 years in power.	Indonesia
22 May	In referendums held in Ireland and Northern Ireland on the Northern Ireland Peace Agreement (see *10 Apr.*) a great majority approves and supports the agreement.	Northern Ireland
27 May	Speaking before the Indian Parliament, Indian Prime Minister Atal Bihari Vajpayee announces that, in India's view, India is now a nuclear weapon state. This is later rejected by the UN Security Council (see *6 June*). He confirms India's moratorium on tests and states that India is willing to 'move towards a de-jure formalization of this declaration'.	India; Nuclear tests; CTBT; Nuclear weapons
28 May	Pakistani Prime Minister Sharif announces that Pakistan has on the same day exploded five nuclear devices at the test site in the Chagai Mountains, near the Afghan border. On 30 May one more explosion is conducted, at a site 100 km south-west of the site used for the first test.	Pakistan; Nuclear tests
5 June	The UN Security Council unanimously adopts Resolution 1171, lifting the sanctions imposed on Sierra Leone following the military coup of 25 May 1997. It further stipulates that states shall prevent the sale or supply of all arms to Sierra Leone other than to the government.	UN; Sierra Leone

6 June	The UN Security Council unanimously adopts Resolution 1172, condemning the nuclear tests conducted by India and Pakistan. It endorses the joint communiqué issued by the permanent members of the Council (the P5) (see *4 May),* demands that India and Pakistan refrain from further nuclear tests and stop their nuclear weapon programmes, recalls that in accordance with the NPT 'India or Pakistan cannot have the status of a nuclear-weapon State' and urges them to become parties to the NPT and the CTBT.	UN/India; Pakistan; Nuclear tests; NPT; CTBT; P5
7 June	Fighting erupts between government forces and army rebels in Guinea-Bissau. On 3–4 July the Economic Community of West African States (ECOWAS) sets up a committee to follow up the implementation of the ECOWAS resolutions concerning the conflict.	Guinea-Bissau; ECOWAS
8 June	The Council of the European Union adopts, in Luxembourg, a Code of Conduct on Arms Exports, establishing criteria designed to curb arms sales to states that have poor human rights records, support terrorism or might use the arms for aggression against their neighbours.	Arms trade; EU
9 June	In a Joint Declaration the foreign ministers of Brazil, Egypt, Ireland, Mexico, New Zealand, Slovenia, South Africa and Sweden pledge that they will spare no efforts to achieve the goal of a world free from nuclear weapons and urge that the preparation for a post-nuclear era start immediately. (Slovenia later withdraws from the declaration.)	Nuclear disarmament
11 June	Pakistan announces a unilateral moratorium on nuclear tests and states that it is ready to constructively engage with India and other members of the international community to formalize the arrangement.	Pakistan; Nuclear tests
22 June	NATO presents proposals for adapting the Treaty on Conventional Armed Forces in Europe (CFE Treaty), including temporary deployments, transits of Treaty-Limited Equipment (TLE) and changes in territorial ceilings.	NATO; CFE
23 June	France formally terminates its testing programme by closing the department responsible for the activities. Its nuclear testing centre in the Pacific is formally closed on 31 July.	France; Nuclear tests
27 June	Chinese President Jiang Zemin and US President Clinton, meeting in Beijing, sign an agreement on the de-targeting of their nuclear weapons so that neither country will be targeted by the other's strategic forces.	USA/China; Nuclear weapons

3 July	The leaders of China, Kazakhstan, Kyrgyzstan, Russia and Tajikistan, meeting in Almaty, state that they will ensure implementation of their 1997 agreement on troop reductions in border areas. On 4 July Chinese President Jiang Zemin and Kazakh President Nazarbayev sign the Second Complementary Agreement which resolves the border issues between the two states.	Central Asia; China/ Kazakhstan
7 July	The UN General Assembly votes (by 124 to 4 with 10 abstentions) to confer additional rights and privileges on Palestine in its capacity as observer to the UN General Assembly, including the right to participate in the Assembly's general debate.	Palestine; UN
8 July	The British Government submits its new Strategic Defence Review (SDR) to Parliament for approval. On the nuclear side, it sets out a significant reduction in the number of operationally available nuclear warheads (to fewer than 200) and a reduced alert state for the Trident submarine force, the sole component of the British nuclear deterrent. The SDR also lists the fissile material holdings of the UK, declaring that the UK is the first nuclear weapon state to achieve transparency in fissile materials.	UK; Nuclear weapons; Fissile material
13 July	The defence ministers of France, Germany, Italy, Spain, Sweden and the UK sign, in London, a letter of intent identifying certain obstacles to the restructuring of the European defence industry and possible solutions for overcoming them. The letter covers security of supply and equipment, removal of export barriers, protection of classified information, transfer of intellectual property rights and harmonization of procurement.	Defence industry; Europe
13 July	The UN Security Council unanimously adopts Resolution 1181, deciding to establish, for an initial period of six months, a UN Observer Mission in Sierra Leone (UNOMSIL) to monitor the military and security situation in the country and the demobilization and disarmament of former combatants.	UN; Sierra Leone
13–14 July	At the invitation of the Norwegian Government a meeting on small arms and light weapons among 21 states, including France, the UK and the USA, is held in Oslo. The participating states agree on an International Agenda on Small Arms and Light Weapons: Elements of a Common Understanding, which includes a series of measures to strengthen controls in the legal trade in small arms and prevent illicit transfers.	Small arms
17 July	A UN Diplomatic Conference, meeting in Rome, decides to establish the International Criminal Court (ICC), with its seat in The Hague. It will try the crime of genocide; crimes against humanity; war crimes and the crime of aggression. The Statute of the Court is adopted on the same day and will enter into force when 60 states have ratified it.	ICC

24 July	Bolivia, Chile and the MERCOSUR (Mercado Común del Sur) states (Argentina, Brazil, Paraguay and Uruguay) sign, in Ushuaia, Argentina, the Political Declaration of MERCOSUR, Bolivia and Chile as a Zone of Peace, in which they agree to strengthen their mechanisms for consultation and cooperation on matters of security and defence and non-proliferation of nuclear weapons and other weapons of mass destruction. They also agree to make progress towards the realization of a zone free from anti-personnel landmines on their territories.	South America; CBM; MERCOSUR
27 July	At the fifth meeting of the ASEAN Regional Forum (ARF), held in Manila, Russian Foreign Minister Primakov presents a series of maritime confidence-building measures (CBMs) to be applied in the Asia–Pacific region.	Russia; ARF; CBM
2–4 Aug.	Rebel troops (mainly Congolese Tutsi soldiers) take control in the eastern part of the Democratic Republic of Congo with the aim of removing President Kabila from power. The Southern African Development Community (SADC) mandates a military intervention on Kabila's behalf.	Congo (Dem. Rep. of); SADC
5 Aug.	The Iraqi National Assembly votes for an immediate suspension of UNSCOM activities. On 9 Aug. UNSCOM suspends its inspections of new sites.	Iraq/UN
11 Aug.	The Conference on Disarmament (CD) decides to establish an ad hoc committee to negotiate a multilateral treaty banning the production of fissile material for nuclear weapons or other nuclear explosive devices.	CD; FMT
15 Aug.	A bomb, killing 28 people and wounding more than 200, is detonated in Omagh, Northern Ireland, by the Real IRA. This is the worst single terrorist incident of the Northern Ireland conflict.	Northern Ireland
20 Aug.	US cruise missiles attack sites in Afghanistan, allegedly used to train terrorists, and a chemical factory in Sudan, allegedly used for production of chemical weapons. The attacks are carried out in retaliation for the bombings of the US embassies in Kenya and Tanzania on 7 Aug.	USA
31 Aug.	North Korea test-fires a three-stage intermediate-range ballistic missile which crosses over Japan before landing in the Pacific. On 1 Sep. Japan announces that it suspends the signing of the agreement on the funding of two nuclear reactors for North Korea, under the 1994 US–North Korean Agreed Framework.	North Korea/ Japan; Agreed Framework

2 Sep.	At a US–Russian summit meeting, held in Moscow, President Clinton and President Yeltsin issue a Joint Statement of Principles for Management and Disposition of Plutonium Designated as no Longer Required for Defense Purposes, affirming their intention to remove approximately 50 tonnes of plutonium from their nuclear weapon programmes and convert it so that it can never be used in nuclear weapons. They also issue a Joint Statement on the Exchange of Information on Missile Launches and Early Warning.	USA/Russia; Plutonium; Missile launches
2–3 Sep.	Recalling the Non-Aligned Movement (NAM) Cartagena summit meeting of 1995, the NAM summit meeting, held in Durban, South Africa, calls for an international conference with the objective of arriving at an agreement before the year 2000 on a phased, time-bound programme for the complete elimination of nuclear weapons and a significant reduction of conventional weapons.	NAM
7–8 Sep.	A summit meeting on the conflict in the Democratic Republic of Congo is held at Victoria Falls, Zimbabwe. The meeting is attended by the OAU Secretary General and the presidents of Angola, the Democratic Republic of Congo, Namibia, Rwanda, Uganda, Zambia and Zimbabwe. The leaders call for a ceasefire in the conflict. Representatives of the rebel movement are also present at the meeting but do not sign the ceasefire communiqué.	Congo (Dem. Rep. of)
9 Sep.	The UN Security Council unanimously adopts Resolution 1194, deciding not to conduct any further reviews of Iraqi sanctions until Iraq rescinds its decision to suspend UNSCOM activities (see *5 Aug.*).	UN; Iraq
16 Sep.	Burkina Faso ratifies, as the 40th state, the 1997 Convention on the Prohibition of the Use, Stockpiling, Production and Transfer of Anti-Personnel Mines and on their Destruction (APM Convention). The convention will enter into force on 1 Mar. 1998.	Burkina Faso; APM Convention
17 Sep.	The Basque separate group ETA (Euzkadi Ta Askatasuna, Basque Homeland and Liberty) announces an indefinite ceasefire as from 18 Sep.	Spain/ETA
22 Sep.	At the IAEA General Conference in Vienna, US Secretary of Energy Richardson and Russian Minister of Atomic Energy Adamov sign an agreement to bring commercial enterprises to Russia's closed 'nuclear cities' and a joint report that outlines a framework to resolve the problems with the 1993 agreement for US purchases of highly enriched uranium (HEU Agreement) from Russian nuclear weapons.	USA/Russia; Conversion; HEU

23 Sep.	The UN Security Council adopts Resolution 1199, demanding that all parties, groups and individuals cease hostilities immediately and maintain a ceasefire in Kosovo and deciding that should these measures not be taken further action and additional measures will be taken to maintain or restore peace and stability in the region.	UN; Yugoslavia/ Kosovo
23 Sep.	Speaking before the UN General Assembly, Pakistani Prime Minister Sharif says that Pakistan is prepared to adhere to the CTBT before the conference of states parties to the treaty, scheduled to be held in Sep. 1999. However, if India resumes testing Pakistan will review its position.	UN; Pakistan; CTBT
24 Sep.	Speaking before the UN General Assembly Indian Prime Minister Vajpayee says that India is prepared to bring discussions on the CTBT to a successful conclusion so that its entry into force is not delayed beyond Sep. 1999.	UN; India; CTBT
12 Oct.	After talks with US Special Envoy Holbrooke on the withdrawal of Serb forces from Kosovo, Yugoslav President Milosevic agrees to accept a 2000-strong OSCE observer force to be posted in Kosovo. In a telephone conversation with UN Secretary-General Annan the president says that Yugoslavia will comply with UN Security Council Resolution 1199 (see *23 Sep.*).	Yugoslavia/ Kosovo; OSCE; UN
13 Oct.	NATO Secretary General Solana announces that as Yugoslavia has not complied fully with UN Security Resolution 1199 (see *23 Sep.*) NATO has decided to issue activation orders for both a phased air campaign and limited air operations in Yugoslavia. On 27 Oct. NATO considers that Yugoslavia has withdrawn sufficient units from Kosovo to comply with the UN demands and decides to suspend its threat.	NATO; Yugoslavia/ Kosovo
16 Oct.	Yugoslav Foreign Minister Jovanovic signs, in Belgrade, an agreement with the OSCE allowing the OSCE Kosovo Verification Mission (KVM) into Kosovo. Its mandate is to verify compliance with UN Security Council Resolutions 1160 (see *31 May*) and 1199 (see *23 Sep.*).	Yugoslavia; OSCE
23 Oct.	Under the supervision of the USA and Jordan, Israeli Prime Minister Netanyahu and Palestinian leader Arafat sign, at Washington, DC, the Wye River Memorandum, worked out at Wye Plantation (Maryland). The memorandum stipulates a further Israeli pull-back from 13 per cent of the West Bank (captured in 1967), a security plan with a timetable for the Palestinians to arrest alleged terrorists and confiscate weapons under CIA supervision and guarantees of safe passage for Palestinians between Gaza and other Palestinian areas.	Israel/Palestine; USA; Jordan

24 Oct.	The UN Security Council adopts Resolution 1203 by a vote of 13 to 0 (China and Russia abstain from voting), demanding that Yugoslavia comply with the UN resolutions on Kosovo. The Council condemns all acts of violence and all external support for such activities in Kosovo, including the supply of arms, and endorses the agreement on an OSCE Kosovo Verification Mission (KVM) (see *16 Oct.*).	UN; Yugoslavia/ Kosovo
25 Oct.	The OSCE Permanent Council takes the decision to establish the Kosovo Verification Mission (KVM).	Yugoslavia; OSCE
25 Oct.	At the EU summit meeting held at Pörtschach, Austria, British Prime Minister Blair discusses different European defence options, including integration of the WEU into the EU and the establishment of flexible European forces.	EU; UK; WEU
26 Oct.	President Fujimori of Peru and President Witt of Ecuador sign, in Brasilia, an agreement which formally ends the territorial dispute between their two countries.	Peru/Ecuador
30–31 Oct.	The summit meeting of the Economic Community of West African States (ECOWAS), held in Abuja, Nigeria, adopts the Declaration of a Moratorium on Importation, Exportation and Manufacture of Light Weapons in West Africa. The moratorium enters into force on 1 Nov. for a three-year renewable period.	ECOWAS; Light weapons
31 Oct.	Iraqi President Hussein announces that Iraq has decided to end all forms of cooperation with UNSCOM until: the UN Security Council has lifted the UN sanctions; the chairman of UNSCOM, Butler, is dismissed; and UNSCOM is restructured in 'a manner that makes it a neutral and professional institution'.	Iraq/UN
1 Nov.	A peace agreement is signed in Abuja, Nigeria, by President Vieira of Guinea-Bissau and representatives of rebel forces loyal to General Mane, ending five months of conflict. (See *7 June.*)	Guinea-Bissau
4 Nov.	The EU defence ministers meet informally in Vienna to discuss the prospects of a European defence policy after the enforcement of the 1997 Treaty of Amsterdam and Europe's role in crisis management and prevention. This is the first EU defence ministers' meeting.	EU
13 Nov.	The NATO Council approves the operation plan (OPLAN) for a rapid intervention force of some 1500 men to be based in the Former Yugoslav Republic of Macedonia. This force should come to the aid, if necessary, of OSCE monitors in Kosovo. The plan is accepted by Macedonia on 2 Dec. (see *16 Oct.* and *25 Oct.).*	NATO; Kosovo; Macedonia; OSCE
28 Nov.	At a Franco-African summit meeting, held in Paris, French President Chirac announces that the presidents of the Democratic Republic of Congo, Rwanda, Uganda and Zimbabwe have agreed to a ceasefire in principle.	France; Congo (Dem. Rep. of)

4 Dec.	At the British–French summit meeting, held in Saint-Malo, France, a declaration on European defence is adopted, stressing the importance of full and rapid implementation of the CFSP in accordance with the 1997 Treaty of Amsterdam. To be able to respond to international crises the EU must have the capacity for autonomous action backed up by credible military forces.	France; UK; EU
4 Dec.	As the last NATO member state to do so, the Netherlands ratifies the Protocols of Accession for admission of the Czech Republic, Hungary and Poland as members of NATO.	NATO
8 Dec.	Setting a framework for its negotiating position regarding the adapted CFE Treaty the members of the North Atlantic Council together with the Czech Republic, Hungary and Poland issue a Statement on the Adaptation of the CFE Treaty: Restraint and Flexibility. In a statement on Kosovo the Council declares that it has authorized an Activation Order (ACTORD) for the NATO-led Extraction Force Operation to be deployed in the Former Yugoslav Republic of Macedonia (see *13 Nov.*) to provide the ability to withdraw personnel of the OSCE Kosovo Verification Mission in an emergency.	NATO; CFE; Kosovo
15 Dec.	In a report to the UN Security Council, the chairman of UNSCOM, Butler, accuses Iraqi authorities of having repeatedly obstructed the work of UNSCOM inspection teams.	UNSCOM/Iraq
17–20 Dec.	The USA and the UK conduct a series of air-strikes (code-named Desert Fox) to degrade Iraqi President Saddam Hussein's military capabilities. At a UN Security Council emergency meeting to consider the military strikes several members (among them China and Russia) condemn the action.	USA; UK/Iraq; UN
21 Dec.	The UN Security Council unanimously adopts Resolution 1216, endorsing the deployment of a border monitoring force by ECOMOG in Guinea-Bissau. (See *7 June* and *1 Nov.*).	UN; Guinea-Bissau
23 Dec.	To protest against US–British air-strikes in Iraq, the Russian Duma Council postpones hearings on START II ratification.	Russia; START II

About the contributors

Bernard Adam (Belgium) is Director of Groupe de Recherche et d'Information sur la Paix et la Sécurité (GRIP) in Brussels, which he founded in 1979. He is also head of the GRIP programme on Conflict Prevention and Arms Transfers. His recent publications include a chapter on arms transfers to countries in Africa in the GRIP volume *Conflicts in Africa. An Analysis of Crises and Crisis Prevention Measures* (1997) and an article on light arms in *Le Monde diplomatique* (April 1998).

Dr Ramses Amer (Sweden) is Associate Professor and Coordinator of the Southeast Asia Programme at the Department of Peace and Conflict Research, Uppsala University. His publications include *Peace-keeping in a Peace Process: The Case of Cambodia* (1995) and *The Cambodian Conflict 1979–1991: From Intervention to Resolution* (1996), which he co-authored with Johan Saravanamuttu and Peter Wallensteen. He has also contributed to international journals and books and has written reports on issues of Asian security. He has contributed to the SIPRI Yearbook since 1993.

Dr Ian Anthony (United Kingdom) is Leader of the SIPRI Project on National Export Controls in the New European Security Environment. In 1992–98 he was Leader of the SIPRI Arms Transfers Project. His most recent publication for SIPRI is *Russia and the Arms Trade* (1998), of which he is editor. He is also the editor of the SIPRI volume *Arms Export Regulations* (1991), the SIPRI Research Report *The Future of Defence Industries in Central and Eastern Europe* (1994), and author of *The Naval Arms Trade* (SIPRI, 1990) and *The Arms Trade and Medium Powers: Case Studies of India and Pakistan 1947–90* (1991). He has written or co-authored chapters for the SIPRI Yearbook since 1988.

Dr Alexei Arbatov (Russia) is a member of the Russian State Duma and Deputy Chairman of the Committee on Defence. He is also part-time Head of the Center for Political and Military Forecasts in the Institute of World Economy and International Relations (IMEMO). He has written extensively on arms control and security issues. His recent publications include a report for the Moscow Public Scientific Foundation, *Rossiyskaya natsionalnaya ideya i vneshnyaya politika* [Russian national idea and foreign policy] (1998) and, with Dag Hartelius, *Russia and the World: A New Deal* (forthcoming, 1999, in English and Russian). He has contributed to the SIPRI volume *Russia and Europe: The Emerging Security Agenda* (1997).

William M. Arkin (United States) is an independent expert on defence matters and a consultant to the Natural Resources Defense Council (NRDC). He is co-editor of the NRDC's *Nuclear Weapons Databook* series and co-author of several of the volumes in the same series. He is a columnist for *Bulletin of the Atomic Scientists* and the Washington Post website. His recent publications include (with Robert S. Norris) *The Internet and the Bomb: A Research Guide to Policy and Information about Nuclear Weapons* (1997), *The US Military Online: A Directory for Online Access to the*

Department of Defense (2nd edn, 1998) and *The Internet and Strategic Studies* (1998). He has contributed to the SIPRI Yearbook since 1985.

Dr Eric Arnett (United States), an engineer, was Leader of the SIPRI Military Technology and International Security Project in 1992–99. He is the editor of the SIPRI volumes *Nuclear Weapons After the Comprehensive Test Ban: Implications for Modernization and Proliferation* (1996), *Military Capacity and the Risk of War: China, India, Pakistan and Iran* (1997), and *Nuclear Weapons and Arms Control in South Asia after the Test Ban* (1998) and has contributed to the SIPRI Yearbook since 1993.

Ylva Isabelle Blondel (Sweden) is a Ph.D. candidate at the Department of Peace and Conflict Research, Uppsala University.

Dr Gennady Chufrin (Russia) is Leader of the SIPRI Project on Russia's Security Agenda. In 1979–97 he was Head of the Department of South-East Asia and Deputy Director of the Institute of Oriental Studies of the Russian Academy of Sciences. He is co-author and editor of *Narco-business: A New Security Threat to Russia from the East* (1996, in Russian) and *Narco-business in the South of Russia: Political Aspects* (1997, in Russian), and author of *Security Concerns of Russia in Asia–Pacific* (1997).

Dr Julian Cooper (United Kingdom) is Director of the Centre for Russian and East European Studies and Professor of Russian Economic Studies at the University of Birmingham. He conducts research on the Russian economy, defence industry, and science and technology policy. He has undertaken studies for the European Commission, the International Labour Organization, NATO, the Organisation for Economic Co-operation and Development (OECD) and other international organizations. Recent publications include chapters on the Russian defence industry and arms exports in *Cascade of Arms* (1997) and *Security Dilemmas in Russia and Eurasia* (1998). He has contributed to the SIPRI Yearbooks 1995, 1997 and 1998.

Agnès Courades Allebeck (France) is Senior Research Officer at the National Board of Trade, Stockholm. She was previously a Research Assistant on the SIPRI Military Expenditure and Arms Production Project where she was responsible for research on military expenditure in NATO, Africa and the Middle East. She is the author of chapters in the SIPRI volumes *Arms Export Regulations* (1991) and *Arms Industry Limited* (1993), and has co-authored several chapters in the SIPRI Yearbook since 1989.

Malcolm Dando (UK) is Professor of International Security at the Department of Peace Studies, University of Bradford. He is the author of *A New Form of Warfare: The Rise of Non-Lethal Weapons* (1996), *Biotechnology, Weapons and Humanity* (1999, co-authored with V. Nathanson and M. Darvell) and *New Biological Weapons* (forthcoming, 2000).

Ragnhild Ferm (Sweden) is Leader of the SIPRI Arms Control and Disarmament Documentary Survey Project. She has published chapters on nuclear explosions, the comprehensive nuclear test-ban and arms control agreements, and the annual chronologies of arms control and political events in the SIPRI Yearbook since 1982. She is the author of fact sheets in Swedish on SIPRI research topics.

Elisabeth M. French (USA) is a Research Assistant on the SIPRI Chemical and Biological Warfare Project and a Ph.D. candidate in Political Science at the State University of New York, Buffalo. She has co-authored (with Jean Pascal Zanders) the paper 'Article XI of the Chemical Weapons Convention: between irrelevance and indispensability' in *Contemporary Security Policy* (1999).

Dr Björn Hagelin (Sweden) is Leader of the SIPRI Arms Transfers Project. Before joining SIPRI in 1998 he was a Researcher at the Department of Peace and Conflict Research, Uppsala University. His recent publications include the report *One for All or All for One? Pentagon Tapping of Foreign Science and Technology* (1997) and a chapter on Sweden in *European Defence Technology in Transition* (1997). He contributed to the *SIPRI Yearbook 1984*.

Ann-Sofi Jakobsson (Sweden) is a Ph.D. student at the Department of Peace and Conflict Research, Uppsala University. She has contributed to the SIPRI Yearbook since 1995.

Andrés Jato (Sweden) is a Ph.D. student at the Department of Peace and Conflict Research, Uppsala University and is currently working in the Policy Planning Department at the Swedish Ministry for Foreign Affairs.

Dr Peter Jones (Canada) was Leader of the SIPRI Middle East Security and Arms Control Project between October 1995 and June 1999, after which he returned to Government Service in Canada with the Privy Council Office. He is author of the SIPRI report *Towards a Regional Security Regime for the Middle East* (1998) and co-author of a SIPRI fact sheet on the United Nations Special Commission's (UNSCOM) experiences in overseeing the elimination of weapons of mass destruction and ballistic missiles in Iraq. He has contributed to the SIPRI Yearbook since 1996.

Anders Jägerskog (Sweden) holds a Masters degree in Political Science. He was an Intern on the SIPRI Middle East Security and Arms Control Project in 1998–99. As well as conducting security-related research on the Middle East, he assisted in the organization of the project's conferences in the region.

Jaana Karhilo (Finland) is a Ph.D. student at the London School of Economics and Political Science. In 1998–99 she was a Research Fellow and in 1994–96 a Research Assistant on the SIPRI Peacekeeping and Regional Security Project. She contributed to the SIPRI Yearbook in 1995 and 1996 and is the author of the ANU Strategic and Defence Studies Centre Working Paper *New Requirements for Multilateral Conflict Management by UN and other Forces: Nordic Responses* (1996). She has also published articles in *Pacific Research* and in the *Nordic Journal of International Law*.

Shannon Kile (United States) is a Researcher on the SIPRI Project on Russia's Security Agenda. He has contributed to most volumes of the SIPRI Yearbook since 1993 on nuclear arms control and is the author of a chapter in the SIPRI Research Report *The Future of the Defence Industries in Central and Eastern Europe* (1994).

Pia Kronestedt (Sweden) was an intern on the SIPRI Programme on Building a Cooperative Security System in and for Europe and the Project on Conventional Arms Control in 1999.

Dr Zdzislaw Lachowski (Poland) is a Researcher on the SIPRI Programme on Building a Cooperative Security System in and for Europe and is responsible for the Project on Conventional Arms Control. He was previously a Researcher at the Polish Institute of International Affairs, where he studied problems of European security and issues concerning West European political integration. He has published extensively on these subjects. He is the author of *Between the Balance of Power and Conventional Arms Control in Europe: Adapting the CFE Regime to the New Security Environment* (1999, in Polish) and has contributed to the SIPRI Yearbook since 1992.

Evamaria Loose-Weintraub (Germany) is a Research Assistant on the SIPRI Military Expenditure and Arms Production Project. She is responsible for research on military expenditure in Europe (except for NATO members), Central and South America, and Oceania. She is the author of chapters in the SIPRI volume *Arms Export Regulations* (1991) and co-author of a chapter in the SIPRI Research Report *The Future of the Defence Industries in Central and Eastern Europe* (1994) and has contributed to most volumes of the SIPRI Yearbook since 1984.

Dr Robert S. Norris (United States) is Senior Staff Analyst with the Natural Resources Defense Council (NRDC) and Director of the Nuclear Weapons Databook Project in Washington, DC. He is co-editor of the NRDC's *Nuclear Weapons Databook* series and co-author of several of the volumes in the series. He has contributed to the SIPRI Yearbook since 1985 and is a columnist for *Bulletin of the Atomic Scientists*. One of his recent works (with William M. Arkin) is *The Internet and the Bomb: A Research Guide to Policy and Information about Nuclear Weapons* (1997).

Natalie Pauwels (Canada) holds a Masters degree in Economics (European Studies) from the London School of Economics. She is currently working as a Junior Researcher at the Bonn International Center for Conversion (BICC). She was a Research Assistant on the SIPRI Chemical and Biological Warfare Project in 1998.

Dr Adam Daniel Rotfeld (Poland) is Director of SIPRI and Leader of the SIPRI Project on Building a Cooperative Security System in and for Europe. He was a member of the Polish Delegation to the Conference on Security and Co-operation in Europe (CSCE) and Personal Representative of the CSCE Chairman-in-Office to examine the settlement of the conflict in the Trans-Dniester region (1992–93). He is the author or editor of over 20 books and more than 300 articles on the legal and political aspects of relations between Germany and the Central and East European states after World War II (recognition of borders, the Munich Agreement and the right of self-determination), human rights, CSBMs, European security and the CSCE process. He has written chapters for the SIPRI Yearbook since 1991.

Johan Sjöberg (Sweden) holds a Masters degree in Peace and Conflict Studies. He was a Research Assistant on the SIPRI Peacekeeping and Regional Security Project in 1998–99.

Elisabeth Sköns (Sweden) is Leader of the SIPRI Military Expenditure and Arms Production Project. She is the author of a chapter on the internationalization of arms production in the SIPRI volume *Arms Industry Limited* (1993) and *Annals of the American Academy of Political and Social Science* (1994) and of a background survey on arms production for the Bonn International Center for Conversion (BICC) *Conversion Survey 1998* (1998). She is co-author (with Reinhilde Weidacher) of a chapter on the economics of arms production for the *Encyclopedia of Violence, Peace and Conflict* (forthcoming, 1999) and of the forthcoming SIPRI Research Report *Arms Production in Western Europe in the 1990s*. She has contributed to most editions of the SIPRI Yearbook since 1983.

Margareta Sollenberg (Sweden) is a Research Assistant on the Uppsala Conflict Data Project at the Department of Peace and Conflict Research, Uppsala University. She has been editor of *States in Armed Conflict* since 1994 and has contributed to the SIPRI Yearbook since 1995.

Petter Stålenheim (Sweden) holds a Masters degree in Political Science and Public Administration. He is a Research Assistant on the SIPRI Military Expenditure and Arms Production Project.

Dr Stefan Troebst (Germany) is Professor of East European Cultural Studies at the University of Leipzig and was Director of the European Centre for Minority Issues (Flensburg) in 1996–98. He is the co-editor of South-Eastern Europe: Society, Politics, Economy and Culture (in German, forthcoming 1999) and is currently writing a book on the OSCE and the Trans-Dniestrian conflict.

Professor Peter Wallensteen (Sweden) has held the Dag Hammarskjöld Chair in Peace and Conflict Research since 1985 and is Head of the Department of Peace and Conflict Research, Uppsala University. He has most recently edited *Preventing Violent Conflicts: Past Record and Future Challenges* (1998) and *International Intervention: New Norms in the Post-Cold War Era?* (1997). He is the author of *From War to Peace: On Conflict Resolution in the Global System* (1994). He has co-authored chapters in the SIPRI Yearbook since 1988.

Dr Shaoguang Wang (China) is Associate Professor of Political Science at Yale University. He has previously worked as a consultant to the World Bank and the UN Development Programme (UNDP). He is the author of *Challenging the Market Myth: The Role of the State Amid Economic Transition* (1997) and co-author, with Hu Angang, of *Regional Disparities in China* (forthcoming, 1999).

Reinhilde Weidacher (Italy) is a Researcher on the SIPRI Military Expenditure and Arms Production Project. She is the author of a report for the Swedish Defence Research Establishment (FOA) on the Italian arms industry (1998) and co-author (with Elisabeth Sköns) of the forthcoming SIPRI Research Report *Arms Production in Western Europe in the 1990s*.

Pieter D. Wezeman (Netherlands) is a Research Assistant on the SIPRI Arms Transfers Project. He has co-authored (with Siemon T. Wezeman) a paper for the Bonn International Center for Conversion (BICC) on Dutch surplus weapon exports (1996) and has published articles on arms export issues in Dutch. He has contributed to the SIPRI Yearbook since 1995 and is responsible for the maintenance of the project's Internet pages.

Siemon T. Wezeman (Netherlands) is a Researcher on the SIPRI Arms Transfers Project. He is the co-author (with Edward J. Laurance and Herbert Wulf) of the SIPRI Research Report *Arms Watch: SIPRI Report on the First Year of the UN Register of Conventional Arms* (1993), (with Bates Gill and J. N. Mak) of *ASEAN Arms Acquisitions: Developing Transparency* (1995) and (with Pieter D. Wezeman) of a paper for BICC on Dutch surplus weapon exports (1996). He has contributed to the SIPRI Research Report *Arms, Transparency and Security in South-East Asia* (1997) and to the SIPRI Yearbook since 1993.

Dr Sten B. Widmalm (Sweden) is Director of the Council for Development and Assistance Studies at Uppsala University. He has written a chapter on the rise and fall of democracy in Jammu and Kashmir in *State and Community Conflict in India* (1998) and is author of a report commissioned by the Swedish Ministry for Foreign Affairs entitled *Defining Partnership with Africa—Sweden's New Africa Policy and Strategies for Relations with Democratic and Authoritarian States* (1999).

Dr Jean Pascal Zanders (Belgium) is Leader of the SIPRI Chemical and Biological Warfare Project. He was previously Research Associate at the Centre for Peace Research at the Free University of Brussels. He has contributed to the SIPRI volume *The Challenge of Old Chemical Munitions and Toxic Armament Wastes* (1997), co-authored a SIPRI fact sheet on the Chemical Weapons Convention (1997) and contributed to the SIPRI Yearbook since 1997. In 1998 he published several papers on regime formation and implementation of the Chemical Weapons Convention as well as on chemical and biological terrorism. He has co-authored (with Elisabeth M. French) the paper 'Article XI of the Chemical Weapons Convention: between irrelevance and indispensability' in *Contemporary Security Policy* (1999).

Professor Irina Zviagelskaya (Russia) is Vice-President of the Russian Center for Strategic Research and International Studies and is a head of section at the Institute of Oriental Studies, Russian Academy of Sciences. She has published extensively on armed conflicts, security issues and international relations, and has contributed to a forthcoming SIPRI volume on Russia and Asia.

Staffan Ångman (Sweden) is a Research Assistant on the Uppsala Conflict Data Project at the Department of Peace and Conflict Research, Uppsala University.

SIPRI Yearbook 1999: Armaments, Disarmament and International Security

Oxford University Press, Oxford, 1999, 772 pp.
(Stockholm International Peace Research Institute)
ISBN 0-19-829646-0

ABSTRACTS

ROTFELD, A. D., 'Introduction: Rethinking the contemporary security system', in *SIPRI Yearbook 1999,* pp. 1–12.

Ten years have passed since profound changes began in the international security system. In spite of all the fairly common expectations cherished at the threshold of the 1980s and still in the 1990s, uncertainty and unpredictability remain as the most serious threats to international security. The course of events in 1998 confirmed this. New concerns are generated by different factors both of an internal and of an international nature. On the one hand, some states, unable to provide basic governance and protection for their own populations, have brought about bloody domestic conflicts, and thus undermine security in different parts of the world; on the other hand, the proliferation of weapons of mass destruction and the spread of dangerous technologies pose a great potential threat to global stability and security.

WIDMALM, S., 'The Kashmir conflict', in *SIPRI Yearbook 1999*, pp. 34–46.

The conflict in the Indian state of Jammu and Kashmir continues despite attempts over the past three years to revitalize democratic institutions. The 1990s has been a decade of violence for Kashmir with continuous fighting between India and Pakistan since 1989. In 1998 no solutions to the conflict were in sight and both separatist-related violence and cross-border firing increased. The 1998 nuclear tests worsened the relationship between India and Pakistan and were followed by a drastic increase in firing across the Line of Control and an escalation of violence in Jammu and Kashmir. Earlier attempts to decrease tensions were reversed and the separatist movement continues its war against the Indian Union.

SOLLENBERG, M., WALLENSTEEN, P. and JATO, A., 'Major armed conflicts', in *SIPRI Yearbook 1999,* pp. 15–25.

In 1998 there were 27 major armed conflicts in 26 locations throughout the world, compared with 25 major armed conflicts in 24 locations in 1997. The increase in the number of conflicts and locations is accounted for by the conflicts on the continent of Africa. All but two of the conflicts in 1998 were internal. The two interstate conflicts were those between India and Pakistan and between Eritrea and Ethiopia. A root cause of the conflicts in Africa is to be found in the weakness of many of its states, where corruption, lack of efficient administration, poor infrastructure and weak national coherence make governance both difficult and costly. The combination of weak states and rich natural resources in Africa has resulted in a dangerous structural environment fuelling conflicts.

TROEBST, S., 'The Kosovo conflict', in *SIPRI Yearbook 1999*, pp. 47–62.

The current conflict between Serbs and Kosovar Albanians over the province of Kosovo is a territorial one, albeit with strong ethno-political, cultural and language factors. Between February and October 1998 the conflict escalated to full-fledged warfare between the Kosovo Liberation Army (KLA) and the Serbian Army and police forces. This was followed by a period of informal ceasefire from mid-October to the end of the year. While both sides in the conflict included outside political factors in their calculations, the actual impact of the international community on the development of military events was modest. By the end of 1998 the long-term solutions to the Kosovo conflict favoured by the Serbian and the Kosovar Albanian sides were even more complex and difficult to reconcile than they were at the beginning of the year.

ZVIAGELSKAYA, I., 'The Tajikistan conflict', in *SIPRI Yearbook 1999*, pp. 63–75.

Tensions and armed conflict were still prevalent in Tajikistan in 1998, in spite of an ongoing reconciliation process between the Tajik Government and the United Tajik Opposition (UTO) in accordance with the June 1997 General Agreement on Peace and National Accord. Several factors obstructed reconciliation in 1998. Most notable were the mounting inter-regional and inter-ethnic controversies. In November the government and the UTO were challenged by a rebellion in the Leninabad region of northern Tajikistan—a region that had been excluded from the power-sharing process. The rebellion and ensuing reactions of the government and the UTO signified a new emerging balance of forces in Tajikistan. While the government and opposition were brought closer together in their efforts to suppress a 'third force', relations between the north and south of the country were aggravated. A positive development was the appointment of several representatives of the UTO to government posts as part of the efforts to achieve a division of power.

ANTHONY, I., 'The Northern Ireland Good Friday Agreement', in *SIPRI Yearbook 1999*, pp. 159–68.

Since 1969 3250 people have died in politically motivated attacks carried out in the context of the disagreement over the legal and political status of Northern Ireland. In April 1998 the Good Friday Agreement was signed and then overwhelmingly approved in simultaneous referendums in the Republic of Ireland and Northern Ireland. The agreement created a framework in which a political settlement to the conflict could be found, but it did not itself resolve the underlying issues at the centre of the dispute. The success of the overall peace process in Northern Ireland was uncertain at the end of 1998.

KARHILO, J., 'Armed conflict prevention, management and resolution', in *SIPRI Yearbook 1999,* pp. 77–136.

There were several major successes in 1998, with peace accords concluded in Northern Ireland, Papua New Guinea and between Ecuador and Peru. Implementation of earlier settlements was moderately successful in the Central African Republic, Eastern Slavonia and Guatemala; troubled in Bosnia and Herzegovina, Georgia, Sierra Leone and Tajikistan; and impossible in Angola. New armed conflict subsided with fragile accords in Guinea-Bissau and Kosovo, stalemated in the Horn of Africa and escalated in the Great Lakes Region. While the UN and regional bodies continued to build their capacity for conflict prevention, management and resolution, international unity of effort was challenged by dissension within the Security Council and by the diversity of regional practices.

JONES, P. and JÄGERSKOG, A., 'The Middle East', in *SIPRI Yearbook 1999*, pp. 169–88.

Developments in the Middle East were largely negative in 1998. The Israeli–Palestinian peace process made progress, but failed to achieve the steps called for by the schedule of the Oslo agreements. The Israeli–Syrian and Israeli–Lebanese tracks of the peace process made no progress and violence continued in south Lebanon. Iranian President Khatami continued to liberalize Iran, although these moves were viewed with suspicion by the conservatives. The situation in Iraq worsened and led to a US–British bombing campaign. In Algeria the bloodshed continued, although at a slower pace than previously. Any of these issues would be a serious challenge to peace and stability in most regions; the Middle East will have to deal simultaneously with all of them. Ultimately, the region requires a new approach to security if it is to move beyond the confrontations and bloodshed which characterized 1998.

ARBATOV, A. G., 'Russia: military reform', in *SIPRI Yearbook 1999*, pp. 195–212.

The drive for military reform in the Russian Federation has been led by economic pressures and the need for savings on operations and for modernization of the armed forces rather than by changes in Russia's threat assessments, dramatic as these have been. For a short period after the spring of 1997, following the appointment of Defence Minister Sergeyev, some momentum built up for cuts and reorganization. Reform, paradoxically, involves costs, particularly those of demobilization and re-equipping the armed forces. With the continuing shrinkage of the Russian economy and after the financial crisis of August 1998 it is unlikely that Russia will now meet its target for reduction in troop numbers to 1.2 million by 1999 or achieve the change to all-professional forces. Procurement and R&D have been particularly hard hit.

CHUFRIN, G., 'The Caspian Sea Basin: the security dimensions', in *SIPRI Yearbook 1999*, pp. 213–34.

In 1998 the security situation in the Caspian Sea region was strongly influenced by a growing competition among regional as well as several extra-regional countries over the vast reserves of natural oil and gas claimed to exist in the Caspian Sea Basin. Among the major obstacles to the use of the Caspian oil and gas resources are the dispute over the existing Caspian Sea legal regime and different approaches to its resolution favoured by the littoral states. Another is connected with the problem of transportation of oil and gas from the Caspian Basin to outside consumers. The conflicting interests of the Caspian littoral states over these issues increased the threat of militarization in the region, which was further exacerbated by unresolved regional conflicts in Nagorno-Karabakh, Abkhazia and Chechnya.

ROTFELD, A. D., 'Europe: the institutionalized security process', in *SIPRI Yearbook 1999*, pp. 235–62.

In 1998 the European security debate focused to a great extent on the future missions and mandates of the major security institutions—NATO, the EU, the Western European Union (WEU) and the Organization for Security and Co-operation in Europe (OSCE)—and their interrelationships as well as on the role of the major powers within these organizations. The European security organizations will need to take creative and bold action if they are to implement the necessary reforms to be able to prepare for and address the security risks and challenges to Europe in the next century. The December 1998 British–French Joint Declaration on European Defence, the Saint-Malo initiative, presented some 'fresh thinking' on and mapped out the future direction of European common defence within the EU.

SKÖNS, E., COURADES ALLEBECK, A., LOOSE-WEINTRAUB, E. and STÅLENHEIM, P., 'Military expenditure', in *SIPRI Yearbook 1999*, pp. 269–99.

SIPRI estimates of world military expenditure show a decrease of about one-third over the period 1989–98 to about $745 billion in 1998. In 1998 the reduction was 3.5 per cent in real terms, a smaller reduction than the ten-year annual average of 4.5 per cent. The deepest cuts took place in Russia, primarily as a result of economic factors. US military expenditure, which accounts for one-third of the world total, declined by 4 per cent in 1998. In most other regions, including Africa, South Asia and Western Europe, military expenditure stayed roughly constant, while East Asian military expenditure continued to increase, although at a slower rate than previously.

WANG, S., 'The military expenditure of China, 1989–98', in *SIPRI Yearbook 1999*, pp. 334–49.

A surprising amount of information is available from open sources on the costs of supporting the Chinese military establishment. Using the SIPRI definition of military expenditure—that is, including the costs of the People's Armed Police, subsidies to military R&D and the arms industry, pensions of retired military, earnings from exports and funding from unknown sources for arms imports—total Chinese military expenditure in 1998 amounted to 141.1 billion yuan in constant 1995 prices. Interestingly, the assumption that arms exports have been used to pay for imports of military technology is not supported by the information available about their respective values.

ARNETT, E., 'Nuclear tests by India and Pakistan', in *SIPRI Yearbook 1999*, pp. 371–86.

The nuclear tests by India and Pakistan served more as a reminder of related problems than a cause of instability in themselves. The greatest risk of nuclear war in South Asia arises from Pakistan's strategy of using nuclear weapons to deter conventional war, while trying to preserve its freedom of action in Kashmir. As long as Indian military planners believe that their nuclear capability will deter Pakistani first use, the risk of nuclear escalation is real. There are encouraging signs that India will limit the size of its arsenal and may not change the nature of its deployment immediately. The situation in Pakistan is less clear, but there are indications that the military may move more decisively towards provocative deployments of nuclear ballistic missiles.

ARNETT, E., 'Military research and development', in *SIPRI Yearbook 1999*, pp. 351–70.

India redoubled its struggle to develop arms indigenously after technology transfer was disrupted in response to the nuclear tests. For the first time Iran, North Korea and Pakistan tested ballistic missiles with estimated ranges greater than 1000 km. Israel initiated new projects in air and missile defence which signal an increase in military technology efforts after a decade of reductions. After cutting its military R&D budget by 20 per cent in 1998, Japan decided to join the US Navy Theater-Wide missile-defence programme. Spain continued a programme of increases in funding for military R&D that could bring about a 1999 level almost six times higher than the 1996 level.

SKÖNS, E. and WEIDACHER, R., 'Arms production', in *SIPRI Yearbook 1999*, pp. 387–411.

During 1998 restructuring of the arms industries continued in most parts of the world. While the declining trend in arms production since the late 1980s appears to have come to a halt, concentration, internationalization and structural change continued in 1998. The arms sales of the top 100 arms-producing companies in the Organisation for Economic Co-operation and Development (OECD) and developing countries (excluding China), at $156 billion in 1997, represented more than three-quarters of total world arms production. The level of Russian arms production, which has declined to one-tenth of its 1991 level, increased by 5 per cent in real terms in 1998. The concentration process has resulted in huge arms-producing companies in the USA and to some extent in Europe. During 1998 there were some efforts in Europe to overcome the political barriers to internationalization.

HAGELIN, B., WEZEMAN, P. D. and WEZEMAN, S. T., 'Transfers of major conventional weapons', in *SIPRI Yearbook 1999*, pp. 421–49.

The global SIPRI trend-indicator value of international transfers of major conventional weapons in 1998 ($21.9 billion) was little more than that in 1994 ($20 billion), the lowest level since 1970. The USA maintained its position as the dominant exporter while Asia accounted for over 40 per cent of all arms imports. The planned delivery of a Russian air defence system to Cyprus put a spotlight on arms dynamics in this part of Europe and showed how a relatively small-scale arms transfer deal can increase regional tensions to a level at which the use of force is considered. The adoption by EU member states of a Common Code of Conduct for Arms Exports marked an important step towards the creation of common European export regulations. In 1998 the UN Register of Conventional Arms (UNROCA) included data on holdings of weapons and procurement from national production for the first time.

ADAM, B., 'Efforts to control the international trade in light weapons', in *SIPRI Yearbook 1999*, pp. 506–16.

Progress was limited to some specific steps—positive regional initiatives by the European Union (EU), the Organization of American States (OAS) and the Economic Community of West African States (ECOWAS)—and practical cooperation developed in southern Africa. Because of lack of support from member states, the only action taken by the UN on the 1997 report of the Group of Governmental Experts on Small Arms was the initiation of a study on ammunition and preparations for an international conference. The fight against arms trafficking will depend on the support of national governments. Support for controls on the 'supply' side is patchy, particularly among the industrialized states, and lack of coordination between national governments is a particular problem in Europe. The next steps are likely to be the introduction of greater transparency (possibly by creating regional registers) and an international system of supplier identification and marking.

KILE, S., 'Nuclear arms control and non-proliferation', in *SIPRI Yearbook 1999*, pp. 519–46.

There was little progress in nuclear arms control in 1998. The nuclear explosions carried out by India and Pakistan in May 1998 violated the emergent norm against nuclear testing and raised international concern about the vitality of the nuclear non-proliferation regime. The implementation of the 1994 US–North Korea Agreed Framework was jeopardized by North Korea's flight-test of a ballistic missile over Japan and by allegations that it is building an underground nuclear weapon-related facility. The centrepiece of US–Russian strategic nuclear arms control endeavours, the 1993 START II Treaty, remained unratified by the Russian Duma. There were some positive developments during the year. In Geneva the Conference on Disarmament formed a committee to negotiate a global Fissile Material Treaty banning the production of fissile material for use in nuclear weapons. The Indian and Pakistani prime ministers indicated that they were willing to consider signing the 1996 Comprehensive Nuclear Test-Ban Treaty.

FERM, R., 'Nuclear explosions, 1945–98', in *SIPRI Yearbook 1999*, pp. 556–64.

Series of nuclear tests were carried out by both India and Pakistan in May 1998. Since the signing of the Comprehensive Nuclear Test-Ban Treaty (CTBT), none of the recognized nuclear weapon states has conducted a nuclear explosion. The fact that not all the explosions announced by India and Pakistan were detected by the CTBT International Monitoring System (IMS) raised questions about the CTBT verification capabilities, especially among those critical of the treaty. However, most scientists agree that the system in fact worked well and will work even better in the region if or when India and Pakistan decide to adhere to the CTBT and provide IMS seismic stations on their territories.

ZANDERS, J. P., FRENCH, E. M. and PAUWELS, N., 'Chemical and biological weapon developments and arms control', in *SIPRI Yearbook 1999*, pp. 565–95.

In 1998 there was definite progress in the development of strong disarmament regimes for chemical and biological weapons (CBW). The 1993 Chemical Weapons Convention (CWC) seems to be well on way to becoming a strong, near-universal disarmament treaty. The experience of the first 18 months of the CWC should generate confidence that a protocol to strengthen the 1972 Biological and Toxin Weapons Convention (BTWC) regime is feasible. Progress in the negotiations was nonetheless modest, because a workable consensus on security and economic matters remains to be achieved between the parties to the BTWC and their biotechnological industries. Terrorism with CBW is emerging as a major threat and major national and international efforts are under way to counter it. Developments in Iraq are also worrying. The UN Special Commission on Iraq (UNSCOM) needs to be maintained in order to disarm the country, but deep divisions within the UN Security Council have paralysed the UNSCOM's work.

DANDO, M., 'Benefits and threats of developments in biotechnology and genetic engineering', in *SIPRI Yearbook 1999*, pp. 596–611.

Concerns about proliferation and possible use of biological weapons (BW) have increased in the 1990s. Current capabilities in genetic engineering could continue to be applied in offensive BW programmes, and the question arises as to what kinds of weapons might be possible in the future as a result of developments in biotechnology. Medical associations have warned that future scientific and technological advances could be misused for such purposes. The norm which promotes peaceful use of the new biotechnology capabilities but prevents misuse in offensive BW programmes must be reinforced. Current indications are that an effective verification protocol to the 1972 Biological and Toxin Weapons Convention (BTWC) could be agreed in 1999–2000. This would considerably strengthen the prohibitions embodied in the BTWC.

LACHOWSKI, Z., 'Conventional arms control', in *SIPRI Yearbook 1999*, pp. 613–43.

Talks on the adaptation of the 1990 Treaty on Conventional Armed Forces in Europe (the CFE Treaty) were deadlocked by controversy in 1998. Neither the adapted treaty nor the planned revisions of the Vienna Document 1994 of the Negotiations on Confidence- and Security-Building Measures in Europe were achieved. At the regional level within Europe, the successful implementation of the 1996 Agreement on Sub-Regional Arms Control (the Florence Agreement) stood in stark contrast to the lack of progress in other fields, the conflict in nearby Kosovo and the failure to begin wider arms control negotiations in the Balkan region. Outside Europe, developments showed a mixed record of arms control-related endeavours, with encouraging developments in South-East Asia and Latin America.

LACHOWSKI, Z. and KRONESTEDT, P., 'Confidence- and security-building measures in Europe', in *SIPRI Yearbook 1999*, pp. 644–54.

The Organization for Security and Co-operation in Europe (OSCE) continued the implementation of and work on confidence- and security-building measures (CSBMs) on the pan-European and regional levels in 1998. Adaptations suggested for the Vienna Document in 1998 aim to enhance transparency, predictability and cooperation, and emphasize deeper security cooperation suited to regional differences. Successful compliance was reported with the 1996 Agreement on Confidence- and Security-Building Measures in Bosnia and Herzegovina, in contrast to the mixed record of implementation of the civilian provisions of the Dayton Agreement.

LACHOWSKI, Z., 'The ban on anti-personnel mines', in *SIPRI Yearbook 1999*, pp. 655–62.

Progress towards a total ban on landmines was made in 1998. Although none of its major opponents had signed the 1997 Convention on the Prohibition of the Use, Stockpiling, Production and Transfer of Anti-Personnel Mines and on their Destruction (the APM Convention), with the required 40 ratifications achieved in September the convention entered into force on 1 March 1999. The Landmine Monitor, a civil society-based global monitoring network, got off to a promising start with the aim of reporting on all activities related to the implementation of a total ban. The entry into force in December 1998 of the 1996 amended Protocol II and Protocol IV of the CCW Convention strengthened efforts to eliminate inhumane weapons.

ANTHONY, I. and FRENCH, E. M., 'Non-cooperative responses to proliferation: multilateral dimensions', in *SIPRI Yearbook 1999*, pp. 667–91.

Events in 1998 further emphasized the need for universal disarmament. Although a comprehensive disarmament framework has not been established, states continue to be concerned with the proliferation of nuclear, biological and chemical (NBC) weapons, increasingly adopting multilateral responses to proliferation. Such responses include military pressure, economic sanctions and non-proliferation export controls. Events in Iraq in 1998 related to UNSCOM inspections and the elimination of its NBC weapon programmes prompted the UN to continue economic sanctions and spurred the USA and the UK to undertake military operations designed to diminish Iraq's military capability. In contrast to international responses to the nuclear tests conducted by India and Pakistan, national responses were divergent and included both economic sanctions and changes in export control practices. The reactions to the events in Iraq and India and Pakistan demonstrate the complex reality of responses to proliferation concerns in pursuit of the desirable ideal of comprehensive disarmament.

Errata

SIPRI Yearbook 1998: Armaments, Disarmament and International Security

Page 39, table 2.1:	Should include: • Gabcikovo-Nagymaros Project (Hungary/Slovakia).
Page 61, line 12:	Should read: 'talks mediated by Egypt, 26 of the 28 Somalian factions signed the Cairo Declaration'.
Page 216, table 6A.2, figure for the Czech Republic, 1995:	Should read: 23 879.
Page 216, table 6A. 2, figures for Czechoslovakia, 1990 and 1992:	Should read: *1990*, 41 900; *1992*, 48 503.
Page 228, table 6A.4, figures for Austria, 1990–1993:	Should read: *1990*, 1.0; *1991*, 1.0; *1992*, 1.0; *1993*, 1.0.
Page 228, table 6A.4, figure for Latvia, 1995:	Should read: 1.0.
Page 228, table 6A.4, figures for Malta, 1992 and 1995–1996:	Should read: *1992*, 1.0; *1995*, 1.0; *1996*, 1.0.
Page 230, table 6A.4, figures for Japan, 1990 and 1992–1996:	Should read: *1990*, 1.0; *1992*, 1.0; *1993*, 1.0; *1994*, 1.0; *1995*, 1.0; *1996*, 1.0.
Page 231, table 6A.4, figure for Gambia, 1989:	Should read: 1.0.
Page 232, table 6A.4, figure for Nigeria, 1989:	Should read: 1.0.
Page 397, line 18:	'the US–Russian Joint Commission on Technological Cooperation' should read 'the US–Russian Joint Commission on Economic and Technological Cooperation'.
Page 520, line 4 from bottom:	'to 31 February 1998' should read 'to 28 February 1998'.

INDEX